CONTENTS

FOREWORD

The names of those who put together the first edition of the *Sporting News Record Book* after the 1908 season are lost to the mists of history. We can imagine without too much difficulty that they were all newspapermen with perhaps a secretary doing some typing and that their boss, Charles Spink, probably parted with no more than a few extra bucks to pay for work that went beyond their usual duties. The book they produced was, in truth, quite small. It measured only 3" by 5 1/4" and had but 36 pages. But it set a precedent that has endured for nearly a century.

That first edition, whose cover said it contained "Information of General Interest to Base Ball Enthusiasts," was not a record book at all. Then as now, major league baseball did not have an official record book, and this little volume did not fill this gap. In fact, there is much more interest now in baseball's early statistical history than there was in 1909. So, those three dozen pages contained the league leaders from 1908, a list of major league no-hitters, an abbreviated version of the *Sporting News* staple "Caught on the Fly," a bunch of miscellaneous notes, the 1909 schedules and the Ernest L. Thayer poem "Casey at the Bat."

The *Record Book* maintained this basic format through the 1940 edition. In that year, the company then known as C.C. Spink & Son introduced a second book, the *Baseball Register*. The following year, perhaps because the *Register* was such a success, the *Record Book* expanded greatly. Its first half, prepared by Ernest J. Lanigan, included some directory information, a review of the 1940 season and a long section summarizing every World Series. The second half, compiled by Leonard Gettelson, was a real record book. It contained 159 pages of fielding, batting, pitching and baserunning records covering individual players, clubs and leagues.

1942 saw the debut of three more titles. Much of Lanigan's work was transferred to the *Baseball Record Book*, and Gettelson's contributions were extended and published as the *Dope Book*. In addition, the right to publish the *Baseball Guide* came to the company when the American Sports Publishing Company, the publishing arm of the Spalding Sporting Goods Company, decided to give up a book it had produced every year since 1877.

The *Register* and the *Guide* have been published continually since their debuts, but the other two books introduced in 1942 immediately went on hiatus. The *Record Book*, which was really not a record book, reappeared in 1948, and was called the *Dope Book*. Gettelson's *Dope Book*, which really was a record book, re-emerged in 1949 and was called *One for the Book* and later, the *Baseball Record Book*.

In 1953, this quartet of titles became a quintet, as Gettelson produced the first edition of *World's Series Records*. And so things remained for more than three decades. In 1986, parts of the *Dope Book*, the *Baseball Record Book*, and *World's Series Records* were incorporated into a new title, the *Complete Baseball Record Book*, the 2005 edition of which is its 20th appearance.

Since 1941, editorial responsibility for these annuals has rested with only five individuals. Ernie Lanigan was a respected baseball statistician. Leonard Gettelson was a New Jersey grocer and a legendary recordkeeper. His reams of handwritten index cards, filling many, many file drawers, survive today in the Sporting News Research Center. In 1972 , the editorship passed to Joe Marcin and in 1978 to Craig Carter, a man of unsurpassed perseverance and dedication.

The 2005 edition of the *Complete Baseball Record Book* is the second to bear my name on the title page, but it is, in many ways, still the product of the labors of those who have gone before. We have made some changes from last year, and we anticipate further changes next year. We hope you like what you see, and we would be pleased to hear from you. Most especially, we encourage communications that point out mistakes, typographical errors and omissions that are an inevitable part of the process. We plan to make next year's *Record Book* even better than this one, and we humbly ask for your assistance.

Steve Gietschier
Editor
Sporting News
10176 Corporate Square Drive
Suite 200
St. Louis, MO 63132

sgietsch@sportingnews.com

HOW TO USE THIS BOOK

The 2005 edition of the *Complete Baseball Record Book* is divided into five sections:

Regular Season
Division Series
Championship Series
World Series
All-Star Game

Category
• *Batting*

Designation
• *Individual*

Section 1
• *World Series*

WORLD SERIES *Individual batting*

Each of these sections can be located by using the table of contents, the index or the vertical gray tabs on the side of each page.

Within these five sections, records are further divided into the following categories:

Results
Service
Batting
Baserunning
Pitching
Fielding
Miscellaneous
Non-Playing Personnel
General Reference

The Regular Season section has the following additional categories:

• Yearly Leaders (year-by-year leaders in various offensive and defensive categories)
• Career Milestones (career leaders in various offensive and defensive categories)
• American League Team Records (team-by-team records for each A.L. club)
• National League Team Records (team-by-team records for each N.L. club)

Finally, the Service, Batting, Baserunning, Pitching and Fielding categories are further designated as Individual, Club or (for the Regular Season) League records.

To look up a record, select the appropriate section, then the correct category and then the proper designation. For example, if you want to learn which players have hit the most home runs in a 7-game World Series, you would locate the World Series section, the Batting category and the Individual designation.

Use the vertical gray tabs on the sides of each page to navigate your way into one of the five sections. Use the tabs again to find the category and the designation you need. From this point, rely on the black and gray horizontal bars to locate the exact record you want. Black bars help narrow your search, and gray bars get even more specific.

Throughout the book, we have tried to arrange records in a sequence such as you would likely see in any standard statistical summary:

Batting: Games played, batting average, on-base percentage, slugging average, at-bats and plate appearances, runs, hits, singles, doubles, triples, home runs, grand slams, total bases, extra base hits, runs batted in, bases on balls, strikeouts, sacrifice hits and flies, hit by pitch and grounding into double plays.

Baserunning: Stolen bases, caught stealing and left on bases.

Pitching: Games, games started, games relieved, complete games, innings, winning percentage, games won, saves, games lost, at-bats and plate appearances, runs, earned runs, ERA, shutouts and scoreless innings, 1-0 games, hits, home runs, total bases, extra base hits, bases on balls, strikeouts, hit batsmen, wild pitches, sacrifice hits and flies, and balks.

Fielding: Games, average, putouts, assists, chances accepted, errors and double plays.

You can follow these sequences by using the black bars. Gray bars sub-divide records even further: records for rookies, righthanders, or switch-hitters, for example, or records for series, games and innings.

Example: To find the record for most regular season home runs by a rookie:

1. Determine which section you need (in this example it is Regular Season), which category within the Regular Season section you need (in this case it is Batting) and whether you are looking for an Individual, Club or League designation (in this case it is Individual).

2. Locate the vertical tab indicating you are in the Regular Season, Individual Batting section (this section runs from page 17 through page 42).

3. Find the horizontal black bar labeled "Home Runs" (which can be found on page 27). Then find the horizontal gray bar labeled "Season" (which can be found on page 28). The record for most home runs by a rookie in the regular season can be found there.

Here are some additional notes to help you use the *Complete Baseball Record Book* efficiently:

1. Most of the records in this book refer to the following leagues: M.L.—major leagues, 1876 to date; N.L.—National League, 1876 to date; A.L.—American League, 1901 to date. Occasionally, National League records are divided in two with N.L. since 1900 identifying the second part. Other major leagues that appear in some places are: A.A—American Association, 1882 to 1891; U.A.—Union Association, 1884; and P.L.—Players League, 1890; and in a few cases, F.L.—Federal League, 1914-1915.

2. In the categories called Service, Batting, Baserunning, Pitching and Fielding, some of the records designated as League records have separate listings depending upon the number of teams in a league. These listings conform to this scheme:

	National League	American League
8 clubs	1900-1961	1901-1960
10 clubs	1962-1968	1961-1968
12 clubs	1969-1992	1969-1976
14 clubs	1993-1997	1977-present
16 clubs	1998-present	

3. Baseball has played two seasons shortened by World War I (1918 and 1919) and four shortened by labor-management difficulties (1972, 1981, 1994 and 1995). We have noted when play in these seasons affected some of the records beginning with the word "Fewest."

4. The category formerly called **long hits** is now called **extra base hits.**

5. **Chances accepted** is the sum of putouts and assists. **Chances offered** is the sum of putouts, assists and errors. **Fielding percentage** is calculated by dividing **chances accepted** by **chances offered**.

7. Many of the records formerly listed separately as having occurred in **extra-inning games** have been consolidated with the same record for **nine-inning games**. The **extra-inning** records are enclosed within parentheses.

8. In editions previous to 2004, records set during the special round of postseason play occasioned by baseball's split season in 1981 were incorporated in the Division Series section. Starting in 2004, these records were removed and placed in an addendum. Records in the Division Series section now commence with games played in 1995.

9. Records for two games in one day with separate admissions are included with doubleheader records.

ACKNOWLEDGEMENTS

The 2005 edition of the *Complete Baseball Record Book* could not have been completed without considerable assistance from a number of people. Obviously, this year's book stands on the shoulders of every previous edition, so thanks are due to Ernie Lanigan, Leonard Gettelson and Joe Marcin, posthumously, and to Craig Carter. In addition, I thank my colleagues at the *Sporting News*, John Rawlings, Dale Bye and Joe Hoppel, for entrusting this assignment to me, and to Chad Painter, who redesigned the book and formatted the pages with skill and alacrity.

My extreme gratitude also goes to the following members of the Society for American Baseball Research, baseball experts, one and all, whose professionalism and willingness, even eagerness, to help were absolutely essential:

Dan Heisman, for sharing lists from his "Baseball's Active Leaders" project;

Trent McCotter, for his enthusiasm for baseball in the 19th century;

Wayne McElreavy, who took on the substantial difficulties associated with checking 1-0 games;

Pete Palmer, who compared the text of the entire book to his substantial statistical database, thereby generating hundreds of additions, changes and corrections;

Dave Smith and the volunteers of Retrosheet (www.retrosheet.org), whose database is an incomparable source of detail and accuracy;

Lyle Spatz, chairman of SABR's Records Committee, who shared his knowledge and his judgment even as the hurricane winds blew; and

David Vincent, custodian of SABR's Tattersall/McConnell Home Run Log, who embraced every home run query I could imagine.

Finally, I thank a group of volunteers who agreed to help revise and extend the "Team Records" section of the book: Derek Adair, Bob Bogart, Steve Elsberry, Steve Ferenchick, Dan Fox, Bill Gilbert, Charlie Hanlon, Ed Hartig, Chris Hauser, Paul Hirsch, Mike Hunssinger, Ron Kaplan, Francis Kinlaw, Henry Kirn, John Matthew IV, Wayne McElreavy, Darren Munk, Cliff Otto, Marty Resnick, Chuck Rodgers, Jeff Sackmann, Mark Schoen, Lyle Spatz, Tom Stillman, Joel Tscherne, Joe Williams, Jim Wohlenhaus and Al Yellon.

Quite simply, there would be no book without them.

REGULAR SEASON

Results: Pennant Winners

Service (Individual, Club, League)

Batting (Individual, Club, League)

Baserunning (Individual, Club, League)

Pitching (Individual, Club, League)

Fielding (Individual, Club, League)

Miscellaneous (Individual, Club, League)

Non-Playing Personnel

Yearly Leaders

Career Milestones

General Reference

American League Team Records

National League Team Records

RESULTS

PENNANT WINNERS
AMERICAN LEAGUE

Year	Club	Manager	W	L	Pct.	GA
1901	Chicago	Clark Griffith	83	53	.610	4.0
1902	Philadelphia	Connie Mack	83	53	.610	5.0
1903	Boston	Jimmy Collins	91	47	.659	14.5
1904	Boston	Jimmy Collins	95	59	.617	1.5
1905	Philadelphia	Connie Mack	92	56	.622	2.0
1906	Chicago	Fielder Jones	93	58	.616	3.0
1907	Detroit	Hughey Jennings	92	58	.613	1.5
1908	Detroit	Hughey Jennings	90	63	.588	0.5
1909	Detroit	Hughey Jennings	98	54	.645	3.5
1910	Philadelphia	Connie Mack	102	48	.680	14.5
1911	Philadelphia	Connie Mack	101	50	.669	13.5
1912	Boston	Jake Stahl	105	47	.691	14.0
1913	Philadelphia	Connie Mack	96	57	.627	6.5
1914	Philadelphia	Connie Mack	99	53	.651	8.5
1915	Boston	Bill Carrigan	101	50	.669	2.5
1916	Boston	Bill Carrigan	91	63	.591	2.0
1917	Chicago	Pants Rowland	100	54	.649	9.0
1918	Boston	Ed Barrow	75	51	.595	1.5
1919	Chicago	Kid Gleason	88	52	.629	3.5
1920	Cleveland	Tris Speaker	98	56	.636	2.0
1921	New York	Miller Huggins	98	55	.641	4.5
1922	New York	Miller Huggins	94	60	.610	1.0
1923	New York	Miller Huggins	98	54	.645	16.0
1924	Washington	Bucky Harris	92	62	.597	2.0
1925	Washington	Bucky Harris	96	55	.636	8.5
1926	New York	Miller Huggins	91	63	.591	3.0
1927	New York	Miller Huggins	110	44	.714	19.0
1928	New York	Miller Huggins	101	53	.656	2.5
1929	Philadelphia	Connie Mack	104	46	.693	18.0
1930	Philadelphia	Connie Mack	102	52	.662	8.0
1931	Philadelphia	Connie Mack	107	45	.704	13.5
1932	New York	Joe McCarthy	107	47	.695	13.0
1933	Washington	Joe Cronin	99	53	.651	7.0
1934	Detroit	Mickey Cochrane	101	53	.656	7.0
1935	Detroit	Mickey Cochrane	93	58	.616	3.0
1936	New York	Joe McCarthy	102	51	.667	19.5
1937	New York	Joe McCarthy	102	52	.662	13.0
1938	New York	Joe McCarthy	99	53	.651	9.5
1939	New York	Joe McCarthy	106	45	.702	17.0
1940	Detroit	Del Baker	90	64	.584	1.0
1941	New York	Joe McCarthy	101	53	.656	17.0
1942	New York	Joe McCarthy	103	51	.669	9.0
1943	New York	Joe McCarthy	98	56	.636	13.5
1944	St. Louis	Luke Sewell	89	65	.578	1.0
1945	Detroit	Steve O'Neill	88	65	.575	1.5
1946	Boston	Joe Cronin	104	50	.675	12.0
1947	New York	Bucky Harris	97	57	.630	12.0
1948	Cleveland†	Lou Boudreau	97	58	.626	1.0
1949	New York	Casey Stengel	97	57	.630	1.0
1950	New York	Casey Stengel	98	56	.636	3.0
1951	New York	Casey Stengel	98	56	.636	5.0
1952	New York	Casey Stengel	95	59	.617	2.0
1953	New York	Casey Stengel	99	52	.656	8.5
1954	Cleveland	Al Lopez	111	43	.721	8.0
1955	New York	Casey Stengel	96	58	.623	3.0
1956	New York	Casey Stengel	97	57	.630	9.0
1957	New York	Casey Stengel	98	56	.636	8.0
1958	New York	Casey Stengel	92	62	.597	10.0
1959	Chicago	Al Lopez	94	60	.610	5.0
1960	New York	Casey Stengel	97	57	.630	8.0
1961	New York	Ralph Houk	109	53	.673	8.0
1962	New York	Ralph Houk	96	66	.593	5.0
1963	New York	Ralph Houk	104	57	.646	10.5
1964	New York	Yogi Berra	99	63	.611	1.0
1965	Minnesota	Sam Mele	102	60	.630	7.0
1966	Baltimore	Hank Bauer	97	63	.606	9.0
1967	Boston	Dick Williams	92	70	.568	1.0
1968	Detroit	Mayo Smith	103	59	.636	12.0
1969	Baltimore (E)	Earl Weaver	109	53	.673	19.0
	Minnesota (W)	Billy Martin	97	65	.599	9.0
1970	Baltimore (E)	Earl Weaver	108	54	.667	15.0
	Minnesota (W)	Bill Rigney	98	64	.605	9.0

Year	Club	Manager	W	L	Pct.	GA
1971	Baltimore (E)	Earl Weaver	101	57	.639	12.0
	Oakland (W)	Dick Williams	101	60	.627	16.0
1972	Detroit (E)	Billy Martin	86	70	.551	0.5
	Oakland (W)	Dick Williams	93	62	.600	5.5
1973	Baltimore (E)	Earl Weaver	97	65	.599	8.0
	Oakland (W)	Dick Williams	94	68	.580	6.0
1974	Baltimore (E)	Earl Weaver	91	71	.562	2.0
	Oakland (W)	Alvin Dark	90	72	.556	5.0
1975	Boston (E)	Darrell Johnson	95	65	.594	4.5
	Oakland (W)	Al Dark	98	64	.605	7.0
1976	New York (E)	Billy Martin	97	62	.610	10.5
	Kansas City (W)	Whitey Herzog	90	72	.556	2.5
1977	New York (E)	Billy Martin	100	62	.617	2.5
	Kansas City (W)	Whitey Herzog	102	60	.630	8.0
1978	New York (E)‡	Billy Martin, Bob Lemon	100	63	.613	1.0
	Kansas City (W)	Whitey Herzog	92	70	.568	5.0
1979	Baltimore (E)	Earl Weaver	102	57	.642	8.0
	California (W)	Jim Fregosi	88	74	.543	3.0
1980	New York	Dick Howser	103	59	.636	3.0
	Kansas City (W)	Jim Frey	97	65	.599	14.0
1981	New York (E)	Gene Michael, Bob Lemon	59	48	.551	§
	Oakland (W)	Billy Martin	64	45	.587	§§
1982	Milwaukee (E)	Buck Rodgers, Harvey Kuenn	95	67	.586	1.0
	California (W)	Gene Mauch	93	69	.574	3.0
1983	Baltimore (E)	Joe Altobelli	98	64	.605	6.0
	Chicago (W)	Tony La Russa	99	63	.611	20.0
1984	Detroit (E)	Sparky Anderson	104	58	.642	15.0
	Kansas City (W)	Dick Howser	84	78	.519	3.0
1985	Toronto (E)	Bobby Cox	99	62	.615	2.0
	Kansas City (W)	Dick Howser	91	71	.562	1.0
1986	Boston (E)	John McNamara	95	66	.590	5.5
	California (W)	Gene Mauch	92	70	.568	5.0
1987	Detroit (W)	Sparky Anderson	98	64	.605	2.0
	Minnesota (W)	Tom Kelly	85	77	.525	2.0
1988	Boston (E)	John McNamara, Joe Morgan	89	73	.549	1.0
	Oakland (W)	Tony La Russa	104	58	.642	13.0
1989	Toronto (E)	Jimy Williams, Cito Gaston	89	73	.549	2.0
	Oakland (W)	Tony La Russa	99	63	.611	7.0
1990	Boston (E)	Joe Morgan	88	74	.543	2.0
	Oakland (W)	Tony La Russa	103	59	.636	9.0
1991	Toronto (E)	Cito Gaston	91	71	.562	7.0
	Minnesota (W)	Tom Kelly	95	67	.586	8.0
1992	Toronto (E)	Cito Gaston	96	66	.593	4.0
	Oakland (W)	Tony La Russa	96	66	.593	6.0
1993	Toronto (E)	Cito Gaston	95	67	.586	7.0
	Chicago (W)	Gene Lamont	94	68	.580	8.0
1994	no pennant winner∞					
1995	Boston (E)	Kevin Kennedy	86	58	.597	7.0
	Cleveland (C)	Mike Hargrove	100	44	.694	30.0
	Seattle (W)††	Lou Piniella	79	66	.545	1.0
1996	New York (E)	Joe Torre	92	70	.568	4.0
	Cleveland (C)	Mike Hargrove	99	62	.615	14.5
	Texas (W)	Johnny Oates	90	72	.556	4.5
1997	Baltimore (E)	Davey Johnson	98	64	.605	2.0
	Cleveland (C)	Mike Hargrove	86	75	.534	6.0
	Seattle (W)	Lou Piniella	90	72	.556	6.0
1998	New York (E)	Joe Torre	114	48	.704	22.0
	Cleveland (C)	Mike Hargrove	89	73	.549	9.0
	Texas (W)	Johnny Oates	88	74	.543	3.0
1999	New York (E)	Joe Torre	98	64	.605	4.0
	Cleveland (C)	Mike Hargrove	97	65	.599	21.5
	Texas (W)	Johnny Oates	95	67	.586	8.0
2000	New York (E)	Joe Torre	87	74	.540	2.5
	Chicago (C)	Jerry Manuel	95	67	.586	5.0
	Oakland (W)	Art Howe	91	70	.565	0.5
2001	New York (E)	Joe Torre	95	65	.594	13.5
	Cleveland (C)	Charlie Manuel	91	71	.562	6.0
	Seattle (W)	Lou Piniella	116	46	.716	14.0
2002	New York (E)	Joe Torre	103	58	.640	10.5
	Minnesota (C)	Ron Gardenhire	94	67	.584	13.5
	Oakland (W)	Art Howe	103	59	.636	4.0
2003	New York (E)	Joe Torre	101	61	.623	6.0
	Minnesota (C)	Ron Gardenhire	90	72	.556	4.0
	Oakland (W)	Ken Macha	96	66	.593	3.0
2004	New York (E)	Joe Torre	101	61	.623	3.0
	Minnesota (C)	Ron Gardenhire	92	70	.568	9.0
	Anaheim (W)	Mike Scioscia	92	70	.568	1.0

†defeated Boston in 1-game playoff; ‡defeated Boston in 1-game playoff to win division; §first half 34-22, second half 25-26; §§first half 37-23, second half 27-22; ∞New York finished the strike-shortened season with the league's best record (70-43, .619). ††defeated California in 1-game playoff to win division

NATIONAL LEAGUE

Year	Club	Manager	W	L	Pct.	GA
1876	Chicago	Al Spalding	52	14	.788	6.0
1877	Boston	Harry Wright	31	17	.646	3.0
1878	Boston	Harry Wright	41	19	.683	4.0
1879	Providence	George Wright	55	23	.705	6.0
1880	Chicago	Cap Anson	67	17	.798	15.0
1881	Chicago	Cap Anson	56	28	.667	9.0
1882	Chicago	Cap Anson	55	29	.655	3.0
1883	Boston	John Morrill	63	35	.643	4.0
1884	Providence	Frank Bancroft	84	28	.750	10.5
1885	Chicago	Cap Anson	87	25	.777	2.0
1886	Chicago	Cap Anson	90	34	.726	2.5
1887	Detroit	Bill Watkins	79	45	.637	3.5
1888	New York	Jim Mutrie	84	47	.641	9.0
1889	New York	Jim Mutrie	83	43	.659	1.0
1890	Brooklyn	Bill McGunnigle	86	43	.667	6.5
1891	Boston	Frank Selee	87	51	.630	3.5
1892	Boston*	Frank Selee	102	48	.680	8.5
1893	Boston	Frank Selee	86	43	.667	5.0
1894	Baltimore	Ned Hanlon	89	39	.695	3.0
1895	Baltimore	Ned Hanlon	87	43	.669	3.0
1896	Baltimore	Ned Hanlon	90	39	.698	9.5
1897	Boston	Frank Selee	93	39	.705	2.0
1898	Boston	Frank Selee	102	47	.685	6.0
1899	Brooklyn	Ned Hanlon	88	42	.677	4.0
1900	Brooklyn	Ned Hanlon	82	54	.603	4.5
1901	Pittsburgh	Fred Clarke	90	49	.647	7.5
1902	Pittsburgh	Fred Clarke	103	36	.741	27.5
1903	Pittsburgh	Fred Clarke	91	49	.650	6.5
1904	New York	John McGraw	106	47	.693	13.0
1905	New York	John McGraw	105	48	.686	9.0
1906	Chicago	Frank Chance	116	36	.763	20.0
1907	Chicago	Frank Chance	107	45	.704	17.0
1908	Chicago	Frank Chance	99	55	.643	1.0
1909	Pittsburgh	Fred Clarke	110	42	.724	6.5
1910	Chicago	Frank Chance	104	50	.675	13.0
1911	New York	John McGraw	99	54	.647	7.5
1912	New York	John McGraw	103	48	.682	10.0
1913	New York	John McGraw	101	51	.664	12.5
1914	Boston	George Stallings	94	59	.614	10.5
1915	Philadelphia	Pat Moran	90	62	.592	7.0
1916	Brooklyn	Wilbert Robinson	94	60	.610	2.5
1917	New York	John McGraw	98	56	.636	10.0
1918	Chicago	Fred Mitchell	84	45	.651	10.5
1919	Cincinnati	Pat Moran	96	44	.686	9.0
1920	Brooklyn	Wilbert Robinson	93	61	.604	7.0
1921	New York	John McGraw	94	59	.614	4.0
1922	New York	John McGraw	93	61	.604	7.0
1923	New York	John McGraw	95	58	.621	4.5
1924	New York	John McGraw	93	60	.608	1.5
1925	Pittsburgh	Bill McKechnie	95	58	.621	8.5
1926	St. Louis	Rogers Hornsby	89	65	.578	2.0
1927	Pittsburgh	Donie Bush	94	60	.610	1.5
1928	St. Louis	Bill McKechnie	95	59	.617	2.0
1929	Chicago	Joe McCarthy	98	54	.645	10.5
1930	St. Louis	Gabby Street	92	62	.597	2.0
1931	St. Louis	Gabby Street	101	53	.656	13.0
1932	Chicago	Rogers Hornsby, Charlie Grimm	90	64	.584	4.0
1933	New York	Bill Terry	91	61	.599	5.0
1934	St. Louis	Frankie Frisch	95	58	.621	2.0
1935	Chicago	Charlie Grimm	100	54	.649	4.0
1936	New York	Bill Terry	92	62	.597	5.0
1937	New York	Bill Terry	95	57	.625	3.0
1938	Chicago	Charlie Grimm, Gabby Hartnett	89	63	.586	2.0
1939	Cincinnati	Bill McKechnie	97	57	.630	4.5
1940	Cincinnati	Bill McKechnie	100	53	.654	12.0
1941	Brooklyn	Leo Durocher	100	54	.649	2.5
1942	St. Louis	Billy Southworth	106	48	.688	2.0
1943	St. Louis	Billy Southworth	105	49	.682	18.0
1944	St. Louis	Billy Southworth	105	49	.682	14.5
1945	Chicago	Charlie Grimm	98	56	.636	3.0
1946	St. Louis†	Eddie Dyer	98	58	.628	2.0
1947	Brooklyn	Burt Shotton	94	60	.610	5.0
1948	Boston	Billy Southworth	91	62	.595	6.5
1949	Brooklyn	Burt Shotton	97	57	.630	1.0
1950	Philadelphia	Eddie Sawyer	91	63	.591	2.0
1951	New York‡	Leo Durocher	98	59	.624	1.0
1952	Brooklyn	Charlie Dressen	96	57	.627	4.5
1953	Brooklyn	Charlie Dressen	105	49	.682	13.0
1954	New York	Leo Durocher	97	57	.630	5.0
1955	Brooklyn	Walter Alston	98	55	.641	13.5
1956	Brooklyn	Walter Alston	93	61	.604	1.0
1957	Milwaukee	Fred Haney	95	59	.617	8.0
1958	Milwaukee	Fred Haney	92	62	.597	8.0
1959	Los Angeles††	Walter Alston	88	68	.564	2.0
1960	Pittsburgh	Danny Murtaugh	95	59	.617	7.0
1961	Cincinnati	Fred Hutchinson	93	61	.604	4.0
1962	San Francisco‡‡	Alvin Dark	103	62	.624	1.0
1963	Los Angeles	Walter Alston	99	63	.611	6.0

Year	Club	Manager	W	L	Pct.	GA
1964	St. Louis	Johnny Keane	93	69	.574	1.0
1965	Los Angeles	Walter Alston	97	65	.599	2.0
1966	Los Angeles	Walter Alston	95	67	.586	1.5
1967	St. Louis	Red Schoendienst	101	60	.627	10.5
1968	St. Louis	Red Schoendienst	97	65	.599	9.0
1969	New York (E)	Gil Hodges	100	62	.617	8.0
	Atlanta (W)	Lum Harris	93	69	.574	3.0
1970	Pittsburgh (E)	Danny Murtaugh	89	73	.549	5.0
	Cincinnati (W)	Sparky Anderson	102	60	.630	14.5
1971	Pittsburgh (E)	Danny Murtaugh	97	65	.599	7.0
	San Francisco (W)	Charlie Fox	90	72	.556	1.0
1972	Pittsburgh (E)	Bill Virdon	96	59	.619	11.0
	Cincinnati (W)	Sparky Anderson	95	59	.617	10.5
1973	New York (E)	Yogi Berra	82	79	.509	1.5
	Cincinnati (W)	Sparky Anderson	99	63	.611	3.5
1974	Pittsburgh (E)	Danny Murtaugh	88	74	.543	1.5
	Los Angeles (W)	Walter Alston	102	60	.630	4.0
1975	Pittsburgh (E)	Danny Murtaugh	92	69	.571	6.5
	Cincinnati (W)	Sparky Anderson	108	54	.667	20.0
1976	Philadelphia (E)	Danny Ozark	101	61	.623	9.0
	Cincinnati (W)	Sparky Anderson	102	60	.630	10.0
1977	Philadelphia (E)	Danny Ozark	101	61	.623	5.0
	Los Angeles (W)	Tommy Lasorda	98	64	.605	10.0
1978	Philadelphia (E)	Danny Ozark	90	72	.556	1.5
	Los Angeles (W)	Tommy Lasorda	95	67	.586	2.5
1979	Pittsburgh (E)	Chuck Tanner	98	64	.605	2.0
	Cincinnati (W)	John McNamara	90	71	.559	1.5
1980	Philadelphia (E)	Dallas Green	91	71	.562	1.0
	Houston (W)**	Bill Virdon	93	70	.571	1.0
1981	Montreal (E)	Dick Williams, Jim Fanning	60	48	.556	§
	Los Angeles (W)	Tommy Lasorda	63	47	.573	§§
1982	St. Louis (E)	Whitey Herzog	92	70	.568	3.0
	Atlanta (W)	Joe Torre	89	73	.549	1.0
1983	Philadelphia (E)	Pat Corrales, Paul Owens	90	72	.556	6.0
	Los Angeles (W)	Tommy Lasorda	91	71	.562	3.0
1984	Chicago (E)	Jim Frey	96	65	.596	6.5
	San Diego (W)	Dick Williams	92	70	.568	12.0
1985	St. Louis (E)	Whitey Herzog	101	61	.623	3.0
	Los Angeles (W)	Tommy Lasorda	95	67	.586	5.5
1986	New York (E)	Davey Johnson	108	54	.667	21.5
	Houston (W)	Hal Lanier	96	66	.593	10.0
1987	St. Louis (E)	Whitey Herzog	95	67	.586	3.0
	San Francisco (W)	Roger Craig	90	72	.556	6.0
1988	New York (E)	Davey Johnson	100	60	.625	15.0
	Los Angeles (W)	Tommy Lasorda	94	67	.584	7.0
1989	Chicago (E)	Don Zimmer	93	69	.571	6.0
	San Francisco (W)	Roger Craig	92	70	.568	3.0
1990	Pittsburgh (E)	Jim Leyland	95	67	.586	4.0
	Cincinnati (W)	Lou Piniella	91	71	.562	5.0
1991	Pittsburgh	Jim Leyland	98	64	.605	14.0
	Atlanta (W)	Bobby Cox	94	68	.580	1.0
1992	Pittsburgh (E)	Jim Leyland	96	66	.593	9.0
	Atlanta (W)	Bobby Cox	98	64	.605	8.0
1993	Philadelphia (E)	Jim Fregosi	97	65	.599	3.0
	Atlanta (W)	Bobby Cox	104	58	.642	1.0
1994	no pennant winner∞					
1995	Atlanta (E)	Bobby Cox	90	54	.625	21.0
	Cincinnati (C)	Davey Johnson	85	59	.590	9.0
	Los Angeles (W)	Tommy Lasorda	78	66	.542	1.0
1996	Atlanta (E)	Bobby Cox	96	66	.593	8.0
	St.Louis (C)	Tony La Russa	88	74	.543	6.0
	San Diego (W)	Bruce Bochy	91	71	.562	1.0
1997	Atlanta (E)	Bobby Cox	101	61	.623	9.0
	Houston (C)	Larry Dierker	84	78	.519	5.0
	San Francisco (W)	Dusty Baker	90	72	.556	2.0
1998	Atlanta (E)	Bobby Cox	106	56	.654	18.0
	Houston (C)	Larry Dierker	102	60	.630	12.5
	San Diego (W)	Bruce Bochy	98	64	.605	9.5
1999	Atlanta (E)	Bobby Cox	103	59	.636	6.5
	Houston (C)	Larry Dierker	97	65	.599	1.5
	Arizona (W)	Buck Showalter	100	62	.617	14.0
2000	Atlanta (E)	Bobby Cox	95	67	.586	1.0
	St. Louis (C)	Tony La Russa	95	67	.586	10.0
	San Francisco (W)	Dusty Baker	97	65	.599	11.0
2001	Atlanta (E)	Bobby Cox	88	74	.543	2.0
	Houston (C)***	Larry Dierker	93	69	.574	(tie)
	Arizona (W)	Bob Brenly	92	70	.568	2.0
2002	Atlanta (E)	Bobby Cox	101	59	.631	19.0
	St. Louis (C)	Tony La Russa	97	65	.599	13.0
	Arizona (W)	Bob Brenly	98	64	.605	2.5
2003	Atlanta (E)	Bobby Cox	101	61	.623	10.0
	Chicago (C)	Dusty Baker	88	74	.543	1.0
	San Francisco (W)	Felipe Alou	100	61	.621	15.5
2004	Atlanta (E)	Bobby Cox	96	66	.593	10.0
	St. Louis (C)	Tony La Russa	105	57	.648	13.0
	Los Angeles (W)	Jim Tracy	93	69	.574	2.0

*Boston won first half, Cleveland won second half, and Boston won playoff, 5 games to none (1 tie); †defeated Brooklyn in playoff, 2 games to none; ‡defeated Brooklyn in playoff, 2 games to 1; ††defeated Milwaukee in playoff, 2 games to none; ‡‡defeated Los Angeles in playoff, 2 games to 1; **defeated Los Angeles in 1-game playoff to win division; §first half 30-25, second half 30-23; §§first half 36-21, second half 27-26; ∞Montreal finished the strike-shortened season with the league's best record (74-40, .649); ***awarded division title over St. Louis by tie-breaker

INDIVIDUAL SERVICE

ALL PLAYERS
YEARS

Most years played
M.L.—27—Nolan Ryan, New York N.L., California A.L., Houston N.L., Texas A.L.; 1966 through 1993, except 1967 (14 in N.L., 13 in A.L.), 807 games.
A.L.—25—Eddie Collins, Philadelphia, Chicago, 1906 through 1930, 2,826 games.
N.L.—24—Pete Rose, Cincinnati, Philadelphia, Montreal, 1963 through 1986, 3,562 games.

For complete lists of 20-year players and pitchers, see page 151.

Most consecutive years played
M.L.—26—Nolan Ryan, New York N.L., California A.L., Houston N.L., Texas A.L.; 1968 through 1993 (13 in N.L., 13 in A.L.), 805 games.
A.L.—25—Eddie Collins, Philadelphia, Chicago, 1906 through 1930, 2,826 games.
N.L.—24—Pete Rose, Cincinnati, Philadelphia, Montreal, 1963 through 1986, 3,562 games.

Most years with one club
A.L.—23—Brooks Robinson, Baltimore, 1955 through 1977, 2,896 games.
Carl Yastrzemski, Boston, 1961 through 1983, 3,308 games.
N.L.—22—Cap Anson, Chicago, 1876 through 1897, 2,253 games.
Mel Ott, New York, 1926 through 1947, 2,730 games.
Stan Musial, St. Louis, 1941 through 1963, except 1945 in military service, 3,026 games.

Most consecutive years with one club
A.L.—23—Brooks Robinson, Baltimore, 1955 through 1977, 2,896 games.
Carl Yastrzemski, Boston, 1961 through 1983, 3,308 games.
N.L.—22—Cap Anson, Chicago, 1876 through 1897, 2,253 games.
Mel Ott, New York, 1926 through 1947, 2,730 games.
(Military service in 1945 interrupted a 22-year streak by Stan Musial, who played for St. Louis from 1941 through 1963, 3,026 games.)

BY POSITION (EXCEPT PITCHERS)

Most years by first baseman
N.L.—22—Willie McCovey, San Francisco, San Diego, 1959 through 1980, 2,045 games.
A.L.—20—Joe Judge, Washington, Boston, 1915 through 1934, 2,084 games.

Most years by second baseman
M.L.—22—Joe Morgan, Houston N.L., Cincinnati N.L., San Francisco N.L., Philadelphia N.L., Oakland A.L., 1963 through 1984, 2,527 games.
A.L.—21—Eddie Collins, Philadelphia, Chicago, 1908 through 1928, 2,651 games.
N.L.—21—Joe Morgan, Houston, Cincinnati, San Francisco, Philadelphia, 1963 through 1983, 2,427 games.

Most years by third baseman
A.L.—23—Brooks Robinson, Baltimore, 1955 through 1977, 2,870 games.
N.L.—18—Mike Schmidt, Philadelphia, 1972 through 1989, 2,212 games.

Most years by shortstop
M.L.—20—Bill Dahlen, Chicago N.L., Brooklyn N.L., New York N.L., Boston N.L., 1891 through 1911, except 1910, 2,139 games.
Bobby Wallace, St. Louis N.L., St. Louis A.L., 1899 through 1918, 1,828 games.
Luke Appling, Chicago A.L., 1930 through 1950, except 1944 in military service, 2,218 games.
Alan Trammell, Detroit, 1977 through 1996, 2,139 games.
A.L.—20—Luke Appling, Chicago, 1930 through 1950, except

1944 in military service, 2,219 games.
Alan Trammell, Detroit, 1977 through 1996, 2,139 games.
N.L.—20—Bill Dahlen, Chicago, Brooklyn, New York, Boston, 1891 through 1911, except 1910, 2,139 games.
N.L. since 1900—19—Rabbit Maranville, Boston, Pittsburgh, Chicago, Brooklyn, St. Louis, 1912 through 1931, except 1924, 2,153 games.
Dave Concepcion, Cincinnati, 1970 through 1988, 2,178 games.
Chris Speier, San Francisco, Montreal, St. Louis, Chicago, 1971 through 1989, 1,888 games.
Ozzie Smith, San Diego, St. Louis, 1978 through 1996, 2,511 games.

Most years by outfielder
M.L.—25—Rickey Henderson, Oakland A.L., New York A.L., Toronto A.L., San Diego N.L., Anaheim A.L., New York N.L., Seattle A.L., Boston A.L., Los Angeles N.L., 1979 through 2003, 2,826 games.
A.L.—24—Ty Cobb, Detroit, Philadelphia, 1905 through 1928, 2,938 games.
N.L.—22—Willie Mays, New York Giants, San Francisco, New York Mets, 1951 through 1973, except 1953 in military service, 2,843 games.

Most years by catcher
M.L.—25—Deacon McGuire, Toledo, Cleveland, Rochester, Washington A.A.; Detroit, Philadelphia, Washington, Brooklyn N.L.; Detroit, New York, Boston, Cleveland A.L., 1884 through 1912, except 1889, 1908, 1909, 1911, 1,608 games.
A.L.—24—Carlton Fisk, Boston, Chicago, 1969 through 1993, except 1970, 2,226 games.
N.L.—21—Bob O'Farrell, Chicago, St. Louis, New York, Cincinnati, 1915 through 1935, 1,338 games.

YOUNGEST AND OLDEST PLAYERS

Youngest player, game
N.L.—15 years, 10 months, 11 days—Joe Nuxhall, Cincinnati, June 10, 1944 (pitcher).
A.L.—16 years, 8 months, 5 days—Carl Scheib, Philadelphia, September 6, 1943, second game (pitcher).

Oldest player, game
A.L.—59 years, 2 months, 18 days—Satchel Paige, Kansas City, September 25, 1965 (pitcher).
N.L.—52 years, 29 days—Jim O'Rourke, New York, September 22, 1904 (catcher).

LEAGUES AND CLUBS

Most leagues played for, career
4— Held by 20 players. Last time—Lave Cross, A.A., P.L., N.L., A.L., 1887 through 1907, 21 years, 2,259 games.

Most leagues played for, season
3— Willie Murphy, 1884, N.L., A.A., U.A.
Walter Prince, 1884, N.L., A.A., U.A.
George Strief, 1884, A.A., U.A., N.L.

Most clubs played for, career
M.L.—12—Deacon McGuire, Toledo, Cleveland, Rochester, Washington, A.A.; Detroit, Philadelphia, Washington, Brooklyn N.L.; Detroit, New York, Boston, Cleveland A.L.; 1884 to 1912, except 1889, 1909, 1911.
Mike Morgan, Oakland A.L., New York A.L., Toronto A.L., Seattle A.L., Baltimore A.L., Los Angeles N.L., Chicago N.L., St. Louis N.L., Cincinnati N.L., Minnesota A.L., Texas A.L., Arizona N.L., 1978 through 2001, except 1980, 1981 and 1984, 21 years.
N.L.—9—Dan Brouthers, Troy, Buffalo, Detroit, Boston, Brooklyn, Baltimore, Louisville, Philadelphia, New York, 1879 through 1889, 1892 through 1896, 1904, 17 years.
N.L. since 1899—7—Jack Barry, Washington, Boston, Philadelphia, Chicago, Cincinnati, St. Louis, New York, 1899 through 1908, 10 years.
Joe Schultz Sr., Boston, Brooklyn, Chicago, Pittsburgh, St. Louis, Philadelphia, Cincinnati, 1912 through 1925, except 1914, 1917 and 1918, 11 years.
Frank J. Thomas, Pittsburgh, Cincinnati, Chicago, Milwaukee, New York, Philadelphia, Houston, 1951 through 1966, 16 years.

A.L.—8—Juan Beniquez, Boston, Texas, New York, Seattle, California, Baltimore, Kansas City, Toronto, 1971 through 1988, except 1973, 17 years.

Most clubs played for, season
M.L.—4—Held by many players. Last player—Dave Martinez, Tampa Bay A.L., Chicago N.L., Texas A.L., Toronto A.L., 132 games, 2000.
N.L.—4—Tom Dowse, Louisville, Cincinnati, Philadelphia, Washington, 63 games, 1892.
A.L.—4—Frank Huelsman, Chicago, Detroit, St. Louis, Washington, 112 games, 1904.
Paul Lehner, Philadelphia, Chicago, St. Louis, Cleveland, 65 games, 1951.
Ted Gray, Chicago, Cleveland, New York, Baltimore, 14 games, 1955.

Most clubs played for, one day
N.L.—2—Max Flack, Chicago, St. Louis, May 30 a.m., p.m., 1922.
Cliff Heathcote, St. Louis, Chicago, May 30 a.m., p.m., 1922.
Joel Youngblood, New York, Montreal, August 4, 1982.

POSITIONS

Most positions played, season
N.L.—9—Sport McAllister, Cleveland, 110 games, 1899.
Jimmy M.T. Walsh, Philadelphia, 84 games, 1911.
Gene Paulette, St. Louis, 125 games, 1918.
Jose Oquendo, St. Louis, 148 games, 1988.
A.L.—9—Sam Mertes, Chicago, 129 games, 1902.
Jack Rothrock, Boston, 117 games, 1928.
Bert Campaneris, Kansas City, 144 games, 1965.
Cesar Tovar, Minnesota, 157 games, 1968.
Scott Sheldon, Texas, 58 games, 2000.
Shane Halter, Detroit, 105 games, 2000.

Most positions played, game
A.L.—9—Bert Campaneris, Kansas City, September 8, 1965; played 8.2 innings of 13-inning game.
Cesar Tovar, Minnesota, September 22, 1968.
Scott Sheldon, Texas, September 6, 2000; played six innings of nine-inning game.
Shane Halter, Detroit, October 1, 2000.

PITCHERS
YEARS

Most years pitched
M.L.—27—Nolan Ryan, New York N.L., California A.L., Houston N.L., Texas A.L., 1966 through 1993, except 1967, 807 games.
A.L.—23—Early Wynn, Washington, Cleveland, Chicago, 1939, 1941 through 1963, except 1945, in military service, 691 games.
N.L.—22—Steve Carlton, St. Louis, Philadelphia, San Francisco, 1965 through 1986, 695 games.

For a complete list of 20-year pitchers, see page 151.

Most consecutive years pitched
M.L.—26—Nolan Ryan, New York N.L., California A.L., Houston N.L., Texas A.L., 1968 through 1993.
A.L.—22—Samuel P. Jones, Cleveland, Boston, New York, St. Louis, Washington, Chicago, 1914 through 1935.
(Military service in 1918 interrupted a 22-year streak by Herb Pennock, who pitched for Philadelphia, Boston and New York from 1912 through 1934; military service in 1945 interrupted a 22-year streak by Early Wynn, who pitched for Washington, Cleveland and Chicago from 1941 through 1963; military service in 1943 and 1944 interrupted a 22-year streak by Red Ruffing, who pitched for Boston, New York and Chicago from 1924 through 1947.)
N.L.—22—Steve Carlton, St. Louis, Philadelphia, San Francisco,

1965 through 1986.

Most years pitched with one club
A.L.—21—Walter Johnson, Washington, 1907 through 1927, 802 games.
Ted Lyons, Chicago, 1923 through 1946, except 1943,1944, 1945, in military service, 594 games.
N.L.—21—Phil Niekro, Milwaukee, Atlanta, 1964 through 1983, 1987, 740 games.

Most consecutive years pitched with one club
A.L.—21—Walter Johnson, Washington, 1907 through 1927, 802 games.
(Military service from 1943 through 1945 interrupted a 21-year streak by Ted Lyons, who pitched for Chicago from 1923 through 1946, 594 games.)
N.L.—20—Phil Niekro, Milwaukee, Atlanta, 1964 through 1983, 739 games.
(Military service from 1943 through 1945 interrupted a 20-year streak for Warren Spahn, who pitched for Boston and Milwaukee from 1942 through 1964, 714 games.)

YOUNGEST AND OLDEST PITCHERS

Youngest pitcher, game
N.L.—15 years, 10 months, 11 days—Joe Nuxhall, Cincinnati, June 10, 1944.
A.L.—16 years, 8 months, 5 days—Carl Scheib, Philadelphia, September 6, 1943, second game.

Oldest pitcher, game
A.L.—60 years, 2 months, 18 days—Satchel Paige, Kansas City, September 25, 1965.
N.L.—50 years, 2 days—Jack Quinn, Cincinnati, July 7, 1933.

LEAGUES AND CLUBS

Most leagues pitched in
4— Jersey Bakely, A.A., U.A., N.L., P.L.
Ed Crane, U.A., N.L., P.L., A.A.
Frank Foreman, U.A., A.A., N.L., A.L.
Con Murphy, U.A., N.L., P.L., A.A.

Most clubs pitched on
M.L.—12—Mike Morgan, Oakland A.L., New York A.L., Toronto A.L., Seattle A.L., Baltimore A.L., Los Angeles N.L., Chicago N.L., St. Louis N.L., Cincinnati N.L., Minnesota A.L., Texas A.L., Arizona N.L., 1978 through 2002, except 1980, 1981 and 1984, 22 years, 597 games.
A.L.—7—Ken Sanders, Kansas City Athletics, 1964, Boston, Kansas City Athletics, 1966, Oakland, 1968, Milwaukee 1970, 1971, 1972, Minnesota, 1973, Cleveland, 1973, 1974, California, 1974, Kansas City Royals, 1976, 9 years, 348 games. (Note: Kansas City Athletics and Oakland are same franchise, not separate clubs).
Ken Brett, Boston, Milwaukee, New York, Chicago, California, Minnesota, Kansas City, 1967, 1969 through 1972, 1976 through 1981, 11 years, 238 games.
Mike Morgan, Oakland, New York, Toronto, Seattle, Baltimore, Minnesota, Texas, 1978, 1979, 1982, 1983, 1985 through 1988, 1998, 1999, 10 years, 209 games.
N.L.—7—Mike Maddux, Philadelphia, Los Angeles, San Diego, New York, Pittsburgh, Montreal, Houston, 1986 through 1995, 1998 through 2000, 13 years, 407 games.

Most clubs pitched on, season
M.L.—4—Willis Hudlin, Cleveland A.L., Washington A.L., St. Louis A.L., New York N.L., 19 games, 1940.
Ted Gray, Chicago A.L., Cleveland A.L., New York A.L., Baltimore A.L., 14 games, 1955.
Mike Kilkenny, Detroit A.L., Oakland A.L., San Diego N.L., Cleveland A.L., 29 games, 1972.
A.L.—4—Ted Gray, Chicago, Cleveland, New York, Baltimore, 14 games, 1955.
N.L.—3—Held by many pitchers. Last pitcher—Willie Banks, Chicago, Los Angeles, Florida, 25 games, 1995.

CLUB SERVICE

PLAYERS USED

Most players used, season
A.L.—59—Cleveland, 2002.
N.L.—59—San Diego, 2002.

Fewest players used, season
N.L.—17—Boston, 1903.
A.L.—18—Boston, 1904.

Most players used, game
A.L.—27—Kansas City vs. California, September 10, 1969.
  (30—Oakland vs. Chicago, September 19, 1972, 15 innings.)
N.L.—25—St. Louis vs. Los Angeles, April 16, 1959.
  Milwaukee vs. Philadelphia, September 26, 1964.
  Philadelphia vs. Chicago, September 27, 1981, second game.
  (27—Philadelphia vs. St. Louis, September 13, 1974, 17 innings.
  Chicago vs. Pittsburgh, September 21, 1978, 14 innings.
  Chicago vs. Houston, September 2, finished September 3, 1986, 18 innings.
  Los Angeles vs. San Francisco, September 28, 1986, 16 innings.)

Most players used by both clubs, game
N.L.—45—Chicago 24, Montreal 21, September 5, 1978.
  Atlanta 24, New York 21, September 29, 2002.
  (53—Chicago 27, Houston 26, September 2, finished September 3, 1986, 18 innings.)
A.L.—44—Oakland 23, Seattle 21, September 21, 2003.
  (54—Seattle 29, Texas 25, September 25, 1992, 16 innings.)

Most players used, doubleheader
A.L.—41—Chicago vs. Oakland, September 7, 1970.
N.L.—41—San Diego vs. San Francisco, May 30, 1977.
  (42—St. Louis vs. Brooklyn, August 29, 1948, 19 innings.
  Montreal vs. Pittsburgh, September 5, 1975, 19 innings.)

Most players used by both clubs, doubleheader
N.L.—74—San Diego 41, San Francisco 33, May 30, 1977.
  (74—Montreal 42, Pittsburgh 32, September 5, 1975, 19 innings.)
A.L.—71—New York 39, Baltimore 32, September 26, 2003.
  (73—Washington 37, Cleveland 36, September 14, finished September 20, 1971, 29 innings.)

PINCH-HITTERS

Most pinch-hitters used, game
N.L.—9—Los Angeles vs. St. Louis, September 22, 1959.
  Montreal vs. Pittsburgh, September 5, 1975, second game.
  Atlanta vs. Montreal, September 21, 1993.
  (9—San Francisco vs. Los Angeles, September 28, 1986, 16 innings.
  St. Louis vs. Cincinnati, September 25, 1997, 14 innings.)
A.L.—8—Baltimore vs. Chicago, May 28, 1954, first game.
  (10—Oakland vs. Chicago, September 19, 1972, 15 innings.)

Most pinch-hitters used by both clubs, game
N.L.—13—Atlanta 9, Montreal 4, September 21, 1993.
  (14—New York 7, Chicago 7, May 2, 1956, 17 innings.
  San Francisco 9, Los Angeles 5, September 28, 1986, 16 innings.)
A.L.—10—Baltimore 6, New York 4, April 26, 1959, second game.
  (14—Oakland 10, Chicago 4, September 19, 1972, 15 innings.)

Most pinch-hitters used, doubleheader
A.L.—10—New York vs. Boston, September 6, 1954.
  Baltimore vs. Washington, April 19, 1959.
N.L.—10—St. Louis vs. Chicago, May 11, 1958.
  St. Louis vs. Pittsburgh, July 13, 1958.
  (15—Montreal vs. Pittsburgh, September 5, 1975, 19 innings.)

Most pinch-hitters used by both clubs, doubleheader
N.L.—15—Milwaukee 8, San Francisco 7, August 30, 1964.
  (19—Montreal 15, Pittsburgh 4, September 5, 1975, 19 innings.)
A.L.—14—New York 10, Boston 4, September 6, 1954.
  (17—New York 9, Washington 8, August 14, 1960, 24 innings.)

Most pinch-hitters used, inning
N.L.—6—San Francisco vs. Pittsburgh, May 5, 1958, ninth inning.
  San Diego vs. San Francisco, September 16, 1986, ninth inning.
  Atlanta vs. Montreal, September 21, 1993, seventh inning.
  Los Angeles vs. Colorado, September 24, 2002, sixth inning.

A.L.—6—Detroit vs. New York, September 5, 1971, seventh inning.

Most consecutive pinch-hitters used, inning
N.L.-A.L.—5—Made in many innings.
  Last N.L. time—Chicago vs. Pittsburgh, September 20, 1996, eighth inning.
  Last A.L. time—New York vs. Milwaukee, September 22, 1987, first game, eighth inning.

Most pinch-hitters used by both clubs, inning
A.L.—8—Chicago 5, Baltimore 3, May 18, 1957, seventh inning.
N.L.—8—Philadelphia 5, St. Louis 3, April 30, 1961, eighth inning.
  New York 5, San Francisco 3, September 16, 1966, ninth inning.

PINCH-RUNNERS

Most pinch-runners used, inning
A.L.—4—Chicago vs. Minnesota, September 16, 1967, ninth inning.
  Oakland vs. Chicago, September 24, 1975, seventh inning.
  Texas vs. California, September 10, 1987, ninth inning.
  Anaheim vs. Texas, September 23, 2000, seventh inning.
N.L.—4—Montreal vs. St. Louis, September 26, 1977, ninth inning.
  San Diego vs. Cincinnati, August 10, 1978, seventh inning.

Most pinch-runners used by both clubs, inning
N.L.—5—Pittsburgh 3, New York 2, September 21, 1981, ninth inning.
A.L.—5—Anaheim 4, Texas 1, September 23, 2000, seventh inning.

NUMBER OF PLAYERS USED BY POSITION
INFIELDERS

Most first basemen used, game
A.L.—5—Chicago vs. New York, June 25, 1953.
N.L.—4—New York vs. Arizona, May 11, 2004.
  New York vs. Philadelphia, July 7, 2004.
  Los Angeles vs. Arizona, July 17, 2004.
  (4—Philadelphia vs. Milwaukee, July 23, 1964, 10 innings.
  Cincinnati vs. Chicago, May 28, 2001, 13 innings

Most first basemen used by both clubs, game
A.L.—6—Chicago 5, New York 1, June 25, 1953.
N.L.—6—Cincinnati 3, New York 3, July 1, 2004.
  New York 4, Philadelphia 2, July 7, 2004.
  (6—Cincinnati 4, Chicago 2, May 28, 2001, 13 innings.)

Most second basemen used, game
A.L.—4—Made in many games.
  (6—Oakland vs. Chicago, September 19, 1972, 15 innings.)
N.L.—4—Made in many games.
  (5—New York vs. Cincinnati, July 20, 1954, 13 innings.)

Most second basemen used by both clubs, game
A.L.—6—Oakland 4, Cleveland 2, May 5, 1973.
  Oakland 4, Cleveland 2, May 6, 1973, first game.
  Oakland 4, Cleveland 2, May 6, 1973, second game.
  (8—Oakland 6, Chicago 2, September 19, 1972, 15 innings.)
N.L.—5—Brooklyn 4, New York 1, April 21, 1948.
  Chicago 4, New York 1, August 21, 1952, second game.
  Houston 3, St. Louis 2, June 15, 1975.
  Montreal 3, Florida 2, July 13, 2003.
  Chicago 4, St. Louis 1, September 3, 2003.
  Los Angeles 3, San Francisco 2, October 3, 2004.
  (7—New York 5, Cincinnati 2, July 20, 1954, 13 innings.)

Most third basemen used, game
N.L.—5—Atlanta vs. Philadelphia, April 21, 1966.
  Philadelphia vs. Pittsburgh, August 6, 1971.
A.L.—4—Held by many clubs.

Most third basemen used by both clubs, game
N.L.—7—Philadelphia 5, Pittsburgh 2, August 6, 1971.
A.L.—5—Minnesota 3, Cleveland 3, July 27, 1969.
  Boston 3, Milwaukee 3, September 14, 1976.
  (6—Detroit 3, Cleveland 3, July 10, 1969, 11 innings.)

Most shortstops used, game
A.L.—4—New York vs. Washington, September 5, 1954.
  Minnesota vs. Oakland, September 22, 1968.

(4—Detroit vs. New York, July 28, 1957, second game, 15 innings.)
Baltimore vs. New York, September 26, 1958, 12 innings.
Texas vs. Seattle, September 25, 1992, 16 innings.)
N.L.—4—San Francisco vs. Cincinnati, September 4, 1989.
(5—Done by many teams in extra innings.)

Most shortstops used by both clubs, game
A.L.—6—Detroit 3, Washington 3, September 21, 1968.
N.L.—5—Cincinnati 3, Houston 2, July 13, 1969.
Montreal 3, Pittsburgh 2, October 1, 1969.
San Francisco 4, Cincinnati 1, September 4, 1989.

OUTFIELDERS

Most right fielders used, game
A.L.—4—Baltimore vs. Washington, September 25, 1955.
(6—Kansas City vs. California, September 8, 1965, 13 innings.)
N.L.—4—Philadelphia vs. St. Louis, June 2, 1928.
Los Angeles vs. Houston, June 10, 1962, first game.
St. Louis vs. Milwaukee, September 17, 2003.
(5—New York vs. Cincinnati, July 22, 1986, 14 innings.)

Most right fielders used by both clubs, game
M.L.—5—Montreal N.L. 3, Anaheim A.L. 2, June 4, 2003.
N.L.—6—Los Angeles 4, Houston 2, June 10, 1962, first game.
(8—San Francisco 4, Los Angeles 4, September 28, 1986, 16 innings.)
A.L.—5—Occurred in many games.
(7—Kansas City 6, California 1, September 8, 1965, 13 innings.)

Most center fielders used, game
A.L.—5—Minnesota vs. Oakland, September 22, 1968.
N.L.—4—Cincinnati vs. St. Louis, May 30, 1942, second game.
(4—Boston vs. Brooklyn, April 25, 1917, 12 innings.
Philadelphia vs. St. Louis, September 25, 1966, 13 innings.
Houston vs. Chicago, September 2, finished September 3, 1986, 18 innings.
Philadelphia vs. Cincinnati, July 20, 1987, 11 innings.)

Most center fielders used by both clubs, game
A.L.—7—Minnesota 5, Oakland 2, September 22, 1968.
N.L.—6—Cincinnati 4, St. Louis 2, May 30, 1942, second game.
New York 3, St. Louis 3, April 30, 2003.
(7—Houston 4, Chicago 3, September 2, finished September 3, 1986, 18 innings.)

Most left fielders used, game
A.L.—5—Seattle vs. Oakland, September 11, 1992.
N.L.—4—Brooklyn vs. Philadelphia, September 26, 1946.
Los Angeles vs. New York, June 4, 1966.
Chicago vs. Philadelphia, September 21, 1977.
Atlanta vs. Philadelphia, September 28, 2003.
St. Louis vs. Milwaukee, October 3, 2004.
(5—Philadelphia vs. Milwaukee, July 23, 1964, 10 innings.)

Most left fielders used by both clubs, game
N.L.—6—New York 3, San Francisco 3, September 22, 1963.
St. Louis 4, Milwaukee 2, October 3, 2004.
(7—Los Angeles 4, St. Louis 3, May 12, 1962, 15 innings.
Chicago 4, St. Louis 3, September 2, 2003, first game, 15 innings.)
A.L.—6—Oakland 4, Cleveland 2, July 20, 1974.
Seattle 5, Oakland 1, September 11, 1992.
(6—Minnesota 3, Baltimore 3, April 16, 1961, second game, 11 innings.
Minnesota 3, Oakland 3, September 6, 1969, 18 innings.)

BATTERY

Most catchers used, game
N.L.—4—Boston vs. New York, October 6, 1929.
Brooklyn vs. St. Louis, May 5, 1940.
New York vs. St. Louis, September 12, 1962.
A.L.—4—Minnesota vs. California, September 27, 1967.
(4—Kansas City vs. Chicago, September 21, 1973, 12 innings.)

Most catchers used by both clubs, game
A.L.—6—Chicago 3, Philadelphia 3, July 10, 1926.
(6—Chicago 3, New York 3, September 10, 1955, 10 innings.
California 3, Oakland 3, September 28, 1969, 11 innings.
Kansas City 4, Chicago 2, September 21, 1972, 12 innings.)
N.L.—6—Boston 4, New York 2, October 6, 1929.
Brooklyn 4, St. Louis 2, May 5, 1940.
New York 4, St. Louis 2, September 2, 1962.

(6—New York 3, Chicago 3, May 2, 1956, 17 innings.)

Most pitchers used, season
N.L.—37—San Diego, 2002.
A.L.—32—Cleveland, 2000.

Fewest pitchers used, season
A.L.—5—Boston, 1904.
N.L.—5—Boston, 1901.

Most relief appearances, season
N.L.—506—Colorado, 2002.
A.L.—494—Texas, 2003.

Most pitchers used, game
A.L.—10—Baltimore vs. New York, September 12, 2004.
(11—Seattle vs. Texas, September 25, 1992, 16 innings.)
N.L.—9—Montreal vs. Chicago, September 10, 1996.
St. Louis vs. Los Angeles, September 8, 2001.
(10—Chicago vs. Pittsburgh, April 20, finished August 11, 1986, 17 innings.
Colorado vs. Atlanta, August 22, 2000, 12 innings.
Atlanta vs. Philadelphia, September 27, 2003, 10 innings.
Philadelphia vs. New York, September 11, 2004, 13 innings.)

Most pitchers used by both clubs, game
N.L.—16—Houston 8, San Francisco 8, September 28, 2002.
(18—Houston 10, Chicago 8, September 28, 1995, 11 innings.
Philadelphia 10, New York 8, September 11, 2004, 13 innings.)
A.L.—15—Detroit 8, Minnesota 7, October 1, 2000.
Baltimore 10, New York 5, September 12, 2004.
(18—Washington 9, Cleveland 9, September 14, finished September 20, 1971, 20 innings.
Seattle 9, Oakland 9, September 20, 1997, 15 innings.)

Most pitchers used by winning club, shutout game
A.L.—8—Boston vs. Baltimore, October 3, 1999, 10 innings (won 1-0).
N.L.—6—Los Angeles vs. Milwaukee, October 3, 1965 (won 3-0).
Florida vs. Chicago, May 15, 1994 (won 3-0).
St. Louis vs. Pittsburgh, May 17, 1994 (won 2-0).
St. Louis vs. Philadelphia, April 19, 1996 (won 1-0).
Florida vs. Philadelphia, June 4, 2002 (won 5-0).

Most pitchers used by winning club, no-hit game
N.L.—6—Houston vs. New York A.L., June 11, 2003 (won 8-0).
A.L.—4—Oakland vs. California, September 28, 1975 (won 5-0).
Baltimore vs. Oakland, July 13, 1991 (won 2-0).

Most pitchers used, doubleheader
N.L.—13—San Diego vs. San Francisco, May 30, 1977.
(13—Milwaukee vs. Philadelphia, May 12, 1963, 23 innings.)
A.L.—12—Cleveland vs. Detroit, September 7, 1959.
California vs. Detroit, September 30, 1967.
(13—Baltimore vs. Texas, August 13, 1991, 21 innings.)

Most pitchers used by both clubs, doubleheader
N.L.—22—Milwaukee 11, New York 11, July 26, 1964.
Chicago 12, Pittsburgh 11, September 19, 2003.
A.L.—21—Detroit 11, Kansas City 10, July 23, 1961.
(22—Washington 12, Cleveland 10, September 14, finished September 20, 1971, 29 innings.)
(M.L.—24—Baltimore A.L. 12, San Francisco N.L. 12, June 12, 2004, 24 innings.)

Most pitchers used, inning
A.L.—6—Oakland vs. Cleveland, September 3, 1983, ninth inning.
N.L.—5—Occurred in many innings. Last time—Philadelphia vs. Atlanta, April 8, 1999, eighth inning.

Most pitchers used by both clubs, inning
N.L.—8—Los Angeles 5, New York 3, August 26, 1987, eighth inning.
A.L.—7—Chicago 4, Baltimore 3, July 16, 1955, ninth inning.
Baltimore 4, Boston 3, June 20, 1975, ninth inning.
Oakland 6, Cleveland 1, September 3, 1983, ninth inning.

FRANCHISE LONGEVITY

Most years in same city by a franchise
N.L.—129—Chicago, 1876 through 2004 (consecutive).
A.L.—104—Boston, Chicago, Cleveland, Detroit, 1901 through 2004 (consecutive).

LEAGUE SERVICE

ALL PLAYERS

Most players, season
N.L. (16 clubs)—699 in 2000.
N.L. (14 clubs)—588 in 1995, 1997.
N.L. (12 clubs)—491 in 1990.
N.L. (10 clubs)—373 in 1967.
N.L. since 1900 (8 clubs)—333 in 1946.
A.L. (14 clubs)—623 in 2004.
A.L. (12 clubs)—440 in 1969.
A.L. (10 clubs)—369 in 1962.
A.L. (8 clubs)—323 in 1955.

Most players in 150 or more games, season
A.L. (14 clubs)—46 in 1998.
A.L. (12 clubs)—32 in 1976.
A.L. (10 clubs)—30 in 1962.
A.L. (8 clubs)—19 in 1921, 1936.
N.L. (16 clubs)—42 in 1998, 2002.
N.L. (14 clubs)—38 in 1997.
N.L. (12 clubs)—40 in 1978, 1979.
N.L. (10 clubs)—34 in 1965.
N.L. since 1900s (8 clubs)—23 in 1953.

Fewest players, season
A.L. (12 clubs)—412 in 1976.
A.L. (8 clubs)—166 in 1904.
N.L. (12 clubs)—420 in 1979.
N.L. since 1900 (8 clubs)—188 in 1905.

Most players playing in all games, season
N.L. since 1900—10 in 1932.
A.L.—10 in 1933.

Fewest players playing in all games, season
A.L.—0—1910, 1963.
N.L. since 1900—0—1914.

Most players with two or more clubs, season
N.L. since 1900—48 in 1998.
A.L.—47 in 1952.

Fewest players with two or more clubs, season
A.L.—2 in 1940.
N.L. since 1900—5 in 1935.

Most players with three or more clubs, season
A.L.—4 in 1952.
N.L. since 1900—3 in 1919.

PITCHERS

Most pitchers in league, season
N.L. (16 clubs)—345 in 2003.
N.L. (14 clubs)—290 in 1995.
N.L. (12 clubs)—228 in 1990.
N.L. (10 clubs)—167 in 1967.
N.L. since 1900 (8 clubs)—152 in 1946.
A.L. (14 clubs)—311 in 2004.
A.L. (12 clubs)—189 in 1970.
A.L. (10 clubs)—170 in 1962.
A.L. (8 clubs)—141 in 1946, 1955.

Most pitchers in league, one day
N.L.—72—September 7, 1964.
A.L.—62—August 9, 1970.

Most pitchers in both leagues, one day
121—September 7, 1964, 72 in N.L. (10 games), 49 in A.L. (eight games).

INDIVIDUAL BATTING

GAMES

Most games, career
N.L.—3,562—Pete Rose, Cincinnati, Philadelphia, Montreal, 24 years, 1963 through 1986.
A.L.—3,308—Carl Yastrzemski, Boston, 23 years, 1961 through 1983.

For a complete list of players playing in 2,400 games in career, see page 151.

Most consecutive games, career
A.L.—2,632—Cal Ripken Jr., Baltimore, May 30, 1982 through September 19, 1998.
N.L.—1,207—Steve Garvey, Los Angeles, San Diego, September 3, 1975, through July 29, 1983, first game.

For a complete list of players playing in 500 consecutive games in career, see page 151.

Most consecutive games from start of career
N.L.—424—Ernie Banks, Chicago, September 17, 1953, through August 10, 1957.
A.L.—394—Al Simmons, Philadelphia, April 15, 1924, through July 20, 1926.

Most games, season
N.L.—165—Maury Wills, Los Angeles, 1962.
A.L.—164—Cesar Tovar, Minnesota, 1967.

Most games with two clubs, season
N.L.—164—Frank Taveras, Pittsburgh, New York, 1979.
A.L.—160—Julio Cruz, Seattle, Chicago, 1983.
Cecil Fielder, Detroit, New York, 1996.

Most games by rookie, season
A.L.—162—Jake Wood, Detroit, 1961.
Bobby Knoop, Los Angeles, 1964.
George Scott, Boston, 1966.
N.L.—162—Dick Allen, Philadelphia, 1964.
Johnny Ray, Pittsburgh, 1982.
Jeff Conine, Florida, 1993.

Most games by righthander, season
N.L.—164—Jose Pagan, San Francisco, 1962.
Ron Santo, Chicago, 1965.
Frank Taveras, Pittsburgh, New York, 1979.
A.L.—164—Cesar Tovar, Minnesota, 1967.

Most games by lefthander, season
N.L.—164—Billy Williams, Chicago, 1965.
A.L.—163—Leon Wagner, Cleveland, 1964.
Al Oliver, Texas, 1980.
Greg Walker, Chicago, 1985.

Most games by switch-hitter, season
N.L.—165—Maury Wills, Los Angeles, 1962.
A.L.—163—Don Buford, Chicago, 1966.
Tony Fernandez, Toronto, 1986.

Most games by pinch-hitter, season
N.L.—95—Lenny Harris, New York, 2001.
A.L.—81—Elmer Valo, New York, Washington, 1960.

Most seasons leading league in games
A.L.—9—Cal Ripken Jr., Baltimore, 1983 (tied), 1984 (tied), 1987, 1989 (tied), 1991 (tied), 1992, 1993, 1996, 1997 (tied).
N.L.—6—Ernie Banks, Chicago, 1954 (tied), 1955 (tied), 1957 (tied), 1958, 1959 (tied), 1960.
Steve Garvey, Los Angeles, 1977 (tied), 1978 (tied), 1980, 1981 (tied), 1982 (tied), San Diego, 1985 (tied).

Most seasons played all club's games
A.L.—15—Cal Ripken Jr., Baltimore, 1983 through 1997 (consecutive).

N.L.—10—Pete Rose, Cincinnati, 1965, 1972, 1974, 1975, 1976, 1977, Philadelphia, 1979, 1980, 1981, 1982.

Most consecutive seasons played all club's games
A.L.—15—Cal Ripken Jr., Baltimore, 1983 through 1997.
N.L.—7—Steve Garvey, Los Angeles, 1976 through 1982.

Most seasons playing 150 or more games
N.L.—17—Pete Rose, Cincinnati, Philadelphia, 1963 through 1983, except 1964, 1967, 1968, 1981.
A.L.—15—Cal Ripken Jr., Baltimore, 1982 through 1998, except 1994 and 1995.

Most consecutive seasons playing 150 or more games
N.L.—13—Willie Mays, New York, San Francisco, 1954 through 1966.
A.L.—12—Cal Ripken Jr., Baltimore, 1982 through 1993.

Most seasons playing 100 or more games
N.L.—23—Pete Rose, Cincinnati, Philadelphia, Montreal, 1963 through 1985.
A.L.—22—Carl Yastrzemski, Boston, 1961 through 1983, except 1981.

Most consecutive seasons playing 100 or more games
N.L.—23—Pete Rose, Cincinnati, Philadelphia, Montreal, 1963 through 1985.
A.L.—20—Carl Yastrzemski, Boston, 1961 through 1980.

Fewest games for leader, season
N.L.—152—Stan Hack, Chicago, 1938.
Billy Herman, Chicago, 1938.
A.L.—154—Held by many players.

BATTING AVERAGE

Highest average, career (15 or more seasons)
A.L.—.366—Ty Cobb, Detroit, Philadelphia, 24 years, 1905 through 1928 (11,434 at-bats, 4,189 hits).
N.L.—.359—Rogers Hornsby, St. Louis, New York, Boston, Chicago, 19 years, 1915 through 1933 (8,058 at-bats, 2,895 hits).

For a complete list of players with .300 career batting averages and 1,500 or more hits, see page 152.

Highest average, season (100 or more games)
N.L.—.440—Hugh Duffy, Boston, 125 games, 1894.
A.A.—.435—Tip O'Neill, St. Louis, 124 games, 1887.
A.L.—.426—Nap Lajoie, Philadelphia, 131 games, 1901.
N.L. since 1900—.424—Rogers Hornsby, St. Louis, 143 games, 1924.

Highest average for non-leader, season (100 or more games)
N.L.—.415—Sam Thompson, Philadelphia, 102 games, 1894.
A.L.—.408—Joe Jackson, Cleveland, 147 games, 1911.
N.L. since 1900—.393—Babe Herman, Brooklyn, 153 games, 1930.

Highest average by rookie, season (100 or more games)
N.L.—.373—George Watkins, St. Louis, 119 games, 1930.
A.L.—.350—Ichiro Suzuki, Seattle, 157 games, 2001.

League leader in batting average, rookie season
A.A.—.378—Pete Browning, Louisville, 69 games, 1882.
A.L.—.323—Tony Oliva, Minnesota, 161 games, 1964.
.350—Ichiro Suzuki, Seattle, 157 games, 2001.
N.L.—Never occurred.

Highest average by righthander, season (100 or more games)
N.L.—.440—Hugh Duffy, Boston, 125 games, 1894.
A.A.—.435—Tip O'Neill, St. Louis, 124 games, 1887.
A.L.—.426—Nap Lajoie, Philadelphia, 131 games, 1910.
N.L. since 1900—.424—Rogers Hornsby, St. Louis, 143 games, 1924.

Highest average by lefthander, season (100 or more games)
N.L.—.424—Willie Keeler, Baltimore, 129 games, 1897.

A.L.—.41979—George Sisler, St. Louis, 142 games, 1922.
(Ty Cobb batted .41962 for Detroit in 146 games in 1911.)
N.L. since 1900—.401—Bill Terry, New York, 154 games, 1930.

Highest average by switch-hitter, season (100 or more games)
A.A.—.372—Tommy Tucker, Baltimore, 134 games, 1889.
A.L.—.365—Mickey Mantle, New York, 144 games, 1957.
N.L.—.355—George Davis, New York, 133 games, 1893.
N.L. since 1900—.353—Willie McGee, St. Louis 152, games, 1985.

Highest average by first baseman, season (100 or more games)
A.L.—.420—George Sisler, St. Louis, 142 games, 1922; 141 games at first base.
N.L.—.401—Bill Terry, New York, 154 games, 1930; 154 games at first base.

Highest average by second baseman, season (100 or more games)
A.L.—.426—Nap Lajoie, Philadelphia, 131 games, 1901; 119 games at second base.
N.L.—.424—Rogers Hornsby, St. Louis, 143 games, 1924; 143 games at second base.

Highest average by third baseman, season (100 or more games)
N.L.—.391—John McGraw, Baltimore, 117 games, 1899; 117 games at third base.
A.L.—.390—George Brett, Kansas City, 117 games, 1980; 112 games at third base.
N.L. since 1900—.379—Fred Lindstrom, New York, 148 games, 1930; 148 games at third base.

Highest average by shortstop, season (100 or more games)
N.L.—.401—Hughie Jennings, Baltimore, 130 games, 1896; 130 games at shortstop.
A.L.—.388—Luke Appling, Chicago, 138 games, 1936; 137 games at shortstop.
N.L. since 1900—.385—Arky Vaughan, Pittsburgh, 137 games, 1935; 137 games at shortstop.

Highest average by outfielder, season (100 or more games)
N.L.—.440—Hugh Duffy, Boston, 125 games, 1894; 124 games in outfield.
A.A.—.435—Tip O'Neill, St. Louis, 124 games, 1887.
A.L.—.420—Ty Cobb, Detroit, 146 games, 1911; 146 games in outfield.
N.L. since 1900—.398—Lefty O'Doul, Philadelphia, 154 games, 1929; 154 games in outfield.

Highest average by catcher, season (100 or more games)
A.L.—.362—Bill Dickey, New York, 112 games, 1936; caught in 107 games.
N.L.—.362—Mike Piazza, Los Angeles, 152 games, 1997; caught in 139 games.

Highest average by pitcher, season (only for games as a pitcher)
A.L.—.440—Walter Johnson, Washington, 36 games, 1925; pitched 30 games.
N.L.—.406—Jack Bentley, New York, 52 games, 1923; pitched 31 games.

Most seasons leading league in batting average
A.L.—12—Ty Cobb, Detroit, 1907, 1908, 1909, 1910, 1911, 1912, 1913, 1914, 1915, 1917, 1918, 1919.
N.L.—8—Honus Wagner, Pittsburgh, 1900, 1903, 1904, 1906, 1907, 1908, 1909, 1911.
Tony Gwynn, San Diego, 1984, 1987, 1988, 1989, 1994, 1995, 1996, 1997.

For a complete list of triple crown winners, see page 162.

Most consecutive seasons leading league in batting average
A.L.—9—Ty Cobb, Detroit, 1907 through 1915.
N.L.—6—Rogers Hornsby, St. Louis, 1920 through 1925.
Most seasons batting .400 or over (50 or more games)
N.L.—3—Ed Delahanty, Philadelphia, 1894, 1895, 1899.

Rogers Hornsby, St. Louis, 1922, 1924, 1925.
A.L.—3—Ty Cobb, Detroit, 1911, 1912, 1922.
Most consecutive seasons batting .400 or over (50 or more games)
N.L.—2—Ed Delahanty, Philadelphia, 1894, 1895.
Jesse Burkett, Cleveland, 1895, 1896.
Rogers Hornsby, St. Louis, 1924, 1925.
A.L.—2—Ty Cobb, Detroit, 1911, 1912.

For a complete list of .400 hitters, see page 162.

Most seasons batting .300 or over (50 or more games)
A.L.—23—Ty Cobb, Detroit, Philadelphia, 1906 through 1928.
N.L.—19—Cap Anson, Chicago, 1876 through 1896, except 1891 and 1892.
N.L. since 1900—18—Tony Gwynn, San Diego, 1983 through 1999, 2001.

For a complete list of batters hitting .300 or better 10 or more times, see page 152.

Most consecutive seasons batting .300 or over (50 or more games)
A.L.—23—Ty Cobb, Detroit, Philadelphia, 1906 through 1928.
N.L.—17—Honus Wagner, Louisville, Pittsburgh, 1897 through 1913.
Tony Gwynn, San Diego, 1983 through 1999.
Most consecutive seasons batting .300 or over from start of career (50 or more games)
N.L.—17—Honus Wagner, Louisville, Pittsburgh, 1897 through 1913.
N.L. since 1900—12—Paul Waner, Pittsburgh, 1926 through 1937.
(Military service in 1945 interrupted a 16-year streak by Stan Musial, who batted .300 for St. Louis from 1942 through 1958.)
A.L.—11—Al Simmons, Philadelphia, Chicago, 1924 through 1934.
(Military service from 1943 through 1945 and most of 1952 and 1953 interrupted a 15-year streak by Ted Williams, who batted .300 for Boston from 1939 through 1958.)
Most seasons batting .300 or over by pitcher
A.L.—8—Red Ruffing, Boston, New York, 1928, 1929, 1930, 1931, 1932, 1935, 1939, 1941.
N.L.—5—Red Lucas, Cincinnati, 1926, 1927, 1928, 1930; Pittsburgh, 1935.
Highest average over five consecutive seasons (100 or more games)
N.L.—.402—Rogers Hornsby, St. Louis, 1921 through 1925.
A.L.—.396—Ty Cobb, Detroit, 1909 through 1913.
Highest average over four consecutive seasons (100 or more games)
N.L.—.404—Rogers Hornsby, St. Louis, 1922 through 1925.
A.L.—.402—Ty Cobb, Detroit, 1910 through 1913.
Highest average over three consecutive seasons (100 or more games)
A.L.—.4084—Ty Cobb, Detroit, 1911, 1912, 1913.
N.L.—.405—Rogers Hornsby, St. Louis, 1923, 1924, 1925.
Highest average over two consecutive seasons (100 or more games)
A.L.—.415—Ty Cobb, Detroit, 1911, 1912.
N.L.—.413—Rogers Hornsby, St. Louis, 1924, 1925.
Lowest average, season (150 or more games)
A.L.—.182—Monte Cross, Philadelphia, 153 games, 1904.
N.L.—.201—Dal Maxvill, St. Louis, 152 games, 1970.
Lowest average for leader, season (100 or more games)
A.L.—.301—Carl Yastrzemski, Boston, 157 games, 1968.
N.L.—.313—Tony Gwynn, San Diego, 133 games, 1988.

ON-BASE PERCENTAGE

Highest on-base percentage, career (15 or more years)
A.L.—.482—Ted Williams, Boston A.L., 19 years, 1939 through 1960, except 1943 through 1945.
N.L.—.443—Barry Bonds, Pittsburgh, San Francisco, 19 years, 1986 through 2004.

Highest on-base percentage, season (100 or more games)
N.L.—.609—Barry Bonds, San Francisco, 147 games, 2004.
A.L.—.553—Ted Williams, Boston, 143 games, 1941.

Highest on-base percentage by rookie, season (100 or more games)
A.L.—.447—Charlie Keller, New York, 111 games, 1939 (If all Keller's 11 sacrifices were sacrifice flies, his OBP would be .437, still the record.)
N.L.—.454—Bernie Carbo, Cincinnati, 125 games, 1970.

Highest on-base percentage by righthander, season (100 or more games)
A.L.—.487—Frank E. Thomas, Chicago, 113 games, 1994.
N.L.—.470—Mark McGwire, St. Louis, 155 games, 1998.

Highest on-base percentage by lefthander, season (100 or more games)
N.L.—.609—Barry Bonds, San Francisco, 147 games, 2004.
A.L.—.553—Ted Williams, Boston, 143 games, 1941.

Highest on-base percentage by switch-hitter, season
A.L.—.512—Mickey Mantle, New York, 144 games, 1957.
N.L.—.449—Augie Galan, Cincinnati, 124 games, 1947.

Lowest on-base percentage, season (100 or more games)
N.L.—.222—Hal Lanier, San Francisco, 151 games, 1968.
A.L.—.201—Juan Bell, Baltimore, 100 games, 1991.

Lowest leading on-base percentage, season (100 or more games)
N.L.—.391—Pete Rose, Cincinnati, 149 games, 1968.
A.L.—.395—Carl Yastrzemski, Boston, 133 games, 1965.

SLUGGING AVERAGE

Highest slugging average, career (15 or more years)
M.L.—.690—Babe Ruth, Boston A.L., New York A.L., Boston N.L., 22 years, 1914 through 1935.
A.L.—.692—Babe Ruth, Boston, New York, 21 years, 1914 through 1934.
N.L.—.611—Barry Bonds, Pittsburgh, San Francisco, 19 years, 1986 through 2004.

For a complete list of career slugging averages of players with 4,000 or more total bases, see page 152.

Highest slugging average, season (100 or more games)
N.L.—.863—Barry Bonds, San Francisco, 153 games, 2001.
A.L.—.847—Babe Ruth, New York, 142 games, 1920.

Highest slugging average by rookie, season (100 or more games)
N.L.—.621—George Watkins, St. Louis, 119 games, 1930.
A.L.—.618—Mark McGwire, Oakland, 151 games, 1987.

Highest slugging average by righthander, season (100 or more games)
N.L.—.756—Rogers Hornsby, St. Louis, 138 games, 1925.
A.L.—.749—Jimmie Foxx, Philadelphia, 154 games, 1932.

Highest slugging average by lefthander, season (100 or more games)
N.L.—.863—Barry Bonds, San Francisco, 153 games, 2001.
A.L.—.847—Babe Ruth, New York, 142 games, 1920.

Highest slugging average by switch-hitter, season (100 or more games)
A.L.—.705—Mickey Mantle, New York, 150 games, 1956.
N.L.—.633—Chipper Jones, Atlanta, 157 games, 1999.

Most seasons leading league in slugging average (100 or more games)
A.L.—13—Babe Ruth, Boston, New York, 1918 through 1931, except 1925. (Played only 95 games in 1918, short season due to war.)
N.L.—9—Rogers Hornsby, St. Louis, Boston, Chicago, 1917, 1920, 1921, 1922, 1923, 1924, 1925, 1928, 1929.

Lowest slugging average, season (150 or more games)
N.L.—.223—Dal Maxvill, St. Louis, 152 games, 1970.
A.L.—.243—George McBride, Washington, 156 games, 1914.

Lowest leading slugging average, season (100 or more games)
N.L.—.436—Hy Myers, Brooklyn, 133 games, 1919.
A.L.—.466—Elmer Flick, Cleveland, 131 games, 1905.

AT-BATS AND PLATE APPEARANCES
CAREER AND SEASON

Most at-bats, career
N.L.—14,053—Pete Rose, Cincinnati, Philadelphia, Montreal, 24 years, 1963 through 1986.
A.L.—11,988—Carl Yastrzemski, Boston, 23 years, 1961 through 1983.

For a complete list of players with 9,000 or more career at-bats, see page 153.

Most plate appearances, career
N.L.—15,890—Pete Rose, Cincinnati, Philadelphia, Montreal, 24 years, 1963 through 1986.
A.L.—13,990—Carl Yastrzemski, Boston, 23 years, 1961 through 1983.

Most at-bats, season
A.L.—705—Willie Wilson, Kansas City, 161 games, 1980.
N.L.—701—Juan Samuel, Philadelphia, 160 games, 1984.

Most plate appearances, season
N.L.—773—Lenny Dykstra, Philadelphia, 161 games, 1993.
A.L.—758—Wade Boggs, Boston, 161 games, 1985.

Most at-bats by rookie, season
N.L.—701—Juan Samuel, Philadelphia, 160 games, 1984.
A.L.—692—Ichiro Suzuki, Seattle, 157 games, 2001.

Most at-bats by righthander, season
N.L.—701—Juan Samuel, Philadelphia, 160 games, 1984.
A.L.—696—Alfonso Soriano, New York, 156 games, 2002.

Most at-bats by lefthander, season
N.L.—698—Matty Alou, Pittsburgh, 162 games, 1969.
A.L.—704—Ichiro Suzuki, Seattle, 161 games, 2004.

Most at-bats by switch-hitter, season
A.L.—705—Willie Wilson, Kansas City, 161 games, 1980.
N.L.—695—Maury Wills, Los Angeles, 165 games, 1962.

Most at-bats by pinch-hitter, season
N.L.—83—Lenny Harris, New York, 95 games, 2001.
A.L.—72—Dave Philley, Baltimore, 79 games, 1961.

Most seasons leading league in at-bats
A.L.—7—Doc Cramer, Philadelphia, Boston, Washington, Detroit, 1933, 1934, 1935, 1938, 1940, 1941, 1942.
N.L.—4—Abner Dalrymple, Chicago, 1880, 1882, 1884, 1885.
Pete Rose, Cincinnati, 1965, 1972, 1973, 1977.

Most consecutive seasons leading league in at-bats
N.L.—3—Sparky Adams, Chicago, 1925, 1926, 1927.
Dave Cash, Philadelphia, 1974, 1975, 1976.
A.L.—3—Doc Cramer, Philadelphia, 1933, 1934, 1935.
Doc Cramer, Boston, Washington, Detroit, 1940, 1941, 1942.
Bobby Richardson, New York, 1962, 1963, 1964.

Most seasons with 600 or more at-bats
N.L.—17—Pete Rose, Cincinnati, 1963 through 1978, except 1964, 1967, Philadelphia, 1979, 1980, 1982.
A.L.—13—Cal Ripken Jr., Baltimore, 1983 through 1993, except 1988; 1996 through 1998.

Most consecutive seasons with 600 or more at-bats
N.L.—13—Pete Rose, Cincinnati, Philadelphia, 1968 through 1980.
A.L.—12—Nellie Fox, Chicago, 1951 through 1962.

Fewest at-bats, season (150 or more games)
N.L.—362—Jim Eisenreich, Philadelphia, 153 games, 1993.
A.L.—389—Tom McCraw, Chicago, 151 games, 1966.

Fewest at-bats for leader, season
N.L.—585—Spike Shannon, New York, 155 games, 1907.
A.L.—588—Ty Cobb, Detroit, 152 games, 1917.

GAME AND INNING

Most at-bats, game
N.L.—8—Held by 18 players. Last player—Barry McCormick, Chicago, June 29, 1897.
N.L. since 1900—7—Held by many players.
  (11—Carson Bigbee, Pittsburgh, August 22, 1917, 22 innings.
  Charlie Pick, Boston, May 1, 1920, 26 innings.
  Tony Boeckel, Boston, May 1, 1920, 26 innings.
  Ralph Garr, Atlanta, May 4, 1973, 20 innings.
  Dave Schneck, New York, September 11, 1974, 25 innings.
  Dave Cash, Montreal, May 21, 1977, 21 innings.)
A.L.—7—Held by many players.
  (11—Johnny Burnett, Cleveland, July 10, 1932, 18 innings.
  Ed Morgan, Cleveland, July 10, 1932, 18 innings.
  Irv Hall, Philadelphia, July 21, 1945, 24 innings.
  Bobby Richardson, New York, June 24, 1962, 22 innings.
  Cecil Cooper, Milwaukee, May 8, completed May 9, 1984, 25 innings.
  Julio Cruz, Chicago, May 8, completed May 9, 1984, 25 innings.
  Carlton Fisk, Chicago, May 8, completed May 9, 1984, 25 innings.
  Rudy Law, Chicago, May 8, completed May 9, 1984, 25 innings.)

Most times faced pitcher as batsman, game
N.L. before 1900—8—Held by many players.
N.L. since 1900—8—Russ Wrightstone, Philadelphia, August 25, 1922.
  Frank Parkinson, Philadelphia, August 25, 1922.
  Taylor Douthit, St. Louis, July 6, 1929, second game.
  Mike Cameron, Cincinnati, May 19, 1999.
  (12—Felix Millan, New York, September 11, 1974, 25 innings.
  John Milner, New York, September 11, 1974, 25 innings.)
A.L.—8—Clyde Vollmer, Boston, June 8, 1950.
  Darryl Hamilton, Milwaukee, August 28, 1992.
  (12—Harold Baines, Chicago, May 8, completed May 9, 1984, 25 innings.
  Carlton Fisk, Chicago, May 8, completed May 9, 1984, 25 innings.
  Rudy Law, Chicago, May 8, completed May 9, 1984, 25 innings.)

Most times faced pitcher with no official at-bats, game
N.L.—6—Pop Smith, Boston, April 17, 1890 (5 bases on balls, 1 hit by pitch).
  Walt Wilmot, Chicago, August 22, 1891 (6 bases on balls).
  Miller Huggins, St. Louis, June 1, 1910 (4 bases on balls, 1 sacrifice hit, 1 sacrifice fly).
  Billy Urbanski, Boston, June 13, 1934 (4 bases on balls, 2 sacrifice hits).
A.L.—6—Jimmie Foxx, Boston, June 16, 1938 (6 bases on balls).

Most at-bats, doubleheader
N.L.—13—Rabbit Maranville, Pittsburgh, August 8, 1922.
  Billy Herman, Chicago, August 21, 1935.
  (14—Jesus Alou, San Francisco, May 31, 1964, 32 innings.
  Joe Christopher, New York, May 31, 1964, 32 innings.
  Jim Hickman, New York, May 31, 1964, 32 innings.
  Ed Kranepool, New York, May 31, 1964, 32 innings.
  Roy McMillan, New York, May 31, 1964, 32 innings.
  Frank J. Thomas, New York, May 31, 1964, 32 innings.
  Dave Cash, Pittsburgh, June 7, 1972, 27 innings.
  Al Oliver, Pittsburgh, June 7, 1972, 27 innings.)
A.L.—13—Dave Philley, Chicago, May 30, 1950.
  (14—Rick Monday, Kansas City, June 17, 1967, 28 innings.
  Ramon Webster, Kansas City, June 17, 1967, 28 innings.
  Dick Billings, Washington, September 14, 1971, 29 innings (second game suspended; completed September 20).
  Ted Uhlaender, Cleveland, September 14, 1971, 29 innings; second game suspended; completed September 20.)

Most times faced pitcher as batsman, inning
A.A.—3—Larry Murphy, Washington, June 17, 1891, first inning.

N.L. before 1900—3—Held by 10 players.
N.L. since 1900—3—Marty Callaghan, Chicago, August 25, 1922, fourth inning.
  Billy Cox, Pee Wee Reese and Duke Snider, Brooklyn, May 21, 1952, first inning.
  Gil Hodges, Brooklyn, August 8, 1954, eighth inning.
  Dusty Baker, Atlanta, September 20, 1972, second inning.
  Mariano Duncan and Luis Quinones, Cincinnati, August 3, 1989, first inning.
  Stan Javier, San Francisco, July 15, 1997, seventh inning.
A.L.—3—Ted Williams, Boston, July 4, 1948, seventh inning.
  Sammy White, Gene Stephens, Tom Umphlett, Johnny Lipon and George Kell, Boston, June 18, 1953, seventh inning.
  Darryl Hamilton, Texas, April 19, 1996, eighth inning.
  Johnny Damon, Boston, June 27, 2003, first inning.

RUNS
CAREER AND SEASON

Most runs, career
M.L.—2,295—Rickey Henderson, Oakland A.L., New York A.L., Toronto A.L., San Diego N.L., Anaheim A.L., New York N.L., Seattle A.L., Boston A.L., Los Angeles N.L., 25 years, 1979 through 2003 (1,939 in A.L., 356 in N.L.).
A.L.—2,246—Ty Cobb, Detroit, Philadelphia, 24 years, 1905 through 1928.
N.L.—2,165—Pete Rose, Cincinnati, Philadelphia, Montreal, 24 years, 1963 through 1986.

For a complete list of players with 1,500 or more career runs, see page 153.

Most runs, season
N.L.—196—Billy Hamilton, Philadelphia, 131 games, 1894.
A.L.—177—Babe Ruth, New York, 152 games, 1921.
N.L. since 1900—158—Chuck Klein, Philadelphia, 156 games, 1930.

Most runs by rookie, season
A.A.—142—Mike Griffin, Baltimore, 136 games, 1887.
N.L.—135—Roy Thomas, Philadelphia, 148 games, 1899.
N.L. since 1900—133—Lloyd Waner, Pittsburgh, 150 games, 1927.
A.L.—132—Joe DiMaggio, New York, 138 games, 1936.

Most runs by righthander, season
A.A.—167—Tip O'Neill, St. Louis, 124 games, 1887.
N.L.—165—Joe Kelley, Baltimore, 129 games, 1894.
N.L. since 1900—156—Rogers Hornsby, Chicago, 156 games, 1929.
A.L.—152—Al Simmons, Philadelphia, 138 games, 1930.

Most runs by lefthander, season
N.L.—198—Billy Hamilton, Philadelphia, 131 games, 1894.
A.L.—177—Babe Ruth, New York, 152 games, 1921.
N.L. since 1900—158—Chuck Klein, Philadelphia, 156 games, 1930.

Most runs by switch-hitter, season
N.L.—140—Max Carey, Pittsburgh, 155 games, 1922.
A.L.—138—Roberto Alomar, Cleveland, 159 games, 1999.

Most seasons leading league in runs
A.L.—8—Babe Ruth, Boston, New York, 1919, 1920, 1921, 1923, 1924, 1926, 1927, 1928.
N.L.—5—George J. Burns, New York, 1914, 1916, 1917, 1919, 1920.
  Rogers Hornsby, St. Louis, New York, Chicago, 1921, 1922, 1924 (tied), 1927 (tied), 1929.
  Stan Musial, St. Louis, 1946, 1948, 1951 (tied), 1952 (tied), 1954 (tied).

Most consecutive seasons leading league in runs
N.L.—3—King Kelly, Chicago, 1884, 1885, 1886.
  Chuck Klein, Philadelphia, 1930, 1931 (tied), 1932.
  Duke Snider, Brooklyn, 1953, 1954 (tied), 1955.
  Pete Rose, Cincinnati, 1974, 1975, 1976.
A.L.—3—Ty Cobb, Detroit, 1909, 1910, 1911.

Eddie Collins, Philadelphia, 1912, 1913, 1914.
Babe Ruth, Boston, 1919, New York, 1920, 1921 and New York, 1926, 1927, 1928.
Ted Williams, Boston, 1940, 1941, 1942 (military service from 1943 through 1945 interrupted a five-year streak by Williams of Boston, who led in runs from 1940 through 1947).
Mickey Mantle, New York, 1956, 1957, 1958.

Most seasons with 150 or more runs
A.L.—6—Babe Ruth, New York, 1920, 1921, 1923, 1927, 1928, 1930.
N.L.—4—Billy Hamilton, Philadelphia, Boston, 1894, 1895, 1896, 1897.
N.L. since 1900—2—Chuck Klein, Philadelphia, 1930, 1932.

Most seasons with 100 or more runs
N.L.—15—Hank Aaron, Milwaukee, Atlanta, 1955 through 1970, except 1968.
A.L.—13—Lou Gehrig, New York, 1926 through 1938.

Most consecutive seasons with 100 or more runs
A.L.—13—Lou Gehrig, New York, 1926 through 1938.
N.L.—13—Hank Aaron, Milwaukee, Atlanta, 1955 through 1967.

Fewest runs for leader, season
N.L.—89—Gavvy Cravath, Philadelphia, 150 games, 1915.
A.L.—92—Harry H. Davis, Philadelphia, 149 games, 1905.

Fewest runs, season (150 or more games)
A.L.—25—Leo Cardenas, California, 150 games, 1972.
N.L.—32—Mike Doolan, Philadelphia, 151 games, 1913.

GAME AND INNING

Most runs, game
A.A.—7—Guy Hecker, Louisville, August 15, 1886, second game.
N.L.—6—Jim Whitney, Boston, June 9, 1883.
  Cap Anson, Chicago, August 24, 1886.
  Mike Tiernan, New York, June 15, 1887.
  King Kelly, Boston, August 27, 1887.
  Ezra Sutton, Boston, August 27, 1887.
  Jimmy Ryan, Chicago, July 25, 1894, seven innings.
  Bobby Lowe, Boston, May 3, 1895.
  Ginger Beaumont, Pittsburgh, July 22, 1899.
  Mel Ott, New York, August 4, 1934, second game; April 30, 1944, first game.
  Frank Torre, Milwaukee, September 2, 1957, first game.
  Edgardo Alfonzo, New York, August 30, 1999.
  Shawn Green, Los Angeles, May 23, 2002.
A.L.—6—Johnny Pesky, Boston, May 8, 1946.
  Spike Owen, Boston, August 21, 1986.
  Joe Randa, Kansas City, September 9, 2004.

Most runs by pitcher, game
A.A.—7—Guy Hecker, Louisville, August 15, 1886, second game.
N.L.—5—Nig Cuppy, Cleveland, August 9, 1895.
N.L. since 1900—4—Held by many pitchers. Last pitcher—Jim Tobin, Boston, September 12, 1940, first game.
A.L.—4—Held by many pitchers. Last pitcher—Billy Hoeft, Detroit, May 5, 1956.

Most runs, doubleheader
N.L.—9—Herman Long, Boston, May 30, 1894.
A.L.—9—Mel Almada, Washington, July 25, 1937.
N.L. since 1900—8—Chuck Klein, Chicago, August 21, 1935.

Most consecutive games scoring one or more runs, season
N.L.—24—Billy Hamilton, Philadelphia, July 6 through August 2, 1894 (35 runs).
A.L.—18—Red Rolfe, New York, August 9 through 25, second game, 1939 (30 runs).
  Kenny Lofton, Cleveland, August 15 through September 3, 2000 (26 runs).
N.L. since 1900—17—Rogers Hornsby, St. Louis, July 3 through 20, 1921 (21 runs).
  Ted Kluszewski, Cincinnati, August 27 through September 13, 1954 (24 runs).

Most times with five or more runs in one game, career
M.L.—6—George Gore, Chicago N.L., 1880, 1881, 1882 (2),

1883, New York P.L. 1890.
  Jimmy Ryan, Chicago N.L., 1887, 1889, 1891, 1894 (2), 1897.
  Willie Keeler, Baltimore N.L., 1895 (2), 1897 (2), Brooklyn N.L., 1901, 1902.
N.L.—6—Jimmy Ryan, Chicago, 1887, 1889, 1891, 1894 (2), 1897.
  Willie Keeler, Baltimore, Brooklyn, 1895 (2), 1897 (2), 1901, 1902.
N.L. since 1900—3—Mel Ott, New York, 1934, 1944 (2).
  Willie Mays, New York, San Francisco, 1954, 1964 (2).
  Craig Biggio, Houston, 1995 (2), 1996.
A.L.—3—Lou Gehrig, New York, 1928, 1936 (2).
  Jimmie Foxx, Philadelphia, Boston, 1932, 1935, 1939.

Most times with five or more runs in one game, season
N.L.—2—Held by many players.
N.L. since 1900—2—Kiki Cuyler, Pittsburgh, May 12, second game, June 20, 1925.
  Mel Ott, New York, April 30, first game, June 12, 1944.
  Phil Weintraub, New York, April 30, first game, June 12, 1944.
  Willie Mays, San Francisco, April 24, September 19, 1964.
  Craig Biggio, Houston, July 4, September 28, 1995.
A.L.—2—Lou Gehrig, New York, May 3, July 28, 1936.

Most runs, inning
A.L.—3—Sammy White, Boston, June 18, 1953, seventh inning.
N.L.—3—Tommy Burns, Chicago, September 6, 1883, seventh inning.
  Ned Williamson, Chicago, September 6, 1883, seventh inning.
N.L. since 1900—2—Held by many players.

HITS
CAREER AND SEASON

Most hits, career
N.L.—4,256—Pete Rose, Cincinnati, Philadelphia, Montreal, 24 years, 1963 through 1986.
A.L.—4,189—Ty Cobb, Detroit, Philadelphia, 24 years, 1905 through 1928.

For a complete list of players with 2,500 or more career hits, see page 153.

Most hits by pinch-hitter, career
N.L.—193—Lenny Harris, Cincinnati, Los Angeles, New York, Colorado, Arizona, Milwaukee, Chicago, Florida, 16 years, 1989 through 2004, 816 games.
A.L.—107—Gates Brown, Detroit, 13 years, 1963 through 1975, 525 games.

Most hits, season (Except 1887, when bases on balls counted as hits)
A.L.—262—Ichiro Suzuki, Seattle, 161 games, 2004.
N.L.—254—Lefty O'Doul, Philadelphia, 154 games, 1929.
  Bill Terry, New York, 154 games, 1930.

Most hits by rookie, season
A.L.—242—Ichiro Suzuki, Seattle, 157 games, 2001.
N.L.—223—Lloyd Waner, Pittsburgh, 150 games, 1927.

For a complete list of rookies with 200 or more hits, see page 162.

Most hits by righthander, season
A.L.—253—Al Simmons, Philadelphia, 153 games, 1925.
N.L.—250—Rogers Hornsby, St. Louis, 154 games, 1922.

Most hits by lefthander, season
A.L.—262—Ichiro Suzuki, Seattle, 161 games, 2004.
N.L.—254—Lefty O'Doul, Philadelphia, 154 games, 1929.
  Bill Terry, New York, 154 games, 1930.

Most hits by switch-hitter, season
N.L.—230—Pete Rose, Cincinnati, 160 games, 1973.
A.L.—230—Willie Wilson, Kansas City, 161 games, 1980.

Switch-hitters with 100 or more hits from each side of plate, season

N.L.—Garry Templeton, St. Louis, 154 games, 1979 (111 hits lefthanded, 100 hits righthanded).

A.L.—Willie Wilson, Kansas City, 161 games, 1980 (130 hits lefthanded, 100 hits righthanded).

Most hits by pinch-hitter, season

N.L.—28—John Vander Wal, Colorado, 92 games, 1995.

A.L.—24—Dave Philley, Baltimore, 79 games, 1961.

Most seasons leading league in hits

A.L.—8—Ty Cobb, Detroit, 1907, 1908, 1909, 1911, 1912, 1915, 1917, 1919 (tied).

N.L.—7—Pete Rose, Cincinnati, 1965, 1968 (tied) 1970 (tied), 1972, 1973, 1976, Philadelphia, 1981.

Tony Gwynn, San Diego, 1984, 1986, 1987, 1989, 1994, 1995 (tied), 1997.

Most consecutive seasons leading league in hits

N.L.—3—Ginger Beaumont, Pittsburgh, 1902, 1903, 1904.

Rogers Hornsby, St. Louis, 1920, 1921, 1922.

Frank McCormick, Cincinnati, 1938, 1939, 1940 (tied).

A.L.—3—Ty Cobb, Detroit, 1907, 1908, 1909.

Tony Oliva, Minnesota, 1964, 1965, 1966.

Kirby Puckett, Minnesota, 1987 (tied), 1988, 1989.

Most games with one or more hits, season

N.L.—135—Rogers Hornsby, St. Louis, 154 games, 1922.

Chuck Klein, Philadelphia, 156 games, 1930.

A.L.—135—Wade Boggs, Boston, 161 games, 1985.

Derek Jeter, New York, 158 games, 1999.

Ichiro Suzuki, Seattle, 157 games, 2001.

Most seasons with 200 or more hits, career

N.L.—10—Pete Rose, Cincinnati, 1965, 1966, 1968, 1969, 1970, 1973, 1975, 1976, 1977, Philadelphia, 1979.

A.L.—9—Ty Cobb, Detroit, 1907, 1909, 1911, 1912, 1915, 1916, 1917, 1922, 1924.

For a complete list of players with 200 or more hits in a seson four or more times, see page 154.

Most consecutive years with 200 or more hits, career

N.L.—8—Willie Keeler, Baltimore, Brooklyn, 1894 through 1901.

A.L.—7—Wade Boggs, Boston, 1983 through 1989.

N.L. since 1900—5—Chuck Klein, Philadelphia, 1929 through 1933.

Most hits, two consecutive seasons

N.L.—485—Rogers Hornsby, St. Louis, 235 in 1921, 250 in 1922.

A.L.—474—Ty Cobb, Detroit, 248 in 1911, 227 in 1912.

Fewest hits, season (150 or more games)

N.L.—80—Dal Maxvill, St. Louis, 152 games, 1970.

A.L.—82—Eddie Brinkman, Washington, 154 games, 1965.

Fewest hits for leader, season

N.L.—171—Sherry Magee, Philadelphia, 146 games, 1914.

A.L.—177—Bert Campaneris, Oakland, 159 games, 1968.

Most at-bats in hitless season

N.L.—70—Bob Buhl, Milwaukee, Chicago, 35 games, 1962.

A.L.—61—Bill Wight, Chicago, 30 games, 1950.

GAME AND DOUBLEHEADER

Most hits, game

N.L.—7—Wilbert Robinson, Baltimore, June 10, 1892, first game (6 singles, 1 double; consecutive).

Rennie Stennett, Pittsburgh, September 16, 1975 (4 singles, 2 doubles, 1 triple; consecutive).

A.L.—6—Held by many players.

(9—Johnny Burnett, Cleveland, July 10, 1932 (7 singles, 2 doubles), 18 innings.)

For a complete list of players with six or more hits in a game, see page 171.

Most times reached base, game (batting 1.000)

N.L.—8—Piggy Ward, Cincinnati, June 18, 1893 (2 singles, 5 bases on balls, 1 hit by pitch).

A.A.—7—Bill Gleason, St. Louis, April 30, 1887 (2 singles, 1 double, 4 bases on balls).

Tip O'Neill, St. Louis, July 13, 1889 (3 singles, one home run, 3 bases on balls).

N.L. since 1900—7—Cliff Heathcote, Chicago, August 25, 1922 (3 singles, 2 doubles, 2 bases on balls).

Cookie Lavagetto, Brooklyn, September 23, 1939, first game (4 singles, 1 double, 1 triple, 1 base on balls).

Mel Ott, New York, April 30, 1944, first game (2 singles, 5 bases on balls).

Rennie Stennett, Pittsburgh, September 16, 1975 (4 singles, 2 doubles, 1 triple).

Sean Casey, Cincinnati, May 19, 1999 (2 singles, 2 home runs, 3 bases on balls).

(9—Max Carey, Pittsburgh, July 7, 1922 (5 singles, 1, double, 3 bases on balls), 18 innings.)

A.L.—7—Ben Chapman, New York, May 24, 1936 (2 doubles, 5 bases on balls).

(7—Cesar Gutierrez, Detroit, June 21, 1970, second game (6 singles, 1 double), 12 innings.

Dwight Evans, Boston, May 4, 1981 (3 singles, 4 bases on balls), 12 innings.

George Brett, Kansas City, June 27, 1985 (2 singles, 1 double, 4 bases on balls), 14 innings.

Tim Raines Sr., Chicago, April 20, 1994 (3 singles, 4 bases on balls), 12 innings.

Mark McGwire, Oakland, April 26, 1997 (1 double, 1 home run, 5 bases on balls), 11 innings.)

Most clubs with one or more hits, one day

N.L.—2—Joel Youngblood, New York, Montreal, August 4, 1982.

Most hits in first major league game

N.L.—5—Fred Clarke, Louisville, June 30, 1894 (4 singles, 1 triple).

N.L. since 1900—4—Casey Stengel, Brooklyn, September 17, 1912 (4 singles).

Ed Freed, Philadelphia, September 11, 1942 (1 single, 2 doubles, 1 triple).

Willie McCovey, San Francisco, July 30, 1959 (2 singles, 2 triples; consecutive).

Mack Jones, Milwaukee, July 13, 1961 (3 singles, 1 double).

Delino DeShields, Montreal, April 9, 1990 (3 singles, 1 double).

Derrick Gibson, Colorado, September 8, 1998 (3 singles, 1 double).

A.L.—4—Ray Jansen, St. Louis, September 30, 1910 (4 singles; only game in major league career).

Art Shires, Chicago, August 20, 1928 (3 singles, 1 triple).

Russ Van Atta, New York, April 25, 1933 (4 singles).

Spook Jacobs, Philadelphia, April 13, 1954 (4 singles).

Ted Cox, Boston, September 18, 1977 (3 singles, 1 double; consecutive).

Kirby Puckett, Minnesota, May 8, 1984 (4 singles).

Billy Bean, Detroit, April 25, 1987 (2 singles, 2 doubles).

(5—Cecil Travis, Washington, May 16, 1933 (5 singles), 12 innings.)

Most hits by pitcher, game

A.A.—6—Guy Hecker, Louisville, August 15, 1886, second game.

N.L.-A.L.—5—Held by many pitchers.

N.L.—Last pitcher—Pete Donohue, Cincinnati, May 22, 1925 (4 singles, 1 home run).

A.L.—Last pitcher—Mel Stottlemyre, New York, September 26, 1964 (4 singles, 1 double).

Most hits, opening day of season

N.L.-A.L.—5—Held by many players.

N.L.—Last player—Craig Biggio, Houston, April 3, 2001 (5 singles).

A.L.—Last player—Nellie Fox, Chicago, April 10, 1959, 14 innings (3 singles, 1 double, 1 home run). Last player in nine-inning game—Harlond Clift, St. Louis, April 21, 1937 (2 singles, 2 doubles, 1 home run).

Most hits comprising all of club's hits, game
A.L.—4—Kid Elberfeld, New York, August 1, 1903 (4 singles).
N.L.—4—Billy Williams, Chicago, September 5, 1969 (2 doubles, 2 home runs).

Most at-bats with no hits, extra-inning game
N.L.—11—Charles Pick, Boston, May 1, 1920, 26 innings.
A.L.—10—George Kell, Philadelphia, July 21, 1945, 24 innings.

Most times with six hits in six times at bat in game, career
M.L.—2—Ed Delahanty, Cleveland, P.L., June 2, 1890; Philadelphia, N.L., June 16, 1894.
Jim Bottomley, St. Louis N.L., September 16, 1924; August 5, 1931, second game.
Doc Cramer, Philadelphia A.L., June 20, 1932; July 13, 1935.
N.L.—2—Jim Bottomley, St. Louis, September 16, 1924; August 5, 1931, second game.
A.L.—2—Doc Cramer, Philadelphia, June 20, 1932; July 13, 1935.

Most times with five or more hits in one game, career
A.L.—14—Ty Cobb, Detroit, Philadelphia, 1908 to 1927.
N.L.—12—Sam Thompson, Detroit, Philadelphia, 1886 through 1895.
N.L. since 1900—10—Pete Rose, Cincinnati, Philadelphia, 1965 to 1986.

Most times with five hits in one game, by pitcher, career
3—Nixey Callahan, Chicago N.L., 1897, Chicago A.L., 1902, 1903.

Most times with five or more hits in one game, season
N.L.—5—Sam Thompson, Detroit, May 16, June 10, July 25, August 9, September 23, 1887.
A.A.—4—Tip O'Neill, St. Louis, April 30, August 24, September 2, September 7, 1887.
N.L. since 1900—4—Stan Musial, St. Louis, April 30, May 19, June 22, September 22, 1948.
Tony Gwynn, San Diego, April 18, July 27, August 4, 1993.
A.L.—4—Ty Cobb, Detroit, May 7, July 7 (second game), July 12, July 17, 1922.
Ichiro Suzuki, Seattle, July 29 (13 innings), August 3, September 4, September 21, 2004.

Most hits, doubleheader
A.A.—9—Fred Carroll, Pittsburgh, July 5, 1886.
N.L.—9—Wilbert Robinson, Baltimore, June 10, 1892.
Joe Kelley, Baltimore, September 3, 1894 (consecutive).
Fred Lindstrom, New York, June 25, 1928.
Bill Terry, New York, June 10, 1929.
A.L.—9—Ray Morehart, Chicago, August 31, 1926.
George Case, Washington, July 4, 1940.
Lee Thomas, Los Angeles, September 5, 1961.
(9—Pete Runnels, Boston, August 30, 1960, 15 and 10 innings.)

Most hits by pinch-hitter, doubleheader
N.L.-A.L.—2—Held by many pinch-hitters.

Most at-bats with no hits, doubleheader
A.L.—11—Albie Pearson, Los Angeles, July 1, 1962.
(13—Brian L. Hunter, Detroit, June 20, 1998, 26 innings.)
N.L.—10—Held by many players.
(12—Red Schoendienst, St. Louis, June 9, 1947, 24 innings.)

HITTING FOR CYCLE
(Single, double, triple, home run in game)

Most times hitting for cycle, career
M.L.—3—John Reilly, Cincinnati A.A., 1883 (2), Cincinnati N.L., 1890.
Bob Meusel, New York A.L., 1921, 1922, 1928.
Babe Herman, Brooklyn N.L., 1931 (2), Chicago N.L., 1933.
A.L.—3—Bob Meusel, New York, 1921, 1922, 1928.
N.L.—3—Babe Herman, Brooklyn, 1931 (2), Chicago, 1933.

For a complete list of players hitting for cycle, see page 169.

Hitting for cycle in American and National Leagues
Bob Watson, Houston N.L., June 24, 1977; Boston A.L., September 15, 1979.

John Olerud, New York N.L., September 11, 1997; Seattle A.L., June 16, 2001.

Most times hitting for cycle, season
A.A.—2—John Reilly, Cincinnati, 1883.
Tip O'Neill, St. Louis, 1887.
N.L.—2—Babe Herman, Brooklyn, 1931.
A.L.—1—Held by many players.

INNING

Most hits, inning
A.L.—3—Gene Stephens, Boston, June 18, 1953, seventh inning (2 singles, 1 double).
Johnny Damon, Boston, June 27, 2003, first inning (1 single, 1 double, 1 triple).
N.L.—3—Tommy Burns, Chicago, September 6, 1883, seventh inning (2 doubles, 1 home run).
Fred Pfeffer, Chicago, September 6, 1883, seventh inning (2 singles, 1 double).
Ned Williamson, Chicago, September 6, 1883, seventh inning (2 singles, 1 double).

Most hits in one inning of first major league game
A.L.—2—Billy Martin, New York, April 18, 1950, eighth inning.
Russ Morman, Chicago, August 3, 1986, fourth inning.
Chad Kreuter, Texas, September 14, 1988, fifth inning.
N.L.—2—Adam LaRoche, Atlanta, April 7, 2004, fourth inning.

Most times with two hits in one inning, game
N.L.—2—Max Carey, Pittsburgh, June 22, 1925, first and eighth innings (2 singles in each inning).
Rennie Stennett, Pittsburgh, September 16, 1975, first inning (single and double); fifth inning (single and single).
A.L.—2—Johnny Hodapp, Cleveland, July 29, 1928, second and sixth innings (2 singles in each inning).
Sherm Lollar, Chicago, April 23, 1955, second inning (single and home run); sixth inning (2 singles).

Most times reached first base safely, inning
N.L.—3—Ned Williamson, Chicago, September 6, 1883, seventh inning.
Tommy Burns, Chicago, September 6, 1883, seventh inning.
Fred Pfeffer, Chicago, September 6, 1883, seventh inning.
Herman Long, Boston, June 18, 1894, a.m. game, first inning.
Bobby Lowe, Boston, June 18, 1894, a.m. game, first inning.
Hugh Duffy, Boston, June 18, 1894, a.m. game, first inning.
Pee Wee Reese, Brooklyn, May 21, 1952, first inning.
A.L.—3—Sammy White, Boston, June 18, 1953, seventh inning.
Gene Stephens, Boston, June 18, 1953, seventh inning.
Tommy Umphlett, Boston, June 18, 1953, seventh inning.
Johnny Damon, Boston, June 27, 2003, first inning.

BATTING STREAKS

Most consecutive hits, season (bases on balls shown in streak)
A.L.—12—Pinky Higgins, Boston, June 19, 19, 21, 21, 1938 (2 B.B.).
Walt Dropo, Detroit, July 14, 15, 15, 1952 (0 B.B.).
N.L.—10—Ed Delahanty, Philadelphia, July 13, 13, 14, 1897 (1 B.B.).
Jake Gettman, Washington, September 10, 11, 11, 1897 (0 B.B.).
Ed Konetchy, Brooklyn, June 28, second game, June 29, July 1, 1919 (0 B.B.).
Kiki Cuyler, Pittsburgh, September 18, 19, 21, 1925 (1 B.B.).
Chick Hafey, St. Louis, July 6, second game, July 8, 9, 1929 (2 B.B.).
Joe Medwick, St. Louis, July 19, 19, 21, 1936 (1 B.B.).
Buddy Hassett, Boston, June 9, second game, June 10, 14, 1940 (1 B.B.).
Woody Williams, Cincinnati, September 5, second game, September 6, 6, 1943 (1 B.B.).
Bip Roberts, Cincinnati, September 19, 20, 22, second game, 23 1992 (1 B.B.).

Most consecutive hits by pitcher, season
N.L.—8—Livan Hernandez, San Francisco, July 31 (1), August 5 (3), 11 (4), 2001.

A.L.—7—Don Larsen, St. Louis, July 24 (1), 28 (3), August 5 (3), 1953.

Most consecutive times reached base safely, season
A.L.—16—Ted Williams, Boston, September 17 (1), 18 (1), 20 (1), 21 (4), 22 (4), 23 (5), 1957 (2 singles, 4 home runs, 9 bases on balls, 1 hit by pitch).
N.L.—15—Barry Bonds, San Francisco, August 31 (1), September 1 (5), 2 (4), 4 (5), 1998 (5 singles, 2 doubles, 2 home runs, 6 bases on balls).
John Olerud, New York, September 16 (1), 18 (5), 19 (4), 20 (4), 22 (1), 1998 (6 singles, 1 double, 2 home runs, 6 bases on balls).

Most consecutive hits from start of career
A.L.—6—Ted Cox, Boston, September 18, 19, 1977.
N.L.—4—John Hale, Los Angeles, October 1, 2, 1974.
Bob Dernier, Philadelphia, September 14, 30, October 5, 1980.
Mike Piazza, Los Angeles, September 1, 4, 1992.
Derrick Gibson, Colorado, September 8, 1988.

Most consecutive hits by pinch-hitter
N.L.—9—Dave Philley, Philadelphia, September 9 through September 28, 1958; April 16, 1959.
A.L.—7—Bill Stein, Texas, April 14 through May 25, 1981.
Randy Bush, Minnesota, July 5 through August 19, 1991.

Most consecutive hits by pinch-hitter, season
N.L.—8—Dave Philley, Philadelphia, September 9 through September 28, 1958.
Rusty Staub, New York, June 11 through June 26, first game, 1983 (1 hit by pitch during streak).
A.L.—7—Bill Stein, Texas, April 14 through May 25, 1981.
Randy Bush, Minnesota, July 5 through August 19, 1991.

Most consecutive games reached base safely during season
A.L.—84—Ted Williams, Boston, July 1 through September 27, 1949.
N.L.—58—Duke Snider, Brooklyn, May 13 through July 11, second game, 1954.
Barry Bonds, San Francisco, June 27 through September 20, 2003.

Most consecutive games batted safely during season
A.L.—56—Joe DiMaggio, New York, May 15 through July 16, 1941.
N.L.—44—Willie Keeler, Baltimore, April 22 through June 18, 1897.
Pete Rose, Cincinnati, June 14 through July 31, 1978.

Most consecutive games batted safely by rookie, season
N.L.—34—Benito Santiago, San Diego, August 25 through October 2, 1987.
A.L.—30—Nomar Garciaparra, Boston, July 26 through August 29, 1997.

Most consecutive games batted safely by righthander, season
A.L.—56—Joe DiMaggio, New York, May 15 through July 16, 1941.
N.L.—42—Bill Dahlen, Chicago, June 20 through August 6, 1894.
N.L. since 1900—34—Benito Santiago, San Diego, August 25 through October 2, 1987.

For a complete list of players with 30-game batting streaks, see page 162. For a detailed breakdown of Joe DiMaggio's 56-game hitting streak, see page 177.

Most consecutive games batted safely by lefthander, season
N.L.—44—Willie Keeler, Baltimore, April 22 to June 18, 1897.
A.L.—41—George Sisler, St. Louis, July 27 to September 17, 1922.
N.L. since 1900—37—Tommy Holmes, Boston, June 6, first game, to July 8, second game, 1945.

Most consecutive games batted safely by switch-hitter, season
N.L.—44—Pete Rose, Cincinnati, June 14 through July 31, 1978.
A.L.—27—Jose Offerman, Kansas City, July 11 through August 7, 1998.

Most consecutive games batted safely from start of season
N.L.—44—Willie Keeler, Baltimore, April 22 through June 18, 1897.
A.L.—34—George Sisler, St. Louis, April 14 through May 19, 1925.

N.L. since 1900—25—Charlie Grimm, Pittsburgh, April 17 through May 16, 1923.

Most 20-game batting streaks, career
N.L.—8—Willie Keeler, Baltimore, Brooklyn, 1894, 1896, 1897, 1898 (2), 1899, 1900, 1902.
N.L. since 1900—7—Pete Rose, Cincinnati, Philadelphia, 1967, 1968, 1977 (2), 1978, 1979, 1982.
A.L.—7—Ty Cobb, Detroit, Philadelphia, 1911, 1912, 1917, 1918, 1920, 1926, 1927.

Most 20-game batting streaks, season
A.L.—3—Tris Speaker, Boston, 1912.
N.L.—2—Held by many players. Last player—Steve Garvey, Los Angeles, 1978.

Most hits in two consecutive games
N.L.—12—Cal McVey, Chicago, July 22 (6), 25 (6), 1876.
N.L. since 1900—10—Rennie Stennett, Pittsburgh, September 16 (7), 17 (3), 1975.
(10—Roberto Clemente, Pittsburgh, August 22 (5), 23 (5), 1970, 25 innings.
Mike Benjamin, San Francisco, June 13 (4), 14 (6), 1995, 22 innings.)
A.L.—10—Kirby Puckett, Minnesota, August 29 (4), 30 (6), 1987.
(11—Johnny Burnett, Cleveland, July 9, second game (2), 10 (9), 1932, 27 innings.)

Most hits by pitcher in two consecutive games
A.A.—10—Guy Hecker, Louisville, August 12, 15, second game, 1886.
A.L.—8—George Earnshaw, Philadelphia, June 9, 12, second game, 1931.
N.L. since 1900—8—Kirby Higbe, Brooklyn, August 11, 17, first game, 1941.

Most hits in three consecutive games
N.L.—15—Cal McVey, Chicago, July 20, 22, 25, 1876.
Cal McVey, Chicago, July 22, 25, 27, 1876.
N.L. since 1900—14—Mike Benjamin, San Francisco, June 11, 13, 14, 1995.
A.L.—13—Joe Cronin, Washington, June 19, 21, 22, 1933.
Walt Dropo, Detroit, July 14, 15, 15, 1952.
Tim Salmon, California, May 10, 11, 13, 1994.

Most hits in four consecutive games
N.L.—18—Cal McVey, Chicago, July 20, 22, 25, 27, 1876.
N.L. since 1900—16—Milt Stock, Brooklyn, June 30, July 1, 2, 3, 1925.
A.A.—17—Guy Hecker, Louisville, August 8, 10, 12, 15, second game, 1886.
A.L.—15—Joe Cronin, Washington, June 18, second game, 19, 21, 22, 1933.
Joe Cronin, Washington, June 19, 21, 22, 23, 1933.
Buddy Lewis, Washington, July 25, 25, 27, 28, 1937.
Walt Dropo, Detroit, July 14, 15, 15, 16, 1952.
Johnny Damon, Kansas City, July 18, 19, 20, 21, 2000.

Most consecutive games with three or more hits, season
A.L.—6—George Brett, Kansas City, May 8, 9, 10, 11, 12, 13, 1976.
N.L.—6—Sam Thompson, Philadelphia, June 11, 14, 14, 19, 20, 21, 1895.
N.L. since 1900—5—Ted Sizemore, August 8, 9, 9, 11, 12, 1970.

Most consecutive games with four or more hits, season
N.L.—4—Milt Stock, Brooklyn, June 30, July 1, 2, 3, 1925.
A.L.—3—Held by many players.

SINGLES

Most singles, career
N.L.—3,215—Pete Rose, Cincinnati, Philadelphia, Montreal, 24 years, 1963 through 1986.
A.L.—3,053—Ty Cobb, Detroit, Philadelphia, 24 years, 1905 through 1928.

For a complete list of players with 2,000 or more career singles, see page 154.

Most singles, season
A.L.—225—Ichiro Suzuki, Seattle, 161 games, 2004.
N.L.—206—Willie Keeler, Baltimore, 129 games, 1898.

N.L. since 1900—198—Lloyd Waner, Pittsburgh, 150 games, 1927.

Most singles by rookie, season
N.L.—198—Lloyd Waner, Pittsburgh, 150 games, 1927.
A.L.—192—Ichiro Suzuki, Seattle, 157 games, 2001.

Most singles by righthander, season
N.L.—178—Curt Flood, St. Louis, 162 games, 1964.
A.L.—174—Al Simmons, Philadelphia, 153 games, 1925.

Most singles by lefthander, season
A.L.—225—Ichiro Suzuki, Seattle, 161 games, 2004.
N.L.—206—Willie Keeler, Baltimore, 129 games, 1898.
N.L. since 1900—198—Lloyd Waner, Pittsburgh, 150 games, 1927.

Most singles by switch-hitter, season
A.L.—184—Willie Wilson, Kansas City, 161 games, 1980.
N.L.—181—Pete Rose, Cincinnati, 160 games, 1973.

Most seasons leading league in singles
A.L.—8—Nellie Fox, Chicago, 1952, 1954, 1955, 1956, 1957, 1958, 1959, 1960.
N.L.—7—Tony Gwynn, San Diego, 1984, 1986 (tied), 1987, 1989, 1994, 1995, 1997.

Most consecutive seasons leading league in singles
A.L.—7—Nellie Fox, Chicago, 1954, 1955, 1956, 1957, 1958, 1959, 1960.
N.L.—4—Brett Butler, San Francisco, 1990, Los Angeles, 1991, 1992, 1993.

Fewest singles, season (150 or more games)
N.L.—49—Barry Bonds, San Francisco, 153 games, 2001.
A.L.—53—Mark McGwire, Oakland, 154 games, 1991.

Fewest singles by leader, season
A.L.—129—Don Buford, Chicago, 155 games, 1965.
N.L.—127—Enos Slaughter, St. Louis, 152 games, 1942.

Most singles, game
M.L.—6—Held by many players.
Last N.L. player—Dave Bancroft, New York, June 28, 1920.
  (6—Done by many players in extra innings. Last player—Willie Davis, Los Angeles, May 24, 1073, 10 innings.
Last A.L. player—Raul Ibanez, Seattle, September 22, 2004.
  (7—Johnny Burnett, Cleveland, July 10, 1932, 18 innings.)

Most singles in a game, each batting in three runs
N.L.-A.L.—1—Held by many players.
Last N.L. player—Willie Montanez, Philadelphia, September 8, 1974, eighth inning.
Last A.L. player—Ernest Riles, Milwaukee, June 5, 1985, third inning.

Most singles, doubleheader
N.L.-A.L.—8—Held by many players.
Last A.L. player—Earl Averill, Cleveland, May 7, 1933.
Last N.L. player—Ken Hubbs, Chicago, May 20, 1962.

Most singles, inning
N.L.-A.L.—2—Held by many players.

DOUBLES
CAREER AND SEASON

Most doubles, career
A.L.—793—Tris Speaker, Boston, Cleveland, Washington, Philadelphia, 22 years, 1907 through 1928.
N.L.—746—Pete Rose, Cincinnati, Philadelphia, Montreal, 24 years, 1963 through 1986.

For a complete list of players with 450 or more career doubles, see page 154.

Most doubles, season
A.L.—67—Earl Webb, Boston, 151 games, 1931.
N.L.—64—Joe Medwick, St. Louis, 155 games, 1936.

Most doubles by rookie, season
N.L.—52—Johnny Frederick, Brooklyn, 148 games, 1929.
A.L.—47—Fred Lynn, Boston, 145 games, 1975.

Most doubles by righthander, season
A.L.—64—George H. Burns, Cleveland, 151 games, 1926.
N.L.—64—Joe Medwick, St. Louis, 155 games, 1936.

Most doubles by lefthander, season
A.L.—67—Earl Webb, Boston, 151 games, 1931.
N.L.—62—Paul Waner, Pittsburgh, 154 games, 1932.

Most doubles by switch-hitter, season
N.L.—55—Lance Berkman, Houston, 156 games, 2001.
A.L.—50—Brian Roberts, Baltimore, 159 games, 2004.

Most doubles by catcher, season
A.L.—45—Ivan Rodriguez, Texas, 146 games, 1996 (had two additional doubles as a designated hitter).
N.L.—40—Johnny Bench, Cincinnati, 154 games, 1968; caught 154 games.
Terry Kennedy, San Diego, 153 games, 1982; caught 139 games (had two additional doubles as first baseman).

Most seasons leading league in doubles
N.L.—8—Stan Musial, St. Louis, 1943, 1944, 1946, 1948, 1949, 1952, 1953, 1954.
A.L.—8—Tris Speaker, Boston, 1912, Cleveland, 1914, 1916 (tied), 1918, 1920, 1921, 1922, 1923.

Most consecutive seasons leading league in doubles
N.L.—4—Honus Wagner, Pittsburgh, 1906, 1907, 1908, 1909.
A.L.—4—Tris Speaker, Cleveland, 1920, 1921, 1922, 1923.

Most seasons with 50 or more doubles, career
A.L.—5—Tris Speaker, Boston, 1912, Cleveland, 1920, 1921, 1923, 1926.
N.L.—3—Paul Waner, Pittsburgh, 1928, 1932, 1936.
Stan Musial, St. Louis, 1944, 1946, 1953.

Fewest doubles, season (150 or more games)
N.L.—5—Dal Maxvill, St. Louis, 152 games, 1970.
A.L.—6—Billy Purtell, Chicago, Boston, 151 games, 1910.

Fewest doubles for leader, season
A.L.—32—Sal Bando, Oakland, 162 games, 1973.
Pedro Garcia, Milwaukee, 160 games, 1973.
N.L.—34—Hank Aaron, Milwaukee, 153 games, 1956.

GAME AND INNING

Most doubles, game
N.L.—4—22 times (held by 22 players). Last player—Adam LaRoche, Atlanta, May 15, 2004.
A.L.—4—22 times (held by 21 players). Last players—Johnny Damon, Kansas City, July 18, 2000, Shannon Stewart, Toronto, July 18, 2000.
A.A.—4—2 times (held by 2 players).

Most consecutive doubles, game
N.L.—4—Frank Bonner, Baltimore, August 4, 1894.
Joe Kelley, Baltimore, September 3, 1894, second game.
Dick Bartell, Philadelphia, April 25, 1933.
Ernie Lombardi, Cincinnati, May 8, 1935, first game.
Bill Werber, Cincinnati, May 13, 1940.
Willie Jones, Philadelphia, April 20, 1949.
Billy Williams, Chicago, April 9, 1969.
Marcus Giles, Atlanta, July 27, 2003.
A.L.—4—Bill Werber, Boston, July 17, 1935, first game.
Mike Kreevich, Chicago, September 4, 1937.
Johnny Lindell, New York, August 17, 1944.
Lou Boudreau, Cleveland, July 14, 1946, first game.
Vic Wertz, Cleveland, September 26, 1956.
Bill Bruton, Detroit, May 19, 1963.
Dave Duncan, Baltimore, June 30, 1975, second game.
Sandy Alomar Jr., Cleveland, June 6, 1997.

Most doubles, opening game of season
A.L.—4—Frank Dillon, Detroit, April 25, 1901.
N.L.—4—Jim Greengrass, Cincinnati, April 13, 1954.

Most doubles by pitcher, game
N.L.—3—George Hemming, Baltimore, August 1, 1895.
Andy Messersmith, Los Angeles, April 25, 1975.
A.L.—3—George Mullin, Detroit, April 27, 1903.
Walter Johnson, Washington, July 29, 1917.
Babe Ruth, Boston, May 9, 1918, 10 innings.
George Uhle, Cleveland, June 1, 1923.
Red Ruffing, Boston, May 25, 1929, second game.
Don Ferrarese, Cleveland, May 26, 1959.

Most doubles, each batting in three runs, game
N.L.—2—Bob Gilks, Cleveland, August 5, 1890 (1 in second, 1 in eighth).
Harry H. Davis, New York, June 27, 1896 (1 in fifth, 1 in ninth).
Klondike Douglass, Philadelphia, July 11, 1898 (1 in second, 1 in sixth).
Gavvy Cravath, Philadelphia, August 8, 1915 (1 in fourth, 1 in eighth).
A.L.—1—Held by many players.
(2—Dan Wilson, Seattle, May 15, 2004 (1 in sixth, 1 in thirteenth.
Carlos Guillen, Detroit, August 21, 2004 (1 in fifth, 1 in sixth in an 11-inning game).

Most doubles, doubleheader
A.L.—6—Hank Majeski, Philadelphia, August 27, 1948.
N.L.—5—Chick Hafey, Cincinnati, July 23, 1933.
Joe Medwick, St. Louis, May 30, 1935.
Red Schoendienst, St. Louis, June 6, 1948.
Mike Ivie, San Diego, May 30, 1977.

Most doubles in two consecutive games
N.L.—6—Cap Anson, Chicago, July 3, 4, a.m. game, 1883.
(6—Sam Thompson, Philadelphia, June 29, July 1, 1895, 22 innings.).
N.L. since 1900—6—Red Schoendienst, St. Louis, June 5, 6, first game, 1948.
A.L.—6—Joe Dugan, Philadelphia, September 24, 25, 1920.
Earl Sheely, Chicago, May 20, 21, 1926.
Hank Majeski, Philadelphia, August 27, 27, 1948.
Kirby Puckett, Minnesota, May 13, 14, 1989.

Most doubles, inning
N.L.-A.L.—2—Held by many players.
Last N.L. player—Craig Wilson, Pittsburgh, June 27, 2004, ninth inning.
Last A.L. player—Gary Sheffield, New York, August 28, 2004, ninth inning.

Most doubles by pitcher, inning
N.L.—2—Fred Goldsmith, Chicago, September 6, 1883, seventh inning.
Hank Borowy, Chicago, May 5, 1946, first game, seventh inning.
A.L.—2—Smokey Joe Wood, Boston, July 4, 1913, a.m. game, fourth inning.
Ted Lyons, Chicago, July 28, 1935, first game, second inning.

TRIPLES
CAREER AND SEASON

Most triples, career
M.L.—312—Sam Crawford, Cincinnati N.L., Detroit A.L., 19 years, 1899 through 1917 (62 in N.L. and 250 in A.L.).
A.L.—295—Ty Cobb, Detroit, Philadelphia, 24 years, 1905 through 1928.
N.L.—252—Honus Wagner, Louisville, Pittsburgh, 21 years, 1897 through 1917.
N.L. since 1900—231—Honus Wagner, Pittsburgh, 18 years, 1900 through 1917.

For a complete list of players with 150 or more career triples, see page 154.

Most triples with bases filled, career
A.L.—8—Shano Collins, Chicago, Boston, 1910, 1915, 1916, 1918 (3), 1920 (2).
N.L.—7—Stan Musial, St. Louis, 1946, 1947 (2), 1948, 1949, 1951, 1954.

Most triples, season
N.L.—36—Owen Wilson, Pittsburgh, 152 games, 1912.
A.L.—26—Joe Jackson, Cleveland, 152 games, 1912.
Sam Crawford, Detroit, 157 games, 1914.

Most triples by rookie, season
N.L.—27—Jimmy Williams, Pittsburgh, 153 games, 1899.
N.L. since 1900—22—Paul Waner, Pittsburgh, 144 games, 1926.
A.L.—19—Joe Cassidy, Washington, 152 games, 1904.
(Home Run Baker collected 19 triples in 148 games in 1909. Baker, however, had 31 at-bats in nine games in 1908. During this period there was no rookie qualification rule.)

Most triples by righthander, season
N.L.—29—Perry Werden, St. Louis, 124 games, 1893.
N.L. since 1900—26—Kiki Cuyler, Pittsburgh, 153 games, 1925.
A.L.—22—Bill Bradley, Cleveland, 136 games, 1903.
Birdie Cree, New York, 137 games, 1911.
George Stirnweiss, New York, 152 games, 1945.

Most triples by lefthander, season
N.L.—36—Owen Wilson, Pittsburgh, 152 games, 1912.
A.L.—26—Joe Jackson, Cleveland, 152 games, 1912.
Sam Crawford, Detroit, 157 games, 1914.

Most triples by switch-hitter, season
N.L.—27—George Davis, New York, 133 games, 1893.
A.L.—21—Willie Wilson, Kansas City, 141 games, 1985.
N.L. since 1900—19—Max Carey, 153 games, 1923.
Garry Templeton, St. Louis, 154 games, 1979.

Most triples with bases filled, season
N.L.—3—George J. Burns, New York, 154 games, 1914.
Ted Sizemore, Los Angeles, 159 games, 1969.
Manny Sanguillen, Pittsburgh, 138 games, 1971.
Alfredo Griffin, Los Angeles, 95 games, 1988.
A.L.—3—Shano Collins, Chicago, 103 games, 1918.
Elmer Valo, Philadelphia, 106 games, 1949.
Jackie Jensen, Boston, 151 games, 1956.

Most seasons leading league in triples (since 1900)
M.L.—6—Sam Crawford, Cincinnati N.L., 1902; Detroit A.L., 1903, 1910, 1913, 1914, 1915.
A.L.—5—Sam Crawford, Detroit, 1903, 1910, 1913, 1914, 1915.
Willie Wilson, Kansas City, 1980 (tied), 1982, 1985, 1987, 1988 (tied).
N.L.—5—Stan Musial, St. Louis, 1943, 1946, 1948, 1949 (tied), 1951 (tied).

Most consecutive seasons leading league in triples (since 1900)
A.L.—4—Lance Johnson, Chicago, 1991 (tied), 1992, 1993, 1994.
N.L.—3—Garry Templeton, St. Louis, 1977, 1978, 1979.

Most seasons with 20 or more triples
M.L.—5—Sam Crawford, Cincinnati N.L., 1902; Detroit A.L., 1903, 1912, 1913, 1914.
A.L.—5—Sam Crawford, Detroit, 1903, 1912, 1913, 1914.
Ty Cobb, Detroit, 1908, 1911, 1912, 1917.
N.L.—3—Roger Connor, New York, 1886, 1887; St. Louis, 1894.
Dan Brouthers, Detroit 1887; Brooklyn, 1892; Baltimore, 1894.
Sam Thompson, Detroit, 1887; Philadelphia, 1894, 1895.
N.L. since 1900—2—Honus Wagner, Pittsburgh, 1900, 1912.
Stan Musial, St. Louis, 1943, 1946.

Most at-bats without a triple, season
A.L.—662—Miguel Tejada, Oakland, 162 games, 2002.
N.L.—643—Sammy Sosa, Chicago, 159 games, 1998.

Fewest triples for league leader, season
A.L.—8—Del Unser, Washington, 153 games, 1969.
N.L.—10—Johnny Callison, Philadelphia, 157 games, 1962.
Willie Davis, Los Angeles, 157 games, 1962.
Bill Virdon, Pittsburgh, 156 games, 1962.
Maury Wills, Los Angeles, 165 games, 1962.
Dickie Thon, Houston, 136 games, 1982.

Jimmy Rollins, Philadelphia, 154 games, 2002.
Steve Finley, Arizona, 147 games, 2003.
Rafael Furcal, Atlanta, 156 games, 2003.

GAME AND INNING

Most triples, game
A.A.—4—George Strief, Philadelphia, June 25, 1885.
N.L.—4—Bill Joyce, New York, May 18, 1897.
N.L. since 1900—3—Held by many players. Last player—Rafael Furcal, Atlanta, April 21, 2002.
A.L.—3—Held by many players. Last player—Lance Johnson, Chicago, September 23, 1995.

Most triples, first major league game
A.L.—2—Ed Irvin, Detroit, May 18, 1912 (only major league game).
Roy Weatherly, Cleveland, June 27, 1936.
N.L.—2—Willie McCovey, San Francisco, July 30, 1959.
John Sipin, San Diego, May 24, 1969 (only major league triples).

Most triples by pitcher, game
N.L.—3—Jouett Meekin, New York, July 4, 1894, first game.

Most consecutive triples, game
N.L.-A.L.—3—Held by many players.
Last N.L. player—Roberto Clemente, Pittsburgh, September 8, 1958.
Last A.L. player—Ben Chapman, Cleveland, July 3, 1939.

Most triples with bases filled, game
N.L.—2—Sam Thompson, Detroit, May 7, 1887.
Heinie Reitz, Baltimore, June 4, 1894, 1 in third inning, 1 in seventh inning.
Willie Clark, Pittsburgh, September 17, 1898, second game, 1 in first inning, 1 in seventh inning.
Bill Bruton, Milwaukee, August 2, 1959, second game, 1 in first inning, 1 in sixth inning.
A.L.—2—Elmer Valo, Philadelphia, May 1, 1949, first game, 1 in third inning, 1 in seventh inning.
Duane Kuiper, Cleveland, July 27, 1978, second game, 1 in first inning, 1 in fifth inning.

Most times with three triples in one game, career
M.L.—2—Harry Stovey, Philadelphia A.A., 1884; Baltimore N.L., 1892.
Billy Hamilton, Kansas City A.A., 1889; Philadelphia N.L., 1891.
N.L.—2—John Reilly, Cincinnati, 1890, 1891.
George Davis, Cleveland, New York, 1891, 1894.
Bill Dahlen, Chicago, 1896, 1898.
Dave Brain, St. Louis, Pittsburgh, 1905 (2).
Jim Bottomley, St. Louis, 1923, 1927.
A.L.—1—Held by many players.

Most times with three triples in one game, season
N.L.—2—Dave Brain, St. Louis, May 29, 1905; Pittsburgh, August 8, 1905.
A.L.—1—Held by many players.

Hitting triple and home run in first major league game
A.L.—Hank Arft, St. Louis, July 27, 1948.
N.L.—Lloyd Merriman, Cincinnati, April 24, 1949, first game.
Frank Ernaga, Chicago, May 24, 1957.
Ken Caminiti, Houston, July 16, 1987.

Hitting triple and home run with bases filled, game
N.L.—Dan Brouthers, Detroit, May 17, 1887.
Kid Nichols, Boston, September 19, 1892.
Jake Stenzel, Pittsburgh, July 15, 1893.
Del Bissonette, Brooklyn, April 21, 1930.
Eddie Phillips, Pittsburgh, May 28, 1931.
Luis Olmo, Brooklyn, May 18, 1945.
Robin Jennings, Cincinnati, August 31, 2001.
A.L.—George Sisler, St. Louis, July 11, 1925.
Harry Heilmann, Detroit, July 26, 1928, second game.

Most triples, doubleheader
A.A.—4—Billy Hamilton, Kansas City, June 28, 1889.

N.L.—4—Mike Donlin, Cincinnati, September 22, 1903.
A.L.—3—Held by many players.

Most triples, inning
N.L.—2—Joe Hornung, Boston, May 6, 1882, eighth inning.
Heinie Peitz, St. Louis, July 2, 1895, first inning.
Frank Shugart, Louisville, July 30, 1895, fifth inning.
Buck Freeman, Boston, July 25, 1900, first inning.
Bill Dahlen, Brooklyn, August 30, 1900, eighth inning.
Curt Walker, Cincinnati, July 22, 1926, second inning.
A.A.—2—Harry Wheeler, Cincinnati, June 28, 1882, 11th inning.
Harry Stovey, Philadelphia, August 18, 1884, eighth inning.
A.L.—2—Al Zarilla, St. Louis, July 13, 1946, fourth inning.
Gil Coan, Washington, April 21, 1951, sixth inning.

HOME RUNS
CAREER

Most home runs, career
M.L.—755—Hank Aaron, Milwaukee N.L., Atlanta N.L., Milwaukee A.L., 23 years, 1954 through 1976 (733 in N.L.; 22 in A.L.).
N.L.—733—Hank Aaron, Milwaukee, Atlanta, 21 years, 1954 through 1974.
A.L.—708—Babe Ruth, Boston, New York, 21 years, 1914 through 1934.

For a complete list of players with 300 or more career home runs, see page 155.

Most home runs with one club, career
N.L.—733—Hank Aaron, Milwaukee, Atlanta, 21 years, 1954 through 1974.
A.L.—659—Babe Ruth, New York, 15 years, 1920 through 1934.

Most home runs by righthander, career
M.L.—755—Hank Aaron, Milwaukee N.L., Atlanta N.L., Milwaukee A.L., 23 years, 1954 through 1976 (733 in N.L.; 22 in A.L.).
N.L.—700—Hank Aaron, Milwaukee, Atlanta, 21 years, 1954 through 1974.
A.L.—573—Harmon Killebrew, Washington, Minnesota, Kansas City, 22 years, 1954 through 1975.

Most home runs by lefthander, career
M.L.—714—Babe Ruth, Boston A.L., New York A.L., Boston N.L., 22 years, 1914 through 1935 (708 in A.L.; 6 in N.L.).
A.L.—708—Babe Ruth, Boston, New York, 21 years, 1914 through 1934.
N.L.—703—Barry Bonds, Pittsburgh, San Francisco, 19 years, 1986 through 2004.

Most home runs by switch-hitter, career
A.L.—536—Mickey Mantle, New York, 18 years, 1951 through 1968.
N.L.—310—Chipper Jones, Atlanta, 11 years, 1993 through 2004, except 1994.

Most home runs by pinch-hitter, career
M.L.—20—Cliff Johnson, Houston N.L., New York A.L., Cleveland A.L., Chicago N.L., Oakland A.L., Toronto A.L., 1974 (5), 1975, 1976, 1977 (3), 1978 (2), 1979, 1980 (3), 1981, 1983, 1984, 1986.
N.L.—18—Jerry Lynch, Cincinnati, Pittsburgh, 1957 (3), 1958, 1959, 1961 (5), 1962, 1963 (4), 1964, 1965, 1966.
A.L.—16—Gates Brown, Detroit, 1963, 1964, 1965, 1966 (2), 1968 (3), 1970, 1971 (2), 1972, 1974 (3), 1975.

For a complete list of players with 10 or more career pinch-hit home runs, see page 155.

Most home runs leading off game, career
M.L.—81—Rickey Henderson, Oakland A.L., New York A.L., Toronto A.L., San Diego N.L., Anaheim A.L., New York N.L., Seattle A.L., Boston A.L., Los Angeles, 25 years, 1979

through 2003 (73 in A.L., 8 in N.L.).

A.L.—73—Rickey Henderson, Oakland, New York, Toronto, Anaheim, Seattle, Boston, 21 years, 1979 through 2002, except 1996, 1999 and 2001.

N.L.—40—Craig Biggio, Houston, 17 years, 1988 through 2004.

Most home runs in extra innings, career

N.L.—22—Willie Mays, New York Giants, San Francisco, New York Mets, 22 years, 1951 through 1973, except 1953 in military service.

A.L.—16—Babe Ruth, Boston, New York, 21 years, 1914 through 1934.

Most home runs in opening games of season, career

M.L.—8—Frank Robinson, Cincinnati N.L., 1959, 1961, 1963; Baltimore A.L., 1966, 1969, 1970; California A.L., 1973; Cleveland A.L., 1975 (5 in A.L., 3 in N.L.).

N.L.—7—Eddie Mathews, Milwaukee, 1954 (2), 1958 (2), 1959, 1961, 1965.

Willie Mays, New York, 1954; San Francisco, 1962, 1963, 1964 (2), 1966, 1971.

A.L.—7—Ken Griffey Jr., Seattle, 1990, 1993, 1995, 1997 (2), 1998, 1999.

Most home runs by first baseman, career

M.L.—566—Mark McGwire, Oakland A.L., St. Louis N.L., 16 years, 1986 through 2001 (349 in A.L., 217 in N.L.).

A.L.—493—Lou Gehrig, New York, 17 years, 1923 through 1939.

N.L.—439—Willie McCovey, San Francisco, San Diego, 22 years, 1959 through 1980.

Most home runs by second baseman, career

M.L.—278—Jeff Kent, Toronto A.L., New York N.L., Cleveland A.L., San Francisco N.L., Houston N.L., 13 years, 1992 through 2004.

N.L.—277—Ryne Sandberg, Philadelphia, Chicago, 16 years, 1981 through 1997, except 1995.

A.L.—246—Joe Gordon, New York, Cleveland, 11 years, 1938 through 1950, except 1944, 1945 in military service.

Most home runs by third baseman, career

N.L.—509—Mike Schmidt, Philadelphia, 18 years, 1972 through 1989.

A.L.—319—Graig Nettles, Minnesota, Cleveland, New York, 16 years, 1968 through 1983.

Most home runs by shortstop, career

A.L.—345—Cal Ripken Jr., Baltimore, 16 years, 1981 through 1996.

N.L.—277—Ernie Banks, Chicago, nine years, 1953 through 1961.

Most home runs by outfielder, career

M.L.—692—Babe Ruth, Boston A.L., New York A.L., Boston N.L., 17 years, 1918 through 1935 (686 in A.L.; 6 in N.L.).

A.L.—686—Babe Ruth, Boston, New York, 17 years, 1918 through 1934.

N.L.—661—Hank Aaron, Milwaukee, Atlanta, 21 years, 1954 through 1974.

Most home runs by catcher, career

N.L.—358—Mike Piazza, Los Angeles, Florida, New York, 13 years, 1992 through 2004.

A.L.—351—Carlton Fisk, Boston, Chicago, 24 years, 1969 through 1993, except 1970.

Most home runs by pitcher, career

A.L.—36—Wes Ferrell, Cleveland, Boston, Washington, New York, 13 years, 1927 through 1939. (Also one home run as pinch-hitter, 1935; one home run as pitcher, Boston N.L., 1941).

N.L.—35—Warren Spahn, Boston, Milwaukee, New York, San Francisco, 21 years, 1942 through 1965, except 1943, 1944, 1945 in military service.

Most major league ballparks, one or more home runs, career (since 1900)

M.L.—43—Fred McGriff, Toronto A.L., San Diego N.L., Atlanta N.L., Tampa Bay A.L., Chicago N.L., Los Angeles N.L., Tampa Bay, A.L., 19 years, 1986 through 2004.

A.L.—31—Rafael Palmeiro, Texas, Baltimore, 15 years, 1989 through 2003.

N.L.—31—Mike Piazza, Los Angeles, Florida, New York, 12 years, 1992 through 2003 (includes one at Tokyo Dome).

Barry Bonds, Pittsburgh, San Francisco, 18 years, 1986 through 2003.

Most consecutive at-bats without hitting a home run, career

N.L.—3,347—Tommy Thevenow, St. Louis, Philadelphia, Pittsburgh, Cincinnati, Boston, September 24, 1926 through October 2, 1938 (end of career).

A.L.—3,278—Eddie Foster, Washington, Boston, St. Louis, April 20, 1916 through August 5, 1923 (end of career).

SEASON

Most home runs, season

N.L.—73—Barry Bonds, San Francisco, 153 games, 2001.

A.L.—61—Roger Maris, New York, 161 games, 1961.

For a complete list of players with 40 or more home runs in a season, see page 162. For complete lists of players combining power and speed (40 HRs, 40 SBs; 30 HRs, 30 SBs; 50 HRs, 20 SBs and 20 HRs, 50 SBs) during a season, see page 168. For detailed breakdowns of Barry Bonds' 73-homer season, Mark McGwire's 70-homer season, Roger Maris' 61-homer season and Babe Ruth's 60-homer season, see page 173.

Most home runs for runner-up, season

N.L.—66—Sammy Sosa, Chicago, 159 games, 1998.

A.L.—54—Mickey Mantle, New York, 153 games, 1961.

Most years leading league in home runs

A.L.—12—Babe Ruth, Boston, New York, 1918 (tied), 1919, 1920, 1921, 1923, 1924, 1926, 1927, 1928, 1929, 1930, 1931 (tied).

N.L.—8—Mike Schmidt, Philadelphia, 1974, 1975, 1976, 1980, 1981, 1983, 1984 (tied), 1986.

Most consecutive years leading league in home runs

N.L.—7—Ralph Kiner, Pittsburgh, 1946, 1947 (tied), 1948 (tied), 1949, 1950, 1951, 1952 (tied).

A.L.—6—Babe Ruth, New York, 1926 through 1931 (tied in 1931).

Most home runs by rookie, season

A.L.—49—Mark McGwire, Oakland, 151 games, 1987.

N.L.—38—Wally Berger, Boston, 151 games, 1930.

Frank Robinson, Cincinnati, 152 games, 1956.

Most home runs by righthander, season

N.L.—70—Mark McGwire, St. Louis, 155 games, 1998.

A.L.—58—Jimmie Foxx, Philadelphia, 154 games, 1932.

Hank Greenberg, Detroit, 155 games, 1938.

Most home runs by lefthander, season

N.L.—73—Barry Bonds, San Francisco, 153 games, 2001.

A.L.—61—Roger Maris, New York, 161 games, 1961.

Most home runs by switch-hitter, season

A.L.—54—Mickey Mantle, New York, 153 games, 1961.

N.L.—45—Chipper Jones, Atlanta, 157 games, 1999.

Most home runs by pinch-hitter, season

N.L.—7—Dave Hansen, Los Angeles, 2000.

Craig Wilson, Pittsburgh, 2001.

A.L.—5—Joe Cronin, Boston, 1943.

Most home runs leading off game, season

A.L.—13—Alfonso Soriano, New York, 156 games, 2003 (38 home runs for season).

N.L.—11—Bobby Bonds, San Francisco, 160 games, 1973 (39 home runs for season).

Most home runs by first baseman, season

N.L.—69—Mark McGwire, St. Louis, 155 games, 1998, 151 games at first base (also had one home run as pinch-hitter).

A.L.—58—Hank Greenberg, Detroit, 155 games, 1938, 154 games at first base.

Most home runs by second baseman, season

N.L.—42—Rogers Hornsby, St. Louis, 154 games, 1922, 154 games at second base.

Dave Johnson, Atlanta, 157 games, 1973, 156 games at second base (also had one home run as pinch-hitter).

A.L.—39—Alfonso Soriano, New York, 156 games, 2002, 155 games at second base.

Most home runs by third baseman, season
N.L.—48—Mike Schmidt, Philadelphia, 150 games, 1980, 149 games at third base.
Adrian Beltre, Los Angeles, 156 games, 2004, 155 games at third base.
A.L.—46—Troy Glaus, Anaheim, 159 games, 2000, 156 games at third base (also had one home run as designated hitter).

Most home runs by shortstop, season
A.L.—57—Alex Rodriguez, Texas, 162 games, 2002, 162 games at shortstop.
N.L.—47—Ernie Banks, Chicago, 154 games, 1958, 154 games at shortstop.

Most home runs by outfielder, season
N.L.—71—Barry Bonds, San Francisco, 153 games, 2001, 143 games in outfield (also had one home run as pinch-hitter and one home run as designated hitter).
A.L.—61—Roger Maris, New York, 161 games, 1961, 160 games in outfield.

Most home runs by catcher, season
N.L.—42—Javy Lopez, Atlanta, 129 games, 2003, caught 120 games.
(Johnny Bench, Cincinnati, 1970, had 38 home runs in 139 games as a catcher and seven additional home runs as an outfielder and first baseman.)
A.L.—35—Ivan Rodriguez, Texas, 144 games, 1999, caught 141 games.
(Carlton Fisk, Chicago, 1985, had 33 home runs in 130 games as a catcher and four additional home runs as a designated hitter.)

Most home runs by pitcher, season (only those hit as pitcher)
A.L.—9—Wes Ferrell, Cleveland, 48 games, 1931, pitched 40 games.
N.L.—7—Don Newcombe, Brooklyn, 57 games, 1955, pitched 34 games.
Don Drysdale, Los Angeles, 47 games, 1958, pitched 44 games.
Don Drysdale, Los Angeles, 58 games, 1965, pitched 44 games.
Mike Hampton, Colorado, 43 games, 2001, pitched 32 games.

Most home runs against one club, season
A.L.—14—Lou Gehrig, New York vs. Cleveland, 1936 (6 at New York, 8 at Cleveland).
N.L.—13—Hank Sauer, Chicago vs. Pittsburgh, 1954 (8 at Chicago, 5 at Pittsburgh).
Joe Adcock, Milwaukee vs. Brooklyn, 1956 (5 at Milwaukee, 7 at Brooklyn, 1 at Jersey City).

Most at-bats without a home run, season
N.L.—672—Rabbit Maranville, Pittsburgh, 155 games, 1922.
A.L.—658—Doc Cramer, Boston, 148 games, 1938.

Fewest home runs by leader, season
N.L.—7—Red Murray, New York, 149 games, 1909.
A.L.—7—Sam Crawford, Detroit, 152 games, 1908.
Braggo Roth, Chicago, Cleveland, 109 games, 1915.

HOME AND ROAD

Most home runs hit at home, season
A.L.—39—Hank Greenberg, Detroit, 1938.
N.L.—38—Mark McGwire, St. Louis, 1998.

Most home runs hit at home by righthander, season
A.L.—39—Hank Greenberg, Detroit, 1938.
N.L.—38—Mark McGwire, St. Louis, 1998.

Most home runs hit at home by lefthander, season
N.L.—37—Barry Bonds, San Francisco, 2001.
A.L.—32—Babe Ruth, New York, 1921.
Ken Williams, St. Louis, 1922.

Most home runs hit at home by switch-hitter, season
A.L.—27—Mickey Mantle, New York, 1956.

N.L.—25—Chipper Jones, Atlanta, 1999.

Most home runs hit at home against one club, season
A.L.—10—Gus Zernial, Philadelphia vs. St. Louis, 1951.
N.L.—9—Stan Musial, St. Louis vs. New York, 1954.

Most home runs hit on road, season
N.L.—36—Barry Bonds, San Francisco, 2001.
A.L.—32—Babe Ruth, New York, 1927.

Most home runs hit on road by righthander, season
N.L.—32—Mark McGwire, St. Louis, 1998.
A.L.—28—Harmon Killebrew, Minnesota, 1962.
George Bell, Toronto, 1987.
Mark McGwire, Oakland, 1987.
Jose Canseco, Oakland, 1991.
Mark McGwire, Oakland, 1996.

Most home runs hit on road by lefthander, season
N.L.—36—Barry Bonds, San Francisco, 2001.
A.L.—32—Babe Ruth, New York, 1927.

Most home runs hit on road by switch-hitter, season
A.L.—30—Mickey Mantle, New York, 1961.
N.L.—23—Howard Johnson, New York, 1987.

Most home runs hit on road against one club, season
A.L.—10—Harry Heilmann, Detroit at Philadelphia, 1922.
N.L.—9—Joe Adcock, Milwaukee at Brooklyn, 1954.
Willie Mays, New York at Brooklyn, 1955.

Most major league ballparks, one or more home runs, season
N.L.—18—Sammy Sosa, Chicago, 1998 (homered in 16 N.L. parks and 2 A.L. parks).
Mike Piazza, New York, 2000 (homered in 14 N.L. parks, 3 A.L. parks and one park in Japan).
A.L.—16—Ken Griffey Jr., Seattle, 1998 (homered in 13 A.L. parks and 3 N.L. parks).
Juan Gonzalez, Texas, 1999 (homered in 13 A.L. parks and 3 N.L. parks).

Most seasons hitting home runs in all parks, career
A.L.—11—Babe Ruth, Boston, New York, 1919, 1920, 1921, 1923, 1924, 1926, 1927, 1928, 1929, 1930, 1931.
N.L.—9—Hank Aaron, Milwaukee, Atlanta, 1954, 1955, 1956, 1957, 1958, 1959, 1960, 1963, 1966.

50, 40, 30 AND 20 IN SEASON

Most seasons with 50 or more home runs
M.L.—4—Babe Ruth, New York A.L., 1920, 1921, 1927, 1928.
Mark McGwire, Oakland A.L., 1996; Oakland A.L. and St. Louis N.L., 1997; St. Louis N.L., 1998, 1999.
Sammy Sosa, Chicago N.L., 1998, 1999, 2000, 2001.
A.L.—4—Babe Ruth, New York, 1920, 1921, 1927, 1928.
N.L.—4—Sammy Sosa, Chicago, 1998, 1999, 2000, 2001.

Most consecutive seasons with 50 or more home runs
M.L.—4—Mark McGwire, Oakland A.L., 1996, Oakland A.L. and St. Louis N.L., 1997, St. Louis N.L., 1998, 1999.
Sammy Sosa, Chicago, 1998, 1999, 2000, 2001.
N.L.—4—Sammy Sosa, Chicago, 1998, 1999, 2000, 2001.
A.L.—2—Babe Ruth, New York, 1920, 1921 and 1927, 1928.
Ken Griffey Jr., Seattle, 1997, 1998.
Alex Rodriguez, Texas, 2001, 2002.

Most seasons with 40 or more home runs
A.L.—11—Babe Ruth, New York, 1920, 1921, 1923, 1924, 1926, 1927, 1928, 1929, 1930, 1931, 1932.
N.L.—8—Hank Aaron, Milwaukee, Atlanta, 1957, 1960, 1962, 1963, 1966, 1969, 1971, 1973.
Barry Bonds, San Francisco, 1993, 1996, 1997, 2000 through 2004.

For a complete list of players with 40 or more home runs in a season, see page 162.

Most consecutive seasons with 40 or more home runs
A.L.—7—Babe Ruth, New York, 1926 through 1932.

N.L.—6—Sammy Sosa, Chicago, 1998 through 2003.

Most seasons with 30 or more home runs
N.L.—15—Hank Aaron, Milwaukee, Atlanta, 1957 through
1973, except 1964, 1968.
A.L.—13—Babe Ruth, New York, 1920 through 1933, except 1925.

Most consecutive seasons with 30 or more home runs
N.L.—13—Barry Bonds, Pittsburgh, San Francisco, 1992
through 2004.
A.L.—12—Jimmie Foxx, Philadelphia, Boston, 1929 through 1940.

Hitting 20 or more home runs for two leagues, season
Mark McGwire, Oakland A.L., 34, St. Louis N.L., 24, 1997.

Most seasons with 20 or more home runs
N.L.—20—Hank Aaron, Milwaukee, Atlanta, 1955 through 1974.
A.L.—16—Babe Ruth, Boston, New York, 1919 through 1934.
Ted Williams, Boston, 1939, 1940, 1941, 1942, 1946, 1947, 1948,
1949, 1950, 1951, 1954, 1955, 1956, 1957, 1958, 1960.
Reggie Jackson, Oakland, Baltimore, New York, California,
1968 through 1980, 1982, 1984, 1985.

Most consecutive seasons with 20 or more home runs
N.L.—20—Hank Aaron, Milwaukee, Atlanta, 1955 through 1974.
A.L.—16—Babe Ruth, Boston, New York, 1919 through 1934.

TWO CONSECUTIVE SEASONS

Most home runs, two consecutive seasons
N.L.—135—Mark McGwire, St. Louis, 70 in 1998, 65 in 1999.
A.L.—114—Babe Ruth, New York, 60 in 1927, 54 in 1928.

Most home runs by righthander, two consecutive seasons
N.L.—135—Mark McGwire, St. Louis, 70 in 1998, 65 in 1999.
A.L.—109—Alex Rodriguez, Texas, 52 in 2001, 57 in 2002.

Most home runs by lefthander, two consecutive seasons
N.L.—122—Barry Bonds, San Francisco, 49 in 2000, 73 in
2001.
A.L.—114—Babe Ruth, New York, 60 in 1927, 54 in 1928.

Most home runs by switch-hitter, two consecutive seasons
A.L.—94—Mickey Mantle, New York, 40 in 1960, 54 in 1961.
N.L.—81—Chipper Jones, Atlanta, 45 in 1999, 36 in 2000.

MONTH AND WEEK

**Most home runs, one month (from first through last day of
month)**
N.L.—20—Sammy Sosa, Chicago, June 1998.
A.L.—18—Rudy York, Detroit, August 1937.

Most home runs by righthander, one month
N.L.—20—Sammy Sosa, Chicago, June 1998.
A.L.—18—Rudy York, Detroit, August 1937.

Most home runs by lefthander, one month
A.L.—17—Babe Ruth, New York, September 1927.
N.L.—17—Barry Bonds, San Francisco, May 2001.

Most home runs by switch-hitter, one month
A.L.—16—Mickey Mantle, New York, May 1956.
N.L.—14—Ken Caminiti, San Diego, August 1996.

Most home runs in March
N.L.—2—Vinny Castilla, Colorado, March 1998.
A.L.—2—Jorge Posada, New York, March 2004.

Most home runs in April
A.L.—13—Ken Griffey Jr., Seattle, April 1997.
N.L.—13—Luis Gonzalez, Arizona, April 2001.

Most home runs through April 30
A.L.—13—Ken Griffey Jr., Seattle, 1997.
N.L.—13—Luis Gonzalez, Arizona, April 2001.

Most home runs in May
N.L.—17—Barry Bonds, San Francisco, May 2001.
A.L.—16—Mickey Mantle, New York, May 1956.

Most home runs through May 31
N.L.—28—Barry Bonds, San Francisco, 2001.
A.L.—24—Ken Griffey Jr., Seattle, 1997.

Most home runs in June
N.L.—20—Sammy Sosa, Chicago, June 1998.
A.L.—15—Babe Ruth, New York, June 1930.
Bob Johnson, Philadelphia, June 1934.
Roger Maris, New York, June 1961.

Most home runs through June 30
N.L.—39—Barry Bonds, San Francisco, 2001.
A.L.—32—Ken Griffey Jr., Seattle, 1994.

Most home runs in July
A.L.—16—Albert Belle, Chicago, July 1998.
N.L.—16—Mark McGwire, St. Louis, July 1999.

Most home runs through July 31
N.L.—45—Mark McGwire, St. Louis, 1998.
Barry Bonds, San Francisco, 2001.
A.L.—41—Babe Ruth, New York, 1928.
Jimmie Foxx, Philadelphia, 1932.

Most home runs in August
A.L.—18—Rudy York, Detroit, August 1937.
N.L.—17—Willie Mays, San Francisco, August 1965.
Sammy Sosa, Chicago, August 2001.

Most home runs through August 31
N.L.—57—Barry Bonds, San Francisco, 2001.
A.L.—51—Roger Maris, New York, 1961.

Most home runs in September
A.L.—17—Babe Ruth, New York, September 1927.
Albert Belle, Cleveland, September 1995.
N.L.—16—Ralph Kiner, Pittsburgh, September 1949.

Most home runs through September 30
N.L.—70—Mark McGwire, St. Louis, 1998.
A.L.—60—Babe Ruth, New York, 1927.
Roger Maris, New York, 1961.

Most home runs in October
N.L.—5—Richie Sexson, Milwaukee, October 2001.
Sammy Sosa, Chicago, October 2001.
A.A.—4—John Milligan, St. Louis, October 1889.
A.L.—4—Gus Zernial, Chicago, October 1950.
George Brett, Kansas City, October 1985.
Ron Kittle, Chicago, October 1985.
Wally Joyner, California, October 1987.
Jose Cruz Jr., Toronto, October 2001.

Most home runs in one week (Sunday through Saturday)
A.L.—10—Frank Howard, Washington, May 12 through 18,
1968, six games.
N.L.—9—Shawn Green, Los Angeles, May 19 through 25,
2002, six games.

GAME, DOUBLEHEADER, INNING

Most home runs, game
N.L.—4—Bobby Lowe, Boston, May 30, 1894, p.m. game (con-
secutive).
Ed Delahanty, Philadelphia, July 13, 1896.
Gil Hodges, Brooklyn, August 31, 1950.
Joe Adcock, Milwaukee, July 31, 1954.
Willie Mays, San Francisco, April 30, 1961.
Bob Horner, Atlanta, July 6, 1986.
Mark Whiten, St. Louis, September 7, 1993, second game.
Shawn Green, Los Angeles, May 23, 2002.
(4—Chuck Klein, Philadelphia, July 10, 1936, 10 innings.
Mike Schmidt, Philadelphia, April 17, 1976, 10 innings (con-
secutive).
A.L.—4—Lou Gehrig, New York, June 3, 1932 (consecutive).
Rocky Colavito, Cleveland, June 10, 1959 (consecutive).
Mike Cameron, Seattle, May 2, 2002 (consecutive).
Carlos Delgado, Toronto, September 25, 2003 (consecutive).
(4—Pat Seerey, Chicago, July 18, 1948, first game, 11
innings.)

**For a complete list of players with three or
more home runs in a game, see page 164.**

Most home runs by pitcher, game
A.A.—3—Guy Hecker, Louisville, August 15, 1886, second game.
N.L.—3—Jim Tobin, Boston, May 13, 1942.
A.L.—2—Held by many pitchers. Last pitcher—Sonny Siebert, Boston, September 2, 1971.

Most home runs, first game in major leagues
A.A.—2—Charlie Reilly, Columbus, October 9, 1889 (on third and fifth times at bat).
A.L.—2—Bob Nieman, St. Louis, September 14, 1951 (on first two times at bat).
  Bert Campaneris, Kansas City, July 23, 1964 (on first and fourth times at bat).
  Mark Quinn, Kansas City, September 14, 1999, second game (on third and fourth times at bat).
N.L.—1—Held by many players.

Most home runs, opening game of season
A.L.—3—George Bell, Toronto, April 4, 1988.
N.L.—3—Karl Rhodes, Chicago, April 4, 1994.

Most inside-the-park home runs, game
N.L.—3—Tom McCreery, Louisville, July 12, 1897.
N.L.-A.L. since 1900—2—Held by many players.
Last N.L. player—Hank Thompson, New York (at Polo Grounds), August 16, 1950.
Last A.L. player—Greg Gagne, Minnesota (at Metrodome), October 4, 1986.

Most home runs in extra innings, game
N.L.—2—Art Shamsky, Cincinnati, August 12, 1966, 10th and 11th innings (consecutive).
  Ralph Garr, Atlanta, May 17, 1971, 10th and 12th innings (consecutive).
A.L.—2—Vern Stephens, St. Louis, September 29, 1943, first game, 11th and 13th innings (consecutive).
  Willie Kirkland, Cleveland, June 14, 1963, second game, 11th and 19th innings.
  Mike Young, Baltimore, May 28, 1987, 10th and 12th innings (consecutive).

Home run winning longest extra-inning game
A.L.—Harold Baines, Chicago, 25 innings, 0 on base, Chicago won vs. Milwaukee, 7-6, May 8, completed May 9, 1984.
N.L.—Rick Dempsey, Los Angeles, 22 innings, 0 on base, Los Angeles won vs. Montreal, 1-0, August 23, 1989.

Home run winning longest 1-0 game
N.L.—Rick Dempsey, Los Angeles, August 23, 1989, 22 innings.
A.L.—Bill Skowron, New York, April 22, 1959, 14 innings.

Home run by pitcher winning 1-0 extra-inning complete game
A.L.—Tom Hughes, Washington, August 3, 1906, 10 innings.
  Red Ruffing, New York, August 13, 1932, 10 innings.
N.L.—Never accomplished—(Johnny Klippstein, Cincinnati, on August 6, 1962, hit home run in 13th inning, after relieving Bob Purkey, who had pitched first 10 innings).

Home run in first major league at-bat
*On first pitch †Not first plate appearance ‡Pitcher
A.A.—George Tebeau, Cincinnati, April 16, 1887.
  Mike Griffin, Baltimore, April 16, 1887.
Total number of players: 2
A.L.—Luke Stuart, St. Louis, August 8, 1921.
  Earl Averill, Cleveland, April 16, 1929.
  Ace Parker, Philadelphia, April 30, 1937.
  Gene Hasson, Philadelphia, September 9, 1937, first game.
  Bill Lefebvre, Boston, June 10, 1938.*‡
  Hack Miller, Detroit, April 23, 1944, second game.
  Eddie Pellagrini, Boston, April 22, 1946.
  George Vico, Detroit, April 20, 1948.*
  Bob Nieman, St. Louis, September 14, 1951.
  Bob Tillman, Boston, May 19, 1962.†
  John Kennedy, Washington, September 5, 1962, first game.
  Buster Narum, Baltimore, May 3, 1963.‡
  Gates Brown, Detroit, June 19, 1963.
  Bert Campaneris, Kansas City, July 23, 1964.*
  Bill Roman, Detroit, September 30, 1964, second game.
  Brant Alyea, Washington, September 12, 1965.*

John Miller, New York, September 11, 1966.
Rick Renick, Minnesota, July 11, 1968.
Joe Keough, Oakland, August 7, 1968, second game.
Gene Lamont, Detroit, September 2, 1970, second game.
Don Rose, California, May 24, 1972.*‡
Reggie J. Sanders, Detroit, September 1, 1974.
Dave McKay, Minnesota, August 22, 1975.
Al Woods, Toronto, April 7, 1977.*
Dave Machemer, California, June 21, 1978.
Gary Gaetti, Minnesota, September 20, 1981.
Andre David, Minnesota, June 29, 1984, first game.
Terry Steinbach, Oakland, September 12, 1986.
Jay Bell, Cleveland, September 29, 1986.*
Junior Felix, Toronto, May 4, 1989.*
Jon Nunnally, Kansas City, April 29, 1995.
Carlos Lee, Chicago, May 7, 1999.
Esteban Yan, Tampa Bay, June 4, 2000.*‡
Marcus Thames, New York, June 10, 2002.*
Miguel Olivo, Chicago, September 15, 2002.
Andy Phillips, New York, September 26, 2004.
Total number of players: 35
N.L.—Joe Harrington, Boston, September 10, 1895.
  Bill Duggleby, Philadelphia, April 21, 1898 (grand slam).‡
  Johnny Bates, Boston, April 12, 1906.
  Walter Mueller, Pittsburgh, May 7, 1922.*
  Clise Dudley, Brooklyn, April 27, 1929.*‡
  Gordon Slade, Brooklyn, May 24, 1930.
  Eddie Morgan, St. Louis, April 14, 1936.*
  Ernie Koy, Brooklyn, April 19, 1938.
  Emmett Mueller, Philadelphia, April 19, 1938.
  Clyde Vollmer, Cincinnati, May 31, 1942, second game.*
  Paul Gillespie, Chicago, September 11, 1942.
  Buddy Kerr, New York, September 8, 1943.
  Whitey Lockman, New York, July 5, 1945.
  Dan Bankhead, Brooklyn, August 26, 1947.‡
  Les Layton, New York, May 21, 1948.
  Ed Sanicki, Philadelphia, September 14, 1949.
  Ted Tappe, Cincinnati, September 14, 1950, first game.
  Hoyt Wilhelm, New York, April 23, 1952.‡
  Wally Moon, St. Louis, April 13, 1954.
  Chuck Tanner, Milwaukee, April 12, 1955.*
  Bill White, New York, May 7, 1956.
  Frank Ernaga, Chicago, May 24, 1957.
  Don Leppert, Pittsburgh, June 18, 1961, first game.
  Cuno Barragan, Chicago, September 1, 1961.
  Benny Ayala, New York, August 27, 1974.
  John Montefusco, San Francisco, September 3, 1974.†‡
  Jose Sosa, Houston, July 30, 1975.‡
  Johnnie LeMaster, San Francisco, September 2, 1975.
  Tim Wallach, Montreal, September 6, 1980.†
  Carmelo Martinez, Chicago, August 22, 1983.†
  Mike Fitzgerald, New York, September 13, 1983.
  Will Clark, San Francisco, April 8, 1986.
  Ricky Jordan, Philadelphia, July 17, 1988.†
  Jose Offerman, Los Angeles, August 19, 1990.
  Dave Eiland, San Diego, April 10, 1992.‡
  Jim Bullinger, Chicago, June 8, 1992, first game.*‡
  Jay Gainer, Colorado, May 14, 1993.*
  Mitch Lyden, Florida, June 16, 1993.
  Garey Ingram, Los Angeles, May 19, 1994.
  Jermaine Dye, Atlanta, May 17, 1996.
  Dustin Hermanson, Montreal, April 16, 1997.‡
  Brad Fullmer, Montreal, September 2, 1997.
  Marlon Anderson, Philadelphia, September 8, 1998.
  Guillermo Mota, Montreal, June 9, 1999.
  Alex Cabrera, Arizona, June 26, 2000.
  Keith McDonald, St. Louis, July 4, 2000.
  Chris Richard, St. Louis, July 17, 2000.*
  Gene Stechschulte, St. Louis, April 17, 2001.*‡ (Was a pitcher batting as a pinch-hitter.)
  Dave Matranga, Houston, June 27, 2003.
Total number of players: 49

Players hitting a pinch home run in first major league at-bat
N.L.—Eddie Morgan, St. Louis, April 14, 1936, seventh inning.
  Les Layton, New York, May 21, 1948, ninth inning.

Ted Tappe, Cincinnati, September 14, 1950, first game, eighth inning.

Chuck Tanner, Milwaukee, April 12, 1955, eighth inning.

Marlon Anderson, Philadelphia, September 8, 1998, seventh inning.

Keith McDonald, St. Louis, July 4, 2000, eighth inning.

Gene Stechschulte, St. Louis, April 17, 2001, sixth inning.

A.L.—Ace Parker, Philadelphia, April 30, 1937, ninth inning.

John Kennedy, Washington, September 5, 1962, first game, sixth inning.

Gates Brown, Detroit, June 19, 1963, fifth inning.

Bill Roman, Detroit, September 30, 1964, second game, seventh inning.

Brant Alyea, Washington, September 12, 1965, sixth inning.

Joe Keough, Oakland, August 7, 1968, second game, eighth inning.

Al Woods, Toronto, April 7, 1977, fifth inning.

Home run in first two major league at-bats

A.L.—Bob Nieman, St. Louis, September 14, 1951 (first two plate appearances).

N.L.—Keith McDonald, St. Louis, July 4, July 6, 2000 (first two plate appearances).

Most home runs, doubleheader (homering in each game)

N.L.—5—Stan Musial, St. Louis, May 2, 1954.

Nate Colbert, San Diego, August 1, 1972.

A.L.—4—Earl Averill, Cleveland, September 17, 1930.

Jimmie Foxx, Philadelphia, July 2, 1933, 19 innings.

Jim Tabor, Boston, July 4, 1939.

Gus Zernial, Chicago, October 1, 1950.

Charlie Maxwell, Detroit, May 3, 1959 (consecutive).

Roger Maris, New York, July 25, 1961.

Rocky Colavito, Detroit, August 27, 1961.

Harmon Killebrew, Minnesota, September 21, 1963.

Bobby Murcer, New York, June 24, 1970 (consecutive).

Graig Nettles, New York, April 14, 1974.

Otto Velez, Toronto, May 4, 1980, 19 innings.

Al Oliver, Texas, August 17, 1980.

Players hitting home runs leading off both games of doubleheader

A.L.—Harry Hooper, Boston, May 30, 1913.

Rickey Henderson, Oakland, July 5, 1993.

Brady Anderson, Baltimore, August 21, 1999.

N.L.—Never accomplished.

Most home runs by pinch-hitter, doubleheader

A.L.—2—Joe Cronin, Boston, June 17, 1943.

N.L.—2—Hal Breeden, Montreal, July 13, 1973.

Most home runs, inning

A.A.—2—Ed Cartwright, St. Louis, September 23, 1890, third inning.

P.L.—2—Lou Bierbauer, Brooklyn, July 12, 1890, third inning.

A.L.—2—Ken Williams, St. Louis, August 7, 1922, sixth inning.

Bill Regan, Boston, June 16, 1928, fourth inning.

Joe DiMaggio, New York, June 24, 1936, fifth inning.

Al Kaline, Detroit, April 17, 1955, sixth inning.

Jim Lemon, Washington, September 5, 1959, third inning.

Joe Pepitone, New York, May 23, 1962, eighth inning.

Rick Reichardt, California, April 30, 1966, eighth inning.

Cliff Johnson, New York, June 30, 1977, eighth inning.

Ellis Burks, Boston, August 27, 1990, fourth inning.

Carlos Baerga, Cleveland, April 8, 1993, seventh inning.

Joe Carter, Toronto, October 3, 1993, second inning.

Dave Nilsson, Milwaukee, May 17, 1996, sixth inning.

Mark McGwire, Oakland, September 22, 1996, fifth inning.

Bret Boone, Seattle, May 2, 2002, first inning.

Mike Cameron, Seattle, May 2, 2002, first inning.

Jared Sandberg, Tampa Bay, June 11, 2002, fifth inning.

Nomar Garciaparra, Boston, July 23, 2002, a.m. game, third inning.

Carl Everett, Texas, July 26, 2002, seventh inning.

N.L.—2—Charley Jones, Boston, June 10, 1880, eighth inning.

Bobby Lowe, Boston, May 30, 1894, p.m. game, third inning.

Jake Stenzel, Pittsburgh, June 6, 1894, third inning.

Hack Wilson, New York, July 1, 1925, second game, third inning.

Hank Leiber, New York, August 24, 1935, second inning.

Andy Seminick, Philadelphia, June 2, 1949, eighth inning.

Sid Gordon, New York, July 31, 1949, second game, second inning.

Willie McCovey, San Francisco, April 12, 1973, fourth inning and June 27, 1977, sixth inning.

John Boccabella, Montreal, July 6, 1973, first game, sixth inning.

Lee May, Houston, April 29, 1974, sixth inning.

Andre Dawson, Montreal, July 30, 1978, third inning and September 24, 1985, fifth inning.

Ray Knight, Cincinnati, May 13, 1980, fifth inning.

Von Hayes, Philadelphia, June 11, 1985, first inning.

Dale Murphy, Atlanta, July 27, 1989, sixth inning.

Jeff Bagwell, Houston, June 24, 1994, sixth inning.

Jeff King, Pittsburgh, August 8, 1995, second inning and April 30, 1996, fourth inning.

Sammy Sosa, Chicago, May 16, 1996, seventh inning.

Mike Lansing, Montreal, May 7, 1997, sixth inning.

Gary Sheffield, Florida, July 13, 1997, fourth inning.

Fernando Tatis, St. Louis, April 23, 1999, third inning.

Eric Karros, Los Angeles, August 22, 2000, sixth inning.

Aaron Boone, Cincinnati, August 9, 2002, first inning.

Mark Bellhorn, Chicago, August 29, 2002, fourth inning.

Reggie L. Sanders, Pittsburgh, August 20, 2003, fifth inning.

Juan Rivera, Montreal, June 19, 2004, second inning.

Most home runs, two consecutive innings (homering each inning)

A.L.—3—Nomar Garciaparra, Boston, July 23, 2002, a.m. game, third inning (2), fourth inning (1).

N.L.—2—Held by many players.

THREE AND TWO IN GAME

Most times hitting three or more home runs in a game, career

M.L.—6—Johnny Mize, St. Louis N.L., 1938 (2), 1940 (2), New York N.L., 1947, New York A.L., 1950.

Sammy Sosa, Chicago N.L., 1996, 1998, 2001 (3), 2002.

N.L.—6—Sammy Sosa, Chicago, 1996, 1998, 2001 (3), 2002.

A.L.—5—Joe Carter, Cleveland, 1986, 1987, 1989 (2); Toronto, 1993.

For a complete list of players with three or more home runs in a game, see page 164.

Most times hitting three or more home runs in a game, season

N.L.—3—Sammy Sosa, August 9, August 22, September 23, 2001.

A.L.—2—Ted Williams, Boston, May 8, June 13, 1957.

Doug DeCinces, California, August 3, August 8, 1982.

Joe Carter, Cleveland, June 24, July 19, 1989.

Cecil Fielder, Detroit, May 6, June 6, 1990.

Geronimo Berroa, Oakland, May 22, August 12, 1996.

Most times hitting three home runs in a doubleheader, career (homering in both games)

A.L.—7—Babe Ruth, New York, 1920, 1922, 1926, 1927, 1930, 1933 (2).

N.L.—5—Mel Ott, New York, 1929, 1931, 1932, 1933, 1944.

Most times hitting three or more consecutive home runs in a game, career

M.L.—4—Johnny Mize, St. Louis, N.L., 1938, 1940, New York, N.L., 1947, New York A.L., 1950.

Sammy Sosa, Chicago N.L., 1996, 2001 (2), 2002.

N.L.—4—Sammy Sosa, Chicago, 1996, 2001 (2), 2002.

A.L.—3—Cecil Fielder, Detroit, 1990 (2), 1996.

Most times hitting two or more home runs in a game, career

M.L.—72—Babe Ruth, Boston A.L., New York A.L., Boston N.L., 22 years, 1914 through 1935 (71 in A.L., 1 in N.L.).

A.L.—71—Babe Ruth, Boston, New York, 21 years, 1914 through 1934.

N.L.—68—Barry Bonds, Pittsburgh, San Francisco, New York Mets, 19 years, 1986 through 2004.

For a complete list of players with 25 or more multiple-home run games, see page 155.

Most times hitting two or more home runs in a game, season
A.L.—11—Hank Greenberg, Detroit, 1938.
N.L.—11—Sammy Sosa, Chicago, 1998.

Most times pitcher hitting two home runs in a game, career
A.L.—5—Wes Ferrell, Cleveland, Boston, 1931, 1934 (2), 1935, 1936.
N.L.—3—Don Newcombe, Brooklyn, 1955 (2), 1956.

Most times pitcher hitting two home runs in a game, season
A.L.—2—Wes Ferrell, Boston, 1934.
　Jack Harshman, Baltimore, 1958.
　Dick Donovan, Cleveland, 1962.
N.L.—2—Don Newcombe, Brooklyn, 1955.
　Tony Cloninger, Atlanta, 1966.
　Rick Wise, Philadelphia, 1971.

Most games hitting home runs from both sides of plate, career
M.L.—11—Eddie Murray, Baltimore A.L., 1977, 1979, 1981, 1982 (2), 1985, 1987 (2); Los Angeles N.L., 1990 (2); Cleveland A.L., 1994.
A.L.—10—Mickey Mantle, New York, 1955 (2), 1956 (2), 1957, 1958, 1959, 1961, 1962, 1964.
N.L.—10—Ken Caminiti, Houston, 1994; San Diego, 1995 (3), 1996 (4), 1998; Houston, 1999.

For a complete list of players hitting home runs from both sides of plate in a game, see page 167.

Most games hitting home runs from both sides of plate, season
N.L.—4—Ken Caminiti, San Diego, 1996.
A.L.—3—Tony Clark, Detroit, 1998.

Hitting home runs from both sides of plate, inning
A.L.—Carlos Baerga, Cleveland, April 8, 1993, seventh inning.
N.L.—Mark Bellhorn, Chicago, August 29, 2002, fourth inning.

CONSECUTIVE AND
IN CONSECUTIVE GAMES

Most consecutive home runs, game
N.L.—4—Bobby Lowe, Boston, May 30, 1894, p.m. game.
　(4—Mike Schmidt, Philadelphia, April 17, 1976, 10 innings.)
A.L.—4—Lou Gehrig, New York, June 3, 1932.
　Rocky Colavito, Cleveland, June 10, 1959.
　Mike Cameron, Seattle, May 2, 2002.
　Carlos Delgado, Toronto, September 25, 2003.

Most consecutive home runs, two games (*also base on balls; †also hit by pitch)
A.L.—4—Jimmie Foxx, Philadelphia, June 7 (1), 8 (3), 1933.
　Hank Greenberg, Detroit, July 26 (2), 27 (2), 1938.
　Charlie Maxwell, Detroit, May 3, first game (1), 3, second game (3), 1959.
　Willie Kirkland, Cleveland, July 9, second game (3), 13 (1), 1961 (also two bases on balls and one sacrifice hit).
　Mickey Mantle, New York, July 4, second game (2), 6 (2), 1962.
　Bobby Murcer, New York, June 24, first game (1), 24, second game (3), 1970.*
　Mike Epstein, Oakland, June 15 (2), 16 (2), 1971.
　Don Baylor, Baltimore, July 1 (1), 2 (3), 1975.*
　Larry Herndon, Detroit, May 16 (1), 18 (3), 1982.
　Bo Jackson, Kansas City, July 17 (3), August 26 (1), 1990.
　Dobby Higginson, Detroit, June 30 (3), July 1 (1), 1997.*
　Manny Ramirez, Cleveland, September 15 (3), 16 (1), 1998.
　Troy Glaus, Anaheim, September 15 (3), 16 (1), 2002.
N.L.—4—Bill Nicholson, Chicago, July 22 (1), 23, first game (3), 1944.*
　Ralph Kiner, Pittsburgh, August 15 (1), 16 (3), 1947.*
　Ralph Kiner, Pittsburgh, September 11 (2), 13 (2), 1949.
　Stan Musial, St. Louis, July 7, second game (1), 8 (3), 1962.*
　Art Shamsky, Cincinnati, August 12 (3), 14 (1), 1966.
　Deron Johnson, Philadelphia, July 10, second game (1), 11 (3), 1971.
　Johnny Bench, Cincinnati, May 8 (1), May 9 (3), 1973.*
　Mike Schmidt, Philadelphia, July 6 (1), 7 (3), 1979.
　Benito Santiago, Philadelphia, September 14 (1), 15 (3), 1996.*

　Barry Bonds, San Francisco, May 19 (2), 20 (2), 2001.*
　Shawn Green, Los Angeles, June 14 (2), 15 (2), 2002.
　Andruw Jones, Atlanta, September 7 (2), 10 (2), 2002.†

Most consecutive home runs, three games (*also base on balls)
A.L.—4
　Johnny Blanchard, New York, July 21 (1), 22 (1), 26 (2), 1961.
　Jeff Manto, Baltimore, June 8 (1), 9 (2), 10 (1), 1995.*
N.L.—Never accomplished.

Most consecutive home runs, four games
A.L.—4—Ted Williams, Boston, September 17, 20, 21, 22, 1957 (four bases on balls in streak).
N.L.—Never accomplished.

Most home runs in consecutive at-bats as a pinch-hitter
N.L.—3—Lee Lacy, Los Angeles, May 2, 6, 17, 1978 (includes one base on balls during streak).
　Del Unser, Philadelphia, June 30, July 5, 10, 1979.
A.L.—2—Ray Caldwell, New York, June 10, 11, 1915.
　Joe Cronin, Boston, June 17, first game, 17, second game, 1943.
　Charlie Keller, New York, September 12, 14, 1948.
　Del Wilber, Boston, May 6, 10, 1953.
　Ted Williams, Boston, September 17, 20, 1957 (includes one base on balls during streak).
　Johnny Blanchard, New York, July 21, 22, 1961.
　Chuck Schilling, Boston, April 30, May 1, 1965.
　Ray Barker, New York, June 20, 22, first game, 1965.
　Curt Motton, Baltimore, May 15, 17, 1968.
　Gates Brown, Detroit, August 9, 11, first game, 1968.
　Gary Alexander, Cleveland, July 5, 6, 1980.
　Daryl Sconiers, California, April 30, May 7, 1983.
　Alex Sanchez, Detroit, July 20, 23, 1985.
　Randy Bush, Minnesota, June 20, 23, 1986.
　Jeromy Burnitz, Milwaukee, August 2, 3, 1997.

Most consecutive games hitting home run in each game
N.L.—8—Dale Long, Pittsburgh, May 19, 20, first game, 20, second game, 22, 23, 25, 26, 28, 1956 (eight home runs).
A.L.—8—Don Mattingly, New York, July 8 (2), 9, 10, 11, 12, 16 (2), 17, 18, 1987 (10 home runs).
　Ken Griffey Jr., Seattle, July 20, 21, 22, 23, 24, 25, 27, 28, 1993 (eight home runs).

Most consecutive games hitting home runs from both sides of plate
A.L.—2—Eddie Murray, Baltimore, May 8, 9, 1987.
N.L.—2—Ken Caminiti, San Diego, September 16, 17, 1995.

Most consecutive games hitting home run by pitcher
N.L.—4—Ken Brett, Philadelphia, June 9, 13, 18, 23, 1973.
A.L.—2—Held by many pitchers.

Most home runs, two consecutive days
A.L.　6—Babe Ruth, New York, May 21 (3), 21 (0), 22 (2), 22, 1930, four games.
　Tony Lazzeri, New York, May 23, 23 (2), 24 (3), 1936, three games.
N.L.—6—Ralph Kiner, Pittsburgh, September 11, 11 (3), 12 (2), 1947, three games.

Most home runs, first two major league games
A.A.—3—Charlie Reilly, Columbus, October 9 (2), 10, 1889.
N.L.—3—Joe Cunningham, St. Louis, June 30, July 1 (2), 1954.
A.L.—2—Earl Averill, Cleveland, April 16, 17, 1929.
　Bob Nieman, St. Louis, September 14 (2), 15 (0), 1951.
　Bert Campaneris, Kansas City, July 23 (2), 24 (0), 1964.
　Curt Blefary, Baltimore, April 14 (0), 17 (2), 1965.
　Joe Lefebvre, New York, May 22, 23, 1980.
　Dave Stapleton, Boston, May 30 (0), 31 (2), 1980.
　Tim Laudner, Minnesota, August 28, 29, 1981.
　Alvin Davis, Seattle, April 11, 13, 1984.
　Sam Horn, Boston, July 25, 26, 1987.
　Mark Quinn, Kansas City, September 14 (2), 15 (0), 1999.

Most home runs in two straight games (homering in each game)
N.L.—5—Cap Anson, Chicago, August 5 (2), 6 (3), 1884.
　Ralph Kiner, Pittsburgh, August 15 (2), 16 (3), 1947.

Ralph Kiner, Pittsburgh, September 11 (3), 12 (2), 1947.
Don Mueller, New York, September 1 (3), 2 (2), 1951.
Stan Musial, St. Louis, May 2, first game (3), 2, second game (2), 1954.
Joe Adcock, Milwaukee, July 30, 31 (4), 1954.
Billy Williams, Chicago, September 8 (2), 10 (3), 1968.
Nate Colbert, San Diego, August 1, first game (2), second game (3), 1972.
Mike Schmidt, Philadelphia, April 17 (4), 18, 1976.
Dave Kingman, Chicago, July 27 (2), 28 (3), 1979.
Gary Carter, New York, September 3 (3), 4 (2), 1985.
Barry Larkin, Cincinnati, June 27 (2), 28 (3), 1991.
Geoff Jenkins, Milwaukee, April 28 (3), 29 (2), 2001.
Barry Bonds, San Francisco, May 19 (3), 20 (2), 2001.
Shawn Green, Los Angeles, May 23 (4), 24 (1), 2002.
A.L.—5—Ty Cobb, Detroit, May 5 (3), 6 (2), 1925.
Tony Lazzeri, New York, May 23, second game (2), 24 (3), 1936.
Carl Yastrzemski, Boston, May 19 (3), 20 (2), 1976.
Mark McGwire, Oakland, June 27 (3), 28 (2), 1987.
Joe Carter, Cleveland, July 18 (2), 19 (3), 1989.
Mark McGwire, Oakland, June 10 (2), 11 (3), 1995.
Albert Belle, Cleveland, September 18 (2), 19 (3), 1995.
Matt Williams, Cleveland, April 25 (3), 26 (2), 1997.
Manny Ramirez, Cleveland, September 15 (3), 16 (2), 1998.
Edgar Martinez, Seattle, May 17 (2), 18 (3), 1999.
Nomar Garciaparra, Boston, July 21 (2), 23, a.m. game (3), 2002.
Alex Rodriguez, Texas, August 17 (3), 18 (2), 2002.
Travis Hafner, Cleveland, July 19 (2 in 10 innings), 20 (3), 2004.

Most home runs in three straight games (homering in each game)
N.L.—7—Shawn Green, Los Angeles, May 23 (4), 24 (1), 25 (2), 2002.
A.L.—6—Tony Lazzeri, New York, May 23, 23 (2), 24 (3), 1936.
Gus Zernial, Philadelphia, May 13, second game (2), 15 (2), 16 (2), 1951.
Manny Ramirez, Cleveland, September 15 (3), 16 (2), 17, 1998.
Alex Rodriguez, Texas, August 16 (1), 17 (3), 18 (2), 2002.
Jeff DaVanon, Anaheim, June 1 (2), 3 (2), 4 (2), 2003.

Most home runs in four straight games (homering in each game)
N.L.—8—Ralph Kiner, Pittsburgh, September 10 (2), 11, 11 (3), 12 (2), 1947.
A.L.—7—Tony Lazzeri, New York, May 21, 23, 23 (2), 24 (3), 1936.
Gus Zernial, Philadelphia, May 13, second game (2), 15 (2), 16 (2), 17, 1951.
Frank Howard, Washington, May 12 (2), 14 (2), 15, 16 (2), 1968.

Players hitting home runs in first four games of season
N.L.—4—Willie Mays, San Francisco, April 6, 7, 8, 10, 1971.
Mark McGwire, St. Louis, March 31, April 2, 3, 4, 1998.
A.L.—Never accomplished.

Most consecutive games with two or more home runs, start of season
N.L.—2—Eddie Mathews, Milwaukee, April 15 (2), 17 (2), 1958.
Barry Bonds, San Francisco, April 2 (2), 3 (2), 2002.
A.L.—1—Held by many players.

Most home runs in five straight games (homering in each game)
A.L.—8—Frank Howard, Washington, May 12 (2), 14 (2), 15, 16 (2), 17, 1968.
Frank Howard, Washington, May 14 (2), 15, 16 (2), 17, 18 (2), 1968.
N.L.—8—Barry Bonds, San Francisco, May 17, 18, 19 (3), 20 (2), 21, 2001.
Barry Bonds, San Francisco, May 18, 19 (3), 20 (2), 21, 22, 2001.

Most home runs in six straight games (homering in each game)
A.L.—10—Frank Howard, Washington, May 12 (2), 14 (2), 15, 16 (2), 17, 18 (2), 1968.
N.L.—9—Barry Bonds, San Francisco, May 17, 18, 19 (3), 20 (2), 21, 22, 2001.

Most home runs in seven straight games (homering in each game)
A.L.—9—Don Mattingly, New York, July 8 (2), 9, 10, 11, 12, 16 (2), 17, 1987.
N.L.—7—Dale Long, Pittsburgh, May 19, 20, 20, 22, 23, 25, 26, 1956.

Most homers in eight straight games (homering in each game)
A.L.—10—Don Mattingly, New York, July 8 (2), 9, 10, 11, 12, 16 (2), 17, 18, 1987.
N.L.—8—Dale Long, Pittsburgh, May 19, 20, 20, 22, 23, 25, 26, 28, 1956.

GRAND SLAMS

Most grand slams, career
A.L.—23—Lou Gehrig, New York, 17 years, 1923 through 1939.
N.L.—18—Willie McCovey, San Francisco, San Diego, 22 years, 1959 through 1980.

For a complete list of players with 10 or more career grand slams, see page 155.

Most grand slams by pinch-hitter, career
A.L.—3—Rich Reese, Minnesota, August 3, 1969, June 7, 1970, July 9, 1972.
N.L.—3—Ron Northey, St. Louis, September 3, 1947; May 30, 1948, second game; Chicago, September 18, 1950.
Willie McCovey, San Francisco, June 12, 1960; September 10, 1965; San Diego, May 30, 1975.

Most grand slams, season
A.L.—6—Don Mattingly, New York, 141 games, 1987.
N.L.—5—Ernie Banks, Chicago, 154 games, 1955.

Most consecutive seasons hitting at least one grand slam
N.L.—9—Willie McCovey, San Francisco, 1964 through 1972 (13 grand slams).
A.L.—8—Manny Ramirez, Cleveland, Boston, 1995 through 2002 (15 grand slams).

Most grand slams by pinch-hitter, season
N.L.—2—Dave Johnson, Philadelphia, April 30, June 3, 1978.
Mike Ivie, San Francisco, May 28, June 30, first game, 1978.
A.L.—2—Darryl Strawberry, New York, May 2, August 4, 1998.
Ben Broussard, Cleveland, June 23, August 12, 2004.

Most grand slams in one month
A.L.—3—Rudy York, Detroit, May 16, 22, 30, first game, 1938.
Jim Northrup, Detroit, June 24 (2), 29, 1968.
Larry Parrish, Texas, July 4, 7, 10, first game, 1982.
Mike Blowers, Seattle, August 3, 14, 18, 1995.
Shane Spencer, New York, September 18, 24, 27, 1998.
N.L.—3—Eric Davis, Cincinnati, May 1, 3, 30, 1987.
Mike Piazza, Los Angeles, April 9, 10, 24, 1998.
Devon White, Milwaukee, May 10, 15, 20, 2001.

Most grand slams in one week (Sunday through Saturday)
A.L.—3—Jim Northrup, Detroit, June 24 (2), 29, 1968. (Lou Gehrig, New York, hit grand slams on Saturday, August 29, Monday, August 31, Tuesday, September 1, 1931, second game.)
Larry Parrish, Texas, July 4, 7, 10, first game, 1982.
N.L.—2—Held by many players. Last players—Fernando Tatis, St. Louis, April 23 (2), 1999; Robin Ventura, New York, May 20, first and second games, 1999.

Most grand slams in one game
A.L.—2—Tony Lazzeri, New York, May 24, 1936, second and fifth innings.
Jim Tabor, Boston, July 4, 1939, second game, third and sixth innings.
Rudy York, Boston, July 27, 1946, second and fifth innings.
Jim Gentile, Baltimore, May 9, 1961, first and second innings.
Jim Northrup, Detroit, June 24, 1968, fifth and sixth innings.
Frank Robinson, Baltimore, June 26, 1970, fifth and sixth innings.
Robin Ventura, Chicago, September 4, 1995, fourth and fifth innings.
Chris Hoiles, Baltimore, August 14, 1998, third and eighth innings.

Nomar Garciaparra, Boston, May 10, 1999, first and eighth innings.
Bill Mueller, Boston, July 29, 2003, seventh and eighth innings (first time from both sides of the plate).
N.L.—2—Tony Cloninger, Atlanta, July 3, 1966, first and fourth innings.
Fernando Tatis, St. Louis, April 23, 1999, both in third inning.

Most grand slams, inning
N.L.—2—Fernando Tatis, St. Louis, April 23, 1999, third inning.
A.L.—1—Held by many players.

Most grand slams in first major league game
N.L.—1—Bill Duggleby, Philadelphia, April 21, 1898, second inning (on first at-bat).
Bobby Bonds, San Francisco, June 25, 1968, sixth inning (on third at-bat).
A.L.—Never accomplished.

Most grand slams, two straight games (homering in each game)
N.L.—2—Jimmy Bannon, Boston, August 6, 7, 1894.
Jim Sheckard, Brooklyn, September 23, 24, 1901.
Phil Garner, Pittsburgh, September 14, 15, 1978.
Fred McGriff, San Diego, August 13, 14, 1991.
Eric Davis, Cincinnati, May 4, 5, 1996.
Mike Piazza, Los Angeles, April 9, 10, 1998.
Sammy Sosa, Chicago, July 27, 28, 1998.
Robin Ventura, New York, May 20, first game, second game, 1999.
A.L.—2—Babe Ruth, New York, September 27, 29, 1927; also August 6, second game, August 7, first game, 1929.
Bill Dickey, New York, August 3, second game, 4, 1937.
Jimmie Foxx, Boston, May 20, 21, 1940.
Jim Busby, Cleveland, July 5, 6, 1956.
Brooks Robinson, Baltimore, May 6, 9, 1962.
Willie Aikens, California, June 13, second game, 14, 1979.
Greg Luzinski, Chicago, June 8, 9, 1984.
Rob Deer, Milwaukee, August 19, 20, 1987.
Mike Blowers, Seattle, May 16, 17, 1993.
Dan Gladden, Detroit, August 10, 11, 1993.
Ken Griffey Jr., Seattle, April 29, 30, 1999.
Albert Belle, Baltimore, June 14, 15, 2000.
David Eckstein, Anaheim, April 27, 28, 2002; second game 14 innings.

Hitting grand slam in both games of doubleheader
N.L.—Robin Ventura, New York, May 20, first game, second game, 1999.
A.L.—Never accomplished.

TOTAL BASES
CAREER AND SEASON

Most total bases, career
M.L.—6,856—Hank Aaron, Milwaukee N.L., Atlanta N.L., Milwaukee A.L., 23 years, 1954 through 1976 (6,591 in N.L., 265 in A.L.).
N.L.—6,591—Hank Aaron, Milwaukee, Atlanta, 21 years, 1954 through 1974.
A.L.—5,854—Ty Cobb, Detroit, Philadelphia, 24 years, 1905 through 1928.

For a complete list of players with 4,000 or more career total bases, see page 156.

Most total bases, season
A.L.—457—Babe Ruth, New York, 152 games, 1921.
N.L.—450—Rogers Hornsby, St. Louis, 154 games, 1922.

For a complete list of players with 400 or more total bases in a season, see page 169.

Most total bases by rookie, season
A.L.—374—Hal Trosky, Cleveland, 154 games, 1934.
Tony Oliva, Minnesota, 161 games, 1964.

N.L.—360—Albert Pujols, St. Louis, 161 games, 2001.

Most total bases by righthander, season
N.L.—450—Rogers Hornsby, St. Louis, 154 games, 1922.
A.L.—438—Jimmie Foxx, Philadelphia, 154 games, 1932.

Most total bases by lefthander, season
A.L.—457—Babe Ruth, New York, 152 games, 1921.
N.L.—445—Chuck Klein, Philadelphia, 156 games, 1930.

Most total bases by switch-hitter, season
A.L.—376—Mickey Mantle, New York, 150 games, 1956.
N.L.—369—Rip Collins, St. Louis, 154 games, 1934.

Most seasons leading league in total bases
N.L.—8—Hank Aaron, Milwaukee, 1956, 1957, 1959, 1960, 1961, 1963, Atlanta, 1967, 1969.
A.L.—6—Ty Cobb, Detroit, 1907, 1908, 1909, 1911, 1915, 1917.
Babe Ruth, Boston, 1919, New York, 1921, 1923, 1924, 1926, 1928.
Ted Williams, Boston, 1939, 1942, 1946, 1947, 1949, 1951.

Most consecutive seasons leading league in total bases
N.L.—4—Honus Wagner, Pittsburgh, 1906, 1907, 1908, 1909.
Chuck Klein, Philadelphia, 1930, 1931, 1932, 1933.
A.L.—3—Ty Cobb, Detroit, 1907, 1908, 1909.
Jim Rice, Boston, 1977, 1978, 1979.
(Military service from 1943 through 1945 interrupted a three-year streak by Ted Williams of Boston, who led in total bases from 1942 through 1947.)

Most seasons with 400 or more total bases
A.L.—5—Lou Gehrig, New York, 1927, 1930, 1931, 1934, 1936.
N.L.—3—Chuck Klein, Philadelphia, 1929, 1930, 1932.

For a complete list of players with 400 or more total bases in a season, see page 169.

Most consecutive seasons with 400 or more total bases
A.L.—2—Lou Gehrig, New York, 1930, 1931.
Jimmie Foxx, Philadelphia, 1932, 1933.
N.L.—2—Chuck Klein, Philadelphia, 1929, 1930.
Todd Helton, Colorado, 2000, 2001.

Most seasons with 300 or more total bases
N.L.—15—Hank Aaron, Milwaukee, Atlanta, 1955 through 1971, except 1964, 1970.
A.L.—13—Lou Gehrig, New York, 1926 through 1938.

Most consecutive seasons with 300 or more total bases
A.L.—13—Lou Gehrig, New York, 1926 through 1938.
N.L.—13—Willie Mays, New York, San Francisco, 1954 through 1966.

Fewest total bases, season (150 or more games)
N.L.—89—Dal Maxvill, St. Louis, 152 games, 1970.
A.L.—114—Eddie Brinkman, Washington, 154 games, 1965.

Fewest total bases for leader
N.L.—237—Honus Wagner, Pittsburgh, 140 games, 1906.
A.L.—260—George Stone, St. Louis, 154 games, 1905.

GAME AND INNING

Most total bases, game
N.L.—19—Shawn Green, Los Angeles, May 23, 2002 (4 home runs, 1 single, 1 double).
A.L.—16—Ty Cobb, Detroit, May 5, 1925 (3 home runs, 1 double, 2 singles).
Lou Gehrig, New York, June 3, 1932 (4 home runs).
Jimmie Foxx, Philadelphia, July 10, 1932, 18 innings (3 home runs, 1 double, 2 singles).
Rocky Colavito, Cleveland, June 10, 1959 (4 home runs).
Fred Lynn, Boston, June 18, 1975 (3 home runs, 1 triple, 1 single).
Mike Cameron, Seattle, May 2, 2002 (4 home runs).
Carlos Delgado, Toronto, September 25, 2003 (4 home runs).
(16—Pat Seerey, Chicago, July 18, 1948, first game (4 home runs), 11 innings).

Most total bases by pitcher, game
A.A.—15—Guy Hecker, Louisville, August 15, 1886, second game (3 home runs, 3 singles).

N.L.—12—Jim Tobin, Boston, May 13, 1942 (3 home runs).

A.L.—10—Snake Wiltse, Philadelphia, August 10, 1901, second game (2 triples, 2 doubles).

Babe Ruth, Boston, May 9, 1918, 10 innings (1 single, 3 doubles, 1 triple).

Red Ruffing, New York, June 17, 1936, first game (2 singles, 2 home runs).

Jack Harshman, Baltimore, September 23, 1958 (2 home runs, 1 double).

Most total bases, doubleheader

N.L.—22—Nate Colbert, San Diego, August 1, 1972.

A.L.—21—Jimmie Foxx, Philadelphia, July 2, 1933, 19 innings.

Al Oliver, Texas, August 17, 1980.

Most total bases, two consecutive games

A.L.—25—Ty Cobb, Detroit, May 5, 6, 1925.

N.L.—25—Joe Adcock, Milwaukee, July 30, 31, 1954.

Shawn Green, Los Angeles, May 23, 24, 2002.

Most total bases, inning

N.L.-A.L.—8—Held by many players.

EXTRA BASE HITS
CAREER AND SEASON

Most extra base hits, career

M.L.—1,477—Hank Aaron, Milwaukee N.L., Atlanta N.L., Milwaukee A.L., 1954 through 1976 (1,429 in N.L.; 48 in A.L.; 624 doubles, 98 triples, 755 home runs).

N.L.—1,429—Hank Aaron, Milwaukee, Atlanta, 21 years, 1954 through 1974 (600 doubles, 96 triples, 733 home runs).

A.L.—1,350—Babe Ruth, Boston, New York, 21 years, 1914 through 1934 (506 doubles, 136 triples, 708 home runs).

For a complete list of players with 800 or more career extra base hits, see page 156.

Most extra base hits, season

A.L.—119—Babe Ruth, New York, 152 games, 1921 (44 doubles, 16 triples, 59 home runs).

N.L.—107—Chuck Klein, Philadelphia, 156 games, 1930 (59 doubles, 8 triples, 40 home runs).

Barry Bonds, San Francisco, 153 games, 2001 (32 doubles, 2 triples, 73 home runs).

For a complete list of players with 100 or more extra base hits in a season, see page 169.

Most extra base hits by rookie, season

A.L.—89—Hal Trosky, Cleveland, 154 games, 1934 (45 doubles, 9 triples, 35 home runs).

N.L.—88—Albert Pujols, St. Louis, 161 games, 2001 (47 doubles, 4 triples, 37 home runs).

Most extra base hits by righthander, season

A.L.—103—Hank Greenberg, Detroit, 154 games, 1937 (49 doubles, 14 triples, 40 home runs).

Albert Belle, Cleveland, 143 games, 1995 (52 doubles, 1 triple, 50 home runs).

N.L.—103—Sammy Sosa, Chicago, 160 games, 2001 (34 doubles, 5 triples, 64 home runs).

Most extra base hits by lefthander, season

A.L.—119—Babe Ruth, New York, 152 games, 1921 (44 doubles, 16 triples, 59 home runs).

N.L.—107—Chuck Klein, Philadelphia, 156 games, 1930 (59 doubles, 8 triples, 40 home runs).

Barry Bonds, San Francisco, 153 games, 2001 (32 doubles, 2 triples, 73 home runs).

Most extra base hits by switch-hitter, season

N.L.—94—Lance Berkman, Houston, 156 games, 2001 (55 doubles, 5 triples, 34 home runs).

A.L.—80—Carlos Beltran, Kansas City, 162 games, 2002 (44 doubles, 7 triples, 29 home runs).

Most seasons leading league in doubles, triples and home runs in same season

A.A.—1—Tip O'Neill, St. Louis, 123 games, 1887 (46 doubles, 24 triples, 13 home runs; also led in batting, .435).

N.L.-A.L.—Never accomplished.

Twenty or more doubles, triples and homers in one season

N.L.—Buck Freeman, Washington, 155 games, 1899 (20 doubles, 26 triples, 25 home runs).

Frank Schulte, Chicago, 154 games, 1911 (30 doubles, 21 triples, 21 homers).

Jim Bottomley, St. Louis, 149 games, 1928 (42 doubles, 20 triples, 31 homers).

Willie Mays, New York, 152 games, 1957 (26 doubles, 20 triples, 35 homers).

A.L.—Jeff Heath, Cleveland, 151 games, 1941 (32 doubles, 20 triples, 24 homers).

George Brett, Kansas City, 154 games, 1979 (42 doubles, 20 triples, 23 homers).

Most seasons leading league in extra base hits

N.L.—7—Honus Wagner, Pittsburgh, 1900, 1902, 1903, 1904, 1907, 1908, 1909.

Stan Musial, St. Louis, 1943, 1944, 1946, 1948, 1949, 1950, 1953.

A.L.—Babe Ruth, Boston, New York, 1918, 1919, 1920, 1921, 1923, 1924, 1928.

Most consecutive seasons leading league in extra base hits

A.L.—4—Babe Ruth, Boston, New York, 1918, 1919, 1920, 1921.

N.L.—3—Held by many players. Last player—Duke Snider, Brooklyn, 1954, 1955 (tied), 1956.

Fewest extra base hits, season (150 or more games)

N.L.—7—Dal Maxvill, St. Louis, 152 games, 1970 (5 doubles, 2 triples).

A.L.—10—Luis Gomez, Toronto, 153 games, 1978 (7 doubles, 3 triples).

Felix Fermin, Cleveland, 156 games, 1989 (9 doubles, 1 triple).

Fewest extra base hits for leader, season

N.L.—50—Sherry Magee, Philadelphia, 154 games, 1906 (36 doubles, 8 triples, 6 home runs).

A.L.—54—Sam Crawford, Detroit, 156 games, 1915 (31 doubles, 19 triples, 4 home runs).

Most consecutive games with one or more extra base hits, season

N.L.—14—Paul Waner, Pittsburgh, June 3 through 19, 1927 (12 doubles, 4 triples, 4 home runs).

A.L.—11—Jesse Barfield, Toronto, August 17 through 27, 1985 (8 doubles, 3 triples, 1 home run).

Most consecutive extra base hits, season

A.L.—7—Elmer Smith, Cleveland, September 4, 5, 5, 1921 (3 doubles, 4 home runs; 2 bases on balls in streak).

Earl Sheely, Chicago, May 20, 21, 1926 (6 doubles, 1 home run; 1 sacrifice hit in streak).

N.L.—6—Larry Walker, Colorado, May 21, 22, 1996 (2 doubles, 3 triples, 1 home run in streak).

GAME AND INNING

Most extra base hits, game

A.A.—5—George Strief, Philadelphia, June 25, 1885 (4 triples, 1 double; consecutive).

N.L.—5—George Gore, Chicago, July 9, 1885 (2 triples, 3 doubles; consecutive).

Larry Twitchell, Cleveland, August 15, 1889 (1 double, 3 triples, 1 home run).

Joe Adcock, Milwaukee, July 31, 1954 (4 home runs, 1 double; consecutive).

Willie Stargell, Pittsburgh, August 1, 1970 (3 doubles, 2 home runs).

Steve Garvey, Los Angeles, August 28, 1977 (3 doubles, 2 home runs; consecutive).

Shawn Green, Los Angeles, May 23, 2002 (1 double, 4 home runs).

A.L.—5—Lou Boudreau, Cleveland, July 14, 1946, first game (4 doubles, 1 home run).

Most extra base hits, opening game of season
N.L.—4—George Myers, Indianapolis, April 20, 1888 (3 doubles, 1 home run).
  Billy Herman, Chicago, April 14, 1936 (3 doubles, 1 home run).
  Jim Greengrass, Cincinnati, April 13, 1954 (4 doubles).
A.L.—4—Frank Dillon, Detroit, April 25, 1901 (4 doubles).
  Don Baylor, Baltimore, April 6, 1973 (2 doubles, 1 triple, 1 home run).

Most extra base hits by pitcher, game
A.A.—4—Bob Caruthers, St. Louis, August 16, 1886 (2 home runs, 1 triple, 1 double).
A.L.—4—Snake Wiltse, Philadelphia, August 10, 1901, second game (2 triples, 2 doubles).
  (4—Babe Ruth, Boston, May 9, 1918 (3 doubles, a triple), 10 innings.)
N.L.—3—Held by many players—Last pitcher—Andy Messersmith, Los Angeles, April 25, 1975 (3 doubles).

Most games with four or more extra base hits, career
A.L.—5—Lou Gehrig, New York, 1926, 1928, 1930, 1932, 1934.
  Joe DiMaggio, New York, 1936, 1937, 1941, 1948, 1950.
N.L.—4—Willie Stargell, Pittsburgh, 1965, 1968, 1970, 1973.

Most games with four extra base hits, season
A.A.—2—Henry Larkin, Philadelphia, June 16, July 29, 1885.
A.L.—2—George H. Burns, Cleveland, June 19, first game, July 23, 1924.
  Jimmie Foxx, Philadelphia, April 24, July 2, second game, 1933.
  Albert Belle, Baltimore, August 29, September 23, second game, 1999.
N.L.—2—Joe Medwick, St. Louis, May 12, August 4, 1937.
  Billy Williams, Chicago, April 9, September 5, 1969.

Most extra base hits, doubleheader
N.L.—6—Joe Medwick, St. Louis, May 30, 1935 (5 doubles, 1 triple).
  Red Schoendienst, St. Louis, June 6, 1948 (5 doubles, 1 HR).
  Larry Walker, Colorado, May 22, 1996 (2 doubles, 3 triples, 2 HR).
  (6—Chick Hafey, St. Louis, July 28, 1928 (4 doubles, 2 home runs), 21 innings.
  Mel Ott, New York, June 19, 1929 (4 doubles, 2 home runs), 20 innings.
  Dusty Rhodes, New York, August 29, 1954 (2 doubles, 2 triples, 2 home runs), 20 innings.
A.L.—6—John Stone, Detroit, April 30, 1933 (4 doubles, 2 HR).
  Hank Majeski, Philadelphia, August 27, 1948 (6 doubles).
  Hal McRae, Kansas City, August 27, 1974 (5 doubles, 1 HR).
  Al Oliver, Texas, August 17, 1980 (1 double, 1 triple, 1 HR).
  (6—Jimmie Foxx, Philadelphia, July 2, 1933 (1 double, 1 triple, 4 home runs), 19 innings.

Most extra base hits in two consecutive games (not DH)
N.L.—7—Ed Delahanty, Philadelphia, July 13, 14, 1896 (2 doubles, 1 triple, 4 HR).
  Red Schoendienst, St. Louis, June 5, 6 (1st G), 1948 (6 doubles, 1 HR).
  Joe Adcock, Milwaukee, July 30, 31, 1954 (2 doubles, 5 HR).
  Jim Edmonds, St. Louis, April 4, 8, 2003 (4 doubles, 3 HR).
A.L.—7—Earl Sheely, Chicago, May 20, 21, 1926 (6 doubles, 1 home run).

Most extra base hits, inning
N.L.—3—Tommy Burns, Chicago, September 6, 1883, seventh inning (2 doubles, 1 home run).
A.L.-N.L. since 1900—2—Held by many players.

Most extra base hits by pitcher, inning
N.L.—2—Fred Goldsmith, Chicago, September 6, 1883, seventh inning (2 doubles).
  Adonis Terry, Chicago, May 19, 1895, third inning (1 home run, 1 double).
  Hank Borowy, Chicago, May 5, 1946, first game, seventh inning (2 doubles).
A.L.—2—Smokey Joe Wood, Boston, July 4, 1913, a.m. game, fourth inning (2 doubles).
  Bob Shawkey, New York, July 12, 1923, third inning (1 triple, 1 double).

Ted Lyons, Chicago, July 28, 1935, first game, second inning (2 doubles).

RUNS BATTED IN
CAREER AND SEASON

Most runs batted in, career
M.L.—2,297—Hank Aaron, Milwaukee N.L., Atlanta N.L., Milwaukee A.L., 23 years, 1954 through 1976 (2,202 in N.L., 95 in A.L.).
N.L.—2,202—Hank Aaron, Milwaukee, Atlanta, 21 years, 1954 through 1974.
A.L.—2,192—Babe Ruth, Boston, New York, 21 years, 1914 through 1934.

For a complete list of players with 1,200 or more career runs batted in, see page 156.

Most runs batted in, season
N.L.—191—Hack Wilson, Chicago, 155 games, 1930.
A.L.—184—Lou Gehrig, New York, 155 games, 1931.

Most runs batted in by rookie, season
A.L.—145—Ted Williams, Boston, 149 games, 1939.
N.L.—130—Albert Pujols, St. Louis, 161 games, 2001.

Most runs batted in by righthander, season
N.L.—191—Hack Wilson, Chicago, 155 games, 1930.
A.L.—183—Hank Greenberg, Detroit, 154 games, 1937.

Most runs batted in by lefthander, season
A.L.—184—Lou Gehrig, New York, 155 games, 1931.
N.L.—170—Chuck Klein, Philadelphia, 156 games, 1930.

Most runs batted in by switch-hitter, season
A.L.—130—Mickey Mantle, New York, 150 games, 1956.
N.L.—130—Ken Caminiti, San Diego, 146 games, 1996.

Most runs batted in by catcher, season
N.L.—142—Roy Campanella, Brooklyn, 144 games, 1953; caught 140 games.
A.L.—133—Bill Dickey, New York, 140 games, 1937; caught 137 games.

Most seasons leading league in runs batted in
N.L.—8—Cap Anson, Chicago, 1880, 1881, 1882, 1884, 1885, 1886, 1888, 1891.
A.L.—6—Babe Ruth, Boston, New York, 1919, 1920, 1921, 1923, 1926, 1928 (tied).
N.L. since 1900—5—Honus Wagner, Pittsburgh, 1901, 1902, 1908, 1909, 1912.

For a complete list of triple crown winners, see page 162.

Most consecutive seasons leading league in runs batted in
A.L.—3—Ty Cobb, Detroit, 1907 through 1909.
  Babe Ruth, Boston, New York, 1919 through 1921.
  Cecil Fielder, Detroit, 1990 through 1992.
N.L.—3—Cap Anson, Chicago, 1880 through 1882, 1884 through 1886.
N.L. since 1900—3—Rogers Hornsby, St. Louis, 1920 (tied), 1921, 1922.
  Joe Medwick, St. Louis, 1936 through 1938.
  George Foster, Cincinnati, 1976 through 1978.

Most seasons with 100 or more runs batted in
A.L.—13—Babe Ruth, Boston, New York, 1919 through 1933, except 1922 and 1925.
  Lou Gehrig, New York, 1926 through 1938.
  Jimmie Foxx, Philadelphia, Boston, 1929 through 1941.
N.L.—13—Barry Bonds, Pittsburgh, San Francisco, 1990 through 2004, except 1994, 1999 and 2003.

Most consecutive seasons with 100 or more runs batted in
A.L.—13—Lou Gehrig, New York, 1926 through 1938.
  Jimmie Foxx, Philadelphia, Boston, 1929 through 1941.
N.L.—9—Sammy Sosa, Chicago, 1995 through 2003.

Most seasons with 150 or more runs batted in
A.L.—7—Lou Gehrig, New York, 1927, 1930, 1931, 1932, 1934, 1936, 1937.

N.L.—2—Hack Wilson, Chicago, 1929, 1930.
Sammy Sosa, Chicago, 1998, 2001.

Most consecutive seasons with 150 or more runs batted in
A.L.—3—Babe Ruth, New York, 1929, 1930, 1931.
Lou Gehrig, New York, 1930, 1931, 1932.
N.L.—2—Hack Wilson, Chicago, 1929, 1930.

Fewest runs batted in, season (150 or more games)
N.L.—20—Richie Ashburn, Philadelphia, 153 games, 1959.
A.L.—19—Morrie Rath, Chicago, 157 games, 1912.

Fewest runs batted in by leader, season (since 1920)
N.L.—94—George Kelly, New York, 155 games, 1920.
Rogers Hornsby, St. Louis, 149 games, 1920.
A.L.—105—Al Rosen, Cleveland, 148 games, 1952.

Most consecutive games with one or more runs batted in, season
N.L.—17—Oscar Grimes, Chicago, June 27 through July 23, 1922 (27 runs batted in).
A.L.—13—Taffy Wright, Chicago, May 4 through May 20, 1941 (22 runs batted in).
Mike Sweeney, Kansas City, June 23 through July 4, 1999 (19 runs batted in).

GAME AND INNING

Most runs batted in, game
N.L.—12—Jim Bottomley, St. Louis, September 16, 1924.
Mark Whiten, St. Louis, September 7, 1993, second game.
A.L.—11—Tony Lazzeri, New York, May 24, 1936.

Most runs batted in by pitcher, game
N.L.—9—Henry Staley, Boston, June 1, 1893*
Tony Cloninger, Atlanta, July 3, 1966.
A.L.—7—Vic Raschi, New York, August 4, 1953.
*RBIs not officially adopted until 1920.

Most runs batted in accounting for all club's runs, game
N.L.—8—George Kelly, New York vs. Cincinnati, June 14, 1924 (New York won, 8-6).
A.L.—8—Bob Johnson, Philadelphia vs. St. Louis, June 12, 1938 (Philadelphia won, 8-3).
(9—Mike Greenwell, Boston vs. Seattle, September 2, 1996, 10 innings; Boston won, 9-8.)

Most runs batted in, two consecutive games
A.L.—15—Tony Lazzeri, New York, May 23, second game (4), May 24 (11), 1936.
N.L.—14—Sammy Sosa, Chicago, August 10 (9), 11 (5), 2002.

Most runs batted in, doubleheader
N.L.—13—Nate Colbert, San Diego, August 1, 1972.
Mark Whiten, St. Louis, September 7, 1993.
A.L.—11—Earl Averill, Cleveland, September 17, 1930, 17 innings.
Jim Tabor, Boston, July 4, 1939, 18 innings.
Boog Powell, Baltimore, July 6, 1966, 20 innings.

Most runs batted in, inning
N.L.—8—Fernando Tatis, St. Louis, April 23, 1999, third inning.
A.A.—7—Ed Cartwright, St. Louis, September 23, 1890, third inning.*
A.L.—6—Bob Johnson, Philadelphia, August 29, 1937, first game, first inning.
Tom McBride, Boston, August 4, 1945, second game, fourth inning.
Joe Astroth, Philadelphia, September 23, 1950, sixth inning.
Gil McDougald, New York, May 3, 1951, ninth inning.
Sam Mele, Chicago, June 10, 1952, fourth inning.
Jim Lemon, Washington, September 5, 1959, third inning.
Carlos Quintana, Boston, July 30, 1991, third inning.
Matt Stairs, Oakland, July 5, 1996, first inning.
Matt Williams, Cleveland, August 27, 1997, fourth inning.
*RBIs not officially adopted until 1920.

Most runs batted in, two consecutive innings (at least one each inning)
A.L.—8—Jim Gentile, Baltimore, May 9, 1961, first and second innings.
Jim Northrup, Detroit, June 24, 1968, fifth and sixth innings.
Frank Robinson, Baltimore, June 26, 1970, fifth and sixth innings.

Robin Ventura, Chicago, September 4, 1995, fourth and fifth innings.
Nomar Garciaparra, Boston, July 23, 2002, a.m. game, third and fourth innings.
N.L.—7—Kid Nichols, Boston, September 19, 1892, fifth and sixth innings.
Tony Piet, Pittsburgh, July 28, 1932, second game, second and third innings.
Johnny Rucker, New York, September 29, 1940, second and third innings.
Del Ennis, Philadelphia, July 27, 1950, seventh and eighth innings.
Earl Torgeson, Boston, June 30, 1951, seventh and eighth innings.
Ralph Kiner, Pittsburgh, July 4, 1951, second game, third and fourth innings.
Joe Morgan, Cincinnati, August 19, 1974, second and third innings.

GAME-WINNING RBIs (1980-1988)

Most game-winning RBIs, career
N.L.—129—Keith Hernandez, St. Louis, New York, 1980 through 1988.
A.L.—117—Eddie Murray, Baltimore, 1980 through 1988.

Most game-winning RBIs, season
N.L.—24—Keith Hernandez, New York, 158 games, 1985.
A.L.—23—Mike Greenwell, Boston, 158 games, 1988.

Most game-winning RBIs by pitcher, season
N.L.—3—Rick Mahler, Atlanta, 39 games, 1985.
Rick Rhoden, Pittsburgh, 35 games, 1985.
(Tim Leary of Los Angeles had 3 in 1988, but 1 came as a pinch-hitter.)
A.L.—Never accomplished.

Most game-winning RBIs by rookie, season
A.L.—14—Jose Canseco, Oakland, 157 games, 1986.
Wally Joyner, California, 154 games, 1986.
Mark McGwire, Oakland, 151 games, 1987.
N.L.—13—Juan Samuel, Philadelphia, 160 games, 1984.
Darryl Strawberry, New York, 122 games, 1983.

Fewest game-winning RBIs in a season (150 or more games)
N.L.—0—Alan Wiggins, San Diego, 158 games, 1984.
Rafael Palmeiro, Chicago, 152 games, 1988.
A.L.—1—Jackie Gutierrez, Boston, 151 games, 1984.
Tony Phillips, Oakland, 154 games, 1984.
Steve Lombardozzi, Minnesota, 156 games, 1986.
Dick Schofield, California, 155 games, 1988.

Most game-winning RBIs, doubleheader
N.L.-A.L.—2—Held by many players.

Most consecutive games with game-winning RBI, season
A.L.—5—Kirk Gibson, Detroit, July 13 through 20, 1986.
N.L.—4—Johnny Ray, Pittsburgh, September 18 through 21, 1984.
Milt Thompson, Philadelphia, August 19 through 21, second game, 1987.
Ozzie Smith, St. Louis, September 8 through 11, 1988.

Most consecutive victories with game-winning RBI, season
N.L.—6—Johnny Ray, Pittsburgh, September 13 through 21, 1984 (two losses in streak).
A.L.—5—Kirk Gibson, Detroit, July 13 through 20, 1986 (no losses in streak).

BASES ON BALLS

Most bases on balls, career
N.L.—2,302—Barry Bonds, Pittsburgh, San Francisco, 19 years, 1986 through 2004.
A.L.—2,042—Babe Ruth, Boston, New York, 21 years, 1914 through 1934.

For a complete list of players with 1,000 or more career bases on balls, see page 157.

Most bases on balls, season
N.L.—232—Barry Bonds, San Francisco, 147 games, 2004.
A.L.—170—Babe Ruth, New York, 152 games, 1923.

Most bases on balls by rookie, season
A.L.—107—Ted Williams, Boston, 149 games, 1939.
N.L.—100—Jim Gilliam, Brooklyn, 151 games, 1953.

Most bases on balls by righthander, season
N.L.—162—Mark McGwire, St. Louis, 155 games, 1998.
A.L.—151—Eddie Yost, Washington, 152 games, 1956.

Most bases on balls lefthander, season
N.L.—232—Barry Bonds, San Francisco, 147 games, 2004.
A.L.—170—Babe Ruth, New York, 152 games, 1923.

Most bases on balls by switch-hitter, season
A.L.—146—Mickey Mantle, New York, 144 games, 1957.
N.L.—126—Chipper Jones, Atlanta, 157 games, 1999.

Most bases on balls by pinch-hitter, season
N.L.—20—Matt Franco, New York, 88 games, 1999.
A.L.—18—Elmer Valo, New York, Washington, 81 games, 1960.

Most seasons leading league in bases on balls
A.L.—11—Babe Ruth, New York, 1920, 1921, 1923, 1924,
1926, 1927, 1928, 1930, 1931, 1932, 1933.
N.L.—10—Barry Bonds, Pittsburgh, San Francisco, 1992, 1994
through 1997, 2000 through 2004.

Most consecutive seasons leading league in bases on balls
N.L.—5—Barry Bonds, San Francisco, 1994 through 1997 and
2000 through 2004.
A.L.—4—Babe Ruth, New York, 1930 through 1933.
Ted Williams, Boston, 1946 through 1949 (military service from
1943 through 1945 interrupted a six-year streak by Williams of
Boston, who led in bases on balls from 1941 through 1949).

Most seasons with 100 or more bases on balls
A.L.—13—Babe Ruth, Boston, New York, 1919 through 1934,
except 1922, 1925 and 1929.
N.L.—12—Barry Bonds, Pittsburgh, San Francisco, 1991
through 2004, except 1994 and 1999.

Most consecutive seasons with 100 or more bases on balls
A.L.—8—Frank E. Thomas, Chicago, 1991 through 1998.
N.L.—7—Mel Ott, New York, 1936 through 1942.
Jeff Bagwell, Houston, 1996 through 2002.

Fewest bases on balls by leader, season
N.L.—69—Hack Wilson, Chicago, 142 games, 1926.
A.L.—89—Whitey Witt, New York, 140 games, 1922.

Fewest bases on balls, season (150 or more games)
A.L.—10—Ozzie Guillen, Chicago, 150 games, 1996.
N.L.—12—Hal Lanier, San Francisco, 151 games, 1968.

Most consecutive bases on balls
A.L.—7—Billy Rogell, Detroit, August 17, second game, August
18, August 19, first game, 1938.
Jose Canseco, Oakland, August 4, 5, 1992.
N.L.—7—Mel Ott, New York, June 16, 17, 18, 1943.
Eddie Stanky, New York, August 29, 30, 1950.
Barry Bonds, San Francisco, September 24, 25, 26, 2004.

Most consecutive games with one or more bases on balls
A.L.—22—Roy Cullenbine, Detroit, July 2 through 22, 1947 (34
bases on balls).
N.L.—20—Barry Bonds, San Francisco, September 9, 2002,
through April 1, 2003 (37 bases on balls).
A.A.—16—Yank Robinson, St. Louis, September 15 through
October 2, 1888 (23 bases on balls).

Most bases on balls, game
N.L.—6—Walt Wilmot, Chicago, August 22, 1891 (consecutive).
A.L.—6—Jimmie Foxx, Boston, June 16, 1938 (consecutive).
(6—Andre Thornton, Cleveland, May 2, 1984, 16 innings.)
N.L. since 1900—5—Held by many players. Last player—Barry
Bonds, September 25, 2004.
(6—Jeff Bagwell, Houston, August 20, 1999, 16 innings.)

Most bases on balls drawn by pitcher, game
A.A.—4—Joe Miller, Philadelphia, September 13, 1886.
A.L.—4—Urban Faber, Chicago, June 18, 1915 (consecutive).

Chuck Stobbs, Boston, June 8, 1950 (consecutive).
N.L.—3—Held by many pitchers.

Most bases on balls, first major league game
A.L.—4—Otto Saltzgaver, New York, April 12, 1932.
Milt Galatzer, Cleveland, June 25, 1933, first game.
N.L.—3—Held by many players.

Most times receiving five bases on balls in one game, career
N.L.—4—Mel Ott, New York, 1929, 1933, 1943, 1944.
A.L.—2—Max Bishop, Philadelphia, 1929, 1930.
Rickey Henderson, Oakland, 1982; Seattle, 2000.
A.A.—2—Dan Brouthers, Boston, 1891.

Most bases on balls, doubleheader
A.L.—8—Max Bishop, Philadelphia, May 21, 1930; Boston, July
8, 1934.
N.L.—6—Mel Ott, New York, October 5, 1929.
Johnny Mize, St. Louis, August 26, 1939.
Mel Ott, New York, April 30, 1944.
Cleon Jones, New York, June 25, 1971.
Jim Wynn, Atlanta, July 31, 1976.
Bobby Bonds, St. Louis, June 8, 1980.
Mark Grace, Chicago, August 10, 1995.
(6—Clay Dalrymple, Philadelphia, July 4, 1967, 19 innings.
Jack Clark, St. Louis, July 8, 1987, 19 innings.)

Most bases on balls, inning
N.L.-A.L.—2—Held by many players.

Most times receiving two bases on balls in one inning, career
A.L.—4—George Selkirk, New York, 1936 (2), 1938, 1940.
N.L.—2—Eddie Stanky, New York, 1950 (2).

Most times receiving two bases on balls in one inning, season
A.L.—2—George Selkirk, New York, June 24, August 28, second game, 1936.
Skeeter Webb, Chicago, July 30, September 3, 1940.
N.L.—2—Eddie Stanky, New York, June 27, August 22, 1950.

INTENTIONAL (SINCE 1955)

Most intentional bases on balls, career
N.L.—604—Barry Bonds, Pittsburgh, San Francisco, 19 years,
1986 through 2004
A.L.—229—George Brett, Kansas City, 21 years, 1973 through
1993.

Most intentional bases on balls, season
N.L.—120—Barry Bonds, San Francisco, 147 games, 2004.
A.L.—33—Ted Williams, Boston, 132 games, 1957.
John Olerud, Toronto, 158 games, 1993.

Most intentional bases on balls by rookie, season
A.L.—16—Alvin Davis, Seattle, 152 games, 1984.
N.L.—14—Willie Montanez, Philadelphia, 158 games, 1971.

Most intentional bases on balls by righthander, season
N.L.—37—Sammy Sosa, Chicago, 160 games, 2001.
A.L.—29—Frank Howard, Washington, 161 games, 1970.
Frank E. Thomas, Chicago, 145 games, 1995.

Most intentional bases on balls by lefthander, season
N.L.—68—Barry Bonds, San Francisco, 143 games, 2002.
A.L.—33—Ted Williams, Boston, 132 games, 1957.
John Olerud, Toronto, 158 games, 1993.

Most intentional bases on balls by switch-hitter, season
N.L.—26—Tim Raines Sr., Montreal, 139 games, 1987.
A.L.—25—Eddie Murray, Baltimore, 162 games, 1984.

Most seasons leading league in intentional bases on balls
N.L.—10—Barry Bonds, Pittsburgh, San Francisco, 1992
through 1998, 2002, 2003, 2004.
A.L.—6—Wade Boggs, Boston, 1987, 1988 (tied), 1989, 1990,
1991, 1992.

Most consecutive seasons leading league in intentional bases on balls
N.L.—7—Barry Bonds, Pittsburgh, San Francisco, 1992
through 1998.

A.L.—6—Wade Boggs, Boston, 1987, 1988 (tied), 1989, 1990, 1991, 1992.

Most seasons with 10 or more intentional bases on balls
N.L.—16—Hank Aaron, Milwaukee, Atlanta, 1957 through 1973, except 1964.
A.L.—11—George Brett, Kansas City, 1979 through 1991, except 1981, 1984.

Most at-bats with no intentional bases on balls, season
A.L.—691—Kirby Puckett, Minnesota, 161 games, 1985.
N.L.—690—Neifi Perez, Colorado, 157 games, 1999.

Most bases on balls with no intentional bases on balls, season
A.L.—118—Rickey Henderson, Oakland, 152 games, 1998.
N.L.—94—Johnny Temple, Cincinnati, 145 games, 1957.

Most intentional bases on balls, game
N.L.—4—Barry Bonds, San Francisco, May 1, 2004.
Barry Bonds, San Francisco, September 22, 2004.
(5—Andre Dawson, Chicago, May 22, 1990, 16 innings.)
A.L.—3—Held by many players.
(4—Roger Maris, New York, May 22, 1962, 12 innings.
Manny Ramirez, Boston, June 5, 2001, 18 innings.)

STRIKEOUTS
CAREER AND SEASON

Most strikeouts, career
A.L.—2,597—Reggie Jackson, Kansas City, Oakland, Baltimore, New York, California, 21 years, 1967 through 1987.
N.L.—1,936—Willie Stargell, Pittsburgh, 21 years, 1962 through 1982.

For a complete list of players with 1,200 or more career strikeouts, see page 157.

Most strikeouts, season
N.L.—195—Adam Dunn, Cincinnati, 161 games, 2004.
A.L.—186—Rob Deer, Milwaukee, 134 games, 1987.

Most strikeouts by rookie, season
A.L.—185—Pete Incaviglia, Texas, 153 games, 1986.
N.L.—168—Juan Samuel, Philadelphia, 160 games, 1984.

Most strikeouts by righthander, season
N.L.—189—Bobby Bonds, San Francisco, 157 games, 1970.
A.L.—186—Rob Deer, Milwaukee, 134 games, 1987.

Most strikeouts by lefthander, season
N.L.—195—Adam Dunn, Cincinnati, 161 games, 2004.
A.L.—185—Jim Thome, Cleveland, 156 games, 2001.

Most strikeouts by switch-hitter, season
A.L.—177—Mark Bellhorn, Boston, 138 games, 2004.
N.L.—146—Todd Hundley, New York, 153 games, 1996.

Most strikeouts by pitcher, season (since 1900)
A.L.—65—Wilbur Wood, Chicago, 49 games, 1972.
N.L.—62—Jerry Koosman, New York, 35 games, 1968.

Most seasons leading league in strikeouts
A.L.—7—Jimmie Foxx, Philadelphia, Boston, 1929, 1930 (tied), 1931, 1933, 1935, 1936, 1941.
N.L.—6—Vince DiMaggio, Boston, Pittsburgh, Philadelphia, 1937, 1938, 1942, 1943, 1944, 1945.

Most consecutive seasons leading league in strikeouts
A.L.—4—Reggie Jackson, Oakland, 1968 through 1971.
N.L.—4—Hack Wilson, Chicago, 1927 through 1930.
Vince DiMaggio, Pittsburgh, Philadelphia, 1942 through 1945.
Juan Samuel, Philadelphia, 1984 through 1987.

Fewest strikeouts by leader, season
N.L.—63—George Grantham, Chicago, 127 games, 1924.
A.L.—66—Jimmie Foxx, Philadelphia, 153 games, 1930.
Ed Morgan, Cleveland, 150 games, 1930.

Most seasons with 100 or more strikeouts
A.L.—18—Reggie Jackson, Oakland, Baltimore, New York, California, 1968 through 1980, 1982 through 1986.
N.L.—13—Willie Stargell, Pittsburgh, 1965 through 1976, 1979.

Most consecutive seasons with 100 or more strikeouts
A.L.—13—Reggie Jackson, Oakland, Baltimore, New York, 1968 through 1980.
N.L.—12—Willie Stargell, Pittsburgh, 1965 through 1976.

Fewest strikeouts, career (14 or more seasons; excludes pitchers)
A.L.—113—Joe Sewell, Cleveland, New York, 14 years, 1920 through 1933, 1,903 games.
N.L.—173—Lloyd Waner, Pittsburgh, Boston, Cincinnati, Philadelphia, Brooklyn, 18 years, 1927 through 1945, except 1943, 1,993 games.

Fewest strikeouts, season (150 or more games)
A.L.—4—Joe Sewell, Cleveland, 155 games, 1925.
Joe Sewell, Cleveland, 152 games, 1929.
N.L.—5—Charlie Hollocher, Chicago, 152 games, 1922.

Fewest strikeouts by rookie, season (150 or more games)
N.L.—17—Buddy Hassett, Brooklyn, 156 games, 1936.
A.L.—25—Tom Oliver, Boston, 154 games, 1930.

Fewest strikeouts by righthander, season (150 or more games)
N.L.—8—Emil Verban, Philadelphia, 155 games, 1947.
A.L.—9—Stuffy McInnis, Boston, 152 games, 1921.
Lou Boudreau, Cleveland, 152 games, 1948.

Fewest strikeouts by lefthander, season (150 or more games)
A.L.—4—Joe Sewell, Cleveland, 155 games, 1925.
Joe Sewell, Cleveland, 152 games, 1929.
N.L.—5—Charlie Hollocher, Chicago, 152 games, 1922.

Fewest strikeouts by switch-hitter, season (150 or more games)
N.L.—10—Frankie Frisch, St. Louis, 153 games, 1927.
A.L.—23—Buck Weaver, Chicago, 151 games, 1920.

Most seasons leading league in fewest strikeouts (150 or more games)
A.L.—11—Nellie Fox, Chicago, 1952 through 1962.
N.L.—4—Stan Musial, St. Louis, 1943, 1948, 1952, 1956 (tied).
Dick Groat, Pittsburgh, St. Louis, 1955, 1958, 1964, 1965 (tied).

Most consecutive games with no strikeouts, season
A.L.—115—Joe Sewell, Cleveland, May 17 through September 19, 1929 (437 at-bats).
N.L.—77—Lloyd Waner, Pittsburgh, Boston, Cincinnati, April 24 through September 16, 1941 (219 at-bats).

GAME AND INNING

Most strikeouts, game (*consecutive)
N.L.—5—Oscar Walker, Buffalo, June 20, 1879.*
Pete Dowling, Louisville, August 15, 1899.*
Floyd Young, Pittsburgh, September 29, 1935, second game.*
Bob Sadowski, Milwaukee, April 20, 1964.*
Dick Allen, Philadelphia, June 28, 1964, first game.*
Ron Swoboda, New York, June 22, 1969, first game.*
Steve Whitaker, San Francisco, April 14, 1970.*
Dick Allen, St. Louis, May 24, 1970.*
Bill Russell, Los Angeles, June 9, 1971.*
Jose Mangual, Montreal, August 11, 1975.*
Frank Taveras, New York, May 1, 1979.*
Bert Blyleven, Pittsburgh, July 27, 1979, second game.*
Dave Kingman, New York, May 28, 1982.*
Darryl Strawberry, Los Angeles, May 1, 1991.*
Delino DeShields, Montreal, September 17, 1991, second game.*
Scott Rolen, Philadelphia, August 23, 1999.*
Richie Sexson, Milwaukee, May 29, 2001.*
Adam Dunn, Cincinnati, August 20, 2002.*
Tony Batista, Montreal, August 31, 2004.*
(6—Don Hoak, Chicago, May 2, 1956, 17 innings.
Geoff Jenkins, Milwaukee, June 8, 2004, 17 innings.)
A.L.—5—Lefty Grove, Philadelphia, June 10, 1933, first game.*
Johnny Broaca, New York, June 25, 1934.*
Chet Laabs, Detroit, October 2, 1938, first game.*
Larry Doby, Cleveland, April 25, 1948.*
Jim Landis, Chicago, July 28, 1957.*
Bob Allison, Minnesota, September 2, 1965.*

Reggie Jackson, Oakland, September 27, 1968.*
Ray Jarvis, Boston, April 20, 1969.*
Rick Monday, Oakland, April 29, 1970.*
Frank Howard, Washington, September 19, 1970, first game.*
Don Buford, Baltimore, August 26, 1971.*
Rick Manning, Cleveland, May 15, 1977.*
Bo Jackson, Kansas City, April 18, 1987.*
Rob Deer, Milwaukee, August 8, 1987, first game.*
Jeffrey Leonard, Milwaukee, August 24, 1988.*
Joey Meyer, Milwaukee, September 20, 1988.*
Phil Bradley, Baltimore, September 7, 1989, first game.
Bernie Williams, New York, August 21, 1991.*
Phil Plantier, Boston, October 1, 1991.*
Bob Hamelin, Kansas City, May 24, 1995.*
Danny Bautista, Detroit, May 28, 1995.
Jose Canseco, Oakland, July 16, 1997.*
Jim Thome, Cleveland, April 9, 2000.
John Jaha, Oakland, April 20, 2000.*
(6—Carl Weilman, St. Louis, July 25, 1913,15 innings *
Rick Reichardt, California, May 31, 1966, 17 innings.
Billy Cowan, California, July 9, 1971, 20 innings.
Cecil Cooper, Boston, June 14, 1974, 15 innings.
Sam Horn, Baltimore, July 17, 1991, 15 innings.
Alex Gonzalez, Toronto, September 9, 1998, 13 innings.*)

Most games with four or more strikeouts, career
A.L.—23—Reggie Jackson, Kansas City, Oakland, Baltimore,
   New York, California, 1967 through 1987.
N.L.—16—Andres Galarraga, Montreal, St. Louis, Colorado,
   Atlanta, San Francisco, 1985 through 2004.

Most games with four or more strikeouts, season
N.L.—7—Dick Allen, Philadelphia, April 13, May 1, 9, June 29,
   July 16, 21, August 19, 1968.
A.L.—5—Reggie Jackson, Oakland, April 7, second game, April
   21, May 18, June 4, September 21, first game, 1971.
   Bobby Darwin, Minnesota, May 12, 13, June 23, July 14,
   August 6, first game, August 10, 1972.

Most strikeouts, first major league game
N.L.—4—Billy Sunday, Chicago, May 22, 1883.
   Wes Bales, Atlanta, August 7, 1966.
A.A.—4—Hercules Burnett, Louisville, June 26, 1888.
   George Goetz, Baltimore, June 17, 1889.
A.L.—4—Rollie Naylor, Philadelphia, September 14, 1917.
   Sam Ewing, Chicago, September 11, 1973.

Most strikeouts, doubleheader
N.L.—7—Mike Vail, New York, September 26, 1975, 24 innings.
A.L.—7—Pat Seerey, Chicago, July 24, 1948, 19 innings.
   Dave Nicholson, Chicago, June 12, 1963, 17 innings.
   Frank Howard, Washington, July 9, 1965, 18 innings.
   Bill Melton, Chicago, July 24, 1970, 18 innings.

Most strikeouts, two consecutive games
A.L.—8—Rick Monday, Oakland, April 28 (3), 29 (5), 1970.
   Gorman Thomas, Milwaukee, July 27, second game (4), 28
   (4), 1975.
   Jay Buhner, Seattle, August 23 (4), 24 (4), 1990.
   Jose Canseco, Oakland, July 14 (3), 16 (5), 1997.
   (8—Pedro Ramos, Cleveland, August 19, 23, 1963, 22
   innings.
   Roy Smalley, Minnesota, August 28, 29, 1976, 26 innings.)
N.L.—8—Wayne Twitchell, Philadelphia, May 16 (4), 22 (4),
   1973.
   Ruppert Jones, San Diego, July 16 (4), 17 (4), 1982.
   (9—Eric Davis, Cincinnati, April 24 (4), 25 (5), 1987, 21
   innings.
   Jack Clark, San Diego, June 11 (5), 13 (4), 1989, 21 innings.)

**Ten or more consecutive strikeouts, season (consecutive plate
   appearances)**
N.L.—12—Sandy Koufax, Brooklyn, June 24 to September 24,
   second game, 1955 (12 at-bats for season, 12 strikeouts).
   10—Tommie Sisk, Pittsburgh, July 27 (2), August 1 (3), 6
   (4), 12 (1), 1966.
A.L.—11—Dean Chance, Los Angeles, July 24 (1), 30 (2),

August 4, first game (3), 9 (4), 13 (1), 1965.
   10—Joe Grzenda, Washington, April 7 (2), 22 (1), May 26
   (4), June 13 (1), 16 (1), August 3 (1), 1970.

**Most consecutive strikeouts, season (not consecutive plate
   appearances)**
N.L.—14—Bill Hands, Chicago, June 9, second game through July
   11, 1968, second game (also one base on balls and two sacrifice
   hits).
   Juan Eichelberger, San Diego, June 30 through August 15,
   1980 (also one sacrifice hit).
A.L.—13—Jim Hannan, Washington, July 24 through August
   13, 1968 (also two bases on balls).

Most strikeouts, inning
A.L.-N.L.—2—Held by many players.

SACRIFICE HITS

Most sacrifices, career
A.L.—511—Eddie Collins, Philadelphia, Chicago, 25 years,
   1906 through 1930.
N.L.—392—Jake Daubert, Brooklyn, Cincinnati, 15 years, 1910
   through 1924.

Most sacrifices, season (including sacrifice scoring flies)
A.L.—67—Ray Chapman, Cleveland, 156 games, 1917.
N.L.—46—Jim Sheckard, Chicago, 148 games, 1909.

Most sacrifices, season (excludes sacrifice flies)
A.L.—46—Bill Bradley, Cleveland, 139 games, 1907.
N.L.—43—Kid Gleason, Philadelphia, 155 games, 1905.

Most sacrifices by rookie, season (includes sacrifice scoring flies)
A.L.—39—Emory Rigney, Detroit, 155 games, 1922.
N.L.—31—Ozzie Smith, San Diego, 159 games, 1978.

**Most sacrifices by rookie, season (since 1931; excludes sacri-
   fice flies)**
A.L.—28—Joe Hoover, Detroit, 144 games, 1943.
N.L.—28—Jackie Robinson, Brooklyn, 151 games, 1947.
   Ozzie Smith, San Diego, 159 games, 1978.

Most sacrifices by righthander, season
A.L.—67—Ray Chapman, Cleveland, 156 games, 1917
   (includes a few sacrifice scoring flies).
N.L.—42—Otto Knabe, Philadelphia, 151 games, 1908 (May
   include some run-scoring flies).
   Bob Fisher, Chicago, 147 games, 1915 (may include some
   run-scoring flies).
   Pie Traynor, Pittsburgh, 144 games, 1928 (may include some
   run-scoring flies).

Most sacrifices by lefthander, season
A.L.—52—Bob Ganley, Washington, 150 games, 1908 (includes
   a few sacrifice scoring flies).
N.L.—46—Jim Sheckard, Chicago, 148 games, 1909 (includes
   a few sacrifice scoring flies).

Most sacrifices by switch-hitter, season
A.L.—52—Donie Bush, Detroit, 157 games, 1909 (includes a
   few sacrifice scoring flies).
N.L.—43—Kid Gleason, Philadelphia, 155 games, 1905 (does
   not include sacrifice flies).

Most seasons leading league in sacrifices
A.L.—6—Mule Haas, Philadelphia, Chicago, 1930, 1931, 1932,
   1933, 1934, 1936.
N.L.—4—Otto Knabe, Philadelphia, 1907, 1908, 1910, 1913.

Most consecutive seasons leading league in sacrifices
A.L.—5—Mule Haas, Philadelphia, Chicago, 1930 through
   1934.
N.L.—2—Held by many players. Last player—Jack Wilson,
   Pittsburgh, 2001 (tied), 2002.

Fewest sacrifices for leader, season (excludes sacrifice flies)
A.L.—13—Billy Martin, Detroit, 131 games, 1958.
   Tony Kubek, New York, 132 games, 1959.
   Jim Landis, Chicago, 149 games, 1959.
   Al Pilarcik, Baltimore, 130 games, 1959.
   Vic Power, Minnesota, 138 games, 1963.
   Paul Blair, Baltimore, 150 games, 1969.

Denny McLain, Detroit, 42 games, 1969.
N.L.—13—Maury Wills, Los Angeles, 148 games, 1961.

Most at-bats with no sacrifice hits, season
N.L.—701—Juan Samuel, Philadelphia, 160 games, 1984.
A.L.—672—Garret Anderson, Anaheim, 161 games, 2001.

Most sacrifice hits, game
A.L.—4—Red Killefer, Washington, August 27, 1910, first
game.
Jack Barry, Boston, August 21, 1916.
Ray Chapman, Cleveland, August 31, 1919.
Felix Fermin, Cleveland, August 22, 1989, 10 innings.
N.L.—4—Jake Daubert, Brooklyn, August 15, 1914, second
game.
Cy Seymour, Cincinnati, July 25, 1902.
Kris Benson, Pittsburgh, April 18, 2004.

Most sacrifice hits, inning
A.L.—2—Al Benton, Detroit, August 6, 1941, third inning.
N.L.—1—Held by many players.

SACRIFICE FLIES

Most sacrifice flies, career
M.L.—128—Eddie Murray, Baltimore A.L., Los Angeles N.L., New
York N.L., Cleveland A.L., Anaheim A.L., 21 years, 1977 through
1997 (92 in A.L., 36 in N.L.).
A.L.—127—Cal Ripken Jr., Baltimore, 21 years, 1981 through
2001.
N.L.—113—Hank Aaron, Milwaukee, Atlanta, 21 years, 1954
through 1974.

Most sacrifice flies, season
N.L.—19—Gil Hodges, Brooklyn, 154 games, 1954. (Pie
Traynor, Pittsburgh, N.L., 144 games, 1928, had 31 sacrifice
flies, advancing runners to second base, third base and
home.)
A.L.—17—Roy White, New York, 147 games, 1971.
Bobby Bonilla, Baltimore, 159 games, 1996.

Most sacrifice flies by rookie, season
N.L.—13—Willie Montanez, Philadelphia, 158 games, 1971.
A.L.—13—Gary Gaetti, Minnesota, 145 games, 1982.

Most sacrifice flies by righthander, season
N.L.—19—Gil Hodges, Brooklyn, 154 games, 1954.
A.L.—16—Chick Gandil, Washington, 145 games, 1914.
Juan Gonzalez, Cleveland, 140 games, 2001.

Most sacrifice flies by lefthander, season
A.L.—16—Sam Crawford, Detroit, 157 games, 1914.
N.L.—14—J.T. Snow, San Francisco, 155 games, 2000.

Most sacrifice flies by switch-hitter, season
A.L.—17—Roy White, New York, 147 games, 1971.
Bobby Bonilla, Baltimore, 159 games, 1996.
N.L.—15—Bobby Bonilla, Pittsburgh, 160 games, 1990.
Howard Johnson, New York, 156 games, 1991.

Most seasons leading league in sacrifice flies
A.L.—4—Brooks Robinson, Baltimore, 1962 (tied), 1964, 1967
(tied), 1968 (tied).
N.L.—3—Ron Santo, Chicago, 1963, 1967, 1969.
Johnny Bench, Cincinnati, 1970, 1972, 1973 (tied).

Most at-bats with no sacrifice flies, season
N.L.—680—Pete Rose, Cincinnati, 160 games, 1973.
Frank Taveras, Pittsburgh, New York, 164 games, 1979.
A.L.—680—Kirby Puckett, Minnesota, 161 games, 1986.

Most sacrifice flies, game
N.L.—3—Harry Steinfeldt, Chicago, May 5, 1909.
Ernie Banks, Chicago, June 2, 1961.
Vince Coleman, St. Louis, May 1, 1986.
Candy Maldonado, San Francisco, August 29, 1987.
A.L.—3—Bob Meusel, New York, September 15, 1926.
Russ Nixon, Boston, August 31, 1965, second game.
Don Mattingly, New York, May 3, 1986.
George Bell, Toronto, August 14, 1990.
Chad Kreuter, Detroit, July 30, 1994.
Juan Gonzalez, Texas, July 3, 1999.
Edgar Martinez, Seattle, August 3, 2002.

HIT BY PITCH

Most hit by pitch, career
A.L.—267—Don Baylor, Baltimore, Oakland, California, New
York, Boston, Minnesota, 19 years, 1970 through 1988.
N.L.—243—Ron Hunt, New York, Los Angeles, San Francisco,
Montreal, St. Louis, 12 years, 1963 through 1974.

Most hit by pitch, season
N.L.—50—Ron Hunt, Montreal, 152 games, 1971.
A.L.—35—Don Baylor, Boston, 160 games, 1986.

Most hit by pitch, rookie, season
A.A.—29—Tommy Tucker, Baltimore, 136 games, 1887.
A.L.—21—David Eckstein, Anaheim, 153 games, 2001.
N.L.—20—Frank Robinson, Cincinnati, 152 games, 1956.

Most hit by pitch, righthander, season
N.L.—50—Ron Hunt, Montreal, 152 games, 1971.
A.L.—35—Don Baylor, Boston, 160 games, 1986.

Most hit by pitch, lefthander, season
N.L.—31—Steve Evans, St. Louis, 151 games, 1910.
A.L.—22—Brady Anderson, Baltimore, 149 games, 1996.

Most hit by pitch, switch-hitter, season
N.L.—25—F.P. Santangelo, Montreal, 130 games, 1997.
A.L.—15—Gene Larkin, Minnesota, 149 games, 1988.

Most seasons leading league in hit by pitch
A.L.—10—Minnie Minoso, Cleveland, Chicago, 1951, 1952,
1953, 1954, 1956, 1957, 1958, 1959, 1960, 1961.
N.L.—7—Ron Hunt, San Francisco, Montreal, St. Louis, 1968,
1969, 1970, 1971, 1972, 1973, 1974.

Most consecutive seasons leading league in hit by pitch
N.L.—7—Ron Hunt, San Francisco, Montreal, St. Louis, 1968
through 1974.
A.L.—6—Minnie Minoso, Chicago, Cleveland, 1956 through
1961.

Fewest hit by pitch for leader, season
A.L.—5—Frank Crosetti, New York, 138 games, 1934.
Frank Pytlak, Cleveland, 91 games, 1934.
N.L.—6—Buddy Blattner, New York, 126 games, 1946.
Andre Dawson, Montreal, 151 games, 1980.
Dan Driessen, Cincinnati, 154 games, 1980.
Tim Foli, Pittsburgh, 127 games, 1980.
Greg Luzinski, Philadelphia, 106 games, 1980.
Elliott Maddox, New York, 130 games, 1980.
Pete Rose, Philadelphia, 162 games, 1980.

Most at-bats with no hit by pitch, season
A.L.—689—Sandy Alomar Sr., California, 162 games, 1971.
N.L.—662—Hugh Critz, Cincinnati, New York, 152 games,
1930.
Granny Hamner, Philadelphia, 154 games, 1949.

Most hit by pitch, game
A.A.—3—5 times (held by 5 players).
N.L.—3—15 times (held by 12 players). Last player—Richard
Hidalgo, Houston, April 19, 2000.
(3—Ron Hunt, San Francisco, April 29, 1969, 13 innings.)
A.L.—3—6 times (held by 6 players). Last player—Corey
Koskie, Minnesota, July 27, 2004.
(3—Jake Stahl, Washington, April 15, 1904, 10 innings.
Craig Kusick, Minnesota, August 27, 1975, 11 innings.)

Most times hit by pitch three times in a game, career
N.L.—3—Hughie Jennings, Baltimore, 1894, 1896, 1898.
N.L. since 1900—2—Frank Chance, Chicago, 1902, 1904.
A.L.—1—Held by five players.

Most hit by pitch, doubleheader
N.L.—5—Frank Chance, Chicago, May 30, 1904.
A.L.—3—Bert Daniels, New York, June 20, 1913.
Al Smith, Chicago, June 21, 1961.

Most hit by pitch, inning
N.L.—2—Willard Schmidt, Cincinnati, April 26, 1959, third
inning.
Frank J. Thomas, New York, April 29, 1962, first game,
fourth inning.
Andres Galarraga, Colorado, July 12, 1996, seventh inning.
A.L.—2—Brady Anderson, Baltimore, May 23, 1999, first inning.

GROUNDING INTO DOUBLE PLAYS

Most grounding into double plays, career
A.L.—350—Cal Ripken Jr., Baltimore, 21 years, 1981 through 2001.
N.L.—305—Hank Aaron, Milwaukee, Atlanta, 21 years, 1954 through 1974.

Most grounding into double plays, season
A.L.—36—Jim Rice, Boston, 159 games, 1984.
N.L.—30—Ernie Lombardi, Cincinnati, 129 games, 1938.
 Brad Ausmus, Houston, 130 games, 2002.

Most grounding into double plays by rookie, season
A.L.—27—Billy Johnson, New York, 155 games, 1943.
 Al Rosen, Cleveland, 155 games, 1950.
N.L.—21—Albert Pujols, St. Louis, 161 games, 2001.

Most grounding into double plays by righthander, season
A.L.—36—Jim Rice, Boston, 159 games, 1984.
N.L.—30—Ernie Lombardi, Cincinnati, 129 games, 1938.
 Brad Ausmus, Houston, 130 games, 2002.

Most grounding into double plays by lefthander, season
A.L.—32—Ben Grieve, Oakland, 158 games, 2000.
N.L.—27—A.J. Pierzynski, San Francisco, 131 games, 2004.

Most grounding into double plays by switch-hitter, season
A.L.—29—Dave Philley, Philadelphia, 151 games, 1952.
N.L.—29—Ted Simmons, St. Louis, 161 games, 1973.

Most seasons leading league in grounding into double plays
N.L.—4—Ernie Lombardi, Cincinnati, New York, 1933, 1934, 1938, 1944.
A.L.—4—Jim Rice, Boston, 1982, 1983 (tied), 1984, 1985.

Fewest grounding into double plays for leader, season
N.L.—19—Andy Seminick, Philadelphia, 124 games, 1946.
 George Kurowski, St. Louis, 146 games, 1947.
 Andy Pafko, Chicago, 129 games, 1947.
A.L.—21—Brooks Robinson, Baltimore, 158 games, 1967.
 John Olerud, Seattle, 159 games, 2001.

Fewest grounding into double plays, season (150 or more games)
N.L.—0—Augie Galan, Chicago, 154 games, 1935.
 Craig Biggio, Houston, 162 games, 1997.
A.L.—0—Dick McAuliffe, Detroit, 151 games, 1968.

Fewest grounding into double plays by rookie, season (150 or more games)
N.L.—3—Vince Coleman, St. Louis, 151 games, 1985.
A.L.—3—Ichiro Suzuki, Seattle, 157 games, 2001.

Fewest grounding into double plays by righthander, season (150 or more games)
N.L.—0—Craig Biggio, Houston, 162 games, 1997.
A.L.—2—Cesar Tovar, Minnesota, 157 games, 1968.
 Mark Belanger, Baltimore, 152 games, 1975.

Fewest grounding into double plays by lefthander, season (150 or more games)
A.L.—0—Dick McAuliffe, Detroit, 151 games, 1968.
N.L.—2—Lou Brock, St. Louis, 155 games, 1965.
 Lou Brock, St. Louis, 157 games, 1969.
 Will Clark, San Francisco, 150 games, 1987.
 Brett Butler, San Francisco, 157 games, 1988.

Fewest grounding into double plays by switch-hitter, season (150 or more games)
N.L.—0—Augie Galan, Chicago, 154 games, 1935.
A.L.—1—Willie Wilson, Kansas City, 154 games, 1979.

Most seasons leading league in fewest grounding into double plays (150 or more games)
N.L.—6—Richie Ashburn, Philadelphia, Chicago, 1951, 1952, 1953, 1954, 1958, 1960 (tied).
A.L.—2—Held by 10 players. Last player—Willie Wilson, Kansas City, 1979, 1980.

Most grounding into double plays, game
A.L.—4—Goose Goslin, Detroit, April 28, 1934 (consecutive).
N.L.—4—Joe Torre, New York, July 21, 1975 (consecutive).

Most grounding into double plays, two consecutive games
N.L.—5—Zeke Bonura, New York, July 8 (3), second game, July 9 (2), 1939.
A.L.—4—Held by many players.

Most grounding into infield triple plays, game or season
N.L.-A.L.—1—Held by many players.

REACHING ON ERRORS OR INTERFERENCE

Most times reaching base on error, game (fair-hit balls)
P.L.—4—Mike Griffin, Philadelphia, June 23, 1890.
N.L.—3—George Gore, New York, August 15, 1887.
 Bill McKechnie, New York, May 9, 1916.
 Al Lopez, Boston, July 16, 1936.
 Jerry Grote, New York, September 5, 1975.
A.L.—3—Phil Bradley, Baltimore, August 4, 1989.
 Ray Durham, Chicago, April 22, 1998.

Most times reaching base on error, inning (fair-hit balls)
A.L.—2—Emory Rigney, Detroit, August 21, 1922, sixth inning.
 Fred Spurgeon, Cleveland, April 14, 1925, eighth inning.
 Johnny Bassler, Detroit, June 17, 1925, sixth inning.
 Sam Rice, Washington, July 10, 1926, eighth inning.
N.L.—2—Stu Martin, St. Louis, June 22, 1940, sixth inning.

Most times reaching base on catcher's interference, season
A.L.—8—Roberto Kelly, New York, 152 games, 1992.
N.L.—7—Dale Berra, Pittsburgh, 161 games, 1983.

Most times reaching base on catcher's interference, nine-inning game
N.L.—2—Ben Geraghty, Brooklyn, April 26, 1936.
 Pat Corrales, Philadelphia, September 29, 1965.
A.L.—2—Dan Meyer, Seattle, May 3, 1977.
 Bob Stinson, Seattle, July 24, 1979.

CLUB BATTING

GAMES

Most games, league
N.L.—19,113—Chicago, 129 years, 1876 to date.
A.L.—16,203—Detroit, 104 years, 1901 to date.

Most games, season
N.L.—165—Los Angeles, 1962 (3 playoffs).
 San Francisco, 1962 (3 playoffs).
A.L.—164—Cleveland, 1964 (2 tied).
 New York, 1964, 1968 (2 tied).
 Minnesota, 1967 (2 tied).
 Detroit, 1968 (2 tied).

Fewest games, season
A.L.—147—Cleveland, 1945 (2 tied, 9 unplayed).
N.L.—149—Philadelphia, 1907 (2 tied, 7 unplayed), 1934 (5 unplayed).

Three games, one day
N.L.—Brooklyn and Pittsburgh, September 1, 1890 (Brooklyn won 3).
 Baltimore and Louisville, September 7, 1896 (Baltimore won 3).
 Pittsburgh and Cincinnati, October 2, 1920 (Cincinnati won 2).
A.L.—Never occurred.

Most doubleheaders, season
A.L.—44—Chicago, 1943. (Won 11, lost 10, split 23).
N.L.—43—Philadelphia, 1943. (Won 11, lost 14, split 18).

Fewest doubleheaders, season
A.L.-N.L.—0—Held by many clubs.
 Last A.L. clubs—Anaheim, Oakland, 2004.
 Last N.L. clubs—Cincinnati, Los Angeles, 2004.

Most consecutive doubleheaders played, season
N.L.—9—Boston, September 4 through September 15, 1928.
A.L.—8—Washington, July 27 through August 5, 1909.

Most consecutive games between same clubs, season
A.L.—11—Detroit vs. St. Louis, September 8 through 14, 1904.
N.L.—10—Chicago vs. Philadelphia, August 7 through 16, 1907.

Most consecutive doubleheaders between same clubs, season
A.L.—5—Philadelphia vs. Washington, August 5, 7, 8, 9, 10, 1901.
N.L.—4—New York vs. Boston, September 10, 11, 13, 14, 1928.

BATTING AVERAGE

Highest batting average, season
N.L.—.350—Philadelphia, 132 games, 1894.
N.L. since 1900—.319—New York, 154 games, 1930.
A.L.—.316—Detroit, 154 games, 1921.

Highest batting average for pennant winner, season
N.L.—.343—Baltimore, 129 games, 1894.
N.L. since 1900—.314—St. Louis, 154 games, 1930.
A.L.—.307—New York, 155 games, 1927.

Highest batting average for an outfield, season
N.L.—.409—Philadelphia, 132 games, 1894.
A.L.—.367—Detroit, 156 games, 1925.
N.L. since 1900—.350—Chicago, 156 games, 1929.

Most years leading league in batting average (since 1900)
N.L.—23—St. Louis, 1915, 1920, 1921, 1934, 1938, 1939, 1942, 1943, 1944, 1946, 1949, 1952, 1954, 1956, 1957, 1963, 1971, 1975, 1979, 1980, 1985, 1992, 2004.
A.L.—22—Boston, 1903, 1938, 1939, 1941, 1942, 1944, 1946, 1949, 1950, 1964, 1967, 1975, 1979, 1981, 1984, 1985, 1987, 1988, 1989, 1990, 1997, 2003.

Most consecutive years leading league in batting average
N.L.—8—Colorado, 1995 through 2002.
A.L.—5—Philadelphia, 1910 through 1914.

Most players batting .400 or over, season (50 or more games)
N.L.—4—Philadelphia, 1894.
N.L. since 1900—1—St. Louis, 1922, 1924, 1925; New York, 1930.
A.L.—1—Philadelphia, 1901; Detroit, 1911, 1912, 1922, 1923; Cleveland, 1911; St. Louis, 1920, 1922; Boston, 1941.

Most players batting .300 or over, season (50 or more games)
A.L.—10—Philadelphia, 1927.
N.L.—10—St. Louis, 1930.

Lowest batting average, season
N.L.—.207—Washington, 136 games, 1888.
A.L.—.212—Chicago, 156 games, 1910.
N.L. since 1900—.213—Brooklyn, 154 games, 1908.

Lowest batting average for a pennant winner, season
A.L.—.228—Chicago, 154 games, 1906; last in batting.
N.L.—.242—New York, 162 games, 1969; tied for seventh in batting.

Lowest batting average for club leader, season
A.L.—.240—Oakland, 163 games, 1968.
N.L.—.254—St. Louis, 157 games, 1915.

ON-BASE PERCENTAGE

Highest on-base percentage, season (since 1900)
N.L.—.418—Baltimore, 129 games, 1894.
A.L.—.385—Boston, 154 games, 1950.
N.L. since 1900—.378—Chicago, 156 games, 1930.

Lowest on-base percentage, season (150 or more games; since 1900)
N.L.—.266—Brooklyn, 154 games, 1908.
A.L.—.274—Washington, 154 games, 1905.

SLUGGING AVERAGE

Highest slugging average, season
A.L.—.491—Boston, 162 games, 2003.
N.L.—.483—Colorado, 162 games, 2001.

Most years leading league in slugging average (since 1900)
A.L.—30—New York, 1901 (franchise in Baltimore), 1920, 1921, 1923, 1924, 1926, 1927, 1928, 1930, 1931, 1936,

1937, 1938, 1939, 1943, 1944, 1945, 1947, 1948, 1951, 1953, 1954, 1955, 1956, 1957, 1958, 1960, 1961, 1962, 1986.
N.L.—21—New York/San Francisco, 1904, 1905, 1908, 1910, 1911, 1919, 1923, 1924, 1927, 1928, 1935, 1945, 1947, 1948, 1952, 1961, 1962, 1963, 1989, 1993, 2002 (15 N.Y., 6 S.F.).

Most consecutive years leading in slugging (since 1900)
A.L.—6—New York, 1953 through 1958.
N.L.—5—Colorado, 1995 through 1999.

Lowest slugging average, season (150 or more games)
A.L.—.261—Chicago, 156 games, 1910.
N.L.—.274—Boston, 155 games, 1909.

AT-BATS AND PLATE APPEARANCES

Most at-bats, season
A.L.—5,781—Boston, 162 games, 1997.
N.L.—5,767—Cincinnati, 163 games, 1968.

Fewest at-bats, season
N.L.—4,725—Philadelphia, 149 games, 1907.
A.L.—4,827—Chicago, 153 games, 1913.

Most at-bats, game
N.L.—66—Chicago vs. Buffalo, July 3, 1883.
N.L. since 1900—58—New York vs. Philadelphia, September 2, 1925, second game.
New York vs. Philadelphia, July 11, 1931, first game.
(89—New York vs. St. Louis, September 11, 1974, 25 innings.)
A.L.—57—Milwaukee vs. Toronto, August 28, 1992
(95—Chicago vs. Milwaukee, May 8, finished May 9, 1984, 25 innings.)

Most plate appearances, game
N.L.—71—Chicago vs. Louisville, June 29, 1897.
N.L. since 1900—66—Philadelphia vs. Chicago, August 25, 1922.
St. Louis vs. Philadelphia, July 6, 1929, second game.
(103—New York vs. St. Louis, September 11, 1974, 25 innings.)
A.L.—65—Milwaukee vs. Toronto, August 28, 1992.
(104—Chicago vs. Milwaukee, May 8, finished May 9, 1984, 25 innings.)

Fewest at-bats, nine-inning game (batting nine times)
A.L.—23—Chicago vs. St. Louis, May 6, 1917.
Cleveland vs. Chicago, May 9, 1961.
Detroit vs. Baltimore, May 6, 1968.
N.L.—24—many times. Last : Pittsburgh vs. Tampa Bay, June 13, 2003.

Fewest at-bats, nine-inning game (batting eight times)
A.L.—19—Baltimore vs. Kansas City, September 12, 1964.
N.L.—21—Pittsburgh vs. St. Louis, September 8, 1908.
Atlanta vs. Pittsburgh, September 6, 1986.

Most at-bats by both clubs, game
N.L.—106—Chicago 64, Louisville 42, July 22, 1876.
N.L. since 1900—99—New York 56, Cincinnati 43, June 9, 1901.
New York 58, Philadelphia 41, July 11, 1931, first game.
Cincinnati 52, Philadelphia 47, August 3, 1969.
(175—New York 89, St. Louis 86, September 11, 1974, 25 innings.)
A.L.—96—Cleveland 51, Philadelphia 45, April 29, 1952.
(175—Chicago 95, Milwaukee 80, May 8, finished May 9, 1984, 25 innings.)

Most plate appearances by both clubs, game
N.L.—125—Philadelphia 66, Chicago 59, August 25, 1922.
(202—New York 103, St. Louis 99, September 11, 1974, 25 innings.)
A.L.—110—Tampa Bay 61, Toronto 49, June 24, 2004.
(198—Chicago 104, Milwaukee 94, May 8, finished May 9, 1984, 25 innings.)

Fewest at-bats by both clubs, nine-inning game
N.L.—48—Boston 25, Philadelphia 23, April 22, 1910.
  Brooklyn 24, Cincinnati 24, July 22, 1911.
A.L.—46—Kansas City 27, Baltimore 19, September 12, 1964.

Most at-bats, doubleheader
A.L.—99—New York vs. Philadelphia, June 28, 1939.
N.L.—98—Pittsburgh vs. Philadelphia, August 8, 1922.

Fewest at-bats, doubleheader
A.L.—50—Boston vs. Chicago, August 28, 1912.
N.L.—52—Brooklyn vs. St. Louis, July 24, 1909.
  St. Louis vs. Montreal, September 29, 1987.

Most at-bats by by both clubs, doubleheader
N.L.—176—Pittsburgh 98, Philadelphia 78, August 8, 1922.
  (234—New York 119, San Francisco 115, May 31, 1964, 32
  innings.)
A.L.—172—Boston 89, Philadelphia 83, July 4, 1939.
  (215—Kansas City 112, Detroit 103, June 17, 1967, 28
  innings.)

Fewest at-bats by both clubs, doubleheader
A.L.—106—Boston 55, Baltimore 51, September 2, 1971.
N.L.—109—St. Louis 57, Brooklyn 52, July 24, 1909.

Most plate appearances, inning
A.L.—23—Boston vs. Detroit, June 18, 1953, seventh inning.
N.L.—23—Chicago vs. Detroit, September 6, 1883, seventh
  inning.
N.L. since 1900—21—Brooklyn vs. Cincinnati, May 21, 1952,
  first inning.

Most batters facing pitcher three times, inning (club)
N.L.—5—Chicago vs. Detroit, September 6, 1883, seventh inning.
A.L.—5—Boston vs. Detroit, June 18, 1953, seventh inning.
N.L. since 1900—3—Brooklyn vs. Cincinnati, May 21, 1952,
  first inning.

RUNS
SEASON AND MONTH

Most runs, season
N.L.—1,220—Boston, 133 games, 1894.
A.L.—1,067—New York, 155 games, 1931.
N.L. since 1900—1,004—St. Louis, 154 games, 1930.

Most runs by pennant winner, season
N.L.—1,170—Baltimore, 129 games, 1894.
A.L.—1,065—New York, 155 games, 1936.
N.L. since 1900—1,004—St. Louis, 154 games, 1930.

Most runs at home, season (since 1900)
N.L.—658—Colorado, 81 games, 1996.
A.L.—625—Boston, 77 games, 1950.

Most runs on road, season (since 1900)
A.L.—591—New York, 78 games, 1930.
N.L.—492—Chicago, 78 games, 1929.

Most runs against one club, season (since 1900)
N.L.—218—Chicago vs. Philadelphia, 24 games, 1930 (117 at
  home, 101 at Philadelphia).
A.L.—216—Boston vs. St. Louis, 22 games, 1950 (118 at
  home, 98 at St. Louis).

Most players scoring 100 or more runs, season
N.L.—7—Boston, 1894.
A.L.—6—New York, 1931.
N.L. since 1900—6—Brooklyn, 1953.

Fewest runs, season
N.L.—372—St. Louis, 154 games, 1908.
A.L.—380—Washington, 156 games, 1909.

Fewest runs scored by leader, season
N.L.—590—St. Louis, 157 games, 1915.
A.L.—622—Philadelphia, 152 games, 1905.

Fewest runs by pennant winner, season
A.L.—550—Boston, 156 games, 1916.
N.L.—571—Chicago, 155 games, 1907.

Most runs scored, month (since 1900)
A.L.—275—New York, August 1938, 36 games.
N.L.—260—New York, June 1929, 33 games.

GAME AND DOUBLEHEADER—ONE CLUB

Most runs, game
N.L.—36—Chicago vs. Louisville (7), June 29, 1897.
A.L.—29—Boston vs. St. Louis (4), June 8, 1950.
  Chicago vs. Kansas City (6), April 23, 1955.
N.L. since 1900—28—St. Louis vs. Philadelphia (7), July 6,
  1929, second game.

Most runs, opening game of season
P.L.—23—Buffalo vs. Cleveland, April 19, 1890 (23-2).
A.L.—21—Cleveland vs. St. Louis, April 14, 1925 (21-14).
N.L.—19—Philadelphia vs. Boston, April 19, 1900, 10 innings
  (19-17).

Most runs scored by infielders, game
N.L.—16—Chicago vs. Philadelphia, June 29, 1897.
  Chicago vs. Boston, July 3, 1945.
A.L.—16—Boston vs. St. Louis, June 8, 1950.

Most runs scored by outfielders, game
A.A.—14—Kansas City vs. Philadelphia, September 30, 1888.
N.L.—14—New York vs. Cincinnati, June 9, 1901.
  New York vs. Brooklyn, April 30, 1944, first game.
A.L.—11—Chicago vs. Philadelphia, September 11, 1936.
  New York vs. Washington, August 12, 1953.

Biggest run deficit overcome to win game
A.L.—12—Detroit vs. Chicago, June 18, 1911, at Detroit.

Chicago	7 0 0		3 3 0		2 0 0—15
Detroit	0 1 0		0 4 3		0 5 3—16

Philadelphia vs. Cleveland, June 15, 1925, at Philadelphia.

Cleveland	0 4 2	2 4 2	1 0 0—15
Philadelphia	0 1 1	0 0 1	1 13 x—17

Seattle vs. Cleveland, August 5, 2001, at Cleveland, 11 innings.

Seattle	0 4 8	0 2 0	0 0 0 0 0—14
Cleveland	0 0 0	2 0 0	3 4 5 0 1—15

N.L.—11—St. Louis vs. New York, June 15, 1952, first game, at
New York.

St. Louis	0 0 0	0 7 0	3 2 2—14
New York	0 5 6	0 0 0	0 0 1—12

Philadelphia vs. Chicago, April 17, 1976, at Chicago, 10 innings.

Philadelphia	0 1 0	1 2 0	3 5 3 3—18
Chicago	0 7 5	1 0 0	0 0 2 1—16

Houston vs. St. Louis, July 18, 1994, at Houston.

St. Louis	3 4 4	0 0 0	0 0 1—12
Houston	0 0 0	2 2 11	0 0 x—15

Most runs scored by two players, game
N.L.—12—Boston vs. Pittsburgh, August 27, 1887 (King Kelly
  6, Ezra Sutton 6).
N.L. since 1900—11—New York vs. Brooklyn, April 30, 1944,
  first game (Mel Ott 6, Joe Medwick 5).
  New York vs. Brooklyn, April 30, 1944, first game (Mel Ott 6,
  Phil Weintraub 5).
A.L.—10—Cleveland vs. Baltimore, September 2, 1902 (Harry
  Bay 5, Bill Bradley 5).
  Chicago vs. Kansas City, April 23, 1955 (Chico Carrasquel 5,
  Minnie Minoso 5).

Longest extra-inning game without a run
N.L.—24 innings—New York vs. Houston, April 15, 1968.
A.L.—20 innings—California vs. Oakland, July 9, 1971.

Most players scoring six runs, game
N.L.—2—Boston vs. Pittsburgh, August 27, 1887 (King Kelly,
  Ezra Sutton).
N.L. since 1900—1—New York vs. Philadelphia, August 4,
  1934, second game (Mel Ott).
  New York vs. Brooklyn, April 30, 1944, first game (Mel Ott).
  Milwaukee vs. Chicago, September 2, 1957, first game (Frank
  Torre).
  New York vs. Houston, August 30, 1999 (Edgardo Alfonzo).
A.L.—1—Boston vs. Chicago, May 8, 1946 (Johnny Pesky).
  Boston vs. Cleveland, August 21, 1986 (Spike Owen).
  Kansas City vs. Detroit, September 9, 2004 (Joe Randa).

Most players scoring five or more runs, game
N.L.—3—Chicago vs. Cleveland, July 24, 1882.
Boston vs. Philadelphia, June 20, 1883.
Boston vs. Pittsburgh, August 27, 1887.
New York vs. Brooklyn, April 30, 1944, first game.
Chicago vs. Boston, July 3, 1945.
A.L.—2—Cleveland vs. Baltimore, September 2, 1902.
Chicago vs. Kansas City, April 23, 1955.

Most players scoring four or more runs, game
N.L.—6—Chicago vs. Cleveland, July 24, 1882.
Chicago vs. Louisville, June 29, 1897.
N.L. since 1900—4—St. Louis vs. Philadelphia, July 6, 1929, second game.
A.L.—4—Boston vs. St. Louis, June 8, 1950.

Most players scoring three or more runs, game
N.L.—9—Chicago vs. Buffalo, July 3, 1883.
A.L.—7—Boston vs. St. Louis, June 8, 1950.
N.L. since 1900—6—New York vs. Philadelphia, September 2, 1925, second game.

Most players scoring two or more runs, game
N.L.—10—Chicago vs. Louisville, June 29, 1897.
N.L. since 1900—9—St. Louis vs. Chicago, April 16, 1912.
Chicago vs. Philadelphia, August 25, 1922.
St. Louis vs. Philadelphia, July 6, 1929, second game.
Chicago vs. Colorado, August 18, 1995.
A.L.—9—Boston vs. Philadelphia, May 2, 1901.
New York vs. Cleveland, July 14, 1904.
Cleveland vs. Boston, July 7, 1923, first game.
New York vs. Chicago, July 26, 1931, second game.
New York vs. Philadelphia, May 24, 1936.
Boston vs. Philadelphia, June 29, 1950.
California vs. Toronto, August 25, 1979.
Minnesota vs. Detroit, June 4, 1994.

Most players scoring one or more runs, game
N.L.—15—Atlanta vs. Florida, October 3, 1999.
A.L.—14—Oakland vs. Texas, September 30, 2000.

Clubs scoring 20 or more runs (most times)
N.L.—41—Chicago, 1876 to date.
A.L.—23—New York, 1903 to date.
N.L. since 1900—15—Brooklyn, 1900 through 1957.

Clubs scoring 20 or more runs (most times), season
N.L.—8—Boston, 1894.
N.L. since 1900—3—Philadelphia, 1900.
A.L.—3—New York, 1939.
Boston, 1950.

Most runs, doubleheader
N.L.—43—Boston vs. Cincinnati, August 21, 1894.
A.L.—36—Detroit vs. St. Louis, August 14, 1937.
N.L. since 1900—34—St. Louis vs. Philadelphia, July 6, 1929.

Longest doubleheader without scoring a run
N.L.—27 innings—St. Louis vs. New York, July 2, 1933.
New York vs. Philadelphia, October 2, 1965.
A.L.—18 innings—Held by many clubs. Last doubleheader—Cleveland vs. Boston, September 26, 1975.

Most runs, two consecutive games
N.L.—53—Chicago, July 22, 25, 1876.
A.L.—49—Boston vs. St. Louis, June 7, 8, 1950.
N.L. since 1900—45—Pittsburgh, June 20, 22, 1925.

Most runs, three consecutive games
N.L.—71—Chicago, July 20, 22, 25, 1876.
N.L. since 1900—54—Pittsburgh, June 19, 20, 22, 1925.
A.L.—56—Boston vs. St. Louis, June 7, 8, 9, 1950.

Most runs, four consecutive games
N.L.—88—Chicago, July 20, 22, 25, 27, 1876.
N.L. since 1900—59—Chicago, June 1, 3, 4, 5, 1930.
A.L.—65—Boston, June 5, 6, 7, 8, 1950.

GAME AND DOUBLEHEADER—BOTH CLUBS

Most runs, game
N.L.—49—Chicago 26, Philadelphia 23, August 25, 1922.
A.L.—36—Boston 22, Philadelphia 14, June 29, 1950.

Most runs, opening game of season
N.L.—36—Philadelphia 19, Boston 17, April 19, 1900, 10 innings.
A.L.—35—Cleveland 21, St. Louis 14, April 14, 1925.

Most players scoring six or more runs, game
N.L.—2—Boston 2 (King Kelly, Ezra Sutton), Pittsburgh 0, August 27, 1887.
A.L.—1—Boston 1 (Johnny Pesky), Chicago 0, May 8, 1946.
Boston 1 (Spike Owen), Cleveland 0, August 21, 1986.
Kansas City 1 (Joe Randa), Detroit 0, September 9, 2004.

Most players scoring five or more runs, game
N.L.—3—Chicago 3, Cleveland 0, July 24, 1882.
Boston 3, Philadelphia 0, June 20, 1883.
Boston 3, Pittsburgh 0, August 27, 1887.
New York 3, Brooklyn 0, April 30, 1944, first game.
Chicago 3, Boston 0, July 3, 1945.
A.L.—2—Cleveland 2, Baltimore 0, September 2, 1902.
Chicago 2, Kansas City 0, April 23, 1955.

Most players scoring four or more runs, game
N.L.—6—Chicago 6, Cleveland 0, July 24, 1882.
Chicago 6, Louisville 0, June 29, 1897.
N.L. since 1900—4—St. Louis 4, Philadelphia 0, July 6, 1929, second game.
A.L.—4—Boston 4, St. Louis 0, June 8, 1950.

Most players scoring three or more runs, game
N.L.—9—Chicago 9, Buffalo 0, July 3, 1883.
A.L.—7—Boston 7, St. Louis 0, June 8, 1950.
N.L. since 1900—6—New York 6, Philadelphia 0, September 2, 1925, second game.
Cincinnati 5, Colorado 1, May 19, 1999.

Most players scoring two or more runs, game
N.L.—16—Chicago 9, Philadelphia 7, August 25, 1922.
A.L.—13—Boston 9, Philadelphia 4, May 2, 1901.
Boston 9, Philadelphia 4, June 29, 1950.

Most players scoring one or more runs, game
N.L.—22—Philadelphia 13, Chicago 9, August 25, 1922.
A.L.—19—Detroit 12, Baltimore 7, August 12, 1993.

Most runs by both teams, doubleheader
A.L.—54—Boston 35, Philadelphia 19, July 4, 1939.
N.L.—54—Boston 43, Cincinnati 11, August 21, 1894.
N.L. since 1900—50—Brooklyn 26, Philadelphia 24, May 18, 1929.
St. Louis 34, Philadelphia 16, July 6, 1929.

Fewest runs by both teams, doubleheader
N.L.—1—Boston 1, Pittsburgh 0, September 4, 1902.
Philadelphia 1, Boston 0, September 5, 1913.
A.L.—2—Washington 1, St. Louis 1, September 25, 1904.
Philadelphia 1, Boston 1, June 1, 1909.
Philadelphia 1, Boston 1, September 11, 1909.
Los Angeles 1, Detroit 1, August 18, 1964.
Washington 1, Kansas City 1, July 2, 1967.
Chicago 1, Milwaukee 1, July 11, 1971.
Baltimore 2, Boston 0, September 2, 1974.

INNING

Most runs, inning
N.L.—18—Chicago vs. Detroit, September 6, 1883, seventh inning.
A.L.—17—Boston vs. Detroit, June 18, 1953, seventh inning.
N.L. since 1900—15—Brooklyn vs. Cincinnati, May 21, 1952, first inning.

Most runs by both clubs, inning
A.L.—19—Cleveland 13, Boston 6, April 10, 1977, eighth inning.
A.A.—19—Washington 14, Baltimore 5, June 17, 1891, first inning.
N.L.—18—Chicago 18, Detroit 0, September 6, 1883, seventh inning.
N.L. since 1900—17—Boston 10, New York 7, June 20, 1912, ninth inning.

Most runs, two consecutive innings
N.L.—21—Pittsburgh vs. Boston, June 6, 1894; 12 in third inning, 9 in fourth inning.
A.L.—19—Boston vs. Philadelphia, May 2, 1901; 9 in second

inning, 10 in third inning.
  Boston vs. Detroit, June 18, 1953; 2 in sixth inning, 17 in seventh inning.
  Milwaukee vs. California, July 8, 1990; 6 in fourth inning, 13 in fifth inning.
N.L. since 1900—18—Montreal vs. San Francisco, May 7, 1997; 5 in fifth inning, 13 in sixth inning.

Most runs, extra inning
A.L.—12—Texas vs. Oakland, July 3, 1983, 15th inning.
N.L.—10—Kansas City vs. Detroit, July 21, 1886, 11th inning.
  Boston vs. New York, June 17, 1887, a.m. game, 10th inning.
  Cincinnati vs. Brooklyn, May 15, 1919, 13th inning.

Most runs by both clubs, extra inning
A.L.—12—Minnesota 11, Oakland 1, June 21, 1969, 10th inning.
  Texas 12, Oakland 0, July 3, 1983, 15th inning.
N.L.—11—New York 8, Pittsburgh 3, June 15, 1929, 14th inning.
  New York 6, Brooklyn 5, April 24, 1955, 10th inning.
  New York 6, Chicago 5, June 30, 1979, 11th inning.

Most runs scored at start of game with none out
N.L.—9—Philadelphia vs. New York, August 13, 1948.
A.L.—10—Boston vs. Florida, June 27, 2003.

Most runs scored at start of inning with none out
N.L.—13—Chicago vs. Detroit, September 6, 1883, seventh inning.
A.L.—11—Detroit vs. New York, June 17, 1925, sixth inning.
N.L. since 1900—12—Brooklyn vs. Philadelphia, May 24, 1953, eighth inning.

Most runs scored in inning with two out
A.L.—13—Cleveland vs. Boston, July 7, 1923, first game, sixth inning.
  Kansas City vs. Chicago, April 21, 1956, second inning.
N.L.—12—Brooklyn vs. Cincinnati, May 21, 1952, first inning.
  Brooklyn vs. Cincinnati, August 8, 1954, eighth inning.

Most runs scored in inning with none on base and two out
N.L.—12—Brooklyn vs. Cincinnati, August 8, 1954, eighth inning.
A.L.—10—Chicago vs. Detroit, September 2, 1959, second game, fifth inning.

Most runs scored by pinch-hitters, inning
N.L.—3—Boston vs. Philadelphia, April 19, 1900, ninth inning.
  Brooklyn vs. Philadelphia, September 9, 1926, ninth inning.
  San Francisco vs. Pittsburgh, May 5, 1958, ninth inning.
A.L.—3—Chicago vs. Philadelphia, September 19, 1916, ninth inning.
  Philadelphia vs. Detroit, September 18, 1940, second game, ninth inning.
  Cleveland vs. Detroit, August 7, 1941, ninth inning.

Most runs scored by pinch-runners, inning
A.L.—3—Chicago vs. Minnesota, September 16, 1967, ninth inning.
  Chicago vs. Oakland, May 19, 1968, second game, fifth inning.
  Oakland vs. California, May 7, 1975, seventh inning.
N.L.—2—Made in many innings.

Most players scoring two or more runs in one inning
N.L.—7—Chicago vs. Detroit, September 6, 1883, seventh inning.
N.L. since 1900—6—Brooklyn vs. Cincinnati, May 21, 1952, first inning.
  Cincinnati vs. Houston, August 3, 1989, first inning.
A.L.—5—New York vs. Washington, July 6, 1920, fifth inning.
  New York vs. Boston, June 21, 1945, fifth inning.
  Boston vs. Philadelphia, July 4, 1948, seventh inning.
  Cleveland vs. Philadelphia, June 18, 1950, second game, first inning.
  Boston vs. Detroit, June 18, 1953, seventh inning.
  Boston vs. Florida, June 27, 2003, first inning.

Clubs scoring in every inning of 9-inning game
A.A.—9—Louisville vs. Pittsburgh, September 22, 1882.
  Columbus vs. Pittsburgh, June 14, 1883.
  Kansas City vs. Brooklyn, May 20, 1889.

N.L.—9—Cleveland vs. Boston, August 15, 1889.
  Washington vs. Boston, June 22, 1894.
  Cleveland vs. Philadelphia, July 12, 1894.
  Chicago vs. Louisville, June 29, 1897.
  New York vs. Philadelphia, June 1, 1923.
  St. Louis vs. Chicago, September 13, 1964.
  Colorado vs. Chicago, May 5, 1999.
A.L.—8—Boston vs. Cleveland, September 16, 1903, did not bat in ninth.
  Cleveland vs. Boston, July 7, 1923, first game, did not bat in ninth.
  New York vs. St. Louis, July 26, 1939, did not bat in ninth.
  Chicago vs. Boston, May 11, 1949, did not bat in ninth.
  Kansas City vs. Oakland, September 14, 1998, did not bat in ninth.

Most innings scored in by both clubs, nine-inning game
N.L.—15—Philadelphia 8, Detroit 7, July 1, 1887.
  Washington 9, Boston 6, June 22, 1894.
A.A.—15—Kansas City 9, Brooklyn 6, May 20, 1889.
P.L.—15—New York 8, Chicago 7, May 23, 1890.
A.L.—14—Baltimore 8, Philadelphia 6, May 7, 1901.
  St. Louis 7, Detroit 7, April 23, 1927.
  Detroit 7, Chicago 7, July 2, 1940.
N.L. since 1900—14—New York 9, Philadelphia 5, June 1, 1923.
  Pittsburgh 8, Chicago 6, July 6, 1975.
  Los Angeles 8, Chicago 6, May 5, 1976.
  Colorado 8, Los Angeles 6, June 30, 1996.

Most consecutive innings scoring runs
A.L.—17—Boston, September 15 (last 3 innings), September 16 (8 innings), September 17 (first 6 innings), 1903, 3 games.
N.L.—14—Pittsburgh, July 31 (last 5 innings), August 1 (8 innings), August 2 (first inning), 1894, 3 games.
  New York, July 18 (last 3 innings), July 19 (8 innings), July 20 (first 3 innings), 1949, 3 games.
  Colorado, May 4 (last 4 innings), May 5 (9 innings), May 7 (first inning), 1999, 3 games.

Most times scoring 10 or more runs in one inning
N.L.—33—Chicago, 1876 to date.
A.L.—29—Boston, 1901 to date.
N.L. since 1900—19—Brooklyn-Los Angeles, 1900 through 1957 in Brooklyn, 1958 to date in Los Angeles.

Most innings scoring 10 or more runs, season
N.L.—5—Boston, 1894.
A.L.—3—Washington, 1930.
N.L. since 1900—3—Brooklyn, 1943.

Most innings scoring 10 or more runs in same game
N.L.—2—Chicago vs. Philadelphia, August 25, 1922; 10 in second, 14 in fourth inning.
  St. Louis vs. Philadelphia, July 6, 1929, second game; 10 in first, 10 in ninth inning.
  Brooklyn vs. Pittsburgh, July 10, 1943; 10 in first, 10 in fourth inning.
A.L.—1—Made in many games.

Most innings with both clubs scoring 10 or more runs in same game (each club scoring)
A.A.—2—St. Louis, 12 in fifth; Baltimore, 10 in eighth; May 12, 1887.
A.L.—2—Philadelphia, 11 in third; New York, 10 in fifth; June 3, 1933.
N.L.—Never accomplished.

Most consecutive games scoring 10 or more runs in one inning, club
N.L.—2—Houston vs. New York, July 30, first game, 11 in ninth; July 30, second game, 10 in third, 1969.
A.L.—2—Baltimore vs. Toronto, September 28, 10 in fourth; vs. New York, September 29, 10 in second, 2000.

FIRST THROUGH 26TH INNINGS

Most runs, first inning
N.L.—16—Boston vs. Baltimore, June 18, 1894, a.m. game.
N.L. since 1900—15—Brooklyn vs. Cincinnati, May 21, 1952.
A.L.—14—Cleveland vs. Philadelphia, June 18, 1950, second

game.
Boston vs. Florida N.L., June 27, 2003, first inning.

Most runs by both clubs, first inning
A.A.—19—Washington 14, Baltimore 5, June 17, 1891.
A.L.—16—Oakland 13, California 3, July 5, 1996.
N.L.—16—Boston 16, Baltimore 0, June 18, 1894, a.m. game.
N.L. since 1900—15—Brooklyn 15, Cincinnati 0, May 21, 1952.

Most runs, second inning
N.L.—13—New York vs. Cleveland, July 19, 1890, first game.
Atlanta vs. Houston, September 20, 1972.
San Diego vs. Pittsburgh, May 31, 1994.
A.L.—13—Kansas City vs. Chicago, April 21, 1956.

Most runs by both clubs, second inning
A.L.—14—Philadelphia 10, Detroit 4, September 23, 1913.
New York 11, Detroit 3, August 28, 1936, second game.
Chicago 8, Cleveland 6, September 2, 2001.
N.L.—13—New York 13, Cleveland 0, July 19, 1890, first game.
Chicago 10, Philadelphia 3, August 25, 1922.
Brooklyn 11, New York 2, April 29, 1930.
Atlanta 13, Houston 0, September 20, 1972.
San Diego 13, Pittsburgh 0, May 31, 1994.

Most runs, third inning
N.L.—14—Cleveland vs. Washington, August 7, 1889.
N.L. since 1900—13—San Francisco vs. St. Louis, May 7, 1966.
A.L.—12—New York vs. Washington, September 11, 1949, first game.

Most runs by both clubs, third inning
N.L.—14—Cleveland 14, Washington 0, August 7, 1889.
N.L. since 1900—13—San Francisco 13, St. Louis 0, May 7, 1966.
St. Louis 7, Atlanta 6, August 21, 1973.
A.L.—13—Boston 8, Detroit 5, July 2, 1995.

Most runs, fourth inning
N.L.—15—Hartford vs. New York, May 13, 1876.
N.L. since 1900—14—Chicago vs. Philadelphia, August 25, 1922.
A.L.—13—Chicago vs. Washington, September 26, 1943, first game.

Most runs by both clubs, fourth inning
N.L.—15—Hartford 15, New York 0, May 13, 1876.
Chicago 14, Philadelphia 1, August 25, 1922.
A.L.—14—Chicago 12, Philadelphia 2, June 10, 1952.

Most runs, fifth inning
A.L.—14—New York vs. Washington, July 6, 1920.
N.L.—13—Chicago vs. Pittsburgh, August 16, 1890.
N.L. since 1900—12—New York vs. Boston, September 3, 1926.
Cincinnati vs. Atlanta, April 25, 1977.
Montreal vs. Chicago, September 24, 1985.

Most runs by both clubs, fifth inning
A.L.—18—Texas 10, Detroit 8, May 8, 2004.
N.L.—16—Brooklyn 11, New York 5, June 3, 1890.
N.L. since 1900—15—Brooklyn 10, Cincinnati 5, June 12, 1949.
Philadelphia 9, Pittsburgh 6, April 16, 1953.

Most runs, sixth inning
P.L.—14—Philadelphia vs. Buffalo, June 26, 1890.
A.L.—13—Cleveland vs. Boston, July 7, 1923, first game.
Detroit vs. New York, June 17, 1925.
N.L.—13—Montreal vs. San Francisco, May 7, 1997.

Most runs by both clubs, sixth inning
A.L.—15—Philadelphia 10, New York 5, September 5, 1912, first game.
Detroit 10, Minnesota 5, June 13, 1967.
N.L.—15—New York 10, Cincinnati 5, June 12, 1979.

Most runs, seventh inning
N.L.—18—Chicago vs. Detroit, September 6, 1883.
N.L. since 1900—13—San Francisco vs. San Diego, July 15, 1997.
A.L.—17—Boston vs. Detroit, June 18, 1953.

Most runs by both clubs, seventh inning
N.L.—18—Chicago 18, Detroit 0, September 6, 1883.

A.L.—17—Boston 17, Detroit 0, June 18, 1953.

Most runs, eighth inning
A.L.—16—Texas vs. Baltimore, April 19, 1996.
N.L.—13—Brooklyn vs. Cincinnati, August 8, 1954.

Most runs by both clubs, eighth inning
A.L.—19—Cleveland 13, Boston 6, April 10, 1977.
N.L.—14—New York 11, Pittsburgh 3, May 25, 1954.
Brooklyn 13, Cincinnati 1, August 8, 1954.
Atlanta 9, San Diego 5, April 27, 1975, first game.
Colorado 8, Los Angeles 6, June 29, 1996.

Most runs, ninth inning
N.L.—14—Baltimore vs. Boston, April 24, 1894.
N.L. since 1900—12—San Francisco vs. Cincinnati, August 23, 1961.
San Diego vs. Colorado, September 12, 2004.
A.L.—13—California vs. Texas, September 14, 1978.
Detroit vs. Texas, August 8, 2001.

Most runs by both clubs, ninth inning
N.L.—17—Boston 10, New York 7, June 20, 1912.
A.L.—15—Toronto 11, Seattle 4, July 20, 1984.

Most runs scored in ninth inning with two out
A.L.—9—Cleveland vs. Washington, May 23, 1901 (won 14-13).
Boston vs. Milwaukee, June 2, 1901 (won 13-2).
Cleveland vs. New York, August 4, 1929, second game (won 14-6).
N.L.—7—Chicago vs. Cincinnati, June 29, 1952, first game (won 9-8).
San Francisco vs. Pittsburgh, May 1, 1973 (won 8-7).
Pittsburgh vs. Houston, July 28, 2001, a.m. game (won 9-8).

Most runs scored in ninth inning with two out and none on base
A.L.—9—Cleveland vs. Washington, May 23, 1901 (won 14-13).
Boston vs. Milwaukee, June 2, 1901 (won 13-2).
N.L.—7—Chicago vs. Cincinnati, June 29, 1952, first game (won 9-8).
Pittsburgh vs. Houston, July 28, 2001, a.m. game (won 9-8).

Most runs, 10th inning
A.L.—11—Minnesota vs. Oakland, June 21, 1969.
N.L.—10—Boston vs. New York, June 17, 1887, a.m. game.
N.L. since 1900—9
Cincinnati vs. Philadelphia, August 24, 1947, first game.
San Diego vs. Philadelphia, May 28, 1995.

Most runs by both clubs, 10th inning
A.L.—12—Minnesota 11, Oakland 1, June 21, 1969.
N.L.—11—New York 6, Brooklyn 5, April 24, 1955.

Most runs, 11th inning
N.L.—10—Kansas City vs. Detroit, July 21, 1886.
N.L. since 1900—9—San Diego vs. Colorado, June 28, 1994, second game.
A.L.—8—Philadelphia vs. Detroit, May 1, 1951.
Texas vs. Seattle, September 23, 1991.
Seattle vs. Kansas City, September 8, 2002.

Most runs by both clubs, 11th inning
A.L.—11—Seattle 6, Boston 5, May 16, 1969.
N.L.—11—New York 6, Chicago 5, June 30, 1979.
Pittsburgh 6, Chicago 5, April 21, 1991.

Most runs, 12th inning
A.L.—11—New York vs. Detroit, July 26, 1928, first game.
N.L.—9—Chicago vs. Pittsburgh, July 23, 1923.

Most runs by both clubs, 12th inning
A.L.—11—New York 8, Detroit 3, May 14, 1923.
New York 11, Detroit 0, July 26, 1928, first game.
N.L.—9—Chicago 9, Pittsburgh 0, July 23, 1923.
New York 8, Brooklyn 1, May 30, 1940, second game.
Houston 8, Cincinnati 1, June 2, 1966.
San Diego 5, Houston 4, July 5, 1969.

Most runs, 13th inning
N.L.—10—Cincinnati vs. Brooklyn, May 15, 1919.
A.L.—9—Cleveland vs. Detroit, August 5, 1933, first game.

Most runs, 14th inning
N.L.—8—New York vs. Pittsburgh, June 15, 1929.
A.L.—7—Cleveland vs. St. Louis, June 3, 1935.

Detroit vs. Milwaukee, May 27, 1991.

Most runs, 15th inning
A.L.—12—Texas vs. Oakland, July 3, 1983.
N.L.—7—St. Louis vs. Boston, September 28, 1928.

Most runs, 16th inning
A.L.—8—Chicago vs. Washington, May 20, 1920.
N.L.—5—Cincinnati vs. New York, August 20, 1973.
  Houston vs. Cincinnati, April 8, 1988.

Most runs, 17th inning
N.L.—7—New York vs. Pittsburgh, July 16, 1920.
A.L.—6—New York vs. Detroit, July 20, 1941.

Most runs, 18th inning
N.L.—5—Chicago vs. Boston, May 14, 1927.
A.L.—4—Minnesota vs. Seattle, July 19, 1969.

Most runs, 19th inning
N.L.—5—New York vs. Atlanta, July 4, 1985.
A.L.—4—Cleveland vs. Detroit, April 27, 1984.

Most runs by both clubs, 19th inning
N.L.—7—New York 5, Atlanta 2, July 4, 1985.
A.L.—5—Chicago 3, Boston 2, July 13, 1951.

Most runs, 20th inning
N.L.—4—Brooklyn vs. Boston, July 5, 1940.
A.L.—3—Boston vs. Seattle, July 27, 1969.
  Washington vs. Cleveland, September 14, second game,
  finished September 20, 1971.

Most runs by both clubs, 20th inning
N.L.—4—Brooklyn 4, Boston 0, July 5, 1940.
A.L.—3—Boston 3, Seattle 1, July 27, 1969.
  Washington 3, Cleveland 1, September 14, second game, fin-
  ished September 20, 1971.

Most runs, 21st inning
A.L.—4—Chicago vs. Cleveland, May 26, finished May 28, 1973.
N.L.—3—San Diego vs. Montreal, May 21, 1977.

Most runs by both clubs, 21st inning
A.L.—6—Milwaukee 3, Chicago 3, May 8, finished May 9, 1984.
N.L.—3—San Diego 3, Montreal 0, May 21, 1977.

Most runs, 22nd inning
A.L.—2—New York vs. Detroit, June 24, 1962.
N.L.—1—Brooklyn vs. Pittsburgh, August 22, 1917.
  Chicago vs. Boston, May 17, 1927.

Most runs, 23rd inning
N.L.—2—San Francisco vs. New York, May 31, 1964, second
  game.
A.L.—0—Boston vs. Philadelphia, September 1, 1906.
  Philadelphia vs. Boston, September 1, 1906.
  Detroit vs. Philadelphia, July 21, 1945.
  Philadelphia vs. Detroit, July 21, 1945.

Most runs, 24th inning
A.L.—3—Philadelphia vs. Boston, September 1, 1906.
N.L.—1—Houston vs. New York, April 15, 1968.

Most runs, 25th inning
N.L.—1—St. Louis vs. New York, September 11, 1974.
A.L.—1—Chicago vs. Milwaukee, May 8, finished May 9, 1984.

Most runs, 26th inning
N.L.—0—Boston vs. Brooklyn, May 1, 1920.
  Brooklyn vs. Boston, May 1, 1920.
A.L.—No 26-inning game.

GAMES BEING SHUT OUT

Most games shut out, season
N.L.—33—St. Louis, 1908.
A.L.—30—Washington, 1909 (includes 1 tie).

Most consecutive games shut out, season
A.L.—4—Boston, August 2 through 6, 1906.
  Philadelphia, September 23 through 25, 1906.
  St. Louis, August 25 through 30, 1913.
  Washington, September 19, 20, 21, 22, 1958.
  Washington, September 1, 2, 4, 5, 1964.
N.L.—4—Boston, May 19 through 23, 1906.
  Cincinnati, July 30 through August 3, 1908.
  Cincinnati, July 31 through August 3, 1931.

Houston, June 20, 21, 22, 23, first game, 1963.
Houston, September 9, 10, 11, 11, 1966.
Chicago, June 16, 16, 19, 20, 1968.

Most games shut out, season (league champion)
N.L.—17—Los Angeles, 1966.
A.L.—16—Chicago, 1906 (includes two ties).

Most consecutive innings shut out by opponent, season
A.L.—48—Philadelphia, September 22 (last seven innings)
  through September 26 (first five innings), 1906.
N.L.—48—Chicago, June 15 (last eight innings) through June
  21 (first two innings), 1968.

Most consecutive games without being shut out, league
A.L.—308—New York, August 3, 1931 through August 2, 1933.
N.L.—208—Cincinnati, April 3, 2000 through May 23, 2001.

Fewest games shut out, season (150 or more games)
A.L.—0—New York, 156 games, 1932.
N.L.—0—Cincinnati, 163 games, 2000.

HITS

SEASON

Most hits, season
N.L.—1,783—Philadelphia, 156 games, 1930.
A.L.—1,724—Detroit, 154 games, 1921.

Fewest hits, season
N.L.—1,044—Brooklyn, 154 games, 1908.
A.L.—1,061—Chicago, 156 games, 1910.

Most players with 200 or more hits, season
N.L.—4—Philadelphia, 1929.
A.L.—4—Detroit, 1937.

Most players with 100 or more hits, season
N.L.—9—Pittsburgh, 1921, 1972, 1976; Philadelphia, 1923;
  New York, 1928; St. Louis, 1979; Arizona, 2001; Florida,
  2001; San Francisco, 2004.
A.L.—10—Detroit, 2004.

Fewest players with 100 or more hits, season
N.L.—0—New York, 1972.
A.L.—2—Washington, 1965.

GAME

Most hits, game
N.L.—36—Philadelphia vs. Louisville, August 17, 1894.
N.L. since 1900—31—New York vs. Cincinnati, June 9, 1901.
A.L.—31—Milwaukee vs. Toronto, August 28, 1992.
  (33—Cleveland vs. Philadelphia, July 10, 1932, 18 innings.)

Most hits by both clubs, game
N.L.—51—Philadelphia 26, Chicago 25, August 25, 1922.
  (52—New York 28, Pittsburgh 24, June 15, 1929, 14
  innings.)
A.L.—45—Philadelphia 27, Boston 18, July 8, 1902.
  Detroit 28, New York 17, September 29, 1928.
  (58—Cleveland 33, Philadelphia 25, July 10, 1932, 18
  innings.)

Most hits by pinch-hitters, game
N.L.—6—Brooklyn vs. Philadelphia, September 9, 1926.
A.L.—4—Cleveland vs. Chicago, April 22, 1930.
  Philadelphia vs. Detroit, September 18, 1940, second game.
  Detroit vs. Chicago, April 22, 1953.
  Kansas City vs. Detroit, September 1, 1958, a.m. game.
  Cleveland vs. Boston, September 21, 1967.
  Oakland vs. Detroit, August 30, 1970.
  Chicago vs. Oakland, September 7, 1970, second game.
  Boston vs. New York, September 8, 1995.

Most hits by infield, game

N.L.—18—Boston vs. St. Louis, May 31, 1897.
A.L.—18—Milwaukee vs. Toronto, August 28, 1992.
N.L. since 1900—16—Pittsburgh vs. Chicago, September 16, 1975.

Most hits by outfield, game

N.L.—16—New York vs. Cincinnati, June 9, 1901.
A.L.—12—Baltimore vs. Detroit, June 24, 1901.
Detroit vs. Washington, July 30, 1917.
Cleveland vs. Philadelphia, April 29, 1952.
Boston vs. Baltimore, July 11, 1969, second game.

Most hits in shutout loss

N.L.—14—New York vs. Chicago, September 14, 1913 (15 total bases; lost 7-0).
(15—Boston vs. Pittsburgh, July 10, 1901 (16 total bases; lost 1-0), 12 innings.)
Boston vs. Pittsburgh, August 1, 1918 (15 total bases; lost 2-0), 21 innings.)
A.L.—14—Cleveland vs. Washington, July 10, 1928, second game (16 total bases; lost 9-0).
(15—Boston vs. Washington, July 3, 1913 (19 total bases; lost 1-0), 15 innings.)

Most consecutive hits, game

N.L.—12—St. Louis vs. Boston, September 17, 1920, fourth and fifth innings.
Brooklyn vs. Pittsburgh, June 23, 1930, sixth and seventh innings.
A.L.—10—Boston vs. Milwaukee, June 2, 1901, ninth inning.
Detroit vs. Baltimore, September 20, 1983, first inning (one walk during streak).
Toronto vs. Minnesota, September 4, 1992, second inning.

Fewest hits, game

N.L., U.A., A.A., A.L.—0—Made in many games.

Fewest hits, extra-inning game

A.A.—0—Toledo vs. Brooklyn, October 4, 1884, 10 innings.
N.L.—0—Philadelphia vs. New York, July 4, 1908, a.m. game, 10 innings.
Chicago vs. Cincinnati, May 2, 1917, 10 innings.
Chicago vs. Cincinnati, August 19, 1965, first game, 10 innings.
N.L.—1—Milwaukee vs. Pittsburgh, May 26, 1959, 13 innings.
A.L.—1—Cleveland vs. Chicago, September 6, 1903, 10 innings.
Boston vs. St. Louis, September 18, 1934, 10 innings.
Los Angeles vs. New York, May 22, 1962, 12 innings.

Fewest hits by both clubs, nine-inning game

N.L.—1—Los Angeles 1, Chicago 0, September 9, 1965.
A.A.—2—Philadelphia 1, Baltimore 1, August 20, 1886.
A.L.—2—Cleveland 1, Washington 1, July 27, 1915.
Cleveland 1, St. Louis 1, April 23, 1952.
Chicago 1, Baltimore 1, June 21, 1956.
Baltimore 1, Kansas City 1, September 12, 1964.
Baltimore 2, Detroit 0, April 30, 1967, first game.

Most games held hitless, season

A.A.—2—Pittsburgh 1884.
N.L.—2—Providence 1885; Boston 1898; Philadelphia 1960; Chicago 1965; Cincinnati 1971; Colorado 1996; San Diego 2001.
A.L.—2—Chicago 1917; Philadelphia 1923; Detroit 1967, 1973; California 1977.

Most consecutive years without being held hitless in a game (nine or more innings)

A.L.—44—New York, 1959 through 2002.
N.L.—40—St. Louis, 1920 through 1959.

Most games held to one hit, season

A.L.—5—St. Louis, 1910.
Cleveland, 1915.
N.L.—4—New York, 1965.

Most players with six hits in a game

A.A.—2—Cincinnati vs. Pittsburgh, September 12, 1883.
N.L.—2—Baltimore vs. St. Louis, September 3, 1897.
A.L.—1—Made in many games.

Most players with five or more hits in a game

N.L.—4—Philadelphia vs. Louisville, August 17, 1894.
N.L. since 1900—3—New York vs. Cincinnati, June 9, 1901.
New York vs. Philadelphia, June 1, 1923.
A.L.—3—Detroit vs. Washington, July 30, 1917.
Chicago vs. Philadelphia, September 11, 1936.
(3—Cleveland vs. Philadelphia, July 10, 1932, 18 innings.
Washington vs. Cleveland, May 16, 1933, 12 innings.)

Most players for both clubs with five or more hits, game

N.L.—4—Philadelphia 4, Louisville 0, August 17, 1894.
N.L. since 1900—3—New York 3, Cincinnati 0, June 9, 1901.
New York 3, Philadelphia 0, June 1, 1923.
A.L.—3—Detroit 3, Washington 0, July 30, 1917.
Chicago 3, Philadelphia 0, September 11, 1936.
(5—Cleveland 3, Philadelphia 2, July 10, 1932, 18 innings.)

Most players with four or more hits, game

N.L.—7—Chicago vs. Cleveland, July 24, 1882.
N.L. since 1900—5—San Francisco vs. Los Angeles, May 13, 1958.
A.L.—4—Detroit vs. New York, September 29, 1928.
Chicago vs. Philadelphia, September 11, 1936.
Boston vs. St. Louis, June 8, 1950.
Milwaukee vs. Toronto, August 28, 1992.
Minnesota vs. Cleveland, June 4, 2002.

Most players for both clubs with four or more hits, game

N.L.—7—Chicago 7, Cleveland 0, July 24, 1882.
N.L. since 1900—5—St. Louis 4, Philadelphia 1, July 6, 1929, second game.
San Francisco 5, Los Angeles 0, May 13, 1958.
A.L.—4—Detroit 4, New York 0, September 29, 1928.
Chicago 4, Philadelphia 0, September 11, 1936.
Boston 4, St. Louis 0, June 8, 1950.
Milwaukee 4, Toronto 0, August 28, 1992.

Most players with three or more hits, game

N.L.—8—Chicago vs. Detroit, September 6, 1883.
N.L. since 1900—7—Cincinnati vs. Philadelphia, May 13, 1902
Pittsburgh vs. Philadelphia, June 12, 1928.
Cincinnati vs. Houston, August 3, 1989.
Cincinnati vs. Colorado, May 19, 1999.
A.L.—7—New York vs. Philadelphia, June 28, 1939, first game.
Chicago vs. Kansas City, April 23, 1955.

Most players with two or more hits, game

A.A.—10—Brooklyn vs. Philadelphia, June 25, 1885.
N.L.—10—Pittsburgh vs. Philadelphia, August 7, 1922.
New York vs. Philadelphia, September 2, 1925, second game.
A.L.—9—Held by many clubs.

Most players with one or more hits, game

N.L.—14—San Francisco vs. San Diego, June 23, 1986.
Chicago vs. Colorado, August 18, 1995.
Florida vs. Atlanta, September 24, 1996.
A.L.—14—Cleveland vs. St. Louis, August 12, 1948, second game.

Most players for both clubs with one or more hits, game

N.L.—23—St. Louis 13, Philadelphia 10, May 11, 1923.
A.L.—22—New York 12, Cleveland 10, July 18, 1934.

Most consecutive games with each player collecting one or more hits

N.L.—5—Pittsburgh, August 5, 7, 8, 9, 10, 1922.

DOUBLEHEADER AND CONSECUTIVE GAMES

Most hits, doubleheader

N.L.—46—Pittsburgh vs. Philadelphia, August 8, 1922.
A.L.—43—New York vs. Philadelphia, June 28, 1939.

Most hits by both clubs, doubleheader

N.L.—73—Washington 41, Philadelphia 32, July 4, 1896.
St. Louis 43, Philadelphia 30, July 6, 1929.
A.L.—65—Boston 35, Philadelphia 30, July 4, 1939.
(65—Baltimore 35, Kansas City 30, June 23, 1991, first game 10 innings, second game 12 innings.)

Most hits by pitchers, doubleheader

A.L.—8—New York vs. Cleveland, June 17, 1936.

Fewest hits, doubleheader

A.L.—2—Cleveland vs. Boston, April 12, 1992.
N.L.—3—Brooklyn vs. St. Louis, September 21, 1934.
New York vs. Philadelphia, June 21, 1964.

Fewest hits by both clubs, doubleheader
A.L.—11—Detroit 7, St. Louis 4, May 30, 1914.
N.L.—12—Chicago 6, Pittsburgh 6, September 3, 1905.
  St. Louis 6, Brooklyn 6, July 24, 1909.

Most hits, two consecutive games
N.L.—55—Philadelphia vs. Louisville, August 16, 17, 1894.
A.L.—51—Boston vs. St. Louis, June 7, 8, 1950.
N.L. since 1900—49—Pittsburgh vs. Philadelphia, August 7, 8,
  first game, 1922.

Most hits by pitchers, two consecutive games
N.L.—9—Chicago, May 19, 20, 1895.

Fewest hits, two consecutive nine-inning games
A.A.—2—Baltimore vs. St. Louis/Louisville, July 28 (1), July 29
  (1), 1886.
N.L.—2—New York vs. Providence, June 17 (1), June 18 (1),
  1884.
  Cincinnati vs. Brooklyn, July 5 (1), July 6 (1), 1900.
  Boston vs. New York, September 28, second game (1);
    September 30, first game (1), 1916.
  New York vs. Milwaukee, September 10 (1), September 11
    (1), 1965.
  Los Angeles vs. Houston, September 26 (0), September 27
    (2), 1981.
A.L.—2—New York vs. Cleveland, September 25 (1), September
  26 (1), 1907.
  St. Louis vs. Washington, September 25, second game (1),
    vs. Philadelphia, September 27, (1), first game, 1910.
  Chicago vs. Washington, August 10 (1), August 11 (1), 1917.
  Milwaukee vs. Kansas City, June 18 (2), June 19 (0), 1974.
  Cleveland vs. Boston, April 12, first game (0), April 12, second
    game (2), 1992.
  Detroit vs. Texas, May 3 (1), May 4 (1), 1996.

INNING

Most hits, inning
N.L.—18—Chicago vs. Detroit, September 6, 1883, seventh
  inning.
N.L. since 1900—16—Cincinnati vs. Houston, August 3, 1989,
  first inning.
A.L.—14—Boston vs. Detroit, June 18, 1953, seventh inning.

Most hits by pinch-hitters, inning
N.L.—4—Chicago vs. Brooklyn, May 21, 1927, second game,
  ninth inning.
  Philadelphia vs. Pittsburgh, September 12, 1974, eighth inning.
A.L.—4—Philadelphia vs. Detroit, September 18, 1940, second
  game, ninth inning.
  Texas vs. Kansas City, June 8, 1995, eighth inning.
  Boston vs. New York, September 8, 1995, eighth inning.

Most consecutive hits, inning
N.L.—10—St. Louis vs. Boston, September 17, 1920, fourth
  inning.
  St. Louis vs. Philadelphia, June 12, 1922, sixth inning.
  Chicago vs. Boston, September 7, 1929, first game, fourth
    inning.
  Brooklyn vs. Pittsburgh, June 23, 1930, sixth inning.
A.L.—10—Boston vs. Milwaukee, June 2, 1901, ninth inning.
  Detroit vs. Baltimore, September 20, 1983, first inning (one
    walk during streak).
  Toronto vs. Minnesota, September 4, 1992, second inning.
  Kansas City vs. Detroit, September 9, 2004, third inning.

Most consecutive hits by pinch-hitters, inning
N.L.-A.L.—3—Made in many innings.
Last N.L. time—Pittsburgh vs. San Francisco, July 2, 1961, first
  game, eighth inning.
Last A.L. time—Boston vs. New York, September 8, 1995, eighth
  inning.

Most consecutive hits before first out of game
N.L.—8—Philadelphia vs. Chicago, August 5, 1975 (4 singles, 2
  doubles, 2 home runs).
  Pittsburgh vs. Atlanta, August 26, 1975 (7 singles, 1 triple).
A.L.—8—Oakland vs. Chicago, September 27, 1981, first game (8
  singles).
  New York vs. Baltimore, September 25, 1990 (6 singles, 2 home
    runs).

Most batters reaching first base safely, inning
A.L.—20—Boston vs. Detroit, June 18, 1953, seventh inning.

N.L.—20—Chicago vs. Detroit, September 6, 1883, seventh
  inning.
N.L. since 1900—19—Brooklyn vs. Cincinnati, May 21, 1952,
  first inning.

Most consecutive batters reaching base safely, inning
N.L.—19—Brooklyn vs. Cincinnati, May 21, 1952, first inning.
A.L.—13—Kansas City vs. Chicago, April 21, 1956, second inning.

Most batters reaching base safely three times, inning
N.L.—3—Chicago vs. Detroit, September 6, 1883, seventh
  inning.
  Boston vs. Baltimore, June 18, 1894, a.m. game, first inning.
N.L. since 1900—1—Brooklyn vs. Cincinnati, May 21, 1952,
  first inning.
A.L.—3—Boston vs. Detroit, June 18, 1953, seventh inning.

Most players making two or more hits, inning
N.L.—7—Cincinnati vs. Houston, August 3, 1989, first inning.
A.L.—5—Philadelphia vs. Boston, July 8, 1902, sixth inning.
  New York vs. Philadelphia, September 10, 1921, ninth inning.

SINGLES

Most singles, season
N.L.—1,338—Philadelphia, 132 games, 1894.
A.L.—1,298—Detroit, 154 games, 1921.
N.L. since 1900—1,297—Pittsburgh, 155 games, 1922.

Fewest singles, season
A.L.—811—Baltimore, 162 games, 1968.
N.L.—843—New York, 156 games, 1972.

Most singles, game
N.L.—28—Philadelphia vs. Louisville, August 17, 1894.
  Boston vs. Baltimore, April 20, 1896.
A.L.—26—Milwaukee vs. Toronto, August 28, 1992.
N.L. since 1900—23—New York vs. Chicago, September 21,
  1931.
  Houston vs. Atlanta, May 30, 1976, second game.
  (23—New York vs. Atlanta, July 4, 1985, 19 innings.)

Most singles by both clubs, game
N.L.—37—Baltimore 21, Washington 16, August 8, 1896.
N.L. since 1900—36—New York 22, Cincinnati 14, June 9, 1901.
  (37—Los Angeles 19, New York 18, May 24, 1973, 19 innings.)
A.L.—36—Chicago 21, Boston 15, August 15, 1922.
  (42—Oakland 25, Texas 17, July 1, 1979, 15 innings.)

Most singles, inning
N.L.—12—Cincinnati vs. Houston, August 3, 1989, first inning.
A.L.—11—Boston vs. Detroit, June 18, 1953, seventh inning.

Most consecutive singles, inning
N.L.—10—St. Louis vs. Boston, September 17, 1920, fourth inning.
A.L.—8—Washington vs. Cleveland, May 7, 1951, fourth
  inning.
  Oakland vs. Chicago, September 27, 1981, first game, first
    inning.
  Baltimore vs. Texas, May 18, 1990, first inning.

DOUBLES

Most doubles, season
N.L.—373—St. Louis, 154 games, 1930.
A.L.—373—Boston, 162 games, 1997.
  Boston, 162 games, 2004.

Fewest doubles, season
N.L.—110—Brooklyn, 154 games, 1908.
A.L.—116—Chicago, 156 games, 1910.

Most consecutive years leading league in doubles
A.L.—8—Cleveland, 1916 through 1923.
N.L.—5—St. Louis, 1920 through 1924.

Most doubles, game
N.L.—14—Chicago vs. Buffalo, July 3, 1883.
N.L. since 1900—13—St. Louis vs. Chicago, July 12, 1931,
  second game.

A.L.—12—Boston vs. Detroit, July 29, 1990.
Cleveland vs. Minnesota, July 13, 1996.

Most doubles by pinch-hitters, game
A.L.—3—Cleveland vs. Washington, June 27, 1948, first game.
Chicago vs. New York, May 7, 1971.
N.L.—3—San Francisco vs. Pittsburgh, May 5, 1958.

Most doubles by both clubs, game
N.L.—23—St. Louis 13, Chicago 10, July 12, 1931, second game.
A.L.—19—Kansas City 11, New York 8, August 11, 2003.

Most doubles, doubleheader
N.L.—17—St. Louis vs. Chicago, July 12, 1931.
A.L.—14—Philadelphia vs. Boston, July 8, 1905.

Most doubles by both clubs, doubleheader
N.L.—32—St. Louis 17, Chicago 15, July 12, 1931.
A.L.—26—Philadelphia 14, Boston 12, July 8, 1905.

Most doubles with bases filled, game
N.L.-A.L.—2—Made in many games.

Most doubles with bases filled by both clubs, game
N.L.-A.L.—2—Made in many games.

Most doubles, inning
N.L.—7—Boston vs. St. Louis, August 25, 1936, first game, first inning.
A.L.—6—Washington vs. Boston, June 9, 1934, eighth inning.
Texas vs. New York, July 31, 2002, second inning.

Most consecutive doubles, inning
A.L.—5—Washington vs. Boston, June 9, 1934, eighth inning.
N.L.—4—Held by many clubs. Last time—Philadelphia vs. Cincinnati, May 4, 2000, first inning.

Most players with two doubles, inning
N.L.—3—Boston vs. St. Louis, August 25, 1936, first game, first inning.
A.L.—2—New York vs. Boston, July 3, 1932, sixth inning.
Toronto vs. Baltimore, June 26, 1978, second inning.

TRIPLES

Most triples, season
N.L.—153—Baltimore, 129 games, 1894.
N.L. since 1900—129—Pittsburgh, 152 games, 1912.
A.L.—112—Baltimore, 134 games, 1901.
Boston, 141 games, 1903.

Fewest triples, season
A.L.—11—Baltimore, 162 games, 1998.
N.L.—14—Los Angeles, 162 games, 1986.
New York, 163 games, 1999.

Most consecutive years leading league in triples
A.L.—7—Washington, 1931 through 1937 (tied 1934).
N.L.—6—Pittsburgh, 1932 through 1937.

Most triples, game
N.L.—9—Baltimore vs. Cleveland, September 3, 1894, first game.
N.L. since 1900—8—Pittsburgh vs. St. Louis, May 30, 1925, second game.
A.L.—6—Chicago vs. Milwaukee, September 15, 1901; second game.
Philadelphia vs. Detroit, May 18, 1912.
Chicago vs. New York, September 17, 1920.
Detroit vs. New York, June 17, 1922.

Most triples by both clubs, game
N.L.—11—Baltimore 9, Cleveland 2, September 3, 1894, first game.
N.L. since 1900—9—Pittsburgh 6, Chicago 3, July 4, 1904, p.m. game.
Pittsburgh 8, St. Louis 1, May 30, 1925, second game.
A.L.—9—Detroit 6, New York 3, June 17, 1922.

Most triples with bases filled, game
N.L.—2—Detroit vs. Indianapolis, May 7, 1887.
Pittsburgh vs. Brooklyn, September 17, 1898.
Chicago vs. Philadelphia, May 14, 1904.

Brooklyn vs. St. Louis, August 25, 1917, first game.
Cincinnati vs. Brooklyn, September 25, 1925.
Pittsburgh vs. St. Louis, September 10, 1938.
Chicago vs. Boston, June 12, 1936.
Brooklyn vs. Philadelphia, May 24, 1953, both in eighth inning.
Milwaukee vs. St. Louis, August 2, 1959, second game.
Montreal vs. Cincinnati, September 1, 1979.
New York vs. Colorado, June 6, 1994.
A.A.—2—Kansas City vs. Philadelphia, August 22, 1889.
A.L.—2—Boston vs. St. Louis, August 16, 1926, second game.
Philadelphia vs. Washington, April 26, 1928.
Philadelphia vs. Washington, May 1, 1949, first game.
Detroit vs. New York, June 9, 1950.
Cleveland vs. New York, July 27, 1978, second game.

Most bases-filled triples by both clubs, game (each club connecting)
N.L.—2—Made in many games. Last time—Chicago 1, St. Louis 1, April 22, 1938.
A.L.—2—Made in many games. Last time—Washington 1, New York 1, July 4, 1950, first game.

Longest extra-inning game without a triple
N.L.—26 innings—Brooklyn vs. Boston, May 1, 1920.
A.L.—25 innings—Milwaukee vs. Chicago, May 8, finished May 9, 1984.
Chicago vs. Milwaukee, May 8, finished May 9, 1984.

Longest extra-inning game without a triple by either club
N.L.—25 innings—New York 0, St. Louis 0, September 11, 1974.
A.L.—25 innings—Milwaukee 0, Chicago 0, May 8, finished May 9, 1984.

Most triples, doubleheader
N.L.—9—Baltimore vs. Cleveland, September 3, 1894.
Cincinnati vs. Chicago, May 27, 1922.
A.L.—9—Chicago vs. Milwaukee, September 15, 1901.

Most triples by both clubs, doubleheader
N.L.—11—Baltimore 9, Cleveland 2, September 3, 1894.
N.L. since 1900—10—Cincinnati 9, Chicago 1, May 27, 1922.
New York 7, Pittsburgh 3, July 30, 1923.
A.L.—10—Chicago 9, Milwaukee 1, September 15, 1901.

Most triples, inning
A.L.—5—Chicago vs. Milwaukee, September 15, 1901, second game, eighth inning.
N.L.—4—Boston vs. Troy, May 6, 1882, eighth inning.
Baltimore vs. St. Louis, July 27, 1892, seventh inning.
St. Louis vs. Chicago, July 2, 1895, first inning.
Chicago vs. St. Louis, April 17, 1899, fourth inning.
Brooklyn vs. Pittsburgh, August 23, 1902, third inning.
Cincinnati vs. Boston, July 22, 1926, second inning.
New York vs. Pittsburgh, July 17, 1936, first inning.

Most consecutive triples, inning
A.L.—4—Boston vs. Detroit, May 6, 1934, fourth inning.
N.L.—3—Made in many games. Last times—Chicago vs. Philadelphia, April 25, 1981, fourth inning; Montreal vs. San Diego, May 6, 1981, ninth inning.

HOME RUNS
SEASON AND MONTH

Most home runs, season
A.L.—264—Seattle, 162 games, 1997 (131 at home, 133 on road).
N.L.—249—Houston, 162 games, 2000 (135 at home, 114 on road).

For a complete list of home runs by club each year beginning in 1901, see page 178.

Fewest home runs, season
N.L.—9—Pittsburgh, 157 games, 1917.
A.L.—3—Chicago, 156 games, 1908.

Most home runs by pinch-hitters, season
N.L.—14—Arizona, 2001.
San Francisco, 2001.

A.L.—11—Baltimore, 1982.

Most home runs at home, season
N.L.—149—Colorado, 1996, 81 games.
A.L.—134—Toronto, 2000, 81 games.

Most home runs on road, season
N.L.—138—San Francisco, 2001, 81 games.
A.L.—136—Baltimore, 1996, 81 games.

Most home runs against one club, season
A.L.—48—New York vs. Kansas City, 1956.
N.L.—44—Cincinnati vs. Brooklyn, 1956.

Most years leading league in home runs (since 1900)
A.L.—35—New York.
N.L.—28—New York/San Francisco (24 by N.Y., 4 by S.F.).

Most consecutive years leading league or tied in home runs
A.L.—12—New York, 1936 through 1947.
N.L.—7—Brooklyn, 1949 through 1955 (1954 tied).

Most years with 200 or more home runs
A.L.—7—Detroit, 209 in 1962; 202 in 1985; 225 in 1987; 209 in 1991; 204 in 1996; 212 in 1999; 201 in 2004.
Cleveland, 207 in 1995; 218 in 1996; 220 in 1997; 209 in 1999; 221 in 2000; 212 in 2001.
N.L.—6—Colorado, 200 in 1995; 221 in 1996; 239 in 1997; 223 in 1999; 213 in 2001; 202 in 2004.

Most consecutive years with 200 or more home runs
A.L.—4—Seattle, 245 in 1996; 264 in 1997; 234 in 1998; 244 in 1999.
N.L.—3—Colorado, 200 in 1995; 221 in 1996; 239 in 1997.

Most years with 100 or more home runs (since 1900)
A.L.—78—New York.
N.L.—67—New York/San Francisco (26 by N.Y., 41 by S.F.).

Most consecutive years with 100 or more home runs
A.L.—35—Boston, 1946 through 1980.
N.L.—29—New York/San Francisco, 1945 through 1957 in New York, 1958 through 1973 in San Francisco.
Cincinnati, 1952 through 1980.

Most home runs by two players, season
A.L.—115—New York, 1961 (Maris 61, Mantle 54).
N.L.—110—San Francisco, 2001 (Bonds 73, Aurilia 37).

Most home runs by three players, season
A.L.—140—New York, 1961 (Maris 61, Mantle, 54, Skowron, 28).
N.L.—132—San Francisco, 2001 (Bonds 73, Aurilia 37, Kent 22).

Most players with 50 or more home runs, season
A.L.—2—New York, 1961 (Maris 61, Mantle 54)
N.L.—1—Held by many clubs.

Most players with 40 or more home runs, season
N.L.—3—Atlanta, 1973 (Johnson 43, Evans 41, Aaron 40).
Colorado, 1996 (Galarraga 47, Burks 40, Castilla 40).
Colorado, 1997 (Walker 49, Galarraga 41, Castilla 40).
A.L.—2—New York, 1927 (Ruth 60, Gehrig 47), 1930 (Ruth 49, Gehrig 41), 1931 (Ruth 46, Gehrig 46), 1961 (Maris 61, Mantle 54).
Detroit, 1961 (Colavito 45, Cash 41).
Boston, 1969 (Petrocelli 40, Yastrzemski 40).
Seattle, 1996 (Griffey 49, Buhner 44).
Seattle, 1997 (Griffey 56, Buhner 40).
Seattle, 1998 (Griffey 56, Rodriguez 42).
Seattle, 1999 (Griffey 48, Rodriguez 42).
Toronto, 1999 (Delgado 44, Green 42).
Toronto, 2000 (Delgado 41, Batista 41).
Texas, 2001 (A. Rodriguez 52, Palmeiro 47).
Texas, 2002 (A. Rodriguez 57, Palmeiro 43).

Most players with 30 or more home runs, season
N.L.—4—Los Angeles, 1977, 1997.
Colorado, 1995, 1996, 1997, 1999.
Atlanta, 1998.
Chicago, 2004.
A.L.—4—Anaheim, 2000.
Toronto, 2000.

Most players with 20 or more home runs, season
A.L.—7—Baltimore, 1996.
Toronto, 2000.
N.L.—6—Milwaukee, 1965.

Most home runs, one month
A.L.—58—Baltimore, May, 1987.
N.L.—55—New York, July, 1947.
St. Louis, April, 2000.
Atlanta, May, 2003.

GAME

Most home runs, game
A.L.—10—Toronto vs. Baltimore, September 14, 1987.
N.L.—9—Cincinnati vs. Philadelphia, September 4, 1999.

Most home runs by both clubs, game
A.L.—12—Detroit 7, Chicago 5, May 28, 1995.
Detroit 6, Chicago 6, July 2, 2002.
N.L.—11—Pittsburgh 6, Cincinnati 5, August 12, 1966, 13 innings.
Chicago 7, New York 4, June 11, 1967, second game.
Chicago 6, Cincinnati 5, July 28, 1977, 13 innings.
Chicago 6, Philadelphia 5, May 17, 1979, 10 innings.

Most home runs, night game
A.L.—10—Toronto vs. Baltimore, September 14, 1987.
N.L.—9—Cincinnati vs. Philadelphia, September 4, 1999.

Most home runs by both clubs, nine-inning night game
A.L.—11—New York 6, Detroit 5, June 23, 1950.
Toronto 10, Baltimore 1, September 14, 1987.
Cleveland 8, Milwaukee 3, April 25, 1997.
N.L.—10—Cincinnati 8, Milwaukee 2, August 18, 1956.
Cincinnati 7, Atlanta 3, April 21, 1970.
Cincinnati 9, Philadelphia 1, September 4, 1999.

Most home runs by pinch-hitters, game
A.L.-N.L.—2—Held by many clubs.

Most home runs by pinch-hitters for both clubs, game
N.L.—3—Philadelphia 2, St. Louis 1, June 2, 1928.
St. Louis 2, Brooklyn 1, July 21, 1930, first game.
A.L.—2—Made in many games. Last times—Cleveland 1, Minnesota 1, May 7, 1989, first game; New York 1, Chicago 1, June 22, 1989.

Most home runs, opening game of season
N.L.—6—New York vs. Montreal, April 4, 1988.
A.L.—5—New York vs. Philadelphia, April 12, 1932.
Boston vs. Washington, April 12, 1965.
Milwaukee vs. Boston, April 10, 1980.
Cleveland vs. Texas, April 27, 1995 (game was not Texas' opener).
Minnesota vs. Kansas City, April 1, 2002.

Most home runs by both clubs, opening game of season
A.L.—7—New York 5, Philadelphia 2, April 12, 1932.
Boston 5, Washington 2, April 12, 1965.
Milwaukee 5, Boston 2, April 10, 1980.
Cleveland 5, Texas 2, April 27, 1995 (game was not Texas' opener).
Milwaukee 4, California 3, April 2, 1996.
N.L.—7—New York 6, Montreal 1, April 4, 1988.
Atlanta 4, Chicago 3, April 5, 1908.
Atlanta 5, San Francisco 2, April 2, 1996.

Most home runs by first-game players for both clubs, game
N.L.—2—Brooklyn 1 (Ernie Koy), Philadelphia 1 (Emmett Mueller), April 19, 1938 (each in first inning).

Most runs, all scoring on solo home runs, club, game
A.L.—6—Oakland vs. Minnesota, August 3, 1991.
N.L.—5—New York vs. Chicago, June 16, 1930.
St. Louis vs. Brooklyn, September 1, 1953.
Cincinnati vs. Milwaukee, April 16, 1955.
Chicago vs. Pittsburgh, April 21, 1964.
Pittsburgh vs. Los Angeles, May 7, 1973.
Colorado vs. San Francisco, May 9, 1994.
Atlanta vs. Colorado, April 19, 1998, first game.

REGULAR SEASON Club batting

Most runs, all scoring on solo home runs, both clubs, game
Both leagues—5—Baltimore A.L. 3, Atlanta N.L. 2, June 5, 1998.
N.L.—5—San Francisco 3, Milwaukee 2, August 30, 1962.
Montreal 3, San Diego 2, May 16, 1986.
A.L.—4—Cleveland 4, New York 0, August 2, 1956.
New York 4, Baltimore 0, May 13, 1973, first game.

Most runs, all scoring on solo home runs, shutout game
A.L.—4—Cleveland vs. New York, August 2, 1956.
New York vs. Baltimore, May 13, 1973, first game.
N.L.—3—St. Louis vs. New York, July 19, 1923.
Philadelphia vs. Cincinnati, August 27, 1951, second game.
San Francisco vs. Milwaukee, August 14, 1964.
Cincinnati vs. Pittsburgh, September 25, 1968.
New York vs. Philadelphia, June 29, 1971.
New York vs. Pittsburgh, September 17, 1971.
New York vs. Cincinnati, August 29, 1972.
San Francisco vs. Philadelphia, September 4, 2000.

Most home runs with none on bases, game
A.L.—7—Boston vs. Toronto, July 4, 1977 (8 home runs in game by Boston).
N.L.—6—New York vs. Philadelphia, August 13, 1939, first game (7 home runs in game by New York).
New York vs. Cincinnati, June 24, 1950 (7 home runs in game by New York).
Atlanta vs. Chicago, August 3, 1967 (7 home runs in game by Atlanta).
Chicago vs. San Diego, August 19, 1970 (7 home runs in game by Chicago).

Most home runs with none on bases, by both clubs, game
A.L.—10—Detroit 5, Chicago 5, May 28, 1995.
N.L.—7—Chicago 6, San Diego 1, August 19, 1970.
Pittsburgh 4, Chicago 3, June 7, 1976.
Philadelphia 5, Colorado 2, May 8, 1999.

Most home runs by infield, game (excluding battery)
N.L.—6—Milwaukee vs. Brooklyn, July 31, 1954.
Montreal vs. Atlanta, July 30, 1978.
A.L.—5—New York vs. Philadelphia, June 3, 1932.
New York vs. Philadelphia, May 24, 1936.
Cleveland vs. Philadelphia, June 18, 1941.
Boston vs. St. Louis, June 8, 1950.

Most home runs by outfield, game
N.L.—6—Cincinnati vs. Milwaukee, August 18, 1956.
San Francisco vs. Milwaukee, April 30, 1961.
A.L.—5—New York vs. Chicago, July 28, 1940, first game.
Cleveland vs. New York, July 13, 1945.
Cleveland vs. Baltimore, June 10, 1959.
New York vs. Boston, May 30, 1961.

Most times with five or more home runs in game, season
A.L.—8—Boston, 1977.
N.L.—6—New York, 1947.

Most players with three or more home runs in game, season
N.L.—4—Brooklyn, 1950 (Snider, Campanella, Hodges, Brown).
Cincinnati, 1956 (Bell, Bailey, Kluszewski, Thurman).
Milwaukee, 2001 (Burnitz 2, Jenkins, Sexson).
A.L.—3—Cleveland, 1987 (Snyder, Carter, Jacoby).
Oakland, 1996 (Berroa 2, Young).
Seattle, 1996 (Wilson, Griffey, Martinez).

Most times with two or more homers by one player in a game, season
A.L.—24—New York, 1961.
N.L.—24—Atlanta, 1966.

Most players with three or more home runs in game
N.L.—2—Milwaukee vs. Arizona, September 25, 2001.
A.L.—1—Held by many clubs.

Most players with three or more home runs by both clubs, game
N.L.—2—Milwaukee 2, Arizona 0, September 25, 2001.
A.L.—1—Occurred in many games.

Most players with two or more home runs, game
N.L.—3—Pittsburgh vs. St. Louis, August 16, 1947.
Chicago vs. St. Louis, April 16, 1955, 14 innings.

New York vs. Pittsburgh, July 8, 1956, first game.
Cincinnati vs. Milwaukee, August 18, 1956.
Philadelphia vs. New York, September 8, 1998.
Colorado vs. Montreal, August 14, 1999.
Houston vs. Chicago, September 9, 2000.
San Francisco vs. Colorado, July 2, 2002.
A.L.—3—Boston vs. St. Louis, June 8, 1950.
New York vs. Boston, May 30, 1961.
Toronto vs. Baltimore, September 14, 1987.
Toronto vs. California, July 14, 1990.
Detroit vs. Chicago, May 28, 1995.
Seattle vs. Milwaukee, July 31, 1996.
Anaheim vs. Tampa Bay, April 21, 2000.
Minnesota vs. Milwaukee N.L., July 12, 2001.

Most players with two or more homers by both clubs, game
N.L.—4—Pittsburgh 3, St. Louis 1, August 16, 1947.
Colorado 3, Montreal 1, August 14, 1999.
A.L.—4—Detroit 3, Chicago 1, May 28, 1995.

Most players with one or more home runs, game
N.L.—8—Cincinnati vs. Philadelphia, September 4, 1999 (9 home runs in game by Cincinnati).
A.L.—7—Baltimore vs. Boston, May 17, 1967 (7 home runs in game by Baltimore).
Oakland vs. California, June 27, 1996 (8 home runs in game by Oakland).
Detroit vs. Toronto, June 20, 2000 (8 home runs in game by Detroit).

Most players with one or more home runs by both clubs, game
N.L.—9—New York 5, Brooklyn 4, September 2, 1939, first game.
New York 6, Pittsburgh 3, July 11, 1954, first game.
Chicago 5, Pittsburgh 4, April 21, 1964.
Cincinnati 6, Atlanta 3, April 21, 1970.
Los Angeles 5, Atlanta 4, April 24, 1977.
Cincinnati 5, Chicago 4, July 28, 1977, 13 innings.
Cincinnati 8, Philadelphia 1, September 4, 1999.
A.L.—9—New York 5, Detroit 4, June 23, 1950.
Minnesota 5, Boston 4, May 25, 1965.
Baltimore 7, Boston 2, May 17, 1967.
California 5, Cleveland 4, August 30, 1970.
Boston 5, Milwaukee 4, May 22, 1977, first game.
California 5, Oakland 4, April 23, 1985.
Detroit 7, Toronto 2, June 20, 2000.
Detroit 5, Chicago 4, July 2, 2002.

Longest extra-inning game without a home run by either club
N.L.—26 innings—Boston 0, Brooklyn 0, May 1, 1920.
A.L.—24 innings—Boston 0, Philadelphia 0, September 1, 1906.
Detroit 0, Philadelphia 0, July 21, 1945.

DOUBLEHEADER AND CONSECUTIVE GAMES

Most home runs, doubleheader
A.L.—13—New York vs. Philadelphia, June 28, 1939.
N.L.—12—Milwaukee vs. Pittsburgh, August 30, 1953.

Most home runs both clubs, doubleheader
N.L.—15—Milwaukee 9, Chicago 6, May 30, 1956.
A.L.—14—New York 9, Philadelphia 5, May 22, 1930.
(14—Chicago 7, Texas 7, August 28, 1998, first game 10 innings.)

Most home runs by pinch-hitters, doubleheader
N.L.—3—Montreal vs. Atlanta, July 13, 1973.
A.L.—2—Made in many doubleheaders.

Most home runs by pinch-hitters for both clubs, doubleheader
N.L.—4—St. Louis 2, Brooklyn 2, July 21, 1930.
A.L.—2—Made in many doubleheaders.

Most consecutive games with one or more home runs
A.L.—27—Texas, August 11 through September 9, 2002 (55 home runs).
N.L.—25—Atlanta, April 18 through May 13, 1998 (45 home runs).

Most home runs in consecutive games in which homers were hit

A.L.—55—Texas, August 11 through September 9, 2002 (27 games).

N.L.—45—Atlanta, April 18 through May 13, 1998 (25 games).

Most consecutive games with one or more homers, start of season

N.L.—13—Chicago, April 13 through May 2, second game, 1954 (28 home runs).

A.L.—10—New York, April 5 through April 16, 1999 (16 home runs).

Most consecutive games with two or more home runs, season

A.L.—9—Cleveland, May 13, first game, through May 21, 1962 (28 home runs).

Baltimore, May 8 through May 16, 1987 (29 home runs).

Baltimore, August 3 through August 11, 1996 (23 home runs).

N.L.—8—Milwaukee, July 19 through July 26, 1956 (20 home runs).

Most home runs, two consecutive games (connecting each game)

N.L.—14—Cincinnati, September 4, 5, 1999.

A.L.—13—New York, June 28, 28, 1939.

Anaheim, June 3, 4, 2003.

Most home runs, three consecutive games

A.L.—16—Boston, June 17 through June 19, 1977.

N.L.—15—Los Angeles, June 29, 30, July 1, 1996.

Cincinnati, September 3, 4, 5, 1999.

Cincinnati, September 4, 5, 6, 1999.

Chicago, August 10, 11, 12, 2002.

Most home runs, four consecutive games

N.L.—18—Houston, August 13 through August 16, 2000.

A.L.—18—Boston, June 16 through June 19, 1977.

Oakland, June 25 through June 29, 1996.

Most home runs, five consecutive games

A.L.—21—Boston, June 14 through June 19, 1977.

N.L.—19—New York, July 7 through July 11, first game, 1954.

Most home runs, six consecutive games

A.L.—24—Boston, June 17 through June 22, 1977.

N.L.—22—New York, July 6 through July 11, first game, 1954.

Most home runs, seven consecutive games

A.L.—26—Boston, June 16 through June 22, 1977.

N.L.—24—New York, July 5, second game through July 11, first game, 1954.

Most home runs, eight consecutive games

A.L.—29—Boston, June 14 through June 22, 1977.

N.L.—26—New York, July 5, first game through July 11, first game, 1954.

Most home runs, nine consecutive games

A.L.—30—Boston June 14 through June 23, 1977.

Boston, June 16 through June 24, 1977.

N.L.—27—New York, July 4, second game through July 11, first game, 1954.

Most home runs, 10 consecutive games

A.L.—33—Boston, June 14 through June 24, 1977.

N.L.—28—New York, July 4, first game through July 11, first game, 1954.

INNING

Most home runs, inning

A.L.—5—Minnesota vs. Kansas City, June 9, 1966, seventh inning.

N.L.—5—New York vs. Cincinnati, June 6, 1939, fourth inning.

Philadelphia vs. Cincinnati, June 2, 1949, eighth inning.

San Francisco vs. Cincinnati, August 23, 1961, ninth inning.

For complete lists of clubs with four or more home runs in an inning and three or more consecutive home runs in an inning, see page 181.

Most home runs by pinch-hitters, inning

N.L.—2—New York vs. St. Louis, June 20, 1954, sixth inning (Hofman, Rhodes).

San Francisco vs. Milwaukee, June 4, 1958, 10th inning, (Sauer, Schmidt; consecutive).

Los Angeles vs. Chicago, August 8, 1963, fifth inning (Howard, Skowron; consecutive).

Los Angeles vs. St. Louis, July 23, 1975, ninth inning (Crawford, Lacy; consecutive).

New York vs. San Francisco, May 4, 1991, ninth inning (Sasser, Carreon; consecutive).

Cincinnati vs. Atlanta, June 22, 1995, eighth inning (Anthony, Taubensee).

New York vs. St. Louis, May 11, 1997, ninth inning (Everett, Huskey; consecutive).

A.L.—2—New York vs. Kansas City, July 23, 1955, ninth inning (Cerv, Howard).

Baltimore vs. Boston, August 26, 1966, ninth inning (Roznovsky, Powell; consecutive).

Seattle vs. New York, April 27, 1979, eighth inning (Stinson, Meyer).

Minnesota vs. Oakland, May 16, 1983, ninth inning (Engle, Hatcher).

Baltimore vs. Cleveland, August 12, 1985, ninth inning (Gross, Sheets; consecutive).

Texas vs. Boston, September 1, 1986, ninth inning (McDowell, Porter; consecutive).

Boston vs. Chicago, September 19, 1997, ninth inning (Pride, Hatteberg).

Toronto vs. Texas, September 11, 2004, eighth inning (Hinske, Gomez).

Most home runs by both clubs, inning

A.L.—5—St. Louis 3, Philadelphia 2, June 8, 1928, ninth inning.

Detroit 4, New York 1, June 23, 1950, fourth inning.

Minnesota 5, Kansas City 0, June 9, 1966, seventh inning.

Baltimore 4, Boston 1, May 17, 1967, seventh inning.

Minnesota 4, Oakland 1, May 16, 1983, ninth inning.

Cleveland 3, Texas 2, June 29, 1984, fifth inning.

Baltimore 3, Boston 2, September 10, 1985, eighth inning.

Cleveland 3, Milwaukee 2, April 25, 1997, fourth inning.

Detroit 3, Baltimore 2, April 7, 2000, fifth inning.

Seattle 3, Kansas City 2, August 27, 2004, fifth inning.

N.L.—5—New York 5, Cincinnati 0, June 6, 1939, fourth inning.

Philadelphia 5, Cincinnati 0, June 2, 1949, eighth inning.

New York 3, Boston 2, July 6, 1951, third inning.

Cincinnati 3, Brooklyn 2, June 11, 1954, seventh inning.

San Francisco 3, Cincinnati 0, August 23, 1961, ninth inning.

Philadelphia 3, Chicago 2, April 17, 1964, fifth inning.

Chicago 3, Atlanta 2, July 3, 1967, first inning.

Pittsburgh 3, Atlanta 2, August 1, 1970, seventh inning.

Cincinnati 3, Chicago 2, July 28, 1977, first inning.

San Francisco 3, Atlanta 2, May 25, 1979, fourth inning.

Cincinnati 4, Atlanta 1, June 19, 1994, first inning.

San Francisco 3, Pittsburgh 2, July 27, 1997, ninth inning.

Colorado 3, St. Louis 2, July 31, 1999, third inning.

Atlanta 4, San Francisco 1, May 20, 2001, seventh inning.

Most consecutive home runs, inning

N.L.—4—Milwaukee vs. Cincinnati, June 8, 1961, seventh inning.

A.L.—4—Cleveland vs. Los Angeles, July 31, 1963, second game, sixth inning.

Minnesota vs. Kansas City, May 2, 1964, 11th inning.

For a complete list of clubs with three or more consecutive home runs in an inning, see page 182.

Most times same players hitting back-to-back home runs, inning

A.L.—2—Seattle vs. Chicago, May 2, 2002, first inning (Boone, Cameron).

N.L.—1—Occurred many times.

Most home runs with two out, inning

N.L.—5—New York vs. Cincinnati, June 6, 1939, fourth inning.

A.L.—4—Boston vs. Detroit, July 18, 1998, fourth inning.

Most home runs with none on base, inning

N.L.—4—New York vs. Philadelphia, August 13, 1939, first game, fourth inning.

A.L.—4—Cleveland vs. Los Angeles, July 31, 1963, second game, sixth inning (consecutive).

Minnesota vs. Kansas City, May 2, 1964, 11th inning (consecutive).

Minnesota vs. Kansas City, June 9, 1966, seventh inning (also one home run with one on base).

Boston vs. New York, June 17, 1977, first inning.

Boston vs. Toronto, July 4, 1977, eighth inning.

Boston vs. Milwaukee, May 31, 1980, fourth inning.

Minnesota vs. New York, May 2, 1992, fifth inning.

Baltimore vs. California, September 5, 1995, second inning.

Seattle vs. Oakland, September 21, 1996, third inning.

Most home runs, start of game

N.L.—3—San Diego vs. San Francisco, April 13, 1987 (Wynne, Gwynn, Kruk).

Atlanta vs. Cincinnati, May 28, 2003 (Furcal, DeRosa, Sheffield.)

A.A.—2—Boston vs. Baltimore, June 25, 1891 (Brown, Joyce).

Philadelphia vs. Boston, August 21, 1891 (McTamany, Larkin).

A.L.—2—Held by many clubs. Last clubs: Boston vs. Detroit, June 3, 2002 (Santiago, Easley); Cleveland vs. Kansas City, July 21, 2002 (Magruder, Vizquel); Minnesota vs. Chicago, August 19, 2002 (Jones, Guzman); Seattle vs. Texas, September 9, 2002 (Suzuki, Relaford).

Most times with three consecutive home runs in an inning (league)

N.L.—17—New York/San Francisco, 1932, 1939 (2), 1948, 1949, 1953, 1954, 1956 in New York, 1963, 1969, 1982, 1998, 1999 (2), 2001, 2002, 2004 in San Francisco.

A.L.—12—Detroit, 1947, 1956, 1961, 1971, 1972, 1974, 1986 (2), 1987, 1990, 1992, 2001.

For a complete list of clubs with three or more consecutive home runs in an inning, see page 182.

Most times with three or more home runs in an inning, season

N.L.—5—New York, 1954.

Chicago, 1955.

A.L.—5—Baltimore, 1996.

Most times hitting two or more consecutive home runs, season

A.L.—18—Seattle, 161 games, 1996.

N.L.—15—Cincinnati, 155 games, 1956.

St. Louis, 162 games, 2000.

GRAND SLAMS

Most grand slams, season

A.L.—14—Oakland, 2000.

N.L.—12—Atlanta, 1997.

St. Louis, 2000.

Most grand slams by pinch-hitters, season

N.L.—3—San Francisco, 1973 (Arnold, Bonds, Goodson).

Chicago, 1975 (Summers, LaCock, Hosley).

San Francisco, 1978 (Ivie 2, Clark).

Philadelphia, 1978 (Johnson 2, McBride).

A.L.—3—Baltimore, 1982 (Ayala, Ford, Crowley).

Most grand slams, game

A.L.—2—Chicago vs. Detroit, May 1, 1901 (Hoy, McFarland).

Boston vs. Chicago, May 13, 1934 (Walters, Morgan).

New York vs. Philadelphia, May 24, 1936 (Lazzeri 2).

Boston vs. Philadelphia, July 4, 1939, second game (Tabor 2).

Boston vs. St. Louis, July 27, 1946 (York 2).

Detroit vs. Philadelphia, June 11, 1954, first game (Boone, Kaline).

Baltimore vs. New York, April 24, 1960 (Pearson, Klaus).

Boston vs. Chicago, May 10, 1960 (Wertz, Repulski).

Baltimore vs. Minnesota, May 9, 1961 (Gentile 2).

Minnesota vs. Cleveland, July 18, 1962 (Allison, Killebrew).

Detroit vs. Cleveland, June 24, 1968 (Northrup 2).

Baltimore vs. Washington, June 26, 1970 (Frank Robinson 2).

Milwaukee vs. Chicago, June 17, 1973 (Porter, Lahoud).

Milwaukee vs. Boston, April 12, 1980 (Cooper, Money).

California vs. Detroit, April 27, 1983 (Lynn, Sconiers).

Boston vs. Detroit, August 7, 1984, first game (Buckner, Armas).

California vs. Oakland, July 31, 1986 (Downing, Boone).

Baltimore vs. Texas, August 6, 1986 (Sheets, Dwyer).

Boston vs. Baltimore, June 10, 1987 (Burks, Barrett).

New York vs. Toronto, June 29, 1987 (Mattingly, Winfield).

Cleveland vs. Minnesota, April 22, 1988 (Snyder, Carter).

Boston vs. New York, May 2, 1995 (Valentin, Vaughn).

Chicago vs. Texas, September 4, 1995 (Ventura 2).

Chicago vs. Detroit, May 19, 1996 (Ventura, Lewis).

Baltimore vs. Cleveland, August 14, 1998 (Hoiles 2).

Boston vs. Seattle, May 10, 1999 (Garciaparra 2).

New York vs. Toronto, September 14, 1999 (Williams, O'Neill).

Cleveland vs. Toronto, September 24, 1999 (Ramirez, Roberts).

Seattle vs. Chicago, August 8, 2000, first game (Buhner, Martinez).

Boston vs. Texas, July 29, 2003 (Mueller, 2).

Oakland vs. Toronto, August 24, 2003 (Hernandez, Tejada).

Texas vs. Houston N.L., July 4, 2004 (Blalock, Teixeira).

Kansas City vs. Oakland, August 13, 2004 (Nunez, Buck).

N.L.—2—Chicago vs. Pittsburgh, August 16, 1890, (Burns, Kittredge).

Brooklyn vs. Cincinnati, September 23, 1901 (Kelley, Sheckard).

Boston vs. Chicago, August 12, 1903, second game (Stanley, Moran).

Philadelphia vs. Boston, April 28, 1921 (Miller, Meadows).

New York vs. Philadelphia, September 5, 1924, second game (Kelly, Jackson).

Pittsburgh vs. St. Louis, June 22, 1925 (Grantham, Traynor).

St. Louis vs. Philadelphia, July 6, 1929, second game (Bottomley, Hafey).

Pittsburgh vs. Philadelphia, May 1, 1933 (Vaughan, Grace).

Boston vs. Philadelphia, April 30, 1938 (Moore, Maggert).

New York vs. Brooklyn, July 4, 1938, second game (Bartell, Mancuso).

New York vs. St. Louis, July 13, 1951 (Westrum, Williams).

Cincinnati vs. Pittsburgh, July 29, 1955 (Thurman, Burgess).

Atlanta vs. San Francisco, July 3, 1966 (Cloninger 2).

Houston vs. New York, July 30, 1969, first game (Menke, Wynn).

San Francisco vs. Montreal, April 26, 1970, first game (McCovey, Dietz).

Pittsburgh vs. Chicago, September 14, 1982 (Hebner, Madlock).

Los Angeles vs. Montreal, August 23, 1985 (Guerrero, Duncan).

Atlanta vs. Houston, May 2, 1987 (Nettles, James).

Chicago vs. Houston, June 3, 1987 (Dayett, Moreland).

Cincinnati vs. Chicago, April 24, 1993 (Sabo, Oliver).

Pittsburgh vs. St. Louis, April 16, 1996 (Merced, Bell).

Montreal vs. Colorado, April 28, 1996 (Fletcher, Segui).

Florida vs. San Diego, April 28, 1997 (Alou, Sheffield).

Atlanta vs. Philadelphia, July 14, 1997 (Spehr, Klesko).

Philadelphia vs. San Francisco, August 18, 1997 (McMillon, Lieberthal).

San Francisco vs. Los Angeles, September 19, 1998 (Mueller, Kent).

St. Louis vs. Los Angeles, April 23, 1999 (Tatis 2).

Cincinnati vs. Montreal, August 21, 1999 (Boone, Taubensee).

Los Angeles vs. Florida, May 21, 2000 (Beltre, Green).

Milwaukee vs. Chicago, May 12, 2002 (Casanova, Sexson).

Philadelphia vs. Atlanta, September 9, 2003 (Perez, Michaels).

Most grand slams by both clubs, game (each club connecting)

A.L.—3—Baltimore 2 (Sheets, Dwyer), Texas 1 (Harrah), August 6, 1986.

N.L.—3—Chicago 2 (Dayett, Moreland), Houston 1 (Hatcher), June 3, 1987.

Most grand slams by pinch-hitters for both clubs, game

N.L.—2—New York 1 (Crawford), Boston 1 (Bell), May 26, 1929.

A.L.—1—Held by many clubs.

Most grand slams, doubleheader
N.L.-A.L.—2—Made in many doubleheaders.
Last N.L. time—New York vs. Milwaukee, May 20, 1999.
Last A.L. time—Baltimore vs. Chicago, August 14, 1976.

Most grand slams by both clubs, doubleheader
N.L.—3—Cincinnati 2, Atlanta 1, September 12, 1974.
A.L.—2—Last time—Seattle 2, Chicago 0, August 8, 2000.
M.L.—2—Kansas City A.L. 1, Colorado N.L. 1, June 7, 2003.

Most grand slams, two consecutive games (connecting each game)
N.L.—3—Brooklyn, September 23 (2), September 24 (1), 1901.
Pittsburgh, June 20 (1), June 22 (2), 1925.
Los Angeles, May 20 (1), May 21 (2), 2000.
A.L.—3—Milwaukee, April 10 (1), April 12 (2), 1980.
Chicago, May 18 (1), May 19 (2), 1996.
Seattle, August 7 (1), August 8, first game (2), 2000.

Most consecutive games, one or more grand slams
A.L.—3—Milwaukee, April 7, 8, 9, 1978. (first three games of season.)
Detroit, August 10, 11, 12, 1993.
N.L.—2—Held by many clubs.

Most grand slams, inning
A.L.—2—Minnesota vs. Cleveland, July 18, 1962, first inning (Allison, Killebrew).
Milwaukee vs. Boston, April 12, 1980, second inning (Cooper, Money).
Baltimore vs. Texas, August 6, 1986, fourth inning (Sheets, Dwyer).
N.L.—2—Chicago vs. Pittsburgh, August 16, 1890, fifth inning (Burns, Kittredge).
Houston vs. New York, July 30, 1969, first game, ninth inning (Menke, Wynn).
St. Louis vs. Los Angeles, April 23, 1999, third inning (Tatis 2).

Most grand slams by both clubs, inning
N.L.—2—Chicago 2 (Burns, Kittredge), Pittsburgh 0, August 16, 1890, fifth inning.
New York 1 (Irvin), Chicago 1 (Walker), May 18, 1950, sixth inning.
Houston 2 (Menke, Wynn), New York 0, July 30, 1969, first game, ninth inning.
Atlanta 1 (Evans), Cincinnati 1, (Geronimo), September 12, 1974, first game, second inning.
Chicago 1 (Sandberg), Pittsburgh 1 (King), September 9, 1992, sixth inning.
St. Louis 2 (Tatis 2), Los Angeles 0, April 23, 1999, third inning.
A.L.—2—Washington 1 (Tasby), Boston 1 (Pagliaroni), June 18, 1961, first game, ninth inning.
Minnesota 2 (Allison, Killebrew), Cleveland 0, July 18, 1962, first inning.
Milwaukee 2 (Cooper, Money), Boston 0, April 12, 1980, second inning.
Cleveland 1 (Orta), Texas 1 (Sundberg), April 14, 1980, first inning.
Baltimore 2 (Sheets, Dwyer), Texas 0, August 6, 1986, fourth inning.
Interleague—2—Anaheim A.L. 1 (Fielder), Arizona N.L. 1 (Benitez), June 9, 1998, third inning.

TOTAL BASES

Most total bases, season
A.L.—2,832—Boston, 162 games, 2003.
N.L.—2,748—Colorado, 162 games, 2001.

Fewest total bases, season
N.L.—1,358—Brooklyn, 154 games, 1908.
A.L.—1,310—Chicago, 156 games, 1910.

Most total bases, game
A.L.—60—Boston vs. St. Louis, June 8, 1950.
N.L.—58—Montreal vs. Atlanta, July 30, 1978.

Most total bases by both clubs, nine-inning game
N.L.—81—Cincinnati 55, Colorado 26, May 19, 1999.
A.L.—77—New York 50, Philadelphia 27, June 3, 1932.

Most total bases by both clubs, extra-inning game
N.L.—97—Chicago 49, Philadelphia 48, May 17, 1979, 10 innings.
A.L.—85—Cleveland 45, Philadelphia 40, July 10, 1932, 18 innings.

Most total bases, doubleheader
A.L.—87—New York vs. Philadelphia, June 28, 1939.
N.L.—73—Milwaukee vs. Pittsburgh, August 30, 1953.

Most total bases by both clubs, doubleheader
A.L.—114—New York 73, Philadelphia 41, May 22, 1930.
N.L.—108—St. Louis 62, Philadelphia 46, July 6, 1929.

Most total bases, two consecutive games
A.L.—102—Boston vs. St. Louis, June 7 (42), June 8 (60), 1950.
N.L.—89—Pittsburgh vs. Brooklyn June 20 (46); vs. St. Louis, June 22 (43), 1925.

Most total bases, inning
N.L.—29—Chicago vs. Detroit, September 6, 1883, seventh inning.
N.L. since 1900—27—San Francisco vs. Cincinnati, August 23, 1961, ninth inning.
A.L.—25—Boston vs. Philadelphia, September 24, 1940, first game, sixth inning.

EXTRA BASE HITS

Most extra base hits, season
A.L.—649—Boston, 162 games, 2003 (371 doubles, 40 triples, 238 home runs).
N.L.—598—Colorado, 162 games, 2001 (324 doubles, 61 triples, 213 home runs).

Fewest extra base hits, season
A.L.—179—Chicago, 156 games, 1910 (116 doubles, 56 triples, 7 home runs).
N.L.—182—Boston, 155 games, 1909 (124 doubles, 43 triples, 15 home runs).

Most extra base hits, game
A.L.—17—Boston vs. St. Louis, June 8, 1950.
N.L.—16—Chicago vs. Buffalo, July 3, 1883.
N.L. since 1900—15—Philadelphia vs. Chicago, June 23, 1986.
Cincinnati vs. Colorado, May 19, 1999.

Most extra base hits by both clubs, game
N.L.—24—St. Louis 13, Chicago 11, July 12, 1931, second game.
A.L.—24—Cleveland 15, Minnesota 9, July 13, 1996.

Longest game without an extra base hit
N.L.—26 innings—Brooklyn vs. Boston, May 1, 1920.
A.L.—19 innings—Detroit vs. New York, August 23, 1968, second game.

Longest game without an extra base by either club
A.L.—18 innings—Chicago 0, New York 0, August 21, 1933.
N.L.—17 innings—Boston 0, Chicago 0, September 21, 1901.

Most extra base hits, doubleheader
N.L.—21—Baltimore vs. Cleveland, September 3, 1894.
N.L. since 1900—18—Chicago vs. St. Louis, July 12, 1931.
A.L.—18—New York vs. Washington, July 4, 1927.
New York vs. Philadelphia, June 28, 1939.

Most extra base hits by both clubs, doubleheader
N.L.—35—Chicago 18, St. Louis 17, July 12, 1931.
A.L.—28—Boston 16, Detroit 12, May 14, 1967.

Longest doubleheader without an extra base hit
A.L.—26—Cleveland vs. Detroit, August 6, 1968.

Most extra base hits, inning
N.L.—8—Chicago vs. Detroit, September 6, 1883, seventh inning.
N.L. since 1900—7—Boston vs. St. Louis, August 25, 1936, first game, first inning.
Philadelphia vs. Cincinnati, June 2, 1949, eighth inning.
Philadelphia vs. Cincinnati, July 6, 1986, third inning.
A.L.—7—St. Louis vs. Washington, August 7, 1922, sixth inning.
Boston vs. Philadelphia, September 24, 1940, first game, sixth inning.

New York vs. St. Louis, May 3, 1951, ninth inning.
Seattle vs. Boston, September 3, 1982, sixth inning.
Texas vs. New York, July 31, 2002, second inning.

RUNS BATTED IN

Most runs batted in, season
A.L.—995—New York, 155 games, 1936.
N.L.—942—St. Louis, 154 games, 1930.

Fewest runs batted in, season (since 1920)
N.L.—354—Philadelphia, 151 games, 1942.
A.L.—424—Texas, 154 games, 1972.

Most players with 100 or more runs batted in, season
A.L.—5—New York, 1936.
N.L.—4—Pittsburgh, 1925; Chicago, 1929; Philadelphia, 1929;
Colorado, 1996, 1997, 1999; Arizona, 1999, Atlanta, 2003.

Most runs batted in, game
A.L.—29—Boston vs. St. Louis, June 8, 1950.
N.L.—26—New York vs. Brooklyn, April 30, 1944, first game.
Chicago vs. Colorado, August 18, 1995.

Most runs batted in by both clubs, nine-inning game
N.L.—43—Chicago 24, Philadelphia 19, August 25, 1922.
(45—Philadelphia 23, Chicago 22, May 17, 1979, 10 innings.)
A.L.—35—Boston 21, Philadelphia 14, June 29, 1950.

Longest game without a run batted in by either club
N.L.—19 innings—Cincinnati 0, Brooklyn 0, September 11, 1946.
A.L.—18 innings—Washington 0, Detroit 0, July 16, 1909.
Washington 0, Chicago 0, May 15, 1918.

Most runs batted in, doubleheader
A.L.—34—Boston vs. Philadelphia, July 4, 1939.
N.L.—31—St. Louis vs. Philadelphia, July 6, 1929.

Most runs batted in by both clubs, doubleheader
A.L.—49—Boston 34, Philadelphia 15, July 4, 1939.
N.L.—45—St. Louis 31, Philadelphia 14, July 6, 1929.

Most runs batted in, two consecutive games
A.L.—49—Boston vs. St. Louis, June 7 (20), 8 (29), 1950.
N.L.—39—Pittsburgh, June 20 (19), June 22 (20), 1925.

Most runs batted in, inning
A.L.—17—Boston vs. Detroit, June 18, 1953, seventh inning.
N.L.—15—Chicago vs. Detroit, September 6, 1883, seventh inning.
Brooklyn vs. Cincinnati, May 21, 1952, first inning.

GAME-WINNING RBIs (1980-1988)

Most game-winning RBIs, season
N.L.—102—New York, 1986 (108 games won).
A.L.—99—Oakland, 1988 (104 games won).

Fewest game-winning RBIs, season
A.L.—48—Baltimore, 1988 (54 games won).
N.L.—51—Atlanta, 1988 (54 games won).

Most games won without game-winning RBIs, season
A.L.—12—Detroit, 1980 (84 games won).
N.L.—12—Houston, 1980 (93 games won).

Fewest games won without game-winning RBIs, season
A.L.—0—New York, 1982 (79 games won).
N.L.—1—Pittsburgh, 1985 (57 games won).
Chicago, 1987 (76 games won).

BASES ON BALLS

Most bases on balls, season
A.L.—835—Boston, 155 games, 1949.
N.L.—732—Brooklyn, 155 games, 1947.

Fewest bases on balls, season
N.L.—283—Philadelphia, 153 games, 1920.
A.L.—356—Philadelphia, 156 games, 1920.

Most bases on balls, game
A.A.—19—Louisville vs. Cleveland, September 21, 1887.
A.L.—18—Detroit vs. Philadelphia, May 9, 1916.
Cleveland vs. Boston, May 20, 1948.
(20—Boston vs. Detroit, September 17, 1920, 12 innings.)
N.L.—17—Chicago vs. New York, May 30, 1887, a.m. game.
Brooklyn vs. Philadelphia, August 27, 1903.
New York vs. Brooklyn, April 30, 1944, first game.
(19—Philadelphia vs. Baltimore A.L., July 2, 2004, 16 innings.)

Most bases on balls by both clubs, game
A.L.—30—Detroit 18, Philadelphia 12, May 9, 1916.
(30—Washington 19, Cleveland 11, September 14, 1971, 2nd game, 20 innings, suspended, finished September 20.)
N.L.—26—Houston 13, San Francisco 13, May 4, 1975, second game.

Most bases on balls, nine-inning game being shut out
A.L.—11—St. Louis vs. New York, August 1, 1941.
N.L.—9—Cincinnati vs. St. Louis, September 1, 1958, first game.
(10—Chicago vs. Cincinnati, August 19, 1965, first game, 10 innings.)

Longest game without a base on balls
N.L.—22 innings—Los Angeles vs. Montreal, August 23, 1989.
A.L.—20 innings—Philadelphia vs. Boston, July 4, 1905, p.m. game.

Longest game without a base on balls by either club
A.L.—13 innings—Washington 0, Detroit 0, July 22, 1904.
Boston 0, Philadelphia 0, September 9, 1907.
N.L.—12 innings—Chicago 0, Los Angeles 0, July 27, 1980.

Most bases on balls, doubleheader
N.L.—25—New York vs. Brooklyn, April 30, 1944.
A.L.—23—Cleveland vs. Philadelphia, June 18, 1950.
(23—Washington vs. Cleveland, September 14, 1971, second game 20 innings, suspended, finished September 20.)

Most bases on balls by both clubs, doubleheader
N.L.—42—Houston 21, San Francisco 21, May 4, 1975.
A.L.—32—Baltimore 18, Chicago 14, May 28, 1954.
Detroit 20, Kansas City 12, August 1, 1962.
Texas 17, Chicago 15, May 24, 1995.
(39—Washington 23, Cleveland 16, September 14, 1971, second game 20 innings; suspended, finished September 20.)

Fewest bases on balls by both clubs, doubleheader
N.L.—1—Cincinnati 1, Brooklyn 0, August 6, 1905.
Cincinnati 1, Pittsburgh 0, September 7, 1924.
Brooklyn 1, St. Louis 0, September 22, 1929.
A.L.—2—Philadelphia 2, Detroit 0, August 28, 1908, 20 innings.
Philadelphia 1, Chicago 1, July 12, 1912.
Cleveland 2, Chicago 0, September 6, 1930.

Longest doubleheader without a base on balls
N.L.—27 innings—St. Louis vs. New York, July 2, 1933.
A.L.—20 innings—Detroit vs. Philadelphia, August 28, 1908.

Most bases on balls, two consecutive games
A.L.—29—Detroit vs. Philadelphia, May 9, 10, 1916.
N.L.—25—New York vs. Brooklyn, April 30, 30, 1944.
Houston vs. Milwaukee, April 28, 29, 2000.
(25—Philadelphia vs. Montreal, July 1; vs. Baltimore A.L., July 2, 2004, 19 innings.)

Most bases on balls by both clubs, two consecutive games
A.L.—48—Detroit 29, Philadelphia 19, May 9, 10, 1916.

Most bases on balls, inning
A.L.—11—New York vs. Washington, September 11, 1949, first game, third inning.
N.L.—9—Cincinnati vs. Chicago, April 24, 1957, fifth inning.

Most consecutive bases on balls, inning
A.L.—7—Chicago vs. Washington, August 28, 1909, first game, second inning.
N.L.—7—Atlanta vs. Pittsburgh, May 25, 1983, third inning.

Most bases on balls by pinch-hitters, inning
N.L.—3—Pittsburgh vs. Philadelphia, June 3, 1911, ninth inning.
Brooklyn vs. New York, April 22, 1922, seventh inning.

Boston vs. Brooklyn, June 2, 1932, first game, ninth inning.
Chicago vs. Philadelphia, July 29, 1947, seventh inning.
Philadelphia vs. Pittsburgh, July 18, 1997, sixth inning.
A.L.—3—Baltimore vs. Washington, April 22, 1955, seventh inning.
Washington vs. Boston, May 14, 1961, second game, ninth inning (consecutive).

Most consecutive bases on balls by pinch-hitters, inning

N.L.—3—Brooklyn vs. New York, April 22, 1922, seventh inning.
Boston vs. Brooklyn, June 2, 1932, first game, ninth inning.
A.L.—3—Washington vs. Boston, May 14, 1961, second game, ninth inning.

Most players with two bases on balls, inning

A.L.—4—New York vs. Washington, September 11, 1949, first game, third inning.
N.L.—2—Made in many innings.

Most consecutive bases on balls at start of game

N.L.—5—New York vs. Cincinnati, June 16, 1941.
A.L.—4—Philadelphia vs. Boston, April 21, 1946.
Toronto vs. Texas, April 18, 1997.
Kansas City vs. Cleveland, June 29, 2000.

INTENTIONAL (SINCE 1955)

Most intentional bases on balls, season

N.L.—153—San Francisco, 162 games, 2004.
A.L.—79—Minnesota, 162 games, 1965.

Fewest intentional bases on balls, season

A.L.—10—Kansas City, 162 games, 1961.
N.L.—22—Los Angeles, 154 games, 1958.
Pittsburgh, 163 games, 1998.

Most intentional bases on balls, game

N.L.—6—San Francisco vs. St. Louis, July 19, 1975.
(7—New York vs. Chicago, May 2, 1956, 17 innings.
Houston vs. Philadelphia, July 15, 1984, 16 innings.
Chicago vs. Cincinnati, May 22, 1990, 16 innings.
Cincinnati vs. San Francisco, April 15, 1969, 12 innings.)
A.L.—5—California vs. New York, May 10, 1967.
Washington vs. Cleveland, September 2, 1970.
(6—Kansas City vs. Texas, June 6, 1991, 12 innings.
Seattle vs. New York, May 15, 2004, 13 innings.)

Most intentional bases on balls by both clubs, game

N.L.—7—New York 4, Pittsburgh 3, June 27, 1979.
(11—New York 7, Chicago 4, May 2, 1956, 17 innings.)
A.L.—6—California 5, New York 1, May 10, 1967.
(7—many times in extra innings. Last: Seattle 6, New York 1, May 15, 2004, 13 innings.)
(M.L.—7—Philadelphia N.L. 4, Baltimore A.L. 3, July 2, 2004, 16 innings.)

Most intentional bases on balls, inning

N.L.-A.L.—3—Made in many innings.

STRIKEOUTS

Most strikeouts, season

N.L.—1,399—Milwaukee, 162 games, 2001.
A.L.—1,268—Detroit, 162 games, 1996.

Fewest strikeouts, season

N.L.—308—Cincinnati, 153 games, 1921.
A.L.—326—Philadelphia, 155 games, 1927.

Most strikeouts, game

A.L.—20—Seattle vs. Boston, April 29, 1986.
Detroit vs. Boston, September 18, 1996.
(26—California vs. Oakland, July 9, 1971, 20 innings.)
N.L.—20—Houston vs. Chicago, May 6, 1998.
(26—Milwaukee vs. Anaheim, June 8, 2004, 17 innings.)
U.A.—19—Boston vs. Chicago, July 7, 1884.

Most strikeouts by both clubs, game

A.L.—31—Texas 18, Seattle 13, July 13, 1997.

(43—California 26, Oakland 17, July 9, 1971, 20 innings.)
N.L.—30—Houston 20, Chicago 10, May 6, 1998.
(40—San Francisco 20, San Diego 20, June 19, 2001, 15 innings.)
U.A.—29—Boston 19, Chicago 10, July 7, 1884.
St. Louis 18, Boston 11, July 19, 1884.

Most strikeouts by pinch-hitters, game

A.L.—5—Detroit vs. New York, September 8, 1979.
N.L.—4—Brooklyn vs. Philadelphia, April 27, 1950.
Philadelphia vs. Milwaukee, September 16, 1960.
Chicago vs. New York, September 21, 1962.
Chicago vs. New York, May 3, 1969.
Cincinnati vs. Houston, September 27, 1969.
Montreal vs. Philadelphia, June 24, 1972.

Most strikeouts by pinch-hitters from both clubs, game

A.L.—5—New York 4, Boston 1, July 4, 1955, first game.
Washington 4, Cleveland 1, May 1, 1957.
Detroit 4, Cleveland 1, August 4, 1967.
Detroit 5, New York 0, September 8, 1979.
N.L.—4—Made in many games. Last time—Montreal 4, Philadelphia 0, June 24, 1972.

Most consecutive strikeouts, game

N.L.—10—San Diego vs. New York, April 22, 1970; 1 in sixth inning, 3 in seventh, eighth and ninth innings.
A.L.—8—Boston vs. California, July 9, 1972; 2 in first inning, 3 in second and third innings.
Milwaukee vs. California, August 7, 1973; 1 in first inning, 3 in second and third innings, 1 in fourth inning.
Seattle vs. Boston, April 29, 1986; 3 in fourth and fifth innings, 2 in sixth inning.
New York vs. Houston, June 11, 2003; 2 in seventh, 4 in eighth, 2 in ninth.

Most consecutive strikeouts at start of game

N.L.—9—Cleveland vs. New York, August 28, 1884.
N.L. since 1900—8—Los Angeles vs. Houston, September 23, 1986.
A.L.—7—Texas vs. Chicago, May 28, 1986.

Longest extra-inning game without a strikeout

N.L.—17—New York vs. Cincinnati, June 26, 1893.
Cincinnati vs. New York, August 27, 1920, first game.
A.L.—16—Cleveland vs. New York, June 7, 1936.

Longest extra-inning game without a strikeout, both clubs

A.L.—12—Chicago 0, St. Louis 0, July 7, 1931.
N.L.—10—Boston 0, New York 0, April 19, 1928.

Most strikeouts, inning (*consecutive)

A.A.—4—Pittsburgh vs. Philadelphia, September 30, 1885, seventh inning.
N.L.—4—Chicago vs. New York, October 4, 1888, fifth inning.*
Cincinnati vs. New York, May 15, 1906, fifth inning *
St. Louis vs. Chicago, May 27, 1956, first game, sixth inning.*
Milwaukee vs. Cincinnati, August 11, 1959, first game, sixth inning.
Cincinnati vs. Los Angeles, April 12, 1962, third inning.*
Philadelphia vs. Los Angeles, April 17, 1965, second inning.*
Pittsburgh vs. St. Louis, June 7, 1966, fourth inning.
Houston vs. St. Louis, July 18, 1972, eighth inning.
Montreal vs. Chicago, July 31, 1974, first game, second inning.*
Pittsburgh vs. Atlanta, July 29, 1977, sixth inning.
Chicago vs. Cincinnati, May 17, 1984, third inning.*
Chicago vs. Houston, September 3, 1986, fifth inning.
St. Louis vs. Atlanta, August 22, 1989, fifth inning.
San Francisco vs. Cincinnati, June 4, 1990, seventh inning.
Chicago vs. Atlanta, June 7, 1995, ninth inning.
San Diego vs. Colorado, September 19, 1995, sixth inning.
Chicago vs. Colorado, July 25, 1996, ninth inning.
Atlanta vs. New York, September 13, 1996, ninth inning.
Montreal vs. Florida, September 16, 1998, fourth inning.*
Chicago vs. Florida, April 28, 1999, seventh inning.
San Diego vs. San Francisco, July 22, 1999, seventh inning.
San Francisco vs. Montreal, August 17, 1999, seventh inning.*
Milwaukee vs. Montreal, May 5, 2000, ninth inning.
Florida vs. Cincinnati, July 22, 2001, seventh inning.
New York vs. Florida, July 5, 2002, first inning.
Milwaukee vs. Chicago, September 2, 2002, fourth inning.*
Colorado vs. Los Angeles, May 22, 2003, second inning.

Milwaukee vs. Houston, June 13, 2004, seventh inning.
Milwaukee vs. New York, August 3, 2004, eighth inning.
A.L.—4—Boston vs. Washington, April 15, 1911, fifth inning.
Philadelphia vs. Cleveland, June 11, 1916, sixth inning.*
Chicago vs. Los Angeles, May 18, 1961, seventh inning.
Washington vs. Cleveland, September 2, 1964, seventh inning.
California vs. Baltimore, May 29, 1970, fourth inning.*
Seattle vs. Cleveland, July 21, 1978, fifth inning.*
Baltimore vs. Texas, August 2, 1987, second inning.*
New York vs. Texas, July 4, 1988, first inning.
Boston vs. Detroit, August 13, 1988, sixth inning.
Boston vs. Seattle, September 9, 1990, first inning.
California vs. Cleveland, April 11, 1994, ninth inning.
Detroit vs. Cleveland, May 14, 1994, ninth inning.
Toronto vs. Kansas City, September 3, 1996, fourth inning.
Detroit vs. Chicago, July 21, 1997, seventh inning.*
Tampa Bay vs. Oakland, July 27, 1998, fourth inning.
New York vs. Anaheim, May 12, 1999, third inning.
Kansas City vs. Boston, August 10, 1999, ninth inning.
Detroit vs. Anaheim, August 15, 1999, first inning.*
Texas vs. Cleveland, April 16, 2000, third inning.*
Texas vs. Oakland, June 30, 2001, seventh inning.
Texas vs. Seattle, April 4, 2003, ninth inning.*
New York vs. Houston, June 11, 2003, eighth.

Most strikeouts by pinch-hitters, inning (*consecutive)
A.L.—3—Philadelphia vs. Washington, September 3, 1910, eighth
inning.*
Chicago vs. Boston, June 5, 1911, ninth inning.*
Detroit vs. Cleveland, September 19, 1945, eighth inning.*
Philadelphia vs. Cleveland, September 9, 1952, ninth inning.
Cleveland vs. New York, May 12, 1953, eighth inning.*
New York vs. Philadelphia, September 24, 1954, ninth inning.*
Detroit vs. Cleveland, August 4, 1967, eighth inning.
California vs. Minnesota, May 17, 1971, ninth inning.*
Cleveland vs. Detroit, June 25, 1975, ninth inning.
Detroit vs. New York, September 8, 1979, ninth inning.
N.L.—3—Pittsburgh vs. Cincinnati, June 5, 1953, ninth inning.*
Cincinnati vs. Brooklyn, August 8, 1953, ninth inning.
St. Louis vs. Cincinnati, May 10, 1961, ninth inning.
Cincinnati vs. Houston, June 2, 1966, eighth inning.*
Atlanta vs. Houston, June 18, 1967, eighth inning.*
Cincinnati vs. Houston, September 27, 1969, eighth inning.
St. Louis vs. Montreal, July 4, 1970, eighth inning.
Philadelphia vs. Pittsburgh, July 6, 1970, ninth inning.

Most strikeouts, doubleheader
N.L.—27—New York vs. Arizona, April 27, 2003.
(31—Pittsburgh vs. Philadelphia, September 22, 1958, 23
innings.
New York vs. Philadelphia, October 2, 1965, 27 innings.)
A.L.—25—Los Angeles vs. Cleveland, July 31, 1963.
(27—Cleveland vs. Boston, August 25, 1963, 24 innings.)

Most strikeouts by both clubs, doubleheader
N.L.—41—Philadelphia 26, New York 15, September 9, 1970.
San Diego 26, New York 15, May 29, 1971.
Chicago 21, New York 20, September 15, 1971.
(51—New York 30, Philadelphia 21, September 26, 1975, 24
innings.)
A.L.—44—Detroit 24, Baltimore 20, September 8, 1980.
(48—Detroit 24, Kansas City 24, June 17, 1967, 28 innings.)

Longest doubleheader without a strikeout
N.L.—21—Pittsburgh vs. Philadelphia, July 12, 1924.
A.L.—20—Boston vs. St. Louis, July 28, 1917.

Fewest strikeouts by both clubs, doubleheader
A.L.—1—Cleveland 1, Boston 0, August 28, 1926.
N.L.—2—Brooklyn 2, New York 0, August 13, 1932.
Pittsburgh 2, St. Louis 0, September 6, 1948.

Most strikeouts, two consecutive games
A.L.—36—Seattle vs. Boston, April 29 (20), April 30 (16), 1986.
N.L.—33—Milwaukee vs. Arizona, April 6 (16), 7 (17), 2002.
(37—Chicago vs. Houston, May 30 (14), 31 (23 in 16
innings), 2003.)

SACRIFICE HITS

Most sacrifice hits, season (includes sacrifice scoring flies)
A.L.—310—Boston, 157 games, 1917.
N.L.—270—Chicago, 158 games, 1908.

Most sacrifice hits, season (no sacrifice flies)
N.L.—231—Chicago, 154 games, 1906.
A.L.—207—Chicago, 154 games, 1906.

Fewest sacrifice hits, season (no sacrifice flies)
A.L.—11—Toronto, 162 games, 2003.
N.L.—29—San Diego, 162 games, 2001.

Most sacrifices, game (includes sacrifice flies)
A.L.—8—New York vs. Boston, May 4, 1918 (two sacrifice scor-
ing flies).
Chicago vs. Detroit, July 11, 1927.
St. Louis vs. Cleveland, July 23, 1928.
Texas vs. Chicago, August 1, 1977.
N.L.—8—Cincinnati vs. Philadelphia, May 6, 1926.

Most sacrifices by both clubs, game (includes sacrifice flies)
A.L.—11—Washington 7, Boston 4, September 1, 1926.
N.L.—9—New York 5, Chicago 4, August 29, 1921.
Cincinnati 8, Philadelphia 1, May 6, 1926.
San Francisco 6, San Diego 3, May 23, 1970, 15 innings (no
sacrifice flies in game).

Longest extra-inning game without a sacrifice
A.L.—24 innings—Detroit vs. Philadelphia, July 21, 1945.
N.L.—23 innings—Brooklyn vs. Boston, June 27, 1939.

Longest extra-inning game without a sacrifice by either club
N.L.—19 innings—Philadelphia 0, Cincinnati 0, September 15,
1950, second game.
A.L.—18 innings—Washington 0, St. Louis 0, June 20, 1952.

Most sacrifices, doubleheader (includes sacrifice flies)
A.L.—10—Detroit vs. Chicago, July 7, 1921.
N.L.—9—Held by many clubs.

**Most sacrifices by both clubs, doubleheader (includes sacrifice
flies)**
A.L.—13—Boston 9, Chicago 4, July 17, 1926.

Fewest sacrifices, doubleheader
N.L.-A.L.—0—Made in many doubleheaders.

Longest doubleheader without a sacrifice by either club
N.L.—28 innings—Cincinnati 0, Philadelphia 0, September 15,
1950.
A.L.—18 innings—Made in many doubleheaders.

Most sacrifice hits, inning (no sacrifice flies)
A.L.—3—Cleveland vs. St. Louis, July 10, 1949, fifth inning.
Detroit vs. Baltimore, July 12, 1970, first game, second inning
(consecutive).
California vs. Detroit, June 5, 1977, eighth inning.
Oakland vs. Kansas City, June 26, 1977, first game, fifth inning.
Cleveland vs. Chicago, June 8, 1980, sixth inning (consecutive).
Seattle vs. California, April 29, 1984, sixth inning.
Minnesota vs. Milwaukee, July 26, 1991, eighth inning.
N.L.—3—Chicago vs. Milwaukee, August 26, 1962, sixth
inning (consecutive).
Philadelphia vs. Los Angeles, September 23, 1967, seventh
inning (consecutive).
Los Angeles vs. San Francisco, May 23, 1972, sixth inning.
Houston vs. San Diego, April 29, 1975, seventh inning.
Houston vs. Atlanta, July 6, 1975, ninth inning.
Pittsburgh vs. St. Louis, September 20, 1988, eighth inning.

SACRIFICE FLIES

Most run-scoring sacrifice flies, season
A.L.—77—Oakland, 162 games, 1984.
N.L.—75—Colorado, 162 games, 2000.

Fewest sacrifice flies, season
N.L.—19—San Diego, 161 games, 1971.
A.L.—23—California, 161 games, 1967.

Most run-scoring sacrifice flies, game
A.L.—5—Seattle vs. Oakland, August 7, 1988.
N.L.—4—New York vs. San Francisco, July 26, 1967.
New York vs. Philadelphia, September 23, 1972.
St. Louis vs. Cincinnati, September 2, 1980.
Cincinnati vs. Houston, May 5, 1982.
San Francisco vs. New York, August 29, 1987.
Pittsburgh vs. Philadelphia, September 9, 1988.
San Francisco vs. San Diego, September 14, 1988.
Montreal vs. Florida, May 24, 1994.
Houston vs. Pittsburgh, May 9, 1995.
Houston vs. Philadelphia, September 8, 1995.
San Diego vs. Colorado, July 3, 2001.
Arizona vs. Pittsburgh, May 18, 2003.
(4—Montreal vs. Chicago, May 28, 1980, 14 innings.
Atlanta vs. San Diego, May 23, 1991, 12 innings.)

Most run-scoring sacrifice flies by both clubs, game
A.L.—5—many games.
N.L.—5—many games.
(5—Los Angeles 3, San Francisco 2, April 15, 1984, 11 innings.)

Most run-scoring sacrifice flies, inning
A.L.—3—Chicago vs. Cleveland, July 1, 1962, second game, fifth inning.
New York vs. Detroit, June 29, 2000, fourth inning.
New York vs. Anaheim, August 19, 2000, third inning.
N.L.—2—Made in many innings.

HIT BY PITCH

Most hit by pitch, season
N.L.—148—Baltimore, 154 games, 1898.
N.L. since 1900—100—Houston, 162 games, 1997.
A.L.—92—Toronto, 162 games, 1996.

Fewest hit by pitch, season
A.L.—5—Philadelphia, 154 games, 1937.
N.L.—9—Philadelphia, 152 games, 1939.
San Diego, 162 games, 1969.

Most hit by pitch, game
A.A.—6—Brooklyn vs. Baltimore, April 25, 1887.
A.L.—6—New York vs. Washington, June 20, 1913, second game.
N.L.—6—Louisville vs. St. Louis, July 31, 1897, first game.
(6—New York vs. Chicago, June 16, 1893, 11 innings.)
N.L. since 1900—5—Atlanta vs. Cincinnati, July 2, 1969.
Houston vs. Los Angeles, April 19, 2000.

Most hit by pitch by both clubs, game
N.L.—8—Washington 5, Pittsburgh 3, May 9, 1896.
Louisville 6, St. Louis 2, July 31, 1897, first game.
N.L. since 1900—6—Brooklyn 4, New York 2, July 17, 1900.
Montreal 4, Florida 2, June 29, 1994.
Pittsburgh 4, Florida 2, May 22, 1999.
(6—Florida 4, Pittsburgh 2, May 16, 1995, 10 innings.
Pittsburgh 4, Houston 2, September 16, 2000, 10 innings.)
A.L.—7—Detroit 4, Washington 3, August 24, 1914, second game.
Minnesota 4, Kansas City 3, April 13, 1971.
Kansas City 5, Texas 2, September 3, 1989.
Oakland 5, Anaheim 2, June 7, 2001.

Most hit by pitch, inning
N.L.—4—Boston vs. Pittsburgh, August 19, 1893, first game, second inning.
N.L. since 1900—3—New York vs. Pittsburgh, September 25, 1905, first inning.

Chicago vs. Boston, September 17, 1928, ninth inning.
Philadelphia vs. Cincinnati, May 15, 1960, first game, eighth inning.
Atlanta vs. Cincinnati, July 2, 1969, second inning.
Cincinnati vs. Pittsburgh, May 1, 1974, first inning, consecutive.
St. Louis vs. Montreal, August 15, 1992, first inning.
San Diego vs. Colorado, June 28, 1994, eleventh inning.
Houston vs. Los Angeles, September 13, 1997, first inning.
Florida vs. Houston, August 3, 1998, eighth inning.
Atlanta vs. San Diego, August 16, 2000, eighth inning.
St. Louis vs. San Diego, September 26, 2000, eighth inning.
Chicago vs. San Diego, April 22, 2003, fourth inning.
Colorado vs. Los Angeles, July 23, 2003, fourth inning.
Pittsburgh vs. Chicago, May 28, 2004, first game, fifth inning.
Milwaukee vs. Colorado, June 22, 2004, seventh inning.
Atlanta vs. Los Angeles, August 21, 2004, first inning.
A.L.—3—New York vs. Washington, June 20, 1913, second game, first inning.
Cleveland vs. New York, August 25, 1921, eighth inning.
Boston vs. New York, June 30, 1954, third inning.
Baltimore vs. California, August 9, 1968, seventh inning.
California vs. Chicago, September 10, 1977, first inning, consecutive.
California vs. Cleveland, July 8, 1988, fourth inning.
Oakland vs. Minnesota, September 28, 1988, second inning.
Oakland vs. Seattle, September 22, 1996, fifth inning.
Toronto vs. Chicago, July 15, 1998, seventh inning.
Tampa Bay vs. Anaheim, May 22, 1999, third inning.
Boston vs. Kansas City, April 30, 2003, ninth inning.
Anaheim vs. Baltimore, May 14, 2004, second inning.

GROUNDING INTO DOUBLE PLAYS

Most grounding into double plays, season
A.L.—174—Boston, 162 games, 1990.
N.L.—166—St. Louis, 154 games, 1958.

Fewest grounding into double plays, season
N.L.—75—St. Louis, 155 games, 1945.
A.L.—79—Kansas City, 161 games, 1967.

Most grounding into double plays, game
N.L.—7—San Francisco vs. Houston, May 4, 1969.
A.L.—6—many teams.
(6—Toronto vs. Minnesota, August 29, 1977, first game, 10 innings.)

Most grounding into double plays by both clubs, game
A.L.—9—Boston 6, California 3, May 1, 1966, first game.
Boston 6, Minnesota 3, July 18, 1990.
N.L.—8—Boston 5, Chicago 3, September 18, 1928.
(10—New York 6, San Francisco 4, August 21, 2004, 12 innings.)

REACHING BASE ON ERRORS

Most times reaching first base on error, game
N.L.—10—Chicago vs. Cleveland, July 24, 1882.
A.L.—8—Detroit vs. Chicago, May 6, 1903.

Most times reaching first base on error by both clubs, game
N.L.—16—Chicago 10, Cleveland 6, July 24, 1882.
A.L.—12—Detroit 8, Chicago 4, May 6, 1903.

Most times reaching first base on error, inning
N.L.—4—St. Louis vs. Pittsburgh, August 5, 1901, eighth inning.
A.L.—4—St. Louis vs. Boston, June 8, 1911, fourth inning.

LEAGUE BATTING

GAMES

Most games, season
N.L. since 1900 (8 clubs)—625 in 1914, 1917
N.L. (10 clubs)—813 in 1965, 1968
N.L. (12 clubs)—974 in 1983
N.L. (14 clubs)—1,135 in 1993
N.L. (16 clubs)—1,298 in 1998
A.L. (8 clubs)—631 in 1914

A.L. (10 clubs)—814 in 1964
A.L. (12 clubs)—973 in 1969, 1970, 1974
A.L. (14 clubs)—1,135 in 1982, 1983, 2003

Fewest games, season
N.L. since 1900 (8 clubs)—560 in 1903 (508 in shortened 1918 and 1919 seasons)
N.L. (10 clubs)—809 in 1966
N.L. (12 clubs)—969 in 1986, 1988 (644 in shortened 1981 season)

N.L. (14 clubs)—1,134 in 1996, 1997 (803 in shortened 1994 season)
N.L. (16 clubs)—1294 in 2002
A.L. (8 clubs)—549 in 1901 (508 in shortened 1918 season)
A.L. (10 clubs)—806 in 1966
A.L. (12 clubs)—963 in 1975 (929 in shortened 1972 season)
A.L. (14 clubs)—1128 in 1979 (750 in shortened 1981 season)

BATTING AVERAGE

Highest batting average, season
N.L. (since 1900)—.303 in 1930
A.L.—.292 in 1921

Lowest batting average, season
N.L. (since 1900)—.239 in 1908
A.L.—.230 in 1968

Most .400 hitters, season (qualifiers for batting championship)
N.L.—4 in 1894
N.L. (since 1900)—1 in 1922, 1924, 1925, 1930
A.L.—2 in 1911, 1922

Most clubs batting .300 or over, season
N.L. (since 1900)—6 in 1930
A.L.—4 in 1921

Most .300 hitters, season (qualifiers for batting championship)
N.L. (since 1900)—33 in 1930
A.L.—27 in 1924

Fewest .300 hitters, season (qualifiers for batting title)
N.L. (since 1900)—4 in 1907
A.L.—1 in 1968

ON-BASE PERCENTAGE

Highest on-base percentage, season
N.L. (since 1900)—.360 in 1930
A.L.—.363 in 1936

Lowest on-base percentage, season (since 1900)
N.L. (since 1900)—.299 in 1908
A.L.—.295 in 1908

SLUGGING AVERAGE

Highest slugging average, season
N.L. (since 1900)—.448 in 1930
A.L.—.445 in 1996

Lowest slugging average, season
N.L. (since 1900)—.306 in 1908
A.L.—.304 in 1908

AT-BATS

Most at-bats, season
N.L. since 1900 (8 clubs)—43, 891 in 1936
N.L. (10 clubs)—55,449 in 1962
N.L. (12 clubs)—66,700 in 1977
N.L. (14 clubs)—77,711 in 1996
N.L. (16 clubs)—89,011 in 1999
A.L. (8 clubs)—43,747 in 1930
A.L. (10 clubs)—55,239 in 1962
A.L. (12 clubs)—66,276 in 1973
A.L. (14 clubs)—79,090 in 1996

Fewest at-bats, season
N.L. since 1900 (8 clubs)—38,005 in 1903 (33,780 in shortened 1918 season)
N.L. (10 clubs)—54,803 in 1963
N.L. (12 clubs)—65,156 in 1978 (43,654 in shortened 1981 season)
N.L. (14 clubs)—77,203 in 1997 (55,068 in shortened 1994 season)
N.L. (16 clubs)—87,794 in 2002
A.L. (8 clubs)—37,434 in 1903 (33,535 in shortened 1918)

A.L. (10 clubs)—54,082 in 1966
A.L. (12 clubs)—64, 641 in 1971 (61,712 in shortened 1972 season)
A.L. (14 clubs)—76,411 in 1978 (50,813 in shortened 1981 season)

Most players with 600 or more at-bats, season
A.L.—22 in 1998
N.L. (since 1900)—19 in 1962

RUNS

Most runs, season
N.L. since 1900 (8 clubs)—7,025 in 1930
N.L. (10 clubs)—7,278 in 1962
N.L. (12 clubs)—8,771 in 1970, 1987
N.L. (14 clubs)—10,623 in 1996
N.L. (16 clubs)—12,976 in 2000
A.L. (8 clubs)—7,009 in 1936
A.L. (10 clubs)—7,342 in 1961
A.L. (12 clubs)—8,314 in 1973
A.L. (14 clubs)—12,208 in 1996

Fewest runs, season
N.L. since 1900 (8 clubs)—4,136 in 1908
N.L. (10 clubs)—5,577 in 1968
N.L. (12 clubs)—7,522 in 1988 (5,035 in shortened 1981 season)
N.L. (14 clubs)—10,190 in 1993 (7,422 in shortened 1994 season)
N.L. (16 clubs)—11,516 in 2002
A.L. (8 clubs)—4,272 in 1909
A.L. (10 clubs)—5,532 in 1968
A.L. (12 clubs)—7,472 in 1971 (6,441 in shortened 1972 season)
A.L. (14 clubs)—9,509 in 1978 (6,112 in shortened 1981 season)

Most players with 100 or more runs, season
N.L. (since 1900)—31 in 1999
A.L.—29 in 1999

Most runs in league, one day
N.L.—159—August 7, 1894
N.L. (since 1900)—123—August 18, 1995
A.L.—128—May 30, 1932

Most runs by both leagues, one day
221 on July 3, 1999; 111 in N.L. (9 games); 110 in A.L. (8 games)

Most players scoring five or more runs in a game, season
N.L. (since 1900)—7 in 1930
A.L.—5 in 1939

Most games with 20 or more runs, league
N.L.—1876 to date—264
N.L. —1900 to date—100
A.L.—1901 to date—107

Most games with 20 or more runs, season
N.L.—32 in 1894
N.L. (since 1900)—5 in 1900, 1925
A.L.—5 in 1923, 1999, 2000

Most games with 10 or more runs, season
N.L.—447 in 1894
N.L. (since 1900)—287 in 2000
A.L.—287 in 2000

Most innings with 10 or more runs, season
N.L.—12 in 1894
N.L. (since 1900)—6 in 1922
A.L.—7 in 1999

HITS

Most hits, season
N.L. since 1900 (8 clubs)—13,260 in 1930
N.L. (10 clubs)—14,453 in 1962
N.L. (12 clubs)—17,465 in 1977
N.L. (14 clubs)—20,427 in 1993
N.L. (16 clubs)—23,880 in 1999
A.L. (8 clubs)—12,657 in 1962
A.L. (10 clubs)—14,068 in 1962
A.L. (12 clubs)—17,193 in 1973
A.L. (14 clubs)—21,922 in 1996

Fewest hits, season
N.L. since 1900 (8 clubs)—9,566 in 1907 (8,583 in shortened 1918 season)
N.L. (10 clubs)—13,351 in 1968
N.L. (12 clubs)—16,215 in 1989 (11,141 in shortened 1981 season)
N.L. (14 clubs)—20,300 in 1997 (14,695 in shortened 1994 season)
N.L. (16 clubs)—22,753 in 2002
A.L. (8 clubs)—9,553 in 1903 (8,502 in shortened 1918 season)
A.L. (10 clubs)—12,359 in 1968
A.L. (12 clubs)—15,957 in 1971 (14,751 in shortened 1972 season)
A.L. (14 clubs)—19,900 in 1990 (13,016 in shortened 1981 season)

Most players with 200 or more hits, season
N.L.—12 in 1929 and 1930
A.L.—9 in 1936 and 1937

Most players with five or more hits in a game, season
N.L. (since 1900)—27 in 1930
A.L.—22 in 1936

Fewest players with five or more hits in a game, season
N.L. (since 1900)—1 in 1914
A.L.—2 in 1913, 1914, 1963

Most hits in league, one day
A.L.—190, July 10, 1932
N.L.—183, July 21, 1963.

Most hits by both leagues, one day
347 on July 3, 1999; 177 in N.L. (9 games); 170 in A.L. (8 games)

SINGLES

Most singles, season
N.L. since 1900 (8 clubs)—9,476 in 1922
N.L. (10 clubs)—10,476 in 1962
N.L. (12 clubs)—12,564 in 1980
N.L. (14 clubs)—14,370 in 1993
N.L. (16 clubs)—15,856 in 1999
A.L. (8 clubs)—9,214 in 1921
A.L. (10 clubs)—9,878 in 1962
A.L. (12 clubs)—12,729 in 1974
A.L. (14 clubs)—15,072 in 1980

Fewest singles, season
N.L. since 1900 (8 clubs)—7,466 in 1956 (6,850 in shortened 1918 season)
N.L. (10 clubs)—9,796 in 1963
N.L. (12 clubs)—11,536 in 1989 (8,187 in shortened 1981 season)
N.L. (14 clubs)—13,745 in 1997 (10,002 in shortened 1994 season)
N.L. (16 clubs)—14,974 in 2001
A.L. (8 clubs)—7,202 in 1903 (6,792 in shortened 1918 season)
A.L. (10 clubs)—9,043 in 1968
A.L. (12 clubs)—11,696 in 1971 (11,000 in shortened 1972 season)
A.L. (14 clubs)—13,404 in 2002 (9,530 in shortened 1981 season)

DOUBLES

Most doubles, season
N.L.N.L. since 1900 (8 clubs)—2,386 in 1930
N.L. (10 clubs)—2,161 in 1964
N.L. (12 clubs)—3,126 in 1987
N.L. (14 clubs)—3,907 in 1997
N.L. (16 clubs)—4,687 in 2004
A.L. (8 clubs)—2,400 in 1936
A.L. (10 clubs)—2,238 in 1962
A.L. (12 clubs)—2,662 in 1975
A.L. (14 clubs)—4,269 in 2000

Fewest doubles, season
N.L. since 1900 (8 clubs)—1,148 in 1907 (1,119 in shortened 1918 season)
N.L. (10 clubs)—1,984 in 1963
N.L. (12 clubs)—2,455 in 1969 (1,881 in shortened 1981 season)
N.L. (14 clubs)—3,588 in 1993 (2,784 in shortened 1994 season)
N.L. (16 clubs)—4,482 in 2002
A.L. (8 clubs)—1,272 in 1909 (1,204 in shortened 1918 season)
A.L. (10 clubs)—1,874 in 1968
A.L. (12 clubs)—2,385 in 1969 (2,260 in shortened 1972 season)
A.L. (14 clubs)—3,325 in 1978 (2,119 in shortened 1981 season)

Most players with 40 or more doubles, season
A.L.—15 in 2000
N.L.—12 in 1920

TRIPLES

Most triples, season
N.L. since 1900 (8 clubs)—684 in 1912
N.L. (10 clubs)—453 in 1962
N.L. (12 clubs)—554 in 1970
N.L. (14 clubs)—513 in 1993
N.L. (16 clubs)—532 in 2000
A.L. (8 clubs)—694 in 1921
A.L. (10 clubs)—408 in 1966
A.L. (12 clubs)—467 in 1976
A.L. (14 clubs)—644 in 1977

Fewest triples, season
N.L. since 1900 (8 clubs)—323 in 1942
N.L. (10 clubs)—359 in 1968
N.L. (12 clubs)—386 in 1973 (354 in shortened 1981 season)
N.L. (14 clubs)—434 in 1996 (377 in shortened 1994 season)
N.L. (16 clubs)—488 in 2001, 2002
A.L. (8 clubs)—267 in 1959
A.L. (10 clubs)—333 in 1964
A.L. (12 clubs)—351 in 1971 (316 in shortened 1972 season)
A.L. (14 clubs)—386 in 1992 (305 in shortened 1981 season)

Most players with 20 or more triples
N.L. (since 1900)—3 in 1911, 1912
A.L.—4 in 1912

HOME RUNS
SEASON

Most home runs, season
N.L. since 1900 (8 clubs)—1,263 in 1955
N.L. (10 clubs)—1,449 in 1962
N.L. (12 clubs)—1,824 in 1987
N.L. (14 clubs)—2,220 in 1996
N.L. (16 clubs)—3,005 in 2000
A.L. (8 clubs)—1,091 in 1959
A.L. (10 clubs)—1,552 in 1962
A.L. (12 clubs)—1,746 in 1970
A.L. (14 clubs)—2,742 in 1996

Most home runs by both leagues, season
5,693 in 2000 (16-club N.L., 14-club A.L.)—3,005 in N.L., 2,688 in A.L.
4,962 in 1996 (14-club leagues)—2,742 in A.L., 2,220 in N.L.
4,458 in 1987 (14-club A.L., 12-club N.L.)—2,634 in A.L., 1,824 in N.L.
3,429 in 1970 (12-club leagues)—1,746 in A.L., 1,683 in N.L.
3,001 in 1962 (10-club leagues)—1,552 in A.L., 1,449 in N.L.

Fewest home runs, season
N.L. since 1900 (8 clubs)—96 in 1902
N.L. (10 clubs)—891 in 1963
N.L. (12 clubs)—1,113 in 1976 (719 in shortened 1981 season)
N.L. (14 clubs)—1,956 in 1993 (1,532 in in shortened 1994 season)
N.L. (16 clubs)—2,565 in 1998
A.L. (8 clubs)—104 in 1907 (96 in shortened 1918 season)
A.L. (10 clubs)—1,104 in 1968
A.L. (12 clubs)—1,122 in 1976
A.L. (14 clubs)—1,680 in 1978 (1,062 in shortened 1981 season)

Most home runs by pinch-hitters, season
N.L. since 1900 (8 clubs)—42 in 1958
N.L. (10 clubs)—45 in 1962
N.L. (12 clubs)—57 in 1986
N.L. (14 clubs)—75 in 1995
N.L. (16 clubs)—95 in 2001
A.L. (8 clubs)—29 in 1953
A.L. (10 clubs)—50 in 1961
A.L. (12 clubs)—24 in 1975
A.L. (14 clubs)—53 in 1980

Most home runs by pinch-hitters in both leagues, season
133 in 2004 (16-club N.L., 14-club A.L.)—93 in N.L., 40 in A.L.
117 in 1996 (14-club leagues)—74 in N.L., 43 in A.L.
95 in 1970 (12-club leagues)—49 in A.L., 46 in N.L.
84 in 1962 (10-club leagues)—45 in N.L., 39 in A.L.

Most clubs with 100 or more home runs, season
N.L. since 1900 (8 clubs)—8 in 1956, 1958, 1959, 1961
N.L. (10 clubs)—10 in 1962
N.L. (12 clubs)—11 in 1970, 1986, 1987
N.L. (14 clubs)—4 in 1996, 1997
N.L. (16 clubs)—16 in 1998 through 2004
A.L. (8 clubs)—8 in 1958, 1960
A.L. (10 clubs)—10 in 1964
A.L. (12 clubs)—11 in 1970, 1973
A.L. (14 clubs)—14 in 1977, 1982, 1985 through 1988, 1990, 1993, 1995 through 2004

Most players with 50 or more home runs, season
N.L.—3 in 1998, 2001
A.L.—2 in 1938, 1961, 1996, 2002

Most players with 40 or more home runs, season
N.L. (16-clubs)—9 in 2000
A.L. (14-clubs)—8 in 1996, 1998

Most players with 30 or more home runs, season
N.L. (16-clubs)—25 in 2001
A.L. (14-clubs)—23 in 2000

Most players with 20 or more home runs, season
N.L. (16-clubs)—54 in 1999
A.L. (14-clubs)—51 in 1987

Most players hitting home runs in all parks, season (8-club league)
N.L.—11 in 1956 (8 parks; 5 of 11 also hit home runs at Jersey City)
A.L.—7 in 1953 (8 parks)

Most players hitting home runs in all parks, season (10-club league)
A.L.—4 in 1962
N.L.—3 in 1963

Most players hitting home runs in all parks, season (12-club league)
N.L.—3 in 1970
A.L.—1 in 1975

ONE DAY

Most players with two or more home runs in a game, season
N.L. (16-clubs)—201 in 1999
N.L. (14-clubs)—137 in 1996
N.L. (12-clubs)—110 in 1987
N.L. (8-clubs)—84 in 1955
A.L. (14-clubs)—180 in 1996
A.L. (10-clubs)—98 in 1964
A.L. (8-clubs)—62 in 1960

Fewest players with two or more home runs in a game, season
N.L.—0 in 1907, 1918
A.L.—0 in 1908, 1915

Most players with two or more home runs in a game, one day
A.L. (14-clubs)—6—August 2, 1983; May 8, 1987
A.L. (10-clubs)—5—June 11, 1961; May 20, 1962
A.L. (8-clubs)—4—April 30, 1933; May 30, 1956
N.L. (16-clubs)—6—July 31, 1999
N.L. (14-clubs)—5—July 14, 1996
N.L. (12-clubs)—5—May 8, 1970
N.L. (10-clubs)—5—June 5, 1966

N.L. (8-clubs)—5—August 16, 1947

Most players with two home runs in a game, both leagues, one day
9 on July 2, 2002; 5 in A.L., 4 in N.L.

Most players with three or more home runs in a game, season
N.L.—16 in 2001
A.L.—11 in 1996

Most players from both leagues with three homers in a game, season
22 in 2001; 16 in N.L., 6 in A.L.

Most times with five or more home runs in a game, season (club)
N.L. (16-club league)—30 in 1999
N.L. (8-club league)—15 in 1954
A.L. (14-club league)—27 in 1999
A.L. (12-club league)—8 in 1969
A.L. (8-club league)—8 in 1950

Most times with three or more home runs in an inning, season
A.L. (14-clubs)—24 in 2000
A.L. (10-clubs)—10 in 1961, 1962
A.L. (8-clubs)—5 in 1936, 1947, 1953, 1954, 1956, 1957, 1959
N.L. (16-clubs)—21 in 2000
N.L. (14-clubs)—18 in 1996
N.L. (8-clubs)—13 in 1954, 1955

Most home runs by pitchers, one day
A.L.—4—July 31, 1935
N.L.—3—June 3, 1892; May 13, 1942; July 2, 1961; June 23, 1971

Most home runs by pinch-hitters, one day
N.L.—4—June 2, 1928; July 21, 1930
A.L.—4—June 28, 1987

Most home runs in league, one day
A.L.—36—April 7, 2000 (7 games)
N.L.—34—May 21, 2000 (8 games)

Most home runs by both leagues, one day
62—July 2, 2002; 32 in N.L. (8 games), 30 in A.L. (8 games)

GRAND SLAMS

Most grand slams, season
N.L. since 1900 (8 clubs)—35 in 1950
N.L. (10 clubs)—37 in 1962
N.L. (12 clubs)—49 in 1970
N.L. (14 clubs)—60 in 1996
N.L. (16 clubs)—87 in 2000
A.L. (8 clubs)—37 in 1938
A.L. (10 clubs)—48 in 1961
A.L. (12 clubs)—39 in 1970, 1973
A.L. (14 clubs)—89 in 2000

Most grand slams by both leagues, season
176 in 2000 (16-club N.L., 14-club A.L.)—89 in A.L.; 87 in N.L.
141 in 1996 (14-club leagues)—81 in A.L.; 60 in N.L.
88 in 1970 (12-club leagues)—49 in N.L.; 39 in A.L.
77 in 1961 (10-club A.L., 8-club N.L.)—48 in A.L.; 29 in N.L.

Fewest grand slams, season
N.L.(since 1900)—1 in 1920
A.L.—1 in 1907, 1909, 1915 (0 in shortened 1918 season)

Fewest grand slams by both leagues, season
3—1907 (2 in N.L., 1 in A.L.)

Most grand slams by pinch-hitters, season
N.L. since 1900 (8-clubs)—4 in 1959.
A.L. (14-clubs)—5 in 1982, 1988

Most grand slams by pinch-hitters in both leagues, season
(14-club A.L.; 12-club N.L.)—13 in 1978 (9 in N.L.; 4 in A.L.).
(12-club leagues)—9 in 1973 (6 in N.L.; 3 in A.L.).
(8-club leagues)—8 in 1953 (5 in A.L.; 3 in N.L.).

Most grand slams, one day
N.L.—4—May 21, 2000

A.L.—4—July 22, 2000

Most grand slams by both leagues, one day
6—May 21, 2000 (4 in N.L., 2 in A.L.)

TOTAL BASES

Most total bases, season
N.L. since 1900 (8 clubs)—19,572 in 1930
N.L. (10 clubs)—21,781 in 1962
N.L. (12 clubs)—26,743 in 1987
N.L. (14 clubs)—31,708 in 1996
N.L. (16 clubs)—38,305 in 2000
A.L. (8 clubs)—18,427 in 1936
A.L. (10 clubs)—21,762 in 1962
A.L. (12 clubs)—25,281 in 1973
A.L. (14 clubs)—35,195 in 1996

Most players with 300 or more total bases, season
N.L. since 1900—20 in 1999, 2001
A.L.—22 in 2000

Most players with 400 or more total bases, season
N.L. since 1900—4 in 2001
A.L.—2 in 1927, 1936

EXTRA BASE HITS

Most extra base hits, season
N.L. since 1900 (8 clubs)—3,903 in 1930
N.L. (10 clubs)—3,977 in 1962
N.L. (12 clubs)—5,385 in 1987
N.L. (14 clubs)—6,555 in 1997
N.L. (16 clubs)—8,169 in 2000
A.L. (8 clubs)—3,706 in 1936
A.L. (10 clubs)—4,190 in 1962
A.L. (12 clubs)—4,611 in 1970
A.L. (14 clubs)—7,377 in 2000

RUNS BATTED IN

Most runs batted in, season
N.L. since 1900 (8 clubs)—6,582 in 1930
N.L. (10 clubs)—6,760 in 1962
N.L. (12 clubs)—8,233 in 1987
N.L. (14 clubs)—9,987 in 1996
N.L. (16 clubs)—12,321 in 1999
A.L. (8 clubs)—6,520 in 1936
A.L. (10 clubs)—6,842 in 1961
A.L. (12 clubs)—7,769 in 1973
A.L. (14 clubs)—11,583 in 1996

Most players with 100 or more runs batted in, season
N.L.—27 in 1999
A.L.—32 in 1999

BASES ON BALLS

Most bases on balls, season
N.L. since 1900 (8 clubs)—4,537 in 1950
N.L. (10 clubs)—5,265 in 1962
N.L. (12 clubs)—6,919 in 1970
N.L. (14 clubs)—7,704 in 1997
N.L. (16 clubs)—9,735 in 2000
A.L. (8 clubs)—5,627 in 1949
A.L. (10 clubs)—5,902 in 1961
A.L. (12 clubs)—7,032 in 1969
A.L. (14 clubs)—8,592 in 1996

Fewest bases on balls, season (since 1900)
N.L. since 1900 (8 clubs)—2,906 in 1921
N.L. (10 clubs)—4,275 in 1968
N.L. (12 clubs)—2,906 in 1921
N.L. (14 clubs)—7,104 in 1993 (5,193 in shortened 1994 season)
N.L. (16 clubs)—8,567 in 2001
A.L. (8 clubs)—3,797 in 1922
A.L. (10 clubs)—4,881 in 1968
A.L. (12 clubs)—6,128 in 1976
A.L. (14 clubs)—7,094 in 1983 (4,761 in shortened 1981 season)

Most players with 100 or more bases on balls, season
A.L.—10 in 2000
N.L.—8 in 2002

INTENTIONAL (SINCE 1955)

Most intentional bases on balls, season
N.L. since 1900 (8 clubs)—504 in 1956
N.L. (10 clubs)—804 in 1967
N.L. (12 clubs)—862 in 1973
N.L. (14 clubs)—743 in 1993
N.L. (16 clubs)—964 in 2002
A.L. (8 clubs)—353 in 1957
A.L. (10 clubs)—534 in 1965
A.L. (12 clubs)—668 in 1969
A.L. (14 clubs)—734 in 1993

Fewest intentional bases on balls, season
N.L. since 1900 (8 clubs)—387 in 1957
N.L. (10 clubs)—452 in 1962
N.L. (12 clubs)—626 in 1991 (505 in shortened 1981 season)
N.L. (14 clubs)—629 in 1997 (559 in shortened 1994 season)
N.L. (16 clubs)—647 in 1998
A.L. (8 clubs)—257 in 1959
A.L. (10 clubs)—290 in 1961
A.L. (12 clubs)—471 in 1976
A.L. (14 clubs)—420 in 1998

STRIKEOUTS

Most strikeouts, season
N.L. since 1900 (8 clubs)—6,824 in 1960
N.L. (10 clubs)—9,649 in 1965
N.L. (12 clubs)—11,657 in 1987
N.L. (14 clubs)—15,320 in 1997
N.L. (16 clubs)—17,908 in 2001
A.L. (8 clubs)—6,081 in 1959
A.L. (10 clubs)—9,956 in 1964
A.L. (12 clubs)—10,957 in 1970
A.L. (14 clubs)—14,617 in 1997

Fewest strikeouts, season
N.L. since 1900 (8 clubs)—3,359 in 1926
N.L. (10 clubs)—9,032 in 1962
N.L. (12 clubs)—9,602 in 1976
N.L. (14 clubs)—13,358 in 1993
N.L. (16 clubs)—16,996 in 2003
A.L. (8 clubs)—3,245 in 1924
A.L. (10 clubs)—8,330 in 1961
A.L. (12 clubs)—9,143 in 1976
A.L. (14 clubs)—10,115 in 1979 (6,905 in shortened 1981 season)

Most players with 100 or more strikeouts, season
N.L.—42 in 2001
A.L.—38 in 1997

SACRIFICE HITS AND FLIES

Most sacrifices including scoring flies, season
N.L. since 1900—1,655 in 1908
A.L.—1,731 in 1917

Most sacrifices with no sacrifice flies, season
N.L. since 1900—1,349 in 1907
A.L.—1,401 in 1906

Fewest sacrifices with no sacrifice flies, season
N.L since 1900—510 in 1957

A.L.—531 in 1958

Most sacrifice flies, season
N.L. since 1900 (8 clubs)—425 in 1954
N.L. (10 clubs)—410 in 1962
N.L. (12 clubs)—589 in 1988
N.L. (14 clubs)—701 in 1993
N.L. (16 clubs)—809 in 2000
A.L. (8 clubs)—370 in 1954
A.L. (10 clubs)—448 in 1961
A.L. (12 clubs)—624 in 1976
A.L. (14 clubs)—765 in 1979

Fewest sacrifice flies, season
N.L. since 1900 (8 clubs)—304 in 1959
N.L. (10 clubs)—363 in 1966
N.L. (12 clubs)—430 in 1969
N.L. (14 clubs)—643 in 1997
N.L. (16 clubs)—660 in 2003
A.L. (8 clubs)—312 in 1959
A.L. (10 clubs)—348 in 1967
A.L. (12 clubs)—484 in 1969
A.L. (14 clubs)—629 in 1987

HIT BY PITCH

Most hit by pitch, season
N.L. since 1900 (8 clubs)—415 in 1903
N.L. (10 clubs)—404 in 1965
N.L. (12 clubs)—43 in 1969
N.L. (14 clubs)—773 in 1997
N.L. (16 clubs)—969 in 2001
A.L. (8 clubs)—454 in 1911
A.L. (10 clubs)—426 in 1968
A.L. (12 clubs)—441 in 1969
A.L. (14 clubs)—921 in 2001

Fewest hit by pitch, season
N.L. since 1900 (8 clubs)—157 in 1943
N.L. (10 clubs)—327 in 1964
N.L. (12 clubs)—249 in 1984 (185 in shortened 1981 season)
N.L. (14 clubs)—567 in 1993 (451 in shortened 1994 season)
N.L. (16 clubs)—799 in 1999
A.L. (8 clubs)—132 in 1947
A.L. (10 clubs)—316 in 1965
A.L. (12 clubs)—374 in 1976
A.L. (14 clubs)—372 in 1982

GROUNDING INTO DOUBLE PLAYS

Most grounding into double plays, season
N.L. since 1900 (8 clubs)—1,105 in 1958
N.L. (10 clubs)—1,251 in 1962
N.L. (12 clubs)—1,547 in 1971
N.L. (14 clubs)—1,699 in 1996
N.L. (16 clubs)—2,085 in 2002
A.L. (8 clubs)—1,181 in 1950
A.L. (10 clubs)—1,256 in 1961
A.L. (12 clubs)—1,608 in 1973
A.L. (14 clubs)—1,968 in 1980

Fewest grounding into double plays, season
N.L. since 1900 (8 clubs)—820 in 1945
N.L. (10 clubs)—1,117 in 1963
N.L. (12 clubs)—1,198 in 1991 (962 in shortened 1981 season)
N.L. (14 clubs)—1,638 in 1993 (1,206 in shortened 1994 season)
N.L. (16 clubs)—1,925 in 2001
A.L. (8 clubs)—890 in 1945
A.L. (10 clubs)—1,060 in 1967
A.L. (12 clubs)—1,442 in 1976
A.L. (14 clubs)—1,708 in 1978 (1,236 in shortened 1994 season)

INDIVIDUAL BASERUNNING

STOLEN BASES

Most stolen bases, career
M.L.—1,406—Rickey Henderson, Oakland A.L., New York A.L., Toronto A.L., San Diego N.L., Anaheim A.L., New York N.L., Seattle A.L., Boston A.L., Los Angeles N.L., 25 years, 1979 through 2003 (1,270 in A.L., 136 in N.L.).
A.L.—1,270—Rickey Henderson, Oakland, New York, Toronto, Anaheim, Seattle, Boston, 21 years, 1979 through 2002, except 1996, 1999 and 2001.
N.L.—938—Lou Brock, Chicago, St. Louis, 19 years, 1961 through 1979.

For a complete list of players with 400 or more career stolen bases, see page 158.

Highest stolen base percentage, career (minimum 300 attempts)
M.L.—.847—Tim Raines Sr., Montreal N.L., Chicago A.L., New York A.L., Oakland A.L., Baltimore A.L., Florida N.L., 1979 through 2002.
N.L.—.857—Tim Raines Sr., Montreal, Florida, 1979 through 1990, 2001, 2002.
A.L.—.833—Willie Wilson, Kansas City, Oakland, 1976 through 1992.

Most consecutive stolen bases with no caught stealing, career
N.L.—50—Vince Coleman, St. Louis, September 18, 1988 through July 26, 1989.
A.L.—40—Tim Raines Sr., Chicago, July 23, 1993 through August 4, 1995.

Most stolen bases, season
A.A.—156—Harry Stovey, Philadelphia, 130 games, 1888.
A.L.—130—Rickey Henderson, Oakland, 149 games, 1982 (42 caught stealing).
N.L.—118—Lou Brock, St. Louis, 153 games, 1974 (33 caught stealing).

For complete lists of players combining power and speed (40 HRs, 40 SBs; 30 HRs, 30 SBs; 50 HRs, 20 SBs and 20 HRs, 50 SBs) during a season, see page 168.

Most stolen bases by rookie, season
N.L.—110—Vince Coleman, St. Louis, 151 games, 1985.
A.A.—98—Mike Griffin, Baltimore, 136 games, 1887.
A.L.—66—Kenny Lofton, Cleveland, 148 games, 1992.

Most stolen bases with no caught stealing, season
N.L.—21—Kevin McReynolds, New York, 147 games, 1988.
A.L.—20—Paul Molitor, Toronto, 115 games, 1994.

Most seasons leading league in stolen bases
A.L.—12—Rickey Henderson, Oakland, New York, 1980 through 1991, except 1987; 1998.
N.L.—10—Max Carey, Pittsburgh, 1913, 1915, 1916, 1917, 1918, 1920, 1922, 1923, 1924, 1925.

Most consecutive seasons leading league in stolen bases
A.L.—9—Luis Aparicio, Chicago, Baltimore, 1956 through 1964.
N.L.—6—Maury Wills, Los Angeles, 1960 through 1965.
Vince Coleman, St. Louis, 1985 through 1990.

Most seasons with 50 or more stolen bases
A.L.—13—Rickey Henderson, Oakland, New York, Toronto, 1980 through 1993, except 1987 and 1992; 1998.
N.L.—12—Lou Brock, St. Louis, 1965 through 1976.

Most consecutive seasons with 50 or more stolen bases
N.L.—12—Lou Brock, St. Louis, 1965 through 1976.
A.L.—7—Rickey Henderson, Oakland, New York, 1980 through 1986.

Fewest stolen bases for leader, season
A.L.—15—Dom DiMaggio, Boston, 141 games, 1950.
N.L.—16—Stan Hack, Chicago, 152 games, 1938.

Most at-bats with no stolen bases, season
A.L.—677—Don Mattingly, New York, 162 games, 1986 (0 caught stealing).
N.L.—662—Pete Rose, Cincinnati, 162 games, 1975 (1 caught stealing).

Most seasons with no stolen bases (150 or more games)
M.L.—5—John Olerud, Toronto A.L., New York N.L., Seattle A.L., 1993, 1997, 2000, 2002, 2003 (4 in A.L., 1 in N.L.).
A.L.—4—Ken Singleton, Baltimore, 1977, 1980, 1982, 1983.
Cecil Fielder, Detroit A.L., 1990, 1991, 1992, 1993.
John Olerud, Toronto, Seattle A.L., 1993, 2000, 2002, 2003.
N.L.—3—Dal Maxvill, St. Louis, 1967, 1968, 1970.
Deron Johnson, Cincinnati, Philadelphia, 1965, 1970, 1971.

Most stolen bases, game
N.L.—7—George Gore, Chicago, June 25, 1881.*
Billy Hamilton, Philadelphia, August 31, 1894, second game.
A.L.—6—Eddie Collins, Philadelphia, September 11, 1912; also September 22, 1912, first game.
N.L. since 1900—6—Otis Nixon, Atlanta, June 16, 1991.
Eric Young, Colorado, June 30, 1996.
*Stolen bases not officially compiled until 1886.

Most stolen bases, two consecutive games
N.L.—8—Walt Wilmot, Chicago, August 6 (4), August 7 (4), 1894.
A.L.—7—Eddie Collins, Philadelphia, September 10 (1), September 11 (6), 1912.
Amos Otis, Kansas City, April 30 (3), May 1 (4), 1975, 13 innings.
Rickey Henderson, Oakland, July 3 (4), 15 innings; July 4 (3), 1983.
Rickey Henderson, New York, August 11 (4), 11 innings; August 12 (3), 1988.
Alex Cole, Cleveland, August 1 (5), 3 (2), 1990.

Most stolen bases, inning
N.L.—3—Held by many players. Last player—Eric Young, Colorado, June 30, 1996, third inning.
A.L.—3—Held by many players. Last player—Chris Stynes, Kansas City, May 12, 1996, first inning.

Most stolen bases by pinch-runner, inning
N.L.—2—Bill O'Hara, New York, September 1, 1909, sixth inning.
Bill O'Hara, New York, September 2, 1909, ninth inning.
Sandy Piez, New York, July 6, 1914, second game, ninth inning.
Jake Pitler, Pittsburgh, May 24, 1918, ninth inning.
Dave Concepcion, Cincinnati, July 7, 1974, first game, seventh inning.
Rodney Scott, Montreal, September 19, 1976, first game, eighth inning.
Ron LeFlore, Montreal, October 5, 1980, eighth inning.
Jerry Royster, Atlanta, May 7, 1981, eighth inning.
Bob Dernier, Philadelphia, July 30, 1983, first game, ninth inning.
Gary Redus, Cincinnati, July 25, 1985, eighth inning.
Eric Davis, Cincinnati, July 22, 1986, 10th inning.
Chris Sabo, Cincinnati, April 12, 1988, ninth inning.
Eric Davis, Cincinnati, May 6, 1988, ninth inning.
A.L.—2—Ray Dowd, Philadelphia, July 9, 1919, second game, ninth inning.
Allan Lewis, Kansas City, July 15, 1967, seventh inning.
Tommy Harper, Cleveland, September 27, 1968, ninth inning.
Bert Campaneris, Oakland, October 4, 1972, fourth inning.
Don Hopkins, Oakland, April 20, 1975, second game, seventh inning.
Claudell Washington, Oakland, June 13, 1976, eighth inning.
Matt Alexander, Oakland, August 8, 1976, second game, eighth inning.
Bert Campaneris, Texas, September 3, 1978, eighth inning.
Bert Campaneris, Texas, September 6, 1978, first game, seventh inning.
Bert Campaneris, California, August 25, 1981, eighth inning.
Billy Sample, Texas, April 29, 1984, ninth inning.
Alfredo Griffin, Toronto, August 27, 1984, ninth inning.
Otis Nixon, Cleveland, August 19, 1985, eighth inning.
Otis Nixon, Cleveland, August 18, 1986, seventh inning.
Gary Pettis, Detroit, June 28, 1989, second inning.
Sammy Sosa, Chicago, September 4, 1990, eighth inning.

Appearing as a pinch-runner and pinch-hitter in the same game (different innings)
A.L.—Pat Collins, St. Louis, June 8, 1923 (pinch-runner in third inning, pinch-hitter in ninth inning).
N.L.—none.

STEALS OF HOME

Most times stole home, career
A.L.—50—Ty Cobb, Detroit, Philadelphia, 24 years, 1905 through 1928.
N.L.—33—Max Carey, Pittsburgh, Brooklyn, 20 years, 1910 through 1929.

Most times stole home, season
A.L.—8—Ty Cobb, Detroit, 140 games, 1912 (61 stolen bases).
N.L.—7—Pete Reiser, Brooklyn, 122 games, 1946 (34 stolen bases).

Most times stole way from first to home in an inning, career
A.L.—4—Ty Cobb, Detroit, 1909, 1911, 1912 (2).
N.L.—3—Honus Wagner, Pittsburgh, 1902, 1907, 1909.
N.L.—Last player—Eric Young, Colorado, June 30, 1996, third inning.
A.L.—Last player—Chris Stynes, Kansas City, May 12, 1996, first inning.

Most times stole home, game
N.L.—2—Honus Wagner, Pittsburgh, June 20, 1901.
Ed Konetchy, St. Louis, September 30, 1907.
Joe Tinker, Chicago, June 28, 1910.
Larry Doyle, New York, September 18, 1911.
Sherry Magee, Philadelphia, July 20, 1912.
Doc Gautreau, Boston, September 3, 1927, first game.
A.L.—2—Joe Jackson, Cleveland, August 11, 1912.
Guy Zinn, New York, August 15, 1912.
Eddie Collins, Philadelphia, September 6, 1913.
Bill Barrett, Chicago, May 1, 1924.
(2—Vic Power, Cleveland, August 14, 1958, 10 innings.)

CAUGHT STEALING

Most caught stealing, career
M.L.—335—Rickey Henderson, Oakland A.L., New York A.L., Toronto A.L., San Diego N.L., Anaheim A.L., New York N.L., Seattle A.L., Boston A.L., Los Angeles N.L., 25 years, 1979 through 2003 (293 in A.L., 42 in N.L.).
N.L.—307—Lou Brock, Chicago, St. Louis, 19 years, 1061 through 1979.
A.L.—293—Rickey Henderson, Oakland, New York, Toronto, Anaheim, Seattle, Boston, 21 years, 1979 through 2002, except 1996, 1999 and 2001.

Most caught stealing, season
A.L.—42—Rickey Henderson, Oakland, 149 games, 1982 (130 stolen bases).
N.L.—36—Miller Huggins, St. Louis, 148 games, 1914 (32 stolen bases).

Most caught stealing by rookie, season
N.L.—25—Vince Coleman, St. Louis, 151 games, 1985 (110 stolen bases).
A.L.—21—Mike Edwards, Oakland, 142 games, 1978 (27 stolen bases).

Most seasons leading league in caught stealing
N.L.—7—Maury Wills, Los Angeles, Pittsburgh, Montreal, 1961, 1962 (tied), 1963, 1965, 1966, 1968, 1969.
Lou Brock, Chicago, St. Louis, 1964, 1967, 1971, 1973, 1974, 1976, 1977 (tied).
A.L.—6—Minnie Minoso, Chicago, Cleveland, 1952, 1953, 1954, 1957, 1958, 1960.

Fewest caught stealing with 50 or more stolen bases, season
N.L.—2—Max Carey, Pittsburgh, 155 games, 1922 (51 stolen bases).
A.L.—8—Luis Aparicio, Chicago, 153 games, 1960 (51 stolen bases).
Bert Campaneris, Oakland, 135 games, 1969 (62 stolen bases).
Amos Otis, Kansas City, 147 games, 1971 (52 stolen bases).
Willie Wilson, Kansas City, 137 games, 1983 (59 stolen bases).
Rickey Henderson, Oakland, Toronto, 134 games, 1993 (53 stolen bases).

Vince Coleman, Kansas City, 104 games, 1994 (50 stolen bases).

Fewest caught stealing, season (150 or more games)
N.L.-A.L.—0—Held by many players.

Fewest caught stealing for leader, season
A.L.—9—Hoot Evers, Detroit, 143 games, 1950 (5 stolen bases).
Jim Rivera, Chicago, 139 games, 1956 (20 stolen bases).
N.L.—10—Willie Mays, New York, 152 games, 1956 (40 stolen bases).

Most consecutive games with no caught stealing, career
M.L.—1,206—Gus Triandos, New York A.L., Baltimore A.L., Detroit A.L., Philadelphia N.L., Houston N.L., August 3, 1953 through August 15, 1965 (1 stolen base).
A.L.—1,079—Gus Triandos, New York, Baltimore, Detroit, August 3, 1953 through September 28, 1963 (1 stolen base).
N.L.—592—Frank Torre, Milwaukee, Philadelphia, April 20, 1956 through August 10, 1962 (4 stolen bases).

Most caught stealing, game
N.L..—3—Held by many players.
(4—Robby Thompson, San Francisco, June 27, 1986, 12 innings.)
A.L.—3—Held by many players.

Most caught stealing, inning
A.L.—2—Don Baylor, Baltimore, June 15, 1974, ninth inning.
Roberto Kelly, New York, April 17, 1990, second inning.
N.L.—2—Jim Morrison, Pittsburgh, June 15, 1987, eighth inning.
Paul Noce, Chicago, June 26, 1987, third inning.
Donell Nixon, San Francisco, July 6, 1988, sixth inning.
Tony Fernandez, San Diego, June 26, 1992, fifth inning.
Eric Young, Colorado, May 1, 1993, eighth inning.
Phil Plantier, San Diego, September 25, 1993, fifth inning.
Derek Bell, Houston, June 19, 1995, fourth inning.
Larry Walker, Colorado, April 30, 1998, eighth inning.

LEFT ON BASE

Most runners left on base, game
N.L.—12—Glenn Beckert, Chicago, September 16, 1972.
Todd Helton, Colorado, April 11, 1998.
A.L.—11—Frank Isbell, Chicago, August 10, 1901.
(11—John Donahue, Chicago, June 23, 1907, 12 innings.)
George Wright, Texas, August 12, 1984, 11 innings.)

Most times out for being hit by batted ball, nine-inning game
N.L.—2—Walt Wilmot, Chicago, September 30, 1890.
A.L.—2—Ernie Shore, Boston, July 28, 1917, second game.

CLUB BASERUNNING

STOLEN BASES

Most stolen bases, season
A.A.—638—Philadelphia, 137 games, 1887.
N.L.—426—New York, 136 games, 1893.
N.L. since 1900—347—New York, 154 games, 1911.
A.L.—341—Oakland, 161 games, 1976.

Most players with 50 or more stolen bases, season
A.L.—3—Oakland, 161 games, 1976. Bill North (75), Bert Campaneris (54), Don Baylor (52).
N.L.—3—San Diego, 163 games, 1980. Gene Richards (61), Ozzie Smith (57), Jerry Mumphrey (52).

Most seasons leading league in stolen bases
A.L.—30—Chicago, 1901 through 1904, 1917, 1919, 1923, 1924, 1926, 1928, 1929, 1939, 1941, 1942, 1943, 1946, 1947, 1949, 1951 through 1961, 1966.
N.L. since 1900—21—Brooklyn/Los Angeles, 1903, 1938, 1942, 1946 through 1953, 1955, 1958 through 1965, 1970 (12 Bkn., 9 L.A.).
St. Louis, 1927, 1931 through 1934, 1936, 1937, 1940, 1954, 1966, 1967, 1971, 1974, 1982 through 1988, 1992.

Fewest stolen bases, season
A.L.—13—Washington, 154 games, 1957.
N.L.—17—St. Louis, 157 games, 1949.

Most stolen bases, game
A.A.—19—Philadelphia vs. Syracuse, April 22, 1890.
N.L.—17—New York vs. Pittsburgh, May 23, 1890.
A.L.—15—New York vs. St. Louis, September 28, 1911.
N.L. since 1900—11—New York vs. Boston, June 20, 1912.
St. Louis vs. Pittsburgh, August 13, 1916, second game, five innings.

Most stolen bases by both clubs, game
A.A.—21—Philadelphia 19, Syracuse 2, April 22, 1890.
N.L.—20—New York 17, Pittsburgh 3, May 23, 1890.
N.L. since 1900—14—New York 9, Boston 5, June 20, 1912.
A.L.—15—New York 15, St. Louis 0, September 28, 1911.
St. Louis 8, Detroit 7, October 1, 1916.

Most triple steals, game
A.L.—2—Philadelphia vs. Cleveland, July 25, 1930, first and fourth innings.
N.L.—1—Made in many games.

Most triples steals by both clubs, game
A.L.—2—Philadelphia 2, Cleveland 0, July 25, 1930.

N.L.—1—Made in many games.

Longest game without a stolen base
N.L.—26 innings—Boston vs. Brooklyn, May 1, 1920.
A.L.—24 innings—Detroit vs. Philadelphia, July 21, 1945.
Philadelphia vs. Detroit, July 21, 1945.

Longest game without a stolen base by either club
A.L.—24 innings—Detroit 0, Philadelphia 0, July 21, 1945.
N.L.—23 innings—San Francisco 0, New York 0, May 31, 1964, second game.

Most stolen bases, inning
A.L.—8—Washington vs. Cleveland, July 19, 1915, first inning.
N.L.—8—Philadelphia vs. New York, July 7, 1919, first game, ninth inning.

STEALS OF HOME

Most times stole home, season
A.L.—18—New York, 153 games, 1912 (245 stolen bases).
N.L.—17—Chicago, 157 games, 1911 (214 stolen bases).
New York, 154 games, 1912 (319 stolen bases).

Most times stole home, game
N.L.—3—St. Louis vs. Boston, September 30, 1907.
Chicago vs. Boston, August 23, 1909.
New York vs. Pittsburgh, September 18, 1911.
A.L.—3—Chicago vs. St. Louis, July 2, 1909.
New York vs. Philadelphia, April 17, 1915.

Most times stole home by both clubs, game
A.L.—3—Chicago 3, St. Louis 0, July 2, 1909.
New York 3, Philadelphia 0, April 17, 1915.
Detroit 2, St. Louis 1, April 22, 1924.
N.L.—3—St. Louis 3, Boston 0, September 30, 1907.
Chicago 3, Boston 0, August 23, 1909.
New York 3, Pittsburgh 0, September 18, 1911.

Most times stole home, inning
N.L.—2—Made in many innings. Last time—St. Louis vs. Brooklyn, September 19, 1925, seventh inning.
A.L.—2—Made in many innings. Last time—Oakland vs. Kansas City, May 28, 1980, first inning.

CAUGHT STEALING

Most caught stealing, season (since 1920)
N.L.—149—Chicago, 154 games, 1924.

A.L.—123—Oakland, 161 games, 1976.

Fewest caught stealing, season
N.L.—8—Milwaukee, 154 games, 1958 (26 stolen bases).
A.L.—11—Kansas City, 155 games, 1960 (16 stolen bases).
Cleveland, 161 games, 1961 (34 stolen bases).

Most caught stealing, game
N.L.—8—Baltimore vs. Washington, May 11, 1897.
N.L. since 1900—6—St. Louis vs. Brooklyn, August 23, 1909,
second game.
A.L.—6—St. Louis vs. Philadelphia, May 12, 1915.
Chicago vs. Philadelphia, June 18, 1915.

Most caught stealing, inning
A.A.—3—Cincinnati vs. Philadelphia, July 26, 1887, third
inning.
A.L.—3—Detroit vs. New York, August 3, 1914, second inning.
N.L.—3—Los Angeles vs. Atlanta, August 6, 1982, fifth inning.

LEFT ON BASE

Most left on base, season
A.L.—1,334—St. Louis, 157 games, 1941.
N.L.—1,328—Cincinnati, 162 games, 1976.

Fewest left on base, season
A.L.—925—Kansas City, 154 games, 1957.
N.L.—964—Chicago, 154 games, 1924.

Most left on base, game
A.L.— 20—New York vs. Boston, September 21, 1956.
(25—Washington vs. Cleveland, September 14, 1971; 20-
inning suspended game completed September 20.
Kansas City vs. Texas, June 6, 1991, 18 innings.)
A.A.—18—Baltimore vs. Cincinnati, July 7, 1891.
N.L.—18—Boston vs. Baltimore, August 15, 1897.
Pittsburgh vs. Cincinnati, September 8, 1905.

Boston vs. St. Louis, July 11, 1923.
St. Louis vs. Philadelphia, September 15, 1928, second game.
New York vs. Philadelphia, August 7, 1943.
St. Louis vs. Cincinnati, June 10, 1944.
St. Louis vs. Philadelphia, September 14, 1950.
Pittsburgh vs. Boston, June 5, 1951.
Atlanta vs. Los Angeles, June 23, 1986.
(27—Atlanta vs. Philadelphia, May 4, 1973, 20 innings.)

Fewest left on base, game
A.L.—0—Made in many games.
(0—Philadelphia vs. New York, June 22, 1929, second game,
14 innings
N.L.—0—Made in many games.

Most left on base by both clubs, game
N.L.—30—Brooklyn 16, Pittsburgh 14, June 30, 1893.
New York 17, Philadelphia 13, July 18, 1943, first game.
(45—New York 25, St. Louis 20, September 11, 1974, 25
innings.)
A.L.—30—New York 15, Chicago 15, August 27, 1935, first
game.
Los Angeles 15, Washington 15, July 21, 1961.
(45—Kansas City 25, Texas 20, June 6, 1991, 18 innings.)

Fewest left on base by both clubs, game
N.L.—1—Los Angeles 1, Chicago 0, September 9, 1965.
(3—Chicago 2, Cincinnati 1, May 2, 1917, 10 innings.)
A.L.—2—Made in many games. Last time—Cleveland 1,
Oakland 1, July 19, 1974.
(4—Made in many games in extra inning.)

Most left on base, nine-inning shutout defeat
N.L.—16—St. Louis vs. Philadelphia, May 24, 1994.
(16—St. Louis vs. Cincinnati, August 30, 1989, 13 innings.)
A.L.—16—Seattle vs. Toronto, May 7, 1998.

LEAGUE BASERUNNING

STOLEN BASES

Most stolen bases, season
N.L. since 1900 (8 clubs)—1,691 in 1911
N.L. (10 clubs)—788 in 1962
N.L. (12 clubs)—1,851 in 1987
N.L. (14 clubs)—1,817 in 1997
N.L. (16-clubs)—1,959 in 1999
A.L. (8 clubs)—1,809 in 1912
A.L. (10 clubs)—811 in 1968
A.L. (12 clubs)—1,690 in 1976
A.L. (14 clubs)—1,734 in 1987

Fewest stolen bases, season
N.L. since 1900 (8 clubs)—37 in 1954
N.L. (10 clubs)—636 in 1964
N.L. (12 clubs)—817 in 1969
N.L. (14 clubs)—1,714 in 1993 (1,141 in shortened 1994 sea-
son)
N.L. (16-clubs)—1,294 in 2003
A.L. (8 clubs)—278 in 1950
A.L. (10 clubs)—540 in 1964
A.L. (12 clubs)—863 in 1970 (853 in shortened 1972 season)
A.L. (14 clubs)—1239 in 2002

CAUGHT STEALING

Most caught stealing, season
N.L. since 1900 (8 clubs)—1001 in 1915
N.L. (10 clubs)—494 in 1966
N.L. (12 clubs)—870 in 1983
N.L. (14 clubs)—841 in 1997
N.L. (16-clubs)—830 in 1999
A.L. (8 clubs)—1372 in 1914
A.L. (10 clubs)—471 in 1968

A.L. (12 clubs)—867 in 1976
A.L. (14 clubs)—1236 in 2002

Fewest caught stealing, season
N.L. since 1900 (8 clubs)—35 in 1944
N.L. (10 clubs)—409 in 1962
N.L. (12 clubs)—492 in 1971
N.L. (14 clubs)—709 in 1996 (529 in shortened 1994 season)
N.L. (16-clubs)—527 in 2004
A.L. (8 clubs)—231 in 1950
A.L. (10 clubs)—270 in 1963
A.L. (12 clubs)—547 in 1971 (539 in shortened 1972 season)
A.L. (14 clubs)—547 in 2003 (503 in shortened 1994 season)

LEFT ON BASE

Most left on bases, season
N.L. since 1900 (8 clubs)—9,424 in 1945
N.L. (10 clubs)—11,416 in 1962
N.L. (12 clubs)—14,468 in 1975
N.L. (14 clubs)—16,195 in 1997
N.L. (16-clubs)—18,939 in 2000
A.L. (8 clubs)—9,628 in 1936
A.L. (10 clubs)—11,680 in 1961
A.L. (12 clubs)—13,925 in 1973
A.L. (14 clubs)—16,711 in 1996

Fewest left on bases, season
N.L. since 1900 (8 clubs)—8,254 in 1920
N.L. (10 clubs)—10,994 in 1966
N.L. (12 clubs)—13,295 in 1988
N.L. (14 clubs)—15,941 in 1993 (11,438 in shortened 1994 season)
N.L. (16-clubs)—18,034 in 2001
A.L. (8 clubs)—7,943 in 1914
A.L. (10 clubs)—10,668 in 1966
A.L. (12 clubs)—13,494 in 1976
A.L. (14 clubs)—15,580 in 1979 (10,377 in shortened 1981 season)

INDIVIDUAL PITCHING

GAMES

Most games, career
M.L.—1,252—Jesse Orosco, New York N.L., Los Angeles, N.L., Cleveland A.L., Milwaukee A.L., Baltimore A.L., St. Louis N.L., San Diego N.L., New York A.L., Minnesota A.L., 24 years, 1979 through 2003, except 1980 (686 in A.L., 566 in N.L.).
N.L.—1,088—John Franco, Cincinnati, New York, 20 years, 1984 through 2004, except 2002.
A.L.—869—Dennis Eckersley, Cleveland, Boston, Oakland, 20 years, 1975 through 1984, 1987 through 1995, 1998.

For a complete list of pitchers with 700 or more career games pitched, see page 158.

Most games with one club
A.L.—802—Walter Johnson, Washington, 21 years, 1907 through 1927.
N.L.—802—Roy Face, Pittsburgh, 15 years, 1953 through 1968, except 1954.

Most games, season
N.L.—106—Mike G. Marshall, Los Angeles, 1974 (208 innings).
A.L.—90—Mike G. Marshall, Minnesota, 1979 (143 innings).

Most seasons leading league in games
M.L.—7—Joe McGinnity, Brooklyn N.L., Baltimore A.L., New York N.L., 1900, 1901, 1903, 1904, 1905, 1906, 1907.
N.L.—6—Joe McGinnity, Brooklyn, New York, 1900, 1903, 1904, 1905, 1906, 1907.
A.L.—6—Fred Marberry, Washington, 1924, 1925, 1926, 1928, 1929, 1932.

Fewest games pitched by leader, season
A.L.—40—Joe Haynes, Chicago, 1942 (103 innings).
N.L.—41—Ray Kremer, Pittsburgh, 1924 (259 innings).
Johnny Morrison, Pittsburgh, 1924 (238 innings).

Most games by rookie, season
A.L.—88—Sean Runyan, Detroit, 1998 (0 complete, 50.1 innings).
N.L.—86—Oscar Villarreal, Arizona, 2003 (0 complete, 98 innings).

GAMES STARTED

Most games started, career
M.L.—818—Cy Young, Cleveland N.L., St. Louis N.L., Boston A.L., Cleveland A.L., Boston N.L., 22 years, 1890 through 1911 (460 in N.L., 358 in A.L.).
N.L.—677—Steve Carlton, St. Louis, Philadelphia, San Francisco, 22 years, 1965 through 1986.
A.L.—666—Walter Johnson, Washington, 21 years, 1907 through 1927.

For a complete list of pitchers with 500 or more career games started, see page 158.

Most games started, season
N.L.—74—Will White, Cincinnati, 1879 (pitched 75 games).
A.L.—51—Jack Chesbro, New York, 1904 (pitched 55 games).
N.L. since 1900—48—Joe McGinnity, New York, 1903 (pitched 55 games).

Most seasons leading league in games started
N.L.—6—Robin Roberts, Philadelphia, 1950 (tied), 1951, 1952, 1953, 1954, 1955.
Tom Glavine, Atlanta, 1993 (tied), 1996, 1999 (tied), 2000 (tied), 2001 (tied), 2002.
Greg Maddux, Chicago, Atlanta, 1990 (tied), 1991, 1992 (tied), 1993 (tied), 2000 (tied), 2003.
A.L.—5—Bob Feller, Cleveland, 1940, 1941, 1946, 1947, 1948.
Early Wynn, Washington, Cleveland, Chicago, 1943 (tied), 1951 (tied), 1954, 1957, 1959 (tied).

Most season-opening games started
M.L.—16—Tom Seaver, New York N.L., Cincinnati N.L., Chicago

A.L., 1968 through 1979, 1981, 1983, 1985, 1986 (14 in N.L., 2 in A.L.).
A.L.—14—Walter Johnson, Washington, 1910 through 1926, except 1911, 1922, 1925.
Jack Morris, Detroit, Minnesota, Toronto, 1980 through 1993.
N.L.—14—Tom Seaver, New York, Cincinnati, 1968 through 1979, 1981, 1983.
Steve Carlton, Philadelphia, 1972 through 1986, except 1976.

Most consecutive starting assignments, career (since 1900)
M.L.—627—Roger Clemens, Boston A.L., Toronto A.L., New York A.L., Houston N.L., July 26, 1984 through 2004 (594 in A.L., 33 in N.L.).
A.L.—594—Roger Clemens, Boston, Toronto, New York, July 26, 1984 through 2003.
N.L.—534—Steve Carlton, St. Louis, Philadelphia, San Francisco, May 15, 1971 through 1986.

Most games started with none complete, season
N.L.—37—Steve Bedrosian, Atlanta, 1985.
A.L.—35—Rick Helling, Texas, 2000.

Most games taken out as starting pitcher, season
N.L.—37—Steve Bedrosian, Atlanta, 1985 (started 37).
A.L.—36—Stan Bahnsen, Chicago, 1972 (started 41).

GAMES RELIEVED

Most games as relief pitcher, career
M.L.—1,248—Jesse Orosco, New York N.L., Los Angeles, N.L., Cleveland A.L., Milwaukee A.L., Baltimore A.L., St. Louis N.L., San Diego N.L., New York A.L., Minnesota A.L., 24 years, 1979 through 2003, except 1980 (686 in A.L., 562 in N.L.).
N.L.—1,088—John Franco, Cincinnati, New York, 20 years, 1984 through 2004, except 2002.
A.L.—807—Sparky Lyle, Boston, New York, Texas, Chicago, 15 years, 1967 through 1982, except 1981.

Most consecutive appearances as relief pitcher, career
M.L.—1,199—Jesse Orosco, New York N.L., Los Angeles N.L., Cleveland A.L., Milwaukee A.L., Baltimore A.L., St. Louis N.L., San Diego N.L., New York A.L., Minnesota A.L., July 20, 1982 through September 27, 2003.
N.L.—1,088—John Franco, Cincinnati, New York, April 24, 1984 through October 3, 2004.
A.L.—807—Sparky Lyle, Boston, New York, Texas, Chicago, July 4, 1967 through September 9, 1980; August 23, 1982 through September 27, second game, 1982.

Most games, none of which were starts, career
N.L.—1,088—John Franco, Cincinnati, New York, 20 years, 1984 through 2004, except 2002.
A.L.—807—Sparky Lyle, Boston, New York, Texas, Chicago, July 4, 1967 through September 9, 1980; August 23, 1982 through September 27, second game, 1982.

Most games as relief pitcher, season
N.L.—106—Mike G. Marshall, Los Angeles, 1974 (started none, 208 innings).
A.L.—89—Mike G. Marshall, Minnesota, 1979 (141 innings; also started one game—two innings).
Mark Eichhorn, Toronto, 1987, started none (127.2 innings).

Most games, none of which were starts, season
N.L.—106—Mike G. Marshall, Los Angeles, 1974 (finished 83, 208 innings).
A.L.—89—Mark Eichhorn, Toronto, 1987 (finished 27, 127.2 innings).

Most consecutive games as relief pitcher
N.L.—13—Mike G. Marshall, Los Angeles, June 18 through July 3, first game, 1974 (26.2 innings).
A.L.—13—Dale Mohorcic, Texas, August 6 through 20, 1986 (14 innings).

COMPLETE GAMES

Most complete games, career
M.L.—751—Cy Young, Cleveland N.L., St. Louis N.L., Boston

A.L., Cleveland A.L., Boston N.L., 22 years, 1890 through 1911 (428 in N.L., 323 in A.L.).
N.L.—557—Pud Galvin, Buffalo, Pittsburgh, St. Louis, 12 years, 1879 through 1892, except 1886, 1890.
A.L.—531—Walter Johnson, Washington, 21 years, 1907 through 1927.
N.L. since 1900—436—Grover Alexander, Philadelphia, Chicago, St. Louis, 20 years, 1911 through 1930.

For a complete list of pitchers with 300 or more career complete games, see page 158.

Most complete games by righthander, career
M.L.—751—Cy Young, Cleveland N.L., St. Louis N.L., Boston A.L., Cleveland A.L., Boston N.L., 22 years, 1890 through 1911 (428 in N.L., 323 in A.L.).
N.L.—557—Pud Galvin, Buffalo, Pittsburgh, St. Louis, 12 years, 1879 through 1892, except 1886, 1890.
A.L.—531—Walter Johnson, Washington, 21 years, 1907 through 1927.
N.L. since 1900—436—Grover Alexander, Philadelphia, Chicago, St. Louis, 20 years, 1911 through 1930.

Most complete games by lefthander, career
A.L.—387—Eddie Plank, Philadelphia, St. Louis, 16 years, 1901 through 1917, except 1915.
N.L.—382—Warren Spahn, Boston, Milwaukee, New York Mets, San Francisco, 21 years, 1942 through 1965, except 1943, 1944, 1945 in military service.

Most complete games, season
N.L.—74—Will White, Cincinnati, 1879; pitched in 75 games.
A.L.—48—Jack Chesbro, New York, 1904; pitched in 55 games.
N.L. since 1900—45—Vic Willis, Boston, 1902; pitched in 51 games.

Most seasons leading league in complete games
N.L.—9—Warren Spahn, Boston, Milwaukee, 1949, 1951, 1957, 1958, 1959, 1960 (tied), 1961, 1962, 1963.
A.L.—6—Walter Johnson, Washington, 1910, 1911, 1913, 1914, 1915, 1916.

Fewest complete games for leader, season
N.L.—6—Curt Schilling, Arizona, 2001.
A.L. 7 David Wells, Toronto, 1999.
Paul Byrd, Kansas City, 2002.

Most consecutive complete games pitched, season (since 1900)
N.L.—39—Jack W. Taylor, St. Louis, April 15 through October 6, first game, 1904 (352 innings, including two games finished in relief).
A.L.—37—Bill Dinneen, Boston, April 16 through October 10, first game, 1904 (337 innings).

Most games, none of which were complete, season
N.L.—106—Mike G. Marshall, Los Angeles, 1974, started none (208 innings).
A.L.—90—Mike G. Marshall, Minnesota, 1979, started one (143 innings).

Most complete games by rookie, season
N.L.—67—Jim Devlin, Louisville, 1876 (67 games).
N.L. since 1900—41—Irv Young, Boston, 1905 (43 games).
A.L.—36—Roscoe Miller, Detroit, 1901 (38 games).

Most complete doubleheaders, career
M.L.—5—Joe McGinnity, Baltimore A.L., 1901 (2); New York N.L., 1903 (3).
N.L.—3—Joe McGinnity, New York, 1903.
A.L.—2—Held by many pitchers.

Most complete doubleheaders, season
N.L.—3—Joe McGinnity, New York, August 1, 8, 31, 1903 (won 3).
A.L.—2—Joe McGinnity, Baltimore, 1901 (split 2).
Mule Watson, Philadelphia, 1918 (split 1, lost 1 game and tied 1 in other doubleheader).

INNINGS

Most innings pitched, career
M.L.—7,377—Cy Young, Cleveland N.L., St. Louis N.L., Boston A.L., Cleveland A.L., Boston N.L., 22 years, 1890 through

---

1911 (4,143 in N.L., 3,234 in A.L.).
A.L.—5,924—Walter Johnson, Washington, 21 years, 1907 through 1927.
N.L.—5,246—Warren Spahn, Boston, Milwaukee, New York Mets, San Francisco, 21 years, 1942 through 1965, except 1943, 1944, 1945 in military service.

For a complete list of pitchers with 3,500 or more career innings, see page 159.

Most innings pitched, season
N.L.—683—Will White, Cincinnati, 75 games, 1879.
A.L.—464—Ed Walsh, Chicago, 66 games, 1908.
N.L. since 1900—434—Joe McGinnity, New York, 55 games, 1903.

Most seasons leading league in innings pitched
N.L.—7—Grover Alexander, Philadelphia, Chicago, 1911, 1912 (tied), 1914, 1915, 1916, 1917, 1920.
A.L.—5—Walter Johnson, Washington, 1910, 1913, 1914, 1915, 1916.
Bob Feller, Cleveland, 1939, 1940, 1941, 1946, 1947.

Fewest innings pitched by leader, season
A.L.—231.2—David Wells, Toronto, 34 games, 1999.
N.L.—233.1—Livan Hernandez, Montreal, 33 games, 2003.

Most consecutive innings without relief, career (since 1900)
N.L.—1,727—Jack W. Taylor, Chicago, St. Louis, June 20, 1901, second game, through August 9, 1906 (203 games, 188 complete games, 15 finished).

Most consecutive innings without relief, season (since 1900)
N.L.—352—Jack W. Taylor, St. Louis, April 15 through October 6, first game, 1904 (complete season, 39 complete games and two games finished).
A.L.—337—Bill Dinneen, Boston, April 16 through October 10, first game, 1904 (complete season, 37 complete games).

Most innings pitched by rookie, season (since 1900)
N.L.—378—Irv Young, Boston, 43 games, 1905.
A.L.—316—Reb Russell, Chicago, 43 games, 1913.

Most years with 200 or more innings pitched
M.L.—19—Cy Young, Cleveland N.L., St. Louis N.L., Boston A.L., Cleveland A.L., 1891 through 1909 (10 in N.L., 9 in A.L.).
Phil Niekro, Milwaukee, N.L., Atlanta N.L., New York A.L., Cleveland A.L., 1967 through 1986, except 1981 (10 in N.L., 3 in A.L.).
A.L.—18—Walter Johnson, Washington, 1908 through 1926, except 1920.
N.L.—17—Warren Spahn, Boston, Milwaukee, 1947 through 1963.

Most years with 300 or more innings pitched
M.L.—16—Cy Young, Cleveland N.L., St. Louis N.L., Boston A.L., 1891 through 1907, except 1906 (10 in N.L., 6 in A.L.).
N.L.—12—Kid Nichols, Boston, 1890 through 1899, 1901, 1904.
N.L. since 1900—11—Christy Mathewson, New York, 1901, 1903, 1904, 1905, 1907, 1908, 1910, 1911, 1912, 1913, 1914.
A.L.—9—Walter Johnson, Washington, 1910 through 1918.

Most consecutive years with 300 or more innings (since 1900)
A.L.—9—Walter Johnson, Washington, 1910 through 1918.
N.L.—7—Grover Alexander, Philadelphia, 1911 through 1917.

Most years with 400 or more innings pitched (since 1900)
N.L.—2—Joe McGinnity, New York, 1903 (434), 1904 (408).
A.L.—2—Ed Walsh, Chicago, 1907 (419), 1908 (464).

Most innings as relief pitcher, career
M.L.—1,870—Hoyt Wilhelm, New York Giants N.L., St. Louis N.L., Cleveland A.L., Baltimore A.L., Chicago A.L., California A.L., Atlanta N.L., Chicago N.L., Los Angeles N.L., 21 years, 1952 through 1972 (916 in N.L., 954 in A.L.).
N.L.—1,436.1—Kent Tekulve, Pittsburgh, Philadelphia, Cincinnati, 16 years, 1974 through 1989.
A.L.—1,265—Sparky Lyle, Boston, New York, Texas, Chicago, 15 years, 1967 through 1982, except 1981.

Most innings pitched as relief pitcher, season
N.L.—208—Mike G. Marshall, Los Angeles, 1974, pitched 106 games as relief pitcher.

A.L.—168.1—Bob Stanley, Boston, 1982, pitched 48 games as relief pitcher. (Bill Campbell, Minnesota, pitched 167.2 innings, rounded to 168, as a relief pitcher in 1976.)

Most innings pitched, game
N.L.—26—Leon Cadore, Brooklyn, May 1, 1920 (1-1 tie). Joe Oeschger, Boston, May 1, 1920 (1-1 tie).
A.L.—24
Jack Coombs, Philadelphia, September 1, 1906 (won 4-1). Joe Harris, Boston, September 1, 1906 (lost 4-1).

WINNING PERCENTAGE

Highest percentage of games won, career (200 or more victories)
A.L.—.690—Whitey Ford, New York, 16 years, 1950 through 1967, except 1951, 1952 in military service (won 236, lost 106).
N.L.—.665—Christy Mathewson, New York, Cincinnati, 17 years, 1900 through 1916 (won 373, lost 188).

Highest percentage of games won, season (70 or more decisions)
N.L.—.833—Hoss Radbourn, Providence, 1884 (won 60, lost 12).

Highest percentage of games won, season (34 or more decisions)
A.L.—.886—Lefty Grove, Philadelphia, 1931 (won 31, lost 4).
N.L.—.824—Jack Chesbro, Pittsburgh, 1902 (won 28, lost 6). Dazzy Vance, Brooklyn, 1924 (won 28, lost 6).

Highest percentage of games won, season (20 or more victories)
A.L.—.893—Ron Guidry, New York, 1978 (won 25, lost 3).
N.L.—.880—Fred Goldsmith, Chicago, 1880 (won 22, lost 3). Preacher Roe, Brooklyn, 1951 (won 22, lost 3).

Highest percentage of games won, season (16 or more decisions)
N.L.—.947—Roy Face, Pittsburgh, 1959 (won 18, lost 1).
A.L.—.938—Johnny Allen, Cleveland, 1937 (won 15, lost 1).

Most seasons leading league in winning percentage (15 or more victories)
A.L.—5—Lefty Grove, Philadelphia, Boston, 1929, 1930, 1931, 1933, 1939.
N.L.—3—Ed Reulbach, Chicago, 1906, 1907, 1908.

GAMES WON
CAREER

Most games won, career
M.L.—511—Cy Young, Cleveland N.L., St. Louis N.L., Boston A.L., Cleveland A.L., Boston N.L., 22 years, 1890 through 1911 (289 in N.L., 222 in A.L.).
A.L.—417—Walter Johnson, Washington, 21 years, 1907 through 1927.
N.L.—373—Christy Mathewson, New York, Cincinnati, 17 years, 1900 through 1916.
Grover Alexander, Philadelphia, Chicago, St. Louis, 20 years, 1911 through 1930.

For a complete list of pitchers with 200 or more career victories, see page 159.

Most games won by righthander, career
M.L.—511—Cy Young, Cleveland N.L., St. Louis N.L., Boston A.L., Cleveland A.L., Boston N.L., 22 years, 1890 through 1911 (289 in N.L., 222 in A.L.).
A.L.—417—Walter Johnson, Washington, 21 years, 1907 through 1927.
N.L.—373—Christy Mathewson, New York, Cincinnati, 17 years, 1900 through 1916.
Grover Alexander, Philadelphia, Chicago, St. Louis, 20 years, 1911 through 1930.

Most games won by lefthander, career
N.L.—363—Warren Spahn, Boston, Milwaukee, New York, San Francisco, 21 years, 1942 through 1965, except 1943, 1944, 1945 in military service.
A.L.—305—Eddie Plank, Philadelphia, St. Louis, 16 years, 1901

through 1917, except 1915.

Most games won as relief pitcher, career
M.L.—124—Hoyt Wilhelm, New York N.L., St. Louis N.L., Cleveland A.L., California A.L., Atlanta N.L., Baltimore A.L., Chicago A.L., Chicago N.L., Los Angeles N.L., 21 years, 1952 through 1972 (73 in A.L., 51 in N.L.).
N.L.—96—Roy Face, Pittsburgh, Montreal, 16 years, 1953 through 1969, except 1954 (lost 82).
A.L.—87—Sparky Lyle, Boston, New York, Texas, Chicago, 15 years, 1967 through 1982, except 1981 (lost 67).

Most games won from one club, career
N.L.—70—Grover Alexander, Philadelphia, Chicago, St. Louis, vs. Cincinnati, 20 years, 1911 through 1930.
A.L.—66—Walter Johnson, Washington, vs. Detroit, 21 years, 1907 through 1927.

Most season-opening games won, career
A.L.—9—Walter Johnson, Washington, 1910, 1913, 1914, 1915, 1916, 1917, 1919, 1924, 1926 (all complete; seven shutouts).
N.L.—8—Grover Alexander, Philadelphia, Chicago, St. Louis, 1914, 1915, 1916, 1917, 1921, 1922, 1925, 1929 (seven complete; one shutout).

SEASON AND MONTH

Most games won by righthander, season
N.L.—60—Hoss Radbourn, Providence, 1884 (lost 12).
A.L.—41—Jack Chesbro, New York, 1904 (lost 13).
N.L. since 1900—37—Christy Mathewson, New York, 1908 (lost 11).

Most games won by lefthander, season
A.A.—46—Matt Kilroy, Baltimore, 1887 (lost 20).
N.L.—42—Charles Baldwin, Detroit, 1886 (lost 14).
A.L.—31—Lefty Grove, Philadelphia, 1931 (lost 4).
N.L. since 1900—27—Sandy Koufax, Los Angeles, 1966 (lost 9).
Steve Carlton, Philadelphia, 1972 (lost 10).

For a complete list of 20-game winners each season, see page 191.

Most games won as relief pitcher, season
N.L.—18—Roy Face, Pittsburgh, 1959 (lost 1).
A.L.—17—John Hiller, Detroit, 1974 (lost 14). Bill Campbell, Minnesota, 1976 (lost 5).

Most seasons leading league in games won
N.L.—8—Warren Spahn, Boston, Milwaukee, 1949, 1950, 1953 (tied), 1957, 1958 (tied), 1959 (tied), 1960 (tied), 1961 (tied).
A.L.—6
Walter Johnson, Washington, 1913, 1914, 1915, 1916, 1918, 1924.
Bob Feller, Cleveland, 1939, 1940, 1941, 1946 (tied), 1947, 1951.

Fewest games won by leader, season
N.L.—18—Rick Sutcliffe, Chicago, 1987 (lost 10).
A.L.—18—Whitey Ford, New York, 1955 (lost 7).
Bob Lemon, Cleveland, 1955 (lost 10).
Frank Sullivan, Boston, 1955 (lost 13).
Chuck Estrada, Baltimore, 1960 (lost 11).
Jim Perry, Cleveland, 1960 (lost 10).

Most games won by rookie, season
N.L.—47—Al Spalding, Chicago, 1876 (lost 13).
N.L. since 1900—28—Grover Alexander, Philadelphia, 1911 (lost 13).
A.L.—26—Russ Ford, New York, 1910 (lost 6).

Most games won from one club, season
N.L.—12—Hoss Radbourn, Providence vs. Cleveland, 1884 (lost 1).
N.L. since 1900—9—Ed Reulbach, Chicago vs. Brooklyn, 1908 (lost 0).
A.L.—9—Frank Smith, Chicago vs. Washington, 1904 (lost 1).
Ed Walsh, Chicago vs. New York, 1908 (lost 1), and vs. Boston, 1908 (lost 0).
Walter Johnson, Washington vs. Chicago, 1912 (lost 1).

Most games won, one month
N.L.—15—John Clarkson, Chicago, June 1885 (lost 1).
N.L. since 1900—9—Christy Mathewson, New York, August

1903 (lost 1).
Christy Mathewson, New York, August, 1904 (lost 1).
Grover Alexander, Chicago, May 1920 (lost 0).
A.L.—10—Rube Waddell, Philadelphia, July 1902 (lost 1, tied 1).

20- AND 30-WIN SEASONS

Most seasons winning 30 or more games
N.L.—7—Kid Nichols, Boston, 1891, 1892, 1893, 1894, 1896, 1897, 1898.
N.L. since 1900—4—Christy Mathewson, New York, 1903, 1904, 1905, 1908.
A.L.—2—Cy Young, Boston, 1901, 1902.
Walter Johnson, Washington, 1912, 1913.

For a complete list of pitchers with two or
more 30-victory seasons, see page 159.

Most seasons winning 20 or more games
M.L.—16—Cy Young, Cleveland N.L., 1891, 1892, 1893, 1894, 1895, 1896, 1897, 1898; St. Louis, N.L., 1899, 1900; Boston A.L., 1901, 1902, 1903, 1904, 1907, 1908 (10 in N.L., 6 in A.L.).
N.L.—13—Christy Mathewson, New York, 1901, 1903, 1904, 1905, 1906, 1907, 1908, 1909, 1910, 1911, 1912, 1913, 1914.
Warren Spahn, Boston, Milwaukee, 1947, 1949, 1950, 1951, 1953, 1954, 1956, 1957, 1958, 1959, 1960, 1961, 1963.
A.L.—12—Walter Johnson, Washington, 1910, 1911, 1912, 1913, 1914, 1915, 1916, 1917, 1918, 1919, 1924, 1925.

For a complete list of 20-game winners
each season, see page 191. For a complete
list of pitchers with five or more 20-victory
seasons, see page 159.

Most seasons winning 20 or more games by righthander
M.L.—16—Cy Young, Cleveland N.L., 1891, 1892, 1893, 1894, 1895, 1896, 1897, 1898; St. Louis, N.L., 1899, 1900; Boston A.L., 1901, 1902, 1903, 1904, 1907, 1908 (10 in N.L., 6 in A.L.).
N.L.—13—Christy Mathewson, New York, 1901, 1903, 1904, 1905, 1906, 1907, 1908, 1909, 1910, 1911, 1912, 1913, 1914.
A.L.—12—Walter Johnson, Washington, 1910, 1911, 1912, 1913, 1914, 1915, 1916, 1917, 1918, 1919, 1924, 1925.

Most seasons winning 20 or more games by lefthander
N.L.—13—Warren Spahn, Boston, Milwaukee, 1947, 1949, 1950, 1951, 1953, 1954, 1956, 1957, 1958, 1959, 1960, 1961, 1963.
A.L.—8—Lefty Grove, Philadelphia, Boston, 1927, 1928, 1929, 1930, 1931, 1932, 1933, 1935.

Most consecutive seasons winning 20 or more games
M.L.—14—Cy Young, Cleveland N.L., St. Louis N.L. Boston A.L., 1891 through 1904 (10 in N.L., 4 in A.L.).
N.L.—12—Christy Mathewson, New York, 1903 through 1914.
A.L.—10—Walter Johnson, Washington, 1910 through 1919.

Most consecutive seasons winning 20 or more games from start of career
N.L.—10—Kid Nichols, Boston, 1890 through 1899.
A.L.—3—Vean Gregg, Cleveland, 1911, 1912, 1913.

DOUBLEHEADER

Most complete-game doubleheaders won, career
N.L.—3—Joe McGinnity, New York, 1903 (lost 0).
A.L.—2—Ed Walsh, Chicago, 1905, 1908 (lost 0).

For a complete list of pitchers with two complete-game victories in one day, see page 189.

Most complete-game doubleheaders won, season
N.L.—3—Joe McGinnity, New York, 1903.
A.L.—1—Held by many pitchers. Last pitcher—Dutch Levsen, Cleveland vs. Boston, August 28, 1926.

CONSECUTIVE

Most consecutive games won, career
N.L.—24—Carl Hubbell, New York, July 17, 1936, through May 27, 1937 (16 in 1936, 8 in 1937).
A.L.—20—Roger Clemens, Toronto, New York, June 3, 1998 through June 1, 1999 (15 with Toronto in 1998, 5 with New York in 1999).

Most consecutive games won from start of career as starting pitcher
N.L.—12—Hooks Wiltse, New York, May 29 through September 15, 1904.
A.L.—9—Whitey Ford, New York, July 17 through September 24, second game, 1950.

Most consecutive games won from start of career as relief pitcher
N.L.—12—Butch Metzger, San Francisco, 1974 (1), San Diego, 1975 (1), 1976 (10), September 21, 1974 through August 8, 1976.
A.L.—9—Joe Pate, Philadelphia, April 15 through August 10, 1926.
Jeff Zimmerman, Texas, April 14 through August 2, 1999.

Most consecutive games won from one club, career
N.L.—24—Christy Mathewson, New York, vs. St. Louis, June 16, 1904 through September 15, 1908.
A.L.—24—Carl Mays, Boston, New York, vs. Philadelphia, August 30, 1918 through July 24, 1923.

Most consecutive games won, season
N.L.—19—Tim Keefe, New York, June 23 through August 10, 1888.
Rube Marquard, New York, April 11 through July 3, first game, 1912.
A.L.—16—Walter Johnson, Washington, July 3, second game, through August 23, first game, 1912.
Joe Wood, Boston, July 8 through September 15, second game, 1912.
Lefty Grove, Philadelphia, June 8 through August 19, 1931.
Schoolboy Rowe, Detroit, June 15 through August 25, 1934.
Roger Clemens, New York, May 26 through September 19, 2001.

For a complete list of pitchers with 12 consecutive victories in one season, see page 190.

Most consecutive games won from start of season
N.L.—19—Rube Marquard, New York, April 11 through July 3, 1912, first game.
A.L.—15—Johnny Allen, Cleveland, April 23, 1937, through September 30, 1937, first game.
Dave McNally, Baltimore, April 12 through July 30, 1969.

Most consecutive games won as relief pitcher, season
N.L.—17—Roy Face, Pittsburgh, April 22 through August 30, second game, 1959.
A.L.—12—Luis Arroyo, New York, July 1 through September 9, 1961.

Most consecutive games won by rookie, season
N.L.—17—Pat Luby, Chicago, August 6, second game, through October 3, 1890.
N.L. since 1900—12—Hooks Wiltse, New York, May 29 through September 15, 1904.
A.L.—12
Atley Donald, New York, May 9 through July 25, 1939.
Russ Ford, New York, August 9 through October 6, 1910.

Most consecutive games won by rookie as starting pitcher, season
N.L.—17—Pat Luby, Chicago, August 6, second game, through October 3, 1890.
N.L. since 1900—12—Hooks Wiltse, New York, May 29 through September 15, 1904.
A.L.—12—Atley Donald, New York, May 9 through July 25, 1939.

Most consecutive games won by rookie as relief pitcher, season
N.L.—10—Eddie Yuhas, St. Louis, June 5 through September 25, 1952 (end of season).
Butch Metzger, San Diego, April 20 through August 8, 1976.

A.L.—9—Joe Pate, Philadelphia, April 15 through August 10, 1926.
Jeff Zimmerman, Texas, April 14 through August 2, 1999.

Most consecutive games won as relief pitcher making consecutive appearances during club's winning streak
A.L.—3—Hal White, Detroit, September 26, second game, 27, 28, 1950, 5.1 innings.
Grant Jackson, Baltimore, September 29, 30, October 1, 1974, 5.1 innings.
Sparky Lyle, New York, August 29, 30, 31, 1977, 7.2 innings.
Chuck McElroy, California, June 10, 11, 12, 1996, three innings.
John Frascatore, Toronto, June 29, 30, July 1, 1999, 2.1 innings.
N.L.—3—Mike G. Marshall, Los Angeles, June 21, 22, 23, 1974, 7 innings.
Gene Garber, Philadelphia, May 15, second game, 16, 17, 1975, 5.2 innings.
Al Hrabosky, St. Louis, July 12, 13, 17, 1975, five innings.
Kent Tekulve, Pittsburgh, May 6, 7, 9, 1980, 5.1 innings.
Mitch Williams, Philadelphia, August 4, 6, 7, 1991, four innings.

Most consecutive games won, end of season
N.L.—17—Pat Luby, Chicago, August 6, second game, through October 3, 1890.
N.L. since 1900—16—Carl Hubbell, New York, July 17 through September 23, 1936.
A.L.—15—Alvin Crowder, Washington, August 2 through September 25, 1932.
Roger Clemens, Toronto, June 3 through September 21, 1998.

SAVES (SINCE 1969)

Most saves, career
M.L.—478—Lee Smith, Chicago N.L., Boston A.L., St. Louis N.L., New York A.L., Baltimore A.L., California A.L., Cincinnati N.L., Montreal N.L., 18 years, 1980 through 1997 (347 in N.L., 131 in A.L.).
N.L.—424—John Franco, Cincinnati, New York, 20 years, 1984 through 2004, except 2002.
A.L.—324—Dennis Eckersley, Cleveland, Boston, Oakland, 20 years, 1975 through 1984, 1987 through 1995, 1998.

For a complete list of pitchers with 150 or more career saves, see page 160.

Most saves, season
A.L.—57—Bobby Thigpen, Chicago, 1990.
N.L.—55—John Smoltz, Atlanta, 2002.
Eric Gagne, Los Angeles, 2003.

Most saves by rookie, season
A.L.—37—Kazuhiro Sasaki, Seattle, 2000.
N.L.—36—Todd Worrell, St. Louis, 1986.

GAMES LOST

Most games lost, career
M.L.—313—Cy Young, Cleveland N.L., St. Louis N.L., Boston A.L., Cleveland A.L., Boston N.L., 22 years, 1890 through 1911 (172 in N.L., 141 in A.L.).
A.L.—279—Walter Johnson, Washington, 21 years, 1907 through 1927.
N.L.—268—Pud Galvin, Buffalo, Pittsburgh, St. Louis, 12 years, 1879 through 1892, except 1886 and 1890.
N.L. since 1900—251—Eppa Rixey, Philadelphia, Cincinnati, 21 years, 1912 through 1933, except 1918 in military service.

Most games lost by righthander, career
M.L.—313—Cy Young, Cleveland N.L., St. Louis N.L., Boston A.L., Cleveland A.L., Boston N.L., 22 years, 1890 through 1911 (172 in N.L., 141 in A.L.).
A.L.—279—Walter Johnson, Washington, 21 years, 1907 through 1927.
N.L.—268—Pud Galvin, Buffalo, Pittsburgh, St. Louis, 12 years, 1879 through 1892, except 1886 and 1890.
N.L. since 1900—230—Phil Niekro, Milwaukee, Atlanta, 21 years, 1964 through 1983, 1987.

Most games lost by lefthander, career
N.L.—251—Eppa Rixey, Philadelphia, Cincinnati, 21 years, 1912 through 1933, except 1918 in military service.

A.L.—221—Frank Tanana, California, Boston, Texas, Detroit, New York, 1973 through 1993, 21 years.

Most consecutive games lost to one club, career
N.L.—13—Don Sutton, Los Angeles vs. Chicago, April 23, 1966 through July 24, 1969 (start of career).
A.L.—10—Dave Morehead, Boston vs. Los Angeles, July 28, 1963 through September 28, 1965 (start of career).

Most games lost, season
N.L.—48—John F. Coleman, Philadelphia, 1883 (won 12).
N.L. since 1900—29—Vic Willis, Boston, 1905 (won 12).
A.L.—26—Jack Townsend, Washington, 1904 (won five).
Bob Groom, Washington, 1909 (won six).

Most games lost as relief pitcher, season
N.L.—16—Gene Garber, Atlanta, 1979 (won six).
A.L.—14—Darold Knowles, Washington, 1970 (won two).
John Hiller, Detroit, 1974 (won 17).
Mike G. Marshall, Minnesota, 1979 (won 10, also lost one game as starter).

Most seasons leading league in games lost
N.L.—4—Phil Niekro, Atlanta, 1977 (tied), 1978, 1979, 1980.
A.L.—4—Bobo Newsom, St. Louis, Washington, Detroit, Philadelphia, 1934, 1935, 1941, 1945.
Pedro Ramos, Washington, Minnesota, 1958, 1959, 1960, 1961.

Fewest games lost for leader, season
A.L.—14—Ted Gray, Detroit, 1951 (won seven).
Alex Kellner, Philadelphia, 1951 (won 11).
Bob Lemon, Cleveland 1951 (won 17).
Billy Pierce, Chicago, 1951 (won 15).
Duane Pillette, St. Louis, 1951 (won six).
Dizzy Trout, Detroit, 1951 (won nine).
N.L.—15—Don Carman, Philadelphia, 1989 (won five).
Orel Hershiser, Los Angeles, 1989 (won 15).
Ken Hill, St. Louis, 1989 (won seven).
Tom Candiotti, Los Angeles, 1992 (won 11).
Orel Hershiser, Los Angeles, 1992 (won 10).

Most games lost by rookie, season
N.L.—48—John F. Coleman, Philadelphia, 1883 (won 12).
N.L. since 1900—25—Harry McIntire, Brooklyn, 1906 (won eight).
A.L.—26—Bob Groom, Washington, 1909 (won six).

Most games lost to one club, season (since 1900)
N.L.—7—Held by seven pitchers. Last time—Cal McLish, Cincinnati vs. Pittsburgh, 1960 (won none).
A.L.—7—Held by 4 pitchers. Last time—Camilo Pascual, Washington vs. New York, 1956 (won none).

Most consecutive games lost, career
N.L.—27—Anthony Young, New York, May 6, 1992 through July 24, 1993 (14 in 1992, 13 in 1993).
A.L.—19—Jack Nabors, Philadelphia, April 28 through September 28, 1916.

Most consecutive games lost from start of career
A.L.—16—Terry Felton, Minnesota, April 18, 1980, second game, through September 12, 1982.
A.A.—13—Charlie Stecher, Philadelphia, September 6 through October 9, 1890.

Most consecutive games lost, season
A.L.—19—Jack Nabors, Philadelphia, April 28 through September 28, 1916.
N.L.—18—Cliff Curtis, Boston, June 13, first game, through September 20, first game, 1910.
Roger Craig, New York, May 4 through August 4, 1963.

For a complete list of pitchers with 12 consecutive games lost in one season, see page 191.

Most consecutive games lost from start of season
A.L.—14—Joe Harris, Boston, May 10 through July 25, 1906.
Matt Keough, Oakland, April 15 through August 8, 1979.
N.L.—13—Anthony Young, New York, April 9 through July 24, 1993.

Most consecutive games lost by rookie, season
N.L.—16—Charles Dean, Cincinnati, July 11 through September 12, 1876.

N.L. since 1900—14—Anthony Young, New York, May 6
through September 29, 1992.
A.L.—13—Guy Morton, Cleveland, June 24 through September
20, 1914.
Terry Felton, Minnesota, April 17 through September 12, 1982.

Most consecutive games lost at end of season
A.L.—19—Jack Nabors, Philadelphia, April 28 through
September 28, 1916.
N.L.—18—Cliff Curtis, Boston, June 13, first game, through
September 20, 1910, first game.

AT-BATS AND PLATE APPEARANCES

Most opponents' at-bats, career (since 1900)
A.L.—21,663—Walter Johnson, Washington, 21 years, 1907
through 1927.
N.L.—19,778—Warren Spahn, Boston, Milwaukee, New York,
San Francisco, 21 years, 1942 through 1965, except 1943,
1944, 1945 in military service.

Most opponents' at-bats, season
N.L.—2,808—Will White, Cincinnati, 75 games, 683 innings, 1879.
N.L. since 1900—1,658—Joe McGinnity, New York, 55 games,
434 innings, 1903.
A.L.—1,690—Ed Walsh, Chicago, 66 games, 464 innings, 1908.

Most seasons leading league in opponents' at-bats
N.L.—6—Grover Alexander, Philadelphia, Chicago, 1911, 1914,
1915, 1916, 1917, 1920.
A.L.—4—Ed Walsh, Chicago, 1908, 1910, 1911, 1912.
Walter Johnson, Washington, 1913, 1914, 1915, 1916.
Bob Lemon, Cleveland, 1948, 1950, 1952, 1953.

Most consecutive seasons leading league in opponents' at-bats
A.L.—4—Walter Johnson, Washington, 1913, 1914, 1915, 1916.
N.L.—4—Grover Alexander, Philadelphia, 1914, 1915, 1916,
1917.
Robin Roberts, Philadelphia, 1952, 1953, 1954, 1955.

Fewest opponents' at-bats for leader, season
A.L.—942—Jim Bunning, Detroit, 250 innings, 1959.
N.L.—890—Livan Hernandez, Montreal, 233.1 innings, 2003.

Most opponents' at-bats, game
N.L.—66—George Derby, Buffalo, July 3, 1883.
N.L. since 1900—49—Doc Parker, Cincinnati, June 21, 1901.
Bill Phillips, Cincinnati, June 24, 1901, second game.
A.L.—53—Roy Patterson, Chicago, May 5, 1901.

Most batters facing pitcher, game
N.L.—67—George Derby, Buffalo, July 3, 1883.
N.L. since 1900—55—Bill Phillips, Cincinnati, June 24, 1901,
second game.
A.L.—57—Roy Patterson, Chicago, May 5, 1901.

Most batters facing pitcher, inning
N.L.—22—Tony Mullane, Baltimore, June 18, 1894, a.m. game,
first inning.
N.L. since 1900—16—Hal Kelleher, Philadelphia, May 5, 1938,
eighth inning.
A.L.—16—Merle Adkins, Boston, July 8, 1902, sixth inning.
Lefty O'Doul, Boston, July 7, 1923, first game, sixth inning.
Howard Ehmke, Boston, September 28, 1923, sixth inning.

RUNS

Most runs allowed, career
M.L.—3,303—Pud Galvin, Buffalo N.L., Pittsburgh A.A.,
Pittsburgh N.L., Pittsburgh P.L., St. Louis N.L., 14 years, 1879
through 1892.
A.L.—2,117—Red Ruffing, Boston, New York, Chicago, 22
years, 1924 through 1947, except 1943, 1944.
N.L.—2,037—Burleigh Grimes, Pittsburgh, Brooklyn, New York,
Boston, St. Louis, Chicago, 19 years, 1916 through 1934.

**For a complete list of pitchers allowing 1,800
or more career runs, see page 160.**

Most runs allowed, season
N.L.—544—John F. Coleman, Philadelphia, 63 games, 538
innings, 1883.
A.L.—226—Snake Wiltse, Philadelphia, Baltimore, 38 games,
302 innings, 1902.
N.L. since 1900—224—Bill Carrick, New York, 45 games, 342
innings, 1900.

Most seasons leading league in runs allowed
N.L.—3—Burleigh Grimes, Brooklyn, Pittsburgh, 1923, 1924,
1928.
Robin Roberts, Philadelphia, 1955, 1956, 1957.
Phil Niekro, Atlanta, 1977, 1978, 1979.
Rick Mahler, Atlanta, Cincinnati, 1986, 1988, 1989.
A.L.—3—Wilbur Wood, Chicago, 1972, 1973, 1975.

Fewest runs allowed for leader, season
N.L.—102—George Smith, New York, Philadelphia, 196
innings, 1919.
A.L.—108—Jim Bagby, Cleveland, 280 innings, 1918.

Most runs allowed, game
N.L.—35—Dave Rowe, Cleveland, July 24, 1882.
N.L. since 1900—21—Doc Parker, Cincinnati, June 21, 1901.
A.L.—24—Al Travers, Detroit, May 18, 1912 (only major league
game).

Most runs allowed, inning
N.L.—16—Tony Mullane, Baltimore, June 18, 1894, a.m. game,
first inning.
N.L. since 1900—12—Hal Kelleher, Philadelphia, May 5, 1938,
eighth inning.
A.L.—13—Lefty O'Doul, Boston, July 7, 1923, first game, sixth
inning.

Fewest runs allowed, doubleheader
N.L.—0—Ed Reulbach, Chicago, September 26, 1908.
A.L.—1—Ed Walsh, Chicago, September 29, 1908.
Carl Mays, Boston, August 30, 1918.

EARNED RUNS

Most earned runs allowed, season (since 1900)
A.L.—186—Bobo Newsom, St. Louis, 330 innings, 1938.
N.L.—165—Guy Bush, Chicago, 225 innings, 1930.

Most seasons leading league in earned runs allowed
N.L.—3—Burleigh Grimes, Brooklyn, 1922, 1924, 1925.
Murry Dickson, St. Louis, Pittsburgh, 1948, 1951, 1952 (tied).
Robin Roberts, Philadelphia, 1955, 1956, 1957.
Jack Fisher, New York, 1964 (tied), 1965 (tied), 1967.
A.L.—3—Bobo Newsom, St. Louis, Washington, Philadelphia,
1938, 1942, 1945.
Wilbur Wood, Chicago, 1972, 1973, 1975.

Fewest earned runs for leader, season
A.L.—83—Willie Adams, Philadelphia, 160 innings, 1918.
Hooks Dauss, Detroit, 250 innings, 1918.
N.L.—85—Pete Schneider, Cincinnati, 217 innings, 1918.
Art Nehf, Boston, 284 innings, 1918.
Wilbur Cooper, Pittsburgh, 287 innings, 1919.

EARNED-RUN AVERAGE

Lowest earned-run average, career (300 or more games won)

A.L.—2.47—Walter Johnson, Washington, 802 games, 21
years, 1907 through 1927. (Johnson's record includes 520
total runs in 1,729 innings from 1907 through 1912, a period
in which earned runs were not compiled. Had earned runs
been compiled for that period, Johnson's earned-run average
would be even lower.)
N.L.—2.61—Grover Alexander, Philadelphia, Chicago, St. Louis,
696 games, 20 years, 1911 through 1930. (Alexander's record
includes 133 total runs in 366 innings in 1911, a year in
which earned runs were not compiled. Had earned runs been
compiled that year, Alexander's earned-run average would be
even lower.)

**For a complete list of pitchers with career
earned-run averages of 3.50 or lower with
3,000 or more innings, see page 160.**

Lowest earned-run average, career (200 or more games won)
A.L.—2.47—Walter Johnson, Washington, 802 games, 21 years, 1907 through 1927. (Johnson's record includes 520 total runs in 1,729 innings from 1907 through 1912, a period in which earned runs were not compiled. Had earned runs been compiled for that period, Johnson's earned-run average would be even lower.)
N.L.—2.61—Grover Alexander, Philadelphia, Chicago, St. Louis, 696 games, 20 years, 1911 through 1930. (Alexander's record includes 133 total runs in 366 innings in 1911, a year in which earned runs were not compiled. Had earned runs been compiled that year, Alexander's earned-run average would be even lower.)

Lowest earned-run average, career (2,000 or more innings)
N.L.—2.33—Hippo Vaughn, Chicago, 2,217 innings, 305 games, nine years, 1913 through 1921.
A.L.—2.47—Walter Johnson, Washington, 5,924 innings, 802 games, 21 years, 1907 through 1927. (Johnson's record includes 520 total runs in 1,729 innings from 1907 through 1912, a period in which earned runs were not compiled. Had earned runs been compiled for that period, Johnson's earned-run average would be even lower.)

Lowest earned-run average, season (300 or more innings)
N.L.—1.12—Bob Gibson, St. Louis, 305 innings, 1968.
A.L.—1.14—Walter Johnson, Washington, 346 innings, 1913.

Lowest earned-run average by righthander, season (300 or more innings)
N.L.—1.12—Bob Gibson, St. Louis, 305 innings, 1968.
A.L.—1.14—Walter Johnson, Washington, 346 innings, 1913.

Lowest earned-run average by lefthander, season (300 or more innings)
N.L.—1.66—Carl Hubbell, New York, 309 innings, 1933.
A.L.—1.75—Babe Ruth, Boston, 324 innings, 1916.

Lowest earned-run average, season (200 or more innings)
A.L.—1.00—Dutch H. Leonard, Boston, 225 innings, 1914.
N.L.—1.12—Bob Gibson, St. Louis, 305 innings, 1968.

Most years leading league in lowest earned-run average
A.L.—9—Lefty Grove, Philadelphia, Boston, 1926, 1929, 1930, 1931, 1932, 1935, 1936, 1938, 1939.
N.L.—5—Grover Alexander, Philadelphia, Chicago, 1915, 1916, 1917, 1919, 1920.
Sandy Koufax, Los Angeles, 1962, 1963, 1964, 1965, 1966.

Most consecutive seasons leading league in lowest earned-run average
N.L.—5—Sandy Koufax, Los Angeles, 1962, 1963, 1964, 1965, 1966.
A.L.—4—Lefty Grove, Philadelphia, 1929, 1930, 1931, 1932.

Highest earned-run average for leader, season
A.L.—3.20—Early Wynn, Cleveland, 214 innings, 1950.
N.L.—3.08—Bill Walker, New York, 178 innings, 1929.

SHUTOUTS

Most shutouts won or tied by righthander, career
A.L.—110—Walter Johnson, Washington, 21 years, 1907 through 1927.
N.L.—90—Grover Alexander, Philadelphia, Chicago, St. Louis, 20 years, 1911 through 1930.

Most shutouts won or tied by lefthander, career
M.L.—69—Eddie Plank, Philadelphia A.L., St. Louis F.L., St. Louis A.L., 17 years, 1901 through 1917.
A.L.—64—Eddie Plank, Philadelphia, St. Louis, 16 years, 1901 through 1917, except 1915.
N.L.—63—Warren Spahn, Boston, Milwaukee, New York, San Francisco, 21 years, 1942 through 1965, except 1943, 1944, 1945 in military service.

For a complete list of pitchers with 40 or more career shutouts, see page 160.

Most shutouts won from one club, career
A.L.—23—Walter Johnson, Washington vs. Philadelphia, 21 years, 1907 through 1927.

N.L.—20—Grover Alexander, Philadelphia, Chicago, St. Louis vs. Cincinnati, 20 years, 1911 through 1930.

Most shutouts won or tied by righthander, season
N.L.—16—George Bradley, St. Louis, 1876.
Grover Alexander, Philadelphia, 1916.
A.L.—13—Jack Coombs, Philadelphia, 1910.

Most shutouts won or tied by lefthander, season
A.A.—12—Ed Morris, Pittsburgh, 1886.
N.L.—11—Sandy Koufax, Los Angeles, 1963.
A.L.—9—Babe Ruth, Boston, 1916.
Ron Guidry, New York, 1978.

Most seasons leading league in shutouts won or tied
N.L.—7—Grover Alexander, Philadelphia, Chicago, 1911 (tied), 1913, 1915, 1916, 1917, 1919, 1921 (tied).
A.L.—7—Walter Johnson, Washington, 1911 (tied), 1913, 1914, 1915, 1918 (tied), 1919, 1924.

Fewest shutouts pitched by leader, season
A.L.-N.L.—3—Held by many pitchers.

Most consecutive shutouts won or tied, season
N.L.—6—Don Drysdale, Los Angeles, May 14, 18, 22, 26, 31, June 4, 1968.
A.L.—5—Doc White, Chicago, September 12, 16, 19, 25, 30, 1904.

Most shutouts won or tied in season openers
A.L.—7—Walter Johnson, Washington, 1910 to 1926.
N.L.—3—Rip Sewell, Pittsburgh, 1943, 1947, 1949.
Chris Short, Philadelphia, 1965, 1968, 1970.
Rick Mahler, Atlanta, 1982, 1986, 1987.

Most shutouts participated in, season
N.L.—20—Grover Alexander, Philadelphia, 1916 (won 16, lost 4).
A.L.—18—Ed Walsh, Chicago, 1908 (won 12, lost 6).

Most shutouts won or tied by rookie, season
N.L.—16—George Bradley, St. Louis, 1876.
N.L. since 1900—8—Fernando Valenzuela, Los Angeles, 1981.
A.L.—8—Russ Ford, New York, 1910.
Reb Russell, Chicago, 1913.

Pitching shutout in first major league game
N.L.—Held by 39 pitchers. Last pitcher—Jason Jennings, Colorado, August 23, 2001.
A.L.—Held by 36 pitchers. Last pitcher—Andy Van Hekken, Detroit, September 3, 2002.

Most seasons with 10 or more shutouts won or tied
A.L.—2—Ed Walsh, Chicago, 1906, 1908.
N.L.—2—Grover Alexander, Philadelphia, 1915, 1916.

Most clubs shut out (won or tied), season
N.L. (10-club league)—8—Bob Gibson, St. Louis, 1968.
N.L. (8-club league)—7—Pud Galvin, Buffalo, 1884.
Christy Mathewson, New York, 1907.
Grover Alexander, Philadelphia, 1913 and 1916; also with Chicago, 1919.
A.L. (12-club league)—8—Nolan Ryan, California, 1972.
A.L. (8-club league)—7—Cy Young, Boston, 1904.
Jack Coombs, Philadelphia, 1910.

Most shutouts won from one club, season
N.L.—5—Charles Baldwin, Detroit vs. Philadelphia, 1886.
Grover Alexander, Philadelphia vs. Cincinnati, 1916.
Larry Jaster, St. Louis vs. Los Angeles, 1966, consecutive.
A.L.—5—Tom Hughes, Washington vs. Cleveland, 1905.
A.A.—5—Tony Mullane, Cincinnati vs. New York, 1887.

Most shutouts won or tied, one month
A.L.—6—Doc White, Chicago, September, 1904.
Ed Walsh, Chicago, August, 1906; September, 1908.
N.L.—5—George Bradley, St. Louis, May, 1876.
Tommy Bond, Hartford, June, 1876.
Pud Galvin, Buffalo, August, 1884.
Ben Sanders, Philadelphia, September, 1888.
Jack Chesbro, Pittsburgh, July, 1902.
Don Drysdale, Los Angeles, May, 1968.
Bob Gibson, St. Louis, June, 1968.
Orel Hershiser, Los Angeles, September, 1988.

Longest complete shutout game pitched
N.L.—18 innings—Monte Ward, Providence, August 17, 1882 (won 1-0).
Carl Hubbell, New York, July 2, 1933, first game (won 1-0).

A.L.—18 innings—Ed Summers, Detroit, July 16, 1909 (0-0 tie).
 Walter Johnson, Washington, May 15, 1918 (won 1-0).

Most shutouts lost, career
A.L.—65—Walter Johnson, Washington, 21 years, 1907 through 1927 (won 109, tied 1).
N.L.—40—Christy Mathewson, New York, Cincinnati, 17 years, 1900 through 1916 (won 83).

Most shutouts lost, season
N.L.—14—Jim Devlin, Louisville, 1876 (won 5).
N.L. since 1900—11—Art Raymond, St. Louis, 1908 (won 5).
A.L.—10—Walter Johnson, Washington, 1909 (won 4).

Most shutouts lost to one club, season
N.L.—5—Jim Devlin, Louisville vs. Hartford, 1876.
A.L.—5—Walter Johnson, Washington vs. Chicago, 1909.
N.L. since 1900—4—Irv Young, Boston vs. Pittsburgh, 1906.

Most shutouts lost, one month
A.L.—5—Walter Johnson, Washington, July, 1909.
N.L.—4—Jim Devlin, Louisville, June, 1876.
 Fred Fitzsimmons, New York, September, 1934.
 Jim McAndrew, New York, August, 1968.

Most consecutive shutouts lost, season
N.L.—4—Jim McAndrew, New York, July 21, first game; August 4, second game; August 10, second game; August 17, 1968.
 Randy Johnson, Arizona, June 25, 30, July 5, 10, 1999.
A.L.—2—Held by many pitchers.

Most doubleheader shutouts
N.L.—1—Ed Reulbach, Chicago vs. Brooklyn, September 26, 1908 (won 5-0, 3-0).
A.L.—None.

CONSECUTIVE SCORELESS INNINGS

Most consecutive scoreless innings by righthander, season
N.L.—59—Orel Hershiser, Los Angeles, from sixth inning, August 30 through 10th inning, September 28, 1988.
A.L.—55.2—Walter Johnson, Washington, from second inning, April 10 through third inning, May 14, 1913 (includes two relief appearances).

Most consecutive scoreless innings by lefthander, season
N.L.—45.1—Carl Hubbell, New York, from seventh inning, July 13 through fifth inning, August 1, 1933 (includes two relief appearances).
A.L.—45—Doc White, Chicago, September 12 through September 30, 1904.

Most consecutive scoreless innings from start of career
N.L.—25—George McQuillan, Philadelphia, from first inning, May 8, through ninth inning, September 29, first game, 1907.
A.L.—22—Dave Ferriss, Boston, from first inning, April 29, through fourth inning, May 13, 1945.

Most consecutive scoreless innings, game
N.L.—21—Joe Oeschger, Boston, May 1, 1920; sixth through 26th innings.
A.L.—20—Joe Harris, Boston, September 1, 1906; fourth through 23rd innings.

1-0 GAMES

Most 1-0 games won, career
A.L.—38—Walter Johnson, Washington, 21 years, 1907 through 1927.
N.L.—17—Grover Alexander, Philadelphia, Chicago, St. Louis, 20 years, 1911 through 1930.

For a complete list of pitchers with 10 or more career 1-0 victories, see page 161.

Most 1-0 complete games won, season
A.L.—5—Reb Russell, Chicago, 1913.
 Walter Johnson, Washington, 1913, 1919.
 Joe Bush, Boston, 1918.
 Dean Chance, Los Angeles, 1964 (also one incomplete game).
N.L.—5—Carl Hubbell, New York, 1933.

Most years leading league in 1-0 games won
A.L.—8—Walter Johnson, Washington, 1913 (tied), 1914, 1915 (tied), 1919, 1920 (tied), 1922, 1923 (tied), 1926 (tied).
N.L.—4—Grover Alexander, Philadelphia, Chicago, 1913 (tied), 1916 (tied), 1917 (tied), 1922 (tied).
 Bill C. Lee, Chicago, Philadelphia, Boston, 1934 (tied), 1936, 1944 (tied), 1945 (tied).

Most 1-0 games won from one club, season
A.L.—3—Stan Coveleski, Cleveland vs. Detroit, 1917.
 Walter Johnson, Washington vs. Philadelphia, 1919.
 Jim Bagby Jr., Cleveland vs. Detroit, 1943.
N.L.—2—Held by many pitchers.

Most 1-0 games lost, career
A.L.—26—Walter Johnson, Washington, 21 years, 1907 through 1927 (won 38).
N.L.—13—Lee Meadows, St. Louis, Philadelphia, Pittsburgh, 15 years, 1915 through 1929 (won 7).

Most 1-0 games lost, season
A.L.—5—Bill Donovan, Detroit, 1903 (won 1).
 Jack Warhop, New York, 1914 (won 0).
N.L.—5—George McQuillan, Philadelphia, 1908 (won 2).
 Roger Craig, New York, 1963 (won 0).
 Jim Bunning, Philadelphia, 1967 (won 1).
 Ferguson Jenkins, Chicago, 1968. (won 0).

Most 1-0 games lost to one club, season
A.L.—3—Jack Warhop, New York vs. Washington, 1914.
N.L.—2—Held by many pitchers.

HITS

Most hits allowed, career
M.L.—7,078—Cy Young, Cleveland N.L., St. Louis N.L., Boston A.L., Cleveland A.L., Boston N.L., 22 years, 1890 through 1911 (4,282 in N.L., 2,796 in A.L.).
N.L.—5,490—Pud Galvin, Buffalo, Pittsburgh, St. Louis, 12 years, 1879 through 1892, except 1886, 1890.
N.L. since 1900—4,868—Grover Alexander, Philadelphia, Chicago, St. Louis, 20 years, 1911 through 1930.
A.L.—4,920—Walter Johnson, Washington, 21 years, 1907 through 1927.

For a complete list of pitchers with 4,000 or more career hits allowed, see page 161.

Most hits allowed, season
N.L.—772—John F. Coleman, Philadelphia, 63 games, 538.1 innings, 1883.
N.L. since 1900—415—Bill Carrick, New York, 45 games, 342 innings, 1900.
A.L.—412—Joe McGinnity, Baltimore, 48 games, 382 innings, 1901.

Most seasons leading league in hits allowed
N.L.—5—Robin Roberts, Philadelphia, 1952, 1953, 1954, 1955, 1956.
A.L.—4—Jim Kaat, Minnesota, Chicago, 1965, 1966, 1967, 1975.

Fewest hits allowed for leader, season
N.L.—230—Andy Benes, San Diego, 231.1 innings, 1992.
A.L.—243—Mel Stottlemyre, New York, 279 innings, 1968.

Most consecutive hitless innings, season
A.L.—24—Cy Young, Boston, from seventh inning, April 25 through sixth inning, May 11, 1904. (Note: On April 30 Young relieved in third inning after another pitcher had given up hits in that inning.)
N.L.—21—Johnny Vander Meer, Cincinnati, from first inning, June 11 through third inning, June 19, first game, 1938.

Most consecutive batsmen retired, season
N.L.—41—Jim Barr, San Francisco, August 23 (last 21), August 29 (first 20), 1972.
A.L.—38—David Wells, New York, May 12 (last 10), May 17 (all 27), May 23 (first 1), 1998.

Most hits allowed, game
N.L.—36—John Wadsworth, Louisville, August 17, 1894.
N.L. since 1900—26—Harley Parker, Cincinnati, June 21, 1901.
A.L.—26—Hod Lisenbee, Philadelphia, September 11, 1936.
  Al Travers, Detroit, May 18, 1912 (only major league game).
  (29—Eddie Rommel, Philadelphia, July 10, 1932, pitched last
  17 innings of 18-inning game.)

Most hits allowed, nine-inning shutout game
N.L.—14—Larry Cheney, Chicago vs. New York, September 14,
  1913 (won 7-0).
A.L.—14—Milt Gaston, Washington vs. Cleveland, July 10,
  1928, second game (won 9-0).

Most hits allowed, inning
N.L.—13—George Weidman, Detroit, September 6, 1883,
  seventh inning.
A.L.—12—Merle Adkins, Boston, July 8, 1902, sixth inning.
N.L. since 1900—11—Reggie Grabowski, Philadelphia, August
  4, 1934, second game, ninth inning.

Most consecutive hits allowed, game
A.L.—10—Bill Reidy, Milwaukee, June 2, 1901, ninth inning.
N.L.—10—Heinie Meine, Pittsburgh, June 23, 1930, sixth
  inning.

Most consecutive hits allowed from start of game
N.L.—7—Bill Bonham, Chicago, August 5, 1975 (3 singles, 2
  doubles, 2 homers).
A.L.—7—Kenny Rogers, Minnesota, June 1, 2003 (6 singles, 1
  triple).

Fewest hits allowed, first major league game (nine innings)
N.L.—0—Charles L. Jones, Cincinnati, October 15, 1892.
N.L. since 1900—1—Juan Marichal, San Francisco, July 19,
  1960 (single in eighth inning).
  Jimmy Jones, San Diego, September 21, 1986 (triple in third
  inning).
A.L.—1—Addie Joss, Cleveland, April 26, 1902 (single in seventh
  inning).
  Mike Fornieles, Washington, September 2, 1952, second
  game (single in second inning).
  Billy Rohr, Boston, April 14, 1967 (single with two out in ninth
  inning).

Fewest hits allowed, opening game of season (nine innings)
A.L.—0—Bob Feller, Cleveland, April 16, 1940.
N.L.—1—Held by many pitchers. Last pitcher—Lon Warneke,
  Chicago, April 17, 1934. (Leon Ames, New York, allowed no
  hits in 9.1 innings on April 15, 1909, but lost on seven hits in
  13 innings.)

NO-HIT AND ONE-HIT GAMES

Most no-hitters pitched, career (nine or more innings)
M.L.—7—Nolan Ryan, California A.L., 1973 (2), 1974, 1975;
  Houston N.L., 1981; Texas A.L., 1990, 1991.
A.L.—6—Nolan Ryan, California, 1973 (2), 1974, 1975; Texas,
  1990, 1991.
N.L.—4—Sandy Koufax, Los Angeles, 1962, 1963, 1964, 1965.

**For a complete list of no-hitters, see
page 184.**

Most no-hit games, season
N.L.—2—Johnny Vander Meer, Cincinnati, June 11, 15, 1938 (con-
  secutive).
  Jim Maloney, Cincinnati, June 14, first 10 innings of 11-inning
  game; August 19, 1965, first game, 10 innings.
A.L.—2—Allie Reynolds, New York, July 12, September 28, first
  game, 1951.
  Virgil Trucks, Detroit, May 15, August 25, 1952.
  Nolan Ryan, California, May 15, July 15, 1973.

Most consecutive no-hit games
N.L.—2—Johnny Vander Meer, Cincinnati, June 11, 15, 1938.
A.L.—Never accomplished.

Longest no-hit complete game
A.A.—10 innings—Sam Kimber, Brooklyn vs. Toledo, October 4,

1884.
N.L.—10 innings—George Wiltse, New York vs. Philadelphia,
  July 4, 1908, a.m. game.
  Fred Toney, Cincinnati vs. Chicago, May 2, 1917.
  Jim Maloney, Cincinnati vs. Chicago, August 19, 1965, first
  game.
A.L.—9—Held by many pitchers.

Most low-hit (no-hit and one-hit) games, career (nine or more innings)
M.L.—19—Nolan Ryan, New York N.L., California A.L., Houston
  N.L., Texas A.L., 1966, 1968 through 1992 (6 no-hit, 9 one-hit
  in A.L.; 1 no-hit, 3 one-hit in N.L.).
A.L.—15—Nolan Ryan, California, Texas, 1972 through 1979,
  1989 through 1992 (6 no-hit, 9 one-hit).
N.L.—8—Hoss Radbourn, Buffalo, Providence, Boston,
  Cincinnati, 1880 through 1889, 1891 (1 no-hit, 7 one-hit).
  Jim Maloney, Cincinnati, 1960 through 1970 (3 no-hit, 5
  one-hit).

Most low-hit (no-hit and one-hit) games, season (nine or more innings)
U.A.—4—Hugh Daily, Chicago, 1884.
N.L.—4—George Bradley, St. Louis, 1876.
N.L. since 1900—4—Grover Alexander, Philadelphia, 1915.
A.L.—3—Addie Joss, Cleveland, 1907.
  Bob Feller, Cleveland, 1946.
  Virgil Trucks, Detroit, 1952.
  Nolan Ryan, California, 1973.
  Dave Stieb, Toronto, 1988.

Longest one-hit complete game
N.L.—12.2 innings—Harvey Haddix, Pittsburgh vs. Milwaukee,
  May 26, 1959 (one double).
A.L.—10—Doc White, Chicago vs. Cleveland, September 6, 1903
  (one double).
  Bobo Newsom, St. Louis vs. Boston, September 18, 1934
  (one single).
  Bert Blyleven, Texas vs. Oakland, June 21, 1976 (one single).

SINGLES, DOUBLES AND TRIPLES

Most singles allowed, game
N.L.—28—John Wadsworth, Louisville, August 17, 1894.
A.L.—23—Charles Baker, Cleveland, April 28, 1901.

Most singles allowed, inning
N.L.—10—Reggie Grabowski, Philadelphia, August 4, 1934,
  second game, ninth inning.
A.L.—10—Eldon Auker, Detroit, September 29, 1935, second
  game, second inning.

Most doubles allowed, game
N.L.—14—George Derby, Buffalo, July 3, 1883.
A.L.—8—Ed LaFitte, Detroit, October 8, 1911, first game.
  Jim Abbott, New York, July 14, 1994.

Most doubles allowed, inning
A.L.—6—Lefty Grove, Boston, June 9, 1934, eighth inning.
  Mike Mussina, New York, July 31, 2002, second inning.
N.L.—6—Dustin Hermanson, Montreal, July 22, 1999, second
  inning.

Most triples allowed, game
N.L.—9—Mike Sullivan, Cleveland, September 3, 1894, first
  game.
A.L.—6—Al Travers, Detroit, May 18, 1912.

Most triples allowed, inning
A.L.—4—Fred Marberry, Detroit, May 6, 1934, fourth inning.
  Al Travers, Detroit, May 18, 1912, fifth inning.
N.L.—3—Held by many pitchers.

HOME RUNS

Most home runs allowed, career
M.L.—505—Robin Roberts, Philadelphia N.L., Baltimore A.L.,
  Houston N.L., Chicago N.L., 19 years, 1948 through 1966
  (418 in N.L., 87 in A.L.).
N.L.—434—Warren Spahn, Boston, Milwaukee, New York, San
  Francisco, 21 years, 1942 through 1965, except 1943, 1944,

1945 in military service.
A.L.—422—Frank Tanana, California, Boston, Texas, Detroit, New York, 21 years, 1973 through 1993.

Most home runs allowed, season
A.L.—50—Bert Blyleven, Minnesota, 36 games, 271.2 innings, 1986.
N.L.—48—Jose Lima, Houston, 33 games, 196.1 innings, 2000.

Most seasons leading league in home runs allowed
M.L.—7—Ferguson Jenkins, Chicago N.L., Texas A.L., 1967, 1968 (tied), 1971, 1972, 1973, 1975, 1979 (5 in N.L., 2 in A.L.).
N.L.—5—Robin Roberts, Philadelphia, 1954, 1955, 1956, 1957, 1960.
 Ferguson Jenkins, Chicago, 1967, 1968 (tied), 1971, 1972, 1973.
A.L.—3—Pedro Ramos, Washington, Minnesota, 1957, 1958, 1961.
 Denny McLain, Detroit, 1966, 1967, 1968.

Most seasons allowing 30 or more home runs
M.L.—9—Robin Roberts, Philadelphia N.L., Baltimore A.L., 1953, 1954, 1955, 1956, 1957, 1958, 1959, 1960, 1963.
N.L.—8—Robin Roberts, Philadelphia, 1953, 1954, 1955, 1956, 1957, 1958, 1959, 1960.
A.L.—4—Mudcat Grant, Cleveland, Minnesota, 1961, 1963, 1964, 1965.
 Denny McLain, Detroit, Washington, 1966, 1967, 1968, 1971.
 Jack Morris, Detroit, 1982, 1983, 1986, 1987.

Most home runs allowed to one club, season
A.L.—15—Jim Perry, Cleveland vs. New York, 1960.
N.L.—13—Warren Hacker, Chicago vs. Brooklyn, 1956.
 Warren Spahn, Milwaukee vs. Chicago, 1958.

Fewest home runs allowed, season (most innings)
A.L.—0—Allen Sothoron, St. Louis, Boston, Cleveland, 29 games, 178 innings, 1921.
N.L.—1—Eppa Rixey, Cincinnati, 40 games, 301 innings, 1921.

Fewest home runs allowed, season (since 1950; 250 or more innings)
N.L.—5—Bob Veale, Pittsburgh, 39 games, 266 innings, 1965.
 Ron Reed, Atlanta, St. Louis, 34 games, 250 innings, 1975.
A.L.—8—Mike Garcia, Cleveland, 45 games, 259 innings, 1954.

Most home runs allowed, game
N.L.—7—Charlie Sweeney, St. Louis, June 12, 1886.
N.L. since 1900—6—Larry Benton, New York, May 12, 1930.
 Hollis Thurston, Brooklyn, August 13, 1932, first game.
 Wayman Kerksieck, Philadelphia, August 13, 1939, first game.
A.L.—6—Al Thomas, St. Louis, June 27, 1936.
 George Caster, Philadelphia, September 24, 1940, first game.
 Tim Wakefield, Boston, August 8, 2004.

Most home runs allowed, inning
N.L.—4—Bill Lampe, Boston, June 6, 1894, third inning.
 Larry Benton, New York, May 12, 1930, seventh inning.
 Wayman Kerksieck, Philadelphia, August 13, 1939, first game, fourth inning.
 Charlie Bicknell, Philadelphia, June 6, 1948, first game, sixth inning.
 Ben Wade, Brooklyn, May 28, 1954, eighth inning.
 Mario Soto, Cincinnati, April 29, 1986, fourth inning.
 John Smoltz, Atlanta, June 19, 1994, first inning.
 Jose Lima, Houston, April 27, 2000, first inning.
 Andy Benes, St. Louis, July 23, 2000, second inning.
 Phil Norton, Chicago, August 8, 2000, fourth inning.
 Steve Trachsel, New York, May 17, 2001, third inning.
 Alan Embree, San Francisco, May 20, 2001, seventh inning.
 Jeff Austin, Cincinnati, May 28, 2003, first inning.
 Jose Acevedo, Cincinnati, September 8, 2004, first inning.
A.L.—4—George Caster, Philadelphia, September 24, 1940, first game, sixth inning.
 Cal McLish, Cleveland, May 22, 1957, sixth inning.
 Paul Foytack, Los Angeles, July 31, 1963, second game, sixth inning (consecutive).
 Catfish Hunter, New York, June 17, 1977, first inning.
 Mike Caldwell, Milwaukee, May 31, 1980, fourth inning.
 Scott Sanderson, New York, May 2, 1992, fifth inning.
 Brian Anderson, California, September 5, 1995, second inning.
 Dave Telgheder, Oakland, September 21, 1996, third inning.

Dave Burba, Cleveland, June 29, 2001, fourth inning.
 Pat Mahomes, Texas, August 17, 2001, sixth inning.

Most consecutive home runs allowed, inning
A.L.—4—Paul Foytack, Los Angeles, July 31, 1963, second game, sixth inning.
N.L.—3—Held by many pitchers. Last pitchers—Josh Beckett, Florida, April 28, 2002, sixth inning; Bruce Chen, Montreal, May 3, 2002, first inning; Jose Cabrera, Milwaukee, May 23, 2002, ninth inning; Kevin Jarvis, San Diego, July 2, 2002, second inning; Todd Jones, Colorado, September 19, 2002, eighth inning.

Most grand slams allowed, career
M.L.—10—Nolan Ryan, New York N.L., California A.L., Houston N.L., Texas A.L., 1970, 1972, 1973, 1977, 1984, 1985, 1988, 1990, 1992 (2) (6 in A.L., 4 in N.L.).
A.L.—9—Ned Garver, St. Louis, Detroit, Kansas City, 1949, 1950 (2), 1951, 1952, 1954, 1955 (2), 1959.
N.L.—9—Jerry Reuss, St. Louis, Houston, Pittsburgh, Los Angeles, 1971 (2), 1972, 1973, 1974, 1976 (2), 1979, 1980.

For a complete list of pitchers with seven or more career grand slams allowed, see page 161.

Most grand slams allowed, season
N.L.—4—Tug McGraw, Philadelphia, 1979.
 Chan Ho Park, Los Angeles, 1999.
 Matt Clement, San Diego, 2000.
A.L.—4—Ray Narleski, Detroit, 1959.
 Mike Schooler, Seattle, 1992.

EXTRA BASE HITS AND TOTAL BASES

Most extra base hits allowed, game
N.L.—16—George Derby, Buffalo, July 3, 1883.
A.L.—10—Dale Gear, Washington, August 10, 1901, second game.
 Luis Tiant, Cleveland, April 18, 1969.

Most total bases allowed, game
N.L.—55—Bill Rhodes, Louisville, June 18, 1893.
N.L. since 1900—39—Dummy Taylor, New York, September 23, 1903.
A.L.—41—Dale Gear, Washington, August 10, 1901, second game.

Most total bases allowed, inning
N.L.—23—Bill Rhodes, Louisville, June 18, 1893, first inning.
A.L.—22—George Caster, Philadelphia, September 24, 1940, first game, sixth inning.
N.L. since 1900—21—Jeff D'Amico, Milwaukee, September 30, 2001, third inning.

BASES ON BALLS

Most bases on balls, career
M.L.—2,795—Nolan Ryan, New York N.L., California A.L., Houston N.L., Texas A.L., 27 years, 1966, 1968 through 1993 (1,655 in A.L., 1,140 in N.L.).
A.L.—1,775—Early Wynn, Washington, Cleveland, Chicago, 23 years, 1939, 1941, through 1963, except 1945 in military service.
N.L.—1,717—Steve Carlton, St. Louis, Philadelphia, San Francisco, 22 years, 1965 through 1986.

For a complete list of pitchers with 1,200 or more career bases on balls allowed, see page 161.

Most bases on balls, season
N.L.—276—Amos Rusie, New York, 64 games, 1890.
N.L. since 1900—185—Sam Jones, Chicago, 242 innings, 1955.
A.L.—208—Bob Feller, Cleveland, 278 innings, 1938.

Most seasons leading league in bases on balls
M.L.—8—Nolan Ryan, California A.L., 1972 through 1978, except 1975; Houston N.L., 1980, 1982.

A.L.—6—Nolan Ryan, California, 1972, 1973, 1974, 1976, 1977, 1978.

N.L.—5—Amos Rusie, New York, 1890, 1891, 1892, 1893, 1894.

N.L. since 1900—4—Jimmy Ring, Philadelphia, 1922, 1923, 1924, 1925.
Kirby Higbe, Chicago, Philadelphia, Pittsburgh, Brooklyn, 1939, 1940, 1941, 1947.
Sam Jones, Chicago, St. Louis, San Francisco, 1955, 1956, 1958, 1959.
Bob Veale, Pittsburgh, 1964, 1965 (tied), 1967, 1968.

Most bases on balls, game

N.L.—16—Bill George, New York, May 30, 1887, first game.
George Van Haltren, Chicago, June 27, 1887.

N.L. since 1900—14—Henry Mathewson, New York, October 5, 1906.

P.L.—16—Henry Gruber, Cleveland, April 19, 1890.

A.L.—16—Bruno Haas, Philadelphia, June 23, 1915 (his first major league game).
(16—Tommy Byrne, St. Louis, August 22, 1951, 13 innings.)

Most bases on balls, nine-inning shutout game

A.L.—11—Lefty Gomez, New York, August 1, 1941.
Mel Stottlemyre, New York, May 21, 1970; pitched first 8.1 innings.

N.L.—9—Vinegar Bend Mizell, St. Louis, September 1, 1958, first game.
(10—Jim Maloney, Cincinnati, August 19, 1965, first game, 10 innings.
J.R. Richard, Houston, July 6, 1976, 10 innings.)

Most bases on balls, inning

A.L.—8—Bill Gray, Washington, August 28, 1909, first game, second inning.

N.L.—7—George Keefe, Washington, May 1, 1889, fifth inning.
Tony Mullane, Baltimore, June 18, 1894, a.m. game, first inning.
Bob Ewing, Cincinnati, April 19, 1902, fourth inning. (His first major league game.)

Most consecutive bases on balls, inning

A.L.—7—Bill Gray, Washington, August 28, 1909, first game, second inning.

N.L.—6—Bill Kennedy, Brooklyn, August 31, 1900, second inning.

Most consecutive bases on balls, from start of game

N.L.—4—Johnny Vander Meer, Cincinnati, June 16, 1941.
Don Warthen, Montreal, May 25, 1977.

A.L.—4—Jim Bagby Jr., Boston, April 21, 1946, second game.
Brian Boehringer, New York, July 5, 1995.
Roger Pavlik, Texas, April 18, 1997.
Bartolo Colon, Cleveland, June 29, 2000.

Most consecutive innings with no bases on balls, season

A.L.—84.1—Bill Fischer, Kansas City, August 3 through September 30, 1962.

N.L.—72.1—Greg Maddux, Atlanta, June 20, third inning, through August 12, second inning, 2001.

Most consecutive innings with no bases on balls from start of season

N.L.—52—Grover Alexander, Chicago, April 18 through May 17, 1923.

Longest game without a base on balls

N.L.—21 innings—Babe Adams, Pittsburgh, July 17, 1914.

A.L.—20 innings—Cy Young, Boston, July 4, 1905, p.m. game.

Fewest bases on balls, season (250 or more innings)

N.L.—18—Babe Adams, Pittsburgh, 263 innings, 1920.

A.L.—28—Cy Young, Boston, 380 innings, 1904.

Most intentional bases on balls, season

N.L.—23—Mike Garman, St. Louis, 66 games, 79 innings, 1975.
Dale Murray, Cincinnati, New York, 68 games, 119 innings, 1978.
Kent Tekulve, Pittsburgh, 85 games, 128.2 innings, 1982.

A.L.—19—John Hiller, Detroit, 59 games, 150 innings, 1974.

STRIKEOUTS
CAREER

Most strikeouts, career

M.L.—5,714—Nolan Ryan, New York N.L., California A.L.,

Houston N.L., Texas A.L., 27 years, 1966, 1968 through 1993 (3,355 in A.L., 2,359 in N.L.).

A.L.—4,099—Roger Clemens, Boston, Toronto, New York, 20 years, 1984 through 2003.

N.L.—4,000—Steve Carlton, St. Louis, Philadelphia, San Francisco, 22 years, 1965 through 1986.

For a complete list of pitchers with 2,000 or more career strikeouts, see page 161.

Most strikeouts by righthander, career

M.L.—5,714—Nolan Ryan, New York N.L., California A.L., Houston N.L., Texas A.L., 27 years, 1966, 1968 through 1993 (3,355 in A.L., 2,359 in N.L.).

A.L.—4,099—Roger Clemens, Boston, Toronto, New York, 20 years, 1984 through 2003.

N.L.—3,272—Tom Seaver, New York, Cincinnati, 17 years, 1967 through 1983.

Most strikeouts by lefthander, career

M.L.—4,161—Randy Johnson, Montreal N.L., Seattle A.L., Houston N.L., Arizona N.L., 17 years, 1988 through 2004.

N.L.—4,000—Steve Carlton, St. Louis, Philadelphia, San Francisco, 22 years, 1965 through 1986.

A.L.—2,679—Mickey Lolich, Detroit, 13 years, 1963 through 1975.

SEASON

Most strikeouts, season

A.A.—505—Matt Kilroy, Baltimore, 65 games, 570 innings, 1886.

N.L.—411—Hoss Radbourn, Providence, 72 games, 679 innings, 1884.

N.L. since 1900—382—Sandy Koufax, Los Angeles, 43 games, 336 innings, 1965.

A.L.—383—Nolan Ryan, California, 41 games, 326 innings, 1973.

Most strikeouts by righthander, season

U.A.—483—Hugh Daily, Chicago, Pittsburgh, Washington, 58 games, 501 innings, 1884.

N.L.—411—Hoss Radbourn, Providence, 72 games, 679 innings, 1884.

N.L. since 1900—319—Curt Schilling, Philadelphia, 35 games, 254.1 innings, 1997.

A.L.—383—Nolan Ryan, California, 41 games, 326 innings, 1973.

Most strikeouts by lefthander, season

A.A.—505—Matt Kilroy, Baltimore, 65 games, 570 innings, 1886.

N.L.—382—Sandy Koufax, Los Angeles, 43 games, 336 innings, 1965.

A.L.—349—Rube Waddell, Philadelphia, 46 games, 384 innings, 1904.

Most seasons leading league in strikeouts

A.L.—12—Walter Johnson, Washington, 1910, 1912, 1913, 1914, 1915, 1916, 1917, 1918, 1919, 1921, 1923, 1924.

N.L.—7—Dazzy Vance, Brooklyn, 1922 through 1928.

Most consecutive seasons leading league in strikeouts

A.L.—8—Walter Johnson, Washington, 1912 through 1919.

N.L.—7—Dazzy Vance, Brooklyn, 1922 through 1928.

Fewest strikeouts for leader, season

A.L.—113—Cecil Hughson, Boston, 281 innings, 1942.
Bobo Newsom, Washington, 214 innings, 1942.

N.L.—133—Rube Waddell, Pittsburgh, 213 innings, 1900.

Most seasons with 400 or more strikeouts

M.L.—1—Fred Shaw, Detroit N.L., Boston U.A., 1884.
Hugh Daily, Chicago U.A., Pittsburgh U.A., Washington U.A., 1884.
Hoss Radbourn, Providence N.L., 1884.
Charlie Buffinton, Boston N.L., 1884.
Matt Kilroy, Baltimore A.A., 1886.
Tom Ramsey, Louisville A.A., 1886.

A.A.—1—Matt Kilroy, Baltimore, 1886.
Tom Ramsey, Louisville, 1886.

U.A.—1—Hugh Daily, Chicago, Pittsburgh, Washington, 1884.

N.L.—1—Hoss Radbourn, Providence, 1884.
Charlie Buffinton, Boston, 1884.

Most seasons with 300 or more strikeouts

M.L.—6—Nolan Ryan, California A.L., 1972 (329), 1973 (383), 1974 (367), 1976 (327), 1977 (341); Texas A.L., 1989 (301). Randy Johnson, Seattle A.L., 1993 (308); Seattle A.L./Houston N.L., 1998 (329—213 with Sea., 113 with Hou.); Arizona N.L., 1999 (364), 2000 (347), 2001 (372), 2002 (334).

A.L.—6—Nolan Ryan, California, 1972 (329), 1973 (383), 1974 (367), 1976 (327), 1977 (341); Texas, 1989 (301).

N.L.—4—Randy Johnson, Arizona, 1999 (364), 2000 (347), 2001 (372), 2002 (334).

Most seasons with 200 or more strikeouts

M.L.—15—Nolan Ryan, California A.L., Houston N.L., Texas A.L., 1972 through 1974, 1976 through 1980, 1982, 1985, 1987 through 1991.

A.L.—11—Roger Clemens, Boston, Toronto, New York, 1986 through 1992, 1996 through 1998, 2001.

N.L.—10—Tom Seaver, New York, Cincinnati, 1968 through 1976, 1978.

Most consecutive seasons with 200 or more strikeouts

N.L.—9—Tom Seaver, New York, 1968 through 1976.

A.L.—7—Rube Waddell, Philadelphia, St. Louis, 1902 through 1908.
Walter Johnson, Washington, 1910 through 1916.
Roger Clemens, Boston, 1986 through 1992.

Most seasons with 100 or more strikeouts

M.L.—24—Nolan Ryan, New York N.L., California A.L., Houston N.L., Texas A.L., 1968 through 1992, except 1969 (12 in N.L., 12 in A.L.).

A.L.—19—Roger Clemens, Boston, Toronto, New York, 1984, 1986 through 2003.

N.L.—18—Steve Carlton, St. Louis, Philadelphia, 1967 through 1984.

Most consecutive years with 100 or more strikeouts

M.L.—23—Nolan Ryan, New York N.L., California A.L., Houston N.L., Texas A.L., 1970 through 1992 (11 in N.L., 12 in A.L.).

N.L.—18—Steve Carlton, St. Louis, Philadelphia, 1967 through 1984.

A.L.—18—Roger Clemens, Boston, Toronto, New York, 1986 through 2003.

Most strikeouts by relief pitcher, season

A.L.—181—Dick Radatz, Boston, 1964, 79 games, 157 innings.
N.L.—153—Dick Selma, Philadelphia, 1970, 73 games, 134 innings.

Most strikeouts by rookie, season (since 1900)

N.L.—276—Dwight Gooden, New York, 218 innings, 1984.
A.L.—245—Herb Score, Cleveland, 227 innings, 1955.

GAME AND INNING

Most strikeouts, game

A.L.—20—Roger Clemens, Boston, April 29, 1986.
Roger Clemens, Boston, September 18, 1996.
(21—Tom Cheney, Washington, September 12, 1962, 16 innings.)

N.L.—20—Kerry Wood, Chicago, May 6, 1998.
(20—Randy Johnson, Arizona, May 8, 2001, pitched first nine innings of 11-inning game.)

U.A.—19—Hugh Daily, Chicago, July 7, 1884.

Most strikeouts by righthander, game

A.L.—20—Roger Clemens, Boston, April 29, 1986.
Roger Clemens, Boston, September 18, 1996.
(21—Tom Cheney, Washington, September 12, 1962, 16 innings.)

N.L.—20—Kerry Wood, Chicago, May 6, 1998.

Most strikeouts by lefthander, game

N.L.—19—Steve Carlton, St. Louis, September 15, 1969.
(20—Randy Johnson, Arizona, May 8, 2001, pitched first nine innings of 11-inning game.)

A.L.—19—Randy Johnson, Seattle, June 24, 1997.
Randy Johnson, Seattle, August 8, 1997.

Most strikeouts, night game

A.L.—20—Roger Clemens, Boston, April 29, 1986.
Roger Clemens, Boston, September 18, 1996.

N.L.—19—Steve Carlton, St. Louis, September 15, 1969.

Most strikeouts by losing pitcher, game

N.L.—19—Steve Carlton, St. Louis, September 15, 1969 (lost 4-3)
(18—Warren Spahn, Boston, June 14, 1952, 15 innings, lost 3-1.
Jim Maloney, Cincinnati, June 14, 1965, 11 innings, lost 1-0.)

A.L.—19—Randy Johnson, Seattle, June 24, 1997 (lost 4-1).
(19—Nolan Ryan, California, August 20, 1974, 11 innings, lost 1-0.)

U.A.—18—Fred Shaw, Boston, July 19, 1884 (lost 1-0).
Henry Porter, Milwaukee, October 3, 1884 (lost 5-4).

A.A.—17—Guy Hecker, Louisville, August 26, 1884 (lost 4-3).

Most strikeouts, first major league game (since 1900)

N.L.—15—Karl Spooner, Brooklyn, September 22, 1954.
J.R. Richard, Houston, September 5, 1971, second game.

A.L.—12—Elmer Myers, Philadelphia, October 6, 1915, second game.
Steve Woodard, Milwaukee, July 28, 1997, first game.

Most strikeouts by relief pitcher, game

N.L.—16—Randy Johnson, Arizona, July 18, finished July 19, 2001, last seven innings of nine-inning game.

A.L.—15—Walter Johnson, Washington, July 25, 1913, last 11.1 innings of 15-inning game.
14—Denny McLain, Detroit, June 15, 1965, 6.2 innings of nine-inning game.

Most games with 15 or more strikeouts, career

M.L.—29—Randy Johnson, Montreal N.L., Seattle A.L., Houston N.L., Arizona N.L., 17 years, 1988 through 2004 (17 in A.L., 12 in N.L.).

A.L.—23—Nolan Ryan, California, 1972 (4), 1973 (2), 1974 (6), 1976 (3), 1977 (2), 1978 (1), 1979 (1); Texas, 1989 (1), 1990 (2), 1991 (1).

N.L.—12—Randy Johnson, Houston, 1998 (1), Arizona, 1999 (2), 2001 (4), 2002 (4), 2004 (1).

Most games with 10 or more strikeouts, career

M.L.—215—Nolan Ryan, New York N.L., California A.L., Houston N.L., Texas A.L., 27 years, 1966 through 1993, except 1967 (148 in A.L., 67 in N.L.).

A.L.—148—Nolan Ryan, California, Texas, 13 years, 1972 through 1979, 1989 through 1993.

N.L.—97—Sandy Koufax, Brooklyn, Los Angeles, 12 years, 1955 through 1966.

Most games with 10 or more strikeouts, season

A.L.—23—Nolan Ryan, California, 1973.
N.L.—23—Randy Johnson, Arizona, 1999, 2000, 2001.

Most strikeouts, inning (*consecutive)

A.A.—4—Bobby Mathews, Philadelphia, September 30, 1885, seventh inning.

N.L.—4—Ed Crane, New York, October 4, 1888, fifth inning.*
Hooks Wiltse, New York, May 15, 1906, fifth inning.*
Jim Davis, Chicago, May 27, 1956, first game, sixth inning.*
Joe Nuxhall, Cincinnati, August 11, 1959, first game, sixth inning.
Pete Richert, Los Angeles, April 12, 1962, third inning.*
Don Drysdale, Los Angeles, April 17, 1965, second inning.*
Bob Gibson, St. Louis, June 7, 1966, fourth inning.
Bill Bonham, Chicago, July 31, 1974, first game, second inning.*
Phil Niekro, Atlanta, July 29, 1977, sixth inning.
Mario Soto, Cincinnati, May 17, 1984, third inning.
Mike Scott, Houston, September 3, 1986, fifth inning.
Paul Assenmacher, Atlanta, August 22, 1989, fifth inning.
Tim Birtsas, Cincinnati, June 4, 1990, seventh inning.
Mark Wohlers, Atlanta, June 7, 1995, ninth inning.
Bruce Ruffin, Colorado, July 25, 1996, ninth inning.
Derek Wallace, New York, September 13, 1996, ninth inning.
Kirt Ojala, Florida, September 16, 1998, fourth inning*
Archie Corbin, Florida, April 28, 1999, seventh inning.
Jerry Spradlin, San Francisco, July 22, 1999, seventh inning.
Steve Kline, Montreal, August 17, 1999, seventh inning.*
Frankie Rodriguez, Cincinnati, July 22, 2001, seventh inning.
A.J. Burnett, Florida, July 5, 2002, first inning.
Kerry Wood, Chicago, September 2, 2002, fourth inning.*
Octavio Dotel, Houston, June 11, 2003, eighth inning.*
Darren Dreifort, Los Angeles, May 22, 2003, second inning.

Brad Lidge, Houston, June 13, 2004, seventh inning.
Mike Stanton, New York, August 3, 2004, eighth inning.
A.L.—4—Walter Johnson, Washington, April 15, 1911, fifth inning.
Guy Morton, Cleveland, June 11, 1916, seventh inning.
Ryne Duren, Los Angeles, May 18, 1961, seventh inning.
Lee Stange, Cleveland, September 2, 1964, seventh inning.
Mike Cuellar, Baltimore, May 29, 1970, fourth inning.*
Mike Paxton, Cleveland, July 21, 1978, fifth inning.*
Bobby Witt, Texas, August 2, 1987, second inning.*
Charlie Hough, Texas, July 4, 1988, first inning.
Matt Young, Seattle, September 9, 1990, first inning.
Paul Shuey, Cleveland, May 14, 1994, ninth inning.
Kevin Appier, Kansas City, September 3, 1996, fourth inning.*
Wilson Alvarez, Chicago, July 21, 1997, seventh inning.*
Blake Stein, Oakland, July 27, 1998, fourth inning.
Chuck Finley, Anaheim, May 12, 1999, third inning.
Tim Wakefield, Boston, August 10, 1999, ninth inning.
Chuck Finley, Anaheim, August 15, 1999, first inning.*
Chuck Finley, Cleveland, April 16, 2000, third inning.*
Erik Hiljus, Oakland, June 30, 2001, seventh inning.
Kazuhiro Sasaki, Seattle, April 4, 2003, ninth inning.*

Three strikeouts on nine pitched balls, inning

A.L.—Rube Waddell, Philadelphia, July 1, 1902, third inning.
Hollis Thurston, Chicago, August 22, 1923, 12th inning.
Lefty Grove, Philadelphia, August 23, 1928, second inning.
Lefty Grove, Philadelphia, September 27, 1928, seventh inning.
Billy Hoeft, Detroit, September 7, 1953, second game, seventh inning.
Jim Bunning, Detroit, August 2, 1959, ninth inning.
Al Downing, New York, August 11, 1967, first game, second inning.
Nolan Ryan, California, July 9, 1972, second inning.
Ron Guidry, New York, August 7, 1984, second game, ninth inning.
Jeff Montgomery, Kansas City, April 29, 1990, eighth inning.
Pedro Martinez, Boston, May 18, 2002, first inning.
N.L.—Pat Ragan, Brooklyn, October 5, 1914, second game, eighth inning.
Hod Eller, Cincinnati, August 21, 1917, ninth inning.
Joe Oeschger, Boston, September 8, 1921, first game, fourth inning.
Dazzy Vance, Brooklyn, September 14, 1924, third inning.
Warren Spahn, Boston, July 2, 1949, second inning.
Sandy Koufax, Los Angeles, June 30, 1962, first inning.
Sandy Koufax, Los Angeles, April 18, 1964, third inning.
Bob Bruce, Houston, April 19, 1964, eighth inning.
Nolan Ryan, New York, April 19, 1968, third inning.
Bob Gibson, St. Louis, May 12, 1969, seventh inning.
Milt Pappas, Chicago, September 24, 1971, fourth inning.
Lynn McGlothen, St. Louis, August 19, 1975, second inning.
Bruce Sutter, Chicago, September 8, 1977, ninth inning.
Jeff Robinson, Pittsburgh, September 7, 1987, eighth inning.
Rob Dibble, Cincinnati, June 4, 1989, eighth inning.
Andy Ashby, Philadelphia, June 15, 1991, fourth inning.
David Cone, New York, August 30, 1991, fifth inning.
Pete Harnisch, Houston, September 6, 1991, seventh inning.
Trevor Wilson, San Francisco, June 7, 1992, ninth inning.
Mel Rojas, Montreal, May 11, 1994, ninth inning.
Mike Magnante, Houston, August 22, 1997, ninth inning.
Randy Johnson, Arizona, August 23, 2001, sixth inning.
Jason Isringhausen, St. Louis, April 13, 2002, ninth inning.
Byung-Hyun Kim, Arizona, May 11, 2002, eighth inning.
Brian Lawrence, San Diego, June 12, 2002, third inning.
Brandon Backe, Houston, April 15, 2004, eighth inning.
Ben Sheets, Milwaukee, June 13, 2004, third inning.
LaTroy Hawkins, Chicago, September 11, 2004, ninth inning.

CONSECUTIVE AND IN CONSECUTIVE GAMES

Most consecutive strikeouts, season

N.L.—10—Tom Seaver, New York, April 22, 1970, 1 in sixth inning, 3 in seventh inning, 3 in eighth inning, 3 in ninth inning.
Eric Gagne, Los Angeles, May 17 (2), 18 (3), 20 (3), 21 (2), 2003.
A.L.—9—Ron Davis, New York, May 4 (8), May 9 (1), 1981.

Most consecutive strikeouts, game

N.L.—10—Tom Seaver, New York, April 22, 1970, 1 in sixth inning, 3 in seventh inning, 3 in eighth inning, 3 in ninth inning.
A.L.—8—Nolan Ryan, California, July 9, 1972, 2 in first inning, 3 in second inning, 3 in third inning.
Nolan Ryan, California, July 15, 1973, 1 in first inning, 3 in second inning, 3 in third inning, 1 in fourth inning.
Ron Davis, New York, May 4, 1981, 2 in seventh inning, 3 in eighth inning, 3 in ninth inning.
Roger Clemens, Boston, April 29, 1986, 3 in fourth inning, 3 in fifth inning, 2 in sixth inning.
Blake Stein, Kansas City, June 17, 2001, 1 in first inning, 3 in second inning, 3 in third inning, 1 in fourth inning.

Most consecutive strikeouts, first major league game

A.L.—7—Sammy Stewart, Baltimore, September 1, 1978, second game, 3 in second inning, 3 in third inning, 1 in fourth inning.
N.L.—6—Karl Spooner, Brooklyn, September 22, 1954, 3 in seventh inning, 3 in eighth inning.
Pete Richert, Los Angeles, April 12, 1962, 1 in second inning, 4 in third inning, 1 in fourth inning (first six batters he faced in majors).

Most consecutive strikeouts by relief pitcher, game

A.L.—8—Ron Davis, New York, May 4, 1981, 2 in seventh inning, 3 in eighth inning, 3 in ninth inning.
N.L.—7—Randy Johnson, Arizona, July 18, finished July 19, 2001 (Johnson actually faced all his batters on July 19, 2 in sixth inning, 3 in seventh inning, 2 in eighth inning.)

Most consecutive strikeouts from start of game

N.L.—9—Mickey Welch, New York, August 28, 1884.
N.L. since 1900—8—Jim Deshaies, Houston, September 23, 1986.
A.L.—7—Joe Cowley, Chicago, May 28, 1986.

Most strikeouts, two consecutive games

U.A.—34—Fred Shaw, Boston, July 19 (18), 21 (16), 1884, 19 innings.
N.L.—33—Kerry Wood, Chicago, May 6 (20), 11 (13), 1998, 16 innings.
A.L.—32—Luis Tiant, Cleveland, June 29, first game (13), July 3 (19), 1968, 19 innings.
Nolan Ryan, California, August 7 (13), 12 (19), 1974, 17.2 innings.
Randy Johnson, Seattle, August 8 (19), 15 (13), 1997, 17 innings.
Pedro Martinez, Boston, May 6 (17), 12 (15), 2000, 18 innings.

HIT BATSMEN

Most hit batsmen, career

A.L.—206—Walter Johnson, Washington, 21 years, 1907 through 1927.
N.L.—195—Emerson Hawley, St. Louis, Pittsburgh, Cincinnati, New York, 9 years, 1892 through 1900.
N.L. since 1900—154—Don Drysdale, Brooklyn, Los Angeles, 14 years, 1956 through 1969.

Most hit batsmen, season

A.A.—54—Phil Knell, Columbus, 58 games, 1891.
N.L.—41—Joe McGinnity, Brooklyn, 45 games, 1900.
A.L.—31—Chick Fraser, Philadelphia, 39 games, 1901.

Most seasons leading league in hit batsmen

A.L.—6—Howard Ehmke, Detroit, Boston, Philadelphia, 1920, 1921 (tied), 1922, 1923 (tied), 1925, 1927.
N.L.—5—Don Drysdale, Los Angeles, 1958, 1959, 1960, 1961, 1965 (tied).

Fewest hit batsmen for leader, season
A.L.—6—Held by five pitchers. Last pitchers—Spud Chandler, New York, 1940; Al Smith, Cleveland, 1940.
N.L.—6—Held by five pitchers. Last pitchers—Rex Barney, Brooklyn, 1948; Sheldon Jones, New York, 1948; Kent Peterson, Cincinnati, 1948.

Most hit batsmen, game
A.A.—6—Ed Knouff, Baltimore, April 25, 1887.
N.L.—6—John Grimes, St. Louis, July 31, 1897, first game.
N.L. since 1900—4—Held by 9 pitchers. Last pitcher—Pedro Astacio, Colorado, April 22, 2001.
A.L.—4—Held by 15 pitchers. Last pitcher—Victor Zambrano, Tampa Bay, July 19, 2003.

Most hit batsmen, inning (*consecutive)
A.L.—3—Bert Gallia, Washington, June 20, 1913, second game, first inning.
Harry Harper, New York, August 25, 1921, eighth inning.
Tom Morgan, New York, June 30, 1954, third inning.
Wilbur Wood, Chicago, September 10, 1977, *first inning.
Bud Black, Cleveland, July 8, 1988, fourth inning.
Bert Blyleven, Minnesota, September 28, 1988, second inning.
Steve Sparks, Anaheim, May 22, 1999, third inning.*
N.L.—3—Pat Luby, Chicago, September 5, 1890, sixth inning.
Emerson Hawley, St. Louis, July 4, 1894, first game, *first inning.
Emerson Hawley, Pittsburgh, May 9, 1896, seventh inning.
Walter Thornton, Chicago, May 18, 1898, *fourth inning.
Deacon Phillippe, Pittsburgh, September 25, 1905, first inning.
Ray Boggs, Boston, September 17, 1928, ninth inning.
Raul Sanchez, Cincinnati, May 15, 1960, first game, eighth inning.
Dock Ellis, Pittsburgh, May 1, 1974, *first inning.
Mark Gardner, Montreal, August 15, 1992, first inning.
Tom Candiotti, Los Angeles, September 13, 1997, first inning.
C.J. Nitkowski, Houston, August 3, 1998, *eighth inning.
Brian Lawrence, San Diego, April 22, 2003, fourth inning.
Kazuhisa Ishii, Los Angeles, July 23, 2003, fourth inning.
Pat Clement, Chicago, May 28, 2004, fifth inning.
Jeff Weaver, Los Angeles, August 21, 2004, *first inning.

Longest game without a hit batsman
N.L.—26 innings—Leon Cadore, Brooklyn, May 1, 1920.
Joe Oeschger, Boston, May 1, 1920.
A.L.—21 innings—Ted Lyons, Chicago, May 24, 1929.

Most innings with no hit batsmen, season
A.L.—327—Alvin Crowder, Washington, 50 games, 1932.
N.L.—323—Sandy Koufax, Los Angeles, 41 games, 1966.

WILD PITCHES

Most wild pitches, career
M.L.—277—Nolan Ryan, New York N.L., California A.L., Houston N.L., Texas A.L., 27 years, 1966, 1968 through 1993.
A.L.—206—Jack Morris, Detroit, Minnesota, Toronto, Cleveland, 18 years, 1977 through 1994.
N.L.—200—Phil Niekro, Milwaukee, Atlanta, 21 years, 1964 through 1983, 1987.

Most wild pitches, season
N.L.—64—Bill Stemmyer, Boston, 41 games, 1886.
N.L. since 1900—30—Leon Ames, New York, 263 innings, 1905.
A.L.—26—Juan Guzman, Toronto, 221 innings, 1993.

Most seasons leading league in wild pitches
M.L.—6—Nolan Ryan, California A.L., Houston N.L., Texas A.L., 1972, 1977, 1978, 1981, 1986, 1989.
Larry Cheney, Chicago N.L., Brooklyn N.L., 1912, 1913, 1914, 1916, 1917 (tied), 1918.
Jack Morris, Detroit A.L., Minnesota A.L., Cleveland A.L., 1983, 1984, 1985, 1987, 1991, 1994 (tied).
N.L.—6—Larry Cheney, Chicago, Brooklyn, 1912, 1913, 1914, 1916, 1917 (tied), 1918.
A.L.—6—Jack Morris, Detroit, Minnesota, Cleveland, 1983, 1984, 1985, 1987, 1991, 1994 (tied).

Fewest wild pitches by leader, season
N.L.—6—Kirby Higbe, Brooklyn, 211 innings, 1946.
Charley Schanz, Philadelphia, 116 innings, 1946.

A.L.—7—Held by eight pitchers. Last pitchers—George Earnshaw, Philadelphia, 1928; Joe Shaute, Cleveland, 1928.

Most wild pitches, game
N.L.—10—Johnny Ryan, Louisville, July 22, 1876.
N.L. since 1900—6—J.R. Richard, Houston, April 10, 1979.
Phil Niekro, Atlanta, August 4, 1979, second game.
Bill Gullickson, Montreal, April 10, 1982.
A.L.—5—Charlie Wheatley, Detroit, September 27, 1912.
Jack Morris, Detroit, August 3, 1987, 10 innings.

Most wild pitches, first major league game
A.A.—5—Tom Seymour, Pittsburgh, September 23, 1882 (his only game in majors).
N.L.—5—Mike Corcoran, Chicago, July 15, 1884 (his only M.L. game).
George Winkelman, Washington, August 2, 1886.

Most wild pitches, opening game of season
N.L.—4—Larry Cheney, Chicago, April 14, 1914.

Most wild pitches, inning
P.L.—5—Bert Cunningham, Buffalo, September 15, 1890, second game, first inning.
A.L.—4—Walter Johnson, Washington, September 21, 1914, fourth inning.
Kevin Gregg, Anaheim, July 25, 2004, eighth inning.
N.L.—4—Phil Niekro, Atlanta, August 4, 1979, second game, fifth inning.

Longest game without a wild pitch
N.L.—26 innings—Leon Cadore, Brooklyn, May 1, 1920.
A.L.—24 innings—Jack Coombs, Philadelphia, September 1, 1906.
Joe Harris, Boston, September 1, 1906.

Most innings with no wild pitches, season
N.L.—340—Joe McGinnity, New York, 1906.
A.L.—327—Alvin Crowder, Washington, 1932.

Most innings with no wild pitches or hit batsmen, season
A.L.—327—Alvin Crowder, Washington, 1932.
N.L.—268—Jesse Barnes, Boston, 1924.

SACRIFICE HITS

Most sacrifices allowed, season (sacrifice hits and sacrifice flies)
A.L.—54—Stan Coveleski, Cleveland, 316 innings, 1921.
Eddie Rommel, Philadelphia, 298 innings, 1923.
N.L.—49—Eppa Rixey, Philadelphia, 284 innings, 1920.
Jack Scott, Philadelphia, 233 innings, 1927.

Most sacrifice hits allowed, season (no sacrifice flies)
N.L.—35—Ed Brandt, Boston, 283 innings, 1933.
A.L.—28—Earl Whitehill, Detroit, 272 innings, 1931.

Most seasons leading league in most sacrifices allowed
N.L.—3—Eppa Rixey, Philadelphia, Cincinnati, 1920, 1921, 1928.
A.L.—3—Earl Whitehill, Detroit, Washington, 1931, 1934, 1935.

Fewest sacrifice hits allowed by leader, season (no sacrifice flies)
A.L.—8—Hector Carrasco, Minnesota-Boston, 78.2 innings, 2000.
Mike Mussina, Baltimore, 237.2 innings, 2000.
N.L.—13—Johnny Antonelli, San Francisco, 242 innings, 1958.
Dick Farrell, Philadelphia, 94 innings, 1958.
Ron Kline, Pittsburgh, 237 innings, 1958.

Most innings by pitcher allowing no sacrifice hits, season
A.L.—238.2—Dan Petry, Detroit, 1985, 34 games.
N.L.—183—Carl Willey, New York, 30 games, 1963.

SACRIFICE FLIES

Most sacrifice flies allowed, career
M.L.—141—Jim Kaat, Washington A.L., Minnesota A.L., Chicago A.L., Philadelphia N.L., New York A.L., St. Louis N.L., 25 years, 1959 through 1983 (108 in A.L., 33 in N.L.).
A.L.—108—Jim Kaat, Washington, Minnesota, Chicago, New York, 19 years, 1959 through 1975, 1979 through 1980.
N.L.—95—Bob Gibson, St. Louis, 17 years, 1959 through 1975.

Most sacrifice flies allowed, season
A.L.—17—Larry Gura, Kansas City, 200.1 innings, 1983.
Jaime Navarro, Milwaukee, 214.1 innings, 1993.

N.L.—15—Randy Lerch, Philadelphia, 214 innings, 1979.

Most innings with no sacrifice flies allowed, season
N.L.—284—Phil Niekro, Atlanta, 40 games, 1969.
A.L.—258.1—Luis Tiant, Cleveland, 34 games, 1968.

BALKS

Most balks, season
A.L.—16—Dave Stewart, Oakland, 275.2 innings, 1988.
N.L.—11—Steve Carlton, Philadelphia, 251 innings, 1979.

Most balks, game
N.L.—5—Bob Shaw, Milwaukee, May 4, 1963.

A.L.—4—Vic Raschi, New York, May 3, 1950.
Bobby Witt, Texas, April 12, 1988.
Rick Honeycutt, Oakland, April 13, 1988.
Gene Walter, Seattle, July 18, 1988.
John Dopson, Boston, June 13, 1989.

Most balks, inning
A.L.—3—Milt Shoffner, Cleveland, May 12, 1930, third inning.
Don Heinkel, Detroit, May 3, 1988, sixth inning.
N.L.—3—Jim Owens, Cincinnati, April 24, 1963, second inning.
Bob Shaw, Milwaukee, May 4, 1963, third inning.
Jim Gott, Pittsburgh, August 6, 1988, eighth inning.

CLUB PITCHING

COMPLETE GAMES

Most complete games, season
A.L.—148—Boston, 157 games, 1904.
N.L.—146—St. Louis, 155 games, 1904.

Fewest complete games, season
A.L.—1—Tampa Bay, 162 games, 2001.
New York, 162 games, 2004.
N.L.—1—Colorado, 162 games, 2002.
Houston, 162 games, 2003.

Most consecutive games, none complete
A.L.—194—Tampa Bay, April 14, 2001 through May 19, 2002.
N.L.—150—Cincinnati, July 29, 2001 through July 14, 2002.

INNINGS

Most innings, season
A.L.—1,507—New York, 164 games, 1964.
N.L.—1,493—Pittsburgh, 163 games, 1979.

Most pitchers with 300 or more innings, season
N.L.—3—Boston, 1905, 1906.
A.L.—3—Detroit, 1904.

GAMES WON

Most games won by two pitchers on same club, season
N.L.—77—Providence, 1884 (Hoss Radbourn, 60, Charlie Sweeney, 17).
N.L. since 1900—68—New York, 1904 (Joe McGinnity, 35, Christy Mathewson, 33).
A.L.—64—New York, 1904 (Jack Chesbro, 41, Jack Powell, 23).

Most pitchers winning 20 or more games, season
A.L.—4—Chicago, 1920.
Baltimore, 1971.
N.L. since 1900—3—Pittsburgh, 1902.
Chicago, 1903.
New York, 1904, 1905, 1913, 1920.
Cincinnati, 1923.

Most consecutive years with pitchers winning 20 or more games
A.L.—13—Baltimore, 1968 through 1980.
N.L.—12—New York, 1903 through 1914.

Most consecutive years without pitchers winning 20 or more games
N.L.—32—Philadelphia, 1918 through 1949.
A.L.—29—California/Anaheim, 1975 through 2003.
Cleveland, 1975 through 2003.

SAVES

Most saves, season
A.L.—68—Chicago, 162 games, 1990.
N.L.—61—Montreal, 163 games, 1993.

Fewest saves, season
A.L.—11—Toronto, 162 games, 1979.
N.L.—13—Chicago, 162 games, 1971.
St. Louis, 156 games, 1972.

GAMES LOST

Most pitchers losing 20 or more games, season
N.L. since 1900—4—Boston, 1905, 1906.
A.L.—3—Washington, 1904.
St. Louis, 1905.
Philadelphia, 1916.

AT-BATS AND PLATE APPEARANCES

Most opponents' at-bats, season
A.L.—5,770—Oakland, 162 games, 1997.
N.L.—5,763—Philadelphia, 156 games, 1930.

Fewest opponents' at-bats, season
A.L.—4,845—Cleveland, 155 games, 1909.
N.L.—4,875—Chicago, 155 games, 1907.

Most batters facing pitcher, season
A.L.—6,713—Detroit, 162 games, 1996.
N.L.—6,574—Colorado, 162 games, 1999.

Fewest batters facing pitcher, season
N.L.—5,478—Philadelphia, 153 games, 1915.
A.L.—6,189—Chicago, 162 games, 2004.

RUNS, EARNED RUNS AND ERA

Most runs allowed, season
N.L.—1,199—Philadelphia, 156 games, 1930.
A.L.—1,103—Detroit, 162 games, 1996.

Fewest runs allowed, season
N.L.—379—Chicago, 154 games, 1906.
A.L.—408—Philadelphia, 153 games, 1909.

Most earned runs allowed, season
N.L.—1,024—Philadelphia, 156 games, 1930.
A.L.—1,015—Detroit, 162 games, 1996.

Fewest earned runs allowed, season
N.L.—332—Philadelphia, 153 games, 1915.
A.L.—343—Chicago, 156 games, 1917.

Lowest earned-run average, season
N.L.—2.12—Brooklyn, 156 games, 1916.
A.L.—2.16—Chicago, 156 games, 1917.

Highest earned-run average, season
N.L.—6.70—Philadelphia, 156 games, 1930.
A.L.—6.38—Detroit, 162 games, 1996.

SHUTOUTS

Most shutout games participated in, season
A.L.—47—Chicago, 1910 (won 22, lost 24, tied 1).
N.L.—47—New York, 1968 (won 25, lost 22).

Fewest shutout games participated in, season
A.L.—4—Texas, 2001 (won 3, lost 1).
N.L.—5—Colorado, 1999 (won 2, lost 3).
San Francisco, 1999 (won 3, lost 2).
Houston, 2000 (won 2, lost 3).

Most shutout games won or tied, season
N.L.—32—Chicago, 1907, 1909.
A.L.—32—Chicago, 1906 (including 2 ties).

Fewest shutout games won or tied, season (150 or more games)
N.L.—0—Brooklyn, 1898.
Washington, 1898.
St. Louis, 1898.
Cleveland, 1899.
Colorado, 1993.
A.L.—1—Chicago, 1924.
Washington, 1956.
Seattle, 1977.
Baltimore, 1996.
Oakland, 1997.
Anaheim, 2001.
Kansas City, 2001.

Most shutouts won from one club, season
N.L.—10—Pittsburgh vs. Boston, 1906 (lost 1).
A.L.—8—Chicago vs. Boston, 1906 (lost 1).
Cleveland vs. Washington, 1956 (lost 0).
Oakland vs. Cleveland 1968 (lost 1).

Most consecutive shutout games won, season
N.L.—6—Pittsburgh, June 2 through 6, 1903 (51 innings).
A.L.—5—
Baltimore, September 2 through 6, 1974 (45 innings).
Baltimore, September 26 through October 1, 1995 (45 innings).

Largest score, shutout day game
N.L.—28-0—Providence vs. Philadelphia, August 21, 1883.
N.L. since 1900—22-0—Pittsburgh vs. Chicago, September 16, 1975.
A.L.—21-0—Detroit vs. Cleveland, September 15, 1901, eight innings.
New York vs. Philadelphia, August 13, 1939, second game, eight innings.
A.A.—23-0—Cincinnati vs. Baltimore, July 6, 1883.

Largest score, shutout night game
N.L.—19-0—Pittsburgh vs. St. Louis, August 3, 1961, at St. Louis.
Los Angeles vs. San Diego, June 28, 1969, at San Diego.
A.L.—17-0—Los Angeles vs. Washington, August 23, 1963, at Washington.

Most runs, doubleheader shutout
A.L.—26—Detroit vs. St. Louis, September 22, 1936 (12-0, 14-0).
N.L.—19—New York vs. Cincinnati, July 31, 1949 (10-0, 9-0).

Doubleheader shutouts since 1900
N.L.—Occurred 101 times. Last time—September 29, 1987, St. Louis vs. Montreal (St. Louis won, 1-0 and 3-0).
A.L.—Occurred 89 times. Last time—June 26, 1988, Minnesota vs. Oakland (Minnesota won, 11-0 and 5-0).

Most consecutive innings shut out opponent, season
N.L.—56—Pittsburgh, June 1 (last two innings) through June 9 (first three innings), 1903.
A.L.—54—Baltimore, September 1, (last inning) through September 7 (first eight innings), 1974.

Most 1-0 games won, season
A.L.—11—Washington, 1914 (lost 4).
N.L.—10—Pittsburgh, 1908 (lost 1).

Fewest 1-0 games won, season
N.L.-A.L.—0—Held by many clubs.
N.L.—Last clubs—Arizona, Colorado, Florida, Los Angeles, Philadelphia, San Diego, 2004.
A.L.—Last clubs—Chicago, Detroit, Tampa Bay, 2004.

Most 1-0 games lost, season
N.L.—10—Pittsburgh, 1914; Chicago, 1916; Philadelphia, 1967.

A.L.—9—New York, 1914; Chicago, 1968.

Fewest 1-0 games lost, season
N.L.-A.L.—0—Held by many clubs.
N.L.—Last clubs—Atlanta, Colorado, Houston, Los Angeles, Philadelphia, St. Louis, San Francisco, 2004.
A.L.—Last clubs—Baltimore, Boston, Kansas City, Tampa Bay, 2004.

Most consecutive 1-0 games won, season
A.L.—3—Chicago, April 25, 26, 27, 1909.
N.L.—3—St. Louis, August 31, second game (five innings), September 1, 1, 1917.

Most consecutive 1-0 games lost, season
N.L.—3—Brooklyn, September 7, 7, 8 (11 innings), 1908.
Pittsburgh, August 31, second game (five innings), September 1, 1, 1917.
Philadelphia, May 11, 12, 13, 1960.
A.L.—3—St. Louis, April 25, 26, 27, 1909.
Washington, May 7, 8, 10 (11 innings), 1909.

Most 1-0 games won from one club, season
N.L.—4—Held by four clubs. Last club—Cincinnati vs. Brooklyn, 1910.
A.L.—4—Held by four clubs. Last club—Detroit vs. Boston, 1917.

Winning two 1-0 games in one day
N.L.—12 times. Last time—Pittsburgh vs. St. Louis, October 3, 1976.
A.L.—1 time—Baltimore vs. Boston, September 2, 1974.

Most hits allowed, season
N.L.—1,993—Philadelphia, 156 games, 1930.
A.L.—1,776—St. Louis, 155 games, 1936.

Fewest hits allowed, season
A.L.—1,069—Philadelphia, 153 games, 1909.
N.L.—1,018—Chicago, 155 games, 1906.

Most home runs allowed, season
A.L.—241—Detroit, 162 games, 1996.
N.L.—239—Colorado, 162 games, 2001.

Most home runs allowed at home, season
N.L.—159—at Colorado, 81 games, 1999.
A.L.—132—at Kansas City, 81 games, 1964.

Most grand slams allowed, season
A.L.—14—Detroit, 162 games, 1996.
N.L.—12—Montreal, 162 games, 2000.

Fewest grand slams allowed, season
N.L.-A.L.—0—Held by many clubs.
N.L.—Last club—Cincinnati, 1999.
A.L.—Last club—Oakland, 2003.

Most no-hit games, season
A.A.—2—Louisville 1882; Columbus 1884; Philadelphia 1888.
A.L.—2—Boston 1904; Cleveland 1908; Chicago 1914; Boston 1916; St. Louis 1917; New York 1951; Detroit 1952; Boston 1962; California 1973.
N.L.—2—Brooklyn 1006; Cincinnati 1930; Brooklyn 1956; Milwaukee 1960; Cincinnati 1965; Chicago 1972.

Most consecutive years with no-hit games by pitchers
N.L.—4—Los Angeles, 1962, 1963, 1964, 1965.
A.L.—3—Boston, 1916, 1917, 1918.
Cleveland, 1946, 1947, 1948.
Baltimore, 1967, 1968, 1969.
California, 1973, 1974, 1975.

Most consecutive years without no-hit games by pitchers
N.L.—57—Philadelphia, 1907 through 1963.
A.L.—39—Detroit, 1913 through 1951.

Most one-hit games, season
A.L.—5—Baltimore, 1964.
N.L.—4—Chicago, 1906, 1909.

Philadelphia, 1907, 1911, 1915, 1979.

Most consecutive one-hit nine-inning games
N.L.—2—Providence vs. New York, June 17, 18, 1884.
Brooklyn vs. Cincinnati, July 5, 6, 1900.
New York vs. Boston, September 28, second game, 30, first game, 1916.
Milwaukee vs. New York, September 10, 11, 1965.
New York vs. Chicago, Philadelphia, May 13, 15, 1970.
Houston vs. Philadelphia, New York, June 18, 19, 1972.
Chicago vs. Cincinnati, Milwaukee, May 24, 25, 2001.
A.L.—2—Cleveland vs. New York, September 25, 26, 1907.
Washington vs. Chicago, August 10, 11, 1917.
Texas vs. Detroit, May 3, 4, 1996.

BASES ON BALLS

Most bases on balls, season
A.L.—827—Philadelphia, 154 games, 1915.
N.L.—737—Colorado, 162 games, 1999.

Fewest bases on balls, season
N.L.—257—Cincinnati, 153 games, 1933.
A.L.—284—Chicago, 156 games, 1908.

Most intentional bases on balls, season
N.L.—116—San Diego, 162 games, 1974.
A.L.—94—Seattle, 163 games, 1980.

Fewest intentional bases on balls, season
N.L.—9—Los Angeles, 162 games, 1974.
A.L.—16—Minnesota, 162 games, 1973.
New York, 159 games, 1976.
Minnesota, 162 games, 2001.

STRIKEOUTS

Most strikeouts, season
N.L.—1,404—Chicago, 162 games, 2003.
A.L.—1,266—New York, 161 games, 2001.

Fewest strikeouts, season
A.L.—310—Boston, 152 games, 1925.
N.L.—357—New York, 153 games, 1921.

HIT BATSMEN AND WILD PITCHES

Most hit batsmen, season
A.L.—95—Tampa Bay, 162 games, 2003.
N.L.—85—Pittsburgh, 134 games, 1895.
N.L. since 1900—84—Colorado, 162 games, 2003.

Fewest hit batsmen, season
A.L.—5—St. Louis, 154 games, 1945.
N.L.—10—St. Louis, 155 games, 1948.

Most wild pitches, season
N.L.—96—Cincinnati, 163 games, 2000.
A.L.—94—Texas, 162 games, 1986.

Fewest wild pitches, season
N.L.—8—Boston, 153 games, 1921.
A.L.—10—Cleveland, 153 games, 1923.
Cleveland, 152 games, 1929.
St. Louis, 154 games, 1930.
Cleveland, 153 games, 1943.

SACRIFICE HITS AND FLIES

Most sacrifice hits allowed, season
A.L.—127—Chicago, 154 games, 1944.
Washington, 154 games, 1949.
N.L.—142—Cincinnati, 154 games, 1931.

Fewest sacrifice hits allowed, season
A.L.—20—Baltimore, 162 games, 2002.
N.L.—44—Montreal, 156 games, 1972.

Most sacrifice flies allowed, season
A.L.—80—Oakland, 162 games, 1997.
N.L.—79—Pittsburgh, 154 games, 1954.

Fewest sacrifice flies allowed, season
N.L.—17—San Francisco, 162 games, 1963.
A.L.—17—Detroit, 164 games, 1968.

BALKS

Most balks, season
A.L.—76—Oakland, 162 games, 1988.
N.L.—41—Montreal, 163 games, 1988.

Fewest balks season
A.L.-N.L.—0—Held by many clubs.

Most balks, game
N.L.—6—Milwaukee vs. Chicago, May 4, 1963.
A.L.—5—Milwaukee vs. New York, April 10, 1988.
Oakland vs. Seattle, April 13, 1988.

Most balks by both clubs, game
N.L.—7—Pittsburgh 4, Cincinnati 3, April 13, 1963.
Milwaukee 6, Chicago 1, May 4, 1963.
A.L.—6—Milwaukee 5, New York 1, April 10, 1988.
Chicago 4, California 2, April 12, 1988.

LEAGUE PITCHING

COMPLETE GAMES AND INNINGS

Most complete games, season
N.L. since 1900 (8 clubs)—1,089 in 1904
N.L. (10 clubs)—471 in 1968
N.L. (12 clubs)—546 in 1972
N.L. (14 clubs)—162 in 1997
N.L. (16 clubs)—128 in 1999
A.L. (8 clubs)—1,097 in 1904
A.L. (12 clubs)—426 in 1968
A.L. (10 clubs)—650 in 1974
A.L. (14 clubs)—645 in 1978

Fewest complete games, season
N.L. since 1900 (8 clubs)—328 in 1961
N.L. (10 clubs)—402 in 1966
N.L. (12 clubs)—150 in 1991
N.L. (14 clubs)—127 in 1996 (102 in shortened 1994 season)
N.L. (16 clubs)—71 in 2004
A.L. (8 clubs)—312 in 1960
A.L. (12 clubs)—323 in 1965
A.L. (10 clubs)—382 in 1970
A.L. (14 clubs)—79 in 2004

Most pitchers with 300 or more innings, season
A.L.—12 in 1904
N.L.—10 in 1905

GAMES WON AND LOST

Most pitchers winning 20 or more games, season
N.L. before 1900—22 in 1892
N.L. since 1900 (8 clubs)—9 in 1903
N.L. (10 clubs)—7 in 1965
N.L. (12 clubs)—9 in 1969
N.L. (14 clubs)—4 in 1993
N.L. (16 clubs)—4 in 2001
A.A.—12 in 1884, 1888
U.A.—9 in 1884
P.L.—9 in 1890
A.L. (8 clubs)—10 in 1907, 1920
A.L. (12 clubs)—5 in 1963
A.L. (10 clubs)—12 in 1973
A.L. (14 clubs)—6 in 1978

Fewest pitchers winning 20 or more games, season
N.L. since 1900—0 in 1931, 1983, 1987 (also the shortened seasons of 1981, 1994, 1995)

A.L.—0 in 1955, 1960, 1982 (also the shortened seasons of 1981, 1994, 1995)

Most pitchers losing 20 or more games, season
N.L.—8 in 1905
A.L.—7 in 1904

SAVES (SINCE 1969)

Most saves, season
NL. (12 clubs)—514 in 1991
N.L. (14 clubs)—599 in 1993
N.L. (16 clubs)—697 in 2004
A.L. (12 clubs)—467 in 1970
A.L. (14 clubs)—637 in 1990

RUNS, EARNED RUNS AND ERA

Most runs, season
N.L. since 1900 (8 clubs)—7,025 in 1930
N.L. (10 clubs)—7,278 in 1962
N.L. (12 clubs)—8,771 in 1970, 1987
N.L. (14 clubs)—10,623 in 1996
N.L. (16 clubs)—13,021 in 2000
A.L. (8 clubs)—7,009 in 1936
A.L. (10 clubs)—7,342 in 1961
A.L. (12 clubs)—8,314 in 1973
A.L. (14 clubs)—12,208 in 1996

Fewest runs, season
N.L. since 1900 (8 clubs)—4,138 in 1908 (3,678 in shortened 1918 season)
N.L. (10 clubs)—5,577 in 1968
N.L. (12 clubs)—7,522 in 1988 (5,035 in shortened 1981 season)
N.L. (14 clubs)—10,190 in 1993 (7,422 in shortened 1993 season)
N.L. (16 clubs)—11,546 in 2002
A.L. (8 clubs)—4,272 in 1909 (3,702 in shortened 1918 season)
A.L. (12 clubs)—5,532 in 1968
A.L. (10 clubs)—7,472 in 1971 (6,441 in shortened 1972 season)
A.L. (14 clubs)—9,509 in 1978 (6,112 in shortened 1981 season)

Most earned runs, season
N.L. since 1900 (8 clubs)—6,049 in 1930
N.L. (10 clubs)—6,345 in 1962
N.L. (12 clubs)—7,878 in 1987
N.L. (14 clubs)—9,500 in 1996
N.L. (16 clubs)—11,884 in 2000
A.L. (8 clubs)—6,120 in 1936
A.L. (10 clubs)—6,451 in 1961
A.L. (12 clubs)—7,376 in 1973
A.L. (14 clubs)—11,241 in 1996

Fewest earned runs, season
N.L. since 1900 (8 clubs)—2,910 in 1908 (2,816 in shortened 1918 season)
N.L. (10 clubs)—4,870 in 1968
N.L. (12 clubs)—6,680 in 1988 (4,512 in shortened 1981 season)
N.L. (14 clubs)—9,057 in 1993 (6,717 in shortened 1994 season)
N.L. (16 clubs)—10,540 in 2002
A.L. (8 clubs)—3,320 in 1917 (2,840 in shortened 1918 season)
A.L. (12 clubs)—4,817 in 1968
A.L. (10 clubs)—6,662 in 1971 (5,682 in shortened 1972 season)
A.L. (14 clubs)—8,433 in 1978 (5,471 in shortened 1981 season)

Lowest earned-run average, season
N.L.—2.62 in 1916
A.L.—2.66 in 1917

Highest earned-run average, season
A.L.—5.04 in 1936
N.L.—4.97 in 1930

SHUTOUTS

(Complete games by one pitcher)

Most shutouts, season
N.L. since 1900 (8 clubs)—164 in 1908
N.L. (10 clubs)—185 in 1968
N.L. (12 clubs)—166 in 1969
N.L. (14 clubs)—117 in 1996

N.L. (16 clubs)—153 in 2002
A.L. (8 clubs)—146 in 1909
A.L. (10 clubs)—154 in 1968
A.L. (12 clubs)—193 in 1972
A.L. (14 clubs)—161 in 1978

Fewest shutouts, season
N.L. since 1900 (8 clubs)—48 in 1925
N.L. (10 clubs)—95 in 1962
N.L. (12 clubs)—98 in 1987
N.L. (14 clubs)—110 in 1993 (78 in shortened 1994 season)
N.L. (16 clubs)—93 in 1999
A.L. (8 clubs)—41 in 1930
A.L. (10 clubs)—100 in 1962
A.L. (12 clubs)—110 in 1970
A.L. (14 clubs)—79 in 1999

Most shutouts, one day
N.L.—5 on July 13, 1888 (six games).
　　　　June 24, 1892 (eight games).
　　　　July 21, 1896 (seven games).
　　　　July 8, 1907 (five games).
　　　　September 7, 1908 (eight games).
　　　　September 9, 1916 (seven games).
　　　　May 31, 1943 (eight games).
　　　　June 17, 1969 (nine games).
　　　　August 9, 1984 (six games).
A.L.—5 on September 7, 1903 (eight games).
　　　　August 5, 1909 (six games).
　　　　May 6, 1945 (eight games).
　　　　June 4, 1972 (nine games).

Most shutouts in both leagues, one day
8—June 4, 1972, 5 in A.L. (nine games), 3 in N.L. (seven games).

1-0 GAMES

Most 1-0 games, season
N.L. since 1900 (8 clubs)—43 in 1907
N.L. (10 clubs)—44 in 1968
A.L. (8 clubs)—41 in 1908
A.L. (12 clubs)—42 in 1971

Fewest 1-0 games, season
N.L. since 1900 (8 clubs)—5 in 1932, 1956
N.L. (10 clubs)—13 in 1962
N.L. (12 clubs)—13 in 1983, 1990
N.L. (14 clubs)—22 in 1993
N.L. (16 clubs)—13 in 1999
A.L. (8 clubs)—4 in 1930, 1936
A.L. (14 clubs)—6 in 1996

Most 1-0 games, one day
A.L.—3—May 14, 1914; July 17, 1962
N.L.—3—July 4, 1918; September 12, 1969; September 1, 1976

NO-HIT AND ONE-HIT GAMES

Most no-hit games of nine or more innings, season
M.L.—8—1884 (4 in A.A., 2 in N.L., 2 in U.A.); 1990 (6 in A.L., 2 in N.L.)
N.L. since 1900 (8 clubs)—4 in 1880
N.L. (12 clubs)—5 in 1969
A.L. (8 clubs)—5 in 1917
A.L. (14 clubs)—6 in 1990

Fewest no-hit games, season
N.L.—0—Made in many seasons. Last season—2002
A.L.—0—Made in many seasons. Last season—2003

Most no-hit games, one day
N.L.—2—April 22, 1898
A.L.—1—Made on many days

Most one-hit games of nine or more innings, season
N.L. since 1900 (8 clubs)—12 in 1906, 1910
N.L. (10 clubs)—13 in 1965
A.L. (8 clubs)—12 in 1910, 1915
A.L. (14 clubs)—13 in 1979, 1988

Fewest one-hit games of nine or more innings, season
N.L. since 1900 (8 clubs)—0—1924, 1929, 1932, 1952
N.L. (12 clubs)—4—1980, 1987

A.L. (8 clubs)—0—1922, 1926, 1927, 1930
A.L. (14 clubs)—3—1998

HOME RUNS

Most home runs allowed, season
N.L. since 1900 (8 clubs)—1,263 in 1955
N.L. (10 clubs)—1,449 in 1962
N.L. (12 clubs)—1,824 in 1987
N.L. (14 clubs)—2,220 in 1996
N.L. (16 clubs)—2,997 in 2000
A.L. (8 clubs)—1,091 in 1959
A.L. (12 clubs)—1,552 in 1962
A.L. (10 clubs)—1,746 in 1970
A.L. (14 clubs)—2,742 in 1996

Most pitchers allowing 30 or more home runs, season
N.L. (16 clubs)—14 in 1999, 2000
A.L (14 clubs).—18 in 1987

BASES ON BALLS

Most bases on balls, season
N.L. since 1900 (8 clubs)—4,537 in 1950
N.L. (10 clubs)—5,265 in 1962
N.L. (12 clubs)—6,919 in 1970
N.L. (14 clubs)—7,807 in 1997
N.L. (16 clubs)—9,847 in 2000
A.L. (8 clubs)—5,627 in 1949
A.L. (10 clubs)—5,902 in 1961
A.L. (12 clubs)—7,032 in 1969
A.L. (14 clubs)—8,592 in 1996

Fewest bases on balls, season
N.L. since 1900 (8 clubs)—2,882 in 1921 (2,522 in shortened 1918 season)
N.L. (10 clubs)—4,275 in 1968
N.L. (12 clubs)—5,793 in 1988 (4,107 in shortened 1981 season)
N.L. (14 clubs)—7,104 in 1993 (5,193 in shortened 1993 season)
N.L. (16 clubs)—8,537 in 2001
A.L. (8 clubs)—2,266 in 1903
A.L. (12 clubs)—4,881 in 1968
A.L. (10 clubs)—6,128 in 1976 (5,742 in shortened 1972 season)
A.L. (14 clubs)—7,094 in 1983 (4,761 in shortened 1981 season)

Most intentional bases on balls, season (since 1955)
N.L. (8 clubs)—504 in 1956
N.L. (10 clubs)—804 in 1967
N.L. (12 clubs)—862 in 1973
N.L. (14 clubs)—743 in 1993
N.L. (16 clubs)—955 in 2002
A.L. (8 clubs)—353 in 1957
A.L. (10 clubs)—534 in 1965
A.L. (12 clubs)—668 in 1969
A.L. (14 clubs)—734 in 1993

STRIKEOUTS

Most strikeouts, season
N.L. since 1900 (8 clubs)—6,824 in 1960
N.L. (10 clubs)—9,649 in 1965
N.L. (12 clubs)—11,657 in 1987
N.L. (14 clubs)—15,497 in 1997
N.L. (16 clubs)—17,930 in 2001
A.L. (8 clubs)—6,081 in 1959
A.L. (10 clubs)—9,956 in 1964
A.L. (12 clubs)—10,957 in 1970
A.L. (14 clubs)—14,474 in 2001

Most pitchers with 300 or more strikeouts, season
N.L.—4 in 1884
A.A.—6 in 1884
U.A.—3 in 1884
N.L. since 1900—2 in 1997, 2002
A.L.—2 in 1971

Most pitchers with 200 or more strikeouts, season
N.L.—12 in 1969
A.L.—7 in 1967, 1973, 1986

Most pitchers with 100 or more strikeouts, season
N.L.—59 in 1998

A.L.—44 in 1998

Fewest strikeouts, season
N.L. since 1900 (8 clubs)—2,697 in 1900
N.L. (10 clubs)—9,032 in 1962
N.L. (12 clubs)—9,602 in 1976 (6,332 in shortened 1981 season)
N.L. (14 clubs)—13,358 in 1993 (10,147 in shortened 1994 season)
N.L. (16 clubs)—17,066 in 2003
A.L. (8 clubs)—2,736 in 1901
A.L. (12 clubs)—8,330 in 1961
A.L. (10 clubs)—9,143 in 1976
A.L. (14 clubs)—10,115 in 1979

HIT BATSMEN

Most hit batsmen, season
N.L. since 1900 (8 clubs)—415 in 1903
N.L. (10 clubs)—404 in 1965
N.L. (12 clubs)—443 in 1969
N.L. (14 clubs)—769 in 1997
N.L. (16 clubs)—956 in 2003
A.L. (8 clubs)—454 in 1911
A.L. (10 clubs)—426 in 1968
A.L. (12 clubs)—439 in 1969
A.L. (14 clubs)—937 in 2001

Fewest hit batsmen, season
N.L. since 1900 (8 clubs)—155 in 1943
N.L. (10 clubs)—327 in 1964
N.L. (12 clubs)—249 in 1984 (185 in shortened 1981 season)
N.L. (14 clubs)—1567 in 1993 (451 in shortened 1994 season)
N.L. (16 clubs)—784 in 1999
A.L. (8 clubs)—132 in 1947
A.L. (12 clubs)—316 in 1965
A.L. (10 clubs)—374 in 1976
A.L. (14 clubs)—372 in 1982 (279 in shortened 1981 season)

WILD PITCHES AND BALKS

Most wild pitches, season
N.L. since 1900 (8 clubs)—356 in 1961
N.L. (10 clubs)—550 in 1965
N.L. (12 clubs)—648 in 1969
N.L. (14 clubs)—884 in 1999
N.L. (16 clubs)—953 in 2001
A.L. (8 clubs)—325 in 1936
A.L. (10 clubs)—513 in 1966
A.L. (12 clubs)—636 in 1969
A.L. (14 clubs)—785 in 1997

Fewest wild pitches, season
N.L. since 1900 (8 clubs)—148 in 1928 (147 in shortened 1918 season)
N.L. (10 clubs)—478 in 1967
N.L. (12 clubs)—443 in 1980 (355 in shortened 1981 season)
N.L. (14 clubs)—697 in 1997 (548 in shortened 1994 season)
N.L. (16 clubs)—718 in 2002
A.L. (8 clubs)—138 in 1928
A.L. (12 clubs)—404 in 1962
A.L. (10 clubs)—491 in 1976 (471 in shortened 1972 season)
A.L. (14 clubs)—553 in 1978 (359 in shortened 1981 season)

Most balks, season
N.L. since 1900 (8 clubs)—76 in 1950
N.L. (10 clubs)—147 in 1963
N.L. (12 clubs)—366 in 1988
N.L. (14 clubs)—195 in 1993
N.L. (16 clubs)—143 in 1998
A.L. (8 clubs)—47 in 1950
A.L. (10 clubs)—51 in 1966
A.L. (12 clubs)—60 in 1976
A.L. (14 clubs)—558 in 1988

Fewest balks, season
N.L. since 1900 (8 clubs)—6 in 1903
N.L. (10 clubs)—25 in 1965
N.L. (12 clubs)—52 in 1971, 1973
N.L. (14 clubs)—1112 in 1997 (106 in shortened 1994 season)
N.L. (16 clubs)—69 in 2004
A.L. (8 clubs)—5 in 1901
A.L. (12 clubs)—29 in 1964
A.L. (10 clubs)—43 in 1973 (29 in shortened 1972 season)
A.L. (14 clubs)—55 in 1979

INDIVIDUAL FIELDING

FIRST BASEMEN
GAMES AND INNINGS

Most games, career
M.L.—2,413—Eddie Murray, Baltimore A.L., Los Angeles N.L., New York N.L., Cleveland A.L., 1977 through 1996, 20 years.
N.L.—2,247—Jake Beckley, Pittsburgh, New York, Cincinnati, St. Louis, 1888 through 1907, except 1890, 19 years.
N.L. since 1900—2,131—Charlie Grimm, St. Louis, Pittsburgh, Chicago, 1918 through 1936, 19 years.
A.L.—2,227—Mickey Vernon, Washington, Cleveland, Boston, 1939 through 1958, except 1944, 1945 in military service, 18 years.

Most consecutive games, career
A.L.—885—Lou Gehrig, New York, June 2, 1925, through September 27, 1930.
N.L.—652—Frank McCormick, Cincinnati, April 19, 1938, through May 24, 1942, second game.

Most games, season
A.L.—162—Norm Siebern, Kansas City, 1962.
  Bill Buckner, Boston, 1985.
  Carlos Delgado, Toronto, 2000.
N.L.—162—Bill White, St. Louis, 1963.
  Ernie Banks, Chicago, 1965.
  Steve Garvey, Los Angeles, 1976, 1979, 1980; San Diego, 1985.
  Pete Rose, Philadelphia, 1980, 1982.
  Jeff Bagwell, Houston, 1996.
  Eric Karros, Los Angeles, 1997.
  Derrek Lee, Florida, 2002.
  Richie Sexson, Milwaukee, 2003.

Most seasons leading league in games
N.L.—9—Steve Garvey, Los Angeles, 1975, 1976, 1977, 1978, 1979, 1980 (tied); 1981; San Diego, 1984, 1985.
A.L.—7—Lou Gehrig, New York, 1926, 1927, 1928 (tied), 1932, 1936, 1937, 1938.

Fewest games for leader, season
A.L.—121—Vic Power, Cleveland, 1959.
N.L.—134—Ed Bouchee, Philadelphia, 1960.

Most innings played, game
N.L.—26—Walter Holke, Boston, May 1, 1920.
  Ed Konetchy, Brooklyn, May 1, 1920.
A.L.—25—Ted Simmons, Milwaukee, May 8, finished May 9, 1984 (fielded 24.1 innings).

AVERAGE

Highest fielding average, career (1,000 or more games)
N.L.—.9959—Steve Garvey, Los Angeles, San Diego, 1972 through 1987, 16 years, 2,059 games.
A.L.—.9958—Don Mattingly, New York, 1983 through 1995, 13 years, 1,634 games.

Highest fielding average, season (150 or more games)
N.L.—1.000—Steve Garvey, San Diego, 159 games, 1984.
A.L.—.9994—Stuffy McInnis, Boston, 152 games, 1921.

Highest fielding average, season (100 or more games)
N.L.—1.000—Steve Garvey, San Diego, 159 games, 1984.
A.L.—.9994—Stuffy McInnis, Boston, 152 games, 1921.

Most seasons leading league in fielding average (100 or more games)
N.L.—9—Charlie Grimm, Pittsburgh, Chicago, 1920, 1922 (tied), 1923, 1924, 1928 (tied), 1930, 1931, 1932 (tied), 1933.
A.L.—6—Joe Judge, Washington, 1923, 1924 (tied), 1925, 1927, 1929, 1930.
  Don Mattingly, New York, 1984 (tied), 1985, 1986 (tied), 1987, 1992, 1993.

Most consecutive seasons leading league in fielding average (100 or more games)
N.L.—5—Ted Kluszewski, Cincinnati, 1951, 1952, 1953, 1954, 1955.
A.L.—4—Chick Gandil, Cleveland, Chicago, 1916, 1917, 1918, 1919.
  Don Mattingly, New York, 1984 (tied), 1985, 1986 (tied), 1987.

Lowest fielding average for leader, season (100 or more games)
N.L.—.978—Alex McKinnon, St. Louis, 100 games, 1885.
A.L.—.981—John Anderson, Milwaukee, 125 games, 1901.
N.L. since 1900—.9836—Dan McGann, St. Louis, 103 games, 1901.

Lowest fielding average, season (100 or more games)
N.L.—.954—Alex McKinnon, New York, 112 games, 1884.
N.L. since 1900—.970—Jack Doyle, New York, 130 games, 1900.
A.L.—.9716—Pat Newnam, St. Louis, 103 games, 1910.

PUTOUTS

Most putouts, career
M.L.—23,696—Jake Beckley, Pittsburgh N.L., Pittsburgh P.L., New York N.L., Cincinnati N.L., St. Louis N.L., 1888 through 1907, 20 years.
N.L.—22,438—Jake Beckley, New York, Pittsburgh, Cincinnati, St. Louis, 1888 through 1907, except 1890, 19 years.
N.L. since 1900—20,700—Charlie Grimm, St. Louis, Pittsburgh, Chicago, 1918 through 1936, 19 years.
A.L.—19,754—Mickey Vernon, Washington, Cleveland, Boston, 1939 through 1958, except 1944, 1945 in military service, 18 years.

Most putouts, season
A.L.—1,846—Jiggs Donahue, Chicago, 157 games, 1907.
N.L.—1,759—George Kelly, New York, 155 games, 1920.

Most seasons leading league in putouts
N.L.—6—Jake Beckley, Pittsburgh, Cincinnati, St. Louis, 1892, 1894, 1895, 1900, 1902, 1904.
  Frank McCormick, Cincinnati, 1939, 1940, 1941, 1942, 1944, 1945.
  Steve Garvey, Los Angeles, San Diego, 1974, 1975, 1976, 1977, 1978, 1985.
A.L.—4—Wally Pipp, New York, 1915, 1919, 1920, 1922.

Fewest putouts for leader, season
A.L.—971—Vic Wertz, Cleveland, 133 games, 1956.
N.L.—1,127—Ed Bouchee, Philadelphia, 134 games, 1959.

Fewest putouts, season (150 or more games)
A.L.—1,154—Tino Martinez, New York, 154 games, 2000.
N.L.—1,162—Gordy Coleman, Cincinnati, 150 games, 1961.

Most putouts, game
A.L.—22—Tom Jones, St. Louis, May 11, 1906.
  Hal Chase, New York, September 21, 1906, first game.
  Don Mattingly, New York, July 20, 1987.
  Alvin Davis, Seattle, May 28, 1988.
  (32—Mike Epstein, Washington, June 12, 1967, 22 innings.
  Rod Carew, California, April 13, finished April 14, 1982, 20 innings.)
N.L.—22—Ernie Banks, Chicago, May 9, 1963.
  (42—Walter Holke, Boston, May 1, 1920, 26 innings.)

ASSISTS

Most assists, career
M.L.—1,865—Eddie Murray, Baltimore A.L., Los Angeles N.L., New York N.L., Cleveland A.L., 1977 through 1996, 20 years.
N.L.—1,690—Jeff Bagwell, Houston, 1991 through 2004, 14 years.
A.L.—1,444—Mickey Vernon, Washington, Cleveland, Washington, Boston, 1939 through 1958, except 1944, 1945 in military service, 18 years.

Most assists, season
A.L.—184—Bill Buckner, Boston, 162 games, 1985.
N.L.—180—Mark Grace, Chicago, 153 games, 1990.

Most seasons leading league in assists
N.L.—8—Fred Tenney, Boston, 1899, 1901, 1902, 1903, 1904, 1905, 1906, 1907.
A.L.—6—George Sisler, St. Louis, 1919, 1920, 1922, 1924, 1925, 1927.
  Vic Power, Kansas City, Cleveland, Minnesota, 1955, 1957, 1959, 1960, 1961, 1962.
  Rafael Palmeiro, Texas, Baltimore, 1989, 1992, 1993, 1995, 1996, 1998.

Fewest assists for leader, season
N.L.—83—Herm Reich, Chicago, 85 games, 1949.
A.L.—85—Wally Pipp, New York, 134 games, 1915.

Fewest assists, season (150 or more games)
N.L.—54—Jim Bottomley, St. Louis, 154 games, 1926.
A.L.—58—Lou Gehrig, New York, 154 games, 1931.

Most assists, game
N.L.—8—Bob Robertson, Pittsburgh, June 21, 1971.
   (8—Bob Skinner, Pittsburgh, July 22, 1954, 14 innings.)
A.L.—7—George Stovall, St. Louis, August 7, 1912.
   (7—Ferris Fain, Philadelphia, June 9, 1949, 12 innings.)

CHANCES ACCEPTED AND OFFERED

Most chances accepted, career
M.L.—25,000—Jake Beckley, Pittsburgh N.L., Pittsburgh P.L., New York N.L., Cincinnati N.L., St. Louis N.L., 1888 through 1907, 20 years.
N.L.—23,687—Jake Beckley, Pittsburgh, New York, Cincinnati, St. Louis, 1888 through 1907, except 1890, 19 years.
N.L. since 1900—21,914—Charlie Grimm, St. Louis, Pittsburgh, Chicago, 1918 through 1936, 19 years.
A.L.—21,198—Mickey Vernon, Washington, Cleveland, Boston, 1939 through 1958, except 1944, 1945 in military service, 18 years.

Most chances accepted, season
A.L.—1,986—Jiggs Donahue, Chicago, 157 games, 1907.
N.L.—1,862—George Kelly, New York, 155 games, 1920.

Most seasons leading league in chances accepted
N.L.—6—Jake Beckley, Pittsburgh, Cincinnati, St. Louis, 1892, 1894, 1895, 1900, 1902, 1904.
   Bill Terry, New York, 1927 (tied), 1928, 1929, 1930, 1932, 1934.
A.L.—4—Wally Pipp, New York, 1915, 1919, 1920, 1922.

Fewest chances accepted by leader, season
A.L.—1,048—Bill Skowron, New York, 120 games, 1956.
   Vic Wertz, Cleveland, 133 games, 1956.
N.L.—1,222—Ed Bouchee, Philadelphia, 134 games, 1959.

Fewest chances accepted, season (150 or more games)
A.L.—1,242—Tino Martinez, New York, 154 games, 2000.
N.L.—1,251—Deron Johnson, Philadelphia, 154 games, 1970.

Most chances accepted, game
A.L.-N.L.—22—Held by many first basemen.
A.L.—Last first baseman—Alvin Davis, Seattle, May 28, 1988 (22 putouts).
   (34—Rudy York, Detroit, July 21, 1945, 24 innings.
   Mike Epstein, Washington, June 12, 1967, 22 innings.
   Rod Carew, California, April 13, finished April 14, 1982, 20 innings.)
N.L.—Last first baseman—Ernie Banks, Chicago, May 9, 1963 (22 putouts).
   (43—Walter Holke, Boston, May 1, 1920, 26 innings.)

Longest game with no chances offered
A.A.—nine innings—Al McCauley, Washington, August 6, 1891.
A.L.—nine innings—Bud Clancy, Chicago, April 27, 1930.
   Gene Tenace, Oakland, September 1, 1974.
N.L.—nine innings—Rip Collins, Chicago, June 29, 1937.

ERRORS

Most errors, career
N.L.—568—Cap Anson, Chicago, 1879 through 1897, 19 years.
A.L.—285—Hal Chase, New York, Chicago, 1905 through 1914, 10 years, 1,175 games.
N.L. since 1900—252—Fred Tenney, Boston, New York, 1900 through 1911, except 1910, 11 years.

Most errors, season
U.A.—62—Joe Quinn, St. Louis, 100 games, 1884.
N.L.—58—Cap Anson, Chicago, 108 games, 1884.
N.L. since 1900—43—Jack Doyle, New York, 130 games, 1900.
A.L.—41—Jerry Freeman, Washington, 154 games, 1908.

Most seasons leading league in errors
M.L.—7—Dick Stuart, Pittsburgh N.L., 1958 (tied), 1959, 1960 (tied), 1961, 1962 (tied); Boston, A.L., 1963, 1964.
   Mo Vaughn, Boston A.L., 1992, 1993, 1994 (tied), 1996, 1997; Anaheim A.L., 2000; New York N.L., 2002.

A.L.—6—Mo Vaughn, Boston, 1992, 1993, 1994 (tied), 1996, 1997; Anaheim, 2000.
N.L.—5—Cap Anson, Chicago, 1882, 1884, 1885, 1886, 1892.
   Dick Stuart, Pittsburgh, 1958 (tied), 1959, 1960 (tied), 1961, 1962 (tied).
   Willie McCovey, San Francisco, 1967 (tied), 1968, 1970, 1971, 1977.

Fewest errors for leader, season
A.L.—10—Vic Power, Kansas City, 144 games, 1955.
   Gus Triandos, Baltimore, 103 games, 1955.
N.L.—12—Fred McGriff, San Diego, 151 games, 1992.
   Eddie Murray, New York, 154 games, 1992.

Fewest errors, season (150 or more games)
N.L.—0—Steve Garvey, San Diego, 159 games, 1984.
A.L.—1—Stuffy McInnis, Boston, 152 games, 1921.

Most consecutive errorless games, career
N.L.—193—Steve Garvey, San Diego, June 26, second game, 1983 through April 14, 1985 (1,623 chances accepted).
A.L.—178—Mike Hegan, Milwaukee, Oakland, September 24, 1970, through May 20, 1973 (758 chances accepted).

Most consecutive errorless games, season
N.L.—159—Steve Garvey, San Diego, April 3 through September 29, 1984 (entire season; 1,319 chances accepted).
A.L.—121—Travis Lee, Tampa Bay, May 9 through September 28, 2003 (1,104 chances accepted).

Most consecutive chances accepted without an error, career
A.L.—1,700—Stuffy McInnis, Boston, Cleveland, May 31, 1921, first game, through June 2, 1922, 163 games (1,300 in 1921, 400 in 1922).
N.L.—1,633—Steve Garvey, San Diego, June 26, first game, 1983 through April 15, 1985 (255 in 1983, 1,319 in 1984, 59 in 1985).

Most consecutive chances accepted without an error, season
N.L.—1,319—Steve Garvey, San Diego, April 3 through September 29, 1984 (entire season; 159 games).
A.L.—1,300—Stuffy McInnis, Boston, May 31, first game, through October 2, 1921, 119 games.

Most errors, game
A.A.—5—Lew Brown, Louisville, September 10, 1883.
U.A.—5—John Gorman, Kansas City, June 28, 1884.
   Joe Quinn, St. Louis, July 4, 1884.
N.L.—5—John Carbine, Louisville, April 29, 1876.
   George Zettlein, Philadelphia, June 22, 1876.
   Everett Mills, Hartford, October 7, 1876.
   Tom Esterbrook, Buffalo, July 27, 1880.
   Roger Connor, Troy City, May 27, 1882.
N.L. since 1900—4—John Menefee, Chicago, October 6, 1901.
   Johnny Lush, Philadelphia, June 11, 1904, and September 15, 1904, second game.
   Fred Tenney, Boston, July 12, 1905, first game.
   Todd Zeile, Philadelphia, August 7, 1996.
A.L.—4—Hal Chase, Chicago, July 23, 1913.
   George Sisler, St. Louis, April 14, 1925.
   Jimmy Wasdell, Washington, May 3, 1939.
   (4—Glenn Davis, Baltimore, April 18, 1991, 10.2 innings.)

Longest game with no errors
N.L.—26 innings—Walter Holke, Boston, May 1, 1920.
   Ed Konetchy, Brooklyn, May 1, 1920.
A.L.—25 innings—Ted Simmons, Milwaukee, May 8, finished May 9, 1984 (fielded 24.1 innings).

Most errors, inning
N.L.—3—Dolph Camilli, Philadelphia, August 2, 1935, first inning.
   Al Oliver, Pittsburgh, May 23, 1969, fourth inning.
   Jack Clark, St. Louis, May 25, 1987, second inning.
A.L.—3—George Metkovich, Boston, April 17, 1945, seventh inning.
   Tom McCraw, Chicago, May 3, 1968, third inning.
   Willie Upshaw, Toronto, July 1, 1986, fifth inning.

DOUBLE PLAYS

Most double plays, career
M.L.—2,044—Mickey Vernon, Washington A.L., Cleveland A.L., Boston A.L., Milwaukee N.L., 1939 through 1959, except 1944, 1945 in military service, 19 years, 2,237 games (2,041 in A.L., 3 in N.L.).
A.L.—2,041—Mickey Vernon, Washington, Cleveland, Boston, 1939 through 1958, except 1944, 1945 in military service, 18 years, 2,227 games.
N.L.—1,708—Charlie Grimm, St. Louis, Pittsburgh, Chicago, 1918 through 1936, 19 years, 2,132 games.

Most double plays, season
A.L.—194—Ferris Fain, Philadelphia, 150 games, 1949.
N.L.—182—Donn Clendenon, Pittsburgh, 152 games, 1966.

Most seasons leading league in double plays
N.L.—6—Keith Hernandez, St. Louis, New York, 1977, 1979, 1980, 1981, 1983, 1984.
A.L.—4—Stuffy McInnis, Philadelphia, Boston, 1912, 1914, 1919, 1920 (tied).
Wally Pipp, New York, 1915, 1916, 1917 (tied), 1920 (tied).
Cecil Cooper, Milwaukee, 1980, 1981, 1982, 1983.

Fewest double plays for leader, season
A.L.—98—Vic Power, Cleveland, 121 games, 1959.
N.L.—109—Bill White, St. Louis, 123 games, 1960.

Fewest double plays, season (150 or more games)
N.L.—82—Mark Grace, Chicago, 156 games, 1998.
A.L.—87—Lou Gehrig, New York, 155 games, 1926.

Most double plays, game
N.L.—7—Curt Blefary, Houston, May 4, 1969.
A.L.—6—Jimmie Foxx, Philadelphia, August 24, 1935, 15 innings.
Ferris Fain, Philadelphia, September 1, 1947, second game.
George Vico, Detroit, May 19, 1948.
Eddie Robinson, Cleveland, August 5, 1948.
Lee Thomas, Los Angeles, August 23, 1963.
Bob Oliver, Kansas City, May 14, 1971.
John Mayberry, Kansas City, May 6, 1972.
Bob Oliver, New York, April 29, 1975.
Dave Bergman, Detroit, April 13, 1984.
Kent Hrbek, Minnesota, July 18, 1990.
Mark McGwire, Oakland, May 17, 1995.
Jason Giambi, New York, June 17, 2003.
(6—Rod Carew, Minnesota, August 29, 1977, first game, 10 innings.)

Most double plays started, game
A.L.—3—Lu Blue, Detroit, September 8, 1922.
Walt Judnich, St. Louis, September 6, 1947.
Vic Power, Philadelphia, September 26, 1954.
Pete O'Brien, Texas, May 22, 1984.
Pat Tabler, Cleveland, April 27, 1985.
(3—Kent Hrbek, Minnesota, August 12, 1986, 12 innings.)
N.L.—3—Frank Hurst, Philadelphia, September 17, 1930.
Tommie Aaron, Milwaukee, May 27, 1962.
Keith Hernandez, St. Louis, August 6, 1976.

Most unassisted double plays, season
A.L.—8—Jim Bottomley, St. Louis, 140 games, 1936.
N.L.—8—Bill White, St. Louis, 151 games, 1961.

Most unassisted double plays, game
N.L.—2—Held by many first basemen. Last first baseman—Richie Sexson, Milwaukee, September 11, 2002.
A.L.—2—Held by many first basemen. Last first baseman—Jason Giambi, Oakland, August 2, 2000.

For a complete list of players turning unassist-ed triple plays, see page 200.

SECOND BASEMEN
GAMES AND INNINGS

Most games, career
A.L.—2,651—Eddie Collins, Philadelphia, Chicago, 1908 through 1928, 21 years.
N.L.—2,427—Joe Morgan, Houston, Cincinnati, San Francisco, Philadelphia, 1963 through 1983, 21 years.

Most consecutive games, career
A.L.—798—Nellie Fox, Chicago, August 7, 1955 through September 3, 1960.
N.L.—443—Dave Cash, Pittsburgh, Philadelphia, September 20, 1973 through August 5, 1976.

Most games, season
A.L.—162—Jake Wood, Detroit, 1961.
Bobby Grich, Baltimore, 1973.
N.L.—163—Bill Mazeroski, Pittsburgh, 1967.

Most seasons leading league in games
A.L.—8—Nellie Fox, Chicago, 1952, 1953, 1954, 1955, 1956, 1957, 1958, 1959.
N.L.—8—Craig Biggio, Houston, 1992, 1993, 1994, 1995, 1996, 1997, 1998, 2001.

Fewest games for leader, season
A.L.—133—Frank LaPorte, St. Louis, 1911.
N.L.—134—George Cutshaw, Pittsburgh, 1917.

Most innings played, game
N.L.—26—Charlie Pick, Boston, May 1, 1920.
Ivy Olson, Brooklyn, May 1, 1920.
A.L.—25—Julio Cruz, Chicago, May 8, finished May 9, 1984.
Jim Gantner, Milwaukee, May 8, finished May 9, 1984 (fielded 24.1 innings).

AVERAGE

Highest fielding average, career (1,000 or more games)
N.L.—.9894—Ryne Sandberg, Philadelphia, Chicago, 16 years, 1981 through 1997, except 1995, 1,995 games.
A.L.—.987—Roberto Alomar, Toronto, Baltimore, Cleveland, 11 years, 1991 through 2001, 1,557 games.

Highest fielding average, season (150 or more games)
N.L.—.996—Jose Oquendo, St. Louis, 150 games, 1990.
A.L.—.995—Bobby Grich, Baltimore, 162 games, 1973.

Highest fielding average, season (100 or more games)
A.L.—.997—Bobby Grich, California, 116 games, 1985.
N.L.—.997—Bret Boone, Cincinnati, 136 games, 1997.

Most seasons leading league in fielding average (100 or more games)
A.L.—9—Eddie Collins, Philadelphia, Chicago, 1909, 1910, 1914, 1915, 1916, 1920, 1921, 1922, 1924.
N.L.—7—Red Schoendienst, St. Louis, New York, Milwaukee, 1946, 1949, 1953, 1955, 1956, 1957 (tied), 1958.

Most consecutive seasons leading league in fielding average (100 or more games)
N.L.—6—Claude Ritchey, Pittsburgh, 1902, 1903, 1904 (tied), 1905, 1906, 1907.
A.L.—4—Charlie Gehringer, Detroit, 1934 (tied), 1935, 1936, 1937.

Lowest fielding average for leader, season (100 or more games)
N.L.—.928—Charley Bassett, Indianapolis, 119 games, 1887.
N.L. since 1900—.953—John Miller, Pittsburgh, 150 games, 1909.
A.L.—.960—Jimmy Williams, New York, 132 games, 1903.

Lowest fielding average, season (100 or more games)
N.L.—.893—Fred Pfeffer, Chicago, 109 games, 1885.
A.L.—.914—Frank Truesdale, St. Louis, 122 games, 1910.
N.L. since 1900—.927—John Farrell, St. Louis, 118 games, 1903.

PUTOUTS

Most putouts, career
A.L.—6,526—Eddie Collins, Philadelphia, Chicago, 1908 through 1928, 21 years.
N.L.—5,541—Joe Morgan, Houston, Cincinnati, San Francisco, Philadelphia, 1963 through 1983, 21 years.

Most putouts, season
A.A.—525—John McPhee, Cincinnati, 140 games, 1886.

A.L.—484—Bobby Grich, Baltimore 160 games, 1974.
N.L.—466—Billy Herman, Chicago, 153 games, 1933.

Most seasons leading league in putouts
A.L.—10—Nellie Fox, Chicago, 1952, 1953, 1954, 1955, 1956, 1957, 1958, 1959, 1960, 1961.
N.L.—7—Fred Pfeffer, Chicago, 1884, 1885, 1886, 1887, 1888, 1889, 1891.
Billy Herman, Chicago, Brooklyn, 1933, 1935, 1936, 1938, 1939, 1940 (tied), 1942.

Fewest putouts for leader, season
A.L.—285—Damion Easley, Detroit, 140 games, 1998.
N.L.—292—Larry Doyle, New York, 144 games, 1909.

Fewest putouts, season (150 or more games)
A.L.—230—Luis Rivas, Minnesota, 150 games, 2001.
N.L.—260—John Miller, Pittsburgh, 150 games, 1909.
Jose Vidro, Montreal, 153 games, 2000.

Most putouts, game
A.A.—12—Lou Bierbauer, Philadelphia, June 22, 1888.
A.L.—12—Bobby Knoop, California, August 30, 1966.
(12—Billy Gardner, Baltimore, May 21, 1957, 16 innings.
Vern Fuller, Cleveland, April 11, 1969, 16 innings.)
N.L.—11—Sam Wise, Washington, August 29, 1893.
John McPhee, Cincinnati, April 21, 1894.
Nap Lajoie, Philadelphia, April 25, 1899.
Billy Herman, Chicago, June 28, 1933, first game.
Gene Baker, Chicago, May 27, 1955.
Charlie Neal, Los Angeles, July 2, 1959.
Julian Javier, St. Louis, June 27, 1964.
(15—Jake Pitler, Pittsburgh, August 22, 1917, 22 innings.)

Longest game with no putouts
A.L.—15 innings—Steve Yerkes, Boston, June 11, 1913.
Denny Doyle, California, June 14, 1974.
Damion Easley, Detroit, July 8, 2000.
N.L.—18 innings—Phil Garner, Pittsburgh, August 10, 1977.

ASSISTS

Most assists, career
A.L.—7,630—Eddie Collins, Philadelphia, Chicago, 21 years, 1908 through 1928.
N.L.—6,738—Joe Morgan, Houston, Cincinnati, San Francisco, Philadelphia, 1963 through 1983, 21 years.

Most assists, season
N.L.—641—Frankie Frisch, St. Louis, 153 games, 1927.
A.L.—572—Oscar Melillo, St. Louis, 148 games, 1930.

Most seasons leading league in assists
N.L.—9—Bill Mazeroski, Pittsburgh, 1958, 1960, 1961, 1962, 1963, 1964, 1966, 1967, 1968.
A.L.—7—Charlie Gehringer, Detroit, 1927, 1928, 1933, 1934, 1935, 1936, 1938.

Fewest assists for leader, season
N.L.—381—Emil Verban, Philadelphia, 138 games, 1946.
A.L.—396—Nellie Fox, Chicago, 154 games, 1956.

Fewest assists, season (150 or more games)
A.L.—310—Joey Cora, Seattle, Cleveland, 151 games, 1998.
N.L.—358—Tony Taylor, Philadelphia, 150 games, 1964.

Most assists, game
N.L. before 1900—12—Fred Dunlap, Cleveland, July 24, 1882.
Monte Ward, Brooklyn, June 10, 1892, first game.
(15—Lave Cross, Philadelphia, August 5, 1897, 12 innings.)
N.L. since 1900—12—Jim Gilliam, Brooklyn, July 21, 1956.
Ryne Sandberg, Chicago, June 12, 1983.
Glenn Hubbard, Atlanta, April 14, 1985.
Juan Samuel, Philadelphia, April 20, 1985.
(13—Morrie Rath, Cincinnati, August 26, 1919, 15 innings.
Davey Lopes, Los Angeles, April 12, 1980, 17 innings.
Mark Loretta, San Diego, May 7, 2003, 9.1 innings.)
A.L.—12—Don Money, Milwaukee, June 24, 1977.
Tony Phillips, Oakland, July 6, 1986.

Harold Reynolds, Seattle, August 27, 1986.
(13—Bobby Avila, Cleveland, July 1, 1952, 19 innings.
Willie Randolph, New York, August 25, 1976, 19 innings.)

CHANCES ACCEPTED AND OFFERED

Most chances accepted, career
A.L.—14,156—Eddie Collins, Philadelphia, Chicago, 1908 through 1928, 21 years.
N.L.—12,279—Joe Morgan, Houston, Cincinnati, San Francisco, Philadelphia, 1963 through 1983, 21 years.

Most chances accepted, season
N.L.—1,037—Frankie Frisch, St. Louis, 153 games, 1927.
A.L.—988—Nap Lajoie, Cleveland, 156 games, 1908.

Most seasons leading league in chances accepted
A.L.—9—Nellie Fox, Chicago, 1952, 1953, 1954, 1955, 1956, 1957, 1958, 1959, 1960.
N.L.—8—Bill Mazeroski, Pittsburgh, 1958, 1960, 1961, 1962, 1963, 1964, 1966, 1967.

Fewest chances accepted by leader, season
N.L.—686—John Miller, Pittsburgh, 150 games, 1909.
A.L.—697—Eddie Collins, Philadelphia, 132 games, 1911.

Fewest chances accepted, season (150 or more games)
A.L.—553—Joey Cora, Seattle, Cleveland, 151 games, 1998.
N.L.—671—Mickey Morandini, Chicago, 151 games, 1998.

Most chances accepted, game
A.A.—18—Clarence Childs, Syracuse, June 1, 1890.
N.L.—18—Fred Dunlap, Cleveland, July 24, 1882.
N.L. since 1900—18—Terry Harmon, Philadelphia, June 12, 1971.
(21—Eddie Moore, Boston vs. Chicago, May 17, 1927, 22 innings.)
A.L.—17—Jimmie Dykes, Philadelphia, August 28, 1921.
Nellie Fox, Chicago, June 12, 1952.
(20—Willie Randolph, New York, August 25, 1976, 19 innings.)

Longest game with no chances offered
A.L.—15 innings—Steve Yerkes, Boston, June 11, 1919.
N.L.—12 innings—Ken Boswell, New York, August 7, 1972 (none out in 13th inning).

ERRORS

Most errors, career
M.L.—828—Fred Pfeffer, Troy N.L., Chicago N.L., Chicago P.L., Louisville N.L., New York N.L., 16 years, 1882 through 1897 (654 in N.L., 74 in P.L.)
N.L.—754—Fred Pfeffer, Troy, Chicago, Louisville, New York, 1882 through 1897, except 1890, 15 years.
N.L. since 1900—443—Larry Doyle, New York, Chicago, 1907 through 1920, 14 years.
A.L.—435—Eddie Collins, Philadelphia, Chicago, 1908 through 1928, 21 years.

Most errors, season
N.L.—88—Charles Smith, Cincinnati, 80 games, 1880.
Bob Ferguson, Philadelphia, 85 games, 1883.
N.L. since 1900—55—George Grantham, Chicago, 150 games, 1923.
A.A.—87—Yank Robinson, St. Louis, 129 games, 1886.
Bill McClellan, Brooklyn, 136 games, 1887.
A.L.—61—Kid Gleason, Detroit, 136 games, 1901.
Hobe Ferris, Boston, 138 games, 1901.

Most seasons leading league in errors
N.L.—5—Fred Pfeffer, Chicago, 1884, 1885, 1886, 1887, 1888.
N.L. since 1900—4
Billy Herman, Chicago, 1932, 1933, 1937, 1939.
Glenn Beckert, Chicago, 1966, 1967, 1969, 1970 (tied).
M.L. since 1900—4—Tito Fuentes, San Francisco N.L., 1971, 1972; San Diego N.L., 1976; Detroit A.L., 1977.
A.L.—4—Bill Wambsganss, Cleveland, Boston, 1917, 1919, 1920, 1924.

Joe Gordon, New York, 1938, 1941, 1942, 1943 (tied).
Harold Reynolds, Seattle, 1987, 1988, 1989, 1990 (tied).

Fewest errors for leader, season
N.L.—13—Luis Castillo, Florida, 133 games, 2001.
A.L.—14—Hector Lopez, Kansas City, 96 games, 1958.

Fewest errors, season (150 or more games)
N.L.—3—Jose Oquendo, St. Louis, 150 games, 1990.
A.L.—5—Jerry Adair, Baltimore, 153 games, 1964.
Bobby Grich, Baltimore, 162 games, 1973.
Roberto Alomar, Toronto, 150 games, 1992.
Roberto Alomar, Cleveland, 157 games, 2001.

Most consecutive errorless games, career
N.L.—123—Ryne Sandberg, Chicago, June 21, 1989 through
May 17, 1990 (577 chances accepted).
A.L.—104—Roberto Alomar, Toronto, June 21, 1994 through
July 3, 1995 (482 chances accepted).

Most consecutive errorless games, season
N.L.—90—Ryne Sandberg, Chicago, June 21 through October
1, 1989 (430 chances accepted).
A.L.—86—Rich Dauer, Baltimore, April 10 through September
29, 1978 (418 chances accepted).

Most consecutive chances accepted without an error, season
N.L.—479—Manny Trillo, Philadelphia, April 8 (part) through
July 31 (part), 1982, 91 games.
A.L.—425—Rich Dauer, Baltimore, April 10 through September
30 (part), 1978, 87 games.

Most errors, game
N.L.—9—Andy Leonard, Boston, June 14, 1876.
N.L. since 1900—4—Held by six second basemen. Last player—
Casey Wise, Chicago, May 3, 1957.
A.L.—5—Charles Hickman, Washington, September 29, 1905.
Nap Lajoie, Philadelphia, April 22, 1915.

Longest game with no errors
N.L.—25 innings—Felix Millan, New York, September 11, 1974.
Ted Sizemore, St. Louis, September 11, 1974.
A.L.—25 innings—Julio Cruz, Chicago, May 8, finished May 9,
1984.
Jim Gantner, Milwaukee, May 8, finished May 9, 1984 (fielded
24.1 innings).

Most errors, inning
N.L.—3—Bid McPhee, Cincinnati, September 23, 1894, first
game, second inning.
Claude Ritchey, Pittsburgh, September 22, 1900, sixth inning.
Bama Rowell, Boston, September 25, 1941, third inning.
Eddie Stanky, Chicago, June 20, 1943, first game, eighth
inning.
George Hausmann, New York, August 13, 1944, second
game, fourth inning.
Kermit Wahl, Cincinnati, September 18, 1945, first game, 11th
inning.
Davey Lopes, Los Angeles, June 2, 1973, first inning.
Ted Sizemore, St. Louis, April 17, 1975, sixth inning.
A.L.—3—Del Pratt, St. Louis, September 1, 1914, second
game, fourth inning.
Bill Wambsganss, Cleveland, May 15, 1923, fourth inning.
Bobby Doerr, Boston, May 11, 1949, second inning.
Tim Cullen, Washington, August 30, 1969, eighth inning
(consecutive).

DOUBLE PLAYS

Most double plays, career
N.L.—1,706—Bill Mazeroski, Pittsburgh, 17 years, 1956
through 1972.
A.L.—1,568—Nellie Fox, Philadelphia, Chicago, 17 years, 1947
through 1963.

Most double plays, season
N.L.—161—Bill Mazeroski, Pittsburgh, 162 games, 1966.
A.L.—150—Gerry Priddy, Detroit, 157 games, 1950.

Most seasons leading league in double plays
N.L.—8—Bill Mazeroski, Pittsburgh, 1960, 1961, 1962, 1963,
1964, 1965, 1966, 1967.
A.L.—5—Nap Lajoie, Cleveland, 1903, 1906, 1907, 1908, 1909
(tied).
Eddie Collins, Philadelphia, Chicago, 1909 (tied), 1910, 1912,
1916, 1919.
Bucky Harris, Washington, 1921, 1922, 1923, 1924 (tied), 1925.
Bobby Doerr, Boston, 1938, 1940, 1943, 1946, 1947.
Nellie Fox, Chicago, 1954, 1956, 1957, 1958, 1960.

Fewest double plays for leader, season
N.L.—81—Rogers Hornsby, St. Louis, 154 games, 1922.
A.L.—84—Charlie Gehringer, Detroit, 121 games, 1927.

Fewest double plays, season (150 or more games)
N.L.—65—George Hausmann, New York, 154 games, 1945.
Jose Oquendo, St. Louis, 150 games, 1990.
A.L.—65—Luis Rivas, Minnesota, 150 games, 2001.

Most double plays, game
A.L.—6—Bobby Knoop, California, May 1, 1966, first game.
Alfonso Soriano, New York, June 17, 2003.
(6—Joe Gordon, Cleveland, August 31, 1949, first game, 14
innings.)
N.L.—6—Bill Doran, Houston, May 8, 1988.
(6—Felix Millan, Atlanta, August 5, 1971, 17 innings.)

Most double plays started, game
A.L.—5—Gerry Priddy, Detroit, May 20, 1950.
N.L.—5—Juan Samuel, Philadelphia, June 14, 1988, first game.
(4—Felix Millan, Atlanta, August 5, 1971, 17 innings.)

Most unassisted double plays, game
N.L.—2—Dave Force, Buffalo, September 15, 1881.
Claude Ritchey, Louisville, July 9, 1899, first game.
A.L.—2—Mike Edwards, Oakland, August 10, 1978.
Luis Alicea, Anaheim, August 8, 1997.

**For a complete list of players turning
unassisted triple plays, see page 200.**

THIRD BASEMEN
GAMES AND INNINGS

Most games, career
A.L.—2,870—Brooks Robinson, Baltimore, 1955 through 1977,
23 years.
N.I—2,212—Mike Schmidt, Philadelphia, 1972 through 1989,
18 years.

Most consecutive games, career
A.L.—576—Eddie Yost, Washington, July 3, 1951, to May 11,
1955.
N.L.—364—Ron Santo, Chicago, April 19, 1964 through May
31, 1966.

Most games, season
N.L.—164—Ron Santo, Chicago, 1965.
A.L.—163—Brooks Robinson, Baltimore, 1961, 1964.

Most seasons leading league in games
A.L.—8—Brooks Robinson, Baltimore, 1960, 1961, 1962, 1963,
1964, 1966 (tied), 1968 (tied), 1970.
N.L.—7—Ron Santo, Chicago, 1961 (tied), 1963, 1965, 1966,
1967, 1968, 1969 (tied).

Fewest games for leader, season
N.L.—111—Art Whitney, Boston, 1934.
A.L.—131—George Kell, Philadelphia, Detroit, 1946.

Most innings played, game
N.L.—26—Tony Boeckel, Boston, May 1, 1920.
Jimmy Johnston, Brooklyn, May 1, 1920.
A.L.—25—Vance Law, Chicago, May 8, finished May 9, 1984.
Randy Ready, Milwaukee, May 8, finished May 9, 1984 (field-
ed 24.1 innings).

AVERAGE

Highest fielding average, career (1,000 or more games)
A.L.—.971—Brooks Robinson, Baltimore, 1955 through 1977, 23 years, 2,870 games.
N.L.—.970—Ken Reitz, St. Louis, San Francisco, Chicago, Pittsburgh, 1972 through 1982, 11 years, 1,321 games.

Highest fielding average, season (150 or more games)
A.L.—.989—Don Money, Milwaukee, 157 games, 1974.
N.L.—.980—Robin Ventura, New York, 160 games, 1999.

Highest fielding average, season (100 or more games)
A.L.—.991—Steve Buechele, Texas, 111 games, 1991.
N.L.—.983—Heinie Groh, New York, 145 games, 1924.

Most seasons leading league in fielding average (100 or more games)
A.L.—11—Brooks Robinson, Baltimore, 1960, 1961, 1962, 1963, 1964, 1966, 1967, 1968, 1969 (tied), 1972, 1975.
N.L.—6—Heinie Groh, Cincinnati, New York, 1915 (tied), 1917, 1918, 1922, 1923, 1924.
Ken Reitz, St. Louis, Chicago, 1973, 1974, 1977, 1978, 1980, 1981.

Most consecutive seasons leading league in fielding average (100 or more games)
A.L.—6—Willie Kamm, Chicago, 1924 through 1929.
N.L.—4—Willie Jones, Philadelphia, 1953 through 1956.

Lowest fielding average for leader, season (100 or more games)
N.L.—.891—Ned Williamson, Chicago, 111 games, 1885.
N.L. since 1900—.912—Bobby Lowe, Boston, 111 games, 1901.
A.L.—.936—Bill Bradley, Cleveland, 133 games, 1901.

Lowest fielding average, season (100 or more games)
N.L.—.836—Charles Hickman, New York, 118 games, 1900.
A.L.—.860—Hunter Hill, Washington, 135 games, 1904.

PUTOUTS

Most putouts, career
A.L.—2,697—Brooks Robinson, Baltimore, 1955 through 1977, 23 years.
N.L.—2,288—Pie Traynor, Pittsburgh, 1921 through 1937, except 1936, 16 years.

Most putouts, season
A.A.—252—Denny Lyons, Philadelphia, 137 games, 1887.
N.L.—252—Jimmy Collins, Boston, 142 games, 1900.
A.L.—243—Willie Kamm, Chicago, 155 games, 1928.

Most seasons leading league in putouts
A.L.—8—Eddie Yost, Washington, Detroit, 1948, 1950, 1951, 1952, 1953, 1954 (tied), 1956, 1959.
N.L.—7—Pie Traynor, Pittsburgh, 1923, 1925, 1926, 1927, 1931, 1933, 1934.
Willie Jones, Philadelphia, 1949, 1950, 1952, 1953, 1954, 1955, 1956.
Ron Santo, Chicago, 1962, 1963, 1964, 1965, 1966, 1967, 1969.

Fewest putouts for leader, season
N.L.—107—Mike Lowell, Florida, 144 games, 2001.
A.L.—111—Joe Randa, Kansas City, 137 games, 2001.

Fewest putouts, season (150 or more games)
N.L.—77—Chipper Jones, Atlanta, 152 games, 1997.
A.L.—79—Travis Fryman, Cleveland, 154 games, 2000.

Most putouts, game
N.L.—10—Willie Kuehne, Pittsburgh, May 24, 1889.
N.L. since 1900—9—Pat Dillard, St. Louis, June 18, 1900.
A.L.—7—Bill Bradley, Cleveland, September 21, 1901, first game; also May 13, 1909.
Harry Riconda, Philadelphia, July 5, 1924, second game.
Ossie Bluege, Washington, June 18, 1927.
Ray Boone, Detroit, April 24, 1954.

Longest game with no putouts
N.L.—21 innings—Larry Parrish, Montreal, May 21, 1977.
Ryne Sandberg, Chicago, August 17, 1982.
A.L.—20 innings—Graig Nettles, Cleveland, September 14, 1971.

ASSISTS

Most assists, career
A.L.—6,205—Brooks Robinson, Baltimore, 23 years, 1955 through 1977.
N.L.—5,045—Mike Schmidt, Philadelphia, 18 years, 1972 through 1989.

Most assists, season
A.L.—412—Graig Nettles, Cleveland, 158 games, 1971.
N.L.—404—Mike Schmidt, Philadelphia, 162 games, 1974.

Most seasons leading league in assists
A.L.—8—Brooks Robinson, Baltimore, 1960, 1963, 1964, 1966, 1967, 1968, 1969, 1974.
N.L.—7—Ron Santo, Chicago, 1962, 1963, 1964, 1965, 1966, 1967, 1968.
Mike Schmidt, Philadelphia, 1974, 1976, 1977, 1980, 1981, 1982, 1983.

Fewest assists for leader, season
N.L.—227—Art Whitney, Boston, 111 games, 1934.
A.L.—258—Ossie Bluege, Washington, 134 games, 1930.

Fewest assists, season (150 or more games)
A.L.—221—Harry Lord, Chicago, 150 games, 1913.
Dean Palmer, Texas, 154 games, 1996.
N.L.—238—Chipper Jones, Atlanta, 156 games, 1999.

Most assists, game
N.L.—11—Deacon White, Buffalo, May 16, 1884.
Jerry Denny, New York, May 29, 1890.
Damon Phillips, Boston, August 29, 1944.
Chris Sabo, Cincinnati, April 7, 1988.
Kevin Young, Pittsburgh, June 25, 1995.
(12—Bobby Byrne, Pittsburgh, June 8, 1910, second game, 11 innings.)
A.L.—11—Ken McMullen, Washington, September 26, 1966, first game.
Mike Ferraro, New York, September 14, 1968.
(11—Home Run Baker, New York, May 24, 1918, 19 innings.
Doug DeCinces, California, May 7, 1983, 12 innings.)

CHANCES ACCEPTED AND OFFERED

Most chances accepted, career
A.L.—8,902—Brooks Robinson, Baltimore, 1955 through 1977, 23 years.
N.L.—6,636—Mike Schmidt, Philadelphia, 1972 through 1989, 18 years.

Most chances accepted, season
A.L.—603—Harlond Clift, St. Louis, 155 games, 1937.
N.L.—593—Jimmy Collins, Boston, 151 games, 1899.
N.L. since 1900—583—Tommy Leach, Pittsburgh, 146 games, 1904.

Most seasons leading league in chances accepted
N.L.—9—Ron Santo, Chicago, 1961, 1962, 1963, 1964, 1965, 1966, 1967, 1968, 1969 (tied).
A.L.—8—Home Run Baker, Philadelphia, New York, 1909, 1910, 1912, 1913, 1914, 1917, 1918, 1919.
Brooks Robinson, Baltimore, 1960, 1963, 1964, 1966, 1967, 1968, 1969, 1974.

Fewest chances accepted for leader, season
N.L.—332—Art Whitney, Boston, 111 games, 1934.
A.L.—372—Robin Ventura, Chicago, 150 games, 1996.

Fewest chances accepted, season (150 or more games)
N.L.—318—Chipper Jones, Atlanta, 152 games, 1997.
A.L.—326—Dean Palmer, Texas, 154 games, 1996.

Most chances accepted, game
A.L.—13—Wid Conroy, Washington, September 25, 1911.
(14—Jimmy Collins, Boston, June 21, 1902, 15 innings.)
Ben Dyer, Detroit, July 16, 1919, 14 innings.
N.L. before 1900—13—Bill Kuehne, Pittsburgh, May 24, 1889.
Jerry Denny, New York, May 19, 1890.
Bill Shindle, Baltimore, September 28, 1893.
Bill Joyce, Washington, May 26, 1894.

(16—Jerry Denny, Providence, August 17, 1882, 18 innings.)
N.L since 1900—Art Devlin, New York, May 23, 1908, first
game.
Tony Cuccinello, Brooklyn, July 12, 1934, first game.
Roy Hughes, Chicago, August 29, 1944, second game.
(14—Don Hoak, Cincinnati, May 4, 1958, second game, 14
innings.)

Longest game with no chances offered
N.L.—20 innings—Jeff Hamilton, Los Angeles, June 3, 1989.
A.L.—15 innings—Toby Harrah, Cleveland, June 20, 1980.

ERRORS

Most errors, career
M.L.—780—Arlie Latham, St. Louis A.A., Chicago P.L.,
Cincinnati N.L., St. Louis N.L., 1883 through 1896, 14 years.
N.L.—533—Jerry Denny, Providence, St. Louis, Indianapolis,
New York, Cleveland, Philadelphia, Louisville, 1881 through
1894, except 1892, 13 years.
N.L. since 1900—324—Pie Traynor, Pittsburgh, 1921 through
1935, 1937, 16 years, 1,864 games.
A.L.—359—Jimmy Austin, New York, St. Louis, 1909 through
1922, 1925, 1926, 1929, 17 years, 1,433 games.

Most errors, season
N.L.—91—Charles Hickman, New York, 118 games, 1900.
A.L.—64—Sammy Strang, Chicago, 137 games, 1902.

Most seasons leading league in errors
N.L.—5—Pie Traynor, Pittsburgh, 1926, 1928 (tied), 1931,
1932, 1933.
A.L.—5—Jim Tabor, Boston, 1939, 1940 (tied), 1941, 1942,
1943 (tied).

Fewest errors for leader, season
N.L.—16.—Eddie Mathews, Milwaukee, 147 games, 1957.
Gene Freese, Pittsburgh, 74 games, 1957.
A.L.—17—Cecil Travis, Washington, 56 games, 1946.

Fewest errors, season (150 or more games)
A.L.—5—Don Money, Milwaukee, 157 games, 1974.
N.L.—8—Ken Reitz, St. Louis, 150 games, 1980.

Most consecutive errorless games, career
M.L.—99—John Wehner, Pittsburgh N.L., August 2, 1992
through September 29, 2000 (202 chances accepted; played
other positions during streak).
Jeff Cirillo, Colorado N.L., Seattle A.L., June 20, 2001 through
April 19, 2002 (255 chances accepted).
N.L.—99—John Wehner, Pittsburgh, August 2, 1992 through
September 29, 2000 (202 chances accepted; played other
positions during streak).
A.L.—88—Don Money, Milwaukee, September 28, 1973, second
game, through July 16, 1974 (261 chances accepted).

Most consecutive errorless games, season
A.L.—86—Don Money, Milwaukee, April 5 through July 16,
1974 (257 chances accepted).
N.L.—85—Jeff Cirillo, Colorado, June 20 through October 7,
2001 (228 chances accepted).

Most consecutive chances accepted without an error, career
A.L.—261—Don Money, Milwaukee, September 28, 1973, first
game, through July 16, 1974, 88 games.
N.L.—246—Jeff Cirillo, Colorado, June 20 through October 7,
2001; San Diego, May 19 through July 21, 2004, 96 games.

Most consecutive chances accepted without an error, season
A.L.—257—Don Money, Milwaukee, April 5 through July 16,
1974, 88 games.
N.L.—230—Vinny Castilla, Colorado, July 5 through October 3,
2004, 75 games.

Most errors, game
U.A.—6—Jim Donnelly, Kansas City, July 16, 1884.
A.A.—6—Joe Moffett, Toledo, August 2, 1884.
Joe Werrick, Louisville, July 28, 1888.
Billy Alvord, Toledo, May 22, 1890.
N.L.—6—Joe Mulvey, Philadelphia, July 30, 1884.

N.L. since 1900—5—Dave Brain, Boston, June 11, 1906.
A.L.—4—Held by 22 third basemen. Last third baseman—
Edgar Martinez, Seattle, May 6, 1990.

Longest game with no errors
N.L.—26 innings—Tony Boeckel, Boston, May 1, 1920.
Jimmy Johnston, Brooklyn, May 1, 1920.
A.L.—25 innings—Vance Law, Chicago, May 8, finished May 9,
1984.

Most errors, Inning
N.L.—4—Lew Whistler, New York, June 19, 1891, fourth
inning.
Bob Brenly, San Francisco, September 14, 1986, fourth inning.
A.L.—4—Jimmy Burke, Milwaukee, May 27, 1901, fourth inning.

DOUBLE PLAYS

Most double plays, career
A.L.—618—Brooks Robinson, Baltimore, 23 years, 1955
through 1977.
N.L.—450—Mike Schmidt, Philadelphia, 18 years, 1972
through 1989.

Most double plays, season
A.L.—54—Graig Nettles, Cleveland, 158 games, 1971.
N.L.—45—Darrell Evans, Atlanta, 160 games, 1974.
Jeff Cirillo, Milwaukee, 149 games, 1998.

Most seasons leading league in double plays
N.L.—6—Heinie Groh, Cincinnati, New York, 1915, 1916, 1918,
1919, 1920 (tied), 1922.
Ron Santo, Chicago, 1961, 1964, 1966, 1967, 1968 (tied), 1971.
Mike Schmidt, 1978, 1979, 1980, 1982 (tied),
1983, 1987.
A.L.—5—Jimmy Austin, New York, St. Louis, 1909, 1911,
1913, 1915, 1917.
Ken Keltner, Cleveland, 1939, 1941, 1942, 1944, 1947.
Frank Malzone, Boston, 1957, 1958, 1959, 1960, 1961.
Dean Palmer, Texas, 154 games, 1996.

Fewest double plays for leader, season
N.L.—17—Joe Stripp, Brooklyn, 140 games, 1933.
Johnny Vergez, New York, 123 games, 1933.
Whitey Kurowski, St. Louis, 138 games, 1946.
Jim Tabor, Philadelphia, 124 games, 1946.
A.L.—23—Marty McManus, Detroit, 130 games, 1930.

Fewest double plays, season (150 or more games)
N.L.—10—Bob Aspromonte, Houston, 155 games, 1964.
Chipper Jones, Atlanta, 156 games, 1999.
A.L.—17—Max Alvis, Cleveland, 156 games, 1965.
Wade Boggs, Boston, 151 games, 1988.

Most double plays, game
N.L.—4—Pie Traynor, Pittsburgh, July 9, 1925, first game.
Johnny Vergez, Philadelphia, August 15, 1935.
Dennis Walling, Houston, My 8, 1988.
Edgardo Alfonzo, New York, May 14, 1997.
Shane Andrews, Chicago, September 23, 2000.
A.L.—4—Andy Carey, New York, July 31, 1955, second game.
Felix Torres, Los Angeles, August 23, 1963.
Ken McMullen, Washington, August 13, 1965.
Wade Boggs, Boston, August 9, 1985.
Jack Howell, California, May 17, 1989.
Scott Brosius, New York, July 6, 2000.

Most double plays started, game
N.L.—5—Dennis Walling, Houston, May 8, 1988.
A.L.—4—Felix Torres, Los Angeles, August 23, 1963.
Ken McMullen, Washington, August 13, 1965.
Jack Howell, California, May 17, 1989.
Scott Brosius, New York, July 6, 2000.

Most unassisted double plays, season
A.L.—4—Joe Dugan, New York, 148 games, 1924.
N.L.—3—Harry Wolverton, Philadelphia, 34 games, 1902.
Heinie Groh, Cincinnati, 131 games, 1915.

Most unassisted double plays, game
N.L.-A.L.—1—Held by many third basemen.

SHORTSTOPS
GAMES AND INNINGS

Most games, career
A.L.—2,581—Luis Aparicio, Chicago, Baltimore, Boston, 1956 through 1973, 18 years.
N.L.—2,511—Ozzie Smith, San Diego, St. Louis, 1978 through 1996, 19 years.

Most consecutive games, career
A.L.—2,216—Cal Ripken Jr., Baltimore, July 1, 1982 through July 14, 1996.
N.L.—584—Roy McMillan, Cincinnati, September 16, 1951, first game, through August 6, 1955.

Most games, season
N.L.—165—Maury Wills, Los Angeles, 1962.
A.L.—163—Tony Fernandez, Toronto, 1986.

Most games, lefthanded shortstop, season
N.L.—73—Billy Hulen, Philadelphia, 1896.

Most seasons leading league in games
A.L.—12—Cal Ripken Jr., Baltimore, 1983, 1984, 1987, 1988, 1989, 1990, 1991, 1992, 1993, 1994, 1995, 1996.
N.L.—6—Mickey Doolan, Philadelphia, 1906, 1909, 1910, 1911, 1912, 1913.
Arky Vaughan, Pittsburgh, 1933 (tied), 1934, 1936, 1938, 1939, 1940.
Roy McMillan, Cincinnati, Milwaukee, 1952, 1953, 1954 (tied), 1956, 1957, 1961.

Fewest games for leader, season
N.L.—141—Rabbit Maranville, Pittsburgh, 1923.
A.L.—142—Luis Aparicio, Chicago, 1957.

Most innings played, game
N.L.—26—Chuck Ward, Brooklyn, May 1, 1920.
Rabbit Maranville, Boston, May 1, 1920.
A.L.—25—Robin Yount, Milwaukee, May 8, finished May 9, 1984, fielded 24.1 innings.

AVERAGE

Highest fielding average, career (1,000 or more games)
A.L.—.984—Omar Vizquel, Seattle, Cleveland, 14 years, 1989 through 2002, 1,914 games.
N.L.—.980—Larry Bowa, Philadelphia, Chicago, 1970 through 1985, 16 years, 2,222 games.

Highest fielding average, season (150 or more games)
A.L.—.996—Cal Ripken Jr., Baltimore, 161 games, 1990.
N.L.—.994—Rey Ordonez, New York, 154 games, 1999.

Highest fielding average, season (100 or more games)
A.L.—.998—Mike Bordick, Baltimore, 117 games, 2002.
N.L.—.994—Rey Ordonez, New York, 154 games, 1999.

Most seasons leading league in fielding average (100 or more games)
A.L.—8—Everett Scott, Boston, New York, 1916, 1917, 1918, 1919, 1920, 1921, 1922, 1923.
Lou Boudreau, Cleveland, 1940, 1941, 1942, 1943, 1944, 1946, 1947, 1948.
Luis Aparicio, Chicago, Baltimore, 1959, 1960, 1961, 1962, 1963, 1964, 1965, 1966.
N.L.—7—Ozzie Smith, San Diego, St. Louis, 1981, 1982, 1984, 1985, 1986, 1987, 1991. (Note: Smith also led N.L. shortstops in fielding in the shortened 1994 season when he played in 96 games.)

Most consecutive seasons leading league in fielding average (100 or more games)
A.L.—8—Everett Scott, Boston, New York, 1916 through 1923.
Luis Aparicio, Chicago, Baltimore, 1959 through 1966.
N.L.—5—Hughie Jennings, Baltimore, 1894 through 1898.
N.L. since 1900—4—Eddie R. Miller, Boston, Cincinnati, 1940 through 1943.
Ozzie Smith, St. Louis, 1984 through 1987.

Lowest fielding average for leader (100 or more games)
N.L.—.90031—Arthur Irwin, Philadelphia, 121 games, 1888.
N.L. since 1900—.936—Tommy Corcoran, Cincinnati, 150 games, 1904.
A.L.—.930—Freddy Parent, Boston, 139 games, 1903.

Lowest fielding average, season (100 or more games)
A.L.—.851—Bill Keister, Baltimore, 112 games, 1901.
N.L.—.884—Tom Burns, Chicago, 111 games, 1885.
N.L. since 1900—.891—Otto Krueger, St. Louis, 107 games, 1902.

PUTOUTS

Most putouts, career
N.L.—5,133—Rabbit Maranville, Boston, Pittsburgh, Chicago, Brooklyn, St. Louis, 1912 through 1931, except 1924, 19 years.
A.L.—4,548—Luis Aparicio, Chicago, Baltimore, Boston, 1956 through 1973, 18 years.

Most putouts, season
N.L.—425—Hughie Jennings, Baltimore, 131 games, 1895.
A.L.—425—Donie Bush, Detroit, 157 games, 1914.
N.L. since 1900—407—Rabbit Maranville, Boston, 156 games, 1914.

Most seasons leading league in putouts
N.L.—6—Rabbit Maranville, Boston, Pittsburgh, 1914, 1915 (tied), 1916, 1917, 1919, 1923.
A.L.—6—Cal Ripken, Baltimore, 1984, 1985, 1988, 1989, 1991, 1992.

Fewest putouts for leader, season
N.L.—230—Barry Larkin, Cincinnati, 151 games, 1996.
A.L.—248—Joe DeMaestri, Kansas City, 134 games, 1957.

Fewest putouts, season (150 or more games)
N.L.—180—Larry Bowa, Philadelphia, 156 games, 1976.
Mark Grudzielanek, Montreal, 153 games, 1996.
A.L.—212—Gary DiSarcina, California, 150 games, 1996.
Derek Jeter, New York, 150 games, 2001.

Most putouts, game
N.L.—11—Shorty Fuller, New York, August 20, 1895.
Hod Ford, Cincinnati, September 18, 1929.
(14—Monte Cross, Philadelphia, July 7, 1899, 11 innings.)
A.L.—11—John Cassidy, Washington, August 30, 1904, first game.

ASSISTS

Most assists, career
N.L.—8,375—Ozzie Smith, San Diego, St. Louis, 1978 through 1996, 19 years.
A.L.—8,016—Luis Aparicio, Chicago, Baltimore, Boston, 1956 through 1973, 18 years.

Most assists, season
N.L.—621—Ozzie Smith, San Diego, 158 games, 1980.
A.L.—583—Cal Ripken Jr., Baltimore, 162 games, 1984.

Most seasons leading league in assists
N.L.—8—Ozzie Smith, San Diego, 1979, 1980, 1981; St. Louis, 1982, 1985, 1987, 1988, 1989.
A.L.—7—Luke Appling, Chicago, 1933, 1935, 1937, 1939, 1941, 1943, 1946.
Luis Aparicio, Chicago, 1956, 1957, 1958, 1959, 1960, 1961, 1968.
Cal Ripken Jr., Baltimore, 1983, 1984, 1986, 1987, 1989, 1991, 1993.

Fewest assists for leader, season
A.L.—438—Joe Sewell, Cleveland, 137 games, 1928.
N.L.—440—Johnny Logan, Milwaukee, 129 games, 1957.

Fewest assists, season (150 or more games)
A.L.—343—Derek Jeter, New York, 150 games, 2001.
N.L.—374—Kevin Elster, New York, 150 games, 1989.

Most assists, game
N.L.—14—Tommy Corcoran, Cincinnati, August 7, 1903.
(14—Herman Long, Boston, May 6, 1892, 14 innings.
Bud Harrelson, New York, May 24, 1973, 19 innings.)

A.L.—13—Bobby Reeves, Washington, August 7, 1927.
Alex Gonzalez, Toronto, April 26, 1996.
(15—Rick Burleson, California, April 13, finished April 14, 1982, 20 innings.)

Longest game with no assists
N.L.—17 innings—Jack Coffey, Boston, July 26, 1909.
A.L.—13 innings—Rick Burleson, Boston, June 29, 1979.

CHANCES ACCEPTED AND OFFERED

Most chances accepted, career
N.L.—12,624—Ozzie Smith, San Diego, St. Louis, 1978 through 1996, 19 years.
A.L.—12,564—Luis Aparicio, Chicago, Baltimore, Boston, 1956 through 1973, 18 years.

Most chances accepted, season
N.L.—984—Dave Bancroft, New York, 156 games, 1922.
A.L.—969—Donie Bush, Detroit, 157 games, 1914.

Most seasons leading league in chances accepted
N.L.—8—Ozzie Smith, San Diego, St. Louis, 1978, 1980, 1981, 1983, 1985, 1987, 1988, 1989.
A.L.—7—Luis Aparicio, Chicago, 1956, 1957, 1958, 1959, 1960, 1961, 1968.

Fewest chances accepted by leader, season
N.L.—683—Mark Grudzielanek, Montreal, 156 games, 1997.
A.L.—695—Luis Aparicio, Chicago, 142 games, 1957.

Fewest chances accepted, season (150 or more games)
A.L.—555—Derek Jeter, New York, 150 games, 2001.
N.L.—609—Kevin Elster, New York, 150 games, 1989.

Most chances accepted, game
N.L.—19—Danny Richardson, Washington, June 20, 1892, first game.
Eddie Joost, Cincinnati, May 7, 1941.
(21—Eddie R. Miller, Boston, June 27, 1939, 23 innings.)
A.L.—17—Bobby Wallace, St. Louis, June 10, 1902.
(20—Roy Smalley, Minnesota, August 25, 1976, 18.2 innings).

Longest game with no chances offered
A.L.—12 innings—John Gochnauer, Cleveland, July 14, 1903.
Billy Rogell, Detroit, June 16, 1937, fielded 11.2 innings.
N.L.—12 innings— Irv Ray, Boston, August 15, 1888.
N.L. since 1900—12 innings—Khalil Greene, San Diego, August 1, 2004.

ERRORS

Most errors, career
M.L.—1,037—Herman Long, Kansas City A.A., Boston N.L., New York A.L., Detroit A.L., 1889 through 1903, 15 years.
N.L.—972—Bill Dahlen, Chicago, Brooklyn, New York, Boston, 1891 through 1911, except 1910, 20 years, 2,139 games.
N.L. since 1900—676—Honus Wagner, Pittsburgh, 1901 through 1917, 17 years, 1,887 games.
A.L.—689—Donie Bush, Detroit, Washington, 1908 through 1921, 14 years, 1,866 games.

Most errors, season
P.L.—115—Bill Shindle, Philadelphia, 132 games, 1890.
N.L.—106—Joe Sullivan, Washington, 127 games, 1893.
N.L. since 1900—81—Rudy Hulswitt, Philadelphia, 138 games, 1903.
A.L.—95—John Gochnauer, Cleveland, 128 games, 1903.

Most seasons leading league in errors
N.L.—6—Dick Groat, Pittsburgh, St. Louis, 1955, 1956, 1959, 1961, 1962, 1964.
Rafael Ramirez, Atlanta, 1981, 1982, 1983, 1984 (tied), 1985, Houston, 1989.
A.L.—5—Luke Appling, Chicago, 1933, 1935, 1937, 1939, 1946.

Fewest errors for leader, season
N.L.—21—Mariano Duncan, Los Angeles, 67 games, 1987.
A.L.—21—Cristian Guzman, Minnesota, 118 games, 2001.

Fewest errors, season (150 or more games)
A.L.—3—Cal Ripken Jr., Baltimore, 161 games, 1990.

Omar Vizquel, Cleveland, 156 games, 2000.
N.L.—4—Rey Ordonez, New York, 154 games, 1999.

Most consecutive errorless games, career
A.L.—110—Mike Bordick, Baltimore, April 11 through September 29, 2002 (541 chances accepted).
N.L.—101—Rey Ordonez, New York, June 14, 1999 through March 29, 2000 (418 chances accepted).

Most consecutive errorless games, season
A.L.—110—Mike Bordick, Baltimore, April 11 through September 29, 2002 (541 chances accepted).
N.L.—100—Rey Ordonez, New York, June 14 through October 4, 1999 (411 chances accepted).

Most consecutive chances accepted without an error, career
A.L.—543—Mike Bordick, Baltimore, April 10 (part) through September 29, 2002.
N.L.—419—Rey Ordonez, New York, June 13 (part) through March 29, 2000.

Most consecutive chances accepted without an error, season
A.L.—543—Mike Bordick, Baltimore, April 10 (part) through September 29, 2002.
N.L.—412—Rey Ordonez, New York, June 13 (part) through October 4, 1999.

Most errors, game
N.L.—7—Jimmy Hallinan, New York, July 29, 1876.
N.L. since 1900—5—Charlie Babb, New York, August 24, 1903, first game; also with Brooklyn, June 20, 1904.
Phil Lewis, Brooklyn, July 20, 1905.
(5—Done by many shortstops in extra innings.)
A.A.—7—Germany Smith, Brooklyn, June 17, 1885.
A.L.—5—Donie Bush, Detroit, August 25, 1911, first game.
(6—Bill O'Neill, Boston, May 21, 1904, 13 innings.)

Longest game with no errors
N.L.—26 innings—Rabbit Maranville, Boston, May 1, 1920.
A.L.—25 innings—Robin Yount, Milwaukee, May 8, finished May 9, 1984, fielded 24.1 innings.

Most errors, inning
N.L.—4—Shorty Fuller, Washington, August 17, 1888, second inning.
Lennie Merullo, Chicago, September 13, 1942, second game, second inning.
A.L.—4—Ray Chapman, Cleveland, June 20, 1914, fifth inning.

DOUBLE PLAYS

Most double plays, career
N.L.—1,590—Ozzie Smith, San Diego, St. Louis, 1978 through 1996, 19 years.
A.L.—1,565—Cal Ripken Jr., Baltimore, 1981 through 1996, 16 years.

Most double plays, season
A.L.—147—Rick Burleson, Boston, 155 games, 1980.
N.L.—137—Bobby Wine, Montreal, 159 games, 1970.

Most seasons leading league in double plays
A.L.—8—Cal Ripken Jr., Baltimore, 1983, 1984, 1985, 1989, 1991, 1992, 1994, 1995.
N.L.—5—Mickey Doolan, Philadelphia, 1907, 1909 (tied), 1910, 1911, 1913.
Dick Groat, Pittsburgh, St. Louis, 1958, 1959, 1961, 1962, 1964.
Ozzie Smith, San Diego, St. Louis, 1980, 1984 (tied), 1986 (tied), 1987, 1991.

Fewest double plays for leader, season
N.L.—79—Ozzie Smith, St. Louis, 150 games, 1991.
A.L.—81—Roger Peckinpaugh, Washington, 155 games, 1924.

Fewest double plays, season (150 or more games)
A.L.—60—Jackie Gutierrez, Boston, 150 games, 1984.
N.L.—63—Kevin Elster, New York, 150 games, 1989.

Most double plays, game
A.L.—5—29 times by 26 shortstops. Last shortstop—Alex

Rodriguez, Texas, July 26, 2002.
(6—Bert Campaneris, Oakland, September 13, 1970, first
game, 11 innings.)
N.L.—5—18 times. Held by 18 shortstops. Last shortstop—
Adam Everett, Houston, May 17, 2003.
(6—Ozzie Smith, San Diego, August 25, 1979, 19 innings.
Rafael Ramirez, Atlanta, June 27, 1982, 14 innings.)

Most double plays started, game
A.L.—5—Charley O'Leary, Detroit, July 23, 1905.
John P. Sullivan, Washington, August 13, 1944, second game.
Jim Fregosi, California, May 1, 1966, first game.
N.L.—4—many players.
(5—Ozzie Smith, San Diego, August 25, 1979, 19 innings.)

Most unassisted double plays, game
A.L.—2—Lee Tannehill, Chicago, August 4, 1911, first game.
N.L.—1—Held by many shortstops.

**For a complete list of players turning
unassisted triple plays, see page 200.**

OUTFIELDERS
GAMES AND INNINGS

Most games, career
A.L.—2,938—Ty Cobb, Detroit, Philadelphia, 1905 through
1928, 24 years.
N.L.—2,843—Willie Mays, New York Giants, San Francisco,
New York Mets, 1951 through 1973, 22 years, except 1953 in
military service.

Most consecutive games, career
N.L.—897—Billy Williams, Chicago, September 22, 1963
through June 13, 1969.
A.L.—511—Clyde Milan, Washington, August 12, 1910,
through October 3, 1913, second game.

Most games, season
A.L.—163—Leon Wagner, Cleveland, 1964.
N.L.—164—Billy Williams, Chicago, 1965.

Most seasons leading league in games
N.L.—6—George J. Burns, New York, Cincinnati, 1914 (tied),
1916 (tied), 1919, 1920 (tied), 1922, 1923 (tied).
Billy Williams, Chicago, 1964 (tied), 1965, 1966, 1967,
1968, 1970 (tied).
Dale Murphy, Atlanta, 1982 (tied), 1983 (tied), 1984 (tied),
1985, 1987, 1988.
A.L.—5—Rocky Colavito, Cleveland, Detroit, 1959, 1961, 1962,
1963, 1965.

Fewest games for leader, season
A.L.—147—Ted Williams, Boston, 1951.
N.L.—149—Max Carey, Pittsburgh, 1924.
Chet Ross, Boston, 1940.

Most innings played, game
N.L.—26—Walt Cruise, Boston, May 1, 1920.
Les Mann, Boston, May 1, 1920.
Bernie Neis, Brooklyn, May 1, 1920.
Ray Powell, Boston, May 1, 1920.
Zack Wheat, Brooklyn, May 1, 1920.
A.L.—25—Harold Baines, Chicago, May 8, finished May 9,
1984.
Rudy Law, Chicago, May 8, finished May 9, 1984.
Ben Oglivie, Milwaukee, May 8, finished May 9, 1984 (fielded
24.1 innings).

AVERAGE

Highest fielding average, career (1,000 or more games)
M.L.—.995—Darryl Hamilton, Milwaukee A.L., Texas A.L., San
Francisco N.L., Colorado N.L., New York N.L., 13 years, 1988,
1990 through 2001, 1,233 games.

N.L.—.993—Terry Puhl, Houston, 14 years, 1977 through
1990, 1,299 games.
A.L.—.9908—Amos Otis, Kansas City, 14 years, 1970 through
1983, 1,845 games.

Highest fielding average, season (150 or more games)
N.L.—1.000—Danny Litwhiler, Philadelphia, 151 games, 1942.
Curt Flood, St. Louis, 159 games, 1966.
Terry Puhl, Houston, 152 games, 1979.
Brett Butler, Los Angeles, 161 games, 1991.
Brett Butler, Los Angeles, 155 games, 1993.
Luis Gonzalez, Arizona, 161 games, 2001.
A.L.—1.000—Rocky Colavito, Cleveland, 162 games, 1965.
Brian Downing, California, 158 games, 1982.

**Most seasons leading league in fielding average (100 or
more games; 162-game season, 108 or more games)**
A.L.—5—Amos Strunk, Philadelphia, Boston, Chicago, 1912,
1914, 1917 (tied), 1918, 1920.
N.L.—4—Joe Hornung, Boston, 1881, 1882, 1883, 1887.
Steve Brodie, Boston, Pittsburgh, Baltimore, 1890, 1891, 1897,
1899.
N.L. since 1900—3—Stan Musial, St. Louis, 1949, 1954, 1961.
Tony Gonzalez, Philadelphia, 1962, 1964, 1967.
Pete Rose, Cincinnati, 1970, 1971 (tied), 1974.

**Most consecutive seasons leading league in fielding average
(100 or more games)**
A.L.—3—Gene Woodling, New York, 1951 (tied), 1952, 1953
(tied).
N.L.—3—Joe Hornung, Boston, 1881, 1882, 1883.
N.L. since 1900—2—Held by many outfielders. Last outfielder—
Pete Rose, Cincinnati, 1970, 1971 (tied).

Lowest fielding average for leader (100 or more games)
N.L.—.941—Pete Gillespie, New York, 102 games, 1885.
N.L. since 1900—.96753—Zack Wheat, Brooklyn, 120 games,
1912.
A.L.—.959—Chick Stahl, Boston, 130 games, 1901.

Lowest fielding average, season (100 or more games)
N.L.—.843—Jack Manning, Philadelphia, 103 games, 1884.
N.L. since 1900—.900—Mike Donlin, Cincinnati, 118 games,
1903.
A.L.—.872—Bill O'Neill, Washington, 112 games, 1904.

PUTOUTS

Most putouts, career
N.L.—7,095—Willie Mays, New York Giants, San Francisco,
New York Mets, 1951 through 1973, except 1953 in military
service, 22 years.
A.L.—6,794—Tris Speaker, Boston, Cleveland, Washington,
Philadelphia, 1907 through 1928, 22 years.

Most putouts, season
N.L.—547—Taylor Douthit, St. Louis, 154 games, 1928.
A.L.—512—Chet Lemon, Chicago, 149 games, 1977.

Most seasons leading league in putouts
N.L.—9—Max Carey, Pittsburgh, 1912, 1913, 1916, 1917,
1918, 1921, 1922, 1923, 1924.
Richie Ashburn, Philadelphia, 1949, 1950, 1951, 1952, 1953,
1954, 1956, 1957, 1958.
A.L.—7—Tris Speaker, Boston, Cleveland, 1909, 1910, 1913,
1914, 1915, 1918, 1919.

Fewest putouts for leader, season
A.L.—319—Tris Speaker, Boston, 142 games, 1909.
N.L.—321—Roy Thomas, Philadelphia, 139 games, 1904.

Fewest putouts, season (150 or more games)
A.L.—182—Ed Hahn, Chicago, 156 games, 1907.
N.L.—210—Sam Thompson, Philadelphia, 151 games, 1892.
N.L. since 1900—217—Al Martin, Pittsburgh, 152 games, 1996.

Most putouts by left fielder, game
N.L.—11—Dick Harley, St. Louis, June 30, 1898.
Topsy Hartsel, Chicago, September 10, 1901.
(12—Fred Treacy, New York, July 10, 1976.
N.L. since 1950—11—Bill Buckner, Los Angeles, July 20,
1973., 15 innings.)

A.L.—11—Paul Lehner, Philadelphia, June 25, 1950, second game.
Willie Horton, Detroit, July 18, 1969.
(12—Tom McBride, Washington, July 2, 1948, 12 innings.
Rickey Henderson, New York, September 11, 1988, 18 innings.
Darin Erstad, Anaheim, July 24, 2000, 12 innings.)

Most putouts by center fielder, game
N.L.—12—Earl Clark, Boston, May 10, 1929.
(12—Carden Gillenwater, Boston, September 11, 1946, 17 innings.
Lloyd Merriman, Cincinnati, September 7, 1951, 18 innings.
Garry Maddox, Philadelphia, June 10, 1984, 12 innings.)
A.L.—12—Lyman Bostock, Minnesota, May 25, 1977, second game.
(12—Harry Bay, Cleveland, July 19, 1904, 12 innings.
Ruppert Jones, Seattle, May 16, 1978, 16 innings.
Rick Manning, Milwaukee, July 11, 1983, 15 innings.
Gary Pettis, California, June 4, 1985, 15 innings.
Oddibe McDowell, Texas, July 20, 1985, 15 innings.
Claudell Washington, New York, May 30, 1988, 13 innings.)

Most putouts by right fielder, game
A.L.—11—Tony Armas, Oakland, June 12, 1982.
N.L.—10—Bill Nicholson, Chicago, September 17, 1945.
(12—Rolando Roomes, Cincinnati, July 28, 1989, 17 innings.)

ASSISTS

Most assists, career
A.L.—450—Tris Speaker, Boston, Cleveland, Washington, Philadelphia, 1907 through 1928, 22 years.
N.L.—356—Jimmy Ryan, Chicago, 1885 through 1900, except 1890, 15 years.
N.L. since 1900—339—Max Carey, Pittsburgh, Brooklyn, 1910 through 1929, 20 years.

Most assists, season
N.L.—45—Hardy Richardson, Buffalo, 78 games, 1881.
N.L. since 1900—44—Chuck Klein, Philadelphia, 156 games, 1930.
A.L.—35—Sam Mertes, Chicago, 123 games, 1902.
Tris Speaker, Boston, 142 games, 1909, also 153 games, 1912.

Most seasons leading league in assists
A.L.—7—Carl Yastrzemski, Boston, 1962, 1963, 1964 (tied), 1966, 1969, 1971, 1977.
N.L.—5—Roberto Clemente, Pittsburgh, 1958, 1960, 1961, 1966, 1967.

Fewest assists for leader, season
A.L.—13—Ken Berry, California, 116 games, 1972.
Carlos May, Chicago, 145 games, 1972.
N.L.—14—Bill Bruton, Milwaukee, 141 games, 1954.
Don Mueller, New York, 153 games, 1954.
Frank J. Thomas, Pittsburgh, 153 games, 1954.
Barry Bonds, Pittsburgh, 150 games, 1990.
Kevin McReynolds, New York, 144 games, 1990.
Vladimir Guerrero, Montreal, 161 games, 2002.
Larry Walker, Colorado, 123 games, 2002.

Fewest assists, season (150 or more games)
A.L.—1—Harmon Killebrew, Minnesota, 157 games, 1964.
Albert Belle, Chicago, 154 games, 1997.
N.L.—2—Lenny Dykstra, Philadelphia, 160 games, 1993.
Brian McRae, Chicago, 155 games, 1996.
Barry Bonds, San Francisco, 155 games, 1998.

Most assists, game
N.L.—4—Harry Schafer, Boston, September 26, 1877.
Bill Crowley, Buffalo, May 24, 1880.
Bill Crowley, Buffalo, August 27, 1880.
Mike Griffin, Brooklyn, July 17, 1893.
(4—Dusty Miller, May 30, 1895, second game, 11 innings.)
N.L. since 1900—4—Fred Clarke, Pittsburgh, August 23, 1910.
A.L.—4—James W. Holmes, Chicago, August 21, 1903.
Lee Magee, New York, June 28, 1916.

Happy Felsch, Chicago, August 14, 1919.
Bob Meusel, New York, September 5, 1921, second game.
Sam Langford, Cleveland, May 1, 1928.

Most assists, outfielder to catcher, game
N.L.—3—Dummy Hoy, Washington, June 19, 1899.
Jim Jones, New York, June 30, 1902.
Jack McCarthy, Chicago, April 26, 1905.
A.L.—2—Held by many outfielders.

Most assists, inning
A.L.-N.L.—2—Held by many outfielders.

CHANCES ACCEPTED AND OFFERED

Most chances accepted, career
N.L.—7,290—Willie Mays, New York Giants, San Francisco, New York Mets, 1951 through 1973, except 1953 in military service, 22 years.
A.L.—7,244—Tris Speaker, Boston, Cleveland, Washington, Philadelphia, 1907 through 1928, 22 years.

Most chances accepted, season
N.L.—557—Taylor Douthit, St. Louis, 154 games, 1928.
A.L.—524—Chet Lemon, Chicago, 149 games, 1977.

Most seasons leading league in chances accepted
N.L.—9—Max Carey, Pittsburgh, 1912, 1913, 1916, 1917, 1918, 1921, 1922, 1923, 1924.
Richie Ashburn, Philadelphia, 1949, 1950, 1951, 1952, 1953, 1954, 1956, 1957, 1958.
A.L.—8—Tris Speaker, Boston, Cleveland, 1909, 1910, 1912, 1913, 1914, 1915, 1918, 1919.

Fewest chances accepted for leader, season
A.L.—333—Sam Crawford, Detroit, 144 games, 1907.
N.L.—342—Roy Thomas, Philadelphia, 139 games, 1904.

Fewest chances accepted, season (150 or more games)
A.L.—206—Ed Hahn, Chicago, 156 games, 1907.
N.L.—222—Al Martin, Pittsburgh, 152 games, 1996.

Most chances accepted by left fielder, game
N.L.—12—Ducky Holmes, Baltimore, September 12, 1899.
N.L. since 1900—11—Topsy Hartsel, Chicago, September 10, 1901.
Phil Clark, San Diego, San Diego, May 1, 1993.
(11—Bill Buckner, Los Angeles, July 20, 1973, 15 innings.)
A.L.—11—Paul Lehner, Philadelphia, June 25, 1950, second game.
Willie Horton, Detroit, July 18, 1969.
(12—Tom McBride, Washington, July 2, 1948, 12 innings.
Darin Erstad, Anaheim, July 24, 2000, 12 innings.)

Most chances accepted by center fielder, game
N.L.—13—Earl Clark, Boston, May 10, 1929.
A.L.—12—Happy Felsch, Chicago, June 23, 1919.
Johnny Mostil, Chicago, May 22, 1928.
Lyman Bostock, Minnesota, May 25, 1977, second game.
(12—Harry Bay, Cleveland, July 19, 1904, 12 innings.
Ruppert Jones, Seattle, May 16, 1978, 16 innings.
Rick Manning, Milwaukee, July 11, 1983, 15 innings.
Gary Pettis, California, June 4, 1985, 15 innings.
Oddibe McDowell, Texas, July 20, 1985, 15 innings.)

Most chances accepted by right fielder, game
A.L.—12—Tony Armas, Oakland, June 12, 1982.
N.L.—10—Greasy Neale, Cincinnati, July 13, 1920.
Casey Stengel, Philadelphia, July 30, 1920.
Bill Nicholson, Chicago, September 17, 1945.
Bake McBride, Philadelphia, September 8, 1978, second game.
Raul Mondesi, Los Angeles, September 25, 1995.
Jeromy Burnitz, Milwaukee, September 17, 2001.

Longest game with no chances offered
A.L.—22 innings—Bill Bruton, Detroit, June 24, 1962.
Cap Peterson, Washington, June 12, 1967.
N.L.—18 innings—Lance Richbourg, Boston, May 14, 1927.
Art Shamsky, Cincinnati, July 19, 1966.

Longest game with no chances offered, left fielder
N.L.—16.1 innings—Larry Stahl, San Diego, July 15, 1971.

A.L.—16 innings—Bob L. Johnson, Philadelphia, June 5, 1942.
Pat Mullin, Detroit, May 9, 1952.
George Hendrick, Cleveland, May 18, 1976.
Rickey Henderson, Oakland, April 8, 1982.

Longest game with no chances offered, center fielder

A.L.—22 innings—Bill Bruton, Detroit, June 24, 1962.
N.L.—17.1 innings—Ernie Orsatti, St. Louis, July 2, 1933, first game.

Longest game with no chances offered, right fielder

A.L.—22 innings—Cap Peterson, Washington, June 12, 1967.
N.L.—18 innings—Lance Richbourg, Boston, May 14, 1927.
Art Shamsky, Cincinnati, July 19, 1966.

ERRORS

Most errors, career

M.L.—384—Dummy Hoy, Washington N.L., Buffalo P.L., St. Louis A.A., Cincinnati N.L., Louisville N.L., Chicago A.L., 1888 through 1902, except 1900, 14 years.
N.L.—347—George Gore, Chicago, New York, St. Louis, 1879 through 1892, except 1890, 13 years.
N.L. since 1900—235—Max Carey, Pittsburgh, Brooklyn, 1910 through 1929, 20 years.
A.L.—271—Ty Cobb, Detroit, Philadelphia, 1905 through 1928, 24 years.

Most errors, season

P.L.—52—Ed Beecher, Buffalo, 125 games, 1890.
N.L.—49—Fred Clarke, Louisville, 132 games, 1895.
N.L. since 1900—36—Cy Seymour, Cincinnati, 135 games, 1903.
A.L.—31—Roy C. Johnson, Detroit, 146 games, 1929.

Most seasons leading league in errors

N.L.—7—Lou Brock, Chicago, St. Louis, 1964, 1965, 1966, 1967, 1968 (tied), 1972, 1973 (tied).
A.L.—5—Burt Shotton, St. Louis, Washington, 1912 (tied), 1914, 1915 (tied), 1916, 1918.
Reggie Jackson, Oakland, Baltimore, 1968, 1970, 1972, 1975, 1976 (tied).

Fewest errors for leader, season

N.L.—8—David Justice, Atlanta, 140 games, 1992.
A.L.—8—Albert Belle, Chicago, 159 games, 1998.
Kenny Lofton, Cleveland, 154 games, 1998.

Fewest errors, season (150 or more games)

N.L.—0—Danny Litwhiler, Philadelphia, 151 games, 1942.
Curt Flood, St. Louis, 159 games, 1966.
Terry Puhl, Houston, 152 games, 1979.
Brett Butler, Los Angeles, 161 games, 1991.
Brett Butler, Los Angeles, 155 games, 1993.
Luis Gonzalez, Arizona, 161 games, 2001.
A.L.—0—Rocky Colavito, Cleveland, 162 games, 1965.
Brian Downing, California, 158 games, 1982.

Most consecutive errorless games, career

M.L.—392—Darren Lewis, Oakland A.L., San Francisco N.L., August 21, 1990 through June 29, 1994 (938 chances accepted).
N.L.—369—Darren Lewis, San Francisco, July 13, 1991 through June 29, 1994 (905 chances accepted).
A.L.—336—Rich Amaral, Seattle, Baltimore, April 30, 1995 through June 14, 2000 (531 chances accepted).

Most consecutive errorless games, season

A.L.—162—Rocky Colavito, Cleveland, April 13 through October 3, 1965 (274 chances accepted).
N.L.—161—Brett Butler, Los Angeles, April 10 through October 6, 1991 (380 chances accepted).
Luis Gonzalez, Arizona, April 3 through October 7, 2001 (288 chances accepted).

Most consecutive chances accepted without an error, career

M.L.—938—Darren Lewis, Oakland A.L., San Francisco N.L., August 21, 1990 through June 29, 1994, 392 games.
N.L.—905—Darren Lewis, San Francisco, July 13, 1991 through June 29, 1994, 369 games.

A.L.—723—Darin Erstad, Anaheim, May 30, 2001 through September 22, 2002, 238 games.

Most errors, game

A.A.—5—Jim Clinton, Baltimore, May 3, 1884.
U.A.—5—Fred Tenney, Washington, May 29, 1884.
A.L.—5—Kip Selbach, Baltimore, August 19, 1902.
N.L.—5—Jack Manning, Boston, May 1, 1876.
Pop Snyder, Louisville, July 29, 1876.
Jim O'Rourke, Boston, June 21, 1877.
Charlie Bennett, Milwaukee, June 15, 1878.
Mike Dorgan, New York, May 24, 1884.
Mike Tiernan, New York, May 16, 1887.
Marty Sullivan, Chicago, May 18, 1887.
N.L. since 1900—4—Fred Nicholson, Boston, June 16, 1922.

Longest game with no errors

N.L.—26 innings—Walt Cruise, Boston, May 1, 1920.
Les Mann, Boston, May 1, 1920.
Bernie Neis, Brooklyn, May 1, 1920.
Ray Powell, Boston, May 1, 1920.
Zack Wheat, Brooklyn, May 1, 1920.
A.L.—25 innings—Harold Baines, Chicago, May 8, finished May 9, 1984.
Rudy Law, Chicago, May 8, finished May 9, 1984.
Ben Oglivie, Milwaukee, May 8, finished May 9, 1984 (fielded 24.1 innings).

Most errors, inning

N.L.—3—George Gore, Chicago, August 8, 1883, first inning.
Larry Herndon, San Francisco, September 6, 1980, fourth inning.
A.A.—3—Jim Donahue, Kansas City, July 4, 1889, p.m. game, first inning.
A.L.—3—Kip Selbach, Washington, June 23, 1904, eighth inning.
Harry Bay, Cleveland, June 29, 1905, second game, ninth inning.
Harry Heilmann, Detroit, May 22, 1914, first inning.
Herschel Bennett, St. Louis, April 14, 1925, eighth inning.
Scott Lusader, Detroit, September 9, 1989, first inning.

DOUBLE PLAYS

Most double plays, career

A.L.—135—Tris Speaker, Boston, Cleveland, Washington, Philadelphia, 1907 through 1928, 22 years.
N.L.—86—Max Carey, Pittsburgh, Brooklyn, 1910 through 1929, 20 years.

Most double plays, season

A.L.—15—Happy Felsch, Chicago, 125 games, 1919.
N.L.—12—Cy Seymour, Cincinnati, 149 games, 1905.
Ginger Beaumont, Boston, 149 games, 1907.
Jimmy Sheckard, Chicago, 156 games, 1911.
Mel Ott, New York, 149 games, 1929.

Most seasons leading league in double plays

A.L.—5—Tris Speaker, Boston, Cleveland, 1909, 1912, 1914, 1915, 1916.
N.L.—4—Willie Mays, New York Giants, San Francisco, 1954, 1955, 1956, 1965.

Fewest double plays for leader, season

N.L.—3—Brett Butler, Los Angeles, 161 games, 1991.
Willie McGee, San Francisco, 128 games, 1991.
A.L.—4—Held by 19 players. Last outfielders—Tony Armas, Oakland, 112 games, 1977; Roy White, New York, 135 games, 1977.

Fewest double plays, season (150 or more games)

N.L.-A.L.—0—Held by many outfielders.
N.L.—Last outfielder—Bobby Abreu, Philadelphia, 158 games, 2003; Lance Berkman, Houston, 153 games, 2003.
A.L.—Last outfielders—Jose Cruz Jr., Tampa Bay, 152 games, 2004.

Most double plays started, game

A.A.—3—Candy Nelson, New York, June 9, 1887.
N.L.—3—Jack McCarthy, Chicago, April 26, 1905.

A.L.—3—Ira Flagstead, Boston, April 19, 1926, p.m. game.

Most unassisted double plays, career
A.L.—6—Tris Speaker, Boston, Cleveland, 1909 (1), 1910 (1), 1914 (2), 1918 (2).
N.L.—2—Held by many outfielders.

Most unassisted double plays, season
A.L.—2—Socks Seybold, Philadelphia, August 15, September 10, first game, 1907.
Tris Speaker, Boston, April 21, August 8, 1914.
Tris Speaker, Cleveland, April 18, April 29, 1918.
Jose Cardenal, Cleveland, June 8, July 16, 1968.
N.L.—2—Adam Comorosky, Pittsburgh, May 31, June 13, 1931.

Most unassisted double plays, game
N.L.-A.L.—1—Held by many outfielders.
N.L.—Last outfielder—Joe McEwing, New York, April 4, 2002.
A.L.—Last outfielder—Mike Cameron, Seattle, May 23, 2003, seventh inning.

Most triple plays started, season
A.L.—2—Charlie Jamieson, Cleveland, May 23, June 9, 1928.
N.L.—1—Held by many outfielders.

CATCHERS
GAMES AND INNINGS

Most games, career
A.L.—2,226—Carlton Fisk, Boston, Chicago, 1969 through 1993, except 1970, 24 years.
N.L.—2,056—Gary Carter, Montreal, New York, San Francisco, Los Angeles, 1974 through 1992, 19 years.

Most consecutive games, career
A.L.—312—Frankie Hayes, St. Louis, Philadelphia, Cleveland, October 2, second game, 1943 through April 21, 1946.
N.L.—233—Ray Mueller, Cincinnati, July 31, 1943, through May 5, 1946, except 1945 in military service.

Most games, season
N.L.—160—Randy Hundley, Chicago, 1968.
A.L.—155—Jim Sundberg, Texas, 1975.
Frankie Hayes, Philadelphia, 1944.

Most games, lefthanded catcher, season
N.L.—105—Jack Clements, Philadelphia, 1891.
A.L.—23—Jiggs Donahue, St. Louis, 1902.

Most games catching all club's games, season
N.L.—155—Ray Mueller, Cincinnati, 1944 (135 complete games).
A.L.—155—Frankie Hayes, Philadelphia, 1944 (135 complete games).

Most seasons leading league in games
A.L.—8—Yogi Berra, New York, 1950, 1951, 1952, 1953, 1954, 1955, 1956, 1957.
N.L.—6—Gary Carter, Montreal, 1977, 1978, 1979, 1980, 1981, 1982.

Most seasons, 100 or more games
M.L.—15—Bob Boone, Philadelphia N.L., California A.L., Kansas City A.L., 1973, 1974, 1976 through 1980, 1982 through 1989.
A.L.—13—Bill Dickey, New York, 1929 through 1941.
N.L.—13—Johnny Bench, Cincinnati, 1968 through 1980.

Most consecutive seasons, 100 or more games
A.L.—13—Bill Dickey, New York, 1929 through 1941.
N.L.—13—Johnny Bench, Cincinnati, 1968 through 1980.

Fewest games for leader, season
N.L.—96—Ernie Lombardi, New York, 1945.
A.L.—98—Jake Early, Washington, 1942.

Most innings caught, game
A.L.—25—Carlton Fisk, Chicago, May 8, finished May 9, 1984.
N.L.—24—Hal King, Houston, April 15, 1968.

Jerry Grote, New York, April 15, 1968 (caught 23.1 innings).

AVERAGE

Highest fielding average, career (1,000 or more games)
A.L.—.9932—Bill Freehan, Detroit, 1961, 1963 through 1976, 15 years, 1,581 games.
N.L.—.992—Johnny Edwards, Cincinnati, St. Louis, Houston, 1961 through 1974, 14 years, 1,392 games.

Highest fielding average, season (150 or more games)
N.L.—.996—Randy Hundley, Chicago, 152 games, 1967.
A.L.—.995—Jim Sundberg, Texas, 150 games, 1979.

Highest fielding average, season (100 or more games)
A.L.—1.000—Buddy Rosar, Philadelphia, 117 games, 1946.
N.L.—1.000—Charles Johnson, Florida, 123 games, 1997.

Most seasons leading league in fielding average (100 or more games)
A.L.—8—Ray Schalk, Chicago, 1913, 1914, 1915, 1916, 1917, 1920, 1921, 1922.
N.L.—7—Gabby Hartnett, Chicago, 1925, 1928, 1930, 1934, 1935, 1936, 1937.

Most consecutive seasons leading league in fielding average (100 or more games)
A.L.—6—Bill Freehan, Detroit, 1965, 1966, 1967 (tied), 1968, 1969 (tied), 1970.
N.L.—4—Johnny Kling, Chicago, 1902 through 1905.
Gabby Hartnett, Chicago, 1934 through 1937.

Lowest fielding average for leader, season (100 or more games, since 1900)
A.L.—.954—Mike Powers, Philadelphia, 111 games, 1901.
N.L.—.958—Gabby Hartnett, Chicago, 110 games, 1925.

Lowest fielding average, season (100 or more games)
A.L.—.934—Sam Agnew, St. Louis, 102 games, 1915.
N.L. since 1900—.947—Red Dooin, Philadelphia, 140 games, 1909.

PUTOUTS

Most putouts, career
N.L.—11,785—Gary Carter, Montreal, New York, San Francisco, Los Angeles, 1974 through 1992, 19 years.
A.L.—11,369—Carlton Fisk, Boston, Chicago, 1969 through 1993, except 1970, 24 years.

Most putouts, season
N.L.—1,135—Johnny Edwards, Houston, 151 games, 1969.
A.L.—1,051—Dan Wilson, Seattle, 144 games, 1997.

Most seasons leading league in putouts
A.L.—9—Ray Schalk, Chicago, 1913, 1914, 1915, 1916, 1917, 1918, 1919, 1920, 1922.
N.L.—8—Gary Carter, Montreal, 1977, 1978, 1979, 1980, 1981, 1982; New York, 1985, 1988.

Fewest putouts for leader, season
N.L.—409—Gabby Hartnett, Chicago, 110 games, 1925.
A.L.—446—Birdie Tebbetts, Detroit, 97 games, 1942.

Fewest putouts, season (150 or more games)
N.L.—471—Ray Mueller, Cincinnati, 155 games, 1944.
A.L.—575—Mike Tresh, Chicago, 150 games, 1945.

Most putouts, game
N.L.—20—Jerry Grote, New York, April 22, 1970 (19 strikeouts).
Sandy Martinez, Chicago, May 6, 1998 (20 strikeouts).
(24—Damian Miller, Chicago, May 15, 2003 (24 strikeouts), 17 innings.)
A.L.—20—Rich Gedman, Boston, April 29, 1986 (20 strikeouts).
Dan Wilson, Seattle, August 8, 1997 (19 strikeouts).
(21—Ellie Rodriguez, California, June 14, 1974 (20 strikeouts), 15 innings.
Dan Wilson, Seattle, March 31, 1996 (21 strikeouts), 12 innings.

Longest game with no putouts
A.L.—14 innings
Wally Schang, Boston, September 13, 1920.

Gene Desautels, Cleveland, August 11, 1942, first game.
N.L.—13 innings—Jimmie Wilson, Philadelphia, August 31, 1927, first game.
Hal Finney, Pittsburgh, September 22, 1931.

Most fouls caught, game
N.L.—6—Wes Westrum, New York, August 24, 1949.
A.L.—6—Sherm Lollar, Chicago, April 10, 1962.

Most fouls caught, inning
N.L.—3—Mickey Owen, Brooklyn, August 4, 1941, third inning.
Wes Westrum, New York, August 24, 1949, ninth inning.
Wes Westrum, New York, September 23, 1956, fifth inning.
A.L.—3—Matt Batts, Detroit, August 2, 1953, second game, fourth game.

ASSISTS

Most assists, career
M.L.—1,835—Deacon McGuire, Toledo, Cleveland, Rochester, Washington A.A., Detroit, Philadelphia, Washington, Brooklyn N.L., Detroit, New York, Boston, Cleveland A.L., 1884 through 1912, except 1889, 1908, 1909, 1911, 25 years.
A.L.—1,810—Ray Schalk, Chicago, 1912 through 1928, 17 years.
N.L.—1,593—Red Dooin, Philadelphia, Cincinnati, New York, 1902 through 1916, 15 years.

Most assists, season
N.L.—214—Pat Moran, Boston, 107 games, 1903.
A.L.—212—Oscar Stanage, Detroit, 141 games, 1911.

Most seasons leading league in assists
N.L.—6—Gabby Hartnett, Chicago, 1925, 1927, 1928 (tied), 1930, 1934, 1935.
Del Crandall, Milwaukee, 1953, 1954, 1957, 1958, 1959, 1960.
A.L.—6—Jim Sundberg, Texas, 1975, 1976, 1977, 1978, 1980, 1981.

Fewest assists for leader, season
N.L.—52—Phil Masi, Boston, 95 games, 1945.
A.L.—58—Terry Kennedy, Baltimore, 142 games, 1987.

Fewest assists, season (150 or more games)
N.L.—59—Randy Hundley, Chicago, 152 games, 1967.
A.L.—68—Brad Ausmus, Detroit, 150 games, 2000.

Most assists, game
N.L.—9—Mike Hines, Boston, May 1, 1883.
A.L.—8—Wally Schang, Boston, May 12, 1920.
N.L. since 1900—7—Ed McFarland, Philadelphia, May 7, 1901.
Fred Jacklitsch, Brooklyn, April 21, 1903.
Bill Bergen, Brooklyn, August 23, 1909, second game.
Jimmy Archer, Pittsburgh, May 24, 1918.
Bert Adams, Philadelphia, August 21, 1919.

Most assists, inning
A.A.—3—Jocko Milligan, Philadelphia, July 26, 1887, third inning.
A.L.—3—Les Nunamaker, New York, August 3, 1914, second inning.
Ray Schalk, Chicago, September 30, 1921, eighth inning.
Bill Dickey, New York, May 13, 1929, sixth inning.
Jim Sundberg, Texas, September 3, 1976, fifth inning.
Sal Butera, Minnesota, September 7, 1981, third inning.
Bob Boone, California, August 29, 1986, fifth inning.
N.L.—3—Bruce Edwards, Brooklyn, August 15, 1946, fourth inning.
Jim Campbell, Houston, June 16, 1963, second game, third inning.
Vic Correll, Atlanta, September 17, 1976, second game, fifth inning.
Bruce Benedict, Atlanta, August 6, 1982, fifth inning.
Alan Ashby, Houston, July 28, 1987, eighth inning.

CHANCES ACCEPTED AND OFFERED

Most chances accepted, career
N.L.—12,988—Gary Carter, Montreal, New York, San Francisco, Los Angeles, 1974 through 1992, 19 years.

A.L.—12,417—Carlton Fisk, Boston, Chicago, 1969 through 1993, except 1970, 24 years.

Most chances accepted, season
N.L.—1,214—Johnny Edwards, Houston, 151 games, 1969.
A.L.—1,044—Bill Freehan, Detroit, 138 games, 1968.

Most seasons leading league in chances accepted
A.L.—8—Ray Schalk, Chicago, 1913, 1914, 1915, 1916, 1917, 1919, 1920, 1922.
Yogi Berra, New York, 1950, 1951, 1952, 1954, 1955, 1956, 1957, 1959.
N.L.—8—Gary Carter, Montreal, 1977, 1978, 1979, 1980, 1981, 1982, New York, 1985, 1988.

Fewest chances accepted by leader, season
N.L.—474—Ernie Lombardi, New York, 96 games, 1945.
A.L.—515—Birdie Tebbetts, Detroit, 97 games, 1942.

Fewest chances accepted, season (150 or more games)
N.L.—536—Ray Mueller, Cincinnati, 155 games, 1944.
A.L.—677—Mike Tresh, Chicago, 150 games, 1945.

Most chances accepted, game
U.A.—23—George Bignell, Milwaukee, October 3, 1884 (18 strikeouts).
N.L.—22—Sandy Nava, Providence, June 7, 1884 (19 strikeouts).
N.L. since 1900—20—Jerry Grote, New York, April 22, 1970 (19 strikeouts).
Sandy Martinez, Chicago, May 6, 1998 (20 strikeouts).
(25—Damian Miller, Chicago, May 15, 2003 (24 strikeouts), 17 innings.)
A.L.—20—Ellie Rodriguez, California, August 12, 1974 (19 strikeouts).
Rich Gedman, Boston, April 29, 1986 (20 strikeouts).
Bill Haselman, Boston, September 18, 1996 (20 strikeouts).
Dan Wilson, Seattle, August 8, 1997 (19 strikeouts).
(25—Mike Powers, Philadelphia, September 1, 1906 (18 strikeouts), 24 innings.)

Longest game with no chances offered
A.L.—14 innings—Gene Desautels, Cleveland, August 11, 1942, first game.
N.L.—13 innings—Jimmie Wilson, Philadelphia, August 31, 1927, first game.

ERRORS

Most errors, career (since 1900)
N.L.—234—Ivy Wingo, St. Louis, Cincinnati, 1911 through 1929, except 1927, 1928, 17 years.
A.L.—218—Wally Schang, Philadelphia, Boston, New York, St. Louis, Detroit, 1913 through 1931, 19 years.

Most errors, season
N.L.—94—Nat Hicks, New York, 45 games, 1876.
A.A.—85—Ed Whiting, Baltimore, 72 games, 1882.
A.L.—41—Oscar Stanage, Detroit, 141 games, 1911.
N.L. since 1900—40—Red Dooin, Philadelphia, 140 games, 1909.

Most seasons leading league in errors
N.L.—7—Ivy Wingo, St. Louis, Cincinnati, 1912 (tied), 1913, 1916, 1917, 1918, 1920, 1921.
A.L.—6—Birdie Tebbetts, Detroit, Boston, 1939, 1940 (tied), 1942 (tied), 1947, 1948, 1949.

Fewest errors for leader, season
A.L.—7—Rick Ferrell, St. Louis, 137 games, 1933.
N.L.—9—Hank Foiles, Pittsburgh, 109 games, 1957.

Fewest errors, season (150 or more games)
N.L.—4—Randy Hundley, Chicago, 152 games, 1967.
A.L.—4—Jim Sundberg, Texas, 150 games, 1979.

Fewest errors, season (100 or more games)
A.L.—0—Buddy Rosar, Philadelphia, 117 games, 1946.
N.L.—0—Charles Johnson, Florida, 123 games, 1997.

Most consecutive errorless games, career
N.L.—252—Mike Matheny, St. Louis, August 2, 2002 through August 1, 2004 (1,631 chances accepted).
A.L.—159—Rick Cerone, New York, Boston, July 5, 1987 through May 8, 1989 (896 chances accepted).

Most consecutive errorless games, season
N.L.—138—Mike Matheny, St. Louis, March 31 through
September 28, 2003 (entire season; 823 chances accepted).
A.L.—117—Buddy Rosar, Philadelphia, April 16 through
September 29, 1946, first game (605 chances accepted).

Most consecutive chances accepted without an error, career
N.L.—1,631—Mike Matheny, St. Louis, August 2, 2002 through
August 1, 2004.
A.L.—950—Yogi Berra, New York, 148 games, July 28, 1957,
second game, through May 10, 1959, second game.

Most consecutive chances accepted without an error, season
N.L.—973—Charles Johnson, Florida, 123 games, April 1
through September 28, 1997.
A.L.—668—Joe Girardi, New York, 98 games, May 7 through
September 29, 1996.

Most errors, game (all fielding errors)
N.L.—7—Jack Rowe, Buffalo, May 16, 1883.
Dickie Lowe, Detroit, June 26, 1884.
A.A.—7—Billy Taylor, Baltimore, May 29, 1886, a.m. game.
N.L. since 1900—4—Gabby Street, Boston, June 7, 1905.
A.L.—4—John Peters, Cleveland, May 16, 1918.
Lena Styles, Philadelphia, July 29, 1921.
Bill Moore, Boston, September 26, 1927, second game.

Longest game with no errors
A.L.—24 innings—Mike R. Powers, Philadelphia, September 1,
1906.
Buddy Rosar, Philadelphia, July 21, 1945.
Bob Swift, Detroit, July 21, 1945.
N.L.—24 innings—Hal King, Houston, April 15, 1968.
Jerry Grote, New York, April 15, 1968 (caught 23.1 innings).

Most errors, inning
N.L.—4—Doggie Miller, St. Louis, May 24, 1895, second
inning.
N.L. since 1900—3—Jeff Reed, Montreal, July 28, 1987, seventh
inning.
A.L.—3—Jeff Sweeney, New York, July 10, 1912, first inning.
John Peters, Cleveland, May 16, 1918, first inning.

PASSED BALLS

Most passed balls, career
M.L.—647—Pop Snyder, Louisville N.L., Boston N.L , Cincinnati
A.A., Cleveland A.A., Cleveland N.L., Cleveland P.L.,
Washington A.A., 1876 through 1879, 1881 through 1891, 15
years.
N.L.—602—Silver Flint, Indianapolis, Chicago, 1878 through
1889, 12 years.
N.L. since 1900—167—Ted Simmons, St. Louis, Atlanta, 1968
through 1980, 1986, 1987, 1988, 16 years.
A.L.—158—Lance Parrish, Detroit, California, Seattle,
Cleveland, Toronto, 1977 through 1986, 1989 through 1993,
1995, 16 years.

Most passed balls, season
N.L.—99—Pop Snyder, Boston, 58 games, 1881.
Michael P. Hines, Boston, 56 games, 1883.
N.L. since 1900—29—Frank Bowerman, New York, 73 games,
1900.
A.L.—35—Geno Petralli, Texas, 63 games, 1987.

Most seasons leading league in passed balls
N.L.—9—Ernie Lombardi, Cincinnati, Boston, New York, 1932,
1935, 1936 (tied), 1937, 1938, 1939, 1940 (tied), 1941, 1945.
A.L.—5—Rick Ferrell, St. Louis, Washington, 1931 (tied), 1939,
1940, 1944, 1945.

Fewest passed balls for leader, season
A.L.—6—Mickey Cochrane, Philadelphia, 117 games, 1931.
Charlie F. Berry, Boston, 102 games, 1931.
Rick Ferrell, St. Louis, 108 games, 1931.
N.L.—7—Held by five catchers.

Fewest passed balls, season (150 or more games)
N.L.—1—Gary Carter, Montreal, 152 games, 1978.
A.L.—3—Brad Ausmus, Detroit, 150 games, 2000.

Fewest passed balls, season (100 or more games)
N.L.—0—Al Todd, Pittsburgh, 128 games, 1937.
Al Lopez, Pittsburgh, 114 games, 1941.
Johnny Bench, Cincinnati, 121 games, 1975.
Benito Santiago, San Diego, 103 games, 1992.
A.L.—0—Bill Dickey, New York, 125 games, 1931.

Most passed balls, game
A.A.—12—Alex Gardner, Washington, May 10, 1884.
N.L.—10—Alamazoo Jennings, Milwaukee, August 15, 1878.
Pat Dealey, Boston, May 1886.
N.L. since 1900—6—Harry Vickers, Cincinnati, October 4,
1902.
Jerry Goff, Houston, May 12, 1996.
A.L.—6—Geno Petralli, Texas, August 30, 1987.

Most passed balls, two consecutive games
N.L.—13—Pete Hotaling, Worcester, September 20, 21, 1881.

Longest game with no passed balls
A.L.—25 innings—Carlton Fisk, Chicago, May 8, finished May
9, 1984.
N.L.—24 innings—Hal King, Houston, April 15, 1968.
Jerry Grote, New York, April 15, 1968 (caught 23.1 innings).

Most passed balls, inning
A.A.—5—Dan Sullivan, St. Louis, August 9, 1885, third inning.
N.L.—4—Ray Katt, New York, September 10, 1954, eighth inning.
A.L.—4—Geno Petralli, Texas, August 22, 1987, seventh inning.

DOUBLE PLAYS

Most double plays, career
A.L.—217—Ray Schalk, Chicago, 1912 through 1928, 17 years.
N.L.—163—Gabby Hartnett, Chicago, New York, 1922 through
1941, 20 years.

Most double plays, season
A.L.—36—Steve O'Neill, Cleveland, 128 games, 1916.
N.L.—23—Tom Haller, Los Angeles, 139 games, 1968.

Most seasons leading league in double plays
N.L.—6—Gabby Hartnett, Chicago, 1926 (tied), 1927, 1930
(tied), 1931, 1934, 1935.
A.L.—6—Yogi Berra, New York, 1949, 1950, 1951, 1952, 1954,
1956.

Fewest double plays for leader, season
N.L.—8—Phil Masi, Boston/Pittsburgh, 81 games, 1949.
Clyde McCullough, Pittsburgh, 90 games, 1949.
A.L.—8—Mike DiFelice, Tampa Bay, 84 games, 1998.
A.J. Hinch, Oakland, 110 games, 1998.

Most double plays, game
N.L.—3—Jack O'Neill, Chicago, April 26, 1905.
Shanty Hogan, New York, August 19, 1931.
Ebba St. Claire, Boston, August 9, 1951.
Eddie Taubensee, Cincinnati, April 23, 1999.
Damian Miller, Arizona, May 25, 1999.
Brian Schneider, Montreal, June 11, 2004 (fielded 8.2
innings).
(3—Bob O'Farrell, Chicago, July 9, 1919, second game, 10.1
innings.
Ron Hodges, New York, April 23, 1978, 11.2 innings.)
A.L.—4—Chris Hoiles, Baltimore, April 9, 1998.

Most double plays started, game
N.L.—3—J. Shanty Hogan, New York, August 19, 1931.
Damian Miller, Arizona, May 25, 1999.
A.L.—3—Rick Dempsey, Baltimore, June 1, 1977.
Bengie Molina, Anaheim, July 29, 2003.
(3—Lance Parrish, California, June 29, 1991, 13 innings.)

Most unassisted double plays, career
A.L.—2—Held by many catchers.

Most unassisted double plays, season
A.L.—2—Frank Crossin, St. Louis, 1914.
Jorge Posada, New York, 2000.
N.L.—1—Held by many catchers.

Most unassisted double plays, game
A.L.-N.L.—1—Held by many players.

BASERUNNERS VS. CATCHERS

Most stolen bases off catcher, game
A.A.—19—Grant Briggs, Syracuse, April 22, 1890.
N.L.—17—Doggie Miller, Pittsburgh, May 23, 1890.
N.L. since 1900—11—Bill Fischer, St. Louis, August 13, 1916, second game, five innings.
A.L.—13—Branch Rickey, New York, June 28, 1907.

Most stolen bases off catcher, inning
A.L.—8—Steve O'Neill, Cleveland, July 19, 1915, first inning.
N.L.—8—Mike Gonzalez, New York, July 7, 1919, first game, ninth inning.

Most runners caught stealing, game
N.L.—8—Duke Farrell, Washington, May 11, 1897.
N.L. since 1900—6—Bill Bergen, Brooklyn, August 23, 1909, second game.
A.L.—6—Wally Schang, Philadelphia, May 12, 1915.

Most runners caught stealing, inning
A.A.—3—Jocko Milligan, Philadelphia, July 26, 1887, third inning.
A.L.—3—Les Nunamaker, New York, August 3, 1914, second inning.
N.L.—2—Held by many catchers.

NO-HITTERS CAUGHT

Most no-hit victories caught, career (entire game; nine or more innings)
Both leagues—3—Jeff Torborg, Los Angeles N.L., 1965, 1970; California A.L., 1973.
N.L.—3—Roy Campanella, Brooklyn, 1952, 1956 (2).
Del Crandall, Milwaukee, 1954, 1960 (2).
Alan Ashby, Houston, 1979, 1981, 1986.
Charles Johnson, Florida, 1996, 1997, 2001.
A.L.—3—Bill Carrigan, Boston, 1911, 1916 (2).
Ray Schalk, Chicago, 1914, 1917, 1922 (Note: In addition, Schalk caught a no-hitter that was broken up in the 10th inning in 1914).
Val Picinich, Philadelphia, 1916, Washington, 1920, Boston, 1923.
Luke Sewell, Cleveland, 1931, Chicago, 1935, 1937.
Jim Hegan, Cleveland, 1947, 1948, 1951.

PITCHERS
GAMES AND INNINGS

Most games, career
M.L.—1,252—Jesse Orosco, New York N.L., Los Angeles, N.L., Cleveland A.L., Milwaukee A.L., Baltimore A.L., St. Louis N.L., San Diego N.L., New York A.L., Minnesota N.L., 24 years, 1979 through 2003, except 1980 (686 in A.L., 566 in N.L.).
N.L.—1,088—John Franco, Cincinnati, New York, 20 years, 1984 through 2004, except 2002..
A.L.—869—Dennis Eckersley, Cleveland, Boston, Oakland, 20 years, 1975 through 1984, 1987 through 1995, 1998.

Most games, season
N.L.—106—Mike Marshall, Los Angeles, 208 innings, 1974.
A.L.—90—Mike Marshall, Minnesota, 143 innings, 1979.

Most seasons leading league in games
M.L.—7—Joe McGinnity, Brooklyn N.L., Baltimore A.L., New York N.L., 1900, 1901, 1903, 1904, 1905, 1906, 1907.
N.L.—6—Joe McGinnity, Brooklyn, New York, 1900, 1903, 1904, 1905, 1906, 1907.
A.L.—6—Firpo Marberry, Washington, 1924, 1925, 1926, 1928, 1929, 1932.

Fewest games for leader, season
A.L.—40—Joe Haynes, Chicago, 1942 (103 innings).
N.L.—41—Ray Kremer, Pittsburgh, 1924 (259 innings).
Johnny Morrison, Pittsburgh, 1924 (238 innings).

Most innings, game
N.L.—26 innings—Leon Cadore, Brooklyn, May 1, 1920.
Joe Oeschger, Boston, May 1, 1920.
A.L.—24 innings—Jack Coombs, Philadelphia, September 1, 1906.
Joe Harris, Boston, September 1, 1906.

AVERAGE

Highest fielding average with most chances accepted, season
N.L.—1.000—Randy Jones, San Diego, 1976, 40 games; 31 putouts, 81 assists, 112 chances accepted.
A.L.—1.000—Walter Johnson, Washington, 1913, 48 games; 21 putouts, 82 assists, 103 chances accepted.

Most seasons leading league in fielding average with most chances accepted
N.L.—4—Claude Passeau, Philadelphia, Chicago, 1939, 1942, 1943, 1945.
Larry Jackson, St. Louis, Chicago, Philadelphia, 1957, 1964, 1965, 1968.
A.L.—3—Walter Johnson, Washington, 1913, 1917, 1922 (tied).

PUTOUTS

Most putouts, career (since 1900)
N.L.—477—Greg Maddux, Chicago, Atlanta, 1986 through 2004, 19 years.
A.L.—387—Jack Morris, Detroit, Minnesota, Toronto, Cleveland, 1977 through 1994, 18 years.

Most putouts, season
N.L.—50—George Bradley, St. Louis, 64 games, 1876.
A.L.—49—Nick Altrock, Chicago, 38 games, 1904.
Mike Boddicker, Baltimore, 34 games, 1984.
N.L. since 1900—41—Kevin Brown, Los Angeles, 35 games, 1999.

Most seasons leading league in putouts
N.L.—8—Greg Maddux, Chicago, 1989, 1990, 1991, 1992, 2004 (tied); Atlanta, 1993, 1996, 1998 (tied).
A.L.—5—Bob Lemon, Cleveland, 1948, 1949, 1952, 1953, 1954.

Fewest putouts for leader, season
N.L.—14—Howie Camnitz, Pittsburgh, 38 games, 1910.
Art Nehf, New York, 37 games, 1922.
Tony Kaufmann, Chicago, 37 games, 1922.
A.L.—16—Roxie Lawson, Detroit, 27 games, 1937.

Most putouts, game
N.L.—7—Greg Maddux, Chicago, April 29, 1990.
A.L.—6—Bert Blyleven, Cleveland, June 24, 1984.
Eric King, Detroit, July 8, 1986.
(7—Dick Fowler, Philadelphia, June 9, 1949, 12 innings.)

ASSISTS

Most assists, career (since 1900)
N.L.—1,489—Christy Mathewson, New York, Cincinnati, 1900 through 1916, 17 years.
A.L.—1,337—Walter Johnson, Washington, 1907 through 1927, 21 years.

Most assists, season
A.L.—227—Ed Walsh, Chicago, 56 games, 1907.
N.L.—168—John Clarkson, Boston, 72 games, 1889.
N.L. since 1900—141—Christy Mathewson, New York, 56 games, 1908.

Most seasons leading league in assists
N.L.—9—Greg Maddux, Chicago, Atlanta, 1990, 1992, 1993, 1995, 1996, 1998, 2000, 2001, 2003.
A.L.—6—Bob Lemon, Cleveland, 1948, 1949, 1951, 1952, 1953, 1956.

Fewest assists for leader, season
A.L.—42—Mark Langston, California, 33 games, 1990.
N.L.—47—Ron Darling, New York, 36 games, 1985.
Ron Darling, New York, 34 games, 1986.
Bob Knepper, Houston, 40 games, 1986.
Fernando Valenzuela, Los Angeles, 34 games, 1986.

Most assists, game
N.L.—11—Rip Sewell, Pittsburgh, June 6, 1941, second game.
(12—Leon Cadore, Brooklyn, May 1, 1920, 26 innings.)
A.L.—11—Al Orth, New York, August 12, 1906.
Ed Walsh, Chicago, April 19, 1907.
Ed Walsh, Chicago, August 12, 1907.
George McConnell, New York, September 2, 1912, second game.
Mellie Wolfgang, Chicago, August 29, 1914.
(12—Nick Altrock, Chicago, June 7, 1908, 10 innings.
Ed Walsh, Chicago, July 16, 1907, 13 innings.)

CHANCES ACCEPTED AND OFFERED

Most chances accepted, career (since 1900)
N.L.—1,761—Christy Mathewson, New York, Cincinnati, 1900 through 1916, 17 years.
A.L.—1,606—Walter Johnson, Washington, 1907 through 1927, 21 years.

Most chances accepted, season
A.L.—262—Ed Walsh, Chicago, 56 games, 1907.
N.L.—206—John Clarkson, Boston, 72 games, 1889.
N.L. since 1900—168—Christy Mathewson, New York, 56 games, 1908.

Most seasons leading league in chances accepted
N.L.—13—Greg Maddux, Chicago, Atlanta, 1989 through 2003, except 1997 and 2002 (tied in 1999).
A.L.—8—Bob Lemon, Cleveland, 1948 through 1956, except 1955.

Fewest chances accepted for leader, season
A.L.—61—Charles Nagy, Cleveland, 34 games, 1997.
N.L.—67—Paul Minner, Chicago, 31 games, 1953.
Robin Roberts, Philadelphia, 44 games, 1953.
Jim Hearn, New York, 39 games, 1955.

Most chances accepted, game
A.L.—13—Nick Altrock, Chicago, August 6, 1904 (3 putouts, 10 assists).
Ed Walsh, Chicago, April 19, 1907 (2 putouts, 11 assists).
(15—Ed Walsh, Chicago, July 16, 1907, 13 innings.)
N.L.—12—Rip Sewell, Pittsburgh, June 6, 1941, second game (1 putout, 11 assists).
(13—Leon Cadore, Brooklyn, May 1, 1920, 26 innings.)

Longest game with no chances offered
N.L.—20 innings—Milt Watson, Philadelphia, July 17, 1918.
A.L.—15 innings— Red Ruffing, New York, July 23, 1932, first game.

ERRORS

Most errors, career (since 1900)
N.L.—64—Hippo Vaughn, Chicago, 1913 through 1921, nine years.
A.L.—55—Ed Walsh, Chicago, 1904 through 1916, 13 years.

Most errors, season
A.A.—63—Tim Keefe, New York, 68 games, 1883.
N.L.—28—Jim Whitney, Boston, 63 games, 1881.
N.L. since 1900—17—Doc Newton, Cincinnati, Brooklyn, 33 games, 1901.
A.L.—15—Jack Chesbro, New York, 55 games, 1904.
Rube Waddell, Philadelphia, 46 games, 1905.
Ed Walsh, Chicago, 62 games, 1912.

Most seasons leading league in errors
N.L.—5—Hippo Vaughn, Chicago, 1914, 1915 (tied), 1917 (tied), 1919, 1920.
Warren Spahn, Boston, Milwaukee, 1949 (tied), 1950, 1952 (tied), 1954 (tied), 1964 (tied).
A.L.—4—Allen Sothoron, St. Louis, 1917, 1918 (tied), 1919, 1920.
Nolan Ryan, California, 1975, 1976, 1977 (tied), 1978.

Fewest errors for leader, season
N.L.-A.L.—4—Held by many pitchers.

Most consecutive errorless games, career
N.L.—546—Lee Smith, Chicago, St. Louis, July 5, 1982 through September 22, 1992 (93 chances accepted).
A.L.—470—Dennis Eckersley, Oakland, May 1, 1987 through May 4, 1995 (76 chances accepted).

Most consecutive errorless games, season
A.L.—88—Wilbur Wood, Chicago, April 10 through September 29, 1968 (32 chances accepted).
N.L.—89—Steve Kline, St. Louis, April 4 through October 7, 2001 (entire season; 13 chances accepted).
Paul Quantrill, Los Angeles, April 1 through September 28, 2003 (entire season; 21 chances accepted).

Most consecutive chances accepted without an error, career
N.L.—273—Claude Passeau, Chicago, September 21, first game, 1941 through May 20, 1946, 145 games.
A.L.—230—Rick Langford, Oakland, April 13, 1977 to October 2, 1980, 142 games.

Most errors, game
N.L.—5—Ed Doheny, New York, August 15, 1899.
N.L. since 1900—4—Doc Newton, Cincinnati, September 13, 1900, first game.
Lave Winham, Pittsburgh, September 21, 1903, first game.
Bill Cramer, Cincinnati, June 25, 1912.
A.L.—4—Buster Ross, Boston, May 17, 1925.

Longest game with no errors
N.L.—26 innings—Leon Cadore, Brooklyn, May 1, 1920.
Joe Oeschger, Boston, May 1, 1920.
A.L.—24 innings—Jack Coombs, Philadelphia, September 1, 1906.
Joe Harris, Boston, September 1, 1906.

Most errors, inning
N.L.—3—Cy Seymour, New York, May 21, 1898, sixth inning.
Jaime Navarro, Chicago, August 18, 1996, third inning.
A.L.—3—Tommy John, New York, July 27, 1988, fourth inning.
Mike Sirotka, Chicago, April 9, 1999, fifth inning.

DOUBLE PLAYS

Most double plays, career
M.L.—83—Phil Niekro, Milwaukee N.L., Atlanta N.L., New York A.L., Cleveland A.L., Toronto A.L., 1964 through 1987, 24 years.
N.L.—82—Warren Spahn, Boston, Milwaukee, New York, San Francisco, 1942 through 1965, except 1943, 1944, 1945 in military service, 21 years.
A.L.—78—Bob Lemon, Cleveland, 1946 through 1958, 13 years.

Most double plays, season
A.L.—15—Bob Lemon, Cleveland, 41 games, 1953.
N.L.—12—Art Nehf, New York, 40 games, 1920.
Curt Davis, Philadelphia, 51 games, 1934.
Randy Jones, San Diego, 40 games, 1976.

Most seasons leading league in double plays
N.L.—5—Bucky Walters, Philadelphia, Cincinnati, 1937, 1939, 1941 (tied), 1943 (tied), 1944 (tied).
Warren Spahn, Milwaukee, 1953 (tied), 1956, 1960 (tied), 1961 (tied), 1963.
Greg Maddux, Chicago, Atlanta, 1987, 1990, 1991 (tied), 1994 (tied), 1996.
A.L.—4—Willis Hudlin, Cleveland, 1929, 1930, 1931, 1934.

Fewest double plays for leader, season
N.L.—4—Bud Black, San Francisco, 1992.
Doug Drabek, Pittsburgh, 1992.
Omar Olivares, St. Louis, 1992.
A.L.—5—Held by many pitchers.

Most double plays, game
A.L.—4—Milt Gaston, Chicago, May 17, 1932.
Hal Newhouser, Detroit, May 19, 1948.
N.L.—3—Held by 5 pitchers. Last pitcher—Larry McWilliams, Pittsburgh, June 3, 1983.

Most unassisted double plays, career
N.L.—2—Tex Carleton, Chicago, Brooklyn, 1935, 1940.
Claude Passeau, Philadelphia, Chicago, 1938, 1945.
A.L.—1—Held by many pitchers.

Most unassisted double plays, game
N.L.—1—Held by many pitchers. Last pitcher—Jason Isringhausen, New York, July 31, 1999, third inning.
A.L.—1—Held by many pitchers. Last pitcher—Jason Boyd, Cleveland, August 9, 2003, second game, sixth inning.

Most triple plays started, season
N.L.—2—Wilbur Cooper, Pittsburgh, July 7, August 21, 1920.
A.L.—1—Held by many pitchers.

CLUB FIELDING

AVERAGE

Highest fielding average, season
N.L.—.989—New York, 163 games, 1999.
A.L.—.989—Seattle, 162 games, 2003.

Lowest fielding average, season (since 1900)
A.L.—.928—Detroit, 136 games, 1901.
N.L.—.936—Philadelphia, 155 games, 1904.

Most consecutive years leading league in fielding
A.L.—6—Boston, 1916 through 1921.
N.L.—6—St. Louis, 1984 through 1989.

PUTOUTS

Most putouts, season
A.L.—4,520—New York, 164 games, 1964.
N.L.—4,480—Pittsburgh, 163 games, 1979.

Fewest putouts, season
N.L.—3,887—Philadelphia, 149 games, 1907.
A.L.—3,907—Cleveland, 147 games, 1945.

Most putouts by infield, game
A.L.—26—Seattle vs. New York, May 28, 1988.
N.L.—25—Chicago vs. Philadelphia, September 24, 1927.
Pittsburgh vs. New York, June 6, 1941, second game.
St. Louis vs. Boston, July 17, 1947.
Chicago vs. Pittsburgh, May 9, 1963.

Most putouts by infielders from both clubs, game
N.L.—46—Cincinnati 24, New York 22, May 7, 1941.
St. Louis 25, Boston 21, July 17, 1947.
A.L.—45—Detroit 24, Washington 21, September 15, 1945, second game.
Boston 24, Cleveland 21, July 11, 1977.

Fewest putouts by infield, game
A.L.—3—St. Louis vs. New York, July 20, 1945, second game.
Boston vs. Seattle, April 29, 1986.
Boston vs. Toronto, June 1, 2003 (fielded eight innings).
Anaheim vs. Boston, August 6, 2003 (fielded eight innings).
N.L.—3—New York vs. San Diego, April 22, 1970.

Most putouts by outfield, game
N.L.—19—Pittsburgh vs. Cincinnati, July 5, 1948, second game.
(23—Brooklyn vs. Boston, May 1, 1920, 26 innings.
Chicago vs. Boston, May 17, 1927, 22 innings.
Florida vs. St. Louis, April 27, 2003, 20 innings.)
A.L.—19—Minnesota vs. Toronto, July 7, 1994.
(22—Chicago vs. Washington, May 15, 1918, 18 innings.)

Most putouts by outfielders from both clubs, game
N.L.—30—Chicago 16, Philadelphia 14, August 7, 1953.
(42—New York 21, Pittsburgh 21, July 17, 1914, 21 innings.)
A.L.—29—Washington 17, St. Louis 12, May 3, 1939.
(38—Washington 20, St. Louis 18, July 19, 1924, 16 innings.)

Longest game with no putouts by outfield
N.L.—13 innings—New York vs. Brooklyn, April 15, 1909.
St. Louis vs. Philadelphia, August 13, 1987.
A.L.—11 innings—St. Louis vs. Cleveland, April 23, 1905.

Fewest putouts by outfielders from both clubs, game
A.A.—1—St. Louis 1, New York 0, June 30, 1886.
N.L.—1—Pittsburgh 1, Brooklyn 0, August 26, 1910.
A.L.—2—New York 2, Detroit 0, May 9, 1930.

Most putouts by outfield, doubleheader
N.L.—27—Pittsburgh vs. Cincinnati, July 5, 1948.
(29—Boston vs. New York, September 3, 1933, 23 innings.)
A.L.—24—Detroit vs. Cleveland, June 28, 1931.

Most putouts by outfielders from both clubs, doubleheader
N.L.—47—Pittsburgh 26, Boston 21, June 26, 1935.
A.L.—43—Detroit 24, Philadelphia 19, June 28, 1931.

ASSISTS

Most assists, season
A.L.—2,446—Chicago, 157 games, 1907.
N.L.—2,293—St. Louis, 154 games, 1917.

Fewest assists, season
A.L.—1,422—Minnesota, 161 games, 2002.
N.L.—1,437—Philadelphia, 156 games, 1957.

Most consecutive years leading league in assists
A.L.—6—Chicago, 1905 through 1910.
N.L.—6—New York, 1933 through 1938.

Most assists, game
N.L.—28—Pittsburgh vs. New York, June 7, 1911.
(41—Boston vs. Brooklyn, May 1, 1920, 26 innings.)
A.L.—27—St. Louis vs. Philadelphia, August 16, 1919.
(38—Detroit vs. Philadelphia, July 21, 1945, 24 innings.
Washington vs. Chicago, June 12, 1967, 22 innings.)

Most assists by both clubs, game
A.L.—44—Cleveland 22, St. Louis 22, May 27, 1909.
(72—Detroit 38, Philadelphia 34, July 21, 1945, 24 innings.)
N.L.—43—Brooklyn 24, New York 19, April 21, 1903.
(72—Boston 41, Brooklyn 31, May 1, 1920, 26 innings.)

Most assists, two consecutive games
N.L.—48—Boston vs. New York, June 24, 25, 1918.
A.L.—43—Washington vs. St. Louis, August 19, 20, 1923.

Fewest assists, game
A.L.—0—St. Louis vs. Cleveland, August 8, 1943, second game (fielded eight innings).
Cleveland vs. New York, July 4, 1945, first game.
New York vs. Cleveland, September 11, 1995.
Baltimore vs. Oakland, June 20, 2000 (fielded eight innings).
Tampa Bay vs. Minnesota, May 1, 2002 (fielded eight innings).
Tampa Bay vs. Baltimore, May 17, 2003 (fielded eight innings).
N.L.—0—New York vs. Philadelphia, June 25, 1989.
Cincinnati vs. Colorado, August 20, 1997.
Milwaukee vs. St. Louis, July 22, 2004 (fielded eight innings).

Fewest assists by both clubs, game
A.L.—5—Baltimore 3, Cleveland 2, August 31, 1955.
Boston 4, New York 1, August 9, 1992.
N.L.—6—Chicago 5, Philadelphia 1, May 2, 1957.
San Francisco 3, Philadelphia 3, May 13, 1959.

Most assists, doubleheader
N.L.—42—New York vs. Boston, September 30, 1914.
A.L.—41—Boston vs. Detroit, September 20, 1927.
Boston vs. Washington, September 26, 1927.

Most assists by both clubs, doubleheader
N.L.—70—Brooklyn 36, Philadelphia 34, September 5, 1922.
A.L.—68—Detroit 34, Philadelphia 34, September 5, 1901.
Cleveland 35, Boston 33, September 7, 1935.
St. Louis 39, Boston 29, July 23, 1939.

Fewest assists, doubleheader
A.L.—8—Philadelphia vs. New York, July 7, 1946.
Minnesota vs. Los Angeles, July 19, 1961, 17.2 innings.
N.L.—7—New York vs. San Diego, May 29, 1971.

Fewest assists by both clubs, doubleheader
N.L.—22—Milwaukee 14, Philadelphia 8, September 12, 1954.
A.L.—25—Washington 13, New York 12, July 4, 1931.

Most assists by infield, game
A.L.—22—Seattle vs. New York, May 28, 1988.
N.L.—21—New York vs. Pittsburgh, July 13, 1919.
Philadelphia vs. Boston, May 30, 1931, p.m. game.
Brooklyn vs. Pittsburgh, August 18, 1935, second game.

Most assists by infielders from both clubs, game
N.L.—38—Brooklyn 20, Cincinnati 18, June 10, 1917.
A.L.—35—Detroit 19, Cleveland 16, April 18, 1924.
Chicago 18, Boston 17, September 17, 1945, second game.

Fewest assists by infield, game
N.L.—0—Pittsburgh vs. Chicago, July 19, 1902.
New York vs. Philadelphia, July 29, 1934, first game.

Chicago vs. Cincinnati, April 26, 1935.
Cincinnati vs. Brooklyn, August 6, 1938.
Boston vs. Pittsburgh, June 17, 1940, first game.
New York vs. Chicago, May 6, 1953.
Philadelphia, vs. Chicago, May 2, 1957.
Houston vs. Cincinnati, September 10, 1968, first game.
Pittsburgh vs. Montreal, September 17, 1977.
New York vs. Philadelphia, June 25, 1989.
A.L.—0—Boston vs. Chicago, August 13, 1924, first game.
Cleveland vs. New York, July 4, 1945, first game.
St. Louis vs. New York, July 20, 1945, second game.
Washington vs. St. Louis, May 20, 1952.
New York vs. Cleveland, September 11, 1995.
Tampa Bay vs. Baltimore, May 17, 2003 (fielded eight innings).

Fewest assists by infielders from both clubs, game
A.L.—2—Philadelphia 2, Washington 0, May 5, 1910, (Washington fielded only eight innings.)
N.L.—2—Chicago 2, Philadelphla 0, May 2, 1957.

Most assists by outfield, game
N.L.—5—Pittsburgh vs. Philadelphia, August 23, 1910.
A.L.—5—New York vs. Boston, September 5, 1921, second game.
Cleveland vs. St. Louis, May 1, 1928.

Most assists from outfielder to catcher with runner thrown out, game
N.L.—3—Washington vs. Indianapolis, June 19, 1889.
New York vs. Boston, June 30, 1902.
Chicago vs. Pittsburgh, April 26, 1905.
St. Louis vs. San Francisco, July 7, 1975.
A.L.—2—Made in many games.

Longest game with no outfield assists
N.L.—26 Innings—Boston vs. Brooklyn, May 1, 1920.
A.L.—24 innings—Boston vs. Philadelphia, September 1, 1906.
Philadclphia vs. Detroit, July 21, 1945.

Longest game with no outfield assists by either club
N.L.—24 innings—Houston 0, New York 0, April 15, 1968.
A.L.—22 innings—Chicago 0, Washington 0, June 12, 1967.

Most assists, inning
A.L.—10—Cleveland vs. Philadelphia, August 17, 1921, first inning.
Boston vs New York, May 10, 1952, fifth inning.
N.L.—8—Boston vs. Philadelphia, May 1, 1911, fourth inning.

CHANCES ACCEPTED AND OFFERED

Most chances accepted, season
A.L.—6,655— Chicago, 157 games, 1907.
N.L.—6,508—Chicago, 162 games, 1977.

Fewest chances accepted, season
A.L.—5,470— Cleveland, 147 games, 1945.
N.L.—5,545—Philadelphia, 154 games, 1955.

Most chances accepted, game
N.L.—55—Pittsburgh vs. New York, June 7, 1911.
(119—Boston vs. Brooklyn, May 1, 1920, 26 innings.)
A.L.—54—St. Louis vs. Philadelphia, August 16, 1919.
(110—Detroit vs. Philadelphia, July 21, 1945, 24 innings.)

Most chances accepted by both clubs, game
N.L.—98—Brooklyn 50, New York 48, April 21, 1903.
New York 52, Cincinnati 46, May 15, 1909.
A.L.—98—Cleveland 49, St. Louis 49, May 7, 1909.

Most chances accepted by infield, game
A.L.—48—Seattle vs. New York, May 28, 1988.
N.L.—45—New York vs. Pittsburgh, July 13, 1919.
Chicago vs. Philadelphia, September 24, 1927.
Chicago vs. Pittsburgh, May 9, 1963.

Most chances accepted by infielders from both clubs, game
N.L.—78—Cincinnati 41, New York 37, May 7, 1941.
A.L.—76—Boston 43, Cleveland 33, June 24, 1931.

Fewest chances offered to infield, game
A.L.—3—St. Louis vs. New York, July 20, 1945, second game.
N.L.—4—New York vs. San Diego, April 22, 1970.

Fewest chances offered to infielders from both clubs, game
A.L.—17—Chicago 10, Cleveland 9, September 6, 2003.
N.L.—18—Houston 13, Chicago 5, August 14, 2003.

Most chances accepted by outfield, game
N.L.—20—Pittsburgh vs. Cincinnati, July 5, 1948, second game.
(25—Florida vs. St. Louis, April 27, 2003, 20 innings.)
A.L.—18—Cleveland vs. St. Louis, September 28, 1929.
New York vs. Boston, October 1, 1933.
Philadelphia vs. Boston, May 27, 1941, second game.
New York vs. Cleveland, June 26, 1955, second game.
(22—Chicago vs. Washington, May 15, 1918, 18 innings.)

Most chances accepted by outfielders from both clubs, game
A.L.—30—Washington 17, St. Louis 13, May 3, 1939.
(40—Washington 21, St. Louis 19, July 19, 1924, 16 innings.)
N.L.—30—Chicago 16, Philadelphia 14, August 7, 1953.
(43—New York 22, Pittsburgh 21, July 17, 1914, 21 innings.)

Fewest chances offered to outfield, game
N.L.—0—Made in many games.
A.L.—0—Made in many games.

Longest game with no outfield chances offered
N.L.—13 innings—St. Louis vs. Philadelphia, August 13, 1987.
A.L.—11 innings—St. Louis vs. Cleveland, April 23, 1905.

Fewest chances offered to outfielders from both clubs, game
A.A.—2—St. Louis 2, New York 0, June 30, 1886.
N.L.—2—Pittsburgh 1, Brooklyn 1, August 26, 1910.
Cincinnati 1, New York 1, May 7, 1941.
A.L.—3—St. Louis 2, Chicago 1, April 24, 1908.
New York 2, Boston 1, May 4, 1911.
New York 2, Detroit 1, May 9, 1930.

Most chances accepted by outfield, doubleheader
N.L.—28—Pittsburgh vs. Cincinnati, July 5, 1948.
A.L.—24—Detroit vs. Philadelphia, June 28, 1931.
Philadelphia vs. Boston, May 27, 1941.

Most chances accepted by outfielders from both clubs, doubleheader
N.L.—48—Pittsburgh 26, Boston 22, June 26, 1935.
A.L.—44—Detroit 24, Philadelphia 20, June 28, 1931.

ERRORS

Most errors, season
N.L.—867—Washington, 122 games, 1000.
A.L.—425—Detroit, 136 games, 1901.
N.L. since 1900—408—Brooklyn, 155 games, 1905.

Fewest errors, season
A.L.—65—Seattle, 162 games, 2003.
N.L.—68—New York, 163 games, 1999.

Most errorless games, season
A.L.—104—Baltimore, 162 games, 1998.
N.L.—104—New York, 163 games, 1999.

Most consecutive years leading league in errors
N.L.—7—Philadelphia, 1930 through 1936.
A.L.—6—Philadelphia, 1936 through 1941.
St. Louis, 1948 through 1953.

Most years leading league with fewest errors
N.L. since 1900—23—Cincinnati.
A.L.—19—St. Louis/Baltimore (2 by St.L., 17 by Balt.).

Most errors, game
N.L.—24—Boston vs. St. Louis, June 14, 1876.
N.L. since 1900—11—St. Louis vs. Pittsburgh, April 19, 1902.
Boston vs. St. Louis, June 11, 1906.
St. Louis vs. Cincinnati, July 3, 1909, second game.
A.L.—12—Detroit vs. Chicago, May 1, 1901.
Chicago vs. Detroit, May 6, 1903.

Most errors by both clubs, game
N.L.—40—Boston 24, St. Louis 16, June 14, 1876.
N.L. since 1900—15—St. Louis 11, Pittsburgh 4, April 19, 1902.
Boston 10, Chicago 5, October 3, 1904.
A.L.—18—Chicago 12, Detroit 6, May 6, 1903.

Longest game with no errors
A.L.—22 innings—Chicago vs. Washington, June 12, 1967.

– 107 –

Washington vs. Chicago, June 12, 1967.
N.L.—21 innings—Boston vs. Pittsburgh, August 1, 1918.
Chicago vs. Philadelphia, July 17, 1918.
Philadelphia vs. Chicago, July 17, 1918 (fielded 20 innings; Chicago scored winning run with none out in 21st inning).
San Francisco vs. Cincinnati, September 1, 1967.
San Diego vs. Montreal, May 21, 1977.

Longest game with no errors by either club
A.L.—22—Chicago 0, Washington 0, June 12, 1967.
N.L.—21—Chicago 0, Philadelphia 0, July 17, 1918
(Philadelphia fielded 20 innings; Chicago scored winning run with none out in 21st inning).

Most consecutive errorless games, season
N.L.—16—St. Louis, July 30 through August 16, 1992.
A.L.—15—Texas, August 4, through 19, 1996.

Most errors, doubleheader (since 1900)
N.L.—17—Cincinnati vs. Brooklyn, September 13, 1900.
Chicago vs. Cincinnati, October 8, 1900.
St. Louis vs. Cincinnati, July 3, 1909.
A.L.—16—Cleveland vs. Washington, September 21, 1901.

Most errors by both clubs, doubleheader (since 1900)
N.L.—25—Chicago 17, Cincinnati 8, October 8, 1900.
A.L.—22—Cleveland 16, Washington 6, September 21, 1901.

Longest doubleheader without an error
A.L.—27 innings—Detroit vs. New York, August 23, 1968, (first game, Detroit fielded eight innings; second game 19 innings).
N.L.—25 innings—Philadelphia vs. Cincinnati, July 8, 1924.

Longest doubleheader without an error by either club
A.L.—24 innings—New York 0, Philadelphia 0, July 4, 1925.
Washington 0, New York 0, August 14, 1960.
N.L.—20 innings—Boston 0, Chicago 0, September 18, 1924.
New York 0, Chicago 0, August 27, 1951.

Most errors by infield, game
N.L.—17—Boston vs. St. Louis, June 14, 1876.
A.L.—10—Detroit vs. Chicago, May 1, 1901.

Most errors by infielders from both clubs, game
N.L.—22—Boston 17, St. Louis 5, June 14, 1876.
A.L.—13—Chicago 8, Detroit 5, May 6, 1903.

Longest game without an error by infield
A.L.—25—Chicago vs. Milwaukee, May 8, finished May 9, 1984.
N.L.—24—Houston vs. New York, April 15, 1968.

Most errors by outfield, game
N.L.—11—Boston vs. Hartford, May 1, 1876.
A.L.—5—Baltimore vs. St. Louis, August 19, 1902.
N.L. since 1900—4—Made in many games. Last time—San Francisco vs. Los Angeles, July 4, 1971.

Most errors, inning (since 1900)
A.L.—7—Cleveland vs. Chicago, September 20, 1905, eighth inning.
N.L.—6—Pittsburgh vs. New York, August 20, 1903, first game, first inning.

PASSED BALLS

Most passed balls, season
N.L.—167—Boston, 98 games, 1883.
A.L.—73—Texas, 162 games, 1987.
N.L. since 1900—42—Boston, 156 games, 1905.
Atlanta, 162 games, 1967.

Fewest passed balls, season
A.L.—0—New York, 155 games, 1931.
N.L.—2—Boston, 153 games, 1943.
New York, 162 games, 1980.
San Diego, 162 games, 1992.

Most passed balls, game
A.A.—12—Washington vs. New York, May 10, 1884.
N.L.—10—Boston vs. Washington, May 3, 1886.
N.L. since 1900—6—Cincinnati vs. Pittsburgh, October 4, 1902.
Houston vs. Montreal, May 12, 1996.
A.L.—6—Texas vs. Detroit, August 30, 1987.

Most passed balls by both clubs, game
A.A.—14—Washington 12, New York 2, May 10, 1884.

N.L.—11—Troy 7, Cleveland 4, June 16, 1880.
N.L. since 1900—6—Cincinnati 6, Pittsburgh 0, October 4, 1902.
Houston 6, Montreal 0, May 12, 1996.
A.L.—6—Texas 6, Detroit 0, August 30, 1987.

Longest game with no passed balls
N.L.—26 innings—Boston vs. Brooklyn, May 1, 1920.
Brooklyn vs. Boston, May 1, 1920.
A.L.—25 innings—Chicago vs. Milwaukee, May 8, finished May 9, 1984.
Milwaukee vs. Chicago, May 8, finished May 9, 1984 (fielded 24.1 innings).

Longest game with no passed balls by either club
N.L.—26 innings—Boston 0, Brooklyn 0, May 1, 1920.
A.L.—25 innings—Chicago 0, Milwaukee 0, May 8, finished May 9, 1984 (Milwaukee fielded 24.1 innings).

DOUBLE PLAYS

Most double plays, season
A.L.—217—Philadelphia, 154 games, 1949.
N.L.—215—Pittsburgh, 162 games, 1966.

Most years with 200 or more double plays
A.L.—3—Philadelphia, 1949 (217), 1950 (208), 1951 (204).
N.L.—1—Pittsburgh, 1966 (215).
Colorado, 1997 (202).

Fewest double plays, season (A.L. since 1912; N.L. since 1919)
A.L.—74—Boston, 151 games, 1913.
N.L.—94—Pittsburgh, 153 games, 1935.

Most times with five or more double plays in a game, season
N.L.—3—New York, 1950.
A.L.—3—Cleveland, 1970.
Kansas City, 1971.

Most double plays, game
A.L.—7—New York vs. Philadelphia, August 14, 1942.
N.L.—7—Houston vs. San Francisco, May 4, 1969.
Atlanta vs. Cincinnati, June 27, 1982, 14 innings.
St. Louis vs. Pittsburgh, June 16, 1994, 10 innings.

Most double plays by both clubs, game
A.L.—10—Minnesota 6, Boston 4, July 18, 1990.
N.L.—9—Chicago 5, Cincinnati 4, July 3, 1929.
Los Angeles 5, Pittsburgh 4, April 15, 1961.
(10—Boston 5, Cincinnati 5, June 7, 1925, 12 innings.
Cincinnati 6, New York 4, May 1, 1955, 16 innings.
San Francisco 6, New Yor, 4, August 21, 2004, 12 innings.)

Most unassisted double plays, nine-inning game
N.L.-A.L.—2—Made in many games.

Most unassisted double plays by both clubs, game
N.L.-A.L.—2—Made in many games.

Most double plays, doubleheader
A.L.—10—Washington vs. Chicago, August 18, 1943, 22.1 innings.
N.L.—9—St. Louis vs. Cincinnati, June 11, 1944, 18 innings.

Most double plays by both clubs, doubleheader
N.L.—13—New York 7, Philadelphia 6, September 28, 1939.
Pittsburgh 8, St. Louis 5, September 6, 1948.
A.L.—12—Philadelphia 9, Cleveland 3, September 14, 1931.
Boston 7, Chicago 5, September 15, 1947.
New York 7, Kansas City 5, July 31, 1955.
California 8, Boston 4, May 1, 1966.
California 7, Baltimore 5, May 19, 1988, 19 innings.

Most consecutive games with one or more double plays
A.L.—25—Boston, May 7 through June 4, second game, 1951 (38 double plays).
Cleveland, August 21, second game, through September 12, 1953 (38 double plays).
N.L.—23—Brooklyn, August 7, second game, through August 27, 1952 (36 double plays).

Most consecutive games with one or more double or triple plays
N.L.—26—New York, August 21 through September 16, second game, 1951 (44 double plays, 1 triple play).
A.L.—25—Boston, May 7 through June 4, second game, 1951 (38 double plays).

Cleveland, August 21, second game, through September 12, 1953 (38 double plays).

Most double plays, two consecutive nine-inning games
N.L.—10—New York vs. Brooklyn, August 12, 13, first game, 1932.
A.L.—10—Detroit vs. Boston, May 18 (4), 19 (6), 1948.
  Cleveland vs. Kansas City, May 3 (5); vs. Chicago, May 5 (5), 1970.
  Kansas City vs. Baltimore, May 5 (4), 6 (6), 1972.

TRIPLE PLAYS

Most triple plays, season
A.A.—3—Cincinnati, 1882.
  Rochester, 1890.

A.L.—3—Detroit, 1911; Boston, 1924, 1979; Oakland, 1979.
N.L.—3—Philadelphia, 1964; Chicago, 1965.

Most triple plays, nine-inning game
A.L.—2—Minnesota vs. Boston, July 17, 1990, fourth and eighth innings.
N.L.—1—Held by many clubs.

Most triple plays by both clubs, game
A.L.—2—Minnesota 2, Boston 0, July 17, 1990.
N.L.—1—Made in many games.

Most consecutive games with triple play
A.L.—2—Detroit vs. Boston, June 6, 7, 1908.
N.L.—Never accomplished.

LEAGUE FIELDING

AVERAGE

Highest fielding percentage, season
N.L.—.9832 in 2004
A.L.—.9827 in 2003

Lowest fielding percentage, season (since 1900)
A.L.—.937 in 1901
N.L.—.949 in 1903

PUTOUTS

Most putouts, season
N.L. since 1900 (8 clubs)—33,724 in 1917
N.L. (10 clubs)—44,042 in 1968
N.L. (12 clubs)—52,630 in 1982
N.L. (14 clubs)—60,867 in 1996
N.L. (16 clubs)—69,720 in 1998
A.L. (8 clubs)—33,830 in 1916
A.L. (10 clubs)—43,847 in 1964
A.L. (12 clubs)—52,510 in 1969
A.L. (14 clubs)—61,146 in 1991

Fewest putouts, season
N.L. since 1900 (8 clubs)—32,296 in 1906
N.L. (10 clubs)—43,470 in 1962
N.L. (12 clubs)—52,000 in 1970
N.L. (14 clubs)—60,767 in 1997
N.L. (16 clubs)—69,223 in 2001
A.L. (8 clubs)—32,235 in 1938
A.L. (10 clubs)—43,281 in 1961
A.L. (12 clubs)—51,821 in 1975
A.L. (14 clubs)—60,155 in 1979

ASSISTS

Most assists, season
N.L. since 1900 (8 clubs)—16,759 in 1920
N.L. (10 clubs)—18,205 in 1968
N.L. (12 clubs)—22,341 in 1980
N.L. (14 clubs)—24,442 in 1993
N.L. (16 clubs)—27,513 in 1998
A.L. (8 clubs)—17,167 in 1910
A.L. (10 clubs)—17,269 in 1961
A.L. (12 clubs)—21,786 in 1976
A.L. (14 clubs)—25,626 in 1980

Fewest assists, season
N.L. since 1900 (8 clubs)—13,345 in 1956
N.L. (10 clubs)—17,681 in 1963
N.L. (12 clubs)—20,351 in 1990
N.L. (14 clubs)—24,198 in 1997
N.L. (16 clubs)—26,279 in 2001
A.L. (8 clubs)—13,219 in 1958
A.L. (10 clubs)—16,999 in 1963
A.L. (12 clubs)—21,001 in 1971
A.L. (14 clubs)—22,740 in 2002

CHANCES ACCEPTED

(Chances accepted equals putouts plus assists)

Most chances accepted, season
N.L. since 1900 (8 clubs)—50,419 in 1920
N.L. (10 clubs)—62,247 in 1968
N.L. (12 clubs)—74,930 in 1980
N.L. (14 clubs)—85,296 in 1993
N.L. (16 clubs)—97,233 in 1998
A.L. (8 clubs)—50,870 in 1910
A.L. (10 clubs)—60,997 in 1964
A.L. (12 clubs)—74,191 in 1976
A.L. (14 clubs)—86,621 in 1980

Fewest chances accepted, season
N.L. since 1900 (8 clubs)—46,404 in 1955
N.L. (10 clubs)—61,302 in 1962
N.L. (12 clubs)—72,495 in 1970
N.L. (14 clubs)—84,965 in 1997
N.L. (16 clubs)—95,502 in 2001
A.L. (8 clubs)—46,086 in 1938
A.L. (10 clubs)—60,450 in 1961
A.L. (12 clubs)—72,875 in 1971
A.L. (14 clubs)—83,232 in 2002 (57,511 in shortened 1981 season)

ERRORS

Most errors, season
N.L. since 1900 (8 clubs)—2,757 in 1900
N.L. (10 clubs)—1,586 in 1964
N.L. (12 clubs)—1,859 in 1975
N.L. (14 clubs)—1,876 in 1993
N.L. (16 clubs)—1,915 in 1999
A.L. (8 clubs)—2,870 in 1901
A.L. (10 clubs)—1,385 in 1966
A.L. (12 clubs)—1,851 in 1975
A.L. (14 clubs)—1,986 in 1977

Fewest errors, season
N.L. since 1900 (8 clubs)—1,082 in 1956
N.L. (10 clubs)—1,389 in 1968
N.L. (12 clubs)—1,401 in 1992 (1,138 in shortened 1981 season)
N.L. (14 clubs)—1,677 in 1997 (1,205 in shortened 1994 season)
N.L. (16 clubs)—1,646 in 2004
A.L. (8 clubs)—1,002 in 1958
A.L. (10 clubs)—1,261 in 1964
A.L. (12 clubs)—1,512 in 1971
A.L. (14 clubs)—1,475 in 2003

PASSED BALLS

Most passed balls, season
N.L. since 1900 (8 clubs)—202 in 1905
N.L. (10 clubs)—216 in 1962
N.L. (12 clubs)—217 in 1969
N.L. (14 clubs)—199 in 1993

N.L. (16 clubs)—192 in 2002
A.L. (8 clubs)—197 in 1911
A.L. (10 clubs)—211 in 1965
A.L. (12 clubs)—247 in 1969
A.L. (14 clubs)—267 in 1987

Fewest passed balls, season
N.L. since 1900 (8 clubs)—65 in 1936
N.L. (10 clubs)—148 in 1968
N.L. (12 clubs)—122 in 1980
N.L. (14 clubs)—154 in 1997 (147 in shortened 1994 season)
N.L. (16 clubs)—163 in 2003, 2004
A.L. (8 clubs)—53 in 1949
A.L. (10 clubs)—147 in 1963, 1966
A.L. (12 clubs)—127 in 1976
A.L. (14 clubs)—128 in 1977

DOUBLE PLAYS

Most double plays, season
N.L. since 1900 (8 clubs)—1,337 in 1951
N.L. (10 clubs)—1,596 in 1962
N.L. (12 clubs)—1,888 in 1971
N.L. (14 clubs)—2,075 in 1997
N.L. (16 clubs)—2,484 in 2002
A.L. (8 clubs)—1,487 in 1949
A.L. (10 clubs)—1,585 in 1961
A.L. (12 clubs)—1,994 in 1973
A.L. (14 clubs)—2,368 in 1980

Fewest double plays, season
N.L. since 1900 (8 clubs)—600 in 1908
N.L. (10 clubs)—1,431 in 1963
N.L. (12 clubs)—1,527 in 1991 (1,177 in shortened 1981 season)

N.L. (14 clubs)—2,028 in 1993
N.L. (16 clubs)—2,340 in 2001
A.L. (8 clubs)—640 in 1905
A.L. (10 clubs)—1,388 in 1967, 1968
A.L. (12 clubs)—1,821 in 1976 (1,770 in shortened 1972 season)
A.L. (14 clubs)—2,081 in 2001

Most double plays, one day
N.L.—29—July 23, 1972
A.L.—28—July 24, 1976

TRIPLE PLAYS

Most triple plays, season
A.L. (14-club league)—10 in 1979
A.L. (8-club league)—7 in 1922, 1936
N.L.—7 in 1891, 1905, 1910, 1929
A.A.—7 in 1890
P.L.—7 in 1890

Fewest triple plays, season
N.L.—0 in 1928, 1938, 1941, 1943, 1945, 1946, 1959, 1961, 1974, 1984, 1994, 2001
A.L.—0 in 1904, 1933, 1942, 1956, 1961, 1962, 1974, 1975, 1987, 1993, 1998, 2003

Fewest triple plays by both leagues, season
0 in 1961, 1974

Most triple plays, one day
N.L.—2—May 29, 1897; August 30, 1921
A.L.—2—July 17, 1990

INDIVIDUAL MISCELLANEOUS

HISTORIC FIRSTS

First player with two clubs in one season
N.L.—Neal Phelps, New York, Philadelphia, 1876.
A.L.—Harry Lockhead, Detroit, Philadelphia, 1901.

First player with three clubs in one season
N.L.—Gus Krock, Chicago, Indianapolis, Washington, 1889.
A.L.—Pat Donahue, Boston, Cleveland, Philadelphia, 1910.
(See next entry: Frank Huelsman played with four clubs in 1904.)

First player with four clubs in one season
N.L.—Tom Dowse, Louisville, Cincinnati, Philadelphia, Washington, 63 games, 1892.
A.L.—Frank Huelsman, Chicago, Detroit, St. Louis, Washington, 112 games, 1904.

First pitcher with two clubs in one season
N.L.—Tom Healey, Providence, Indianapolis, 1878.
A.L.—Charles Baker, Cleveland, Philadelphia, 1901.

First pitcher with three clubs in one season
N.L.—Gus Krock, Chicago, Indianapolis, Washington, 1889.
A.L.—Bill James, Detroit, Boston, Chicago, 1919.

First player to enter military service in World War I
Hank Gowdy, Boston N.L., June 27, 1917.

First player to enter military service in World War II
Hugh Mulcahy, Philadelphia N.L., March 8, 1941.

First player to come to bat three times in one inning
N.L.—Tom Carey, Hartford, May 13, 1876, fourth inning.
A.L.—Ted Williams, Boston, July 4, 1948, seventh inning.

First player with seven at-bats in nine-inning game
N.L.—Jack Burdock, Hartford, May 13, 1876.
A.L.—Billy Gilbert, Milwaukee, May 5, 1901.

First player with eight at-bats in nine-inning game
N.L.—Ross Barnes, Chicago, July 22, 1876.

First player to score five runs in nine-inning game
N.L.—George Hall, Philadelphia, June 17, 1876.
A.L.—Mike Donlin, Baltimore, June 24, 1901.

First player to score six runs in nine-inning game
N.L.—Jim Whitney, Boston, June 9, 1883.
A.L.—Johnny Pesky, Boston, May 8, 1946.

First player with five hits in nine-inning game
N.L.—Joe Battin, St. Louis, May 13, 1876.
Jack Burdock, Hartford, May 13, 1876.
Tom Carey, Hartford, May 13, 1876.
A.L.—Irv Waldron, Milwaukee, April 28, 1901.

First player with six hits in nine-inning game
N.L.—Dave Force, Philadelphia, June 27, 1876 (six at-bats).
A.L.—Mike Donlin, Baltimore, June 24, 1901 (six at-bats).

First player with eight hits in a doubleheader
A.A.—Henry Simon, Syracuse, October 11, 1890. (See next entry: Fred Carroll had nine hits in doubleheader in 1886.)
N.L.—Joe Quinn, St. Louis, September 30, 1893. (See next entry: Wilbert Robinson had nine hits in doubleheader in 1892.)
A.L.—Charles Hickman, Washington, September 7, 1905.

First player with nine hits in a doubleheader
A.A.—Fred Carroll, Pittsburgh, July 5, 1886.
N.L.—Wilbert Robinson, Baltimore, June 10, 1892.
A.L.—Ray Morehart, Chicago, August 31, 1926.

First player with four long hits in nine-inning game
N.L.—George Hall, Philadelphia, June 14, 1876 (3 triples, 1 home run).
A.L.—Frank Dillon, Detroit, April 25, 1901 (4 doubles).

First player with five long hits in nine-inning game
A.A.—George Strief, Philadelphia, June 25, 1885 (4 triples, 1 double).
N.L.—George Gore, Chicago, July 9, 1885 (2 triples, 3 doubles).
A.L.—Lou Boudreau, Cleveland, July 14, 1946, first game (4 doubles, 1 home run).

First player with four doubles in nine-inning game
N.L.—John O'Rourke, Boston, September 15, 1880.
A.L.—Frank Dillon, Detroit, April 25, 1901.

First player with three triples in nine-inning game
N.L.—George Hall, Philadelphia, June 14, 1876.

Ezra Sutton, Philadelphia, June 14, 1876.
A.L.—Elmer Flick, Cleveland, July 6, 1902.

First player with four triples in nine-inning game
A.A.—George Strief, Philadelphia, June 25, 1885.
N.L.—Bill Joyce, New York, May 18, 1897.
A.L.—Never accomplished.

First player to hit home run
N.L.—Ross Barnes, Chicago, May 2, 1876.
Charley Jones, Cincinnati, May 2, 1876.
A.L.—Erve Beck, Cleveland, April 25, 1901.

First player to hit two homers in nine-inning game
N.L.—George Hall, Philadelphia, June 17, 1876.
A.L.—Buck Freeman, Boston, June 1, 1901.

First player to hit three homers in nine-inning game
N.L.—Ned Williamson, Chicago, May 30, 1884, p.m. game.
A.L.—Kenny Williams, St. Louis, April 22, 1922.

First player to hit four homers in nine-inning game
N.L.—Bobby Lowe, Boston, May 30, 1894, p.m. game.
A.L.—Lou Gehrig, New York, June 3, 1932.

First player to hit two homers in one inning
N.L.—Charley Jones, Boston, June 10, 1880, eighth inning.
A.L.—Ken Williams, St. Louis, August 7, 1922, sixth inning.

First player to hit grand slam
N.L.—Roger Connor, Troy, September 10, 1881.
A.L.—Herm McFarland, Chicago, May 1, 1901.

First player to hit grand slam as pinch-hitter
N.L.—Mike O'Neill, St. Louis, June 3, 1902, ninth inning.
A.L.—Marty Kavanagh, Cleveland, September 24, 1916, fifth inning.

First player to hit home run in night game
N.L.—Babe Herman, Cincinnati, July 10, 1935.
A.L.—Frankie Hayes, Philadelphia, May 16, 1939.

First player to hit for cycle
N.L.—Curry Foley, Buffalo, May 25, 1882.
A.L.—Harry Davis, Philadelphia, July 10, 1901.

First player to receive five bases on balls in nine-inning game
A.A.—Henry Larkin, Philadelphia, May 2, 1887.
N.L.—Fred Carroll, Pittsburgh, July 4, 1889, a.m. game.
A.L.—Sammy Strang, Chicago, April 27, 1902.

First player to receive six bases on balls in nine-inning game
N.L.—Walt Wilmot, Chicago, August 22, 1891.
A.L.—Jimmie Foxx, Boston, June 16, 1938.

First player to receive two bases on balls in one inning
N.L.—Elmer Smith, Pittsburgh, April 22, 1892, first inning.
A.L.—Donie Bush, Detroit, August 27, 1909, fourth inning.

First player to strike out four times in nine-inning game
N.L.—George Derby, Detroit, August 6, 1881. (See next item: Oscar Walker had five strikeouts in game in 1879.)
A.L.—Emmett Heidrick, St. Louis, May 16, 1902.

First player to strike out five times in nine-inning game
N.L.—Oscar Walker, Buffalo, June 20, 1879.
A.L.—Lefty Grove, Philadelphia, June 10, 1933, first game.

First player to strike out twice in one inning
A.L.—Billy Purtell, Chicago, May 10, 1910, sixth inning.
N.L.—Edd Roush, Cincinnati, July 22, 1916, sixth inning.

First pinch-hitter
N.L.—Mickey Welch, New York, August 10, 1889 (struck out).
A.L.—Larry McLean, Boston, April 26, 1901 (doubled).

First hit by pinch-hitter
N.L.—Tom Daly, Brooklyn, May 14, 1892 (homered).
A.L.—Larry McLean, Boston, April 26, 1901 (doubled).

First pitcher to lose doubleheader (two complete games)
N.L.—Dave Anderson, Pittsburgh vs. Brooklyn, September 1, 1890; lost 3-2, 8-4 (pitched 2 games of tripleheader).

First player to be intentionally walked with bases filled
A.L.—Nap Lajoie, Philadelphia, May 23, 1901, ninth inning.

First manager ejected from two games in one day by umpires
N.L.—Mel Ott, New York vs. Pittsburgh, June 9, 1946, doubleheader.
A.L.—Jimmie Dykes, Baltimore vs. New York, June 6, 1954, doubleheader.

First lefthanded catcher
Bill Harbidge, Hartford N.L., May 6, 1876.

First lefthanded pitcher
Bobby Mitchell, Cincinnati N.L., 1877.

First pitcher to wear glasses
Will White, Boston N.L., 1877.

First infielder to wear glasses
George Toporcer, St. Louis N.L., 1921.

First catcher to wear glasses
Clint Courtney, New York A.L., 1951.

CLUB MISCELLANEOUS

HISTORIC FIRSTS

First shutout game
N.L.—April 25, 1876, Chicago 4, Louisville 0.
A.L.—May 15, 1901, Washington 4, Boston 0.

First 1-0 game
N.L.—May 5, 1876, St. Louis 1, Chicago 0.
A.L.—July 27, 1901, Detroit 1, Baltimore 0.

First tie game
N.L.—May 25, 1876, Philadelphia 2, Louisville 2, 14 innings (darkness).
A.L.—May 31, 1901, Washington 3, Milwaukee 3, 7 innings (darkness).

First extra-inning game
N.L.—April 29, 1876, Hartford 3, Boston 2, 10 innings.
A.L.—April 30, 1901, Boston 8, Philadelphia 6, 10 innings.

First extra-inning shutout game
N.L.—May 25, 1876, Boston 4, Cincinnati 0, 10 innings.
A.L.—August 11, 1902, Philadelphia 1, Detroit 0, 13 innings.

First extra-inning 1-0 game
N.L.—June 10, 1876, New York Mutuals 1, Cincinnati 0, 10 innings.
A.L.—August 11, 1902, Philadelphia 1, Detroit 0, 13 innings.

First extra-inning tie game
N.L.—May 25, 1876, Philadelphia 2, Louisville 2, 14 innings (darkness).
A.L.—August 27, 1901, Milwaukee 5, Baltimore 5, 11 innings (darkness).

First time two games played in one day
N.L.—September 9, 1876, Hartford 14, Cincinnati 6; Hartford 8, Cincinnati 3.
A.L.—May 30, 1901, Baltimore 10, Detroit 7; Detroit 4, Baltimore 1.
Chicago 8, Boston 3; Chicago 5, Boston 3.
Milwaukee 5, Washington 2; Milwaukee 14, Washington 3.
Philadelphia 3, Cleveland 1; Philadelphia 8, Cleveland 2, eight innings.

First doubleheader
N.L.—September 25, 1882, Worcester 4, Providence 3; Providence 8, Worcester 6.
A.L.—July 15, 1901, Washington 3, Baltimore 2; Baltimore 7, Washington 3.

First doubleheader shutout victory
N.L.—July 13, 1888, Pittsburgh 4, Boston 0; Pittsburgh 6,

Boston 0.

A.L.—September 3, 1901, Cleveland 1, Boston 0; Cleveland 4, Boston 0.

First forfeited game

N.L.—August 21, 1876, St. Louis 7, Chicago 6, at St. Louis; forfeited to St. Louis.

A.L.—May 2, 1901, Detroit 7, Chicago 5, at Chicago; forfeited to Detroit.

Last forfeited game

N.L.—August 10, 1995, St. Louis 2, Los Angeles 1, at Los Angeles; forfeited to St. Louis.

A.L.—July 12, 1979, second game, Detroit 9, Chicago 0, at Chicago; forfeited to Detroit.

First game played by

Boston N.L.—April 22, 1876—Boston 6, Philadelphia Athletics 5 (A).

Philadelphia Athletics N.L.—April 22, 1876—Boston 6, Philadelphia 5 (H).

New York Mutuals N.L.—April 25, 1876—Boston 7, New York Mutuals 6 (H).

Chicago N.L.—April 25, 1876—Chicago 4, Louisville 0 (A).

Cincinnati N.L.—April 25, 1876—Cincinnati 2, St. Louis 1 (H).

St. Louis N.L.—April 25, 1876—Cincinnati 2, St. Louis 1 (A).

Philadelphia N.L.—May 1, 1883—Providence 4, Philadelphia 3 (H).

New York N.L. (Original Club)—May 1, 1883—New York 7, Boston 5 (H).

Pittsburgh N.L.—April 30, 1887—Pittsburgh 6, Chicago 2 (H).

Brooklyn N.L.—April 19, 1890—Boston 15, Brooklyn 9 (A).

Chicago A.L.—April 24, 1901—Chicago 8, Cleveland 2 (H).

Cleveland A.L.—April 24, 1901—Chicago 8, Cleveland 2 (A).

Detroit A.L.—April 25, 1901—Detroit 14, Milwaukee 13 (H).

Baltimore A.L.—April 26, 1901—Baltimore 10, Boston 6 (H).

Boston A.L.—April 26, 1901—Baltimore 10, Boston 6 (A).

Philadelphia A.L.—April 26, 1901—Washington 5, Philadelphia 1 (H).

Washington A.L. (Original Club)—April 26, 1901—Washington 5, Philadelphia 1 (A).

Milwaukee A.L.—April 25, 1901—Detroit 14, Milwaukee 13 (A).

St. Louis A.L.—April 23, 1902—St. Louis 5, Cleveland 2 (H).

New York A.L.—April 22, 1903—Washington 3, New York 1 (A).

Milwaukee N.L. since 1900—April 13, 1953—Milwaukee 2, Cincinnati 0 (A).

Baltimore A.L. (Present Club)—April 13, 1954—Detroit 3, Baltimore 0 (A).

Kansas City A.L.—April 12, 1955—Kansas City 6, Detroit 2 (H).

Los Angeles N.L.—April 15, 1958—San Francisco 8, Los Angeles 0 (A).

San Francisco N.L.—April 15, 1958—San Francisco 8, Los Angeles 0 (H).

Los Angeles A.L.—April 11, 1961—Los Angeles 7, Baltimore 2 (A).

Minnesota A.L.—April 11, 1961—Minnesota 6, New York 0 (A).

Washington A.L. (Second Club)—April 10, 1961—Chicago 4, Washington 3 (A).

Houston N.L.—April 10, 1962—Houston 11, Chicago 2 (H).

New York N.L. (Present Club)—April 11, 1962—St. Louis 11, New York 4 (A).

Atlanta N.L.—April 12, 1966—Pittsburgh 3, Atlanta 2, 13 innings (H).

Oakland A.L.—April 10, 1968—Baltimore 3, Oakland 1 (A).

San Diego N.L.—April 8, 1969—San Diego 2, Houston 1 (H).

Seattle A.L. (Original Club)—April 8, 1969—Seattle 4, California 3 (A).

Montreal N.L.—April 8, 1969—Montreal 11, New York 10 (A).

Kansas City A.L. (Present Club)—April 8, 1969—Kansas City 4, Minnesota 3, 12 innings (H).

Milwaukee A.L. (Present Club)—April 7, 1970—California 12, Milwaukee 0 (H).

Texas A.L.—April 15, 1972—California 1, Texas 0 (A).

Seattle A.L. (Present Club)—April 6, 1977—California 7, Seattle 0 (H).

Toronto A.L.—April 7, 1977—Toronto 9, Chicago 5 (H).

Florida N.L.—April 5, 1993—Florida 6, Los Angeles 3 (H).

Colorado N.L.—April 5, 1993—New York 3, Colorado 0 (A).

Tampa Bay A.L.—March 31, 1998—Detroit 11, Tampa Bay 6 (H).

Arizona N.L.—March 31, 1998—Colorado 9, Arizona 2 (H).

First game played

At Sportsman's Park, St. Louis—May 5, 1876—St. Louis N.L. 1,

Chicago 0.

By St. Louis A.L.—April 23, 1902—St. Louis 5, Cleveland 2.

By St. Louis N.L. (since 1900)—July 1, 1920—Pittsburgh 6, St. Louis 2, 10 innings.

At Shibe Park (later Connie Mack Stadium), Philadelphia—April 12, 1909—Philadelphia A.L. 8, Boston 1.

At Shibe Park (later Connie Mack Stadium), Philadelphia—May 16, 1927—St. Louis N.L. 2, Philadelphia N.L. 1.

At Forbes Field, Pittsburgh—June 30, 1909—Chicago N.L. 3, Pittsburgh 2.

At Comiskey Park (old), Chicago—July 1, 1910—St. Louis A.L. 2, Chicago 0.

At League Park, Cleveland—April 21, 1910—Detroit A.L. 5, Cleveland 0.

At Griffith Stadium, Washington—April 12, 1911—Washington A.L. 8, Boston 5.

At Polo Grounds, New York (first game after fire)—June 28, 1911—New York N.L. 3, Boston 0.

Formal opening—April 19, 1912—New York N.L. 6, Brooklyn 2.

At Redland Field (later Crosley Field), Cincinnati—April 11, 1912—Cincinnati N.L. 10, Chicago 6.

At Navin Field (later Tiger Stadium), Detroit—April 20, 1912—Detroit A.L. 6, Cleveland 5, 11 innings.

At Fenway Park, Boston—April 20, 1912—Boston A.L. 7, New York 6 (11 innings).

Formal opening—May 17, 1912—Chicago A.L. 5, Boston 2.

At Ebbets Field, Brooklyn—April 9, 1913—Philadelphia N.L. 1, Brooklyn 0.

At Wrigley Field, Chicago—April 23, 1914—Chicago F.L. 9, Kansas City 1.

By Chicago N.L.—April 20, 1916—Chicago 7, Cincinnati 6, 11 innings.

At Braves Field, Boston—August 18, 1915—Boston N.L. 3, St. Louis 1.

At Yankee Stadium, New York—April 18, 1923, New York A.L. 4, Boston 1.

At Municipal Stadium, Cleveland—July 31, 1932, Philadelphia A.L. 1, Cleveland 0.

At Milwaukee County Stadium—April 14, 1953, Milwaukee N.L. 3, St. Louis 2, 10 innings.

At Memorial Stadium, Baltimore—April 15, 1954, Baltimore A.L. 3, Chicago 1.

At Municipal Stadium, Kansas City—April 12, 1955, Kansas City A.L. 6, Detroit 2.

At Roosevelt Stadium, Jersey City—April 19, 1956, Brooklyn N.L. 5, Philadelphia 4, 10 innings.

At Seals Stadium, San Francisco—April 15, 1958—San Francisco N.L. 8, Los Angeles 0.

At Memorial Coliseum, Los Angeles—April 18, 1958—Los Angeles N.L. 6, San Francisco 5.

At Candlestick Park, San Francisco—April 12, 1960—San Francisco N.L. 3, St. Louis 1.

At Metropolitan Stadium, Minnesota—April 21, 1961—Washington A.L. 5, Minnesota 3.

At Wrigley Field, Los Angeles—April 27, 1961—Minnesota A.L. 4, Los Angeles 2.

At Dodger Stadium, Los Angeles—April 10, 1962—Cincinnati N.L. 6, Los Angeles 3.

At Colt Stadium, Houston—April 10, 1962—Houston N.L. 11, Chicago 2.

At District of Columbia Stadium, Washington—April 9, 1962, Washington A.L. 4, Detroit 1.

At Shea Stadium, New York—April 17, 1964—Pittsburgh N.L. 4, New York 3.

At Astrodome, Houston—April 12, 1965—Philadelphia N.L. 2, Houston 0.

At Atlanta Stadium, Atlanta—April 12, 1966—Pittsburgh N.L. 3, Atlanta 2, 13 innings.

At Anaheim Stadium, California—April 19, 1966—Chicago A.L. 3, California 1.

At Busch Memorial Stadium, St. Louis—May 12, 1966—St. Louis N.L. 4, Atlanta 3, 12 innings.

At Oakland-Alameda County Coliseum—April 17, 1968—Baltimore A.L. 4, Oakland 1.

At San Diego Stadium—April 8, 1969—San Diego N.L. 2, Houston 1.

At Sicks' Stadium, Seattle—April 11, 1969—Seattle A.L. 7, Chicago 0.

At Jarry Park, Montreal—April 14, 1969—Montreal N.L. 8, St. Louis 7.

At Riverfront Stadium, Cincinnati—June 30, 1970—Atlanta N.L. 8, Cincinnati 2.

At Three Rivers Stadium, Pittsburgh—July 16, 1970—Cincinnati N.L. 3, Pittsburgh 2.

At Veterans Stadium, Philadelphia—April 10, 1971—Philadelphia N.L. 4, Montreal 1.

At Arlington Stadium, Texas—April 21, 1972—Texas A.L. 7, California 6.

At Royals Stadium, Kansas City—April 10, 1973—Kansas City A.L. 12, Texas 1.

At Kingdome, Seattle—April 6, 1977—California A.L. 7, Seattle 0.

At Exhibition Stadium, Toronto—April 7, 1977—Toronto A.L. 9, Chicago 5.

At Olympic Stadium, Montreal—April 15, 1977—Philadelphia N.L. 7, Montreal 2.

At Metrodome, Minnesota—April 6, 1982—Seattle A.L. 11, Minnesota 7.

At SkyDome, Toronto—June 5, 1989—Milwaukee A.L. 5, Toronto 3.

At Comiskey Park (new), Chicago—April 18, 1991—Detroit A.L. 16, Chicago 0.

At Oriole Park at Camden Yards, Baltimore—April 6, 1992—Baltimore A.L. 2, Cleveland 0.

At Joe Robbie Stadium, Florida—April 5, 1993—Florida N.L. 6, Los Angeles 3.

At Mile High Stadium, Colorado—April 9, 1993—Colorado N.L. 11, Montreal 4.

At Jacobs Field, Cleveland—April 4, 1994—Cleveland A.L. 4, Seattle 3 (11 innings).

At The Ballpark in Arlington, Texas—April 11, 1994—Milwaukee A.L. 4, Texas 3.

At Coors Field, Colorado—April 26, 1995—Colorado N.L. 11, New York 9 (11 innings).

At Cashman Field, Las Vegas—April 1, 1996—Toronto A.L. 9, Oakland 6.

At Monterrey Stadium, Mexico—August 16, 1996—San Diego N.L. 15, New York 10.

At Turner Field, Atlanta—April 4, 1997—Atlanta N.L. 5, Chicago 4.

At Aloha Stadium, Honolulu—April 19, 1997, first game, St. Louis N.L. 1, San Diego 0.

At Tropicana Field, Tampa Bay—March 31, 1998—Detroit A.L. 11, Tampa Bay 6.

At Bank One Ballpark, Arizona—March 31, 1998—Colorado N.L. 9, Arizona 2.

At Safeco Field, Seattle—July 15, 1999—San Diego N.L. 3, Seattle A.L. 2.

At Tokyo Dome, Japan—March 29, 2000—Chicago N.L. 5, New York N.L. 3.

At Enron Field, Houston—April 7, 2000—Philadelphia N.L. 4, Houston 1.

At Pacific Bell Park, San Francisco—April 11, 2000—Los Angeles N.L. 6, San Francisco 5.

At Comerica Park, Detroit—April 11, 2000—Detroit A.L. 5, Seattle 2.

At Hiram Bithorn Stadium, San Juan, Puerto Rico—April 1, 2001—Toronto A.L. 8, Texas 1.

At Miller Park, Milwaukee—April 6, 2001—Milwaukee N.L. 5, Cincinnati 4.

At PNC Park, Pittsburgh—April 9, 2001—Cincinnati N.L. 8, Pittsburgh 2.

At Great American Ball Park, Cincinnati—March 31, 2003—Pittsburgh N.L. 10, Cincinnati 1.

First Sunday game

A.A.—At. Louisville—May 7, 1882, Louisville 10, St. Louis 3.

N.L.—At St. Louis—April 17, 1892, Cincinnati 5, St. Louis 1.

A.L.—At Detroit—April 28, 1901, Detroit 12, Milwaukee 11.
  At Chicago, A.L.—April 28, 1901, Chicago 13, Cleveland 1.

First night game

At Cincinnati—May 24, 1935, Cincinnati 2, Philadelphia 1.

By Pittsburgh (at Cincinnati)—May 31, 1935, Pittsburgh 4, Cincinnati 1.

By Chicago N.L. (at Cincinnati)—July 1, 1935, Chicago 8, Cincinnati 4.

By Brooklyn (at Cincinnati)—July 10, 1935, Cincinnati 15, Brooklyn 2.

By Boston N.L. (at Cincinnati)—July 24, 1935, Cincinnati 5, Boston 4.

By St. Louis N.L. (at Cincinnati)—July 31, 1935, Cincinnati 4, St. Louis 3, 10 innings.

At Brooklyn—June 15, 1938, Cincinnati 6, Brooklyn 0.

At Philadelphia A.L.—May 16, 1939, Cleveland 8, Philadelphia 3, 10 innings.

By Chicago A.L. (at Philadelphia)—May 24, 1939, Chicago 4, Philadelphia 1.

At Philadelphia N.L.—June 1, 1939, Pittsburgh 5, Philadelphia 2.

By St. Louis A.L. (at Philadelphia)—June 14, 1939, St. Louis 6, Philadelphia 0.

By Detroit (at Philadelphia)—June 20, 1939, Detroit 5, Philadelphia 0.

By New York A.L. (at Philadelphia)—June 26, 1939, Philadelphia 3, New York 2.

At Cleveland—June 27, 1939, Cleveland 5, Detroit 0.

By Washington (at Philadelphia)—July 6, 1939, Philadelphia 9, Washington 3.

At Chicago A.L.—August 14, 1939, Chicago 5, St. Louis 2.

By Boston A.L. (at Cleveland)—July 13, 1939, Boston 6, Cleveland 5, 10 innings.

At New York N.L.—May 24, 1940, New York 8, Boston 1.

By New York N.L.—May 24, 1940, New York 8, Boston 1.

At St. Louis A.L.—May 24, 1940, Cleveland 3, St. Louis 2.

At Pittsburgh—June 4, 1940, Pittsburgh 14, Boston 2.

At St. Louis N.L.—June 4, 1940, Brooklyn 10, St. Louis 1.

At Washington—May 28, 1941, New York 6, Washington 5.

At Boston N.L.—May 11, 1946, New York 5, Boston 1.

At New York A.L.—May 28, 1946, Washington 2, New York 1.

At Boston A.L.—June 13, 1947, Boston 5, Chicago 3.

At Detroit—June 15, 1948, Detroit 4, Philadelphia 1.

By Milwaukee N.L. (at St. Louis)—April 20, 1953, St. Louis 9, Milwaukee 4.

At Milwaukee N.L.—May 8, 1953, Milwaukee 2, Chicago 0.

At Baltimore—April 21, 1954, Cleveland 2, Baltimore 1.

At Kansas City—April 18, 1955, Cleveland 11, Kansas City 9.

At San Francisco—April 16, 1958, Los Angeles 13, San Francisco 1.

At Los Angeles N.L.—April 22, 1958, Los Angeles 4, Chicago 2.

By Minnesota—April 14, 1961, Minnesota 3, Baltimore 2.

At Minnesota—May 18, 1961, Kansas City 4, Minnesota 3.

At Los Angeles A.L.—April 28, 1961, Los Angeles 6, Minnesota 5, 12 innings.

At Houston—April 11, 1962, Houston 2, Chicago 0.

At Atlanta—April 12, 1966, Pittsburgh 3, Atlanta 2, 13 innings.

At Oakland—April 17, 1968, Baltimore 4, Oakland 1.

At San Diego—April 8, 1969, San Diego 2, Houston 1.

By Seattle—April 8, 1969, Seattle 4, California 3.

By Montreal—April 17, 1969, Montreal 7, Philadelphia 0.

At Seattle—April 12, 1969, Seattle 5, Chicago 1.

At Montreal—April 30, 1969, New York 2, Montreal 1.

By Milwaukee A.L.—April 13, 1970, Oakland 2, Milwaukee 1.

At Milwaukee A.L.—May 5, 1970, Boston 6, Milwaukee 0.

At Texas—April 21, 1972, Texas 7, California 6.

At Toronto—May 2, 1977, Milwaukee 3, Toronto 1.

At Chicago N.L.—August 9, 1988, Chicago 6, New York 4.

At Florida—April 6, 1993, Los Angeles 4, Florida 2.

At Colorado—April 13, 1993, New York 8, Colorado 4.

At Tampa Bay—March 31, 1998, Detroit 11, Tampa Bay 6.

At Arizona—March 31, 1998, Colorado 9, Arizona 2.

First night opening game

N.L.—At St. Louis—April 18, 1950, St. Louis 4, Pittsburgh 2.

A.L.—At Philadelphia—April 17, 1951, Washington 6, Philadelphia 1.

First ladies day

N.L.—At Cincinnati, 1876 season.

A.L.—At St. Louis, 1912 season.

First ladies night

N.L.—At New York, June 27, 1941, New York 7, Philadelphia 4.

A.L.—At Boston, August 17, 1950, Boston 10, Philadelphia 6.

First day games completed with lights

N.L.—At Boston, April 23, 1950, second game, Philadelphia 6, Boston 5.

A.L.—At New York, August 29, 1950, New York 6, Cleveland 5.

First time all games played at night

(8-club leagues)—August 9, 1946 (4 in N.L., 4 in A.L.).

(12-club leagues)—April 25, 1969 (6 in N.L., 6 in A.L.).

First time all games were twi-night doubleheaders

N.L.—August 25, 1953.

First time uniforms were numbered
N.L.—Cincinnati, 1883 season.
A.L.—New York, 1929 season, complete (Cleveland vs. Chicago at Cleveland, June 26, 1916 wore numbers on the sleeves of their uniforms).

First team with 1,000,000 home attendance
A.L.—New York, 1920 (1,289,422).
N.L.—Chicago, 1927 (1,159,168).

First team with 2,000,000 home attendance
A.L.—New York, 1946 (2,265,512).
N.L.—Milwaukee, 1954 (2,131,388).

First team with 3,000,000 home attendance
N.L.—Los Angeles, 1978 (3,347,845).
A.L.—Minnesota, 1988 (3,030,672).

First team with 4,000,000 home attendance
A.L.—Toronto, 1991 (4,001,527).
N.L.—Colorado, 1993 (4,483,350).

NIGHT GAMES AND POSTPONEMENTS

Most night games, season (includes twilight games)
A.L.—135—Texas, 1979 (won 68, lost 67).
N.L.—127—Florida, 1993 (won 49, lost 78).

Most games postponed at start of season
A.L.—5—Chicago, April 6 through 10, 1982.
New York, April 6 through 10, 1982.
N.L.—4—New York, April 12 through 15, 1933.

Most consecutive games postponed, season
N.L.—9—Philadelphia, August 10 through 19, 1903.
A.L.—7—Detroit, May 14 through 18, 1945.
Philadelphia, May 14 through 18, 1945.
Washington, April 23 through 29, 1952.

TIES AND ONE-RUN DECISIONS

Most tie games, season
A.L.—10—Detroit, 1904.
N.L.—9—St. Louis, 1911.

Fewest tie games, season
A.L.-N.L.—0—By all clubs in many seasons.
Last A.L. season—2002.
Last N.L. season—2003.

Most games decided by one run, season
A.L.—74—Chicago, 1968 (won 30, lost 44).
N.L.—75—Houston, 1971 (won 32, lost 43).

Fewest games decided by one run, season
A.L.—27—Cleveland, 1948 (won 9, lost 18).
N.L.—28—Brooklyn, 1949 (won 16, lost 12).

LENGTH OF GAMES
BY INNINGS

Longest game
N.L.—26 innings—Brooklyn 1, Boston 1, May 1, 1920, at Boston.
A.L.—25 innings—Chicago 7, Milwaukee 6, May 8, finished May 9, 1984, at Chicago.

For a complete list of games of 18 or more innings, see page 207.

Longest night game
N.L.—25 innings—St. Louis 4, New York 3, September 11, 1974, at New York.
A.L.—25 innings—Chicago 7, Milwaukee 6, May 8, finished May 9, 1984, at Chicago.

Longest opening game
A.L.—15 innings—Washington 1, Philadelphia 0, April 13, 1926

at Washington.
Detroit 4, Cleveland 2, April 19, 1960, at Cleveland.
N.L.—14 innings—Philadelphia 5, Brooklyn 5, April 17, 1923, at Brooklyn.
New York 1, Brooklyn 1, April 16, 1933, at Brooklyn (opener for New York only).
Pittsburgh 4, Milwaukee 3, April 15, 1958, at Milwaukee.
Pittsburgh 6, St. Louis 2, April 8, 1969, at St. Louis.
Cincinnati 2, Los Angeles 1, April 7, 1975, at Cincinnati.
New York 1, Philadelphia 0, March 31, 1998, at New York.

Longest 0-0 game
N.L.—19 innings—Brooklyn vs. Cincinnati, September 11, 1946, at Brooklyn.
A.L.—18 innings—Detroit vs. Washington, July 16, 1909, at Detroit.

Longest 0-0 night game
N.L.—18 innings—Philadelphia vs. New York, October 2, 1965, second game, at New York.
A.L.—None.

Longest 1-0 day game
N.L.—18 innings—Providence 1, Detroit 0, August 17, 1882, at Providence.
New York 1, St. Louis 0, July 2, 1933, first game, at New York.
A.L.—18 innings—Washington 1, Chicago 0, May 15, 1918, at Washington.
Washington 1, Chicago 0, June 8, 1947, first game, at Chicago.

Longest 1-0 night game
N.L.—24 innings—Houston 1, New York 0, April 15, 1968, at Houston.
A.L.—20 innings—Oakland 1, California 0, July 9, 1971, at Oakland.

Longest shutout game
N.L.—24 innings—Houston 1, New York 0, April 15, 1968, at Houston.
A.L.—20 innings—Oakland 1, California 0, July 9, 1971, at Oakland.

Longest tie game
N.L.—26 innings—Boston 1, Brooklyn 1, May 1, 1920, at Boston.
A.L.—24 innings—Detroit 1, Philadelphia 1, July 21, 1945, at Philadelphia.

Most innings, one day
N.L.—32—San Francisco at New York, May 31, 1964.
A.L.—29—Boston at Philadelphia, July 4, 1905.
Boston at New York, August 29, 1967.

Most extra-inning games, season
A.L.—31—Boston, 1943 (won 15, lost 14, tied 2).
N.L.—27—Boston, 1943 (won 14, lost 13).
Los Angeles, 1967 (won 10, lost 17).

Most consecutive extra-inning games, one club
A.L.—5—Detroit, September 9 through 13, 1908 (54 innings).
N.L.—4—Pittsburgh, August 18 through 22, 1917 (59 innings).
San Francisco, July 7 through 10, 1987 (49 innings).

Most consecutive extra-inning games between same clubs
A.L.—4—Chicago and Detroit, September 9 through 12, 1908 (43 innings).
Cleveland and St. Louis, May 1, 2, 4, 5, 1910 (46 innings).
Boston and St. Louis, May 31, first game, to June 2, second game, 1943 (45 innings).
N.L.—4—New York and Pittsburgh, May 24, 25, June 23, 24, 1978 (44 innings; both clubs played other teams between these contests).
N.L.—3—Brooklyn and Pittsburgh, August 20, 21, 22, 1917 (45 innings).
Chicago and Pittsburgh, August 18, 19, 20, 1961 (33 innings).
Cincinnati and New York, May 5, 6, 7, 1980 (36 innings).

Most innings, two consecutive extra-inning games
N.L.—45—Boston, May 1 (26), 3 (19), 1920.
A.L.—37—Minnesota vs. Milwaukee May 12 (22), May 13 (15), 1972.

Most innings between same clubs, two consecutive extra-inning games
N.L.—40—Boston and Chicago, May 14 (18), May 17 (22), 1927.
A.L.—37—Minnesota and Milwaukee, May 12 (22), May 13 (15), 1972.

Most innings, three consecutive extra-inning games
N.L.—58—Brooklyn, May 1 through 3, 1920.
A.L.—41—Cleveland, April 16 through 21, 1935.
Boston, April 8 through 11, 1969.

Most innings between same clubs, three consecutive extra-inning games
N.L.—45—Brooklyn and Pittsburgh, August 20 through 22, 1917.
A.L.—40—Chicago and Washington, August 24 through 26, 1915.
Detroit and Philadelphia, May 12 through 14, 1943.

Most innings, four consecutive extra-inning games
N.L.—59—Pittsburgh, August 18 through 22, 1917.
A.L.—51—Chicago, August 23 through 26, 1915.
Detroit, May 11, second game, through May 14, 1943.

Most innings between same clubs, four consecutive extra-inning games
A.L.—46—Cleveland and St. Louis, May 1, 2, 4, 5, 1910.
N.L.—No performance.

BY TIME

Longest nine-inning game
N.L.—4 hours, 27 minutes—Los Angeles 11, San Francisco 10, October 5, 2001.
A.L.—4 hours, 22 minutes—Baltimore 13, New York 9, September 5, 1997.

Longest extra-inning game
A.L.—8 hours, 6 minutes—Chicago 7, Milwaukee 6, May 8, finished May 9, 1984, 25 innings.
N.L.—7 hours, 23 minutes—San Francisco 8, New York 6, May 31, 1964, second game, 23 innings.

Longest nine-inning 1-0 game
A.L.—3 hours, 20 minutes—Milwaukee 1, Oakland 0, May 7, 1997.
Interleague—3 hours, 16 minutes—Anaheim A.L. 1, Los Angeles N.L. 0, June 8, 2001.
N.L.—3 hours, 7 minutes—New York 1, San Diego 0, May 17, 1988.

Longest extra-inning 1-0 game
N.L.—6 hours, 14 minutes—Los Angeles 1, Montreal 0, August 23, 1989, 22 innings.
A.L.—5 hours, 5 minutes—Oakland 1, California 0, July 9, 1971, 20 innings.

Longest extra-inning 1-0 night game
N.L.—6 hours, 14 minutes—Los Angeles 1, Montreal 0, August 23, 1989, 22 innings.
A.L.—5 hours, 5 minutes—Oakland 1, California 0, July 9, 1971, 20 innings.

Longest nine-inning night game
N.L.—4 hours, 27 minutes—Los Angeles 11, San Francisco 10, October 5, 2001.
A.L.—4 hours, 22 minutes—Baltimore 13, New York 9, September 5, 1997.

Longest extra-inning night game
A.L.—8 hours, 6 minutes—Chicago 7, Milwaukee 6, at Chicago, May 8, finished May 9, 1984, 25 innings.
N.L.—7 hours, 14 minutes—Houston 5, Los Angeles 4, at Houston, June 3, 1989, 22 innings.

Longest doubleheader (18 innings)
A.L.—7 hours, 39 minutes—Texas at Chicago, May 24, 1995.
N.L.—6 hours, 46 minutes—Brooklyn at New York, August 7, 1952.

Longest doubleheader (more than 18 innings)
N.L.—9 hours, 52 minutes—San Francisco at New York, May 31, 1964, 32 innings.
A.L.—9 hours, 5 minutes—Kansas City at Detroit, June 17, 1967, 28 innings.

Shortest nine-inning game
N.L.—51 minutes—New York 6, Philadelphia 1, September 28, first game, 1919.
A.L.—55 minutes—St. Louis 6, New York 2, September 26, second game, 1926.

Shortest nine-inning night game
N.L.—1 hour, 15 minutes—Boston 2, Cincinnati 0, August 10, 1944.
A.L.—1 hour, 29 minutes—Chicago 1, Washington 0, May 21, 1943.

Shortest 1-0 game
N.L.—57 minutes—New York 1, Brooklyn 0, August 30, 1918.
A.L.—1 hour, 13 minutes—Detroit 1, New York 0, August 8, 1920.

Shortest doubleheader (18 innings)
A.L.—2 hours, 7 minutes—New York at St. Louis, September 26, 1926.
N.L.—2 hours, 20 minutes—Chicago at Brooklyn, August 14, 1919.

GAMES WON

Most games won, league
N.L.—9,756—Chicago, 129 years, 1876 through 2004.
A.L.—8,979—New York, 102 years, 1903 through 2004.

For a complete list of franchise won-lost records, see page 201.

Most games won, season
N.L.—116—Chicago, 1906 (lost 36).
A.L.—116—Seattle, 2001 (lost 46).

For a complete list of clubs with 100 or more victories in a season, see page 202.

Fewest games won, season
N.L.—20—Cleveland, 1899 (lost 134).
N.L. since 1900—38—Boston, 1935 (lost 115).
A.L.—36—Philadelphia, 1916 (lost 117).

Most games won, two consecutive seasons
N.L.—223—Chicago, 1906, 1907 (lost 81).
A.L.—217—Baltimore, 1969, 1970 (lost 107).

Most games won, three consecutive seasons
N.L.—322—Chicago, 1906, 1907, 1908 (lost 130).
A.L.—318—Baltimore, 1969, 1970, 1971 (lost 164).

Most years winning 100 or more games
A.L.—18—New York, 1927, 1928, 1932, 1936, 1937, 1939, 1941, 1942, 1954, 1961, 1963, 1977, 1978, 1980, 1998, 2002, 2003, 2004.
N.L.—8—Boston/Milwaukee/Atlanta, 1892, 1898 in Boston, none in Milwaukee; 1993, 1997, 1998, 1999, 2002, 2003 in Atlanta.

Most consecutive years winning 100 or more games
A.L.—3—Philadelphia, 1929, 1930, 1931.
Baltimore, 1969, 1970, 1971.
New York, 2002, 2003, 2004.
N.L.—3—St. Louis, 1942, 1943, 1944.
Atlanta, 1997, 1998, 1999.

Most games won at home, season
A.L.—65—New York, 1961 (lost 16).
N.L.—64—Cincinnati, 1975 (lost 17).

Most games won on road, season
N.L.—60—Chicago, 1906 (lost 15).
A.L.—59—Seattle, 2001 (lost 22).

Most games won from one club, season
N.L. (8 clubs)—21—Chicago vs. Boston, 1909 (lost 1).
Pittsburgh vs. Cincinnati, 1937 (lost 1).
Chicago vs. Cincinnati, 1945 (lost 1).
N.L. (12 clubs)—17—Atlanta vs. San Diego, 1974 (lost 1).
New York vs. Pittsburgh, 1986 (lost 1).

A.L. (8 clubs)—21—New York vs. St. Louis, 1927 (lost 1).
A.L. (12 clubs)—15—Baltimore vs. Milwaukee, 1973 (lost 3).

Most games won from one club at home
N.L.—16—Brooklyn vs. Pittsburgh, 1890 (lost 2).
 Philadelphia vs. Pittsburgh, 1890 (lost 1).
N.L. since 1900—13—New York vs. Philadelphia, 1904 (lost 2).
A.L.—12—Chicago vs. St. Louis, 1915 (lost 0).

Most games won from one club on road
N.L. (8 clubs)—11—Pittsburgh vs. St. Louis, 1908 (lost 0).
 Chicago vs. Boston, 1909 (lost 0).
 Brooklyn vs. Philadelphia, 1945 (lost 0).
A.L. (8 clubs)—11—Chicago vs. Philadelphia, 1915 (lost 0).
 New York vs. St. Louis, 1927 (lost 0).
 New York vs. St. Louis, 1939 (lost 0).
 Cleveland vs. Boston, 1954 (lost 0).

Most games won by one run, season
N.L.—42—San Francisco, 1978 (lost 26).
A.L.—40—Baltimore, 1970 (lost 15).
 Baltimore, 1974 (lost 21).

Fewest games won by one run, season
A.L.—9—Cleveland, 1948 (lost 18).
N.L.—9—New York, 1953 (lost 24).

Most games won from league champions, season
N.L.—16—St. Louis vs. Chicago, 1945 (lost 6).
A.L.—14—Philadelphia vs. Detroit, 1909 (lost 8).
 Minnesota vs. Oakland, 1973 (lost 4).

Most games won from one club, two consecutive seasons
N.L. (8 clubs)—40—Pittsburgh vs. St. Louis, 1907, 1908.
A.L. (8 clubs)—37—Philadelphia vs. St. Louis, 1910, 1911.
 Chicago vs. Philadelphia, 1915, 1916.
 New York vs. Philadelphia, 1919, 1920.
 New York vs. St. Louis, 1926, 1927.

Fewest games won from one club, season (excludes interleague games)
A.L.—0—Kansas City vs. Baltimore, 1970 (lost 12).
 Oakland vs. Baltimore, 1978 (lost 11).
 Baltimore vs. Kansas City, 1988 (lost 12).
 New York vs. Oakland, 1990 (lost 12).
 Detroit vs. Cleveland, 1996 (lost 12).
 Kansas City vs. New York, 1998 (lost 10).
 Minnesota vs. Texas, 1999 (lost 12).
 Kansas City vs. New York, 2001 (lost 6).
 Kansas City vs. Baltimore, 2002 (lost 7).
 Detroit vs. Toronto, 2002 (lost 6).
 Minnesota vs. New York, 2002 (lost 6).
 Minnesota vs. New York, 2003 (lost 7).
 Tampa Bay vs. Minnesota, 2003 (lost 6).
N.L.—0—Philadelphia vs. Boston, 1883 (lost 14).
 Buffalo vs. Chicago, 1885 (lost 16).
 Baltimore vs. Boston, 1892 (lost 13).
 Cleveland vs. Brooklyn, 1899 (lost 14).
 Cleveland vs. Cincinnati, 1899 (lost 14).
 Colorado vs. Atlanta, 1993 (lost 13; 14).
 San Diego vs. Montreal, 1994 (lost 12). (Note: Teams completed the schedule against each other. Los Angeles was 0-6 against Atlanta in 1994, but seven games were cancelled.)
 Florida vs. Cincinnati, 1998 (lost 9).
 Florida vs. Milwaukee, 1998 (lost 9).
 Florida vs. San Francisco, 1998 (lost 9).
 San Diego vs. St. Louis, 2000 (lost 9).
 Montreal vs. Houston, 2001 (lost 6).
 Cincinnati vs. Arizona, 2002 (lost 6).
 New York vs. San Francisco, 2002 (lost 6).
 Colorado vs. Atlanta, 2003 (lost 6).
 Milwaukee vs. Montreal, 2003 (lost 6).
 San Francisco vs. Montreal, 2003 (lost 7).
A.A.—1—Cleveland vs. St. Louis, 1887 (lost 18).
 Louisville vs. Brooklyn, 1889 (lost 19).

Most times winning two games in one day, season
N.L.—20—Chicago, 1945 (lost 3).

A.L.—15—Chicago, 1961 (lost 7).

Most times winning two games in one day, from one club, season
A.L.—7—Chicago vs. Philadelphia, 1943 (lost 0).
N.L.—7—Chicago vs. Cincinnati, 1945 (lost 0).

Fewest times winning two games in one day, season
A.L.-N.L.—0—Held by many clubs.

Most games won, one month
N.L.—29—New York, September, 1916 (lost 5).
A.L.—28—New York, August, 1938 (lost 8).

Most games won, two consecutive days
N.L.—5—Baltimore, September 7 (3), September 8 (2), 1896.
A.L.—4—Made on many days.

CONSECUTIVE

Most consecutive games won, season
N.L.—26—New York, September 7 through 30, first game, 1916 (1 tie).
A.L.—20—Oakland, August 13 through September 4, 2002.

For a complete list of clubs with 13 or more consecutive victories in a season, see page 204.

Most consecutive games won with no tie games, season
N.L.—21—Chicago, June 2 through July 8, 1880.
 Chicago, September 4 through 27, second game, 1935.
A.L.—20—Oakland, August 13 through September 4, 2002.

Most consecutive games won at start of season
U.A.—20—St. Louis, April 20 through May 22, 1884.
N.L.—13—Atlanta, April 6 through 21, 1982.
A.L.—13—Milwaukee, April 6 through 20, 1987.

For a complete list of clubs with eight or more consecutive victories at the start of a season, see page 206.

Most consecutive home games won, season
A.A.—27—St. Louis, April 26 through July 16, 1885.
N.L.—26—New York, September 7 through 30, first game, 1916 (1 tie).
A.L.—24—Boston, June 25 through August 13, 1988.

Most consecutive road games won, season
N.L.—17—New York, May 9 through 29, 1916.
A.L.—17—Detroit, April 3 through May 24, 1984 (start of season).

Most consecutive games won from one club, league
A.L. (12 clubs)—23—Baltimore vs. Kansas City, May 10, 1969 through August 2, 1970 (last 11 in 1969, all 12 in 1970).
N.L. (8 clubs)—22—Boston vs. Philadelphia, May 4, 1883 through June 3, 1884 (all 14 in 1883, first 8 in 1884).
N.L. since 1900 (8 clubs)—20—Pittsburgh vs. Cincinnati, May 31, second game, 1937 through April 24, 1938 (last 17 in 1937, first 3 in 1938).
A.L. (8 clubs)—22—Boston vs. Washington, August 31, 1903 through September 6, first game, 1904 (last 6 in 1903, first 16 in 1904).

Most consecutive games won from one club at home, league
N.L.—32—Baltimore vs. Louisville, June 7, 1894 through July 11, 1899 (last 6 in 1894, all 6 in 1895, 1896 and 1897, all 7 in 1898, first 1 in 1899).
N.L. since 1900—25—St. Louis vs. Cincinnati, April 27, 1929, second game through May 31, 1931, first game (last 9 in 1929, all 11 in 1930, first 5 in 1931).
A.L.—27—Cleveland vs. St. Louis/Baltimore, August 13, 1952, second game through August 15, 1954, second game (last 5 in 1952, all 11 in 1953 and 1954).

Most consecutive games won from one club on road, league
N.L.—18—Brooklyn vs. Philadelphia, May 5, first game, 1945

– 116 –

through August 10, 1946 (all 11 in 1945; first 7 in 1946).
St. Louis vs. Pittsburgh, May 7, 1964 through April 15, 1966 (last 8 in 1964, all 9 in 1965, first in 1966).
A.L.—18—Boston vs. New York, October 3, first game, 1911 through June 2, second game, 1913 (last 3 in 1911; all 10 in 1912; first 6, excluding one tie, in 1913).

Most consecutive doubleheaders won, season (no other games between)
A.L.—5—New York, August 30 through September 4, 1906.
N.L.—4—Brooklyn, September 1 through 4, 1924.
New York, September 10 through 14, 1928.

GAMES LOST

Most games lost, league
N.L.—9,805—Philadelphia, 122 years, 1883 through 2004.
A.L.—7,959—Detroit, 104 years, 1901 through 2004.

For a complete list of franchise won-lost records, see page 201.

Most games lost, season
N.L.—134—Cleveland, 1899 (won 20).
N.L. since 1900—120—New York, 1962 (won 40).
A.L.—119—Detroit, 2003 (won 43).

For a complete list of clubs with 100 or more games lost in a season, see page 203.

Most games lost, two consecutive seasons
N.L.—231—New York, 1962, 1963 (won 91).
A.L.—226—Philadelphia, 1915, 1916 (won 79).

Most games lost, three consecutive seasons
N.L.—340—New York, 1962 through 1964 (won 144).
A.L.—324—Philadelphia, 1915 through 1917 (won 134).

Most years losing 100 or more games
A.L.—15—Philadelphia/Kansas City, 1915, 1916, 1919, 1920, 1921, 1936, 1940, 1943, 1946, 1950, 1954 in Philadelphia, 1956, 1961, 1964, 1965 in Kansas City.
N.L.—14—Philadelphia, 1904, 1921, 1923, 1927, 1928, 1930, 1936, 1938, 1939, 1940, 1941, 1942, 1945, 1961.

Most consecutive years losing 100 or more games
N.L.—5—Philadelphia, 1938 through 1942.
A.L.—4—Washington, 1961 through 1964.

Most night games lost, season
A.L.—83—Seattle, 1980 (won 44).
N.L.—82—Atlanta, 1977 (won 43).

Most games lost at home, season
A.L.—59—St. Louis, 1939 (won 18).
N.L.—58—New York, 1962 (won 22).

Most games lost on road, season
N.L.—102—Cleveland, 1899 (won 11).
N.L. since 1900—65—Boston, 1935 (won 13).
A.L.—64—Philadelphia, 1916 (won 13).

Most games lost by one run, season
A.L.—44—Chicago, 1968 (won 30).
N.L.—43—Houston, 1971 (won 32).

Fewest games lost by one run, season
A.L.—10—Boston, 1986 (won 24).
New York, 1998 (won 21).
N.L.—12—Brooklyn, 1949 (won 16).
San Francisco, 2003 (won 28).

Most times losing two games in one day, season
N.L.—19—Chicago, 1950 (won 4).
A.L.—18—Philadelphia, 1943 (won 4).

Fewest times losing two games in one day, season
N.L.-A.L.—0—Held by many clubs.

Most games lost, one month
A.L.—29—Washington, July, 1909 (won 5).
N.L.—27—Pittsburgh, August, 1890 (won 1).
Cleveland, September, 1899 (won 1).
St. Louis, September, 1908 (won 7).
Brooklyn, September, 1908 (won 6).
Philadelphia, September, 1939 (won 6).

Most games lost, two consecutive days
N.L.—5—Louisville, September 7 (3), September 8 (2), 1896.
A.L.—4—Made on many days.

CONSECUTIVE

Most consecutive games lost, season
A.A.—26—Louisville, May 22 through June 22, second game, 1889.
N.L.—24—Cleveland, August 26 through September 16, 1899.
N.L. since 1900—23—Philadelphia, July 29 through August 20, first game, 1961.
A.L.—21—Baltimore, April 4 through 28, 1988.

For a complete list of clubs with 13 or more consecutive games lost in a season, see page 205.

Most consecutive games lost at start of season
A.L.—21—Baltimore, April 4 through 28, 1988.
N.L.—14—Chicago, April 1 through 20, first game, 1997.

For a complete list of clubs with eight or more consecutive games lost at the start of a season, see page 206.

Most consecutive home games lost, season
A.L.—20—St. Louis, June 3 through July 7, 1953.
N.L.—14—Boston, May 8 through 24, 1911.

Most consecutive road games lost, season
N.L.—41—Pittsburgh, July 18 through September 12, second game, 1890.
N.L. since 1900—22—New York, June 16, first game, through July 28, 1963.
A.L.—19—Philadelphia, July 25 through August 8, 1916.

Most consecutive games lost to one club, league
A.L. (12 clubs)—23—Kansas City vs. Baltimore, May 9, 1969 through August 2, 1970; last 11 in 1969, all 12 in 1970.
A.L. (8 clubs)—22—Washington vs. Boston, August 31, 1903 through September 6, first game, 1904; last 6 in 1903, first 16 in 1904.
N.L. (8 clubs)—22—Philadelphia vs. Boston, May 4, 1883 through June 3, 1884; all 14 in 1883, first 8 in 1884.
N.L. since 1900 (8 clubs)—20—Cincinnati vs. Pittsburgh, May 31, second game, 1937 through April 24, 1938; last 17 in 1937, first 3 in 1938.

Most consecutive doubleheaders lost, season (no other games between)
N.L.—5—Boston, September 8 through 14, 1928.
A.L.—4—Boston, June 29 through July 5, 1921.

WINNING PERCENTAGE
HIGHEST

Highest percentage games won, season
U.A.—.850—St. Louis, 1884 (won 91, lost 16).
N.L.—.798—Chicago, 1880 (won 67, lost 17).
N.L. since 1900—.763—Chicago, 1906 (won 116, lost 36).
A.L.—.721—Cleveland, 1954 (won 111, lost 43).

Highest percentage games won, season, for league champions since 1969
A.L.—.704—New York, 1998 (won 114, lost 48).
N.L.—.667—Cincinnati, 1975 (won 108, lost 54).
New York, 1986 (won 108, lost 54).

LOWEST

Lowest percentage games won, season
N.L.—.130—Cleveland, 1899 (won 20, lost 134).
N.L. since 1900—.248—Boston, 1935 (won 38, lost 115).
A.L.—.235—Philadelphia, 1916 (won 36, lost 117).

Lowest percentage games won, pennant winner, through 1968
N.L.—.564—Los Angeles, 1959 (won 88, lost 68).
A.L.—.568—Boston, 1967 (won 92, lost 70).

Lowest percentage games won, league champion, since 1969
N.L.—.509—New York, 1973 (won 82, lost 79).
A.L.—.525—Minnesota, 1987 (won 85, lost 77).

CHAMPIONSHIPS

Most championships won, club
A.L.—39—New York, 1921, 1922, 1923, 1926, 1927, 1928, 1932, 1936, 1937, 1938, 1939, 1941, 1942, 1943, 1947, 1949, 1950, 1951, 1952, 1953, 1955, 1956, 1957, 1958, 1960, 1961, 1962, 1963, 1964, 1976, 1977, 1978, 1981, 1996, 1998, 1999, 2000, 2001, 2003.
N.L.—21—Brooklyn/Los Angeles, 1890, 1899, 1900, 1916, 1920, 1941, 1947, 1949, 1952, 1953, 1955, 1956 in Brooklyn, 1959, 1963, 1965, 1966, 1974, 1977, 1978, 1981, 1988 in Los Angeles.
N.L. since 1900—19—Brooklyn/Los Angeles, 1900, 1916, 1920, 1941, 1947, 1949, 1952, 1953, 1955, 1956 in Brooklyn, 1959, 1963, 1965, 1966, 1974, 1977, 1978, 1981, 1988 in Los Angeles.

Most consecutive championships won, club
A.L.—5—New York, 1949, 1950, 1951, 1952, 1953.
New York, 1960, 1961, 1962, 1963, 1964.
A.A.—4—St. Louis, 1885, 1886, 1887, 1888.
N.L.—4—New York, 1921, 1922, 1923, 1924.

Most consecutive years without winning championship, league
N.L.—58—Chicago, 1946 through 2003.
A.L.—44—Chicago, 1960 through 2003.

Most consecutive years with first-division finishes, through 1968
A.L.—39—New York, 1926 through 1964.
N.L.—14—Chicago, 1878 through 1891.
Pittsburgh, 1900 through 1913.
Chicago, 1926 through 1939.

LAST-PLACE AND SECOND-DIVISION FINISHES

Most times finished in overall last place, league
A.L.—26—Philadelphia/Kansas City/Oakland, 1915, 1916, 1917, 1918, 1919, 1920, 1921, 1935, 1936, 1938, 1940, 1941, 1942, 1943, 1945, 1946, 1950, 1954 in Philadelphia, 1956, 1960, 1961 (tied), 1964, 1965, 1967 in Kansas City, 1993, 1997 in Oakland.
N.L.—27—Philadelphia, 1883, 1904, 1919, 1920, 1921, 1923, 1926, 1927, 1928, 1930, 1936, 1938, 1939, 1940, 1941, 1942, 1944, 1945, 1947 (tied), 1958, 1959, 1960, 1961, 1972, 1996, 1997, 2000 (tied).

Most consecutive last-place finishes, through 1968
A.L.—7—Philadelphia, 1915 through 1921.
N.L.—5—Philadelphia, 1938 through 1942.

Most consecutive times with lowest winning percentage, through 1968
A.L.—7—Philadelphia, 1915 through 1921.
N.L.—5—Philadelphia, 1938 through 1942.

Most consecutive years with second-division finishes, through 1968
N.L.—20—Chicago, 1947 through 1966.
A.L.—16—Philadelphia/Kansas City/Oakland, 1953 through 1968.

Most consecutive years without lowest winning percentage, season
N.L.—86—Brooklyn/Los Angeles, 1906 through 1991.
A.L.—72—Boston, 1933 through 2004.

GAMES FINISHED AHEAD AND BEHIND

Best gain in games from previous season, pennant winner
A.A.—64 games—Louisville, 1889 to 1890
1889—won 27, lost 111, .196, 8th place
1890—won 88, lost 44, .667
N.L.—41.5 games—Brooklyn, 1898 to 1899*
1898—won 54, lost 91, .372, 10th place
1899—won 88, lost 42, .677 (*some sources list 1899 record as 101-47, but N.L. president threw out 18 Brooklyn games for using an illegal player)
N.L. (12 clubs)—29 games—Atlanta, 1990 to 1991
1990—won 65, lost 97, .401, 6th place
1991—won 94, lost 68, .580
N.L. (8-clubs)—27 games—New York, 1953 to 1954
1953—won 70, lost 84, .455, 5th place
1954—won 97, lost 57, .630
A.L. (8-clubs)—33 games—Boston, 1945 to 1946
1945—won 71, lost 83, .461, 7th place
1946—won 104, lost 50, .675

Best gain in games by any club from previous season
A.A.—64—Louisville, 1889 to 1890
1889—won 27, lost 111, .196, 8th place
1890—won 88, lost 44, .667, 1st place
N.L.—41.5—Brooklyn, 1898 to 1899*
1898—won 54, lost 91, .372, 10th place
1899—won 88, lost 42, .677, 1st place (*some sources list 1899 record as 101-47, but N.L. president threw out 18 Brooklyn games for using an illegal player)
N.L. since 1900 (8-clubs)—34.5—New York, 1902 to 1903
1902—won 48, lost 88, .353, 8th place
1903—won 84, lost 55, .604, 2nd place
N.L. (10-clubs)—27.5—Chicago, 1966 to 1967
1966—won 59, lost 103, .364, 10th place
1967—won 87, lost 74, .540, 3rd place
N.L. (12-clubs)—29—Atlanta, 1990 to 1991
1990—won 65, lost 97, .401, 6th place
1991—won 94, lost 68, .580, 1st place
N.L. (14-clubs)—31—San Francisco, 1992 to 1993
1992—won 72, lost 90, .444, 5th place
1993—won 103, lost 59, .636, 2nd place
N.L. (16-clubs)—35—Arizona, 1998 to 1999
1998—won 65, lost 97, .401, 5th place
1999—won 100, lost 62, .617, 1st place
A.L.—33—Boston, 1945 to 1946
1945—won 71, lost 83, .461, 7th place
1946—won 104, lost 50, .675, 1st place

Best gain in position from previous season, any club, through 1968
N.L.—10th to 1st—Brooklyn, 1898 to 1899*
1898—won 54, lost 91, .372, 41.5 games behind
1899—won 88, lost 42, .677 (*some sources list 1899 record as 101-47, but N.L. president threw out 18 Brooklyn games for using an illegal player)
N.L. since 1900 (8-clubs)—7th to 1st—Los Angeles, 1958 to 1959
1958—won 71, lost 83, .461, 16 games behind
1959—won 88, lost 68, .564
N.L. (12-clubs)—9th to 1st—New York, 1968 to 1969
1968—won 73, lost 89, .451, 27 games behind
1969—won 100, lost 62, .617
A.A.—8th to 1st—Louisville, 1889 to 1890

1889—won 27, lost 111, .196, 64 games behind
1890—won 88, lost 44, .667
A.L. (8-clubs)—7th to 1st—New York, 1925 to 1926
  1925—won 69, lost 85, .448, 22 games behind
  1926—won 91, lost 63, .591
  Boston, 1945 to 1946
  1945—won 71, lost 83, .461, 33 games behind
  1946—won 104, lost 50, .675
A.L. (10-clubs)—9th to 1st—Boston, 1966 to 1967
  1966—won 72, lost 90, .444, 20 games behind
  1967—won 92, lost 70, .568

Most games leading league or division at end of season
A.L.—30—Cleveland, 1995.
N.L.—27.5—Pittsburgh, 1902.

Fewest games leading league or division at end of season (before any playoff)
N.L.—0—St. Louis and Brooklyn, 1946 (8-club league).
  New York and Brooklyn, 1951 (8-club league).
  Los Angeles and Milwaukee, 1959 (8-club league).
  San Francisco and Los Angeles, 1962 (10-club league).
  Houston and Los Angeles, 1980 (12-club league).
  Houston and St. Louis, 2001 (16-club league).
A.L.—0—Cleveland and Boston, 1948 (8-club league).
  New York and Boston, 1978 (14-club league).

Largest lead (in games) for pennant winner on July 4, p.m., through 1968
N.L.—14.5—New York, 1912.
A.L.—12—New York, 1928.

Most games behind, eventual pennant winner, on July 4, p.m., through 1968
N.L.—15—Boston, 1914 (8th place).
A.L.—6.5—Detroit, 1907 (4th place).

Most games behind pennant winner, last-place club, through 1968
N.L. (12-club league)—80—Cleveland, 1899.
N.L. since 1900 (8-club league)—66.5—Boston, 1906.
A.L. (8-club league)—64.5—St. Louis, 1939.

Fewest games behind pennant winner, last-place club, through 1968
N.L. (8-club league)—21—New York, 1915.
A.L. (8-club league)—25—Washington, 1944. (24
  Philadelphia in shortened 1918 season)

Most games behind Eastern Division leader, last-place club, since 1969
N.L.—52—Florida, 1998.
A.L.—51—Tampa Bay, 1998.

Most games behind Central Division leader, last-place club, since 1994
A.L.—47—Detroit, 2003.
N.L.—41—Milwaukee, 2002.

Most games behind Western Division leader, last-place club, since 1969
N.L.—43.5—Houston, 1975.
A.L.—43—Texas, 2001.

Fewest games behind Eastern Division leader, last-place club, since 1969
N.L.—11.5—Philadelphia, 1973.
A.L.—17—Toronto, 1982.
  Cleveland, 1982.

Fewest games behind Central Division leader, last-place club, since 1994
N.L.—15—Pittsburgh, 1996.
A.L.—19—Kansas City, 1997 (15—Milwaukee in shortened 1994 season)

Western Division leader, last-place club, since 1969
A.L.—10—California, 1987.
  Texas, 1987.
N.L.—19.5—San Diego, 1980.

PENNANT-CLINCHING DATES

Fewest games played before clinching pennant
A.L.—136—New York, September 4, 1941 (won 91, lost 45, .669).
N.L.—137—New York, September 22, 1904 (won 100, lost 37, .730).

Earliest date for pennant clinching, through 1968
A.L.—September 4, 1941—New York (won 91, lost 45, .669, 136th game).
N.L.—September 8, 1955—Brooklyn (won 92, lost 46, .667, 138th game).

Earliest date for Western Division pennant clinching, since 1969
A.L.—September 15, 1971, first game—Oakland (won 94, lost 55, .631, 148th game).
N.L.—September 7, 1975—Cincinnati (won 95, lost 47, .669, 142nd game).

Earliest date for Eastern Division pennant clinching, since 1969
A.L.—September 13, 1969—Baltimore (won 101, lost 45, .690, 146th game).
N.L.—September 17, 1986—New York (won 95, lost 50, .655, 145th game).

DAYS IN FIRST PLACE

Leading or tied for first place for entire season
A.L.—New York, 1927.
  Detroit (East), 1984.
  Baltimore (East), 1997.
  Cleveland (Central), 1998.
  Seattle (West), 2001.
N.L.—New York, 1923.
  Brooklyn Dodgers, 1955.
  Cincinnati Reds (West), 1990.
  San Francisco (West), 2003.

Fewest days in first place, season, for pennant winner, through 1968
N.L.—3—New York, 1951 (before playoff).
A.L.—20—Boston, 1967 (6 days alone).

ATTENDANCE

Highest home attendance, season
N.L.—4,483,350—Colorado, 1993.
A.L.—4,057,947—Toronto, 1993

For a complete list of clubs with 3,200,000 or higher home attendance, see page 206.

Highest road attendance, season
N.L.—3,016,074—Cincinnati, 2000.
A.L.—2,940,048—New York, 2002.

Largest crowd, day game
N.L.—80,227—Montreal at Colorado, April 9, 1993 (home opener).
A.L.—74,420—Detroit at Cleveland, April 7, 1973 (home opener).

Largest crowd, night game
A.L.—78,382—Chicago at Cleveland, August 20, 1948.
N.L.—72,208—San Francisco at Colorado, July 31, 1993.

Largest crowd, doubleheader
A.L.—84,587—New York at Cleveland, September 12, 1954.
N.L.—72,140—Cincinnati at Los Angeles, August 16, 1961.

Largest crowd, opening day
N.L.—80,227—Montreal at Colorado, April 9, 1993.
A.L.—74,420—Detroit at Cleveland, April 7, 1973.

LEAGUE MISCELLANEOUS

NIGHT GAMES

Most night games, season

A.L. (14-club league)—822 in 1982.
A.L. (12-club league)—661 in 1976.
A.L. (10-club league)—472 in 1965.
N.L. (12-club league)—799 in 1983.
N.L. (10-club league)—487 in 1968.
Note: N.L. had record of 864-876 in night games (including interleague games) in 1998.

Most night games in both leagues, season

1,675 in 1998 (16-club N.L.; 14-club A.L.; includes interleague games).
1,530 in 1993 (14-club leagues; 765 in A.L., 765 in N.L.).
1,432 in 1983 (14-club A.L.; 12-club N.L.; 633 in A.L., 799 in N.L.).
1,274 in 1975 (12-club leagues; 651 in A.L., 623 in N.L.).
960 in 1968 (10-club leagues; 487 in N.L., 473 in A.L.).

CANCELED AND POSTPONED GAMES

Most unplayed games, season (since 1900, except 1918)

A.L.—19 in 1901.
N.L.—14 in 1938.

Fewest unplayed scheduled games, season (since 1900)

N.L.-A.L.—0—Made in many years.

Fewest unplayed games in both leagues, season

0 in 1930, 1947, 1949, 1951, 1954, 1956, 1959, 1960, 1964, 1972, 1982, 1983, 1992, 1993 (14 years).

Most postponed games, season

A.L. (8-club league)—97 in 1935.
N.L.—49
in 1956 (8-club league).
in 1967 (10-club league).

Fewest postponed dates, season

A.L.—15 in 1987.
N.L.—12 in 1987.

Most postponed doubleheaders, season

A.L.—14 in 1945.
N.L.—5 in 1959.

Fewest postponed doubleheaders, season

A.L.—0 in 1914, 1957.
N.L.—0 in 1961, 1966, 1970.

TIE GAMES

Most tie games, season

A.L.—19 in 1910.
N.L.—16 in 1913.

Most tie games, one day

N.L.—3, April 6, 1897.
A.L.—2, made on many days.

Fewest tie games, season

N.L.—0 in 1925, 1954, 1958, 1970, 1976, 1977, 1978, 1982, 1984, 1986, 1987, 1990, 1991, 1992, 1995, 1996, 1997, 1999, 2001, 2003 (20 years).
A.L.—0 in 1930, 1963, 1965, 1971, 1972, 1973, 1975, 1976, 1977, 1978, 1979, 1987, 1988, 1989, 1990, 1991, 1992, 1993, 1994, 1997, 2000, 2002 (22 years).

Most 0-0 games, season

A.L.—6 in 1904.
N.L.—3 in 1917.

EXTRA-INNING GAMES

Most extra-inning games, season

A.L. (14-club league)—117 in 1991.
A.L. (12-club league)—116 in 1976.
A.L. (10-club league)—91 in 1965.
A.L. (8-club league)—91 in 1943.
N.L. (12-club league)—116 in 1986.
N.L. (10-club league)—93 in 1967.
N.L. (8-club league)—86 in 1916.
Note: N.L. had record of 126-121 in extra-inning games (including interleague games) in 1998.

Most extra-inning games, one day

N.L.—5—May 30, 1892, May 11, 1988.
A.L.—4—June 11, 1969, June 4, 1976.

Most extra-inning games in both leagues, one day

6 on August 22, 1951; 3 in N.L. (five games), 3 in A.L. (five games).
6 on May 12, 1963; 4 in N.L. (eight games), 2 in A.L. (seven games).
6 on May 11, 1988; 5 in N.L. (six games), 1 in A.L. (six games).

100- AND 90-WIN AND LOSS SEASONS

Most clubs winning 100 or more games, season

A.L. (14-club league)—2 in 1977, 1980, 2001, 2002.
A.L. (12-club league)—2 in 1971.
A.L. (10-club league)—2 in 1961.
A.L. (8-club league)—2 in 1915, 1954.
N.L. (16-club league)—2 in 1998, 1999, 2003.
N.L. (14-club league)—2 in 1993.
N.L. (12-club league)—2 in 1976.
N.L. (10-club league)—2 in 1962.
N.L. (8-club league)—2 in 1909, 1942.

For a complete list of clubs with 100 or more victories in a season, see page 202.

Most clubs winning 90 or more games, season

A.L. (14-club league)—6 in 1977, 2002.
A.L. (12-club league)—4 in 1975.
A.L. (8-club league)—4 in 1950.
N.L. (16-club league)—5 in 1999, 2002.
N.L. (14-club league)—4 in 1993.
N.L. (12-club league)—4 in 1969, 1976, 1980, 1987.
N.L. (10-club league)—4 in 1962, 1964.
N.L. (8-club league)—3 in many seasons.

Most clubs losing 100 or more games, season

A.L. (14-club league)—3 in 2002.
A.L. (10-club league)—2 in 1961, 1964, 1965.
A.L. (8-club league)—2 in 1912, 1932, 1949, 1954.
N.L. (16-club league—1 in 2001, 2002.
N.L. (14-club league)—2 in 1993.
N.L. (12-club league)—2 in 1969, 1985.
N.L. (10-club league)—2 in 1962.
N.L. (8-club league)—2 in 1898, 1905, 1908, 1923, 1938.

HOME AND ROAD VICTORIES

Most games won by home clubs, season

N.L. (16-club league)—720 in 2003 (lost 575; includes interleague games).
N.L. (14-club league)—641 in 1996 (lost 493).
N.L. (12-club league)—556 in 1978 (lost 415), 1980 (lost 416).
N.L. (10-club league)—464 in 1967 (lost 345).
N.L. (8-club league)—358 in 1931 (lost 256), 1955 (lost 257).
A.L. (14-club league)—649 in 1978 (lost 482).
A.L. (12-club league)—540 in 1969 (lost 431).
A.L. (10-club league)—454 in 1961 (lost 353).
A.L. (8-club league)—360 in 1945 (lost 244), 1949 (lost 256).

Most games won by home clubs, one day

N.L.-A.L. (8-club leagues)—8—Made on many days.

Most games won by home clubs in both leagues, one day

14 on May 30, 1903 (A.L. won 8, lost 0; N.L. won 6, lost 2).

Most games won by visiting clubs, season

N.L. (16-club league)—622 in 1999 (lost 674); 622 in 2004 (lost 673).
N.L. (14-club league)—532 in 1993 (lost 602).
N.L. (12-club league)—473 in 1982 (lost 499).
N.L. (10-club league)—400 in 1968 (lost 410).
N.L. (8-club league)—307 in 1948 (lost 308).
A.L. (14-club league)—547 in 1980 (lost 582).
A.L. (12-club league)—469 in 1971 (lost 497).
A.L. (10-club league)—391 in 1968 (lost 418).
A.L. (8-club league)—312 in 1953 (lost 301).

Most games won by visiting clubs, one day

N.L.-A.L. (8-club league)—8—Made on many days.

Most games won by visiting clubs in both leagues, one day

(8-club leagues)—12 on July 4, 1935 (N.L. won 7, lost 1; A.L. won 5, lost 3).
12 on August 5, 1951 (N.L. won 7, lost 0; A.L. won 5, lost 2).
12 on June 15, 1958 (A.L. won 8, lost 0; N.L. won 4, lost 1).

ONE-RUN DECISIONS

Most games won by one run, season

N.L. (16-club league)—413 in 1998.
N.L. (14-club league)—356 in 1993.
N.L. (12-club league)—346 in 1980.
N.L. (10-club league)—294 in 1968.
N.L. (8-club league)—223 in 1946.
A.L. (14-club league)—368 in 1978.
A.L. (12-club league)—332 in 1969.
A.L. (10-club league)—281 in 1967, 1968.
A.L. (8-club league)—217 in 1943.

Fewest games won by one run, season

A.L. (8-club league)—157 in 1938.
A.L. (12-club league)—279 in 1973.
A.L. (14-club league)—272 in 2003 (includes interleague games).
N.L. (8-club league)—170 in 1949.
N.L. (12-club league)—294 in 1970.
N.L. (14-club league)—351 in 1996.
N.L. (16-club league)—355 in 2001.

Most games won by one run, one day

A.L.—6—May 30, 1967 (10 games); August 22, 1967 (nine games).
N.L.—6—June 6, 1967 (seven games); June 8, 1969 (six games).

Most games won by one run both leagues, one day

10 on May 30, 1967, A.L. 6 (10 games), N.L. 4 (seven games)

ATTENDANCE

Highest attendance, season

N.L. (16-club league)—39,851,427 in 2000.
N.L. (14-club league)—36,923,856 in 1993.
N.L. (12-club league)—25,323,834 in 1989.
N.L. (10-club league)—15,015,471 in 1966.
N.L. (8-club league)—10,684,963 in 1960.
A.L. (14-club league)—33,332,603 in 1993.
A.L. (12-club league)—14,657,802 in 1976.
A.L. (10-club league)—11,336,923 in 1967.
A.L. (8-club league)—11,150,099 in 1948.

NON-PLAYING PERSONNEL

MANAGERS
INDIVIDUAL

Most years as manager

M.L.—53—Connie Mack, Pittsburgh N.L. (1894 through 1896), Philadelphia A.L. (1901 through 1950).
A.L.—50—Connie Mack, Philadelphia, 1901 through 1950.
N.L.—32—John McGraw, Baltimore, 1899; New York, 1902 through 1932.

Most clubs managed, career

M.L.—7—Frank Bancroft, Worcester N.L., Detroit N.L., Cleveland N.L., Providence N.L., Philadelphia A.A., Indianapolis N.L., Cincinnati N.L.
M.L. since 1900—6—Rogers Hornsby, St. Louis N.L., New York N.L., Boston N.L., Chicago N.L., St. Louis A.L., Cincinnati N.L.
Jimmie Dykes, Chicago A.L., Philadelphia A.L., Baltimore A.L., Cincinnati N.L., Detroit A.L., Cleveland A.L.
Dick Williams, Boston A.L., Oakland A.L., California A.L., Montreal N.L., San Diego N.L., Seattle A.L.

John McNamara, Oakland A.L., San Diego N.L., Cincinnati N.L., California A.L., Boston A.L., Cleveland A.L.
N.L.—6—Frank Bancroft, Worcester, Detroit, Cleveland, Providence, Indianapolis, Cincinnati.
N.L. since 1900—5—Rogers Hornsby, St. Louis, New York, Boston, Chicago, Cincinnati.
A.L.—5—Jimmie Dykes, Chicago, Philadelphia, Baltimore, Detroit, Cleveland.
Billy Martin, Minnesota, Detroit, Texas, New York, Oakland.

Most clubs managed in one season

U.A.—2—Ted Sullivan, St. Louis, Kansas City, 1884.
A.A.—2—Billy Barnie, Baltimore, Philadelphia, 1891.
N.L.—2—Leo Durocher, Brooklyn, New York, 1948.
Leo Durocher, Chicago, Houston, 1972.
A.L.—2—Jimmie Dykes, Detroit, Cleveland, 1960.
Joe Gordon, Cleveland, Detroit, 1960.
Billy Martin, Detroit, Texas, 1973.
Billy Martin, Texas, New York, 1975.
Bob Lemon, Chicago, New York, 1978.
Tony La Russa, Chicago, Oakland, 1986.

Most clubs managed in different major leagues, season

2—Joe Battin, 1884 (Pittsburgh A.A., Pittsburgh U.A.).
Bill Watkins, 1888 (Detroit N.L., Kansas City A.A.).
Gus Schmelz, 1890 (Cleveland N.L., Columbus A.A.).
John McGraw, 1902 (Baltimore A.L., New York N.L.).
Rogers Hornsby, 1952 (St. Louis A.L., Cincinnati N.L.).
Bill Virdon, 1975 (New York A.L., Houston N.L.).
Pat Corrales, 1983 (Philadelphia N.L., Cleveland A.L.).
Buck Rodgers, 1991 (Montreal N.L., California A.L.).

Most different times as manager for one major league club

A.L.—5—Billy Martin, New York, 1975 (part) through 1978
(part), 1979 (part), 1983 (complete), 1985 (part), 1988 (part).
N.L.—4—Danny Murtaugh, Pittsburgh, 1957 (part) through 1964;
1967 (part), 1970 through 1971, 1973 (part) through 1976.

Most years managing championship club, league

N.L.—10—John McGraw, New York, 1904, 1905, 1911, 1912,
1913, 1917, 1921, 1922, 1923, 1924.
A.L.—10—Casey Stengel, New York, 1949, 1950, 1951, 1952,
1953, 1955, 1956, 1957, 1958, 1960.

Most consecutive years as championship manager

A.L.—5—Casey Stengel, New York, 1949 through 1953 (first
five years as New York manager).
A.A.—4—Charlie Comiskey, St. Louis, 1885 through 1888.
N.L.—4—John McGraw, New York, 1921 through 1924.

Most years managed without winning championship, career

M.L.—26—Gene Mauch, Philadelphia N.L., 1960 to 1968;
Montreal N.L., 1969 through 1975; Minnesota A.L., 1976 to
1980; California A.L., 1981 through 1982, 1985 through 1987.
A.L.—20—Jimmie Dykes, Chicago, 1934 through 1946,
Philadelphia, 1951 through 1953, Baltimore, 1954, Detroit,
1959, 1960, Cleveland, 1960, 1961.
N.L.—16—Gene Mauch, Philadelphia, 1960 to 1968; Montreal,
1969 through 1975.

Most consecutive years managed without winning championship

M.L.—23—Gene Mauch, Philadelphia N.L., 1960 to 1968;
Montreal N.L., 1969 through 1975; Minnesota A.L., 1976 to
1980; California A.L., 1981 through 1982.
A.L.—19—Connie Mack, Philadelphia, 1932 through 1950.
N.L.—16—Gene Mauch, Philadelphia, 1960 to 1968; Montreal,
1969 through 1975.

Youngest manager to start season

Lou Boudreau, Cleveland A.L., appointed November 25, 1941;
24 years, 4 months, 8 days when appointed.

Youngest manager to finish season

Roger Peckinpaugh, New York A.L., appointed September 16,
1914; 23 years, 7 months, 11 days.

Oldest to make debut as manager

Tom Sheehan, San Francisco N.L., appointed June 18, 1960;
66 years, 2 months, 18 days.

CLUB

Most managers on one club, season

A.A.—7—Louisville, 1889.
N.L.—4—Washington, 1892, 1898.
St. Louis, 1895, 1896, 1897, 1980.
Chicago, 1961.
A.L.—4—Texas, 1977.

LEAGUE

Most managers, season (since 1900)

A.L. (14-club league)—19 in 1977, 1981, 1986 (Tony La Russa,

Chicago, Oakland, counted as one), 1988.
A.L. (12-club league)—16 in 1969, 1975.
A.L. (10-club league)—15 in 1966.
A.L. (8-club league)—12 in 1933, 1946.
N.L. (12-club league)—16 in 1972, 1991 (Leo Durocher,
Chicago, Houston, counted as one in 1972).
N.L. (14-club league)—16 in 1993.
N.L. (16-club league)—18 in 2001, 2003.
N.L. (8-club league)—12 in 1902, 1948 (Leo Durocher,
Brooklyn, New York, counted as one in 1948).
N.L. (10-club league)—12 in 1965, 1966, 1967, 1968.

Most player/managers in both leagues, season

10 in 1934 (8-club leagues)—6 in N.L., 4 in A.L.

Most managerial changes, start of season

A.L.—6 in 1955.
N.L.—5 in 2001.

UMPIRES

Most years umpired

N.L.—37—Bill Klem, 1905 through 1941.
A.L.—31—Tommy Connolly, 1901 through 1931 (also umpired
three years in the National League, 1898 through 1900).

Longest game, plate umpire by time

A.L.—8 hours, 6 minutes—Jim Evans, Milwaukee at Chicago,
May 8, 1984, finished May 9 (Chicago won 7-6.)
N.L.—7 hours, 23 minutes—Ed Sudol, San Francisco at New
York, May 31, 1964, second game, 23 innings (San Francisco
won 8-6.)

YEARLY LEADERS

BATTING

BATTING AVERAGE

AMERICAN LEAGUE

Year	Player, Club	BA
1901	Nap Lajoie, Philadelphia	.426
1902	Ed Delahanty, Washington	.376
1903	Nap Lajoie, Cleveland	.344
1904	Nap Lajoie, Cleveland	.376
1905	Elmer Flick, Cleveland	.308
1906	George Stone, St. Louis	.358
1907	Ty Cobb, Detroit	.350
1908	Ty Cobb, Detroit	.324
1909	Ty Cobb, Detroit	.377
1910	Ty Cobb, Detroit	.383
1911	Ty Cobb, Detroit	.420
1912	Ty Cobb, Detroit	.409
1913	Ty Cobb, Detroit	.390
1914	Ty Cobb, Detroit	.368
1915	Ty Cobb, Detroit	.369
1916	Tris Speaker, Cleveland	.386
1917	Ty Cobb, Detroit	.383
1918	Ty Cobb, Detroit	.382
1919	Ty Cobb, Detroit	.384
1920	George Sisler, St. Louis	.407
1921	Harry Heilmann, Detroit	.394
1922	George Sisler, St. Louis	.420
1923	Harry Heilmann, Detroit	.403
1924	Babe Ruth, New York	.378
1925	Harry Heilmann, Detroit	.393
1926	Heinie Manush, Detroit	.378
1927	Harry Heilmann, Detroit	.398
1928	Goose Goslin, Washington	.379
1929	Lew Fonseca, Cleveland	.369
1930	Al Simmons, Philadelphia	.381
1931	Al Simmons, Philadelphia	.390
1932	Dale Alexander, Detroit/Boston	.367
1933	Jimmie Foxx, Philadelphia	.356
1934	Lou Gehrig, New York	.363
1935	Buddy Myer, Washington	.349
1936	Luke Appling, Chicago	.388
1937	Charlie Gehringer, Detroit	.371
1938	Jimmie Foxx, Boston	.349
1939	Joe DiMaggio, New York	.381
1940	Joe DiMaggio, New York	.352
1941	Ted Williams, Boston	.406
1942	Ted Williams, Boston	.356
1943	Luke Appling, Chicago	.328
1944	Lou Boudreau, Cleveland	.327
1945	George Stirnweiss, New York	.309
1946	Mickey Vernon, Washington	.353
1947	Ted Williams, Boston	.343
1948	Ted Williams, Boston	.369
1949	George Kell, Detroit	.343
1950	Billy Goodman, Boston	.354
1951	Ferris Fain, Philadelphia	.344
1952	Ferris Fain, Philadelphia	.327
1953	Mickey Vernon, Washington	.337
1954	Bobby Avila, Cleveland	.341
1955	Al Kaline, Detroit	.340
1956	Mickey Mantle, New York	.353
1957	Ted Williams, Boston	.388
1958	Ted Williams, Boston	.328
1959	Harvey Kuenn, Detroit	.353
1960	Pete Runnels, Boston	.320
1961	Norm Cash, Detroit	.361
1962	Pete Runnels, Boston	.326
1963	Carl Yastrzemski, Boston	.321
1964	Tony Oliva, Minnesota	.323
1965	Tony Oliva, Minnesota	.321
1966	Frank Robinson, Baltimore	.316
1967	Carl Yastrzemski, Boston	.326
1968	Carl Yastrzemski, Boston	.301
1969	Rod Carew, Minnesota	.332
1970	Alex Johnson, California	.329
1971	Tony Oliva, Minnesota	.337
1972	Rod Carew, Minnesota	.318

Year	Player, Club	Avg.
1973	Rod Carew, Minnesota	.350
1974	Rod Carew, Minnesota	.364
1975	Rod Carew, Minnesota	.359
1976	George Brett, Kansas City	.333
1977	Rod Carew, Minnesota	.388
1978	Rod Carew, Minnesota	.333
1979	Fred Lynn, Boston	.333
1980	George Brett, Kansas City	.390
1981	Carney Lansford, Boston	.336
1982	Willie Wilson, Kansas City	.332
1983	Wade Boggs, Boston	.361
1984	Don Mattingly, New York	.343
1985	Wade Boggs, Boston	.368
1986	Wade Boggs, Boston	.357
1987	Wade Boggs, Boston	.363
1988	Wade Boggs, Boston	.366
1989	Kirby Puckett, Minnesota	.339
1990	George Brett, Kansas City	.329
1991	Julio Franco, Texas	.341
1992	Edgar Martinez, Seattle	.343
1993	John Olerud, Toronto	.363
1994	Paul O'Neill, New York	.359
1995	Edgar Martinez, Seattle	.356
1996	Alex Rodriguez, Seattle	.358
1997	Frank E. Thomas, Chicago	.347
1998	Bernie Williams, New York	.339
1999	Nomar Garciaparra, Boston	.357
2000	Nomar Garciaparra, Boston	.372
2001	Ichiro Suzuki, Seattle	.350
2002	Manny Ramirez, Boston	.349
2003	Bill Mueller, Boston	.326
2004	Ichiro Suzuki, Seattle	.372

NATIONAL LEAGUE

Year	Player, Club	BA
1876	Ross Barnes, Chicago	.429
1877	Deacon White, Boston	.387
1878	Abner Dalrymple, Milwaukee	.354
1879	Cap Anson, Chicago	.317
1880	George Gore, Chicago	.360
1881	Cap Anson, Chicago	.399
1882	Dan Brouthers, Buffalo	.368
1883	Dan Brouthers, Buffalo	.374
1884	Jim O'Rourke, Buffalo	.347
1885	Roger Connor, New York	.371
1886	King Kelly, Chicago	.388
1887	Cap Anson, Chicago	.347
1888	Cap Anson, Chicago	.344
1889	Dan Brouthers, Boston	.373
1890	Jack Glasscock, New York	.336
1891	Billy Hamilton, Philadelphia	.340
1892	Dan Brouthers, Brooklyn	.335
1893	Hugh Duffy, Boston	.363
1894	Hugh Duffy, Boston	.440
1895	Jesse Burkett, Cleveland	.405
1896	Jesse Burkett, Cleveland	.410
1897	Willie Keeler, Baltimore	.424
1898	Willie Keeler, Baltimore	.385
1899	Ed Delahanty, Philadelphia	.410
1900	Honus Wagner, Pittsburgh	.381
1901	Jesse Burkett, St. Louis	.376
1902	Ginger Beaumont, Pittsburgh	.357
1903	Honus Wagner, Pittsburgh	.355
1904	Honus Wagner, Pittsburgh	.349
1905	Cy Seymour, Cincinnati	.377
1906	Honus Wagner, Pittsburgh	.339
1907	Honus Wagner, Pittsburgh	.350
1908	Honus Wagner, Pittsburgh	.354
1909	Honus Wagner, Pittsburgh	.339
1910	Sherry Magee, Philadelphia	.331
1911	Honus Wagner, Pittsburgh	.334
1912	Heinie Zimmerman, Chicago	.372
1913	Jake Daubert, Brooklyn	.350
1914	Jake Daubert, Brooklyn	.329
1915	Larry Doyle, New York	.320
1916	Hal Chase, Cincinnati	.339
1917	Edd Roush, Cincinnati	.341
1918	Zack Wheat, Brooklyn	.335

Year	Player, Club	BA
1919	Edd Roush, Cincinnati	.321
1920	Rogers Hornsby, St. Louis	.370
1921	Rogers Hornsby, St. Louis	.397
1922	Rogers Hornsby, St. Louis	.401
1923	Rogers Hornsby, St. Louis	.384
1924	Rogers Hornsby, St. Louis	.424
1925	Rogers Hornsby, St. Louis	.403
1926	Bubbles Hargrave, Cincinnati	.353
1927	Paul Waner, Pittsburgh	.380
1928	Rogers Hornsby, Boston	.387
1929	Lefty O'Doul, Philadelphia	.398
1930	Bill Terry, New York	.401
1931	Chick Hafey, St. Louis	.349
1932	Lefty O'Doul, Brooklyn	.368
1933	Chuck Klein, Philadelphia	.368
1934	Paul Waner, Pittsburgh	.362
1935	Arky Vaughan, Pittsburgh	.385
1936	Paul Waner, Pittsburgh	.373
1937	Joe Medwick, St. Louis	.374
1938	Ernie Lombardi, Cincinnati	.342
1939	Johnny Mize, St. Louis	.349
1940	Debs Garms, Pittsburgh	.355
1941	Pete Reiser, Brooklyn	.343
1942	Ernie Lombardi, Boston	.330
1943	Stan Musial, St. Louis	.357
1944	Dixie Walker, Brooklyn	.357
1945	Phil Cavarretta, Chicago	.355
1946	Stan Musial, St. Louis	.365
1947	Harry Walker, St. Louis/Philadelphia	.363
1948	Stan Musial, St. Louis	.376
1949	Jackie Robinson, Brooklyn	.342
1950	Stan Musial, St. Louis	.346
1951	Stan Musial, St. Louis	.355
1952	Stan Musial, St. Louis	.336
1953	Carl Furillo, Brooklyn	.344
1954	Willie Mays, New York	.345
1955	Richie Ashburn, Philadelphia	.338
1956	Hank Aaron, Milwaukee	.328
1957	Stan Musial, St. Louis	.351
1958	Richie Ashburn, Philadelphia	.350
1959	Hank Aaron, Milwaukee	.355
1960	Dick Groat, Pittsburgh	.325
1961	Roberto Clemente, Pittsburgh	.351
1962	Tommy Davis, Los Angeles	.346
1963	Tommy Davis, Los Angeles	.326
1964	Roberto Clemente, Pittsburgh	.339
1965	Roberto Clemente, Pittsburgh	.329
1966	Matty Alou, Pittsburgh	.342
1967	Roberto Clemente, Pittsburgh	.357
1968	Pete Rose, Cincinnati	.335
1969	Pete Rose, Cincinnati	.348
1970	Rico Carty, Atlanta	.366
1971	Joe Torre, St. Louis	.363
1972	Billy Williams, Chicago	.333
1973	Pete Rose, Cincinnati	.338
1974	Ralph Garr, Atlanta	.353
1975	Bill Madlock, Chicago	.354
1976	Bill Madlock, Chicago	.339
1977	Dave Parker, Pittsburgh	.338
1978	Dave Parker, Pittsburgh	.334
1979	Keith Hernandez, St. Louis	.344
1980	Bill Buckner, Chicago	.324
1981	Bill Madlock, Pittsburgh	.341
1982	Al Oliver, Montreal	.331
1983	Bill Madlock, Pittsburgh	.323
1984	Tony Gwynn, San Diego	.351
1985	Willie McGee, St. Louis	.353
1986	Tim Raines Sr., Montreal	.334
1987	Tony Gwynn, San Diego	.370
1988	Tony Gwynn, San Diego	.313
1989	Tony Gwynn, San Diego	.336
1990	Willie McGee, St. Louis	*.335
1991	Terry Pendleton, Atlanta	.319
1992	Gary Sheffield, San Diego	.330
1993	Andres Galarraga, Colorado	.370
1994	Tony Gwynn, San Diego	.394
1995	Tony Gwynn, San Diego	.368
1996	Tony Gwynn, San Diego	†.353
1997	Tony Gwynn, San Diego	.372
1998	Larry Walker, Colorado	.363
1999	Larry Walker, Colorado	.379
2000	Todd Helton, Colorado	.372

Year	Player, Club	BA
2001	Larry Walker, Colorado	.350
2002	Barry Bonds, San Francisco	.370
2003	Albert Pujols, St. Louis	.359
2004	Barry Bonds, San Francisco	.362

Note—bases on balls counted as hits in 1887

*Eddie Murray of Los Angeles hit .330 in 1990, the highest batting average in the majors. McGee won the N.L. title, but was traded to Oakland on August 29 and finished the season with a combined .324 in for both leagues.

†Gwynn's 498 plate appearances were four short of the qualifying mark. Under Rule 10.23 (a), if Gwynn were charged with four more at-bats, his subsequent batting average of .349 would still be higher than the next-highest mark of .344, achieved by Ellis Burks of Colorado.

SLUGGING AVERAGE

AMERICAN LEAGUE

Year	Player, Club	SLG
1901	Nap Lajoie, Philadelphia	.643
1902	Ed Delahanty, Washington	.590
1903	Nap Lajoie, Cleveland	.518
1904	Nap Lajoie, Cleveland	.546
1905	Elmer Flick, Cleveland	.462
1906	George Stone, St. Louis	.501
1907	Ty Cobb, Detroit	.468
1908	Ty Cobb, Detroit	.475
1909	Ty Cobb, Detroit	.517
1910	Ty Cobb, Detroit	.551
1911	Ty Cobb, Detroit	.621
1912	Ty Cobb, Detroit	.584
1913	Joe Jackson, Cleveland	.551
1914	Ty Cobb, Detroit	.513
1915	Jack Fournier, Chicago	.491
1916	Tris Speaker, Cleveland	.502
1917	Ty Cobb, Detroit	.570
1918	Babe Ruth, Boston	.555
1919	Babe Ruth, Boston	.657
1920	Babe Ruth, New York	.847
1921	Babe Ruth, New York	.846
1922	Babe Ruth, New York	.672
1923	Babe Ruth, New York	.764
1924	Babe Ruth, New York	.739
1925	Ken Williams, St. Louis	.613
1926	Babe Ruth, New York	.737
1927	Babe Ruth, New York	.772
1928	Babe Ruth, New York	.709
1929	Babe Ruth, New York	.697
1930	Babe Ruth, New York	.732
1931	Babe Ruth, New York	.700
1932	Jimmie Foxx, Philadelphia	.749
1933	Jimmie Foxx, Philadelphia	.703
1934	Lou Gehrig, New York	.706
1935	Jimmie Foxx, Philadelphia	.636
1936	Lou Gehrig, New York	.696
1937	Joe DiMaggio, New York	.673
1938	Jimmie Foxx, Boston	.704
1939	Jimmie Foxx, Boston	.694
1940	Hank Greenberg, Detroit	.670
1941	Ted Williams, Boston	.735
1942	Ted Williams, Boston	.648
1943	Rudy York, Detroit	.527
1944	Bobby Doerr, Boston	.528
1945	George Stirnweiss, New York	.476
1946	Ted Williams, Boston	.667
1947	Ted Williams, Boston	.634
1948	Ted Williams, Boston	.615
1949	Ted Williams, Boston	.650
1950	Joe DiMaggio, New York	.585
1951	Ted Williams, Boston	.556
1952	Larry Doby, Cleveland	.541
1953	Al Rosen, Cleveland	.613
1954	Ted Williams, Boston	.635
1955	Mickey Mantle, New York	.611
1956	Mickey Mantle, New York	.705
1957	Ted Williams, Boston	.731
1958	Rocky Colavito, Cleveland	.620
1959	Al Kaline, Detroit	.530
1960	Roger Maris, New York	.581

Year	Player, Club	SLG
1961	Mickey Mantle, New York	.687
1962	Mickey Mantle, New York	.605
1963	Harmon Killebrew, Minnesota	.555
1964	Boog Powell, Baltimore	.606
1965	Carl Yastrzemski, Boston	.536
1966	Frank Robinson, Baltimore	.637
1967	Carl Yastrzemski, Boston	.622
1968	Frank Howard, Washington	.552
1969	Reggie Jackson, Oakland	.608
1970	Carl Yastrzemski, Boston	.592
1971	Tony Oliva, Minnesota	.546
1972	Dick Allen, Chicago	.603
1973	Reggie Jackson, Oakland	.531
1974	Dick Allen, Chicago	.563
1975	Fred Lynn, Boston	.566
1976	Reggie Jackson, Baltimore	.502
1977	Jim Rice, Boston	.593
1978	Jim Rice, Boston	.600
1979	Fred Lynn, Boston	.637
1980	George Brett, Kansas City	.664
1981	Bobby Grich, California	.543
1982	Robin Yount, Milwaukee	.578
1983	George Brett, Kansas City	.563
1984	Harold Baines, Chicago	.541
1985	George Brett, Kansas City	.585
1986	Don Mattingly, New York	.573
1987	Mark McGwire, Oakland	.618
1988	Jose Canseco, Oakland	.569
1989	Ruben Sierra, Texas	.543
1990	Cecil Fielder, Detroit	.592
1991	Danny Tartabull, Kansas City	.593
1992	Mark McGwire, Oakland	.585
1993	Juan Gonzalez, Texas	.632
1994	Frank E. Thomas, Chicago	.729
1995	Albert Belle, Cleveland	.690
1996	Mark McGwire, Oakland	.730
1997	Ken Griffey Jr., Seattle	.646
1998	Albert Belle, Chicago	.655
1999	Manny Ramirez, Cleveland	.663
2000	Manny Ramirez, Cleveland	.697
2001	Jason Giambi, Oakland	.660
2002	Jim Thome, Cleveland	.677
2003	Alex Rodriguez, Texas	.600
2004	Manny Ramirez, Boston	.613

NATIONAL LEAGUE

Year	Player, Club	SLG
1900	Honus Wagner, Pittsburgh	.573
1901	Jimmy Sheckard, Brooklyn	.534
1902	Honus Wagner, Pittsburgh	.463
1903	Fred Clarke, Pittsburgh	.532
1904	Honus Wagner, Pittsburgh	.520
1905	Cy Seymour, Cincinnati	.559
1906	Harry Lumley, Brooklyn	.477
1907	Honus Wagner, Pittsburgh	.513
1908	Honus Wagner, Pittsburgh	.542
1909	Honus Wagner, Pittsburgh	.489
1910	Sherry Magee, Philadelphia	.507
1911	Frank Schulte, Chicago	.534
1912	Heinie Zimmerman, Chicago	.571
1913	Gavvy Cravath, Philadelphia	.568
1914	Sherry Magee, Philadelphia	.509
1915	Gavvy Cravath, Philadelphia	.510
1916	Zack Wheat, Brooklyn	.461
1917	Rogers Hornsby, St. Louis	.484
1918	Edd Roush, Cincinnati	.455
1919	Hy Myers, Brooklyn	.436
1920	Rogers Hornsby, St. Louis	.559
1921	Rogers Hornsby, St. Louis	.659
1922	Rogers Hornsby, St. Louis	.722
1923	Rogers Hornsby, St. Louis	.627
1924	Rogers Hornsby, St. Louis	.696
1925	Rogers Hornsby, St. Louis	.756
1926	Cy Williams, Philadelphia	.569
1927	Chick Hafey, St. Louis	.590
1928	Rogers Hornsby, Boston	.632
1929	Rogers Hornsby, Chicago	.679
1930	Hack Wilson, Chicago	.723
1931	Chuck Klein, Philadelphia	.584
1932	Chuck Klein, Philadelphia	.646

Year	Player, Club	SLG
1933	Chuck Klein, Philadelphia	.602
1934	Rip Collins, St. Louis	.615
1935	Arky Vaughan, Pittsburgh	.607
1936	Mel Ott, New York	.588
1937	Joe Medwick, St. Louis	.641
1938	Johnny Mize, St. Louis	.614
1939	Johnny Mize, St. Louis	.626
1940	Johnny Mize, St. Louis	.636
1941	Pete Reiser, Brooklyn	.558
1942	Johnny Mize, New York	.521
1943	Stan Musial, St. Louis	.562
1944	Stan Musial, St. Louis	.549
1945	Tommy Holmes, Boston	.577
1946	Stan Musial, St. Louis	.587
1947	Ralph Kiner, Pittsburgh	.639
1948	Stan Musial, St. Louis	.702
1949	Ralph Kiner, Pittsburgh	.658
1950	Stan Musial, St. Louis	.596
1951	Ralph Kiner, Pittsburgh	.627
1952	Stan Musial, St. Louis	.538
1953	Duke Snider, Brooklyn	.627
1954	Willie Mays, New York	.667
1955	Willie Mays, New York	.659
1956	Duke Snider, Brooklyn	.598
1957	Willie Mays, New York	.626
1958	Ernie Banks, Chicago	.614
1959	Hank Aaron, Milwaukee	.636
1960	Frank Robinson, Cincinnati	.595
1961	Frank Robinson, Cincinnati	.611
1962	Frank Robinson, Cincinnati	.624
1963	Hank Aaron, Milwaukee	.586
1964	Willie Mays, San Francisco	.607
1965	Willie Mays, San Francisco	.645
1966	Dick Allen, Philadelphia	.632
1967	Hank Aaron, Atlanta	.573
1968	Willie McCovey, San Francisco	.545
1969	Willie McCovey, San Francisco	.656
1970	Willie McCovey, San Francisco	.612
1971	Hank Aaron, Atlanta	.669
1972	Billy Williams, Chicago	.606
1973	Willie Stargell, Pittsburgh	.646
1974	Mike Schmidt, Philadelphia	.546
1975	Dave Parker, Pittsburgh	.541
1976	Joe Morgan, Cincinnati	.576
1977	George Foster, Cincinnati	.631
1978	Dave Parker, Pittsburgh	.585
1979	Dave Kingman, Chicago	.613
1980	Mike Schmidt, Philadelphia	.624
1981	Mike Schmidt, Philadelphia	.644
1982	Mike Schmidt, Philadelphia	.547
1983	Dale Murphy, Atlanta	.540
1984	Dale Murphy, Atlanta	.547
1985	Pedro Guerrero, Los Angeles	.577
1986	Mike Schmidt, Philadelphia	.547
1987	Jack Clark, St. Louis	.597
1988	Darryl Strawberry, New York	.545
1989	Kevin Mitchell, San Francisco	.635
1990	Barry Bonds, Pittsburgh	.565
1991	Will Clark, San Francisco	.536
1992	Barry Bonds, Pittsburgh	.624
1993	Barry Bonds, San Francisco	.677
1994	Jeff Bagwell, Houston	.750
1995	Dante Bichette, Colorado	.620
1996	Ellis Burks, Colorado	.639
1997	Larry Walker, Colorado	.720
1998	Mark McGwire, St. Louis	.752
1999	Larry Walker, Colorado	.710
2000	Todd Helton, Colorado	.698
2001	Barry Bonds, San Francisco	.863
2002	Barry Bonds, San Francisco	.799
2003	Barry Bonds, San Francisco	.749
2004	Barry Bonds, San Francisco	.812

ON-BASE PERCENTAGE

AMERICAN LEAGUE

Year	Player, Club	OBP
1931	Babe Ruth, New York	.495
1932	Babe Ruth, New York	.489
1933	Mickey Cochrane, Philadelphia	.459

Year	Player, Club	OBP
1934	Lou Gehrig, New York	.465
1935	Lou Gehrig, New York	.466
1936	Lou Gehrig, New York	.478
1937	Lou Gehrig, New York	.473
1938	Jimmie Foxx, Boston	.462
1939	none	
1940	Ted Williams, Boston	.442
1941	Ted Williams, Boston	.553
1942	Ted Williams, Boston	.499
1943	Luke Appling, Chicago	.419
1944	Bob Johnson, Boston	.431
1945	Eddie Lake, Boston	.412
1946	Ted Williams, Boston	.497
1947	Ted Williams, Boston	.499
1948	Ted Williams, Boston	.497
1949	Ted Williams, Boston	.490
1950	Larry Doby, Cleveland	.442
1951	Ted Williams, Boston	.464
1952	Ferris Fain, Philadelphia	.438
1953	Gene Woodling, New York	.429
1954	Ted Williams, Boston	.513
1955	Mickey Mantle, New York	.431
1956	Ted Williams, Boston	.479
1957	Ted Williams, Boston	.526
1958	Ted Williams, Boston	.458
1959	Eddie Yost, Detroit	.435
1960	Eddie Yost, Detroit	.414
1961	Norm Cash, Detroit	.487
1962	Mickey Mantle, New York	.486
1963	Carl Yastrzemski, Boston	.418
1964	Mickey Mantle, New York	.423
1965	Carl Yastrzemski, Boston	.395
1966	Frank Robinson, Baltimore	.410
1967	Carl Yastrzemski, Boston	.418
1968	Carl Yastrzemski, Boston	.426
1969	Harmon Killebrew, Minnesota	.427
1970	Carl Yastrzemski, Boston	.452
1971	Bobby Murcer, New York	.427
1972	Dick Allen, Chicago	.420
1973	John Mayberry, Kansas City	.417
1974	Rod Carew, Minnesota	.433
1975	Rod Carew, Minnesota	.421
1976	Hal McRae, Kansas City	.407
1977	Rod Carew, Minnesota	.449
1978	Rod Carew, Minnesota	.411
1979	Fred Lynn, Boston	.423
1980	George Brett, Kansas City	.454
1981	Mike Hargrove, Cleveland	.424
1982	Dwight Evans, Boston	.402
1983	Wade Boggs, Boston	.444
1984	Eddie Murray, Baltimore	.410
1985	Wade Boggs, Boston	.450
1986	Wade Boggs, Boston	.453
1987	Wade Boggs, Boston	.461
1988	Wade Boggs, Boston	.476
1989	Wade Boggs, Boston	.430
1990	Rickey Henderson, Oakland	.439
1991	Frank Thomas, Chicago	.453
1992	Frank Thomas, Chicago	.439
1993	John Olerud, Toronto	.473
1994	Frank Thomas, Chicago	.487
1995	Edgar Martinez, Seattle	.479
1996	Mark McGwire, Oakland	.467
1997	Frank Thomas, Chicago	.456
1998	Edgar Martinez, Seattle	.429
1999	Edgar Martinez, Seattle	.447
2000	Jason Giambi, Oakland	.476
2001	Jason Giambi, Oakland	.477
2002	Manny Ramirez, Boston	.450
2003	Manny Ramirez, Boston	.427
2004	Melvin Mora, Baltimore	.419

Year	Player, Club	OBP
1937	Dolf Camilli, Philadelphia	.446
1938	Mel Ott, New York	.462
1939	none	
1940	Elbie Fletcher, Pittsburgh	.418
1941	Elbie Fletcher Pittsburgh	.421
1942	Elbie Fletcher, Pittsburgh	.417
1943	Stan Musial, St. Louis	.425
1944	Stan Musial, St. Louis	.440
1945	Phil Cavaretta, Chicago	.449
1946	Eddie Stanky, Brooklyn	.436
1947	Augie Galan, Cincinnati	.449
1948	Stan Musial, St. Louis	.450
1949	Stan Musial, St. Louis	.438
1950	Eddie Stanky, New York	.460
1951	Ralph Kiner, Pittsburgh	.452
1952	Jackie Robinson, Brooklyn	.440
1953	Stan Musial, St. Louis	.437
1954	Richie Ashburn, Philadelphia	.441
1955	Richie Ashburn, Philadelphia	.449
1956	Duke Snider, Brooklyn	.399
1957	Stan Musial, St. Louis	.422
1958	Richie Ashburn, Philadelphia	.440
1959	Joe Cunningham, St. Louis	.453
1960	Richie Ashburn, Chicago	.415
1961	Wally Moon, Los Angeles	.434
1962	Frank Robinson, Cincinnati	.421
1963	Eddie Mathews, Milwaukee	.399
1964	Ron Santo, Chicago	.398
1965	Willie Mays, San Francisco	.398
1966	Ron Santo, Chicago	.412
1967	Dick Allen, Philadelphia	.404
1968	Pete Rose, Cincinnati	.391
1969	Willie McCovey, San Francisco	.453
1970	Rico Carty, Atlanta	.454
1971	Willie Mays, San Francisco	.425
1972	Joe Morgan, Cincinnati	.417
1973	Ken Singleton, Montreal	.425
1974	Joe Morgan, Cincinnati	.427
1975	Joe Morgan, Cincinnati	.466
1976	Joe Morgan, Cincinnati	.444
1977	Reggie Smith, Los Angeles	.427
1978	Jeff Burroughs, Atlanta	.432
1979	Pete Rose, Philadelphia	.418
1980	Keith Hernandez, St. Louis	.408
1981	Mike Schmidt, Philadelphia	.435
1982	Mike Schmidt, Philadelphia	.403
1983	Mike Schmidt, Philadelphia	.399
1984	Gary Matthews, Chicago	.410
1985	Pedro Guerrero, Los Angeles	.422
1986	Tim Raines, Montreal	.413
1987	Jack Clark, St. Louis	.459
1988	Kal Daniels, Cincinnati	.397
1989	Lonnie Smith, Atlanta	.415
1990	Lennie Dykstra, Philadelphia	.418
1991	Barry Bonds, Pittsburgh	.410
1992	Barry Bonds, Pittsburgh	.456
1993	Barry Bonds, San Francisco	.458
1994	Tony Gwynn, San Diego	.454
1995	Barry Bonds, San Francisco	.431
1996	Gary Sheffield, Florida	.465
1997	Larry Walker, Colorado	.452
1998	Mark McGwire, St. Louis	.470
1999	Larry Walker, Colorado	.458
2000	Todd Helton, Colorado	.463
2001	Barry Bonds, San Francisco	.515
2002	Barry Bonds, San Francisco	.582
2003	Barry Bonds, San Francisco	.529
2004	Barry Bonds, San Francisco	.609

Note—official statistic since 1984; calculated from official statistics, 1931-1983 except for 1939 for which there is no official tabulation of sacrifice flies

NATIONAL LEAGUE

Year	Player, Club	OBP
1931	Chick Hafey, St. Louis	.404
1932	Mel Ott, New York	.424
1933	Chuck Klein, Philadelphia	.422
1934	Arky Vaughan, Pittsburgh	.431
1935	Arky Vaughan, Pittsburgh	.491
1936	Arky Vaughan, Pittsburgh	.453

RUNS

AMERICAN LEAGUE

Year	Player, Club	No.
1901	Nap Lajoie, Philadelphia	145
1902	Dave Fultz, Philadelphia	109
	Topsy Hartsel, Philadelphia	109
1903	Patsy Dougherty, Boston	107

Year	Player, Club	No.
1904	Patsy Dougherty, Boston/New York	113
1905	Harry Davis, Philadelphia	93
1906	Elmer Flick, Cleveland	98
1907	Sam Crawford, Detroit	102
1908	Matty McIntyre, Detroit	105
1909	Ty Cobb, Detroit	116
1910	Ty Cobb, Detroit	106
1911	Ty Cobb, Detroit	147
1912	Eddie Collins, Philadelphia	137
1913	Eddie Collins, Philadelphia	125
1914	Eddie Collins, Philadelphia	122
1915	Ty Cobb, Detroit	144
1916	Ty Cobb, Detroit	113
1917	Donie Bush, Detroit	112
1918	Ray Chapman, Cleveland	84
1919	Babe Ruth, Boston	103
1920	Babe Ruth, New York	158
1921	Babe Ruth, New York	177
1922	George Sisler, St. Louis	134
1923	Babe Ruth, New York	151
1924	Babe Ruth, New York	143
1925	Johnny Mostil, Chicago	135
1926	Babe Ruth, New York	139
1927	Babe Ruth, New York	158
1928	Babe Ruth, New York	163
1929	Charlie Gehringer, Detroit	131
1930	Al Simmons, Philadelphia	152
1931	Lou Gehrig, New York	163
1932	Jimmie Foxx, Philadelphia	151
1933	Lou Gehrig, New York	138
1934	Charlie Gehringer, Detroit	134
1935	Lou Gehrig, New York	125
1936	Lou Gehrig, New York	167
1937	Joe DiMaggio, New York	151
1938	Hank Greenberg, Detroit	144
1939	Red Rolfe, New York	139
1940	Ted Williams, Boston	134
1941	Ted Williams, Boston	135
1942	Ted Williams, Boston	141
1943	George Case, Washington	102
1944	George Stirnweiss, New York	125
1945	George Stirnweiss, New York	107
1946	Ted Williams, Boston	142
1947	Ted Williams, Boston	125
1948	Tommy Henrich, New York	138
1949	Ted Williams, Boston	150
1950	Dom DiMaggio, Boston	131
1951	Dom DiMaggio, Boston	113
1952	Larry Doby, Cleveland	104
1953	Al Rosen, Cleveland	115
1954	Mickey Mantle, New York	129
1955	Al Smith, Cleveland	123
1956	Mickey Mantle, New York	132
1957	Mickey Mantle, New York	121
1958	Mickey Mantle, New York	127
1959	Eddie Yost, Detroit	115
1960	Mickey Mantle, New York	119
1961	Mickey Mantle, New York	132
	Roger Maris, New York	132
1962	Albie Pearson, Los Angeles	115
1963	Bob Allison, Minnesota	99
1964	Tony Oliva, Minnesota	109
1965	Zoilo Versalles, Minnesota	126
1966	Frank Robinson, Baltimore	122
1967	Carl Yastrzemski, Boston	112
1968	Dick McAuliffe, Detroit	95
1969	Reggie Jackson, Oakland	123
1970	Carl Yastrzemski, Boston	125
1971	Don Buford, Baltimore	99
1972	Bobby Murcer, New York	102
1973	Reggie Jackson, Oakland	99
1974	Carl Yastrzemski, Boston	93
1975	Fred Lynn, Boston	103
1976	Roy White, New York	104
1977	Rod Carew, Minnesota	128
1978	Ron LeFlore, Detroit	126
1979	Don Baylor, California	120
1980	Willie Wilson, Kansas City	133
1981	Rickey Henderson, Oakland	89
1982	Paul Molitor, Milwaukee	136
1983	Cal Ripken, Baltimore	121
1984	Dwight Evans, Boston	121
1985	Rickey Henderson, New York	146
1986	Rickey Henderson, New York	130
1987	Paul Molitor, Milwaukee	114
1988	Wade Boggs, Boston	128
1989	Wade Boggs, Boston	113
	Rickey Henderson, New York/Oakland	113
1990	Rickey Henderson, Oakland	119
1991	Paul Molitor, Milwaukee	133
1992	Tony Phillips, Detroit	114
1993	Rafael Palmeiro, Texas	124
1994	Frank E. Thomas, Chicago	106
1995	Albert Belle, Cleveland	121
	Edgar Martinez, Seattle	121
1996	Alex Rodriguez, Seattle	141
1997	Ken Griffey Jr., Seattle	125
1998	Derek Jeter, New York	127
1999	Roberto Alomar, Cleveland	138
2000	Johnny Damon, Kansas City	136
2001	Alex Rodriguez, Texas	133
2002	Alfonso Soriano, New York	128
2003	Alex Rodriguez, Texas	124
2004	Vladimir Guerrero, Anaheim	124

NATIONAL LEAGUE

Year	Player, Club	No.
1900	Roy Thomas, Philadelphia	132
1901	Jesse Burkett, St. Louis	142
1902	Honus Wagner, Pittsburgh	105
1903	Ginger Beaumont, Pittsburgh	137
1904	George Browne, New York	99
1905	Mike Donlin, New York	124
1906	Frank Chance, Chicago	103
	Honus Wagner, Pittsburgh	103
1907	Spike Shannon, New York	104
1908	Fred Tenney, New York	101
1909	Tommy Leach, Pittsburgh	126
1910	Sherry Magee, Philadelphia	110
1911	Jimmy Sheckard, Chicago	121
1912	Bob Bescher, Cincinnati	120
1913	Max Carey, Pittsburgh	99
	Tommy Leach, Chicago	99
1914	George J. Burns, New York	100
1915	Gavvy Cravath, Philadelphia	89
1916	George J. Burns, New York	105
1917	George J. Burns, New York	103
1918	Heinie Groh, Cincinnati	88
1919	George J. Burns, New York	86
1920	George J. Burns, New York	115
1921	Rogers Hornsby, St. Louis	131
1922	Rogers Hornsby, St. Louis	141
1923	Ross Youngs, New York	121
1924	Frankie Frisch, New York	121
	Rogers Hornsby, St. Louis	121
1925	Kiki Cuyler, Pittsburgh	144
1926	Kiki Cuyler, Pittsburgh	113
1927	Lloyd Waner, Pittsburgh	133
	Rogers Hornsby, New York	133
1928	Paul Waner, Pittsburgh	142
1929	Rogers Hornsby, Chicago	156
1930	Chuck Klein, Philadelphia	158
1931	Bill Terry, New York	121
	Chuck Klein, Philadelphia	121
1932	Chuck Klein, Philadelphia	152
1933	Pepper Martin, St. Louis	122
1934	Paul Waner, Pittsburgh	122
1935	Augie Galan, Chicago	133
1936	Arky Vaughan, Pittsburgh	122
1937	Joe Medwick, St. Louis	111
1938	Mel Ott, New York	116
1939	Bill Werber, Cincinnati	115
1940	Arky Vaughan, Pittsburgh	113
1941	Pete Reiser, Brooklyn	117
1942	Mel Ott, New York	118
1943	Arky Vaughan, Brooklyn	112
1944	Bill Nicholson, Chicago	116
1945	Eddie Stanky, Brooklyn	128
1946	Stan Musial, St. Louis	124
1947	Johnny Mize, New York	137
1948	Stan Musial, St. Louis	135
1949	Pee Wee Reese, Brooklyn	132
1950	Earl Torgeson, Boston	120

Year	Player, Club	No.
1951	Stan Musial, St. Louis	124
	Ralph Kiner, Pittsburgh	124
1952	Stan Musial, St. Louis	105
	Solly Hemus, St. Louis	105
1953	Duke Snider, Brooklyn	132
1954	Stan Musial, St. Louis	120
	Duke Snider, Brooklyn	120
1955	Duke Snider, Brooklyn	126
1956	Frank Robinson, Cincinnati	122
1957	Hank Aaron, Milwaukee	118
1958	Willie Mays, San Francisco	121
1959	Vada Pinson, Cincinnati	131
1960	Billy Bruton, Milwaukee	112
1961	Willie Mays, San Francisco	129
1962	Frank Robinson, Cincinnati	134
1963	Hank Aaron, Milwaukee	121
1964	Dick Allen, Philadelphia	125
1965	Tommy Harper, Cincinnati	126
1966	Felipe Alou, Atlanta	122
1967	Hank Aaron, Atlanta	113
	Lou Brock, St. Louis	113
1968	Glenn Beckert, Chicago	98
1969	Bobby Bonds, San Francisco	120
	Pete Rose, Cincinnati	120
1970	Billy Williams, Chicago	137
1971	Lou Brock, St. Louis	126
1972	Joe Morgan, Cincinnati	122
1973	Bobby Bonds, San Francisco	131
1974	Pete Rose, Cincinnati	110
1975	Pete Rose, Cincinnati	112
1976	Pete Rose, Cincinnati	130
1977	George Foster, Cincinnati	124
1978	Ivan DeJesus, Chicago	104
1979	Keith Hernandez, St. Louis	116
1980	Keith Hernandez, St. Louis	111
1981	Mike Schmidt, Philadelphia	78
1982	Lonnie Smith, St. Louis	120
1983	Tim Raines Sr., Montreal	133
1984	Ryne Sandberg, Chicago	114
1985	Dale Murphy, Atlanta	118
1986	Tony Gwynn, San Diego	107
	Von Hayes, Philadelphia	107
1987	Tim Raines Sr., Montreal	123
1988	Brett Butler, San Francisco	109
1989	Will Clark, San Francisco	104
	Howard Johnson, New York	104
	Ryne Sandberg, Chicago	104
1990	Ryne Sandberg, Chicago	116
1991	Brett Butler, Los Angeles	112
1992	Barry Bonds, Pittsburgh	109
1993	Lenny Dykstra, Philadelphia	143
1994	Jeff Bagwell, Houston	104
1995	Craig Biggio, Houston	123
1996	Ellis Burks, Colorado	142
1997	Craig Biggio, Houston	146
1998	Sammy Sosa, Chicago	134
1999	Jeff Bagwell, Houston	143
2000	Jeff Bagwell, Houston	152
2001	Sammy Sosa, Chicago	146
2002	Sammy Sosa, Chicago	122
2003	Albert Pujols, St. Louis	137
2004	Albert Pujols, St. Louis	133

HITS

AMERICAN LEAGUE

Year	Player, Club	No.
1901	Nap Lajoie, Philadelphia	232
1902	Charles Hickman, Boston/Cleveland	193
1903	Patsy Dougherty, Boston	195
1904	Nap Lajoie, Cleveland	208
1905	George Stone, St. Louis	187
1906	Nap Lajoie, Cleveland	214
1907	Ty Cobb, Detroit	212
1908	Ty Cobb, Detroit	188
1909	Ty Cobb, Detroit	216
1910	Nap Lajoie, Cleveland	227
1911	Ty Cobb, Detroit	248
1912	Ty Cobb, Detroit	226
	Joe Jackson, Cleveland	226
1913	Joe Jackson, Cleveland	197
1914	Tris Speaker, Boston	193
1915	Ty Cobb, Detroit	208
1916	Tris Speaker, Cleveland	211
1917	Ty Cobb, Detroit	225
1918	George H. Burns, Philadelphia	178
1919	Ty Cobb, Detroit	191
	Bobby Veach, Detroit	191
1920	George Sisler, St. Louis	257
1921	Harry Heilmann, Detroit	237
1922	George Sisler, St. Louis	246
1923	Charlie Jamieson, Cleveland	222
1924	Sam Rice, Washington	216
1925	Al Simmons, Philadelphia	253
1926	George H. Burns, Cleveland	216
	Sam Rice, Washington	216
1927	Earle Combs, New York	231
1928	Heinie Manush, St. Louis	241
1929	Dale Alexander, Detroit	215
	Charlie Gehringer, Detroit	215
1930	Johnny Hodapp, Cleveland	225
1931	Lou Gehrig, New York	211
1932	Al Simmons, Philadelphia	216
1933	Heinie Manush, Washington	221
1934	Charlie Gehringer, Detroit	214
1935	Joe Vosmik, Cleveland	216
1936	Earl Averill Sr., Cleveland	232
1937	Beau Bell, St. Louis	218
1938	Joe Vosmik, Boston	201
1939	Red Rolfe, New York	213
1940	Rip Radcliff, St. Louis	200
	Barney McCosky, Detroit	200
	Doc Cramer, Boston	200
1941	Cecil Travis, Washington	218
1942	Johnny Pesky, Boston	205
1943	Dick Wakefield, Detroit	200
1944	George Stirnweiss, New York	205
1945	George Stirnweiss, New York	195
1946	Johnny Pesky, Boston	208
1947	Johnny Pesky, Boston	207
1948	Bob Dillinger, St. Louis	207
1949	Dale Mitchell, Cleveland	203
1950	George Kell, Detroit	218
1951	George Kell, Detroit	191
1952	Nellie Fox, Chicago	192
1953	Harvey Kuenn, Detroit	209
1954	Nellie Fox, Chicago	201
	Harvey Kuenn, Detroit	201
1955	Al Kaline, Detroit	200
1956	Harvey Kuenn, Detroit	196
1957	Nellie Fox, Chicago	196
1958	Nellie Fox, Chicago	187
1959	Harvey Kuenn, Detroit	198
1960	Minnie Minoso, Chicago	184
1961	Norm Cash, Detroit	193
1962	Bobby Richardson, New York	209
1963	Carl Yastrzemski, Boston	183
1964	Tony Oliva, Minnesota	217
1965	Tony Oliva, Minnesota	185
1966	Tony Oliva, Minnesota	191
1967	Carl Yastrzemski, Boston	189
1968	Bert Campaneris, Oakland	177
1969	Tony Oliva, Minnesota	197
1970	Tony Oliva, Minnesota	204
1971	Cesar Tovar, Minnesota	204
1972	Joe Rudi, Oakland	181
1973	Rod Carew, Minnesota	203
1974	Rod Carew, Minnesota	218
1975	George Brett, Kansas City	195
1976	George Brett, Kansas City	215
1977	Rod Carew, Minnesota	239
1978	Jim Rice, Boston	213
1979	George Brett, Kansas City	212
1980	Willie Wilson, Kansas City	230
1981	Rickey Henderson, Oakland	135
1982	Robin Yount, Milwaukee	210
1983	Cal Ripken, Baltimore	211
1984	Don Mattingly, New York	207
1985	Wade Boggs, Boston	240
1986	Don Mattingly, New York	238
1987	Kirby Puckett, Minnesota	207
	Kevin Seitzer, Kansas City	207

Year	Player, Club	No.
1988	Kirby Puckett, Minnesota	234
1989	Kirby Puckett, Minnesota	215
1990	Rafael Palmeiro, Texas	191
1991	Paul Molitor, Milwaukee	216
1992	Kirby Puckett, Minnesota	210
1993	Paul Molitor, Toronto	211
1994	Kenny Lofton, Cleveland	160
1995	Lance Johnson, Chicago	186
1996	Paul Molitor, Minnesota	225
1997	Nomar Garciaparra, Boston	209
1998	Alex Rodriguez, Seattle	213
1999	Derek Jeter, New York	219
2000	Darin Erstad, Anaheim	240
2001	Ichiro Suzuki, Seattle	242
2002	Alfonso Soriano, New York	209
2003	Vernon Wells, Toronto	215
2004	Ichiro Suzuki, Seattle	262

NATIONAL LEAGUE

Year	Player, Club	No.
1900	Willie Keeler, Brooklyn	204
1901	Jesse Burkett, St. Louis	226
1902	Ginger Beaumont, Pittsburgh	193
1903	Ginger Beaumont, Pittsburgh	209
1904	Ginger Beaumont, Pittsburgh	185
1905	Cy Seymour, Cincinnati	219
1906	Harry Steinfeldt, Chicago	176
1907	Ginger Beaumont, Boston	187
1908	Honus Wagner, Pittsburgh	201
1909	Larry Doyle, New York	172
1910	Honus Wagner, Pittsburgh	178
	Bobby Byrne, Pittsburgh	178
1911	Doc Miller, Boston	192
1912	Heinie Zimmerman, Chicago	207
1913	Gavvy Cravath, Philadelphia	179
1914	Sherry Magee, Philadelphia	171
1915	Larry Doyle, New York	189
1916	Hal Chase, Cincinnati	184
1917	Heinie Groh, Cincinnati	182
1918	Charlie Hollocher, Chicago	161
1919	Ivy Olson, Brooklyn	164
1920	Rogers Hornsby, St. Louis	218
1921	Rogers Hornsby, St. Louis	235
1922	Rogers Hornsby, St. Louis	250
1923	Frankie Frisch, New York	223
1924	Rogers Hornsby, St. Louis	227
1925	Jim Bottomley, St. Louis	227
1926	Eddie Brown, Boston	201
1927	Paul Waner, Pittsburgh	237
1928	Fred Lindstrom, New York	231
1929	Lefty O'Doul, Philadelphia	254
1930	Bill Terry, New York	254
1931	Lloyd Waner, Pittsburgh	214
1932	Chuck Klein, Philadelphia	226
1933	Chuck Klein, Philadelphia	223
1934	Paul Waner, Pittsburgh	217
1935	Billy Herman, Chicago	227
1936	Joe Medwick, St. Louis	223
1937	Joe Medwick, St. Louis	237
1938	Frank McCormick, Cincinnati	209
1939	Frank McCormick, Cincinnati	209
1940	Stan Hack, Chicago	191
	Frank McCormick, Cincinnati	191
1941	Stan Hack, Chicago	186
1942	Enos Slaughter, St. Louis	188
1943	Stan Musial, St. Louis	220
1944	Stan Musial, St. Louis	197
	Phil Cavarretta, Chicago	197
1945	Tommy Holmes, Boston	224
1946	Stan Musial, St. Louis	228
1947	Tommy Holmes, Boston	191
1948	Stan Musial, St. Louis	230
1949	Stan Musial, St. Louis	207
1950	Duke Snider, Brooklyn	199
1951	Richie Ashburn, Philadelphia	221
1952	Stan Musial, St. Louis	194
1953	Richie Ashburn, Philadelphia	205
1954	Don Mueller, New York	212
1955	Ted Kluszewski, Cincinnati	192
1956	Hank Aaron, Milwaukee	200
1957	Red Schoendienst, New York/Milwaukee	200

Year	Player, Club	No.
1958	Richie Ashburn, Philadelphia	215
1959	Hank Aaron, Milwaukee	223
1960	Willie Mays, San Francisco	190
1961	Vada Pinson, Cincinnati	208
1962	Tommy Davis, Los Angeles	230
1963	Vada Pinson, Cincinnati	204
1964	Roberto Clemente, Pittsburgh	211
	Curt Flood, St. Louis	211
1965	Pete Rose, Cincinnati	209
1966	Felipe Alou, Atlanta	218
1967	Roberto Clemente, Pittsburgh	209
1968	Felipe Alou, Atlanta	210
	Pete Rose, Cincinnati	210
1969	Matty Alou, Pittsburgh	231
1970	Pete Rose, Cincinnati	205
	Billy Williams, Chicago	205
1971	Joe Torre, St. Louis	230
1972	Pete Rose, Cincinnati	198
1973	Pete Rose, Cincinnati	230
1974	Ralph Garr, Atlanta	214
1975	Dave Cash, Philadelphia	213
1976	Pete Rose, Cincinnati	215
1977	Dave Parker, Pittsburgh	215
1978	Steve Garvey, Los Angeles	202
1979	Garry Templeton, St. Louis	211
1980	Steve Garvey, Los Angeles	200
1981	Pete Rose, Philadelphia	140
1982	Al Oliver, Montreal	204
1983	Jose Cruz, Houston	189
	Andre Dawson, Montreal	189
1984	Tony Gwynn, San Diego	213
1985	Willie McGee, St. Louis	216
1986	Tony Gwynn, San Diego	211
1987	Tony Gwynn, San Diego	218
1988	Andres Galarraga, Montreal	184
1989	Tony Gwynn, San Diego	203
1990	Brett Butler, San Francisco	*192
	Lenny Dykstra, Philadelphia	*192
1991	Terry Pendleton, Atlanta	187
1992	Terry Pendleton, Atlanta	199
	Andy Van Slyke, Pittsburgh	199
1993	Lenny Dykstra, Philadelphia	194
1994	Tony Gwynn, San Diego	165
1995	Dante Bichette, Colorado	197
	Tony Gwynn, San Diego	197
1996	Lance Johnson, New York	227
1997	Tony Gwynn, San Diego	220
1998	Dante Bichette, Colorado	219
1999	Luis Gonzalez, Arizona	206
2000	Todd Helton, Colorado	216
2001	Rich Aurilia, San Francisco	206
2002	Vladimir Guerrero, Montreal	206
2003	Albert Pujols, St. Louis	212
2004	Juan Pierre, Florida	221

*Willie McGee led the majors with 199 hits in 1990, collecting 168 with St. Louis (N.L.) and another 31 with Oakland (A.L.) following an August 29 trade.

SINGLES
AMERICAN LEAGUE

Year	Player, Club	No.
1901	Nap Lajoie, Philadelphia	156
1902	Fielder Jones, Chicago	150
1903	Patsy Dougherty, Boston	160
1904	Willie Keeler, New York	162
1905	Willie Keeler, New York	147
1906	Willie Keeler, New York	167
1907	Ty Cobb, Detroit	163
1908	Matty McIntyre, Detroit	131
	George Stone, St. Louis	131
1909	Ty Cobb, Detroit	164
1910	Nap Lajoie, Cleveland	165
1911	Ty Cobb, Detroit	169
1912	Ty Cobb, Detroit	167
1913	Eddie Collins, Philadelphia	145
1914	Stuffy McInnis, Philadelphia	160
1915	Ty Cobb, Detroit	161
1916	Tris Speaker, Cleveland	160
1917	Ty Cobb, Detroit	151

Year	Player, Club	No.
	Clyde Milan, Washington	151
1918	George H. Burns, Philadelphia	141
1919	Sam Rice, Washington	144
1920	George Sisler, St. Louis	171
1921	Jack Tobin, St. Louis	179
1922	George Sisler, St. Louis	178
1923	Charlie Jamieson, Cleveland	172
1924	Charlie Jamieson, Cleveland	168
1925	Sam Rice, Washington	182
1926	Sam Rice, Washington	167
1927	Earle Combs, New York	166
1928	Heinie Manush, St. Louis	161
1929	Earle Combs, New York	151
1930	Sam Rice, Washington	158
1931	Oscar Melillo, St. Louis	142
	John Stone, Detroit	142
1932	Heinie Manush, Washington	145
1933	Heinie Manush, Washington	167
1934	Doc Cramer, Philadelphia	158
1935	Doc Cramer, Philadelphia	170
1936	Rip Radcliff, Chicago	161
1937	Buddy Lewis, Washington	162
1938	Mel Almada, Washington/St. Louis	158
1939	Doc Cramer, Boston	147
1940	Doc Cramer, Boston	160
1941	Cecil Travis, Washington	153
1942	Johnny Pesky, Boston	165
1943	Doc Cramer, Detroit	159
1944	George Stirnweiss, New York	146
1945	Irv Hall, Philadelphia	139
1946	Johnny Pesky, Boston	159
1947	Johnny Pesky, Boston	172
1948	Dale Mitchell, Cleveland	162
1949	Dale Mitchell, Cleveland	161
1950	Phil Rizzuto, New York	150
1951	George Kell, Detroit	150
1952	Nellie Fox, Chicago	157
1953	Harvey Kuenn, Detroit	167
1954	Nellie Fox, Chicago	167
1955	Nellie Fox, Chicago	157
1956	Nellie Fox, Chicago	158
1957	Nellie Fox, Chicago	155
1958	Nellie Fox, Chicago	160
1959	Nellie Fox, Chicago	149
1960	Nellie Fox, Chicago	139
1961	Bobby Richardson, New York	148
1962	Bobby Richardson, New York	158
1963	Albie Pearson, Los Angeles	139
1964	Bobby Richardson, New York	148
1965	Don Buford, Chicago	129
1966	Luis Aparicio, Baltimore	143
1967	Horace Clarke, New York	140
1968	Bert Campaneris, Oakland	139
1969	Horace Clarke, New York	146
1970	Alex Johnson, California	156
1971	Cesar Tovar, Minnesota	171
1972	Rod Carew, Minnesota	143
1973	Rod Carew, Minnesota	156
1974	Rod Carew, Minnesota	180
1975	Thurman Munson, New York	151
1976	George Brett, Kansas City	160
1977	Rod Carew, Minnesota	171
1978	Ron LeFlore, Detroit	153
1979	Willie Wilson, Kansas City	148
1980	Willie Wilson, Kansas City	184
1981	Willie Wilson, Kansas City	115
1982	Willie Wilson, Kansas City	157
1983	Wade Boggs, Boston	154
1984	Wade Boggs, Boston	162
1985	Wade Boggs, Boston	187
1986	Tony Fernandez, Toronto	161
1987	Kevin Seitzer, Kansas City	151
1988	Kirby Puckett, Minnesota	163
1989	Steve Sax, New York	171
1990	Rafael Palmeiro, Texas	136
1991	Julio Franco, Texas	156
1992	Carlos Baerga, Cleveland	152
1993	Kenny Lofton, Cleveland	148
1994	Kenny Lofton, Cleveland	107
	Paul Molitor, Toronto	107
1995	Otis Nixon, Texas	151
1996	Paul Molitor, Minnesota	167

Year	Player, Club	No.
1997	Garret Anderson, Anaheim	142
	Derek Jeter, New York	142
1998	Derek Jeter, New York	151
1999	Randy Velarde, Anaheim/Oakland	152
2000	Darin Erstad, Anaheim	170
2001	Ichiro Suzuki, Seattle	192
2002	Ichiro Suzuki, Seattle	165
2003	Ichiro Suzuki, Seattle	162
2004	Ichiro Suzuki, Seattle	225

NATIONAL LEAGUE

Year	Player, Club	No.
1900	Willie Keeler, Brooklyn	175
1901	Jesse Burkett, St. Louis	181
1902	Ginger Beaumont, Pittsburgh	166
1903	Ginger Beaumont, Pittsburgh	166
1904	Ginger Beaumont, Pittsburgh	158
1905	Mike Donlin, New York	162
1906	Miller Huggins, Cincinnati	141
	Spike Shannon, St. Louis/New York	141
1907	Ginger Beaumont, Pittsburgh	150
1908	Mike Donlin, New York	153
1909	Eddie Grant, Philadelphia	147
1910	Eddie Grant, Philadelphia	134
1911	Jake Daubert, Brooklyn	146
	Doc Miller, Boston	146
1912	Bill Sweeney, Boston	159
1913	Jake Daubert, Brooklyn	152
1914	Beals Becker, Philadelphia	128
1915	Larry Doyle, New York	135
1916	Dave Robertson, New York	142
1917	Benny Kauff, New York	141
	Edd Roush, Cincinnati	141
1918	Charlie Hollocher, Chicago	130
1919	Ivy Olson, Brooklyn	140
1920	Milt Stock, St. Louis	170
1921	Carson Bigbee, Pittsburgh	161
1922	Carson Bigbee, Pittsburgh	166
1923	Frankie Frisch, New York	169
1924	Zack Wheat, Brooklyn	149
1925	Milt Stock, Brooklyn	164
1926	Eddie Brown, Boston	160
1927	Lloyd Waner, Pittsburgh	198
1928	Lloyd Waner, Pittsburgh	180
1929	Lefty O'Doul, Philadelphia	181
	Lloyd Waner, Pittsburgh	181
1930	Bill Terry, New York	177
1931	Lloyd Waner, Pittsburgh	172
1932	Lefty O'Doul, Brooklyn	158
1933	Chick Fullis, Philadelphia	162
1934	Bill Terry, New York	169
1935	Woody Jensen, Pittsburgh	160
1936	Joe Moore, New York	160
1937	Paul Waner, Pittsburgh	178
1938	Frank McCormick, Cincinnati	160
1939	Buddy Hassett, Boston	162
1940	Burgess Whitehead, New York	141
1941	Stan Hack, Chicago	141
1942	Enos Slaughter, St. Louis	127
1943	Mickey Witek, New York	172
1944	Phil Cavarretta, Chicago	142
1945	Stan Hack, Chicago	155
1946	Stan Musial, St. Louis	142
1947	Tommy Holmes, Boston	146
1948	Stan Rojek, Pittsburgh	150
1949	Red Schoendienst, St. Louis	160
1950	Eddie Waitkus, Philadelphia	143
1951	Richie Ashburn, Philadelphia	181
1952	Bobby Adams, Cincinnati	145
1953	Richie Ashburn, Philadelphia	169
1954	Don Mueller, New York	165
1955	Don Mueller, New York	152
1956	Johnny Temple, Cincinnati	157
1957	Richie Ashburn, Philadelphia	152
1958	Richie Ashburn, Philadelphia	176
1959	Don Blasingame, St. Louis	144
1960	Dick Groat, Pittsburgh	154
1961	Vada Pinson, Cincinnati	150
	Maury Wills, Los Angeles	150
1962	Maury Wills, Los Angeles	179
1963	Curt Flood, St. Louis	152

Year	Player, Club	No.
1964	Curt Flood, St. Louis	178
1965	Maury Wills, Los Angeles	165
1966	Sonny Jackson, Houston	160
1967	Maury Wills, Pittsburgh	162
1968	Curt Flood, St. Louis	160
1969	Matty Alou, Pittsburgh	183
1970	Matty Alou, Pittsburgh	171
1971	Ralph Garr, Atlanta	180
1972	Lou Brock, St. Louis	156
1973	Pete Rose, Cincinnati	181
1974	Dave Cash, Philadelphia	167
1975	Dave Cash, Philadelphia	166
1976	Willie Montanez, San Francisco/Atlanta	164
1977	Garry Templeton, St. Louis	155
1978	Larry Bowa, Philadelphia	153
1979	Pete Rose, Philadelphia	159
1980	Gene Richards, San Diego	155
1981	Pete Rose, Philadelphia	117
1982	Bill Buckner, Chicago	147
1983	Rafael Ramirez, Atlanta	160
1984	Tony Gwynn, San Diego	177
1985	Willie McGee, St. Louis	162
1986	Tony Gwynn, San Diego	157
	Steve Sax, Los Angeles	157
1987	Tony Gwynn, San Diego	162
1988	Steve Sax, Los Angeles	147
1989	Tony Gwynn, San Diego	165
1990	Brett Butler, San Francisco	160
1991	Brett Butler, Los Angeles	162
1992	Brett Butler, Los Angeles	143
1993	Brett Butler, Los Angeles	149
1994	Tony Gwynn, San Diego	117
1995	Tony Gwynn, San Diego	154
1996	Lance Johnson, New York	166
1997	Tony Gwynn, San Diego	152
1998	Tony Womack, Pittsburgh	149
1999	Doug Glanville, Philadelphia	149
2000	Luis Castillo, Florida	158
2001	Juan Pierre, Colorado	163
2002	Luis Castillo, Florida	160
2003	Juan Pierre, Florida	168
2004	Juan Pierre, Florida	184

DOUBLES

AMERICAN LEAGUE

Year	Player, Club	No.
1901	Nap Lajoie, Philadelphia	48
1902	Harry Davis, Philadelphia	43
	Ed Delahanty, Washington	43
1903	Socks Seybold, Philadelphia	45
1904	Nap Lajoie, Cleveland	49
1905	Harry Davis, Philadelphia	47
1906	Nap Lajoie, Cleveland	48
1907	Harry Davis, Philadelphia	35
1908	Ty Cobb, Detroit	36
1909	Sam Crawford, Detroit	35
1910	Nap Lajoie, Cleveland	51
1911	Ty Cobb, Detroit	47
1912	Tris Speaker, Boston	53
1913	Joe Jackson, Cleveland	39
1914	Tris Speaker, Boston	46
1915	Bobby Veach, Detroit	40
1916	Jack Graney, Cleveland	41
	Tris Speaker, Cleveland	41
1917	Ty Cobb, Detroit	44
1918	Tris Speaker, Cleveland	33
1919	Bobby Veach, Detroit	45
1920	Tris Speaker, Cleveland	50
1921	Tris Speaker, Cleveland	52
1922	Tris Speaker, Cleveland	48
1923	Tris Speaker, Cleveland	59
1924	Joe Sewell, Cleveland	45
	Harry Heilmann, Detroit	45
1925	Marty McManus, St. Louis	44
1926	George H. Burns, Cleveland	64
1927	Lou Gehrig, New York	52
1928	Heinie Manush, St. Louis	47
	Lou Gehrig, New York	47

Year	Player, Club	No.
1929	Heinie Manush, St. Louis	45
	Roy Johnson, Detroit	45
	Charlie Gehringer, Detroit	45
1930	Johnny Hodapp, Cleveland	51
1931	Earl Webb, Boston	67
1932	Eric McNair, Philadelphia	47
1933	Joe Cronin, Washington	45
1934	Hank Greenberg, Detroit	63
1935	Joe Vosmik, Cleveland	47
1936	Charlie Gehringer, Detroit	60
1937	Beau Bell, St. Louis	51
1938	Joe Cronin, Boston	51
1939	Red Rolfe, New York	46
1940	Hank Greenberg, Detroit	50
1941	Lou Boudreau, Cleveland	45
1942	Don Kolloway, Chicago	40
1943	Dick Wakefield, Detroit	38
1944	Lou Boudreau, Cleveland	45
1945	Wally Moses, Chicago	35
1946	Mickey Vernon, Washington	51
1947	Lou Boudreau, Cleveland	45
1948	Ted Williams, Boston	44
1949	Ted Williams, Boston	39
1950	George Kell, Detroit	56
1951	George Kell, Detroit	36
	Eddie Yost, Washington	36
	Sam Mele, Washington	36
1952	Ferris Fain, Philadelphia	43
1953	Mickey Vernon, Washington	43
1954	Mickey Vernon, Washington	33
1955	Harvey Kuenn, Detroit	38
1956	Jimmy Piersall, Boston	40
1957	Minnie Minoso, Chicago	36
	Billy Gardner, Baltimore	36
1958	Harvey Kuenn, Detroit	39
1959	Harvey Kuenn, Detroit	42
1960	Tito Francona, Cleveland	36
1961	Al Kaline, Detroit	41
1962	Floyd Robinson, Chicago	45
1963	Carl Yastrzemski, Boston	40
1964	Tony Oliva, Minnesota	43
1965	Zoilo Versalles, Minnesota	45
	Carl Yastrzemski, Boston	45
1966	Carl Yastrzemski, Boston	39
1967	Tony Oliva, Minnesota	34
1968	Reggie Smith, Boston	37
1969	Tony Oliva, Minnesota	39
1970	Tony Oliva, Minnesota	36
	Amos Otis, Kansas City	36
	Cesar Tovar, Minnesota	36
1971	Reggie Smith, Boston	33
1972	Lou Piniella, Kansas City	33
1973	Sal Bando, Oakland	32
	Pedro Garcia, Milwaukee	32
1974	Joe Rudi, Oakland	39
1975	Fred Lynn, Boston	47
1976	Amos Otis, Kansas City	40
1977	Hal McRae, Kansas City	54
1978	George Brett, Kansas City	45
1979	Chet Lemon, Chicago	44
	Cecil Cooper, Milwaukee	44
1980	Robin Yount, Milwaukee	49
1981	Cecil Cooper, Milwaukee	35
1982	Hal McRae, Kansas City	46
	Robin Yount, Milwaukee	46
1983	Cal Ripken, Baltimore	47
1984	Don Mattingly, New York	44
1985	Don Mattingly, New York	48
1986	Don Mattingly, New York	53
1987	Paul Molitor, Milwaukee	41
1988	Wade Boggs, Boston	45
1989	Wade Boggs, Boston	51
1990	George Brett, Kansas City	45
	Jody Reed, Boston	45
1991	Rafael Palmeiro, Texas	49
1992	Edgar Martinez, Seattle	46
	Frank Thomas, Chicago	46
1993	John Olerud, Toronto	54
1994	Chuck Knoblauch, Minnesota	45
1995	Albert Belle, Cleveland	52
	Edgar Martinez, Seattle	52
1996	Alex Rodriguez, Seattle	54

Year	Player, Club	No.
1997	John Valentin, Boston	47
1998	Juan Gonzalez, Texas	50
1999	Shawn Green, Toronto	45
2000	Carlos Delgado, Toronto	57
2001	Jason Giambi, Oakland	47
2002	Garret Anderson, Anaheim	56
	Nomar Garciaparra, Boston	56
2003	Garret Anderson, Anaheim	49
	Vernon Wells, Toronto	49
2004	Brian Roberts, Baltimore	50

NATIONAL LEAGUE

Year	Player, Club	No.
1876	Ross Barnes, Chicago	21
	Dick Higham, Hartford	21
	Paul Hines, Chicago	21
1877	Cap Anson, Chicago	19
1878	Dick Higham, Providence	22
1879	Charlie Eden, Cleveland	31
1880	Fred Dunlap, Cleveland	27
1881	Paul Hines, Providenc	27
	King Kelly, Chicago	27
1882	King Kelly, Chicago	37
1883	Ned Williamson, Chicago	49
1884	Paul Hines, Providence	36
1885	Cap Anson, Chicago	35
1886	Dan Brouthers, Detroit	40
1887	Dan Brouthers, Detroit	36
1888	Dan Brouthers, Detroit	33
	Jimmy Ryan, Chicago	33
1889	King Kelly, Boston	41
1890	Sam Thompson, Philadelphia	41
1891	Mike Griffin, Brooklyn	36
1892	Roger Connor, Philadelphia	37
1893	Sam Thompson, Philadelphia	37
1894	Hugh Duffy, Boston	51
1895	Ed Delahanty, Philadelphia	49
1896	Ed Delahanty, Philadelphia	44
1897	Jake Stenzel, Baltimore	43
1898	Nap Lajoie, Philadelphia	43
1899	Ed Delahanty, Philadelphia	55
1900	Honus Wagner, Pittsburgh	45
1901	Tom Daly, Brooklyn	38
	Ed Delahanty, Philadelphia	38
1902	Honus Wagner, Pittsburgh	30
1903	Fred Clarke, Pittsburgh	32
	Sam Mertes, New York	32
	Harry Steinfeldt, Cincinnati	32
1904	Honus Wagner, Pittsburgh	44
1905	Cy Seymour, Cincinnati	40
1906	Honus Wagner, Pittsburgh	38
1907	Honus Wagner, Pittsburgh	38
1908	Honus Wagner, Pittsburgh	39
1909	Honus Wagner, Pittsburgh	39
1910	Bobby Byrne, Pittsburgh	43
1911	Ed Konetchy, St. Louis	38
1912	Heinie Zimmerman, Chicago	41
1913	Red Smith, Brooklyn	40
1914	Sherry Magee, Philadelphia	39
1915	Larry Doyle, New York	40
1916	Bert Niehoff, Philadelphia	42
1917	Heinie Groh, Cincinnati	39
1918	Heinie Groh, Cincinnati	28
1919	Ross Youngs, New York	31
1920	Rogers Hornsby, St. Louis	44
1921	Rogers Hornsby, St. Louis	44
1922	Rogers Hornsby, St. Louis	46
1923	Edd Roush, Cincinnati	41
1924	Rogers Hornsby, St. Louis	43
1925	Jim Bottomley, St. Louis	44
1926	Jim Bottomley, St. Louis	40
1927	Riggs Stephenson, Chicago	46
1928	Paul Waner, Pittsburgh	50
1929	Johnny Frederick, Brooklyn	52
1930	Chuck Klein, Philadelphia	59
1931	Sparky Adams, St. Louis	46
1932	Paul Waner, Pittsburgh	62
1933	Chuck Klein, Philadelphia	44
1934	Kiki Cuyler, Chicago	42
	Ethan Allen, Philadelphia	42
1935	Billy Herman, Chicago	57

Year	Player, Club	No.
1936	Joe Medwick, St. Louis	64
1937	Joe Medwick, St. Louis	56
1938	Joe Medwick, St. Louis	47
1939	Enos Slaughter, St. Louis	52
1940	Frank McCormick, Cincinnati	44
1941	Pete Reiser, Brooklyn	39
	Johnny Mize, St. Louis	39
1942	Marty Marion, St. Louis	38
1943	Stan Musial, St. Louis	48
1944	Stan Musial, St. Louis	51
1945	Tommy Holmes, Boston	47
1946	Stan Musial, St. Louis	50
1947	Eddie Miller, Cincinnati	38
1948	Stan Musial, St. Louis	46
1949	Stan Musial, St. Louis	41
1950	Red Schoendienst, St. Louis	43
1951	Alvin Dark, New York	41
1952	Stan Musial, St. Louis	42
1953	Stan Musial, St. Louis	53
1954	Stan Musial, St. Louis	41
1955	Johnny Logan, Milwaukee	37
	Hank Aaron, Milwaukee	37
1956	Hank Aaron, Milwaukee	34
1957	Don Hoak, Cincinnati	39
1958	Orlando Cepeda, San Francisco	38
1959	Vada Pinson, Cincinnati	47
1960	Vada Pinson, Cincinnati	37
1961	Hank Aaron, Milwaukee	39
1962	Frank Robinson, Cincinnati	51
1963	Dick Groat, St. Louis	43
1964	Lee Maye, Milwaukee	44
1965	Hank Aaron, Milwaukee	40
1966	Johnny Callison, Philadelphia	40
1967	Rusty Staub, Houston	44
1968	Lou Brock, St. Louis	46
1969	Matty Alou, Pittsburgh	41
1970	Wes Parker, Los Angeles	47
1971	Cesar Cedeno, Houston	40
1972	Cesar Cedeno, Houston	39
	Willie Montanez, Philadelphia	39
1973	Willie Stargell, Pittsburgh	43
1974	Pete Rose, Cincinnati	45
1975	Pete Rose, Cincinnati	47
1976	Pete Rose, Cincinnati	42
1977	Dave Parker, Pittsburgh	44
1978	Pete Rose, Cincinnati	51
1979	Keith Hernandez, St. Louis	48
1980	Pete Rose, Philadelphia	42
1981	Bill Buckner, Chicago	35
1982	Al Oliver, Montreal	43
1983	Bill Buckner, Chicago	38
	Al Oliver, Montreal	38
	Johnny Ray, Pittsburgh	38
1984	Tim Raines Sr., Montreal	38
	Johnny Ray, Pittsburgh	38
1985	Dave Parker, Cincinnati	42
1986	Von Hayes, Philadelphia	46
1987	Tim Wallach, Montreal	42
1988	Andres Galarraga, Montreal	42
1989	Pedro Guerrero, St. Louis	42
	Tim Wallach, Montreal	42
1990	Gregg Jefferies, New York	40
1991	Bobby Bonilla, Pittsburgh	44
1992	Andy Van Slyke, Pittsburgh	45
1993	Charlie Hayes, Colorado	45
1994	Craig Biggio, Houston	44
	Larry Walker, Montreal	44
1995	Mark Grace, Chicago	51
1996	Jeff Bagwell, Houston	48
1997	Mark Grudzielanek, Montreal	54
1998	Craig Biggio, Houston	51
1999	Craig Biggio, Houston	56
2000	Todd Helton, Colorado	59
2001	Lance Berkman, Houston	55
2002	Bobby Abreu, Philadelphia	50
2003	Albert Pujols, St. Louis	51
2004	Lyle Overbay, Milwaukee	53

TRIPLES

AMERICAN LEAGUE

Year	Player, Club	No.
1901	Bill Keister, Baltimore	21
	Jimmy Williams, Baltimore	21
1902	Jimmy Williams, Baltimore	21
1903	Sam Crawford, Detroit	25
1904	Joe Cassidy, Washington	19
	Buck Freeman, Boston	19
	Chick Stahl, Boston	19
1905	Elmer Flick, Cleveland	18
1906	Elmer Flick, Cleveland	22
1907	Elmer Flick, Cleveland	18
1908	Ty Cobb, Detroit	20
1909	Home Run Baker, Philadelphia	19
1910	Sam Crawford, Detroit	19
1911	Ty Cobb, Detroit	24
1912	Joe Jackson, Cleveland	26
1913	Sam Crawford, Detroit	23
1914	Sam Crawford, Detroit	26
1915	Sam Crawford, Detroit	19
1916	Joe Jackson, Chicago	21
1917	Ty Cobb, Detroit	24
1918	Ty Cobb, Detroit	14
1919	Bobby Veach, Detroit	17
1920	Joe Jackson, Chicago	20
1921	Howard Shanks, Washington	18
	George Sisler, St. Louis	18
	Jack Tobin, St. Louis	18
1922	George Sisler, St. Louis	18
1923	Sam Rice, Washington	18
	Goose Goslin, Washington	18
1924	Wally Pipp, New York	19
1925	Goose Goslin, Washington	20
1926	Lou Gehrig, New York	20
1927	Earle Combs, New York	23
1928	Earle Combs, New York	21
1929	Charlie Gehringer, Detroit	19
1930	Earle Combs, New York	22
1931	Roy Johnson, Detroit	19
1932	Joe Cronin, Washington	18
1933	Heinie Manush, Washington	17
1934	Ben Chapman, New York	13
1935	Joe Vosmik, Cleveland	20
1936	Earl Averill Sr., Cleveland	15
	Joe DiMaggio, New York	15
	Red Rolfe, New York	15
1937	Dixie Walker, Chicago	16
	Mike Kreevich, Chicago	16
1938	Jeff Heath, Cleveland	18
1939	Buddy Lewis, Washington	16
1940	Barney McCosky, Detroit	19
1941	Jeff Heath, Cleveland	20
1942	Stan Spence, Washington	15
1943	Johnny Lindell, New York	12
	Wally Moses, Chicago	12
1944	Johnny Lindell, New York	16
	George Stirnweiss, New York	16
1945	George Stirnweiss, New York	22
1946	Hank Edwards, Cleveland	16
1947	Tommy Henrich, New York	13
1948	Tommy Henrich, New York	14
1949	Dale Mitchell, Cleveland	23
1950	Dom DiMaggio, Boston	11
	Bobby Doerr, Boston	11
	Hoot Evers, Detroit	11
1951	Minnie Minoso, Cleveland/Chicago	14
1952	Bobby Avila, Cleveland	11
1953	Jim Rivera, Chicago	16
1954	Minnie Minoso, Chicago	18
1955	Mickey Mantle, New York	11
	Andy Carey, New York	11
1956	Minnie Minoso, Chicago	11
	Jackie Jensen, Boston	11
	Harry Simpson, Kansas City	11
	Jim Lemon, Washington	11
1957	Gil McDougald, New York	9
	Hank Bauer, New York	9
	Harry Simpson, New York	9
1958	Vic Power, Kansas City/Cleveland	10

Year	Player, Club	No.
1959	Bob Allison, Washington	9
1960	Nellie Fox, Chicago	10
1961	Jake Wood, Detroit	14
1962	Gino Cimoli, Kansas City	15
1963	Zoilo Versalles, Minnesota	13
1964	Rich Rollins, Minnesota	10
	Zoilo Versalles, Minnesota	10
1965	Bert Campaneris, Kansas City	12
	Zoilo Versalles, Minnesota	12
1966	Bobby Knoop, California	11
1967	Paul Blair, Baltimore	12
1968	Jim Fregosi, California	13
1969	Del Unser, Washington	8
1970	Cesar Tovar, Minnesota	13
1971	Fred Patek, Kansas City	11
1972	Carlton Fisk, Boston	9
	Joe Rudi, Oakland	9
1973	Al Bumbry, Baltimore	11
	Rod Carew, Minnesota	11
1974	Mickey Rivers, California	11
1975	George Brett, Kansas City	13
	Mickey Rivers, California	13
1976	George Brett, Kansas City	14
1977	Rod Carew, Minnesota	16
1978	Jim Rice, Boston	15
1979	George Brett, Kansas City	20
1980	Alfredo Griffin, Toronto	15
	Willie Wilson, Kansas City	15
1981	John Castino, Minnesota	9
1982	Willie Wilson, Kansas City	15
1983	Robin Yount, Milwaukee	10
1984	Dave Collins, Toronto	15
	Lloyd Moseby, Toronto	15
1985	Willie Wilson, Kansas City	21
1986	Brett Butler, Cleveland	14
1987	Willie Wilson, Kansas City	15
1988	Harold Reynolds, Seattle	11
	Willie Wilson, Kansas City	11
	Robin Yount, Milwaukee	11
1989	Ruben Sierra, Texas	14
1990	Tony Fernandez, Toronto	17
1991	Lance Johnson, Chicago	13
	Paul Molitor, Milwaukee	13
1992	Lance Johnson, Chicago	12
1993	Lance Johnson, Chicago	14
1994	Lance Johnson, Chicago	14
1995	Kenny Lofton, Cleveland	13
1996	Chuck Knoblauch, Minnesota	14
1997	Nomar Garciaparra, Boston	11
1998	Jose Offerman, Kansas City	13
1999	Jose Offerman, Boston	11
2000	Cristian Guzman, Minnesota	20
2001	Cristian Guzman, Minnesota	14
2002	Johnny Damon, Boston	11
2003	Cristian Guzman, Minnesota	14
2004	Carl Crawford, Tampa Bay	19

NATIONAL LEAGUE

Year	Player, Club	No.
1876	Ross Barnes, Chicago	14
1877	Deacon White, Boston	11
1878	Tom York, Providence	10
1879	Buttercup Dickerson, Cincinnati	14
1880	Harry Stovey, Worcester	14
1881	Jack Rowe, Buffalo	11
1882	Roger Connor, Troy	18
1883	Dan Brouthers, Buffalo	17
1884	Buck Ewing, New York	20
1885	Jim O'Rourke, New York	16
1886	Roger Connor, New York	20
1887	Sam Thompson, Detroit	23
1888	Dick Johnston, Boston	18
1889	Walt Wilmot, Washington	19
1890	John Reilly, Cincinnati	26
1891	Harry Stovey, Boston	20
1892	Ed Delahanty, Philadelphia	21
1893	Perry Werden, St. Louis	29
1894	Heinie Reitz, Baltimore	31
1895	Kip Selbach, Washington	22
1896	Tom McCreery, Louisville	21
	George Van Haltren, New York	21

Year	Player, Club	No.
1897	Harry Davis, Pittsburgh	28
1898	John Anderson, Brooklyn/Washington	22
1899	Jimmy Williams, Pittsburgh	27
1900	Honus Wagner, Pittsburgh	22
1901	Jimmy Sheckard, Brooklyn	19
1902	Sam Crawford, Cincinnati	22
	Tommy Leach, Pittsburgh	22
1903	Honus Wagner, Pittsburgh	19
1904	Harry Lumley, Brooklyn	18
1905	Cy Seymour, Cincinnati	21
1906	Fred Clarke, Pittsburgh	13
	Frank Schulte, Chicago	13
1907	John Ganzel, Cincinnati	16
	Whitey Alperman, Brooklyn	16
1908	Honus Wagner, Pittsburgh	19
1909	Mike Mitchell, Cincinnati	17
1910	Mike Mitchell, Cincinnati	18
1911	Larry Doyle, New York	25
1912	Chief Wilson, Pittsburgh	36
1913	Vic Saier, Chicago	21
1914	Max Carey, Pittsburgh	17
1915	Tommy Long, St. Louis	25
1916	Bill Hinchman, Pittsburgh	16
1917	Rogers Hornsby, St. Louis	17
1918	Jake Daubert, Brooklyn	15
1919	Hy Myers, Brooklyn	14
	Billy Southworth, Pittsburgh	14
1920	Hy Myers, Brooklyn	22
1921	Rogers Hornsby, St. Louis	18
	Ray Powell, Boston	18
1922	Jake Daubert, Cincinnati	22
1923	Max Carey, Pittsburgh	19
	Pie Traynor, Pittsburgh	19
1924	Edd Roush, Cincinnati	21
1925	Kiki Cuyler, Pittsburgh	26
1926	Paul Waner, Pittsburgh	22
1927	Paul Waner, Pittsburgh	18
1928	Jim Bottomley, St. Louis	20
1929	Lloyd Waner, Pittsburgh	20
1930	Adam Comorosky, Pittsburgh	23
1931	Bill Terry, New York	20
1932	Babe Herman, Cincinnati	19
1933	Arky Vaughan, Pittsburgh	19
1934	Joe Medwick, St. Louis	18
1935	Ival Goodman, Cincinnati	18
1936	Ival Goodman, Cincinnati	14
1937	Arky Vaughan, Pittsburgh	17
1938	Johnny Mize, St. Louis	16
1939	Billy Herman, Chicago	18
1940	Arky Vaughan, Pittsburgh	15
1941	Pete Reiser, Brooklyn	17
1942	Enos Slaughter, St. Louis	17
1943	Stan Musial, St. Louis	20
1944	Johnny Barrett, Pittsburgh	19
1945	Luis Olmo, Brooklyn	13
1946	Stan Musial, St. Louis	20
1947	Harry Walker, St. Louis/Philadelphia	16
1948	Stan Musial, St. Louis	18
1949	Stan Musial, St. Louis	13
	Enos Slaughter, St. Louis	13
1950	Richie Ashburn, Philadelphia	14
1951	Stan Musial, St. Louis	12
	Gus Bell, Pittsburgh	12
1952	Bobby Thomson, New York	14
1953	Jim Gilliam, Brooklyn	17
1954	Willie Mays, New York	13
1955	Willie Mays, New York	13
	Dale Long, Pittsburgh	13
1956	Billy Bruton, Milwaukee	15
1957	Willie Mays, New York	20
1958	Richie Ashburn, Philadelphia	13
1959	Wally Moon, Los Angeles	11
	Charlie Neal, Los Angeles	11
1960	Billy Bruton, Milwaukee	13
1961	George Altman, Chicago	12
1962	Johnny Callison, Philadelphia	10
	Bill Virdon, Pittsburgh	10
	Willie Davis, Los Angeles	10
	Maury Wills, Los Angeles	10
1963	Vada Pinson, Cincinnati	14
1964	Dick Allen, Philadelphia	13
	Ron Santo, Chicago	13

Year	Player, Club	No.
1965	Johnny Callison, Philadelphia	16
1966	Tim McCarver, St. Louis	13
1967	Vada Pinson, Cincinnati	13
1968	Lou Brock, St. Louis	14
1969	Roberto Clemente, Pittsburgh	12
1970	Willie Davis, Los Angeles	16
1971	Joe Morgan, Houston	11
	Roger Metzger, Houston	11
1972	Larry Bowa, Philadelphia	13
1973	Roger Metzger, Houston	14
1974	Ralph Garr, Atlanta	17
1975	Ralph Garr, Atlanta	11
1976	Dave Cash, Philadelphia	12
1977	Garry Templeton, St. Louis	18
1978	Garry Templeton, St. Louis	13
1979	Garry Templeton, St. Louis	19
1980	Omar Moreno, Pittsburgh	13
	Rodney Scott, Montreal	13
1981	Craig Reynolds, Houston	12
	Gene Richards, San Diego	12
1982	Dickie Thon, Houston	10
1983	Brett Butler, Atlanta	13
1984	Juan Samuel, Philadelphia	19
	Ryne Sandberg, Chicago	19
1985	Willie McGee, St. Louis	18
1986	Mitch Webster, Montreal	13
1987	Juan Samuel, Philadelphia	15
1988	Andy Van Slyke, Pittsburgh	15
1989	Robby Thompson, San Francisco	11
1990	Mariano Duncan, Cincinnati	11
1991	Ray Lankford, St. Louis	15
1992	Deion Sanders, Atlanta	14
1993	Steve Finley, Houston	13
1994	Brett Butler, Los Angeles	9
	Darren Lewis, San Francisco	9
1995	Brett Butler, New York/Los Angeles	9
	Eric Young, Colorado	9
1996	Lance Johnson, New York	21
1997	Delino DeShields, St. Louis	14
1998	David Dellucci, Arizona	12
1999	Bobby Abreu, Philadelphia	11
	Neifi Perez, Colorado	11
2000	Tony Womack, Arizona	14
2001	Jimmy Rollins, Philadelphia	12
2002	Jimmy Rollins, Philadelphia	10
2003	Steve Finley, Arizona	10
	Rafael Furcal, Atlanta	10
2004	Juan Pierre, Florida	12
	Jimmy Rollins, Philadelphia	12
	Jack Wilson, Pittsburgh	12

HOME RUNS

AMERICAN LEAGUE

Year	Player, Club	No.
1901	Nap Lajoie, Philadelphia	14
1902	Socks Seybold, Philadelphia	16
1903	Buck Freeman, Boston	13
1904	Harry Davis, Philadelphia	10
1905	Harry Davis, Philadelphia	8
1906	Harry Davis, Philadelphia	12
1907	Harry Davis, Philadelphia	8
1908	Sam Crawford, Detroit	7
1909	Ty Cobb, Detroit	9
1910	Jake Stahl, Boston	10
1911	Home Run Baker, Philadelphia	11
1912	Home Run Baker, Philadelphia	10
	Tris Speaker, Boston	10
1913	Home Run Baker, Philadelphia	12
1914	Home Run Baker, Philadelphia	9
1915	Braggo Roth, Chicago/Cleveland	7
1916	Wally Pipp, New York	12
1917	Wally Pipp, New York	9
1918	Babe Ruth, Boston	11
	Tilly Walker, Philadelphia	11
1919	Babe Ruth, Boston	29
1920	Babe Ruth, New York	54
1921	Babe Ruth, New York	59
1922	Ken Williams, St. Louis	39
1923	Babe Ruth, New York	41

Year	Player, Club	No.
1924	Babe Ruth, New York	46
1925	Bob Meusel, New York	33
1926	Babe Ruth, New York	47
1927	Babe Ruth, New York	60
1928	Babe Ruth, New York	54
1929	Babe Ruth, New York	46
1930	Babe Ruth, New York	49
1931	Babe Ruth, New York	46
	Lou Gehrig, New York	46
1932	Jimmie Foxx, Philadelphia	58
1933	Jimmie Foxx, Philadelphia	48
1934	Lou Gehrig, New York	49
1935	Jimmie Foxx, Philadelphia	36
	Hank Greenberg, Detroit	36
1936	Lou Gehrig, New York	49
1937	Joe DiMaggio, New York	46
1938	Hank Greenberg, Detroit	58
1939	Jimmie Foxx, Boston	35
1940	Hank Greenberg, Detroit	41
1941	Ted Williams, Boston	37
1942	Ted Williams, Boston	36
1943	Rudy York, Detroit	34
1944	Nick Etten, New York	22
1945	Vern Stephens, St. Louis	24
1946	Hank Greenberg, Detroit	44
1947	Ted Williams, Boston	32
1948	Joe DiMaggio, New York	39
1949	Ted Williams, Boston	43
1950	Al Rosen, Cleveland	37
1951	Gus Zernial, Chicago/Philadelphia	33
1952	Larry Doby, Cleveland	32
1953	Al Rosen, Cleveland	43
1954	Larry Doby, Cleveland	32
1955	Mickey Mantle, New York	37
1956	Mickey Mantle, New York	52
1957	Roy Sievers, Washington	42
1958	Mickey Mantle, New York	42
1959	Rocky Colavito, Cleveland	42
	Harmon Killebrew, Washington	42
1960	Mickey Mantle, New York	40
1961	Roger Maris, New York	61
1962	Harmon Killebrew, Minnesota	48
1963	Harmon Killebrew, Minnesota	45
1964	Harmon Killebrew, Minnesota	49
1965	Tony Conigliaro, Boston	32
1966	Frank Robinson, Baltimore	49
1967	Harmon Killebrew, Minnesota	44
	Carl Yastrzemski, Boston	44
1968	Frank Howard, Washington	44
1969	Harmon Killebrew, Minnesota	49
1970	Frank Howard, Washington	44
1971	Bill Melton, Chicago	33
1972	Dick Allen, Chicago	37
1973	Reggie Jackson, Oakland	32
1974	Dick Allen, Chicago	32
1975	Reggie Jackson, Oakland	36
	George Scott, Milwaukee	36
1976	Graig Nettles, New York	32
1977	Jim Rice, Boston	39
1978	Jim Rice, Boston	46
1979	Gorman Thomas, Milwaukee	45
1980	Reggie Jackson, New York	41
	Ben Oglivie, Milwaukee	41
1981	Tony Armas, Oakland	22
	Dwight Evans, Boston	22
	Bobby Grich, California	22
	Eddie Murray, Baltimore	22
1982	Reggie Jackson, California	39
	Gorman Thomas, Milwaukee	39
1983	Jim Rice, Boston	39
1984	Tony Armas, Boston	43
1985	Darrell Evans, Detroit	40
1986	Jesse Barfield, Toronto	40
1987	Mark McGwire, Oakland	49
1988	Jose Canseco, Oakland	42
1989	Fred McGriff, Toronto	36
1990	Cecil Fielder, Detroit	51
1991	Jose Canseco, Oakland	44
	Cecil Fielder, Detroit	44
1992	Juan Gonzalez, Texas	43
1993	Juan Gonzalez, Texas	46
1994	Ken Griffey Jr., Seattle	40

Year	Player, Club	No.
1995	Albert Belle, Cleveland	50
1996	Mark McGwire, Oakland	52
1997	Ken Griffey Jr., Seattle	56
1998	Ken Griffey Jr., Seattle	56
1999	Ken Griffey Jr., Seattle	48
2000	Troy Glaus, Anaheim	47
2001	Alex Rodriguez, Texas	52
2002	Alex Rodriguez, Texas	57
2003	Alex Rodriguez, Texas	47
2004	Manny Ramirez, Boston	43

NATIONAL LEAGUE

Year	Player, Club	No.
1876	George Hall, Philadelphia	5
1877	Lipman Pike, Cincinnati	4
1878	Paul Hines, Providence	4
1879	Charley Jones, Boston	9
1880	Jim O'Rourke, Boston	6
	Harry Stovey, Worcester	6
1881	Dan Brouthers, Buffalo	8
1882	George Wood, Detroit	7
1883	Buck Ewing, New York	10
1884	Ned Williamson, Chicago	27
1885	Abner Dalrymple, Chicago	11
1886	Dan Brouthers, Detroit	11
	Hardy Richardson, Detroit	11
1887	Billy O'Brien, Washington	19
1888	Jimmy Ryan, Chicago	16
1889	Sam Thompson, Philadelphia	20
1890	Walt Wilmot, Chicago	13
1891	Harry Stovey, Boston	16
	Mike Tiernan, New York	16
1892	Bug Holliday, Cincinnati	13
1893	Ed Delahanty, Philadelphia	19
1894	Hugh Duffy, Boston	18
1895	Sam Thompson, Philadelphia	18
1896	Ed Delahanty, Philadelphia	13
	Bill Joyce, Washington/New York	13
1897	Hugh Duffy, Boston	11
1898	Jimmy Collins, Boston	15
1899	Buck Freeman, Washington	25
1900	Herman Long, Boston	12
1901	Sam Crawford, Cincinnati	16
1902	Tommy Leach, Pittsburgh	6
1903	Jimmy Sheckard, Brooklyn	9
1904	Harry Lumley, Brooklyn	9
1905	Fred Odwell, Cincinnati	9
1906	Tim Jordan, Brooklyn	12
1907	Dave Brain, Boston	10
1908	Tim Jordan, Brooklyn	12
1909	Red Murray, New York	7
1910	Fred Beck, Boston	10
	Frank Schulte, Chicago	10
1911	Frank Schulte, Chicago	21
1912	Heinie Zimmerman, Chicago	14
1913	Gavvy Cravath, Philadelphia	19
1914	Gavvy Cravath, Philadelphia	19
1915	Gavvy Cravath, Philadelphia	24
1916	Dave Robertson, New York	12
	Cy Williams, Chicago	12
1917	Dave Robertson, New York	12
	Gavvy Cravath, Philadelphia	12
1918	Gavvy Cravath, Philadelphia	8
1919	Gavvy Cravath, Philadelphia	12
1920	Cy Williams, Philadelphia	15
1921	George Kelly, New York	23
1922	Rogers Hornsby, St. Louis	42
1923	Cy Williams, Philadelphia	41
1924	Jack Fournier, Brooklyn	27
1925	Rogers Hornsby, St. Louis	39
1926	Hack Wilson, Chicago	21
1927	Hack Wilson, Chicago	30
	Cy Williams, Philadelphia	30
1928	Hack Wilson, Chicago	31
	Jim Bottomley, St. Louis	31
1929	Chuck Klein, Philadelphia	43
1930	Hack Wilson, Chicago	56
1931	Chuck Klein, Philadelphia	31
1932	Chuck Klein, Philadelphia	38
	Mel Ott, New York	38
1933	Chuck Klein, Philadelphia	28
1934	Rip Collins, St. Louis	35

Year	Player, Club	No.
	Mel Ott, New York	35
1935	Wally Berger, Boston	34
1936	Mel Ott, New York	33
1937	Mel Ott, New York	31
	Joe Medwick, St. Louis	31
1938	Mel Ott, New York	36
1939	Johnny Mize, St. Louis	28
1940	Johnny Mize, St. Louis	43
1941	Dolf Camilli, Brooklyn	34
1942	Mel Ott, New York	30
1943	Bill Nicholson, Chicago	29
1944	Bill Nicholson, Chicago	33
1945	Tommy Holmes, Boston	28
1946	Ralph Kiner, Pittsburgh	23
1947	Ralph Kiner, Pittsburgh	51
	Johnny Mize, New York	51
1948	Ralph Kiner, Pittsburgh	40
	Johnny Mize, New York	40
1949	Ralph Kiner, Pittsburgh	54
1950	Ralph Kiner, Pittsburgh	47
1951	Ralph Kiner, Pittsburgh	42
1952	Ralph Kiner, Pittsburgh	37
	Hank Sauer, Chicago	37
1953	Eddie Mathews, Milwaukee	47
1954	Ted Kluszewski, Cincinnati	49
1955	Willie Mays, New York	51
1956	Duke Snider, Brooklyn	43
1957	Hank Aaron, Milwaukee	44
1958	Ernie Banks, Chicago	47
1959	Eddie Mathews, Milwaukee	46
1960	Ernie Banks, Chicago	41
1961	Orlando Cepeda, San Francisco	46
1962	Willie Mays, San Francisco	49
1963	Hank Aaron, Milwaukee	44
	Willie McCovey, San Francisco	44
1964	Willie Mays, San Francisco	47
1965	Willie Mays, San Francisco	52
1966	Hank Aaron, Atlanta	44
1967	Hank Aaron, Atlanta	39
1968	Willie McCovey, San Francisco	36
1969	Willie McCovey, San Francisco	45
1970	Johnny Bench, Cincinnati	45
1971	Willie Stargell, Pittsburgh	48
1972	Johnny Bench, Cincinnati	40
1973	Willie Stargell, Pittsburgh	44
1974	Mike Schmidt, Philadelphia	36
1975	Mike Schmidt, Philadelphia	38
1976	Mike Schmidt, Philadelphia	38
1977	George Foster, Cincinnati	52
1978	George Foster, Cincinnati	40
1979	Dave Kingman, Chicago	48
1980	Mike Schmidt, Philadelphia	48
1981	Mike Schmidt, Philadelphia	31
1982	Dave Kingman, New York	37
1983	Mike Schmidt, Philadelphia	40
1984	Dale Murphy, Atlanta	36
	Mike Schmidt, Philadelphia	36
1985	Dale Murphy, Atlanta	37
1986	Mike Schmidt, Philadelphia	37
1987	Andre Dawson, Chicago	49
1988	Darryl Strawberry, New York	39
1989	Kevin Mitchell, San Francisco	47
1990	Ryne Sandberg, Chicago	40
1991	Howard Johnson, New York	38
1992	Fred McGriff, San Diego	35
1993	Barry Bonds, San Francisco	46
1994	Matt Williams, San Francisco	43
1995	Dante Bichette, Colorado	40
1996	Andres Galarraga, Colorado	47
1997	Larry Walker, Colorado	*49
1998	Mark McGwire, St. Louis	70
1999	Mark McGwire, St. Louis	65
2000	Sammy Sosa, Chicago	50
2001	Barry Bonds, San Francisco	73
2002	Sammy Sosa, Chicago	49
2003	Jim Thome, Philadelphia	47
2004	Adrian Beltre, Los Angeles	48

*Mark McGwire led the majors with 58 home runs in 1997, 34 with Oakland (A.L.) and 24 with St. Louis (N.L.) following a July 31 trade.

TOTAL BASES

AMERICAN LEAGUE

Year	Player, Club	No.
1901	Nap Lajoie, Philadelphia	350
1902	Charlie Hickman, Boston/Cleveland	288
1903	Buck Freeman, Boston	281
1904	Nap Lajoie, Cleveland	302
1905	George Stone, St. Louis	259
1906	George Stone, St. Louis	291
1907	Ty Cobb, Detroit	283
1908	Ty Cobb, Detroit	276
1909	Ty Cobb, Detroit	296
1910	Nap Lajoie, Cleveland	304
1911	Ty Cobb, Detroit	367
1912	Joe Jackson, Cleveland	331
1913	Sam Crawford, Detroit	298
1914	Tris Speaker, Boston	287
1915	Ty Cobb, Detroit	274
1916	Joe Jackson, Chicago	293
1917	Ty Cobb, Detroit	335
1918	George H. Burns, Philadelphia	236
1919	Babe Ruth, Boston	284
1920	George Sisler, St. Louis	399
1921	Babe Ruth, New York	457
1922	Ken Williams, St. Louis	367
1923	Babe Ruth, New York	399
1924	Babe Ruth, New York	391
1925	Al Simmons, Philadelphia	392
1926	Babe Ruth, New York	365
1927	Lou Gehrig, New York	447
1928	Babe Ruth, New York	380
1929	Al Simmons, Philadelphia	373
1930	Lou Gehrig, New York	419
1931	Lou Gehrig, New York	410
1932	Jimmie Foxx, Philadelphia	438
1933	Jimmie Foxx, Philadelphia	403
1934	Lou Gehrig, New York	409
1935	Hank Greenberg, Detroit	389
1936	Hal Trosky, Cleveland	405
1937	Joe DiMaggio, New York	418
1938	Jimmie Foxx, Boston	398
1939	Ted Williams, Boston	344
1940	Hank Greenberg, Detroit	384
1941	Joe DiMaggio, New York	348
1942	Ted Williams, Boston	338
1943	Rudy York, Detroit	301
1944	Johnny Lindell, New York	297
1945	George Stirnweiss, New York	301
1946	Ted Williams, Boston	343
1947	Ted Williams, Boston	335
1948	Joe DiMaggio, New York	355
1949	Ted Williams, Boston	368
1950	Walt Dropo, Boston	326
1951	Ted Williams, Boston	295
1952	Al Rosen, Cleveland	297
1953	Al Rosen, Cleveland	367
1954	Minnie Minoso, Chicago	304
1955	Al Kaline, Detroit	321
1956	Mickey Mantle, New York	376
1957	Roy Sievers, Washington	331
1958	Mickey Mantle, New York	307
1959	Rocky Colavito, Cleveland	301
1960	Mickey Mantle, New York	294
1961	Roger Maris, New York	366
1962	Rocky Colavito, Detroit	309
1963	Dick Stuart, Boston	319
1964	Tony Oliva, Minnesota	374
1965	Zoilo Versalles, Minnesota	308
1966	Frank Robinson, Baltimore	367
1967	Carl Yastrzemski, Boston	360
1968	Frank Howard, Washington	330
1969	Frank Howard, Washington	340
1970	Carl Yastrzemski, Boston	335
1971	Reggie Smith, Boston	302
1972	Bobby Murcer, New York	314
1973	Dave May, Milwaukee	295
	George Scott, Milwaukee	295
	Sal Bando, Oakland	295
1974	Joe Rudi, Oakland	287
1975	George Scott, Milwaukee	318

Year	Player, Club	No.
1976	George Brett, Kansas City	298
1977	Jim Rice, Boston	382
1978	Jim Rice, Boston	406
1979	Jim Rice, Boston	369
1980	Cecil Cooper, Milwaukee	335
1981	Dwight Evans, Boston	215
1982	Robin Yount, Milwaukee	367
1983	Jim Rice, Boston	344
1984	Tony Armas, Boston	339
1985	Don Mattingly, New York	370
1986	Don Mattingly, New York	388
1987	George Bell, Toronto	369
1988	Kirby Puckett, Minnesota	358
1989	Ruben Sierra, Texas	344
1990	Cecil Fielder, Detroit	339
1991	Cal Ripken, Baltimore	368
1992	Kirby Puckett, Minnesota	313
1993	Ken Griffey Jr., Seattle	359
1994	Albert Belle, Cleveland	294
1995	Albert Belle, Cleveland	377
1996	Alex Rodriguez, Seattle	379
1997	Ken Griffey Jr., Seattle	393
1998	Albert Belle, Chicago	399
1999	Shawn Green, Toronto	361
2000	Carlos Delgado, Toronto	378
2001	Alex Rodriguez, Texas	393
2002	Alex Rodriguez, Texas	389
2003	Vernon Wells, Toronto	373
2004	Vladimir Guerrero, Anaheim	366

NATIONAL LEAGUE

Year	Player, Club	No.
1900	Elmer Flick, Philadelphia	302
1901	Jesse Burkett, St. Louis	306
1902	Sam Crawford, Cincinnati	256
1903	Ginger Beaumont, Pittsburgh	272
1904	Honus Wagner, Pittsburgh	255
1905	Cy Seymour, Cincinnati	325
1906	Honus Wagner, Pittsburgh	237
1907	Honus Wagner, Pittsburgh	264
1908	Honus Wagner, Pittsburgh	308
1909	Honus Wagner, Pittsburgh	242
1910	Sherry Magee, Philadelphia	263
1911	Frank Schulte, Chicago	308
1912	Heinie Zimmerman, Chicago	318
1913	Gavvy Cravath, Philadelphia	298
1914	Sherry Magee, Philadelphia	277
1915	Gavvy Cravath, Philadelphia	266
1916	Zack Wheat, Brooklyn	262
1917	Rogers Hornsby, St. Louis	253
1918	Charlie Hollocher, Chicago	202
1919	Hy Myers, Brooklyn	223
1920	Rogers Hornsby, St. Louis	329
1921	Rogers Hornsby, St. Louis	378
1922	Rogers Hornsby, St. Louis	450
1923	Frankie Frisch, New York	311
1924	Rogers Hornsby, St. Louis	373
1925	Rogers Hornsby, St. Louis	381
1926	Jim Bottomley, St. Louis	305
1927	Paul Waner, Pittsburgh	342
1928	Jim Bottomley, St. Louis	362
1929	Rogers Hornsby, Chicago	409
1930	Chuck Klein, Philadelphia	445
1931	Chuck Klein, Philadelphia	347
1932	Chuck Klein, Philadelphia	420
1933	Chuck Klein, Philadelphia	365
1934	Rip Collins, St. Louis	369
1935	Joe Medwick, St. Louis	365
1936	Joe Medwick, St. Louis	367
1937	Joe Medwick, St. Louis	406
1938	Johnny Mize, St. Louis	326
1939	Johnny Mize, St. Louis	353
1940	Johnny Mize, St. Louis	368
1941	Pete Reiser, Brooklyn	299
1942	Enos Slaughter, St. Louis	292
1943	Stan Musial, St. Louis	347
1944	Bill Nicholson, Chicago	317
1945	Tommy Holmes, Boston	367
1946	Stan Musial, St. Louis	366
1947	Ralph Kiner, Pittsburgh	361
1948	Stan Musial, St. Louis	429

Year	Player, Club	No.
1949	Stan Musial, St. Louis	382
1950	Duke Snider, Brooklyn	343
1951	Stan Musial, St. Louis	355
1952	Stan Musial, St. Louis	311
1953	Duke Snider, Brooklyn	370
1954	Duke Snider, Brooklyn	378
1955	Willie Mays, New York	382
1956	Hank Aaron, Milwaukee	340
1957	Hank Aaron, Milwaukee	369
1958	Ernie Banks, Chicago	379
1959	Hank Aaron, Milwaukee	400
1960	Hank Aaron, Milwaukee	334
1961	Hank Aaron, Milwaukee	358
1962	Willie Mays, San Francisco	382
1963	Hank Aaron, Milwaukee	370
1964	Dick Allen, Philadelphia	352
1965	Willie Mays, San Francisco	360
1966	Felipe Alou, Atlanta	355
1967	Hank Aaron, Atlanta	344
1968	Billy Williams, Chicago	321
1969	Hank Aaron, Atlanta	332
1970	Billy Williams, Chicago	373
1971	Joe Torre, St. Louis	352
1972	Billy Williams, Chicago	348
1973	Bobby Bonds, San Francisco	341
1974	Johnny Bench, Cincinnati	315
1975	Greg Luzinski, Philadelphia	322
1976	Mike Schmidt, Philadelphia	306
1977	George Foster, Cincinnati	388
1978	Dave Parker, Pittsburgh	340
1979	Dave Winfield, San Diego	333
1980	Mike Schmidt, Philadelphia	342
1981	Mike Schmidt, Philadelphia	228
1982	Al Oliver, Montreal	317
1983	Andre Dawson, Montreal	341
1984	Dale Murphy, Atlanta	332
1985	Dave Parker, Cincinnati	350
1986	Dave Parker, Cincinnati	304
1987	Andre Dawson, Chicago	353
1988	Andres Galarraga, Montreal	329
1989	Kevin Mitchell, San Francisco	345
1990	Ryne Sandberg, Chicago	344
1991	Will Clark, San Francisco	303
	Terry Pendleton, Atlanta	303
1992	Gary Sheffield, San Diego	323
1993	Barry Bonds, San Francisco	365
1994	Jeff Bagwell, Houston	300
1995	Dante Bichette, Colorado	359
1996	Ellis Burks, Colorado	392
1997	Larry Walker, Colorado	409
1998	Sammy Sosa, Chicago	416
1999	Sammy Sosa, Chicago	397
2000	Todd Helton, Colorado	405
2001	Sammy Sosa, Chicago	425
2002	Vladimir Guerrero, Montreal	364
2003	Albert Pujols, St. Louis	394
2004	Albert Pujols, St. Louis	389

RUNS BATTED IN

AMERICAN LEAGUE

Year	Player, Club	No.
1907	Ty Cobb, Detroit	119
1908	Ty Cobb, Detroit	108
1909	Ty Cobb, Detroit	107
1910	Sam Crawford, Detroit	120
1911	Ty Cobb, Detroit	127
1912	Home Run Baker, Philadelphia	130
1913	Home Run Baker, Philadelphia	117
1914	Sam Crawford, Detroit	104
1915	Sam Crawford, Detroit	112
	Bobby Veach, Detroit	112
1916	Del Pratt, St. Louis	103
1917	Bobby Veach, Detroit	103
1918	Bobby Veach, Detroit	78
1919	Babe Ruth, Boston	114
1920	Babe Ruth, New York	137
1921	Babe Ruth, New York	171
1922	Ken Williams, St. Louis	155
1923	Babe Ruth, New York	131

Year	Player, Club	No.
1924	Goose Goslin, Washington	129
1925	Bob Meusel, New York	138
1926	Babe Ruth, New York	146
1927	Lou Gehrig, New York	175
1928	Babe Ruth, New York	142
	Lou Gehrig, New York	142
1929	Al Simmons, Philadelphia	157
1930	Lou Gehrig, New York	174
1931	Lou Gehrig, New York	184
1932	Jimmie Foxx, Philadelphia	169
1933	Jimmie Foxx, Philadelphia	163
1934	Lou Gehrig, New York	165
1935	Hank Greenberg, Detroit	170
1936	Hal Trosky, Cleveland	162
1937	Hank Greenberg, Detroit	183
1938	Jimmie Foxx, Boston	175
1939	Ted Williams, Boston	145
1940	Hank Greenberg, Detroit	150
1941	Joe DiMaggio, New York	125
1942	Ted Williams, Boston	137
1943	Rudy York, Detroit	118
1944	Vern Stephens, St. Louis	109
1945	Nick Etten, New York	111
1946	Hank Greenberg, Detroit	127
1947	Ted Williams, Boston	114
1948	Joe DiMaggio, New York	155
1949	Ted Williams, Boston	159
	Vern Stephens, Boston	159
1950	Walt Dropo, Boston	144
	Vern Stephens, Boston	144
1951	Gus Zernial, Chicago-Philadelphia	129
1952	Al Rosen, Cleveland	105
1953	Al Rosen, Cleveland	145
1954	Larry Doby, Cleveland	126
1955	Ray Boone, Detroit	116
	Jackie Jensen, Boston	116
1956	Mickey Mantle, New York	130
1957	Roy Sievers, Washington	114
1958	Jackie Jensen, Boston	122
1959	Jackie Jensen, Boston	112
1960	Roger Maris, New York	112
1961	Roger Maris, New York	142
1962	Harmon Killebrew, Minnesota	126
1963	Dick Stuart, Boston	118
1964	Brooks Robinson, Baltimore	118
1965	Rocky Colavito, Cleveland	108
1966	Frank Robinson, Baltimore	122
1967	Carl Yastrzemski, Boston	121
1968	Ken Harrelson, Boston	109
1969	Harmon Killebrew, Minnesota	140
1970	Frank Howard, Washington	126
1971	Harmon Killebrew, Minnesota	119
1972	Dick Allen, Chicago	113
1973	Reggie Jackson, Oakland	117
1974	Jeff Burroughs, Texas	118
1975	George Scott, Milwaukee	109
1976	Lee May, Baltimore	109
1977	Larry Hisle, Minnesota	119
1978	Jim Rice, Boston	139
1979	Don Baylor, California	139
1980	Cecil Cooper, Milwaukee	122
1981	Eddie Murray, Baltimore	78
1982	Hal McRae, Kansas City	133
1983	Cecil Cooper, Milwaukee	126
	Jim Rice, Boston	126
1984	Tony Armas, Boston	123
1985	Don Mattingly, New York	145
1986	Joe Carter, Cleveland	121
1987	George Bell, Toronto	134
1988	Jose Canseco, Oakland	124
1989	Ruben Sierra, Texas	119
1990	Cecil Fielder, Detroit	132
1991	Cecil Fielder, Detroit	133
1992	Cecil Fielder, Detroit	124
1993	Albert Belle, Cleveland	129
1994	Kirby Puckett, Minnesota	112
1995	Albert Belle, Cleveland	126
	Mo Vaughn, Boston	126
1996	Albert Belle, Cleveland	148
1997	Ken Griffey Jr., Seattle	147
1998	Juan Gonzalez, Texas	157
1999	Manny Ramirez, Cleveland	165
2000	Edgar Martinez, Seattle	145
2001	Bret Boone, Seattle	141
2002	Alex Rodriguez, Texas	142
2003	Carlos Delgado, Toronto	145
2004	Miguel Tejada, Baltimore	150

NATIONAL LEAGUE

Year	Player, Club	No.
1907	Sherry Magee, Philadelphia	85
1908	Honus Wagner, Pittsburgh	109
1909	Honus Wagner, Pittsburgh	100
1910	Sherry Magee, Philadelphia	123
1911	Frank Schulte, Chicago	107
	Chief Wilson, Pittsburgh	107
1912	Honus Wagner, Pittsburgh	102
1913	Gavvy Cravath, Philadelphia	128
1914	Sherry Magee, Philadelphia	103
1915	Gavvy Cravath, Philadelphia	115
1916	Heinie Zimmerman, Chicago/New York	83
1917	Heinie Zimmerman, New York	102
1918	Sherry Magee, Cincinnati	76
1919	Hy Myers, Brooklyn	73
1920	George Kelly, New York	94
	Rogers Hornsby, St. Louis	94
1921	Rogers Hornsby, St. Louis	126
1922	Rogers Hornsby, St. Louis	152
1923	Irish Meusel, New York	125
1924	George Kelly, New York	136
1925	Rogers Hornsby, St. Louis	143
1926	Jim Bottomley, St. Louis	120
1927	Paul Waner, Pittsburgh	131
1928	Jim Bottomley, St. Louis	136
1929	Hack Wilson, Chicago	159
1930	Hack Wilson, Chicago	191
1931	Chuck Klein, Philadelphia	121
1932	Don Hurst, Philadelphia	143
1933	Chuck Klein, Philadelphia	120
1934	Mel Ott, New York	135
1935	Wally Berger, Boston	130
1936	Joe Medwick, St. Louis	138
1937	Joe Medwick, St. Louis	154
1938	Joe Medwick, St. Louis	122
1939	Frank McCormick, Cincinnati	128
1940	Johnny Mize, St. Louis	137
1941	Dolf Camilli, Brooklyn	120
1942	Johnny Mize, New York	110
1943	Bill Nicholson, Chicago	128
1944	Bill Nicholson, Chicago	122
1945	Dixie Walker, Brooklyn	124
1946	Enos Slaughter, St. Louis	130
1947	Johnny Mize, New York	138
1948	Stan Musial, St. Louis	131
1949	Ralph Kiner, Pittsburgh	127
1950	Del Ennis, Philadelphia	126
1951	Monte Irvin, New York	121
1952	Hank Sauer, Chicago	121
1953	Roy Campanella, Brooklyn	142
1954	Ted Kluszewski, Cincinnati	141
1955	Duke Snider, Brooklyn	136
1956	Stan Musial, St. Louis	109
1957	Hank Aaron, Milwaukee	132
1958	Ernie Banks, Chicago	129
1959	Ernie Banks, Chicago	143
1960	Hank Aaron, Milwaukee	126
1961	Orlando Cepeda, San Francisco	142
1962	Tommy Davis, Los Angeles	153
1963	Hank Aaron, Milwaukee	130
1964	Ken Boyer, St. Louis	119
1965	Deron Johnson, Cincinnati	130
1966	Hank Aaron, Atlanta	127
1967	Orlando Cepeda, St. Louis	111
1968	Willie McCovey, San Francisco	105
1969	Willie McCovey, San Francisco	126
1970	Johnny Bench, Cincinnati	148
1971	Joe Torre, St. Louis	137
1972	Johnny Bench, Cincinnati	125
1973	Willie Stargell, Pittsburgh	119
1974	Johnny Bench, Cincinnati	129
1975	Greg Luzinski, Philadelphia	120
1976	George Foster, Cincinnati	121

Year	Player, Club	No.
1977	George Foster, Cincinnati	149
1978	George Foster, Cincinnati	120
1979	Dave Winfield, San Diego	118
1980	Mike Schmidt, Philadelphia	121
1981	Mike Schmidt, Philadelphia	91
1982	Dale Murphy, Atlanta	109
	Al Oliver, Montreal	109
1983	Dale Murphy, Atlanta	121
1984	Gary Carter, Montreal	106
	Mike Schmidt, Philadelphia	106
1985	Dave Parker, Cincinnati	125
1986	Mike Schmidt, Philadelphia	119
1987	Andre Dawson, Chicago	137
1988	Will Clark, San Francisco	109
1989	Kevin Mitchell, San Francisco	125
1990	Matt Williams, San Francisco	122
1991	Howard Johnson, New York	117
1992	Darren Daulton, Philadelphia	109
1993	Barry Bonds, San Francisco	123
1994	Jeff Bagwell, Houston	116
1995	Dante Bichette, Colorado	128
1996	Andres Galarraga, Colorado	150
1997	Andres Galarraga, Colorado	140
1998	Sammy Sosa, Chicago	158
1999	Mark McGwire, St. Louis	147
2000	Todd Helton, Colorado	147
2001	Sammy Sosa, Chicago	160
2002	Lance Berkman, Houston	128
2003	Preston Wilson, Colorado	141
2004	Vinnie Castilla, Colorado	131

Note—official statistic since 1920

Year	Player, Club	No.
1955	Mickey Mantle, New York	113
1956	Eddie Yost, Washington	151
1957	Mickey Mantle, New York	146
1958	Mickey Mantle, New York	129
1959	Eddie Yost, Detroit	135
1960	Eddie Yost, Detroit	125
1961	Mickey Mantle, New York	126
1962	Mickey Mantle, New York	122
1963	Carl Yastrzemski, Boston	95
1964	Norm Siebern, Baltimore	106
1965	Rocky Colavito, Cleveland	93
1966	Harmon Killebrew, Minnesota	103
1967	Harmon Killebrew, Minnesota	131
1968	Carl Yastrzemski, Boston	119
1969	Harmon Killebrew, Minnesota	145
1970	Frank Howard, Washington	132
1971	Harmon Killebrew, Minnesota	114
1972	Dick Allen, Chicago	99
	Roy White, New York	99
1973	John Mayberry, Kansas City	122
1974	Gene Tenace, Oakland	110
1975	John Mayberry, Kansas City	119
1976	Mike Hargrove, Texas	97
1977	Toby Harrah, Texas	109
1978	Mike Hargrove, Texas	107
1979	Darrell Porter, Kansas City	121
1980	Willie Randolph, New York	119
1981	Dwight Evans, Boston	85
1982	Rickey Henderson, Oakland	116
1983	Rickey Henderson, Oakland	103
1984	Eddie Murray, Baltimore	107
1985	Dwight Evans, Boston	114
1986	Wade Boggs, Boston	105
1987	Brian Downing, California	106
	Dwight Evans, Boston	106
1988	Wade Boggs, Boston	125
1989	Rickey Henderson, New York/Oakland	126
1990	Mark McGwire, Oakland	110
1991	Frank Thomas, Chicago	138
1992	Mickey Tettleton, Detroit	122
	Frank Thomas, Chicago	122
1993	Tony Phillips, Detroit	132
1994	Frank Thomas, Chicago	109
1995	Frank Thomas, Chicago	136
1996	Tony Phillips, Chicago	125
1997	Jim Thome, Cleveland	120
1998	Rickey Henderson, Oakland	118
1999	Jim Thome, Cleveland	127
2000	Jason Giambi, Oakland	137
2001	Jason Giambi, Oakland	129
2002	Jim Thome, Cleveland	122
2003	Jason Giambi, New York	129
2004	Eric Chavez, Oakland	95

BASES ON BALLS

AMERICAN LEAGUE

Year	Player, Club	No.
1913	Burt Shotton, St. Louis	99
1914	Donie Bush, Detroit	112
1915	Eddie Collins, Chicago	119
1916	Burt Shotton, St. Louis	110
1917	Jack Graney, Cleveland	94
1918	Ray Chapman, Cleveland	84
1919	Jack Graney, Cleveland	105
1920	Babe Ruth, New York	150
1921	Babe Ruth, New York	145
1922	Whitey Witt, New York	89
1923	Babe Ruth, New York	170
1924	Babe Ruth, New York	142
1925	Willie Kamm, Chicago	90
	Johnny Mostil, Chicago	90
1926	Babe Ruth, New York	144
1927	Babe Ruth, New York	138
1928	Babe Ruth, New York	135
1929	Max Bishop, Philadelphia	128
1930	Babe Ruth, New York	136
1931	Babe Ruth, New York	128
1932	Babe Ruth, New York	130
1933	Babe Ruth, New York	114
1934	Jimmie Foxx, Philadelphia	111
1935	Lou Gehrig, New York	132
1936	Lou Gehrig, New York	130
1937	Lou Gehrig, New York	127
1938	Jimmie Foxx, Boston	119
	Hank Greenberg, Detroit	119
1939	Harlond Clift, St. Louis	111
1940	Charlie Keller, New York	106
1941	Ted Williams, Boston	147
1942	Ted Williams, Boston	145
1943	Charlie Keller, New York	106
1944	Nick Etten, New York	97
1945	Roy Cullenbine, Cleveland/Detroit	112
1946	Ted Williams, Boston	156
1947	Ted Williams, Boston	162
1948	Ted Williams, Boston	126
1949	Ted Williams, Boston	162
1950	Eddie Yost, Washington	141
1951	Ted Williams, Boston	144
1952	Eddie Yost, Washington	129
1953	Eddie Yost, Washington	123
1954	Ted Williams, Boston	136

NATIONAL LEAGUE

Year	Player, Club	No.
1910	Miller Huggins, St. Louis	116
1911	Jimmy Sheckard, Chicago	147
1912	Jimmy Sheckard, Chicago	122
1913	Bob Bescher, Cincinnati	94
1914	Miller Huggins, St. Louis	105
1915	Gavvy Cravath, Philadelphia	86
1916	Heinie Groh, Cincinnati	84
1917	George J. Burns, New York	75
1918	Max Carey, Pittsburgh	62
1919	George J. Burns, New York	82
1920	George J. Burns, New York	76
1921	George J. Burns, New York	80
1922	Max Carey, Pittsburgh	80
1923	George J. Burns, New York	101
1924	Rogers Hornsby, St. Louis	89
1925	Jack Fournier, Brooklyn	86
1926	Hack Wilson, Chicago	69
1927	Rogers Hornsby, New York	86
1928	Rogers Hornsby, Boston	107
1929	Mel Ott, New York	113
1930	Hack Wilson, Chicago	105
1931	Mel Ott, New York	80
1932	Mel Ott, New York	100
1933	Mel Ott, New York	75
1934	Arky Vaughan, Pittsburgh	94

Year	Player, Club	No.
1935	Arky Vaughan, Pittsburgh	97
1936	Arky Vaughan, Pittsburgh	118
1937	Mel Ott, New York	102
1938	Dolf Camilli, Brooklyn	119
1939	Dolf Camilli, Brooklyn	110
1940	Elbie Fletcher, Pittsburgh	119
1941	Elbie Fletcher, Pittsburgh	118
1942	Mel Ott, New York	109
1943	Augie Galan, Brooklyn	103
1944	Augie Galan, Brooklyn	101
1945	Eddie Stanky, Brooklyn	148
1946	Eddie Stanky, Brooklyn	137
1947	Hank Greenberg, Pittsburgh	104
	Pee Wee Reese, Brooklyn	104
1948	Bob Elliott, Boston	131
1949	Ralph Kiner, Pittsburgh	117
1950	Eddie Stanky, New York	144
1951	Ralph Kiner, Pittsburgh	137
1952	Ralph Kiner, Pittsburgh	110
1953	Stan Musial, St. Louis	105
1954	Richie Ashburn, Philadelphia	125
1955	Eddie Mathews, Milwaukee	109
1956	Duke Snider, Brooklyn	99
1957	Richie Ashburn, Philadelphia	94
	Johnny Temple, Cincinnati	94
1958	Richie Ashburn, Philadelphia	97
1959	Jim Gilliam, Los Angeles	96
1960	Richie Ashburn, Chicago	116
1961	Eddie Mathews, Milwaukee	93
1962	Eddie Mathews, Milwaukee	101
1963	Eddie Mathews, Milwaukee	124
1964	Ron Santo, Chicago	86
1965	Joe Morgan, Houston	97
1966	Ron Santo, Chicago	95
1967	Ron Santo, Chicago	96
1968	Ron Santo, Chicago	96
1969	Jim Wynn, Houston	148
1970	Willie McCovey, San Francisco	137
1971	Willie Mays, San Francisco	112
1972	Joe Morgan, Cincinnati	115
1973	Darrell Evans, Atlanta	124
1974	Darrell Evans, Atlanta	126
1975	Joe Morgan, Cincinnati	132
1976	Jim Wynn, Atlanta	127
1977	Gene Tenace, San Diego	125
1978	Jeff Burroughs, Atlanta	117
1979	Mike Schmidt, Philadelphia	120
1980	Dan Driessen, Cincinnati	93
	Joe Morgan, Houston	93
1981	Mike Schmidt, Philadelphia	73
1982	Mike Schmidt, Philadelphia	107
1983	Mike Schmidt, Philadelphia	128
1984	Gary Matthews, Chicago	103
1985	Dale Murphy, Atlanta	90
1986	Keith Hernandez, New York	94
1987	Jack Clark, St. Louis	136
1988	Will Clark, San Francisco	100
1989	Jack Clark, San Diego	132
1990	Jack Clark, San Diego	104
1991	Brett Butler, Los Angeles	108
1992	Barry Bonds, Pittsburgh	127
1993	Lenny Dykstra, Philadelphia	129
1994	Barry Bonds, San Francisco	74
1995	Barry Bonds, San Francisco	120
1996	Barry Bonds, San Francisco	151
1997	Barry Bonds, San Francisco	145
1998	Mark McGwire, St. Louis	162
1999	Jeff Bagwell, Houston	149
2000	Barry Bonds, San Francisco	117
2001	Barry Bonds, San Francisco	177
2002	Barry Bonds, San Francisco	198
2003	Barry Bonds, San Francisco	148
2004	Barry Bonds, San Francisco	232

Note—not included in batting records in A.L. prior to 1913 and N.L. prior to 1910

STRIKEOUTS

AMERICAN LEAGUE

Year	Player, Club	No.
1913	Danny Moeller, Washington	103

Year	Player, Club	No.
1914	Gus Williams, St. Louis	120
1915	Doc Lavan, St. Louis	83
1916	Wally Pipp, New York	82
1917	Braggo Roth, Cleveland	73
1918	Babe Ruth, Boston	58
1919	Red Shannon, Philadelphia/Boston	70
1920	Aaron Ward, New York	84
1921	Bob Meusel, New York	88
1922	Jimmie Dykes, Philadelphia	98
1923	Babe Ruth, New York	93
1924	Babe Ruth, New York	81
1925	Marty McManus, St. Louis	69
1926	Tony Lazzeri, New York	96
1927	Babe Ruth, New York	89
1928	Babe Ruth, New York	87
1929	Jimmie Foxx, Philadelphia	70
1930	Jimmie Foxx, Philadelphia	66
	Ed Morgan, Cleveland	66
1931	Jimmie Foxx, Philadelphia	84
1932	Bruce Campbell, Chicago/St. Louis	104
1933	Jimmie Foxx, Philadelphia	93
1934	Harlond Clift, St. Louis	100
1935	Jimmie Foxx, Philadelphia	99
1936	Jimmie Foxx, Boston	119
1937	Frank Crosetti, New York	105
1938	Frank Crosetti, New York	97
1939	Hank Greenberg, Detroit	95
1940	Sam Chapman, Philadelphia	96
1941	Jimmie Foxx, Boston	103
1942	Joe Gordon, New York	95
1943	Chet Laabs, St. Louis	105
1944	Pat Seerey, Cleveland	99
1945	Pat Seerey, Cleveland	97
1946	Charlie Keller, New York	101
	Pat Seerey, Cleveland	101
1947	Eddie Joost, Philadelphia	110
1948	Pat Seerey, Cleveland/Chicago	102
1949	Dick Kokos, St. Louis	91
1950	Gus Zernial, Chicago	110
1951	Gus Zernial, Chicago/Philadelphia	101
1952	Larry Doby, Cleveland	111
	Mickey Mantle, New York	111
1953	Larry Doby, Cleveland	121
1954	Mickey Mantle, New York	107
1955	Norm Zauchin, Boston	105
1956	Jim Lemon, Washington	138
1957	Jim Lemon, Washington	94
1958	Jim Lemon, Washington	120
	Mickey Mantle, New York	120
1959	Mickey Mantle, New York	126
1960	Mickey Mantle, New York	125
1961	Jake Wood, Detroit	141
1962	Harmon Killebrew, Minnesota	142
1963	Dave Nicholson, Chicago	175
1964	Nelson Mathews, Kansas City	143
1965	Zoilo Versalles, Minnesota	122
1966	George Scott, Boston	152
1967	Frank Howard, Washington	155
1968	Reggie Jackson, Oakland	171
1969	Reggie Jackson, Oakland	142
1970	Reggie Jackson, Oakland	135
1971	Reggie Jackson, Oakland	161
1972	Bobby Darwin, Minnesota	145
1973	Bobby Darwin, Minnesota	137
1974	Bobby Darwin, Minnesota	127
1975	Jeff Burroughs, Texas	155
1976	Jim Rice, Boston	123
1977	Butch Hobson, Boston	162
1978	Gary Alexander, Oakland/Cleveland	166
1979	Gorman Thomas, Milwaukee	175
1980	Gorman Thomas, Milwaukee	170
1981	Tony Armas, Oakland	115
1982	Reggie Jackson, California	156
1983	Ron Kittle, Chicago	150
1984	Tony Armas, Boston	156
1985	Steve Balboni, Kansas City	166
1986	Pete Incaviglia, Texas	185
1987	Rob Deer, Milwaukee	186
1988	Rob Deer, Milwaukee	153
	Pete Incaviglia, Texas	153
1989	Bo Jackson, Kansas City	172
1990	Cecil Fielder, Detroit	182

Year	Player, Club	No.
1991	Rob Deer, Detroit	175
1992	Dean Palmer, Texas	154
1993	Rob Deer, Detroit/Boston	169
1994	Travis Fryman, Detroit	128
1995	Mo Vaughn, Boston	150
1996	Jay Buhner, Seattle	159
1997	Jay Buhner, Seattle	175
1998	Jose Canseco, Toronto	159
1999	Jim Thome, Cleveland	171
2000	Mo Vaughn, Anaheim	181
2001	Jim Thome, Cleveland	185
2002	Mike Cameron, Seattle	176
2003	Jason Giambi, New York	140
2004	Mark Bellhorn, Boston	177

NATIONAL LEAGUE

Year	Player, Club	No.
1910	John Hummel, Brooklyn	81
1911	Bob Bescher, Cincinnati	78
	Bob Coulson, Brooklyn	78
1912	Ed McDonald, Boston	91
1913	George J. Burns, New York	74
1914	Fred Merkle, New York	80
1915	Doug Baird, Pittsburgh	88
1916	Gavvy Cravath, Philadelphia	89
1917	Cy Williams, Chicago	78
1918	Ross Youngs, New York	49
	Dode Paskert, Chicago	49
1919	Ray Powell, Boston	79
1920	George Kelly, New York	92
1921	Ray Powell, Boston	85
1922	Frank Parkinson, Philadelphia	93
1923	George Grantham, Chicago	92
1924	George Grantham, Chicago	63
1925	Gabby Hartnett, Chicago	77
1926	Barney Friberg, Philadelphia	77
1927	Hack Wilson, Chicago	70
1928	Hack Wilson, Chicago	94
1929	Hack Wilson, Chicago	83
1930	Hack Wilson, Chicago	84
1931	Nick Cullop, Cincinnati	86
1932	Hack Wilson, Brooklyn	85
1933	Wally Berger, Boston	77
1934	Dolf Camilli, Chicago/Philadelphia	94
1935	Dolf Camilli, Philadelphia	113
1936	Bill Brubaker, Pittsburgh	96
1937	Vince DiMaggio, Boston	111
1938	Vince DiMaggio, Boston	134
1939	Dolf Camilli, Brooklyn	107
1940	Chet Ross, Boston	128
1941	Dolf Camilli, Brooklyn	115
1942	Vince DiMaggio, Pittsburgh	87
1943	Vince DiMaggio, Pittsburgh	126
1944	Vince DiMaggio, Pittsburgh	83
1945	Vince DiMaggio, Philadelphia	91
1946	Ralph Kiner, Pittsburgh	109
1947	Bill Nicholson, Chicago	83
1948	Hank Sauer, Cincinnati	85
1949	Duke Snider, Brooklyn	92
1950	Roy Smalley, Chicago	114
1951	Gil Hodges, Brooklyn	99
1952	Eddie Mathews, Boston	115
1953	Steve Bilko, St. Louis	125
1954	Duke Snider, Brooklyn	96
1955	Wally Post, Cincinnati	102
1956	Wally Post, Cincinnati	124
1957	Duke Snider, Brooklyn	104
1958	Harry Anderson, Philadelphia	95
1959	Wally Post, Philadelphia	101
1960	Frank Herrera, Philadelphia	136
1961	Dick Stuart, Pittsburgh	121
1962	Ken Hubbs, Chicago	129
1963	Donn Clendenon, Pittsburgh	136
1964	Dick Allen, Philadelphia	138
1965	Dick Allen, Philadelphia	150
1966	Byron Browne, Chicago	143
1967	Jim Wynn, Houston	137
1968	Donn Clendenon, Pittsburgh	163
1969	Bobby Bonds, San Francisco	187
1970	Bobby Bonds, San Francisco	189
1971	Willie Stargell, Pittsburgh	154

Year	Player, Club	No.
1972	Lee May, Houston	145
1973	Bobby Bonds, San Francisco	148
1974	Mike Schmidt, Philadelphia	138
1975	Mike Schmidt, Philadelphia	180
1976	Mike Schmidt, Philadelphia	149
1977	Greg Luzinski, Philadelphia	140
1978	Dale Murphy, Atlanta	145
1979	Dave Kingman, Chicago	131
1980	Dale Murphy, Atlanta	133
1981	Dave Kingman, New York	105
1982	Dave Kingman, New York	156
1983	Mike Schmidt, Philadelphia	148
1984	Juan Samuel, Philadelphia	168
1985	Dale Murphy, Atlanta	141
	Juan Samuel, Philadelphia	141
1986	Juan Samuel, Philadelphia	142
1987	Juan Samuel, Philadelphia	162
1988	Andres Galarraga, Montreal	153
1989	Andres Galarraga, Montreal	158
1990	Andres Galarraga, Montreal	169
1991	Delino DeShields, Montreal	151
1992	Ray Lankford, St. Louis	147
1993	Cory Snyder, Los Angeles	147
1994	Reggie Sanders, Cincinnati	114
1995	Andres Galarraga, Colorado	146
1996	Henry Rodriguez, Montreal	160
1997	Sammy Sosa, Chicago	174
1998	Sammy Sosa, Chicago	171
1999	Sammy Sosa, Chicago	171
2000	Preston Wilson, Florida	187
2001	Jose Hernandez, Milwaukee	185
2002	Jose Hernandez, Milwaukee	188
2003	Jim Thome, Philadelphia	162
2004	Adam Dunn, Cincinnati	195

Note—not included in batting records in A.L. prior to 1913 and N.L. prior to 1910.

BASERUNNING
STOLEN BASES
AMERICAN LEAGUE

Year	Player, Club	No.
1901	Frank Isbell, Chicago	52
1902	Topsy Hartsel, Philadelphia	47
1903	Harry Bay, Cleveland	45
1904	Harry Bay, Cleveland	38
	Elmer Flick, Cleveland	38
1905	Danny Hoffman, Philadelphia	46
1906	Elmer Flick, Cleveland	39
	John Anderson, Washington	39
1907	Ty Cobb, Detroit	53
1908	Patsy Dougherty, Chicago	47
1909	Ty Cobb, Detroit	76
1910	Eddie Collins, Philadelphia	81
1911	Ty Cobb, Detroit	83
1912	Clyde Milan, Washington	88
1913	Clyde Milan, Washington	75
1914	Fritz Maisel, New York	74
1915	Ty Cobb, Detroit	96
1916	Ty Cobb, Detroit	68
1917	Ty Cobb, Detroit	55
1918	George Sisler, St. Louis	45
1919	Eddie Collins, Chicago	33
1920	Sam Rice, Washington	63
1921	George Sisler, St. Louis	35
1922	George Sisler, St. Louis	51
1923	Eddie Collins, Chicago	48
1924	Eddie Collins, Chicago	42
1925	Johnny Mostil, Chicago	43
1926	Johnny Mostil, Chicago	35
1927	George Sisler, St. Louis	27
1928	Buddy Myer, Boston	30
1929	Charlie Gehringer, Detroit	27
1930	Marty McManus, Detroit	23
1931	Ben Chapman, New York	61
1932	Ben Chapman, New York	38
1933	Ben Chapman, New York	27
1934	Bill Werber, Boston	40
1935	Bill Werber, Boston	29
1936	Lyn Lary, St. Louis	37

Year	Player, Club	No.
1937	Bill Werber, Philadelphia	35
	Ben Chapman, Washington/Boston	35
1938	Frank Crosetti, New York	27
1939	George Case, Washington	51
1940	George Case, Washington	35
1941	George Case, Washington	33
1942	George Case, Washington	44
1943	George Case, Washington	61
1944	George Stirnweiss, New York	55
1945	George Stirnweiss, New York	33
1946	George Case, Cleveland	28
1947	Bob Dillinger, St. Louis	34
1948	Bob Dillinger, St. Louis	28
1949	Bob Dillinger, St. Louis	20
1950	Dom DiMaggio, Boston	15
1951	Minnie Minoso, Cleveland/Chicago	31
1952	Minnie Minoso, Chicago	22
1953	Minnie Minoso, Chicago	25
1954	Jackie Jensen, Boston	22
1955	Jim Rivera, Chicago	25
1956	Luis Aparicio, Chicago	21
1957	Luis Aparicio, Chicago	28
1958	Luis Aparicio, Chicago	29
1959	Luis Aparicio, Chicago	56
1960	Luis Aparicio, Chicago	51
1961	Luis Aparicio, Chicago	53
1962	Luis Aparicio, Chicago	31
1963	Luis Aparicio, Baltimore	40
1964	Luis Aparicio, Baltimore	57
1965	Bert Campaneris, Kansas City	51
1966	Bert Campaneris, Kansas City	52
1967	Bert Campaneris, Kansas City	55
1968	Bert Campaneris, Oakland	62
1969	Tommy Harper, Seattle	73
1970	Bert Campaneris, Oakland	42
1971	Amos Otis, Kansas City	52
1972	Bert Campaneris, Oakland	52
1973	Tommy Harper, Boston	54
1974	Billy North, Oakland	54
1975	Mickey Rivers, California	70
1976	Billy North, Oakland	75
1977	Fred Patek, Kansas City	53
1978	Ron LeFlore, Detroit	68
1979	Willie Wilson, Kansas City	83
1980	Rickey Henderson, Oakland	100
1981	Rickey Henderson, Oakland	56
1982	Rickey Henderson, Oakland	130
1983	Rickey Henderson, Oakland	108
1984	Rickey Henderson, Oakland	66
1985	Rickey Henderson, New York	80
1986	Rickey Henderson, New York	87
1987	Harold Reynolds, Seattle	60
1988	Rickey Henderson, New York	93
1989	Rickey Henderson, New York/Oakland	77
1990	Rickey Henderson, Oakland	65
1991	Rickey Henderson, Oakland	58
1992	Kenny Lofton, Cleveland	66
1993	Kenny Lofton, Cleveland	70
1994	Kenny Lofton, Cleveland	60
1995	Kenny Lofton, Cleveland	54
1996	Kenny Lofton, Cleveland	75
1997	Brian L. Hunter, Detroit	74
1998	Rickey Henderson, Oakland	66
1999	Brian L. Hunter, Detroit/Seattle	44
2000	Johnny Damon, Kansas City	46
2001	Ichiro Suzuki, Seattle	56
2002	Alfonso Soriano, New York	41
2003	Carl Crawford, Tampa Bay	55
2004	Carl Crawford, Tampa Bay	59

NATIONAL LEAGUE

Year	Player, Club	No.
1886	Ed Andrews, Philadelphia	56
1887	Monte Ward, New York	111
1888	Dummy Hoy, Washington	82
1889	Jim Fogarty, Philadelphia	99
1890	Billy Hamilton, Philadelphia	102
1891	Billy Hamilton, Philadelphia	111
1892	Monte Ward, Brooklyn	88
1893	Tom Brown, Louisville	66
1894	Billy Hamilton, Philadelphia	100
1895	Billy Hamilton, Philadelphia	97
1896	Joe Kelley, Baltimore	87
1897	Bill Lange, Chicago	73
1898	Ed Delahanty, Philadelphia	58
1899	Jimmy Sheckard, Baltimore	77
1900	Patsy Donovan, St. Louis	45
	George Van Haltren, New York	45
1901	Honus Wagner, Pittsburgh	49
1902	Honus Wagner, Pittsburgh	42
1903	Jimmy Sheckard, Brooklyn	67
	Frank Chance, Chicago	67
1904	Honus Wagner, Pittsburgh	53
1905	Billy Maloney, Chicago	59
	Art Devlin, New York	59
1906	Frank Chance, Chicago	57
1907	Honus Wagner, Pittsburgh	61
1908	Honus Wagner, Pittsburgh	53
1909	Bob Bescher, Cincinnati	54
1910	Bob Bescher, Cincinnati	70
1911	Bob Bescher, Cincinnati	81
1912	Bob Bescher, Cincinnati	67
1913	Max Carey, Pittsburgh	61
1914	George J. Burns, New York	62
1915	Max Carey, Pittsburgh	36
1916	Max Carey, Pittsburgh	63
1917	Max Carey, Pittsburgh	46
1918	Max Carey, Pittsburgh	58
1919	George J. Burns, New York	40
1920	Max Carey, Pittsburgh	52
1921	Frankie Frisch, New York	49
1922	Max Carey, Pittsburgh	51
1923	Max Carey, Pittsburgh	51
1924	Max Carey, Pittsburgh	49
1925	Max Carey, Pittsburgh	46
1926	Kiki Cuyler, Pittsburgh	35
1927	Frankie Frisch, St. Louis	48
1928	Kiki Cuyler, Chicago	37
1929	Kiki Cuyler, Chicago	43
1930	Kiki Cuyler, Chicago	37
1931	Frankie Frisch, St. Louis	28
1932	Chuck Klein, Philadelphia	20
1933	Pepper Martin, St. Louis	26
1934	Pepper Martin, St. Louis	23
1935	Augie Galan, Chicago	22
1936	Pepper Martin, St. Louis	23
1937	Augie Galan, Chicago	23
1938	Stan Hack, Chicago	16
1939	Stan Hack, Chicago	17
	Lee Handley, Pittsburgh	17
1940	Lonny Frey, Cincinnati	22
1941	Danny Murtaugh, Philadelphia	18
1942	Pete Reiser, Brooklyn	20
1943	Arky Vaughan, Brooklyn	20
1944	Johnny Barrett, Pittsburgh	28
1945	Red Schoendienst, St. Louis	26
1946	Pete Reiser, Brooklyn	34
1947	Jackie Robinson, Brooklyn	29
1948	Richie Ashburn, Philadelphia	32
1949	Jackie Robinson, Brooklyn	37
1950	Sam Jethroe, Boston	35
1951	Sam Jethroe, Boston	35
1952	Pee Wee Reese, Brooklyn	30
1953	Billy Bruton, Milwaukee	26
1954	Billy Bruton, Milwaukee	34
1955	Billy Bruton, Milwaukee	25
1956	Willie Mays, New York	40
1957	Willie Mays, New York	38
1958	Willie Mays, San Francisco	31
1959	Willie Mays, San Francisco	27
1960	Maury Wills, Los Angeles	50
1961	Maury Wills, Los Angeles	35
1962	Maury Wills, Los Angeles	104
1963	Maury Wills, Los Angeles	40
1964	Maury Wills, Los Angeles	53
1965	Maury Wills, Los Angeles	94
1966	Lou Brock, St. Louis	74
1967	Lou Brock, St. Louis	52
1968	Lou Brock, St. Louis	62
1969	Lou Brock, St. Louis	53
1970	Bobby Tolan, Cincinnati	57
1971	Lou Brock, St. Louis	64
1972	Lou Brock, St. Louis	63

Year	Player, Club	No.
1973	Lou Brock, St. Louis	70
1974	Lou Brock, St. Louis	118
1975	Dave Lopes, Los Angeles	77
1976	Dave Lopes, Los Angeles	63
1977	Frank Taveras, Pittsburgh	70
1978	Omar Moreno, Pittsburgh	71
1979	Omar Moreno, Pittsburgh	77
1980	Ron LeFlore, Montreal	97
1981	Tim Raines Sr., Montreal	71
1982	Tim Raines Sr., Montreal	78
1983	Tim Raines Sr., Montreal	90
1984	Tim Raines Sr., Montreal	75
1985	Vince Coleman, St. Louis	110
1986	Vince Coleman, St. Louis	107
1987	Vince Coleman, St. Louis	109
1988	Vince Coleman, St. Louis	81
1989	Vince Coleman, St. Louis	65
1990	Vince Coleman, St. Louis	77
1991	Marquis Grissom, Montreal	76
1992	Marquis Grissom, Montreal	78
1993	Chuck Carr, Florida	58
1994	Craig Biggio, Houston	39
1995	Quilvio Veras, Florida	56
1996	Eric Young, Colorado	53
1997	Tony Womack, Pittsburgh	60
1998	Tony Womack, Pittsburgh	58
1999	Tony Womack, Arizona	72
2000	Luis Castillo, Florida	62
2001	Juan Pierre, Colorado	46
	Jimmy Rollins, Philadelphia	46
2002	Luis Castillo, Florida	48
2003	Juan Pierre, Florida	65
2004	Scott Podsednik, Milwaukee	70

Note—not compiled prior to 1886

PITCHING
WINNING PERCENTAGE
AMERICAN LEAGUE

Year	Pitcher, Club	W	L	Pct.
1901	Clark Griffith, Chicago	24	7	.774
1902	Bill Bernhard, Philadelphia/Cleveland	18	5	.783
1903	Cy Young, Boston	28	9	.757
1904	Jack Chesbro, New York	41	12	.774
1905	Rube Waddell, Philadelphia	27	10	.730
1906	Eddie Plank, Philadelphia	19	6	.760
1907	Bill Donovan, Detroit	25	4	.862
1908	Ed Walsh Sr., Chicago	40	15	.727
1909	George Mullin, Detroit	29	8	.784
1910	Chief Bender, Philadelphia	23	5	.821
1911	Chief Bender, Philadelphia	17	5	.773
1912	Joe Wood, Boston	34	5	.872
1913	Walter Johnson, Washington	36	7	.837
1914	Chief Bender, Philadelphia	17	3	.850
1915	Joe Wood, Boston	15	5	.750
1916	Ed Cicotte, Chicago	15	7	.682
1917	Reb Russell, Chicago	15	5	.750
1918	Sam Jones, Boston	16	5	.762
1919	Ed Cicotte, Chicago	29	7	.806
1920	Jim Bagby Sr., Cleveland	31	12	.721
1921	Carl Mays, New York	27	9	.750
1922	Joe Bush, New York	26	7	.788
1923	Herb Pennock, New York	19	6	.760
1924	Walter Johnson, Washington	23	7	.767
1925	Stan Coveleski, Washington	20	5	.800
1926	George Uhle, Cleveland	27	11	.711
1927	Waite Hoyt, New York	22	7	.759
1928	Alvin Crowder, St. Louis	21	5	.808
1929	Lefty Grove, Philadelphia	20	6	.769
1930	Lefty Grove, Philadelphia	28	5	.848
1931	Lefty Grove, Philadelphia	31	4	.886
1932	Johnny Allen, New York	17	4	.810
1933	Lefty Grove, Philadelphia	24	8	.750
1934	Lefty Gomez, New York	26	5	.839
1935	Eldon Auker, Detroit	18	7	.720
1936	Monte Pearson, New York	19	7	.731
1937	Johnny Allen, Cleveland	15	1	.938
1938	Red Ruffing, New York	21	7	.750
1939	Lefty Grove, Boston	15	4	.789

Year	Pitcher, Club	W	L	Pct.
1940	Schoolboy Rowe, Detroit	16	3	.842
1941	Lefty Gomez, New York	15	5	.750
1942	Tiny Bonham, New York	21	5	.808
1943	Spud Chandler, New York	20	4	.833
1944	Tex Hughson, Boston	18	5	.783
1945	Hal Newhouser, Detroit	25	9	.735
1946	Boo Ferriss, Boston	25	6	.806
1947	Allie Reynolds, New York	19	8	.704
1948	Jack Kramer, Boston	18	5	.783
1949	Ellis Kinder, Boston	23	6	.793
1950	Vic Raschi, New York	21	8	.724
1951	Bob Feller, Cleveland	22	8	.733
1952	Bobby Shantz, Philadelphia	24	7	.774
1953	Eddie Lopat, New York	16	4	.800
1954	Sandy Consuegra, Chicago	16	3	.842
1955	Tommy Byrne, New York	16	5	.762
1956	Whitey Ford, New York	19	6	.760
1957	Dick Donovan, Chicago	16	6	.727
	Tom Sturdivant, New York	16	6	.727
1958	Bob Turley, New York	21	7	.750
1959	Bob Shaw, Chicago	18	6	.750
1960	Jim Perry, Cleveland	18	10	.643
1961	Whitey Ford, New York	25	4	.862
1962	Ray Herbert, Chicago	20	9	.690
1963	Whitey Ford, New York	24	7	.774
1964	Wally Bunker, Baltimore	19	5	.792
1965	Mudcat Grant, Minnesota	21	7	.750
1966	Sonny Siebert, Cleveland	16	8	.667
1967	Joe Horlen, Chicago	19	7	.731
1968	Denny McLain, Detroit	31	6	.838
1969	Jim Palmer, Baltimore	16	4	.800
1970	Mike Cuellar, Baltimore	24	8	.750
1971	Dave McNally, Baltimore	21	5	.808
1972	Catfish Hunter, Oakland	21	7	.750
1973	Catfish Hunter, Oakland	21	5	.808
1974	Mike Cuellar, Baltimore	22	10	.688
1975	Mike Torrez, Baltimore	20	9	.690
1976	Bill Campbell, Minnesota	17	5	.773
1977	Paul Splittorff, Kansas City	16	6	.727
1978	Ron Guidry, New York	25	3	.893
1979	Mike Caldwell, Milwaukee	16	6	.727
1980	Steve Stone, Baltimore	25	7	.781
1981	Pete Vuckovich, Milwaukee	14	4	.778
1982	Pete Vuckovich, Milwaukee	18	6	.750
1983	Rich Dotson, Chicago	22	7	.759
1984	Doyle Alexander, Toronto	17	6	.739
1985	Ron Guidry, New York	22	6	.700
1986	Roger Clemens, Boston	24	4	.857
1987	Roger Clemens, Boston	20	9	.690
1988	Frank Viola, Minnesota	24	7	.774
1989	Bret Saberhagen, Kansas City	23	6	.793
1990	Bob Welch, Oakland	27	6	.818
1991	Scott Erickson, Minnesota	20	8	.714
1992	Mike Mussina, Baltimore	18	5	.783
1993	Jimmy Key, New York	18	6	.750
1994	Jason Bere, Chicago	12	2	.857
1995	Randy Johnson, Seattle	18	2	.900
1996	Charles Nagy, Cleveland	17	5	.773
1997	Randy Johnson, Seattle	20	4	.833
1998	David Wells, New York	18	4	.818
1999	Pedro Martinez, Boston	23	4	.852
2000	Tim Hudson, Oakland	20	6	.769
2001	Roger Clemens, New York	20	3	.870
2002	Pedro Martinez, Boston	20	4	.833
2003	Roy Halladay, Toronto	22	7	.759
2004	Curt Schilling, Boston	21	6	.778

NATIONAL LEAGUE

Year	Pitcher, Club	W	L	Pct.
1876	Al Spalding, Chicago	47	12	.797
1877	Tommy Bond, Boston	40	17	.702
1878	Tommy Bond, Boston	40	19	.678
1879	Monte Ward, Providence	47	19	.712
1880	Fred Goldsmith, Chicago	21	3	.875
1881	Hoss Radbourn, Providence	25	11	.694
1882	Larry Corcoran, Chicago	27	12	.692
1883	Jim McCormick, Cleveland	28	12	.700
1884	Hoss Radbourn, Providence	59	12	.831
1885	Mickey Welch, New York	44	11	.800
1886	Jocko Flynn, Chicago	23	6	.793
1887	Charlie Getzien, Detroit	29	13	.690

Year	Pitcher, Club	W	L	Pct.
1888	Tim Keefe, New York	35	12	.745
1889	John Clarkson, Boston	49	19	.721
1890	Tom Lovett, Brooklyn	30	11	.732
1891	John Ewing, New York	21	8	.724
1892	Cy Young, Cleveland	36	12	.750
1893	Hank Gastright, Pittsburgh/Boston	15	5	.750
1894	Jouett Meekin, New York	33	9	.786
1895	Bill Hoffer, Baltimore	31	6	.838
1896	Bill Hoffer, Baltimore	25	7	.781
1897	Fred Klobedanz, Boston	26	7	.788
1898	Ted Lewis, Boston	26	8	.765
1899	Jim Hughes, Brooklyn	28	6	.824
1900	Joe McGinnity, Brooklyn	28	8	.778
1901	Jack Chesbro, Pittsburgh	21	10	.677
1902	Jack Chesbro, Pittsburgh	28	6	.824
1903	Sam Leever, Pittsburgh	25	7	.781
1904	Joe McGinnity, New York	35	8	.814
1905	Sam Leever, Pittsburgh	20	5	.800
1906	Ed Reulbach, Chicago	19	4	.826
1907	Ed Reulbach, Chicago	17	4	.810
1908	Ed Reulbach, Chicago	24	7	.774
1909	Christy Mathewson, New York	25	6	.806
	Howie Camnitz, Pittsburgh	25	6	.806
1910	King Cole, Chicago	20	4	.833
1911	Rube Marquard, New York	24	7	.774
1912	Claude Hendrix, Pittsburgh	24	9	.727
1913	Bert Humphries, Chicago	16	4	.800
1914	Bill James, Boston	26	7	.788
1915	Grover Alexander, Philadelphia	31	10	.756
1916	Tom Hughes, Boston	16	3	.842
1917	Ferdie Schupp, New York	21	7	.750
1918	Claude Hendrix, Chicago	20	7	.741
1919	Dutch Ruether, Cincinnati	19	6	.760
1920	Burleigh Grimes, Brooklyn	23	11	.676
1921	Bill Doak, St. Louis	15	6	.714
1922	Pete Donohue, Cincinnati	18	9	.667
1923	Dolf Luque, Cincinnati	27	8	.771
1924	Emil Yde, Pittsburgh	16	3	.842
1925	Willie Sherdel, St. Louis	15	6	.714
1926	Ray Kremer, Pittsburgh	20	6	.769
1927	Larry Benton, Boston/New York	17	7	.708
1928	Larry Benton, New York	25	9	.735
1929	Charlie Root, Chicago	19	6	.760
1930	Freddie Fitzsimmons, New York	19	7	.731
1931	Paul Derringer, St. Louis	18	8	.692
1932	Lon Warneke, Chicago	22	6	.786
1933	Ben Cantwell, Boston	20	10	.667
1934	Dizzy Dean, St. Louis	30	7	.811
1935	Bill Lee, Chicago	20	6	.769
1936	Carl Hubbell, New York	26	6	.813
1937	Carl Hubbell, New York	22	8	.733
1938	Bill Lee, Chicago	22	9	.710
1939	Paul Derringer, Cincinnati	25	7	.781
1940	Freddie Fitzsimmons, Brooklyn	16	2	.889
1941	Elmer Riddle, Cincinnati	19	4	.826
1942	Larry French, Brooklyn	15	4	.789
1943	Mort Cooper, St. Louis	21	8	.724
1944	Ted Wilks, St. Louis	17	4	.810
1945	Harry Brecheen, St. Louis	15	4	.789
1946	Murry Dickson, St. Louis	15	6	.714
1947	Larry Jansen, New York	21	5	.808
1948	Harry Brecheen, St. Louis	20	7	.741
1949	Preacher Roe, Brooklyn	15	6	.714
1950	Sal Maglie, New York	18	4	.818
1951	Preacher Roe, Brooklyn	22	3	.880
1952	Hoyt Wilhelm, New York	15	3	.833
1953	Carl Erskine, Brooklyn	20	6	.769
1954	Johnny Antonelli, New York	21	7	.750
1955	Don Newcombe, Brooklyn	20	5	.800
1956	Don Newcombe, Brooklyn	27	7	.794
1957	Bob Buhl, Milwaukee	18	7	.720
1958	Warren Spahn, Milwaukee	22	11	.667
	Lew Burdette, Milwaukee	20	10	.667
1959	Roy Face, Pittsburgh	18	1	.947
1960	Ernie Broglio, St. Louis	21	9	.700
1961	Johnny Podres, Los Angeles	18	5	.783
1962	Bob Purkey, Cincinnati	23	5	.821
1963	Ron Perranoski, Los Angeles	16	3	.842
1964	Sandy Koufax, Los Angeles	19	5	.792
1965	Sandy Koufax, Los Angeles	26	8	.765
1966	Juan Marichal, San Francisco	25	6	.806
1967	Dick Hughes, St. Louis	16	6	.727

Year	Pitcher, Club	W	L	Pct.
1968	Steve Blass, Pittsburgh	18	6	.750
1969	Tom Seaver, New York	25	7	.781
1970	Bob Gibson, St. Louis	23	7	.767
1971	Don Gullett, Cincinnati	16	6	.727
1972	Gary Nolan, Cincinnati	15	5	.750
1973	Tommy John, Los Angeles	16	7	.696
1974	Andy Messersmith, Los Angeles	20	6	.769
1975	Don Gullett, Cincinnati	15	4	.789
1976	Steve Carlton, Philadelphia	20	7	.741
1977	John Candelaria, Pittsburgh	20	5	.800
1978	Gaylord Perry, San Diego	21	6	.778
1979	Tom Seaver, Cincinnati	16	6	.727
1980	Jim Bibby, Pittsburgh	19	6	.760
1981	Tom Seaver, CIncinnati	14	2	.875
1982	Phil Niekro, Atlanta	17	4	.810
1983	John Denny, Philadelphia	19	6	.760
1984	Rick Sutcliffe, Chicago	16	1	.941
1985	Orel Hershiser, Los Angeles	19	3	.864
1986	Bob Ojeda, New York	18	5	.783
1987	Dwight Gooden, New York	15	7	.682
1988	David Cone, New York	20	3	.870
1989	Mike Bielecki, Chicago	18	7	.720
1990	Doug Drabek, Pittsburgh	22	6	.786
1991	John Smiley, Pittsburgh	20	8	.714
	Jose Rijo, Cincinnati	15	6	.714
1992	Bob Tewksbury, St. Louis	16	5	.762
1993	Mark Portugal, Houston	18	4	.818
1994	Marvin Freeman, Colorado	10	2	.833
1995	Greg Maddux, Atlanta	19	2	.905
1996	John Smoltz, Atlanta	24	8	.750
1997	Greg Maddux, Atlanta	19	4	.826
1998	John Smoltz, Atlanta	17	3	.850
1999	Mike Hampton, Houston	22	4	.846
2000	Randy Johnson, Arizona	19	7	.731
2001	Curt Schilling, Arizona	22	6	.786
2002	Randy Johnson, Arizona	24	5	.828
2003	Jason Schmidt, San Francisco	17	5	.773
2004	Roger Clemens, Houston	18	4	.818

Note—based on 15 or more victories, except for 1981 and 1994 percentages, which are based on 10 or more victories

EARNED RUN AVERAGE

AMERICAN LEAGUE

Year	Pitcher, Club	G	IP	ERA
1913	Walter Johnson, Washington	48	346	1.14
1914	Dutch Leonard, Boston	36	225	0.96
1915	Joe Wood, Boston	25	157	1.49
1916	Babe Ruth, Boston	44	324	1.75
1917	Ed Cicotte, Chicago	49	346	1.53
1918	Walter Johnson, Washington	39	325	1.27
1919	Walter Johnson, Washington	39	290	1.49
1920	Bob Shawkey, New York	38	267	2.45
1921	Red Faber, Chicago	43	331	2.48
1922	Red Faber, Chicago	43	352	2.81
1923	Stan Coveleski, Cleveland	33	228	2.76
1924	Walter Johnson, Washington	38	278	2.72
1925	Stan Coveleski, Washington	32	241	2.84
1926	Lefty Grove, Philadelphia	45	258	2.51
1927	Wilcy Moore, New York	50	213	2.28
1928	Garland Braxton, Washington	38	218	2.51
1929	Lefty Grove, Philadelphia	42	275	2.81
1930	Lefty Grove, Philadelphia	50	291	2.54
1931	Lefty Grove, Philadelphia	41	289	2.06
1932	Lefty Grove, Philadelphia	44	292	2.84
1933	Monte Pearson, Cleveland	19	135	2.33
1934	Lefty Gomez, New York	38	282	2.33
1935	Lefty Grove, Boston	35	273	2.70
1936	Lefty Grove, Boston	35	253	2.81
1937	Lefty Gomez, New York	34	278	2.33
1938	Lefty Grove, Boston	24	164	3.07
1939	Lefty Grove, Boston	23	191	2.54
1940	Bob Feller, Cleveland	43	320	2.62
1941	Thornton Lee, Chicago	35	300	2.37
1942	Ted Lyons, Chicago	20	180	2.10
1943	Spud Chandler, New York	30	253	1.64
1944	Dizzy Trout, Detroit	49	352	2.12
1945	Hal Newhouser, Detroit	40	313	1.81
1946	Hal Newhouser, Detroit	37	293	1.94
1947	Spud Chandler, New York	17	128	2.46

Year	Pitcher, Club	G	IP	ERA
1948	Gene Bearden, Cleveland	37	230	2.43
1949	Mel Parnell, Boston	39	295	2.78
1950	Early Wynn, Cleveland	32	214	3.20
1951	Saul Rogovin, Detroit/Chicago	27	217	2.78
1952	Allie Reynolds, New York	35	244	2.07
1953	Eddie Lopat, New York	25	178	2.43
1954	Mike Garcia, Cleveland	45	259	2.64
1955	Billy Pierce, Chicago	33	206	1.97
1956	Whitey Ford, New York	31	226	2.47
1957	Bobby Shantz, New York	30	173	2.45
1958	Whitey Ford, New York	30	219	2.01
1959	Hoyt Wilhelm, Baltimore	32	226	2.19
1960	Frank Baumann, Chicago	47	185	2.68
1961	Dick Donovan, Washington	23	169	2.40
1962	Hank Aguirre, Detroit	42	216	2.21
1963	Gary Peters, Chicago	41	243	2.33
1964	Dean Chance, Los Angeles	46	278	1.65
1965	Sam McDowell, Cleveland	42	273	2.18
1966	Gary Peters, Chicago	30	205	1.98
1967	Joe Horlen, Chicago	35	258	2.06
1968	Luis Tiant, Cleveland	34	258	1.60
1969	Dick Bosman, Washington	31	193	2.19
1970	Diego Segui, Oakland	47	162	2.56
1971	Vida Blue, Oakland	39	312	1.82
1972	Luis Tiant, Boston	43	179	1.91
1973	Jim Palmer, Baltimore	38	296	2.40
1974	Catfish Hunter, Oakland	41	318	2.49
1975	Jim Palmer, Baltimore	39	323	2.09
1976	Mark Fidrych, Detroit	31	250	2.34
1977	Frank Tanana, California	31	241	2.54
1978	Ron Guidry, New York	35	274	1.74
1979	Ron Guidry, New York	33	236	2.78
1980	Rudy May, New York	41	175	2.47
1981	Steve McCatty, Oakland	22	186	2.32
1982	Rick Sutcliffe, Cleveland	34	216	2.96
1983	Rick Honeycutt, Texas	25	174.2	2.42
1984	Mike Boddicker, Baltimore	34	261.1	2.79
1985	Dave Stieb, Toronto	36	265.0	2.48
1986	Roger Clemens, Boston	33	254.0	2.48
1987	Jimmy Key, Toronto	36	261.0	2.76
1988	Allan Anderson, Minnesota	30	202.1	2.45
1989	Bret Saberhagen, Kansas City	36	262.1	2.16
1990	Roger Clemens, Boston	31	228.1	1.93
1991	Roger Clemens, Boston	35	271.1	2.62
1992	Roger Clemens, Boston	32	246.2	2.41
1993	Kevin Appier, Kansas City	34	238.2	2.56
1994	Steve Ontiveros, Oakland	27	115.1	2.65
1995	Randy Johnson, Seattle	30	214.1	2.48
1996	Juan Guzman, Toronto	27	187.2	2.93
1997	Roger Clemens, Toronto	34	264.0	2.05
1998	Roger Clemens, Toronto	33	234.2	2.65
1999	Pedro Martinez, Boston	31	213.1	2.07
2000	Pedro Martinez, Boston	29	217.0	1.74
2001	Freddy Garcia, Seattle	34	238.2	3.05
2002	Pedro Martinez, Boston	30	199.1	2.26
2003	Pedro Martinez, Boston	29	186.2	2.22
2004	Johan Santana, Minnesota	34	228.0	2.61

NATIONAL LEAGUE

Year	Pitcher, Club	G	IP	ERA
1912	Jeff Tesreau, New York	36	243	1.96
1913	Christy Mathewson, New York	40	306	2.06
1914	Bill Doak, St. Louis	36	256	1.72
1915	Grover Alexander, Philadelphia	49	376	1.22
1916	Grover Alexander, Philadelphia	48	390	1.55
1917	Grover Alexander, Philadelphia	45	388	1.83
1918	Hippo Vaughn, Chicago	35	290	1.74
1919	Grover Alexander, Chicago	30	235	1.72
1920	Grover Alexander, Chicago	46	363	1.91
1921	Bill Doak, St. Louis	32	209	2.59
1922	Phil Douglas, New York	24	158	2.63
1923	Dolf Luque, Cincinnati	41	322	1.93
1924	Dazzy Vance, Brooklyn	35	309	2.16
1925	Dolf Luque, Cincinnati	36	291	2.63
1926	Ray Kremer, Pittsburgh	37	231	2.61
1927	Ray Kremer, Pittsburgh	35	226	2.47
1928	Dazzy Vance, Brooklyn	38	280	2.09
1929	Bill Walker, New York	29	178	3.09
1930	Dazzy Vance, Brooklyn	35	259	2.61
1931	Bill Walker, New York	37	239	2.26
1932	Lon Warneke, Chicago	35	277	2.37
1933	Carl Hubbell, New York	45	309	1.66
1934	Carl Hubbell, New York	49	313	2.30
1935	Cy Blanton, Pittsburgh	35	254	2.59
1936	Carl Hubbell, New York	42	304	2.31
1937	Jim Turner, Boston	33	257	2.38
1938	Bill Lee, Chicago	44	291	2.66
1939	Bucky Walters, Cincinnati	39	319	2.29
1940	Bucky Walters, Cincinnati	36	305	2.48
1941	Elmer Riddle, Cincinnati	33	217	2.24
1942	Mort Cooper, St. Louis	37	279	1.77
1943	Howie Pollet, St. Louis	16	118	1.75
1944	Ed Heusser, Cincinnati	30	193	2.38
1945	Hank Borowy, Chicago	15	122	2.14
1946	Howie Pollet, St. Louis	40	266	2.10
1947	Warren Spahn, Boston	40	290	2.33
1948	Harry Brecheen, St. Louis	33	233	2.24
1949	Dave Koslo, New York	38	212	2.50
1950	Jim Hearn, St. Louis/New York	22	134	2.49
1951	Chet Nichols, Boston	33	156	2.88
1952	Hoyt Wilhelm, New York	71	159	2.43
1953	Warren Spahn, Milwaukee	35	266	2.10
1954	Johnny Antonelli, New York	39	259	2.29
1955	Bob Friend, Pittsburgh	44	200	2.84
1956	Lew Burdette, Milwaukee	39	256	2.71
1957	Johnny Podres, Brooklyn	31	196	2.66
1958	Stu Miller, San Francisco	41	182	2.47
1959	Sam Jones, San Francisco	50	271	2.82
1960	Mike McCormick, San Francisco	40	253	2.70
1961	Warren Spahn, Milwaukee	38	263	3.01
1962	Sandy Koufax, Los Angeles	28	184	2.54
1963	Sandy Koufax, Los Angeles	40	311	1.88
1964	Sandy Koufax, Los Angeles	29	223	1.74
1965	Sandy Koufax, Los Angeles	43	336	2.04
1966	Sandy Koufax, Los Angeles	41	323	1.73
1967	Phil Niekro, Atlanta	46	207	1.87
1968	Bob Gibson, St. Louis	34	305	1.12
1969	Juan Marichal, San Francisco	37	300	2.10
1970	Tom Seaver, New York	37	291	2.81
1971	Tom Seaver, New York	36	286	1.76
1972	Steve Carlton, Philadelphia	41	346	1.98
1973	Tom Seaver, New York	36	290	2.08
1974	Buzz Capra, Atlanta	39	217	2.28
1975	Randy Jones, San Diego	37	285	2.24
1976	John Denny, St. Louis	30	207	2.52
1977	John Candelaria, Pittsburgh	33	231	2.34
1978	Craig Swan, New York	29	207	2.43
1979	J.R. Richard, Houston	38	292	2.71
1980	Don Sutton, Los Angeles	32	212	2.21
1981	Nolan Ryan, Houston	21	149	1.69
1982	Steve Rogers, Montreal	35	277	2.40
1983	Atlee Hammaker, San Francisco	23	172.1	2.25
1984	Alejandro Pena, Los Angeles	28	199.1	2.48
1985	Dwight Gooden, New York	35	276.2	1.53
1986	Mike Scott, Houston	37	275.1	2.22
1987	Nolan Ryan, Houston	34	211.2	2.76
1988	Joe Magrane, St. Louis	24	165.1	2.18
1989	Scott Garrelts, San Francisco	30	193.1	2.28

Year	Pitcher, Club	G	IP	ERA
1990	Danny Darwin, Houston	48	162.2	2.21
1991	Dennis Martinez, Montreal	31	222.0	2.39
1992	Bill Swift, San Francisco	30	164.2	2.08
1993	Greg Maddux, Atlanta	36	267.0	2.36
1994	Greg Maddux, Atlanta	25	202.0	1.56
1995	Greg Maddux, Atlanta	28	209.2	1.63
1996	Kevin Brown, Florida	32	233.0	1.89
1997	Pedro J. Martinez, Montreal	31	241.1	1.90
1998	Greg Maddux, Atlanta	34	251.0	2.22
1999	Randy Johnson, Arizona	35	271.2	2.48
2000	Kevin Brown, Los Angeles	33	230.0	2.58
2001	Randy Johnson, Arizona	35	249.2	2.49
2002	Randy Johnson, Arizona	35	260.0	2.32
2003	Jason Schmidt, San Francisco	29	207.2	2.34
2004	Jake Peavy, San Diego	27	166.1	2.27

Note—not tabulated in N.L. prior to 1912 and in A.L. prior to 1913; based on 10 CG through 1950; 154 IP until 1961 in A.L. and 1962 in N.L.; 162 IP since 1962, except 1981 leaders based on one IP per game played by team; all IP rounded to nearest whole

Note—In 1916, Ferdie Schupp, New York N.L., appeared in 30 games and had a 0.90 ERA, but pitched only 8 CG. He was recognized as the league leader at the time.

Note—In 1927, Wilcy Moore, New York A.L., appeared in 50 games but had only 6 CG. He is recognized as the leader because he had 213 IP.

Note—In 1940, Tiny Bonham, New York A.L., had 10 complete games and a 1.91 ERA, but he appeared in only 12 games and had only 99.1 IP. Bob Feller is recognized as the leader.

WINS

For the list of pitchers who led each league in wins, see page 191.

SHUTOUTS

AMERICAN LEAGUE

Year	Pitcher, Club	No.
1901	Clark Griffith, Chicago	5
	Cy Young, Boston	5
1902	Addie Joss, Cleveland	5
1903	Cy Young, Boston	7
1904	Cy Young, Boston	10
1905	Ed Killian, Detroit	8
1906	Ed Walsh Sr., Chicago	10
1907	Eddie Plank, Philadelphia	8
1908	Ed Walsh Sr., Chicago	11
1909	Ed Walsh Sr., Chicago	8
1910	Jack Coombs, Philadelphia	13
1911	Walter Johnson, Washington	6
	Eddie Plank, Philadelphia	6
1912	Joe Wood, Boston	10
1913	Walter Johnson, Washington	11
1914	Walter Johnson, Washington	9
1915	Walter Johnson, Washington	7
	Jim Scott, Chicago	7
1916	Babe Ruth, Boston	9
1917	Stan Coveleski, Cleveland	9
1918	Walter Johnson, Washington	8
	Carl Mays, Boston	8
1919	Walter Johnson, Washington	7
1920	Carl Mays, New York	6
1921	Sam P. Jones, Boston	5
1922	George Uhle, Cleveland	5
1923	Stan Coveleski, Cleveland	5
1924	Walter Johnson, Washington	6
1925	Ted Lyons, Chicago	5

Year	Pitcher, Club	No.
1926	Ed Wells, Detroit	4
1927	Hod Lisenbee, Washington	4
1928	Herb Pennock, New York	5
1929	George Blaeholder, St. Louis	4
	Alvin Crowder, St. Louis	4
	Sam Gray, St. Louis	4
	Danny MacFayden, Boston	4
1930	Clint Brown, Cleveland	3
	George Earnshaw, Philadelphia	3
	George Pipgras, New York	3
1931	Lefty Grove, Philadelphia	4
	Vic Sorrell, Detroit	4
1932	Tommy Bridges, Detroit	4
	Lefty Grove, Philadelphia	4
1933	Oral Hildebrand, Cleveland	6
1934	Lefty Gomez, New York	6
	Mel Harder, Cleveland	6
1935	Schoolboy Rowe, Detroit	6
1936	Lefty Grove, Boston	6
1937	Lefty Gomez, New York	6
1938	Lefty Gomez, New York	4
1939	Red Ruffing, New York	5
1940	Bob Feller, Cleveland	4
	Ted Lyons, Chicago	4
	Al Milnar, Cleveland	4
1941	Bob Feller, Cleveland	6
1942	Tiny Bonham, New York	6
1943	Spud Chandler, New York	5
	Dizzy Trout, Detroit	5
1944	Dizzy Trout, Detroit	7
1945	Hal Newhouser, Detroit	8
1946	Bob Feller, Cleveland	10
1947	Bob Feller, Cleveland	5
1948	Bob Lemon, Cleveland	10
1949	Mike Garcia, Cleveland	6
	Ellis Kinder, Boston	6
	Virgil Trucks, Detroit	6
1950	Art Houtteman, Detroit	4
1951	Allie Reynolds, New York	7
1952	Mike Garcia, Cleveland	6
	Allie Reynolds, New York	6
1953	Bob Porterfield, Washington	9
1954	Mike Garcia, Cleveland	5
	Virgil Trucks, Chicago	5
1955	Billy Hoeft, Detroit	7
1956	Herb Score, Cleveland	5
1957	Jim Wilson, Chicago	5
1958	Whitey Ford, New York	7
1959	Camilo Pascual, Washington	6
1960	Whitey Ford, New York	4
	Jim Perry, Cleveland	4
	Early Wynn, Chicago	4
1961	Steve Barber, Baltimore	8
	Camilo Pascual, Minnesota	8
1962	Dick Donovan, Cleveland	5
	Jim Kaat, Minnesota	5
	Camilo Pascual, Minnesota	5
1963	Ray Herbert, Chicago	7
1964	Dean Chance, Los Angeles	11
1965	Mudcat Grant, Minnesota	6
1966	Tommy John, Chicago	5
	Sam McDowell, Cleveland	5
	Luis Tiant, Cleveland	5
1967	Steve Hargan, Cleveland	6
	Joe Horlen, Chicago	6
	Tommy John, Chicago	6
	Mickey Lolich, Detroit	6
	Jim McGlothlin, California	6
1968	Luis Tiant, Cleveland	9

Year	Pitcher, Club	No.
1969	Denny McLain, Detroit	9
1970	Chuck Dobson, Oakland	5
	Jim Palmer, Baltimore	5
1971	Vida Blue, Oakland	8
1972	Nolan Ryan, California	9
1973	Bert Blyleven, Minnesota	9
1974	Luis Tiant, Boston	7
1975	Jim Palmer, Baltimore	10
1976	Nolan Ryan, California	7
1977	Frank Tanana, California	7
1978	Ron Guidry, New York	9
1979	Nolan Ryan, California	5
	Mike Flanagan, Baltimore	5
	Dennis Leonard, Kansas City	5
1980	Tommy John, New York	6
1981	Rich Dotson, Chicago	4
	Ken Forsch, California	4
	Steve McCatty, Oakland	4
	Doc Medich, Texas	4
1982	Dave Stieb, Toronto	5
1983	Mike Boddicker, Baltimore	5
1984	Bob Ojeda, Boston	5
	Geoff Zahn, California	5
1985	Bert Blyleven, Cleveland/Minnesota	5
1986	Jack Morris, Detroit	6
1987	Roger Clemens, Boston	7
1988	Roger Clemens, Boston	8
1989	Bert Blyleven, California	5
1990	Roger Clemens, Boston	4
	Dave Stewart, Oakland	4
1991	Roger Clemens, Boston	4
1992	Roger Clemens, Boston	5
1993	Jack McDowell, Chicago	4
1994	Randy Johnson, Seattle	4
1995	Mike Mussina, Baltimore	4
1996	Pat Hentgen, Toronto	3
	Ken Hill, Texas	3
	Rich Robertson, Minnesota	3
1997	Roger Clemens, Toronto	3
	Pat Hentgen, Toronto	3
1998	David Wells, New York	5
1999	Scott Erickson, Baltimore	3
2000	Pedro Martinez, Boston	4
2001	Mark Mulder, Oakland	4
2002	Jeff Weaver, Detroit/New York	3
2003	Roy Halladay, Toronto	2
	Tim Hudson, Oakland	2
	John Lackey, Anaheim	2
	Mark Mulder, Oakland	2
	Joel Pineiro, Seattle	2
2004	Jeremy Bonderman, Detroit	2
	Tim Hudson, Oakland	2
	Sidney Ponson, Baltimore	2

NATIONAL LEAGUE

Year	Pitcher, Club	No.
1900	Clark Griffith, Chicago	4
	Noodles Hahn, Cincinnati	4
	Kid Nichols, Boston	4
	Cy Young, St. Louis	4
1901	Jack Chesbro, Pittsburgh	6
	Al Orth, Philadelphia	6
	Vic Willis, Boston	6
1902	Jack Chesbro, Pittsburgh	8
	Christy Mathewson, New York	8
1903	Sam Leever, Pittsburgh	7
1904	Joe McGinnity, New York	9
1905	Christy Mathewson, New York	8
1906	Mordecai Brown, Chicago	9

Year	Pitcher, Club	No.
1907	Christy Mathewson, New York	8
	Orval Overall, Chicago	8
1908	Christy Mathewson, New York	11
1909	Orval Overall, Chicago	9
1910	Mordecai Brown, Chicago	6
	Al Mattern, Boston	6
	Earl Moore, Philadelphia	6
	Nap Rucker, Brooklyn	6
1911	Grover Alexander, Philadelphia	7
1912	Nap Rucker, Brooklyn	6
1913	Grover Alexander, Philadelphia	9
1914	Jeff Tesreau, New York	8
1915	Grover Alexander, Philadelphia	12
1916	Grover Alexander, Philadelphia	16
1917	Grover Alexander, Philadelphia	8
1918	Lefty Tyler, Chicago	8
	Hippo Vaughn, Chicago	8
1919	Grover Alexander, Chicago	9
1920	Babe Adams, Pittsburgh	8
1921	Grover Alexander, Chicago	3
	Phil Douglas, New York	3
	Dana Fillingim, Boston	3
	Dolf Luque, Cincinnati	3
	Clarence Mitchell, Brooklyn	3
	Johnny Morrison, Pittsburgh	3
	Joe Oeschger, Boston	3
	Jesse Haines, St. Louis	3
1922	Dazzy Vance, Brooklyn	6
1923	Dolf Luque, Cincinnati	6
1924	Jesse Barnes, Boston	4
	Wilbur Cooper, Pittsburgh	4
	Ray Kremer, Pittsburgh	4
	Eppa Rixey, Cincinnati	4
	Allen Sothoron, St. Louis	4
	Emil Yde, Pittsburgh	4
1925	Hal Carlson, Philadelphia	4
	Dolf Luque, Cincinnati	4
	Dazzy Vance, Brooklyn	4
1926	Pete Donohue, Cincinnati	5
1927	Jesse Haines, St. Louis	6
1928	Sheriff Blake, Chicago	4
	Burleigh Grimes, Pittsburgh	4
	Red Lucas, Cincinnati	4
	Doug McWeeny, Brooklyn	4
	Dazzy Vance, Brooklyn	4
1929	Pat Malone, Chicago	5
1930	Charlie Root, Chicago	4
	Dazzy Vance, Brooklyn	4
1931	Bill Walker, New York	6
1932	Lon Warneke, Chicago	4
	Dizzy Dean, St. Louis	4
	Steve Swetonic, Pittsburgh	4
1933	Carl Hubbell, New York	10
1934	Dizzy Dean, St. Louis	7
1935	Cy Blanton, Pittsburgh	4
	Freddie Fitzsimmons, New York	4
	Larry French, Chicago	4
	Van Lingle Mungo, Brooklyn	4
	Jim Weaver, Pittsburgh	4
1936	Cy Blanton, Pittsburgh	4
	Tex Carleton, Chicago	4
	Larry French, Chicago	4
	Bill Lee, Chicago	4
	Al Smith, New York	4
	Bucky Walters, Philadelphia	4
	Lon Warneke, Chicago	4
1937	Lou Fette, Boston	5
	Lee Grissom, Cincinnati	5
	Jim Turner, Boston	5

Year	Pitcher, Club	No.
1938	Bill Lee, Chicago	9
1939	Lou Fette, Boston	6
1940	Bill Lohrman, New York	5
	Manny Salvo, Boston	5
	Whitlow Wyatt, Brooklyn	5
1941	Whitlow Wyatt, Brooklyn	7
1942	Mort Cooper, St. Louis	10
1943	Hi Bithorn, Chicago	7
1944	Mort Cooper, St. Louis	7
1945	Claude Passeau, Chicago	5
1946	Ewell Blackwell, Cincinnati	6
1947	Warren Spahn, Boston	7
1948	Harry Brecheen, St. Louis	7
1949	Ken Heintzelman, Philadelphia	5
	Don Newcombe, Brooklyn	5
	Howie Pollet, St. Louis	5
	Ken Raffensberger, Cincinnati	5
1950	Jim Hearn, New York	5
	Larry Jansen, New York	5
	Sal Maglie, New York	5
	Robin Roberts, Philadelphia	5
1951	Warren Spahn, Boston	7
1952	Ken Raffensberger, Cincinnati	6
	Curt Simmons, Philadelphia	6
1953	Harvey Haddix, St. Louis	6
1954	Johnny Antonelli, New York	6
1955	Joe Nuxhall, Cincinnati	5
1956	Johnny Antonelli, New York	6
	Lew Burdette, Milwaukee	6
1957	Johnny Podres, Brooklyn	6
1958	Carl Willey, Milwaukee	4
1959	Johnny Antonelli, San Francisco	4
	Bob Buhl, Milwaukee	4
	Lew Burdette, Milwaukee	4
	Roger Craig, Los Angeles	4
	Don Drysdale, Los Angeles	4
	Sam Jones, San Francisco	4
	Warren Spahn, Milwaukee	4
1960	Jack Sanford, San Francisco	6
1961	Joey Jay, Cincinnati	4
	Warren Spahn, Milwaukee	4
1962	Bob Friend, Pittsburgh	5
	Bob Gibson, St. Louis	5
1963	Sandy Koufax, Los Angeles	11
1964	Sandy Koufax, Los Angeles	7
1965	Juan Marichal, San Francisco	10
1966	Jim Bunning, Philadelphia	5
	Bob Gibson, St. Louis	5
	Larry Jackson, Philadelphia	5
	Larry Jaster, St. Louis	5
	Sandy Koufax, Los Angeles	5
	Jim Maloney, Cincinnati	5
1967	Jim Bunning, Philadelphia	6
1968	Bob Gibson, St. Louis	13
1969	Juan Marichal, San Francisco	8
1970	Gaylord Perry, San Francisco	5
1971	Steve Blass, Pittsburgh	5
	Al Downing, Los Angeles	5
	Bob Gibson, St. Louis	5
	Milt Pappas, Chicago	5
1972	Don Sutton, Los Angeles	9
1973	Jack Billingham, Cincinnati	7
1974	Jon Matlack, New York	7
1975	Andy Messersmith, Los Angeles	7
1976	Jon Matlack, New York	6
	John Montefusco, San Francisco	6
1977	Tom Seaver, New York/Cincinnati	7
1978	Bob Knepper, San Francisco	6
1979	Tom Seaver, Cincinnati	5

Year	Pitcher, Club	No.
	Joe Niekro, Houston	5
	Steve Rogers, Montreal	5
1980	Jerry Reuss, Los Angeles	6
1981	Fernando Valenzuela, Los Angeles	8
1982	Steve Carlton, Philadelphia	6
1983	Steve Rogers, Montreal	5
1984	Joaquin Andujar, St. Louis	4
	Orel Hershiser, Los Angeles	4
	Alejandro Pena, Los Angeles	4
1985	John Tudor, St. Louis	10
1986	Bob Knepper, Houston	5
	Mike Scott, Houston	5
1987	Rick Reuschel, Pittsburgh/San Francisco	4
	Bob Welch, Los Angeles	4
1988	Orel Hershiser, Los Angeles	8
1989	Tim Belcher, Los Angeles	8
1990	Bruce Hurst, San Diego	4
	Mike Morgan, Los Angeles	4
1991	Dennis Martinez, Montreal	5
1992	David Cone, New York	5
	Tom Glavine, Atlanta	5
1993	Pete Harnisch, Houston	4
1994	Greg Maddux, Atlanta	3
	Ramon Martinez, Los Angeles	3
1995	Greg Maddux, Atlanta	3
	Hideo Nomo, Los Angeles	3
1996	Kevin Brown, Florida	3
1997	Carlos Perez, Montreal	5
1998	Greg Maddux, Atlanta	5
1999	Andy Ashby, San Diego	3
2000	Randy Johnson, Arizona	3
	Greg Maddux, Atlanta	3
2001	Greg Maddux, Atlanta	3
	Javier Vazquez, Montreal	3
2002	A.J. Burnett, Florida	5
2003	Kevin Millwood, Philadelphia	3
	Matt Morris, St. Louis	3
	Jason Schmidt, San Francisco	3
2004	Cory Lidle, Philadelphia	3
	Jason Schmidt, San Francisco	3

SAVES

AMERICAN LEAGUE

Year	Pitcher, Club	No.
1969	Ron Perranoski, Minnesota	31
1970	Ron Perranoski, Minnesota	34
1971	Ken Sanders, Milwaukee	31
1972	Sparky Lyle, New York	35
1973	John Hiller, Detroit	38
1974	Terry Forster, Chicago	24
1975	Rich Gossage, Chicago	26
1976	Sparky Lyle, New York	23
1977	Bill Campbell, Boston	31
1978	Rich Gossage, New York	27
1979	Mike Marshall, Minnesota	32
1980	Rich Gossage, New York	33
	Dan Quisenberry, Kansas City	33
1981	Rollie Fingers, Milwaukee	28
1982	Dan Quisenberry, Kansas City	35
1983	Dan Quisenberry, Kansas City	45
1984	Dan Quisenberry, Kansas City	44
1985	Dan Quisenberry, Kansas City	37
1986	Dave Righetti, New York	46
1987	Tom Henke, Toronto	34
1988	Dennis Eckersley, Oakland	45
1989	Jeff Russell, Texas	38
1990	Bobby Thigpen, Chicago	57

Year	Pitcher, Club	No.
1991	Bryan Harvey, California	46
1992	Dennis Eckersley, Oakland	51
1993	Jeff Montgomery, Kansas City	45
	Duane Ward, Toronto	45
1994	Lee Smith, Baltimore	33
1995	Jose Mesa, Cleveland	46
1996	John Wetteland, New York	43
1997	Randy Myers, Baltimore	45
1998	Tom Gordon, Boston	46
1999	Mariano Rivera, New York	45
2000	Todd Jones, Detroit	42
	Derek Lowe, Boston	42
2001	Mariano Rivera, New York	50
2002	Eddie Guardado, Minnesota	45
2003	Keith Foulke, Oakland	43
2004	Mariano Rivera, New York	53

NATIONAL LEAGUE

Year	Pitcher, Club	No.
1969	Fred Gladding, Houston	29
1970	Wayne Granger, Cincinnati	35
1971	Dave Giusti, Pittsburgh	30
1972	Clay Carroll, Cincinnati	37
1973	Mike Marshall, Montreal	31
1974	Mike Marshall, Los Angeles	21
1975	Rawly Eastwick, Cincinnati	22
	Al Hrabosky, St. Louis	22
1976	Rawly Eastwick, Cincinnati	26
1977	Rollie Fingers, San Diego	35
1978	Rollie Fingers, San Diego	37
1979	Bruce Sutter, Chicago	37
1980	Bruce Sutter, Chicago	28
1981	Bruce Sutter, St. Louis	25
1982	Bruce Sutter, St. Louis	36
1983	Lee Smith, Chicago	29
1984	Bruce Sutter, St. Louis	45
1985	Jeff Reardon, Montreal	41
1986	Todd Worrell, St. Louis	36
1987	Steve Bedrosian, Philadelphia	40
1988	John Franco, Cincinnati	39
1989	Mark Davis, San Diego	44
1990	John Franco, New York	33
1991	Lee Smith, St. Louis	47
1992	Lee Smith, St. Louis	43
1993	Randy Myers, Chicago	53
1994	John Franco, New York	30
1995	Randy Myers, Chicago	38
1996	Jeff Brantley, Cincinnati	44
	Todd Worrell, Los Angeles	44
1997	Jeff Shaw, Cincinnati	42
1998	Trevor Hoffman, San Diego	53
1999	Ugueth Urbina, Montreal	41
2000	Antonio Alfonseca, Florida	45
2001	Robb Nen, San Francisco	45
2002	John Smoltz, Atlanta	55
2003	Eric Gagne, Los Angeles	55
2004	Armando Benitez, Florida	47
	Jason Isringhausen, St. Louis	47

STRIKEOUTS

AMERICAN LEAGUE

Year	Pitcher, Club	No.
1901	Cy Young, Boston	158
1902	Rube Waddell, Philadelphia	210
1903	Rube Waddell, Philadelphia	302
1904	Rube Waddell, Philadelphia	349
1905	Rube Waddell, Philadelphia	287

Year	Pitcher, Club	No.
1906	Rube Waddell, Philadelphia	196
1907	Rube Waddell, Philadelphia	232
1908	Ed Walsh, Chicago	269
1909	Frank Smith, Chicago	177
1910	Walter Johnson, Washington	313
1911	Ed Walsh, Chicago	255
1912	Walter Johnson, Washington	303
1913	Walter Johnson, Washington	243
1914	Walter Johnson, Washington	225
1915	Walter Johnson, Washington	203
1916	Walter Johnson, Washington	228
1917	Walter Johnson, Washington	188
1918	Walter Johnson, Washington	162
1919	Walter Johnson, Washington	147
1920	Stan Coveleski, Cleveland	133
1921	Walter Johnson, Washington	143
1922	Urban Shocker, St. Louis	149
1923	Walter Johnson, Washington	130
1924	Walter Johnson, Washington	158
1925	Lefty Grove, Philadelphia	116
1926	Lefty Grove, Philadelphia	194
1927	Lefty Grove, Philadelphia	174
1928	Lefty Grove, Philadelphia	183
1929	Lefty Grove, Philadelphia	170
1930	Lefty Grove, Philadelphia	209
1931	Lefty Grove, Philadelphia	175
1932	Red Ruffing, New York	190
1933	Lefty Gomez, New York	163
1934	Lefty Gomez, New York	158
1935	Tommy Bridges, Detroit	163
1936	Tommy Bridges, Detroit	175
1937	Lefty Gomez, New York	194
1938	Bob Feller, Cleveland	240
1939	Bob Feller, Cleveland	246
1940	Bob Feller, Cleveland	261
1941	Bob Feller, Cleveland	260
1942	Bobo Newsom, Washington	113
	Tex Hughson, Boston	113
1943	Allie Reynolds, Cleveland	151
1944	Hal Newhouser, Detroit	187
1945	Hal Newhouser, Detroit	212
1946	Bob Feller, Cleveland	348
1947	Bob Feller, Cleveland	196
1948	Bob Feller, Cleveland	164
1949	Virgil Trucks, Detroit	153
1950	Bob Lemon, Cleveland	170
1951	Vic Raschi, New York	164
1952	Allie Reynolds, New York	160
1953	Billy Pierce, Chicago	186
1954	Bob Turley, Baltimore	185
1955	Herb Score, Cleveland	245
1956	Herb Score, Cleveland	263
1957	Early Wynn, Cleveland	184
1958	Early Wynn, Chicago	179
1959	Jim Bunning, Detroit	201
1960	Jim Bunning, Detroit	201
1961	Camilo Pascual, Minnesota	221
1962	Camilo Pascual, Minnesota	206
1963	Camilo Pascual, Minnesota	202
1964	Al Downing, New York	217
1965	Sam McDowell, Cleveland	325
1966	Sam McDowell, Cleveland	225
1967	Jim Lonborg, Boston	246
1968	Sam McDowell, Cleveland	283
1969	Sam McDowell, Cleveland	279
1970	Sam McDowell, Cleveland	304
1971	Mickey Lolich, Detroit	308
1972	Nolan Ryan, California	329
1973	Nolan Ryan, California	383

Year	Pitcher, Club	No.
1974	Nolan Ryan, California	367
1975	Frank Tanana, California	269
1976	Nolan Ryan, California	327
1977	Nolan Ryan, California	341
1978	Nolan Ryan, California	260
1979	Nolan Ryan, California	223
1980	Len Barker, Cleveland	187
1981	Len Barker, Cleveland	127
1982	Floyd Bannister, Seattle	209
1983	Jack Morris, Detroit	232
1984	Mark Langston, Seattle	204
1985	Bert Blyleven, Cleveland/Minnesota	206
1986	Mark Langston, Seattle	245
1987	Mark Langston, Seattle	262
1988	Roger Clemens, Boston	291
1989	Nolan Ryan, Texas	301
1990	Nolan Ryan, Texas	232
1991	Roger Clemens, Boston	241
1992	Randy Johnson, Seattle	241
1993	Randy Johnson, Seattle	308
1994	Randy Johnson, Seattle	204
1995	Randy Johnson, Seattle	294
1996	Roger Clemens, Boston	257
1997	Roger Clemens, Toronto	292
1998	Roger Clemens, Toronto	271
1999	Pedro Martinez, Boston	313
2000	Pedro Martinez, Boston	284
2001	Hideo Nomo, Boston	220
2002	Pedro Martinez, Boston	239
2003	Esteban Loaiza, Chicago	207
2004	Johan Santana, Minnesota	265

NATIONAL LEAGUE

Year	Pitcher, Club	No.
1900	Noodles Hahn, Cincinnati	132
1901	Noodles Hahn, Cincinnati	239
1902	Vic Willis, Boston	225
1903	Christy Mathewson, New York	267
1904	Christy Mathewson, New York	212
1905	Christy Mathewson, New York	206
1906	Fred Beebe, Chicago/St. Louis	171
1907	Christy Mathewson, New York	178
1908	Christy Mathewson, New York	259
1909	Orval Overall, Chicago	205
1910	Earl Moore, Philadelphia	185
1911	Rube Marquard, New York	237
1912	Grover Alexander, Philadelphia	195
1913	Tom Seaton, Philadelphia	168
1914	Grover Alexander, Philadelphia	214
1915	Grover Alexander, Philadelphia	241
1916	Grover Alexander, Philadelphia	167
1917	Grover Alexander, Philadelphia	200
1918	Hippo Vaughn, Chicago	148
1919	Hippo Vaughn, Chicago	141
1920	Grover Alexander, Chicago	173
1921	Burleigh Grimes, Brooklyn	136
1922	Dazzy Vance, Brooklyn	134
1923	Dazzy Vance, Brooklyn	197
1924	Dazzy Vance, Brooklyn	262
1925	Dazzy Vance, Brooklyn	221
1925	Dazzy Vance, Brooklyn	140
1927	Dazzy Vance, Brooklyn	184
1928	Dazzy Vance, Brooklyn	200
1929	Pat Malone, Chicago	166
1930	Bill Hallahan, St. Louis	177
1931	Bill Hallahan, St. Louis	159
1932	Dizzy Dean, St. Louis	191
1933	Dizzy Dean, St. Louis	199
1934	Dizzy Dean, St. Louis	195
1935	Dizzy Dean, St. Louis	182
1936	Van Lingle Mungo, Brooklyn	238
1937	Carl Hubbell, New York	159
1938	Clay Bryant, Chicago	135
1939	Claude Passeau, Philadelphia/Chicago	137

Year	Pitcher, Club	No.
	Bucky Walters, Cincinnati	137
1940	Kirby Higbe, Philadelphia	137
1941	Johnny Vander Meer, Cincinnati	202
1942	Johnny Vander Meer, Cincinnati	186
1943	Johnny Vander Meer, Cincinnati	174
1944	Bill Voiselle, New York	161
1945	Preacher Roe, Pittsburgh	148
1946	Johnny Schmitz, Chicago	135
1947	Ewell Blackwell, Cincinnati	193
1948	Harry Brecheen, St. Louis	149
1949	Warren Spahn, Boston	151
1950	Warren Spahn, Boston	191
1951	Warren Spahn, Boston	164
	Don Newcombe, Brooklyn	164
1952	Warren Spahn, Boston	183
1953	Robin Roberts, Philadelphia	198
1954	Robin Roberts, Philadelphia	185
1955	Sam Jones, Chicago	198
1956	Sam Jones, Chicago	176
1957	Jack Sanford, Philadelphia	188
1958	Sam Jones, St. Louis	225
1959	Don Drysdale, Los Angeles	242
1960	Don Drysdale, Los Angeles	246
1961	Sandy Koufax, Los Angeles	269
1962	Don Drysdale, Los Angeles	232
1963	Sandy Koufax, Los Angeles	306
1964	Bob Veale, Pittsburgh	250
1965	Sandy Koufax, Los Angeles	382
1966	Sandy Koufax, Los Angeles	317
1967	Jim Bunning, Philadelphia	253
1968	Bob Gibson, St. Louis	268
1969	Ferguson Jenkins, Chicago	273
1970	Tom Seaver, New York	283
1971	Tom Seaver, New York	289
1972	Steve Carlton, Philadelphia	310
1973	Tom Seaver, New York	251
1974	Steve Carlton, Philadelphia	240
1975	Tom Seaver, New York	243
1976	Tom Seaver, New York	235
1977	Phil Niekro, Atlanta	262
1978	J.R. Richard, Houston	303
1979	J.R. Richard, Houston	313
1980	Steve Carlton, Philadelphia	286
1981	Fernando Valenzuela, Los Angeles	180
1982	Steve Carlton, Philadelphia	286
1983	Steve Carlton, Philadelphia	275
1984	Dwight Gooden, New York	276
1985	Dwight Gooden, New York	268
1986	Mike Scott, Houston	306
1987	Nolan Ryan, Houston	270
1988	Nolan Ryan, Houston	228
1989	Jose DeLeon, St. Louis	201
1990	David Cone, New York	233
1991	David Cone, New York	241
1992	John Smoltz, Atlanta	*215
1993	Jose Rijo, Cincinnati	227
1994	Andy Benes, San Diego	189
1995	Hideo Nomo, Los Angeles	236
1996	John Smoltz, Atlanta	276
1997	Curt Schilling, Philadelphia	319
1998	Curt Schilling, Philadelphia	†300
1999	Randy Johnson, Arizona	364
2000	Randy Johnson, Arizona	347
2001	Randy Johnson, Arizona	372
2002	Randy Johnson, Arizona	334
2003	Kerry Wood, Chicago	266
2004	Randy Johnson, Arizona	290

*David Cone led the majors with 261 strikeouts in 1992, compiling 214 with New York (N.L.) and another 47 with Toronto (A.L.) following an August 27 trade.

†Randy Johnson led the majors with 329 strikeouts in 1998, compiling 213 with Seattle (A.L.) and another 116 with Houston (N.L.) following a July 31 trade.

CAREER MILESTONES

SERVICE
20-YEAR PLAYERS
(does not include pitchers)

Player	Yrs.	Games
1. Deacon McGuire	26	1,782
2. Rickey Henderson	25	3,081
3. Eddie Collins	25	2,826
Bobby Wallace	25	2,383
5. Pete Rose	24	3,562
Ty Cobb	24	3,035
Carlton Fisk	24	2,499
Rick Dempsey	24	1,766
9. Carl Yastrzemski	23	3,308
Hank Aaron	23	3,298
Rusty Staub	23	2,951
Rabbit Maranville	23	2,670
Brooks Robinson	23	2,896
Tony Perez	23	2,777
Tim Raines Sr.	23	2,502
Rogers Hornsby	23	2,259
17. Stan Musial	22	3,026
Willie Mays	22	2,992
Dave Winfield	22	2,973
Al Kaline	22	2,834
Harold Baines	22	2,830
Tris Speaker	22	2,789
Mel Ott	22	2,730
Graig Nettles	22	2,700
Joe Morgan	22	2,649
Willie McCovey	22	2,588
Bill Buckner	22	2,517
Babe Ruth	22	2,503
Harmon Killebrew	22	2,435
Jimmie Dykes	22	2,282
Cap Anson	22	2,277
Phil Cavarretta	22	2,030
Kid Gleason	22	1,968
Harry H. Davis	22	1,755
35. Eddie Murray	21	3,026
Cal Ripken Jr.	21	3,001
Reggie Jackson	21	2,820
Frank Robinson	21	2,808
Honus Wagner	21	2,794
George Brett	21	2,707
Darrell Evans	21	2,687
Paul Molitor	21	2,683
Andre Dawson	21	2,627
Nap Lajoie	21	2,480
Ted Simmons	21	2,456
Bill Dahlen	21	2,444
Ron Fairly	21	2,442
Willie Stargell	21	2,360
Lave Cross	21	2,278
Fred Clarke	21	2,246
Tim McCarver	21	1,909
Bob O'Farrell	21	1,492
Jack O'Connor	21	1,452
54. Robin Yount	20	2,856
Dwight Evans	20	2,606
Paul Waner	20	2,549
Gary Gaetti	20	2,507
Max Carey	20	2,476
Tony Gwynn	20	2,440
Luke Appling	20	2,422
Mickey Vernon	20	2,409
Sam Rice	20	2,404
Jake Beckley	20	2,389
George Davis	20	2,372
Brian Downing	20	2,344
Jimmie Foxx	20	2,317
Alan Trammell	20	2,293
Julio Franco	**20**	**2,269**
Doc Cramer	20	2,239
Al Simmons	20	2,215
Joe Judge	20	2,171
Charlie Grimm	20	2,166
Joe Cronin	20	2,124
Gabby Hartnett	20	1,990

Player	Yrs.	Games
Elmer Valo	20	1,806
Jay Johnstone	20	1,748
Luke Sewell	20	1,630
Manny Mota	20	1,536
Johnny Cooney	20	1,172

20-YEAR PITCHERS

Pitcher	Yrs.	Games
1. Nolan Ryan	27	807
2. Tommy John	26	760
3. Jim Kaat	25	898
Charlie Hough	25	858
5. Jesse Orosco	24	1,252
Dennis Eckersley	24	1,071
Phil Niekro	24	864
Steve Carlton	24	741
9. Don Sutton	23	774
Jack Quinn	23	756
Dennis Martinez	23	692
Early Wynn	23	691
13. Rich Gossage	22	1,002
Cy Young	22	906
Gaylord Perry	22	777
Joe Niekro	22	702
Bert Blyleven	22	692
Sam Jones	22	647
Jerry Reuss	22	628
Red Ruffing	22	624
Herb Pennock	22	617
Mike Morgan	22	597
23. Hoyt Wilhelm	21	1,070
Lindy McDaniel	21	987
Walter Johnson	21	802
Rick Honeycutt	21	797
Warren Spahn	21	750
Danny Darwin	21	716
Eppa Rixey	21	692
Waite Hoyt	21	674
Roger Clemens	**21**	**640**
Frank Tanana	21	638
Ted Lyons	21	594
34. John Franco	**20**	**1,088**
Grover Alexander	20	696
Red Faber	20	669
Tom Seaver	20	656
Dutch Leonard	20	640
Bobo Newsom	20	600
Mel Harder	20	582
Curt Simmons	20	569
Dolf Luque	20	550
Clark Griffith	20	453

BATTING
2,400 GAMES
(does not include pitchers)

Player	No.
1. Pete Rose	3,562
2. Carl Yastrzemski	3,308
3. Hank Aaron	3,298
4. Rickey Henderson	3,081
5. Ty Cobb	3,035
6. Eddie Murray	3,026
Stan Musial	3,026
8. Cal Ripken Jr.	3,001
9. Willie Mays	2,992
10. Dave Winfield	2,973
11. Rusty Staub	2,951
12. Brooks Robinson	2,896
13. Robin Yount	2,856
14. Al Kaline	2,834
15. Eddie Collins	2,826
16. Reggie Jackson	2,820
17. Frank Robinson	2,808
18. Harold Baines	2,830
19. Honus Wagner	2,794

Player	No.
20. Tris Speaker	2,789
21. Tony Perez	2,777
22. Mel Ott	2,730
23. Rafael Palmeiro	**2,721**
24. Barry Bonds	**2,716**
25. George Brett	2,707
26. Graig Nettles	2,700
27. Darrell Evans	2,687
28. Paul Molitor	2,683
29. Rabbit Maranville	2,670
30. Joe Morgan	2,649
31. Andre Dawson	2,627
32. Lou Brock	2,616
33. Dwight Evans	2,606
34. Luis Aparicio	2,599
35. Willie McCovey	2,588
36. Ozzie Smith	2,573
37. Paul Waner	2,549
38. Ernie Banks	2,528
39. Bill Buckner	2,517
Sam Crawford	2,517
41. Gary Gaetti	2,507
42. Babe Ruth	2,503
43. Tim Raines Sr.	2,502
44. Carlton Fisk	2,499
45. Billy Williams	2,488
Dave Concepcion	2,488
47. Nap Lajoie	2,480
48. Max Carey	2,476
49. Vada Pinson	2,469
Rod Carew	2,469
51. Dave Parker	2,466
52. Fred McGriff	**2,460**
53. Ted Simmons	2,456
54. Bill Dahlen	2,444
55. Ron Fairly	2,442
56. Wade Boggs	2,440
Tony Gwynn	2,440
58. Chili Davis	2,436
59. Harmon Killebrew	2,435
60. Roberto Clemente	2,433
61. Willie Davis	2,429
62. Luke Appling	2,422
63. Zack Wheat	2,410
64. Craig Biggio	**2,409**
Mickey Vernon	2,409
66. Buddy Bell	2,405
67. Sam Rice	2,404
Mike Schmidt	2,404
69. Mickey Mantle	2,401

500 CONSECUTIVE GAMES

Player	No.
1. Cal Ripken Jr.	2,632
2. Lou Gehrig	2,130
3. Everett Scott	1,307
4. Steve Garvey	1,207
5. Billy Williams	1,117
6. Joe Sewell	1,103
7. Stan Musial	895
8. Eddie Yost	829
9. Gus Suhr	822
10. Nellie Fox	798
11. Miguel Tejada	****756**
12. Pete Rose*	745
13. Dale Murphy	740
14. Richie Ashburn	730
15. Ernie Banks	717
16. Pete Rose*	678
17. Earl Averill	673
18. Frank McCormick	652
19. Sandy Alomar Sr.	648
20. Eddie Brown	618
21. Roy McMillan	585
22. George Pinckney	577
23. Steve Brodie	574

Player	No.
24. Aaron Ward	.565
25. Alex Rodriguez	**.546**
26. Candy LaChance	.540
27. Buck Freeman	.535
28. Fred Luderus	.533
29. Charlie Gehringer*	.511
Clyde Milan	.511
31. Vada Pinson	.508
32. Joe Carter	.507
33. Tony Cuccinello	.504
Charlie Gehringer*	.504
35. Omar Moreno	.503

*Only players with two streaks;
**Ongoing streak

BATTING .300, 10 TIMES

(50 or more games, season)

Player	Yrs.	Consec.
1. Ty Cobb	23	23
2. Tony Gwynn	18	17
Cap Anson	18	*11
Tris Speaker	18	10
5. Honus Wagner	17	*17
Stan Musial	†17	*16
Eddie Collins	17	9
Babe Ruth	17	8
Ted Williams	†16	*15
10. Rod Carew	15	15
Dennis Brouthers	15	14
Wade Boggs	15	*10
Nap Lajoie	15	10
Pete Rose	15	9
15. Rogers Hornsby	14	12
Paul Waner	14	*12
Luke Appling	14	9
Hank Aaron	14	5
Willie Keeler	13	13
Frankie Frisch	13	11
Al Simmons	13	*11
George Sisler	13	9
George Van Haltren	13	9
Roberto Clemente	13	8
Charlie Gehringer	13	8
Jim Ryan	13	7
Jake Beckley	13	6
Zack Wheat	13	6
Jim O'Rourke	13	5
Sam Rice	13	5
31. Ed Delahanty	12	12
Lou Gehrig	12	12
Billy Hamilton	12	12
Harry Heilmann	12	12
Edd Roush	12	11
Joe Medwick	12	*10
Arky Vaughan	12	*10
Riggs Stephenson	12	8
Roger Connor	12	6
Jimmie Foxx	12	5
Paul Molitor	12	4
42. Joe Kelley	11	11
Jesse Burkett	11	10
Hugh Duffy	11	10
Bill Terry	11	10
Al Oliver	11	9
Joe DiMaggio	11	7
Goose Goslin	11	7
Heinie Manush	11	7
Bill Dickey	11	6
Barry Bonds	**11**	**5**
George Brett	11	5
Fred Clarke	11	5
Stuffy McInnis	11	5
55. Buck Ewing	11	8
Frank Thomas	**10**	***8**
Pete Browning	10	7
Spud Davis	10	7
Edgar Martinez	**10**	**7**
Willie Mays	10	7
Kenny Williams	10	7
Jake Daubert	10	6
Patsy Donovan	10	6
Pie Traynor	10	6
Dixie Walker	10	6

Player	Yrs.	Consec.
Lloyd Waner	10	6
Ernie Lombardi	10	5
Mickey Mantle	10	5
Enos Slaughter	10	5
Sam Crawford	10	4
Kiki Cuyler	10	4
Mel Ott	10	3

*From start of career
†Streak interrupted by military service

.300 BATTING AVERAGE

(1,500 or more hits)

Player	Hits	Avg.
1. Ty Cobb	4,189	.366
2. Rogers Hornsby	2,930	.358
3. Joe Jackson	1,772	.356
4. Ed Delahanty	2,597	.346
5. Tris Speaker	3,514	.345
6. Billy Hamilton	2,164	.344
7. Ted Williams	2,654	.344
8. Dan Brouthers	2,296	.342
9. Babe Ruth	2,873	.342
10. Harry Heilmann	2,660	.342
11. Pete Browning	1,646	.341
12. Willie Keeler	2,932	.341
13. Bill Terry	2,193	.341
14. George Sisler	2,812	.340
15. Lou Gehrig	2,721	.340
16. Jesse Burkett	2,850	.338
17. Tony Gwynn	3,141	.338
18. Nap Lajoie	3,242	.338
19. Riggs Stephenson	1,515	.336
20. Al Simmons	2,927	.334
21. Paul Waner	3,152	.333
22. Eddie Collins	3,315	.333
23. Sam Thompson	1,988	.331
24. Cap Anson	3,012	.331
25. Stan Musial	3,630	.331
26. Heinie Manush	2,524	.330
27. Wade Boggs	3,010	.328
28. Rod Carew	3,053	.328
29. Honus Wagner	3,420	.328
30. Hugh Duffy	2,293	.326
31. Jimmie Foxx	2,646	.325
32. Earle Combs	1,866	.325
33. Joe DiMaggio	2,214	.325
34. Babe Herman	1,818	.324
35. Joe Medwick	2,471	.324
36. Edd Roush	2,376	.323
37. Sam Rice	2,987	.322
38. Kiki Cuyler	2,299	.321
39. Charlie Gehringer	2,839	.320
40. Chuck Klein	2,076	.320
41. Pie Traynor	2,416	.320
42. Mickey Cochrane	1,652	.320
43. Kenny Williams	1,552	.319
44. Kirby Puckett	2,304	.318
45. Earl Averill	2,019	.318
46. Arky Vaughan	2,103	.318
47. Roberto Clemente	3,000	.317
48. Joe Kelley	2,220	.317
49. Zack Wheat	2,884	.317
50. Roger Connor	2,467	.316
51. Lloyd Waner	2,459	.316
52. George Van Haltren	2,544	.316
53. Frankie Frisch	2,880	.316
54. Goose Goslin	2,735	.316
55. Manny Ramirez	**1,760**	**.316**
56. Mike Piazza	**1,829**	**.315**
57. Derek Jeter	**1,734**	**.315**
58. Cecil Travis	1,544	.314
59. Larry Walker	**2,069**	**.314**
60. Hank Greenberg	1,628	.313
61. Jack Fournier	1,631	.313
62. Elmer Flick	1,767	.315
63. Bill Dickey	1,969	.313
64. Johnny Mize	2,011	.312
65. Joe Sewell	2,226	.312
66. Fred Clarke	2,678	.312
67. Hughey Jennings	1,526	.312
68. Edgar Martinez	**2,247**	**.312**
69. Fred Lindstrom	1,747	.311
70. Bing Miller	1,934	.311

Player	Hits	Avg.
71. Jackie Robinson	1,518	.311
72. Baby Doll Jacobson	1,714	.311
73. Ginger Beaumont	1,759	.311
74. Mike Tiernan	1,838	.311
75. Luke Appling	2,749	.310
76. Irish Meusel	1,521	.310
77. Bobby Veach	2,063	.310
78. Jim O'Rourke	2,304	.310
79. Jim Bottomley	2,313	.310
80. Sam Crawford	2,961	.309
81. Bob Meusel	1,693	.309
82. Jack Tobin	1,906	.309
83. Frank Thomas	**2,113**	**.308**
84. Richie Ashburn	2,574	.308
85. Jake Beckley	2,934	.308
86. King Kelly	1,813	.308
87. Jim Ryan	2,513	.308
88. Stuffy McInnis	2,405	.307
89. Don Mattingly	2,153	.307
90. Joe Vosmik	1,682	.307
91. Home Run Baker	1,838	.307
92. George Burns	2,018	.307
93. Matty Alou	1,777	.307
94. George Kell	2,054	.306
95. Ivan Rodriguez	**2,051**	**.306**
96. Paul Molitor	3,319	.306
97. Dixie Walker	2,064	.306
98. Cupid Childs	1,721	.306
99. Ernie Lombardi	1,792	.306
100. Ralph Garr	1,562	.306
101. Alex Rodriguez	**1,707**	**.305**
102. Hank Aaron	3,771	.305
103. Chick Stahl	1,546	.305
104. George Brett	3,154	.305
105. Bill Madlock	2,008	.305
106. Billy Herman	2,345	.304
107. Tony Oliva	1,917	.304
108. Mel Ott	2,876	.304
109. Chipper Jones	**1,705**	**.304**
110. Deacon White	1,619	.303
111. Will Clark	2,176	.303
112. Charlie Jamieson	1,990	.303
113. Cy Seymour	1,724	.303
114. Mark Grace	2,445	.303
115. Jake Daubert	2,326	.303
116. Al Oliver	2,743	.303
117. Buck Ewing	1,625	.303
118. Steve Brodie	1,728	.303
119. Pete Rose	4,256	.303
120. Buddy Myer	2,131	.303
121. Harvey Kuenn	2,092	.303
122. Hal Trosky	1,561	.302
123. Ed McKean	2,084	.302
124. George Grantham	1,508	.302
125. Ben Chapman	1,958	.302
126. Tommy Holmes	1,507	.302
127. Willie Mays	3,283	.302
128. Joe Cronin	2,285	.301
129. Stan Hack	2,193	.301
130. Bernie Williams	**2,097**	**.301**
131. George Gore	1,612	.301
132. Paul Hines	1,881	.301
133. Patsy Donovan	2,256	.301
134. Roberto Alomar	**2,724**	**.300**
135. Wally Berger	1,550	.300
136. Pedro Guerrero	1,618	.300
137. Barry Bonds	**2,730**	**.300**
138. Julio Franco	**2,457**	**.300**
139. Enos Slaughter	2,383	.300
140. Billy Goodman	1,691	.300
141. Moises Alou	**1,764**	**.300**

(in strict numerical order rounded to three places)

.500 SLUGGING AVERAGE

(2,500 or more total bases)

Player	TB	Slg.
1. Babe Ruth	5,793	.690
2. Ted Williams	4,884	.634
3. Lou Gehrig	5,060	.632
4. Barry Bonds	**5,556**	**.611**
5. Jimmie Foxx	4,956	.609
6. Hank Greenberg	3,142	.605

Player	TB	Slg.
7. Manny Ramirez	3,339	.599
8. Vlad Guerrero	2,577	.589
9. Mark McGwire	3,639	.588
10. Joe DiMaggio	3,948	.579
11. Rogers Hornsby	4,712	.577
12. Alex Rodriguez	3,207	.574
13. Jim Thome	3,259	.569
14. Larry Walker	3,746	.568
15. Frank Thomas	3,887	.567
16. Albert Belle	3,300	.564
17. Johnny Mize	3,621	.562
18. Mike Piazza	3,260	.562
19. Juan Gonzalez	3,676	.561
20. Ken Griffey Jr.	4,131	.560
21. Stan Musial	6,134	.559
22. Willie Mays	6,066	.557
23. Mickey Mantle	4,511	.557
24. Carlos Delgado	2,786	.556
25. Hank Aaron	6,856	.555
26. Ralph Kiner	2,852	.548
27. Hack Wilson	2,593	.545
28. Sammy Sosa	4,368	.545
29. Jim Edmonds	2,767	.544
30. Chuck Klein	3,522	.543
31. Jeff Bagwell	4,175	.542
32. Jason Giambi	2,568	.540
33. Duke Snider	3,865	.540
34. Frank Robinson	5,373	.537
35. Chipper Jones	3,014	.537
36. Al Simmons	4,685	.535
37. Dick Allen	3,379	.534
38. Earl Averill	3,390	.534
39. Mel Ott	5,041	.533
40. Babe Herman	2,980	.532
41. Ken Williams	2,579	.530
42. Willie Stargell	4,190	.529
43. Gary Sheffield	3,854	.528
44. Mike Schmidt	4,404	.527
45. Mo Vaughn	2,894	.523
46. Hal Trosky	2,692	.522
47. Wally Berger	2,693	.522
48. Harry Heilmann	4,053	.520
49. Dan Brouthers	3,484	.519
50. Joe Jackson	2,577	.517
51. Rafael Palmeiro	5,223	.517
52. Edgar Martinez	3,718	.515
53. Willie McCovey	4,219	.515
54. Jose Canseco	3,361	.515
55. Moises Alou	3,020	.513
56. Ty Cobb	5,854	.512
57. Ellis Burks	3,691	.510
58. Eddie Mathews	4,349	.509
59. Fred McGriff	4,458	.509
60. Jeff Heath	2,512	.509
61. Harmon Killebrew	4,143	.509
62. Shawn Green	2,804	.508
63. Bob Johnson	3,501	.506
64. Bill Terry	3,252	.506
65. Jeff Kent	3,338	.505
66. Darryl Strawberry	2,738	.505
67. Sam Thompson	3,031	.505
68. Ed Delahanty	3,794	.505
69. Joe Medwick	3,852	.505
70. Jim Rice	4,129	.502
71. Tris Speaker	5,101	.500
72. David Justice	2,814	.500
73. Tim Salmon	2,863	.500
74. Jim Bottomley	3,737	.500
75. Goose Goslin	4,325	.500
76. Ernie Banks	4,706	.500

(in strict numerical order rounded to three places)

9,000 AT-BATS

Player	No.
1. Pete Rose	14,053
2. Hank Aaron	12,364
3. Carl Yastrzemski	11,988
4. Cal Ripken Jr.	11,551
5. Ty Cobb	11,434
6. Eddie Murray	11,336
7. Robin Yount	11,008
8. Dave Winfield	11,003
9. Stan Musial	10,972
10. Rickey Henderson	10,961
11. Willie Mays	10,881
12. Paul Molitor	10,835
13. Brooks Robinson	10,654
14. Honus Wagner	10,439
15. George Brett	10,349
16. Lou Brock	10,332
17. Luis Aparicio	10,230
18. Tris Speaker	10,195
19. Al Kaline	10,116
20. Rafael Palmeiro	10,103
21. Rabbit Maranville	10,078
22. Frank Robinson	10,006
23. Eddie Collins	9,949
24. Andre Dawson	9,927
25. Harold Baines	9,908
26. Reggie Jackson	9,864
27. Tony Perez	9,778
28. Rusty Staub	9,720
29. Vada Pinson	9,645
30. Nap Lajoie	9,589
31. Sam Crawford	9,570
32. Jake Beckley	9,538
33. Paul Waner	9,459
34. Mel Ott	9,456
35. Roberto Clemente	9,454
36. Ernie Banks	9,421
37. Bill Buckner	9,397
38. Ozzie Smith	9,396
39. Max Carey	9,363
40. Dave Parker	9,358
41. Billy Williams	9,350
42. Rod Carew	9,315
43. Tony Gwynn	9,288
44. Joe Morgan	9,277
45. Sam Rice	9,269
46. Nellie Fox	9,232
47. Craig Biggio	9,221
48. Wade Boggs	9,180
49. Willie Davis	9,174
50. Roger Cramer	9,140
51. Frankie Frisch	9,112
52. Zack Wheat	9,106
53. Cap Anson	9,104
54. Barry Bonds	9,098
55. Lave Cross	9,085
56. Roberto Alomar	9,073
57. Al Oliver	9,049
58. George Davis	9,046
59. Bill Dahlen	9,036

1,500 RUNS

Player	No.
1. Rickey Henderson	2,295
2. Ty Cobb	2,246
3. Hank Aaron	2,174
Babe Ruth	2,174
5. Pete Rose	2,165
6. Barry Bonds	2,070
7. Willie Mays	2,062
8. Stan Musial	1,949
9. Lou Gehrig	1,888
10. Tris Speaker	1,882
11. Mel Ott	1,859
12. Frank Robinson	1,829
13. Eddie Collins	1,821
14. Carl Yastrzemski	1,816
15. Ted Williams	1,798
16. Paul Molitor	1,782
17. Charlie Gehringer	1,774
18. Jimmie Foxx	1,751
19. Honus Wagner	1,739
20. Cap Anson	1,722
21. Jesse Burkett	1,720
22. Willie Keeler	1,719
23. Billy Hamilton	1,697
24. Bid McPhee	1,684
25. Mickey Mantle	1,677
26. Dave Winfield	1,669
27. Joe Morgan	1,650
28. Cal Ripken Jr.	1,647
29. Jim Ryan	1,643
30. George Van Haltren	1,642
31. Robin Yount	1,632
32. Eddie Murray	1,627
Paul Waner	1,627
34. Fred Clarke	1,622
Al Kaline	1,622
36. Roger Connor	1,620
37. Rafael Palmeiro	1,616
38. Lou Brock	1,610
39. Craig Biggio	1,603
40. Jake Beckley	1,602
41. Ed Delahanty	1,600
42. Bill Dahlen	1,590
43. George Brett	1,583
44. Rogers Hornsby	1,579
45. Tim Raines Sr.	1,571
46. Hugh Duffy	1,554
47. Reggie Jackson	1,551
48. Max Carey	1,545
George Davis	1,545
50. Frankie Frisch	1,532
51. Dan Brouthers	1,523
Tom Brown	1,523
53. Sam Rice	1,514
54. Wade Boggs	1,513
55. Eddie Mathews	1,509
56. Roberto Alomar	1,508
57. Al Simmons	1,507
58. Jeff Bagwell	1,506
Mike Schmidt	1,506
60. Nap Lajoie	1,504

2,500 HITS

Player	No.
1. Pete Rose	4,256
2. Ty Cobb	4,189
3. Hank Aaron	3,771
4. Stan Musial	3,630
5. Tris Speaker	3,514
6. Honus Wagner	3,420
7. Carl Yastrzemski	3,419
8. Paul Molitor	3,319
9. Eddie Collins	3,315
10. Willie Mays	3,283
11. Eddie Murray	3,255
12. Nap Lajoie	3,242
13. Cal Ripken Jr.	3,184
14. George Brett	3,154
15. Paul Waner	3,152
16. Robin Yount	3,142
17. Tony Gwynn	3,141
18. Dave Winfield	3,110
19. Rickey Henderson	3,055
20. Rod Carew	3,053
21. Lou Brock	3,023
22. Cap Anson	3,012
23. Wade Boggs	3,010
24. Al Kaline	3,007
25. Roberto Clemente	3,000
26. Sam Rice	2,987
27. Sam Crawford	2,961
28. Frank Robinson	2,943
29. Jake Beckley	2,934
30. Willie Keeler	2,932
31. Rogers Hornsby	2,930
32. Al Simmons	2,927
33. Rafael Palmeiro	2,922
34. Zack Wheat	2,884
35. Frankie Frisch	2,880
36. Mel Ott	2,876
37. Babe Ruth	2,873
38. Harold Baines	2,866
39. Jesse Burkett	2,850
40. Brooks Robinson	2,848
41. Charlie Gehringer	2,839
42. George Sisler	2,812
43. Andre Dawson	2,774
44. Vada Pinson	2,757
45. Luke Appling	2,749
46. Al Oliver	2,743
47. Goose Goslin	2,735
48. Tony Perez	2,732
49. Barry Bonds	2,730

Player	No.
50. **Roberto Alomar**	**2,724**
51. Lou Gehrig	2,721
52. Rusty Staub	2,716
53. Bill Buckner	2,715
54. Dave Parker	2,712
55. Billy Williams	2,711
56. Roger Cramer	2,705
57. Fred Clarke	2,678
58. Luis Aparicio	2,677
59. Max Carey	2,665
George Davis	2,665
61. Nellie Fox	2,663
62. Harry Heilmann	2,660
63. Lave Cross	2,651
64. Ted Williams	2,654
65. Jimmie Foxx	2,646
66. **Craig Biggio**	**2,639**
67. Rabbit Maranville	2,605
Tim Raines Sr.	2,605
69. Steve Garvey	2,597
70. Ed Delahanty	2,593
71. Reggie Jackson	2,584
72. Ernie Banks	2,583
73. Richie Ashburn	2,574
74. Willie Davis	2,561
75. George Van Haltren	2,544
76. Heinie Manush	2,524
77. Joe Morgan	2,517
78. Buddy Bell	2,514
79. Jim Ryan	2,513

200-HIT SEASONS, 4 TIMES

Player	Yrs.
1. Pete Rose	10
2. Ty Cobb	9
3. Lou Gehrig	8
Willie Keeler	8
Paul Waner	8
6. Wade Boggs	7
Charlie Gehringer	7
Rogers Hornsby	7
9. Jesse Burkett	6
Steve Garvey	6
Stan Musial	6
Sam Rice	6
Al Simmons	6
George Sisler	6
Bill Terry	6
16. Tony Gwynn	5
Chuck Klein	5
Kirby Puckett	5
19. **Ichiro Suzuki**	**4**
Lou Brock	4
Rod Carew	4
Roberto Clemente	4
Ed Delahanty	4
Harry Heilmann	4
Joe Jackson	4
Nap Lajoie	4
Heinie Manush	4
Joe Medwick	4
Paul Molitor	4
Vada Pinson	4
Jim Rice	4
Tris Speaker	4
Jack Tobin	4
Lloyd Waner	4

2,000 SINGLES

Player	No.
1. Pete Rose	3,215
2. Ty Cobb	2,643
Eddie Collins	2,643
4. Willie Keeler	2,513
5. Honus Wagner	2,424
6. Rod Carew	2,404
7. Tris Speaker	2,383
8. Tony Gwynn	2,378
9. Paul Molitor	2,366
10. Nap Lajoie	2,340
11. Hank Aaron	2,294

Player	No.
12. Jesse Burkett	2,273
13. Sam Rice	2,271
14. Cap Anson	2,262
Carl Yastrzemski	2,262
16. Wade Boggs	2,253
Stan Musial	2,253
18. Lou Brock	2,247
19. Paul Waner	2,243
20. Rickey Henderson	2,182
Robin Yount	2,182
22. Frankie Frisch	2,171
23. Roger Cramer	2,163
24. Luke Appling	2,162
25. Nellie Fox	2,161
26. Eddie Murray	2,156
27. Roberto Clemente	2,154
28. Jake Beckley	2,130
29. George Sisler	2,121
30. Richie Ashburn	2,119
31. Luis Aparicio	2,108
32. Cal Ripken	2,106
33. Zack Wheat	2,104
34. Sam Crawford	2,097
35. Lave Cross	2,056
36. George Brett	2,035
37. Al Kaline	2,035
38. Lloyd Waner	2,033
39. Brooks Robinson	2,030
Fred Clarke	2,030
41. George Van Haltren	2,028
42. Rabbit Maranville	2,020
43. Max Carey	2,017
44. Dave Winfield	2,017

450 DOUBLES

Player	No.
1. Tris Speaker	792
2. Pete Rose	746
3. Stan Musial	725
4. Ty Cobb	724
5. George Brett	665
6. Nap Lajoie	657
7. Carl Yastrzemski	646
8. Honus Wagner	643
9. Hank Aaron	624
10. Paul Molitor	605
Paul Waner	605
12. Cal Ripken Jr.	603
13. Robin Yount	583
14. Wade Boggs	578
15. Charlie Gehringer	574
16. **Rafael Palmeiro**	**572**
17. **Craig Biggio**	**564**
18. **Barry Bonds**	**563**
19. Eddie Murray	560
20. Tony Gwynn	543
21. Harry Heilmann	542
22. Rogers Hornsby	541
23. Joe Medwick	540
Dave Winfield	540
25. Al Simmons	539
26. Lou Gehrig	534
27. Cap Anson	529
Al Oliver	529
29. Frank Robinson	528
30. Dave Parker	526
31. Ted Williams	525
32. Willie Mays	523
33. Ed Delahanty	522
34. Joe Cronin	515
35. **Edgar Martinez**	**514**
36. Mark Grace	511
37. Rickey Henderson	510
38. Babe Ruth	506
39. Tony Perez	505
40. **Roberto Alomar**	**504**
41. Andre Dawson	503
42. Goose Goslin	500
43. Rusty Staub	499
44. Bill Buckner	498
Al Kaline	498
Sam Rice	498
47. **John Olerud**	**493**

Player	No.
48. Heinie Manush	491
49. Mickey Vernon	490
50. Harold Baines	488
Mel Ott	488
52. Lou Brock	486
Billy Herman	486
54. Vada Pinson	485
55. **Jeff Bagwell**	**484**
Hal McRae	484
57. Dwight Evans	483
Ted Simmons	483
59. Brooks Robinson	482
60. Zack Wheat	476
61. Jake Beckley	473
62. Frankie Frisch	466
63. Jim Bottomley	465
64. Reggie Jackson	463
65. Dan Brouthers	460
66. **Luis Gonzalez**	**458**
Sam Crawford	458
Jimmie Foxx	458
69. George Davis	453
Jimmie Dykes	453
71. **Larry Walker**	**451**
Paul O'Neill	451
Jimmy Ryan	451

150 TRIPLES

Player	No.
1. Sam Crawford	309
2. Ty Cobb	295
3. Honus Wagner	252
4. Jake Beckley	244
5. Roger Connor	233
6. Tris Speaker	222
7. Fred Clarke	220
8. Dan Brouthers	205
9. Joe Kelley	194
10. Paul Waner	191
11. Bid McPhee	189
12. Eddie Collins	187
13. Ed Delahanty	186
14. Sam Rice	184
15. Jesse Burkett	182
Ed Konetchy	182
Edd Roush	182
18. Buck Ewing	178
19. Rabbit Maranville	177
Stan Musial	177
21. Harry Stovey	174
22. Goose Goslin	173
23. Zack Wheat	172
Tommy Leach	172
25. Rogers Hornsby	169
26. Joe Jackson	168
27. Roberto Clemente	166
Sherry Magee	166
29. Jake Daubert	165
30. Elmer Flick	164
George Sisler	164
Pie Traynor	164
33. Bill Dahlen	163
George Davis	163
Lou Gehrig	163
Nap Lajoie	163
37. Mike Tiernan	162
38. Sam Thompson	161
George Van Haltren	161
40. Harry Hooper	160
Heinie Manush	160
42. Max Carey	159
Joe Judge	159
44. Ed McKean	158
45. Kiki Cuyler	157
Jim Ryan	157
47. Tommy Corcoran	155
48. Earle Combs	154
49. Jim Bottomley	151
Harry Heilmann	151

300 HOME RUNS

Player	No.
1. Hank Aaron	755
2. Babe Ruth	714
3. **Barry Bonds**	**703**
4. Willie Mays	660
5. Frank Robinson	586
6. Mark McGwire	583
7. **Sammy Sosa**	**574**
8. Harmon Killebrew	573
9. Reggie Jackson	563
10. **Rafael Palmeiro**	**551**
11. Mike Schmidt	548
12. Mickey Mantle	536
13. Jimmie Foxx	534
14. Willie McCovey	521
Ted Williams	521
16. Ernie Banks	512
Eddie Mathews	512
18. Mel Ott	511
19. Eddie Murray	504
20. **Ken Griffey Jr.**	**501**
21. **Fred McGriff**	**493**
Lou Gehrig	493
23. Stan Musial	475
Willie Stargell	475
25. Dave Winfield	465
26. Jose Canseco	462
27. Carl Yastrzemski	452
28. **Jeff Bagwell**	**446**
29. Dave Kingman	442
30. Andre Dawson	438
31. **Frank Thomas**	**436**
32. **Juan Gonzalez**	**434**
33. Cal Ripken Jr.	431
34. Billy Williams	426
35. **Jim Thome**	**423**
36. **Gary Sheffield**	**415**
37. Darrell Evans	414
38. Duke Snider	407
39. **Andres Galarraga**	**399**
Al Kaline	399
41. Dale Murphy	398
42. Joe Carter	396
43. **Manny Ramirez**	**390**
Graig Nettles	390
45. Johnny Bench	389
46. Dwight Evans	385
47. Harold Baines	384
48. Frank Howard	382
Jim Rice	382
50. **Alex Rodriguez**	**381**
Albert Belle	381
52. Orlando Cepeda	379
Tony Perez	379
54. **Mike Piazza**	**378**
Matt Williams	378
56. Norm Cash	377
57. Carlton Fisk	376
58. Rocky Colavito	374
59. Gil Hodges	370
60. Ralph Kiner	369
61. **Larry Walker**	**368**
62. Joe DiMaggio	361
63. Gary Gaetti	360
64. Johnny Mize	359
65. Yogi Berra	358
66. Greg Vaughn	355
67. Lee May	354
68. **Ellis Burks**	**352**
69. Dick Allen	351
70. Chili Davis	350
71. George Foster	348
72. Ron Santo	342
73. Jack Clark	340
74. Dave Parker	339
Boog Powell	339
76. Don Baylor	338
77. **Carlos Delgado**	**336**
Joe Adcock	336
79. Darryl Strawberry	335
80. Bobby Bonds	332
81. Hank Greenberg	331
82. Mo Vaughn	328

Player	No.
83. Willie Horton	325
84. Gary Carter	324
Lance Parrish	324
86. **Tino Martinez**	**322**
87. Ron Gant	321
88. Cecil Fielder	319
89. Roy Sievers	318
90. George Brett	317
91. Ron Cey	316
92. Reggie Smith	314
93. **Chipper Jones**	**310**
Jay Buhner	310
95. **Edgar Martinez**	**309**
96. Greg Luzinski	307
Al Simmons	307
98. Fred Lynn	306
99. David Justice	305
100. **Vinny Castilla**	**303**
101. **Jim Edmonds**	**302**
Jeff Kent	**302**
Ruben Sierra	**302**
104. Rogers Hornsby	301
105. Chuck Klein	300

10 PINCH HOME RUNS

Player	No.
1. Cliff Johnson	20
2. Jerry Lynch	18
3. **John Vander Wal**	**17**
4. Gates Brown	16
Smoky Burgess	16
Willie McCovey	16
7. **Dave Hansen**	**15**
8. George Crowe	14
9. Glenallen Hill	13
10. Joe Adcock	12
Bob Cerv	12
Jose Morales	12
Graig Nettles	12
14. **Mark Sweeney**	**11**
Craig Wilson	**11**
Jeff Burroughs	11
Jay Johnstone	11
Candy Maldonado	11
Orlando Merced	11
Fred Whitfield	11
Cy Williams	11
22. Mark Carreon	10
Dave Clark	10
Jim Dwyer	10
Mike Lum	10
Ken McMullen	10
Don Mincher	10
Wally Post	10
Champ Summers	10
Jerry Turner	10
Gus Zernial	10

25 MULTIPLE-HR GAMES

Player	No.
1. Babe Ruth	72
2. **Barry Bonds**	**68**
3. Mark McGwire	67
4. **Sammy Sosa**	**66**
5. Willie Mays	63
6. Hank Aaron	62
7. Jimmie Foxx	55
8. Frank Robinson	54
9. **Ken Griffey Jr.**	**50**
10. Eddie Mathews	49
Mel Ott	49
12. **Juan Gonzalez**	**48**
13. Harmon Killebrew	46
Mickey Mantle	46
15. Willie McCovey	44
Mike Schmidt	44
Dave Kingman	43
18. Ernie Banks	42
Lou Gehrig	42
Reggie Jackson	42
21. **Fred McGriff**	**40**

Player	No.
Ralph Kiner	40
23. **Manny Ramirez**	**39**
Albert Belle	39
Andre Dawson	39
26. **Carlos Delgado**	**37**
Stan Musial	37
Ted Williams	37
29. **Alex Rodriguez**	**36**
Jose Canseco	36
Willie Stargell	36
32. **Jim Thome**	**35**
Joe DiMaggio	35
Hank Greenberg	35
Lee May	35
Jim Rice	35
37. **Rafael Palmeiro**	**34**
Mike Piazza	**34**
Joe Carter	34
Cecil Fielder	34
Duke Snider	34
42. **Vinny Castilla**	**32**
Dick Allen	32
Rocky Colavito	32
Dale Murphy	32
Billy Williams	32
Gus Zernial	32
48. **Jeff Bagwell**	**31**
Gary Sheffield	**31**
Eddie Murray	31
Hank Sauer	31
Greg Vaughn	31
Matt Williams	31
54. **Andres Galarraga**	**30**
Chipper Jones	**30**
Gil Hodges	30
Willie Horton	30
Johnny Mize	30
Darryl Strawberry	30
Mo Vaughn	30
Dave Winfield	30
62. **Larry Walker**	**29**
63. Joe Adcock	28
Gary Carter	28
Chili Davis	28
Chuck Klein	28
67. **Moises Alou**	**27**
Shawn Green	**27**
Graig Nettles	27
Roy Sievers	27
Hack Wilson	27
Carl Yastrzemski	27
73. **Frank Thomas**	**26**
Bob Horner	26
Frank Howard	26
Ron Santo	26
77. Norm Cash	25
Roger Maris	25
Ryne Sandberg	25
Hal Trosky	25

10 GRAND SLAMS

Player	No.
1. Lou Gehrig	23
2. Eddie Murray	19
3. **Robin Ventura**	**18**
Willie McCovey	18
5. **Manny Ramirez**	**17**
6. Jimmie Foxx	17
Ted Williams	17
8. Hank Aaron	16
Dave Kingman	16
Babe Ruth	16
11. **Ken Griffey Jr.**	**14**
Mike Piazza	**14**
Gil Hodges	14
Mark McGwire	14
15. Harold Baines	13
Albert Belle	13
Joe DiMaggio	13
George Foster	13
Ralph Kiner	13
20. Ernie Banks	12
Don Baylor	12

Player	No.
Rogers Hornsby	12
Joe Rudi	12
Rudy York	12
25. Barry Bonds	11
Jeff Kent	11
Rafael Palmeiro	11
Johnny Bench	11
Gary Carter	11
Eric Davis	11
Cecil Fielder	11
Gary Gaetti	11
Hank Greenberg	11
Reggie Jackson	11
Harmon Killebrew	11
Lee May	11
Willie Stargell	11
Danny Tartabull	11
Devon White	11
Matt Williams	11
Dave Winfield	11
42. Ellis Burks	10
Andres Galarraga	10
Jason Giambi	10
Tino Martinez	10
Alex Rodriguez	10
Joe Adcock	10
George Bell	10
Jay Buhner	10
Jeff Burroughs	10
Joe Carter	10
Darrell Evans	10
John Milner	10
Roy Sievers	10
Al Simmons	10
Vern Stephens	10
Mo Vaughn	10
Vic Wertz	10

4,000 TOTAL BASES

Player	No.
1. Hank Aaron	6,856
2. Stan Musial	6,134
3. Willie Mays	6,066
4. Ty Cobb	5,854
5. Babe Ruth	5,793
6. Pete Rose	5,752
7. Barry Bonds	5,556
8. Carl Yastrzemski	5,539
9. Eddie Murray	5,397
10. Frank Robinson	5,373
11. Rafael Palmeiro	5,223
12. Dave Winfield	5,221
13. Cal Ripken Jr.	5,168
14. Tris Speaker	5,101
15. Lou Gehrig	5,060
16. George Brett	5,044
17. Mel Ott	5,041
18. Jimmie Foxx	4,956
19. Ted Williams	4,884
20. Honus Wagner	4,870
21. Paul Molitor	4,854
22. Al Kaline	4,852
23. Reggie Jackson	4,834
24. Andre Dawson	4,787
25. Robin Yount	4,730
26. Rogers Hornsby	4,712
27. Ernie Banks	4,706
28. Al Simmons	4,685
29. Harold Baines	4,604
30. Billy Williams	4,599
31. Rickey Henderson	4,588
32. Tony Perez	4,532
33. Mickey Mantle	4,511
34. Roberto Clemente	4,492
35. Paul Waner	4,478
36. Nap Lajoie	4,471
37. Fred McGriff	4,458
38. Dave Parker	4,405
39. Mike Schmidt	4,404
40. Sammy Sosa	4,368
41. Eddie Mathews	4,349
42. Sam Crawford	4,328
43. Goose Goslin	4,325

Player	No.
44. Brooks Robinson	4,270
45. Eddie Collins	4,268
46. Vada Pinson	4,264
47. Tony Gwynn	4,259
48. Charlie Gehringer	4,257
49. Lou Brock	4,238
50. Dwight Evans	4,230
51. Willie McCovey	4,219
52. Willie Stargell	4,190
53. Rusty Staub	4,185
54. Jeff Bagwell	4,175
55. Jake Beckley	4,156
56. Harmon Killebrew	4,143
57. Ken Griffey Jr.	4,131
58. Jim Rice	4,129
59. Zack Wheat	4,100
60. Al Oliver	4,083
61. Cap Anson	4,080
62. Wade Boggs	4,064
63. Harry Heilmann	4,053
64. Andres Galarraga	4,038
65. Roberto Alomar	4,018
66. Craig Biggio	4,007

800 EXTRA BASE HITS

Player	No.
1. Hank Aaron	1,477
2. Stan Musial	1,377
3. Babe Ruth	1,356
4. Barry Bonds	1,343
5. Willie Mays	1,323
6. Lou Gehrig	1,190
7. Frank Robinson	1,186
8. Rafael Palmeiro	1,161
9. Carl Yastrzemski	1,157
10. Ty Cobb	1,136
11. Tris Speaker	1,131
12. George Brett	1,119
13. Jimmie Foxx	1,117
Ted Williams	1,117
15. Eddie Murray	1,099
16. Dave Winfield	1,093
17. Cal Ripken Jr.	1,078
18. Reggie Jackson	1,075
19. Mel Ott	1,071
20. Pete Rose	1,041
21. Andre Dawson	1,039
22. Mike Schmidt	1,015
23. Rogers Hornsby	1,011
24. Ernie Banks	1,009
25. Honus Wagner	996
26. Al Simmons	995
27. Al Kaline	972
28. Tony Perez	963
29. Jeff Bagwell	962
30. Robin Yount	960
31. Fred McGriff	958
32. Sammy Sosa	957
33. Paul Molitor	953
Willie Stargell	953
35. Mickey Mantle	952
36. Billy Williams	948
37. Dwight Evans	941
38. Dave Parker	940
39. Eddie Mathews	938
40. Ken Griffey Jr.	937
41. Harold Baines	921
Goose Goslin	921
43. Willie McCovey	920
44. Paul Waner	909
45. Charlie Gehringer	904
46. Nap Lajoie	902
47. Frank Thomas	891
48. Harmon Killebrew	887
49. Joe Carter	881
Joe DiMaggio	881
51. Larry Walker	880
52. Harry Heilmann	876
53. Andres Galarraga	875
54. Rickey Henderson	873
55. Vada Pinson	868
56. Sam Crawford	864
57. Joe Medwick	858

Player	No.
58. Duke Snider	850
59. Craig Biggio	849
60. Juan Gonzalez	847
61. Roberto Clemente	846
62. Carlton Fisk	844
63. Gary Gaetti	842
64. Mark McGwire	841
65. Edgar Martinez	838
Rusty Staub	838
67. Jim Bottomley	835
68. Jim Rice	834
69. Gary Sheffield	825
Al Oliver	825
71. Orlando Cepeda	823
72. Brooks Robinson	818
73. Ellis Burks	817
74. Jose Canseco	816
75. Luis Gonzalez	813
Joe Morgan	813
77. Roger Connor	812
78. Ed Delahanty	809
Johnny Mize	809
80. Jake Beckley	804
Chili Davis	804
82. Joe Cronin	803

1,200 RUNS BATTED IN

Player	No.
1. Hank Aaron	2,297
2. Babe Ruth	2,213
3. Lou Gehrig	1,995
4. Stan Musial	1,951
5. Ty Cobb	1,938
6. Jimmie Foxx	1,922
7. Eddie Murray	1,917
8. Willie Mays	1,903
9. Cap Anson	1,880
10. Mel Ott	1,860
11. Carl Yastrzemski	1,844
12. Barry Bonds	1,843
13. Ted Williams	1,839
14. Dave Winfield	1,833
15. Al Simmons	1,827
16. Frank Robinson	1,812
17. Rafael Palmeiro	1,775
18. Honus Wagner	1,733
19. Reggie Jackson	1,702
20. Cal Ripken Jr.	1,695
21. Tony Perez	1,652
22. Ernie Banks	1,636
23. Harold Baines	1,628
24. Goose Goslin	1,609
25. Nap Lajoie	1,599
26. George Brett	1,595
Mike Schmidt	1,595
28. Andre Dawson	1,591
29. Harmon Killebrew	1,584
Rogers Hornsby	1,584
31. Al Kaline	1,583
32. Jake Beckley	1,578
33. Willie McCovey	1,555
34. Fred McGriff	1,550
35. Willie Stargell	1,540
36. Harry Heilmann	1,539
37. Joe DiMaggio	1,537
38. Sammy Sosa	1,530
39. Tris Speaker	1,529
40. Sam Crawford	1,525
41. Jeff Bagwell	1,510
42. Mickey Mantle	1,509
43. Dave Parker	1,493
44. Billy Williams	1,475
45. Ed Delahanty	1,466
Rusty Staub	1,466
47. Eddie Mathews	1,453
48. Jim Rice	1,451
49. Ken Griffey Jr.	1,444
50. Joe Carter	1,445
51. George Davis	1,440
52. Frank Thomas	1,439
53. Yogi Berra	1,430
54. Charlie Gehringer	1,427
55. Andres Galaragga	1,425

Player	No.
56. Joe Cronin	1,424
57. Jim Bottomley	1,422
58. Mark McGwire	1,414
59. Jose Canseco	1,407
60. Robin Yount	1,406
61. Juan Gonzalez	**1,404**
62. Ted Simmons	1,389
63. Dwight Evans	1,384
64. Joe Medwick	1,383
65. Lave Cross	1,378
66. Johnny Bench	1,376
67. Chili Davis	1,372
68. Orlando Cepeda	1,365
69. Brooks Robinson	1,357
70. Darrell Evans	1,354
71. Gary Sheffield	**1,353**
72. Gary Gaetti	1,341
73. Johnny Mize	1,337
74. Duke Snider	1,333
75. Ron Santo	1,331
76. Carlton Fisk	1,330
77. Al Oliver	1,326
78. Roger Connor	1,323
79. Graig Nettles	1,314
Pete Rose	1,314
81. Mickey Vernon	1,311
82. Paul Waner	1,309
83. Steve Garvey	1,308
84. Paul Molitor	1,307
85. Roberto Clemente	1,305
Sam Thompson	1,305
87. Enos Slaughter	1,304
88. Hugh Duffy	1,302
89. Eddie Collins	1,300
90. Dan Brouthers	1,296
91. Ruben Sierra	**1,289**
92. Del Ennis	1,284
93. Bob Johnson	1,283
94. Don Baylor	1,276
Hank Greenberg	1,276
96. Gil Hodges	1,274
97. Pie Traynor	1,273
98. Manny Ramirez	**1,270**
99. Paul O'Neill	1,269
100. Dale Murphy	1,266
101. Edgar Martinez	**1,261**
102. Larry Walker	**1,259**
103. Ty Cobb	1,249
104. Zack Wheat	1,248
105. Bobby Doerr	1,247
106. Frankie Frisch	1,244
Lee May	1,244
108. Albert Belle	1,239
George Foster	1,239
110. Bill Dahlen	1,234
111. Gary Carter	1,225
112. Tino Martinez	**1,222**
113. Matt Williams	1,218
114. Dave Kingman	1,210
115. Bill Dickey	1,209
116. Bill Buckner	1,208
117. Jeff Kent	**1,207**
118. Ellis Burks	**1,206**
119. Will Clark	1,205
120. Chuck Klein	1,201

1,000 WALKS

Player	No.
1. Barry Bonds	**2,302**
2. Rickey Henderson	2,190
3. Babe Ruth	2,062
4. Ted Williams	2,021
5. Joe Morgan	1,865
6. Carl Yastrzemski	1,845
7. Mickey Mantle	1,733
8. Mel Ott	1,708
9. Eddie Yost	1,614
10. Darrell Evans	1,605
11. Stan Musial	1,599
12. Pete Rose	1,566
13. Harmon Killebrew	1,559
14. Lou Gehrig	1,507
15. Mike Schmidt	1,507

Player	No.
16. Eddie Collins	1,499
17. Willie Mays	1,464
18. Jimmie Foxx	1,452
19. Frank Thomas	**1,450**
20. Eddie Mathews	1,444
21. Frank Robinson	1,420
22. Wade Boggs	1,412
23. Hank Aaron	1,402
24. Dwight Evans	1,391
25. Jeff Bagwell	**1,383**
26. Tris Speaker	1,381
27. Reggie Jackson	1,375
28. Willie McCovey	1,345
29. Eddie Murray	1,333
30. Tim Raines, Sr.,	1,330
31. Tony Phillips	1,319
32. Mark McGwire	1,317
33. Rafael Palmeiro	**1,310**
34. Fred McGriff	**1,305**
35. Luke Appling	1,302
36. Edgar Martinez	**1,283**
37. Al Kaline	1,277
38. Ken Singleton	1,263
39. Jack Clark	1,262
40. John Olerud	**1,259**
41. Rusty Staub	1,255
42. Willie Randolph	1,243
43. Jim Wynn	1,224
44. Dave Winfield	1,216
45. Jim Thome	**1,212**
46. Pee Wee Reese	1,210
47. Gary Sheffield	**1,202**
48. Richie Ashburn	1,198
49. Brian Downing	1,197
Lou Whitaker	1,197
51. Chili Davis	1,194
52. Billy Hamilton	1,189
53. Charlie Gehringer	1,186
54. Donie Bush	1,158
55. Max Bishop	1,156
56. Toby Harrah	1,153
57. Harry Hooper	1,136
58. Jimmy Sheckard	1,135
59. Brett Butler	1,129
Cal Ripken Jr.	1,129
61. Ron Santo	1,108
62. George Brett	1,096
63. Paul Molitor	1,094
64. Lu Blue	1,092
Stan Hack	1,092
66. Paul Waner	1,091
67. Graig Nettles	1,088
68. Bobby Grich	1,087
69. Robin Ventura	**1,075**
Mark Grace	1,075
Bob Johnson	1,075
72. Ozzie Smith	1,072
73. Harlond Clift	1,070
Keith Hernandez	1,070
75. Bill Dahlen	1,064
76. Harold Baines	1,062
77. Craig Biggio	**1,060**
78. Joe Cronin	1,059
79. Ron Fairly	1,052
80. Billy Williams	1,045
81. Norm Cash	1,043
Eddie Joost	1,043
83. Roy Thomas	1,042
84. Max Carey	1,040
85. Rogers Hornsby	1,038
86. Jim Gilliam	1,036
87. Roberto Alomar	**1,032**
88. Sal Bando	1,031
89. Jesse Burkett	1,029
90. Rod Carew	1,018
Enos Slaughter	1,018
92. Ron Cey	1,012
93. Ralph Kiner	1,011
94. Dummy Hoy	1,006
95. Miller Huggins	1,003
96. Roger Connor	1,002
87. Boog Powell	1,001

1,200 STRIKEOUTS

Player	No.
1. Reggie Jackson	2,597
2. Sammy Sosa	**2,110**
3. Andres Galarraga	**2,003**
4. Jose Canseco	1,942
5. Willie Stargell	1,936
6. Mike Schmidt	1,883
7. Fred McGriff	**1,882**
8. Tony Perez	1,867
9. Dave Kingman	1,816
10. Bobby Bonds	1,757
11. Dale Murphy	1,748
12. Lou Brock	1,730
13. Mickey Mantle	1,710
14. Jim Thome	**1,703**
15. Harmon Killebrew	1,699
16. Chili Davis	1,698
17. Dwight Evans	1,697
18. Rickey Henderson	1,694
19. Dave Winfield	1,686
20. Gary Gaetti	1,602
21. Mark McGwire	1,596
22. Lee May	1,570
23. Dick Allen	1,556
24. Ray Lankford	**1,550**
25. Willie McCovey	1,550
26. Jeff Bagwell	**1,537**
Dave Parker	1,537
28. Frank Robinson	1,532
29. Lance Parrish	1,527
30. Willie Mays	1,526
Devon White	1,526
32. Eddie Murray	1,516
33. Rick Monday	1,513
Greg Vaughn	1,513
35. Andre Dawson	1,509
36. Tony Phillips	1,499
37. Greg Luzinski	1,495
38. Eddie Mathews	1,487
39. Craig Biggio	**1,467**
40. Frank Howard	1,460
41. Jay Bell	1,443
42. Juan Samuel	1,442
43. Harold Baines	1,441
Jack Clark	1,441
45. Reggie Sanders	**1,438**
46. Mo Vaughn	1,429
47. Barry Bonds	**1,428**
48. Jim Wynn	1,427
49. Jim Rice	1,423
50. George Foster	1,419
51. George Scott	1,418
52. Ron Gant	1,411
53. Darrell Evans	1,410
54. Rob Deer	1,409
55. Jay Buhner	1,406
56. Eric Davis	1,398
57. Carl Yastrzemski	1,393
58. Joe Carter	1,387
59. Carlton Fisk	1,386
60. Hank Aaron	1,383
61. Travis Fryman	1,369
62. Matt Williams	1,363
63. Danny Tartabull	1,362
64. Larry Parrish	1,359
65. Darryl Strawberry	1,352
66. Robin Yount	1,350
67. Ron Santo	1,343
68. Ellis Burks	**1,340**
69. Gorman Thomas	1,339
70. Dean Palmer	1,332
71. Babe Ruth	1,330
72. Ken Griffey Jr.	**1,323**
73. Deron Johnson	1,318
74. Tim Salmon	**1,316**
Cecil Fielder	1,316
76. Willie Horton	1,313
77. Jimmie Foxx	1,311
78. Mickey Tettleton	1,307
Tim Wallach	1,307
80. Rafael Palmeiro	**1,305**
Cal Ripken Jr.	1,305
82. Jose Hernandez	**1,291**

Player	No.
83. Kirk Gibson	1,285
84. Todd Zeile	**1,279**
85. Johnny Bench	1,278
Bobby Grich	1,278
87. Pete Incaviglia	1,277
88. Juan Gonzalez	**1,273**
89. Jim Edmonds	**1,272**
90. Benito Santiago	**1,267**
91. Claudell Washington	1,266
92. Ryne Sandberg	1,260
93. Jeff Kent	**1,255**
94. Ken Singleton	1,246
95. Paul Molitor	1,244
96. Carlos Delgado	**1,242**
97. Willie McGee	1,238
98. Duke Snider	1,237
99. Ernie Banks	1,236
100. Ron Cey	1,235
101. Jesse Barfield	1,234
102. Bret Boone	**1,230**
Manny Ramirez	**1,230**
Roberto Clemente	1,230
105. Boog Powell	1,226
106. Marquis Grissom	**1,222**
107. Julio Franco	**1,212**
108. Graig Nettles	1,209
109. Bobby Bonilla	1,204
110. Edgar Martinez	**1,202**
111. Tony Armas	1,201

BASERUNNING
400 STOLEN BASES

Player	No.
1. Rickey Henderson	1,406
2. Lou Brock	938
3. Billy Hamilton	914
4. Ty Cobb	897
5. Tim Raines, Sr.	808
6. Vince Coleman	752
7. Arlie Latham	742
8. Eddie Collins	741
9. Max Carey	738
10. Honus Wagner	723
11. Joe Morgan	689
12. Willie Wilson	668
13. Tom Brown	657
14. Bert Campaneris	649
15. Otis Nixon	620
16. George Davis	619
17. Dummy Hoy	596
18. Maury Wills	586
19. George Van Haltren	583
20. Ozzie Smith	580
21. Hugh Duffy	574
22. Bid McPhee	568
23. Brett Butler	558
24. Dave Lopes	557
25. Cesar Cedeno	550
26. Bill Dahlen	548
27. Kenny Lofton	**545**
28. Monte Ward	540
29. Herman Long	537
30. Patsy Donovan	518
Jack Doyle	518
32. Fred Clarke	509
Harry Stovey	509
34. Barry Bonds	**506**
Luis Aparicio	506
36. Paul Molitor	504
37. Willie Keeler	495
Clyde Milan	495
39. Omar Moreno	487
40. Roberto Alomar	**474**
41. Mike Griffin	473
42. Tom McCarthy	468
43. Jim Sheckard	465
44. Delino DeShields	463
45. Bobby Bonds	461
46. Ed Delahanty	455
Ron LeFlore	455
48. Curt Welch	453
49. Eric Young	**450**
50. Steve Sax	444
51. Joe Kelley	443

Player	No.
52. Sherry Magee	441
53. John McGraw	436
Tris Speaker	436
55. Marquis Grissom	**428**
Bob Bescher	428
Mike Tiernan	428
58. Frankie Frisch	419
Jim Ryan	419
60. Charlie Comiskey	416
61. Tommy Harper	408
62. Chuck Knoblauch	407
63. Donie Bush	406
64. Frank Chance	403
65. Bill Lange	400

PITCHING
700 GAMES

Pitcher	Yrs.	Games
1. Jesse Orosco	24	1,252
2. John Franco	**20**	**1,088**
3. Dennis Eckersley	24	1,071
4. Hoyt Wilhelm	21	1,070
5. Dan Plesac	18	1,064
6. Kent Tekulve	16	1,050
7. Lee Smith	18	1,022
8. Mike Jackson	**17**	**1,005**
9. Rich Gossage	22	1,002
10. Lindy McDaniel	21	987
11. Mike Stanton	**16**	**968**
12. Rollie Fingers	17	944
13. Gene Garber	19	931
14. Cy Young	22	906
15. Sparky Lyle	16	899
16. Jim Kaat	25	898
17. Paul Assenmacher	14	884
18. Jeff Reardon	16	880
19. Don McMahon	18	874
20. Phil Niekro	24	864
21. Charlie Hough	25	858
22. Roy Face	16	848
23. Doug Jones	16	846
24. Jose Mesa	**16**	**832**
25. Roberto Hernandez	**14**	**825**
26. Tug McGraw	19	824
27. Mike Timlin	**14**	**812**
28. Nolan Ryan	27	807
29. Steve Reed	**13**	**803**
30. Walter Johnson	21	802
31. Rick Honeycutt	21	797
32. Paul Quantrill	**13**	**791**
33. Gaylord Perry	22	777
34. Don Sutton	23	774
35. Mark Guthrie	15	765
Darold Knowles	16	765
37. Tommy John	26	760
38. John Quinn	23	756
39. Ron Reed	19	751
40. Warren Spahn	21	750
41. Tom Burgmeier	17	745
Gary Lavelle	13	745
43. Todd Jones	**12**	**744**
Willie Hernandez	13	744
45. Jeff Nelson	**13**	**743**
46. Steve Carlton	24	741
47. Buddy Groom	**13**	**739**
48. Ron Perranoski	13	737
49. Ron Kline	17	736
50. Rick Aguilera	16	732
51. Steve Bedrosian	14	732
52. Clay Carroll	15	731
53. Randy Myers	14	728
54. Mike G. Marshall	14	723
Roger McDowell	12	723
56. Dave Righetti	16	718
57. Danny Darwin	21	716
58. Eric Plunk	14	714
59. Johnny Klippstein	18	711
60. Greg Minton	16	710
61. Rod Beck	**13**	**704**
Stu Miller	16	704
63. Greg A. Harris	15	703
64. Joe Niekro	22	702

Pitcher	Yrs.	Games
65. Bill Campbell	15	700
Jeff Montgomery	13	700

500 GAMES STARTED

Pitcher	No.
1. Cy Young	815
2. Nolan Ryan	773
3. Don Sutton	756
4. Phil Niekro	716
5. Steve Carlton	709
6. Tommy John	700
7. Gaylord Perry	690
8. Bert Blyleven	685
9. Pud Galvin	681
10. Walter Johnson	666
11. Warren Spahn	665
12. Tom Seaver	647
13. Roger Clemens	**639**
14. Jim Kaat	625
15. Frank Tanana	616
16. Early Wynn	612
17. Robin Roberts	609
18. Greg Maddux	**604**
19. Grover Alexander	600
20. Ferguson Jenkins	594
Tim Keefe	594
22. Tom Glavine	**570**
23. Kid Nichols	562
Dennis Martinez	562
25. Eppa Rixey	554
26. Christy Mathewson	552
27. Mickey Welch	549
28. Jerry Reuss	547
29. Red Ruffing	538
30. Eddie Plank	529
Rick Reuschel	529
32. Jerry Koosman	527
Jack Morris	527
34. Jim Palmer	521
35. Jim Bunning	519
36. John Clarkson	518
37. Jack Powell	516
38. Gus Weyhing	505
39. Tony Mullane	504
40. Hoss Radbourn	502
41. Joe Niekro	500

300 COMPLETE GAMES

Pitcher	No.
1. Cy Young	749
2. Pud Galvin	639
3. Tim Keefe	554
4. Kid Nichols	532
5. Walter Johnson	531
6. Mickey Welch	525
7. Hoss Radbourn	488
8. John Clarkson	485
9. Tony Mullane	468
10. Jim McCormick	466
11. Gus Weyhing	449
12. Grover Alexander	437
13. Christy Mathewson	435
14. Jack Powell	422
15. Eddie Plank	410
16. Will White	394
17. Amos Rusie	393
18. Vic Willis	388
19. Warren Spahn	382
20. Jim Whitney	377
21. Adonis Terry	367
22. Ted Lyons	356
23. George Mullin	353
24. Charlie Buffinton	351
25. Chick Fraser	342
26. Clark Griffith	337
27. Red Ruffing	335
28. Silver King	328
29. Al Orth	324
30. Bill Hutchinson	321
31. Burleigh Grimes	314
Joe McGinnity	314
33. Red Donahue	312
Guy Hecker	312
35. Bill Dinneen	306

Player	No.
36. Robin Roberts	305
37. Gaylord Perry	303
38. Ted Breitenstein	301

3,500 INNINGS

Pitcher	No.
1. Cy Young	7,356.0
2. Pud Galvin	5,941.1
3. Walter Johnson	5,914.1
4. Phil Niekro	5,404.1
5. Nolan Ryan	5,386.0
6. Gaylord Perry	5,350.1
7. Don Sutton	5,282.1
8. Warren Spahn	5,243.2
9. Steve Carlton	5,217.1
10. Grover Alexander	5,190.0
11. Kid Nichols	5,067.1
12. Tim Keefe	5,049.2
13. Bert Blyleven	4,970.0
14. Mickey Welch	4,802.0
15. Christy Mathewson	4,788.2
16. Tom Seaver	4,782.2
17. Tommy John	4,710.1
18. Robin Roberts	4,688.2
19. Early Wynn	4,564.0
20. John Clarkson	4,536.1
21. Tony Mullane	4,531.1
22. Jim Kaat	4,530.1
23. Hoss Radbourn	4,527.1
24. Roger Clemens	4,493.0
25. Ferguson Jenkins	4,400.2
26. Eddie Plank	4,495.2
27. Eppa Rixey	4,494.2
28. Jack Powell	4,389.0
29. Red Ruffing	4,344.0
30. Gus Weyhing	4,337.0
31. Jim McCormick	4,275.2
32. Frank Tanana	4,188.1
33. Greg Maddux	4,181.1
34. Burleigh Grimes	4,179.2
35. Ted Lyons	4,161.0
36. Red Faber	4,086.2
37. Dennis Martinez	3,999.2
38. Vic Willis	3,996.0
39. Jim Palmer	3,947.1
40. Lefty Grove	3,940.2
41. Jack Quinn	3,920.1
42. Bob Gibson	3,884.1
43. Sam Jones	3,883.0
44. Jerry Koosman	3,839.1
45. Bob Feller	3,827.0
46. Jack Morris	3,824.0
47. Charlie Hough	3,801.1
48. Amos Rusie	3,778.2
49. Waite Hoyt	3,762.1
50. Jim Bunning	3,760.1
51. Bobo Newsom	3,759.1
52. Tom Glavine	3,740.1
53. George Mullin	3,686.2
54. Jerry Reuss	3,669.2
55. Paul Derringer	3,645.0
56. Mickey Lolich	3,638.1
57. Bob Friend	3,611.0
58. Carl Hubbell	3,590.1
59. Joe Niekro	3,584.0
60. Herb Pennock	3,571.2
61. Earl Whitehill	3,564.2
62. Rick Reuschel	3,548.1
63. Will White	3,542.2
64. Adonis Terry	3,514.1
65. Juan Marichal	3,507.1

200 VICTORIES

Pitcher	W	L
1. Cy Young	511	316
2. Walter Johnson	417	279
3. Christy Mathewson	373	188
Grover Alexander	373	208
5. Warren Spahn	363	245
6. Kid Nichols	361	208
Pud Galvin	361	308
8. Tim Keefe	342	225
9. Steve Carlton	329	244
10. Roger Clemens	328	164

Pitcher	W	L
11. John Clarkson	328	178
12. Eddie Plank	326	194
13. Don Sutton	324	256
Nolan Ryan	324	292
15. Phil Niekro	318	274
16. Gaylord Perry	314	265
17. Tom Seaver	311	205
18. Hoss Radbourn	309	194
19. Mickey Welch	307	210
20. Greg Maddux	305	174
21. Lefty Grove	300	141
Early Wynn	300	244
23. Tommy John	288	231
24. Bert Blyleven	287	250
25. Robin Roberts	286	245
26. Tony Mullane	284	220
27. Ferguson Jenkins	284	226
28. Jim Kaat	283	237
29. Red Ruffing	273	225
30. Burleigh Grimes	270	212
31. Jim Palmer	268	152
32. Bob Feller	266	162
Eppa Rixey	266	251
34. Jim McCormick	265	214
Gus Weyhing	264	232
36. Tom Glavine	262	171
37. Ted Lyons	260	230
38. Jack Morris	254	186
Red Faber	254	213
40. Carl Hubbell	253	154
41. Bob Gibson	251	174
42. Vic Willis	249	205
Jack Quinn	247	218
44. Randy Johnson	246	128
Joe McGinnity	246	142
46. Amos Rusie	246	174
47. Dennis Martinez	245	193
48. Jack Powell	245	254
49. Juan Marichal	243	142
50. Herb Pennock	241	162
51. Frank Tanana	240	236
52. Mordecai Brown	239	130
53. Clark Griffith	237	146
Waite Hoyt	237	182
55. Whitey Ford	236	106
56. Charlie Buffinton	233	152
57. Will White	229	166
Luis Tiant	229	172
Sam Jones	229	217
60. George Mullin	228	196
61. Catfish Hunter	224	166
Jim Bunning	224	184
63. Hooks Dauss	223	182
64. Mel Harder	223	186
Paul Derringer	223	212
66. Jerry Koosman	222	209
67. Joe Niekro	221	204
68. Jerry Reuss	220	191
69. Bob Caruthers	218	99
Earl Whitehill	218	185
71. Fred Fitzsimmons	217	146
Mickey Lolich	217	191
73. Wilbur Cooper	216	178
Charlie Hough	216	216
75. Stan Coveleski	215	142
Jim Perry	215	174
77. Rick Reuschel	214	191
78. Chief Bender	212	127
David Wells	212	136
80. Mike Mussina	211	119
Bob Welch	211	146
Billy Pierce	211	169
Bobo Newsom	211	222
84. Jesse Haines	210	158
85. Ed Cicotte	209	148
Vida Blue	209	161
Milt Pappas	209	164
Don Drysdale	209	166
89. Carl Mays	208	126
90. Bob Lemon	207	128
Kevin Brown	207	137
Hal Newhouser	207	150
93. Orel Hershiser	204	150
Al Orth	204	189
95. Jack Stivetts	203	132
Silver King	203	154
97. Lew Burdette	203	144

Pitcher	W	L
98. Charlie Root	201	160
Rube Marquard	201	177
100. George Uhle	200	166
Chuck Finley	200	173

20 VICTORIES, 5 TIMES

Pitcher	No.
1. Cy Young	16
2. Christy Mathewson	13
Warren Spahn	13
4. Walter Johnson	12
5. Kid Nichols	11
6. Pud Galvin	10
7. Grover Alexander	9
Hoss Radbourn	9
Mickey Welch	9
10. John Clarkson	8
Lefty Grove	8
Jim McCormick	8
Joe McGinnity	8
Tony Mullane	8
Jim Palmer	8
Amos Rusie	8
17. Charlie Buffinton	7
Clark Griffith	7
Ferguson Jenkins	7
Tim Keefe	7
Bob Lemon	7
Eddie Plank	7
Gus Weyhing	7
Vic Willis	7
25. Mordecai Brown	6
Steve Carlton	6
Bob Caruthers	6
Roger Clemens	6
Bob Feller	6
Wes Ferrell	6
Juan Marichal	6
Robin Roberts	6
Jack Stivetts	6
Jesse Tannehill	6
35. Tommy Bond	5
Jack Chesbro	5
Larry Corcoran	5
Stan Coveleski	5
Bob Gibson	5
Tom Glavine	5
Burleigh Grimes	5
Carl Hubbell	5
Catfish Hunter	5
Charles King	5
Carl Mays	5
John McMahon	5
George Mullin	5
Gaylord Perry	5
Deacon Phillippe	5
Tom Seaver	5
Hippo Vaughn	5
Will White	5
Jim Whitney	5
Early Wynn	5

30 VICTORIES, 2 TIMES

Pitcher	Yrs.
1. Kid Nichols	7
2. John Clarkson	6
Tim Keefe	6
4. Tony Mullane	5
Cy Young	5
6. Tommy Bond	4
Larry Corcoran	4
Silver King	4
Christy Mathewson	4
Jim McCormick	4
Mickey Welch	4
Will White	4
13. Grover Alexander	3
Bob Caruthers	3
Pud Galvin	3
Bill Hutchison	3
Bobby Mathews	3

Pitcher	Yrs.
Ed Morris	3
Hoss Radbourn	3
Amos Rusie	3
21. Dave Foutz	2
George Haddock	2
Guy Hecker	2
Walter Johnson	2
Frank Killen	2
Joe McGinnity	2
John McMahon	2
Tom Ramsey	2
Jack Stivetts	2
Monte Ward	2
Gus Weyhing	2
Jim Whitney	2

150 SAVES

(Since 1969)

Pitcher	No.
1. Lee Smith	478
2. **John Franco**	**424**
3. **Trevor Hoffman**	**393**
4. Dennis Eckersley	390
5. Jeff Reardon	367
6. Randy Myers	347
7. Rollie Fingers	341
8. **Mariano Rivera**	**336**
9. John Wetteland	330
10. **Roberto Hernandez**	**320**
11. Rick Aguilera	318
12. **Troy Percival**	**316**
13. Robb Nen	314
14. Tom Henke	311
15. Rich Gossage	310
16. Jeff Montgomery	304
17. Doug Jones	303
18. Bruce Sutter	300
19. **Jose Mesa**	**292**
20. **Rod Beck**	**286**
21. Todd Worrell	256
22. Dave Righetti	252
23. **Billy Wagner**	**246**
24. **Armando Benitez**	**244**
Dan Quisenberry	244
26. **Ugueth Urbina**	**227**
27. Sparky Lyle	222
28. Gene Garber	218
29. Gregg Olson	217
30. Dave Smith	216
31. Jeff Shaw	203
32. Bobby Thigpen	201
33. Mike Henneman	193
34. Mitch Williams	192
35. **Todd Jones**	**186**
Jeff Russell	186
37. Steve Bedrosian	184
Kent Tekulve	184
39. Tug McGraw	179
40. Mike G. Marshall	178
41. **Jason Isringhausen**	**177**
Bryan Harvey	177
43. **Keith Foulke**	**175**
44. **Danny Graves**	**172**
Jeff Brantley	172
46. **Bob Wickman**	**169**
47. **Bill Koch**	**163**
48. Roger McDowell	159
49. Dan Plesac	158
50. Jay Howell	155
51. **John Smoltz**	**154**
52. **Eric Gagne**	**152**
53. Greg Minton	150

1,800 RUNS ALLOWED

Pitcher	No.
1. Pud Galvin	3,315
2. Cy Young	3,167
3. Gus Weyhing	2,796
4. Mickey Welch	2,556
5. Tony Mullane	2,523
6. Kid Nichols	2,480

Pitcher	No.
7. Tim Keefe	2,471
8. John Clarkson	2,384
9. Phil Niekro	2,337
10. Adonis Terry	2,303
11. Hoss Radbourn	2,273
12. Nolan Ryan	2,178
13. Steve Carlton	2,130
14. Gaylord Perry	2,128
15. Red Ruffing	2,115
16. Don Sutton	2,104
17. Jim McCormick	2,095
18. Amos Rusie	2,068
19. Ted Lyons	2,056
20. Burleigh Grimes	2,050
21. Jim Kaat	2,038
22. Early Wynn	2,037
23. Bert Blyleven	2,029
24. Jim Whitney	2,026
25. Earl Whitehill	2,018
26. Tommy John	2,017
27. Warren Spahn	2,016
28. Sam Jones	2,008
29. Chick Fraser	1,995
30. Jack Powell	1,991
31. Eppa Rixey	1,986
32. Robin Roberts	1,962
33. Bert Cunningham	1,942
34. Pink Hawley	1,927
35. Bill Hutchinson	1,913
36. Frank Tanana	1,910
37. Bobo Newsom	1,908
38. Walter Johnson	1,902
39. Red Ehret	1,881
40. Brickyard Kennedy	1,863
41. Ferguson Jenkins	1,853
42. Grover Alexander	1,852
Clark Griffith	1,852
44. Ted Breitenstein	1,848
45. Will White	1,844
46. Jack Quinn	1,837
47. Jack Stivetts	1,836
48. Dennis Martinez	1,835
49. Charlie Buffinton	1,824
50. Mark Baldwin	1,816
51. Jack Morris	1,815
52. Red Faber	1,813
53. Charlie Hough	1,807
54. Silver King	1,803

3.50 OR UNDER ERA

(Pitchers with 3,000 or more innings pitched)

Pitcher	IP	ERA
1. Mordecai Brown	3,172.1	2.06
2. Christy Mathewson	4,788.2	2.13
3. Walter Johnson	5,914.0	2.17
4. Will White	3,542.2	2.28
5. Eddie Plank	4,495.2	2.35
6. Eddie Cicotte	3,226.0	2.38
7. Doc White	3,041.0	2.39
8. Jim McCormick	4,275.2	2.43
9. Chief Bender	3,017.0	2.46
10. Grover Alexander	5,190.0	2.56
11. Tim Keefe	5,049.2	2.63
12. Cy Young	7,356.0	2.63
13. Vic Willis	3,996.0	2.63
14. Red Ames	3,198.0	2.63
15. Joe McGinnity	3,441.1	2.66
16. Hoss Radbourn	4,527.1	2.68
17. Mickey Welch	4,802.0	2.71
18. Whitey Ford	3,171.1	2.75
19. John Clarkson	4,536.1	2.81
20. George Mullin	3,686.2	2.82
21. Jim Palmer	3,948.0	2.86
22. Tom Seaver	4,782.2	2.86
23. Pud Galvin	5,941.1	2.87
24. Juan Marichal	3,507.1	2.89
25. Stan Coveleski	3,082.0	2.89
26. Wilbur Cooper	3,480.0	2.89
27. Bob Gibson	3,884.1	2.91
28. Carl Mays	3,021.1	2.92
29. Don Drysdale	3,432.0	2.95
30. **Greg Maddux**	**4,181.1**	**2.95**
31. Kid Nichols	5,067.1	2.96
32. Charlie Buffinton	3,404.0	2.96
33. Jim Whitney	3,496.1	2.97

Pitcher	IP	ERA
34. Jack Powell	4,389.0	2.97
35. Carl Hubbell	3,590.1	2.98
36. Bill Dinneen	3,074.2	3.01
37. Tony Mullane	4,531.1	3.05
38. Lefty Grove	3,940.2	3.06
39. **Randy Johnson**	**3,368.0**	**3.07**
40. Amos Rusie	3,778.2	3.07
41. Rube Marquard	3,306.2	3.08
42. Warren Spahn	5,243.2	3.09
43. Gaylord Perry	5,350.1	3.11
44. Eppa Rixey	4,494.2	3.15
45. Red Faber	4,086.2	3.15
46. Silver King	3,180.2	3.18
47. **Roger Clemens**	**4,493.0**	**3.18**
48. Nolan Ryan	5,386.0	3.19
49. **Kevin Brown**	**3,183.0**	**3.20**
50. Steve Carlton	5,217.1	3.22
51. Dolf Luque	3,220.1	3.24
52. Dutch Leonard	3,218.1	3.25
53. Bob Feller	3,827.0	3.25
54. Catfish Hunter	3,449.1	3.26
55. Vida Blue	3,343.1	3.26
56. Don Sutton	5,282.1	3.26
57. Billy Pierce	3,306.2	3.27
58. Jim Bunning	3,760.1	3.27
59. Jack Quinn	3,920.1	3.29
60. Claude Osteen	3,460.1	3.30
61. Bucky Walters	3,104.2	3.30
62. Luis Tiant	3,486.1	3.30
63. Hooks Dauss	3,390.2	3.30
64. Clark Griffith	3,385.2	3.31
65. Bert Blyleven	4,970.0	3.31
66. Ferguson Jenkins	4,500.2	3.34
67. Tommy John	4,710.1	3.34
68. Phil Niekro	5,404.1	3.35
69. Jerry Koosman	3,839.1	3.36
70. Al Orth	3,354.2	3.37
71. Rick Reuschel	3,548.1	3.37
72. Lee Meadows	3,160.2	3.37
73. Milt Pappas	3,186.0	3.40
74. Larry Jackson	3,262.0	3.40
75. Robin Roberts	4,688.2	3.41
76. Mickey Lolich	3,638.1	3.44
77. **Tom Glavine**	**3,740.1**	**3.44**
78. Larry French	3,152.0	3.44
79. Jim Perry	3,285.2	3.45
80. Jim Kaat	4,530.1	3.45
81. Paul Derringer	3,645.0	3.46
82. Bob Welch	3,092.0	3.47
83. Orel Hershiser	3,130.1	3.48
84. Dennis Eckersley	3,285.2	3.50

(in strict numerical order rounded to three places)

40 SHUTOUTS

Pitcher	No.
1. Walter Johnson	110
2. Grover Alexander	90
3. Christy Mathewson	79
4. Cy Young	76
5. Eddie Plank	69
6. Warren Spahn	63
7. Nolan Ryan	61
Tom Seaver	61
9. Bert Blyleven	60
10. Don Sutton	58
11. Pud Galvin	57
Ed Walsh	57
13. Bob Gibson	56
14. Mordecai Brown	55
Steve Carlton	55
16. Jim Palmer	53
Gaylord Perry	53
18. Juan Marichal	52
19. Rube Waddell	50
Vic Willis	50
21. Don Drysdale	49
Ferguson Jenkins	49
Luis Tiant	49
Early Wynn	49
25. Kid Nichols	48
26. **Roger Clemens**	**46**
Tommy John	46
Jack Powell	46
29. Whitey Ford	45

Pitcher	No.
Addie Joss	45
Phil Niekro	45
Robin Roberts	45
Red Ruffing	45
Doc White	45
35. Babe Adams	44
Bob Feller	44
37. Milt Pappas	43
38. Catfish Hunter	42
Bucky Walters	42
40. Mickey Lolich	41
Hippo Vaughn	41
Mickey Welch	41
43. Chief Bender	40
Jim Bunning	40
Larry French	40
Sandy Koufax	40
Claude Osteen	40
Ed Reulbach	40
Mel Stottlemyre	40

TEN 1-0 VICTORIES

(complete games)

Pitcher	No.
1. Walter Johnson	38
2. Grover Alexander	17
3. Bert Blyleven	15
4. Christy Mathewson	14
Eddie Plank	14
6. Dean Chance	13
Ed Au. Walsh	13
Doc White	13
Cy Young	13
10. Steve Carlton	12
Stan Coveleski	12
Gaylord Perry	12
13. Greg Maddux	**11**
Mordecai Brown	11
Ferguson Jenkins	11
Kid Nichols	11
Nap Rucker	11
Nolan Ryan	11
18. Joe Bush	10
Paul Derringer	10
Bill Doak	10
Addie Joss	10
Sandy Koufax	10
Dick Rudolph	10
Warren Spahn	10
Virgil Trucks	10
Hippo Vaughn	10

4,000 HITS ALLOWED

Pitcher	No.
1. Cy Young	7,092
2. Pud Galvin	6,352
3. Phil Niekro	5,044
4. Gaylord Perry	4,938
5. Kid Nichols	4,929
6. Walter Johnson	4,913
7. Grover Alexander	4,868
8. Warren Spahn	4,830
9. Tommy John	4,783
10. Don Sutton	4,692
11. Steve Carlton	4,672
12. Eppa Rixey	4,633
13. Bert Blyleven	4,632
14. Jim Kaat	4,620
15. Mickey Welch	4,588
16. Robin Roberts	4,582
17. Gus Weyhing	4,576
18. Ted Lyons	4,489
19. Tim Keefe	4,438
20. Burleigh Grimes	4,412
21. Hoss Radbourn	4,328
22. Jack Powell	4,319
23. John Clarkson	4,295
24. Early Wynn	4,291
25. Red Ruffing	4,284
26. Jack Quinn	4,238
27. Christy Mathewson	4,219
28. Tony Mullane	4,195
29. Ferguson Jenkins	4,142

Pitcher	No.
30. Red Faber	4,106
31. Jim McCormick	4,092
32. Sam Jones	4,084
33. Frank Tanana	4,063
34. Waite Hoyt	4,037

7 GRAND SLAMS ALLOWED

Pitcher	No.
1. Mike Jackson	10
Nolan Ryan	10
3. Ned Garver	9
Milt Pappas	9
Jerry Reuss	9
Lee Smith	9
Frank Viola	9
8. Brian Boehringer	**8**
Jimmy Haynes	**8**
Kenny Rogers	**8**
Willie Blair	8
Bert Blyleven	8
Jim Brewer	8
Roy Face	8
Bob Feller	8
Alex Fernandez	8
Mike Jackson	8
Jim Kaat	8
Johnny Klippstein	8
Lindy McDaniel	8
Tug McGraw	8
Jesse Orosco	8
Gaylord Perry	8
Frank Tanana	8
Early Wynn	8
26. Tom Gordon	**7**
Jamie Moyer	**7**
Terry Mulholland	**7**
Denny Neagle	**7**
Doug Bair	7
Steve Bedrosian	7
Tim Belcher	7
Ricky Bones	7
David Cone	7
Larry French	7
Jim Hearn	7
Charlie Hough	7
Ramon Martinez	7
Phil Niekro	7
Dennis Rasmussen	7
Ray Sadecki	7
Jack Sanford	7
Bill Sherdel	7
Don Sutton	7
Mike Torrez	7
Lon Warneke	7
Bobby Witt	7
Mike Witt	7
Matt Young	7

1,200 BASES ON BALLS

Pitcher	No.
1. Nolan Ryan	2,795
2. Steve Carlton	1,833
3. Phil Niekro	1,809
4. Early Wynn	1,775
5. Bob Feller	1,764
6. Bobo Newsom	1,732
7. Amos Rusie	1,707
8. Charlie Hough	1,665
9. Gus Weyhing	1,570
10. Red Ruffing	1,541
11. Roger Clemens	**1,458**
12. Bump Hadley	1,442
13. Warren Spahn	1,434
14. Earl Whitehill	1,431
15. Tony Mullane	1,408
16. Sam Jones	1,396
17. Jack Morris	1,390
Tom Seaver	1,390
19. Gaylord Perry	1,379
20. Bobby Witt	1,375
21. Mike Torrez	1,371
22. Walter Johnson	1,363
23. Don Sutton	1,343
24. Chick Fraser	1,338
25. Bob Gibson	1,336

Pitcher	No.
26. Chuck Finley	1,332
27. Bert Blyleven	1,322
28. Sam McDowell	1,312
29. Jim Palmer	1,311
30. Mark Baldwin	1,307
31. Randy Johnson	**1,302**
32. Adonis Terry	1,298
33. Mickey Welch	1,297
34. Burleigh Grimes	1,295
35. Mark Langston	1,289
36. Tom Glavine	**1,276**
37. Kid Nichols	1,272
38. Joe Bush	1,263
39. Joe Niekro	1,262
40. Allie Reynolds	1,261
41. Tommy John	1,259
42. Frank Tanana	1,255
43. Bob Lemon	1,251
44. Hal Newhouser	1,249
45. George Mullin	1,238
46. Tim Keefe	1,233
47. Cy Young	1,217
48. Red Faber	1,213
49. Vic Willis	1,212
50. Ted Breitenstein	1,207
51. Brickyard Kennedy	1,203

2,000 STRIKEOUTS

Pitcher	No.
1. Nolan Ryan	5,714
2. Roger Clemens	**4,317**
3. Randy Johnson	**4,161**
4. Steve Carlton	4,136
5. Bert Blyleven	3,701
6. Tom Seaver	3,640
7. Don Sutton	3,574
8. Gaylord Perry	3,534
9. Walter Johnson	3,509
10. Phil Niekro	3,342
11. Ferguson Jenkins	3,192
12. Bob Gibson	3,117
13. Greg Maddux	**2,916**
14. Jim Bunning	2,855
15. Mickey Lolich	2,832
16. Cy Young	2,803
17. Frank Tanana	2,773
18. Curt Schilling	**2,745**
19. David Cone	2,668
20. Pedro Martinez	**2,653**
21. Chuck Finley	2,610
22. Warren Spahn	2,583
23. Bob Feller	2,581
24. Tim Keefe	2,564
25. Jerry Koosman	2,556
26. Christy Mathewson	2,507
27. Don Drysdale	2,486
28. Jack Morris	2,478
29. Mark Langston	2,464
30. Jim Kaat	2,461
31. Luis Tiant	2,416
32. Dennis Eckersley	2,401
34. John Smoltz	**2,398**
35. Sandy Koufax	2,396
36. Charlie Hough	2,362
37. Robin Roberts	2,357
38. Kevin Brown	**2,347**
39. Early Wynn	2,334
40. Rube Waddell	2,316
41. Juan Marichal	2,303
42. Dwight Gooden	2,293
43. Lefty Grove	2,266
44. Mike Mussina	**2,258**
45. Eddie Plank	2,246
46. Tom Glavine	**2,245**
Tommy John	2,245
48. Jim Palmer	2,212
49. Grover Alexander	2,198
50. Vida Blue	2,175
51. Camilo Pascual	2,167
52. Dennis Martinez	2,149
53. Bobo Newsom	2,082
54. Fernando Valenzuela	2,074
55. Dazzy Vance	2,045
56. Rick Reuschel	2,015
57. Orel Hershiser	2,014
58. Catfish Hunter	2,012
59. Andy Benes	2,000

GENERAL REFERENCE

BATTING

TRIPLE CROWN HITTERS

AMERICAN LEAGUE

Year	Player, Club	Avg.	HR	RBI
1901	Napoleon Lajoie, Philadelphia	.426	14	125
1909	Ty Cobb, Detroit	.377	9	107
1933	Jimmie Foxx, Philadelphia	.356	48	163
1934	Lou Gehrig, New York	.363	49	165
1942	Ted Williams, Boston	.356	36	137
1947	Ted Williams, Boston	.343	32	114
1956	Mickey Mantle, New York	.353	52	130
1966	Frank Robinson, Baltimore	.316	49	122
1967	Carl Yastrzemski, Boston	.326	44	121

Total number of occurrences: 9

NATIONAL LEAGUE

Year	Player, Club	Avg.	HR	RBI
1922	Rogers Hornsby, St. Louis	.401	42	152
1925	Rogers Hornsby, St. Louis	.403	39	143
1933	Chuck Klein, Philadelphia	.368	28	120
1937	Joe Medwick, St. Louis	.374	31	154

Total number of occurrences: 4

.400 HITTERS

Year	Player, Club	Avg.
1894	Hugh Duffy, Boston N.L.	.440
1887	Tip O'Neill, St. Louis A.A.	.435
1876	Ross Barnes, Chicago N.L	.429
1901	Nap Lajoie, Philadelphia A.L.	.426
1897	Willie Keeler, Baltimore N.L.	.424
1924	Rogers Hornsby, St. Louis N.L	.424
1911	Ty Cobb, Detroit A.L	.420
1922	George Sisler, St. Louis A.L.	.420
1894	Sam Thompson, Philadelphia N.L.	.415
1884	Fred Dunlap, St. Louis U.A.	.412
1896	Jesse Burkett, Cleveland N.L	.410
1899	Ed Delahanty, Philadelphia N.L	.410
1912	Ty Cobb, Detroit A.L	.409
1911	Joe Jackson, Cleveland A.L	.408
1920	George Sisler, St. Louis A.L.	.407
1941	Ted Williams, Boston A.L.	.406
1895	Jesse Burkett, Cleveland N.L	.405
1894	Ed Delahanty, Philadelphia N.L	.404
1895	Ed Delahanty, Philadelphia N.L	.404
1894	Billy Hamilton, Philadelphia N.L.	.403
1923	Harry Heilmann, Detroit A.L.	.403
1925	Rogers Hornsby, St. Louis N.L.	.403
1887	Pete Browning, Louisville A.A.	.402
1896	Hughie Jennings, Baltimore N.L	.401
1922	Ty Cobb, Detroit A.L	.401
1922	Rogers Hornsby, St. Louis N.L	.401
1930	Bill Terry, New York N.L.	.401

Total number of occurrences: 27

200 HITS BY ROOKIES IN SEASON

AMERICAN LEAGUE

Year	Player, Club	G	H
2001	Ichiro Suzuki, Seattle	157	242
1964	Tony Oliva, Minnesota	161	217
1929	Dale Alexander, Detroit	155	215
1997	Nomar Garciaparra, Boston	153	209
1953	Harvey Kuenn, Detroit	155	209
1987	Kevin Seitzer, Kansas City	161	207
1936	Joe DiMaggio, New York	138	206
1934	Hal Trosky, Cleveland	154	206
1942	Johnny Pesky, Boston	147	205
1929	Roy Johnson, Detroit	148	201
1943	Dick Wakefield, Detroit	155	200

NATIONAL LEAGUE

Year	Player, Club	G	H
1927	Lloyd Waner, Pittsburgh	150	223
1899	Jimmy Williams, Pittsburgh	153	219
1929	Johnny Frederick, Brooklyn	148	206
1964	Dick Allen, Philadelphia	162	201

30-GAME BATTING STREAKS

Year	Player, Club	G
1941	Joe DiMaggio, New York A.L.	56
1897	Willie Keeler, Baltimore N.L.*	44
1978	Pete Rose, Cincinnati N.L.	44
1894	Bill Dahlen, Chicago N.L.	42
1922	George Sisler, St. Louis N.L.	41
1911	Ty Cobb, Detroit A.L.	40
1987	Paul Molitor, Milwaukee A.L.	39
1945	Tommy Holmes, Boston N.L.	37
1895	Fred Clarke, Louisville N.L.	35
1917	Ty Cobb, Detroit A.L.	35
2002	Luis Castillo, Florida N.L.	35
1925	George Sisler, St. Louis A.L.*	34
1938	George McQuinn, St. Louis A.L.	34
1949	Dom DiMaggio, Boston A.L.	34
1987	Benito Santiago, San Diego N.L.	34
1893	George Davis, New York N.L.	33
1907	Hal Chase, New York A.L.	33
1922	Rogers Hornsby, St. Louis N.L.	33
1933	Heinie Manush, Washington A.L.	33
1899	Ed Delahanty, Philadelphia N.L.	31
1906	Nap Lajoie, Cleveland A.L.	31
1924	Sam Rice, Washington A.L.	31
1969	Willie Davis, Los Angeles N.L.	31
1970	Rico Carty, Atlanta N.L.	31
1980	Ken Landreaux, Minnesota A.L.	31
1999	Vladimir Guerrero, Montreal N.L.	31
1876	Cal McVey, Chicago N.L.	30
1898	Elmer E. Smith, Cincinnati N.L.	30
1912	Tris Speaker, Boston A.L.	30
1934	Goose Goslin, Detroit A.L.	30
1950	Stan Musial, St. Louis N.L.	30
1976	Ron LeFlore, Detroit A.L.*	30
1980	George Brett, Kansas City A.L.	30
1989	Jerome Walton, Chicago N.L.	30
1997	Sandy Alomar Jr., Cleveland A.L.	30
1997	Nomar Garciaparra, Boston A.L.	30
1998	Eric Davis, Baltimore A.L.	30
1999	Luis Gonzalez, Arizona N.L.	30
2003	Albert Pujols, St. Louis N.L.	30

*From start of season.

Total number of occurrences: 39

40 HOME RUNS IN SEASON

AMERICAN LEAGUE

Year	Player, Club	No.
1961	Roger Maris, New York	61
1927	Babe Ruth, New York	60
1921	Babe Ruth, New York	59
1932	Jimmie Foxx, Philadelphia	58
1938	Hank Greenberg, Detroit	58
2002	Alex Rodriguez, Texas	57
1997	Ken Griffey Jr., Seattle	56
1998	Ken Griffey Jr., Seattle	56
1920	Babe Ruth, New York	54
1928	Babe Ruth, New York	54
1961	Mickey Mantle, New York	54
1956	Mickey Mantle, New York	52
1996	Mark McGwire, Oakland	52
2001	Alex Rodriguez, Texas	52
2002	Jim Thome, Cleveland	52
1990	Cecil Fielder, Detroit	51
1938	Jimmie Foxx, Boston	50
1995	Albert Belle, Cleveland	50
1996	Brady Anderson, Baltimore	50
1930	Babe Ruth, New York	49
1934	Lou Gehrig, New York	49
1936	Lou Gehrig, New York	49
1964	Harmon Killebrew, Minnesota	49
1966	Frank Robinson, Baltimore	49
1969	Harmon Killebrew, Minnesota	49
1987	Mark McGwire, Oakland	49
1996	Ken Griffey Jr., Seattle	49
1998	Albert Belle, Chicago	49
2001	Jim Thome, Cleveland	49
1933	Jimmie Foxx, Philadelphia	48

Year	Player, Club	No.
1962	Harmon Killebrew, Minnesota	48
1969	Frank Howard, Washington	48
1996	Albert Belle, Cleveland	48
1999	Ken Griffey Jr., Seattle	48
1926	Babe Ruth, New York	47
1927	Lou Gehrig, New York	47
1969	Reggie Jackson, Oakland	47
1987	George Bell, Toronto	47
1996	Juan Gonzalez, Texas	47
1999	Rafael Palmeiro, Texas	47
2000	Troy Glaus, Anaheim	47
2001	Rafael Palmeiro, Texas	47
2003	Alex Rodriguez, Texas	47
1924	Babe Ruth, New York	46
1929	Babe Ruth, New York	46
1931	Lou Gehrig, New York	46
1931	Babe Ruth, New York	46
1937	Joe DiMaggio, New York	46
1961	Jim Gentile, Baltimore	46
1961	Harmon Killebrew, Minnesota	46
1978	Jim Rice, Boston	46
1993	Juan Gonzalez, Texas	46
1998	Jose Canseco, Toronto	46
1961	Rocky Colavito, Detroit	45
1963	Harmon Killebrew, Minnesota	45
1979	Gorman Thomas, Milwaukee	45
1993	Ken Griffey Jr., Seattle	45
1998	Juan Gonzalez, Texas	45
1998	Manny Ramirez, Cleveland	45
1934	Jimmie Foxx, Philadelphia	44
1946	Hank Greenberg, Detroit	44
1967	Harmon Killebrew, Minnesota	44
1967	Carl Yastrzemski, Boston	44
1968	Frank Howard, Washington	44
1970	Frank Howard, Washington	44
1991	Jose Canseco, Oakland	44
1991	Cecil Fielder, Detroit	44
1996	Jay Buhner, Seattle	44
1996	Mo Vaughn, Boston	44
1997	Tino Martinez, New York	44
1999	Carlos Delgado, Toronto	44
1999	Manny Ramirez, Cleveland	44
1949	Ted Williams, Boston	43
1953	Al Rosen, Cleveland	43
1984	Tony Armas, Boston	43
1992	Juan Gonzalez, Texas	43
1998	Rafael Palmeiro, Baltimore	43
2000	Jason Giambi, Oakland	43
2000	Frank Thomas, Chicago	43
2002	Rafael Palmeiro, Texas	43
2004	Manny Ramirez, Boston	43
1936	Hal Trosky, Cleveland	42
1953	Gus Zernial, Philadelphia	42
1957	Roy Sievers, Washington	42
1958	Mickey Mantle, New York	42
1959	Rocky Colavito, Cleveland	42
1959	Harmon Killebrew, Washington	42
1963	Dick Stuart, Boston	42
1988	Jose Canseco, Oakland	42
1992	Mark McGwire, Oakland	42
1997	Juan Gonzalez, Texas	42
1998	Alex Rodriguez, Seattle	42
1999	Shawn Green, Toronto	42
1999	Alex Rodriguez, Seattle	42
2003	Carlos Delgado, Toronto	42
2003	Frank Thomas, Chicago	42
1923	Babe Ruth, New York	41
1930	Lou Gehrig, New York	41
1932	Babe Ruth, New York	41
1936	Jimmie Foxx, Boston	41
1940	Hank Greenberg, Detroit	41
1958	Rocky Colavito, Cleveland	41
1961	Norm Cash, Detroit	41
1970	Harmon Killebrew, Minnesota	41
1980	Reggie Jackson, New York	41
1980	Ben Oglivie, Milwaukee	41
1993	Frank Thomas, Chicago	41
2000	Tony Batista, Toronto	41
2000	Carlos Delgado, Toronto	41
2000	David Justice, Cleveland-New York	41
2000	Alex Rodriguez, Seattle	41
2001	Troy Glaus, Anaheim	41
2001	Manny Ramirez, Boston	41
2002	Jason Giambi, New York	41
2003	Jason Giambi, New York	41
2004	Paul Konerko, Chicago	41
2004	David Ortiz, Boston	41
1937	Hank Greenberg, Detroit	40
1960	Mickey Mantle, New York	40
1969	Rico Petrocelli, Boston	40
1969	Carl Yastrzemski, Boston	40
1970	Carl Yastrzemski, Boston	40
1985	Darrell Evans, Detroit	40
1986	Jesse Barfield, Toronto	40
1994	Ken Griffey Jr., Seattle	40
1995	Jay Buhner, Seattle	40
1995	Frank Thomas, Chicago	40
1996	Frank Thomas, Chicago	40
1997	Jay Buhner, Seattle	40
1997	Jim Thome, Cleveland	40
1998	Mo Vaughn, Boston	40

Total number of occurrences: 131

NATIONAL LEAGUE

Year	Player, Club	No.
2001	Barry Bonds, San Francisco	73
1998	Mark McGwire, St. Louis	70
1998	Sammy Sosa, Chicago	66
1999	Mark McGwire, St. Louis	65
2001	Sammy Sosa, Chicago	64
1999	Sammy Sosa, Chicago	63
2001	Luis Gonzalez, Arizona	57
1930	Hack Wilson, Chicago	56
1949	Ralph Kiner, Pittsburgh	54
1965	Willie Mays, San Francisco	52
1977	George Foster, Cincinnati	52
1947	Ralph Kiner, Pittsburgh	51
1947	Johnny Mize, New York	51
1955	Willie Mays, New York	51
1998	Greg Vaughn, San Diego	50
2000	Sammy Sosa, Chicago	50
1954	Ted Kluszewski, Cincinnati	49
1962	Willie Mays, San Francisco	49
1987	Andre Dawson, Chicago	49
1997	Larry Walker, Colorado	49
2000	Barry Bonds, San Francisco	49
2001	Todd Helton, Colorado	49
2001	Shawn Green, Los Angeles	49
2002	Sammy Sosa, Chicago	49
1971	Willie Stargell, Pittsburgh	48
1979	Dave Kingman, Chicago	48
1980	Mike Schmidt, Philadelphia	48
2004	Adrian Beltre, Los Angeles	48
1950	Ralph Kiner, Pittsburgh	47
1953	Eddie Mathews, Milwaukee	47
1955	Ted Kluszewski, Cincinnati	47
1958	Ernie Banks, Chicago	47
1964	Willie Mays, San Francisco	47
1971	Hank Aaron, Atlanta	47
1989	Kevin Mitchell, San Francisco	47
1996	Andres Galarraga, Colorado	47
2000	Jeff Bagwell, Houston	47
2003	Jim Thome, Philadelphia	47
1959	Eddie Mathews, Milwaukee	46
1961	Orlando Cepeda, San Francisco	46
1993	Barry Bonds, San Francisco	46
1998	Vinny Castilla, Colorado	46
2002	Barry Bonds, San Francisco	46
2004	Adam Dunn, Cincinnati	46
2004	Albert Pujols, St. Louis	46
1959	Ernie Banks, Chicago	45
1962	Hank Aaron, Milwaukee	45
1969	Willie McCovey, San Francisco	45
1970	Johnny Bench, Cincinnati	45
1979	Mike Schmidt, Philadelphia	45
1999	Chipper Jones, Atlanta	45
1999	Greg Vaughn, Cincinnati	45
2001	Richie Sexson, Milwaukee	45
2003	Barry Bonds, San Francisco	45
2003	Richie Sexson, Milwaukee	45
2004	Barry Bonds, San Francisco	45
1955	Ernie Banks, Chicago	44
1957	Hank Aaron, Milwaukee	44
1963	Hank Aaron, Milwaukee	44
1963	Willie McCovey, San Francisco	44
1966	Hank Aaron, Atlanta	44
1969	Hank Aaron, Atlanta	44
1973	Willie Stargell, Pittsburgh	44
1987	Dale Murphy, Atlanta	44
1998	Andres Galarraga, Atlanta	44

Year	Player, Club	No.
2000	Vladimir Guerrero, Montreal	44
2000	Richard Hidalgo, Houston	44
1929	Chuck Klein, Philadelphia	43
1940	Johnny Mize, St. Louis	43
1956	Duke Snider, Brooklyn	43
1957	Ernie Banks, Chicago	43
1973	Dave Johnson, Atlanta	43
1994	Matt Williams, San Francisco	43
1997	Jeff Bagwell, Houston	43
2000	Gary Sheffield, Los Angeles	43
2003	Javier Lopez, Atlanta	43
2003	Albert Pujols, St. Louis	43
1922	Rogers Hornsby, St. Louis	42
1929	Mel Ott, New York	42
1951	Ralph Kiner, Pittsburgh	42
1953	Duke Snider, Brooklyn	42
1954	Gil Hodges, Brooklyn	42
1955	Duke Snider, Brooklyn	42
1970	Billy Williams, Chicago	42
1996	Barry Bonds, San Francisco	42
1996	Gary Sheffield, Florida	42
1999	Jeff Bagwell, Houston	42
1999	Vladimir Guerrero, Montreal	42
2000	Jim Edmonds, St. Louis	42
2000	Todd Helton, Colorado	42
2002	Lance Berkman, Houston	42
2002	Shawn Green, Los Angeles	42
2004	Jim Edmonds, St. Louis	42
2004	Jim Thome, Philadelphia	42
1923	Fred Williams, Philadelphia	41
1953	Roy Campanella, Brooklyn	41
1954	Hank Sauer, Chicago	41
1954	Willie Mays, New York	41
1955	Eddie Mathews, Milwaukee	41
1960	Ernie Banks, Chicago	41
1973	Darrell Evans, Atlanta	41
1977	Jeff Burroughs, Atlanta	41
1996	Todd Hundley, New York	41
1997	Andres Galarraga, Colorado	41
2001	Phil Nevin, San Diego	41
1930	Chuck Klein, Philadelphia	40
1948	Ralph Kiner, Pittsburgh	40
1948	Johnny Mize, New York	40
1951	Gil Hodges, Brooklyn	40
1953	Ted Kluszewski, Cincinnati	40
1954	Duke Snider, Brooklyn	40
1954	Eddie Mathews, Milwaukee	40
1955	Wally Post, Cincinnati	40
1957	Duke Snider, Brooklyn	40
1960	Hank Aaron, Milwaukee	40
1961	Willie Mays, San Francisco	40
1966	Dick Allen, Philadelphia	40
1970	Tony Perez, Cincinnati	40
1972	Johnny Bench, Cincinnati	40
1973	Hank Aaron, Atlanta	40
1978	George Foster, Cincinnati	40
1983	Mike Schmidt, Philadelphia	40
1990	Ryne Sandberg, Chicago	40
1993	David Justice, Atlanta	40
1995	Dante Bichette, Colorado	40
1996	Ellis Burks, Colorado	40
1996	Vinny Castilla, Colorado	40
1996	Ken Caminiti, San Diego	40
1996	Sammy Sosa, Chicago	40
1997	Barry Bonds, San Francisco	40
1997	Vinny Castilla, Colorado	40
1997	Mike Piazza, Los Angeles	40
1999	Mike Piazza, New York	40
2000	Ken Griffey Jr., Cincinnati	40
2003	Sammy Sosa, Chicago	40

Total number of occurences: 129

TWO LEAGUES IN SEASON

Year	Player, Club	No.
1997	Mark McGwire, Oakland A.L. (34), St. Louis, N.L. (24)	58
1996	Greg Vaughn, Milwaukee A.L. (31), San Diego N.L. (10)	41

Total number of occurrences: 2

PLAYERS WITH FOUR HOMERS IN GAME

NATIONAL LEAGUE

BOBBY LOWE, Boston, May 30, 1894, second game (H).
Ed Delahanty, Philadelphia, July 13, 1896 (A) (three consecutive).
Chuck Klein, Philadelphia, July 10, 1936, 10 innings (A) (three consecutive).
Gil Hodges, Brooklyn, August 31, 1950 (H).
Joe Adcock, Milwaukee, July 31, 1954 (A) (three consecutive).
Willie Mays, San Francisco, April 30, 1961 (A).
MIKE SCHMIDT, Philadelphia, April 17, 1976, 10 innings (A).
Bob Horner, Atlanta, July 6, 1986 (H).
Mark Whiten, St. Louis, September 7, 1993 (A) (three consecutive).
Shawn Green, Los Angeles, May 23, 2002 (A) (three consecutive).
Note—Capitalized name denotes four consecutive homers (bases on balls excluded); parentheses denotes home or away games.
Total number of occurrences: 10

AMERICAN LEAGUE

LOU GEHRIG, New York, June 3, 1932 (A).
Pat Seerey, Chicago, July 18, 1948, first game, 11 innings (A) (three consecutive).
ROCKY COLAVITO, Cleveland, June 10, 1959 (A).
MIKE CAMERON, Seattle, May 2, 2002 (A).
CARLOS DELGADO, Toronto, September 25, 2003 (H)
Note—Capitalized name denotes four consecutive homers (bases on balls excluded); parentheses denotes home or away games.
Total number of occurrences: 5

PLAYERS WITH THREE HOMERS IN GAME

AMERICAN ASSOCIATION

Guy Hecker, Louisville, August 15, 1886, second game (H).
Total number of occurrences: 1

AMERICAN LEAGUE

Ken Williams, St. Louis, April 22, 1922 (H).
Joe Hauser, Philadelphia, August 2, 1924 (A).
Goose Goslin, Washington, June 19, 1925, 12 innings (A).
Ty Cobb, Detroit, May 5, 1925 (A).
Mickey Cochrane, Philadelphia, May 21, 1925 (A).
Tony Lazzeri, New York, June 8, 1927 (H).
Lou Gehrig, New York, June 23, 1927 (A).
Lou Gehrig, New York, May 4, 1929 (A).
Babe Ruth, New York, May 21, 1930, first game (A).
Lou Gehrig, New York, May 22, 1930, second game (A).
CARL REYNOLDS, Chicago, July 2, 1930, second game (A).
GOOSE GOSLIN, St. Louis, August 19, 1930 (A).
EARL AVERILL, Cleveland, September 17, 1930, first game (H).
Goose Goslin, St. Louis, June 23, 1932 (H).
Ben Chapman, New York, July 9, 1932, second game (H).
Jimmie Foxx, Philadelphia, July 10, 1932, 18 innings (A).
Al Simmons, Philadelphia, July 15, 1932 (H).
JIMMIE FOXX, Philadelphia, June 8, 1933 (H).
HAL TROSKY, Cleveland, May 30, 1934, second game (H).
ED COLEMAN, Philadelphia, August 17, 1934, first game (H).
FRANK HIGGINS, Philadelphia, June 27, 1935 (H).
MOOSE SOLTERS, St. Louis, July 7, 1935 (A).
Tony Lazzeri, New York, May 24, 1936 (A).
JOE DiMAGGIO, New York, June 13, 1937, second game, 11 innings (A).
Hal Trosky, Cleveland, July 5, 1937, first game (A).
MERV CONNORS, Chicago, September 17, 1938, second game (H).
KEN KELTNER, Cleveland, May 25, 1939 (A).
Jim Tabor, Boston, July 4, 1939, second game (A).
BILL DICKEY, New York, July 26, 1939 (H).
FRANK HIGGINS, Detroit, May 20, 1940 (H).
Charlie Keller, New York, July 28, 1940, first game (A).
Rudy York, Detroit, September 1, 1941, first game (H).
Pat Seerey, Cleveland, July 13, 1945 (A).
Ted Williams, Boston, July 14, 1946, first game (H).
Sam Chapman, Philadelphia, August 15, 1946 (H).
JOE DiMAGGIO, New York, May 23, 1948, first game (A).
Pat Mullin, Detroit, June 26, 1949, second game (A).
Bobby Doerr, Boston, June 8, 1950 (H).
LARRY DOBY, Cleveland, August 2, 1950 (H).
Joe DiMaggio, New York, September 10, 1950 (A).
JOHNNY MIZE, New York, September 15, 1950 (A).
Gus Zernial, Chicago, October 1, 1950, second game (H).

Bobby Avila, Cleveland, June 20, 1951 (A).
Clyde Vollmer, Boston, July 26, 1951 (H).
Al Rosen, Cleveland, April 29, 1952 (A).
BILL GLYNN, Cleveland, July 5, 1954, first game (A).
Al Kaline, Detroit, April 17, 1955 (H).
Mickey Mantle, New York, May 13, 1955 (H).
Norm Zauchin, Boston, May 27, 1955 (H).
JIM LEMON, Washington, August 31, 1956 (H).
Ted Williams, Boston, May 8, 1957 (H).
Ted Williams, Boston, June 13, 1957 (A).
Hector Lopez, Kansas City, June 26, 1958 (H).
PRESTON WARD, Kansas City, September 9, 1958 (H).
CHARLIE MAXWELL, Detroit, May 3, 1959, second game (H).
Bob Cerv, Kansas City, August 20, 1959 (H).
WILLIE KIRKLAND, Cleveland, July 9, 1961, second game (H).
Rocky Colavito, Detroit, August 27, 1961, second game (A).
Lee Thomas, Los Angeles, September 5, 1961, second game (A).
ROCKY COLAVITO, Detroit, July 5, 1962 (A).
Steve Boros, Detroit, August 6, 1962 (A).
DON LEPPERT, Washington, April 11, 1963 (H).
BOB ALLISON, Minnesota, May 17, 1963 (A).
BOOG POWELL, Baltimore, August 10, 1963 (A).
Harmon Killebrew, Minnesota, September 21, 1963, first game (A).
Jim King, Washington, June 8, 1964 (H).
Boog Powell, Baltimore, June 27, 1964 (A).
MANNY JIMENEZ, Kansas City, July 4, 1964 (A).
TOM TRESH, New York, June 6, 1965, second game (H).
Boog Powell, Baltimore, August 15, 1966 (A).
Tom McGraw, Chicago, May 24, 1967 (A).
Curt Blefary, Baltimore, June 6, 1967, first game (A).
KEN HARRELSON, Boston, June 14, 1968 (A).
Mike Epstein, Washington, May 16, 1969 (A).
Joe Lahoud, Boston, June 11, 1969 (A).
BILL MELTON, Chicago, June 24, 1969, second game (A).
Reggie Jackson, Oakland, July 2, 1969 (H).
Paul Blair, Baltimore, April 29, 1970 (A).
Tony Horton, Cleveland, May 24, 1970, second game (H).
Willie Horton, Detroit, June 9, 1970 (H).
BOBBY MURCER, New York, June 24, 1970, second game (H).
Bill Freehan, Detroit, August 9, 1971 (A).
GEORGE HENDRICK, Cleveland, June 19, 1973 (H).
Tony Oliva, Minnesota, July 3, 1973 (A).
Leroy Stanton, California, July 10, 1973, 10 innings (A).
Bobby Murcer, New York, July 13, 1973 (H).
BOBBY GRICH, Baltimore, June 18, 1974 (H).
Fred Lynn, Boston, June 18, 1975 (A).
John Mayberry, Kansas City, July 1, 1975 (A).
DON BAYLOR, Baltimore, July 2, 1975 (A).
TONY SOLAITA, Kansas City, September 7, 1975, 11 innings (A).
Carl Yastrzemski, Boston, May 19, 1976 (A).
Willie Horton, Texas, May 15, 1977 (A).
JOHN MAYBERRY, Kansas City, June 1, 1977 (A).
CLIFF JOHNSON, New York, June 30, 1977 (A).
Jim Rice, Boston, August 29, 1977 (H).
Al Oliver, Texas, May 23, 1979 (H).
Ben Oglivie, Milwaukee, July 8, 1979, first game (H).
Claudell Washington, Chicago, July 14, 1979 (H).
George Brett, Kansas City, July 22, 1979 (A).
Cecil Cooper, Milwaukee, July 27, 1979 (H).
EDDIE MURRAY, Baltimore, August 29, 1979, second game (A).
CARNEY LANSFORD, California, September 1, 1979 (A).
Otto Velez, Toronto, May 4, 1980, first game, 10 innings (H).
Fred Patek, California, June 20, 1980 (A).
AL OLIVER, Texas, August 17, 1980, second game (A).
Eddie Murray, Baltimore, September 14, 1980, 13 innings (A).
Jeff Burroughs, Seattle, August 14, 1981, second game (A).
Paul Molitor, Milwaukee, May 12, 1982 (A).
LARRY HERNDON, Detroit, May 18, 1982 (H).
BEN OGLIVIE, Milwaukee, June 20, 1982 (A).
HAROLD BAINES, Chicago, July 7, 1982 (H).
DOUG DeCINCES, California, August 3, 1982 (H).
Doug DeCinces, California, August 8, 1982 (A).
George Brett, Kansas City, April 20, 1983 (H).
Ben Oglivie, Milwaukee, May 14, 1983 (H).
Dan Ford, Baltimore, July 20, 1983 (A).
Jim Rice, Boston, August 29, 1983, second game (A).
DAVE KINGMAN, Oakland, April 16, 1984 (A).
Harold Baines, Chicago, September 17, 1984 (A).
GORMAN THOMAS, Seattle, April 11, 1985 (H).
LARRY PARRISH, Texas, April 29, 1985 (H).
Eddie Murray, Baltimore, August 26, 1985 (A).
Leon Lacy, Baltimore, June 8, 1986 (H).
JUAN BENIQUEZ, Baltimore, June 12, 1986 (H).

Joe Carter, Cleveland, August 29, 1986 (A).
Jim Presley, Seattle, September 1, 1986 (H).
Reggie Jackson, California, September 18, 1986 (H).
Cory Snyder, Cleveland, May 21, 1987 (H).
Joe Carter, Cleveland, May 28, 1987 (A).
Mark McGwire, Oakland, June 27, 1987 (A).
Bill Madlock, Detroit, June 28, 1987, 11 innings (H).
BROOK JACOBY, Cleveland, July 3, 1987 (H).
Dale Sveum, Milwaukee, July 17, 1987 (H).
Mike Brantley, Seattle, September 14, 1987 (H).
Ernie Whitt, Toronto, September 14, 1987 (H).
Wally Joyner, California, October 3, 1987 (H).
George Bell, Toronto, April 4, 1988 (A).
Jose Canseco, Oakland, July 3, 1988 (A).
JOE CARTER, Cleveland, June 24, 1989 (A).
Joe Carter, Cleveland, July 19, 1989 (A).
CECIL FIELDER, Detroit, May 6, 1990 (A).
CECIL FIELDER, Detroit, June 6, 1990 (A).
RANDY MILLIGAN, Baltimore, June 9, 1990 (H).
BO JACKSON, Kansas City, July 17, 1990 (A).
TOM BRUNANSKY, Boston, September 29, 1990 (H).
DAVE WINFIELD, California, April 13, 1991 (A).
Harold Baines, Oakland, May 7, 1991 (H).
Danny Tartabull, Kansas City, July 6, 1991 (H).
Jack Clark, Boston, July 31, 1991 (H).
DAVE HENDERSON, Oakland, August 3, 1991 (H).
Juan Gonzalez, Texas, June 7, 1992 (H).
Albert Belle, Cleveland, September 6, 1992 (H).
Carlos Baerga, Cleveland, June 17, 1993 (A).
Joe Carter, Toronto, August 23, 1993 (H).
Juan Gonzalez, Texas, August 28, 1993 (H).
Tim Raines Sr., Chicago, April 18, 1994 (A).
Jose Canseco, Texas, June 13, 1994 (H).
Darnell Coles, Toronto, July 5, 1994 (A).
JIM THOME, Cleveland, July 22, 1994 (H).
John Valentin, Boston, June 2, 1995 (H).
MARK McGWIRE, Oakland, June 11, 1995 (A).
MIKE STANLEY, New York, August 10, 1995, first game (H).
PAUL O'NEILL, New York, August 31, 1995 (H).
ALBERT BELLE, Cleveland, September 19, 1995 (A).
Dan Wilson, Seattle, April 11, 1996 (A).
CECIL FIELDER, Detroit, April 16, 1996 (A).
Ernie Young, Oakland, May 10, 1996 (H).
Geronimo Berroa, Oakland, May 22, 1996 (A).
KEN GRIFFEY JR., Seattle, May 24, 1996 (H).
Cal Ripken Jr., Baltimore, May 28, 1996 (A).
EDGAR MARTINEZ, Seattle, July 6, 1996 (A).
DARRYL STRAWBERRY, New York, August 6, 1996 (H).
Geronimo Berroa, Oakland, August 12, 1996 (H).
FRANK THOMAS, Chicago, September 15, 1996 (A).
MO VAUGHN, Boston, September 24, 1996 (H).
TINO MARTINEZ, New York, April 2, 1997 (A).
Matt Williams, Cleveland, April 25, 1997 (A).
Ken Griffey Jr., Seattle, April 25, 1997 (A).
ROBERTO ALOMAR, Baltimore, April 26, 1997 (A).
MO VAUGHN, Boston, May 30, 1997 (H).
BOB HIGGINSON, Detroit, June 30, 1997 (H).
IVAN RODRIGUEZ, Texas, September 11, 1997 (H).
Lee Stevens, Texas, April 13, 1998 (H).
CARLOS DELGADO, Toronto, August 4, 1998 (A).
MANNY RAMIREZ, Cleveland, September 15, 1998 (H).
Nomar Garciaparra, Boston, May 10, 1999 (H).
EDGAR MARTINEZ, Seattle, May 18, 1999 (H).
Miguel Tejada, Oakland, June 11, 1999 (H).
Trot Nixon, Boston, July 24, 1999 (A).
Albert Belle, Baltimore, July 25, 1999 (H).
Carlos Delgado, Toronto, August 6, 1999 (A).
Manny Ramirez, Cleveland, August 25, 1999 (A).
JUAN GONZALEZ, Texas, September 24, 1999 (A).
Alex Rodriguez, Seattle, April 16, 2000 (A).
BOBBY HIGGINSON, Detroit, June 24, 2000 (A).
Darrin Fletcher, Toronto, August 27, 2000 (A).
CARLOS DELGADO, Toronto, April 4, 2001 (A).
Carlos Delgado, Toronto, April 20, 2001 (A).
Jason Varitek, Boston, May 20, 2001 (A).
Ellis Burks, Cleveland, June 19, 2001 (H).
Miguel Tejada, Oakland, June 30, 2001 (A).
Jim Thome, Cleveland, July 6, 2001 (H).
NOMAR GARCIAPARRA, Boston, July 23, 2002, a.m. game (H).
CHRIS WOODWARD, Toronto, August 7, 2002 (H).
Alex Rodriguez, Texas, August 17, 2002 (H).
TROY GLAUS, Anaheim, September 15, 2002 (H).
CARLOS PENA, Detroit, May 19, 2003 (A).

Garret Anderson, Anaheim, July 4, 2003 (A).
Bill Mueller, Boston, July 29, 2003 (A).
JOSE VALENTIN, Chicago, July 30, 2003 (A).
Victor Martinez, Cleveland, July 16, 2004 (A).
TRAVIS HAFNER, Cleveland, July 20, 2004 (H).
KEVIN MILLAR, Boston, July 23, 2004 (H).
ERUBIEL DURAZO, Oakland, August 18, 2004 (A).
TONY CLARK, New York, August 28, 2004 (A).
Note—Capitalized name denotes three consecutive homers (bases on balls excluded); parentheses denotes home or away games.
Total number of occurrences: 216

NATIONAL LEAGUE

Ned Williamson, Chicago, May 30, 1884, second game (H).
CAP ANSON, Chicago, August 6, 1884 (H).
JACK MANNING, Philadelphia, October 9, 1884 (A).
Dennis Brouthers, Detroit, September 10, 1886 (A).
Roger Connor, New York, May 9, 1888 (A).
Frank Shugart, St. Louis, May 10, 1894 (A).
BILL JOYCE, Washington, August 20, 1894 (H).
Tom McCreery, Louisville, July 12, 1897 (A).
Jake Beckley, Cincinnati, September 26, 1897, first game (A).
Butch Henline, Philadelphia, September 15, 1922 (H).
Fred Williams, Philadelphia, May 11, 1923 (H).
GEORGE KELLY, New York, September 17, 1923 (A).
George Kelly, New York, June 14, 1924 (H).
Jack Fournier, Brooklyn, July 13, 1926 (A).
Les Bell, Boston, June 2, 1928 (H).
GEORGE HARPER, St. Louis, September 20, 1928, first game (A).
Hack Wilson, Chicago, July 26, 1930 (A).
MEL OTT, New York, August 31, 1930, second game (H).
ROGERS HORNSBY, Chicago, April 24, 1931 (A).
GEORGE WATKINS, St. Louis, June 24, 1931, second game (A).
Bill Terry, New York, August 13, 1932, first game (H).
Babe Herman, Chicago, July 20, 1933 (H).
Hal Lee, Boston, July 6, 1934 (A).
Babe Ruth, Boston, May 25, 1935 (A).
JOHNNY MOORE, Philadelphia, July 22, 1936 (H).
Alex Kampouris, Cincinnati, May 9, 1937 (A).
JOHNNY MIZE, St. Louis, July 13, 1938 (H).
Johnny Mize, St. Louis, July 20, 1938, second game (H).
HANK LEIBER, Chicago, July 4, 1939, first game (H).
Johnny Mize, St. Louis, May 13, 1940, 14 innings (A).
JOHNNY MIZE, St. Louis, September 8, 1940, first game (H).
JIM TOBIN, Boston, May 13, 1942 (H).
CLYDE McCULLOUGH, Chicago, July 26, 1942, first game (A).
BILL NICHOLSON, Chicago, July 23, 1944, first game (A).
JOHNNY MIZE, New York, April 24, 1947 (A).
WILLARD MARSHALL, New York, July 18, 1947 (H).
RALPH KINER, Pittsburgh, August 16, 1947 (H).
RALPH KINER, Pittsburgh, September 11, 1947, second game (H).
Ralph Kiner, Pittsburgh, July 5, 1948, first game (H).
GENE HERMANSKI, Brooklyn, August 5, 1948 (H).
Andy Seminick, Philadelphia, June 2, 1949 (H).
Walker Cooper, Cincinnati, July 6, 1949 (H).
BOB ELLIOTT, Boston, September 24, 1949 (A).
DUKE SNIDER, Brooklyn, May 30, 1950, second game (H).
Wes Westrum, New York, June 24, 1950 (H).
ANDY PAFKO, Chicago, August 2, 1950, second game (A).
ROY CAMPANELLA, Brooklyn, August 26, 1950 (A).
HANK SAUER, Chicago, August 28, 1950, first game (H).
TOMMY BROWN, Brooklyn, September 18, 1950 (H).
Ralph Kiner, Pittsburgh, July 18, 1951 (A).
DEL WILBER, Philadelphia, August 27, 1951, second game (H).
Don Mueller, New York, September 1, 1951 (H).
Hank Sauer, Chicago, June 11, 1952 (H).
EDDIE MATHEWS, Boston, September 27, 1952 (A).
DUSTY RHODES, New York, August 26, 1953 (H).
Jim Pendleton, Milwaukee, August 30, 1953, first game (A).
Stan Musial, St. Louis, May 2, 1954, first game (H).
HANK THOMPSON, New York, June 3, 1954 (A).
DUSTY RHODES, New York, July 28, 1954 (H).
Duke Snider, Brooklyn, June 1, 1955 (H).
GUS BELL, Cincinnati, July 21, 1955 (A).
Del Ennis, Philadelphia, July 23, 1955 (H).
Smoky Burgess, Cincinnati, July 29, 1955 (H).
Ernie Banks, Chicago, August 4, 1955 (H).
GUS BELL, Cincinnati, May 29, 1956 (A).
Ed Bailey, Cincinnati, June 24, 1956, first game (A).
Ted Kluszewski, Cincinnati, July 1, 1956, first game, 10 innings (A).
BOB THURMAN, Cincinnati, August 18, 1956 (H).
ERNIE BANKS, Chicago, September 14, 1957, second game (H).
Lee Walls, Chicago, April 24, 1958 (A).

Roman Mejias, Pittsburgh, May 4, 1958, first game (A).
Walt Moryn, Chicago, May 30, 1958, second game (A).
FRANK THOMAS, Pittsburgh, August 16, 1958 (A).
Don Demeter, Los Angeles, April 21, 1959, 11 innings (H).
Hank Aaron, Milwaukee, June 21, 1959 (A).
FRANK ROBINSON, Cincinnati, August 22, 1959 (H).
DICK STUART, Pittsburgh, June 30, 1960, second game (H).
Willie Mays, San Francisco, June 29, 1961, 10 innings (A).
BILL WHITE, St. Louis, July 5, 1961 (A).
Don Demeter, Philadelphia, September 12, 1961 (A).
ERNIE BANKS, Chicago, May 29, 1962 (H).
STAN MUSIAL, St. Louis, July 8, 1962 (A).
Willie Mays, San Francisco, June 2, 1963 (A).
Ernie Banks, Chicago, June 9, 1963 (H).
WILLIE McCOVEY, San Francisco, September 22, 1963, (H).
WILLIE McCOVEY, San Francisco, April 22, 1964 (A).
JOHNNY CALLISON, Philadelphia, September 27, 1964 (H).
Johnny Callison, Philadelphia, June 6, 1965, second game (A).
Willie Stargell, Pittsburgh, June 24, 1965 (A).
JIM HICKMAN, New York, September 3, 1965 (A).
Gene Oliver, Atlanta, July 30, 1966, second game (H).
ART SHAMSKY, Cincinnati, August 12, 1966, 13 innings (H).
Willie McCovey, San Francisco, September 17, 1966, 10 innings (H).
Roberto Clemente, Pittsburgh, May 15, 1967, 10 innings (A).
ADOLFO PHILLIPS, Chicago, June 11, 1967, second game (H).
JIM WYNN, Houston, June 15, 1967 (H).
Willie Stargell, Pittsburgh, May 22, 1968 (A).
Billy Williams, Chicago, September 10, 1968 (H).
DICK ALLEN, Philadelphia, September 29, 1968 (A).
BOB TILLMAN, Atlanta, July 30, 1969, first game (A).
ROBERTO CLEMENTE, Pittsburgh, August 13, 1969 (A).
Rico Carty, Atlanta, May 31, 1970 (H).
Mike Lum, Atlanta, July 3, 1970, first game (H).
JOHNNY BENCH, Cincinnati, July 26, 1970 (H).
ORLANDO CEPEDA, Atlanta, July 26, 1970, first game (A).
Willie Stargell, Pittsburgh, April 10, 1971, 12 innings (A).
WILLIE STARGELL, Pittsburgh, April 21, 1971 (H).
DERON JOHNSON, Philadelphia, July 11, 1971 (H).
RICK MONDAY, Chicago, May 16, 1972 (A).
Nate Colbert, San Diego, August 1, 1972, second game (A).
Johnny Bench, Cincinnati, May 9, 1973 (A).
Lee May, Houston, June 21, 1973 (A).
George Mitterwald, Chicago, April 17, 1974 (H).
Jim Wynn, Los Angeles, May 11, 1974 (A).
Dave Lopes, Los Angeles, August 20, 1974 (A).
Reggie Smith, St. Louis, May 22, 1976 (A).
Dave Kingman, New York, June 4, 1976 (A).
Bill Robinson, Pittsburgh, June 5, 1976, 15 innings (H).
Gary Matthews, San Francisco, September 25, 1976 (H).
GARY CARTER, Montreal, April 20, 1977 (H).
LARRY PARRISH, Montreal, May 29, 1977 (H).
GEORGE FOSTER, Cincinnati, July 14, 1977 (H).
Pete Rose, Cincinnati, April 29, 1978 (A).
Dave Kingman, Chicago, May 14, 1978 (A).
LARRY PARRISH, Montreal, July 30, 1978 (A).
Dave Kingman, Chicago, May 17, 1979 (H).
Dale Murphy, Atlanta, May 18, 1979 (H).
MIKE SCHMIDT, Philadelphia, July 7, 1979 (H).
DAVE KINGMAN, Chicago, July 28, 1979 (A).
Larry Parrish, Montreal, April 25, 1980 (A).
Johnny Bench, Cincinnati, May 29, 1980 (A).
Claudell Washington, New York, June 22, 1980 (A).
Darrell Evans, San Francisco, June 15, 1983 (A).
DARRYL STRAWBERRY, New York, August 5, 1985 (A).
GARY CARTER, New York, September 3, 1985 (A).
Andre Dawson, Montreal, September 24, 1985 (A).
Ken Griffey Sr., Atlanta, July 22, 1986, 11 innings (H).
Eric Davis, Cincinnati, September 10, 1986 (A).
ERIC DAVIS, Cincinnati, May 3, 1987 (A).
Tim Wallach, Montreal, May 4, 1987 (A).
MIKE SCHMIDT, Philadelphia, June 14, 1987 (A).
Andre Dawson, Chicago, August 1, 1987 (H).
GLENN DAVIS, Houston, September 10, 1987 (A).
Darnell Coles, Pittsburgh, September 30, 1987, second game (H).
Von Hayes, Philadelphia, August 29, 1989 (A).
KEVIN MITCHELL, San Francisco, May 25, 1990 (A).
Jeff Treadway, Atlanta, May 26, 1990 (A).
GLENN DAVIS, Houston, June 1, 1990 (A).
BARRY LARKIN, Cincinnati, June 28, 1991 (H).
Jeff Blauser, Atlanta, July 12, 1992, 10 innings (A).
KARL RHODES, Chicago, April 4, 1994 (H).
Cory Snyder, Los Angeles, April 17, 1994 (A).

JEFF BAGWELL, Houston, June 24, 1994 (H).
Barry Bonds, San Francisco, August 2, 1994 (H).
ANDRES GALARRAGA, Colorado, June 25, 1995 (A).
REGGIE SANDERS, Cincinnati, August 15, 1995 (H).
SAMMY SOSA, Chicago, June 5, 1996 (H).
Mike Piazza, Los Angeles, June 29, 1996 (A).
BENITO SANTIAGO, Philadelphia, September 15, 1996 (A).
Willie Greene, Cincinnati, September 24, 1996 (H).
LARRY WALKER, Colorado, April 5, 1997 (A).
Steve Finley, San Diego, May 19, 1997 (A).
Steve Finley, San Diego, June 23, 1997 (A).
Bobby Estalella, Philadelphia, September 4, 1997 (A).
JOSE VALENTIN, Milwaukee, April 3, 1998 (A).
MARK McGWIRE, St. Louis, April 14, 1998 (H).
Mark McGwire, St. Louis, May 19, 1998 (A).
Sammy Sosa, Chicago, June 15, 1998 (H).
Brant Brown, Chicago, June 18, 1998 (H).
Ken Caminiti, San Diego, July 12, 1998 (A).
BRET BOONE, Cincinnati, September 20, 1998 (A).
Mike Lansing, Colorado, September 22, 1998 (H).
Jeff Bagwell, Houston, April 21, 1999 (A).
Larry Walker, Colorado, April 28, 1999 (A).
Jeffrey Hammonds, Cincinnati, May 19, 1999 (A).
Vinny Castilla, Colorado, June 5, 1999 (H).
JEFF BAGWELL, Houston, June 9, 1999 (H).
Edgardo Alfonzo, New York, August 30, 1999 (A).
GREG VAUGHN, Cincinnati, September 7, 1999, second game (A).
STEVE FINLEY, Arizona, September 8, 1999 (A).
Kevin Elster, Los Angeles, April 11, 2000 (A).
Todd Helton, Colorado, May 1, 2000 (H).
Mark McGwire, St. Louis, May 18, 2000 (A).
BRET BOONE, San Diego, June 23, 2000 (A).
Jeff Cirillo, Colorado, June 28, 2000 (H).
TYLER HOUSTON, Milwaukee, July 9, 2000 (H).
ARAMIS RAMIREZ, Pittsburgh, April 8, 2001 (A).
TODD HOLLANDSWORTH, Colorado, April 15, 2001 (H).
GEOFF JENKINS, Milwaukee, April 28, 2001 (H).
Jeromy Burnitz, Milwaukee, May 10, 2001 (H).
Barry Bonds, San Francisco, May 19, 2001 (A).
Luis Gonzalez, Arizona, June 8, 2001 (A).
Vinny Castilla, Houston, July 28, 2001, first game (A).
SAMMY SOSA, Chicago, August 9, 2001 (H).
Shawn Green, Los Angeles, August 15, 2001 (A).
JOSE ORTIZ, Colorado, August 17, 2001 (H).
Sammy Sosa, Chicago, August 22, 2001 (H).
Barry Bonds, San Francisco, September 9, 2001 (A).
SAMMY SOSA, Chicago, September 23, 2001 (A).
RICHIE SEXSON, Milwaukee, September 25, 2001 (A).
JEROMY BURNITZ, Milwaukee, September 25, 2001 (A).
Phil Nevin, San Diego, October 6, 2001 (H).
LANCE BERKMAN, Houston, April 16, 2002 (A).
Erubiel Durazo, Colorado, May 17, 2002 (H).
Russell Branyan, Cincinnati, August 4, 2002 (A).
AARON BOONE, Cincinnati, August 9, 2002 (H).
MIKE LIEBERTHAL, Philadelphia, August 10, 2002 (A).
SAMMY SOSA, Chicago, August 10, 2002 (A).
BARRY BONDS, San Francisco, August 27, 2002 (A).
Andruw Jones, Atlanta, September 25, 2002 (A).
Richie Sexson, Milwaukee, April 25, 2003 (A).
Aaron Boone, Cincinnati, May 8, 2003 (H).
GEOFF JENKINS, Milwaukee, May 21, 2003 (H).
Todd Helton, Colorado, May 29, 2003 (H).
Moises Alou, Chicago, July 4, 2003 (H).
SHEA HILLENBRAND, Arizona, July 7, 2003 (H).
RICHARD HIDALGO, Houston, September 16, 2003 (A).
Mike Lowell, Florida, April 21, 2004 (A).
Steve Finley, Arizona, April 28, 2004 (H).
LUIS GONZALEZ, Arizona, May 10, 2004 (H).
Larry Walker, Colorado, June 25, 2004 (A).
Albert Pujols, St. Louis, July 20, 2004 (A).
Aramis Ramirez, Chicago, July 30, 2004 (H).
J.T. SNOW, San Francisco, August 13, 2004 (A).
Aramis Ramirez, Chicago, September 16, 2004 (A).
Note—Capitalized name denotes three consecutive homers (bases on balls excluded); parentheses denotes home or away games.
Total number of occurrences: 225

SWITCH-HIT HOME RUNS IN GAME

(players hitting home runs from both sides of plate in game)

A.L.—Wally Schang, Philadelphia, September 8, 1916.

Johnny Lucadello, St. Louis, September 16, 1940.
Mickey Mantle, New York, May 13, 1955 (1 righthanded, 2 lefthanded).
Mickey Mantle, New York, August 15, 1955, second game.
Mickey Mantle, New York, May 18, 1956.
Mickey Mantle, New York, July 1, 1956, second game.
Mickey Mantle, New York, June 12, 1957.
Mickey Mantle, New York, July 28, 1958.
Mickey Mantle, New York, September 15, 1959.
Mickey Mantle, New York, April 26, 1961.
Mickey Mantle, New York, May 6, 1962, second game.
Tom Tresh, New York, September 1, 1963.
Tom Tresh, New York, July 13, 1964.
Mickey Mantle, New York, August 12, 1964.
Tom Tresh, New York, June 6, 1965, second game (1 righthanded, 2 lefthanded).
Reggie Smith, Boston, August 20, 1967, first game.
Reggie Smith, Boston, August 11, 1968, second game.
Don Buford, Baltimore, April 9, 1970.
Roy White, New York, May 7, 1970.
Reggie Smith, Boston, July 2, 1972, first game.
Reggie Smith, Boston, April 16, 1973.
Roy White, New York, August 13, 1973.
Roy White, New York, April 23, 1975.
Ken Henderson, Chicago, August 29, 1975.
Roy White, New York, August 18, 1976.
Eddie Murray, Baltimore, August 3, 1977.
Roy White, New York, June 13, 1978.
Larry Milbourne, Seattle, July 15, 1978.
Willie Wilson, Kansas City, June 15, 1979.
Eddie Murray, Baltimore, August 29, 1979, second game (2 righthanded, 1 lefthanded).
U.L. Washington, Kansas City, September 21, 1979.
Eddie Murray, Baltimore, August 16, 1981.
Eddie Murray, Baltimore, April 24, 1982.
Ted Simmons, Milwaukee, May 2, 1982.
Eddie Murray, Baltimore, August 26, 1982.
Roy Smalley, New York, September 5, 1982.
Donnie Scott, Seattle, April 29, 1985.
Mike Young, Baltimore, August 13, 1985.
Eddie Murray, Baltimore, August 26, 1985 (1 righthanded, 2 lefthanded).
Nelson Simmons, Detroit, September 16, 1985.
Roy Smalley, Minnesota, May 30, 1986.
Tony Bernazard, Cleveland, July 1, 1986.
Ruben Sierra, Texas, September 13, 1986.
Eddie Murray, Baltimore, May 8, 1987.
Eddie Murray, Baltimore, May 9, 1987.
Devon White, California, June 23, 1987.
Dale Sveum, Milwaukee, July 17, 1987 (1 righthanded, 2 lefthanded).
Dale Sveum, Milwaukee, June 12, 1988.
Mickey Tettleton, Baltimore, June 13, 1988.
Chili Davis, California, July 30, 1988.
Ruben Sierra, Texas, August 27, 1988.
Ruben Sierra, Texas, June 8, 1989.
Chili Davis, California, July 1, 1989.
Devon White, California, June 29, 1990.
Roberto Alomar, Toronto, May 10, 1991.
Devon White, Toronto, June 1, 1992.
Chili Davis, Minnesota, October 2, 1992.
Carlos Baerga, Cleveland, April 8, 1993.
Mickey Tettleton, Detroit, May 7, 1993, 12 innings.
Tim Raines Sr., Chicago, August 31, 1993.
Chad Kreuter, Detroit, September 7, 1993.
Eddie Murray, Cleveland, April 21, 1994.
Chili Davis, California, May 11, 1994.
Bernie Williams, New York, June 6, 1994.
Ruben Sierra, Oakland, June 7, 1994.
Chili Davis, California, July 30, 1994.
Mickey Tettleton, Texas, April 28, 1995.
Roberto Alomar, Toronto, May 3, 1995, 10 innings.
Luis Alicea, Boston, July 28, 1995.
Raul Casanova, Detroit, June 6, 1996.
J.T. Snow, California, June 9, 1996, 13 innings.
Ruben Sierra, New York, June 22, 1996.
Melvin Nieves, Detroit, July 15, 1996.
Roberto Alomar, Baltimore, July 25, 1996.
Roberto Alomar, Baltimore, August 14, 1996.
Melvin Nieves, Detroit, August 20, 1996.
Chili Davis, California, August 21, 1996.
Bernie Williams, New York, September 12, 1996.
Tony Clark, Detroit, April 5, 1997.
Chili Davis, Kansas City, June 7, 1997.
Jose Cruz Jr., Toronto, August 24, 1997, 13 innings.

David Segui, Seattle, April 1, 1998.
Tony Clark, Detroit, June 17, 1998.
Tony Clark, Detroit, July 26, 1998.
Tony Clark, Detroit, August 1, 1998.
Jorge Posada, New York, August 23, 1998.
Bernie Williams, New York, September 4, 1998.
Brian Simmons, Chicago, September 26, 1998.
Bernie Williams, New York, May 4, 1999.
Jorge Posada, New York, July 10, 1999.
Tony Clark, Detroit, July 18, 1999.
Tony Clark, Detroit, July 25, 1999.
Carl Everett, Boston, April 11, 2000.
Bernie Williams, New York, April 23, 2000.
Jorge Posada, New York, April 23, 2000.
Bernie Williams, New York, May 17, 2000.
Carlos Beltran, Kansas City, June 29, 2000.
Carl Everett, Boston, August 29, 2000.
Jose Valentin, Chicago, September 30, 2000.
Ruben Sierra, Texas, June 13, 2001.
Bernie Williams, New York, June 30, 2001.
Roberto Alomar, Cleveland, July 16, 2001.
Bernie Williams, New York, May 17, 2002, 14 innings.
Jorge Posada, New York, June 28, 2002.
Jose Valentin, Chicago, August 13, 2002.
Carlos Beltran, Kansas City, September 6, 2002.
Jeff DaVanon, Anaheim, June 3, 2003.
Jeff DaVanon, Anaheim, June 4, 2003.
Bill Mueller, Boston, July 4, 2003.
Bill Mueller, Boston, July 29, 2003.
Jose Valentin, Chicago, July 29, 2003.
Jorge Posada, New York, March 31, 2004.
Geoff Blum, Tampa Bay, May 4, 2004.
Carlos Guillen, Detroit, May 31, 2004.
Mark Texeira, Texas, July 4, 2004.
Victor Martinez, Cleveland, July 16, 2004 (2 righthanded, 1 lefthanded).
Carlos Guillen, Detroit, July 24, 2004.
Tony Clark, New York, August 28, 2004 (2 lefthanded, 1 righthanded).
Dmitri Young, Detroit, September 18, 2004, 12 innings.
Total number of occurrences: 119

N.L.—Augie Galan, Chicago, June 25, 1937.
Jim Russell, Boston, June 7, 1948.
Jim Russell, Brooklyn, July 26, 1950.
Red Schoendienst, St. Louis, July 8, 1951, second game.
Maury Wills, Los Angeles, May 30, 1962, first game.
Ellis Burton, Chicago, August 1, 1963.
Ellis Burton, Chicago, September 7, 1964, first game.
Jim Lefebvre, Los Angeles, May 7, 1966.
Wes Parker, Los Angeles, June 5, 1966, first game.
Pete Rose, Cincinnati, August 30, 1966.
Pete Rose, Cincinnati, August 2, 1967.
Ted Simmons, St. Louis, April 17, 1975.
Reggie Smith, St. Louis, May 4, 1975.
Reggie Smith, St. Louis, May 22, 1976 (2 righthanded, 1 lefthanded).
Lee Mazzilli, New York, September 3, 1978.
Ted Simmons, St. Louis, June 11, 1979.
Alan Ashby, Houston, September 27, 1982.
Chili Davis, San Francisco, June 5, 1983.
Mark Bailey, Houston, September 16, 1984.
Chili Davis, San Francisco, June 27, 1987.
Bobby Bonilla, Pittsburgh, July 3, 1987.
Kevin Bass, Houston, August 3, 1987, 13 innings.
Kevin Bass, Houston, September 2, 1987.
Chili Davis, San Francisco, September 15, 1987.
Bobby Bonilla, Pittsburgh, April 6, 1988, 14 innings.
Tim Raines Sr., Montreal, July 16, 1988.
Steve Jeltz, Philadelphia, June 8, 1989.
Kevin Bass, Houston, August 20, 1989.
Eddie Murray, Los Angeles, April 18, 1990.
Eddie Murray, Los Angeles, June 9, 1990.
Bret Barberie, Montreal, August 2, 1991.
Howard Johnson, New York, August 31, 1991.
Kevin Bass, San Francisco, August 2, 1992, second game.
Bobby Bonilla, New York, April 23, 1993.
Bobby Bonilla, New York, June 10, 1993.
Todd Benzinger, San Francisco, August 30, 1993.
Mark Whiten, St. Louis, September 14, 1993.
Geronimo Pena, St. Louis, April 17, 1994.
Bobby Bonilla, New York, May 4, 1994.
Todd Hundley, New York, June 18, 1994.

Ken Caminiti, Houston, July 3, 1994.
Bobby Bonilla, New York, May 12, 1995.
Ken Caminiti, San Diego, September 16, 1995.
Ken Caminiti, San Diego, September 17, 1995.
Ken Caminiti, San Diego, September 19, 1995.
Todd Hundley, New York, May 18, 1996.
Todd Hundley, New York, June 10, 1996.
Ken Caminiti, San Diego, August 1, 1996.
Ken Caminiti, San Diego, August 21, 1996.
Ken Caminiti, San Diego, August 28, 1996, 12 innings.
Ken Caminiti, San Diego, September 11, 1996.
Carl Everett, New York, April 20, 1997, first game.
Todd Hundley, New York, May 5, 1997.
F.P. Santangelo, Montreal, June 7, 1997.
Todd Hundley, New York, July 20, 1997.
Carl Everett, Houston, April 24, 1998.
Ken Caminiti, San Diego, July 12, 1998.
Chipper Jones, Atlanta, May 1, 1999.
Jose Valentin, Milwaukee, July 1, 1999.
Chipper Jones, Atlanta, August 1, 1999.
Carl Everett, Houston, August 7, 1999.
Dale Sveum, Pittsburgh, August 18, 1999.
Ken Caminiti, Houston, August 20, 1999.
Chipper Jones, Atlanta, September 21, 1999.
Chipper Jones, Atlanta, May 14, 2000.
Jose Vidro, Montreal, July 3, 2000.
Chipper Jones, Atlanta, July 5, 2000.
Geoff Blum, Montreal, July 5, 2001.
Tomas Perez, Philadelphia, July 24, 2001.
Mark Bellhorn, Chicago, June 30, 2002.
Mark Bellhorn, Chicago, August 29, 2002.
Tony Clark, New York, August 3, 2003.
Jose Reyes, New York, August 28, 2003.
Aaron Miles, Colorado, April 14, 2004.
Carlos Beltran, Houston, July 1, 2004, 10 innings.
Alex Citron, Arizona, July 8, 2004.
Total number of occurrences: 76

40 STOLEN BASES AND 40 HOMERS IN SEASON

AMERICAN LEAGUE

Player, Club	Year	G	SB	HR
Jose Canseco, Oakland	1988	158	40	42
Alex Rodriguez, Seattle	1998	161	46	42
Total number of occurrences: 2				

NATIONAL LEAGUE

Player, Club	Year	G	SB	HR
Barry Bonds, San Francisco	1996	158	40	42
Total number of occurrences: 1				

30 STOLEN BASES AND 30 HOMERS IN SEASON

AMERICAN LEAGUE

Player, Club	Year	G	SB	HR
Kenny Williams, St. Louis	1922	153	37	39
Tommy Harper, Milwaukee	1970	154	38	31
Bobby Bonds, New York	1975	145	30	32
Bobby Bonds, California	1977	158	41	37
Bobby Bonds, Chicago/Texas	1978	156	43	31
Joe Carter, Cleveland	1987	149	31	32
Jose Canseco, Oakland	1988	158	40	42
Alex Rodriguez, Seattle	1998	161	46	42
Shawn Green, Toronto	1998	158	35	35
Jose Cruz Jr., Toronto	2001	146	32	34
Alfonso Soriano, New York	2002	156	41	39
Alfonso Soriano, New York	2003	156	35	38
Total number of occurrences: 12				

NATIONAL LEAGUE

Player, Club	Year	G	SB	HR
Willie Mays, New York	1956	152	40	36
Willie Mays, New York	1957	152	38	35
Hank Aaron, Milwaukee	1963	161	31	44
Bobby Bonds, San Francisco	1969	158	45	32
Bobby Bonds, San Francisco	1973	160	43	39
Dale Murphy, Atlanta	1983	162	30	36
Eric Davis, Cincinnati	1987	129	50	37
Howard Johnson, New York	1987	157	32	36
Darryl Strawberry, New York	1987	154	36	39

Howard Johnson, New York	1989	153	41	36
Ron Gant, Atlanta	1990	152	33	32
Barry Bonds, Pittsburgh	1990	151	52	33
Ron Gant, Atlanta	1991	154	34	32
Howard Johnson, New York	1991	156	30	38
Barry Bonds, Pittsburgh	1992	140	39	34
Sammy Sosa, Chicago	1993	159	36	33
Sammy Sosa, Chicago	1995	144	34	36
Barry Bonds, San Francisco	1995	144	31	33
Dante Bichette, Colorado	1996	159	31	31
Barry Bonds, San Francisco	1996	158	40	42
Ellis Burks, Colorado	1996	156	32	40
Barry Larkin, Cincinnati	1996	152	36	33
Larry Walker, Colorado	1997	153	33	49
Jeff Bagwell, Houston	1997	162	31	43
Barry Bonds, San Francisco	1997	159	37	40
Raul Mondesi, Los Angeles	1997	159	32	30
Jeff Bagwell, Houston	1999	162	30	42
Raul Mondesi, Los Angeles	1999	159	36	33
Preston Wilson, Florida	2000	161	36	31
Vladimir Guerrero, Montreal	2001	159	37	34
Bobby Abreu, Philadelphia	2001	162	36	31
Vladimir Guerrero, Montreal	2002	161	40	39
Bobby Abreu, Philadelphia	2004	159	40	30

Total number of occurrences: 33

BOTH LEAGUES

Player, Club	Year	G	SB	HR
Carlos Beltran, KC/Hou	2004	159	42	38
KC 14/15, Hou 28/23				

20 STOLEN BASES AND 50 HOMERS IN SEASON

AMERICAN LEAGUE

Player, Club	Year	G	SB	HR
Brady Anderson, Baltimore	1996	149	21	50
Ken Griffey Jr., Seattle	1998	161	20	56

Total number of occurrences: 2

NATIONAL LEAGUE

Player, Club	Year	G	SB	HR
Willie Mays, New York	1955	152	24	51

Total number of occurrences: 1

50 STOLEN BASES AND 20 HOMERS IN SEASON

AMERICAN LEAGUE

Player, Club	Year	G	SB	HR
Rickey Henderson, New York	1985	143	80	24
Rickey Henderson, New York	1986	153	87	28
Rickey Henderson, Oakland	1990	136	65	28
Brady Anderson, Baltimore	1992	159	53	21
Rickey Henderson, Oak.-Tor.	1993	134	53	21

Total number of occurrences: 5

NATIONAL LEAGUE

Player, Club	Year	G	SB	HR
Lou Brock, St. Louis	1967	159	52	21
Cesar Cedeno, Houston	1972	139	55	22
Cesar Cedeno, Houston	1973	139	56	25
Joe Morgan, Cincinnati	1973	157	67	26
Cesar Cedeno, Houston	1974	160	57	26
Joe Morgan, Cincinnati	1974	149	58	22
Joe Morgan, Cincinnati	1976	141	60	27
Ryne Sandberg, Chicago	1985	153	54	26
Eric Davis, Cincinnati	1986	132	80	27
Eric Davis, Cincinnati	1987	129	50	37
Barry Bonds, Pittsburgh	1990	151	52	33
Craig Biggio, Houston	1998	160	50	20

Total number of occurrences: 12

400 TOTAL BASES IN SEASON

AMERICAN LEAGUE

Year	Player, Club	No.
1921	Babe Ruth, New York	457
1927	Lou Gehrig, New York	447
1932	Jimmie Foxx, Philadelphia	438

Year	Player, Club	No.
1930	Lou Gehrig, New York	419
1937	Joe DiMaggio, New York	418
1927	Babe Ruth, New York	417
1931	Lou Gehrig, New York	410
1934	Lou Gehrig, New York	409
1978	Jim Rice, Boston	406
1936	Hal Trosky, Cleveland	405
1936	Lou Gehrig, New York	403
1933	Jimmie Foxx, Philadelphia	403

Total number of occurrences: 12

NATIONAL LEAGUE

Year	Player, Club	No.
1922	Rogers Hornsby, St. Louis	450
1930	Chuck Klein, Philadelphia	445
1948	Stan Musial, St. Louis	429
2001	Sammy Sosa, Chicago	425
1930	Hack Wilson, Chicago	423
1932	Chuck Klein, Philadelphia	420
2001	Luis Gonzalez, Arizona	419
1930	Babe Herman, Brooklyn	416
1998	Sammy Sosa, Chicago	416
2001	Barry Bonds, San Francisco	411
1929	Rogers Hornsby, Chicago	409
1997	Larry Walker, Colorado	409
1937	Joe Medwick, St. Louis	406
1929	Chuck Klein, Philadelphia	405
2000	Todd Helton, Colorado	405
2001	Todd Helton, Colorado	402
1959	Hank Aaron, Milwaukee	400

Total number of occurrences: 17

100 EXTRA BASE HITS IN SEASON

AMERICAN LEAGUE

Year	Player, Club	2B	3B	HR	EBH
1921	Babe Ruth, New York	44	16	59	119
1927	Lou Gehrig, New York	52	18	47	117
1937	Hank Greenberg, Detroit	49	14	40	103
1995	Albert Belle, Cleveland	52	1	50	103
1930	Lou Gehrig, New York	42	17	41	100
1932	Jimmie Foxx, Philadelphia	33	9	58	100

Total number of occurrences: 6

NATIONAL LEAGUE

Year	Player, Club	2B	3B	HR	EBH
1930	Chuck Klein, Philadelphia	59	8	40	107
2001	Barry Bonds, San Francisco	32	2	73	107
2001	Todd Helton, Colorado	54	2	49	105
1932	Chuck Klein, Philadelphia	50	15	38	103
1948	Stan Musial, St. Louis	46	18	39	103
2000	Todd Helton, Colorado	59	2	42	103
2001	Sammy Sosa, Chicago	34	5	64	103
1922	Rogers Hornsby, St. Louis	46	14	42	102
2001	Luis Gonzalez, Arizona	36	7	57	100

Total number of occurrences: 9

PLAYERS HITTING FOR CYCLE

(single, double, triple and home run in game)

AMERICAN ASSOCIATION

Al Knight, Philadelphia, July 30, 1883.
John Reilly, Cincinnati, September 12, 1883.
John Reilly, Cincinnati, September 19, 1883.
Dave Orr, New York, June 12, 1885.
Henry Larkin, Philadelphia, June 16 ,1885.
Pete Browning, Louisville, August 8, 1886.
Jim McGarr, Philadelphia, September 23, 1886.
Tip O'Neill, St. Louis, April 30, 1887.
Tip O'Neill, St. Louis, May 7 ,1887.
Dave Orr, New York, August 10, 1887.
Bid McPhee, Cincinnati, August 26, 1887.
Harry Stovey, Philadelphia, May 15, 1888.
Sam Barkley, Kansas City, June 13, 1888.
Pete Browning, Louisville, June 7, 1889.
Bill Van Dyke, Toledo, July 5, 1890.
Jim Davis, Brooklyn, July 18, 1890.
Bill Weaver, Louisville, August 12, 1890.
Abner Dalrymple, Milwaukee, September 12, 1891.
Total number of occurrences: 18

PLAYERS LEAGUE

Roger Conner, New York, July 21, 1890.
Total number of occurrences: 1

AMERICAN LEAGUE

Harry Davis, Philadelphia, July 10, 1901.
Nap Lajoie, Philadelphia, July 30, 1901.
Patsy Dougherty, Boston, July 29, 1903.
Bill Bradley, Cleveland, September 24, 1903.
Otis Clymer, Washington, October 2, 1908.
Danny Murphy, Philadelphia, August 25, 1910.
Home Run Baker, Philadelphia, July 3, 1911, second game.
Tris Speaker, Boston, June 9, 1912.
Bert Daniels, New York, July 25, 1912.
George Sisler, St. Louis, August 8, 1920, second game.
Bobby Veach, Detroit, September 17, 1920, 12 innings.
Bob Meusel, New York, May 7, 1921.
George Sisler, St. Louis, August 13, 1921, 10 innings.
Ray Schalk, Chicago, June 27, 1922.
Bob Meusel, New York, July 3, 1922.
Bill Jacobson, St. Louis, April 17, 1924.
Goose Goslin, Washington, August 28, 1924.
Roy Carlyle, Boston, July 21, 1925, first game.
Bob Fothergill, Detroit, September 26, 1926, first game.
Bob Meusel, New York, July 26, 1928, first game, 12 innings.
Oscar Melillo, St. Louis, May 23, 1929, second game.
Joe Cronin, Washington, September 2, 1929, first game.
Tony Lazzeri, New York, June 3, 1932.
Mickey Cochrane, Philadelphia, July 22, 1932.
Mickey Cochrane, Philadelphia, August 2, 1933.
Pinky Higgins, Philadelphia, August 6, 1933.
Jimmie Foxx, Philadelphia, August 14, 1933.
Earl Averill, Cleveland, August 17, 1933.
Doc Cramer, Philadelphia, June 10, 1934.
Lou Gehrig, New York, June 25, 1934.
Moose Solters, Boston, August 19, 1934, first game.
Gee Walker, Detroit, April 20, 1937.
Joe DiMaggio, New York, July 9, 1937.
Lou Gehrig, New York, August 1, 1937.
Odell Hale, Cleveland, July 12, 1938.
Sam Chapman, Philadelphia, May 5, 1939.
Charlie Gehringer, Detroit, May 27, 1939.
Buddy Rosar, New York, July 19, 1940.
Joe Cronin, Boston, August 2, 1940.
Joe Gordon, New York, September 8, 1940.
George McQuinn, St. Louis, July 19, 1941, first game.
Leon Culberson, Boston, July 3, 1943.
Bobby Doerr, Boston, May 17, 1944, second game.
Bob Johnson, Boston, July 6, 1944.
Mickey Vernon, Washington, May 19, 1946, second game.
Ted Williams, Boston, July 21, 1946, second game.
Bobby Doerr, Boston, May 13, 1947.
Vic Wertz , Detroit, September 14, 1947, first game.
Joe DiMaggio, New York, May 20, 1948.
George Kell, Detroit, June 2, 1950, second game.
Elmer Valo, Philadelphia, August 2, 1950.
Hoot Evers, Detroit, September 7, 1950, 10 innings.
Larry Doby, Cleveland, June 4, 1952.
Mickey Mantle, New York, July 23, 1957.
Brooks Robinson, Baltimore, July 15, 1960.
Lu Clinton, Boston, July 13, 1962, 15 innings.
Jim King, Washington, May 26, 1964.
Jim Fregosi, Los Angeles, July 28, 1964.
Carl Yastrzemski, Boston, May 14, 1965, 10 innings.
Jim Fregosi, California, May 20, 1968, 11 innings.
Rod Carew, Minnesota, May 20, 1970.
Tony Horton, Cleveland, July 2, 1970.
Fred Patek, Kansas City, July 9, 1971.
Bobby Murcer, New York, August 29, 1972, first game, 11 innings.
Cesar Tovar, Minnesota, September 19, 1972.
Larry Hisle, Minnesota, June 4, 1976, 10 innings.
Lyman Bostock, Minnesota, July 24, 1976.
Mike Hegan, Milwaukee, September 3, 1976.
John Mayberry, Kansas City, August 5, 1977.
Jack Brohamer, Chicago, September 24, 1977.
Andre Thornton, Cleveland, April 22, 1978.
Mike Cubbage, Minnesota, July 27, 1978.
George Brett, Kansas City, May 28, 1979, 16 innings.
Dan Ford, California, August 10, 1979, 14 innings.
Bob Watson, Boston, September 15, 1979.
Frank White, Kansas City, September 26, 1979.
Fred Lynn, Boston, May 13, 1980.

Gary Ward, Minnesota, September 18, 1980, first game.
Charlie Moore, Milwaukee, October 1, 1980.
Frank White, Kansas City, August 3, 1982.
Cal Ripken, Baltimore, May 6, 1984.
Carlton Fisk, Chicago, May 16, 1984.
Dwight Evans, Boston, June 28, 1984, 11 innings.
Oddibe McDowell, Texas, July 23, 1985.
Rich Gedman, Boston, September 18, 1985.
Tony Phillips, Oakland, May 16, 1986.
Kirby Puckett, Minnesota, August 1, 1986.
Robin Yount, Milwaukee, June 12, 1988.
Mike Greenwell, Boston, September 14, 1988.
Kelly Gruber, Toronto, April 16, 1989.
George Brett, Kansas City, July 25, 1990.
Paul Molitor, Milwaukee, May 15, 1991.
Dave Winfield, California, June 24, 1991.
Jay Buhner, Seattle, June 23, 1993, 14 innings.
Travis Fryman, Detroit, July 28, 1993.
Scott Cooper, Boston, April 12, 1994.
Tony Fernandez, New York, September 3, 1995, 10 innings.
John Valentin, Boston, June 6, 1996.
Alex Rodriguez, Seattle, June 5, 1997.
Mike Blowers, Oakland, May 18, 1998.
Chris Singleton, Chicago, July 6, 1999, 10 innings.
Jose Valentin, Chicago, April 27, 2000.
Eric Chavez, Oakland, June 21, 2000.
Damion Easley, Detroit, June 8, 2001.
John Olerud, Seattle, June 16, 2001.
Jeff Frye, Toronto, August 17, 2001.
Miguel Tejada, Oakland, September 29, 2001.
Eric Byrnes, Oakland, June 29, 2003.
Travis Hafner, Cleveland, August 14, 2003.
Mark Texeira, Texas, August 17, 2004.
Jeff DeVanon, Anaheim, August 25, 2004.
Total number of occurrences: 111

NATIONAL LEAGUE

Charles Foley, Buffalo, May 25, 1882.
Jim O'Rourke, Buffalo, June 16, 1884.
George Wood, Detroit, June 13, 1885.
Bill McQuery, Detroit, September 28, 1885.
Fred Dunlap, St. Louis, May 24, 1886.
John Rowe, Detroit, August 21, 1886.
Fred Carroll, Pittsburgh, May 2, 1887.
Jimmy Ryan, Chicago, July 28, 1888.
Mike Tiernan, New York, August 25, 1888.
John Glasscock, Indianapolis, August 8, 1889.
Larry Twitchell, Cleveland, August 15, 1889.
Tom Burns, Brooklyn, August 1, 1890, second game.
John Reilly, Cincinnati, August 6, 1890.
Jimmy Ryan, Chicago, July 1, 1891.
Lave Cross, Philadelphia, April 24, 1894.
Bill Hassamaer, Washington, June 13, 1894.
Sam Thompson, Philadelphia, August 17, 1894.
Tom Parrett, Cincinnati, September 28, 1894.
Tom Dowd, St. Louis, August 16,1895.
Ed Cartwright, Washington, September 30, 1895, first game.
Herman Long, Boston, May 9, 1896.
Bill Joyce, Washington, May 30, 1896, first game.
Fred Clarke, Pittsburgh, July 23, 1901.
Fred Clarke, Pittsburgh, May 7, 1903.
Rich Cooley, Boston, June 20, 1904, second game.
Sam Mertes, New York, October 4, 1904, first game.
John Bates, Boston, April 26, 1907.
Chief Wilson, Pittsburgh, July 3, 1910.
Bill Collins, Boston, October 6, 1910.
Mike Mitchell, Cincinnati, August 19, 1911, second game.
Chief Meyers, New York, June 10, 1912.
Honus Wagner, Pittsburgh, August 22, 1912, second game.
Heinie Groh, Cincinnati, July 5, 1915, second game.
Cliff Heathcote, St. Louis, June 13, 1918, 19 innings.
George Burns, New York, September 17, 1920, 10 innings.
Dave Bancroft, New York, June 1, 1921, second game.
Dave Robertson, Pittsburgh, August 30, 1921.
Ross Youngs, New York, April 29, 1922.
Jimmy Johnston, Brooklyn, May 25, 1922, first game.
Pie Traynor, Pittsburgh, July 7, 1923.
Kiki Cuyler, Pittsburgh, June 4, 1925.
Max Carey, Pittsburgh, June 20, 1925.
Jim Bottomley, St. Louis, July 15, 1927.
Cy Williams, Philadelphia, August 5, 1927.
Bill Terry, New York, May 29, 1928.
Mel Ott, New York, May 16, 1929, second game.
Fred Lindstrom, New York, May 8, 1930.

Hack Wilson, Chicago, June 23, 1930.
Chick Hafey, St. Louis, August 21, 1930.
Babe Herman, Brooklyn, May 18, 1931.
Chuck Klein, Philadelphia, July 1, 1931.
Babe Herman, Brooklyn, July 24, 1931.
Pepper Martin, St. Louis, May 5, 1933.
Chuck Klein, Philadelphia, May 26, 1933, 14 innings.
Arky Vaughan, Pittsburgh, June 24, 1933.
Babe Herman, Chicago, September 30, 1933.
Joe Medwick, St. Louis, June 29, 1935.
Sam Leslie, New York, May 24, 1936.
Arky Vaughan, Pittsburgh, July 19, 1939.
Harry Craft, Cincinnati, June 8, 1940.
Harry Danning, New York, June 15, 1940.
Johnny Mize, St. Louis, July 13, 1940, first game.
Dixie Walker, Brooklyn, September 2, 1944.
Bob Elliott, Pittsburgh, July 15, 1945, second game.
Bill Salkeld, Pittsburgh, August 4, 1945.
Wally Westlake, Pittsburgh, July 30, 1948.
Jackie Robinson, Brooklyn, August 29, 1948, first game.
Wally Westlake, Pittsburgh, June 14, 1949.
Gil Hodges, Brooklyn, June 25, 1949.
Stan Musial, St. Louis, July 24, 1949.
Ralph Kiner, Pittsburgh, June 25, 1950.
Roy Smalley, Chicago, June 28, 1950.
Gus Bell, Pittsburgh, June 4, 1951.
Don Mueller, New York, July 11, 1954, first game.
Lee Walls, Chicago, July 2, 1957, 10 innings.
Frank Robinson, Cincinnati, May 2, 1959.
Bill White, St. Louis, August 14, 1960, first game.
Ken Boyer, St. Louis, September 14, 1961, second game, 11 innings.
Johnny Callison, Philadelphia, June 27, 1963.
Jim Hickman, New York, August 7, 1963.
Ken Boyer, St. Louis, June 16, 1964.
Willie Stargell, Pittsburgh, July 22, 1964.
Billy Williams, Chicago, July 17, 1966, second game.
Randy Hundley, Chicago, August 11, 1966, first game, 11 innings.
Wes Parker, Los Angeles, May 7, 1970, 10 innings.
Tommie Agee, New York, July 6, 1970.
Jim Hart, San Francisco, July 8, 1970.
Dave Kingman, San Francisco, April 16, 1972.
Cesar Cedeno, Houston, August 2, 1972.
Joe Torre, St. Louis, June 27, 1973.
Richie Zisk, Pittsburgh, June 9, 1974.
Lou Brock, St. Louis, May 27, 1975.

Tim Foli, Montreal, April 21, 1976, suspended game completed April 22.
Mike Phillips, New York, June 25, 1976.
Cesar Cedeno, Houston, August 9, 1976.
Bob Watson, Houston, June 24, 1977, 11 innings.
Chris Speier, Montreal, July 20, 1978.
Ivan DeJesus, Chicago, April 22, 1980.
Mike Easler, Pittsburgh, June 12, 1980.
Willie McGee, St. Louis, June 23, 1984, 11 innings.
Jeff Leonard, San Francisco, June 27, 1985.
Keith Hernandez, New York, July 4, 1985, 19 innings.
Andre Dawson, Chicago, April 29, 1987.
Candy Maldonado, San Francisco, May 4, 1987.
Tim Raines Sr., Montreal, August 16, 1987.
Albert Hall, Atlanta, September 23, 1987.
Chris Speier, San Francisco, July 9, 1988.
Eric Davis, Cincinnati, June 2, 1989.
Kevin McReynolds, New York, August 1, 1989.
Gary Redus, Pittsburgh, August 25, 1989.
Robby Thompson, San Francisco, April 22, 1991.
Ray Lankford, St. Louis, September 15, 1991.
Andujar Cedeno, Houston, August 25, 1992.
Mark Grace, Chicago, May 9, 1993.
Rondell White, Montreal, June 11, 1995, 13 innings.
Gregg Jefferies, Philadelphia, August 25, 1995.
John Mabry, St. Louis, May 18, 1996.
Alex Ochoa, New York, July 3, 1996.
John Olerud, New York, September 11, 1997.
Dante Bichette, Colorado, June 10, 1998.
Neifi Perez, Colorado, July 25, 1998.
Jeff Kent, San Francisco, May 3, 1999.
Todd Helton, Colorado, June 19, 1999.
Jason Kendall, Pittsburgh, May 19, 2000.
Mike Lansing, Colorado, June 18, 2000.
Luis Gonzalez, Arizona, July 5, 2000.
Jeff Bagwell, Houston, July 18, 2001.
Craig Biggio, Houston, April 8, 2002.
Greg Colbrunn, Arizona, September 18, 2002.
Brad Wilkerson, Montreal, June 24, 2003.
Vladimir Guerrero, Montreal, September 14, 2003.
Chad Moeller, Milwaukee, April 27, 2004.
David Bell, Philadelphia, June 28, 2004.
Daryle Ward, Pittsburgh, May 26, 2004.
Eric Valent, New York, July 29, 2004.
Total number of occurrences: 135

SIX HITS IN ONE GAME

AMERICAN ASSOCIATION

Player	Club, Date	Place	AB	R	H	2B	3B	HR
Hick Carpenter	Cincinnati, September 12, 1883	H	7	5	6	0	0	0
John Reilly	Cincinnati, September 12, 1883	H	7	6	6	1	1	1
Oscar Walker	Brooklyn, May 31, 1884	H	6	2	6	1	1	0
Lon Knight	Philadelphia, July 30, 1884	H	6	5	6	0	1	0
Dave Orr	New York, June 12, 1885	H	6	4	6	2	1	1
Henry Larkin	Philadelphia, June 16, 1885	H	6	4	6	2	1	1
George Pinckney	Brooklyn, June 25, 1885	H	6	5	6	0	0	0
Arlie Latham	St. Louis, April 24, 1886	H	6	5	6	0	1	0
Guy Hecker	Louisville, August 15, 1886†	H	7	7	6	0	0	3
Denny Lyons	Philadelphia, April 26, 1887	H	6	4	6	2	1	0
Pete Hotaling	Cleveland, June 6, 1888	H	7	5	6	0	1	0
Jim McTamany	Kansas City, June 15, 1888	H	6	3	6	0	0	1
Darby O'Brien	Brooklyn, August 8, 1889	A	6	1	6	3	0	0
Farmer Weaver	Louisville, August 12, 1890	H	6	3	6	1	2	1
Frank Sheibeck	Toledo, September 27, 1890	H	6	4	6	1	1	0
Reddy Mack	Louisville, May 26, 1887	H	6	5	6	0	0	0

†Pitcher.
Total number of occurrences: 16

PLAYERS LEAGUE

Player	Club, Date	Place	AB	R	H	2B	3B	HR
Ed Delahanty	Cleveland, June 2, 1890	H	6	4	6	1	1	0
Bill Shindle	Philadelphia, August 26, 1890	H	6	3	6	2	1	0

Total number of occurrences: 2

AMERICAN LEAGUE

Player	Club, Date	Place	AB	R	H	2B	3B	HR
Mike Donlin	Baltimore, June 24, 1901	H	6	5	6	2	2	0
Doc Nance	Detroit, July 13, 1901	H	6	3	6	1	0	0

Player	Club, Date	Place	AB	R	H	2B	3B	HR
Erwin Harvey	Cleveland, April 25, 1902	A	6	3	6	0	0	0
Danny Murphy	Philadelphia, July 8, 1902	A	6	3	6	0	0	1
Jimmy Williams	Baltimore, August 25, 1902	H	6	1	6	1	1	0
Bobby Veach	Detroit, September 17, 1920, 12 innings	H	6	2	6	1	1	1
George Sisler	St. Louis, August 9, 1921, 19 innings	A	9	2	6	0	1	0
Frank Brower	Cleveland, August 7, 1923	A	6	3	6	1	0	0
George Burns	Cleveland, June 19, 1924, first game	A	6	2	6	3	1	0
Ty Cobb	Detroit, May 5, 1925	A	6	4	6	1	0	3
Jimmie Foxx	Philadelphia, May 30, 1930, first game, 13 innings	H	7	0	6	2	1	0
Roger Cramer	Philadelphia, June 20, 1932	A	6	3	6	0	0	0
Jimmie Foxx	Philadelphia, July 10, 1932, 18 innings	A	9	4	6	1	0	3
Johnny Burnett	Cleveland, July 10, 1932, 18 innings	H	11	4	9	2	0	0
Sam West	St. Louis, April 13, 1933, 11 innings	H	6	2	6	1	0	0
Myril Hoag	New York, June 6, 1934, first game	A	6	3	6	0	0	0
Bob Johnson	Philadelphia, June 16, 1934, second game, 11 innings	A	6	3	6	1	0	2
Roger Cramer	Philadelphia, July 13, 1935, first game	A	6	3	6	1	0	0
Bruce Campbell	Cleveland, July 2, 1936, first game	A	6	1	6	1	0	0
Ray Radcliff	Chicago, July 18, 1936, second game	A	7	4	6	2	0	0
Henry Steinbacher	Chicago, June 22, 1938	H	6	3	6	1	0	0
George Myatt	Washington, May 1, 1944	A	6	3	6	1	0	0
Stan Spence	Washington, June 1, 1944	A	6	2	6	0	0	1
George Kell	Detroit, September 20, 1946	A	7	4	6	1	0	0
Jim Fridley	Cleveland, April 29, 1952	A	6	4	6	0	0	0
Jimmy Piersall	Boston, June 10, 1953, first game	A	6	2	6	1	0	0
Joe DeMaestri	Kansas City, July 8, 1955, 11 innings	A	6	2	6	0	0	0
Pete Runnels	Boston, August 30, 1960, first game, 15 innings	H	7	1	6	1	0	0
Rocky Colavito	Detroit, June 24, 1962, 22 innings	A	10	1	7	0	1	0
Floyd Robinson	Chicago, July 22, 1962	A	6	1	6	0	0	0
Bob Oliver	Kansas City, May 4, 1969	A	6	2	6	1	0	1
Jim Northrup	Detroit, August 28, 1969, 13 innings	H	6	2	6	0	0	0
Cesar Gutierrez	Detroit, June 21, 1970, second game, 12 innings	A	7	3	7	1	0	0
John Briggs	Milwaukee, August 4, 1973	A	6	2	6	2	0	0
Jorge Orta	Cleveland, June 15, 1980	H	6	4	6	1	0	0
Jerry Remy	Boston, September 3, 1981, 20 innings	H	10	2	6	0	0	0
Kevin Seitzer	Kansas City, August 2, 1987	H	6	4	6	1	0	2
Kirby Puckett	Minnesota, August 30, 1987	A	6	4	6	2	0	2
Kirby Puckett	Minnesota, May 23, 1991, 11 innings	H	7	2	6	0	1	0
Carlos Baerga	Cleveland, April 11, 1992, 19 innings	H	9	1	6	0	0	0
Kevin Reimer	Milwaukee, August 24, 1993, second game	H	6	4	6	2	0	0
Lance Johnson	Chicago, September 23, 1995	A	6	4	6	0	3	0
Gerald Williams	New York, May 1, 1996, 15 innings	A	8	1	6	0	0	1
Garret Anderson	California, September 27, 1996, 15 innings	A	7	0	6	0	0	0
Cal Ripken Jr.	Baltimore, June 13, 1999	A	6	5	6	1	0	2
Damion Easley	Detroit, August 8, 2001	A	6	3	6	0	0	1
Nomar Garciaparra	Boston, June 21, 2003, 13 innings	A	6	1	6	0	0	0
Frank Catalanotto	Toronto, May 1, 2004	A	6	2	6	1	0	0
Alfonso Soriano	Texas, May 8, 2004, 10 innings	H	6	1	6	2	0	0
Carlos Pena	Detroit, May 27, 2004	A	6	4	6	1	0	2
Omar Vizquel	Cleveland, August 31, 2004	A	7	3	6	2	0	0
Joe Randa	Kansas City, September 9, 2004	A	7	6	6	1	0	0
Raul Ibanez	Seattle, September 22, 2004	A	6	1	6	0	0	0

Total number of occurrences: 53

NATIONAL LEAGUE

Player	Club, Date	Place	AB	R	H	2B	3B	HR
David Force	Philadelphia, June 27, 1876	H	6	3	6	1	0	0
Cal McVey	Chicago, July 22, 1876	H	7	4	6	1	0	0
Cal McVey	Chicago, July 25, 1876	H	7	4	6	1	0	0
Ross Barnes	Chicago, July 27, 1876	H	6	3	6	1	1	0
Paul Hines	Providence, August 26, 1879, 10 innings	H	6	1	6	0	0	0
George Gore	Chicago, May 7, 1880	H	6	5	6	0	0	0
Lew Dickerson	Worcester, June 16, 1881	H	6	3	6	0	1	0
Sam Wise	Boston, June 20, 1883	H	7	5	6	1	1	0
Dennis Brouthers	Buffalo, July 19, 1883	H	6	3	6	2	0	0
Danny Richardson	New York, June 11, 1887	H	7	2	6	0	0	0
King Kelly	Boston, August 27, 1887	H	7	6	6	1	0	1
Jerry Denny	Indianapolis, May 4, 1889	H	6	3	6	1	0	1
Larry Twitchell	Cleveland, August 15, 1889	H	6	5	6	1	3	1
John Glasscock	New York, September 27, 1890	A	6	2	6	0	0	0
Bobby Lowe	Boston, June 11, 1891	H	6	4	6	1	0	1
Henry Larkin	Washington, June 7, 1892	H	7	3	6	0	1	0
Wilbert Robinson	Baltimore, June 10, 1892, first game	H	7	1	7	1	0	0
John Boyle	Philadelphia, July 6, 1893, 11 innings	A	6	1	6	1	0	0
Duff Cooley	St. Louis, September 30, 1893, second game	A	6	1	6	1	1	0
Ed Delahanty	Philadelphia, June 16, 1894	H	6	4	6	1	0	0
Steve Brodie	Baltimore, July 9, 1894	H	6	2	6	2	1	0
Chief Zimmer	Cleveland, July 11, 1894, 10 innings	H	6	3	6	2	0	0
Sam Thompson	Philadelphia, August 17, 1894	H	7	4	6	1	1	1
Roger Connor	St. Louis, June 1, 1895	A	6	4	6	2	1	0
George Davis	New York, August 15, 1895	H	6	3	6	2	1	0
Jacob Stenzel	Pittsburgh, May 14, 1896	H	6	3	6	0	0	0
Fred Tenney	Boston, May 31, 1897	H	8	3	6	1	0	0
Dick Harley	St. Louis, June 24, 1897, 12 innings	H	6	2	6	1	0	0
Barry McCormick	Chicago, June 29, 1897	H	8	5	6	0	1	1

Player	Club, Date	Place	AB	R	H	2B	3B	HR
Tommy Tucker	Washington, July 15, 1897	A	6	1	6	1	0	0
Willie Keeler	Baltimore, September 3, 1897	H	6	5	6	0	1	0
Jack Doyle	Baltimore, September 3, 1897	H	6	2	6	2	0	0
Chick Stahl	Boston, May 31, 1899	H	6	4	6	0	0	0
Ginger Beaumont	Pittsburgh, July 22, 1899	H	6	6	6	0	0	0
Kip Selbach	New York, June 9, 1901	A	7	4	6	2	0	0
George Cutshaw	Brooklyn, August 9, 1915	A	6	2	6	0	0	0
Carson Bigbee	Pittsburgh, August 22, 1917, 22 innings	A	11	0	6	0	0	0
Dave Bancroft	New York, June 28, 1920	A	6	2	6	0	0	0
Johnny Gooch	Pittsburgh, July 7, 1922, 18 innings	H	8	1	6	1	0	0
Max Carey	Pittsburgh, July 7, 1922, 18 innings	H	6	3	6	1	0	0
Jack Fournier	Brooklyn, June 29, 1923	A	6	1	6	2	0	1
Kiki Cuyler	Pittsburgh, August 9, 1924, first game	A	6	3	6	3	1	0
Frankie Frisch	New York, September 10, 1924, first game	A	7	3	6	0	0	1
Jim Bottomley	St. Louis, September 16, 1924	A	6	3	6	1	0	2
Paul Waner	Pittsburgh, August 26, 1926	H	6	1	6	2	1	0
Lloyd Waner	Pittsburgh, June 15, 1929, 14 innings	H	8	2	6	1	1	0
Hank DeBerry	Brooklyn, June 23, 1929, 14 innings	H	7	0	6	0	0	0
Wally Gilbert	Brooklyn, May 30, 1931, second game	A	7	3	6	1	0	0
Jim Bottomley	St. Louis, August 5, 1931, second game	A	6	2	6	1	0	0
Tony Cuccinello	Cincinnati, August 13, 1931, first game	A	6	4	6	2	1	0
Terry Moore	St. Louis, September 5, 1935	H	6	2	6	1	0	0
Ernie Lombardi	Cincinnati, May 9, 1937	A	6	3	6	1	0	0
Frank Demaree	Chicago, July 5, 1937, first game, 14 innings	H	7	2	6	3	0	0
Cookie Lavagetto	Brooklyn, September 23, 1939, first game	A	6	4	6	1	1	0
Walker Cooper	Cincinnati, July 6, 1949	H	7	5	6	0	0	3
Johnny Hopp	Pittsburgh, May 14, 1950, second game	A	6	3	6	0	0	2
Connie Ryan	Philadelphia, April 16, 1953	A	6	3	6	2	0	0
Dick Groat	Pittsburgh, May 13, 1960	A	6	2	6	3	0	0
Jesus Alou	San Francisco, July 10, 1964	A	6	1	6	0	0	1
Joe Morgan	Houston, July 8, 1965, 12 innings	A	6	4	6	0	1	2
Felix Millan	Atlanta, July 6, 1970	H	6	2	6	1	1	0
Don Kessinger	Chicago, June 17, 1971, 10 innings	H	6	3	6	1	0	0
Willie Davis	Los Angeles, May 24, 1973, 19 innings	H	9	1	6	0	0	0
Bill Madlock	Chicago, July 26, 1975, 10 innings	H	6	1	6	0	1	0
Rennie Stennett	Pittsburgh, September 16, 1975	A	7	5	7	2	1	0
Jose Cardenal	Chicago, May 2, 1976, first game, 14 innings	A	7	2	6	1	0	1
Gene Richards	San Diego, July 26, 1977, second game, 15 innings	H	7	1	6	1	0	0
Joe Lefebvre	San Diego, September 13, 1982, 16 innings	A	8	1	6	1	0	1
Wally Backman	Pittsburgh, April 27, 1990	A	6	1	6	1	0	0
Sammy Sosa	Chicago, July 2, 1993	A	6	2	6	1	0	0
Tony Gwynn	San Diego, August 4, 1993, 12 innings	H	7	2	6	2	0	0
Rondell White	Montreal, June 11, 1995, 13 innings	A	7	5	6	2	1	1
Mike Benjamin	San Francisco, June 14, 1995, 13 innings	A	7	0	6	1	0	0
Andres Galarraga	Colorado, July 3, 1995	H	6	4	6	1	0	2
Edgardo Alfonzo	New York, August 30, 1999	A	6	6	6	1	0	3
Paul Lo Duca	Los Angeles, May 28, 2001, 11 innings	H	6	3	6	0	0	1
Shawn Green	Los Angeles, May 23, 2002	A	6	6	6	1	0	4

Total number of occurrences: 77

BARRY BONDS' 73 HOME RUNS—2001

HR No.	Team game No.	Date		Opposing pitcher, Club	Place	Inning	On base
1.	1	April	2	Woody Williams (righthander), San Diego	H	5	0
2.	9	April	12	Adam Eaton (righthander), San Diego	A	4	0
3.	10	April	13	Jamey Wright (righthander), Milwaukee	A	1	1
4.	11	April	14	Jimmy Haynes (righthander), Milwaukee	A	5	2
5.	12	April	15	Dave Weathers (righthander), Milwaukee	A	8	0
6.	13	April	17	Terry Adams (righthander), Los Angeles	H	8	1
7.	14	April	18	Chan Ho Park (righthander), Los Angeles	H	7	0
8.	16	April	20	Jimmy Haynes (righthander), Milwaukee	H	4	1
9.	19	April	24	Jim Brower (righthander), Cincinnati	H	3	1
10.	21	April	26	Scott Sullivan (righthander), Cincinnati	H	8	1
11.	24	April	29	Manny Aybar (righthander), Chicago N.L.	H	4	0
12.	26	May	2	Todd Ritchie (righthander), Pittsburgh	A	5	1
13.	27	May	3	Jimmy Anderson (lefthander), Pittsburgh	A	1	1
14.	28	May	4	Bruce Chen (lefthander), Philadelphia	A	6	1
15.	35	May	11	Steve Trachsel (righthander), New York N.L.	H	4	0
16.	40	May	17	Chuck Smith (righthander), Florida	A	3	1
17.	41	May	18	Mike Remlinger (lefthander), Atlanta	A	8	0
18.	42	May	19	Odalis Perez (lefthander), Atlanta	A	3	0
19.	42	May	19	Jose Cabrera (righthander), Atlanta	A	7	0
20.	42	May	19	Jason Marquis (righthander), Atlanta	A	8	0
21.	43	May	20	John Burkett (righthander), Atlanta	A	1	0
22.	43	May	20	Mike Remlinger (lefthander), Atlanta	A	7	0
23.	44	May	21	Curt Schilling (righthander), Arizona	A	4	0
24.	45	May	22	Russ Springer (righthander), Arizona	A	9	1
25.	47	May	24	John Thomson (righthander), Colorado	H	3	0
26.	50	May	27	Denny Neagle (lefthander), Colorado	H	1	1
27.	53	May	30	Robert Ellis (righthander), Arizona	H	2	0
28.	53	May	30	Robert Ellis (righthander), Arizona	H	6	1

HR No.	Team game No.	Date		Opposing pitcher, Club	Place	Inning	On base
29.	54	June	1	Shawn Chacon (righthander), Colorado	A	3	1
30.	57	June	4	Bobby J. Jones (righthander), San Diego	H	4	0
31.	58	June	5	Wascar Serrano (righthander), San Diego	H	3	1
32.	60	June	7	Brian Lawrence (righthander), San Diego	H	7	1
33.	64	June	12	Pat Rapp (righthander), Anaheim	H	1	0
34.	66	June	14	Lou Pote (righthander), Anaheim	H	6	0
35.	67	June	15	Mark Mulder (lefthander), Oakland	H	1	0
36.	67	June	15	Mark Mulder (lefthander), Oakland	H	6	0
37.	70	June	19	Adam Eaton (righthander), San Diego	A	5	0
38.	71	June	20	Rodney Myers (righthander), San Diego	A	8	1
39.	74	June	23	Darryl Kile (righthander), St. Louis	A	1	1
40.	89	July	12	Paul Abbott (righthander), Seattle	A	1	0
41.	95	July	18	Mike Hampton (lefthander), Colorado	H	4	0
42.	95	July	18	Mike Hampton (lefthander), Colorado	H	5	1
43.	103	July	26	Curt Schilling (righthander), Arizona	A	4	0
44.	103	July	26	Curt Schilling (righthander), Arizona	A	5	3
45.	104	July	27	Brian Anderson (lefthander), Arizona	A	4	0
46.	108	Aug.	1	Joe Beimel (lefthander), Pittsburgh	H	1	0
47.	111	Aug.	4	Nelson Figueroa (righthander), Philadelphia	H	6	1
48.	113	Aug.	7	Danny Graves (righthander), Cincinnati	A	11	0
49.	115	Aug.	9	Scott Winchester (righthander), Cincinnati	A	3	0
50.	117	Aug.	11	Joe Borowski (righthander), Chicago N.L.	A	2	2
51.	119	Aug.	14	Ricky Bones (righthander), Florida	H	6	3
52.	121	Aug.	16	A.J. Burnett (righthander), Florida	H	4	0
53.	121	Aug.	16	Vic Darensbourg (lefthander), Florida	H	8	2
54.	123	Aug.	18	Jason Marquis (righthander), Atlanta	H	8	0
55.	127	Aug.	23	Graeme Lloyd (lefthander), Montreal	H	9	0
56.	131	Aug.	27	Kevin Appier (righthander), New York N.L.	A	5	0
57.	135	Aug.	31	John Thomson (righthander), Colorado	H	8	1
58.	138	Sept.	3	Jason Jennings (righthander), Colorado	H	4	0
59.	139	Sept.	4	Miguel Batista (righthander), Arizona	H	7	0
60.	141	Sept.	6	Albie Lopez (righthander), Arizona	H	2	0
61.	144	Sept.	9	Scott Elarton (righthander), Colorado	A	1	0
62.	144	Sept.	9	Scott Elarton (righthander), Colorado	A	5	0
63.	144	Sept.	9	Todd Belitz (lefthander), Colorado	A	11	2
64.	147	Sept.	20	Wade Miller (righthander), Houston	H	5	1
65.	150	Sept.	23	Jason Middlebrook (righthander), San Diego	A	2	0
66.	150	Sept.	23	Jason Middlebrook (righthander), San Diego	A	4	0
67.	151	Sept.	24	James Baldwin (righthander), Los Angeles	H	7	0
68.	154	Sept.	28	Jason Middlebrook (righthander), San Diego	A	2	0
69.	155	Sept.	29	Chuck McElroy (lefthander), San Diego	H	6	0
70.	159	Oct.	4	Wilfredo Rodriguez (lefthander), Houston	A	9	0
71.	160	Oct.	5	Chan Ho Park (righthander), Los Angeles	H	1	0
72.	160	Oct.	5	Chan Ho Park (righthander), Los Angeles	H	3	0
73.	162	Oct.	7	Dennis Springer (righthander), Los Angeles	H	1	0

Bonds played in 153 games.

MARK McGWIRE'S 70 HOME RUNS—1998

HR No.	Team game No.	Date		Opposing pitcher, Club	Place	Inning	On base
1.	1	March	31	Ramon Martinez (righthander), Los Angeles	H	5	3
2.	2	April	2	Frank Lankford (righthander), Los Angeles	H	12	2
3.	3	April	3	Mark Langston (lefthander), San Diego	H	5	1
4.	4	April	4	Don Wengert (righthander), San Diego	H	6	2
5.	13	April	14	Jeff Suppan (righthander), Arizona	H	3	1
6.	13	April	14	Jeff Suppan (righthander), Arizona	H	5	0
7.	13	April	14	Barry Manuel (righthander), Arizona	H	8	1
8.	16	April	17	Matt Whiteside (righthander), Philadelphia	H	4	1
9.	19	April	21	Trey Moore (lefthander), Montreal	A	3	1
10.	23	April	25	Jerry Spradlin (righthander), Philadelphia	A	7	1
11.	27	April	30	Marc Pisciotta (righthander), Chicago N.L.	A	8	1
12.	28	May	1	Rod Beck (righthander), Chicago N.L.	A	9	1
13.	34	May	8	Rick Reed (righthander), New York N.L.	A	3	1
14.	36	May	12	Paul Wagner (righthander), Milwaukee	H	5	2
15.	38	May	14	Kevin Millwood (righthander), Atlanta	H	4	0
16.	40	May	16	Livan Hernandez (righthander), Florida	H	4	0
17.	42	May	18	Jesus Sanchez (lefthander), Florida	H	4	0
18.	43	May	19	Tyler Green (righthander), Philadelphia	A	3	1
19.	43	May	19	Tyler Green (righthander), Philadelphia	A	5	1
20.	43	May	19	Wayne Gomes (righthander), Philadelphia	A	8	1
21.	46	May	22	Mark Gardner (righthander), San Francisco	H	6	1
22.	47	May	23	Rich Rodriguez (lefthander), San Francisco	H	4	0
23.	47	May	23	John Johnstone (righthander), San Francisco	H	5	2
24.	48	May	24	Robb Nen (righthander), San Francisco	H	12	1
25.	49	May	25	John Thomson (righthander), Colorado	H	1	0
26.	52	May	29	Dan Miceli (righthander), San Diego	A	9	1
27.	53	May	30	Andy Ashby (righthander), San Diego	A	1	0
28.	59	June	5	Orel Hershiser (righthander), San Francisco	H	1	1

HR No.	Team game No.	Date	Opposing pitcher, Club	Place	Inning	On base
29.	62	June 8	Jason Bere (righthander), Chicago A.L.	A	4	1
30.	64	June 10	Jim Parque (lefthander), Chicago A.L.	A	3	2
31.	65	June 12	Andy Benes (righthander), Arizona	A	3	3
32.	69	June 17	Jose Lima (righthander), Houston	A	3	0
33.	70	June 18	Shane Reynolds (righthander), Houston	A	5	0
34.	76	June 24	Jaret Wright (righthander), Cleveland	A	4	0
35.	77	June 25	Dave Burba (righthander), Cleveland	A	1	0
36.	79	June 27	Mike Trombley (righthander), Minnesota	A	7	1
37.	81	June 30	Glendon Rusch (lefthander), Kansas City	H	7	0
38.	89	July 11	Billy Wagner (lefthander), Houston	H	11	1
39.	90	July 12	Sean Bergman (righthander), Houston	H	1	0
40.	90	July 12	Scott Elarton (righthander), Houston	H	7	0
41.	95	July 17	Brian Bohanon (lefthander), Los Angeles	H	1	0
42.	95	July 17	Antonio Osuna (righthander), Los Angeles	H	8	0
43.	98	July 20	Brian Boehringer (righthander), San Diego	A	5	1
44.	104	July 26	John Thomson (righthander), Colorado	A	4	0
45.	105	July 28	Mike Myers (lefthander), Milwaukee	H	8	0
46.	115	Aug. 8	Mark Clark (righthander), Chicago N.L.	H	4	0
47.	118	Aug. 11	Bobby J. Jones (righthander), New York N.L.	H	4	0
48.	124	Aug. 19	Matt Karchner (righthander), Chicago N.L.	A	8	0
49.	124	Aug. 19	Terry Mulholland (lefthander), Chicago N.L.	A	10	0
50.	125	Aug. *20	Willie Blair (righthander), New York N.L.	A	7	0
51.	126	Aug. †20	Rick Reed (righthander), New York N.L.	A	1	0
52.	129	Aug. 22	Francisco Cordova (righthander), Pittsburgh	A	1	0
53.	130	Aug. 23	Ricardo Rincon (lefthander), Pittsburgh	A	8	0
54.	133	Aug. 26	Justin Speier (righthander), Florida	H	8	1
55.	137	Aug. 30	Dennis Martinez (righthander), Atlanta	H	7	2
56.	139	Sept. 1	Livan Hernandez (righthander), Florida	A	7	0
57.	139	Sept. 1	Donn Pall (righthander), Florida	A	9	0
58.	140	Sept. 2	Brian Edmondson (righthander), Florida	A	7	1
59.	140	Sept. 2	Rob Stanifer (righthander), Florida	A	8	1
60.	142	Sept. 5	Dennis Reyes (lefthander), Cincinnati	H	1	1
61.	144	Sept. 7	Mike Morgan (righthander), Chicago N.L.	H	1	0
62.	145	Sept. 8	Steve Trachsel (righthander), Chicago N.L.	H	4	0
63.	153	Sept. *15	Jason Christiansen (lefthander), Pittsburgh	H	9	0
64.	155	Sept. 18	Rafael Roque (lefthander), Milwaukee	A	4	1
65.	157	Sept. 20	Scott Karl (lefthander), Milwaukee	A	1	1
66.	161	Sept. 25	Shayne Bennett (righthander), Montreal	H	5	1
67.	162	Sept. 26	Dustin Hermanson (righthander), Montreal	H	4	0
68.	162	Sept. 26	Kirk Bullinger (righthander), Montreal	H	7	1
69.	163	Sept. 27	Mike Thurman (righthander), Montreal	H	3	0
70.	163	Sept. 27	Carl Pavano (righthander), Montreal	H	7	2

*First game of doubleheader. †Second game of doubleheader. St. Louis played 163 games in 1998 (one tie on August 24). McGwire did not play in this game. McGwire played in 155 games.

ROGER MARIS' 61 HOME RUNS—1961

HR No.	Team game No.	Date	Opposing pitcher, Club	Place	Inning	On base
1.	11	April 26	Paul Foytack (righthander), Detroit	A	5	0
2.	17	May 3	Pedro Ramos (righthander), Minnesota	A	7	2
3.	20	May 6	Eli Grba (righthander), Los Angeles	A	5	0
4.	29	May 17	Pete Burnside (lefthander), Washington	H	8	1
5.	30	May 19	Jim Perry (righthander), Cleveland	H	1	1
6.	31	May 20	Gary Bell (righthander), Cleveland	A	3	0
7.	32	May 21	Chuck Estrada (righthander), Baltimore	H	1	0
8.	35	May 24	Gene Conley (righthander), Boston	H	4	1
9.	38	May †28	Cal McLish (righthander), Chicago	H	2	1
10.	40	May 30	Gene Conley (righthander), Boston	A	3	0
11.	40	May 30	Mike Fornieles (righthander), Boston	A	8	2
12.	41	May 31	Billy Muffett (righthander), Boston	A	3	0
13.	43	June 2	Cal McLish (righthander), Chicago	A	3	2
14.	44	June 3	Bob Shaw (righthander), Chicago	A	8	2
15.	45	June 4	Russ Kemmerer (righthander), Chicago	A	3	0
16.	48	June 6	Ed Palmquist (righthander), Minnesota	H	6	2
17.	49	June 7	Pedro Ramos (righthander), Minnesota	H	3	2
18.	52	June 9	Ray Herbert (righthander), Kansas City	H	7	1
19.	55	June †11	Eli Grba (righthander), Los Angeles	H	3	0
20.	55	June †11	Johnny James (righthander), Los Angeles	H	7	0
21.	57	June 13	Jim Perry (righthander), Cleveland	A	6	0
22.	58	June 14	Gary Bell (righthander), Cleveland	A	4	1
23.	61	June 17	Don Mossi (lefthander), Detroit	A	4	0
24.	62	June 18	Jerry Casale (righthander), Detroit	A	8	1
25.	63	June 19	Jim Archer (lefthander), Kansas City	A	9	0
26.	64	June 20	Joe Nuxhall (lefthander), Kansas City	A	1	0
27.	66	June 22	Norm Bass (righthander), Kansas City	A	2	1
28.	74	July 1	Dave Sisler (righthander), Washington	H	9	1
29.	75	July 2	Pete Burnside (lefthander), Washington	H	3	2
30.	75	July 2	Johnny Klippstein (righthander), Washington	H	7	1

HR No.	Team game No.	Date		Opposing pitcher, Club	Place	Inning	On base
31.	77	July	†4	Frank Lary (righthander), Detroit	H	8	1
32.	78	July	5	Frank Funk (righthander), Cleveland	H	7	0
33.	82	July	*9	Bill Monbouquette (righthander), Boston	H	7	0
34.	84	July	13	Early Wynn (righthander), Chicago	A	1	1
35.	86	July	15	Ray Herbert (righthander), Chicago	A	3	0
36.	92	July	21	Bill Monbouquette (righthander), Boston	A	1	0
37.	95	July	*25	Frank Baumann (lefthander), Chicago	H	4	1
38.	95	July	*25	Don Larsen (righthander), Chicago	H	8	0
39.	96	July	†25	Russ Kemmerer (righthander), Chicago	H	4	0
40.	96	July	†25	Warren Hacker (righthander), Chicago	H	6	2
41.	106	Aug.	4	Camilo Pascual (righthander), Minnesota	H	1	2
42.	114	Aug.	11	Pete Burnside (lefthander), Washington	A	5	0
43.	115	Aug.	12	Dick Donovan (righthander), Washington	A	4	0
44.	116	Aug.	*13	Bennie Daniels (righthander), Washington	A	4	0
45.	117	Aug.	†13	Marty Kutyna (righthander), Washington	A	1	1
46.	118	Aug.	15	Juan Pizarro (lefthander), Chicago	H	4	0
47.	119	Aug.	16	Billy Pierce (lefthander), Chicago	H	1	1
48.	119	Aug.	16	Billy Pierce (lefthander), Chicago	H	3	1
49.	124	Aug.	*20	Jim Perry (righthander), Cleveland	A	3	1
50.	125	Aug.	22	Ken McBride (righthander), Los Angeles	A	6	1
51.	129	Aug.	26	Jerry Walker (righthander), Kansas City	A	6	0
52.	135	Sept.	2	Frank Lary (righthander), Detroit	H	6	0
53.	135	Sept.	2	Hank Aguirre (lefthander), Detroit	H	8	1
54.	140	Sept.	6	Tom Cheney (righthander), Washington	H	4	0
55.	141	Sept.	7	Dick Stigman (lefthander), Cleveland	H	3	0
56.	143	Sept.	9	Mudcat Grant (righthander), Cleveland	H	7	0
57.	151	Sept.	16	Frank Lary (righthander), Detroit	A	3	1
58.	152	Sept.	17	Terry Fox (righthander), Detroit	A	12	1
59.	155	Sept.	20	Milt Pappas (righthander), Baltimore	A	3	0
60.	159	Sept.	26	Jack Fisher (righthander), Baltimore	H	3	0
61.	163	Oct.	1	Tracy Stallard (righthander), Boston	H	4	0

*First game of doubleheader .†Second game of doubleheader. New York played 163 games in 1961 (one tie on April 22). Maris did not hit a home run in this game. Maris played in 161 games.

BABE RUTH'S 60 HOME RUNS—1927

HR No.	Team game No.	Date		Opposing pitcher, Club	Place	Inning	On base
1.	4	April	15	Howard Ehmke (righthander), Philadelphia	H	1	0
2.	11	April	23	Rube Walberg (lefthander), Philadelphia	A	1	0
3.	12	April	24	Sloppy Thurston (righthander), Washington	A	6	0
4.	14	April	29	Slim Harriss (righthander), Boston	A	5	0
5.	16	May	1	Jack Quinn (righthander), Philadelphia	H	1	1
6.	16	May	1	Rube Walberg (lefthander), Philadelphia	H	8	0
7.	24	May	10	Milt Gaston (righthander), St. Louis	A	1	2
8.	25	May	11	Ernie Nevers (righthander), St. Louis	A	1	1
9.	29	May	17	Rip H. Collins (righthander), Detroit	A	8	0
10.	33	May	22	Benn Karr (righthander), Cleveland	A	6	1
11.	34	May	23	Sloppy Thurston (righthander), Washington	A	1	0
12.	37	May	*28	Sloppy Thurston (righthander), Washington	H	7	2
13.	39	May	29	Danny MacFayden (righthander), Boston	H	8	0
14.	41	May	‡30	Rube Walberg (lefthander), Philadelphia	A	11	0
15.	42	May	*31	Jack Quinn (righthander), Philadelphia	A	1	1
16.	43	May	†31	Howard Ehmke (righthander), Philadelphia	A	5	1
17.	47	June	5	Earl Whitehill (lefthander), Detroit	H	6	0
18.	48	June	7	Tommy Thomas (righthander), Chicago	H	4	0
19.	52	June	11	Garland Buckeye (lefthander), Cleveland	H	3	1
20.	52	June	11	Garland Buckeye (lefthander), Cleveland	H	5	0
21.	53	June	12	George Uhle (righthander), Cleveland	H	7	0
22.	55	June	16	Tom Zachary (lefthander), St. Louis	H	1	1
23.	60	June	*22	Hal Wiltse (lefthander), Boston	A	5	0
24.	60	June	*22	Hal Wiltse (lefthander), Boston	A	7	1
25.	70	June	30	Slim Harriss (righthander), Boston	H	4	1
26.	73	July	3	Hod Lisenbee (righthander), Washington	A	1	0
27.	78	July	†8	Don Hankins (righthander), Detroit	A	2	2
28.	79	July	*9	Ken Holloway (righthander), Detroit	A	1	1
29.	79	July	*9	Ken Holloway (righthander), Detroit	A	4	2
30.	83	July	12	Joe Shaute (lefthander), Cleveland	A	9	1
31.	94	July	24	Tommy Thomas (righthander), Chicago	A	3	0
32.	95	July	*26	Milt Gaston (righthander), St. Louis	H	1	1
33.	95	July	*26	Milt Gaston (righthander), St. Louis	H	6	0
34.	98	July	28	Lefty Stewart (lefthander), St. Louis	H	8	1
35.	106	Aug.	5	George S. Smith (righthander), Detroit	H	8	0
36.	110	Aug.	10	Tom Zachary (lefthander), Washington	A	3	2
37.	114	Aug.	16	Tommy Thomas (righthander), Chicago	A	5	0
38.	115	Aug.	17	Sarge Connally (righthander), Chicago	A	11	0
39.	118	Aug.	20	Jake Miller (lefthander), Cleveland	A	1	1
40.	120	Aug.	22	Joe Shaute (lefthander), Cleveland	A	6	0
41.	124	Aug.	27	Ernie Nevers (righthander), St. Louis	A	8	1

HR No.	Team game No.	Date	Opposing pitcher, Club	Place	Inning	On base
42.	125	Aug. 28	Ernie Wingard (lefthander), St. Louis	A	1	1
43.	127	Aug. 31	Tony Welzer (righthander), Boston	H	8	0
44.	128	Sept. 2	Rube Walberg (lefthander), Philadelphia	A	1	0
45.	132	Sept. *6	Tony Welzer (righthander), Boston	A	6	2
46.	132	Sept. *6	Tony Welzer (righthander), Boston	A	7	1
47.	133	Sept. †6	Jack Russell (righthander), Boston	A	9	0
48.	134	Sept. 7	Danny MacFayden (righthander), Boston	A	1	0
49.	134	Sept. 7	Slim Harriss (righthander), Boston	A	8	1
50.	138	Sept. 11	Milt Gaston (righthander), St. Louis	H	4	0
51.	139	Sept. *13	Willis Hudlin (righthander), Cleveland	H	7	1
52.	140	Sept. †13	Joe Shaute (lefthander), Cleveland	H	4	0
53.	143	Sept. 16	Ted Blankenship (righthander), Chicago	H	3	0
54.	147	Sept. †18	Ted Lyons (righthander), Chicago	H	5	1
55.	148	Sept. 21	Sam Gibson (righthander), Detroit	H	9	0
56.	149	Sept. 22	Ken Holloway (righthander), Detroit	H	9	1
57.	152	Sept. 27	Lefty Grove (lefthander), Philadelphia	H	6	3
58.	153	Sept. 29	Hod Lisenbee (righthander), Washington	H	1	0
59.	153	Sept. 29	Paul Hopkins (righthander), Washington	H	5	3
60.	154	Sept. 30	Tom Zachary (lefthander), Washington	H	8	1

*First game of doubleheader. †Second game of doubleheader. ‡Afternoon game of split doubleheader. New York A.L. played 155 games in 1927 (one tie on April 14), with Ruth participating in 151 games. (No home run for Ruth in game No. 155 on October 1.)

JOE DIMAGGIO'S 56-GAME HITTING STREAK—1941

Date	Opposing pitcher, Club	AB	R	H	2B	3B	HR	RBI
May 15	Eddie Smith, Chicago	4	0	1	0	0	0	1
16	Thornton Lee, Chicago	4	2	2	0	1	1	1
17	Johnny Rigney, Chicago	3	1	1	0	0	0	0
18	Bob Harris (2), Johnny Niggeling (1), St. Louis	3	3	3	1	0	0	1
19	Denny Galehouse, St. Louis	3	0	1	1	0	0	0
20	Eldon Auker, St. Louis	5	1	1	0	0	0	1
21	Schoolboy Rowe (1), Al Benton (1), Detroit	5	0	2	0	0	0	1
22	Archie McKain, Detroit	4	0	1	0	0	0	1
23	Dick Newsome, Boston	5	0	1	0	0	0	2
24	Earl Johnson, Boston	4	2	1	0	0	0	2
25	Lefty Grove, Boston	4	0	1	0	0	0	0
27	Ken Chase (1), Red Anderson (2), Alex Carrasquel (1), Washington	5	3	4	0	0	1	3
28	Sid Hudson, Washington	4	1	1	0	1	0	0
29	Steve Sundra, Washington	3	1	1	0	0	0	0
30	Earl Johnson, Boston	2	1	1	0	0	0	0
30	Mickey Harris, Boston	3	0	1	1	0	0	0
June 1	Al Milnar, Cleveland	4	1	1	0	0	0	0
1	Mel Harder, Cleveland	4	0	1	0	0	0	0
2	Bob Feller, Cleveland	4	2	2	1	0	0	0
3	Dizzy Trout, Detroit	4	1	1	0	0	1	1
5	Hal Newhouser, Detroit	5	1	1	0	1	0	1
7	Bob Muncrief (1), Johnny Allen (1), George Caster (1), St. Louis	5	2	3	0	0	0	1
8	Elden Auker, St. Louis	4	3	2	0	0	2	4
8	George Caster (1), Jack Kramer (1), St. Louis	4	1	2	1	0	1	3
10	Johnny Rigney, Chicago	5	1	1	0	0	0	0
12	Thornton Lee, Chicago	4	1	2	0	0	1	1
14	Bob Feller, Cleveland	2	0	1	1	0	0	1
15	Jim Bagby, Cleveland	3	1	1	0	0	1	1
16	Al Milnar, Cleveland	5	0	1	0	0	0	0
17	Johnny Rigney, Chicago	4	1	1	0	0	0	0
18	Thornton Lee, Chicago	3	0	1	0	0	0	0
19	Eddie Smith (1), Buck Ross (2), Chicago	3	2	3	0	0	1	2
20	Bobo Newsom (2), Archie McKain (2), Detroit	5	3	4	1	0	0	1
21	Dizzy Trout, Detroit	4	0	1	0	0	0	1
22	Hal Newhouser (1), Bobo Newsom (1), Detroit	5	1	2	1	0	1	2
24	Bob Muncrief, St. Louis	4	1	1	0	0	0	0
25	Denny Galehouse, St. Louis	4	1	1	0	0	1	3
26	Elden Auker, St. Louis	4	0	1	0	0	0	1
27	Chubby Dean, Philadelphia	3	1	2	0	0	1	2
28	Johnny Babich (1), Lum Harris (1), Philadelphia	5	1	2	1	0	0	1
29	Dutch E. Leonard, Washington	4	1	1	1	0	0	0
29	Red Anderson, Washington	5	1	1	0	0	0	1
July 1	Mickey Harris (1), Mike Ryba (1), Boston	4	0	2	0	0	0	1
1	Jack Wilson, Boston	3	1	1	0	0	0	1
2	Dick Newsome, Boston	5	1	1	0	0	1	3
5	Phil Marchildon, Philadelphia	4	2	1	0	0	1	2
6	Johnny Babich (1), Bump Hadley (3), Phi.	5	2	4	1	0	0	2
6	Jack Knott, Philadelphia	4	0	2	0	1	0	2
10	Johnny Niggeling, St. Louis	2	0	1	0	0	0	0
11	Bob Harris (3), Jack Kramer (1), St. Louis	5	1	4	0	0	1	2
12	Elden Auker (1), Bob Muncrief (1), St. Louis	5	1	2	1	0	0	1

Date	Opposing pitcher, Club	AB	R	H	2B	3B	HR	RBI
July 13	Ted Lyons (2), Jack Hallett (1), Chicago	4	2	3	0	0	0	0
13	Thornton Lee, Chicago	4	0	1	0	0	0	0
14	Johnny Rigney, Chicago	3	0	1	0	0	0	0
15	Eddie Smith, Chicago	4	1	2	1	0	0	2
16	Al Milnar (2), Joe Krakauskas (1), Cleveland	4	3	3	1	0	0	0
Totals for 56 games		**223**	**56**	**91**	**16**	**4**	**15**	**55**

Note—Numbers in parentheses refer to hits off each pitcher. Streak stopped July 17 at Cleveland, New York won, 4-3. First inning, Al Smith pitching, thrown out by Ken Keltner; fourth inning, Smith pitching, received base on balls; seventh inning, Smith pitching, thrown out by Keltner; eighth inning, Jim Bagby Jr., pitching, grounded into double play.

HOME RUNS BY CLUBS, EACH YEAR

AMERICAN LEAGUE (1901-2004)

*denotes leader or tie

Year	Ana.	Bal.	Bos.	Chi.	Cle.	Det.	K.C.	Mil.	Min.	N.Y.	Oak.	Sea.	T.B.	Tex.	Tor.	Total
1901	..	..	*37	32	12	29	..	..	33	..	35	..	..	..	..	228
1902	..	29	42	14	33	22	..	..	*47	..	38	..	..	..	..	258
1903	..	12	*48	14	31	12	..	..	17	18	32	..	..	..	..	184
1904	..	10	26	14	27	11	..	..	10	27	*31	..	..	..	..	156
1905	..	16	*29	11	18	13	..	..	22	23	24	..	..	..	..	156
1906	..	20	13	7	12	10	..	..	26	17	*32	..	..	..	..	137
1907	..	10	18	5	11	11	..	..	12	15	*22	..	..	..	..	104
1908	..	*20	14	3	18	19	..	..	8	13	21	..	..	..	..	116
1909	..	10	*20	4	10	19	..	..	9	16	21	..	..	..	..	109
1910	..	12	*43	7	9	28	..	..	9	20	19	..	..	..	..	147
1911	..	17	*35	20	20	30	..	..	16	25	*35	..	..	..	..	198
1912	..	19	*29	17	12	19	..	..	20	18	22	..	..	..	..	156
1913	..	18	17	24	16	24	..	..	19	8	*33	..	..	..	..	159
1914	..	17	18	19	10	25	..	..	18	12	*29	..	..	..	..	148
1915	..	19	14	25	20	23	..	..	12	*31	16	..	..	..	..	160
1916	..	14	14	17	16	17	..	..	12	*35	19	..	..	..	..	144
1917	..	15	14	18	13	25	..	..	4	*27	17	..	..	..	..	133
1918	..	5	15	8	9	13	..	..	4	20	*22	..	..	..	..	96
1919	..	31	33	25	24	23	..	..	24	*45	35	..	..	..	..	240
1920	..	50	22	37	35	30	..	..	36	*115	44	..	..	..	..	369
1921	..	67	17	35	42	58	..	..	42	*134	82	..	..	..	..	477
1922	..	98	45	45	32	54	..	..	45	95	*111	..	..	..	..	525
1923	..	82	34	42	59	41	..	..	26	*105	53	..	..	..	..	442
1924	..	67	30	41	41	35	..	..	22	*98	63	..	..	..	..	397
1925	..	*110	41	38	52	50	..	..	56	*110	76	..	..	..	..	533
1926	..	72	32	32	27	36	..	..	43	*121	61	..	..	..	..	424
1927	..	55	28	36	26	51	..	..	29	*158	56	..	..	..	..	439
1928	..	63	38	24	34	62	..	..	40	*133	89	..	..	..	..	483
1929	..	46	28	37	62	110	..	..	48	*142	122	..	..	..	..	595
1930	..	75	47	63	72	82	..	..	57	*152	125	..	..	..	..	673
1931	..	76	37	27	71	43	..	..	49	*155	118	..	..	..	..	576
1932	..	67	53	36	78	80	..	..	61	160	*172	..	..	..	..	707
1933	..	64	50	43	50	57	..	..	60	*144	139	..	..	..	..	607
1934	..	62	51	71	100	74	..	..	51	135	*144	..	..	..	..	688
1935	..	73	69	74	93	106	..	..	32	104	*112	..	..	..	..	663
1936	..	79	86	60	123	94	..	..	62	*182	72	..	..	..	..	758
1937	..	71	100	67	103	150	..	..	47	*174	94	..	..	..	..	806
1938	..	92	98	67	113	137	..	..	85	*174	98	..	..	..	..	864
1939	..	91	124	64	85	124	..	..	44	*166	98	..	..	..	..	796
1940	..	118	145	73	101	134	..	..	52	*155	105	..	..	..	..	883
1941	..	91	124	47	103	81	..	..	52	*151	85	..	..	..	..	734
1942	..	98	103	25	50	76	..	..	40	*108	33	..	..	..	..	533
1943	..	78	57	33	55	77	..	..	47	*100	26	..	..	..	..	473
1944	..	72	69	23	70	60	..	..	33	*96	36	..	..	..	..	459
1945	..	63	50	22	65	77	..	..	27	*93	33	..	..	..	..	430
1946	..	84	109	37	79	108	..	..	60	*136	40	..	..	..	..	653
1947	..	90	103	53	112	103	..	..	42	*115	61	..	..	..	..	679
1948	..	63	121	55	*155	78	..	..	31	139	68	..	..	..	..	710
1949	..	117	*131	43	112	88	..	..	81	115	82	..	..	..	..	769
1950	..	106	161	93	*164	114	..	..	76	159	100	..	..	..	..	973
1951	..	86	127	86	*140	104	..	..	54	*140	102	..	..	..	..	839
1952	..	82	113	80	*148	103	..	..	50	129	89	..	..	..	..	794
1953	..	112	101	74	*160	108	..	..	69	139	116	..	..	..	..	879
1954	..	52	123	94	*156	90	..	..	81	133	94	..	..	..	..	823
1955	..	54	137	116	148	130	..	..	80	*175	121	..	..	..	..	961
1956	..	91	139	128	153	150	..	..	112	*190	112	..	..	..	..	1,075
1957	..	87	153	106	140	116	..	..	111	145	*166	..	..	..	..	1,024
1958	..	108	155	101	161	109	..	..	121	*164	138	..	..	..	..	1,057
1959	..	109	125	97	*167	160	..	..	163	153	117	..	..	..	..	1,091
1960	..	123	124	112	127	150	..	..	147	*193	110	..	..	..	..	1,086
1961	189	149	112	138	150	180	..	..	167	*240	90	..	..	119	..	1,534
1962	137	156	146	92	180	*209	..	..	185	199	116	..	..	132	..	1,552
1963	95	146	171	114	169	148	..	..	*225	188	95	..	..	138	..	1,489
1964	102	162	186	106	164	157	..	..	*221	162	166	..	..	125	..	1,551
1965	92	125	*165	125	156	162	..	..	150	149	110	..	..	136	..	1,370

Year	Ana.	Bal.	Bos.	Chi.	Cle.	Det.	K.C.	Mil.	Min.	N.Y.	Oak.	Sea.	T.B.	Tex.	Tor.	Total
1966	122	175	145	87	155	*179	..	..	144	162	70	..	..	126	..	1,365
1967	114	138	*158	89	131	152	..	..	131	100	69	..	..	115	..	1,197
1968	83	133	125	71	75	*185	..	..	105	109	94	..	..	124	..	1,104
1969	88	175	*197	112	119	182	98	†125	163	94	148	..	..	148	..	1,649
1970	114	179	*203	123	183	148	97	126	153	111	171	..	..	138	..	1,746
1971	96	158	161	138	109	*179	80	104	116	97	160	..	..	86	..	1,484
1972	78	100	124	108	91	122	78	88	93	103	*134		..	..	56	..	1,175
1973	93	119	147	111	*158	157	114	145	120	131	147	..	..	110	..	1,552
1974	95	116	109	*135	131	131	89	120	111	101	132	..	..	99	..	1,369
1975	55	124	134	94	*153	125	118	146	121	110	151	..	..	134	..	1,465
1976	63	119	*134	73	85	101	65	88	81	120	113	..	..	80	..	1,122
1977	131	148	*213	192	100	166	146	125	123	184	117	133	..	135	100	2,013
1978	108	154	172	106	106	129	98	*173	82	125	100	97	..	132	98	1,680
1979	164	181	*194	127	138	164	116	185	112	150	108	132	..	140	95	2,006
1980	106	156	162	91	89	143	115	*203	99	189	137	104	..	124	126	1,844
1981	97	88	90	76	39	65	61	96	47	100	*104	89	..	49	61	1,062
1982	186	179	136	136	109	177	132	*216	148	161	149	130	..	115	106	2,080
1983	154	*168	142	157	86	156	109	132	141	153	121	111	..	106	167	1,903
1984	150	160	181	172	123	*187	117	96	114	130	158	129	..	120	143	1,980
1985	153	*214	162	146	116	202	154	101	141	176	155	171	..	129	158	2,178
1986	167	169	144	121	157	*198	137	127	196	188	163	158	..	184	181	2,290
1987	172	211	174	173	187	*225	168	163	196	196	199	161	..	194	215	2,634
1988	124	137	124	132	134	143	121	113	151	148	156	148	..	112	*158	1,901
1989	*145	129	108	94	127	116	101	126	117	130	127	134	..	122	142	1,718
1990	147	132	106	106	110	*172	100	128	100	147	164	107	..	110	167	1,796
1991	115	170	126	139	79	*209	117	116	140	147	159	126	..	177	133	1,953
1992	88	148	84	110	127	*182	75	82	104	163	142	149	..	159	163	1,776
1993	114	157	114	162	141	178	125	125	121	178	158	161	..	*181	159	2,074
1994	120	139	120	121	*167	161	100	99	103	139	113	153	..	124	115	1,774
1995	186	173	175	146	*207	159	119	128	120	122	169	182	..	138	140	2,164
1996	192	*257	209	195	218	204	123	178	118	162	243	245	..	221	177	2,742
1997	161	196	185	158	220	176	158	135	132	161	197	*264	..	187	147	2,477
1998	147	214	205	198	198	165	134	...	115	207	149	*234	111	201	221	2,499
1999	158	203	176	162	209	212	151	...	105	193	235	*244	145	230	212	2,635
2000	236	184	167	216	221	177	150	...	116	205	239	198	162	173	*244	2,688
2001	158	136	198	214	212	139	152	...	164	203	199	169	121	*246	195	2,506
2002	152	165	177	217	192	124	140	...	167	223	205	152	133	*230	187	2,464
2003	150	152	238	220	158	153	162	...	155	230	176	139	137	*239	190	2,499
2004	162	169	222	*242	184	201	150	...	191	*242	189	136	145	227	145	2,605
Totals	**5,759**	**10,601**	**10,900**	**8,766**	**10,548**	**11,263**	**4,270**	**3,789**	**8,690**	**12,983**	**10,763**	**4,356**	**954**	**6,371**	**4,435**	**114,441**

Note: Figures in Baltimore column 1902-1953 are for St. Louis (3,014); in Oakland column 1901-54 are for Philadelphia (3,502), Kansas City, 1955-67 (1,480); Minnesota column 1901-1960 are for old Washington club (2,786). Texas column represents second Washington club, 1961 through 1971. Second Milwaukee club totals include only those homers in American League. Figures in Totals column are all inclusive. (Baltimore had 24 in 1901 and 33 in 1902 and Milwaukee had 26 in 1901); these are included in League Totals but not in Club Totals. †Predecessor Seattle club. Anaheim column represents the Los Angeles Angels for 1961 through September 1, 1965 and California Angels through 1996.

NATIONAL LEAGUE (1900-2004)

*denotes leader or tie

Year	Ariz.	Atl.	Chi.	Cin.	Col.	Fla.	Hou.	L.A.	Mil.	Mon.	N.Y.	Phi.	Pit.	St.L.	S.D.	S.F.	Total
1900	..	*48	33	33	..	..	..	26	..	..	..	29	26	36	..	23	254
1901	..	28	18	38	..	..	..	32	..	..	..	24	29	*39	..	19	227
1902	..	14	6	18	..	..	..	*19	..	..	..	5	18	10	..	6	96
1903	..	25	9	28	..	..	..	15	..	..	..	12	*34	8	..	20	151
1904	..	24	22	21	..	..	..	15	..	..	..	23	15	24	..	*31	175
1905	..	17	12	27	..	..	..	29	..	..	..	16	22	20	..	*39	182
1906	..	16	20	16	..	..	..	*25	..	..	..	12	12	10	..	15	126
1907	..	22	13	15	..	..	..	18	..	..	..	12	19	18	..	*23	140
1908	..	17	19	14	..	..	..	*28	..	..	..	11	25	17	..	20	151
1909	..	14	20	22	..	..	..	16	..	..	..	12	25	15	..	*26	150
1910	..	31	*34	23	..	..	..	25	..	..	..	22	33	15	..	31	214
1911	..	37	54	21	..	..	..	28	..	..	..	*60	49	26	..	41	316
1912	..	35	42	21	..	..	..	32	..	..	..	43	39	27	..	*47	286
1913	..	32	59	27	..	..	..	39	..	..	..	*73	35	15	..	30	310
1914	..	35	42	16	..	..	..	31	..	..	..	*62	18	33	..	30	267
1915	..	17	53	15	..	..	..	14	..	..	..	*58	24	20	..	24	225
1916	..	22	*46	14	..	..	..	28	..	..	..	42	20	25	..	42	239
1917	..	22	17	26	..	..	..	25	..	..	..	38	9	26	..	*39	202
1918	..	13	21	15	..	..	..	10	..	..	..	25	15	*27	..	13	139
1919	..	24	21	20	..	..	..	25	..	..	..	*42	17	18	..	40	207
1920	..	23	34	18	..	..	..	28	..	..	..	*64	16	32	..	46	261
1921	..	61	37	20	..	..	..	59	..	..	..	*88	37	83	..	75	460
1922	..	32	42	45	..	..	..	56	..	..	..	*116	52	107	..	80	530
1923	..	32	90	45	..	..	..	62	..	..	..	*112	49	63	..	85	538
1924	..	25	66	36	..	..	..	72	..	..	..	94	44	67	..	*95	499
1925	..	41	86	44	..	..	..	64	..	..	..	100	78	109	..	*114	636
1926	..	16	66	35	..	..	..	40	..	..	..	75	44	*90	..	73	439
1927	..	37	74	29	..	..	..	39	..	..	..	57	54	84	..	*109	483
1928	..	52	92	32	..	..	..	66	..	..	..	85	52	113	..	*118	610

Year	Ariz.	Atl.	Chi.	Cin.	Col.	Fla.	Hou.	L.A.	Mil.	Mon.	N.Y.	Phi.	Pit.	St.L.	S.D.	S.F.	Total
1929	..	33	139	34	..	..	..	99	..	..	..	*153	60	100	..	136	754
1930	..	66	*171	74	..	..	..	122	..	..	..	126	86	104	..	143	892
1931	..	34	84	21	..	..	..	71	..	..	..	81	41	60	..	*101	493
1932	..	63	69	47	..	..	..	110	..	..	..	*122	48	76	..	116	651
1933	..	54	72	34	..	..	..	62	..	..	..	60	39	57	..	*82	460
1934	..	83	101	55	..	..	..	79	..	..	..	56	52	104	..	*126	656
1935	..	75	88	73	..	..	..	59	..	..	..	92	66	86	..	*123	662
1936	..	67	76	82	..	..	..	33	..	..	..	*103	60	88	..	97	606
1937	..	63	96	73	..	..	..	37	..	..	..	103	47	94	..	*111	624
1938	..	54	65	110	..	..	..	61	..	..	..	40	65	91	..	*125	611
1939	..	56	91	98	..	..	..	78	..	..	..	49	63	98	..	*116	649
1940	..	59	86	89	..	..	..	93	..	..	..	75	76	*119	..	91	688
1941	..	48	99	64	..	..	..	*101	..	..	..	64	56	70	..	95	597
1942	..	68	75	66	..	..	..	62	..	..	..	44	54	60	..	*109	538
1943	..	39	52	43	..	..	..	39	..	..	..	66	42	70	..	*81	432
1944	..	79	71	51	..	..	..	56	..	..	..	55	70	*100	..	93	575
1945	..	101	57	56	..	..	..	57	..	..	..	56	72	64	..	*114	577
1946	..	44	56	65	..	..	..	55	..	..	..	80	60	81	..	*121	562
1947	..	85	71	95	..	..	..	83	..	..	..	60	156	115	..	*221	886
1948	..	95	87	104	..	..	..	91	..	..	..	91	108	105	..	*164	845
1949	..	103	97	86	..	..	..	*152	..	..	..	122	126	102	..	147	935
1950	..	148	161	99	..	..	..	*194	..	..	..	125	138	102	..	133	1,100
1951	..	130	103	88	..	..	..	*184	..	..	..	108	137	95	..	179	1,024
1952	..	110	107	104	..	..	..	*153	..	..	..	93	92	97	..	151	907
1953	..	156	137	166	..	..	..	*208	..	..	..	115	99	140	..	176	1,197
1954	..	139	159	147	..	..	..	*186	..	..	..	102	76	119	..	*186	1,114
1955	..	182	164	181	..	..	..	*201	..	..	..	132	91	143	..	169	1,263
1956	..	177	142	*221	..	..	..	179	..	..	..	121	110	124	..	145	1,219
1957	..	*199	147	187	..	..	..	147	..	..	..	117	92	132	..	157	1,178
1958	..	167	*182	123	..	..	..	172	..	..	..	124	134	111	..	170	1,183
1959	..	*177	163	161	..	..	..	148	..	..	..	113	112	118	..	167	1,159
1960	..	*170	119	140	..	..	..	126	..	..	..	99	120	138	..	130	1,042
1961	..	*188	176	158	..	..	..	157	..	..	..	103	128	103	..	183	1,196
1962	..	181	126	167	..	..	105	140	..	..	139	142	108	137	..	*204	1,449
1963	..	139	127	122	..	..	62	110	..	..	96	126	108	128	..	*197	1,215
1964	..	159	145	130	..	..	70	79	..	..	103	130	121	109	..	*165	1,211
1965	..	*196	134	183	..	..	97	78	..	..	107	144	111	109	..	159	1,318
1966	..	*207	140	149	..	..	112	108	..	..	98	117	158	108	..	181	1,378
1967	..	*158	128	109	..	..	93	82	..	..	83	103	91	115	..	140	1,102
1968	..	80	*130	106	..	..	66	67	..	..	81	100	80	73	..	108	891
1969	..	141	142	*171	..	..	104	97	..	125	109	137	119	90	99	136	1,470
1970	..	160	179	*191	..	..	129	87	..	136	120	101	130	113	172	165	1,683
1971	..	153	128	138	..	..	71	95	..	88	98	123	*154	95	96	140	1,379
1972	..	144	133	124	..	..	134	98	..	91	105	98	110	70	102	*150	1,359
1973	..	*206	117	137	..	..	134	110	..	125	85	134	154	75	112	161	1,550
1974	..	120	110	135	..	..	110	*139	..	86	96	95	114	83	99	93	1,280
1975	..	107	95	124	..	..	84	118	..	98	101	125	*138	81	78	84	1,233
1976	..	82	105	*141	..	..	66	91	..	94	102	110	110	63	64	85	1,113
1977	..	139	111	181	..	..	114	*191	..	138	88	186	133	96	120	134	1,631
1978	..	123	72	136	..	..	70	*149	..	121	86	133	115	79	75	117	1,276
1979	..	126	135	132	..	..	49	*183	..	143	74	119	148	100	93	125	1,427
1980	..	144	107	113	..	..	75	*148	..	114	61	117	116	101	67	80	1,243
1981	..	64	57	64	..	..	45	*82	..	81	57	69	55	50	32	63	719
1982	..	*146	102	82	..	..	74	138	..	133	97	112	134	67	81	133	1,299
1983	..	130	140	107	..	..	97	*146	..	102	112	125	121	83	93	142	1,398
1984	..	111	136	106	..	..	79	102	..	96	107	*147	98	75	109	112	1,278
1985	..	126	*150	114	..	..	121	129	..	118	134	141	80	87	109	115	1,424
1986	..	138	*155	144	..	..	125	130	..	110	148	154	111	58	136	114	1,523
1987	..	152	*209	192	..	..	122	125	..	120	192	169	131	94	113	205	1,824
1988	..	96	113	122	..	..	96	99	..	107	*152	106	110	71	94	113	1,279
1989	..	128	124	128	..	..	97	89	..	100	*147	123	95	73	120	141	1,365
1990	..	162	136	125	..	..	94	129	..	114	*172	103	138	73	123	152	1,521
1991	..	141	159	*164	..	..	79	108	..	95	117	111	126	68	121	141	1,430
1992	..	*138	104	99	..	..	96	72	..	102	93	118	106	94	135	105	1,262
1993	..	*169	161	137	142	94	138	130	..	122	158	156	110	118	153	168	1,956
1994	..	*137	109	124	125	94	120	115	..	108	117	80	80	108	92	123	1,532
1995	..	168	158	161	*200	144	109	140	..	118	125	94	125	107	116	152	1,917
1996	..	197	175	191	*221	150	129	150	..	148	147	132	138	142	147	153	2,220
1997	..	174	127	142	*239	136	133	174	..	172	153	116	129	144	152	172	2,163
1998	159	215	212	138	183	114	166	159	152	147	136	126	107	*223	167	161	2,565
1999	216	197	189	209	*223	128	168	187	165	163	181	161	171	194	153	188	2,893
2000	179	179	183	200	161	160	249	211	177	178	198	144	168	235	157	226	3,005
2001	208	174	194	176	213	166	208	206	209	131	147	164	161	199	161	*235	2,952
2002	165	164	*200	169	152	146	167	155	139	162	160	165	142	175	136	198	2,595
2003	152	*235	172	182	198	157	191	124	196	144	124	166	163	196	128	180	2,708
2004	135	178	*235	194	202	148	187	203	135	151	185	215	142	214	139	183	2,846
Totals	**1,214**	**10,608**	**10,775**	**10,088**	**2,259**	**1,637**	**4,835**	**10,094**	**1,173**	**4,381**	**5,191**	**9,999**	**8,945**	**9,216**	**4,144**	**12,111**	**106,670**

Note: Figures in Atlanta column 1900-1952 are for Boston (2,569) and 1953-1965 for Milwaukee (2,230); in Los Angeles column 1900-1957 are for Brooklyn (4,018); San Francisco column 1900-1957 are for New York Giants (5,162); New York column represents the present Mets franchise. Figures in Totals columns are all inclusive. Milwaukee Brewers totals are as National League club.

CLUBS WITH FIVE HOME RUNS IN INNING

AMERICAN LEAGUE

Date	Inn.	Club (Players)
June 9, 1966	7	Minnesota (Rollins, Versalles, OLIVA, MINCHER, KILLEBREW).

Total number of clubs: 1

NATIONAL LEAGUE

Date	Inn.	Club (Players)
June 6, 1939	4	New York (Danning, Demaree, WHITEHEAD, SALVO, MOORE).
June 2, 1949	8	Philadelphia (Ennis, Seminick, Jones, Rowe, Seminick).
Aug. 23, 1961	9	San Francisco (Cepeda, F. Alou, Davenport, Mays, Orsino).

Note—Capitalized letters denote three or more consecutive homers.
Total number of clubs: 3

CLUBS WITH FOUR HOME RUNS IN INNING

AMERICAN LEAGUE

Date	Inn.	Club (Players)
Sept. 24, 1940*	6	Boston (WILLIAMS, FOXX, CRONIN, Tabor).
June 23, 1950	4	Detroit (Trout, Priddy, Wertz, Evers).
May 22, 1957	6	Boston (Mauch, Williams, Gernert, Malzone).
Aug. 26, 1957	7	Boston (Zauchin, Lepcio, Piersall, Malzone).
July 31, 1963†	6	Cleveland (HELD, RAMOS, FRANCONA, BROWN).
May 2, 1964	11	Minnesota (OLIVA, ALLISON, HALL, KILLEBREW).
May 17, 1967	7	Baltimore (Etchebarren, Bowens, Powell, D. Johnson).
July 29, 1974	1	Detroit (KALINE, FREEHAN, STANLEY, Brinkman).
June 17, 1977	1	Boston (Burleson, Lynn, Fisk, Scott).
July 4, 1977	8	Boston (LYNN, RICE, YASTRZEMSKI, Scott).
May 31, 1980	4	Boston (Stapleton, PEREZ, FISK, HOBSON).
May 16, 1983	9	Minnesota (Engle, Mitchell, Gaetti, Hatcher).
Sept. 10, 1986	4	Detroit (Lemon, Heath, Gibson, Coles).
May 2, 1992	5	Minnesota (Mack, Puckett, Hrbek, Bush).
Sept. 5, 1995	2	Baltimore (Hoiles, MANTO, SMITH, ANDERSON).
May 26, 1996	8	Chicago (THOMAS, BAINES, VENTURA, Kreuter).
Sept. 21, 1996	3	Seattle (RODRIGUEZ, GRIFFEY, MARTINEZ, Sorrento).
Aug. 21, 1997	3	Oakland (Giambi, Young, McDonald, Canseco).
July 18, 1998	4	Boston (Sadler, Lewis, Garciaparra, Vaughn).
Aug. 1, 1999	4	Oakland (Tejada, Chavez, Giambi, Jaha).
May 3, 2000	6	Chicago (Johnson, VALENTIN, THOMAS, KONERKO).
May 26, 2000	6	Kansas City (Dye, Quinn, Johnson, Febles).
May 28, 2000	5	Anaheim (Erstad, VAUGHN, SALMON, ANDERSON).
July 3, 2000	4	Boston (Everett, O'Leary, Varitek, Burkhart).
June 29, 2001	4	Kansas City (Sweeney, DYE, IBANEZ, BELTRAN)
Aug. 17, 2001	6	Toronto (Frye, Cruz, Stewart, Delgado).
Apr. 27, 2002	3	Oakland (Hatteberg, Long, Pena, Menechino).
May 2, 2002	1	Seattle (Boone 2, Cameron 2).
July 23, 2002‡	3	Boston (Damon, Garciaparra 2, Ramirez).
July 16, 2004	9	Cleveland (Broussard, Martinez, Hafner, Gerut).

Total number of clubs: 30

NATIONAL LEAGUE

Date	Inn.	Club (Players)
June 6, 1894	3	Pittsburgh (Stenzel, Lyons, Bierbauer, Stenzel).
May 12, 1930	7	Chicago (Heathcote, Wilson, Grimm, Beck).
Aug. 13, 1939*	4	New York (Bonura, KAMPOURIS, LOHRMAN, MOORE).
June 6, 1948*	6	St. Louis (Dusak, Schoendienst, Slaughter, Jones).
May 28, 1954	8	New York (Williams, Dark, Irvin, Gardner).
July 8, 1956*	4	New York (Mays, THOMPSON, SPENCER, WESTRUM).
June 8, 1961	7	Milwaukee (MATHEWS, AARON, ADCOCK, THOMAS).
June 8, 1965	10	Milwaukee (Torre, Mathews, Aaron, Oliver).
July 10, 1970	9	San Diego (Murrell, Spiezio, Campbell, Gaston).
June 21, 1971*	8	Atlanta (Lum, King, H. Aaron, Evans).
July 30, 1978	3	Montreal (Dawson, Parrish, Cash, Dawson).
Aug. 17, 1985	7	Philadelphia (SAMUEL, WILSON, SCHMIDT, Daulton).
Apr. 29, 1986	4	Montreal (Dawson, Brooks, Wallach, Fitzgerald).
Sept. 20, 1992	6	Atlanta (JUSTICE, HUNTER, GANT, Lemke).
June 19, 1994	1	Cincinnati (Morris, Mitchell, Branson, Taubensee).
Aug. 8, 1995	2	Pittsburgh (King, Merced, King, Cummings).
Aug. 17, 1996	8	Cincinnati (Taubensee, Sanders, Branson, Larkin).
June 22, 1997	3	Atlanta (Blauser, C. Jones, McGriff, Tucker).
Aug. 26, 1998	9	Florida (LEE, FLOYD, ORIE, Kotsay).
June 6, 1999	7	Colorado (Blanco, Perez, Bichette, Echevarria).
Apr. 27, 2000	1	Chicago (Young, Gutierrez, Rodriguez, Buford).
July 23, 2000	2	Houston (Spiers, Bagwell, Berkman, Hidalgo).
Aug. 8, 2000	4	Los Angeles (Elster, Dreifort, Sheffield, Green).
May 17, 2001	3	San Diego (Arias, Henderson, Klesko, Trammell).
May 20, 2001	7	Atlanta (A. Jones, Jordan, Lopez, Helms).
May 28, 2003	1	Atlanta (FURCAL, DEROSA, SHEFFIELD, Lopez).
Aug. 20, 2003	5	Pittsburgh (KENDALL, GILES, SANDERS, Sanders).
Sept 8, 2004	1	Houston (Biggio, Bagwell, Berkman, Lamb).

Note—Capitalized letters denote three or more consecutive homers.
*first game; †second game; ‡a.m. game
Total number of clubs: 28

CLUBS WITH THREE CONSECUTIVE HOME RUNS IN INNING

PLAYERS LEAGUE

Date	Inn.	Club (Players)
May 31, 1890	8	New York (GORE, EWING, CONNOR).

Total number of clubs: 1

AMERICAN LEAGUE

Date	Inn.	Club (Players)
June 30, 1902*	6	Cleveland (LAJOIE, HICKMAN, BRADLEY).
May 2, 1922	4	Philadelphia (WALKER, PERKINS, MILLER).
Sept. 10, 1925*	4	New York (MEUSEL, RUTH, GEHRIG).
May 4, 1929	7	New York (RUTH, GEHRIG, MEUSEL).
June 18, 1930	5	Philadelphia (SIMMONS, FOXX, MILLER).
July 17, 1934	4	Philadelphia (JOHNSON, FOXX, HIGGINS).
June 25, 1939*	7	Cleveland (CHAPMAN, TROSKY, HEATH).
Sept. 24, 1940*‡	6	Boston (WILLIAMS, FOXX, CRONIN).
May 23, 1946	5	New York (DiMAGGIO, ETTEN, GORDON).
April 23, 1947	8	Detroit (CULLENBINE, WAKEFIELD, EVERS).
May 13, 1947	6	New York (KELLER, DiMAGGIO, LINDELL).
April 19, 1948*	2	Boston (SPENCE, STEPHENS, DOERR).
June 6, 1948†	6	Boston (WILLIAMS, SPENCE, STEPHENS).
July 28, 1950	3	Cleveland (DOBY, ROSEN, EASTER).
Sept. 2, 1951	1	Cleveland (SIMPSON, ROSEN, EASTER).
July 16, 1953†	5	St. Louis (COURTNEY, KRYHOSKI, DYCK).
July 7, 1956	7	Detroit (KUENN, TORGESON, MAXWELL).
Sept. 7, 1959	2	Boston (BUDDIN, CASALE, GREEN).
April 30, 1961†	7	Baltimore (GENTILE, TRIANDOS, HANSEN).
May 23, 1961	9	Detroit (CASH, BOROS, BROWN).
June 27, 1961	1	Washington (GREEN, TASBY, LONG).
June 17, 1962*	2	Cleveland (KINDALL, PHILLIPS, MAHONEY).
Aug. 19, 1962	7	Kansas City (CIMOLI, CAUSEY, BRYAN).
Aug. 28, 1962	4	Los Angeles (J. L. THOMAS, WAGNER, RODGERS).
July 31, 1963†‡	6	Cleveland (HELD, RAMOS, FRANCONA, BROWN).
May 2, 1964‡	11	Minnesota (OLIVA, ALLISON, HALL, KILLEBREW).
Sept. 10, 1965	8	Baltimore (ROBINSON, BLEFARY, ADAIR).
June 9, 1966‡	7	Minnesota (OLIVA, MINCHER, KILLEBREW).
June 29, 1966	3	New York (RICHARDSON, MANTLE, PEPITONE).
July 2, 1966	6	Washington (HOWARD, LOCK, McMULLEN).
June 22, 1969*	3	Oakland (KUBIAK, JACKSON, BANDO).
Aug. 10, 1969	6	New York (MURCER, MUNSON, MICHAEL).
Sept. 4, 1969	9	Baltimore (F. ROBINSON, POWELL, B. C. ROBINSON).
Aug. 22, 1970	6	Cleveland (SIMS, NETTLES, LEON).
April 17, 1971	7	Detroit (NORTHRUP, CASH, HORTON).
June 27, 1972	1	Detroit (RODRIGUEZ, KALINE, HORTON).
July 15, 1973	8	Minnesota (MITTERWALD, LIS, HOLT).
July 29, 1974‡	1	Detroit (KALINE, FREEHAN, STANLEY).
May 11, 1977	2	California (BONDS, BAYLOR, JACKSON).
July 4, 1977‡	8	Boston (LYNN, RICE, YASTRZEMSKI).
Aug. 13, 1977	6	Boston (SCOTT, HOBSON, EVANS).
May 8, 1979	6	Baltimore (MURRAY, MAY, ROENICKE).
June 19, 1979	4	Oakland (GROSS, REVERING, HEATH).
May 31, 1980‡	4	Boston (PEREZ, FISK, HOBSON).
June 3, 1980	9	Oakland (REVERING, PAGE, ARMAS).
May 28, 1982	6	Milwaukee (COOPER, MONEY, THOMAS).
June 5, 1982	7	Milwaukee (YOUNT, COOPER, OGLIVIE).
June 7, 1982	8	Minnesota (WASHINGTON, BRUNANSKY, HRBEK).
Sept. 12, 1982	3	Milwaukee (COOPER, SIMMONS, OGLIVIE).
Aug. 2, 1983	3	Seattle (S. HENDERSON, D. HENDERSON, RAMOS).
Sept. 9, 1983	1	Chicago (FISK, PACIOREK, LUZINSKI).
April 24, 1984	4	California (R.M. JACKSON, DOWNING, GRICH).
April 26, 1984	6	Toronto (UPSHAW, BELL, BARFIELD).
May 29, 1984	6	New York (MATTINGLY, BAYLOR, WINFIELD).
June 3, 1984	4	New York (GAMBLE, KEMP, HARRAH).
June 29, 1984	5	Cleveland (THORNTON, HALL, WILLARD).
Aug. 19, 1984	7	Kansas City (MOTLEY, WHITE, BALBONI).
Aug. 24, 1985	9	Chicago (LAW, LITTLE, BAINES).
Sept. 16, 1985	8	Baltimore (RIPKEN, MURRAY, LYNN).
July 8, 1986	4	Detroit (GIBSON, PARRISH, EVANS).
July 31, 1986	5	Detroit (TRAMMELL, GIBSON, GRUBB).
Sept. 28, 1986	4	Kansas City (BRETT, WHITE, QUIRK).
June 28, 1987	9	Detroit (GRUBB, NOKES, MADLOCK).
Sept. 12, 1987	8	Toronto (WHITT, BARFIELD, GRUBER).
July 9, 1988*	4	Chicago (PASQUA, WALKER, BOSTON).
May 16, 1990	4	Oakland (CANSECO, McGWIRE, HASSEY).
June 17, 1990	7	Cleveland (MALDONADO, JACOBY, SNYDER).
July 6, 1990†	3	Oakland (R. HENDERSON, LANSFORD, CANSECO).
Aug. 7, 1990	9	Detroit (TRAMMELL, FIELDER, WARD).
April 20, 1992	3	Detroit (TRAMMELL, FIELDER, TETTLETON).
May 8, 1994	6	New York (TARTABULL, STANLEY, G. WILLIAMS).

Date		Inn.	Club (Players)
May 28,	1995	4	Chicago (DURHAM, KARKOVICE, GREBECK).
Sept. 5,	1995‡	2	Baltimore (MANTO, SMITH, ANDERSON).
May 26,	1996‡	8	Chicago (THOMAS, BAINES, VENTURA).
Sept. 12,	1996	7	Cleveland (THOME, BELLE, FRANCO).
Sept. 21,	1996‡	3	Seattle (RODRIGUEZ, GRIFFEY, MARTINEZ).
Aug. 28,	1998	4	Texas (GONZALEZ, CLARK, RODRIGUEZ).
May 19,	1999	5	Texas (RODRIGUEZ, PALMEIRO, ZEILE).
May 28,	1999	1	Texas (GONZALEZ, PALMEIRO, RODRIGUEZ).
Apr. 9,	2000	6	Minnesota (COOMER, JONES, LeCROY).
Apr. 9,	2000	8	Kansas City (BELTRAN, DYE, SWEENEY).
Apr. 18,	2000	6	Toronto (GREBECK, MONDESI, DELGADO).
May 3,	2000	6	Chicago (VALENTIN, THOMAS, KONERKO).
May 28,	2000	5	Anaheim (VAUGHN, SALMON, ANDERSON).
June 16,	2000	8	Oakland (CHAVEZ, TEJADA, HERNANDEZ).
June 23,	2000	2	Oakland (VELARDE, JA. GIAMBI, GRIEVE).
June 24,	2000	2	Anaheim (ANDERSON, GLAUS, SPIEZIO).
June 24,	2001	2	Detroit (FICK, ENCARNACION, HALTER).
June 29,	2001	4	Kansas City (DYE, IBANEZ, BELTRAN).
July 12,	2001	3	Minnesota (MIENTKIEWICZ, KOSKIE, HUNTER).
July 26,	2001	1	Anaheim (GLAUS, ERSTAD, ANDERSON).
Aug. 21,	2001	6	Toronto (STEWART, DELGADO, MONDESI).
May 31,	2002	11	Kansas City (BELTRAN, SWEENEY, RANDA).
Apr. 18,	2004	6	Texas (NIX, BARAJAS, GONZALEZ).
May 24,	2004	3	Anaheim (GUERRERO, GUILLEN, DaVANON).
July 16,	2004	3	Cleveland (LAWTON, MARTINEZ, BLAKE).
Aug. 27,	2004	5	Seattle (OLIVO, LOPEZ, BOCACHICA).

Total number of clubs: 97

NATIONAL LEAGUE

Date		Inn.	Club (Players)
May 10,	1894	7	St. Louis (SHUGART, MILLER, PEITZ).
Aug. 13,	1932*	4	New York (TERRY, OTT, LINDSTROM).
June 10,	1935	8	Pittsburgh (P. WANER, VAUGHAN, YOUNG).
July 9,	1938	3	Boston (CUCCINELLO, WEST, FLETCHER).
June 6,	1939‡	4	New York (WHITEHEAD, SALVO, MOORE).
Aug. 13,	1939*‡	4	New York (KAMPOURIS, LOHRMAN, MOORE).
Aug. 11,	1941	5	Chicago (CAVARRETTA, HACK, NICHOLSON).
June 11,	1944†	8	St. Louis (W. COOPER, KUROWSKI, LITWHILER).
Aug. 11,	1946*	8	Cincinnati (HATTON, WEST, MUELLER).
June 20,	1948†	8	New York (MIZE, MARSHALL, GORDON).
June 4,	1949	6	New York (LOCKMAN, GORDON, MARSHALL).
April 19,	1952	7	Brooklyn (CAMPANELLA, PAFKO, SNIDER).
Sept. 27,	1952	7	Pittsburgh (KINER, GARAGIOLA, BELL).
Sept. 4,	1953	4	New York (WESTRUM, CORWIN, LOCKMAN).
June 20,	1954	6	New York (HOFMAN, WESTRUM, RHODES).
Aug. 15,	1954	9	Cincinnati (BELL, KLUSZEWSKI, GREENGRASS).
April 16,	1955	2	Chicago (JACKSON, BANKS, FONDY).
July 6,	1955*	6	Pittsburgh (LYNCH, THOMAS, LONG).
May 30,	1956*	1	Milwaukee (MATHEWS, AARON, THOMSON).
May 31,	1956	9	Cincinnati (BELL, KLUSZEWSKI, ROBINSON)
June 29,	1956	9	Brooklyn (SNIDER, JACKSON, HODGES).
July 0,	1956*‡	4	New York (THOMPSON, SPENCER, WESTRUM).
April 21,	1957*	3	Pittsburgh (THOMAS, SMITH, GROAT).
June 26,	1957	5	Milwaukee (AARON, MATHEWS, COVINGTON).
May 7,	1958	5	Pittsburgh (SKINNER, KLUSZEWSKI, THOMAS).
May 31,	1958	1	Milwaukee (AARON, MATHEWS, COVINGTON).
June 8,	1961‡	7	Milwaukee (MATHEWS, AARON, ADCOCK, THOMAS).
June 18,	1961	3	Milwaukee (AARON, ADCOCK, THOMAS).
April 28,	1962	6	New York (THOMAS, NEAL, HODGES).
Aug. 27,	1963	3	San Francisco (MAYS, CEPEDA, F. ALOU).
July 18,	1964	8	St. Louis (BOYER, WHITE, McCARVER).
Aug. 5,	1969*	5	San Francisco (MARSHALL, HUNT, BONDS).
May 18,	1970	8	New York (MARSHALL, FOY, GROTE).
Aug. 1,	1970	7	Pittsburgh (ROBERTSON, STARGELL, PAGAN).
July 16,	1974	9	San Diego (COLBERT, McCOVEY, WINFIELD).
July 20,	1974	5	New York (THEODORE, STAUB, JONES).
May 17,	1977	5	Chicago (BIITTNER, MURCER, MORALES).
Sept. 30,	1977	2	Philadelphia (LUZINSKI, HEBNER, MADDOX).
Aug. 14,	1978	3	Atlanta (MATTHEWS, BURROUGHS, HORNER).
June 17,	1979	4	Montreal (PEREZ, CARTER, VALENTINE).
July 11,	1979	1	San Diego (TURNER, WINFIELD, TENACE).
May 27,	1980	3	Cincinnati (GRIFFEY, FOSTER, DRIESSEN).
Aug. 31,	1980†	2	Los Angeles (CEY, MONDAY, FERGUSON).
July 11,	1982	2	San Francisco (SMITH, MAY, SUMMERS).
June 24,	1984	5	Houston (CABELL, GARNER, CRUZ).
Aug. 17,	1985‡	7	Philadelphia (SAMUEL, WILSON, SCHMIDT).
July 27,	1986	3	New York (CARTER, STRAWBERRY, MITCHELL).
April 13,	1987	1	San Diego (WYNNE, GWYNN, KRUK).
July 26,	1987	8	Philadelphia (THOMPSON, HAYES, SCHMIDT).
May 1,	1988	5	New York (TEUFEL, HERNANDEZ, STRAWBERRY).
April 17,	1989	3	New York (STRAWBERRY, McREYNOLDS, HERNANDEZ).
June 16,	1990	5	Cincinnati (SABO, LARKIN, DAVIS).
Sept. 14,	1991	4	Cincinnati (DUNCAN, MORRIS, O'NEILL).
Sept. 20,	1992‡	6	Atlanta (JUSTICE, HUNTER, GANT).
Sept. 6,	1993	6	Chicago (BUECHELE, WILSON, LAKE).

– 183 –

Date		Inn.	Club (Players)
April 15,	1994	1	Atlanta (McGRIFF, PENDLETON, TARASCO).
April 18,	1994	1	Atlanta (KLESKO, McGRIFF, JUSTICE).
July 7,	1995	2	Colorado (WALKER, GALARRAGA, CASTILLA).
Aug. 8,	1995‡	2	Pittsburgh (MERCED, KING, CUMMINGS).
April 19,	1996	6	Chicago (McRAE, SANDBERG, GRACE).
June 30,	1996	3	Los Angeles (PIAZZA, KARROS, MONDESI).
July 23,	1996	1	Colorado (BICHETTE, GALARRAGA, CASTILLA).
April 1,	1997	6	San Diego (GOMEZ, HENDERSON, VERAS).
April 9,	1997	6	Cincinnati (LARKIN, GREENE, SANDERS).
May 29,	1997	6	Colorado (WALKER, GALARRAGA, BICHETTE).
June 1,	1997	4	Los Angeles (PIAZZA, KARROS, ZEILE).
June 7,	1997*	6	Colorado (WALKER, GALARRAGA, BICHETTE).
Aug. 23,	1997	9	Montreal (STANKIEWICZ, GRUDZIELANEK, LANSING).
Aug. 2,	1998	2	San Francisco (BURKS, BONDS, KENT).
Aug. 10,	1998	5	Chicago (SOSA, GRACE, RODRIGUEZ).
Aug. 26,	1998‡	9	Florida (LEE, FLOYD, ORIE).
April 28,	1999	1	Philadelphia (ROLEN, BROGNA, GANT).
June 18,	1999	8	Chicago (SOSA, GRACE, RODRIGUEZ).
Aug. 20,	1999	4	San Francisco (MARTINEZ, BONDS, BURKS).
Aug. 22,	1999	1	San Francisco (BONDS, KENT, BURKS).
Aug. 22,	1999	1	Arizona (GONZALEZ, WILLIAMS, DURAZO).
Sept. 17,	1999	4	St. Louis (McGWIRE, T. HOWARD, TATIS).
Apr. 6,	2000	3	St. Louis (TATIS, DREW, MATHENY).
May 13,	2000	8	Cincinnati (TUCKER, GRIFFEY, YOUNG).
June 14,	2000	8	Houston (ALOU, HIDALGO, EUSEBIO).
July 22,	2001	5	San Francisco (KENT, DAVIS, SANTIAGO).
Aug. 3,	2001	6	Cincinnati (YOUNG, LaRUE, REESE).
Sept. 29,	2001	1	Chicago (McGRIFF, WHITE, HUNDLEY).
Apr. 28,	2002	6	Arizona (FINLEY, MILLER, GRACE).
May 3,	2002	1	Arizona (BAUTISTA, FINLEY, MILLER).
May 23,	2002	9	Los Angeles (BELTRE, GREEN, HANSEN).
June 11,	2002	5	Atlanta (A. JONES, CASTILLA, M. FRANCO).
June 22,	2002	5	Colorado (BUTLER, WALKER, HELTON).
July 2,	2002	2	St. Louis (POLANCO, EDMONDS, PUJOLS).
Aug. 4,	2002	6	San Francisco (SNOW, SANDERS, BELL).
Sept. 19,	2002	8	St. Louis (MARRERO, EDMONDS, PUJOLS).
Apr. 7,	2003	6	Atlanta (SHEFFIELD, C. JONES, A. JONES).
May 28,	2003‡	1	Atlanta (FURCAL, DEROSA, SHEFFIELD).
June 24,	2003	6	Chicago (WOOD, GRUDZIELANEK, GONZALEZ).
July 19,	2003	1	Houston (BERKMAN, HIDALGO, ENSBERG).
Aug. 20,	2003‡	5	Pittsburgh (KENDALL, GILES, SANDERS).
Sept. 21,	2003	4	Los Angeles (VENTURA, BELTRE, BURNITZ).
Apr. 18,	2004	5	Los Angeles (BELTRE, ENCARNACION, ROSS).
Apr. 27,	2004	4	Colorado (BURNITZ, JOHNSON, HOLLIDAY).
May 4,	2004	5	Philadelphia (ABREU, THOME, BURRELL).
May 18,	2004	4	Philadelphia (ABREU, BURRELL, THOME).
Aug. 3,	2004	7	San Francisco (SNOW, BONDS, FELIZ).
Aug. 5,	2004	1	Los Angeles (WERTH, BRADLEY, BELTRE).
Aug. 31,	2004	5	Houston (BELTRAN, BAGWELL, BERKMAN).
Sept. 15,	2004	1	Chicago (LEE, SOSA, BARRETT).

*first game; †second game; ‡Club had more than three homers in inning.
Total number of clubs: 105

PITCHING
NO-HIT GAMES

PERFECT GAMES OF NINE OR MORE INNINGS
AMERICAN LEAGUE

Year		Score
1904	Cy Young, Boston vs. Philadelphia, May 5	3-0
1908	Addie Joss, Cleveland vs. Chicago, October 2	1-0
1922	Charlie Robertson, Chicago at Detroit, April 30	2-0
1968	Catfish Hunter, Oakland vs. Minnesota, May 8	4-0
1981	Len Barker, Cleveland vs. Toronto, May 15	3-0
1984	Mike Witt, California at Texas, September 30	1-0
1994	Kenny Rogers, Texas vs. California, July 28	4-0
1998	David Wells, New York vs. Minnesota, May 17	4-0
1999	David Cone, New York vs. Montreal N.L., July 18	6-0

Note: Ernie Shore of Boston is often included in the list of perfect game pitchers. In the first game of a June 23, 1917 doubleheader at Boston, Babe Ruth, the starting Red Sox pitcher, was removed for arguing with umpire Brick Owens after giving a base on balls to Washington's Ray Morgan, the first batter. Shore, without warming up, took Ruth's place. Morgan was retired trying to steal second. From then on, Shore faced 26 batters, with none reaching base. Shore won the game, 4-0. He and Ruth are listed under the category "No-hit games of nine or more innings."

Note: Don Larsen of the New York Yankees pitched a perfect game in the World Series, defeating the Brooklyn Dodgers, 2-0, at Yankee Stadium on October 8, 1956.

Total number of games (excluding Shore's and Larsen's): 9

NATIONAL LEAGUE

Year		Score
1880	Lee Richmond, Worcester vs. Cleveland, June 12	1-0
	Monte Ward, Providence vs. Buffalo, June 17	5-0

Year		Score
1964	Jim Bunning, Philadelphia at New York, June 21, first game	6-0
1965	Sandy Koufax, Los Angeles vs. Chicago, September 9	1-0
1988	Tom Browning, Cincinnati vs. Los Angeles, September 16	1-0
1991	Dennis Martinez, Montreal at Los Angeles, July 28	2-0
2004	Randy Johnson, Arizona at Atlanta, May 18	2-0

Total number of games: 7

PERFECT GAMES FOR NINE INNINGS THAT WERE BROKEN UP IN EXTRA INNINGS
NATIONAL LEAGUE

Year		Score
1959	Harvey Haddix, Pittsburgh at Milwaukee, May 26 (Haddix pitched 12 perfect innings before Felix Mantilla, leading off the 13th, reached base on third baseman Don Hoak's throwing error. After Eddie Mathews sacrificed and Hank Aaron was walked intentionally, Joe Adcock doubled to score Mantilla, ending the game.)	0-1
1995	Pedro J. Martinez Montreal at San Diego, June 3 (Martinez pitched nine perfect innings before Bip Roberts doubled leading off the 10th. Mel Rojas then relieved and retired the game's final three batters.)	1-0

Total number of games: 2

PERFECT GAMES OF LESS THAN NINE INNINGS
AMERICAN LEAGUE

Year		Score
1907	Rube Vickers, Philadelphia at Washington, October 5, second game, five innings	4-0
1967	Dean Chance, Minnesota vs. Boston, August 6, five innings	2-0

Total number of games: 2

NATIONAL LEAGUE

Year		Score
1907	Ed Karger, St. Louis vs. Boston, August 11, second game, seven innings	4-0
1984	David Palmer, Montreal at St. Louis, April 21, second game, five innings	4-0

Total number of games: 2

NO-HIT GAMES OF NINE OR MORE INNINGS
AMERICAN ASSOCIATION

Year		Score
1882	Tony Mullane, Louisville at Cincinnati, September 11 (first no-hitter at 50-foot distance)	2-0
	Guy Hecker, Louisville at Pittsburgh, September 19	3-1
1884	Al Atkinson, Philadelphia vs. Pittsburgh, May 24	10-1
	Ed Morris, Columbus at Pittsburgh, May 29	5-0
	Frank Mountain, Columbus at Washington, June 5	12-0
	Sam Kimber, Brooklyn vs. Toledo, October 4, 10 innings	0-0
1886	Al Atkinson, Philadelphia vs. New York, May 1	3-2
	Adonis Terry, Brooklyn vs. St. Louis, July 24	1-0
	Matt Kilroy, Baltimore at Pittsburgh, October 6	6-0
1888	Adonis Terry, Brooklyn vs. Louisville, May 27	4-0
	Henry Porter, Kansas City at Baltimore, June 6	4-0
	Ed Seward, Philadelphia vs. Cincinnati, July 26	12-2
	Gus Weyhing, Philadelphia vs. Kansas City, July 31	4-0
1890	Cannonball Titcomb, Rochester vs. Syracuse, September 15	7-0
1891	Ted Breitenstein, St. Louis vs. Louisville, October 4, first game (first major league start)	8-0

Total number of games: 15

UNION ASSOCIATION

Year		Score
1884	Dick Burns, Cincinnati at Kansas City, August 26	3-1
1884	Ed Cushman, Milwaukee vs. Washington, September 28	5-0

Total number of games: 2

AMERICAN LEAGUE

Year		Score
1902	Nixey Callahan, Chicago vs. Detroit, September 20, first game	3-0
1904	Jesse Tannehill, Boston at Chicago, August 17	6-0
1905	Weldon Henley, Philadelphia at St. Louis, July 22, first game	6-0
	Frank E. Smith, Chicago at Detroit, September 6, second game	15-0
	Bill Dinneen, Boston vs. Chicago, September 27, first game	2-0
1908	Cy Young, Boston at New York, June 30	8-0
	Bob Rhoads, Cleveland vs. Boston, September 18	2-1
	Frank Smith, Chicago vs. Philadelphia, September 20	1-0
1910	Addie Joss, Cleveland at Chicago, April 20	1-0
	Chief Bender, Philadelphia vs. Cleveland, May 12	4-0
1911	Joe Wood, Boston vs. St. Louis, July 29, first game	5-0
	Ed Walsh Sr., Chicago vs. Boston, August 27	5-0
1912	George Mullin, Detroit vs. St. Louis, July 4, second game	7-0
	Earl Hamilton, St. Louis at Detroit, August 30	5-1
1914	Joe Benz, Chicago vs. Cleveland, May 31	6-1
1916	Rube Foster, Boston vs. New York, June 21	2-0
	Bullet Joe Bush, Philadelphia vs. Cleveland, August 26	5-0
	Dutch H. Leonard, Boston vs. St. Louis, August 30	4-0
1917	Eddie Cicotte, Chicago at St. Louis, April 14	11-0
	George Mogridge, New York at Boston, April 24	2-1

Year		Score
	Ernie Koob, St. Louis vs. Chicago, May 5	1-0
	Bob Groom, St. Louis vs. Chicago, May 6, second game	3-0
	Babe Ruth (0 innings) and Ernie Shore (9 innings), Boston vs. Washington, June 23, first game (see note under American League "perfect games of nine or more innings")	4-0
1918	Dutch H. Leonard, Boston at Detroit, June 3	5-0
1919	Ray Caldwell, Cleveland at New York, September 10, first game	3-0
1920	Walter Johnson, Washington at Boston, July 1	1-0
1923	Sad Sam Jones, New York at Philadelphia, September 4	2-0
	Howard Ehmke, Boston at Philadelphia, September 7	4-0
1926	Ted Lyons, Chicago at Boston, August 21	6-0
1931	Wes Ferrell, Cleveland vs. St. Louis, April 29	9-0
	Bobby Burke, Washington vs. Boston, August 8	5-0
1935	Vern Kennedy, Chicago vs. Cleveland, August 31	5-0
1937	Bill Dietrich, Chicago vs. St. Louis, June 1	8-0
1938	Monte Pearson, New York vs. Cleveland, August 27, second game....................	13-0
1940	Bob Feller, Cleveland at Chicago, April 16 (season opener for both clubs)	1-0
1945	Dick Fowler, Philadelphia vs. St. Louis, September 9, second game	1-0
1946	Bob Feller, Cleveland at New York, April 30	1-0
1947	Don Black, Cleveland vs. Philadelphia, July 10, first game	3-0
	Bill McCahan, Philadelphia vs. Washington, September 3	3-0
1948	Bob Lemon, Cleveland at Detroit, June 30	2-0
1951	Bob Feller, Cleveland vs. Detroit, July 1, first game	2-1
	Allie Reynolds, New York at Cleveland, July 12	1-0
	Allie Reynolds, New York vs. Boston, September 28, first game	8-0
1952	Virgil Trucks, Detroit vs. Washington, May 15	1-0
	Virgil Trucks, Detroit at New York, August 25	1-0
1953	Bobo Holloman, St. Louis vs. Philadelphia, May 6 (first major league start)	6-0
1956	Mel Parnell, Boston vs. Chicago, July 14	4-0
1957	Bob Keegan, Chicago vs. Washington, August 20, second game	6-0
1958	Jim Bunning, Detroit at Boston, July 20, first game	3-0
	Hoyt Wilhelm, Baltimore vs. New York, September 20	1-0
1962	Bo Belinsky, Los Angeles vs. Baltimore, May 5	2-0
	Earl Wilson, Boston vs. Los Angeles, June 26	2-0
	Bill Monbouquette, Boston at Chicago, August 1	1-0
	Jack Kralick, Minnesota vs. Kansas City, August 26	1-0
1965	Dave Morehead, Boston vs. Cleveland, September 16	2-0
1966	Sonny Siebert, Cleveland vs. Washington, June 10	2-0
1967	Steve Barber (8.2 innings) and Stu Miller (.1 inning), Baltimore vs. Detroit, April 30, first game	1-2
	Dean Chance, Minnesota at Cleveland, August 25, second game	2-1
	Joel Horlen, Chicago vs. Detroit, September 10, first game..............................	6-0
1968	Tom Phoebus, Baltimore vs. Boston, April 27	6-0
1969	Jim Palmer, Baltimore vs. Oakland, August 13	8-0
1970	Clyde Wright, California vs. Oakland, July 3	4-0
	Vida Blue, Oakland vs. Minnesota, September 21	6-0
1973	Steve Busby, Kansas City at Detroit, April 27	3-0
	Nolan Ryan, California at Kansas City, May 15	3-0
	Nolan Ryan, California at Detroit, July 15	6-0
	Jim Bibby, Texas at Oakland, July 30	6-0
1974	Steve Busby, Kansas City at Milwaukee, June 19	2-0
	Dick Bosman, Cleveland at Oakland, July 19	4-0
	Nolan Ryan, California vs. Minnesota, September 28	4-0
1975	Nolan Ryan, California vs. Baltimore, June 1	1-0
	Vida Blue (five innings), Glenn Abbott (one inning), Paul Lindblad (one inning) and Rollie Fingers (two innings), Oakland vs. California, September 28	5-0
1976	Blue Moon Odom (five innings) and Francisco Barrios (four innings), Chicago at Oakland, July 28..........	2-1
1977	Jim Colborn, Kansas City vs. Texas, May 14	6-0
	Dennis Eckersley, Cleveland vs. California, May 30...	1-0
	Bert Blyleven, Texas at California, September 22	6-0
1983	Dave Righetti, New York vs. Boston, July 4	4-0
	Mike Warren, Oakland vs. Chicago, September 29	3-0
1984	Jack Morris, Detroit at Chicago, April 7	4-0
1986	Joe Cowley, Chicago at California, September 19	7-1
1987	Juan Nieves, Milwaukee at Baltimore, April 15	7-0
1990	Mark Langston (seven innings) and Mike Witt (two innings), California vs. Seattle, April 11	1-0
	Randy Johnson, Seattle vs. Detroit, June 2	2-0
	Nolan Ryan, Texas at Oakland, June 11	5-0
	Dave Stewart, Oakland at Toronto, June 29	5-0
	Dave Stieb, Toronto at Cleveland, September 2	3-0
1991	Nolan Ryan, Texas vs. Toronto, May 1	3-0
	Bob Milacki (six innings), Mike Flanagan (one inning), Mark Williamson (one inning) and Gregg Olson (one inning), Baltimore at Oakland, July 13	2-0
	Wilson Alvarez, Chicago at Baltimore, August 11	7-0
	Bret Saberhagen, Kansas City vs. Chicago, August 26	7-0
1993	Chris Bosio, Seattle vs. Boston, April 22	2-0
	Jim Abbott, New York vs. Cleveland, September 4	4-0
1994	Scott Erickson, Minnesota vs. Milwaukee, April 27	6-0
1996	Dwight Gooden, New York vs. Seattle, May 14	2-0

Year		Score
1999	Eric Milton, Minnesota vs. Anaheim, September 11	7-0
2001	Hideo Nomo, Boston at Baltimore, April 4	3-0
2002	Derek Lowe, Boston vs. Tampa Bay, April 27	10-0

Note—Andy Hawkins (1990) and Matt Young (1992), as visiting teams' pitchers, pitched all eight innings of nine-inning, no-hit losses. Both are listed under the category "No-hit games of less than nine innings."

Total number of games (excluding Hawkins' and M. Young's): 97

NATIONAL LEAGUE

Year		Score
1876	George Bradley, St. Louis vs. Hartford, July 15	2-0
1880	Larry Corcoran, Chicago vs. Boston, August 19	6-0
	Pud Galvin, Buffalo at Worcester, August 20	1-0
1882	Larry Corcoran, Chicago vs. Worcester, September 20	5-0
1883	Hoss Radbourn, Providence at Cleveland, July 25	8-0
	Hugh Daily, Cleveland at Philadelphia, September 13	1-0
1884	Larry Corcoran, Chicago vs. Providence, June 27	6-0
	Pud Galvin, Buffalo at Detroit, August 4	18-0
1885	John Clarkson, Chicago at Providence, July 27	4-0
	Charlie J. Ferguson, Philadelphia vs. Providence, August 29	1-0
1891	Tom Lovett, Brooklyn vs. New York, June 22	4-0
	Amos Rusie, New York vs. Brooklyn, July 31	6-0
1892	Jack Stivetts, Boston vs. Brooklyn, August 6	11-0
	Ben Sanders, Louisville vs. Baltimore, August 22	6-2
	Bumpus Jones, Cincinnati vs. Pittsburgh, October 15 (first major league game)	7-1
1893	Bill Hawke, Baltimore vs. Washington, August 16 (first no-hitter at 60-foot, 6-inch distance)	5-0
1897	Cy Young, Cleveland vs. Cincinnati, September 18, first game	6-0
1898	Ted Breitenstein, Cincinnati vs. Pittsburgh, April 22	11-0
	Jim J. Hughes, Baltimore vs. Boston, April 22	8-0
	Frank Donahue, Philadelphia vs. Boston, July 8	5-0
	Walter Thornton, Chicago vs. Brooklyn, August 21, second game	2 0
1899	Deacon Phillippe, Louisville vs. New York, May 25	7-0
	Vic Willis, Boston vs. Washington, August 7	7-1
1900	Noodles Hahn, Cincinnati vs. Philadelphia, July 12	4-0
1901	Christy Mathewson, New York at St. Louis, July 15	5-0
1903	Chick Fraser, Philadelphia at Chicago, September 18, second game	10-0
1905	Christy Mathewson, New York at Chicago, June 13	1-0
1906	Johnny Lush, Philadelphia at Brooklyn, May 1	6-0
	Mal Eason, Brooklyn at St. Louis, July 20	2-0
1907	Frank Pfeffer, Boston vs. Cincinnati, May 8	6-0
	Nick Maddox, Pittsburgh vs. Brooklyn, September 20	2-1
1908	Hooks Wiltse, New York vs. Philadelphia, July 4, first game, 10 innings	1-0
	Nap Rucker, Brooklyn vs. Boston, September 5, second game	6-0
1912	Jeff Tesreau, New York at Philadelphia, September 6, first game	3-0
1914	George A. Davis, Boston vs. Philadelphia, September 9, second game	7-0
1915	Rube Marquard, New York vs. Brooklyn, April 15	2-0
	Jimmy Lavender, Chicago at New York, August 31, first game	2-0
1916	Tom L. Hughes, Boston vs. Pittsburgh, June 16	2-0
1917	Fred Toney, Cincinnati at Chicago, May 2, 10 innings (Hippo Vaughn of Chicago pitched 9.1 hitless innings in the same game before his no-hitter was spoiled.)	1-0
1919	Hod Eller, Cincinnati vs. St. Louis, May 11	6-0
1922	Jesse Barnes, New York vs. Philadelphia, May 7	6-0
1924	Jesse Haines, St. Louis vs. Boston, July 17	5-0
1925	Dazzy Vance, Brooklyn vs. Philadelphia, September 13, first game	10-1
1929	Carl Hubbell, New York vs. Pittsburgh, May 8	11-0
1934	Paul Dean, St. Louis at Brooklyn, September 21, second game	3-0
1938	Johnny Vander Meer, Cincinnati vs. Boston, June 11	3-0
	Johnny Vander Meer, Cincinnati at Brooklyn, June 15 (His two no-hitters were consecutive.)	6-0
1940	Tex Carleton, Brooklyn at Cincinnati, April 30	3-0
1941	Lon Warneke, St. Louis at Cincinnati, August 30	2-0
1944	Jim Tobin, Boston vs. Brooklyn, April 27	2-0
	Clyde Shoun, Cincinnati vs. Boston, May 15	1-0
1946	Ed Head, Brooklyn vs. Boston, April 23	5-0
1947	Ewell Blackwell, Cincinnati vs. Boston, June 18	6-0
1948	Rex Barney, Brooklyn at New York, September 9	2-0
1950	Vern Bickford, Boston vs. Brooklyn, August 11	7-0
1951	Cliff Chambers, Pittsburgh at Boston, May 6, second game	3-0
1952	Carl Erskine, Brooklyn vs. Chicago, June 19	5-0
1954	Jim Wilson, Milwaukee vs. Philadelphia, June 12	2-0
1955	Sam Jones, Chicago vs. Pittsburgh, May 12	4-0
1956	Carl Erskine, Brooklyn vs. New York, May 12	3-0
	Sal Maglie, Brooklyn vs. Philadelphia, September 25	5-0
1960	Don Cardwell, Chicago vs. St. Louis, May 15, second game	4-0
	Lew Burdette, Milwaukee vs. Philadelphia, August 18	1-0
	Warren Spahn, Milwaukee vs. Philadelphia, September 16	4-0
1961	Warren Spahn, Milwaukee vs. San Francisco, April 28	1-0
1962	Sandy Koufax, Los Angeles vs. New York, June 30	5-0
1963	Sandy Koufax, Los Angeles vs. San Francisco, May 11	8-0
	Don Nottebart, Houston vs. Philadelphia, May 17	4-1

Year		Score
	Juan Marichal, San Francisco vs. Houston, June 15	1-0
1964	Ken Johnson, Houston vs. Cincinnati, April 23	0-1
	Sandy Koufax, Los Angeles at Philadelphia, June 4	3-0
1965	Jim Maloney, Cincinnati at Chicago, August 19, first game, 10 innings	1-0
1967	Don Wilson, Houston vs. Atlanta, June 18	2-0
1968	George Culver, Cincinnati at Philadelphia, July 29, second game	6-1
	Gaylord Perry, San Francisco vs. St. Louis, September 17	1-0
	Ray Washburn, St. Louis at San Francisco, September 18	2-0
1969	Bill Stoneman, Montreal at Philadelphia, April 17	7-0
	Jim Maloney, Cincinnati vs. Houston, April 30	10-0
	Don Wilson, Houston at Cincinnati, May 1	4-0
	Ken Holtzman, Chicago vs. Atlanta, August 19	3-0
	Bob Moose, Pittsburgh at New York, September 20	4-0
1970	Dock Ellis, Pittsburgh at San Diego, June 12, first game	2-0
	Bill Singer, Los Angeles vs. Philadelphia, July 20	5-0
1971	Ken Holtzman, Chicago at Cincinnati, June 3	1-0
	Rick Wise, Philadelphia at Cincinnati, June 23	4-0
	Bob Gibson, St. Louis at Pittsburgh, August 14	11-0
1972	Burt Hooton, Chicago vs. Philadelphia, April 16	4-0
	Milt Pappas, Chicago vs. San Diego, September 2	8-0
	Bill Stoneman, Montreal vs. New York, October 2, first game	7-0
1973	Phil Niekro, Atlanta vs. San Diego, August 5	9-0
1975	Ed Halicki, San Francisco vs. New York, August 24, second game	6-0
1976	Larry Dierker, Houston vs. Montreal, July 9	6-0
	John Candelaria, Pittsburgh vs. Los Angeles, August 9	2-0
	John Montefusco, San Francisco at Atlanta, September 29	9-0
1978	Bob Forsch, St. Louis vs. Philadelphia, April 16	5-0
	Tom Seaver, Cincinnati vs. St. Louis, June 16	4-0
1979	Ken Forsch, Houston vs. Atlanta, April 7	6-0
1980	Jerry Reuss, Los Angeles at San Francisco, June 27	8-0
1981	Charlie Lea, Montreal vs. San Francisco, May 10, second game	4-0
	Nolan Ryan, Houston vs. Los Angeles, September 26	5-0
1983	Bob Forsch, St. Louis vs. Montreal, September 26	3-0
1986	Mike Scott, Houston vs. San Francisco, September 25	2-0
1990	Fernando Valenzuela, Los Angeles vs. St. Louis, June 29	6-0
	Terry Mulholland, Philadelphia vs. San Francisco, August 15	6-0
1991	Tommy Greene, Philadelphia at Montreal, May 23	2-0
	Kent Mercker (six innings), Mark Wohlers (two innings) and Alejandro Pena (one inning), Atlanta vs. San Diego, September 11	1-0
1992	Kevin Gross, Los Angeles vs. San Francisco, August 17	2-0
1993	Darryl Kile, Houston vs. New York, September 8	7-1
1994	Kent Mercker, Atlanta vs. Los Angeles, April 8	6-0
1995	Ramon Martinez, Los Angeles vs. Florida, July 14	7-0
1996	Al Leiter, Florida vs. Colorado, May 11	11-0
	Hideo Nomo, Los Angeles at Colorado, September 17	9-0
1997	Kevin Brown, Florida at San Francisco, June 10	9-0
	Francisco Cordova (nine innings) and Ricardo Rincon (one inning), Pittsburgh vs. Houston, July 12, 10 innings	3-0
1999	Jose Jimenez, St. Louis at Arizona, June 25	1-0
2001	A.J. Burnett, Florida at San Diego, May 12	3-0
	Bud Smith, St. Louis at San Diego, September 3	4-0
2003	Kevin Millwood, Philadelphia vs. San Francisco, April 27	1-0
	Roy Oswalt (one inning), Peter Munro (two innings), Kirk Saarloos (one inning), Brad Lidge (two innings), Octavio Dotel (one inning) and Billy Wagner (one inning), Houston at New York A.L., June 11	8-0

Total number of games: 119

NO-HIT GAMES FOR NINE OR MORE INNINGS THAT WERE BROKEN UP IN EXTRA INNINGS
AMERICAN LEAGUE

Year		Score
1901	Earl Moore, Cleveland vs. Chicago, May 9 (Moore pitched nine hitless innings before Sam Mertes singled; lost on two hits in 10 innings.)	2-4
1910	Tom L. Hughes, New York vs. Cleveland, August 30, second game (Hughes pitched 9.1 hitless innings before Harry Niles singled; lost on seven hits in 11 innings.)	0-5
1914	Jim Scott, Chicago at Washington, May 14 (Scott pitched nine hitless innings before Chick Gandil singled; lost on two hits in 10 innings)	0-1
1934	Bobo Newsom, St. Louis vs. Boston, September 18 (Newsom pitched 9.2 hitless innings before Roy Johnson singled; lost on one hit in 10 innings.)	1-2

Total number of games: 4

NATIONAL LEAGUE

Year		Score
1904	Bob Wicker, Chicago at New York, June 11 (pitched 9.1 hitless innings before Sam Mertes singled; won on one hit in 12 innings.)	1-0
1906	Harry McIntire, Brooklyn vs. Pittsburgh, August 1 (pitched 10.2 hitless innings before Claude Ritchey singled; lost on four hits in 13 innings.)	0-1
1909	Red Ames, New York vs. Brooklyn, April 15 (pitched 9.1 hitless innings before Whitey Alperman singled; lost on seven hits in 13 innings. The game was both teams' season opener.)	0-3
1917	Hippo Vaughn, Chicago vs. Cincinnati, May 2 (pitched 9.1 hitless innings before Larry Kopf singled; lost on two hits in 10 innings. Fred Toney of Cincinnati pitched 10 no-hit innings in the same game.)	0-1

Year		Score
1956	Johnny Klippstein (seven innings), Hershell Freeman (one inning) and Joe Black (three innings), Cincinnati at Milwaukee, May 26 (Jack Dittmer doubled for the first hit with two outs in the 10th inning and Black lost on three hits in 11 innings.)	...1-2
1965	Jim Maloney, Cincinnati vs. New York, June 14 (pitched 10 hitless innings before Johnny Lewis homered; lost on two hits in 11 innings.)	0-1
1991	Mark Gardner (nine innings) and Jeff Fassero (no innings), Montreal at Los Angeles, July 26 (Lenny Harris singled off Gardner in the 10th inning; Gardner allowed another hit and Fassero allowed one hit; Gardner lost the game in the 10th inning.)	0-1

Total number of games: 7

NO-HIT GAMES OF LESS THAN NINE INNINGS
AMERICAN ASSOCIATION

Year		Score
1884	Larry McKeon, Indianapolis at Cincinnati, May 6, six innings	0-0
1889	Matt Kilroy, Baltimore vs. St. Louis, July 29, second game, seven innings	0-0
1890	George Nicol, St. Louis vs. Philadelphia, September 23, seven innings	21-2
	Hank Gastright, Columbus vs. Toledo, October 12, eight innings	6-0

Total number of games: 4

PLAYERS LEAGUE

Year		Score
1890	Charles King, Chicago vs. Brooklyn, June 21, eight innings	0-1

Total number of games: 1

UNION ASSOCIATION

Year		Score
1884	Charlie Geggus, Washington vs. Wilmington, August 21, eight innings	12-1
	Charlie Sweeney (two innings) and Henry Boyle (three innings), St. Louis vs. St. Paul, October 5, five innings	0-1

Total number of games: 2

AMERICAN LEAGUE

Year		Score
1905	Rube Waddell, Philadelphia vs. St. Louis, August 15, five innings	2-0
1907	Ed Walsh Sr., Chicago vs. New York, May 26, five innings	8-1
1912	Jay Cashion, Washington vs. Cleveland, August 20, second game, six innings	2-0
1924	Walter Johnson, Washington vs. St. Louis, August 25, seven innings	2-0
1940	John Whitehead, St. Louis vs. Detroit, August 5, second game, six innings	4-0
1990	Andy Hawkins, New York at Chicago, July 1 (As a visiting team's pitcher, he pitched all eight innings of a nine-inning, no-hit loss.)	0-4
	Melido Perez, Chicago at New York, July 12, six innings	8-0
1992	Matt Young, Boston at Cleveland, April 12 (As a visiting team's pitcher, he pitched all eight innings of a nine-inning, no-hit loss.)	1-2

Total number of games: 8

NATIONAL LEAGUE

Year		Score
1884	Charlie Getzien, Detroit vs. Philadelphia, October 1, six innings	1-0
1885	Fred Shaw, Providence at Buffalo, October 7, first game, five innings	4-0
1888	George Van Haltren, Chicago vs. Pittsburgh, June 21, six innings	1-0
	Cannonball Crane, New York vs. Washington, September 27, seven innings	3-0
1892	Jack Stivetts, Boston at Washington, October 15, second game, five innings	4-0
1893	Elton Chamberlain, Cincinnati vs. Boston, September 23, second game, seven innings	6-0
1894	Ed Stein, Brooklyn vs. Chicago, June 2, six innings	1-0
1903	Red Ames, New York at St. Louis, September 14, second game, five innings (first major league game)	5-0
1906	Jake Weimer, Cincinnati vs. Brooklyn, August 24, second game, seven innings	1-0
	Stoney McGlynn, St. Louis vs. Brooklyn, September 24, second game, seven innings	1-1
	Lefty Leifield, Pittsburgh at Philadelphia, September 26, second game, six innings	8-0
1907	Howie Camnitz, Pittsburgh at New York, August 23, second game, five innings	1-0
1908	Johnny Lush, St. Louis at Brooklyn, August 6, six innings	2-0
1910	King Cole, Chicago at St. Louis, July 31, second game, seven innings	4-0
1937	Fred Frankhouse, Brooklyn vs. Cincinnati, August 27, eight innings	5-0
1944	Jim Tobin, Boston vs. Philadelphia, June 22, second game, five innings	7-0
1959	Mike McCormick, San Francisco at Philadelphia, June 12, five innings (McCormick allowed a single to Richie Ashburn in the sixth inning, but the game was halted because of rain before completion of the inning. The hit was erased because, under existing rules, records reverted to the last completed inning.)	3-0
	Sam Jones, San Francisco at St. Louis, September 26, seven innings	4-0
1988	Pascual Perez, Montreal at Philadelphia, September 24, five innings	1-0

Total number of games: 19

<table>
<tr><td colspan="4">

TWO COMPLETE-GAME VICTORIES IN ONE DAY

PLAYERS LEAGUE
</td></tr>
</table>

		Scores	
July 26, 1890	Henry Gruber, Cleveland	6-1	8-7
Aug. 20, 1890	Bert Cunningham, Buffalo	6-2	7-0
Sept. 27, 1890	Ed Crane, New York	9-8	8-3

Total number of occurrences: 3

AMERICAN ASSOCIATION

		Scores	
July 4, 1883	Tim Keefe, New York	9-1	3-0
July 4, 1884	Guy Hecker, Louisville	5-4	8-2
July 26, 1887	Matt Kilroy, Baltimore	‡8-0	9-1
Oct. 1, 1887	Matt Kilroy, Baltimore	5-2	‡8-1
Sept. 20, 1888	Tony Mullane, Cincinnati	1-0	2-1

Total number of occurrences: 5

AMERICAN LEAGUE

		Scores	
July 1, 1905	Frank Owen, Chicago	3-2	2-0
Sept. 26, 1905	Ed Walsh, Chicago	10-5	§3-1
Sept. 22, 1906	George Mullin, Detroit	5-3	4-3
Sept. 25, 1908	Ed Summers, Detroit	7-2	∞1-0
Sept. 29, 1908	Ed Walsh, Chicago	5-1	2-0
Sept. 22, 1914	Ray Collins, Boston	5-3	§5-0
July 29, 1916	Dave Davenport, St. Louis	3-1	3-2
Aug. 30, 1918	Carl Mays, Boston	12-0	4-1
Sept. 6, 1924	Urban Shocker, St. Louis	6-2	6-2
Aug. 28, 1926	Dutch Levsen, Cleveland	6-1	5-1

Total number of occurrences: 10

NATIONAL LEAGUE

		Scores	
Sept. 19, 1876	Candy Cummings, Hartford	14-4	8-4
Aug. 9, 1878	Monte Ward, Providence	12-6	8-5
July 12, 1879	Pud Galvin, Buffalo	4-3	◆5-4
July 4, 1881	Mickey Welch, Troy	8-0	12-3
July 4, 1882	Pud Galvin, Buffalo	9-5	18-8
May 30, 1884	Hoss Radbourn, Providence	12-9	9-2
Oct. 7, 1885	Fred Shaw, Providence	*4-0	*6-1
Oct. 10, 1885	Fred Shaw, Providence	†3-0	*7-3
Oct. 9, 1886	Charlie Ferguson, Philadelphia	5-1	†6-1
Aug. 20, 1887	Jim Whitney, Washington	3-1	4-3
Sept. 12, 1889	John Clarkson, Boston	3-2	5-0
May 30, 1890	Bill Hutchinson, Chicago	6-4	11-7
Oct. 4, 1890	Cy Young, Cleveland	5-1	7-3
Sept. 12, 1891	Mark Baldwin, Pittsburgh	13-3	8-4
Sept. 28, 1891	Amos Rusie, New York	10-4	†13-5
May 30, 1892	Mark Baldwin, Pittsburgh	11-1	4-3
Sept. 5, 1892	Jack Stivetts, Boston	▲2-1	5-2
Oct. 4, 1892	Amos Rusie, New York	6-4	9-5
May 30, 1893	William Kennedy, Brooklyn	3-0	6-2
June 3, 1897	Cy Seymour, New York	6-1	‡10-6
Oct. 13, 1898	Al Orth, Philadelphia	5-1	*9-6
Aug. 1, 1903	Joe McGinnity, New York	4-1	5-2
Aug. 8, 1903	Joe McGinnity, New York	6-1	4-3
Aug. 31, 1903	Joe McGinnity, New York	4-1	9-2
Oct. 3, 1905	Doc Scanlan, Brooklyn	4-0	3-2
Sept. 26, 1908	Ed Reulbach, Chicago	5-0	3-0
Sept. 9, 1916	Pol Perritt, New York	3-1	3-0
Sept. 20, 1916	Al Demaree, Philadelphia	7-0	3-2
Sept. 23, 1916	Grover Alexander, Philadelphia	7-3	4-0
July 1, 1917	Fred Toney, Cincinnati	4-1	5-1
Sept. 3, 1917	Grover Alexander, Philadelphia	5-0	9-3
Sept. 18, 1917	Bill Doak, St. Louis	2-0	12-4
Aug. 13, 1921	Mule Watson, Boston	4-3	8-0
July 10, 1923	Johnny Stuart, St. Louis	11-1	6-3
July 19, 1924	Herman Bell, St. Louis	6-1	2-1

*5 innings. †6 innings. ‡7 innings. §8 innings. ∞10 innings.
▲11 innings. ◆12 innings.

Total number of occurrences: 35

PITCHERS WITH 12 STRAIGHT VICTORIES IN SEASON

AMERICAN ASSOCIATION

Year	Pitcher	Won
1890	Scott Stratton, Louisville	15
1884	John Lynch, New York	14
1882	Will White, Cincinnati	12

Total number of occurrences: 3

UNION ASSOCIATION

Year	Pitcher	Won
1884	Jim McCormick, Cincinnati	14

Total number of occurrences: 1

AMERICAN LEAGUE

Year	Pitcher	Won
1912	Walter Johnson, Washington	16
1912	Joe Wood, Boston	16
1931	Lefty Grove, Philadelphia	16
1934	Schoolboy Rowe, Detroit	16
2001	Roger Clemens, New York	16
1932	Alvin Crowder, Washington	15

Year	Pitcher	Won
1937	Johnny Allen, Cleveland	15
1969	Dave McNally, Baltimore	15
1974	Gaylord Perry, Cleveland	15
1998	Roger Clemens, Toronto	15
2003	Roy Halladay, Toronto	15
1904	Jack Chesbro, New York	14
1913	Walter Johnson, Washington	14
1914	Chief Bender, Philadelphia	14
1928	Lefty Grove, Philadelphia	14
1961	Whitey Ford, New York	14
1980	Steve Stone, Baltimore	14
1986	Roger Clemens, Boston	14
1924	Walter Johnson, Washington	13
1925	Stan Coveleski, Washington	13
1930	Wes Ferrell, Cleveland	13
1940	Bobo Newsom, Detroit	13
1949	Ellis Kinder, Boston	13
1971	Dave McNally, Baltimore	13
1973	Catfish Hunter, Oakland	13
1978	Ron Guidry, New York	13
1983	LaMarr Hoyt, Chicago	13
1901	Cy Young, Boston	12
1910	Russ Ford, New York	12
1914	Dutch H. Leonard, Boston	12
1929	Tom Zachary, New York	12
1931	George Earnshaw, Philadelphia	12
1938	Johnny Allen, Cleveland	12
1939	Atley Donald, New York	12
1946	Dave Ferriss, Boston	12
1961	Luis Arroyo, New York	12
1963	Whitey Ford, New York	12
1968	Dave McNally, Baltimore	12
1971	Pat Dobson, Baltimore	12
1985	Ron Guidry, New York	12
1990	Bobby Witt, Texas	12
1991	Scott Erickson, Minnesota	12
1997	Brad Radke, Minnesota	12
2002	Jarrod Washburn, Anaheim	12
2004	Johan Santana, Minnesota	12

Total number of occurrences: 45

NATIONAL LEAGUE

Year	Pitcher	Won
1888	Tim Keefe, New York	19
1912	Rube Marquard, New York	19
1884	Hoss Radbourn, Providence	18
1885	Mickey Welch, New York	17
1890	Pat Luby, Chicago	17
1959	Elroy Face, Pittsburgh	17
1886	Jim McCormick, Chicago	16
1936	Carl Hubbell, New York	16
1947	Ewell Blackwell, Cincinnati	16
1962	Jack Sanford, San Francisco	16
1924	Dazzy Vance, Brooklyn	15
1968	Bob Gibson, St. Louis	15
1972	Steve Carlton, Philadelphia	15
1885	Jim McCormick, Chicago	14
1886	John Flynn, Chicago	14
1904	Joe McGinnity, New York	14
1909	Ed Reulbach, Chicago	14
1984	Rick Sutcliffe, Chicago	14
1985	Dwight Gooden, New York	14
1996	John Smoltz, Atlanta	14
1880	Larry Corcoran, Chicago	13
1884	Charlie Buffinton, Boston	13
1885	John Clarkson, Chicago	13
1892	Cy Young, Cleveland	13
1893	Frank Killen, Pittsburgh	13
1896	Frank Dwyer, Cincinnati	13
1897	Fred Klobedanz, Boston	13
1898	Ted Lewis, Boston	13
1909	Christy Mathewson, New York	13
1910	Deacon Phillippe, Pittsburgh	13
1927	Burleigh Grimes, New York	13
1956	Brooks Lawrence, Cincinnati	13
1966	Phil Regan, Los Angeles	13
1971	Dock Ellis, Pittsburgh	13
1992	Tom Glavine, Atlanta	13
1886	Charlie Ferguson, Philadelphia	12

Year	Pitcher	Won
1902	Jack Chesbro, Pittsburgh	12
1904	George Wiltse, New York	12
1906	Ed Reulbach, Chicago	12
1975	Burt Hooton, Los Angeles	12
1993	Mark Portugal, Houston	12
2002	Wade Miller, Houston	12

Total number of occurrences: 42

PITCHERS WITH 12 STRAIGHT LOSSES IN SEASON

AMERICAN ASSOCIATION

Year	Pitcher	Lost
1882	Fred Nichols, Baltimore	12
1887	Billy Crowell, Cleveland	12

Total number of occurrences: 2

AMERICAN LEAGUE

Year	Pitcher	Lost
1916	John Nabors, Philadelphia	19
1980	Mike Parrott, Seattle	16
1909	Bob Groom, Washington	15
1906	Joe Harris, Boston	14
1949	Howard Judson, Chicago	14
1949	Paul Calvert, Washington	14
1979	Matt Keough, Oakland	14
1914	Guy Morton, Cleveland	13
1920	Roy Moore, Philadelphia	13
1930	Frank Henry, Chicago	13
1943	Luman Harris, Philadelphia	13
1982	Terry Felton, Minnesota	13
1901	Bill Carrick, Washington	12
1929	Red Ruffing, Boston	12
1940	Walt Masterson, Washington	12
1945	Bobo Newsom, Philadelphia	12
1945	Steve Gerkin, Philadelphia	12
1953	Charlie Bishop, Philadelphia	12

Total number of occurrences: 18

NATIONAL LEAGUE

Year	Pitcher	Lost
1910	Cliff Curtis, Boston	18
1963	Roger Craig, New York	18
1876	Dory Dean, Cincinnati	16
1899	Jim Hughey, Cleveland	16
1962	Craig Anderson, New York	16
1887	Frank Gilmore, Washington	14
1899	Fred Bates, Cleveland	14
1908	Jim Pastorius, Brooklyn	14
1911	Buster Brown, Boston	14
1992	Anthony Young, New York	14
1884	Sam Moffett, Cleveland	13
1917	Burleigh Grimes, Pittsburgh	13
1922	Joe Oeschger, Boston	13
1935	Ben Cantwell, Boston	13
1948	Bob McCall, Chicago	13
1993	Anthony Young, New York	13
2000	Jose Lima, Houston	13
1880	William Purcell, Cincinnati	12
1883	John Coleman, Philadelphia	12
1897	Bill Hart, St. Louis	12
1902	Henry Thielman, Cincinnati	12
1905	Mal Eason, Brooklyn	12
1914	Rube Marquard, New York	12
1914	Pete Schneider, Cincinnati	12
1928	Russ Miller, Philadelphia	12
1933	Silas Johnson, Cincinnati	12
1939	Max Butcher, Philadelphia-Pittsburgh	12
1940	Hugh Mulcahy, Philadelphia	12
1962	Bob Miller, New York	12
1972	Ken Reynolds, Philadelphia	12

Total number of occurrences: 30

20-GAME WINNERS

(Numbers in parentheses after club denote
position of team at close of season)

AMERICAN ASSOCIATION

	W	L
1882 (5)		
Will White, Cincinnati (1)	40	12
Tony Mullane, Louisville (2)	30	24
Sam Weaver, Philadelphia (3)	26	15
George McGinnis, St. Louis (5)	25	21
Harry Salisbury, Pittsburgh (5)	20	19
1883 (8)		
Will White, Cincinnati (3)	43	22
Tim Keefe, New York (4)	41	27
Tony Mullane, St. Louis (2)	35	15
Bobby Mathews, Philadelphia (1)	30	14
George McGinnis, St. Louis (2)	29	15
Guy Hecker, Louisville (5)	28	25
Frank Mountain, Columbus (6)	26	33
Sam Weaver, Louisville (5)	24	20
1884 (12)		
Guy Hecker, Louisville (3)	52	20
Jack Lynch, New York (1)	37	15
Tim Keefe, New York (1)	37	17
Ed Morris, Columbus (2)	35	13
Tony Mullane, Toledo (8)	35	25
Will White, Cincinnati (5)	34	18
Bob Emslie, Baltimore (6)	32	18
Bobby Mathews, Philadelphia (7)	30	18
Hardie Henderson, Baltimore (6)	27	22
George McGinnis, St. Louis (4)	24	16
Frank Mountain, Columbus (2)	24	17
Billy Mountjoy, Cincinnati (5)	20	12
1885 (9)		
Bob Caruthers, St. Louis (1)	40	13
Ed Morris, Pittsburgh (3)	39	24
Dave Foutz, St. Louis (1)	33	14
Henry Porter, Brooklyn (5T)	33	21
Bobby Mathews, Philadelphia (4)	30	17
Guy Hecker, Louisville (5T)	30	24
Hardie Henderson, Baltimore (8)	26	35
Jack Lynch, New York (7)	23	21
Larry McKeon, Cincinnati (2)	20	15
1886 (11)		
Dave Foutz, St. Louis (1)	41	16
Ed Morris, Pittsburgh (2)	41	20
Tom Ramsey, Louisville (4)	37	27
Tony Mullane, Cincinnati (5)	31	27
Bob Caruthers, St. Louis (1)	30	14
Pud Galvin, Pittsburgh (2)	29	21
Matt Kilroy, Baltimore (8)	29	34
Henry Porter, Brooklyn (3)	28	20
Guy Hecker, Louisville (4)	27	23
Al Atkinson, Philadelphia (6)	25	17
Jack Lynch, New York (7)	20	20
1887 (10)		
Matt Kilroy, Baltimore (3)	46	20
Tom Ramsey, Louisville (4)	39	27
Charles King, St. Louis (1)	34	11
Elmer Smith, Cincinnati (2)	33	18
Tony Mullane, Cincinnati (2)	31	17
Bob Caruthers, St. Louis (1)	29	9
John Smith, Baltimore (3)	29	29
Gus Weyhing, Philadelphia (5)	26	25
Ed Seward, Philadelphia (5)	25	24
Dave Foutz, St. Louis (1)	24	12
1888 (12)		
Charles King, St. Louis (1)	45	21
Ed Seward, Philadelphia (3)	34	19
Bob Caruthers, Brooklyn (2)	29	15
Gus Weyhing, Philadelphia (3)	29	19
Lee Viau, Cincinnati (4)	27	14
Tony Mullane, Cincinnati (4)	26	16
Nat Hudson, St. Louis (1)	25	11
Elton Chamberlain, 9-8 Louisville (7), 16-4 St. Louis (1)	25	12
Mickey Hughes, Brooklyn (2)	25	13
Ed Bakely, Cleveland (6)	25	33

	W	L
Elmer Smith, Cincinnati (4)	22	17
Bert Cunningham, Baltimore (5)	22	29

1889 (11)

	W	L
Bob Caruthers, Brooklyn (1)	40	12
Elton Chamberlain, St. Louis (2)	35	15
Charles King, St. Louis (2)	33	17
Jesse Duryea, Cincinnati (4)	32	21
Gus Weyhing, Philadelphia (3)	28	19
Matt Kilroy, Baltimore (5)	28	25
Mark Baldwin, Columbus (6)	26	24
Frank Foreman, Baltimore (5)	25	21
Adonis Terry, Brooklyn (1)	21	16
Ed Seward, Philadelphia (3)	21	16
Lee Viau, Cincinnati (4)	21	19

1890 (8)

	W	L
John McMahon, 29-19 Philadelphia (8), 7-2 Baltimore (6)	36	21
Scott Stratton, Louisville (1)	34	13
Hank Gastright, Columbus (2)	29	13
Bob Barr, Rochester (5)	28	25
Jack Stivetts, St. Louis (3)	27	21
Tom Ramsey, St. Louis (3)	26	16

1890 (8)

	W	L
Red Ehret, Louisville (1)	25	14
Egyptian Healy, Toledo (4)	22	23

1891 (8)

	W	L
John McMahon, Baltimore (3)	35	24
George Haddock, Boston (1)	34	11
Jack Stivetts, St. Louis (2)	33	22
Gus Weyhing, Philadelphia (4)	31	20
Charlie Buffinton, Boston (1)	29	9
Phil Knell, Columbus (5)	27	26
Elton Chamberlain, Philadelphia (4)	23	23
Willie McGill, 2-5 Cincinnati (5), 19-10 St. Louis (2)	21	15

PLAYERS LEAGUE

1890 (9)

	W	L
Mark Baldwin, Chicago (4)	32	24
Gus Weyhing, Brooklyn (2)	30	16
Charles King, Chicago (4)	30	22
Hoss Radbourn, Boston (1)	27	12
Adison Gumbert, Boston (1)	23	12
Hank O'Day, New York (3)	22	13
Henry Gruber, Cleveland (7)	22	23
Phil Knell, Philadelphia (5)	21	10
Harry Staley, Pittsburgh (6)	21	23

UNION ASSOCIATION

1884 (9)

	W	L
Bill Sweeney, Baltimore (3)	40	21
Hugh Daily, 22-25 Chicago (6), 1-1 Washington (5), 5-4 Pittsburgh (8)	28	30
Billy Taylor, St. Louis (1)	25	4
Dick Burns, Cincinnati (2)	25	15
Charlie Sweeney, St. Louis (1)	24	8
Bill Wise, Washington (5)	23	20
Jim McCormick, Cincinnati (2)	22	4
Fred Shaw, Boston (4)	22	15
George Bradley, Cincinnati (2)	21	13

AMERICAN LEAGUE

1901 (5)

	W	L
Cy Young, Boston (2)	33	10
Joe McGinnity, Baltimore (5)	26	21
Clark Griffith, Chicago (1)	24	7
Roscoe Miller, Detroit (3)	23	13
Chick Fraser, Philadelphia (4)	20	15

1902 (7)

	W	L
Cy Young, Boston (3)	32	11
Rube Waddell, Philadelphia (1)	23	7
Frank Donahue, St. Louis (2)	22	11
Jack Powell, St. Louis (2)	22	17
Bill Dinneen, Boston (3)	21	21
Roy Patterson, Chicago (4)	20	12
Eddie Plank, Philadelphia (1)	20	15

1903 (7)

	W	L
Cy Young, Boston (1)	28	9
Eddie Plank, Philadelphia (2)	23	16
Bill Dinneen, Boston (1)	21	13
Willie Sudhoff, St. Louis (6)	21	15

	W	L
Jack Chesbro, New York (4)	21	15
Rube Waddell, Philadelphia (2)	21	16
Tom Hughes, Boston (1)	20	7

1904 (9)

	W	L
Jack Chesbro, New York (2)	41	13
Cy Young, Boston (1)	26	16
Eddie Plank, Philadelphia (1)	26	17
Rube Waddell, Philadelphia (5)	25	19
Bill Bernhard, Cleveland (4)	23	13
Bill Dinneen, Boston (1)	23	14
Jack Powell, New York (2)	23	19
Jesse Tannehill, Boston (1)	21	11
Frank Owen, Chicago (3)	21	15

1905 (9)

	W	L
Rube Waddell, Philadelphia (1)	26	11
Eddie Plank, Philadelphia (1)	25	12
Nick Altrock, Chicago (2)	24	12
Ed Killian, Detroit (3)	23	13
Jesse Tannehill, Boston (4)	22	9
Frank Owen, Chicago (2)	21	13
George Mullin, Detroit (3)	21	20
Addie Joss, Cleveland (5)	20	11
Frank Smith, Chicago (2)	20	14

1906 (8)

	W	L
Al Orth, New York (2)	27	17
Jack Chesbro, New York (2)	24	16
Bob Rhoads, Cleveland (3)	22	10
Frank Owen, Chicago (1)	22	13
Addie Joss, Cleveland (3)	21	9
George Mullin, Detroit (6)	21	18
Nick Altrock, Chicago (1)	20	13
Otto Hess, Cleveland (3)	20	17

1907 (10)

	W	L
Addie Joss, Cleveland (4)	27	10
Guy White, Chicago (3)	27	13
Bill Donovan, Detroit (1)	25	4
Ed Killian, Detroit (1)	25	13
Eddie Plank, Philadelphia (2)	24	16
Ed Walsh, Chicago (3)	24	18
Frank Smith, Chicago (3)	22	11
Cy Young, Boston (7)	22	15
Jimmy Dygert, Philadelphia (2)	20	9
George Mullin, Detroit (1)	20	20

1908 (4)

	W	L
Ed Walsh, Chicago (3)	40	15
Addie Joss, Cleveland (2)	24	11
Ed Summers, Detroit (1)	24	12
Cy Young, Boston (5)	21	11

1909 (3)

	W	L
George Mullin, Detroit (1)	29	8
Frank Smith, Chicago (4)	25	17
Ed Willett, Detroit (1)	22	9

1910 (5)

	W	L
Jack Coombs, Philadelphia (1)	31	9
Russ Ford, New York (2)	26	6
Walter Johnson, Washington (7)	25	17
Chief Bender, Philadelphia (1)	23	5
George Mullin, Detroit (3)	21	12

1911 (7)

	W	L
Jack Coombs, Philadelphia (1)	28	12
Ed Walsh, Chicago (4)	27	18
Walter Johnson, Washington (7)	25	13
Vean Gregg, Cleveland (3)	23	7
Joe Wood, Boston (5)	23	17
Eddie Plank, Philadelphia (1)	22	8
Russ Ford, New York (6)	22	11

1912 (9)

	W	L
Joe Wood, Boston (1)	34	5
Walter Johnson, Washington (2)	33	12
Ed Walsh, Chicago (4)	27	17
Eddie Plank, Philadelphia (3)	26	6
Bob Groom, Washington (2)	24	13
Jack Coombs, Philadelphia (3)	21	10
Hugh Bedient, Boston (1)	20	9
Vean Gregg, Cleveland (5)	20	13
Tom O'Brien, Boston (1)	20	13

1913 (6)

	W	L
Walter Johnson, Washington (2)	36	7
Fred Falkenberg, Cleveland (3)	23	10
Ewell Russell, Chicago (5)	22	16

	W	L
Chief Bender, Philadelphia (1)	21	10
Vean Gregg, Cleveland (3)	20	13
Jim Scott, Chicago (5)	20	20
1914 (3)		
Walter Johnson, Washington (3)	28	18
Harry Coveleski, Detroit (4)	22	12
Ray Collins, Boston (2)	20	13
1915 (5)		
Walter Johnson, Washington (4)	27	13
Jim Scott, Chicago (3)	24	11
Hooks Dauss, Detroit (2)	24	13
Red Faber, Chicago (3)	24	14
Harry Coveleski, Detroit (2)	22	13
1916 (4)		
Walter Johnson, Washington (7)	25	20
Bob Shawkey, New York (4)	24	14
Babe Ruth, Boston (1)	23	12
Harry Coveleski, Detroit (3)	21	11
1917 (5)		
Ed Cicotte, Chicago (1)	28	12
Babe Ruth, Boston (2)	24	13
Jim Bagby, Cleveland (3)	23	13
Walter Johnson, Washington (5)	23	16
Carl Mays, Boston (2)	22	9
1918 (4)		
Walter Johnson, Washington (3)	23	13
Stan Coveleski, Cleveland (2)	22	13
Carl Mays, Boston (1)	21	13
Scott Perry, Philadelphia (8)	20	19
1919 (7)		
Ed Cicotte, Chicago (1)	29	7
Lefty Williams, Chicago (1)	23	11
Stan Coveleski, Cleveland (2)	23	12
Hooks Dauss, Detroit (4)	21	9
Allen Sothoron, St. Louis (5)	21	11
Bob Shawkey, New York (3)	20	13
Walter Johnson, Washington (7)	20	14
1920 (10)		
Jim Bagby, Cleveland (1)	31	12
Carl Mays, New York (3)	26	11
Stan Coveleski, Cleveland (1)	24	14
Red Faber, Chicago (2)	23	13
Lefty Williams, Chicago (2)	22	14
Dickie Kerr, Chicago (2)	21	9
Ed Cicotte, Chicago (2)	21	10
Ray Caldwell, Cleveland (1)	20	10
Urban Shocker, St. Louis (4)	20	10
Bob Shawkey, New York (3)	20	13
1921 (5)		
Carl Mays, New York (1)	27	9
Urban Shocker, St. Louis (3)	27	12
Red Faber, Chicago (7)	25	15
Stan Coveleski, Cleveland (2)	23	13
Sam Jones, Boston (5)	23	16
1922 (6)		
Eddie Rommel, Philadelphia (7)	27	13
Joe Bush, New York (1)	26	7
Urban Shocker, St. Louis (2)	24	17
George Uhle, Cleveland (4)	22	16
Red Faber, Chicago (5)	21	17
Bob Shawkey, New York (1)	20	12
1923 (5)		
George Uhle, Cleveland (3)	26	16
Sam Jones, New York (1)	21	8
Hooks Dauss, Detroit (2)	21	13
Urban Shocker, St. Louis (5)	20	12
Howard Ehmke, Boston (8)	20	17
1924 (4)		
Walter Johnson, Washington (1)	23	7
Herb Pennock, New York (2)	21	9
Sloppy Thurston, Chicago (8)	20	14
Joe Shaute, Cleveland (6)	20	17
1925 (4)		
Eddie Rommel, Philadelphia (2)	21	10
Ted Lyons, Chicago (5)	21	11
Stan Coveleski, Washington (1)	20	5
Walter Johnson, Washington (1)	20	7
1926 (2)		
George Uhle, Cleveland (2)	27	11
Herb Pennock, New York (1)	23	11

	W	L
1927 (3)		
Waite Hoyt, New York (1)	22	7
Ted Lyons, Chicago (5)	22	14
Lefty Grove, Philadelphia (2)	20	13
1928 (5)		
Lefty Grove, Philadelphia (2)	24	8
George Pipgras, New York (1)	24	13
Waite Hoyt, New York (1)	23	7
Alvin Crowder, St. Louis (3)	21	5
Sam Gray, St. Louis (3)	20	12
1929 (3)		
George Earnshaw, Philadelphia (1)	24	8
Wes Ferrell, Cleveland (3)	21	10
Lefty Grove, Philadelphia (1)	20	6
1930 (5)		
Lefty Grove, Philadelphia (1)	28	5
Wes Ferrell, Cleveland (4)	25	13
George Earnshaw, Philadelphia (1)	22	13
Ted Lyons, Chicago (7)	22	15
Walter Stewart, St. Louis (6)	20	12
1931 (5)		
Lefty Grove, Philadelphia (1)	31	4
Wes Ferrell, Cleveland (4)	22	12
George Earnshaw, Philadelphia (1)	21	7
Lefty Gomez, New York (2)	21	9
Rube Walberg, Philadelphia (1)	20	12
1932 (5)		
Alvin Crowder, Washington (3)	26	13
Lefty Grove, Philadelphia (2)	25	10
Lefty Gomez, New York (1)	24	7
Wes Ferrell, Cleveland (4)	23	13
Monte Weaver, Washington (3)	22	10
1933 (3)		
Lefty Grove, Philadelphia (3)	24	8
Alvin Crowder, Washington (1)	24	15
Earl Whitehill, Washington (1)	22	8
1934 (4)		
Lefty Gomez, New York (2)	26	5
Schoolboy Rowe, Detroit (1)	24	8
Tommy Bridges, Detroit (1)	22	11
Mel Harder, Cleveland (3)	20	12
1935 (4)		
Wes Ferrell, Boston (4)	25	14
Mel Harder, Cleveland (3)	22	11
Tommy Bridges, Detroit (1)	21	10
Lefty Grove, Boston (4)	20	12
1936 (5)		
Tommy Bridges, Detroit (2)	23	11
Vern Kennedy, Chicago (3)	21	9
Johnny Allen, Cleveland (5)	20	10
Red Ruffing, New York (1)	20	12
Wes Ferrell, Boston (6)	20	15
1937 (2)		
Lefty Gomez, New York (1)	21	11
Red Ruffing, New York (1)	20	7
1938 (2)		
Red Ruffing, New York (1)	21	7
Bobo Newsom, St. Louis (7)	20	16
1939 (4)		
Bob Feller, Cleveland (3)	24	9
Red Ruffing, New York (1)	21	7
Dutch E. Leonard, Washington (6)	20	8
Bobo Newsom, 3-1 St. Louis (8)		
17-10 Detroit (5)	20	11
1940 (2)		
Bob Feller, Cleveland (2)	27	11
Bobo Newsom, Detroit (1)	21	5
1941 (2)		
Bob Feller, Cleveland (4T)	25	13
Thornton Lee, Chicago (3)	22	11
1942 (2)		
Cecil Hughson, Boston (2)	22	6
Ernie Bonham, New York (1)	21	5
1943 (2)		
Spud Chandler, New York (1)	20	4
Dizzy Trout, Detroit (5)	20	12
1944 (2)		
Hal Newhouser, Detroit (2)	29	9
Dizzy Trout, Detroit (2)	27	14

1945 (3)	W	L
Hal Newhouser, Detroit (1)	25	9
Dave Ferriss, Boston (7)	21	10
Roger Wolff, Washington (2)	20	10

1946 (5)
Hal Newhouser, Detroit (2) | 26 | 9
Bob Feller, Cleveland (6) | 26 | 15
Dave Ferriss, Boston (1) | 25 | 6
Spud Chandler, New York (3) | 20 | 8
Cecil Hughson, Boston (1) | 20 | 11

1947 (1)
Bob Feller, Cleveland (4) | 20 | 11

1948 (3)
Hal Newhouser, Detroit (5) | 21 | 12
Gene Bearden, Cleveland (1) | 20 | 7
Bob Lemon, Cleveland (1) | 20 | 14

1949 (5)
Mel Parnell, Boston (2) | 25 | 7
Ellis Kinder, Boston (2) | 23 | 6
Bob Lemon, Cleveland (3) | 22 | 10
Vic Raschi, New York (1) | 21 | 10
Alex Kellner, Philadelphia (5) | 20 | 12

1950 (2)
Bob Lemon, Cleveland (4) | 23 | 11
Vic Raschi, New York (1) | 21 | 8

1951 (6)
Bob Feller, Cleveland (2) | 22 | 8
Eddie Lopat, New York (1) | 21 | 9
Vic Raschi, New York (1) | 21 | 10
Ned Garver, St. Louis (8) | 20 | 12
Mike Garcia, Cleveland (2) | 20 | 13
Early Wynn, Cleveland (2) | 20 | 13

1952 (5)
Bobby Shantz, Philadelphia (4) | 24 | 7
Early Wynn, Cleveland (2) | 23 | 12
Mike Garcia, Cleveland (2) | 22 | 11
Bob Lemon, Cleveland (2) | 22 | 11
Allie Reynolds, New York (1) | 20 | 8

1953 (4)
Bob Porterfield, Washington (5) | 22 | 10
Mel Parnell, Boston (4) | 21 | 8
Bob Lemon, Cleveland (2) | 21 | 15
Virgil Trucks, 5-4 St. Louis (8)
  15-6 Chicago (3) | 20 | 10

1954 (3)
Bob Lemon, Cleveland (1) | 23 | 7
Early Wynn, Cleveland (1) | 23 | 11
Bob Grim, New York (2) | 20 | 6

1955 (0)
Whitey Ford, New York, Bob Lemon, Cleveland, and Frank Sullivan, Boston, each had 18 wins.

1956 (6)
Frank Lary, Detroit (5) | 21 | 13
Herb Score, Cleveland (2) | 20 | 9
Early Wynn, Cleveland (2) | 20 | 9
Billy Pierce, Chicago (3) | 20 | 9
Bob Lemon, Cleveland (2) | 20 | 14
Billy Hoeft, Detroit (5) | 20 | 14

1957 (2)
Jim Bunning, Detroit (4) | 20 | 8
Billy Pierce, Chicago (2) | 20 | 12

1958 (1)
Bob Turley, New York (1) | 21 | 7

1959 (1)
Early Wynn, Chicago (1) | 22 | 10

1960 (0)
Chuck Estrada, Baltimore, and Jim Perry, Cleveland, each had 18 wins.

1961 (2)
Whitey Ford, New York (1) | 25 | 4
Frank Lary, Detroit (2) | 23 | 9

1962 (4)
Ralph Terry, New York (1) | 23 | 12
Ray Herbert, Chicago (5) | 20 | 9
Dick Donovan, Cleveland (6) | 20 | 10
Camilo Pascual, Minnesota (2) | 20 | 11

1963 (5)
Whitey Ford, New York (1) | 24 | 7
Jim Bouton, New York (1) | 21 | 7

	W	L
Camilo Pascual, Minnesota (3)	21	9
Bill Monbouquette, Boston (7)	20	10
Steve Barber, Baltimore (4)	20	13

1964 (2)
Dean Chance, Los Angeles (5) | 20 | 9
Gary Peters, Chicago (2) | 20 | 8

1965 (2)
Mudcat Grant, Minnesota (1) | 21 | 7
Mel Stottlemyre, New York (6) | 20 | 9

1966 (2)
Jim Kaat, Minnesota (2) | 25 | 13
Denny McLain, Detroit (3) | 20 | 14

1967 (3)
Jim Lonborg, Boston (1) | 22 | 9
Earl Wilson, Detroit (2T) | 22 | 11
Dean Chance, Minnesota (2T) | 20 | 14

1968 (4)
Denny McLain, Detroit (1) | 31 | 6
Dave McNally, Baltimore (2) | 22 | 10
Luis Tiant, Cleveland (3) | 21 | 9
Mel Stottlemyre, New York (5) | 21 | 12

1969 (6)
Denny McLain, Detroit (2E) | 24 | 9
Mike Cuellar, Baltimore (1E) | 23 | 11
Jim Perry, Minnesota (1W) | 20 | 6
Dave McNally, Baltimore (1E) | 20 | 7
Dave Boswell, Minnesota (1W) | 20 | 12
Mel Stottlemyre, New York (5E) | 20 | 14

1970 (7)
Mike Cuellar, Baltimore (1E) | 24 | 8
Dave McNally, Baltimore (1E) | 24 | 9
Jim Perry, Minnesota (1W) | 24 | 12
Clyde Wright, California (3W) | 22 | 12
Jim Palmer, Baltimore (1E) | 20 | 10
Fritz Peterson, New York (2E) | 20 | 11
Sam McDowell, Cleveland (5E) | 20 | 12

1971 (10)
Mickey Lolich, Detroit (2E) | 25 | 14
Vida Blue, Oakland (1W) | 24 | 8
Wilbur Wood, Chicago (3W) | 22 | 13
Dave McNally, Baltimore (1E) | 21 | 5
Catfish Hunter, Oakland (1W) | 21 | 11
Pat Dobson, Baltimore (1E) | 20 | 8
Jim Palmer, Baltimore (1E) | 20 | 9
Mike Cuellar, Baltimore (1E) | 20 | 9
Joe Coleman, Detroit (2E) | 20 | 9
Andy Messersmith, California (4W) | 20 | 13

1972 (6)
Gaylord Perry, Cleveland (5W) | 24 | 16
Wilbur Wood, Chicago (2W) | 24 | 17
Mickey Lolich, Detroit (1E) | 22 | 14
Catfish Hunter, Oakland (1W) | 21 | 7
Jim Palmer, Baltimore (3E) | 21 | 10
Stan Bahnsen, Chicago (2W) | 21 | 16

1973 (12)
Wilbur Wood, Chicago (5W) | 24 | 20
Joe Coleman, Detroit (3E) | 23 | 15
Jim Palmer, Baltimore (1E) | 22 | 9
Catfish Hunter, Oakland (1W) | 21 | 5
Ken Holtzman, Oakland (1W) | 21 | 13
Nolan Ryan, California (4W) | 21 | 16
Vida Blue, Oakland (1W) | 20 | 9
Paul Splittorff, Kansas City (2W) | 20 | 11
Jim Colborn, Milwaukee (5E) | 20 | 12
Luis Tiant, Boston (2E) | 20 | 13
Bill Singer, California (4W) | 20 | 14
Bert Blyleven, Minnesota (3W) | 20 | 17

1974 (9)
Catfish Hunter, Oakland (1W) | 25 | 12
Ferguson Jenkins, Texas (2W) | 25 | 12
Mike Cuellar, Baltimore (1E) | 22 | 10
Luis Tiant, Boston (3E) | 22 | 13
Steve Busby, Kansas City (5W) | 22 | 14
Nolan Ryan, California (6W) | 22 | 16
Jim Kaat, Chicago (4W) | 21 | 13
Gaylord Perry, Cleveland (4E) | 21 | 13
Wilbur Wood, Chicago (4W) | 20 | 19

1975 (5)
Jim Palmer, Baltimore (2E) | 23 | 11

	W	L
Catfish Hunter, New York (3E)	23	14
Vida Blue, Oakland (1W)	22	11
Mike Torrez, Baltimore (2E)	20	9
Jim Kaat, Chicago (5W)	20	14
1976 (3)		
Jim Palmer, Baltimore (2E)	22	13
Luis Tiant, Boston (3E)	21	12
Wayne Garland, Baltimore (2E)	20	7
1977 (3)		
Jim Palmer, Baltimore (2TE)	20	11
Dave Goltz, Minnesota (4W)	20	11
Dennis Leonard, Kansas City (1W)	20	12
1978 (6)		
Ron Guidry, New York (1E)	25	3
Mike Caldwell, Milwaukee (3E)	22	9
Jim Palmer, Baltimore (4E)	21	12
Dennis Leonard, Kansas City (1W)	21	17
Dennis Eckersley, Boston (2E)	20	8
Ed Figueroa, New York (1E)	20	9
1979 (3)		
Mike Flanagan, Baltimore (1E)	23	9
Tommy John, New York (4E)	21	9
Jerry Koosman, Minnesota (4W)	20	13
1980 (5)		
Steve Stone, Baltimore (2E)	25	7
Tommy John, New York (1E)	22	9
Mike Norris, Oakland (2W)	22	9
Scott McGregor, Baltimore (2E)	20	8
Dennis Leonard, Kansas City (1W)	20	11
1981 (0)		

1981 (0)
Dennis Martinez, Baltimore, Steve McCatty, Oakland, Jack Morris, Detroit, and Pete Vukovich, Milwaukee, each had 14 wins.

1982 (0)
La Marr Hoyt, Chicago, had 19 wins.

1983 (4)	W	L
LaMarr Hoyt, Chicago (1W)	24	10
Rich Dotson, Chicago (1W)	22	7
Ron Guidry, New York (3E)	21	9
Jack Morris, Detroit (2E)	20	13
1984 (1)		
Mike Boddicker, Baltimore (5E)	20	11
1985 (2)		
Ron Guidry, New York (2E)	22	6
Bret Saberhagen, Kansas City (1W)	20	6
1986 (3)		
Roger Clemens, Boston (1E)	24	4
Jack Morris, Detroit (3E)	21	8
Ted Higuera, Milwaukee (6E)	20	11
1987 (2)		
Roger Clemens, Boston (5E)	20	9
Dave Stewart, Oakland (3W)	20	13
1988 (3)		
Frank Viola, Minnesota (2W)	24	7
Dave Stewart, Oakland (1W)	21	12
Mark Gubicza, Kansas City (3W)	20	8
1989 (2)		
Bret Saberhagen, Kansas City (2W)	23	6
Dave Stewart, Oakland (1W)	21	9
1990 (3)		
Bob Welch, Oakland (1W)	27	6
Dave Stewart, Oakland (1W)	22	11
Roger Clemens, Boston (1E)	21	6
1991 (2)		
Scott Erickson, Minnesota (1W)	20	8
Bill Gullickson, Detroit (2TE)	20	9
1992 (3)		
Jack Morris, Toronto (1E)	21	6
Kevin Brown, Texas (4W)	21	11
Jack McDowell, Chicago (3W)	20	10
1993 (1)		
Jack McDowell, Chicago (1W)	22	10
1994 (0)		

1994 (0)
Jimmy Key, New York, had 17 wins.

1995 (0)
Mike Mussina, Baltimore, had 19 wins.

1996 (2)		
Andy Pettitte, New York (1E)	21	8
Pat Hentgen, Toronto (4E)	20	10

1997 (3)	W	L
Roger Clemens, Toronto (5E)	21	7
Randy Johnson, Seattle (1W)	20	4
Brad Radke, Minnesota (4C)	20	10
1998 (3)		
Roger Clemens, Toronto (3E)	20	6
David Cone, New York (1E)	20	7
Rick Helling, Texas (1W)	20	7
1999 (1)		
Pedro Martinez, Boston (2E)	23	4
2000 (2)		
Tim Hudson, Oakland (1W)	20	6
David Wells, Toronto (3E)	20	8
2001 (3)		
Mark Mulder, Oakland (2W)	21	8
Roger Clemens, New York (1E)	20	3
Jamie Moyer, Seattle (1W)	20	6
2002 (3)		
Barry Zito, Oakland (1W)	23	5
Derek Lowe, Boston (2E)	21	8
Pedro Martinez, Boston (2E)	20	4
2003 (4)		
Roy Halladay, Toronto (3E)	22	7
Esteban Loaiza, Chicago (2C)	21	9
Jamie Moyer, Seattle (2W)	21	7
Andy Pettitte, New York (1E)	21	8
2004 (2)		
Curt Schilling, Boston (2E)	21	6
Johan Santana, Minnesota (1C)	20	6

NATIONAL LEAGUE

1876 (5)	W	L
Al Spalding, Chicago (1)	47	13
George Bradley, St. Louis (2)	45	19
Tommy Bond, Hartford (3)	32	13
Jim Devlin, Louisville (5)	30	34
Bobby Mathews, New York (6)	21	34
1877 (3)		
Tommy Bond, Boston (1)	31	17
Jim Devlin, Louisville (2)	28	20
Terry Larkin, Hartford (3)	22	21
1878 (4)		
Tommy Bond, Boston (1)	40	19
Will White, Cincinnati (2)	29	21
Terry Larkin, Chicago (4)	29	26
Monte Ward, Providence (3)	22	13
1879 (6)		
Monte Ward, Providence (1)	44	18
Tommy Bond, Boston (2)	43	19
Will White, Cincinnati (5)	43	31
Pud Galvin, Buffalo (3T)	37	27
Terry Larkin, Chicago (3T)	30	23
Jim McCormick, Cleveland (6)	20	40
1880 (8)		
Jim McCormick, Cleveland (3)	45	28
Larry Corcoran, Chicago (1)	43	14
Monte Ward, Providence (2)	40	23
Mickey Welch, Troy (4)	34	30
Lee Richmond, Worcester (5)	31	33
Tommy Bond, Boston (6)	26	29
Fred Goldsmith, Chicago (1)	22	3
Pud Galvin, Buffalo (7)	20	37
1881 (9)		
Larry Corcoran, Chicago (1)	31	14
Jim Whitney, Boston (6)	31	33
Pud Galvin, Buffalo (3)	29	24
George Derby, Detroit (4)	29	26
Jim McCormick, Cleveland (7)	26	30
Hoss Radbourn, Providence (2)	25	11
Fred Goldsmith, Chicago (1)	25	13
Lee Richmond, Worcester (8)	25	27
Mickey Welch, Troy (5)	21	18
1882 (7)		
Jim McCormick, Cleveland (5)	36	29
Hoss Radbourn, Providence (2)	31	19
Pud Galvin, Buffalo (3T)	28	22
Fred Goldsmith, Chicago (1)	28	16
Larry Corcoran, Chicago (1)	27	13
George Weidman, Detroit (6)	26	20

	W	L
Jim Whitney, Boston (3T)	24	22

1883 (9)

	W	L
Hoss Radbourn, Providence (3)	49	25
Pud Galvin, Buffalo (5)	46	29
Jim Whitney, Boston (3)	37	21
Larry Corcoran, Chicago (2)	31	21
Fred Goldsmith, Chicago (2)	28	18
Jim McCormick, Cleveland (4)	27	13
Charlie Buffinton, Boston (1)	25	14
Mickey Welch, New York (6)	25	23
Hugh Daily, Cleveland (4)	24	18

1884 (7)

	W	L
Hoss Radbourn, Providence (1)	60	12
Charlie Buffinton, Boston (2)	48	16
Pud Galvin, Buffalo (3)	46	22
Mickey Welch, New York (4T)	39	21
Larry Corcoran, Chicago (4T)	35	23
Jim Whitney, Boston (2)	23	14
Charlie Ferguson, Philadelphia (6)	21	24

1885 (9)

	W	L
John Clarkson, Chicago (1)	53	16
Mickey Welch, New York (2)	44	11
Tim Keefe, New York (2)	32	13
Charlie Ferguson, Philadelphia (3)	26	19
Hoss Radbourn, Providence (4)	26	20
Ed Daily, Philadelphia (3)	26	22
Fred Shaw, Providence (4)	23	26
Charlie Buffinton, Boston (5)	22	27
Jim McCormick, 1-3 Providence (4) 20-4 Chicago (1)	21	7

1886 (11)

	W	L
Charles Baldwin, Detroit (2)	42	13
Tim Keefe, New York (3)	42	20
John Clarkson, Chicago (1)	35	17
Mickey Welch, New York (3)	33	22
Charlie Ferguson, Philadelphia (4)	32	9
Charlie Getzien, Detroit (2)	31	11
Jim McCormick, Chicago (1)	31	11
Hoss Radbourn, Boston (5)	27	30
Dan Casey, Philadelphia (4)	25	19
John Flynn, Chicago (1)	24	6
Bill Stemmeyer, Boston (5)	22	18

1887 (11)

	W	L
John Clarkson, Chicago (3)	38	21
Tim Keefe, New York (4)	35	19
Charlie Getzien, Detroit (1)	29	13
Dan Casey, Philadelphia (2)	28	13
Pud Galvin, Pittsburgh (6)	28	21
Jim Whitney, Washington (7)	24	21
Hoss Radbourn, Boston (5)	24	23
Mickey Welch, New York (4)	22	15
Michael Madden, Boston (5)	22	14
Charlie Ferguson, Philadelphia (2)	21	10
Charlie Buffinton, Philadelphia (2)	21	17

1888 (8)

	W	L
Tim Keefe, New York (1)	35	12
John Clarkson, Boston (4)	33	20
Pete Conway, Detroit (5)	30	14
Ed Morris, Pittsburgh (6)	29	23
Charlie Buffinton, Philadelphia (3)	28	17
Mickey Welch, New York (1)	26	19
Gus Krock, Chicago (2)	25	14
Pud Galvin, Pittsburgh (6)	23	25

1889 (10)

	W	L
John Clarkson, Boston (2)	49	19
Tim Keefe, New York (1)	28	13
Mickey Welch, New York (1)	27	12
Charlie Buffinton, Philadelphia (4)	26	17
Pud Galvin, Pittsburgh (5)	23	16
John O'Brien, Cleveland (6)	22	17
Harry Staley, Pittsburgh (5)	21	26
Hoss Radbourn, Boston (2)	20	11
Ed Beatin, Cleveland (6)	20	14
Henry Boyle, Indianapolis (7)	20	23

1890 (13)

	W	L
Bill Hutchison, Chicago (2)	42	25
Kid Gleason, Philadelphia (3)	38	16
Tom Lovett, Brooklyn (1)	32	11
Amos Rusie, New York (6)	29	30
Billy Rhines, Cincinnati (4)	28	17
Kid Nichols, Boston (5)	27	19

	W	L
John Clarkson, Boston (5)	26	18
Adonis Terry, Brooklyn (1)	25	16
Bob Caruthers, Brooklyn (1)	23	11
Charlie Getzien, Boston (5)	23	17
Tom Vickery, Philadelphia (3)	22	23
Ed Beatin, Cleveland (7)	22	31
Pat Luby, Chicago (2)	21	9

1891 (12)

	W	L
Bill Hutchison, Chicago (2)	43	19
John Clarkson, Boston (1)	33	19
Amos Rusie, New York (3)	32	19
Kid Nichols, Boston (1)	30	17
Cy Young, Cleveland (5)	27	20
Harry Staley, 4-5 Pittsburgh (8) 20-8 Boston (1)	24	13
Kid Gleason, Philadelphia (4)	24	19
Tony Mullane, Cincinnati (7)	24	25
John Ewing, New York (3)	22	8
Tom Lovett, Brooklyn (6)	21	20
Mark Baldwin, Pittsburgh (8)	21	27
Charles Esper, Philadelphia (4)	20	14

1892 (22)

	W	L
Bill Hutchison, Chicago (7)	37	34
Cy Young, Cleveland (2)	36	11
Kid Nichols, Boston (1)	35	16
Jack Stivetts, Boston (1)	35	16
George Haddock, Brooklyn (3)	31	13
Amos Rusie, New York (8)	31	28
Frank Killen, Washington (10)	30	23
George Cuppy, Cleveland (2)	28	12
Gus Weyhing, Philadelphia (4)	28	18
Mark Baldwin, Pittsburgh (6)	27	20
Ed Stein, Brooklyn (3)	26	16
John Clarkson, 8-6 Boston (1) 17-10 Cleveland (2)	25	16
Ad Gumbert, Chicago (7)	23	21
Harry Staley, Boston (1)	22	10
Charles King, New York (8)	22	24
Tony Mullane, Cincinnati (5)	21	10
Adonis Terry 2-4, Baltimore (12) 19-6 Pittsburgh (6)	21	10
Frank Dwyer 3-11, St. Louis (11) 18-8 Cincinnati (8)	21	19
Scott Stratton, Louisville (9)	21	19
Elton Chamberlain, Cincinnati (5)	20	22
Kid Gleason, St. Louis (11)	20	24
John McMahon, Baltimore (12)	20	25

1893 (8)

	W	L
Frank Killen, Pittsburgh (2)	36	14
Kid Nichols, Boston (1)	34	14
Cy Young, Cleveland (3)	32	16
Amos Rusie, New York (5)	29	18
William Kennedy, Brooklyn (6T)	26	19
John McMahon, Baltimore (8)	24	16
Gus Weyhing, Philadelphia (4)	24	16
Jack Stivetts, Boston (1)	20	12

1894 (13)

	W	L
Amos Rusie, New York (2)	36	13
Jouett Meekin, New York (2)	34	9
Kid Nichols, Boston (3)	32	13
Ted Breitenstein, St. Louis (9)	27	22
Jack Stivetts, Boston (3)	26	14
John McMahon, Baltimore (1)	25	8
Ed Stein, Brooklyn (5)	25	15
Cy Young, Cleveland (6)	25	22
George Cuppy, Cleveland (3)	23	17
John B. Taylor, Philadelphia (4)	22	11
William Kennedy, Brooklyn (5)	22	20
Clark Griffith, Chicago (8)	21	11
Frank Dwyer, Cincinnati (10)	20	18

1895 (13)

	W	L
Cy Young, Cleveland (2)	35	10
Emerson Hawley, Pittsburgh (7)	32	21
Bill Hoffer, Baltimore (1)	30	7
John B. Taylor, Philadelphia (3)	26	13
Kid Carsey, Philadelphia (3)	26	15
Kid Nichols, Boston (5T)	26	16
Clark Griffith, Chicago (4)	25	13
George Cuppy, Cleveland (2)	25	15
Adonis Terry, Chicago (2)	23	13
Amos Rusie, New York (9)	22	21

	W	L
George Hemming, Baltimore (1)	20	10
Billy Rhines, Cincinnati (8)	20	10
Ted Breitenstein, St. Louis (11)	20	29
1896 (12)		
Kid Nichols, Boston (4)	30	14
Frank Killen, Pittsburgh (6)	29	15
Cy Young, Cleveland (2)	29	16
Bill Hoffer, Baltimore (1)	26	7
Jouett Meekin, New York (7)	26	13
Frank Dwyer, Cincinnati (3)	25	10
George Cuppy, Cleveland (2)	25	15
George Mercer, Washington (9T)	25	19
Clark Griffith, Chicago (5)	22	13
Jack Stivetts, Boston (4)	22	14
John B. Taylor, Philadelphia (8)	21	20
Emerson Hawley, Pittsburgh (6)	21	21
1897 (13)		
Kid Nichols, Boston (1)	31	11
Amos Rusie, New York (3)	29	8
Fred Klobedanz, Boston (1)	26	7
Joe Corbett, Baltimore (2)	24	8
George Mercer, Washington (6T)	24	21
Ted Breitenstein, Cincinnati (4)	23	12
Bill Hoffer, Baltimore (2)	22	10
Ed Lewis, Boston (1)	21	12
Cy Young, Cleveland (5)	21	18
Clark Griffith, Chicago (9)	21	19
Jerry Nops, Baltimore (2)	20	7
Jouett Meekin, New York (3)	20	11
Cy Seymour, New York (3)	20	14
1898 (17)		
Kid Nichols, Boston (1)	31	12
Bert Cunningham, Louisville (9)	28	15
James McJames, Baltimore (2)	27	14
Ed Lewis, Boston (1)	26	8
Clark Griffith, Chicago (4)	26	10
Emerson Hawley, Cincinnati (3)	26	12
Vic Willis, Boston (1)	25	13
Cy Young, Cleveland (5)	25	14
Cy Seymour, New York (7)	25	17
Wiley Piatt, Philadelphia (6)	24	14
Jesse Tannehill, Pittsburgh (8)	24	14
Jack Powell, Cleveland (5)	24	15
Jim Hughes, Baltimore (2)	21	11
Ted Breitenstein, Cincinnati (3)	21	14
Al Maul, Baltimore (2)	20	7
Amos Rusie, New York (7)	20	10
Jim Callahan, Chicago (4)	20	11
1899 (17)		
Jim Hughes, Brooklyn (1)	28	6
Joe McGinnity, Baltimore (4)	28	17
Vic Willis, Boston (2)	27	8
Cy Young, St. Louis (5)	26	15
Frank Hahn, Cincinnati (6)	23	7
Jim Callahan, Chicago (8)	23	12
Jesse Tannehill, Pittsburgh (7)	23	14
Wiley Piatt, Philadelphia (3)	23	15
Jack Powell, St. Louis (5)	23	21
Frank Donahue, Philadelphia (3)	22	7
Clark Griffith, Chicago (8)	22	13
Jack Dunn, Brooklyn (1)	21	12
Charles Fraser, Philadelphia (3)	21	13
Kid Nichols, Boston (2)	21	19
Frank Kitson, Baltimore (4)	20	16
Deacon Phillippe, Louisville (9)	20	17
Sam Leever, Pittsburgh (7)	20	23
1900 (5)		
Joe McGinnity, Brooklyn (1)	29	9
William Kennedy, Brooklyn (1)	22	15
Bill Dinneen, Boston (4)	21	15
Jesse Tannehill, Pittsburgh (2)	20	7
Cy Young, St. Louis (5T)	20	18
1901 (9)		
Bill Donovan, Brooklyn (3)	25	15
Deacon Phillippe, Pittsburgh (1)	22	12
Frank Hahn, Cincinnati (8)	22	19
Jack Chesbro, Pittsburgh (1)	21	9
Al Orth, Philadelphia (2)	20	12
Jack Harper, St. Louis (4)	20	12
Frank Donahue, Philadelphia (2)	20	13

	W	L
Christy Mathewson, New York (7)	20	17
Vic Willis, Boston (5)	20	17
1902 (7)		
Jack Chesbro, Pittsburgh (1)	28	6
Charlie Pittinger, Boston (3)	27	16
Vic Willis, Boston (3)	27	20
John W. Taylor, Chicago (5)	22	10
Frank Hahn, Cincinnati (4)	22	12
Jesse Tannehill, Pittsburgh (1)	20	6
Deacon Phillippe, Pittsburgh (1)	20	9
1903 (9)		
Joe McGinnity, New York (2)	31	20
Christy Mathewson, New York (2)	30	13
Sam Leever, Pittsburgh (1)	25	7
Deacon Phillippe, Pittsburgh (1)	25	9
Frank Hahn, Cincinnati (4)	22	12
Henry Schmidt, Brooklyn (5)	22	13
John W. Taylor, Chicago (3)	21	14
Jacob Weimer, Chicago (3)	20	8
Bob Wicker, 0-0 St. Louis (8)		
20-9 Chicago (3)	20	9
1904 (7)		
Joe McGinnity, New York (1)	35	8
Christy Mathewson, New York (1)	33	12
Jack Harper, Cincinnati (3)	23	9
Kid Nichols, St. Louis (5)	21	13
Luther Taylor, New York (1)	21	15
Jacob Weimer, Chicago (2)	20	14
John W. Taylor, St. Louis (5)	20	19
1905 (8)		
Christy Mathewson, New York(1)	31	9
Charlie Pittinger, Philadelphia (4)	23	14
Leon Ames, New York (1)	22	8
Joe McGinnity, New York (1)	21	15
Sam Leever, Pittsburgh (2)	20	5
Bob Ewing, Cincinnati (5)	20	11
Deacon Phillippe, Pittsburgh (2)	20	13
Irv Young, Boston (7)	20	21
1906 (8)		
Joe McGinnity, New York (2)	27	12
Mordecai Brown, Chicago (1)	26	6
Vic Willis, Pittsburgh (3)	23	13
Sam Leever, Pittsburgh (3)	22	7
Christy Mathewson, New York (2)	22	12
Jack Pfiester, Chicago (1)	20	8
John W. Taylor, 8-9 St. Louis (7),		
12-3 Chicago (1)	20	12
Jacob Weimer, Cincinnati (6)	20	14
1907 (6)		
Christy Mathewson, New York (4)	24	12
Orval Overall, Chicago (1)	23	8
Frank Sparks, Philadelphia (3)	22	8
Vic Willis, Pittsburgh (2)	21	11
Mordecai Brown, Chicago (1)	20	6
Lefty Leifield, Pittsburgh (2)	20	16
1908 (7)		
Christy Mathewson, New York (2T)	37	11
Mordecai Brown, Chicago (1)	29	9
Ed Reulbach, Chicago (1)	24	7
Nick Maddox, Pittsburgh (2T)	23	8
Vic Willis, Pittsburgh (2T)	23	11
George Wiltse, New York (2T)	23	14
George McQuillan, Philadelphia (4)	23	17
1909 (6)		
Mordecai Brown, Chicago (2)	27	9
Howie Camnitz, Pittsburgh (1)	25	6
Christy Mathewson, New York (3)	25	6
Vic Willis, Pittsburgh (1)	22	11
George Wiltse, New York (3)	20	11
Orval Overall, Chicago (1)	20	11
1910 (5)		
Christy Mathewson, New York (2)	27	9
Mordecai Brown, Chicago (1)	25	14
Earl Moore, Philadelphia (4)	22	15
Leonard Cole, Chicago (1)	20	4
George Suggs, Cincinnati (5)	20	12
1911 (8)		
Grover Alexander, Philadelphia (4)	28	13

	W	L
Christy Mathewson, New York (1)	26	13
Rube Marquard, New York (1)	24	7
Bob Harmon, St. Louis (5)	23	16
Babe Adams, Pittsburgh (3)	22	12
George Rucker, Brooklyn (7)	22	18
Mordecai Brown, Chicago (2)	21	11
Howie Camnitz, Pittsburgh (3)	20	15
1912 (5)		
Larry Cheney, Chicago (3)	26	10
Rube Marquard, New York (1)	26	11
Claude Hendrix, Pittsburgh (2)	24	9
Christy Mathewson, New York (1)	23	12
Howie Camnitz, Pittsburgh (2)	22	12
1913 (7)		
Tom Seaton, Philadelphia (2)	27	12
Christy Mathewson, New York (1)	25	11
Rube Marquard, New York (1)	23	10
Grover Alexander, Philadelphia (2)	22	8
Jeff Tesreau, New York (1)	22	13
Babe Adams, Pittsburgh (4)	21	10
Larry Cheney, Chicago (3)	21	14
1914 (9)		
Grover Alexander, Philadelphia (6)	27	15
Dick Rudolph, Boston (1)	26	10
Bill James, Boston (1)	26	7
Jeff Tesreau, New York (2)	26	10
Christy Mathewson, New York (2)	24	13
Jeff Pfeffer, Brooklyn (5)	23	12
Hippo Vaughn, Chicago (4)	21	13
Erskine Mayer, Philadelphia (6)	21	19
Larry Cheney, Chicago (4)	20	18
1915 (5)		
Grover Alexander, Philadelphia (1)	31	10
Dick Rudolph, Boston (2)	22	19
Al Mamaux, Pittsburgh (5)	21	8
Erskine Mayer, Philadelphia (1)	21	15
Hippo Vaughn, Chicago (4)	20	12
1916 (4)		
Grover Alexander, Philadelphia (2)	33	12
Jeff Pfeffer, Brooklyn (1)	25	11
Eppa Rixey, Philadelphia (2)	22	10
Al Mamaux, Pittsburgh (6)	21	15
1917 (5)		
Grover Alexander, Philadelphia (2)	30	13
Fred Toney, Cincinnati (4)	24	16
Hippo Vaughn, Chicago (5)	23	13
Ferdie Schupp, New York (1)	21	7
Pete Schneider, Cincinnati (4)	20	19
1918 (2)		
Hippo Vaughn, Chicago (1)	22	10
Claude Hendrix, Chicago (1)	20	7
1919 (3)		
Jesse Barnes, New York (2)	25	9
Harry Sallee, Cincinnati (1)	21	7
Hippo Vaughn, Chicago (3)	21	14
1920 (7)		
Grover Alexander, Chicago (5T)	27	14
Wilbur Cooper, Pittsburgh (4)	24	15
Burleigh Grimes, Brooklyn (1)	23	11
Fred Toney, New York (2)	21	11
Art Nehf, New York (2)	21	12
Bill Doak, St. Louis (5T)	20	12
Jesse Barnes, New York (2)	20	15
1921 (4)		
Burleigh Grimes, Brooklyn (5)	22	13
Wilbur Cooper, Pittsburgh (2)	22	14
Art Nehf, New York (1)	20	10
Joe Oeschger, Boston (4)	20	14
1922 (3)		
Eppa Rixey, Cincinnati (2)	25	13
Wilbur Cooper, Pittsburgh (3T)	23	14
Walt Ruether, Brooklyn (6)	21	12
1923 (7)		
Dolf Luque, Cincinnati (2)	27	8
Johnny Morrison, Pittsburgh (3)	25	13
Grover Alexander, Chicago (4)	22	12
Pete Donohue, Cincinnati (2)	21	15

	W	L
Burleigh Grimes, Brooklyn (6)	21	18
Jesse Haines, St. Louis (5)	20	13
Eppa Rixey, Cincinnati (2)	20	15
1924 (4)		
Dazzy Vance, Brooklyn (2)	28	6
Burleigh Grimes, Brooklyn (2)	22	13
Carl Mays, Cincinnati (4)	20	9
Wilbur Cooper, Pittsburgh (3)	20	14
1925 (3)		
Dazzy Vance, Brooklyn (6T)	22	9
Eppa Rixey, Cincinnati (3)	21	11
Pete Donohue, Cincinnati (3)	21	14
1926 (4)		
Remy Kremer, Pittsburgh (3)	20	6
Flint Rhem, St. Louis (1)	20	7
Lee Meadows, Pittsburgh (3)	20	9
Pete Donohue, Cincinnati (2)	20	14
1927 (4)		
Charlie Root, Chicago (4)	26	15
Jesse Haines, St. Louis (2)	24	10
Carmen Hill, Pittsburgh (1)	22	11
Grover Alexander, St. Louis (2)	21	10
1928 (6)		
Larry Benton, New York (2)	25	9
Burleigh Grimes, Pittsbrugh (4)	25	14
Dazzy Vance, Brooklyn (6)	22	10
Bill Sherdel, St. Louis (1)	21	10
Jesse Haines, St. Louis (1)	20	8
Fred Fitzsimmons, New York (2)	20	9
1929 (1)		
Pat Malone, Chicago (1)	22	10
1930 (2)		
Pat Malone, Chicago (2)	20	9
Remy Kremer, Pittsburgh (5)	20	12
1931 (0)		

Jumbo Elliott, Philadelphia, Bill Hallahan, St. Louis, and Heinie Meine, Pittsburgh, each had 19 wins.

	W	L
1932 (2)		
Lon Warneke, Chicago (1)	22	6
Watty Clark, Brooklyn (3)	20	12
1933 (4)		
Carl Hubbell, New York (1)	23	12
Ben Cantwell, Boston (4)	20	10
Guy Bush, Chicago (3)	20	12
Dizzy Dean, St. Louis (5)	20	18
1934 (4)		
Dizzy Dean, St. Louis (1)	30	7
Hal Schumacher, New York (2)	23	10
Lon Warneke, Chicago (3)	22	10
Carl Hubbell, New York (2)	21	12
1935 (5)		
Dizzy Dean, St. Louis (2)	28	12
Carl Hubbell, New York (3)	23	12
Paul Derringer, Cincinnati (6)	22	13
Bill Lee, Chicago (1)	20	6
Lon Warneke, Chicago (1)	20	13
1936 (2)		
Carl Hubbell, New York (1)	26	6
Dizzy Dean, St. Louis (2T)	24	13
1937 (4)		
Carl Hubbell, New York (1)	22	8
Cliff Melton, New York (1)	20	9
Lou Fette, Boston (5)	20	10
Jim Turner, Boston (5)	20	11
1938 (2)		
Bill Lee, Chicago (1)	22	9
Paul Derringer, Cincinnati (4)	21	14
1939 (4)		
Bucky Walters, Cincinnati (1)	27	11
Paul Derringer, Cincinnati (1)	25	7
Curt Davis, St. Louis (2)	22	16
Luke Hamlin, Brooklyn (3)	20	13
1940 (3)		
Bucky Walters, Cincinnati (1)	22	10
Paul Derringer, Cincinnati (1)	20	12
Claude Passeau, Chicago (5)	20	13
1941 (2)		
Kirby Higbe, Brooklyn (1)	22	9
Whit Wyatt, Brooklyn (1)	22	10

1942 (2)	W	L
Mort Cooper, St. Louis (1)	22	7
Johnny Beazley, St. Louis (1)	21	6

1943 (3)

	W	L
Mort Cooper, St. Louis (1)	21	8
Rip Sewell, Pittsburgh (4)	21	9
Elmer Riddle, Cincinnati (2)	21	11

1944 (4)

	W	L
Bucky Walters, Cincinnati (3)	23	8
Mort Cooper, St. Louis (1)	22	7
Rip Sewell, Pittsburgh (2)	21	12
Bill Voiselle, New York (5)	21	16

1945 (2)

	W	L
Red Barrett, 2-3 Boston (6) 21-9 St. Louis (2)	23	12
Hank Wyse, Chicago (1)	22	10

1946 (2)

	W	L
Howie Pollet, St. Louis (1)	21	10
Johnny Sain, Boston (4)	20	14

1947 (5)

	W	L
Ewell Blackwell, Cincinnati (5)	22	8
Larry Jansen, New York (4)	21	5
Warren Spahn, Boston (3)	21	10
Ralph Branca, Brooklyn (1)	21	12
Johnny Sain, Boston (3)	21	12

1948 (2)

	W	L
Johnny Sain, Boston (1)	24	15
Harry Brecheen, St. Louis (2)	20	7

1949 (2)

	W	L
Warren Spahn, Boston (4)	21	14
Howie Pollet, St. Louis (2)	20	9

1950 (3)

	W	L
Warren Spahn, Boston (4)	21	17
Robin Roberts, Philadelphia (1)	20	11
Johnny Sain, Boston (4)	20	13

1951 (7)

	W	L
Sal Maglie, New York (1)	23	6
Larry Jansen, New York (1)	23	11
Preacher Roe, Brooklyn (2)	22	3
Warren Spahn, Boston (4)	22	14
Robin Roberts, Philadelphia (5)	21	15
Don Newcombe, Brooklyn (2)	20	9
Murry Dickson, Pittsburgh (7)	20	16

1952 (1)

	W	L
Robin Roberts, Philadelphia (4)	28	7

1953 (4)

	W	L
Warren Spahn, Milwaukee (2)	23	7
Robin Roberts, Philadelphia (3T)	23	16
Carl Erskine, Brooklyn (1)	20	6
Harvey Haddix, St. Louis (3T)	20	9

1954 (3)

	W	L
Robin Roberts, Philadelphia (4)	23	15
Johnny Antonelli, New York (1)	21	7
Warren Spahn, Milwaukee (3)	21	12

1955 (2)

	W	L
Robin Roberts, Philadelphia (4)	23	14
Don Newcombe, Brooklyn (1)	20	5

1956 (3)

	W	L
Don Newcombe, Brooklyn (1)	27	7
Warren Spahn, Milwaukee (2)	20	11
Johnny Antonelli, New York (6)	20	13

1957 (1)

	W	L
Warren Spahn, Milwaukee (1)	21	11

1958 (3)

	W	L
Warren Spahn, Milwaukee (1)	22	11
Bob Friend, Pittsburgh (2)	22	14
Lew Burdette, Milwaukee (1)	20	10

1959 (3)

	W	L
Lew Burdette, Milwaukee (2)	21	15
Warren Spahn, Milwaukee (2)	21	15
Sam Jones, San Francisco (3)	21	15

1960 (3)

	W	L
Ernie Broglio, St. Louis (3)	21	9
Warren Spahn, Milwaukee (2)	21	10
Vernon Law, Pittsburgh (1)	20	9

1961 (2)

	W	L
Joey Jay, Cincinnati (1)	21	10
Warren Spahn, Milwaukee (4)	21	13

1962 (4)

	W	L
Don Drysdale, Los Angeles (2)	25	9
Jack Sanford, San Francisco (1)	24	7

	W	L
Bob Purkey, Cincinnati (3)	23	5
Joey Jay, Cincinnati (3)	21	14

1963 (5)

	W	L
Sandy Koufax, Los Angeles (1)	25	5
Juan Marichal, San Francisco (3)	25	8
Jim Maloney, Cincinnati (5)	23	7
Warren Spahn, Milwaukee (6)	23	7
Dick Ellsworth, Chicago (7)	22	10

1964 (3)

	W	L
Larry Jackson, Chicago (8)	24	11
Juan Marichal, San Francisco (4)	21	8
Ray Sadecki, St. Louis (1)	20	11

1965 (7)

	W	L
Sandy Koufax, Los Angeles (1)	26	8
Tony Cloninger, Milwaukee (5)	24	11
Don Drysdale, Los Angeles (1)	23	12
Sammy Ellis, Cincinnati (4)	22	10
Juan Marichal, San Francisco (2)	22	13
Jim Maloney, Cincinnati (4)	20	9
Bob Gibson, St. Louis (7)	20	12

1966 (5)

	W	L
Sandy Koufax, Los Angeles (1)	27	9
Juan Marichal, San Francisco (2)	25	6
Gaylord Perry, San Francisco (2)	21	8
Bob Gibson, St. Louis (6)	21	12
Chris Short, Philadelphia (4)	20	10

1967 (2)

	W	L
Mike McCormick, San Francisco (2)	22	10
Ferguson Jenkins, Chicago (3)	20	13

1968 (3)

	W	L
Juan Marichal, San Francisco (2)	26	9
Bob Gibson, St. Louis (1)	22	9
Ferguson Jenkins, Chicago (3)	20	15

1969 (9)

	W	L
Tom Seaver, New York (1E)	25	7
Phil Niekro, Atlanta (1W)	23	13
Juan Marichal, San Francisco (2W)	21	11
Ferguson Jenkins, Chicago (2E)	21	15
Bill Singer, Los Angeles (4W)	20	12
Larry Dierker, Houston (5W)	20	13
Bob Gibson, St. Louis (4E)	20	13
Bill Hands, Chicago (2E)	20	14
Claude Osteen, Los Angeles (4W)	20	15

1970 (4)

	W	L
Bob Gibson, St. Louis (4E)	23	7
Gaylord Perry, San Francisco (3W)	23	13
Ferguson Jenkins, Chicago (2E)	22	16
Jim Merritt, Cincinnati (1W)	20	12

1971 (4)

	W	L
Ferguson Jenkins, Chicago (3ET)	24	13
Al Downing, Los Angeles (2W)	20	9
Steve Carlton, St. Louis (2E)	20	9
Tom Seaver, New York (3ET)	20	10

1972 (4)

	W	L
Steve Carlton, Philadelphia (6E)	27	10
Tom Seaver, New York (3E)	21	12
Claude Osteen, Los Angeles (3W)	20	11
Ferguson Jenkins, Chicago (2E)	20	12

1973 (1)

	W	L
Ron Bryant, San Francisco (3W)	24	12

1974 (2)

	W	L
Andy Messersmith, Los Angeles (1W)	20	6
Phil Niekro, Atlanta (3W)	20	13

1975 (2)

	W	L
Tom Seaver, New York (3ET)	22	9
Randy Jones, San Diego (4W)	20	12

1976 (5)

	W	L
Randy Jones, San Diego (5W)	22	14
Jerry Koosman, New York (3E)	21	10
Don Sutton, Los Angeles (2W)	21	10
Steve Carlton, Philadelphia (1E)	20	7
J.R. Richard, Houston (3W)	20	15

1977 (6)

	W	L
Steve Carlton, Philadelphia (1E)	23	10
Tom Seaver, 7-3, New York (6E),		

	W	L
14-3, Cincinnati (2W)	21	6
John Candelaria, Pittsburgh (2E)	20	5
Bob Forsch, St. Louis (3E)	20	7
Tommy John, Los Angeles (1W)	20	7
Rick Reuschel, Chicago (4E)	20	10
1978 (2)		
Gaylord Perry, San Diego (3W)	21	6
Ross Grimsley, Montreal (4E)	20	11
1979 (2)		
Joe Niekro, Houston (2W)	21	11
Phil Niekro, Atlanta (6W)	21	20
1980 (2)		
Steve Carlton, Philadelphia (1E)	24	9
Joe Niekro, Houston (1W)	20	12
1981 (0)		
Tom Seaver, Cincinnati, had 14 wins.		
1982 (1)		
Steve Carlton, Philadelphia (2E)	23	11
1983 (0)		
John Denny, Philadelphia, had 19 wins.		
1984 (1)		
Joaquin Andujar, St. Louis (3E)	20	14
1985 (4)		
Dwight Gooden, New York (2E)	24	4
John Tudor, St. Louis (1E)	21	8
Joaquin Andujar, St. Louis (1E)	21	12
Tom Browning, Cincinnati (2W)	20	9
1986 (2)		
Fernando Valenzuela, Los Angeles (5W)	21	11
Mike Krukow, San Francisco (3W)	20	9
1987 (0)		
Rick Sutcliffe, Chicago, had 18 wins.		
1988 (3)		
Orel Hershiser, Los Angeles (1W)	23	8
Danny Jackson, Cincinnati (2W)	23	8
David Cone, New York (1E)	20	3
1989 (1)		
Mike Scott, Houston (3W)	20	10
1990 (3)		
Doug Drabek, Pittsburgh (1E)	22	6
Ramon Martinez, Los Angeles (2W)	20	6
Frank Viola, New York (2E)	20	12
1991 (2)		
John Smiley, Pittsburgh (1E)	20	8
Tom Glavine, Atlanta (1W)	20	11
1992 (2)		
Tom Glavine, Atlanta (1W)	20	8
Greg Maddux, Chicago (4E)	20	11
1993 (4)		
Tom Glavine, Atlanta (1W)	22	6
John Burkett, San Francisco (2W)	22	7
Bill Swift, San Francisco (2W)	21	8
Greg Maddux, Atlanta (1W)	20	10

	W	L
1994 (0)		
Ken Hill, Montreal, and Greg Maddux, Atlanta, each had 16 wins.		
1995 (0)		
Greg Maddux, Atlanta, had 19 wins.		
1996 (1)		
John Smoltz, Atlanta (1E)	24	8
1997 (1)		
Denny Neagle, Atlanta (1E)	20	5
1998 (1)		
Tom Glavine, Atlanta (1E)	20	6
1999 (2)		
Mike Hampton, Houston (1C)	22	4
Jose Lima, Houston (1C)	21	10
2000 (2)		
Tom Glavine, Atlanta (1E)	21	9
Darryl Kile, St. Louis (1C)	20	9
2001 (4)		
Curt Schilling, Arizona (1W)	22	6
Matt Morris, St. Louis (2C)	22	8
Randy Johnson, Arizona (1W)	21	6
Jon Lieber, Chicago (3C)	20	6
2002 (2)		
Randy Johnson, Arizona (1W)	24	5
Curt Schilling, Arizona (1W)	23	7
2003 (1)		
Russ Ortiz, Atlanta (1E)	21	7
2004 (1)		
Roy Oswalt, Houston (2C)	20	10

TWO LEAGUES IN SEASON

	W	L
1884 (4)		
Billy Taylor, 25-4 St. Louis U.A. (1),		
18-12 Philadelphia A.A. (7)	43	16
Charlie Sweeney, 17-7 Providence N.L. (1),		
24-8 St. Louis U.A. (1)	41	15
Jim McCormick, 19-22 Cleveland N.L. (7),		
22-4 Cincinnati U.A. (2)	41	26
Fred Shaw, 8-18 Detroit N.L. (8),		
22-15 Boston U.A. (4)	30	33
1902 (1)		
Joe McGinnity, 13-10 Baltimore A.L. (8),		
8-8 New York N.L. (8)	21	18
1904 (1)		
Patsy Flaherty, 2-2 Chicago A.L. (3),		
19-9 Pittsburgh N.L. (4)	21	11
1945 (1)		
Hank Borowy, 10-5 New York A.L. (4),		
11-2 Chicago N.L. (1)	21	7
1984 (1)		
Rick Sutcliffe, 4-5 Cleveland A.L. (6E),		
16-1 Chicago N.L. (1E)	20	6
2002 (1)		
Bartolo Colon, 10-4 Cleveland A.L. (3C),		
10-4 Montreal N.L. (2E)	20	8

FIELDING
UNASSISTED TRIPLE PLAYS

Neal Ball, shortstop, Cleveland A.L. vs. Boston at Cleveland, July 19, 1909, first game, second inning. Ball caught McConnell's liner, touched second, retiring Wagner, who was on his way to third base, and then tagged Stahl as he came up to second.

George H. Burns, first baseman, Boston A.L. vs. Cleveland at Boston, September 14, 1923, second inning. Burns caught Brower's liner, tagged Lutzke off first and then ran to second and reached that bag before Stephenson could return from third base.

Ernie Padgett, shortstop, Boston N.L. vs. Philadelphia at Boston, October 6, 1923, second game, fourth inning. Padgett caught Holke's liner, ran to second to retire Tierney, then tagged Lee before he could return to first.

Glenn Wright, shortstop, Pittsburgh N.L. vs. St. Louis at Pittsburgh, May 7, 1925, ninth inning. Wright caught Bottomley's liner, ran to second to retire Cooney and then tagged Hornsby, who was on his way to second.

Jimmy E. Cooney, shortstop, Chicago N.L. vs. Pittsburgh at Pittsburgh, May 30, 1927, a.m. game, fourth inning. Cooney caught Paul Waner's liner, stepped on second to retire Lloyd Waner, then tagged Barnhart off first.

Johnny Neun, first baseman, Detroit A.L. vs. Cleveland at Detroit, May 31, 1927, ninth inning. Neun caught Summa's liner, ran over and tagged Jamieson between first and second and then touched second base before Myatt could return.

Ron Hansen, shortstop, Washington A.L. vs. Cleveland at Cleveland, July 30, 1968, first inning. With the count 3-and-2 on Azcue, Nelson broke for third base. Hansen caught Azcue's liner, stepped on second to double Nelson and then tagged Snyder going into second.

Mickey Morandini, second baseman, Philadelphia N.L. vs. Pittsburgh at Pittsburgh, September 20, 1992, sixth inning. Morandini caught King's liner, stepped on second to retire Van Slyke, then tagged Bonds coming from first.

John Valentin, shortstop, Boston A.L. vs. Seattle at Boston, July 8, 1994, sixth inning. Valentin caught Newfield's line drive, stepped on second to retire Blowers, then tagged Mitchell coming from first.

Randy Velarde, second baseman, Oakland A.L. vs. New York

A.L. at New York, May 29, 2000, sixth inning. Velarde caught Spencer's line drive, tagged Posada off first, then stepped on second to retire Martinez.

Rafael Furcal, shortstop, Atlanta N.L. vs. St. Louis at St. Louis, August 10, 2003, fifth inning. Furcal caught Williams' line drive, stepped on second to retire Matheny, then tagged Palmeiro coming from first.

(Note: All above unassisted triple plays made with runners on first and second bases only. In addition to the 11 regular-season unassisted triple plays, Bill Wambsganss turned one in the 1920 World Series. For details see World Series General Reference section.)

Total number of occurrences (excluding Wambsganss'): 11

CLUB MISCELLANEOUS

ALL-TIME FRANCHISE WON-LOST RECORDS

CURRENT AMERICAN LEAGUE CLUBS (1901 THROUGH 2004)

Present franchise	Years	Total Games	Won	Lost	Tied	Pct.
Anaheim (Los Angeles, 1961-1965, California 1966-1996)	1961-2004	7,001	3,412	3,586	3	.487
Baltimore	1954-2004	8,063	4,206	3,845	12	.522
Boston	1901-2004	16,164	8,263	7,817	84	.514
Chicago	1901-2004	16,171	8,111	7,957	103	.505
Cleveland	1901-2004	16,177	8,209	7,877	91	.510
Detroit	1901-2004	16,203	8,150	7,959	94	.506
Kansas City	1969-2004	5,695	2,186	2,877	2	.495
Minnesota	1961-2004	6,995	3,482	3,505	8	.498
New York	1903-2004	15,876	8,979	6,809	88	.569
Oakland	1968-2004	5,865	3,067	2,797	1	.523
Seattle	1977-2004	4,413	2,080	2,331	2	.472
Tampa Bay	1998-2004	1,131	451	680	0	.399
Texas	1972-2004	5,214	2,5177	2,692	5	.483
Toronto	1977-2004	4,413	2,178	2,233	2	.494
Present Totals		**129,381**	**65,921**	**62,965**	**495**	**.511**

DEFUNCT AMERICAN LEAGUE CLUBS (1901 THROUGH 1997)

Extinct franchise	Years	Total Games	Won	Lost	Tied	Pct.
Baltimore	1901-1902	276	118	153	5	.435
Kansas City	1955-1967	2,060	829	1,224	7	.404
Milwaukee (original club)	1901	139	48	89	2	.350
Milwaukee (second club)	1970-1997	4,407	2,136	2,269	2	.485
Philadelphia	1901-1954	8,213	3,886	4,248	79	.478
St. Louis	1902-1953	7,974	3,414	4,465	95	.433
Seattle	1969	163	64	98	1	.395
Washington (original club)	1901-1960	9,188	4,223	4,864	101	.465
Washington (second club)	1961-1971	1,773	740	1,032	1	.418
Extinct totals		**34,193**	**15,458**	**18,442**	**293**	**.456**
American League totals		**163,786**	**81,379**	**81,407**	**788**	**.500**

CURRENT NATIONAL LEAGUE CLUBS (1876 THROUGH 2004)

Present franchise	Years	Total Games	Won	Lost	Tied	Pct.
Arizona	1998-2004	1,134	575	559	0	.507
Atlanta	1966-2004	6,183	3,179	2,996	8	.515
Chicago	1876-2004	19,113	9,756	9,203	154	.514
Cincinnati	1890-2004	17,742	8,898	8,719	125	.505
Colorado	1993-2004	1,881	882	999	0	.469
Florida	1993-2004	1,877	880	997	0	.469
Houston	1962-2004	6,842	3,408	3,430	4	.498
Los Angeles	1958-2004	7,464	4,011	3,447	6	.538
Milwaukee	1998-2004	1,133	480	652	1	.424
Montreal	1969-2004	5,702	2,755	2,943	4	.484
New York	1962-2004	6,834	3,228	3,598	8	.473
Philadelphia	1883-2004	18,509	8,591	9,805	113	.467
Pittsburgh	1887-2004	18,120	9,186	8,805	129	.511
St. Louis	1892-2004	17,469	8,801	8,539	129	.508
San Diego	1969-2004	5,707	2,611	3,094	2	.458
San Francisco	1958-2004	7,464	3,895	3,563	6	.522
Present Totals		**143,174**	**71,136**	**71,349**	**689**	**.499**

NOTE: Totals for the current Milwaukee Brewers franchise include its American League totals in the Extinct American League Clubs chart and its National League totals in the Current National League Clubs.

DEFUNCT NATIONAL LEAGUE CLUBS (1876 THROUGH 1965)

Extinct franchise	Years	Total Games	Won	Lost	Tied	Pct.
Baltimore	1892-1899	1,117	644	447	26	.590
Boston	1876-1952	10,852	5,118	5,598	136	.478

	Years	Total Games	Won	Lost	Tied	Pct.
Brooklyn	1890-1957	10,253	5,214	4,926	113	.514
Buffalo	1879-1885	656	314	333	9	.485
Cincinnati	1876-1880	348	125	217	6	.365
Cleveland	1879-1884	549	242	299	8	.447
Cleveland	1889-1899	1,534	738	764	32	.491
Detroit	1881-1888	879	426	437	16	.494
Hartford	1876-1877	129	78	48	3	.619
Indianapolis	1878	63	24	36	3	.400
Indianapolis	1887-1889	398	146	249	3	.370
Kansas City	1886	126	30	91	5	.250
Louisville	1876-1877	130	65	61	4	.516
Louisville	1892-1899	1,121	419	683	19	.380
Milwaukee	1878	61	15	45	1	.250
Milwaukee	1953-1965	2,044	1,146	890	8	.563
New York	1876	57	21	35	1	.375
New York	1883-1957	11,116	6,067	4,898	151	.553
Philadelphia	1876	60	14	45	1	.237
Providence	1878-1885	725	438	278	9	.612
St. Louis	1876-1877	124	73	51	0	.589
St. Louis	1885-1886	236	79	151	6	.343
Syracuse	1879	71	22	48	1	.314
Troy	1879-1882	330	134	191	5	.412
Washington	1886-1889	514	163	337	14	.326
Washington	1892-1899	1,125	410	697	18	.370
Worcester	1880-1882	252	90	159	3	.361
Extinct totals		**44,870**	**22,255**	**22,014**	**601**	**.503**
National League totals		**188,044**	**93,391**	**93,363**	**1,290**	**.500**

AMERICAN ASSOCIATION CLUBS (1882 THROUGH 1891)

Extinct franchise	Years	Total Games	Won	Lost	Tied	Pct.
Baltimore	1882-1889	944	403	519	22	.439
Baltimore	1890-1891	174	87	81	6	.517
Boston	1891	139	93	42	4	.684
Brooklyn	1884-1889	783	410	354	19	.536
Brooklyn	1890	101	26	74	1	.262
Cincinnati	1882-1889	957	549	396	12	.580
Cincinnati	1891	102	43	57	2	.431
Cleveland	1887-1888	268	89	519	5	.341
Columbus	1883-1884	207	101	104	2	.493
Columbus	1889-1891	418	200	209	9	.489
Indianapolis	1884	110	29	78	3	.277
Kansas City	1888-1889	271	98	171	2	.365
Louisville	1882-1891	1,233	575	638	20	.475
Milwaukee	1891	36	21	15	0	.583
New York	1883-1887	592	270	309	13	.467
Philadelphia	1882-1891	1,223	633	564	26	.528
Pittsburgh	1882-1886	538	236	296	6	.444
Richmond	1884	46	12	30	4	.304
Rochester	1890	133	63	63	7	.500
St. Louis	1882-1891	1,235	782	433	20	.641
Syracuse	1890	128	55	72	1	.434
Toledo	1884	110	46	58	6	.446
Toledo	1890	134	68	64	2	.515
Washington	1884	63	12	51	0	.191
Washington	1891	139	43	92	4	.324
American Association totals		**10,084**	**4,944**	**4,944**	**196**	**.500**

CLUBS WITH 100 VICTORIES IN SEASON

AMERICAN LEAGUE

Year	Club	Won	Lost	Pct.
2001	Seattle	116	46	.716
1998	New York	114	48	.704
1954	Cleveland	111	43	.721
1927	New York	110	44	.714
1961	New York	109	53	.673
1969	Baltimore	109	53	.673
1970	Baltimore	108	54	.667
1931	Philadelphia	107	45	.704
1932	New York	107	47	.695
1939	New York	106	45	.702
1912	Boston	105	47	.691
1929	Philadelphia	104	46	.693
1946	Boston	104	50	.675
1963	New York	104	57	.646
1984	Detroit	104	58	.642
1988	Oakland	104	58	.642
1942	New York	103	51	.669
1954	New York	103	51	.669
2002	New York	103	58	.640
1968	Detroit	103	59	.636
1980	New York	103	59	.636
1990	Oakland	103	59	.636
2002	Oakland	103	59	.636
1910	Philadelphia	102	48	.680

Year	Club	Won	Lost	Pct.
1936	New York	102	51	.667
1930	Philadelphia	102	52	.662
1937	New York	102	52	.662
1979	Baltimore	102	57	.642
1965	Minnesota	102	60	.630
1977	Kansas City	102	60	.630
2001	Oakland	102	60	.630
1911	Philadelphia	101	50	.669
1915	Boston	101	50	.669
1928	New York	101	53	.656
1934	Detroit	101	53	.656
1941	New York	101	53	.656
1971	Baltimore	101	57	.639
1971	Oakland	101	60	.627
1961	Detroit	101	61	.623
2003	New York	101	61	.623
2004	New York	101	61	.623
1995	Cleveland	100	44	.694
1915	Detroit	100	54	.649
1917	Chicago	100	54	.649
1977	New York	100	62	.617
1980	Baltimore	100	62	.617
1978	New York	100	63	.613

NATIONAL LEAGUE

Year	Club	Won	Lost	Pct.
1906	Chicago	116	36	.763
1909	Pittsburgh	110	42	.724
1975	Cincinnati	108	54	.667
1986	New York	108	54	.667
1907	Chicago	107	45	.704
1904	New York	106	47	.693
1942	St. Louis	106	48	.688
1998	Atlanta	106	56	.654
1905	New York	105	48	.686
1943	St. Louis	105	49	.682
1944	St. Louis	105	49	.682
1953	Brooklyn	105	49	.682
2004	St. Louis	105	47	.648
1909	Chicago	104	49	.680
1910	Chicago	104	50	.675
1942	Brooklyn	104	50	.675
1993	Atlanta	104	58	.642
1902	Pittsburgh	103	36	.741
1912	New York	103	48	.682
1993	San Francisco	103	59	.636
1999	Atlanta	103	59	.636
1962	San Francisco	103	62	.624
1898	Boston	102	47	.685
1892	Boston	102	48	.680
1970	Cincinnati	102	60	.630
1998	Houston	102	60	.630
1974	Los Angeles	102	60	.630
1976	Cincinnati	102	60	.630
1962	Los Angeles	102	63	.618
1899	Brooklyn	101	47	.682
1913	New York	101	51	.664
1931	St. Louis	101	53	.656
2002	Atlanta	101	59	.631
1967	St. Louis	101	60	.627
1976	Philadelphia	101	61	.623
1977	Philadelphia	101	61	.623

Year	Club	Won	Lost	Pct.
1985	St. Louis	101	61	.623
1997	Atlanta	101	61	.623
2003	Atlanta	101	61	.623
1940	Cincinnati	100	53	.654
1935	Chicago	100	54	.649
1941	Brooklyn	100	54	.649
1988	New York	100	60	.625
2003	San Francisco	100	61	.621
1969	New York	100	62	.617
1999	Arizona	100	62	.617

CLUBS WITH 100 LOSSES IN SEASON

AMERICAN ASSOCIATION

Year	Club	Won	Lost	Pct.
1890	Pittsburgh	23	113	.169
1889	Louisville	27	111	.196

AMERICAN LEAGUE

Year	Club	Won	Lost	Pct.
1916	Philadelphia	36	117	.235
1904	Washington	38	113	.251
2003	Detroit	43	119	.265
1932	Boston	43	111	.279
1939	St. Louis	43	111	.279
1909	Washington	42	110	.276
1915	Philadelphia	43	109	.283
1996	Detroit	53	109	.327
1979	Toronto	53	109	.327
1937	St. Louis	46	108	.299
1979	Oakland	54	108	.333
1911	St. Louis	45	107	.296
1926	Boston	46	107	.301
1910	St. Louis	47	107	.305
1988	Baltimore	54	107	.335
1977	Toronto	54	107	.335
1920	Philadelphia	48	106	.312
2002	Tampa Bay	55	106	.342
2002	Detroit	55	106	.342
1970	Chicago	56	106	.346
1963	Washington	56	106	.346
1925	Boston	47	105	.309
1906	Boston	49	105	.318
1943	Philadelphia	49	105	.318
1946	Philadelphia	49	105	.318
1991	Cleveland	57	105	.352
1964	Kansas City	57	105	.352
1973	Texas	57	105	.352
1919	Philadelphia	36	104	.257
1952	Detroit	50	104	.325
1949	Washington	50	104	.325
1978	Seattle	56	104	.350
2004	Kansas City	58	104	.358
1927	Boston	51	103	.331
1908	New York	51	103	.331
1954	Philadelphia	51	103	.331
1989	Detroit	59	103	.364
1965	Kansas City	59	103	.364
1980	Seattle	59	103	.364
1932	Chicago	49	102	.325
1907	Washington	49	102	.325
1912	New York	50	102	.329

Year	Club	Won	Lost	Pct.
1914	Cleveland	51	102	.333
1930	Boston	52	102	.338
1956	Kansas City	52	102	.338
1950	Philadelphia	52	102	.338
1951	St. Louis	52	102	.338
1975	Detroit	57	102	.358
1978	Toronto	59	102	.366
1971	Cleveland	60	102	.370
1985	Cleveland	60	102	.370
1982	Minnesota	60	102	.370
1983	Seattle	60	102	.370
1948	Chicago	51	101	.336
1912	St. Louis	53	101	.344
1949	St. Louis	53	101	.344
1955	Washington	53	101	.344
1962	Washington	60	101	.373
1987	Cleveland	61	101	.377
1921	Philadelphia	53	100	.346
1936	Philadelphia	53	100	.346
1954	Baltimore	54	100	.351
1940	Philadelphia	54	100	.351
1953	St. Louis	54	100	.351
1972	Texas	54	100	.351
1961	Kansas City	61	100	.379
1961	Washington	61	100	.379
1965	Boston	62	100	.383
1964	Washington	62	100	.383
2001	Tampa Bay	62	100	.383
2002	Kansas City	62	100	.383

Year	Club	Won	Lost	Pct.
1940	Philadelphia	50	103	.327
1905	Boston	51	103	.331
1921	Philadelphia	51	103	.331
1927	Philadelphia	51	103	.331
1917	Pittsburgh	51	103	.331
1962	Chicago	59	103	.364
1966	Chicago	59	103	.364
1993	New York	59	103	.364
1897	St. Louis	29	102	.221
1906	Boston	49	102	.325
1930	Philadelphia	52	102	.338
1973	San Diego	60	102	.370
1974	San Diego	60	102	.370
1892	Baltimore	46	101	.313
1898	Washington	51	101	.336
1912	Boston	52	101	.340
1907	St. Louis	52	101	.340
1908	Brooklyn	53	101	.344
1954	Pittsburgh	53	101	.344
1977	Atlanta	61	101	.377
1982	Cincinnati	61	101	.377
1967	New York	61	101	.377
1993	San Diego	61	101	.377
1904	Philadelphia	52	100	.342
1910	Boston	53	100	.346
1922	Boston	53	100	.346
1924	Boston	53	100	.346
1923	Boston	54	100	.351
1936	Philadelphia	54	100	.351
1971	San Diego	61	100	.379
1985	San Francisco	62	100	.383
2001	Pittsburgh	62	100	.383

NATIONAL LEAGUE

Year	Club	Won	Lost	Pct.
1899	Cleveland	20	134	.130
1962	New York	40	120	.250
1935	Boston	38	115	.248
1952	Pittsburgh	42	112	.273
1965	New York	50	112	.309
1898	St. Louis	39	111	.260
1941	Philadelphia	43	111	.279
1963	New York	51	111	.315
2004	Arizona	51	111	.315
1969	Montreal	52	110	.321
1969	San Diego	52	110	.321
1942	Philadelphia	42	109	.278
1928	Philadelphia	43	109	.283
1964	New York	53	109	.327
1909	Boston	45	108	.294
1945	Philadelphia	46	108	.299
1998	Florida	54	108	.333
1911	Boston	44	107	.291
1961	Philadelphia	47	107	.305
1976	Montreal	55	107	.340
1939	Philadelphia	45	106	.298
1988	Atlanta	54	106	.338
2002	Milwaukee	56	106	.346
1938	Philadelphia	45	105	.300
1908	St. Louis	49	105	.318
1905	Brooklyn	48	104	.316
1923	Philadelphia	50	104	.325
1953	Pittsburgh	50	104	.325
1985	Pittsburgh	57	104	.354
1928	Boston	50	103	.327

CLUBS WITH 13 STRAIGHT VICTORIES IN SEASON

AMERICAN ASSOCIATION

Year	Club	G	Home	Away
1885	St. Louis	17	14	3
1887	St. Louis	15	15	0
1889	Philadelphia (1 tie)	14	13	1

UNION ASSOCIATION

Year	Club	G	Home	Away
1884	St. Louis	20	16	4
1884	Baltimore	16	7	9

AMERICAN LEAGUE

Year	Club	G	Home	Away
2002	Oakland	20	10	10
1906	Chicago (1 tie)	19	11	8
1947	New York	19	6	13
1953	New York	18	3	15
1912	Washington	17	1	16
1931	Philadelphia	17	5	12
1926	New York	16	12	4
1977	Kansas City	16	9	7
1906	New York	15	12	3
1913	Philadelphia	15	13	2
1946	Boston	15	11	4
1960	New York	15	9	6
1991	Minnesota	15	10	5
2001	Seattle	15	10	5

Year	Club	Won	Lost	Pct.
1909	Detroit	14	14	0
1916	St. Louis	14	13	1
1934	Detroit	14	9	5
1941	New York	14	6	8
1951	Chicago	14	3	11
1973	Baltimore	14	10	4
1988	Oakland	14	5	9
1991	Texas	14	7	7
1994	Kansas City	14	12	2
1908	Chicago	13	12	1
1910	Philadelphia (1 tie)	13	12	1
1927	Detroit (1 tie)	13	13	0
1931	Philadelphia	13	13	0
1933	Washington	13	1	12
1942	Cleveland	13	4	9
1948	Boston	13	12	1
1951	Cleveland	13	7	6
1954	New York	13	8	5
1961	New York	13	12	1
1978	Baltimore	13	3	10
1987	Milwaukee	13	6	7
1999	Baltimore	13	5	8

Year	Club	Won	Lost	Pct.
1905	New York	13	8	5
1911	Pittsburgh	13	9	4
1922	Pittsburgh	13	2	11
1928	Chicago	13	13	0
1938	Pittsburgh	13	5	8
1947	Brooklyn	13	2	11
1953	Brooklyn	13	7	6
1962	Los Angeles	13	8	5
1965	Los Angeles	13	7	6
1977	Philadelphia	13	8	5
1982	Atlanta	13	5	8
1991	Philadelphia	13	9	4
1992	Atlanta	13	3	10

CLUBS WITH 13 STRAIGHT LOSSES IN SEASON

AMERICAN ASSOCIATION

Year	Club	G	Home	Away
1889	Louisville	26	5	21
1890	Philadelphia	22	6	16
1882	Baltimore	15	0	15
1884	Washington	15	0	15
1891	Louisville	15	0	15
1889	Louisville	14	14	0
1886	Louisville	13	0	13
1890	Brooklyn	13	0	13

UNION ASSOCIATION

Year	Club	G	Home	Away
1884	Kansas City (1 tie)	15	3	12
1884	Kansas City	14	0	14

AMERICAN LEAGUE

Year	Club	G	Home	Away
1988	Baltimore	21	8	13
1906	Boston	20	19	1
1916	Philadelphia	20	1	19
1943	Philadelphia	20	3	17
1975	Detroit	19	9	10
1920	Philadelphia	18	0	18
1948	Washington	18	8	10
1959	Washington	18	3	15
1926	Boston	17	14	3
1907	Boston (2 ties)	16	9	7
1927	Boston	15	10	5
1937	Philadelphia (1 tie)	15	10	5
1972	Texas	15	5	10
2002	Tampa Bay	15	9	6
1911	St. Louis	14	6	8
1930	Boston	14	3	11
1940	St. Louis	14	0	14
1945	Philadelphia	14	0	14
1953	St. Louis	14	14	0
1954	Baltimore	14	7	7
1961	Washington	14	11	3
1970	Washington	14	4	10
1977	Oakland	14	9	5
1982	Minnesota	14	6	8
1992	Seattle	14	4	10
1994	Milwaukee	14	6	8
1904	Washington (1 tie)	13	7	6
1913	New York	13	7	6

NATIONAL LEAGUE

Year	Club	G	Home	Away
1916	New York (1 tie)	26	26	0
1880	Chicago (1 tie)	21	11	10
1935	Chicago	21	18	3
1884	Providence	20	16	4
1885	Chicago	18	14	4
1891	Boston (1 tie)	18	16	2
1894	Baltimore	18	13	5
1904	New York	18	13	5
1897	Boston	17	16	1
1907	New York	17	14	3
1916	New York	17	0	17
1887	Philadelphia (1 tie)	16	5	11
1890	Philadelphia	16	14	2
1892	Philadelphia	16	11	5
1909	Pittsburgh	16	12	4
1912	New York	16	11	5
1951	New York	16	13	3
1886	Detroit	15	12	3
1903	Pittsburgh	15	11	4
1924	Brooklyn	15	3	12
1936	Chicago	15	11	4
1936	New York	15	7	8
2000	Atlanta	15	9	6
1886	Chicago	14	13	1
1895	Baltimore	14	13	1
1899	Cincinnati	14	10	4
1903	Pittsburgh (1 tie)	14	7	7
1906	Chicago	14	14	0
1909	Pittsburgh	14	12	2
1913	New York	14	6	8
1932	Chicago	14	14	0
1935	St. Louis	14	12	2
1965	San Francisco	14	6	8
1999	San Diego	14	10	4
1880	Chicago	13	9	4
1890	Cincinnati	13	13	0
1892	Chicago	13	11	2

Year	Club	G	Home	Away
1920	Detroit	13	5	8
1924	Chicago	13	2	11
1935	Philadelphia	13	10	3
1936	St. Louis	13	2	11
1953	Detroit (2 ties)	13	12	1
1958	Washington	13	4	9
1959	Kansas City	13	4	9
1961	Minnesota	13	0	13
1962	Washington	13	7	6

NATIONAL LEAGUE

Year	Club	G	Home	Away
1899	Cleveland	24	5	19
1890	Pittsburgh	23	1	22
1961	Philadelphia	23	6	17
1894	Louisville	20	0	20
1969	Montreal	20	12	8
1906	Boston	19	3	16
1914	Cincinnati	19	6	13
1876	Cincinnati	18	9	9
1894	Louisville	18	0	18
1897	St. Louis	18	4	14
1894	Washington	17	4	13
1962	New York	17	7	10
1977	Atlanta	17	8	9
1882	Troy (1 tie)	16	5	11
1885	Buffalo	16	12	4
1888	Detroit	16	5	11
1899	Cleveland	16	0	16
1907	Boston	16	5	11
1911	Boston	16	8	8
1944	Brooklyn	16	0	16
1895	Louisville	15	10	5
1909	Boston	15	0	15
1909	St. Louis	15	11	4
1927	Boston	15	0	15
1935	Boston	15	0	15
1963	New York	15	8	7
1982	New York	15	6	9
1878	Milwaukee	14	9	5
1882	Worcester	14	2	12
1883	Philadelphia	14	4	10
1896	St. Louis (1 tie)	14	9	5
1898	Washington	14	3	11
1899	Cleveland	14	1	13
1905	St. Louis	14	9	5
1911	Boston	14	14	0
1916	St. Louis	14	0	14
1927	Philadelphia	14	1	13
1935	Boston	14	4	10
1936	Philadelphia	14	10	4
1937	Brooklyn	14	0	14
1937	Cincinnati	14	10	4
1997	Chicago	14	6	8
2004	Arizona	14	11	3
1876	Cincinnati	13	6	7
1877	Cincinnati	13	3	10
1884	Cleveland	13	1	12
1885	Detroit	13	1	12
1885	Providence	13	2	11
1886	Washington	13	13	0

Year	Club	G	Home	Away
1886	Kansas City (2 ties)	13	0	13
1888	Indianapolis	13	0	13
1890	Pittsburgh	13	2	11
1892	Baltimore	13	2	11
1899	Cleveland	13	3	10
1902	New York	13	4	9
1909	Boston	13	13	0
1910	St. Louis	13	5	8
1919	Philadelphia	13	0	13
1919	Philadelphia	13	7	6
1930	Cincinnati	13	1	12
1942	Philadelphia	13	4	9
1944	Chicago	13	7	6
1944	New York	13	0	13
1945	Cincinnati	13	2	11
1955	Philadelphia	13	9	4
1962	New York	13	9	4
1976	Atlanta	13	6	7
1980	New York	13	3	10
1982	Chicago	13	7	6
1985	Chicago	13	4	9
1993	Colorado	13	7	6
1994	San Diego	13	4	9

CLUBS WINNING FIRST EIGHT GAMES OF SEASON

AMERICAN ASSOCIATION

Never accomplished

UNION ASSOCIATION

Year	Club	G	Home	Away
1884	St. Louis	20	16	4

AMERICAN LEAGUE

Year	Club	G	Home	Away
1987	Milwaukee	13	6	7
1981	Oakland	11	3	8
1966	Cleveland	10	8	2
1944	St. Louis	9	5	4
1984	Detroit	9	3	6
2003	Kansas City	9	5	4
1982	Chicago	8	3	5

NATIONAL LEAGUE

Year	Club	G	Home	Away
1982	Atlanta	13	5	8
1884	New York	12	12	0
1955	Brooklyn	10	3	7
1962	Pittsburgh	10	3	7
1888	Boston	9	0	9
1918	New York	9	6	3
1940	Brooklyn	9	3	6
1990	Cincinnati	9	3	6
1881	Worcester	8	3	5
1915	Philadelphia	8	2	6
1980	Cincinnati	8	1	7

CLUBS LOSING FIRST EIGHT GAMES OF SEASON

AMERICAN ASSOCIATION

Year	Club	G	Home	Away
1884	Toledo	8	0	8
1887	New York	10	0	10

UNION ASSOCIATION

Year	Club	G	Home	Away
1884	Altoona	11	4	7

AMERICAN LEAGUE

Year	Club	G	Home	Away
1988	Baltimore	21	8	13
1904	Washington (1 tie)	13	7	6
1920	Detroit	13	5	8
2002	Detroit	11	5	6
1968	Chicago	10	4	6
2003	Detroit	9	6	3
1914	Cleveland	8	1	7
1945	Boston	8	3	5
1952	Detroit	8	3	5

NATIONAL LEAGUE

Year	Club	G	Home	Away
1997	Chicago	14	6	8
1884	Detroit	11	0	11
1988	Atlanta	10	8	2
1918	Brooklyn	9	3	6
1919	Boston	9	5	4
1962	New York	9	6	3
1983	Houston	9	6	3
1883	Philadelphia	8	6	2
1889	Washington	8	4	4
1955	Pittsburgh	8	4	4
1963	New York	8	2	6

GAMES OF 18 OR MORE INNINGS

AMERICAN LEAGUE

25 Innings—(1)
Chicago 7 vs. Milwaukee 6, May 8, finished May 9, 1984.
24 Innings—(2)
Philadelphia 4 at Boston 1, September 1, 1906.
Detroit 1 at Philadelphia 1 (tie), July 21, 1945.
22 Innings—(4)
New York 9 at Detroit 7, June 24, 1962.
Washington 6 vs. Chicago 5, June 12, 1967.
Milwaukee 4 at Minnesota 3, May 12, finished May 13, 1972.
Minnesota 5 vs. Cleveland 4, August 31, 1993.
21 innings—(3)
Detroit 6 at Chicago 5, May 24, 1929.
Oakland 5 at Washington 3, June 4, 1971.
Chicago 6 vs. Cleveland 3, May 26, finished May 28, 1973.
20 Innings—(8)
Philadelphia 4 at Boston 2, July 4, 1905, p.m. game.
Washington 9 at Minnesota 7, August 9, 1967.
New York 4 vs. Boston 3, August 29, 1967, second game.
Boston 5 at Seattle 3, July 27, 1969.
Oakland 1 vs. California 0, July 9, 1971.
Washington 8 at Cleveland 6, September 14, second game, finished
September 20, 1971 (game completed at Washington).
Seattle 8 at Boston 7, September 3, finished September 4, 1981.
California 4 vs. Seattle 3, April 13, finished April 14, 1982.
19 Innings—(15)
Washington 5 at Philadelphia 4, September 27, 1912.
Chicago 5 at Cleveland 4, June 24, 1915.
Cleveland 3 at New York 2, May 24, 1918.
St. Louis 8 at Washington 6, August 9, 1921.

Chicago 5 vs. Boston 4, July 13, 1951.
Cleveland 4 vs. St. Louis 3, July 1, 1952.
Cleveland 3 vs. Washington 2, June 14, 1963, second game.
Baltimore 7 vs. Washington 5, June 4, 1967.
Kansas City 6 at Detroit 5, June 17, 1967, second game.
Detroit 3 at New York 3 (tie), August 23, 1968, second game.
Oakland 5 vs. Chicago 3, August 10, finished August 11, 1972.
New York 5 vs. Minnesota 4, August 25, 1976.
Cleveland 8 at Detroit 4, April 27, 1984.
Milwaukee 10 vs. Chicago 9, May 1, 1991.
Boston 7 at Cleveland 5, April 11, 1992.
Seattle 5 vs. Boston 4, August 1, 2000.
18 Innings—(25)
Chicago 6 vs. New York 6 (tie), June 25, 1903.
Washington 0 at Detroit 0 (tie), July 16, 1909.
Washington 1 vs. Chicago 0, May 15, 1918.
Detroit 7 vs. Washington 6, August 4, 1918.
Boston 12 vs. New York 11, September 5, 1927, first game.
Philadelphia 18 at Cleveland 17, July 10, 1932.
New York 3 at Chicago 3 (tie), August 21, 1933.
Washington 1 at Chicago 0, June 8, 1947, first game.
Washington 5 at St. Louis 5 (tie), June 20, 1952.
Chicago 1 at Baltimore 1 (tie), August 6, 1959.
New York 7 vs. Boston 6, April 16, 1967.
Minnesota 3 at New York 2, July 26, 1967, second game.
Baltimore 3 vs. Boston 2, August 25, 1960.
Minnesota 11 at Seattle 7, July 19, finished July 20, 1969.
Oakland 9 vs. Baltimore 8, August 24, 1969, second game.
Minnesota 8 at Oakland 6, September 6, 1969.
Washington 2 vs. New York 1, April 22, 1970.
Texas 4 at Kansas City 3, May 17, 1972.
Detroit 4 vs. Cleveland 3, June 9, finished September 24, 1982.
New York 5 vs. Detroit 4, September 11, 1988.
Kansas City 4 vs. Texas 3, June 6, 1001.
Boston 4 vs. Detroit 3, June 5, 2001.
Texas 8 vs. Boston 7, August 25, 2001.
Texas 9 vs. Seattle 7, June 24, 2004.
Oakland 6 at Minnesota 5, August 8, 2004.

NATIONAL LEAGUE

26 Innings—(1)
Brooklyn 1 at Boston 1 (tie), May 1, 1920.
25 Innings—(1)
St. Louis 4 at New York 3, September 11, 1974.
24 Innings—(1)
Houston 1 vs. New York 0, April 15, 1968.
23 Innings—(2)
Brooklyn 2 at Boston 2 (tie), June 27, 1939.
San Francisco 8 at New York 6, May 31, 1964, second game.
22 Innings—(4)
Brooklyn 6 vs. Pittsburgh 5, August 22, 1917.
Chicago 4 at Boston 3, May 17, 1927.
Houston 5 vs. Los Angeles 4, June 3, 1989.
Los Angeles 1 at Montreal 0, August 23, 1989.
21 Innings—(7)
New York 3 at Pittsburgh 1, July 17, 1914.
Chicago 2 vs. Philadelphia 1, July 17, 1918.
Pittsburgh 2 at Boston 0, August 1, 1918.
San Francisco 1 at Cincinnati 0, September 1, 1967.
Houston 2 at San Diego 1, September 24, 1971, first game.
San Diego 11 at Montreal 8, May 21, 1977.
Los Angeles 2 at Chicago 1, August 17, finished August 18, 1982.
20 Innings—(10)
Chicago 7 at Cincinnati 7 (tie), June 30, 1892.

Chicago 2 at Philadelphia 1, August 24, 1905.
Brooklyn 9 at Philadelphia 9 (tie), April 30, 1919.
St. Louis 8 at Chicago 7, August 28, 1930.
Brooklyn 6 at Boston 2, July 5, 1940.
Philadelphia 5 vs. Atlanta 4, May 4, 1973.
Pittsburgh 5 vs. Chicago 4, July 6, 1980.
Houston 3 at San Diego 1, August 15, 1980.
Philadelphia 7 vs. Los Angeles 6, July 7, 1993.
St. Louis 7 at Florida 6, April 27, 2003.

19 Innings—(16)

Chicago 3 vs. Pittsburgh 2, June 22, 1902.
Pittsburgh 7 at Boston 6, July 31, 1912.
Chicago 4 vs. Brooklyn 3, June 17, 1915.
St. Louis 8 at Philadelphia 8 (tie), June 13, 1918.
Boston 2 vs. Brooklyn 1, May 3, 1920.
Chicago 3 vs. Boston 2, August 17, 1932.
Brooklyn 9 at Chicago 9 (tie), May 17, 1939.
Cincinnati 0 at Brooklyn 0 (tie), September 11, 1946.
Philadelphia 8 vs. Cincinnati 7, September 15, 1950, second game.
Pittsburgh 4 vs. Milwaukee 3, July 19, 1955.
Cincinnati 2 vs. Los Angeles 1, August 8, 1972.
New York 7 at Los Angeles 3, May 24, 1973.
Pittsburgh 4 at San Diego 3, August 25, 1979.
New York 16 at Atlanta 13, July 4, 1985.
Montreal 6 at Houston 3, July 7, 1985.
Atlanta 7 at St. Louis 5, May 14, 1988.

18 Innings—(33)

Providence 1 vs. Detroit 0, August 17, 1882.
Brooklyn 7 at St. Louis 7 (tie), August 17, 1902.
Chicago 2 at St. Louis 1, June 24, 1905.
Pittsburgh 3 at Chicago 2, June 28, 1916, second game.
Philadelphia 10 at Brooklyn 9, June 1, 1919.
New York 9 at Pittsburgh 8, July 7, 1922.
Chicago 2 at Boston 2, May 14, 1927.
New York 1 vs. St. Louis 0, July 2, 1933, first game.
St. Louis 8 at Cincinnati 6, July 1, 1934, first game.
Chicago 10 at Cincinnati 8, August 9, 1942, first game.
Philadelphia 4 vs. Pittsburgh 3, June 9, 1949.
Cincinnati 7 vs. Chicago 6, September 7, 1951.
Philadelphia 0 at New York 0 (tie), October 2, 1965, second game.
Cincinnati 3 at Chicago 2, July 19, 1966.
Philadelphia 2 vs. Cincinnati 1, May 21, 1967.
Pittsburgh 1 at San Diego 0, June 7, 1972, second game.
New York 3 vs. Philadelphia 2, August 1, 1972, first game.
Montreal 5 at Chicago 4, June 27, 1973, finished June 28, 1973.
Chicago 8 at Montreal 7, June 28, 1974, first game.
New York 4 vs. Montreal 3, September 16, 1975.
Pittsburgh 2 vs. Chicago 1, August 10, 1977.
Chicago 9 vs. Cincinnati 8, May 10, finished July 23.
Houston 3 vs. New York 2, June 18, 1979.
San Diego 8 at New York 6, August 26, 1980.
St. Louis 3 at Houston 1, May 27, 1983.
Pittsburgh 4 vs. San Francisco 3, July 13, 1984, second game.
Atlanta 3 at Los Angeles 2, September 6, 1984.
New York 5 vs. Pittsburgh 4, April 28, 1985.
San Francisco 5 at Atlanta 4, June 11, 1985.
Houston 8 at Chicago 7, September 2, finished September 3, 1986.
Pittsburgh 5 vs. Chicago 4, August 6, 1989.
Atlanta 5 at Los Angeles 3, August 3, 1996.
Arizona 1 at San Francisco 0, May 29, 2001.

CLUBS WITH 3,200,000 HOME ATTENDANCE

AMERICAN LEAGUE

Year	Club	Attendance
1993	Toronto Blue Jays	4,057,947
1992	Toronto Blue Jays	4,028,318
1991	Toronto Blue Jays	4,001,527
1990	Toronto Blue Jays	3,885,284

Year	Club	Attendance
2004	New York Yankees	3,775,292
2004	Anaheim Angels	3,375,677
1997	Baltimore Orioles	3,711,132
1998	Baltimore Orioles	3,685,194
1996	Baltimore Orioles	3,646,950
1993	Baltimore Orioles	3,644,965
1992	Baltimore Orioles	3,567,819
2002	Seattle Mariners	3,540,482
2001	Seattle Mariners	3,507,975
1999	Cleveland Indians	3,468,456
1998	Cleveland Indians	3,467,299
2002	New York Yankees	3,461,644
2000	Cleveland Indians	3,456,278
1999	Baltimore Orioles	3,433,150
1997	Cleveland Indians	3,404,750
1989	Toronto Blue Jays	3,375,883
2003	New York Yankees	3,335,293
1996	Cleveland Indians	3,318,174
2000	Baltimore Orioles	3,295,128
1999	New York Yankees	3,292,736
2003	Seattle Mariners	3,268,509
2001	New York Yankees	3,264,777
2000	New York Yankees	3,227,657

NATIONAL LEAGUE

Year	Club	Attendance
1993	Colorado Rockies	4,483,350
1996	Colorado Rockies	3,891,014
1997	Colorado Rockies	3,888,453
1993	Atlanta Braves	3,884,725
1998	Colorado Rockies	3,789,347
1982	Los Angeles Dodgers	3,608,881
1998	Arizona Diamondbacks	3,600,412
1983	Los Angeles Dodgers	3,510,313
2004	Los Angeles Dodgers	3,488,283
1999	Colorado Rockies	3,481,065
1997	Atlanta Braves	3,464,488
1995	Colorado Rockies	3,390,037
1998	Atlanta Braves	3,361,350
1991	Los Angeles Dodgers	3,348,170
1978	Los Angeles Dodgers	3,347,845
2000	St. Louis Cardinals	3,336,493
1997	Los Angeles Dodgers	3,319,504
2000	San Francisco Giants	3,315,330
2000	Colorado Rockies	3,285,710
1999	Atlanta Braves	3,284,897
1994	Colorado Rockies	3,281,511
2001	San Francisco Giants	3,277,244
1985	Los Angeles Dodgers	3,264,593
2004	San Francisco Giants	3,258,864
2002	San Francisco Giants	3,253,205
1980	Los Angeles Dodgers	3,249,287
2000	Atlanta Braves	3,234,301
1999	St. Louis Cardinals	3,225,334
2003	San Francisco Giants	3,222,706
2004	Philadelphia Phillies	3,206,532
2002	Arizona Diamondbacks	3,200,725

NON-PLAYING PERSONNEL

COMMISSIONERS

Kenesaw Landis, January 12, 1921 to November 25, 1944
Happy Chandler, April 24, 1945 to July 15, 1951

Ford Frick, October 8, 1951 through December 14, 1965
William Eckert, December 15, 1965 to February 4, 1969
Bowie Kuhn, February 4, 1969 through September 30, 1984
Peter Ueberroth, October 1, 1984 through March 31, 1989
Bart Giamatti, April 1 through September 1, 1989
Fay Vincent, September 2, 1989 through September 7, 1992
Bud Selig, September 9, 1992 through July 9, 1998, acting; July 9, 1998 to present

PRESIDENTS

NATIONAL LEAGUE

Morgan Bulkeley, 1876
William Hulbert, 1876 to 1882
Arthur Soden, 1882
A. G. Mills, 1882 to 1884
Nicholas Young, 1884 to 1902
Harry Pulliam, 1902 to July 29, 1909
John Heydler, July 30, 1909 to December 15, 1909

Thomas Lynch, December 15, 1909 to December 9, 1913
John Tener, December 9, 1913 to August 6, 1918
John Heydler, December 10, 1918 to December 11, 1934
Ford Frick, December 11, 1934 to October 8, 1951
Warren Giles, October 8, 1951 through December 31, 1969
Chub Feeney, January 1, 1970 to December 11, 1986
Bart Giamatti, December 11, 1986 through March 31, 1989
Bill White, April 1, 1989 through February 28, 1994
Leonard Coleman Jr., March 1, 1994 through October 31, 1999

AMERICAN LEAGUE

Byron Bancroft Johnson, 1901 to October 17, 1927
Ernest Barnard, October 31, 1927 to March 27, 1931
Will Harridge, May 27, 1931 through January 31, 1959
Joe Cronin, February 1, 1959 through 1973
Lee MacPhail Jr., January 1, 1974 through 1983
Bobby Brown, 1984 through July 31, 1994
Gene Budig, August 1, 1994 through December 31, 1999

AMERICAN LEGUE TEAM RECORDS

ANAHEIM ANGELS
YEARLY FINISHES

(American League expansion franchise known as Los Angeles Angels until September 1965
and California Angels from September 1965 to 1996)

Year	Position	W	L	Pct.	GB	Manager	Attendance
1961	8th	70	91	.435	38.5	Bill Rigney	603,510
1962	3rd	86	76	.531	10.0	Bill Rigney	1,144,063
1963	9th	70	91	.435	34.0	Bill Rigney	821,015
1964	5th	82	80	.506	17.0	Bill Rigney	760,439
1965	7th	75	87	.463	27.0	Bill Rigney	566,727
1966	6th	80	82	.494	18.0	Bill Rigney	1,400,321
1967	5th	84	77	.522	7.5	Bill Rigney	1,317,713
1968	8th	67	95	.414	36.0	Bill Rigney	1,025,956

WEST DIVISION

Year	Position	W	L	Pct.	GB	Manager	Attendance
1969	3rd	71	91	.438	26.0	Bill Rigney, Lefty Phillips	758,388
1970	3rd	86	76	.531	12.0	Lefty Phillips	1,077,741
1971	4th	76	86	.469	25.5	Lefty Phillips	926,373
1972	5th	75	80	.484	18.0	Del Rice	744,190
1973	4th	79	83	.488	15.0	Bobby Winkles	1,058,206
1974	6th	68	94	.420	22.0	Bobby Winkles, Dick Williams	917,269
1975	6th	72	89	.447	25.5	Dick Williams	1,058,163
1976	4th (tied)	76	86	.469	14.0	Dick Williams, Norm Sherry	1,006,774
1977	5th	74	88	.457	28.0	Norm Sherry, Dave Garcia	1,432,633
1978	2nd (tied)	87	75	.537	5.0	Dave Garcia, Jim Fregosi	1,755,386
1979	1st (c)	88	74	.543	+3.0	Jim Fregosi	2,523,575
1980	6th	65	95	.406	31.0	Jim Fregosi	2,297,327
1981	4th/7th	51	59	.464	*	Jim Fregosi, Gene Mauch	1,441,545
1982	1st (c)	93	69	.574	+3.0	Gene Mauch	2,807,360
1983	5th (tied)	70	92	.432	29.0	John McNamara	2,555,016
1984	2nd (tied)	81	81	.500	3.0	John McNamara	2,402,997
1985	2nd	90	72	.556	1.0	Gene Mauch	2,567,427
1986	1st (c)	92	70	.568	+5.0	Gene Mauch	2,655,872
1987	6th (tied)	75	87	.463	10.0	Gene Mauch	2,696,299
1988	4th	75	87	.463	29.0	Cookie Rojas	2,340,925
1989	3rd	91	71	.562	8.0	Doug Rader	2,647,291
1990	4th	80	82	.494	23.0	Doug Rader	2,555,688
1991	7th	81	81	.500	14.0	Doug Rader, Buck Rodgers	2,416,236
1992	5th (tied)	72	90	.444	24.0	Buck Rodgers	2,065,444
1993	5th (tied)	71	91	.438	23.0	Buck Rodgers	2,057,460
1994	4th	47	68	.409	5.5	Buck Rodgers, Marcel Lachemann	1,512,622
1995	2nd (p)	78	67	.538	1.0	Marcel Lachemann	1,748,680
1996	4th	70	91	.435	19.5	Marcel Lachemann, John McNamara, Joe Maddon	1,820,521
1997	2nd	84	78	.519	6.0	Terry Collins	1,767,330
1998	2nd	85	77	.525	3.0	Terry Collins	2,519,210
1999	4th	70	92	.432	25.0	Terry Collins, Joe Maddon	2,253,123
2000	3rd	82	80	.506	9.5	Mike Scioscia	2,066,977
2001	3rd	75	87	.463	41.0	Mike Scioscia	2,000,917
2002	2nd (D,C,S)	99	63	.611	4.0	Mike Scioscia	2,305,565
2003	3rd	77	85	.475	19.0	Mike Scioscia	3,061,090
2004	1st (d)	92	70	.568	+1.0	Mike Scioscia	3,375,677

(c) lost League Championship Series; *first half 31-29, second half 20-30; (p) lost division playoff; (D) won Division Series; (C) won League Championship Series; (S) won World Series; (d) lost Division Series

INDIVIDUAL AND CLUB RECORDS
BATTING

	Individual		Club
	Season	Career	Season
Games	162—Bobby Knoop, 1964 Jim Fregosi, 1966 Sandy Alomar, 1970, 1971 Don Baylor, 1979	1,661—Brian Downing	163 (1969, 1974)
At-bats	689—Sandy Alomar, 162 g, 1971	5,897—Garret Anderson	5,686 (1996)
Runs	124—Vlad Guerrero, 157 g, 2004	956—Tim Salmon	866 (1979) Fewest—498 (1968)
Hits	240—Darin Erstad, 157 g, 2000	1,766—Garret Anderson	1,603 (2002, 2004) Fewest—1,209 (1968)
Hitting streak	28 g—Garret Anderson, 1998		
Singles	170—Darin Erstad, 157 g, 2000	1,162—Garret Anderson	1,132 (2004)

	Individual		Club
	Season	**Career**	**Season**
Doubles	56—Garret Anderson, 158 g, 2002	369—Garret Anderson	333 (2002)
Triples	17—Chone Figgins, 148 g, 2004	70—Jim Fregosi	54 (1966)

HOME RUNS

	Season	Career	Season
			236 (2000)
			Fewest—55 (1975)
Righthander	47—Troy Glaus, 159 g, 2000	290—Tim Salmon	
Lefthander	39—Reggie Jackson, 153 g, 1982	207—Garret Anderson	
Switch-hitter	28—Chili Davis, 145 g, 1996	156—Chili Davis	
Rookie	31—Tim Salmon, 142 g, 1993		
Home	24—Troy Glaus, 2000	155—Tim Salmon	130 (2000)
Road	24—Leon Wagner, 1962, 1963	135—Tim Salmon	106 (2000)
Month	13—Tim Salmon, Jun 1996		50 (May 2000)
	Mo Vaughn, May 2000		
Pinch	4—Jack Howell, 1996	7—Jack Howell	9 (1987)
Grand slams	3—Joe Rudi, 133 g, 1978	7—Joe Rudi	8 (1979, 1983)
	Joe Rudi, 90 g, 1979		
	David Eckstein, 152 g, 2002		
Home runs at Wrigley Field, all teams			248 (1961)
Home runs at Chavez Ravine, all teams			102 (1964)
Home runs at Angel Field, all teams			243 (2000)
Total bases	366—Darin Erstad, 157 g, 2000	2,863—Tim Salmon	2,659 (2000)
	Vlad Guerrero, 156 g, 2004		
Extra base hits	88—Garret Anderson, 158 g, 2002	643—Tim Salmon	579 (2000)
Sacrifice hits	26—Tim Foli, 150 g, 1982	90—Bob Boone	114 (1982)
Sacrifice flies	13—Dan Ford, 142 g, 1979	67—Tim Salmon	64 (2002)
Bases on balls	113—Tony Phillips, 139 g, 1995	941—Tim Salmon	681 (1961)
			Fewest—416 (1992)
Strikeouts	181—Mo Vaughn, 161 g, 2000	1,316—Tim Salmon	1,080 (1968)
	Fewest—22—Tim Foli, 150 g, 1982		Fewest—602 (1970)
Hit by pitch	27—David Eckstein, 152 g, 2002	105—Brian Downing	77 (2001)
			Fewest—22 (1965)
Runs batted in	139—Don Baylor, 162 g, 1982	989—Tim Salmon	837 (2000)
			Fewest—453 (1968)
Grounded into double plays	26—Lyman Bostock, 147 g, 1978	152—Brian Downing	148 (1966)
	Fewest—5—Leon Wagner, 160 g, 1962		Fewest—98 (1975)
	Albie Pearson, 154 g, 1963		
	Dick Schofield, 155 g, 1988		
Left on base			1,209 (1966)
			Fewest—975 (1992)
Batting average	.355—Darin Erstad, 157 g, 2000	.314—Rod Carew	.282 (2002, 2004)
			Lowest—.227 (1968)
Most .300 hitters			2 (1963, 1964, 1979,
			1982, 1995, 1998, 2002)
Slugging average	.604—Troy Glaus, 159 g, 2000	.506—Tim Salmon	.472 (2000)
			Lowest—.318 (1968, 1976)
On-base percentage	.429—Tim Salmon, 143 g, 1995	.393—Rod Carew	.352 (2000)
	Chili Davis, 119 g, 1995		Lowest—.290 (1971)

BASERUNNING

	Season	Career	Season
Stolen bases	70—Mickey Rivers, 155 g, 1975	186—Gary Pettis	220 (1975)
Caught stealing	24—Chad Curtis, 152 g, 1993	82—Luis Polonia	108 (1975)

PITCHING

	Season	Career	Season
Games	72—Minnie Rojas, 1967	579—Troy Percival	
Games started	41—Nolan Ryan, 1974	379—Chuck Finley	
Complete games	26—Nolan Ryan, 1973, 1974	156—Nolan Ryan	72 (1973)

PITCHING (Cont.)

	Individual Season	Career	Club Season
Wins	22—Clyde Wright, 1970 Nolan Ryan, 1974	165—Chuck Finley	
Percentage	.773—Bert Blyleven (17-5), 1989	.567—Frank Tanana	
Winning streak	12—Jarrod Washburn, 2002		
20-win seasons		2—Nolan Ryan	
Losses	19—George Brunet, 1967 Clyde Wright, 1973 Frank Tanana, 1974 Kirk McCaskill, 1991	140—Chuck Finley	
Losing streak	11—Andy Hassler, 1975 Jim Abbott, 1996		
Saves	46—Bryan Harvey, 1991	316—Troy Percival	54 (2002)
Innings	333—Nolan Ryan, 1974	2,675—Chuck Finley	1,481 (1971)
Hits	287—Tommy John, 1983	2,544—Chuck Finley	1,636 (1983)
Runs	130—Mike Witt, 1988	1,234—Chuck Finley	943 (1996)
Earned runs	118—Jim Abbott, 1996	1,107—Chuck Finley	847 (1996)
Bases on balls	204—Nolan Ryan, 1977	1,302—Nolan Ryan	713 (1961)
Strikeouts	383—Nolan Ryan, 1973	2,416—Nolan Ryan	1,091 (1998)
Strikeouts, game	19—Nolan Ryan, Aug 12, 1974 Nolan Ryan, Jun 14, 1974 (pitched first 13 inn of 15-inn game) Nolan Ryan, Aug 20, 1974, 11 inn Nolan Ryan, Jun 8, 1977 (pitched first 11 inn of 13-inn game)		
Hit batsmen	21—Tom Murphy, 1969	71—Chuck Finley	84 (1996)
Wild pitches	21—Nolan Ryan, 1977	117—Chuck Finley	80 (1996)
Home runs	40—Shawn Boskie, 1996 Ramon Ortiz, 2002	254—Chuck Finley	228 (2000)
Sacrifice hits	22—Nolan Ryan, 1977 Nolan Ryan	90—Chuck Finley	89 (1965)
Sacrifice flies	14—Nolan Ryan, 1978	70—Chuck Finley	67 (1988)
Earned run average	1.65—Dean Chance, 278 inn, 1964	3.07—Nolan Ryan	2.91 (1964)
Shutouts	11—Dean Chance, 1964	40—Nolan Ryan	28 (1964) Lost—23 (1971)
1-0 games won	5—Dean Chance, 1964	9—Dean Chance	10 (1964) Lost—5 (1968)

TEAM FIELDING

Putouts	4,443 (1971) Fewest—4,133 (1972)	Assists	2,077 (1983) Fewest—1,511 (2004)
Chances accepted	6,499 (1983) Fewest—5,740 (1972)	Errors	192 (1961) Fewest—87 (2002)
Double plays	202 (1985) Fewest—126 (2004)	Passed balls	30 (1969) Fewest—4 (1982, 1984)
Errorless games	95 (2004) Consecutive—14 (1991)	Fielding average.	.986 (2002) Lowest—.969 (1961)

MISCELLANEOUS

Most players, season 52 (1996)

Fewest players, season 33 (1963)

Games won 99 (2002)
Month 22 (Jun 1998)
Consecutive 11 (1964)

Winning percentage .611 (2002), 99-63
Lowest .406 (1980), 65-95

Number of league championships 1
Most recent 2002

Runs, game 24 vs Toronto, Aug 25, 1979
Opponents' 21 by Seattle, Sept 30, 2000

Most seasons, non-pitcher 13—Brian Downing
Tim Salmon

Most seasons, pitcher 14—Chuck Finley

Games lost 95 (1968, 1980)
Month 22 (Jun 1961, May 1964, Aug 1968)
Consecutive 12 (1988)

Overall record 3,412-3,586 (44 seasons)
Interleague play 71-69

Number of times worst record in league 2
Most recent 1994

Runs, inning 13 vs Texas, Sept 14, 1978, 9th
vs Chicago, May 12, 1997, 7th

Hits, game 26 vs Toronto, Aug 25, 1979
vs Boston, Jun 20, 1980
Home runs, game 7 vs Montreal, Jun 4, 2003
Runs, shutout 19 vs Chicago, May 10, 2003
Opponents' 14 by Seattle, Aug 7, 1987
Longest 1-0 win 15 inn, vs Chicago, Apr 13, 1963

Total bases, game 52 vs Boston, Jun 20, 1980
Consecutive games with one or more home runs 18 (30 hrs), 1982
Longest shutout 16 inn, 3-0 vs Chicago, Sept 22, 1975
Longest 1-0 loss 20 inn, vs Oakland, Jul 9, 1971

ATTENDANCE

Highest home attendance		Largest crowds	
Wrigley Field	605,510 (1961)	**Day**	63,132 vs Kansas City, Jul 4, 1983
Chavez Ravine	1,400,321 (1965)	**Night**	63,073 vs Baltimore, Apr 23, 1983
Angel Field	3,375,677 (2004)	**Doubleheader**	43,461 vs Chicago, Aug 5, 1988
		Home opener	51,145 vs Detroit, Apr 26, 1995
Highest road attendance	2,491,562 (2001)		

BALTIMORE ORIOLES (1901-1902)
YEARLY FINISHES

(Original American League franchise moved to New York after the 1902 season)

Year	Position	W	L	Pct.	GB	Manager	Attendance
1901	5th	68	65	.511	13.5	John McGraw	141,952
1902	8th	50	88	.362	34.0	John McGraw, Wilbert Robinson	174,606

INDIVIDUAL AND CLUB RECORDS
BATTING

	Individual		Club
	Season	**Career**	**Season**
Games	134—Cy Seymour, 1901	255—Jimmy Williams	141 (1902)
At-bats	547—Cy Seymour, 134 g, 1901	999—Jimmy Williams	4,760 (1902)
Runs	113—Jimmy Williams, 130 g, 1901	196—Jimmy Williams	760 (1901)
			Fewest—715 (1902)
Hits	166—Cy Seymour, 134 g, 1901	315—Jimmy Williams	1,348 (1901)
			Fewest—1,318 (1902)
Hitting streak	unknown		
Singles	138—Cy Seymour, 134 g, 1901	205—Jimmy Williams	1,034 (1901)
Doubles	27—Kip Selbach, 128 g, 1902	53—Jimmy Williams	202 (1902)
	Jimmy Williams, 125 g, 1902		
Triples	21—Bill Keisler, 115 g, 1901	42—Jimmy Williams	111 (1901)
	Jimmy Williams, 130 g, 1901		
	Jimmy Williams, 125 g, 1902		

HOME RUNS

			33 (1902)
			Fewest—24 (1901)
Righthander	8—Jimmy Williams, 125 g, 1902	15—Jimmy Williams	
Lefthander	5—Mike Donlin, 121 g, 1901	5—Mike Donlin	
Switch-hitter	0	0	
Rookie	2—Harry Arndt, 68 g, 1902		
	Frank Foutz, 20 g, 1901		
	Jim Jackson, 99 g, 1901		
	Snake Wiltse, 19 g, 1902		
Home	3—Mike Donlin, 1901	6—Jimmy Williams	16 (1902)
	Cy Seymour, 1902		
	Jimmy Williams, 1901		
	Jimmy Williams, 1902		
Road	5—Jimmy Williams, 1902	9—Jimmy Williams	17 (1902)
Month	3—Mike Donlin, May 1901		10 (Sep 1902)
	Jimmy Williams, Jul 1901		
	Jimmy Williams, Jul 1902		
Pinch	0	0	0
Grand slams	1—Herm McFarland, 61 g, 1902	1—Herm McFarland	2 (1902)
	Jimmy Williams, 125 g, 1901	Jimmy Williams	
	Snake Wiltse, 19 g, 1902	Snake Wiltse	
Home runs at American League Park, all teams			34 (1902)

	Individual		Club
	Season	**Career**	**Season**
Total bases	249—Jimmy Williams, 125 g, 1902	497—Jimmy Williams	1,833 (1902)
Extra base hits	56—Jimmy Williams, 125 g, 1902	110—Jimmy Williams	342 (1902)
Sacrifice hits	20—Billy Gilbert, 129 g, 1902	21—Cy Seymour	115 (1902)
Bases on balls	61—John McGraw, 73 g, 1901	92—Jimmy Williams	417 (1902)
			Fewest—369 (1901)
Strikeouts	unknown	unknown	429 (1902)
	Fewest—unknown		Fewest—377 (1901)
Hit by pitch	14—John McGraw, 73 g, 1901	16—John McGraw	54 (1902)
			Fewest—52 (1901)
Runs batted in	96—Jimmy Williams, 130 g, 1901	179—Jimmy Williams	633 (1901)
			Fewest—598 (1902)
Grounded into	unknown	unknown	unknown
double plays	Fewest—unknown		Fewest—unknown
Left on base			unknown
Batting average	.340—Mike Donlin, 121 g, 1901	.315—Jimmy Williams	.294 (1901)
			Lowest—.277 (1902)
Most .300 hitters			4 (1901)
Slugging average	.500—Jimmy Williams, 125 g, 1901	.497—Jimmy Williams	.397 (1901)
			Lowest—.385 (1902)
On-base percentage	.409—Mike Donlin, 121 g, 1901	.375—Jimmy Williams	.353 (1901)
			Lowest—.342 (1902)

BASERUNNING

	Individual		Club
Stolen bases	38—Cy Seymour, 134 g, 1901	50—Cy Seymour	207 (1901)
	Billy Gilbert, 129 g, 1902		
Caught stealing	unknown	unknown	unknown

PITCHING

	Individual		Club
Games	48—Joe McGinnity, 1901	73—Joe McGinnity	
Games started	43—Joe McGinnity, 1901	66—Joe McGinnity, 1901	
Complete games	39—Joe McGinnity, 1901	58—Joe McGinnity, 1901	119 (1902)
Wins	26—Joe McGinnity, 1901	39—Joe McGinnity, 1901	
Percentage	.565—Joe McGinnity, (26-20), 1901	.565—Joe McGinnity	
Winning streak	unknown		
20-win seasons		1—Joe McGinnity	
Losses	21—Harry Howell, 1901	36—Harry Howell	
Losing streak	unknown		
Innings	382—Joe McGinnity, 1901	580.2—Joe McGinnity	1,210.1 (1902)
Hits	412—Joe McGinnity, 1901	631—Joe McGinnity	1,531 (1902)
Runs	219—Joe McGinnity, 1901	324—Harry Howell	848 (1902)
Earned runs	151—Joe McGinnity, 1901	227—Joe McGinnity	582 (1902)
Bases on balls	96—Joe McGinnity, 1901	142—Joe McGinnity	354 (1902)
Strikeouts	93—Harry Howell, 1901	126—Harry Howell	271 (1901)
Strikeouts, game	unknown		
Hit batsmen	21—Joe McGinnity, 1901	29—Joe McGinnity	48 (1901)
Wild pitches	10—Jerry Nops, 1901	10—Jerry Nops	29 (1901)
Home runs	7—Joe McGinnity, 1901	10—Joe McGinnity	30 (1902)
	Charlie Shields, 1902	Harry Howell	
Sacrifice hits	28—Harry Howell, 1901	41—Joe McGinnity	unknown
Earned run average	3.44—Joe McGinnity, 198.2 inn, 1902	3.52—Joe McGinnity	3.73 (1901)
Shutouts	1—held by many players	2—Harry Howell	4 (1901)
			Lost—7 (1902)
1-0 games won	1—Frank Foreman, 1901	1—Frank Foreman	1 (1901)
			Lost—1 (1901, 1902)

TEAM FIELDING

Putouts	3,622 (1902)	**Assists**	1,763 (1902)
	Fewest—3,472 (1901)		Fewest—1,560 (1901)
Chances accepted	5,385 (1902)	**Errors**	401 (1901)
	Fewest—5,032 (1901)		Fewest—357 (1902)
Double plays	109 (1902)	**Passed balls**	26 (1902)
	Fewest—76 (1901)		Fewest—20 (1901)
Errorless games	unknown	**Fielding average**	.947 (1902)
	Consecutive—unknown		Lowest—.935 (1901)

MISCELLANEOUS

Most players, season 39 (1902)
Fewest players, season 23 (1901)
Games won 68 (1901)
  Month 16 (Jul 1901)
  Consecutive 11 (1901)
Winning percentage .511 (1901), 68-65
  Lowest .362 (1902), 50-88
Number of league championships 0
  Most recent ---
Runs, game 21 vs Chicago, Aug 25, 1902
  Opponents' 23 by Cleveland, Sept 2, 1902
Hits, game unknown
Home runs, game unknown
Runs, shutout 13 vs Washington, Jul 7, 1902
  Opponents' 12 by Chicago, Jun 13, 1901
Longest 1-0 win none over 9 inn

Most seasons, non-pitcher 2—many players
Most seasons, pitcher 2—many players
Games lost 88 (1902)
  Month 23 (Sept 1902)
  Consecutive 9 (1902)
Overall record 118-153 (2 seasons)

Number of times worst record in league 1
  Most recent 1902
Runs, inning unknown

Total bases, game unknown
Consecutive games with one or more home runs unknown
Longest shutout none over 9 inn

Longest 1-0 loss 10 inn vs St. Louis, Aug 28, 1902

ATTENDANCE

Highest home attendance	174,606 (1901)	**Largest crowds**	
		Day	unknown
Highest road attendance	unknown	Night	none
		Doubleheader	unknown
		Home opener	unknown

BALTIMORE ORIOLES (1954-   )
YEARLY FINISHES

(Original American League franchise moved from Milwaukee to St. Louis after the 1901 season
and to Baltimore after the 1953 season)

Year	Position	W	L	Pct.	GB	Manager	Attendance
1954	7th	54	100	.351	57.0	Jimmie Dykes	1,060,910
1955	7th	57	97	.370	39.0	Paul Richards	852,039
1956	6th	69	85	.448	28.0	Paul Richards	901,201
1957	5th	76	76	.500	21.0	Paul Richards	1,029,581
1958	6th	74	79	.484	17.5	Paul Richards	829,991
1959	6th	74	80	.481	20.0	Paul Richards	891,926
1960	2nd	89	65	.578	8.0	Paul Richards	1,187,849
1961	3rd	95	67	.586	14.0	Paul Richards, Luman Harris	951,089
1962	7th	77	85	.475	19.0	Billy Hitchcock	790,254
1963	4th	86	76	.531	18.5	Billy Hitchcock	774,343
1964	3rd	97	65	.599	2.0	Hank Bauer	1,116,215
1965	3rd	94	68	.580	8.0	Hank Bauer	781,649
1966	1st (S)	97	63	.606	+9.0	Hank Bauer	1,203,366
1967	6th (tied)	76	85	.472	15.5	Hank Bauer	955,053
1968	2nd	91	71	.562	12.0	Hank Bauer, Earl Weaver	943,977

EAST DIVISION

Year	Position	W	L	Pct.	GB	Manager	Attendance
1969	1st (C,s)	109	53	.673	+19.0	Earl Weaver	1,058,168
1970	1st (C,S)	108	54	.667	+15.0	Earl Weaver	1,057,069
1971	1st (C,s)	101	57	.639	+12.0	Earl Weaver	1,023,037
1972	3rd	80	74	.519	5.0	Earl Weaver	899,950
1973	1st (c)	97	65	.599	+8.0	Earl Weaver	958,667
1974	1st (c)	91	71	.562	+2.0	Earl Weaver	962,572
1975	2nd	90	69	.566	4.5	Earl Weaver	1,002,157
1976	2nd	88	74	.543	10.5	Earl Weaver	1,058,609
1977	2nd (tied)	97	64	.602	2.5	Earl Weaver	1,195,769
1978	4th	90	71	.559	9.0	Earl Weaver	1,051,724
1979	1st (C,s)	102	57	.642	+8.0	Earl Weaver	1,681,009

Year	Position	W	L	Pct.	GB	Manager	Attendance
1980	2nd	100	62	.617	3.0	Earl Weaver	1,797,438
1981	2nd/4th	59	46	.562	*	Earl Weaver	1,024,652
1982	2nd	94	68	.580	1.0	Earl Weaver	1,613,031
1983	1st (C,S)	98	64	.605	+6.0	Joe Altobelli	2,042,071
1984	5th	85	77	.525	19.0	Joe Altobelli	2,045,784
1985	4th	83	78	.516	16.0	Joe Altobelli, Earl Weaver	2,132,387
1986	7th	73	89	.451	22.5	Earl Weaver	1,973,176
1987	6th	67	95	.414	31.0	Cal Ripken Sr.	1,835,692
1988	7th	54	107	.335	34.5	Cal Ripken Sr., Frank Robinson	1,660,738
1989	2nd	87	75	.537	2.0	Frank Robinson	2,535,208
1990	5th	76	85	.472	11.5	Frank Robinson	2,415,189
1991	6th	67	95	.414	24.0	Frank Robinson, Johnny Oates	2,552,753
1992	3rd	89	73	.549	7.0	Johnny Oates	3,567,819
1993	3rd (tied)	85	77	.525	10.0	Johnny Oates	3,644,965
1994	2nd	63	49	.563	6.5	Johnny Oates	2,535,359
1995	3rd	71	73	.493	15.0	Phil Regan	3,098,475
1996	2nd (D,c)	88	74	.543	4.0	Dave Johnson	3,646,950
1997	1st (D,c)	98	64	.605	+2.0	Dave Johnson	3,711,132
1998	4th	79	83	.488	35.0	Ray Miller	3,685,194
1999	4th	78	84	.481	20.0	Ray Miller	3,433,150
2000	4th	74	88	.457	13.5	Mike Hargrove	3,295,128
2001	4th	63	98	.391	32.5	Mike Hargrove	3,094,841
2002	4th	67	95	.414	36.5	Mike Hargrove	2,682,917
2003	4th	71	91	.438	30.0	Mike Hargrove	2,454,523
2004	3rd	78	84	.481	23.0	Lee Mazzilli	2,744,013

(S) won World Series; (C) won League Championship Series; (s) lost World Series; *first half 31-23, second 28-23; (D) won Division Series; (c) lost League Championship Series

INDIVIDUAL AND CLUB RECORDS

BATTING

	Individual		Club
	Season	Career	Season
Games	163—Brooks Robinson, 1961, 1964 Cal Ripken Jr., 1996	3,001—Cal Ripken Jr.	163 (1961, 1964, 1982, 1996, 2003)
At-bats	673—B.J. Surhoff, 162 g, 1999	11,551—Cal Ripken Jr.	5,736 (2004)
Runs	132—Roberto Alomar, 153 g, 1996	1,647—Cal Ripken Jr.	949 (1996) Fewest—483 (1954)
Hits	211—Cal Ripken Jr., 162 g, 1983	3,184—Cal Ripken Jr.	1,614 (2004) Fewest—1,187 (1968)
Hitting streak	30 g—Eric Davis, 1998		
Singles	158—Al Bumbry, 160 g, 1980	2,106—Cal Ripken Jr.	1,108 (2004)
Doubles	50—Brian Roberts, 159 g, 2004	603—Cal Ripken Jr.	319 (2004)
Triples	12—Paul Blair, 151 g, 1967	68—Brooks Robinson	49 (1954)

HOME RUNS

257 (1996)
Fewest—52 (1954)

Righthander	49—Frank Robinson, 155 g, 1966	431—Cal Ripken Jr.	
Lefthander	50—Brady Anderson, 149 g, 1996	303—Boog Powell	
Switch-hitter	35—Ken Singleton, 159 g, 1979	343—Eddie Murray	
Rookie	28—Cal Ripken Jr., 160 g, 1982		
Home	27—Frank Robinson, 1966	214—Cal Ripken Jr.	121(1996)
Road	31—Brady Anderson, 1996	217—Cal Ripken Jr.	136 (1996)
Month	15—Jim Gentile, Aug 1961		58 (May 1987)
Pinch	3—Sam Bowens, 1967 Jim Dwyer, 1986 Whitey Herzog, 1962 Sam Horn, 1991 Pat Kelly, 1979	9—Jim Dwyer	11 (1982)
Grand slams	5—Jim Gentile, 148 g, 1961	16—Eddie Murray	11 (1996)
Home runs at Memorial Stadium, all teams			235 (1987)
Home runs at Oriole Park at Camden Yards, all teams			229 (1996)
Total bases	369—Brady Anderson, 149 g, 1996	5,168—Cal Ripken Jr.	2,685 (1996)
Extra base hits	92—Brady Anderson, 149 g, 1996	1,078—Cal Ripken Jr.	585 (1996)
Sacrifice hits	23—Mark Belanger, 152 g, 1975	153—Mark Belanger	110 (1957)
Sacrifice flies	17—Bobby Bonilla, 159 g, 1996	127—Cal Ripken Jr.	67 (1996)
Bases on balls	118—Ken Singleton, 155 g, 1975	1,129—Cal Ripken Jr.	717 (1970) Fewest—431 (2003)

	Individual		Club
	Season	Career	Season
Strikeouts	160—Mickey Tettleton, 135 g, 1990	1,305—Cal Ripken Jr.	1,019 (1964, 1968)
	Fewest—19—Rick Dauer, 152 g, 1980		Fewest—634 (1954)
Hit by pitch	24—Brady Anderson, 150 g, 1999	148—Brady Anderson	77 (2001)
			Fewest—19 (1955, 1985)
Runs batted in	150—Miguel Tejada, 162 g, 2004	1,695—Cal Ripken Jr.	914 (1996)
			Fewest—451 (1954)
Grounded into	32—Cal Ripken Jr., 161 g, 1985	350—Cal Ripken Jr.	159 (1986)
double plays	Fewest—1—Brady Anderson, 151 g, 1997		Fewest—102 (1968)
Left on base			1,262 (1970)
			Fewest—1,037 (2002)
Batting average	.340—Melvin Mora, 140 g, 2004	.294—Eddie Murray	.281 (2004)
			Lowest—.225 (1968)
Most .300 hitters			3 (1980, 2004)
Slugging average	.646—Jim Gentile, 148 g, 1961	.545—Rafael Palmeiro	.472 (1996)
			Lowest—.320 (1955)
On-base percentage	.442—Bob Nieman, 114 g, 1956	.401—Frank Robinson	.353 (1999)

BASERUNNING

	Season	Career	Season
Stolen bases	57—Luis Aparicio, 146 g, 1964	307—Brady Anderson	150 (1976)
Caught stealing	18—Don Buford, 144 g, 1969	98—Brady Anderson	65 (2000)

PITCHING

	Season	Career	Season
Games	76—Tippy Martinez, 1982	558—Jim Palmer	
	B.J. Ryan, 2003, 2004		
Games started	40—Dave McNally, 1969	521—Jim Palmer	
	Mike Cuellar, 1970		
	Dave McNally, 1970		
	Jim Palmer, 1976		
	Mike Flanagan, 1978		
Complete games	25—Jim Palmer, 1975	211—Jim Palmer	71 (1971)
Wins	25—Steve Stone, 1980	268—Jim Palmer	
Percentage	.808—Dave McNally (21-5), 1971	.645—Mike Mussina	
Winning streak	15—Dave McNally, 1969		
Winning streak, two seasons	17—Dave McNally, 1968 (2), 1969 (15)		
20-win seasons		8—Jim Palmer	
Losses	21—Don Larsen, 1954	152—Jim Palmer	
Losing streak	10—Jay Tibbs, 1988		
Saves	45—Randy Myers, 1997	160—Gregg Olson	59 (1997)
Innings	323—Jim Palmer, 1975	3,948—Jim Palmer	1,478.2 (1970)
Hits	284—Scott Erickson, 1996	3,349—Jim Palmer	1,604 (1996)
Runs	137—Scott Erickson, 1996	1,395—Jim Palmer	913 (2000)
	Mike Mussina, 1996		
Earned runs	130—Mike Mussina, 1996	1,253—Jim Palmer	855 (2000)
Bases on balls	181—Bob Turley, 1954	1,311—Jim Palmer	688 (1954)
Strikeouts	218—Mike Mussina, 1997	2,212—Jim Palmer	1,139 (1997)
Strikeouts, game	15—Mike Mussina, Aug 1, 2000		
	Mike Mussina, Sept 24, 2000		
Hit batsmen	15—Chuck Estrada, 1960	68—Dave McNally	80 (2003)
Wild pitches	14—Milt Pappas, 1959	85—Jim Palmer	68 (2004)
Home runs	35—Robin Roberts, 1963	303—Jim Palmer	226 (1987)
	Scott McGregor, 1986		
	Sidney Ponson, 1999		
Sacrifice hits	20—Mike Cuellar, 1975	133—Jim Palmer	100 (1955)
Sacrifice flies	14—Jim Palmer, 1976	84—Jim Palmer	63 (1955, 1976)
	David Wells, 1996		
Earned run average	1.95—Dave McNally, 273 inn, 1968	2.86—Jim Palmer	2.53 (1972)
Shutouts	10—Jim Palmer, 1975	53—Jim Palmer	21 (1961)
			Lost—22 (1955)
1-0 games won	3—Mike Cuellar, 1974	9—Jim Palmer	8 (1974)
	Ross Grimsley, 1974		Lost—5 (1973)
	Jim Palmer, 1975, 1978		

TEAM FIELDING

Putouts	4,436 (1970)	**Assists**	1,974 (1975)
	Fewest—4,082 (1956)		Fewest—1,516 (1958)
Chances accepted	6,344 (1974)	**Errors**	167 (1955)
	Fewest—5,625 (1958)		Fewest—81 (1998)
Double plays	191 (1999)	**Passed balls**	49 (1959)
	Fewest—131 (1968)		Fewest—4 (1985)
Errorless games	104 (1998)	**Fielding average**	.987 (1998)
	Consecutive—13 (1991)		Lowest—.972 (1955)

MISCELLANEOUS

Most players, season 54 (1955)
Fewest players, season 30 (1969)
Games won 109 (1969)
  Month 25 (Jun 1966)
  Consecutive 14 (1973)
Winning percentage .673 (1969), 109-53
  Lowest .335 (1988), 54-107
Number of league championships 6
  Most recent 1983
Runs, game 23 vs Toronto, Sept 28, 2000
  Opponents' 26 by Texas, Apr 19, 1996
Hits, game 26 vs California, Aug 28, 1980
Home runs, game 7 vs Boston, May 17, 1967
  vs California, Aug 26, 1985
Runs, shutout 17 vs Chicago, Jul 27, 1969
  Opponents' 16 by New York, Apr 30, 1960
Longest 1-0 win 17 inn, vs Milwaukee, Sept 27, 1974

Most seasons, non-pitcher 23—Brooks Robinson
Most seasons, pitcher 19—Jim Palmer
Games lost 107 (1988)
  Month 25 (Aug 1954)
  Consecutive 21 (1988)
Overall record 4,206-3,845 (51 seasons)
  Interleague play 56-83
Number of times worst record in league 1
  Most recent 1988
Runs, inning 12 vs Tampa Bay, April 11, 2002, 6th
  vs Chicago, May 12, 1997, 7th
Total bases, game 44 vs Atlanta N.L., Jun 13, 1999
Consecutive games with one or more home runs 20 (38 hrs), 1998

Longest shutout unknown

Longest 1-0 loss 15 inn, vs Cleveland, May 14, 1961, 1st game

ATTENDANCE

Highest home attendance
  Memorial Stadium 3,711,132 (1997)
  Oriole Park at Camden Yards 3,711,132 (1997)

Highest road attendance 2,333,664 (2001)

Largest crowds
  Day 52,395 vs Milwaukee, Apr 4, 1988
  Night 52,159 vs Boston, Jun 27, 1986
  Doubleheader 51,883 vs Milwaukee, Oct 1, 1982
Home opener 52,395 vs Milwaukee, Apr 4, 1988

BOSTON RED SOX
YEARLY FINISHES

(Original American League franchise)

Year	Position	W	L	Pct.	GB	Manager	Attendance
1901	2nd	79	57	.581	4.0	Jimmy Collins	289,448
1902	3rd	77	60	.562	6.5	Jimmy Collins	348,567
1903	1st (S)	91	47	.659	+14.5	Jimmy Collins	379,338
1904	1st (n)	95	59	.617	+1.5	Jimmy Collins	623,295
1905	4th	78	74	.513	16.0	Jimmy Collins	468,828
1906	8th	49	105	.318	45.5	Jimmy Collins, Chick Stahl	410,209
1907	7th	59	90	.396	32.5	George Huff, Bob Unglaub, Deacon McGuire	436,777
1908	5th	75	79	.487	15.5	Deacon McGuire, Fred Lake	473,048
1909	3rd	88	63	.583	9.5	Fred Lake	668,965
1910	4th	81	72	.529	22.5	Patsy Donovan	584,619
1911	5th	78	75	.510	24.0	Patsy Donovan	503,961
1912	1st (S)	105	47	.691	+14.0	Jake Stahl	597,096
1913	4th	79	71	.527	15.5	Jake Stahl, Bill Carrigan	437,194
1914	2nd	91	62	.595	8.5	Bill Carrigan	481,359
1915	1st (S)	101	50	.669	+2.5	Bill Carrigan	539,885
1916	1st (S)	91	63	.591	+2.0	Bill Carrigan	496,397
1917	2nd	90	62	.592	9.0	Jack Barry	387,856
1918	1st (S)	75	51	.595	+2.5	Ed Barrow	249,513
1919	6th	66	71	.482	20.5	Ed Barrow	417,291
1920	5th	72	81	.471	25.5	Ed Barrow	402,445
1921	5th	75	79	.487	23.5	Hugh Duffy	279,273
1922	8th	61	93	.396	33.0	Hugh Duffy	259,184
1923	8th	61	91	.401	37.0	Frank Chance	229,668
1924	7th	67	87	.435	25.0	Lee Fohl	448,556
1925	8th	47	105	.309	49.5	Lee Fohl	267,782
1926	8th	46	107	.301	44.5	Lee Fohl	285,155
1927	8th	51	103	.331	59.0	Bill Carrigan	305,275
1928	8th	57	96	.373	43.5	Bill Carrigan	396,920

Year	Position	W	L	Pct.	GB	Manager	Attendance
1929	8th	58	96	.377	48.0	Bill Carrigan	394,620
1930	8th	52	102	.338	50.0	Heinie Wagner	444,045
1931	6th	62	90	.408	45.0	Shano Collins	350,975
1932	8th	43	111	.279	64.0	Shano Collins, Marty McManus	182,150
1933	7th	63	86	.423	34.5	Marty McManus	268,715
1934	4th	76	76	.500	24.0	Bucky Harris	610,640
1935	4th	78	75	.510	16.0	Joseph Cronin	558,568
1936	6th	74	80	.481	28.5	Joe Cronin	626,895
1937	5th	80	72	.526	21.0	Joe Cronin	559,659
1938	2nd	88	61	.591	9.5	Joe Cronin	646,459
1939	2nd	89	62	.589	17.0	Joe Cronin	573,070
1940	4th (tied)	82	72	.532	8.0	Joe Cronin	716,234
1941	2nd	84	70	.545	17.0	Joe Cronin	718,497
1942	2nd	93	59	.612	9.0	Joe Cronin	730,340
1943	7th	68	84	.447	29.0	Joe Cronin	358,275
1944	4th	77	77	.500	12.0	Joe Cronin	506,975
1945	7th	71	83	.461	17.5	Joe Cronin	603,794
1946	1st (s)	104	50	.675	+12.0	Joe Cronin	1,416,944
1947	3rd	83	71	.539	14.0	Joe Cronin	1,427,315
1948	2nd (l)	96	59	.619	1.0	Joe McCarthy	1,558,798
1949	2nd	96	58	.623	1.0	Joe McCarthy	1,596,650
1950	3rd	94	60	.610	4.0	Joe McCarthy, Steve O'Neill	1,344,080
1951	3rd	87	67	.565	11.0	Steve O'Neill	1,312,282
1952	6th	76	78	.494	19.0	Lou Boudreau	1,115,750
1953	4th	84	69	.549	16.0	Lou Boudreau	1,026,133
1954	4th	69	85	.448	42.0	Lou Boudreau	931,127
1955	4th	84	70	.545	12.0	Pinky Higgins	1,203,200
1956	4th	84	70	.545	13.0	Pinky Higgins	1,137,158
1957	3rd	82	72	.532	16.0	Pinky Higgins	1,181,087
1958	3rd	79	75	.513	13.0	Pinky Higgins	1,077,047
1959	5th	75	79	.487	19.0	Pinky Higgins, Billy Jurges	984,102
1960	7th	65	89	.422	32.0	Billy Jurges, Pinky Higgins	1,129,866
1961	6th	76	86	.469	33.0	Pinky Higgins	850,509
1962	8th	76	84	.475	19.0	Pinky Higgins	733,080
1963	7th	76	85	.472	28.0	Johnny Pesky	942,642
1964	8th	72	90	.444	27.0	Johnny Pesky, Billy Herman	883,276
1965	9th	62	100	.383	40.0	Billy Herman	652,201
1966	9th	72	90	.444	26.0	Billy Herman, Pete Runnels	811,172
1967	1st	92	70	.568	+1.0	Dick Williams	1,727,832
1968	4th	86	76	.531	17.0	Dick Williams	1,940,788

EAST DIVISION

Year	Position	W	L	Pct.	GB	Manager	Attendance
1969	3rd	87	75	.537	22.0	Dick Williams, Eddie Popowski	1,833,246
1970	3rd	87	75	.537	21.0	Eddie Kasko	1,595,278
1971	3rd	85	77	.525	18.0	Eddie Kasko	1,678,732
1972	2nd	85	70	.548	0.5	Eddie Kasko	1,441,718
1973	2nd	89	73	.549	8.0	Eddie Kasko	1,401,002
1974	3rd	84	78	.519	7.0	Darrell Johnson	1,556,411
1975	1st (C,s)	95	65	.594	+4.5	Darrell Johnson	1,748,587
1976	3rd	83	79	.512	15.5	Darrell Johnson, Don Zimmer	1,895,846
1977	2nd (tied)	97	64	.602	2.5	Don Zimmer	2,074,549
1978	2nd (p)	99	64	.607	1.0	Don Zimmer	2,320,643
1979	3rd	91	69	.569	11.5	Don Zimmer	2,353,114
1980	4th	83	77	.519	19.0	Don Zimmer, Johnny Pesky	1,956,092
1981	5th/2nd (tied)	59	49	.546	*	Ralph Houk	1,060,379
1982	3rd	89	73	.549	6.0	Ralph Houk	1,950,124
1983	6th	78	84	.481	20.0	Ralph Houk	1,782,285
1984	4th	86	76	.531	18.0	Ralph Houk	1,661,618
1985	5th	81	81	.500	18.5	John McNamara	1,786,633
1986	1st (C,s)	95	66	.590	+5.5	John McNamara	2,147,641
1987	5th	78	84	.481	20.0	John McNamara	2,231,551
1988	1st (c)	89	73	.549	+1.0	John McNamara, Joe Morgan	2,464,851
1989	3rd	83	79	.512	6.0	Joe Morgan	2,510,012
1990	1st (c)	88	74	.543	+2.0	Joe Morgan	2,528,986
1991	2nd (tied)	84	78	.519	7.0	Joe Morgan	2,562,435
1992	7th	73	89	.451	23.0	Butch Hobson	2,468,574
1993	5th	80	82	.494	15.0	Butch Hobson	2,422,021
1994	4th	54	61	.470	17.0	Butch Hobson	1,775,818
1995	1st (d)	86	58	.597	+7.0	Kevin Kennedy	2,164,410
1996	3rd	85	77	.525	7.0	Kevin Kennedy	2,315,231
1997	4th	78	84	.481	20.0	Jimy Williams	2,226,136
1998	2nd (d)	92	70	.568	22.0	Jimy Williams	2,343,947
1999	2nd (D,c)	94	68	.580	4.0	Jimy Williams	2,446,162
2000	2nd	85	77	.525	2.5	Jimy Williams	2,586,032
2001	2nd	82	79	.509	13.5	Jimy Williams, Joe Kerrigan	2,625,333
2002	2nd	93	69	.574	10.5	Grady Little	2,650,063
2003	2nd (D,c)	95	67	.586	6.0	Grady Little	2,724,165
2004	2nd (D,C,S)	98	64	.605	3.0	Terry Francona	2,837,304

(S) won World Series; (n) no World Series; (s) lost World Series; (l) lost league playoff; (C) won League Championship Series; (p) lost division playoff; *first half 30-26, second half 29-23; (c) lost League Championship Series; (d) lost Division Series; (D) won Division Series

INDIVIDUAL AND CLUB RECORDS
BATTING

	Individual		Club
	Season	**Career**	**Season**
Games	163—Jim Rice, 1978	3,308—Carl Yastrzemski	163 (1961, 1978, 1985)
At-bats	684—Nomar Garciaparra, 153 g, 1997	11,988—Carl Yastrzemski	5,781 (1997)
Runs	150—Ted Williams, 155 g, 1949	1,816—Carl Yastrzemski	1,027 (1950)
			Fewest—463 (1906)
Hits	240—Wade Boggs, 161 g, 1985	3,419—Carl Yastrzemski	1,684 (1997)
			Fewest—1,175 (1905)
Hitting streak	34 g—Dom DiMaggio, 1949		
Singles	187—Wade Boggs, 161 g, 1985	2,262—Carl Yastrzemski	1,156 (1950)
Doubles	67—Earl Webb, 151 g, 1931	646—Carl Yastrzemski	373 (1997, 2004)
Triples	22—Chick Stahl, 157 g, 1904	130—Harry Hooper	112 (1903)
	Tris Speaker, 141 g, 1913		

HOME RUNS

			124 (1941)
			Fewest—13 (1906)
Righthander	50—Jimmie Foxx, 149 g, 1938	382—Jim Rice	
Lefthander	44—Carl Yastrzemski, 161 g, 1967	521—Ted Williams	
	Mo Vaughn, 161 g, 1996		
Switch-hitter	34—Carl Everett, 137 g, 2000	149—Reggie Smith	
Rookie	34—Walt Dropo, 136 g, 1950		
Home	35—Jimmie Foxx, 1938	248—Ted Williams	124 (1977)
Road	26—Ted Williams, 1957	273—Ted Williams	127 (2003)
Month	14—Jackie Jensen, Jun 1958		55 (Jul 2003)
Pinch	5—Joe Cronin, 1943	7—Ted Williams	6 (1953)
Grand slams	4—Babe Ruth, 130 g, 1919	17—Ted Williams	9 (1941, 1950, 1987, 2001)
Home runs at Huntington Avenue Grounds, all teams			53 (1910)
Home runs at Fenway Park, all teams			219 (1977)
Total bases	406—Jim Rice, 163 g, 1978	5,539—Carl Yastrzemski	2,832 (2003)
Extra base hits	92—Jimmie Foxx, 149 g, 1938	1,157—Carl Yastrzemski	649 (2003)
Sacrifice hits	35—Freddy Parent, 153 g, 1905	218—Duffy Lewis	142 (1906)
Sacrifice flies	12—Jackie Jensen, 152 g, 1955	105—Carl Yastrzemski	64 (2003)
	Jimmy Piersall, 155 g, 1956		
	Jackie Jensen, 148 g, 1959		
Bases on balls	162—Ted Williams, 156 g, 1947	2,021—Ted Williams	835 (1949)
	Ted Williams, 155, 1949		Fewest—262 (1903)
Strikeouts	177—Mark Bellhorn, 138 g, 2004	1,643—Dwight Evans	1,189 (2004)
	Fewest—9—Stuffy McInnis, 152 g, 1921		Fewest—329 (1921)
Hit by pitch	35—Don Baylor, 160 g, 1986	71—Mo Vaughn	72 (2002)
			Fewest—11 (1934)
Runs batted in	175—Jimmie Foxx, 149 g, 1938	1,844—Carl Yastrzemski	974 (1950)
			Fewest—405 (1907)
Grounded into	36—Jim Rice, 159 g, 1984	323—Carl Yastrzemski	174 (1990)
double plays	Fewest—3—Tony Lupien, 154 g, 1943		Fewest—94 (1942)
Left on base			1,308 (1989)
			Fewest—1,015 (1929)
Batting average	.406—Ted Williams, 143 g, 1941	.344—Ted Williams	.302 (1950)
			Lowest—.234 (1905, 1907)
Most .300 hitters			9 (1950)
Slugging average	.735—Ted Williams, 143 g, 1941	.634—Ted Williams	.491 (2003)
			Lowest—.318 (1916, 1917)
On-base percentage	.551—Ted Williams, 143 g, 1941	.482—Ted Williams	.385 (1950)
			Lowest—.281 (1907)

BASERUNNING

Stolen bases	54—Tommy Harper, 147 g, 1973	300—Harry Hooper	215 (1909)
Caught stealing	19—Mike Menosky, 141 g, 1920	116—Carl Yastrzemski	111 (1920)

PITCHING

	Individual		Club
	Season	**Career**	**Season**
Games	80—Greg A. Harris, 1993	637—Bob Stanley	
Games started	43—Cy Young, 1902	382—Roger Clemens	
Complete games	41—Cy Young, 1902	275—Cy Young	148 (1904)
Wins	34—Joe Wood, 1912	192—Cy Young	
		Roger Clemens	
Percentage	.882—Bob Stanley (15-2), 1978	.765—Pedro Martinez	
Winning streak	16—Joe Wood, 1912		
20-win seasons		6—Cy Young	
Losses	25—Red Ruffing, 1928	112—Cy Young	
Losing streak	14—Joe W. Harris, 1906		
Saves	46—Tom Gordon, 1998	132—Bob Stanley	53 (1998)
Innings	386—Cy Young, 1902	2,776—Roger Clemens	1,472.2 (1978)
Hits	343—Bill Dinneen, 1902	2,359—Roger Clemens	1,615 (1925)
Runs	162—Red Ruffing, 1929	1,045—Roger Clemens	922 (1925)
	Jack Russell, 1930		
Earned runs	140—Wes Ferrell, 1936	943—Roger Clemens	807 (1996)
Bases on balls	134—Mel Parnell, 1949	856—Roger Clemens	748 (1950)
Strikeouts	313—Pedro Martinez, 1999	2,590—Roger Clemens	1,259 (2001)
Strikeouts, game	20—Roger Clemens, Apr 29, 1986		
	Roger Clemens, Sept 18, 1996		
Hit batsmen	20—Howard Ehmke, 1923	15—Tim Wakefield	93 (2001)
	Bronson Arroyo, 2004		
Wild pitches	21—Earl Wilson, 1963	72—Roger Clemens	73 (1968)
Home runs	38—Tim Wakefield, 1996	244—Tim Wakefield	190 (1987)
Sacrifice hits	24—Tex Hughson, 1943	208—Cy Young	2288 (1926)
	Gordon Rhodes, 1934		
Sacrifice Flies	14—Dave Morehead, 1964	68—Tim Wakefield	67 (1996)
Earned run average	1.00—Dutch Leonard, 225 inn, 1914	2.00—Cy Young	2.12 (1904)
Shutouts	10—Cy Young, 1904	38—Cy Young	26 (1918)
	Joe Wood, 1912	Roger Clemens	Lost 20 (1900)
1 0 games won	5—Joe Bush, 1918	7—Tex Hughson	8 (1918)
			Lost—7 (1909, 1914)

TEAM FIELDING

Putouts	4,418 (1978)	**Assists**	2,195 (1907)
	Fewest—3,940 (1938)		Fewest—1,542 (1988)
Chances accepted	6,425 (1907)	**Errors**	337 (1901)
	Fewest—5,667 (1938)		Fewest—93 (1988)
Double plays	207 (1949)	**Passed balls**	36 (1997)
	Fewest—74 (1913)		Fewest—3 (1933, 1975)
Errorless games	92 (1988, 1998)	**Fielding average**	.984 (1988)
	Consecutive—10 (1986)		Lowest—.943 (1901)

MISCELLANEOUS

Most players, season 55 (1996)
Fewest players, season 18 (1904)

Games won 105 (1912)
  Month 25 (Jul 1048)
  Consecutive 15 (1946)
Winning percentage .691 (1912), 105-47
  Lowest .279 (1932), 43-111
Number of league championships 11
  Most recent 2004
Runs, game 29 vs St. Louis, Jun 8, 1950
  Opponents' 27 by Cleveland, Jul 7, 1923, 1st game
Hits, game 28 vs St. Louis, Jun 8, 1950
  vs Florida, Jun 27, 2003
Home runs, game 8 vs Toronto, Jul 4, 1977
Runs, shutout 19 vs Philadelphia, Apr 30, 1950, 1st game
  Opponents' 19 by Cleveland, Aug 21, 1920
Longest 1-0 win 15 inn, vs Detroit, May 11, 1904

Most seasons, non-pitcher 23—Carl Yastrzemski
Most seasons, pitcher 13—Bob Stanley
      Roger Clemens
Games lost 111 (1932)
  Month 24 (Jul 1925, Jun 1927, Jul 1928)
  Consecutive 20 (1906)
Overall record 8,263-7,817 (104 seasons)
  Interleague play 65-74
Number of times worst record in league 10
  Most recent 1932
Runs, inning 17 vs Detroit, Jun 18, 1953, 7th

Total bases, game 60 vs St. Louis, Jun 8, 1950

Consecutive games with one or more home runs 19 (30 hrs), 1996
Longest shutout 1-0, vs Detroit, May 11, 1904

Longest 1-0 loss 15 inn, vs Washington, Jul 3, 1915

Highest home attendance		Largest crowds	
Huntington Avenue Grounds	668,965 (1909)	Day	36,388 vs Cleveland, Apr 22, 1978
Fenway Park	2,837,304 (2004)	Night	36,228 vs New York, Jun 28, 1949
		Doubleheader	47,627 vs New York, Sept 22, 1935
Highest road attendance	2,695,389 (2001)	Home opener	35,343 vs Baltimore, Apr 14, 1969

CHICAGO WHITE SOX
YEARLY FINISHES

(Original American League franchise)

Year	Position	W	L	Pct.	GB	Manager	Attendance
1901	1st	83	53	.610	+4.0	Clark Griffith	354,350
1902	4th	74	60	.552	8.0	Clark Griffith	337,898
1903	7th	60	77	.438	30.5	Nixey Callahan	286,183
1904	3rd	89	65	.578	6.0	Nixey Callahan, Fielder Jones	557,123
1905	2nd	92	60	.605	2.0	Fielder Jones	687,419
1906	1st (S)	93	58	.616	+3.0	Fielder Jones	585,202
1907	3rd	87	64	.576	5.5	Fielder Jones	666,307
1908	3rd	88	64	.579	1.5	Fielder Jones	636,096
1909	4th	78	74	.513	20.0	Billy Sullivan	478,400
1910	6th	68	85	.444	35.5	Hugh Duffy	552,084
1911	4th	77	74	.510	24.0	Hugh Duffy	583,208
1912	4th	78	76	.506	28.0	Nixey Callahan	602,241
1913	5th	78	74	.513	17.5	Nixey Callahan	644,501
1914	6th (tied)	70	84	.455	30.0	Nixey Callahan	469,290
1915	3rd	93	61	.604	9.5	Pants Rowland	539,461
1916	2nd	89	65	.578	2.0	Pants Rowland	679,923
1917	1st (S)	100	54	.649	+9.0	Pants Rowland	684,521
1918	6th	57	67	.460	17.0	Pants Rowland	195,081
1919	1st (s)	88	52	.629	+3.5	Kid Gleason	627,186
1920	2nd	96	58	.623	2.0	Kid Gleason	833,492
1921	7th	62	92	.403	36.5	Kid Gleason	543,650
1922	5th	77	77	.500	17.0	Kid Gleason	602,860
1923	7th	69	85	.448	30.0	Kid Gleason	573,778
1924	8th	66	87	.431	25.5	Johnny Evers	606,658
1925	5th	79	75	.513	18.5	Eddie Collins	832,231
1926	5th	81	72	.529	9.5	Eddie Collins	710,339
1927	5th	70	83	.458	29.5	Ray Schalk	614,423
1928	5th	72	82	.468	29.0	Ray Schalk, Lena Blackburne	494,152
1929	7th	59	93	.388	46.0	Lena Blackburne	426,795
1930	7th	62	92	.403	40.0	Donie Bush	406,123
1931	8th	56	97	.366	51.0	Donie Bush	403,550
1932	7th	49	102	.325	56.5	Lew Fonseca	233,198
1933	6th	67	83	.447	31.0	Lew Fonseca	397,789
1934	8th	53	99	.349	47.0	Lew Fonseca, Jimmie Dykes	236,559
1935	5th	74	78	.487	19.5	Jimmie Dykes	470,281
1936	3rd	81	70	.536	20.0	Jimmie Dykes	440,810
1937	3rd	86	68	.558	16.0	Jimmie Dykes	589,245
1938	6th	65	83	.439	32.0	Jimmie Dykes	338,278
1939	4th	85	69	.552	22.5	Jimmie Dykes	594,104
1940	4th (tied)	82	72	.532	8.0	Jimmie Dykes	660,336
1941	3rd	77	77	.500	24.0	Jimmie Dykes	677,077
1942	6th	66	82	.446	34.0	Jimmie Dykes	425,734
1943	4th	82	72	.532	16.0	Jimmie Dykes	508,962
1944	7th	71	83	.461	18.0	Jimmie Dykes	563,539
1945	6th	71	78	.477	15.0	Jimmie Dykes	657,981
1946	5th	74	80	.481	30.0	Jimmie Dykes, Ted Lyons	983,403
1947	6th	70	84	.455	27.0	Ted Lyons	876,948
1948	8th	51	101	.336	44.5	Ted Lyons	777,844
1949	6th	63	91	.409	34.0	Jack Onslow	937,151
1950	6th	60	94	.390	38.0	Jack Onslow, Red Corriden	781,330
1951	4th	81	73	.526	17.0	Paul Richards	1,328,234
1952	3rd	81	73	.526	14.0	Paul Richards	1,231,675
1953	3rd	89	65	.578	11.5	Paul Richards	1,191,353
1954	3rd	94	60	.610	17.0	Paul Richards, Marty Marion	1,231,629
1955	3rd	91	63	.591	5.0	Marty Marion	1,175,684
1956	3rd	85	69	.552	12.0	Marty Marion	1,000,090
1957	2nd	90	64	.584	8.0	Al Lopez	1,135,668
1958	2nd	82	72	.532	10.0	Al Lopez	797,451
1959	1st (s)	94	60	.610	+5.0	Al Lopez	1,423,144
1960	3rd	87	67	.565	10.0	Al Lopez	1,644,460
1961	4th	86	76	.531	23.0	Al Lopez	1,146,019
1962	5th	85	77	.525	11.0	Al Lopez	1,131,562
1963	2nd	94	68	.580	10.5	Al Lopez	1,158,848
1964	2nd	98	64	.605	1.0	Al Lopez	1,250,053

Year	Position	W	L	Pct.	GB	Manager	Attendance
1965	2nd	95	67	.586	7.0	Al Lopez	1,130,519
1966	4th	83	79	.512	15.0	Eddie Stanky	990,016
1967	4th	89	73	.549	3.0	Eddie Stanky	985,634
1968	8th (tied)	67	95	.414	36.0	Eddie Stanky, Al Lopez	803,775

WEST DIVISION

Year	Position	W	L	Pct.	GB	Manager	Attendance
1969	5th	68	94	.420	29.0	Al Lopez, Don Gutteridge	589,546
1970	6th	56	106	.346	42.0	Don Gutteridge, Chuck Tanner	495,355
1971	3rd	79	83	.488	22.5	Chuck Tanner	833,891
1972	2nd	87	67	.565	5.5	Chuck Tanner	1,177,318
1973	5th	77	85	.475	17.0	Chuck Tanner	1,302,527
1974	4th	80	80	.500	9.0	Chuck Tanner	1,149,596
1975	5th	75	86	.466	22.5	Chuck Tanner	750,802
1976	6th	64	97	.398	25.5	Paul Richards	914,945
1977	3rd	90	72	.556	12.0	Bob Lemon	1,657,135
1978	5th	71	90	.441	20.5	Bob Lemon, Larry Doby	1,491,100
1979	5th	73	87	.456	14.0	Don Kessinger, Tony La Russa	1,280,702
1980	5th	70	90	.438	26.0	Tony La Russa	1,200,365
1981	3rd/6th	54	52	.509	*	Tony La Russa	946,651
1982	3rd	87	75	.537	6.0	Tony La Russa	1,567,787
1983	1st (c)	99	63	.611	+20.0	Tony La Russa	2,132,821
1984	5th (tied)	74	88	.457	10.0	Tony La Russa	2,136,988
1985	3rd	85	77	.525	6.0	Tony La Russa	1,669,888
1986	5th	72	90	.444	20.0	Tony La Russa, Jim Fregosi	1,424,313
1987	5th	77	85	.475	8.0	Jim Fregosi	1,208,060
1988	5th	71	90	.441	32.5	Jim Fregosi	1,115,749
1989	7th	69	92	.429	29.5	Jeff Torborg	1,045,651
1990	2nd	94	68	.580	9.0	Jeff Torborg	2,002,357
1991	2nd	87	75	.537	8.0	Jeff Torborg	2,934,154
1992	3rd	86	76	.531	10.0	Gene Lamont	2,681,156
1993	1st (c)	94	68	.580	+8.0	Gene Lamont	2,581,091

CENTRAL DIVISION

Year	Position	W	L	Pct.	GB	Manager	Attendance
1994	1st	67	46	.593	+1.0	Gene Lamont	1,697,398
1995	3rd	68	76	.472	32.0	Gene Lamont, Terry Bevington	1,609,773
1996	2nd	85	77	.525	14.5	Terry Bevington	1,676,403
1997	2nd	80	81	.497	6.0	Terry Bevington	1,864,782
1998	2nd	80	82	.494	9.0	Jerry Manuel	1,391,146
1999	2nd	75	86	.466	21.5	Jerry Manuel	1,338,851
2000	1st (d)	95	67	.586	+5.0	Jerry Manuel	1,947,799
2001	3rd	83	79	.512	8.0	Jerry Manuel	1,766,172
2002	2nd	81	81	.500	13.5	Jerry Manuel	1,670,004
2003	2nd	86	76	.531	4.0	Jerry Manuel	1,939,611
2004	2nd	83	79	.512	9.0	Ozzie Guillen	1,930,537

(S) won World Series; (s) lost World Series; *first half 31-22, second half 23-30; (c) lost League Championship Series; (d) lost Division Series

INDIVIDUAL AND CLUB RECORDS

BATTING

	Individual		Club
	Season	**Career**	**Season**
Games	163—Don Buford, 1966 Greg Walker, 1985 Albert Belle, 1998	2,422—Luke Appling	163 (1961, 1966, 1974, 1985, 199
At-bats	649—Nellie Fox, 154 g, 1956	8,856—Luke Appling	5,646 (2000)
Runs	135—Johnny Mostil, 153 g, 1925	1,319—Luke Appling	978 (2000) Fewest—457 (1910)
Hits	224—Eddie Collins, 153 g, 1920	2,749—Luke Appling	1,615 (2000) Fewest—1,061 (1910)
Hitting streak	28 g—Carlos Lee, 2004		
Singles	170—Eddie Collins, 153 g, 1920	2,162—Luke Appling	1,199 (1936)
Doubles	48—Albert Belle, 163 g, 1998	444—Frank Thomas	325 (2000)
Triples	21—Joe Jackson, 153 g, 1916	104—Shano Collins Nellie Fox	102 (1915)

	Individual		Club
	Season	**Career**	**Season**
HOME RUNS			242 (2004)
			Fewest—3 (1908)
Righthander	49—Albert Belle, 163 g, 1998	436—Frank Thomas	
Lefthander	34—Robin Ventura, 158 g, 1996	221—Harold Baines	
Switch-hitter	28—Jose Valentin, 124 g, 2001	106—Ray Durham	
	Jose Valentin, 144 g, 2003	106—Jose Valentin	
Rookie	35—Ron Kittle, 145 g, 1983		
Home	30—Frank Thomas, 2000	254—Frank Thomas	145 (2004)
Road	25—Frank Thomas, 1995	182—Frank Thomas	119 (1996)
Month	16—Albert Belle, July 1998		51 (Aug 2001, Jul 2003)
Pinch	3—Oscar Gamble, 1977	7—Jerry Hairston	9 (1984)
	Ron Northey, 1956		
	John Romano, 1959		
Grand slams	4—Albert Belle, 161 g, 1997	10—Robin Ventura	8 (1996, 2002)
Home runs at South Side Park, all teams			25 (1901)
Home runs at Comiskey Park, all teams			175 (1970)
Home runs at U.S. Cellular Field, all teams			277 (2004)
Total bases	399—Albert Belle, 163 g, 1998	3,887—Frank Thomas	2,654 (2000)
Extra base hits	99—Albert Belle, 163 g, 1998	891—Frank Thomas	574 (2000)
Sacrifice hits	40—George Davis, 151 g, 1905	342—Eddie Collins	207 (1906)
Sacrifice flies	15—Albert Belle, 163 g, 1998	106—Frank Thomas	69 (1992)
	Magglio Ordonez, 153 g, 2000		
Bases on balls	138—Frank Thomas, 158 g, 1991	1,450—Frank Thomas	702 (1949)
			Fewest—325 (1903)
Strikeouts	175—Dave Nicholson, 126 g, 1963	1,134—Frank Thomas	1,030 (2004)
	Fewest—11—Nellie Fox, 155 g, 1958		Fewest—355 (1920)
Hit by pitch	23—Minnie Minoso, 151 g, 1956	145—Minnie Minoso	75 (1956)
			Fewest—10 (1940)
Runs batted in	152—Albert Belle, 163 g, 1998	1,439—Frank Thomas	926 (2000)
			Fewest—351 (1910)
Grounded into	29—George Bell, 155 g, 1992	188—Frank Thomas	156 (1950, 1974)
double plays	Fewest—3—Tony Lupien, 154 g, 1948		Fewest—94 (1966)
	Don Buford, 163 g, 1966		
	Don Buford, 156 g, 1967		
Left on base			1,279 (1936)
			Fewest—1,009 (1985)
Batting average	.388—Luke Appling, 138 g, 1936	.340—Joe Jackson	.295 (1920)
			Lowest—.212 (1910)
Most .300 hitters			8 (1924)
Slugging average	.729—Frank Thomas, 113 g, 1994	.567—Frank Thomas	.470 (2000)
			Lowest—.261 (1910)
On-base percentage	.487—Frank Thomas, 113 g, 1994	.429—Frank Thomas	.373 (1936)
			Lowest—.275 (1910)

BASERUNNING

Stolen bases	77—Rudy Law, 141 g, 1983	368—Eddie Collins	275 (1901)
Caught stealing	29—Eddie Collins, 145 g, 1923	141—Eddie Collins	119 (1923)

PITCHING

Games	88—Wilbur Wood, 1968	669—Red Faber	
Games started	49—Ed Au. Walsh, 1908	484—Ted Lyons	
	Wilbur Wood, 1972		
Complete games	42—Ed Au. Walsh, 1908	356—Ted Lyons	134 (1904)
Wins	40—Ed Au. Walsh, 1908	260—Ted Lyons	
Percentage	.842—Sandy Consuegra (16-3), 1954	.609—Ed Au. Walsh	
Winning streak	13—LaMarr Hoyt, 1983		
20-win seasons		4—Ed Au. Walsh	
		Red Faber	
		Wilbur Wood	

	Individual		Club
	Season	Career	Season
Losses	25—Patrick Flaherty, 1903	230—Ted Lyons	
Losing streak	14—Howard Judson, 1949		
Saves	57—Bobby Thigpen, 1990	201—Bobby Thigpen	68 (1990)
Innings	464—Ed Au. Walsh, 1908	4,161—Ted Lyons	1,490.1 (1967)
Hits	381—Wilbur Wood, 1973	4,489—Ted Lyons	1,635 (1924)
Runs	182—Dick Kerr, 1921	2,056—Ted Lyons	946 (1934)
Earned runs	162—Dick Kerr, 1921	1,696—Ted Lyons	835 (1998)
Bases on balls	147—Vern Kennedy, 1936	1,213—Red Faber	734 (1950)
Strikeouts	269—Ed A. Walsh, 1908	1,796—Billy Pierce	1,056 (2003)
Strikeouts, game	16—Jack Harshman, Jul 25, 1954, 1st game		
Hit batsmen	16—Jim Scott, 1909	103—Red Faber	88 (2001)
Wild pitches	18—Jaime Navarro, 1998	83—Ed Au. Walsh	71 (1997)
Home runs	38—Floyd Bannister, 1987	241—Billy Pierce	224 (2004)
Sacrifice hits	27—Bill Dietrich, 1944	519—Red Faber	232 (23)
Sacrifice flies	16—Charlie Hough, 1991	64—Wilbur Wood	61 (1976, 1988)
Earned run average	1.53—Ed Cicotte, 346 inn, 1917	1.81—Ed Au. Walsh	1.99 (1905)
Shutouts	12—Ed Au. Walsh, 1908	58—Ed Au. Walsh	32 (1906)
			Lost—24 (1910)
1-0 games won	5—Reb Russell, 1913	13—Doc White	9 (1909, 1967)
		Ed Au. Walsh	Lost—9 (1968)

TEAM FIELDING

Putouts	4,471 (1967)	Assists	2,446 (1907)
	Fewest—3,943 (1942)		Fewest—1,439 (1997)
Chances accepted	6,655 (1907)	Errors	358 (1901)
	Fewest—5,670 (1942)		Fewest—93 (2003)
Double plays	190 (2000)	Passed balls	45 (1965)
	Fewest—94 (1915)		Fewest—3 (1922)
Errorless games	93 (2003)	Fielding average	.984 (2002, 2003, 2004)
	Consecutive—9 (1955, 1964, 1995)		Lowest—.938 (1901)

MISCELLANEOUS

Most players, season 50 (1932)
Fewest players, season 19 (1905)
Games won 100 (1917)
  Month 23 (Sept 1905)
  Consecutive 19 (1906)
Winning percentage .649 (1917), 100-54
  Lowest .325 (1932), 49-102
Number of league championships 5
  Most recent 1959
Runs, game 29 vs Kansas City, Apr 23, 1955
  Opponents' 22 by New York, Jul 26, 1931, 2nd game
Hits, game 29 vs Kansas City, Apr 23, 1955
Home runs, game 7 vs Kansas City, Apr 23, 1955
Runs, shutout 17 vs Washington, Sept 19, 1925, 2nd game
                vs Cleveland, Jul 5, 1987
  Opponents' 19 by Anaheim, May 10, 2002
Longest 1-0 win 15 inn, vs Chicago, Apr 13, 1963

Most seasons, non-pitcher 20—Luke Appling
Most seasons, pitcher 21—Ted Lyons
Games lost 106 (1970)
  Month 24 (Jun 1934, Aug 1968)
  Consecutive 13 (1924)
Overall record 8,111-7,957 (104 seasons)
  Interleague play 73-65
Number of times worst record in league 6
  Most recent 1976
Runs, inning 13 vs Washington, Sept 26, 1943, 1st game, 4th

Total bases, game 55 vs Kansas City, Apr 23, 1955
Consecutive games with one or more home runs 17 (28 hrs), 2000
Longest shutout 1-0, vs Cleveland, Sept 13, 1967

Longest 1-0 loss 18 inn, vs Washington, May 15, 1918
                vs Washington, Jun 8, 1947, 1st game

ATTENDANCE

Highest home attendance		Largest crowds	
South Side Park	687,419 (1905)	Day	51,560 vs Milwaukee, Apr 14, 1981
Comiskey Park	2,136,988 (1984)	Night	53,940 vs New York, Jun 8, 1951
U.S. Cellular Field	2,934,154 (1991)	Doubleheader	55,555 vs Minnesota, May 20, 1973
		Home opener	51,560 vs Milwaukee, Apr 14, 1981
Highest road attendance	2,571,969 (1993)		

(Original American League franchise)

REGULAR SEASON A.L.—*Cleveland Indians*

Year	Position	W	L	Pct.	GB	Manager	Attendance
1901	7th	54	82	.397	29.0	James McAleer	131,380
1902	5th	69	67	.507	14.0	Bill Armour	275,395
1903	3rd	77	63	.550	15.0	Bill Armour	311,280
1904	4th	86	65	.570	7.5	Bill Armour	264,749
1905	5th	76	78	.494	19.0	Nap Lajoie	316,306
1906	3rd	89	64	.582	5.0	Nap Lajoie	325,733
1907	4th	85	67	.559	8.0	Nap Lajoie	382,046
1908	2nd	90	64	.584	0.5	Nap Lajoie	422,242
1909	6th	71	82	.464	27.5	Nap Lajoie, Deacon McGuire	354,627
1910	5th	71	81	.467	32.0	Deacon McGuire	293,456
1911	3rd	80	73	.523	22.0	Deacon McGuire, George Stovall	406,296
1912	5th	75	78	.490	30.5	Harry Davis, J.L. Birmingham	336,844
1913	3rd	86	66	.566	9.5	J.L. Birmingham	541,000
1914	8th	51	102	.333	48.5	J.L. Birmingham	185,997
1915	7th	57	95	.375	44.5	J.L. Birmingham, Lee Fohl	159,285
1916	6th	77	77	.500	14.0	Lee Fohl	492,106
1917	3rd	88	66	.571	12.0	Lee Fohl	477,298
1918	2nd	73	54	.575	2.5	Lee Fohl	295,515
1919	2nd	84	55	.604	3.5	Lee Fohl, Tris Speaker	538,135
1920	1st (S)	98	56	.636	+2.0	Tris Speaker	912,832
1921	2nd	94	60	.610	4.5	Tris Speaker	748,705
1922	4th	78	76	.506	16.0	Tris Speaker	528,145
1923	3rd	82	71	.536	16.5	Tris Speaker	558,856
1924	6th	67	86	.438	24.5	Tris Speaker	481,905
1925	6th	70	84	.455	27.5	Tris Speaker	419,005
1926	2nd	88	66	.571	3.0	Tris Speaker	627,426
1927	6th	66	87	.431	43.5	Jack McAllister	373,138
1928	7th	62	92	.403	39.0	Roger Peckinpaugh	375,907
1929	3rd	81	71	.533	24.0	Roger Peckinpaugh	536,210
1930	4th	81	73	.526	21.0	Roger Peckinpaugh	528,657
1931	4th	78	76	.506	30.0	Roger Peckinpaugh	483,027
1932	4th	87	65	.572	19.0	Roger Peckinpaugh	468,953
1933	4th	75	76	.497	23.5	Roger Peckinpaugh, Walter Johnson	387,936
1934	3rd	85	69	.552	16.0	Walter Johnson	391,338
1935	3rd	82	71	.536	12.0	Walter Johnson, Steve O'Neill	397,615
1936	5th	80	74	.519	22.5	Steve O'Neill	500,391
1937	4th	83	71	.539	19.0	Steve O'Neill	564,849
1938	3rd	86	66	.566	13.0	Ossie Vitt	652,006
1939	3rd	87	67	.565	20.5	Ossie Vitt	563,926
1940	2nd	89	65	.578	1.0	Ossie Vitt	902,576
1941	4th (tied)	75	79	.487	26.0	Roger Peckinpaugh	745,948
1942	4th	75	79	.487	28.0	Lou Boudreau	459,447
1943	3rd	82	71	.536	15.5	Lou Boudreau	438,894
1944	5th (tied)	72	82	.468	17.0	Lou Boudreau	475,272
1945	5th	73	72	.503	11.0	Lou Boudreau	558,182
1946	6th	68	86	.442	36.0	Lou Boudreau	1,057,289
1947	4th	80	74	.519	17.0	Lou Boudreau	1,521,978
1948	1st (L,S)	97	58	.626	+1.0	Lou Boudreau	2,620,627
1949	3rd	89	65	.578	8.0	Lou Boudreau	2,233,771
1950	4th	92	62	.597	6.0	Lou Boudreau	1,727,464
1951	2nd	93	61	.604	5.0	Al Lopez	1,704,984
1952	2nd	93	61	.604	2.0	Al Lopez	1,444,607
1953	2nd	92	62	.597	8.5	Al Lopez	1,069,176
1954	1st (s)	111	43	.721	+8.0	Al Lopez	1,335,472
1955	2nd	93	61	.604	3.0	Al Lopez	1,221,780
1956	2nd	88	66	.571	9.0	Al Lopez	865,467
1957	6th	76	77	.497	21.5	Kerby Farrell	722,256
1958	4th	77	76	.503	14.5	Bobby Bragan, Joe Gordon	663,805
1959	2nd	89	65	.578	5.0	Joe Gordon	1,497,976
1960	4th	76	78	.494	21.0	Joe Gordon, Jimmie Dykes	950,985
1961	5th	78	83	.484	30.5	Jimmie Dykes	725,547
1962	6th	80	82	.494	16.0	Mel McGaha	716,076
1963	5th (tied)	79	83	.488	25.5	Birdie Tebbetts	562,507
1964	6th (tied)	79	83	.488	20.0	Birdie Tebbetts	653,293
1965	5th	87	75	.537	15.0	Birdie Tebbetts	934,786
1966	5th	81	81	.500	17.0	Birdie Tebbetts, George Strickland	903,359
1967	8th	75	87	.463	17.0	Joe Adcock	662,980
1968	3rd	86	75	.534	16.5	Alvin Dark	857,994

– 226 –

EAST DIVISION

Year	Position	W	L	Pct.	GB	Manager	Attendance
1969	6th	62	99	.385	46.5	Alvin Dark	619,970
1970	5th	76	86	.469	32.0	Alvin Dark	729,752
1971	6th	60	102	.370	43.0	Alvin Dark, John Lipon	591,361
1972	5th	72	84	.462	14.0	Ken Aspromonte	626,354
1973	6th	71	91	.438	26.0	Ken Aspromonte	615,107
1974	4th	77	85	.475	14.0	Ken Aspromonte	1,114,262
1975	4th	79	80	.497	15.5	Frank Robinson	977,039
1976	4th	81	78	.509	16.0	Frank Robinson	948,776
1977	5th	71	90	.441	28.5	Frank Robinson, Jeff Torborg	900,365
1978	6th	69	90	.434	29.0	Jeff Torborg	800,584
1979	6th	81	80	.503	22.0	Jeff Torborg, Dave Garcia	1,011,644
1980	6th	79	81	.494	23.0	Dave Garcia	1,033,827
1981	6th/5th	52	51	.505	*	Dave Garcia	661,395
1982	6th (tied)	78	84	.481	17.0	Dave Garcia	1,044,021
1983	7th	70	92	.432	28.0	Mike Ferraro, Pat Corrales	768,941
1984	6th	75	87	.463	29.0	Pat Corrales	734,079
1985	7th	60	102	.370	39.5	Pat Corrales	655,181
1986	5th	84	78	.519	11.5	Pat Corrales	1,471,805
1987	7th	61	101	.377	37.0	Pat Corrales, Doc Edwards	1,077,898
1988	6th	78	84	.481	11.0	Doc Edwards	1,411,610
1989	6th	73	89	.451	16.0	Doc Edwards, John Hart	1,285,542
1990	4th	77	85	.475	11.0	John McNamara	1,225,240
1991	7th	57	105	.352	34.0	John McNamara, Mike Hargrove	1,051,863
1992	4th (tied)	76	86	.469	20.0	Mike Hargrove	1,224,274
1993	6th	76	86	.469	19.0	Mike Hargrove	2,177,908

CENTRAL DIVISION

Year	Position	W	L	Pct.	GB	Manager	Attendance
1994	2nd	66	47	.584	1.0	Mike Hargrove	1,995,174
1995	1st (D,C,s)	100	44	.694	+30.0	Mike Hargrove	2,842,745
1996	1st (d)	99	62	.615	+14.5	Mike Hargrove	3,318,174
1997	1st (D,C,s)	86	75	.534	+6.0	Mike Hargrove	3,404,750
1998	1st (D,c)	89	73	.549	+9.0	Mike Hargrove	3,467,299
1999	1st (d)	97	65	.599	+21.5	Mike Hargrove	3,468,456
2000	2nd	90	72	.556	5.0	Charlie Manuel	3,456,278
2001	1st (d)	91	71	.562	+6.0	Charlie Manuel	3,175,523
2002	3rd	74	88	.457	20.5	Charlie Manuel, Joel Skinner	2,616,940
2003	4th	68	94	.420	22.0	Eric Wedge	1,730,001
2004	3rd	80	82	.494	12.0	Eric Wedge	1,814,401

(S) won World Series; (L) won league playoff; (s) lost World Series; *first half 26-24, second half 26-27; (D) won Division Series; (C) won League Championship Series; (d) lost Division Series; (c) lost League Championship Series

INDIVIDUAL AND CLUB RECORDS

BATTING

	Individual		Club
	Season	Career	Season
Games	163—Loon Wagner, 1964	1,626—Terry Turner	164 (1964)
At-bats	663—Joe Carter, 162 g, 1986	6,034—Nap Lajoie	5,702 (1986)
Runs	140—Earl Averill, 155 g, 1931	1,154—Earl Averill	1,009 (1999)
			Fewest—493 (1909)
Hits	233—Joe Jackson, 147 g, 1911	2,046—Nap Lajoie	1,715 (1936)
			Fewest—1,210 (1915)
Hitting streak	31 g—Nap Lajoie, 1906		
Singles	172—Charlie Jamieson, 152 g, 1923	1,511—Nap Lajoie	1,218 (1925)
Doubles	64—George Burns, 151 g, 1926	486—Tris Speaker	358 (1930)
Triples	26—Joe Jackson, 152 g, 1912	121—Earl Averill	95 (1920)

HOME RUNS

			221 (2000)
			Fewest—9 (1910)
Righthander	50—Albert Belle, 143 g, 1995	242—Albert Belle	
Lefthander	52—Jim Thome, 147 g, 2002	334—Jim Thome	
Switch-hitter	24—Roberto Alomar, 159 g, 1999	104—Carlos Baerga	
Rookie	37—Al Rosen, 155 g, 1950		
Home	30—Hal Trosky, 1936	182—Jim Thome	133 (1970)
	Jim Thome, 2001, 2002		
Road	26—Albert Belle, 1996	152—Jim Thome	124 (1997)
Month	17—Albert Belle, Sept 1995		50 (Jun 1950, Aug 1997)
Pinch	3—Gene Green, 1962	8—Fred Whitfield	9 (1965, 1970)
	Ron Kittle, 1988		
	Ted Uhlaender, 1970		
	Fred Whitfield, 1965		

	Individual		Club
	Season	**Career**	**Season**
Grand slams	4—Al Rosen, 154 g, 1951	13—Manny Ramirez	12 (1999)
Home runs at Municipal Stadium, all teams			236 (1970)
Home runs at Jacobs Field, all teams			219 (1999)
Total bases	405—Hal Trosky, 151 g, 1936	3,200—Earl Averill	2,700 (1996)
Extra base hits	103—Albert Belle, 143 g, 1995	724—Earl Averill	576 (1996)
Sacrifice hits	46—Bill Bradley, 139 g, 1907	340—Ray Chapman	195 (1906)
Sacrifice flies	16—Juan Gonzalez, 140 g, 2001	62—Omar Vizquel	74 (1980)
Bases on balls	127—Jim Thome, 146 g, 1999	997—Jim Thome	743 (1999)
			Fewest—243 (1901)
Strikeouts	185—Jim Thome, 156 g, 2001	1,377—Jim Thome	1,102 (1963)
	Fewest—4—Joe Sewell, 155 g, 1925		Fewest—331 (1922, 1926)
	Joe Sewell, 152 g, 1929		
Hit by pitch	17—Minnie Minoso, 148 g, 1959	79—Nap Lajoie	78 (2004)
	Travis Hafner, 140 g, 2004		Fewest—11 (1943, 1976)
Runs batted in	165—Manny Ramirez, 147 g, 1999	1,084—Earl Averill	960 (1999)
			Fewest—407 (1909)
Grounded into double plays	28—Julio Franco, 149 g, 1986	165—Julio Franco	165 (1980)
	Fewest—3—Jose Cardenal, 157 g, 1986		Fewest—94 (1941)
	Cory Snyder, 157 g, 1987		
Left on base			1,260 (2000)
			Fewest—995 (1959)
Batting average	.408—Joe Jackson, 147 g, 1911	.375—Joe Jackson	.308 (1921)
			Lowest—.234 (1968, 1972)
Most .300 hitters			9 (1921)
Slugging average	.697—Manny Ramirez, 118 g, 2000	.592—Manny Ramirez	.484 (1994)
			Lowest—.305 (1910)
On-base percentage	.483—Tris Speaker, 150 g, 1920	.444—Tris Speaker	.383 (1921)
			Lowest—.288 (1909)

BASERUNNING

	Season	**Career**	**Season**
Stolen bases	75—Kenny Lofton, 154 g, 1996	450—Kenny Lofton	210 (1917)
Caught stealing	23—Bobby Bonds, 146 g, 1979	109—Charlie Jamieson	92 (1920)

PITCHING

	Season	**Career**	**Season**
Games	76—Sid Monge, 1979	582—Mel Harder	
Games started	44—George Uhle, 1923	484—Bob Feller	
Complete games	36—Bob Feller, 1946	279—Bob Feller	141 (1904)
Wins	31—Jim Bagby Sr., 1920	266—Bob Feller	
Percentage	.938—Johnny Allen (15-1), 1937	.623—Addie Joss	
Winning streak	15—Johnny Allen, 1937		
	Gaylord Perry, 1974		
Winning streak, two seasons	17—Johnny Allen 1936 (2), 1937 (15)		
20-win seasons		7—Bob Lemon	
Losses	22—Pete Dowling, 1901	186—Mel Harder	
Losing streak	13—Guy Morton, 1914		
Saves	46—Jose Mesa, 1995	129—Doug Jones	50 (1995)
Innings	371—Bob Feller, 1946	3,827—Bob Feller	1,487.2 (1964)
Hits	378—George Uhle, 1923	3,706—Mel Harder	1,663 (1930)
Runs	167—George Uhle, 1923	1,714—Mel Harder	957 (1987)
Earned runs	150—George Uhle, 1923	1,447—Mel Harder	835 (1987)
Bases on balls	208—Bob Feller, 1938	1,764—Bob Feller	770 (1971)
Strikeouts	348—Bob Feller, 1946	2,581—Bob Feller	1,218 (2001)
Strikeouts, game	18—Bob Feller, Oct 2, 1938, 1st game		
	(19—Luis Tiant, Jul 3, 1968, 10 inn)		
Hit batsmen	20—Otto Hess, 1906	95—George Uhle	73 (1901)
Wild pitches	18—Sam McDowell, 1967	114—Sam McDowell	87 (1973)
Home runs	37—Luis Tiant, 1969	224—Bob Feller	219 (1987)
Sacrifice hits	25—Bob Feller, 1946	301—George Uhle	216 (1927)

	Individual			Club
	Season		**Career**	**Season**
Sacrifice flies	13—Bob Lemon, 1954		55—Charles Nagy	73 (1984)
Earned run average	1.60—Luis Tiant, 258 inn, 1968		1.89—Addie Joss	2.02 (1908)
Shutouts	10—Bob Feller, 1946		45—Addie Joss	27 (1906)
	Bob Lemon, 1948			Lost—24 (1914)
1-0 games won	3—Addie Joss, 1908		10—Addie Joss	7 (1989)
	Stan Coveleski, 1917			Lost—7 (1918, 1955)
	Jim Bagby Jr., 1943			
	Bob Feller, 1946			
	Steve Hargan, 1967			

TEAM FIELDING

Putouts	4,463 (1964)	Assists	2,267 (1907)
	Fewest—3,907 (1945)		Fewest—1,468 (1968)
Chances accepted	6,663 (1910)	Errors	329 (1901)
	Fewest—5,470 (1945)		Fewest—72 (2000)
Double plays	197 (1953)	Passed balls	35 (1958)
	Fewest—77 (1915)		Fewest—3 (1943)
Errorless games	99 (2000)	Fielding average	.988 (2000)
	Consecutive—11 (1967)		Lowest—.941 (1901)

MISCELLANEOUS

Most players, season 59 (2002)
Fewest players, season 24 (1904)
Games won 111 (1954)
  Month 26 (Aug 1954)
  Consecutive 13 (1942, 1951)
Winning percentage .721 (1954), 111-43
  Lowest .333 (1914), 51-102
Number of league championships 5
  Most recent 1997
Runs, game 27 vs Boston, Jul 7, 1923
  Opponents' 24 by Boston, Aug 21, 1986
Hits, game 29 vs St. Louis, Aug 12, 1948, 2nd game
  vs Boston, Jun 20, 1980
Home runs, game 8 vs Milwaukee, Apr 25, 1997
  vs Seattle, Jul 16, 2004
Runs, shutout 22 vs New York, Aug 31, 2004
  Opponents' 21 by Detroit, Sept 15, 1901, 8 inn
Longest 1-0 win 16 inn, vs Baltimore, May 14, 1961, 1st game

Most seasons, non-pitcher 15—Terry Turner
Most seasons, pitcher 20—Mel Harder
Games lost 105 (1991)
  Month 24 (Jul 1914)
  Consecutive 12 (1931)
Overall record 8,209-7,877 (104 seasons)
  Interleague play 70-69
Number of times worst record in league 6
  Most recent 1991
Runs, inning 14 vs Philadelphia, Jun 18, 1950, 2nd game, 1st

Total bases, game 50 vs Seattle, Jul 16, 2004

Consecutive games with one or more home runs 19 (40 hrs), 2000

Longest shutout 16 inn, 3-0 vs Chicago, Sept 22, 1975

Longest 1-0 loss 17 inn, vs Chicago, Sept 13, 1967

ATTENDANCE

Highest home attendance
  League Park 912,832 (1920)
  Municipal Stadium 2,620,627 (1948)
  Jacobs Field 3,468,456 (1999)

Highest road attendance 2,449,537 (1999)

Largest crowds
  Day 74,420 vs Detroit, Apr 7, 1973
  Night 78,382 vs Chicago, Aug 20, 1948
  Doubleheader 84,587 vs New York, Sept 12, 1954
  Home opener 74,420 vs Detroit, Apr 7, 1973

DETROIT TIGERS
YEARLY FINISHES

(Original American League franchise)

Year	Position	W	L	Pct.	GB	Manager	Attendance
1901	3rd	74	61	.548	8.5	George Stallings	259,430
1902	7th	52	83	.385	30.5	Frank Dwyer	189,469
1903	5th	65	71	.478	25.0	Ed Barrow	224,523
1904	7th	62	90	.408	32.0	Ed Barrow, Bobby Lowe	177,796
1905	3rd	79	74	.516	15.5	Bill Armour	193,384
1906	6th	71	78	.477	21.0	Bill Armour	174,043
1907	1st (s)	92	58	.613	+1.5	Hughey Jennings	297,079
1908	1st (s)	90	63	.588	+.5	Hughey Jennings	436,199
1909	1st (s)	98	54	.645	+3.5	Hughey Jennings	490,490
1910	3rd	86	68	.558	18.0	Hughey Jennings	391,288
1911	2nd	89	65	.578	13.5	Hughey Jennings	484,988
1912	6th	69	84	.451	36.5	Hughey Jennings	402,870
1913	6th	66	87	.431	30.0	Hughey Jennings	398,502

Year	Position	W	L	Pct.	GB	Manager	Attendance
1914	4th	80	73	.523	19.5	Hughey Jennings	416,225
1915	2nd	100	54	.649	2.5	Hughey Jennings	476,105
1916	3rd	87	67	.565	4.0	Hughey Jennings	616,772
1917	4th	78	75	.510	21.5	Hughey Jennings	457,289
1918	7th	55	71	.437	20.0	Hughey Jennings	203,719
1919	4th	80	60	.571	8.0	Hughey Jennings	643,805
1920	7th	61	93	.396	37.0	Hughey Jennings	579,650
1921	6th	71	82	.464	27.0	Ty Cobb	661,527
1922	3rd	79	75	.513	15.0	Ty Cobb	861,206
1923	2nd	83	71	.539	16.0	Ty Cobb	911,377
1924	3rd	86	68	.558	6.0	Ty Cobb	1,015,136
1925	4th	81	73	.526	16.5	Ty Cobb	820,766
1926	6th	79	75	.513	12.0	Ty Cobb	711,914
1927	4th	82	71	.536	27.5	George Moriarty	773,716
1928	6th	68	86	.442	33.0	George Moriarty	474,323
1929	6th	70	84	.455	36.0	Bucky Harris	869,318
1930	5th	75	79	.487	27.0	Bucky Harris	649,450
1931	7th	61	93	.396	47.0	Bucky Harris	434,056
1932	5th	76	75	.503	29.5	Bucky Harris	397,157
1933	5th	75	79	.487	25.0	Del Baker	320,972
1934	1st (s)	101	53	.656	+7.0	Mickey Cochrane	919,161
1935	1st (S)	93	58	.616	+3.0	Mickey Cochrane	1,034,929
1936	2nd	83	71	.539	19.5	Mickey Cochrane	875,948
1937	2nd	89	65	.578	13.0	Mickey Cochrane	1,072,276
1938	4th	84	70	.545	16.0	Mickey Cochrane, Del Baker	799,557
1939	5th	81	73	.526	26.5	Del Baker	836,279
1940	1st (s)	90	64	.584	+1.0	Del Baker	1,112,693
1941	4th (tied)	75	79	.487	26.0	Del Baker	684,915
1942	5th	73	81	.474	30.0	Del Baker	580,087
1943	5th	78	76	.506	20.0	Steve O'Neill	606,287
1944	2nd	88	66	.571	1.0	Steve O'Neill	923,176
1945	1st (S)	88	65	.575	+1.5	Steve O'Neill	1,280,341
1946	2nd	92	62	.597	12.0	Steve O'Neill	1,722,590
1947	2nd	85	69	.552	12.0	Steve O'Neill	1,398,093
1948	5th	78	76	.506	18.5	Steve O'Neill	1,743,035
1949	4th	87	67	.565	10.0	Red Rolfe	1,821,204
1950	2nd	95	59	.617	3.0	Red Rolfe	1,951,474
1951	5th	73	81	.474	25.0	Red Rolfe	1,132,641
1952	8th	50	104	.325	45.0	Red Rolfe, Fred Hutchinson	1,026,846
1953	6th	60	94	.390	40.5	Fred Hutchinson	884,658
1954	5th	68	86	.442	43.0	Fred Hutchinson	1,079,847
1955	5th	79	75	.513	17.0	Bucky Harris	1,181,838
1956	5th	82	72	.532	15.0	Bucky Harris	1,051,182
1957	4th	78	76	.506	20.0	Jack Tighe	1,272,346
1958	5th	77	77	.500	15.0	Jack Tighe, Bill Norman	1,098,924
1959	4th	76	78	.494	18.0	Bill Norman, Jimmie Dykes	1,221,221
1960	6th	71	83	.461	26.0	Jimmie Dykes, Billy Hitchcock, Joe Gordon	1,167,669
1961	2nd	101	61	.623	8.0	Bob Scheffing	1,600,710
1962	4th	85	76	.528	10.5	Bob Scheffing	1,207,881
1963	5th (tied)	79	83	.488	25.5	Bob Scheffing, Charlie Dressen	821,952
1964	4th	85	77	.525	14.0	Charlie Dressen	816,139
1965	4th	89	73	.549	13.0	Charlie Dressen, Bob Swift	1,029,645
1966	3rd	88	74	.543	10.0	Charlie Dressen, Bob Swift, Frank Skaff	1,124,293
1967	2nd (tied)	91	71	.562	1.0	Mayo Smith	1,447,143
1968	1st (S)	103	59	.636	+12.0	Mayo Smith	2,031,847

EAST DIVISION

Year	Position	W	L	Pct.	GB	Manager	Attendance
1969	2nd	90	72	.556	19.0	Mayo Smith	1,577,481
1970	4th	79	83	.488	29.0	Mayo Smith	1,501,293
1971	2nd	91	71	.562	12.0	Billy Martin	1,591,073
1972	1st (c)	86	70	.551	+0.5	Billy Martin	1,892,386
1973	3rd	85	77	.525	12.0	Billy Martin, Joe Schultz	1,724,146
1974	6th	72	90	.444	19.0	Ralph Houk	1,243,080
1975	6th	57	102	.358	37.5	Ralph Houk	1,058,836
1976	5th	74	87	.460	24.0	Ralph Houk	1,467,020
1977	4th	74	88	.457	26.0	Ralph Houk	1,359,856
1978	5th	86	76	.531	13.5	Ralph Houk	1,714,893
1979	5th	85	76	.528	18.0	Les Moss, Dick Tracewski, Sparky Anderson	1,630,929
1980	5th	84	78	.519	19.0	Sparky Anderson	1,785,293
1981	4th/2nd (tied)	60	49	.550	*	Sparky Anderson	1,149,144
1982	4th	83	79	.512	12.0	Sparky Anderson	1,636,058
1983	2nd	92	70	.568	6.0	Sparky Anderson	1,829,636
1984	1st (C,S)	104	58	.642	+15.0	Sparky Anderson	2,704,794
1985	3rd	84	77	.522	15.0	Sparky Anderson	2,286,609
1986	3rd	87	75	.537	8.5	Sparky Anderson	1,899,437
1987	1st†	98	64	.605	+2.0	Sparky Anderson	2,061,830
1988	2nd	88	74	.543	1.0	Sparky Anderson	2,081,162
1989	7th	59	103	.364	30.0	Sparky Anderson	1,543,656

Year	Position	W	L	Pct.	GB	Manager	Attendance
1990	3rd	79	83	.488	9.0	Sparky Anderson	1,495,785
1991	2nd	84	78	.519	7.0	Sparky Anderson	1,641,661
1992	6th	75	87	.463	21.0	Sparky Anderson	1,423,963
1993	3rd (tied)	85	77	.525	10.0	Sparky Anderson	1,971,421
1994	5th	53	62	.461	18.0	Sparky Anderson	1,184,783
1995	4th	60	84	.417	26.0	Sparky Anderson	1,180,979
1996	5th	53	109	.327	39.0	Buddy Bell	1,168,610
1997	3rd	79	83	.488	19.0	Buddy Bell	1,365,157

CENTRAL DIVISION

Year	Position	W	L	Pct.	GB	Manager	Attendance
1998	5th	65	97	.401	24.0	Buddy Bell, Larry Parrish	1,409,391
1999	3rd	69	92	.429	27.5	Larry Parrish	2,026,441
2000	3rd	79	83	.488	16.0	Phil Garner	2,533,753
2001	4th	66	96	.407	25.0	Phil Garner	1,921,305
2002	4th	55	106	.342	39.0	Phil Garner, Luis Pujols	1,503,623
2003	5th	43	119	.265	47.0	Alan Trammell	1,368,285
2004	4th	72	90	.444	20.0	Alan Trammell	1,917,004

(s) lost World Series; (S) won World Series; (c) lost League Championship Series; *first half 31-26, second half 29-23; (C) won League Championship Series

INDIVIDUAL AND CLUB RECORDS
BATTING

	Individual		Club
	Season	Career	Season
Games	163—Rocky Colavito, 1961	2,834—Al Kaline	164 (1968)
At-bats	679—Harvey Kuenn, 155 g, 1953	10,586—Ty Cobb	5,664 (1998)
Runs	147—Ty Cobb, 146 g, 1911	2,087—Ty Cobb	958 (1934)
			Fewest—499 (1904)
Hits	248—Ty Cobb, 146 g, 1911	3,902—Ty Cobb	1,724 (1921)
			Fewest—1,204 (1905)
Hitting streak	40 g—Ty Cobb, 1911		
Singles	169—Ty Cobb, 146 g, 1911	2,839—Ty Cobb	1,298 (1921)
Doubles	63—Hank Greenberg, 153 g, 1934	665—Ty Cobb	349 (1934)
Triples	26—Sam Crawford, 157 g, 1914	286—Ty Cobb	102 (1913)

HOME RUNS

			225 (1987)
			Fewest—9 (1906)
Righthander	58—Hank Greenberg, 155 g, 1938	399—Al Kaline	
Lefthander	41—Norm Cash, 159 g, 1961	373—Norm Cash	
Switch-hitter	34—Tony Clark, 157 g, 1998	158—Tony Clark	
Rookie	35—Rudy York, 104 g, 1937		
Home	39—Hank Greenberg, 1938	226—Al Kaline	125 (1987)
Road	27—Rocky Colavito, 1961	173—Al Kaline	108 (2000)
Month	18—Rudy York, Aug 1937		49 (Aug 1937)
Pinch	3—many players	16—Gates Brown	8 (1971)
Grand slams	4—Rudy York, 135 g, 1938	10—Rudy York	10 (1938)
	Jim Northrup,155 g, 1968	Hank Greenberg	
		Cecil Fielder	
Home runs at Tiger Stadium, all teams			235 (1999)
Home runs at Comerica Park, all teams			162 (2003)
Total bases	397—Hank Greenberg, 154 g, 1937	5,475—Ty Cobb	2,548 (1987)
Extra base hits	103—Hank Greenberg, 154 g, 1937	1,063—Ty Cobb	546 (1929)
Sacrifice hits	36—Bill Coughlin, 147 g, 1906	327—Donie Bush	182 (1906)
Sacrifice flies	16—Sam Crawford, 157 g, 1914	104—Al Kaline	59 (1983)
Bases on balls	137—Roy Cullenbine, 142 g, 1947	1,277—Al Kaline	765 (1993)
			Fewest—292 (1903)
Strikeouts	182—Cecil Fielder, 159 g, 1990	1,099—Lou Whitaker	1,268 (1996)
	Fewest—13—Charlie Gehringer, 154 g, 1936		Fewest—376 (1921)
	Harvey Kuenn, 155 g, 1954		
Hit by pitch	24—Bill Freehan, 155 g, 1968	114—Bill Freehan	82 (1999)
			Fewest—9 (1945)
Runs batted in	183—Hank Greenberg, 154 g, 1937	1,828—Ty Cobb	873 (1937)
			Fewest—404 (1906)
Grounded into	29—Jimmy Bloodworth, 129 g, 1943	271—Al Kaline	164 (1949)
double plays	Fewest—0—Dick McAuliffe, 151 g, 1968		Fewest—81 (1985)

	Individual		Club
	Season	Career	Season
Left on base			1,312 (1993)
			Fewest—1,021 (1917)
Batting average	.420—Ty Cobb, 146 g, 1911	.367—Ty Cobb	.316 (1921)
			Lowest—.231 (1904)
Most .300 hitters			8 (1922, 1924, 1934)
Slugging average	.683—Hank Greenberg, 155 g, 1938	.616—Hank Greenberg	.454 (1994)
			Lowest—.321 (1918)
On-base percentage	.487—Norm Cash, 159 g, 1961	.434—Ty Cobb	.385 (1921)
			Lowest—.282 (1904)

BASERUNNING

Stolen bases	96—Ty Cobb, 156 g, 1915	865—Ty Cobb	281 (1909)
Caught stealing	38—Ty Cobb, 156 g, 1915	188—Ty Cobb	92 (1921)

PITCHING

Games	88—Mike Myers, 1997	545—John Hiller	
	Sean Runyan, 1998		
Games started	45—Mickey Lolich, 1971	459—Mickey Lolich	
Complete games	42—George Mullin, 1904	336—George Mullin	143 (1904)
Wins	31—Denny McLain, 1968	222—Hooks Dauss	
Percentage	.862—Bill Donovan (25-4), 1907	.654—Denny McLain	
Winning streak	16—Schoolboy Rowe, 1934		
Winning streak, two seasons	16—Bill Donovan, 1907 (8), 1908 (8)		
20-win seasons		5—George Mullin	
Losses	23—George Mullin, 1904	182—Hooks Dauss	
Losing streak	10—Mickey Lolich, 1967		
	Mike Moore, 1995		
Saves	42—Todd Jones, 2000	154—Mike Henneman	51 (1984)
Innings	382—George Mullin, 1904	3,394—George Mullin	1,489.2 (1968)
Hits	346—George Mullin, 1904	3,407—Hooks Dauss	1,699 (1996)
Runs	160—Joe Coleman Jr., 1974	1,594—Hooks Dauss	1,103 (1996)
Earned runs	142—Mickey Lolich, 1974	1,289—Mickey Lolich	1,015 (1996)
Bases on balls	158—Joe Coleman Jr., 1974	1,227—Hal Newhouser	784 (1996)
Strikeouts	308—Mickey Lolich, 1971	2,679—Mickey Lolich	1,115 (1968)
Strikeouts, game	16—Mickey Lolich, May 23, 1969		
	Mickey Lolich, Jun 9, 1969 (pitched first 9 inn of 10-inn game)		
Hit batsmen	23—Howard Ehmke, 1922	121—Hooks Dauss	84 (1922)
Wild pitches	24—Jack Morris, 1987	155—Jack Morris	82 (1996)
Home runs	42—Denny McLain, 1966	329—Mickey Lolich	241 (1996)
Sacrifice hits	28—Earl Whitehill, 1931	423—George Mullin	222 (1927)
Sacrifice flies	13—Jack Morris, 1980	90—Jack Morris	72 (1996)
Earned run average	1.81—Hal Newhouser, 313 inn, 1945	2.38—Ed Killian	2.26 (1909)
Shutouts	9—Denny McLain, 1969	39—Mickey Lolich	20 (1917, 1944, 1969)
			Lost—22 (1904)
1-0 games won	4—Ed Summers, 1908	9—Bill Donovan	9 (1908)
			Lost—7 (1903, 1943)

TEAM FIELDING

Putouts	4,469 (1968)	Assists	2,272 (1914)
	Fewest—4,006 (1906)		Fewest—1,443 (1962)
Chances accepted	6,504 (1914)	Errors	425 (1901)
	Fewest—5,594 (1959)		Fewest—92 (1997)
Double plays	194 (1950, 2003)	Passed balls	30 (2001)
	Fewest—94 (1912, 1917)		Fewest—4 (1924)
Errorless games	92 (1997)	Fielding average	.985 (1997)
	Consecutive—12 (1963)		Lowest—.922 (1901)

MISCELLANEOUS

Most players, season 57 (2002)

Fewest players, season 24 (1906, 1907)
Games won 104 (1984)
 Month 23 (Jul 1908, Aug 1915, Aug 1934, Aug 1935)
 Consecutive 14 (1909, 1934)
Winning percentage .656 (1934), 101-53
 Lowest .265 (2003), 43-119
Number of league championships   9
 Most recent 1984
Runs, game 21 vs Cleveland, Sept 15, 1901, 8 inn
          vs Philadelphia, Jul 17, 1908
          vs St. Louis, Jul 25, 1920
          vs Chicago, Jul 1, 1936
 Opponents' 26 by Kansas City, Sept 9, 2004
Hits, game 27 vs New York, Sept 29, 1928
          vs Kansas City, May 27, 2004
Home runs, game 8 vs Toronto, Jun 20, 2000
Runs, shutout 21 vs Cleveland, Sept 15, 1901, 8 inn
 Opponents' 16 by St. Louis, Sept 9, 1922
Longest 1-0 win 12 inn, vs St. Louis, Sept 8, 1917
          vs Cleveland, Jun 26, 1919
          vs Chicago, Sept 10, 1950, 1st game

Most seasons, non-pitcher 22—Ty Cobb
                              Al Kaline
Most seasons, pitcher 16—Tommy Bridges
Games lost 119 (2003)
 Month 24 (Jun 1975)
 Consecutive 19 (1975)
Overall record 8,150-7,959 (104 seasons)
 Interleague play 62-77
Number of times worst record in league 6 (inc. 1 tie)
 Most recent 2003
Runs, inning 13 vs New York, Sept 22, 1936, 6th
          vs Texas, Aug 8, 2001, 9th

Total bases, game 47 vs Toronto, Jun 20, 2000

Consecutive games with one or more home runs 25 (46 hrs), 1994
Longest shutout 16 inn, 3-0 vs Chicago, Sept 22, 1975

Longest 1-0 loss 16 inn, vs Chicago, Aug 14, 1954

ATTENDANCE

Highest home attendance		**Largest crowds**	
Tiger Stadium	2,704,794 (1984)	**Day**	57,888 vs Cleveland, Sept 26, 1948
Comerica Park	2,533,752 (2000)	**Night**	56,586 vs Cleveland, Aug 9, 1948
		Doubleheader	58,369 vs New York, Jul 20, 1947
Highest road attendance	2,396,528 (1991)	**Home opener**	54,089 vs Cleveland, Apr 6, 1971

KANSAS CITY ATHLETICS
YEARLY FINISHES

**(Original American League franchise moved from Philadelphia to Kansas City after the 1954 season
and to Oakland after the 1967 season)**

Year	Position	W	L	Pct.	GB	Manager	Attendance
1955	6th	63	91	.409	33.0	Lou Boudreau	1,393,054
1956	8th	52	102	.338	45.0	Lou Boudreau	1,015,154
1957	7th	59	94	.386	38.5	Lou Boudreau, Harry Craft	901,067
1958	7th	73	81	.474	19.0	Harry Craft	925,090
1959	7th	66	88	.429	28.0	Harry Craft	963,683
1960	8th	58	96	.377	39.0	Bob Elliott	774,944
1961	9th (tied)	61	100	.379	47.5	Joe Gordon, Hank Bauer	683,817
1962	9th	72	90	.444	24.0	Hank Bauer	635,675
1963	8th	73	89	.451	31.5	Ed Lopat	762,364
1964	10th	57	105	.352	42.0	Ed Lopat, Mel McGaha	642,478
1965	10th	59	103	.364	43.0	Mel McGaha, Haywood Sullivan	528,344
1966	7th	74	86	.463	23.0	Alvin Dark	773,929
1967	10th	62	99	.385	29.5	Alvin Dark, Luke Appling	726,639

INDIVIDUAL AND CLUB RECORDS
BATTING

	Individual		Club
	Season	**Career**	**Season**
Games	162—Norm Siebern, 1962	726—Ed Charles	163 (1964)
At-bats	641—Jerry Lumpe, 156 g, 1962	2,782—Jerry Lumpe	5,576 (1962)
Runs	114—Norm Siebern, 162 g, 1962	361—Jerry Lumpe	745 (1962)
			Fewest—533 (1967)
Hits	193—Jerry Lumpe, 156 g, 1962	775—Jerry Lumpe	1,467 (1962)
			Fewest—1,244 (1967)
Hitting streak	22 g—Hector Lopez, 1957		
	Vic Power, 1958		
Singles	139—Jerry Lumpe, 156 g, 1962	593—Jerry Lumpe	1,073 (1962)
Doubles	36—Norm Siebern, 153 g, 1961	119—Jerry Lumpe	231 (1959)
Triples	15—Gino Cimoli, 152 g, 1962	34—Jerry Lumpe	59 (1965)

	Individual		Club
	Season	Career	Season
HOME RUNS			138 (1958)
			Fewest—70 (1966)
Righthander	38—Bob Cerv, 141 g, 1958	75—Bob Cerv	
Lefthander	28—Jim Gentile, 136 g, 1964	78—Norm Siebern	
Switch-hitter	3—Jerry Walker, 36 g, 1962	3—Jerry Walker	
		Tommie Reynolds	
Rookie	20—Woodie Held, 92 g, 1957		
Home	22—Rocky Colavito, 1964	44—Bob Cerv	107 (1964)
		Hector Lopez	
Road	17—Bob Cerv, 1958	43—Norm Siebern	75 (1957)
Month	10—Rocky Colavito, May 1964		38 (June 1957)
Pinch	3—Bob Cerv, 1957	4—George Alusik	7 (1964)
		Bob Cerv	
Grand slams	2—Gus Zernial, 120 g, 1955	3—Marv Throneberry	4 (1958, 1959, 1960)
	Harry Simpson, 141 g, 1956	Roger Maris	
	Roger Maris, 99 g, 1958		
	Marv Throneberry, 104 g, 1960		
	Nelson Mathews, 157 g, 1964		
Home runs at Municipal Stadium, all teams			239 (1964)
Total bases	305—Bob Cerv, 141 g, 1958	1,065—Ed Charles	2,151 (1962)
Extra base hits	67—Rocky Colavito, 160 g, 1964	214—Norm Siebern	411 (1964)
Sacrifice hits	11—Dick Williams, 130 g, 1959	27—Wayne Causey	89 (1961)
Sacrifice flies	12—Leo Posada, 116 g, 1961	25—Norm Siebern	50 (1962)
Bases on balls	110—Norm Siebern, 162 g, 1962	343—Norm Siebern	580 (1961)
			Fewest—364 (1957)
Strikeouts	143—Nelson Mathews, 157 g, 1964	379—Ed Charles	1,104 (1964)
	Fewest—16—Vic Power, 127 g, 1956		Fewest—725 (1955)
Hit by pitch	13—Bobby Del Greco, 132 g, 1962	25—Bert Campaneris	42 (1962, 1964, 1967)
			Fewest—12 (1960)
Runs batted in	117—Norm Siebern, 162 g, 1962	367—Norm Siebern	691 (1962)
			Fewest—481 (1967)
Grounded into	23—Hector Lopez, 151 g, 1958	73—Ed Charles	154 (1960)
double plays	Fewest—4—Norm Siebern, 153 g, 1961		Fewest—79 (1967)
Left on base			1,224 (1962)
			Fewest—925 (1957)
Batting average	.319—Vic Power, 147 g, 1955	.289—Norm Siebern	.263 (1959, 1962)
			Lowest—.233 (1967)
Most .300 hitters			4 (1955)
Slugging average	.592—Bob Cerv, 148 g, 1958	.463—Norm Siebern	.394 (1957)
			Lowest—.330 (1967)
On-base percentage	.412—Norm Siebern, 162 g, 1962	.381—Norm Siebern	.332 (1962)
			Lowest—.294 (1966)

BASERUNNING

	Individual		Club
Stolen bases	55—Bert Campaneris, 147 g, 1967	168—Bert Campaneris	132 (1966, 1967)
Caught stealing	19—Bert Campaneris, 144 g, 1965	47—Bert Campaneris	59 (1967)

PITCHING

	Individual		Club
Games	81—John Wyatt, 1964	292—John Wyatt	
Games started	35—Bud Daley, 1960	99—Diego Segui	
	Ed Rakow, 1962		
	Diego Segui, 1964		
	Catfish Hunter, 1967		
Complete games	14—Art Ditmar, 1956	32—Ray Herbert	44 (1959, 1960)
	Ray Herbert, 1960		
Wins	16—Bud Daley, 1959, 1960	39—Bud Daley	
Percentage	.552—Bud Daley (16-13), 1959	none with 1,500 inn	
Winning streak	9—Bud Daley, 1960		
20-win seasons		none	

	Individual		Club
	Season	**Career**	**Season**
Losses	22—Art Ditmar, 1956	48—Ray Herbert	
Losing streak	11—Troy Herriage, 1956		
Innings	259.2—Catfish Hunter, 1967	782.2—Ray Herbert	1458 (1963)
Hits	256—Ray Herbert, 1960	815—Ray Herbert	1519 (1961)
Runs	141—Art Ditmar, 1956	411—Ray Herbert	911 (1955)
Earned runs	125—Art Ditmar, 1956	370—Ray Herbert	822 (1955)
Bases on balls	108—Art Ditmar, 1956	311—Diego Segui	707 (1955)
Strikeouts	196—Catfish Hunter, 1967	513—Diego Segui	990 (1967)
Strikeouts, game	12—Jim Nash, Jul 13, 1967		
	Jim Nash, Jul 23, 1967, 2nd game		
	Catfish Hunter, Sept 12, 1967		
Hit batsmen	12—Johnny Kucks, 1959	32—Bud Daley	54 (1964)
Wild pitches	13—John Wyatt, 1965	35—John Wyatt	67 (1965)
Home runs	40—Orlando Pena, 1964	85—Diego Segui	220 (1964)
Sacrifice hits	16—Ray Herbert, 1960	48—Ray Herbert	110 (1960)
	Jim Archer, 1961		
Sacrifice flies	10—Ray Herbert, 1959, 1960	36—Ray Herbert	64 (1961)
	Dave Wickersham, 1963		
	Jim Nash, 1967		
Earned run average	2.80—Catfish Hunter, 260 inn, 1967	none with 1,500 inn	3.56 (1966)
Shutouts	5—Catfish Hunter, 1967	8—Ned Garver	11 (1963, 1966)
			Lost—19 (1967)
1-0 games won	2—Alex Kellner, 1955	2—Catfish Hunter	4 (1966)
	Ed Radow, 1962	Alex Kellner	Lost— 5 (1967)
	Catfish Hunter, 1967	John O'Donoghue	
		Ed Rakow	
		Ralph Terry	

TEAM FIELDING

Putouts	4,374 (1963)	**Assists**	1,785 (1956)
	Fewest—4,086 (1959)		Fewest—1,533 (1967)
Chances accepted	6,095 (1963)	**Errors**	175 (1961)
	Fewest—5,755 (1959)		Fewest—125 (1957, 1958)
Double plays	187 (1956)	**Passed balls**	34 (1958)
	Fewest—120 (1967)		Fewest—11 (1963)
Errorless games	78 (1963)	**Fielding average**	.980 (1963)
	Consecutive—8 (1960, 1964)		Lowest—.972 (1961)

MISCELLANEOUS

Most players, season 52 (1955, 1961)

Fewest players, season 38 (1957)
Games won 74 (1966)
  Month 19 (Jul 1959)
  Consecutive 11 (1959)
Winning percentage .474 (1958), 73-81
  Lowest .338 (1956), 52-102
Number of league championships 0
  Most recent ---
Runs, game 20 vs Minnesota, Apr 25, 1961
  Opponents' 29 by Chicago, Apr 23, 1955
Hits, game 21 vs Washington, Jun 13, 1956
    vs Chicago, May 23, 1959
    vs Cleveland, May 5, 1962, 1st game
    26 vs New York, Jul 27, 1956, 14 inn)
Home runs, game 5 vs Cleveland, Apr 18, 1955
    vs Cleveland, Apr 24, 1957
    vs Baltimore, Sept 9, 1958
Runs, shutout 16 vs Chicago, May 23, 1959
  Opponents' 16 by Detroit, Apr 17, 1955
    by Boston, Aug 26, 1957
Longest 1-0 win 11 inn, vs Cleveland, Sept 15, 1966

Most seasons, non-pitcher 6—Billy Bryan
    Ed Charles
    Wayne Causey
Most seasons, pitcher 6—John Wyatt
Games lost 105 (1964)
  Month 26 (Aug 1961)
  Consecutive 13 (1959)
Overall record 829-1,224 (13 seasons)

Number of times worst record in league 6 (inc. 1 tie)
  Most recent 1967
Runs, inning 13 vs Chicago, Apr 21, 1956, 2nd

Total bases, game vs Washington, Jun 13, 1956
    vs Chicago, May 23, 1959
    vs Cleveland, May 5, 1962, 1st game
    vs New York, Jun 27, 1956, 14 inn)
Consecutive games with one or more home runs 11 (13 hrs), 1964

Longest shutout unknown

Longest 1-0 loss none over nine innings

ATTENDANCE

Highest home attendance	1,393,054 (1955)	**Largest crowds**	
		Day	34,065 vs New York, Aug 27, 1961
Highest road attendance	938,214 (1967)	Night	33,471 vs New York, Apr 29, 1955
		Doubleheader	35,147 vs New York, Aug 18, 1962
		Home opener	32,147 vs Detroit, Apr 12, 1955

KANSAS CITY ROYALS
YEARLY FINISHES

(American League expansion franchise)

WEST DIVISION

Year	Position	W	L	Pct.	GB	Manager	Attendance
1969	4th	69	93	.426	28.0	Joe Gordon	902,414
1970	4th (tied)	65	97	.401	33.0	Charlie Metro, Bob Lemon	693,047
1971	2nd	85	76	.528	16.0	Bob Lemon	910,784
1972	4th	76	78	.494	16.5	Bob Lemon	707,656
1973	2nd	88	74	.543	6.0	Jack McKeon	1,345,341
1974	5th	77	85	.475	13.0	Jack McKeon	1,173,292
1975	2nd	91	71	.562	7.0	Jack McKeon, Whitey Herzog	1,151,836
1976	1st (c)	90	72	.556	+2.5	Whitey Herzog	1,680,265
1977	1st (c)	102	60	.630	+8.0	Whitey Herzog	1,852,603
1978	1st (c)	92	70	.568	+5.0	Whitey Herzog	2,255,493
1979	2nd	85	77	.525	3.0	Whitey Herzog	2,261,845
1980	1st (C,s)	97	65	.599	+14.0	Jim Frey	2,288,714
1981	5th/1st (i)	50	53	.485	*	Jim Frey, Dick Howser	1,279,403
1982	2nd	90	72	.556	3.0	Dick Howser	2,284,464
1983	2nd	79	83	.488	20.0	Dick Howser	1,963,875
1984	1st (c)	84	78	.519	+3.0	Dick Howser	1,810,018
1985	1st (C,S)	91	71	.562	+1.0	Dick Howser	2,162,717
1986	3rd (tied)	76	86	.469	16.0	Dick Howser, Mike Ferraro	2,320,794
1987	2nd	83	79	.512	2.0	Billy Gardner, John Wathan	2,392,471
1988	3rd	84	77	.522	19.5	John Wathan	2,350,181
1989	2nd	92	70	.568	7.0	John Wathan	2,477,700
1990	6th	75	86	.466	27.5	John Wathan	2,244,956
1991	6th	82	80	.506	13.0	John Wathan, Hal McRae	2,161,537
1992	5th (tied)	72	90	.444	24.0	Hal McRae	1,867,689
1993	3rd	84	78	.519	10.0	Hal McRae	1,934,578

CENTRAL DIVISION

Year	Position	W	L	Pct.	GB	Manager	Attendance
1994	3rd	64	51	.557	4.0	Hal McRae	1,400,494
1995	2nd	70	74	.486	30.0	Bob Boone	1,233,530
1996	5th	75	86	.466	24.0	Bob Boone	1,435,997
1997	5th	67	94	.416	19.0	Bob Boone, Tony Muser	1,517,638
1998	3rd	72	89	.447	16.5	Tony Muser	1,494,875
1999	4th	64	97	.398	32.5	Tony Muser	1,506,068
2000	4th	77	85	.475	18.0	Tony Muser	1,677,915
2001	5th	65	97	.401	26.0	Tony Muser	1,536,371
2002	4th	62	100	.383	32.5	Tony Muser, Tony Pena	1,323,034
2003	3rd	83	79	.512	7.0	Tony Pena	1,779,895
2004	5th	58	104	.358	34.0	Tony Pena	1,661,478

(c) lost League Championship Series; (C) won League Championship Series; (s) lost World Series; (i) lost intra-divisional playoff; *first half 20-30, second half 30-23; (S) won World Series

INDIVIDUAL AND CLUB RECORDS
BATTING

	Individual		Club
	Season	**Career**	**Season**
Games	162—Al Cowens, 1977 Hal McRae, 1977 Carlos Beltran, 2002	2,707—George Brett	163 (1969, 1983)
At-bats	705—Willie Wilson, 161 g, 1980	10,349—George Brett	5,714 (1980)
Runs	136—Johnny Damon, 159 g, 2000	1,583—George Brett	879 (2000) Fewest—586 (1969)
Hits	230—Willie Wilson, 161 g, 1980	3,154—George Brett	1,644 (2000) Fewest—1,311 (1969)
Hitting streak	30 g—George Brett, 1980		
Singles	184—Willie Wilson, 161 g, 1980	2,035—George Brett	1,193 (1980)

	Individual Season	Individual Career	Club Season
Doubles	54—Hal McRae, 162 g, 1977	665—George Brett	316 (1990)
Triples	21—Willie Wilson, 141 g, 1985	137—George Brett	79 (1979)

HOME RUNS

	Individual Season	Individual Career	Club Season
			168 (1987) / Fewest—65 (1976)
Righthander	36—Steve Balboni, 160 g, 1985	193—Amos Otis	
Lefthander	34—John Mayberry, 156 g, 1975	317—George Brett	
Switch-hitter	30—Chili Davis, 140 g, 1997	123—Carlos Beltran	
Rookie	24—Bob Hamelin, 101 g, 1994		
Home	21—Chili Davis, 1997 / Dean Palmer, 1998	136—George Brett	88 (1997, 2002)
Road	23—John Mayberry, 1975	181—George Brett	95 (1987)
Month	12—John Mayberry, Jul 1975 / Chili Davis, Aug 1997		43 (Aug 1987, Aug 1997)
Pinch	2—Steve Balboni, 1987 / Carmelo Martinez, 1991	2—many players	6 (1995)
Grand slams	3—Danny Tartabull, 146 g, 1988	6—Frank White	7 (1991)
Home runs at Municipal Stadium, all teams			102 (1969)
Home runs at Royals Stadium, all teams			209 (2002)
Total bases	363—George Brett, 154 g, 1979	5,044—George Brett	2,440 (1977)
Extra base hits	86—Hal McRae, 162 g, 1977	1,119—George Brett	522 (1977)
Sacrifice hits	21—Tom Goodwin, 143 g, 1996	101—Frank White	72 (1972)
Sacrifice flies	13—Darrell Porter, 157 g, 1979 / Dean Palmer, 152 g, 1998 / Mike Sweeney, 159 g, 2000	120—George Brett	76 (1979)
Bases on balls	122—John Mayberry, 152 g, 1973	1,096—George Brett	644 (1973) / Fewest—397 (1983)
Strikeouts	172—Bo Jackson, 135 g, 1989 / Fewest—29—Gregg Jefferies, 152 g, 1992	1,035—Frank White	1,061 (1997) / Fewest—644 (1997)
Hit by pitch	18—Mike Macfarlane, 92 g, 1994 / Angel Berroa, 158 g, 2003	78—Mike Macfarlane	76 (2004) / Fewest—21 (1970)
Runs batted in	144—Mike Sweeney, 159 g, 2000	1,595—George Brett	831 (2000) / Fewest—538 (1969)
Grounded into double plays	26—John Wathan, 121 g, 1982 / Fewest—1—Willie Wilson, 154 g, 1979	235—George Brett	156 (1999) / Fewest—95 (1978)
Left on base			1,209 (1980) / Fewest—1,057 (1985)
Batting average	.390—George Brett, 117 g, 1980	.305—George Brett / Mike Sweeney	.288 (2000) / Lowest—.240 (1969)
Most .300 hitters			4 (2000)
Slugging average	.664—George Brett, 117 g, 1980	.518—Danny Tartabull	.436 (1977) / Lowest—.338 (1969)
On-base percentage	.454—George Brett, 117 g, 1980	.377—Mike Sweeney	.348 (1999, 2000) / Lowest—.309 (1969, 1970)

BASERUNNING

	Individual Season	Individual Career	Club Season
Stolen bases	83—Willie Wilson, 154 g, 1979	612—Willie Wilson	218 (1976)
Caught stealing	22—Tom Goodwin, 143 g, 1996	119—Willie Wilson	106 (1976)

PITCHING

	Individual Season	Individual Career	Club Season
Games	84—Dan Quisenberry, 1985	686—Jeff Montgomery	
Games started	40—Dennis Leonard, 1978	392—Paul Splittorff	
Complete games	21—Dennis Leonard, 1977	103—Dennis Leonard	54 (1974)
Wins	23—Bret Saberhagen, 1989	166—Paul Splittorff	
Percentage	.800—Larry Gura (16-4), 1978	.587—Larry Gura	
Winning streak	11—Rich Gale, 1980		
Winning streak, two seasons	11—Paul Splittorff, 1977 (7), 1978 (4)		
20-win seasons		3—Dennis Leonard	

	Individual		Club
	Season	Career	Season
Losses	19—Paul Splittorff, 1974 Darrell May, 2004	143—Paul Splittorff	
Losing streak	9—Jeff Suppan, 2002 Brian Anderson, 2004		
Saves	45—Dan Quisenberry, 1983 Jeff Montgomery, 1993	304—Jeff Montgomery	50 (1984)
Innings	294.2—Dennis Leonard, 1978	2,554.2—Paul Splittorff	1,472.1 (1976)
Hits	284—Steve Busby, 1974	2,644—Paul Splittorff	1,638 (2004)
Runs	137—Larry Gura, 1979 Paul Splittorff, 1979	1,243—Paul Splittorff	930 (2000)
Earned runs	123—Jeff Suppan, 2002	1,082—Paul Splittorff	876 (2000)
Bases on balls	120—Mark Gubicza, 1987	783—Mark Gubicza	694 (2000)
Strikeouts	244—Dennis Leonard, 1977	1,458—Kevin Appier	1,006 (1990)
Strikeouts, game	14—Mark Gubicza, Aug 27, 1988		
Hit batsmen	13—Jim Colborn, 1977 Mike Boddicker, 1991	58—Mark Gubicza	68 (1999)
Wild pitches	18—Dan Reichert, 2000	107—Mark Gubicza	77 (2000)
Home runs	38—Darrell May, 2004	202—Dennis Leonard	239 (2000)
Sacrifice hits	18—Larry Gura, 1978	122—Paul Splittorff	92 (1970)
Sacrifice flies	17—Larry Gura, 1983	92—Paul Splittorff	69 (2002)
Earned run average	2.08—Roger Nelson, 173 inn, 1972	3.21—Bret Saberhagen	3.21 (1976)
Shutouts	6—Roger Nelson, 1972	23—Dennis Leonard	16 (1972) Lost—18 (1971, 1989)
1-0 games won	2—Dick Drago, 1971 Roger Nelson, 1972 Al Fitzmorris, 1974 Dennis Leonard, 1979 Larry Gura, 1982	4—Dennis Leonard	5 (1972) Lost—4 (1971, 1989, 1992)

TEAM FIELDING

Putouts	4,417 (1976) Fewest—4,144 (1972)	Assists	1,912 (1973) Fewest—1,598 (1990)
Chances accepted	6,290 (1974, 1985) Fewest—5,860 (1990)	Errors	167 (1973) Fewest—91 (1997)
Double plays	204 (2001) Fewest—114 (1969)	Passed balls	29 (1974) Fewest—3 (1984)
Errorless games	95 (1993) Consecutive—11 (1997)	Fielding average	.985 (1997) Lowest—.974 (1973, 1983)

MISCELLANEOUS

Most players, season 58 (2004)
Fewest players, season 32 (1975)
Games won 102 (1977)
  Month 25 (Sept 1977)
  Consecutive 16 (1977)
Winning percentage .630 (1977), 102-60
  Lowest .358 (2004), 58-104
Number of league championships 2
  Most recent 1985
Runs, game 26 vs Detroit, Sept 9, 2004, 1st game
  Opponents' 22 by Boston, Apr 12, 1994
Hits, game 26 vs Detroit, Sept 9, 2004, 1st game
Home runs, game 6 vs Detroit, Jul 14, 1991
Runs, shutout 16 vs Oakland, Jun 25, 1984
  Opponents' 17 by Detroit, Jul 19, 1991
Longest 1-0 win 15 inn, vs Minnesota, May 23, 1981

Most seasons, non-pitcher 21—George Brett
Most seasons, pitcher 15—Paul Splittorff
Games lost 104 (2004)
  Month 21 (Aug 1999)
  Consecutive 12 (1997)
Overall record 2,816-2,877 (36 seasons)
  Interleague play 57-82
Number of times worst record in league 1
  Most recent 2004
Runs, inning 12 vs Minnesota, Jun 17, 2003, 6th

Total bases, game 37 vs Chicago, Jul 18, 2000
Consecutive games with one or more home runs 12 (19 hrs), 1985
Longest shutout 16 inn, 3-0 vs Chicago, Sept 22, 1975

Longest 1-0 loss 14 inn, vs Cleveland, Jul 23, 1992

ATTENDANCE

Highest home attendance		**Largest crowds**	
Municipal Stadium	910,784 (1971)	Day	41,575 vs Chicago, Apr 5, 2004
Kauffman Stadium	2,477,700 (1989)	Night	41,860 vs New York, Jul 26, 1980
		Doubleheader	42,039 vs Milwaukee, Aug 8, 1983
Highest road attendance	2,378,624 (1993)	Home opener	41,575 vs Chicago, Apr 5, 2004

MILWAUKEE BREWERS (1901)
YEARLY FINISH

(Original American League franchise moved from Milwaukee to St. Louis after the 1901 season)

Year	Position	W	L	Pct.	GB	Manager	Attendance
1901	8th	48	89	.350	35.5	Hugh Duffy	139,034

INDIVIDUAL AND CLUB RECORDS
BATTING

	Individual	Club
	Season	**Season**
Games	139—Bill Hallman	139
At-bats	576—John Anderson, 138 g	4,795
Runs	90—John Anderson, 138 g	641
Hits	190—John Anderson, 138 g	1,250
Hitting streak	unknown	
Singles	129—John Anderson, 138 g	966
Doubles	46—John Anderson, 138 g	192
Triples	9—Hugh Duffy, 79 g	66

HOME RUNS

		26
Righthander	5—Wid Conroy, 131 g	
Lefthander	4—Bill Friel, 106 g	
Switch-hitter	8—John Anderson, 138 g	
Rookie	5—Wid Conroy, 131 g	
Home	6—John Anderson	15
Road	3—Davy Jones	11
Month	3—John Anderson, Jul	9 (Sept)
	John Anderson, Sept	
	Davy Jones, Sept	
Pinch	0	0
Grand slams	0	0
Home runs at Milwaukee Park (Lloyd Street Grounds), all teams		29

Total bases	274—John Anderson, 138 g	1,662
Extra base hits	61—John Anderson, 100 g	284
Sacrifice hits	15—Billy Gilbert, 127 g	122
Bases on balls	41—Bill Hallman, 139 g	325
Strikeouts	unknown	385
Hit by pitch	8—Wid Conroy, 131 g	46
	Billy Maloney, 86 g	
Runs batted in	99—John Anderson, 138 g	513
Grounded into double plays	unknown	unknown
Left on base		unknown
Batting average	.330—John Anderson, 138 g	.261
Most .300 hitters		1
Slugging average	.476—John Anderson, 138 g	.345
On-base percentage	.360—John Anderson, 138 g	.314

BASERUNNING

Stolen bases	35—John Anderson, 138 g	176
Caught stealing	unknown	unknown

PITCHING

Games	37—Ned Garvin	
	Bill Reidy	
Games started	33—Bill Reidy	
Complete games	28—Bill Reidy	107
Wins	16—Bill Reidy	
Percentage	.444—Bill Reidy (16-20)	
Winning streak	unknown	
20-win seasons		none

	Individual		Club
	Season		**Season**
Losses	20—Ned Garvin		
	Bill Reidy		
Losing streak	unknown		
Innings	301.1—Bill Reidy		1,218
Hits	364—Bill Reidy		1,383
Runs	183—Bill Reidy		828
Earned runs	141—Bill Reidy		549
Bases on balls	95—Bert Husting		395
Strikeouts	122—Ned Garvin		376
Strikeouts, game	unknown		
Hit batsmen	14—Ned Garvin		63
	Tully Sparks		
Wild pitches	13—Ned Garvin		34
Home runs	14—Bill Reidy		32
Sacrifice hits	unknown		unknown
Earned run average	3.46—Ned Garvin, 257.1 inn		4.06
Shutouts	2—Bill Reidy		3
			Lost—13
1-0 games won	1—Ned Garvin		2
	Bill Reidy		Lost—0

TEAM FIELDING

Putouts	3,650	**Assists**	1,886
Chances accepted	5,536	**Errors**	393
Double plays	106	**Passed balls**	30
Errorless games	unknown	**Fielding average**	.934
	Consecutive—unknown		

MISCELLANEOUS

Most players, season 17
Games won 48
   Month 11 (May, Jul)
   Consecutive 4
Winning percentage .350, 48-89
Number of league championships 0
Runs, game 21 vs Chicago, May 5
   Opponents' 20 by Washington, Sept 7
Hits, game unknown
Home runs, game unknown
Runs, shutout 2 vs Cleveland, Jul 7
   Opponents' 14 by Seattle, Aug 7, 1987
Longest 1-0 win 9 inn vs Washington, Jul 28
                vs Washington, Aug 24

Games lost 89
   Month 18 (Jun, Jul, Sept)
   Consecutive 8
Overall record 48-89 (1 season)
Number of times worst record in league 1
Runs, inning unknown

Total bases, game unknown
Consecutive games with one or more home runs unknown
Longest shutout none more than 9 inn

Longest 1-0 loss none

ATTENDANCE

Highest home attendance	139,034	**Largest crowds**	
		Day	10,000 vs Philadelphia, May 26
Highest road attendance	unknown	**Doubleheader**	unknown
		Home opener	4,000 vs Chicago, May 3

MINNESOTA TWINS
YEARLY FINISHES

(Original American League franchise moved from Washington to Minnesota after the 1960 season)							
Year	**Position**	**W**	**L**	**Pct.**	**GB**	**Manager**	**Attendance**
1961	7th	70	90	.438	38.0	Cookie Lavagetto, Sam Mele	1,256,723
1962	2nd	91	71	.562	5.0	Sam Mele	1,433,116
1963	3rd	91	70	.565	13.0	Sam Mele	1,406,652
1964	6th (tied)	79	83	.488	20.0	Sam Mele	1,207,514
1965	1st (s)	102	60	.630	+7.0	Sam Mele	1,463,258
1966	2nd	89	73	.549	9.0	Sam Mele	1,259,374
1967	2nd (tied)	91	71	.562	1.0	Sam Mele, Cal Ermer	1,483,547
1968	7th	79	83	.488	24.0	Cal Ermer	1,143,257

WEST DIVISION

Year	Position	W	L	Pct.	GB	Manager	Attendance
1969	1st (c)	97	65	.599	+9.0	Billy Martin	1,349,328
1970	1st (c)	98	64	.605	+9.0	Bill Rigney	1,261,887
1971	5th	74	86	.463	26.5	Bill Rigney	940,858
1972	3rd	77	77	.500	15.5	Bill Rigney, Frank Quilici	797,901
1973	3rd	81	81	.500	13.0	Frank Quilici	907,499
1974	3rd	82	80	.506	8.0	Frank Quilici	662,401
1975	4th	76	83	.478	20.5	Frank Quilici	737,156
1976	3rd	85	77	.525	5.0	Gene Mauch	715,394
1977	4th	84	77	.522	17.5	Gene Mauch	1,162,727
1978	4th	73	89	.451	19.0	Gene Mauch	787,878
1979	4th	82	80	.506	6.0	Gene Mauch	1,070,521
1980	3rd	77	84	.478	19.5	Gene Mauch, Johnny Goryl	769,206
1981	7th/4th	41	68	.376	*	Johnny Goryl, Billy Gardner	469,090
1982	7th	60	102	.370	33.0	Billy Gardner	921,186
1983	5th (tied)	70	92	.432	29.0	Billy Gardner	858,939
1984	2nd (tied)	81	81	.500	3.0	Billy Gardner	1,598,422
1985	4th (tied)	77	85	.475	14.0	Billy Gardner, Ray Miller	1,651,814
1986	6th	71	91	.438	21.0	Ray Miller, Tom Kelly	1,255,453
1987	1st (C,S)	85	77	.525	+2.0	Tom Kelly	2,081,976
1988	2nd	91	71	.562	13.0	Tom Kelly	3,030,672
1989	5th	80	82	.494	19.0	Tom Kelly	2,277,438
1990	7th	74	88	.457	29.0	Tom Kelly	1,751,584
1991	1st (C,S)	95	67	.586	+8.0	Tom Kelly	2,293,842
1992	2nd	90	72	.556	6.0	Tom Kelly	2,482,428
1993	5th (tied)	71	91	.438	23.0	Tom Kelly	2,048,673

CENTRAL DIVISION

Year	Position	W	L	Pct.	GB	Manager	Attendance
1994	4th	53	60	.469	14.0	Tom Kelly	1,398,565
1995	5th	56	88	.389	44.0	Tom Kelly	1,057,667
1996	4th	78	84	.481	21.5	Tom Kelly	1,437,352
1997	4th	68	94	.420	18.5	Tom Kelly	1,411,064
1998	4th	70	92	.432	19.0	Tom Kelly	1,165,980
1999	5th	63	97	.394	33.0	Tom Kelly	1,202,829
2000	5th	69	93	.426	26.0	Tom Kelly	1,059,715
2001	2nd	85	77	.525	6.0	Tom Kelly	1,782,926
2002	1st (D,c)	94	67	.584	+13.5	Ron Gardenhire	1,924,473
2003	1st (d)	90	72	.556	+4.0	Ron Gardenhire	1,946,011
2004	1st (d)	92	70	.568	+9.0	Ron Gardenhire	1,879,222

(s) lost World Series; (c) lost League Championoip Series; *first half 17-39, second half 24-29; (C) won League Championship Series; (S) won World Series; (D) won Division Series; (d) lost Division Series

INDIVIDUAL AND CLUB RECORDS

BATTING

	Individual		Club
	Season	Career	Season
Games	164—Cesar Tovar, 1967	1,939—Harmon Killebrew	164 (1967)
At-bats	691—Kirby Puckett, 161 g, 1985	7,244—Kirby Puckett	5,677 (1969)
Runs	140—Chuck Knoblauch, 153 g, 1996	1,071—Kirby Puckett	877 (1996)
			Fewest—562 (1968)
Hits	239—Rod Carew, 155 g, 1977	2,304—Kirby Puckett	1,633 (1966)
			Fewest—1,274 (1968)
Hitting streak	31 g—Ken Landreaux, 1980		
Singles	180—Rod Carew, 153 g, 1974	1,626—Kirby Puckett	1,192 (1974)
Doubles	46—Marty Cordova, 145 g, 1996	414—Kirby Puckett	348 (2002)
Triples	20—Christian Guzman, 156 g, 2000	90—Rod Carew	60 (1977)

HOME RUNS

	Individual	Career	Club Season
			225 (1963)
			Fewest—81 (1976)
Righthander	49—Harmon Killebrew, 158 g, 1964	475—Harmon Killebrew	
	Harmon Killebrew, 162 g, 1969		
Lefthander	34—Kent Hrbek, 143 g, 1987	293—Kent Hrbek	
Switch-hitter	29—Chili Davis, 153 g, 1991	110—Roy Smalley	
Rookie	33—Jimmie Hall, 156 g, 1963		
Home	29—Harmon Killebrew, 1961	244—Harmon Killebrew	116 (1986)
Road	28—Harmon Killebrew, 1962	231—Harmon Killebrew	113 (1963)
Month	14—Harmon Killebrew, Jun 1964		55 (May 1964)

	Individual		Club
	Season	**Career**	**Season**
Pinch	4—Don Mincher, 1964	8—Bob Allison	7 (1964, 1967)
	Matt LeCroy, 2004		
Grand slams	3—Bob Allison, 159 g, 1961	10—Harmon Killebrew	8 (1961)
	Rod Carew, 156 g, 1976		
	Kent Hrbek, 158 g, 1985		
	Kirby Puckett, 160 g, 1992		
Home runs at Metropolitan Stadium, all teams			211 (1963)
Home runs at Metrodome, all teams			223 (1986)
Total bases	374—Tony Oliva, 161 g, 1964	3,453—Kirby Puckett	2,440 (2003)
Extra base hits	84—Tony Oliva, 161 g, 1964	728—Harmon Killebrew	551 (2002)
Sacrifice hits	25—Rob Wilfong, 140 g, 1979	79—Roy Smalley	142 (1979)
Sacrifice flies	13—Gary Gaetti, 145 g, 1982	66—Kent Hrbek	63 (1996)
	Tom Brunansky, 157 g, 1985	Harmon Killebrew	
Bases on balls	145—Harmon Killebrew, 162 g, 1969	1,321—Harmon Killebrew	649 (1962)
			Fewest—436 (1980)
Strikeouts	145—Bobby Darwin, 145 g, 1972	1,314—Harmon Killebrew	1,121 (1997)
	Fewest—22—Brian Harper, 140 g, 1992		Fewest—684 (1978)
Hit by pitch	19—Chuck Knoblauch, 153 g, 1996	74— Chuck Knoblauch	65 (1996)
			Fewest—21 (1980)
Runs batted in	140—Harmon Killebrew, 162 g, 1969	1,325—Harmon Killebrew	812 (1996)
			Fewest—522 (1968)
Grounded into	28—Harmon Killebrew, 157 g, 1970	210—Harmon Killebrew	172 (11996)
double plays	Fewest—2—Cesar Tovar, 157 g, 1968		Fewest—93 (1965)
Left on base			1,263 (1974)
			Fewest—1,041 (1987)
Batting average	.388—Rod Carew, 155 g, 1977	.334—Rod Carew	.288 (1996)
			Lowest—.237 (1968)
Most .300 hitters			3 (1977, 1988, 1992, 1996, 2003)
Slugging average	.606—Harmon Killebrew, 150 g, 1961	.518—Harmon Killebrew	.437 (2002)
			Lowest—.338 (1981)
On-base percentage	.449—Rod Carew, 155 g, 1977	.393—Rod Carew	.357 (1996)
			Lowest—.293 (1981)

BASERUNNING

Stolen bases	62—Chuck Knoblauch, 156 g, 1997	276—Chuck Knoblauch	151 (1997)
Caught stealing	22—Rod Carew, 156 g, 1976	123—Rod Carew	75 (1976)

PITCHING

Games	90—Mike Marshall, 1979	639—Eddie Guardado	
Games started	42—Jim Kaat, 1965	422—Jim Kaat	
Complete games	25—Bert Blyleven, 1973	141—Bert Blyleven	58 (1963, 1967)
Wins	25—Jim Kaat, 1966	189—Jim Kaat	
Percentage	.774—Frank Viola (24-7), 1988	.587—Jim Perry	
Winning streak	13—Johan Santana, 2004		
20-win seasons		2—Camilo Pascual, Jim Perry	
Losses	20—Pedro Ramos, 1961	152—Jim Kaat	
Losing streak	13—Terry Felton, 1982		
Saves	45—Eddie Guardado, 2002	254—Rick Aguilera	58 (1970)
Innings	325—Bert Blyleven, 1973	2,959.1—Jim Kaat	1,497.2 (1969)
Hits	296—Bert Blyleven, 1973	2,927—Jim Kaat	1,634 (2000)
Runs	141—Frank Viola, 1983	1,295—Jim Kaat	900 (1996)
Earned runs	129—LaTroy Hawkins, 1999	1,080—Jim Kaat	844 (1996)
Bases on balls	127—Jim Hughes, 1975	694—Jim Kaat	643 (1982)
Strikeouts	265—Johan Santana, 2004	2,035—Bert Blyleven	1,123 (2004)

	Individual		Club
	Season	Career	Season
Strikeouts, game	15—Camilo Pascual, Jul 19, 1961, 1st game		
	Joe Decker, Jun 26, 1973		
	Jerry Koosman, Jun 23, 1980		
	Bert Blyleven, Aug 1, 1986		
Hit batsmen	18—Jim Katt, 1962	89—Jim Kaat	56 (2001)
Wild pitches	15—Dave Goltz, 1976	104—Jim Kaat	73 (1964)
	Mike Smithson, 1986		
	Jack Morris, 1991		
	Johan Santana, 2002		
Home runs	50—Bert Blyleven, 1986	270—Jim Kaat	233 (1996)
Sacrifice hits	17—Dean Chance, 1968	104—Jim Kaat	76 (1964, 1978)
	Jerry Koosman, 1980		
Sacrifice flies	13—Bert Blyleven, 1973	79—Jim Kaat	68 (1998)
	Scott Erickson, 1993		
Earned run average	2.45—Allan Anderson, 202.1 inn, 1988	3.15—Jim Perry	2.84 (1972)
Shutouts	9—Bert Blyleven, 1973	29—Bert Blyleven	18 (1967, 1973)
			Lost—14 (1964, 1972, 1990)
1-0 games won	3—Bert Blyleven, 1971	8—Bert Blyleven	5 (1966)
			Lost—5 (1974)

TEAM FIELDING

Putouts	4,493 (1969)	**Assists**	2,007 (1979)
	Fewest—4,198 (1972)		Fewest—1,422 (2002)
Chances accepted	6,349 (1969)	**Errors**	174 (1961)
	Fewest—5,756 (12002)		Fewest—74 (2002)
Double plays	203 (1979)	**Passed balls**	21 (1987, 1993)
	Fewest—114 (2003)		Fewest—4 (1984, 2001)
Errorless games	103 (2002)	**Fielding average**	.987 (2002)
	Consecutive—12 (2002)		Lowest—.972 (1961)

MISCELLANEOUS

Most players, season 46 (1995)
Fewest players, season 31 (1976)
Games won 102 (1965)
  Month 23 (Jul 1969)
  Consecutive 15 (1991)
Winning percentage .630 (1965), 102-60
  Lowest .370 (1982), 60-102
Number of league championships 3
  Most recent 1991
Runs, game 24 vs Detroit, Apr 24, 1996
  Opponents' 23 by Kansas City, Apr 6, 1974

Hits, game 25 vs Cleveland, Jun 4, 2002
  vs Boston, Jun 20, 1980
Home runs, game 8 vs Washington, Aug 29, 1963, 1st game
Runs, shutout 16 vs Boston, May 25, 1990
  Opponents' 17 by California, Apr 23, 1980
Longest 1-0 win 13 inn, vs Texas, Sept 22, 1992

Most seasons, non-pitcher 15—Tony Oliva
Most seasons, pitcher 13—Jim Kaat
Games lost 102 (1982)
  Month 26 (May 1982)
  Consecutive 14 (1982)
Overall record 3,482-3,505 (44 seasons)
  Interleague play 71-67
Number of times worst record in league 4 (inc. 1 tie)
  Most recent 2000
Runs, inning 11 vs Cleveland, Jul 18, 1962, 1st
  vs Oakland, Jun 21, 1969, 10th
  vs Cleveland, Aug 5, 1977, 4th
  vs Boston, May 20, 1994, 5th
Total bases, game 47 vs Washington, Aug 29, 1963, 1st game

Consecutive games with one or more home runs 16 (28 hrs), 1979
Longest shutout 13 inn, 1-0 vs Texas, Sept 22, 1992

Longest 1-0 loss 15 inn, vs Kansas City, May 23, 1981

ATTENDANCE

Highest home attendance		**Largest crowds**	
Metropolitan Stadium	1,483,547 (1967)	Day	53,106 vs Kansas City, Sept 27, 1987
Metrodome	3,030,672 (1988)	Night	53,067 vs Toronto, Apr 8, 1988
		Doubleheader	51,017 vs Oakland, Jul 28, 1990
Highest road attendance	2,332,786 (1988)	Home opener	53,067 vs Toronto, Apr 8, 1988

NEW YORK YANKEES
YEARLY FINISHES

(Original American League franchise moved from Baltimore to New York after the 1902 season)

Year	Position	W	L	Pct.	GB	Manager	Attendance
1903	4th	72	62	.537	17.0	Clark Griffith	211,808
1904	2nd	92	59	.609	1.5	Clark Griffith	438,919
1905	6th	71	78	.477	21.5	Clark Griffith	309,100
1906	2nd	90	61	.596	3.0	Clark Griffith	434,709
1907	5th	70	78	.473	21.0	Clark Griffith	350,020
1908	8th	51	103	.331	39.5	Clark Griffith, Kid Elberfeld	305,500
1909	5th	74	77	.490	23.5	George Stallings	501,000
1910	2nd	88	63	.583	14.5	George Stallings, Hal Chase	355,857
1911	6th	76	76	.500	25.5	Hal Chase	302,444
1912	8th	50	102	.329	55.0	Harry Wolverton	242,194
1913	7th	57	94	.377	38.0	Frank Chance	357,551
1914	6th (tied)	70	84	.455	30.0	Frank Chance, Roger Peckinpaugh	359,477
1915	5th	69	83	.454	32.5	Bill Donovan	256,035
1916	4th	80	74	.519	11.0	Bill Donovan	469,211
1917	6th	71	82	.464	28.5	Bill Donovan	330,294
1918	4th	60	63	.488	13.5	Miller Huggins	282,047
1919	3rd	80	59	.576	7.5	Miller Huggins	619,164
1920	3rd	95	59	.617	3.0	Miller Huggins	1,289,422
1921	1st (s)	98	55	.641	+4.5	Miller Huggins	1,230,696
1922	1st (s)	94	60	.610	+1.0	Miller Huggins	1,026,134
1923	1st (S)	98	54	.645	+16.0	Miller Huggins	1,007,066
1924	2nd	89	63	.586	2.0	Miller Huggins	1,053,533
1925	7th	69	85	.448	30.0	Miller Huggins	697,267
1926	1st (s)	91	63	.591	+3.0	Miller Huggins	1,027,095
1927	1st (S)	110	44	.714	+19.0	Miller Huggins	1,164,015
1928	1st (S)	101	53	.656	+2.5	Miller Huggins	1,072,132
1929	2nd	88	66	.571	18.0	Miller Huggins, Art Fletcher	960,148
1930	3rd	86	68	.558	16.0	Bob Shawkey	1,169,230
1931	2nd	94	59	.614	13.5	Joe McCarthy	912,437
1932	1st (S)	107	47	.695	+13.0	Joe McCarthy	962,320
1933	2nd	91	59	.607	7.0	Joe McCarthy	728,014
1934	2nd	94	60	.610	7.0	Joe McCarthy	854,682
1935	2nd	89	60	.597	3.0	Joe McCarthy	657,508
1936	1st (S)	102	51	.667	+19.5	Joe McCarthy	976,913
1937	1st (S)	102	52	.662	+13.0	Joe McCarthy	998,148
1938	1st (S)	99	53	.651	+9.5	Joe McCarthy	970,916
1939	1st (S)	106	45	.702	+17.0	Joe McCarthy	859,785
1940	3rd	88	66	.571	2.0	Joe McCarthy	988,975
1941	1st (S)	101	53	.656	+17.0	Joe McCarthy	964,722
1942	1st (s)	103	51	.669	+9.0	Joe McCarthy	988,251
1943	1st (S)	98	56	.636	+13.5	Joe McCarthy	645,006
1944	3rd	83	71	.539	6.0	Joe McCarthy	822,864
1945	4th	81	71	.533	6.5	Joe McCarthy	881,846
1946	3rd	87	67	.565	17.0	Joe McCarthy, Bill Dickey, Johnny Neun	2,265,512
1947	1st (S)	97	57	.630	+12.0	Bucky Harris	2,178,937
1948	3rd	94	60	.610	2.5	Bucky Harris	2,373,901
1949	1st (S)	97	57	.630	+1.0	Casey Stengel	2,281,676
1950	1st (S)	98	56	.636	+3.0	Casey Stengel	2,081,380
1951	1st (S)	98	56	.636	+5.0	Casey Stengel	1,950,107
1952	1st (S)	95	59	.617	+2.0	Casey Stengel	1,629,665
1953	1st (S)	99	52	.656	+8.5	Casey Stengel	1,537,811
1954	2nd	103	51	.669	8.0	Casey Stengel	1,475,171
1955	1st (s)	96	58	.623	+3.0	Casey Stengel	1,490,138
1956	1st (S)	97	57	.630	+9.0	Casey Stengel	1,491,784
1957	1st (s)	98	56	.636	+8.0	Casey Stengel	1,497,134
1958	1st (S)	92	62	.597	+10.0	Casey Stengel	1,428,438
1959	3rd	79	75	.513	15.0	Casey Stengel	1,552,030
1960	1st (s)	97	57	.630	+8.0	Casey Stengel	1,627,349

1961	1st (S)	109	53	.673	+8.0	Ralph Houk	1,747,725
1962	1st (S)	96	66	.593	+5.0	Ralph Houk	1,493,574
1963	1st (s)	104	57	.646	+10.5	Ralph Houk	1,308,920
1964	1st (s)	99	63	.611	+1.0	Yogi Berra	1,305,638
1965	6th	77	85	.475	25.0	Johnny Keane	1,213,552
1966	10th	70	89	.440	26.5	Johnny Keane, Ralph Houk.	1,124,648
1967	9th	72	90	.444	20.0	Ralph Houk	1,259,514
1968	5th	83	79	.512	20.0	Ralph Houk	1,185,666

EAST DIVISION

Year	Position	W	L	Pct.	GB	Manager	Attendance
1969	5th	80	81	.497	28.5	Ralph Houk	1,067,996
1970	2nd	93	69	.574	15.0	Ralph Houk	1,136,879
1971	4th	82	80	.506	21.0	Ralph Houk	1,070,771
1972	4th	79	76	.510	6.5	Ralph Houk	966,328
1973	4th	80	82	.494	17.0	Ralph Houk	1,262,103
1974	2nd	89	73	.549	2.0	Bill Virdon	1,273,075
1975	3rd	83	77	.519	12.0	Bill Virdon, Billy Martin	1,288,048
1976	1st (C,s)	97	62	.610	+10.5	Billy Martin	2,012,434
1977	1st (C,S)	100	62	.617	+2.5	Billy Martin	2,103,092
1978	1st (P,C,S)	100	63	.613	+1.0	Billy Martin, Bob Lemon	2,335,871
1979	4th	89	71	.556	13.5	Bob Lemon, Billy Martin	2,537,765
1980	1st (c)	103	59	.636	+3.0	Dick Howser	2,627,417
1981	1st/6th (I,C,s)	59	48	.551	*	Gene Michael, Bob Lemon	1,614,533
1982	5th	79	83	.488	16.0	Bob Lemon, Gene Michael, Clyde King	2,041,219
1983	3rd	91	71	.562	7.0	Billy Martin	2,257,976
1984	3rd	87	75	.537	17.0	Yogi Berra	1,821,815
1985	2nd	97	64	.602	2.0	Yogi Berra, Billy Martin	2,214,587
1986	2nd	90	72	.556	5.5	Lou Piniella	2,268,030
1987	4th	89	73	.549	9.0	Lou Piniella	2,427,672
1988	5th	85	76	.528	3.5	Billy Martin, Lou Piniella	2,633,701
1989	5th	74	87	.460	14.5	Dallas Green, Bucky Dent	2,170,485
1990	7th	67	95	.414	21.0	Bucky Dent, Stump Merrill	2,006,436
1991	5th	71	91	.438	20.0	Stump Merrill	1,863,733
1992	4th (tied)	76	86	.469	20.0	Buck Showalter	1,748,733
1993	2nd	88	74	.543	7.0	Buck Showalter	2,410,905
1994	1st (n)	70	43	.619	+6.5	Buck Showalter	1,675,556
1995	2nd (d)	79	65	.549	7.0	Buck Showalter	1,705,263
1996	1st (D,C,S)	92	70	.568	+4.0	Joe Torre	2,250,877
1997	2nd (d)	96	66	.593	2.0	Joe Torre	2,580,325
1998	1ot (D,C,O)	114	48	.704	+22.0	Joe Torre	2,949,734
1999	1st (D,C,S)	98	64	.605	+4.0	Joe Torre	3,292,736
2000	1st (D,C,S)	87	74	.540	+2.5	Joe Torre	3,227,657
2001	1st (D,C,s)	95	65	.594	+13.5	Joe Torre	3,264,777
2002	1st (d)	103	58	.640	+10.5	Joe Torre	3,461,644
2003	1st (D,C,s)	101	61	.623	+6.0	Joe Torre	3,465,585
2004	1st (D,c)	101	61	.623	+3.0	Joe Torre	3,775,292

(s) lost World Series; (S) won World Series; (C) won League Championship Series; (P) won division playoff; (c) lost League Championship Series; (I) won intra-divisional playoff; *first half 34-22, second half 25-26; (n) no World Series; (d) lost Division Series; (D) won Division Series

INDIVIDUAL AND CLUB RECORDS
BATTING

	Individual		Club
	Season	**Career**	**Season**
Games	163—Hideki Matsui, 2003	2,401—Mickey Mantle	164 (1964, 1968)
At-bats	696—Alfonso Soriano, 156 g, 2002	8,102—Mickey Mantle	5,710 (1997)
Runs	177—Babe Ruth, 152 g, 1921	1,959—Babe Ruth	1,067 (1931)
			Fewest—459 (1908)
Hits	238—Don Mattingly, 162 g, 1986	2,721—Lou Gehrig	1,683 (1930)
			Fewest—1,137 (1968)
Hitting streak	56 g—Joe DiMaggio, 1941		
Singles	171—Steve Sax, 158 g, 1989	1,531—Lou Gehrig	1,157 (1931)
Doubles	53—Don Mattingly, 162 g, 1986	534—Lou Gehrig	325 (199)

Triples	23—Earle Combs, 152 g, 1927	163—Lou Gehrig	110 (1930)

HOME RUNS

			242 (2004)
			Fewest—8 (1913)
Righthander	46—Joe DiMaggio, 151 g, 1937	361—Joe DiMaggio	
Lefthander	61—Roger Maris, 161 g, 1961	659—Babe Ruth	
Switch-hitter	54—Mickey Mantle, 153 g, 1961	536—Mickey Mantle	
Rookie	29—Joe DiMaggio, 138 g, 1936		
Home	32—Babe Ruth, 1921	334—Babe Ruth	117 (2000)
Road	32—Babe Ruth, 1927	325—Babe Ruth	128 (1961)
Month	17—Babe Ruth, Sept 1927		54 (Jul 1940, Aug 1998)
Pinch	4—Johnny Blanchard, 1961	9—Yogi Berra	10 (1961)
Grand slams	6—Don Mattingly, 141 g, 1987	23—Lou Gehrig	10 (1987)
Home runs at Hilltop Park, all teams			48 (1904)
Home runs at the Polo Grounds, all teams			117 (1921)
Home runs at Yankee Stadium, all teams			209 (2000)

Total bases	457—Babe Ruth, 152 g, 1921	5,131—Babe Ruth	2,703 (1936)
Extra base hits	119—Babe Ruth, 152 g, 1921	1,190—Lou Gehrig	580 (1936)
Sacrifice hits	42—Willie Keeler, 149 g, 1905	225—Wally Pipp	178 (1906)
Sacrifice flies	17—Roy White, 147 g, 1971	96—Don Mattingly	72 (1974, 1996)
Bases on balls	170—Babe Ruth, 152 g, 1923	1,852—Babe Ruth	766 (1932)
			Fewest—288 (1908)
Strikeouts	157—Alfonso Soriano, 156 g, 2002	1,710—Mickey Mantle	1,171 (2002)
	Fewest—12—Yogi Berra, 151 g, 1950		Fewest—420 (1924)
Hit by pitch	24—Don Baylor, 142 g, 1985	114—Frankie Crosetti	81 (2003)
			Fewest—14 (1969)
Runs batted in	184—Lou Gehrig, 155 g, 1931	1,995—Lou Gehrig	995 (1936)
			Fewest—372 (1908)
Grounded into	30—Dave Winfield, 152 g, 1983	193—Bernie Williams	157 (2004)
double plays	Fewest—2—Mickey Mantle, 153 g, 1961		Fewest—91 (1963)
Left on base			1,276 (1997)
			Fewest—1,010 (1920)
Batting average	.393—Babe Ruth, 152 g, 1923	.349—Babe Ruth	.309 (1930)
			Lowest—.214 (1968)
Most .300 hitters			9 (1930)
Slugging average	.847—Babe Ruth, 142 g, 1920	.711—Babe Ruth	.489 (1927)
			Lowest—.287 (1914)
On-base percentage	.545—Babe Ruth, 152 g, 1923	.484—Babe Ruth	.384 (1930)
			Lowest—.283 (1908)

BASERUNNING

Stolen bases	93—Rickey Henderson, 140 g, 1988	326—Rickey Henderson	289 (1910)
Caught stealing	23—Ben Chapman, 149 g, 1931	117—Babe Ruth	82 (1920)

PITCHING

Games	86—Paul Quantrill, 2004	586—Mariano Rivera	
Games started	51—Jack Chesbro, 1904	438—Whitey Ford	
Complete games	48—Jack Chesbro, 1904	261—Red Ruffing	123 (1904)
Wins	41—Jack Chesbro, 1904	236—Whitey Ford	
Percentage	.893—Ron Guidry (25-3), 1978	.717—Spud Chandler	
Winning streak	16—Roger Clemens, 2001		
20-win seasons		4—Bob Shawkey	
		Lefty Gomez	
		Red Ruffing	
Losses	21—Al Orth, 1907	139—Mel Stottlemyre Sr.	
	Sam Jones, 1925		

	Individual		Club
	Season	**Career**	**Season**
	Joe Lake, 1908		
	Russ Ford, 1912		
Losing streak	11—George Mogridge, 1916		
Saves	50—Mariano Rivera, 2001	334—Mariano Rivera	59 (2004)
Innings	454—Jack Chesbro, 1904	3,170.1—Whitey Ford	1,506.2 (1964)
Hits	340—Jack Powell, 1904	2,995—Red Ruffing	1,566 (1930)
Runs	165—Russ Ford, 1912	1,406—Red Ruffing	898 (1930)
Earned runs	127—Sam Jones, 1925	1,222—Red Ruffing	753 (2000)
Bases on balls	179—Tommy Byrne, 1949	1,090—Lefty Gomez	812 (1949)
Strikeouts	248—Ron Guidry, 1978	1,956—Whitey Ford	1,266 (2001)
Strikeouts, game	18—Ron Guidry, Jun 17, 1978		
Hit batsmen	26—Jack Warhop, 1909	114—Jack Warhop	71 (1908)
Wild pitches	23—Tim Leary, 1990	75—Whitey Ford	83 (1990)
Home runs	40—Ralph Terry, 1962	228—Whitey Ford	179 (1987)
Sacrifice hits	23—Ed Lopat, 1948	239—Waite Hoyt	202 (1926)
Sacrifice flies	15—Doc Medich, 1975	65—Ron Guidry	59 (1982, 1983)
Earned run average	1.64—Spud Chandler, 253 inn, 1943	2.58—Jack Chesbro	2.57 (1904)
Shutouts	9—Ron Guidry, 1978	45—Whitey Ford	24 (1951)
			Lost—27 (1914)
1-0 games won	2—many pitchers	7—Whitey Ford	6 (1908, 1968)
		Bob Shawkey	Lost—9 (1914)

TEAM FIELDING

Putouts	4,520 (1964)	**Assists**	2,086 (1904)
	Fewest—3,993 (1935)		Fewest—1,487 (2000)
Chances accepted	6,377 (1968)	**Errors**	386 (1912)
	Fewest—5,551 (1935)		Fewest—91 (1996)
Double plays	214 (1956)	**Passed balls**	32 (1913)
	Fewest—81 (1912)		Fewest—0 (1931)
Errorless games	94 (1996)	**Fielding average**	.986 (1995)
	Consecutive—10 (1977, 1993, 1995)		Lowest—.939 (1912)

MISCELLANEOUS

Most players, season 49 (1989, 2003)

Fewest players, season 25 (1923, 1927)
Games won 114 (1998)
  Month 28 (Aug 1938)
  Consecutive 19 (1947)
Winning percentage .714 (1927), 110-44
  Lowest .329 (1912), 50-102
Number of league championships 39
  Most recent 2003
Runs, game 25 vs Philadelphia, May 24, 1936
  Opponents' 24 by Cleveland, Jul 29, 1928
Hits, game 30 vs Boston, Sept 28, 1923
Home runs, game 8 vs Philadelphia, Jun 28, 1939, 1st game
Runs, shutout 21 vs Philadelphia, Aug 13, 1939, 2nd game, 8 inn
  Opponents' 22 by Cleveland, Aug 31, 2004
Longest 1-0 win 15 inn, vs Philadelphia, Jul 4, 1925, 1st game

Most seasons, non-pitcher 18—Yogi Berra
      Mickey Mantle
Most seasons, pitcher 16—Whitey Ford
Games lost 103 (1908)
  Month 24 (Jul 1908)
  Consecutive 13 (1913)
  Overall record 8,979-6,809 (102 seasons)
  Interleague play 82-56
Number of times worst record in league 5
  Most recent 1990
Runs, inning 14 vs Washington, Jul 6, 1920, 5th

Total bases, game 53 vs Philadelphia, Jun 28, 1939, 1st game
Consecutive games with one or more home runs 25 (40 hrs), 1941
Longest shutout unknown

Longest 1-0 loss 14 inn, vs Boston, Sept 24, 1969

ATTENDANCE

Highest home attendance		**Largest crowds**	
Hilltop Park	501,000 (1909)	Day	73,205 vs Philadelphia, Apr 19, 1931
Polo Grounds	1,289,422 (1920)	Night	74,747 vs Boston, May 26, 1947
Yankee Stadium	3,775,292 (2004)	Doubleheader	81,841 vs Boston, May 30, 1938
Highest road attendance	2,940,048 (2002)	Home opener	51,145 vs Oakland, Apr 10, 1998

OAKLAND ATHLETICS
YEARLY FINISHES

(Original American League franchise moved from Philadelphia to Kansas City after the 1954 season
and to Oakland after the 1967 season)

Year	Position	W	L	Pct.	GB	Manager	Attendance
1968	6th	82	80	.506	21.0	Bob Kennedy	837,466

WEST DIVISION

Year	Position	W	L	Pct.	GB	Manager	Attendance
1969	2nd	88	74	.543	9.0	Hank Bauer, John McNamara	778,232
1970	2nd	89	73	.549	9.0	John McNamara	778,355
1971	1st (c)	101	60	.627	+16.0	Dick Williams	914,993
1972	1st (C,S)	93	62	.600	+5.5	Dick Williams	921,323
1973	1st (C,S)	94	68	.580	+6.0	Dick Williams	1,000,763
1974	1st (C,S)	90	72	.556	+5.0	Alvin Dark	845,693
1975	1st (c)	98	64	.605	+7.0	Alvin Dark	1,075,518
1976	2nd	87	74	.540	2.5	Chuck Tanner	780,593
1977	7th	63	98	.391	38.5	Jack McKeon, Bobby Winkles	495,599
1978	6th	69	93	.426	23.0	Bobby Winkles, Jack McKeon	526,999
1979	7th	54	108	.333	34.0	Jim Marshall	306,763
1980	2nd	83	79	.512	14.0	Billy Martin	842,259
1981	1st/2nd (I,c)	64	45	.587	*	Billy Martin	1,304,054
1982	5th	68	94	.420	25.0	Billy Martin	1,735,489
1983	4th	74	88	.457	25.0	Steve Boros	1,294,941
1984	4th	77	85	.475	7.0	Steve Boros, Jackie Moore	1,353,281
1985	4th (tied)	77	85	.475	14.0	Jackie Moore	1,334,599
1986	3rd (tied)	76	86	.469	16.0	Jackie Moore, Tony La Russa	1,314,646
1987	3rd	81	81	.500	4.0	Tony La Russa	1,678,921
1988	1st (C,s)	104	58	.642	+13.0	Tony La Russa	2,287,335
1989	1st (C,S)	99	63	.611	+7.0	Tony La Russa	2,667,225
1990	1st (C,s)	103	59	.636	+9.0	Tony La Russa	2,900,217
1991	4th	84	78	.519	11.0	Tony La Russa	2,713,493
1992	1st (c)	96	66	.593	+6.0	Tony La Russa	2,494,160
1993	7th	68	94	.420	26.0	Tony La Russa	2,035,025
1994	2nd	51	63	.447	1.0	Tony La Russa	1,242,692
1995	4th	67	77	.465	11.5	Tony La Russa	1,174,310
1996	3rd	78	84	.481	12.0	Art Howe	1,148,380
1997	4th	65	97	.401	25.0	Art Howe	1,264,218
1998	4th	74	88	.457	14.0	Art Howe	1,232,339
1999	2nd	87	75	.537	8.0	Art Howe	1,434,610
2000	1st (d)	91	70	.565	+0.5	Art Howe	1,728,888
2001	2nd (d)	102	60	.630	14.0	Art Howe	2,133,277
2002	1st (d)	103	59	.636	+4.0	Art Howe	2,169,811
2003	1st (d)	96	66	.593	+3.0	Ken Macha	2,216,596
2004	2nd	91	71	.562	1.0	Ken Macha	2,201,516

(c) lost League Championship Series; (C) won League Championship Series; (S) won World Series; (I) won intra-divisional playoff; *first half 37-23, second 27-22; (d) lost Division Series

INDIVIDUAL AND CLUB RECORDS
BATTING

	Individual		Club
	Season	**Career**	**Season**
Games	162—Sal Bando, 1968, 1969, 1973	1,704—Rickey Henderson	163 (1968)
	Alfredo Griffin, 1985, 1986		
	Terrence Long, 2001, 2002		
	Miguel Tejada, 2001, 2002, 2003		
At-bats	662—Miguel Tejada, 162 g, 2002	6,140—Rickey Henderson	5,728 (2004)
Runs	123—Reggie Jackson, 152 g, 1969	1,270—Rickey Henderson	947 (2000)
			Fewest—532 (1978)
Hits	204—Miguel Tejada, 162 g, 2002	1,768—Rickey Henderson	1,545 (2004)
			Fewest—1,276 (1979)
Hitting streak	25 g—Jason Giambi, 1997		
Singles	153—Carney Lansford, 148 g, 1989	1,271—Rickey Henderson	1,061 (1983)
Doubles	47—Jason Giambi, 154 g, 2001	289—Rickey Henderson	336 (2004)
Triples	12—Phil Garner, 159 g, 1976	41—Rickey Henderson	40 (1968)

HOME RUNS

			243 (1996)
			Fewest—94 (1968)
Righthander	52—Mark McGwire, 130 g, 1996	363—Mark McGwire	
Lefthander	47—Reggie Jackson, 152 g, 1969	268—Reggie Jackson	
Switch-hitter	23—Ruben Sierra, 110 g, 1994	60—Ruben Sierra	

	Individual		Club
	Season	**Career**	**Season**
Rookie	49—Mark McGwire, 151 g, 1987		
Home	27—Jason Giambi, 2001	166—Mark McGwire	126 (2000)
Road	28—Mark McGwire, 1987, 1996	197—Mark McGwire	130 (1996)
	Jose Canseco, 1991		
Month	15—Mark McGwire, May 1987		55 (Jun 1996, Aug 1999)
Pinch	4—Jeff Burroughs, 1982	5—Mike Aldrete	8 (1970)
		Jeff Burroughs	
		Mark McGwire	
		Terry Steinbach	
Grand slams	4—Jason Giambi, 152 g, 2000	9—Mark McGwire	14 (2000)
Home runs at Network Associates Coliseum, all teams			215 (1996)
			(inc. 23 at Las Vegas)
Total bases	347—Jose Canseco, 158 g, 1988	2,640—Reggie Jackson	2,546 (1996)
Extra base hits	87—Jason Giambi, 154 g, 2001	563—Mark McGwire	555 (2001)
Sacrifice hits	22—Dwayne Murphy, 159 g, 1980	101—Bert Campaneris	108 (1978)
Sacrifice flies	14—Dave Kingman, 147 g, 1984	59—Mark McGwire	77 (1984)
Bases on balls	137—Jason Giambi, 152 g, 2000	1,227—Rickey Henderson	770 (1999)
			Fewest—433 (1978)
Strikeouts	175—Jose Canseco, 157 g, 1986	1,180—Reggie Jackson	1,181 (1997)
	Fewest—31—Felipe Alou, 154 g, 1970		Fewest—751 (1979)
Hit by pitch	20—Don Baylor, 157 g, 1976	59—Sal Bando	88 (2001)
			Fewest—16 (1985)
Runs batted in	137—Jason Giambi, 152 g, 2000	941—Mark McGwire	908 (2000)
			Fewest—492 (1978)
Grounded into	32—Ben Grieve, 158 g, 2000	137—Terry Steinbach	163 (1989)
double plays	Fewest—3—Reggie Jackson, 154 g, 1968		Fewest—87 (1968)
Left on base			1,274 (2004)
			Fewest—1,030 (1979)
Batting average	.342—Jason Giambi, 154 g, 2001	.308—Jason Giambi	.270 (2000, 2004)
			Lowest—.236 (1982)
Most .300 hitters			2 (1988)
Slugging average	.730—Mark McGwire, 130 g, 1996	.551—Mark McGwire	.458 (2000)
			Lowest—.343 (1968)
On base percentage	.477—Jason Giambi, 154 g, 2001	.409—Rickey Henderson	.360 (2000)
			Lowest—.302 (1979)

BASERUNNING

Stolen bases	130—Rickey Henderson, 149 g, 1982	867—Rickey Henderson	341 (1976)
Caught stealing	42—Rickey Henderson, 149 g, 1982	219—Rickey Henderson	123 (1976)

PITCHING

Games	84—Billy Koch, 2002	525—Dennis Eckersley	
Games started	41—Catfish Hunter, 1974	262—Vida Blue	
Complete games	28—Rick Langford, 1980	105—Vida Blue	94 (1980)
Wins	27—Bob Welch, 1990	131—Catfish Hunter	
Percentage	.821—Barry Zito (23-5), 1990	.630—Catfish Hunter	
Winning streak	13—Catfish Hunter, 1973		
20-win seasons		4—Catfish Hunter	
		Dave Stewart	
Losses	20—Brian Kingman, 1980	105—Rick Langford	
Losing streak	14—Matt Keough, 1979		
Saves	51—Dennis Eckersley, 1992	320—Dennis Eckersley	64 (1988, 1990)
Innings	318—Catfish Hunter, 1974	1,946—Vida Blue	1,489.1 (1988)
Hits	284—Vida Blue, 1977	1,650—Vida Blue	1,734 (1997)
Runs	144—Matt Keough, 1982	784—Dave Stewart	943 (1996)
Earned runs	133—Matt Keough, 1982	712—Dave Stewart	880 (1997)
Bases on balls	112—John Odom, 1969	655—Dave Stewart	680 (1993)
Strikeouts	301—Vida Blue, 1971	1,315—Vida Blue	1,117 (2001)
Strikeouts, game	17—Vida Blue, Jul 9, 1971 (pitched first 11 inn of 20-inn game)		
	16—Jose Rijo, Apr 19, 1986 (pitched first 8 inn of 9-inn game)		

	Individual		Club
	Season	**Career**	**Season**
Hit batsmen	13—Barry Zito, 2001	46—Tim Hudson	64 (1997)
Wild pitches	22—Mike Moore, 1992	78—Dave Stewart	72 (1979)
Home runs	39—Catfish Hunter, 1973	207—Catfish Hunter	205 (1996)
Sacrifice hits	17—Bob Lacey, 1977	77—Vida Blue	92 (1978)
Sacrifice flies	15—Dave Stewart, 1991	64—Dave Stewart	80 (1997)
Earned run average	1.82—Vida Blue, 312 inn, 1971	2.94—Vida Blue	2.58 (1972)
Shutouts	8—Vida Blue, 1971	28—Vida Blue	23 (1972)
			Lost—19 (1978)
1-0 games won	2—Vida Blue, 1971	3—Vida Blue	5 (1971)
	Catfish Hunter, 1971		Lost—5 (1971, 1978)
	Mike Torrez, 1976, 1978		

TEAM FIELDING

Putouts	4,468 (1988)	**Assists**	1,821 (1976)
	Fewest—4,288 (1979)		Fewest—1,508 (1984)
Chances accepted	6,230 (1969)	**Errors**	190 (1977)
	Fewest—5,798 (1984)		Fewest—87 (1990)
Double plays	195 (1997)	**Passed balls**	26 (1969)
	Fewest—115 (1980)		Fewest—4 (2001)
Errorless games	97 (2004)	**Fielding average**	.986 (1990, 2004)
	Consecutive—12 (2002)		Lowest—.970 (1977)

MISCELLANEOUS

Most players, season 49 (1997)
Fewest players, season 34 (1968, 1980)

Games won 104 (1988)
Month 24 (Aug 2002)
Consecutive 20 (2002)
Winning percentage .642 (1988), 104-58
Lowest .333 (1979), 54-108
Number of league championships 6
Most recent 1990
Runs, game 23 vs Texas, Sept 30, 2000
Opponents' 20 by Minnesota, Apr 27, 1980
by Cleveland, May 4, 1991
by Detroit, Apr 13, 1993
Hits, game 25 vs Boston, Jun 14, 1969
(29 vs Texas, Jul 1, 1979, 15 inn)
Home runs, game 8 vs California, Jun 27, 1996
Runs, shutout 15 vs Baltimore, Aug 30, 2001
Opponents' 16 by Kansas City, Jun 25, 1984
Longest 1-0 win 20 inn, vs California, Jul 9, 1971

Most seasons, non-pitcher 14—Rickey Henderson
Most seasons, pitcher 10—Rick Langford
Mike Norris
Curt Young
Games lost 108 (1979)
Month 24 (Jun 1979)
Consecutive 14 (1977)
Overall record 3,067-2,797 (37 seasons)
Interleague play 85-55
Number of times worst record in league 2
Most recent 1997
Runs, inning 13 vs California, Jul 5, 1996, 1st
vs Chicago, May 12, 1997, 7th

Total bases, game 44 vs California, Jun 27, 1996

Consecutive games with one or more home runs 23 (50 hrs), 1996
Longest shutout 16 inn, 3-0 vs Chicago, Sept 22, 1975

Longest 1-0 loss 13 inn, vs Detroit, May 25, 1973

ATTENDANCE

Highest home attendance	2,900,217 (1990)	**Largest crowds**	
		Day	55,413 vs San Francisco N.L., Jun 22, 2003
Highest road attendance	2,636,157 (1991)	**Night**	55,601 vs Anaheim, Jul 5, 2003
		Doubleheader	48,592 vs New York, May 3, 1981
		Home opener	53,498 vs Detroit, Apr 3, 2000

PHILADELPHIA ATHLETICS
YEARLY FINISHES

(Original American League franchise moved to Kansas City after the 1954 season)

Year	Position	W	L	Pct.	GB	Manager	Attendance
1901	4th	74	62	.544	9.0	Connie Mack	206,329
1902	1st	83	53	.610	+5.0	Connie Mack	442,473
1903	2nd	75	60	.556	14.5	Connie Mack	420,078
1904	5th	81	70	.536	12.5	Connie Mack	512,294
1905	1st (s)	92	56	.622	+2.0	Connie Mack	554,576
1906	4th	78	67	.538	12.0	Connie Mack	489,129
1907	2nd	88	57	.607	1.5	Connie Mack	625,581
1908	6th	68	85	.444	22.0	Connie Mack	455,062

Year	Position	W	L	Pct.	GB	Manager	Attendance
1909	2nd	95	58	.621	3.5	Connie Mack	674,915
1910	1st (S)	102	48	.680	+14.5	Connie Mack	588,905
1911	1st (S)	101	50	.669	+13.5	Connie Mack	605,749
1912	3rd	90	62	.592	15.0	Connie Mack	517,653
1913	1st (S)	96	57	.627	+6.5	Connie Mack	571,896
1914	1st (s)	99	53	.651	+8.5	Connie Mack	346,641
1915	8th	43	109	.283	58.5	Connie Mack	146,223
1916	8th	36	117	.235	54.5	Connie Mack	184,471
1917	8th	55	98	.359	44.5	Connie Mack	221,432
1918	8th	52	76	.406	24.0	Connie Mack	177,926
1919	8th	36	104	.257	52.0	Connie Mack	225,209
1920	8th	48	106	.312	50.0	Connie Mack	287,888
1921	8th	53	100	.346	45.0	Connie Mack	344,430
1922	7th	65	89	.422	29.0	Connie Mack	425,356
1923	6th	69	83	.454	29.0	Connie Mack	534,122
1924	5th	71	81	.467	20.0	Connie Mack	531,992
1925	2nd	88	64	.579	8.5	Connie Mack	869,703
1926	3rd	83	67	.553	6.0	Connie Mack	714,308
1927	2nd	91	63	.591	19.0	Connie Mack	605,529
1928	2nd	98	55	.641	2.5	Connie Mack	689,756
1929	1st (S)	104	46	.693	+18.0	Connie Mack	839,176
1930	1st (S)	102	52	.662	+8.0	Connie Mack	721,663
1931	1st (s)	107	45	.704	+13.5	Connie Mack	627,464
1932	2nd	94	60	.610	13.0	Connie Mack	405,500
1933	3rd	79	72	.523	19.5	Connie Mack	297,138
1934	5th	68	82	.453	31.0	Connie Mack	305,847
1935	8th	58	91	.389	34.0	Connie Mack	233,173
1936	8th	53	100	.346	49.0	Connie Mack	285,173
1937	7th	54	97	.358	46.5	Connie Mack	430,733
1938	8th	53	99	.349	46.0	Connie Mack	385,357
1939	7th	55	97	.362	51.5	Connie Mack	395,022
1940	8th	54	100	.351	36.0	Connie Mack	432,145
1941	8th	64	90	.416	37.0	Connie Mack	528,894
1942	8th	55	99	.357	48.0	Connie Mack	423,487
1943	8th	49	105	.318	49.0	Connie Mack	376,735
1944	5th (tied)	72	82	.468	17.0	Connie Mack	505,322
1945	8th	52	98	.347	34.5	Connie Mack	462,631
1946	8th	49	105	.318	55.0	Connie Mack	621,793
1947	5th	78	76	.506	19.0	Connie Mack	911,566
1948	4th	84	70	.545	12.5	Connie Mack	945,076
1949	5th	81	73	.526	16.0	Connie Mack	816,514
1950	8th	52	102	.338	46.0	Connie Mack	309,805
1951	6th	70	84	.455	28.0	Jimmie Dykes	465,469
1952	4th	79	75	.513	16.0	Jimmie Dykes	627,100
1953	7th	59	95	.383	41.5	Jimmie Dykes	362,113
1954	8th	51	103	.331	60.0	Ed Joost	304,666

(s) lost World Series; (S) won World Series

INDIVIDUAL AND CLUB RECORDS
BATTING

	Individual		Club
	Season	Career	Season
Games	157—Dave Philley, 1953	1,702—Jimmie Dykes	158 (1914)
At-bats	670—Al Simmons, 154 g, 1932	6,023—Jimmie Dykes	5,537 (1932)
Runs	152—Al Simmons, 138 g, 1930	997—Bob Johnson	981 (1932)
			Fewest—447 (1916)
Hits	253—Al Simmons, 153 g, 1925	1,827—Al Simmons	1,659 (1925)
	Fewest—1,131 (1908)		
Hitting streak	29 g—Bill Lamar, 1925		
Singles	174—Al Simmons, 153 g, 1925	1,181—Jimmie Dykes	1,206 (1925)
Doubles	53—Al Simmons, 147 g, 1926	365—Jimmie Dykes	323 (1928)
Triples	21—Home Run Baker, 149 g, 1912	102—Danny Murphy	108 (1912)

HOME RUNS

			172 (1932)
			Fewest—76 (1925)
Righthander	58—Jimmie Foxx, 154 g, 1932	302—Jimmie Foxx	
Lefthander	27—Joe Hauser, 149 g, 1924	108—Mickey Cochrane	
Switch-hitter	9—Dave Philley, 157 g, 1953	23—Dave Philley	
Rookie	21—Bob Johnson, 142 g, 1933		
Home	31—Jimmie Foxx, 1932	169—Jimmie Foxx	109 (1932)
	Jimmie Foxx, 1933		

	Individual		Club
	Season	**Career**	**Season**
Road	27—Jimmie Foxx, 1932	133—Jimmie Foxx	67 (1953)
Month	15—Bob Johnson, June 1934		34 (Jun 1932, Jul 1932, Jun 1934)
Pinch	3—Allie Clark, 1952 Kite Thomas, 1952	3—Allie Clark Frankie Hayes Kite Thomas Tilly Walker	6 (1952)
Grand slams	3—Jimmie Foxx, 154 g, 1932 Jimmie Foxx, 150 g, 1934 Bob Johnson, 152 g, 1938 Gus Zernial, 145 g, 1952	9—Jimmie Foxx Sam Chapman	8 (1932)
Home runs at Columbia Park, all teams			34 (1902)
Home runs at Shibe Park, all teams			189 (1932)
Total bases	438—Jimmie Foxx, 154 g, 1932	2,998—Al Simmons	2,529 (1932)
Extra base hits	100—Jimmie Foxx, 154 g, 1932	655—Al Simmons	527 (1932)
Sacrifice hits	43—Roy Grover, 141 g, 1917	188—Jimmie Dykes	248 (1909)
Sacrifice flies	7—Joe DeMaestri, 146 g, 1954	7—Joe DeMaestri	31 (1954)
Bases on balls	149—Ed Joost, 144 g, 1949	1,043—Max Bishop	783 (1949) Fewest—268 (1903)
Strikeouts	110—Ed Joost, 151 g, 1947 Fewest—7—Mickey Cochrane, 126 g, 1927	706—Jimmie Dykes	677 (1954) Fewest—293 (1902)
Hit by pitch	15—Eddie Collins, 132 g, 1911	87—Jimmie Dykes	65 (1911, 1913) Fewest—5 (1937)
Runs batted in	169—Jimmie Foxx, 154 g, 1932	1,178—Al Simmons	923 (1932) Fewest—380 (1916)
Grounded into double plays	29—Dave Philley, 151 g, 1952 Fewest—4—Wally Moses, 142 g, 1938 Wally Moses, 142 g, 1940 Eddie Joost, 135 g, 1948 Dave Philley, 125 g, 1951	157—Pete Suder	170 (1950) Fewest—105 (1945)
Left on base			1,235 (1949) Fewest—999 (1924)
Batting average	.426—Nap Lajoie, 131 g, 1901	.356—Al Simmons	.307 (1925) Lowest—.223 (1908)
Most .300 hitters			11 (1927)
Slugging average	.749—Jimmie Foxx, 154 g, 1932	.640—Jimmie Foxx	.457 (1932) Lowest—.292 (1908)
On-base percentage	.469—Jimmie Foxx, 154 g, 1932	.440—Jimmie Foxx	.372 (1927) Lowest—.281 (1908)

BASERUNNING

Stolen bases	81—Eddie Collins, 153 g, 1910	376—Eddie Collins	258 (1912)
Caught stealing	32—Eddie Murphy, 148 g, 1914	70—Amos Strunk	188 (1914)

PITCHING

Games	58—Morrie Martin, 1953	524—Eddie Plank	
Games started	46—Rube Waddell, 1904	459—Eddie Plank	
Complete games	39—Rube Waddell, 1904	362—Eddie Plank	136 (1904)
Wins	31—Jack Coombs, 1910 Lefty Grove, 1931	284—Eddie Plank	
Percentage	.886—Lefty Grove (31-4), 1931	.712—Lefty Grove	
Winning streak	16—Lefty Grove, 1931		
20-win seasons		7—Eddie Plank Lefty Grove	
Losses	25—Scott Perry, 1920	162—Eddie Plank	
Losing streak	19—Jack Nabors, 1916		
Innings	383—Rube Waddell, 1904	3,860.2—Eddie Plank	1421.2 (1910)
Hits	360—Jack Coombs, 1911	3,438—Eddie Plank	1,687 (1939)
Runs	210—Chick Fraser, 1901	1,374—Eddie Plank	1,045 (1936)

	Individual		Club
	Season	**Career**	**Season**
Earned runs	146—George Earnshaw, 1930	1,025—Eddie Plank	913 (1936)
Bases on balls	168—Elmer Myers, 1916	913—Eddie Plank	827 (1915)
Strikeouts	349—Rube Waddell, 1904	1,985—Eddie Plank	895 (1905)
Strikeouts, game	14—Rube Waddell, Jul 14, 1903		
	Rube Waddell, Sept 6, 1904, 1st game		
	Rube Waddell, Aug 2, 1905		
	(18—Jack Coombs, Sept 1, 1906, 24 inn		
	Jack Coombs, Aug 4, 1910, 16 inn)		
Hit batsmen	32—Chick Fraser, 1901	185—Eddie Plank	81 (1911)
Wild pitches	16—Stu Flythe, 1936	80—Eddie Plank	68 (1915)
Home runs	29—Lynn Nelson, 1938	138—Eddie Rommel	148 (1939)
Sacrifice hits	54—Eddie Rommel, 1923	343—Eddie Plank	217 (1921)
Sacrifice flies	17—Arnie Portocarrero, 1954	17—Arnie Portocarrero	69 (1954)
Earned run average	1.30—Jack Coombs, 353 inn, 1910	1.97—Rube Waddell	1.79 (1910)
Shutouts	13—Jack Coombs, 1910	59—Eddie Plank	27 (1907, 1909-plus 1 tie)
			Lost—24 (1943)
1-0 games won	4—Harry Krause, 1909	12—Eddie Plank	9 (1909)
			Lost—7 (1908, 1909)

TEAM FIELDING

Putouts	4,255 (1910)	**Assists**	2,173 (1920)
	Fewest—3,600 (1901)		Fewest—1,594 (1946)
Chances accepted	6,293 (1920)	**Errors**	338 (1915)
	Fewest—5,601 (1938)		Fewest—113 (1948)
Double plays	217 (1949)	**Passed balls**	25 (1914)
	Fewest—64 (1905)		Fewest—5 (1947)
Errorless games	unknown	**Fielding average**	.981 (1948)
	Consecutive—7 (1951)		Lowest—.942 (1901)

MISCELLANEOUS

Most players, season 56 (1915)
Fewest players, season 19 (1905)
Games won 107 (1931)
  Month 28 (Jul 1931)
  Consecutive 17 (1931)
Winning percentage .704 (1931), 107-45
  Lowest .235 (1916), 36-117
Number of league championships 9
  Most recent 1931
Runs, game 24 vs Detroit, May 18, 1912
    vs Boston, May 1, 1929
  Opponents' 25 by Cleveland, May 11, 1930
    by New York, May 24, 1936
Hits, game 29 vs Boston, May 1, 1929
Home runs, game 7 vs Detroit, Jun 3, 1921
Runs, shutout 16 vs Chicago, Jul 25, 1928, 1st game
    vs Chicago, Aug 29, 1937, 1st game
  Opponents' 21 by New York, Aug 13, 1939, 2nd game, 8 inn
Longest 1-0 win 13 inn, vs Detroit, Aug 11, 1902
    vs Boston, Sept 10, 1904
    vs Chicago, May 16, 1909
    vs Cleveland, May 14, 1914

Most seasons, non-pitcher 16—Harry Davis
Most seasons, pitcher 14—Eddie Plank
Games lost 117 (1916)
  Month 28 (Jul 1916)
  Consecutive 20 (1916, 1943)
Overall record 3,886-4,248 (54 seasons)

Number of times worst record in league 18
  Most recent 1954
Runs, inning 13 vs Cleveland, Jun 15, 1925, 8th

Total bases, game 44 vs Boston, May 1, 1929
Consecutive games with one or more home runs 12 (20 hrs), 1951
  Longest shutout unknown

Longest 1-0 loss 16 inn, vs St. Louis, Jun 5, 1942

ATTENDANCE

Highest home attendance		**Largest crowds**	
Columbia Park	625,076 (1907)	Day	37,534 vs New York, May 16, 1937
Shibe Park	945,076 (1948)	Night	37,383 vs New York, Jun 27, 1947
		Doubleheader	38,800 vs New York, Jul 13, 1931
Highest road attendance	1,562,360 (1948)	Home opener	32,825 vs New York, Apr 20, 1927

ST. LOUIS BROWNS
YEARLY FINISHES

(Original American League franchise moved from Milwaukee to St. Louis after the 1901 season

and to Baltimore after the 1953 season)

Year	Position	W	L	Pct.	GB	Manager	Attendance
1902	2nd	78	58	.574	5.0	Jimmy McAleer	272,283
1903	6th	65	74	.468	26.5	Jimmy McAleer	380,405
1904	6th	65	87	.428	29.0	Jimmy McAleer	318,108
1905	8th	54	99	.353	40.5	Jimmy McAleer	339,112
1906	5th	76	73	.510	16.0	Jimmy McAleer	389,157
1907	6th	69	83	.454	24.0	Jimmy McAleer	419,025
1908	4th	83	69	.546	6.5	Jimmy McAleer	618,947
1909	7th	61	89	.407	36.0	Jimmy McAleer	366,274
1910	8th	47	107	.305	57.0	Jack O'Connor	249,889
1911	8th	45	107	.296	56.5	Bobby Wallace	207,984
1912	7th	53	101	.344	53.0	Bobby Wallace, George Stovall	214,070
1913	8th	57	96	.373	39.0	George Stovall, Branch Rickey	250,330
1914	5th	71	82	.464	28.5	Branch Rickey	244,714
1915	6th	63	91	.409	39.5	Branch Rickey	150,358
1916	5th	79	75	.513	12.0	Fielder Jones	335,740
1917	7th	57	97	.370	43.0	Fielder Jones	210,486
1918	5th	58	64	.475	15.0	Fielder Jones, Jimmy Austin, Jimmy Burke	122,076
1919	5th	67	72	.482	20.5	Jimmy Burke	349,350
1920	4th	76	77	.497	21.5	Jimmy Burke	419,311
1921	3rd	81	73	.526	17.5	Lee Fohl	355,978
1922	2nd	93	61	.604	1.0	Lee Fohl	712,918
1923	5th	74	78	.487	24.0	Lee Fohl, Jimmy Austin	430,296
1924	4th	74	78	.487	17.0	George Sisler	533,349
1925	3rd	82	71	.536	15.0	George Sisler	462,898
1926	7th	62	92	.403	29.0	George Sisler	283,986
1927	7th	59	94	.386	50.5	Dan Howley	247,879
1928	3rd	82	72	.532	19.0	Dan Howley	339,497
1929	4th	79	73	.520	26.0	Dan Howley	280,697
1930	6th	64	90	.416	38.0	Bill Killefer	152,088
1931	5th	63	91	.409	45.0	Bill Killefer	179,126
1932	6th	63	91	.409	44.0	Bill Killefer	112,558
1933	8th	55	96	.364	43.5	Bill Killefer, Allen Sothoron, Rogers Hornsby	88,113
1934	6th	67	85	.441	33.0	Rogers Hornsby	115,305
1935	7th	65	87	.428	28.5	Rogers Hornsby	80,922
1936	7th	57	95	.375	44.5	Rogers Hornsby	93,267
1937	8th	46	108	.299	56.0	Rogers Hornsby, Jim Bottomley	123,121
1938	7th	55	97	.362	44.0	Gabby Street	130,417
1939	8th	43	111	.279	64.5	Fred Haney	109,159
1940	6th	67	87	.435	23.0	Fred Haney	239,591
1941	6th (tied)	70	84	.455	31.0	Fred Haney, Luke Sewell	176,240
1942	3rd	82	69	.543	19.5	Luke Sewell	255,617
1943	6th	72	80	.474	25.0	Luke Sewell	214,392
1944	1st (s)	89	65	.578	+1.0	Luke Sewell	508,644
1945	3rd	81	70	.536	6.0	Luke Sewell	482,986
1946	7th	66	88	.429	38.0	Luke Sewell, Zack Taylor	526,435
1947	8th	59	95	.383	38.0	Muddy Ruel	320,474
1948	6th	59	94	.386	37.0	Zack Taylor	335,546
1949	7th	53	101	.344	44.0	Zack Taylor	270,936
1950	7th	58	96	.377	40.0	Zack Taylor	247,131
1951	8th	52	102	.338	46.0	Zack Taylor	293,790
1952	7th	64	90	.416	31.0	Rogers Hornsby, Marty Marion	518,796
1953	8th	54	100	.351	46.5	Marty Marion	297,238

(s) lost World Series

INDIVIDUAL AND CLUB RECORDS
BATTING

	Individual		Club
	Season	Career	Season
Games	159—Del Pratt, 1915	1,647—George Sisler	159 (1914, 1915)
At-bats	671—Jack Tobin, 150 g, 1921	6,667—George Sisler	5,510 (1937)
Runs	145—Harlond Clift, 152 g, 1936	1,091—George Sisler	900 (1925)
			Fewest—441 (1909)
Hits	257—George Sisler, 154 g, 1920	2,295—George Sisler	1,693 (1922)
			Fewest—1,105 (1910)

	Individual		Club
	Season	**Career**	**Season**
Hitting streak	41 g—George Sisler, 1922		
Singles	179—Jack Tobin, 150 g, 1921	1,714—George Sisler	1,239 (1920)
Doubles	51—Beau Bell, 156 g, 1937	343—George Sisler	327 (1937)
Triples	20—Heinie Manush, 154 g, 1928 George Stone, 154 g, 1906	145—George Sisler	106 (1921)

HOME RUNS

			98 (1922)
			Fewest—10 (1904, 1907, 1909)
Righthander	34—Harlond Clift, 149 g, 1938	170—Harlond Clift	
Lefthander	39—Ken Williams, 153 g, 1922	185—Ken Williams	
Switch-hitter	14—Lu Blue, 154 g, 1928	24—Lu Blue	
Rookie	24—Wally Judnich, 137 g, 1940		
Home	32—Ken Williams, 1922	137—Ken Williams	73 (1925)
Road	16—Goose Goslin, 1930	82—Harlond Clift	54 (1950, 1953)
Month	15—Harlond Clift, Aug 1938		36 (Jun 1940)
Pinch	2—Hank Arft, 1951 Pat Collins, 1922 Pat Collins, 1923 Les Moss, 1950	4—Pat Collins	4 (1950, 1951)
Grand slams	2—many players	5—Ken Williams Harlond Clift Vern Stephens	5 (1922, 1940, 1950)
Home runs at Sportman's Park, all teams			146 (1925)
Total bases	399—George Sisler, 154 g, 1920	3,207—George Sisler	2,466 (1922)
Extra base hits	86—George Sisler, 154 g, 1920	581—George Sisler	482 (1922, 1925)
Sacrifice hits	48—Joe Gedeon, 153 g, 1920	222—Jimmy Austin	223 (1908)
Bases on balls	126—Lu Blue, 151 g, 1929	986—Harlond Clift	775 (1941) Fewest—271 (1903)
Strikeouts	120—Gus Williams, 143 g, 1914 Fewest—9—Hank Severeid, 143 g, 1921	649—Harlond Clift	863 (1914) Fewest—339 (1920)
Hit by pitch	18—Dick Padden, 132 g, 1904	40—George Sisler	56 (190-4) Fewest—12 (1931)
Runs batted in	155—Ken Williams, 153 g, 1922	959—George Sisler	798 (1925) Fewest—347 (1910)
Grounded into double plays	21—Glenn McQuillen, 100 g, 1942 Fewest—1—George McQuinn, 146 g, 1944	66—John Berardino	151 (1951) Fewest—93 (1944)
Left on base			1,334 (1941) Fewest—1,055 (1951)
Batting average	.420—George Sisler, 142 g, 1922	.344—George Sisler	.313 (1922) Lowest—.218 (1910)
Most .300 hitters			8 (1922)
Slugging average	.632—George Sisler, 154 g, 1920	.558—Ken Williams	.455 (1922) Lowest—.274 (1910)
On-base percentage	.467—George Sisler, 142 g, 1922	.403—Ken Williams	.372 (1922) Lowest—.281 (1910)

BASERUNNING

Stolen bases	51—George Sisler, 142 g, 1922	351—George Sisler	234 (1916)
Caught stealing	32—Burt Shotton, 156 g, 1915	126—George Sisler	189 (1914)

PITCHING

Games	60—Marlin Stuart, 1953	323—Elam Vangilder	
Games started	40—Bobo Newsom, 1938	264—Jack Powell	
Complete games	36—Jack Powell, 1902	210—Jack Powell	135 (1904)
Wins	27—Urban Shocker, 1922	126—Urban Shocker	
Percentage	.808—Alvin Crowder (21-5), 1928	.612—Urban Shocker	
Winning streak	10—Alvin Crowder, 1928		

	Individual		Club
	Season	Career	Season
Winning streak, two seasons	10—Bill Dinneen, 1907 (1), 1908 (9)		
20-win seasons		4—Urban Shocker	
Losses	25—Fred Glade, 1905	142—Jack Powell	
Losing streak	9—Walter Leverenz, 1913, 1914 Earl Hamilton, 1917		
Losing streak, two seasons	12—Earl Hamilton, 1916 (3), 1917 (9)		
Innings	348—Urban Shocker, 1922	2,229.2—Jack Powell	1,443.2 (1916)
Hits	365—Urban Shocker, 1922	2,083—Jack Powell	1,776 (1936)
Runs	205—Bobo Newsom, 1938	958—George Blaeholder	1,064 (1936)
Earned runs	186—Bobo Newsom, 1938	824—George Blaeholder	935 (1936)
Bases on balls	192—Bobo Newsom, 1938	640—Dixie Davis	801 (1951)
Strikeouts	232—Rube Waddell, 1908	884—Jack Powell	639 (1953)
Strikeouts, game	16—Rube Waddell, Jul 29, 1908 (17—Rube Waddell, Sept 20, 1908, 10 inn)		
Hit batsmen	20—Barney Pelty, 1904	103—Barney Pelty	64 (1915)
Wild pitches	11—Dave Davenport, 1917 Bill James, 1914 Jack Knott, 1936 Carl Weilman, 1913	42—Barney Pelty	47 (1948)
Home runs	30—Bobo Newsom, 1938	142—George Blaeholder	143 (1937)
Sacrifice hits	53—Tom Zachary, 1926	224—Elam Vangilder	258 (1926)
Earned run average	1.59—Barney Pelty, 260.2 inn, 1906	2.06—Harry Howell	2.15 (1908)
Shutouts	6—Fred Glade, 1904 Harry Howell, 1906	27—Jack Powell	21 (1909) Lost—25 (1904, 1906, 1910)
1-0 games won	3—Fred Glade, 1904	6—Jack Powell	6 (1909) Lost—7 (1907)

TEAM FIELDING

Putouts	4,328 (1916) Fewest—3,993 (1911)	**Assists**	2,189 (1910) Fewest—1,584 (1938)
Chances accepted	6,516 (1916) Fewest—5,618 (1972)	**Errors**	378 (1910) Fewest—134 (1947)
Double plays	190 (1948) Fewest—116 (1914)	**Passed balls**	30 (1914, 1915) Fewest—4 (1930, 1933)
Errorless games	unknown Consecutive—8 (1928)	**Fielding average**	.977 (1947) Lowest—.943 (1910)

MISCELLANEOUS

Most players, season 52 (1951)
Fewest players, season 19 (1906)

Games won 93 (1922)
Month 23 (Aug 1945)
Consecutive 14 (1916)
Winning percentage .604 (1922), 93-61
Lowest .279 (1939), 43-111
Number of league championships 1
Most recent 1944
Runs, game 20 vs Detroit, Aug 18, 1951
Opponents' 29 by Boston, Jun 8, 1950
vs Detroit, Aug 18, 1951, 7th
Hits, game 24 vs Philadelphia, Sept 17, 1920
vs Washington, Jun 14, 1932
Home runs, game 5 vs New York, Sept 16, 1940
Runs, shutout 16 vs Detroit, Sept 9, 1922
Opponents' 18 by Detroit, Apr 29, 1935
Longest 1-0 win 16 inn, vs Philadelphia, Jun 5, 1942

Most seasons, non-pitcher 16—Jimmy Austin
Most seasons, pitcher 10—George Blaeholder
Barney Pelty
Jack Powell

Games lost 111 (1939)
Month 24 (Sept 1939, Jul 1952)
Consecutive 14 (1911, 1953)
Overall record 3,414-4,465 (52 seasons)

Number of times worst record in league 11
Most recent 1953
Runs, inning 11 vs Philadelphia, Jul 21, 1949, 1st game, 6th

Total bases, game 40 vs Chicago, May 31, 1925

Consecutive games with one or more home runs 11 (20 hrs), 1922
Longest shutout unknown

Longest 1-0 loss 15 inn, vs Washington, Aug 14, 1903, 1st game
vs Washington, Jul 25, 1918

ATTENDANCE

Highest home attendance	712,918 (1922)	**Largest crowds**	
		Day	34,625 vs New York, Oct 1, 1944
Highest road attendance	1,170,349 (1948)	Night	22,847 vs Cleveland, May 24, 1940
		Doubleheader	31,932 vs New York, Jun 17, 1928
		Home opener	19,561 vs Detroit, Apr 18, 1923

SEATTLE MARINERS
YEARLY FINISHES

(American League expansion franchise)

WEST DIVISION

Year	Position	W	L	Pct.	GB	Manager	Attendance
1977	6th	64	98	.395	38.0	Darrell Johnson	1,338,511
1978	7th	56	104	.350	35.0	Darrell Johnson	877,440
1979	6th	67	95	.414	21.0	Darrell Johnson	844,447
1980	7th	59	103	.364	38.0	Darrell Johnson, Maury Wills	836,204
1981	6th/5th	44	65	.404	*	Maury Wills, Rene Lachemann	636,276
1982	4th	76	86	.469	17.0	Rene Lachemann	1,070,404
1983	7th	60	102	.370	39.0	Rene Lachemann, Del Crandall	813,537
1984	5th (tied)	74	88	.457	10.0	Del Crandall, Chuck Cottier	870,372
1985	6th	74	88	.457	17.0	Chuck Cottier	1,128,696
1986	7th	67	95	.414	25.0	Chuck Cottier, Marty Martinez, Dick Williams	1,029,045
1987	4th	78	84	.481	7.0	Dick Williams	1,134,255
1988	7th	68	93	.422	35.5	Dick Williams, Jim Snyder	1,022,398
1989	6th	73	89	.451	26.0	Jim Lefebvre	1,298,443
1990	5th	77	85	.475	26.0	Jim Lefebvre	1,509,727
1991	5th	83	79	.512	12.0	Jim Lefebvre	2,147,905
1992	7th	64	98	.395	32.0	Bill Plummer	1,651,398
1993	4th	82	80	.506	12.0	Lou Piniella	2,051,853
1994	3rd	49	63	.438	2.0	Lou Piniella	1,104,206
1995	1st (P,D,c)	79	66	.545	+1.0	Lou Piniella	1,643,203
1996	2nd	85	76	.528	4.5	Lou Piniella	2,723,850
1997	1st (d)	90	72	.556	+6.0	Lou Piniella	3,192,237
1998	3rd	76	85	.472	11.5	Lou Piniella	2,644,166
1999	3rd	79	83	.488	16.0	Lou Piniella	2,916,346
2000	2nd (D,c)	91	71	.562	0.5	Lou Piniella	3,148,317
2001	1st (D,c)	116	46	.716	+14.0	Lou Piniella	3,507,975
2002	3rd	93	69	.574	10.0	Lou Piniella	3,540,482
2003	2nd	93	69	.574	3.0	Bob Melvin	3,268,864
2004	4th	63	99	.389	29.0	Bob Melvin	2,940,731

*first half 21-36, second half 23-29; (P) won division playoff; (D) won Division Series, (c) lost League Championship Series; (d) lost Division Series

INDIVIDUAL AND CLUB RECORDS
BATTING

	Individual		Club
	Season	**Career**	**Season**
Games	162—Ruppert Jones, 1979 Willie Horton, 1979	2,055—Edgar Martinez	163 (1980)
At-bats	704—Ichiro Suzuki, 161 g, 2004	7,213—Edgar Martinez	5,722 (2004)
Runs	141—Alex Rodriguez, 146 g, 1996	1,219—Edgar Martinez	993 (1996) Fewest—558 (1983)
Hits	262—Ichiro Suzuki, 161 g, 2004	2,247—Edgar Martinez	1,637 (2001) Fewest—1,280 (1983)
Hitting streak	24 g—Joey Cora, 1997		
Singles	225—Ichiro Suzuki, 161 g, 2004	1,409—Edgar Martinez	1,120 (2001)
Doubles	54—Alex Rodriguez, 146 g, 1996	514—Edgar Martinez	343 (1996)
Triples	11—Harold Reynolds, 158 g, 1988	48—Harold Reynolds	52 (1979)

HOME RUNS

			264 (1997) Fewest—97 (1978)
Righthander	44—Jay Buhner, 150 g, 1996	309—Edgar Martinez	
Lefthander	56—Ken Griffey Jr., 157 g, 1997 Ken Griffey Jr., 161 g, 1998	398—Ken Griffey	
Switch-hitter	19—David Segui, 143 g, 1998	29—Carlos Guillen	
Rookie	27—Alvin Davis, 152 g, 1984		

	Individual		Club
	Season	**Career**	**Season**
Home	30—Ken Griffey Jr., 1998	212—Ken Griffey Jr.	131 (1997)
Road	29—Ken Griffey Jr., 1997	186—Ken Griffey Jr.	133 (1997)
Month	15—Ken Griffey Jr., May 1994		58 (May 1999)
Pinch	2—Greg Briley, 1992	4—Ken Phelps	5 (1994, 1996)
	Gary Gray, 1981		
	Ken Phelps, 1986		
	Leon Roberts, 1978		
	Paul Sorrento, 1997		
Grand slams	4—Edgar Martinez, 153 g, 2000	12—Ken Griffey Jr.	11 (1996, 2000)
Home runs at Kingdome, all teams			237 (1996)
Home runs at Safeco Field, all teams			179 (2004)
Total bases	393—Ken Griffey Jr., 157 g, 1997	3,718—Edgar Martinez	2,741 (1996)
Extra base hits	93—Ken Griffey Jr., 157 g, 1997	838—Edgar Martinez	607 (1996)
Sacrifice hits	15—Craig Reynolds, 135 g, 1977	85—Dan Wilson	106 (1980)
	Larry Milbourne, 106 g, 1980		
Sacrifice flies	13—Bret Boone, 158 g, 2001	77—Edgar Martinez	72 (2002)
	Mike Cameron, 150 g, 2001		
Bases on balls	123—Edgar Martinez, 139 g, 1996	1,283—Edgar Martinez	775 (2000)
			Fewest—426 (1977)
Strikeouts	176—Mike Cameron, 158 g, 2002	1,375—Jay Buhner	1,148 (1986)
	Fewest—34—Harold Reynolds, 160 g, 1987		Fewest—702 (1978)
Hit by pitch	17—Dave Valle, 135 g, 1993	89—Edgar Martinez	75 (1996)
			Fewest—19 (1980)
Runs batted in	147—Ken Griffey Jr., 157 g, 1997	1,261—Edgar Martinez	954 (1996)
			Fewest—536 (1983)
Grounded into double plays	29—Jim Presley, 155 g, 1985	190—Edgar Martinez	158 (1979)
	Fewest—3—Ichiro Suzuki, 157 g, 2001		Fewest—101 (1984)
	Ichiro Suzuki, 159 g, 2003		
Left on base			1,257 (2001)
			Fewest—1,034 (1983)
Batting average	.372—Ichiro Suzuki, 116 g, 2004	.312—Edgar Martinez	.288 (2001)
			Lowest—.240 (1983)
Most .300 hitters			4 (1997, 2001)
Slugging average	.646—Ken Griffey Jr., 157 g, 1997	.569—Ken Griffey Jr.	.485 (1997)
			Lowest—.356 (1980)
On-base percentage	.479—Edgar Martinez, 145 g, 1995	.418—Edgar Martinez	.366 (1996)
			Lowest—.301 (1983)

BASERUNNING

	Individual Season	Career	Club Season
Stolen bases	60—Harold Reynolds, 160 g, 1987	290—Julio Cruz	174 (1987, 2001)
Caught stealing	29—Harold Reynolds, 158 g, 1988	120—Harold Reynolds	82 (1982)

PITCHING

	Individual Season	Career	Club Season
Games	78—Ed Vande Berg, 1982	383—Jeff Nelson	
Games started	37—Mike Moore, 1986	266—Randy Johnson	
		Jamie Moyer	
Complete games	14—Mike Moore, 1985	56—Mike Moore	39 (1987)
	Mark Langston, 1987		
Wins	21—Jamie Moyer, 2003	130—Randy Johnson	
Percentage	.900—Randy Johnson (18-2), 1995	.649—Jamie Moyer	
Winning streak	10—Paul Abbott, 2001		
	Jamie Moyer, 2001		
Winning streak, two seasons	12—Randy Johnson, 1995 (7), 1996 (5)		
Winning streak, three seasons	16—Randy Johnson, 1995 (7), 1996 (5), 1997 (4)		
20-win seasons		2—Jamie Moyer	
Losses	19—Matt Young, 1985	96—Mike Moore	
	Mike Moore, 1987		

	Individual		Club
	Season	**Career**	**Season**
Losing streak	16—Mike Parrott, 1980		
Saves	45—Kazuhiro Sasaki, 1991	129—Kazuhiro Sasaki	56 (2001)
Innings	272—Mark Langston, 1987	1,838.1—Randy Johnson	1,476.1 (1982)
Hits	279—Mike Moore, 1986	1,696—Jamie Moyer	1,613 (1999)
Runs	145—Mike Moore, 1987	811—Jamie Moyer	943 (1996)
Earned runs	129—Mark Langston, 1986	751—Jamie Moyer	834 (1999)
Bases on balls	152—Randy Johnson, 1991	884—Randy Johnson	684 (1999)
Strikeouts	308—Randy Johnson, 1993	2,162—Randy Johnson	1,207 (1997)
Strikeouts, game	19—Randy Johnson, Jun 24, 1997		
	Randy Johnson, Aug 8, 1997		
Hit batsmen	18—Randy Johnson, 1992	89—Randy Johnson	72 (2004)
Wild pitches	16—Matt Young, 1990	66—Randy Johnson	82 (1991)
Home runs	44—Jamie Moyer, 2004	208—Jamie Moyer	216 (1996)
Sacrifice hits	15—Shane Rawley, 1980	49—Randy Johnson	75 (1979, 1980)
Sacrifice flies	14—Rich DeLucia, 1991	42—Randy Johnson	64 (1978)
		Jamie Moyer	
Earned run average	2.28—Randy Johnson, 213 inn, 1997	3.42—Randy Johnson	3.54 (2001)
Shutouts	4—Dave Fleming, 1992	19—Randy Johnson	15 (2003)
	Randy Johnson, 1992		Lost—15 (1978, 1983, 1990)
1-0 games won	1—many pitchers	3—Mark Langston	3 (1979, 2002)
			Lost—4 (1980, 1989, 1990)

TEAM FIELDING

Putouts	4,429 (1982)	**Assists**	1930 (1980)
	Fewest—4,255 (1982)		Fewest—1,450 (2003)
Chances accepted	6,302 (1980)	**Errors**	156 (1986)
	Fewest—5,773 (2003)		Fewest—65 (2003)
Double plays	191 (1986)	**Passed balls**	24 (1991)
	Fewest—134 (2002)		Fewest—3 (1997)
Errorless games	112 (2003)	**Fielding average**	.989 (2003)
	Consecutive—11 (1993)		Lowest—.975 (1986)

MISCELLANEOUS

Most players, season 51 (1999)
Fewest players, season 34 (1978, 1980)
Games won 116 (2001)
  Month 20 (Jun 1997, Apr 2001, May 2001, Aug 2001)
  Consecutive 15 (2001)
Winning percentage .716 (2001), 116-46
  Lowest .350 (1978), 56-104
Number of league championships 0
  Most recent ---
Runs, game 22 vs Detroit, Apr 29, 1999
  Opponents 20 by Detroit, Apr 17, 1993
Hits, game 24 vs Minnesota, Jun 11, 1996
  Anaheim, Sept 22, 2004
  (24 vs Boston, Sept 3, 1981, 20 inn)
Home runs, game 7 vs Oakland, Apr 11, 1985
  vs Milwaukee, Jul 31, 1996
  vs Anaheim, Jul 5, 1999
  vs Chicago, May 2, 2002
Runs, shutout 14 vs California, Aug 7, 1987
  vs Minnesota, May 15, 2000
  vs Baltimore, Sept 16, 2000
  Opponents' 15 by Minnesota, Jul 10, 1977
Longest 1-0 win none over 9 inn

Most seasons, non-pitcher 18—Edgar Martinez
Most seasons, pitcher 10—Randy Johnson
Games lost 104 (1978)
  Month 22 (Aug 1977)
  Consecutive 14 (1992)
Overall record 2,080-2,331 (28 seasons)
  Interleague play 74-66
Number of times worst record in league 5
  Most recent 1992
Runs, inning 11 vs Detroit, Apr 29, 1999, 5th
  vs Chicago, May 12, 1997, 7th
Total bases, game 44 vs Toronto, Apr 16, 2000

Consecutive games with one or more home runs 19 (29 hrs), 1999

Longest shutout unknown

Longest 1-0 loss 12 inn, vs Texas, Jun 29, 1988

ATTENDANCE

Highest home attendance
  Kingdome — 3,192,237 (1997)
  Safeco Field — 3,540,482 (2002)

Highest road attendance — 2,572,882 (2001)

Largest crowds
  Day — 57,822 vs Cleveland, Mar 31, 1998
  Night — 57,806 vs Minnesot, Apr 11, 1994
  Doubleheader — 32,597 vs California, Aug 12, 1985
  Home opener — 57,822 vs Cleveland, Mar 31, 1998

SEATTLE PILOTS
YEARLY FINISH

(American League expansion franchise moved to Milwaukee after the 1969 season)

WEST DIVISION

Year	Position	W	L	Pct.	GB	Manager	Attendance
1969	6th	64	98	.395	33	Joe Schultz	677,944

INDIVIDUAL AND CLUB RECORDS
BATTING

	Individual	Club
	Season	**Season**
Games	148—Tommy Harper	163
At-bats	537—Tommy Harper, 148 g	5,444
Runs	88—Wayne Comer, 147 g	639
Hits	126—Tommy Harper, 148 g	1,276
Hitting streak	18 g—Tommy Davis	
Singles	105—Tommy Harper, 148 g	945
Doubles	29—Tommy Davis, 123 g	179
Triples	6—Mike Hegan, 95 g	27

HOME RUNS

		125
Righthander	15—Wayne Comer, 147 g	
Lefthander	25—Don Mincher, 140	
Switch-hitter	none	
Rookie	15—Wayne Comer	
Home	13—Don Mincher	74
Road	12—Don Mincher	51
Month	8—Don Mincher, Jul	28 (May)
Pinch	1—Greg Goossen	4
	Mike Hegan	
	Don Mincher	
	Jim Pagliaroni	
Grand slams	1—Don Mincher, 140 g	3
	Rich Rollins, 58 g	
	Fred Talbot, 27 g	
Home runs at Sick's Stadium, all teams		167
Total bases	194—Don Mincher, 140 g	1,884
Extra base hits	39—Don Mincher, 140 g	331
Sacrifice hits	9—Jerry McNertney, 128 g	72
Sacrifice flies	5—Tommy Davis, 123 g	29
Bases on balls	95—Tommy Harper, 148 g	626
Strikeouts	90—Tommy Harper, 148 g	1,015
	Fewest—46—Tommy Davis, 123 g	
Hit by pitch	5—Don Mincher, 140 g	34
	Rich Rollins, 58 g	
Runs batted in	80—Tommy Davis, 123 g	583
Grounded into	17—Tommy Davis, 123 g	111
double plays	Fewest—8—Tommy Harper, 148 g	
Left on base		1,130
Batting average	.271—Tommy Davis, 123 g	.234
Most .300 hitters		none
Slugging average	.454—Don Mincher, 140 g	.346
On-base percentage	.366—Don Mincher, 140 g	.316

BASERUNNING

Stolen bases	73—Tommy Harper, 148 g	167
Caught stealing	18—Tommy Harper, 148 g	59

PITCHING

	Individual Season	Club Season
Games	66—Diego Segui	
Games started	29—Gene Brabender	
Complete games	7—Gene Brabender	21
Wins	13—Gene Brabender	
Percentage	.667—Diego Segui (12-6)	
Winning streak	5—Diego Segui	
20-win seasons	none	
Losses	14—Gene Brabender	
Losing streak	9—John Gelnar	
Saves	12—Diego Segui	33
Innings	202—Gene Brabender	1,463.2
Hits	193—Gene Brabender	1,490
Runs	111—Gene Brabender	799
Earned runs	99—Marty Pattin	707
Bases on balls	103—Gene Brabender	653
Strikeouts	139—Gene Brabender	963
Strikeouts, game	11—Marty Pattin, Apr 29	
Hit batsmen	13—Gene Brabender	47
Wild pitches	8—Jim Bouton	61
Home runs	29—Marty Pattin	172
Sacrifice hits	10—Diego Segui	60
Sacrifice flies	6—Gene Brabender	40
Earned run average	3.36—Diego Segui, 142 inn	4.35
Shutouts	1—held by 5 pitchers	6
1-0 games won	1—Gene Brabender	2
	Marty Pattin	Lost—0

TEAM FIELDING

Putouts	4,391	Assists	1,763
Chances accepted	6,154	Errors	167
Double plays	14	Passed balls	21
Errorless games	66	Fielding average	.974
	Consecutive—4		

MISCELLANEOUS

Players, season 53

Games won 64
  Month 14 (Jun, Sept)
  Consecutive 5
Winning percentage .395 (1969), 64-98
Number of league championships 0
Runs, game 16 vs Washington, May 10
  Opponents' 15 by Baltimore, Aug 16
Hits, game 16 vs Oakland, Sept 10
Hits, extra inn 20 vs Minnesota, Jul 19, 18 inn
Home runs, game 4 vs Boston, May 16, 11 inn
Runs, shutout 8 vs California, Jul 9, 1st game
  Opponents' 10 by Baltimore, Jun 7
Longest 1-0 win none over 9 inn

Games lost 98
  Month 22 (Aug)
  Consecutive 10
Overall record 64-98 (1 season)
Number of times worst record in league 0
Runs, inning 6 vs Boston, May 16, 11th

Total bases, game 31 vs Boston, May 16, 11 inn

Consecutive games with one or more home runs 5 (8 hrs)
Longest shutout none over 9 inn

Longest 1-0 loss none

ATTENDANCE

Highest home attendance	677,944	Largest crowds	
		Day	23,657 vs New York, Aug 3
Highest road attendance	889,578	Night	20,490 vs Baltimore, May 28
		Doubleheader	18,413 vs Kansas City, Jun 20
		Home opener	14,993 vs Chicago, Apr 11

TAMPA BAY DEVIL RAYS
YEARLY FINISHES
(American League expansion franchise)

EAST DIVISION

Year	Position	W	L	Pct.	GB	Manager	Attendance
1998	5th	63	99	.389	51.0	Larry Rothschild	2,506,023
1999	5th	69	93	.426	29.0	Larry Rothschild	1,562,827
2000	5th	69	92	.429	18.0	Larry Rothschild	1,549,052
2001	5th	62	100	.383	34.0	Larry Rothschild, Hal McRae	1,227,673
2002	5th	55	106	.342	48.0	Hal McRae	1,065,762
2003	5th	63	99	.389	38.0	Lou Piniella	1,058,622
2004	4th	70	91	.435	30.5	Lou Piniella	1,275,011

INDIVIDUAL AND CLUB RECORDS
BATTING

	Individual Season	Career	Club Season
Games	162—Aubrey Huff, 2003	582—Aubrey Huff	162 (1998, 1999, 2001, 2003)
At-bats	637—Rocco Baldelli, 156 g, 2003	2,223—Aubrey Huff	5,654 (2003)
Runs	104—Carl Crawford, 152 g, 2004	304—Aubrey Huff	772 (1999) Fewest—620 (1998)
Hits	198—Aubrey Huff, 162 g, 2003	655—Aubrey Huff	1,531 (1999) Fewest—1,414 (2000)
Hitting streak	18 g—Quinton McCracken, 1998		
Singles	145—Carl Crawford, 151 g, 2003	420—Aubrey Huff	1,085 (1999)
Doubles	47—Aubrey Huff, 162 g, 2003	131—Aubrey Huff	333 (2002)
Triples	19—Carl Crawford, 152 g, 2004	34—Carl Crawford	46 (2004)

HOME RUNS

	Individual Season	Career	Club Season
			162 (2000) Fewest—111 (1998)
Righthander	34—Jose Canseco, 113 g, 1999	60—Greg Vaughn	
Lefthander	34—Aubrey Huff, 162 g, 2003	99—Fred McGriff	
Switch-hitter	21—Jose Cruz Jr, 153 g, 2004	24—Randy Winn	
Rookie	12—Bubba Trammell, 59 g, 1998		
Home	18—Fred McGriff, 1999	56—Aubrey Huff	76 (2000)
Road	22—Jose Canseco, 1999	47—Fred McGriff	86 (2000)
Month	10—Jose Canseco, April 1999 Aubrey Huff, May 2003		32 (Aug 2002)
Pinch	3—Bubba Trammell, 2000	4—Bubba Trammell	3 (1998, 2000, 2003)
Grand slams	2—Paul Sorrento, 137 g, 1998 Fred McGriff, 158 g, 2000 Ben Grieve, 154 g, 2001 Greg Vaughn, 136 g, 2001	2—Paul Sorrento Fred McGriff Ben Grieve Greg Vaughn Randy Winn	4 (2000, 2001)
Home runs at Tropicana Field, all teams			185 (2000)

	Individual Season	Career	Club Season
Total bases	353—Aubrey Huff, 162 g, 2003	1,092—Aubrey Huff	2,296 (1999)
Extra base hits	84—Aubrey Huff, 162 g, 2003	235—Aubrey Huff	473 (2003)
Sacrifice hits	12—Felix Martinez, 106 g, 2000	24—Miguel Cairo	53 (1998)
Sacrifice flies	10—John Flaherty, 117 g, 1999	20—John Flaherty	56 (2004)
Bases on balls	91—Fred McGriff, 158 g, 2000	305—Fred McGriff	558 (2000) Fewest—420 (2003)
Strikeouts	159—Ben Grieve, 154 g, 2001 Fewest—44—Miguel Cairo, 150 g, 1998	433—Fred McGriff	1,116 (2001) Fewest—944 (2004)
Hit by pitch	13—Jose Guillen, 105 g, 2000	23—Jose Guillen	64 (1999) Fewest—37 (1998)
Runs batted in	107—Aubrey Huff, 162 g, 2003	359—Fred McGriff	728 (1999) Fewest—579 (1998)
Grounded into double plays	20—Toby Hall, 119 g, 2004 Fewest—2—Carl Crawford, 152 g, 2004	69—Aubrey Huff	157 (1999) Fewest—97 (2004)
Left on base			1,169 (1999) Fewest—1,096 (2004)

	Individual		Club
	Season	**Career**	**Season**
Batting average	.311—Aubrey Huff, 162 g, 2003	.295—Aubrey Huff	.274 (1999)
			Lowest—.253 (2002)
Most .300 hitters			1 (1999, 2003)
Slugging average	.563—Jose Canseco, 113 g, 1999	.491—Aubrey Huff	.411 (1999)
			Lowest—.385 (1998)
On-base percentage	.405—Fred McGriff, 144 g, 1999	.380—Fred McGriff	.343 (1999)
			Lowest—.314 (2002)

BASERUNNING

	Season	**Career**	**Season**
Stolen bases	59—Carl Crawford, 152 g, 2004	123—Carl Crawford	142 (2003)
Caught stealing	15—Carl Crawford, 152 g, 2004	46—Randy Winn	73 (1998)

PITCHING

	Season	**Career**	**Season**
Games	72—Roberto Hernandez, 1999	266—Esteban Yan	
Games started	33—Tanyon Sturtze, 2002	83—Ryan Rupe	
Complete games	5—Joe Kennedy, 2002	6—Joe Kennedy	12 (2002)
Wins	14—Rolando Arrojo, 1998	35—Victor Zambrano	
Percentage	.545—Victor Zambrano (12-10), 2003	none with 1,500 inn	
	(no pitcher with 15 wins in any season)		
Winning streak	6—Victor Zambrano, 2004		
20-win seasons		none	
Losses	18—Tanyon Sturtze, 2002	37—Bryan Rekar	
		Ryan Rupe	
Losing streak	10—Albie Lopez, 2001		
Saves	43—Roberto Hernandez, 1999	101—Roberto Hernandez	45 (1999)
Innings	224.0—Tanyon Sturtze, 2002	495.1—Bryan Rekar	1,443 (1998)
Hits	271—Tanyon Sturtze, 2002	583—Bryan Rekar	1,606 (1999)
Runs	141—Tanyon Sturtze, 2002	327—Ryan Rupe	943 (1996)
Earned runs	129—Tanyon Sturtze, 2002	303—Ryan Rupe	846 (2002)
Bases on balls	111—Tony Saunders, 1998	288—Victor Zambrano	695 (1999)
Strikeouts	172—Tony Saunders, 1998	372—Victor Zambrano	1,055 (1999)
Strikeouts, game	12—Dan Wheeler, Sept 12, 1999		
Hit batsmen	20—Victor Zambrano, 2003	43—Victor Zambrano	95 (2003)
Wild pitches	15—Victor Zambrano, 2003	34—Victor Zambrano	76 (2001)
Home runs	33—Tanyon Sturtze, 2002	77—Ryan Rupe	215 (2002)
Sacrifice hits	7—Bobby Witt, 1999	16—Albie Lopez	42 (1999, 2000)
	Roberto Hernandez, 2000	Esteban Yan	
	Tanyon Sturtze, 2002		
	Victor Zambrano, 2002		
	Travis Harper, 2003		
Sacrifice flies	12—Paul Wilson, 2001	28—Victor Zambrano	65 (2003)
Earned run average	3.56—Rolando Arrojo, 202 inn, 1998	none with 1,500 inn	4.35 (1998)
Shutouts	2—Rolando Arrojo, 1998	2—Rolando Arrojo	8 (2000)
	Bobby Witt, 1999	Albie Lopez	Lost—17 (1998)
		Joe Kennedy	
		Bobby Witt	
1-0 games won	1—Steve Trachsel, 2000	2—Steve Trachsel	3 (2000)
	Joe Kennedy, 2003	Joe Kennedy	Lost—2 (2003)
	Jorge Sosa, 2003	Jorge Sosa	

TEAM FIELDING

Putouts	4,329 (1998)	**Assists**	1,814 (2000)
	Fewest—4,251 (2004)		Fewest—1,530 (2004)
Chances accepted	6,108 (2000)	**Errors**	139 (2001)
	Fewest—5,781 (2004)		Fewest—94 (1998)
Double plays	198 (1999)	**Passed balls**	19 (1998)
	Fewest—139 (2004)		Fewest—8 (2001, 2004)
Errorless games	91 (2003)	**Fielding average**	.985 (1998)
	Consecutive—8 (2003)		Lowest—.977 (2001)

MISCELLANEOUS

Most players, season 51 (2003)

Fewest players, season 42 (1998)

Games won 70 (2004)
  Month 20 (Jun 2004)
  Consecutive 12 (2004)
Winning percentage .435 (2004), 70-91
  Lowest .342 (2002), 55-106
Number of league championships 0
  Most recent ---
Runs, game 19 vs Toronto, Jun 24, 2004
  Opponents 22 by Boston, Jul 23, 2002, a.m. game
Hits, game 24 vs Toronto, Jun 24, 2004

Home runs, game 6 vs Kansas City, Aug 10, 2002
Runs, shutout 10 vs Seattle, Sept 8, 1998
           vs Montreal N.L., Jul 12, 2001
  Opponents' 14 by Toronto, Jul 1, 2004
Longest 1-0 win none over 9 inn

Most seasons, non-pitcher 5—John Flaherty
           Toby Hall
           Aubrey Huff
           Fred McGriff
           Damian Rolls
           Bobby Smith
           Randy Winn
Most seasons, pitcher 5—Travis Harper
           Esteban Yan
Games lost 106 (2002)
  Month 21 (Jun 2003)
  Consecutive 15 (2002)
Overall record 451-680 (7 seasons)
  Interleague play 53-71
Number of times worst record in league 3 (inc. 1 tie)
  Most recent 2002 (tie)
Runs, inning 11 vs Seattle, May 28, 2000, 8th

Total bases, game 37 vs Toronto, Jun 24, 2004
           vs Kansas City, Aug 10, 2002
Consecutive games with one or more home runs 12 (21 hrs), 2003
Longest shutout none over 9 inn

Longest 1-0 loss 12 inn, vs New York, Jun 18, 2003

ATTENDANCE

Highest home attendance   2,261,158 (1998)

Highest road attendance   2,289,235 (2001)

Largest crowds
  Day   43,373 vs New York, Jul 12, 1998
  Night   45,369 vs Detroit, Mar 31, 1998
  Doubleheader   none
  Home opener   45,369 vs Detroit, Mar 31, 1998
           (Devil Rays drew 55,000 to their 2004
           "home opener" in Tokyo, Mar 30)

TEXAS RANGERS
YEARLY FINISHES

(American League expansion franchise moved from Washington to Texas after the 1971 season)

WEST DIVISION

Year	Position	W	L	Pct.	GB	Manager	Attendance
1972	6th	54	100	.351	38.5	Ted Williams	662,974
1973	6th	57	105	.352	37.0	Whitey Herzog, Del Wilber, Billy Martin	686,085
1974	2nd	84	76	.525	5.0	Billy Martin	1,193,902
1975	3rd	79	83	.488	19.0	Billy Martin, Frank Lucchesi	1,127,924
1976	4th (tied)	76	86	.469	14.0	Frank Lucchesi	1,164,982
1977	2nd	94	68	.580	8.0	Frank Lucchesi, Eddie Stanky, Connie Ryan, Billy Hunter	1,250,722
1978	2nd (tied)	87	75	.537	5.0	Billy Hunter, Pat Corrales	1,447,963
1979	3rd	83	79	.512	5.0	Pat Corrales	1,519,671
1980	4th	76	85	.472	20.5	Pat Corrales	1,198,175
1981	2nd/3rd	57	48	.543	*	Don Zimmer	850,076
1982	6th	64	98	.395	29.0	Don Zimmer, Darrell Johnson	1,154,432
1983	3rd	77	85	.475	22.0	Doug Rader	1,363,469
1984	7th	69	92	.429	14.5	Doug Rader	1,102,471
1985	7th	62	99	.385	28.5	Doug Rader, Bobby Valentine	1,112,497
1986	2nd	87	75	.537	5.0	Bobby Valentine	1,692,002
1987	6th (tied)	75	87	.463	10.0	Bobby Valentine	1,763,053
1988	6th	70	91	.435	33.5	Bobby Valentine	1,581,901
1989	4th	83	79	.512	16.0	Bobby Valentine	2,043,993
1990	3rd	83	79	.512	20.0	Bobby Valentine	2,057,911
1991	3rd	85	77	.525	10.0	Bobby Valentine	2,297,720
1992	4th	77	85	.475	19.0	Bobby Valentine, Toby Harrah	2,198,231
1993	2nd	86	76	.531	8.0	Kevin Kennedy	2,244,616
1994	1st (n)	52	62	.456	+1.0	Kevin Kennedy	2,503,198
1995	3rd	74	70	.514	4.5	Johnny Oates	1,985,910
1996	1st (d)	90	72	.556	+4.5	Johnny Oates	2,889,020
1997	3rd	77	85	.475	13.0	Johnny Oates	2,945,228
1998	1st (d)	88	74	.543	+3.0	Johnny Oates	2,927,409
1999	1st (d)	95	67	.586	+8.0	Johnny Oates	2,771,469
2000	4th	71	91	.438	20.5	Johnny Oates	2,800,147
2001	4th	73	89	.451	43.0	Johnny Oates, Jerry Narron	2,831,111

Year	Position	W	L	Pct.	GB	Manager	Attendance
2002	4th	72	90	.444	31.0	Jerry Narron	2,352,447
2003	4th	71	91	.438	25.0	Buck Showalter	2,095,132
2004	3rd	89	73	.549	3.0	Buck Showalter	2,513,685

*first half 33-22, second half 24-26; (n) no World Series; (d) lost Division Series

INDIVIDUAL AND CLUB RECORDS
BATTING

	Individual		Club
	Season	Career	Season
Games	163—Al Oliver, 1980	1,573—Rafael Palmeiro	163 (1980, 1983, 1996)
At-bats	690—Michael Young, 160 g, 2004	5,830—Rafael Palmeiro	5,703 (1991)
Runs	133—Alex Rodriguez, 162 g, 2001	958—Rafael Palmeiro	945 (1999)
			Fewest—590 (1982)
Hits	216—Michael Young, 160 g, 2004	1,723—Ivan Rodriguez	1,653 (1999)
			Fewest—1,353 (1978)
Hitting streak	28 g—Gabe Kapler, 2000		
Singles	165—Mickey Rivers, 147 g, 1980	1,136—Ivan Rodriguez	1,202 (1980)
Doubles	50—Juan Gonzalez, 154 g, 1998	344—Ivan Rodriguez	330 (2000)
Triples	14—Ruben Sierra, 162 g, 1989	44—Ruben Sierra	46 (1989)

HOME RUNS

			246 (2001)
			Fewest—80 (1976)
Righthander	57—Alex Rodriguez, 162 g, 2002	372—Juan Gonzalez	
Lefthander	47—Rafael Palmeiro, 158 g, 1999	321—Rafael Palmeiro	
	Rafael Palmeiro, 160 g, 2001		
Switch-hitter	38—Mark Texeira, 145 g, 2004	180—Ruben Sierra	
Rookie	30—Pete Incaviglia, 153 g, 1986		
Home	34—Alex Rodriguez, 2002	176—Rafael Palmeiro	140 (2003)
Road	26—Alex Rodriguez, 2001	206—Juan Gonzalez	127 (1999)
Month	15—Juan Gonzalez, July 1996		55 (Aug 1999)
	Rafael Palmeiro, Aug 1999		
	Alex Rodriguez, Aug 2003		
Pinch	3—Darrell Porter, 1987	6—Geno Petralli	7 (1980)
Grand slams	3—Jeff Burroughs, 161 g, 1973	7—Juan Gonzalez	8 (1999)
	Larry Parrish, 128 g, 1982	Rafael Palmeiro	
	Rafael Palmeiro, 158 g, 1999		
	Hank Blalock, 159 g, 2004		
Home runs at Arlington Stadium, all teams			204 (1987)
Home runs at Ameriquest Field in Arlington, all teams			245 (2002, 2003)

Total bases	393—Alex Rodriguez, 162 g, 2001	3,073—Juan Gonzalez	2,705 (1999)
Extra base hits	97—Juan Gonzalez, 154 g, 1998	713—Juan Gonzalez	595 (2001)
Sacrifice hits	40—Bert Campaneris, 150 g, 1977	102—Jim Sundberg	116 (1977)
Sacrifice flies	12—Jeff Burroughs, 152 g, 1974	66—Ruben Sierra	69 (1979)
	Ruben Sierra, 158 g, 1987		
	Juan Gonzalez, 144 g, 1999		
Bases on balls	113—Toby Harrah, 126 g, 1985	805—Rafael Palmeiro	660 (1996)
			Fewest—420 (1984)
Strikeouts	185—Pete Incaviglia, 153 g, 1986	1,076—Juan Gonzalez	1,116 (1997)
	Fewest—33—Cesar Tovar, 138 g, 1974		Fewest—589 (1980)
Hit by pitch	16—Alex Rodriguez, 162 g, 2001	54—Rafael Palmeiro	75 (2001, 2003)
			Fewest—20 (1984)
Runs batted in	157—Juan Gonzalez, 154 g, 1998	1,180—Juan Gonzalez	897 (1999)
			Fewest—558 (1982)
Grounded into double plays	31—Ivan Rodriguez, 144 g, 1999	187—Ivan Rodriguez	161 (2000)
	Fewest—2—Cecil Espy, 142 g, 1989		Fewest—91 (2004)
	Tom Goodwin, 154 g, 1998		
Left on base			1,253 (1996)
			Fewest—1,034 (1993)
Batting average	.341—Julio Franco, 146 g, 1983	.3046—Ivan Rodriguez	.293 (1999)
		.3045—Rusty Greer	Lowest—.249 (1982)
Most .300 hitters			4 (1998, 1999)

	Individual		Club
	Season	**Career**	**Season**
Slugging average	.643—Juan Gonzalez, 134 g, 1996	.565—Juan Gonzalez	.479 (1999) Lowest—.290 (1972)
On-base percentage	.432—Toby Harrah, 126 g, 1985	.399—Mike Hargrove	.361 (1999) Lowest—.290 (1972)

BASERUNNING

Stolen bases	52—Bump Wills, 157 g, 1978	161—Bump Wills	196 (1978)
Caught stealing	21—Otis Nixon, 139 g, 1995	60—Toby Harrah	91 (1978)

PITCHING

Games	85—Mitch Williams, 1987	498—Kenny Rogers	
Games started	41—Jim Bibby, 1974 Ferguson Jenkins, 1974	313—Charlie Hough	
Complete games	29—Ferguson Jenkins, 1974	98—Charlie Hough	63 (1976)
Wins	25—Ferguson Jenkins, 1974	139—Charlie Hough	
Percentage	.741—Rick Helling (20-7), 1998	.575—Kenny Rogers	
Winning streak	12—Bobby Witt, 1990		
20-win seasons		1—Ferguson Jenkins Kevin Brown Rick Helling	
Losses	19—Jim Bibby, 1974	123—Charlie Hough	
Losing streak	9—David Clyde, 1974		
Saves	49—Francisco Cordero, 2004	150—John Wetteland	52 (2004)
Innings	328.1—Ferguson Jenkins, 1974	2,308—Charlie Hough	1,479 (1991)
Hits	286—Ferguson Jenkins, 1974	1,995—Charlie Hough	1,683 (2000)
Runs	159—Charlie Hough, 1987	1,086—Charlie Hough	974 (2000)
Earned runs	139—Jim Bibby, 1974	943—Charlie Hough	913 (2001)
Bases on balls	143—Bobby Witt, 1986	1,001—Bobby Witt	760 (1987)
Strikeouts	301—Nolan Ryan, 1989	1,452—Charlie Hough	1,112 (1989)
Strikeouts, game	16—Nolan Ryan, Apr 26, 1990 Nolan Ryan, May 1, 1991		
Hit batsmen	19—Charlie Hough, 1987	89—Charlie Hough	81 (2004)
Wild pitches	22—Bobby Witt, 1986	99—Charlie Hough	94 (1986)
Home runs	41—Rick Helling, 1999	238—Charlie Hough	222 (2001)
Sacrifice hits	16—Jim Umbarger, 1976	53—Kenny Rogers	90 (1976)
Sacrifice flies	14—Charlie Hough, 1987	66—Bobby Witt	73 (2001)
Earned run average	2.17—Mike Paul, 162 inn, 1972	3.68—Charlie Hough	3.31 (2001)
Shutouts	6—Ferguson Jenkins, 1974 Bert Blyleven, 1976	17—Ferguson Jenkins	17 (1977) Lost—27 (1972)
1-0 games won	4—Ferguson Jenkins, 1974 Bert Blyleven, 1976	7—Ferguson Jenkins	5 (1974, 1975, 1976, 1990) Lost—7 (1976)

TEAM FIELDING

Putouts	4,437 (1991) Fewest—4,235 (1985)	**Assists**	1,980 (1975) Fewest—1,580 (1998)
Chances accepted	6,377 (1975) Fewest—5,874 (1998)	**Errors**	191 (1975) Fewest—87 (1996)
Double plays	173 (1975) Fewest—137 (1989)	**Passed balls**	73 (1987) Fewest—2 (1999, 2001)
Errorless games	95 (1996) Consecutive—15 (1996)	**Fielding average**	.986 (1996) Lowest—.971 (1975)

MISCELLANEOUS

Most players, season 52 (1992, 2003, 2004)
Fewest players, season 35 (1984)

Most seasons, non-pitcher 13—Juan Gonzalez
Most seasons, pitcher 11—Charlie Hough
Kenny Rogers
Bobby Witt

Games won 95 (1999)
  Month 21 (Sept 1978)
  Consecutive 14 (1991)
Winning percentage .586 (1999), 95-67
  Lowest .351 (1972), 54-100
Number of league championships 0
  Most recent ---
Runs, game 26 vs Baltimore, Apr 19, 1996
  Opponents' 23 by Oakland, Sept 30, 2000
Hits, game 23 vs Chicago, Apr 2, 1998
                   vs Seattle, Jun 24, 2004
Home runs, game 7 vs Minnesota, Sept 13, 1986
                   vs Cleveland, Aug 1, 2003
Runs, shutout   14 vs Oakland, Jul 26, 1977
  Opponents'   14 by Chicago, Apr 18, 1972
                        by Chicago, Sept 4, 1973
Longest 1-0 win 14 inn, vs Boston, Apr 17, 1983

Games lost 105 (1973)
  Month 24 (Aug 1973)
  Consecutive 15 (1972)
Overall record 2,517-2,692 (33 seasons)
  Interleague play 66-74
Number of times worst record in league 2
  Most recent 1973
Runs, inning 16 vs Baltimore, Apr 19, 1996, 8th

Total bases, game 43 vs Minnesota, Sept 13, 1986

Consecutive games with one or more home runs 27 (55 hrs), 2002

Longest shutout 16 inn, 3-0 vs Chicago, Sept 22, 1975

Longest 1-0 loss 13 inn, vs Minnesota, Sept 22, 1992

ATTENDANCE

Highest home attendance
  Arlington Stadium   2,244,616 (1993)
  Ameriquest Field in Arlington   2,945,228 (1997)

Highest road attendance   2,406,986 (2000)

Largest crowds
  Day   49,617 vs Anaheim, Apr 5, 2002
  Night   49,603 vs Houston N.L., Jun 9, 2001
  Doubleheader   42,163 vs Detroit, Jul 10, 1982
  Home opener   49,617 vs Anaheim, Apr 5, 2002

TORONTO BLUE JAYS
YEARLY FINISHES

(American League expansion franchise)

EAST DIVISION

Year	Position	W	L	Pct.	GB	Manager	Attendance
1977	7th	54	107	.335	45.5	Roy Hartsfield	1,701,052
1978	7th	59	102	.366	40.0	Roy Hartsfield	1,562,585
1979	7th	53	109	.327	50.5	Roy Hartsfield	1,431,651
1980	7th	67	95	.414	36.0	Bobby Mattick	1,400,327
1981	7th/7th	37	69	.349	*	Bobby Mattick	755,083
1982	6th (tied)	78	84	.481	17.0	Bobby Cox	1,275,978
1983	4th	89	73	.549	9.0	Bobby Cox	1,930,415
1984	2nd	89	73	.549	15.0	Bobby Cox	2,110,009
1985	1st (c)	99	62	.615	+2.0	Bobby Cox	2,468,925
1986	4th	86	76	.531	9.5	Jimy Williams	2,455,477
1987	2nd	96	66	.593	2.0	Jimy Williams	2,778,429
1988	3rd (tied)	87	75	.537	2.0	Jimy Williams	2,595,175
1989	1st (c)	89	73	.549	+2.0	Jimy Williams, Cito Gaston	3,375,883
1990	2nd	86	76	.531	2.0	Cito Gaston	3,885,284
1991	1st (c)	91	71	.562	+7.0	Cito Gaston	4,001,527
1992	1st (C,S)	96	66	.593	+4.0	Cito Gaston	4,028,318
1993	1st (C,S)	95	67	.586	+7.0	Cito Gaston	4,057,947
1994	3rd	55	60	.478	16.0	Cito Gaston	2,907,933
1995	5th	56	88	.389	30.0	Cito Gaston	2,826,483
1996	4th	74	88	.457	18.0	Cito Gaston	2,559,573
1997	5th	76	86	.469	22.0	Cito Gaston, Mel Queen	2,589,297
1998	3rd	88	74	.543	26.0	Tim Johnson	2,454,183
1999	3rd	84	78	.519	14.0	Jim Fregosi	2,163,464
2000	3rd	83	79	.512	4.5	Jim Fregosi	1,819,886
2001	3rd	80	82	.494	16.0	Buck Martinez	1,915,438
2002	3rd	78	84	.481	25.5	Buck Martinez, Carlos Tosca	1,636,904
2003	3rd	86	76	.531	15.0	Carlos Tosca	1,799,458
2004	5th	67	94	.416	33.5	Carlos Tosca, John Gibbons	1,900,041

*first half 16-42, second half 21-27; (c) lost League Championship Series; (C) won League Championship Series; (S) won World Series

INDIVIDUAL AND CLUB RECORDS
BATTING

	Individual		Club
	Season	**Career**	**Season**
Games	163—Tony Fernandez, 1986	1,450—Tony Fernandez	163 (1984, 1986, 1998)
At-bats	687—Tony Fernandez, 163 g, 1986	5,335—Tony Fernandez	5,716 (1986)
Runs	134—Shawn Green, 153 g, 1999	889—Carlos Delgado	894 (2003)
			Fewest—590 (1978)

	Individual		Club
	Season	Career	Season
Hits	215—Vernon Wells, 161 g, 2003	1,583—Tony Fernandez	1,580 (1999, 2003)
			Fewest—1,333 (1997)
Hitting streak	28 g—Shawn Green, 1999		
Singles	161—Tony Fernandez, 163 g, 1986	1,160—Tony Fernandez	1,069 (1984)
Doubles	57—Carlos Delgado, 162 g, 2000	343—Carlos Delgado	357 (2003)
Triples	17—Tony Fernandez, 161 g, 1990	72—Tony Fernandez	68 (1984)

HOME RUNS

	Season	Career	Season
			244 (2000)
			Fewest—95 (1979)
Righthander	47—George Bell, 156 g, 1987	203—Joe Carter	
Lefthander	44—Carlos Delgado, 152 g, 1999	336—Carlos Delgado	
Switch-hitter	34—Jose Cruz Jr., 146 g, 2001	122—Jose Cruz Jr.	
Rookie	24—Eric Hinske, 151 g, 2002		
Home	30—Carlos Delgado, 2000	175—Carlos Delgado	134 (2000)
Road	28—George Bell, 1987	161—Carlos Delgado	116 (1999)
Month	12—Carlos Delgado, Aug 1999		48 (June 2000)
	Jose Cruz Jr., Aug 2001		
Pinch	3—Willie Greene, 1999	4—Jesse Bartfield	6 (1984)
		Ernie Whitt	
Grand slams	3—Carlos Delgado, 153 g, 1997	9—Carlos Delgado	9 (2000)
	Darrin Fletcher, 122 g, 2000		
Home runs at Exhibition Stadium, all teams			185 (1983)
Home runs at SkyDome, all teams			226 (2000)

	Season	Career	Season
Total bases	378—Carlos Delgado, 162 g, 2000	2,786—Carlos Delgado	2,664 (2000)
Extra base hits	99—Carlos Delgado, 162 g, 2000	690—Carlos Delgado	593 (2000)
Sacrifice hits	19—Luis Gomez, 153 g, 1978	74—Alfredo Griffin	81 (1977)
Sacrifice flies	14—George Bell, 153 g, 1989	65—Joe Carter	65 (1991)
Bases on balls	123—Carlos Delgado, 162 g, 2000	827—Carlos Delgado	588 (1993)
			Fewest—415 (1982)
Strikeouts	159—Jose Canseco, 151 g, 1998	1,242—Carlos Delgado	1,142 (2002)
	Fewest—21—Bob Bailor, 154 g, 1978		Fewest—645 (1978)
Hit by pitch	20—Reed Johnson, 114 g, 2003	122—Carlos Delgado	92 (1996)
			Fewest—23 (1977, 1978)
Runs batted in	145—Carlos Delgado, 161 g, 2003	1,058—Carlos Delgado	856 (1999)
			Fewest—551 (1978)
Grounded into	23—Ed Sprague, 150 g, 1993	112—George Bell	156 (1977)
double plays	Fewest—5—Alfredo Griffin, 162 g, 1983		Fewest—91 (1984)
	Willie Upshaw, 155 g, 1986		
	Roberto Alomar, 161 g, 1991		
Left on base			1,187 (1993)
			Fewest—1,064 (1979)
Batting average	.363—John Olerud, 158 g, 1993	.307—Roberto Alomar	.280 (1999)
			Lowest—.244 (1997)
Most .300 hitters			4 (1999)
Slugging average	.558—Carlos Delgado, 162 g, 2000	.556—Carlos Delgado	.469 (2000)
			Lowest—.359 (1978)
On-base percentage	.473—John Olerud, 158 g, 1993	.392—Carlos Delgado	.352 (1999)
			Lowest—.286 (1981)

BASERUNNING

	Season	Career	Season
Stolen bases	60—Dave Collins, 128 g, 1984	255—Lloyd Moseby	193 (1984)
Caught stealing	23—Alfredo Griffin, 155 g, 1980	86—Tony Fernandez	81 (1982, 1998)
		Damaso Garcia	
		Lloyd Moseby	

PITCHING

	Season	Career	Season
Games	89—Mark Eichhorn, 1987	452—Duane Ward	
Games started	40—Jim Clancy, 1982	408—Dave Stieb	
Complete games	19—Dave Stieb, 1982	103—Dave Stieb	44 (1979)

	Individual		Club
	Season	**Career**	**Season**
Wins	22—Roy Halladay, 2003	175—Dave Stieb	
Percentage	.778—Jack Morris (21-6), 1992	.589—Jimmy Key	
Winning streak	15—Roger Clemens, 1998		
	Roy Halladay, 2003		
20-win seasons		2—Roger Clemens	
Losses	18—Jerry Garvin, 1977	140—Jim Clancy	
	Phil Huffman, 1979		
Losing streak	10—Jerry Garvin, 1977, 1978		
	Paul Mirabella, 1980		
Saves	45—Duane Ward, 1993	217—Tom Henke	60 (1991)
Innings	288.1—Dave Stieb, 1982	2,873—Dave Stieb	1,476 (1986)
Hits	278—Dave Lemanczyk, 1977	2,545—Dave Stieb	1,615 (2000)
Runs	143—Dave Lemanczyk, 1977	1,208—Dave Stieb	908 (2000)
	Erik Hanson, 1996		
Earned runs	129—Erik Hanson, 1996	1,091—Dave Stieb	821 (2000)
Bases on balls	128—Jim Clancy, 1980	1,020—Dave Stieb	654 (1995)
Strikeouts	292—Roger Clemens, 1997	1,658—Dave Stieb	1,154 (1998)
Strikeouts, game	18—Roger Clemens, Aug 25, 1998		
Hit batsmen	16—Chris Carpenter, 2001	129—Dave Stieb	76 (2001)
Wild pitches	26—Juan Guzman, 1993	88—Juan Guzman	83 (1993)
Home runs	36—Woody Williams, 1998	224—Dave Stieb	195 (2000)
Sacrifice hits	16—Jerry Garvin, 1977	96—Dave Stieb	92 (1980)
Sacrifice flies	12—Jim Clancy, 1983	72—Jim Clancy	70 (1977)
	Doyle Alexander, 1984		
Earned run average	2.05—Roger Clemens, 264 inn, 1997	3.42—Jimmy Key	3.31 (1985)
		Dave Stieb	
Shutouts	5—Dave Stieb, 1982	30—Dave Stieb	17 (1988)
			Lost—20 (1981)
1-0 games won	2—Jim Clancy, 1980	3—Pat Hentgen	5 (1980)
	Jimmy Key, 1988	Jimmy Key	Lost—3 (1979, 1992)
	Dave Stieb		

TEAM FIELDING

Putouts	4,428 (1986)	**Assists**	1,939 (1980)
	Fewest—4,251 (1979)		Fewest—1,502 (1990)
Chances accepted	6,337 (1980)	**Errors**	164 (1977)
	Fewest—5,864 (1997)		Fewest—86 (1990)
Double plays	206 (1980)	**Passed balls**	31 (1995)
	Fewest—109 (1992)		Fewest—3 (1985)
Errorless games	103 (1990)	**Fielding average**	.986 (1990)
	Consecutive—11 (1986)		Lowest—.974 (1977)

MISCELLANEOUS

Most players, season 53 (1999)

Fewest players, season 33 (1983)
Games won 99 (1985)
  Month 21 (May 2003)
  Consecutive 11 (1987, 1998)
Winning percentage .615 (1985), 99-62
  Lowest .327 (1979), 53-109
Number of league championships 2
  Most recent 1993
Runs, game 24 vs Baltimore, Jun 26, 1978
  Opponents' 24 by California, Aug 25, 1979
Hits, game 25 vs Texas, Aug 9, 1999
  vs Boston, Jun 20, 1980
Home runs, game 10 vs Baltimore, Sept 14, 1987
Runs, shutout 15 vs Detroit, Jul 6, 1996
  Opponents' 15 by New York, Sept 25, 1977, 1st game
Longest 1-0 win 12 inn, vs Boston, Sept 26, 1986

Most seasons, non-pitcher 12—Carlos Delgado
  Tony Fernandez
  Ernie Whitt
Most seasons, pitcher 15—Dave Stieb
Games lost 109 (1979)
  Month 23 (May 1979)
  Consecutive 12 (1981)
Overall record 2,178-2,233 (28 seasons)
  Interleague play 66-73
Number of times worst record in league 4 (inc. 1 tie)
  Most recent 1995 (tie)
Runs, inning 11 vs Seattle, Jul 20, 1984, 9th
  vs Chicago, May 12, 1997, 7th
Total bases, game 53 vs Baltimore, Sept 14, 1987

Consecutive games with one or more home runs 23 (44 hrs), 2000
Longest shutout 16 inn, 3-0 vs Chicago, Sept 22, 1975

Longest 1-0 loss 15 inn, vs Oakland, Jul 27, 1986

ATTENDANCE

Highest home attendance		**Largest crowds**	
Exhibition Stadium	2,778,429 (1987)	Day	50,533 vs Cleveland, Apr 9, 1993
Skydome	4,057,947 (1993)	Night	50,532 vs Boston, Sept 22, 1993
		Doubleheader	48,641 vs California, Jul 17, 1989
Highest road attendance	2,549,898 (1993)	Home opener	50,533 vs Cleveland, Apr 9, 1993

WASHINGTON SENATORS (1901-1960)
YEARLY FINISHES

(Original American League franchise moved to Minnesota after the 1960 season)

Year	Position	W	L	Pct.	GB	Manager	Attendance
1901	6th	61	72	.459	20.5	Jimmy Manning	161,661
1902	6th	61	75	.449	22.0	Tom Loftus	188,158
1903	8th	43	94	.314	47.5	Tom Loftus	128,878
1904	8th	38	113	.252	55.5	Patsy Donovan	131,744
1905	7th	64	87	.424	29.5	Jake Stahl	252,027
1906	7th	55	95	.367	37.5	Jake Stahl	129,903
1907	8th	49	102	.325	43.5	Joe Cantillon	221,929
1908	7th	67	85	.441	22.5	Joe Cantillon	264,252
1909	8th	42	110	.276	56.0	Joe Cantillon	205,199
1910	7th	66	85	.437	36.5	Jimmy McAleer	254,591
1911	7th	64	90	.416	38.5	Jimmy McAleer	244,884
1912	2nd	91	61	.599	14.0	Clark Griffith	350,663
1913	2nd	90	64	.584	6.5	Clark Griffith	325,831
1914	3rd	81	73	.526	19.0	Clark Griffith	243,888
1915	4th	85	68	.556	17.0	Clark Griffith	167,332
1916	7th	76	77	.497	14.5	Clark Griffith	177,265
1917	5th	74	79	.484	25.5	Clark Griffith	89,682
1918	3rd	72	56	.563	4.0	Clark Griffith	182,122
1919	7th	56	84	.400	32.0	Clark Griffith	234,096
1920	6th	68	84	.447	29.0	Clark Griffith	359,260
1921	4th	80	73	.523	18.0	George McBride	456,069
1922	6th	69	85	.448	25.0	Clyde Milan	458,552
1923	4th	75	78	.490	23.5	Donie Bush	357,406
1924	1st (S)	92	62	.597	+2.0	Bucky Harris	534,310
1925	1st (s)	96	55	.636	+8.5	Bucky Harris	817,199
1926	4th	81	69	.540	8.0	Bucky Harris	551,580
1927	3rd	85	69	.552	25.0	Bucky Harris	528,976
1928	4th	75	79	.487	26.0	Bucky Harris	378,501
1929	5th	71	81	.467	34.0	Walter Johnson	355,506
1930	2nd	94	60	.610	8.0	Walter Johnson	614,474
1931	3rd	92	62	.597	16.0	Walter Johnson	492,657
1932	3rd	93	61	.604	14.0	Walter Johnson	371,396
1933	1st (s)	99	53	.651	+7.0	Joe Cronin	437,533
1934	7th	66	86	.434	34.0	Joe Cronin	330,074
1935	6th	67	86	.438	27.0	Bucky Harris	255,011
1936	4th	82	71	.536	20.0	Bucky Harris	379,525
1937	6th	73	80	.477	28.5	Bucky Harris	397,799
1938	5th	75	76	.497	23.5	Bucky Harris	522,694
1939	6th	65	87	.428	41.5	Bucky Harris	339,257
1940	7th	64	90	.416	26.0	Bucky Harris	381,241
1941	6th (tied)	70	84	.455	31.0	Bucky Harris	415,663
1942	7th	62	89	.411	39.5	Bucky Harris	403,493
1943	2nd	84	69	.549	13.5	Ossie Bluege	574,694
1944	8th	64	90	.416	25.0	Ossie Bluege	525,235
1945	2nd	87	67	.565	1.5	Ossie Bluege	652,660
1946	4th	76	78	.494	28.0	Ossie Bluege	1,027,216
1947	7th	64	90	.416	33.0	Ossie Bluege	850,758
1948	7th	56	97	.366	40.0	Joe Kuhel	795,254
1949	8th	50	104	.325	47.0	Joe Kuhel	770,745
1950	5th	67	87	.435	31.0	Bucky Harris	699,697
1951	7th	62	92	.403	36.0	Bucky Harris	695,167
1952	5th	78	76	.506	17.0	Bucky Harris	699,457
1953	5th	76	76	.500	23.5	Bucky Harris	595,594
1954	6th	66	88	.429	45.0	Bucky Harris	503,542
1955	8th	53	101	.344	43.0	Chuck Dressen	425,238
1956	7th	59	95	.383	38.0	Chuck Dressen	431,647
1957	8th	55	99	.357	43.0	Chuck Dressen, Cookie Lavagetto	457,079
1958	8th	61	93	.396	31.0	Cookie Lavagetto	475,288
1959	8th	63	91	.409	31.0	Cookie Lavagetto	615,372
1960	5th	73	81	.474	24.0	Cookie Lavagetto	743,404

(S) won World Series; (s) lost World Series

INDIVIDUAL AND CLUB RECORDS
BATTING

	Individual		Club
	Season	**Career**	**Season**
Games	158—Eddie Foster, 1916	2,307—Sam Rice	159 (1916)
At-bats	668—Buddy Lewis, 156 g, 1937	8,934—Sam Rice	5,592 (1935)
Runs	127—Joe Cronin, 154 g, 1930	1,466—Sam Rice	892 (1930)
			Fewest—380 (1909)
Hits	227—Sam Rice, 152 g, 1925	2,889—Sam Rice	1,620 (1930)
			Fewest—1,112 (1909)
Hitting streak	33 g—Heinie Manush, 1933		
Singles	182—Sam Rice, 152 g, 1925	2,195—Sam Rice	1,209 (1935)
Doubles	51—Mickey Vernon, 148 g, 1946	479—Sam Rice	308 (1931)
Triples	20—Goose Goslin, 150 g, 1925	183—Sam Rice	100 (1932)

HOME RUNS

	Individual		Club
			85 (1938)
			Fewest—42 (1947)
Righthander	42—Roy Sievers, 152 g, 1957	180—Roy Sievers	
	Harmon Killebrew, 153, 1959		
Lefthander	20—Mickey Vernon, 151 g, 1954	127—Goose Goslin	
Switch-hitter	6—Danny Moeller, 132 g, 1912	15—Danny Moeller	
Rookie	30—Bob Allison, 150 g, 1959		
Home	26—Roy Sievers, 1957	88—Jim Lemon	83 (1959)
Road	21—Roy Sievers, 1958	100—Roy Sievers	80 (1959)
Month	15—Harmon Killebrew, May 1959		38 (May 1959, Jun 1959)
Pinch	2—Carlos Paula, 1955	3—Clint Courtney	4 (1955, 1957)
		Goose Goslin	
		Carlos Paula	
		Roy Sievers	
Grand slams	2—many players	4—Roy Sievers	8 (1938)
Home runs at American League Park, all teams			74 (1902)
Home runs at Griffith Stadium, all teams			158 (1956)

	Individual		Club
Total bases	331—Roy Sievers, 152 g, 1957	3,833—Sam Rice	2,287 (1930)
Extra base hits	76—Stan Spence, 152 g, 1946	694—Sam Rice	464 (1932)
Sacrifice hits	36—Hunter Hill, 100 g, 1905	249—Joe Judge	135 (1906)
Sacrifice flies	11—Roy Sievers, 145 g, 1954	33—Roy Sievers	42 (1954)
Bases on balls	151—Eddie Yost, 152 g, 1956	927—Tim Salmon	690 (1956)
			Fewest—257 (1903)
Strikeouts	138—Jim Lemon, 146 g, 1956	1,274—Eddie Yost	883 (1960)
	Fewest—9—Sam Rice, 150 g, 1929		Fewest—359 (1927)
Hit by pitch	24—Kid Elberfeld, 127 g, 1911	99—Bucky Harris	80 (1911)
			Fewest—8 (1947)
Runs batted in	129—Goose Goslin, 154 g, 1924	1,044—Sam Rice	822 (1936)
			Fewest—306 (1909)
Grounded into double plays	25—Sam Dente, 155 g, 1950	144—Mickey Vernon	145 (1951)
	Fewest—5—George Case, 154 g, 1940		Fewest—94 (1943)
	George Case, 153 g, 1941		
	Stan Spence, 153 g, 1944		
	Eddie Yost, 155 g, 1954		
Left on base			1,305 (1935)
			Fewest—998 (1959)
Batting average	.379—Goose Goslin, 135 g, 1923	.328—Heinie Manush	.303 (1925)
			Lowest—.223 (1909)
Most .300 hitters			9 (1925)
Slugging average	.614—Goose Goslin, 135 g, 1928	.502—Goose Goslin	.426 (1930)
			Lowest—.287 (1910)
On-base percentage	.454—Buddy Myer, 127 g, 1938	.392—Buddy Myer	.372 (1925)
			Lowest—.274 (1905)

BASERUNNING

	Individual		Club
	Season	**Career**	**Season**
Stolen bases	88—Clyde Milan, 154 g, 1912	494—Clyde Milan	291 (1913)
Caught stealing	30—Sam Rice, 153 g, 1920	142—Sam Rice	56 (1975)

PITCHING

	Season	Career	Club Season
Games	64—Firpo Marberry, 1926	802—Walter Johnson	
Games started	42—Walter Johnson, 1910	666—Walter Johnson	
Complete games	38—Walter Johnson, 1910	531—Walter Johnson	137 (1904)
Wins	36—Walter Johnson, 1913	417—Walter Johnson	
Percentage	.837—Walter Johnson (36-7), 1913	.622—Firpo Marberry	
Winning streak	16—Walter Johnson, 1912		
Winning streak, two seasons	16—Alvin Crowder, 1932 (15), 1933 (1)		
20-win seasons		12—Walter Johnson	
Losses	26—Jack Townsend, 1904 Bob Groom, 1909	279—Walter Johnson	
Losing streak	15—Bob Groom, 1909		
Innings	374—Walter Johnson, 1910	5,923—Walter Johnson	1,430.2 (1916)
Hits	367—Bill Carrick, 1901 Al Orth, 1902 Case Patten, 1904	4,921—Walter Johnson	1,672 (1935)
Runs	172—Al Orth, 1903	1,902—Walter Johnson	943 (1996)
Earned runs	144—Jimmie DeShong, 1937	1,424—Walter Johnson	811 (1956)
Bases on balls	146—Bobo Newsom, 1936	1,353—Walter Johnson	779 (1949)
Strikeouts	313—Walter Johnson, 1910	3,508—Walter Johnson	828 (1912)
Strikeouts, game	15—Camilo Pascual, Apr 18, 1960		
Hit batsmen	20—Walter Johnson, 1923	203—Walter Johnson	69 (1913)
Wild pitches	21—Walter Johnson, 1910	155—Walter Johnson	57 (1911)
Home runs	43—Pedro Ramos, 1957	170—Pedro Ramos	171 (1956)
Sacrifice hits	42—Beany Jacobson, 1904 Jack Townsend, 1904	534—Walter Johnson	218 (1926)
Sacrifice flies	12—Camilo Pascual, 1957	42—Pedro Ramos	60 (1955)
Earned run average	1.14—Walter Johnson, 346 inn, 1913	2.16—Walter Johnson	2.14 (1918)
Shutouts	12—Walter Johnson, 1913	110—Walter Johnson	25 (1914) Lost—29 (1909)
1-0 games won	5—Walter Johnson, 1913, 1919	38—Walter Johnson	11 (1914) Lost—7 (1915)

TEAM FIELDING

Putouts	4,291 (1916) Fewest—3,944 (1906)	**Assists**	2,232 (1911) Fewest—1,587 (1951)
Chances accepted	6,363 (1910) Fewest—5,672 (1953)	**Errors**	325 (1901) Fewest—118 (1958)
Double plays	186 (1935) Fewest—93 (1912)	**Passed balls**	40 (1945) Fewest—3 (1927)
Errorless games	91 (1989) Consecutive—9 (1952)	**Fielding average**	.980 (1958) Lowest—.936 (1902)

MISCELLANEOUS

Most players, season 44 (1909)
Fewest players, season 25 (1908, 1917)
Games won 99 (1933)
  Month 24 (Aug 1945)
  Consecutive 17 (1912)
Winning percentage .651 (1933), 99-53
  Lowest .252 (1904), 38-113
Number of league championships 3
  Most recent 1933
Runs, game 21 vs Detroit, Aug 5, 1929
  Opponents' 24 by Boston, Sept 27, 1940

Most seasons, non-pitcher 19—Sam Rice
Most seasons, pitcher 21—Walter Johnson
Games lost 113 (1904)
  Month 29 (Jul 1909)
  Consecutive 18 (1948, 1959)
Overall record 4,223-4,864 (60 seasons)

Number of times worst record in league 10
  Most recent 1959
Runs, inning 12 vs St. Louis, Jul 10, 1926, 8th
  vs Chicago, May 12, 1997, 7th

Hits, game 24 vs Detroit, Jul 9, 1903
vs Cleveland, Jul 18, 1925
Home runs, game 5 vs Detroit, May 2, 1959
(7 vs Chicago, May 3, 1949, 10 inn)
Runs, shutout 14 vs Boston, Sept 11, 1905, 2nd game, 7 inn
vs Chicago, Sept 3, 1942, 2nd game
Opponents' 17 by New York, Apr 24, 1909
by New York, Jul 6, 1920
by Chicago, Sept 19, 1925, 2nd game
Longest 1-0 win 18 inn, vs Chicago, May 15, 1918
vs Chicago, Jun 8, 1947, 1st game

Total bases, game 41 vs Detroit, Jul 9, 1904

Consecutive games with one or more home runs 8 (14 hrs), 1959

Longest shutout 16 inn, 3-0 vs Chicago, Sept 22, 1975

Longest 1-0 loss 13 inn, vs Boston, Aug 15, 1916
vs Chicago, Jul 29, 1918

ATTENDANCE

Highest home attendance	1,027,216 (1946)	**Largest crowds**	
		Day	31,728 vs New York, Apr 19, 1948
Highest road attendance	1,055,171 (1948)	**Night**	30,701 vs Cleveland, Jun 17, 1947
		Doubleheader	35,563 vs New York, Jul 4, 1936
		Home opener	31,728 vs New York, Apr 19, 1948

REGULAR SEASON A.L.—Washington Senators

WASHINGTON SENATORS (1961-1971)
YEARLY FINISHES

(American League expansion club moved to Texas after the 1971 season)

Year	Position	W	L	Pct.	GB	Manager	Attendance
1961	9th (tied)	61	100	.379	47.5	Mickey Vernon	597,287
1962	10th	60	101	.373	35.5	Mickey Vernon	729,775
1963	10th	56	106	.346	48.5	Mickey Vernon, Gil Hodges	535,604
1964	9th	62	100	.383	37.0	Gil Hodges	600,106
1965	8th	70	92	.432	32.0	Gil Hodges	560,083
1966	8th	71	88	.447	25.5	Gil Hodges	576,260
1967	6th (tied)	76	85	.472	15.5	Gil Hodges	770,863
1968	10th	65	96	.404	37.5	Jim Lemon	546,661

EAST DIVISION

Year	Position	W	L	Pct.	GB	Manager	Attendance
1969	4th	86	76	.531	23.0	Ted Williams	918,106
1970	6th	70	92	.432	38.0	Ted Williams	824,789
1971	5th	63	96	.396	38.5	Ted Williams	655,156

INDIVIDUAL AND CLUB RECORDS
BATTING

	Individual		Club
	Season	**Career**	**Season**
Games	161—Frank Howard, 1969, 1970	1,142—Eddie Brinkman	162 (1962, 1963, 1964, 1966, 1969, 1970)
At-bats	635—Del Unser, 156 g, 1968	3,845—Eddie Brinkman	5,484 (1962)
Runs	111—Frank Howard, 161 g, 1969	516—Frank Howard	694 (1969) Fewest—524 (1968)
Hits	175—Frank Howard, 161 g, 1969	1,071—Frank Howard	1,370 (1962) Fewest—1,209 (1968)
Hitting streak	19 g—Ken McMullen, 1967		
Singles	144—Eddie Brinkman, 158 g, 1970	685—Eddie Brinkman	1,006 (1969)
Doubles	31—Aurelio Rodriguez, 142 g, 1970	146—Frank Howard	217 (1961)
Triples	12—Chuck Hinton, 150 g, 1963	30—Chuck Hinton	44 (1961)

HOME RUNS

119 (1961)
Fewest—124 (1968)

Righthander	48—Frank Howard, 161 g, 1969	237—Frank Howard	
Lefthander	30—Mike Epstein, 131 g, 1969	89—Jim King	
Switch-hitter	16—Fred Valentine, 146 g, 1966	34—Fred Valentine	
Rookie	13—Paul Casanova, 122 g, 1966		
Home	27—Frank Howard, 1969	116—Frank Howard	77 (1969)
Road	26—Frank Howard, 1968	121—Frank Howard	85 (1961)
Month	15—Frank Howard, May 1968		37 (May 1965)
Pinch	3—Brant Alyea, 1969	6—Brant Alyea	8 (1965, 1966)
	Don Lock, 1966		
	Tommy McCraw, 1971		
	Rick Reichardt, 1970		

	Individual		Club
	Season	**Career**	**Season**
Grand slams	2—Don Zimmer, 121 g, 1963	3—Mike Epstein Don Zimmer	4 (1961, 1963, 1967)
Home runs at Griffith Stadium, all teams			87 (1961)
Home runs at Robert F. Kennedy Memorial Stadium, all teams			166 (1964)
Total bases	340—Frank Howard, 161 g, 1969	1,968—Frank Howard	2,060 (1969)
Extra base hits	75—Frank Howard, 158 g, 1968	403—Frank Howard	380 (1961)
Sacrifice hits	15—Danny O'Connell, 138 g, 1961	34—Eddie Brinkman	84 (1966)
Sacrifice flies	8—Ken McMullen, 158 g, 1959	26—Ken McMullen	44 (1961)
Bases on balls	132—Frank Howard, 161 g, 1970	533—Frank Howard	635 (1970) Fewest—450 (1966)
Strikeouts	155—Frank Howard, 149 g, 1967 Fewest—41—Eddie Brinkman, 158 g, 1970	854—Frank Howard	1,125 (1965) Fewest—789 (1962)
Hit by pitch	13—Mike Epstein, 123 g, 1968	42—Mike Epstein	46 (1970) Fewest—15 (1962)
Runs batted in	126—Frank Howard, 161 g, 1970	670—Frank Howard	640 (1969) Fewest—489 (1968)
Grounded into double plays	29—Frank Howard, 161 g, 1969 Frank Howard, 153 g, 1971 Fewest—4—Del Unser, 153 g, 1971	131—Frank Howard	148 (1966) Fewest—98 (1975)
Left on base			1,196 (1970) Fewest—1,054 (1966)
Batting average	.310—Chuck Hinton, 151 g, 1962	.280—Chuck Hinton	.251 (1969) Lowest—.223 (1967)
Most .300 hitters			1 (1961, 1962)
Slugging average	.574—Frank Howard, 161 g, 1969	.513—Frank Howard	.378 (1969) Lowest—.326 (1967, 1971)
On-base percentage	.416—Frank Howard, 161 g, 1970	.369—Frank Howard	.330 (1969) Lowest—.287 (1968)

BASERUNNING

Stolen bases	29—Ed Stroud, 129 g, 1970	92—Chuck Hinton	99 (1962)
Caught stealing	10—Willie Tasby, 141 g, 1961 Chuck Hinton, 150 g, 1962 Fred Valentine, 146 g, 1966 Del Unser, 153 g, 1969	30—Eddie Brinkman Chuck Hinton	53 (1962)

PITCHING

Games	74—Ron Kline, 1965	267—Casey Cox	
Games started	36—Claude Osteen, 1964 Joe Coleman, 1969	123—Joe Coleman	
Complete games	13—Claude Osteen, 1964	36—Joe Coleman	39 (1961)
Wins	16—Dick Bosman, 1970	49—Dick Bosman	
Percentage	.571—Dick Bosman (16-12), 1970	none over 1,500 inn	
Winning streak	8—Dick Bosman, 1969		
20-win seasons		none	
Losses	22—Denny McLain, 1971	60—Bennie Daniels	
Losing streak	10—Bennie Daniels, 1962		
Saves	27—Darold Knowles, 1970	40—Darold Knowles	41 (1969)
Innings	257—Claude Osteen, 1964	889.2—Dick Bosman	1,473.1 (1967)
Hits	256—Claude Osteen, 1964	850—Dick Bosman	1,486 (1963)
Runs	115—Denny McLain, 1971	428—Bennie Daniels	812 (1963)
Earned runs	103—Denny McLain, 1971	378—Bennie Daniels	710 (1963)
Bases on balls	100—Joe Coleman, 1969	378—Jim Hannan	656 (1969)

	Individual		Club
	Season	**Career**	**Season**
Strikeouts	195—Pete Richert, 1966	561—Joe Coleman	878 (1967)
Strikeouts, game	13—Jim Duckworth, Sept 25, 1965, 2nd game		
	(21—Tom Cheney, Sept 12, 1962, 16 inn)		
Hit batsmen	12—Joe Coleman, 1968	31—Joe Coleman	45 (1971)
Wild pitches	17—Frank Bertaina, 1968	43—Joe Coleman	61 (1968)
Home runs	36—Pete Richert, 1966	90—Phil Ortega	176 (1963)
Sacrifice hits	20—Buster Narum, 1965	51—Jim Hannan	97 (1968)
Sacrifice flies	12—Casey Cox, 1970	29—Joe Coleman	59 (1963)
	Joe McClain, 1961	Casey Cox	
	Denny McLain, 1971		
Earned run average	2.19—Dick Bosman, 193 inn, 1969	none with 1,500 inn	3.38 (1967)
Shutouts	4—Tom Cheney, 1963	7—Tom Cheney	14 (1967)
	Frank Bertaina, 1967		Lost—22 (1964)
	Camilo Pascual, 1968		
	Joe Coleman, 1969		
1-0 games won	2—Dick Donovan, 1961	3—Phil Ortega	4 (1962, 1967, 1968)
	Dave Stenhouse, 1962		Lost—5 (1963, 1971)

TEAM FIELDING

Putouts	4,420 (1967)	**Assists**	1,946 (1970)
	Fewest—4,1256 (1971)		Fewest—1,647 (1965)
Chances accepted	6,319 (1970)	**Errors**	182 (1963)
	Fewest—5,949 (1966)		Fewest—116 (1970)
Double plays	173 (1970)	**Passed balls**	23 (1961, 1971)
	Fewest—139 (1966)		Fewest—12 (1970)
Errorless games	83 (1964)	**Fielding average**	.982 (1970)
	Consecutive—6 (1970)		Lowest—.971 (1963)

MISCELLANEOUS

Most players, season 43 (1963)
Fewest players, season 36 (1969)
Games won 86 (1969)
  Month 19 (Jul 1967)
  Consecutive 8 (1967)
Winning percentage .531 (1969), 86-76
  Lowest .346 (1963), 56-106
Number of league championships 0
  Most recent ---
Runs, game 15 vs Detroit, May 18, 1965
    vs Cleveland, Jul 5, 1971
  Opponents' 18 by Baltimore, Apr 22, 1965
Hits, game 20 vs Boston, Jul 27, 1962, 2nd game

Home runs, game 5 vs Detroit, May 20, 1965
    vs Chicago, May 16, 1969
    vs Chicago, Jun 13, 1970
Runs, shutout 13 vs Los Angeles, Jun 2, 1965, 1st game
  Opponents' 17 by Los Angeles, Aug 23, 1963
Longest 1-0 win 10 inn, vs Chicago, Jun 9, 1961, 1st game
    vs Chicago, Sept 19, 1964

Most seasons, non-pitcher 10—Eddie Brinkman
Most seasons, pitcher 9—Jim Hannan
Games lost 106 (1963)
  Month 24 (Aug 1961)
  Consecutive 14 (1961, 1970)
Overall record 740-1,032 (11 seasons)

Number of times worst record in league 4 (inc. 1 tie)
  Most recent 1968
Runs, inning 11 vs Baltimore, May 11, 1962, 6th

Total bases, game 32 vs Boston, Jul 27, 1962, 2nd game
    vs Chicago, Jun 13, 1970
Consecutive games with one or more home runs 10 (16 hrs), 1970

Longest shutout 16 inn, 3-0 vs Chicago, Sept 22, 1975

Longest 1-0 loss 10 inn, vs Chicago, Sept 9, 1966

ATTENDANCE

Highest home attendance	918,106 (1969)	**Largest crowds**	
		Day	45,125 vs New York, Apr 7, 1969
Highest road attendance	1,042,638 (1968)	Night	30,421 vs New York, Jul 31, 1962
		Doubleheader	40,359 vs Minnesota, Jun 14, 1964
		Home opener	45,125 vs New York, Apr 7, 1969

NATIONAL LEAGUE TEAM RECORDS

ARIZONA DIAMONDBACKS
YEARLY FINISHES

(National League expansion franchise)

WEST DIVISION

Year	Position	W	L	Pct.	GB	Manager	Attendance
1998	5th	65	97	.401	33.0	Buck Showalter	3,600,412
1999	1st (d)	100	62	.617	+14.0	Buck Showalter	3,019,654
2000	3rd	85	77	.525	12.0	Buck Showalter	2,942,516
2001	1st (D,C,S)	92	70	.556	2.0	Bob Brenly	2,740,554
2002	1st (d)	98	64	.605	+2.5	Bob Brenly	3,200,725
2003	3rd	84	78	.519	16.5	Bob Brenly	2,805,202
2004	5th	51	111	.315	42.0	Bob Brenly, Al Pedrique	2,519,560

(d) lost Division Series; (D) won Division Series; (C) won League Championship Series; (S) won World Series

INDIVIDUAL AND CLUB RECORDS
BATTING

	Individual		Club
	Season	**Career**	**Season**
Games	162—Luis Gonzalez, 2000, 2001	886—Luis Gonzalez	162 (1998-2004)
At-bats	627—Matt Williams, 154 g, 1999	3,323—Luis Gonzalez	5,658 (1999)
Runs	132—Jay Bell, 151 g, 1999	597—Luis Gonzalez	908 (1999)
			Fewest—615 (2004)
Hits	206—Luis Gonzalez, 153 g, 1999	1,021—Luis Gonzalez	1,566 (1999)
			Fewest—1,353 (1999)
Hitting streak	30 g—Luis Gonzalez, 1999		
Singles	131—Luis Gonzalez, 153 g, 1999	590—Luis Gonzalez	1,015 (1999)
	Tony Womack, 144 g, 1999		
Doubles	47—Luis Gonzalez, 162 g, 2000	221—Luis Gonzalez	303 (2003)
Triples	14—Tony Womack, 146 g, 2000	37—Tony Womack	47 (2003)

HOME RUNS

			216 (1999)
			Fewest—135 (2004)
Righthander	38—Jay Bell, 151 g, 1999	99—Matt Williams	
Lefthander	57—Luis Gonzalez, 162 g, 2001	185—Luis Gonzalez	
Switch-hitter	22—Devon White, 146 g, 1998	22—Devon White	
Rookie	22—Travis Lee, 146 g, 1998		
Home	26—Luis Gonzalez, 2001	80—Steve Finley	107 (2001)
Road	31—Luis Gonzalez, 2001	108—Luis Gonzalez	115 (1999)
Month	13—Luis Gonzalez, April 2001		44 (Apr 2000, Apr 2001)
Pinch	5—David Dellucci, 2001	6—David Dellucci	14 (2001)
	Erubiel Durazo, 2001	Erubiel Durazo	
Grand slams	2—Matt Williams, 135 g, 1998	7—Matt Williams	9 (2001)
	Travis Lee, 120 g, 1999		
	Matt Williams, 154 g, 1999		
	Luis Gonzalez, 162 g, 2001		
Home runs at Bank One Ballpark, all teams			228 (2001)
Total bases	419—Luis Gonzalez, 162 g, 2001	1,847—Luis Gonzalez	2,595 (1999)
Extra base hits	100—Luis Gonzalez, 162 g, 2001	431—Luis Gonzalez	551 (1999)
Sacrifice hits	14—Curt Schilling, 35 g, 2001	33—Curt Schilling	71 (2001)
Sacrifice flies	12—Luis Gonzalez, 162 g, 2000	34—Luis Gonzalez	60 (1999)
Bases on balls	100—Luis Gonzalez, 162 g, 2001	503—Luis Gonzalez	643 (2002)
			Fewest—441 (2004)
Strikeouts	132—Jay Bell, 151 g, 1999	467—Steve Finley	1,239 (1998)
	Fewest—49—Shea Hillenbrand, 148 g, 2004		Fewest—975 (2000)
Hit by pitch	18—Andy Fox, 139 g, 1998	43—Luis Gonzalez	64 (1998)
			Fewest—35 (2004)
Runs batted in	142—Matt Williams, 154 g, 1999	622—Luis Gonzalez	865 (1999)
	Luis Gonzalez, 162 g, 2001		Fewest—582 (2004)
Grounded into double plays	20—Danny Bautista, 141 g, 2004	79—Luis Gonzalez	137 (2004)
	Fewest—4—Steve Finley, 156 g, 1999		Fewest—94 (1999)

– 276 –

	Individual		Club
	Season	Career	Season
Left on base			1,230 (2004)
			Fewest—1,104 (1998)
Batting average	.336—Luis Gonzalez, 153 g, 1999	.307—Luis Gonzalez	.277 (1999)
			Lowest—.246 (1998)
Most .300 hitters			2 (1999)
Slugging average	.688—Luis Gonzalez, 162 g, 2001	.556—Luis Gonzalez	.459 (1999)
			Lowest—.393 (1998, 2004)
On-base percentage	.429—Luis Gonzalez, 162 g, 2001	.401—Luis Gonzalez	.347 (1999)
			Lowest—.310 (2004)

BASERUNNING

	Season	Career	Season
Stolen bases	72—Tony Womack, 144 g, 1999	182—Tony Womack	137 (1999)
Caught stealing	13—Tony Womack, 144 g, 1999	46—Tony Womack	46 (2002)

PITCHING

	Season	Career	Season
Games	86—Oscar Villarreal, 2003	243—Byung-Hyun Kim	
Games started	35—Randy Johnson, 1999, 2000, 2002, 2004	192—Randy Johnson	
	Curt Schilling, 2001, 2002		
	Brandon Webb, 2004		
Complete games	12—Randy Johnson, 1999	36—Randy Johnson	16 (1999, 2000)
Wins	24—Randy Johnson, 2002	103—Randy Johnson	
Percentage	.828—Randy Johnson (24-5), 2002	.678—Randy Johnson	
Winning streak	9—Curt Schilling, 2002		
20-win seasons		2—Randy Johnson	
		Curt Schilling	
Losses	16—Brandon Webb, 2004	49—Randy Johnson	
Losing streak	9—Edgar Gonzalez, 2004		
Saves	36—Byung-Hyun Kim, 2002	74—Matt Mantei	42 (1999, 2000)
Innings	271.2—Randy Johnson, 1999	1,389.2—Randy Johnson	1,467.1 (1999)
Hits	237—Curt Schilling, 2001	1,089—Randy Johnson	1,480 (2004)
Runs	117—Andy Benes, 1999	476—Randy Johnson	899 (2004)
Earned runs	106—Andy Benes, 1999	422—Brian Johnson	794 (2004)
Bases on balls	119—Brandon Webb, 2004	359—Randy Johnson	668 (2004)
Strikeouts	372—Randy Johnson, 2001	1,832—Randy Johnson	1,303 (2002)
Strikeouts, game	20—Randy Johnson, May 8, 2001 (pitched first 9 inn of 11-inn game)		
	17—Randy Johnson, Jun 30, 1999		
	Curt Schilling, Apr 7, 2002		
	Randy Johnson, Apr 21, 2002		
	Randy Johnson, Sept 14, 2002		
Hit batsmen	18—Randy Johnson, 2001	64—Randy Johnson	75 (2004)
Wild pitches	17—Brandon Webb, 2004	26—Brandon Webb	71 (2004)
Home runs	39—Brian Anderson, 1998	143—Brian Anderson	197 (2004)
Sacrifice hits	14—Randy Johnson, 2000	43—Randy Johnson	81 (2003)
	Brandon Webb, 2004		
Sacrifice flies	8—Andy Benes, 1998	23—Randy Johnson	47 (2004)
	Brian Anderson, 2002		
	Miguel Batista, 2002		
Earned run average	2.32—Randy Johnson, 260 inn, 2002	2.65—Randy Johnson	3.77 (1999)
Shutouts	4—Randy Johnson, 2002	14—Randy Johnson	13 (2001)
			Lost—16 (1998)
1-0 games won	1—Brian Anderson, 1998	1—Brian Anderson	2 (2003)
	Randy Johnson, 2000	Randy Johnson	Lost—3 (1998, 2001, 2002)

TEAM FIELDING

Putouts	4,402 (1999)	Assists	1,721 (1998)
	Fewest—4,297 (1998)		Fewest—1,506 (2002)
Chances accepted	6,058 (2003)	Errors	139 (2004)
	Fewest—5,846 (2002)		Fewest—84 (2001)
Double plays	148 (2001)	Passed balls	18 (2004)
	Fewest—116 (2002)		Fewest—4 (2000)
Errorless games	94 (2001)	Fielding average	.986 (2001)
	Consecutive—9 (1999)		Lowest—.977 (2004)

MISCELLANEOUS

Most players, season 52 (2004)

Fewest players, season 41 (2000)

Games won 100 (1999)
  Month 22 (Aug 1998)
  Consecutive 12 (2003)
Winning percentage .617 (1999), 100-62
  Lowest .315 (2004), 51-111
Number of league championships 1
  Most recent 2001
Runs, game 17 vs St. Louis, Jul 4, 1999
              vs St. Louis, Jul 27, 2000
              vs St. Louis, Apr 17, 2001
              vs Colorado, Sept 28, 2002
  Opponents' 20 by Colorado, Sept 23, 2003
Hits, game 20 vs Montreal, Jun 2, 1999
         vs Los Angeles, May 8, 2000
         vs Milwaukee, Apr 22, 2004
         (21 vs Los Angeles, Apr 13, 1999, 16 inn)
Home runs, game 5, many times
Runs, shutout 12 vs San Diego, Jul 26, 2002
  Opponents' 12 by San Diego, Sept 3, 2003
Longest 1-0 win 18 inn, vs San Francisco, May 29, 2001

Most seasons, non-pitcher 6—David Dellucci
                                Steve Finley
                                Luis Gonzalez
                                Matt Williams
Most seasons, pitcher 6—Randy Johnson
                         Matt Mantei

Games lost 111 (2004)
  Month 23 (Jul 2004)
  Consecutive 14 (2004)
Overall record 575-559 (7 seasons)
  Interleague play 53-56
Number of times worst record in league 1
  Most recent 2004
Runs, inning 8 vs Florida, Aug 26, 1999, 9th
               vs Chicago, Aug 19, 2000, 3rd
               vs Kansas City A.L., Jun 10, 2001, 4th
               vs Atlanta, Apr 25, 2002, 5th

Total bases, game 40 vs St. Louis, Apr 17, 2001

Consecutive games with one or more home runs 13 (21 hrs), 1999
Longest shutout 18 inn, vs. San Francisco, May 29, 2001

Longest 1-0 loss 13 inn, by San Diego, Sept 2, 2001

ATTENDANCE

Highest home attendance	3,600,412 (1998)	**Largest crowds**	
		Day	48,277 vs Los Angeles, May 24, 1998
Highest road attendance	2,689,308 (2002)	**Night**	48,389 vs Seattle, Jun 27, 1998
		Doubleheader	none
		Home opener	47,465 vs Colorado, Mar 31, 1998

ATLANTA BRAVES
YEARLY FINISHES

(Original National League franchise moved from Boston to Milwaukee after the 1952 season and to Atlanta after the 1965 season)

Year	Position	W	L	Pct.	GB	Manager	Attendance
1966	5th	85	77	.525	10.0	Bobby Bragan, Billy Hitchcock	1,539,801
1967	7th	77	85	.475	24.5	Billy Hitchcock, Ken Silvestri	1,389,222
1968	5th	81	81	.500	16.0	Lum Harris	1,126,540

WEST DIVISION

Year	Position	W	L	Pct.	GB	Manager	Attendance
1969	1st (c)	93	69	.574	+3.0	Lum Harris	1,458,320
1970	5th	76	86	.469	26.0	Lum Harris	1,078,848
1971	3rd	82	80	.506	8.0	Lum Harris	1,006,320
1972	4th	70	84	.455	25.0	Lum Harris, Eddie Mathews	752,973
1973	5th	76	85	.472	22.5	Eddie Mathews	800,655
1974	3rd	88	74	.543	14.0	Eddie Mathews, Clyde King	981,085
1975	5th	67	94	.416	40.5	Clyde King, Connie Ryan	534,672
1976	6th	70	92	.432	32.0	Dave Bristol	818,179
1977	6th	61	101	.377	37.0	Dave Bristol, Ted Turner	872,464
1978	6th	69	93	.426	26.0	Bobby Cox	904,494
1979	6th	66	94	.413	23.5	Bobby Cox	769,465
1980	4th	81	80	.503	11.0	Bobby Cox	1,048,411
1981	4th/5th	50	56	.472	*	Bobby Cox	535,418
1982	1st (c)	89	73	.549	+1.0	Joe Torre	1,801,985
1983	2nd	88	74	.543	3.0	Joe Torre	2,119,935
1984	2nd (tied)	80	82	.494	12.0	Joe Torre	1,724,892
1985	5th	66	96	.407	29.0	Eddie Haas, Bobby Wine	1,350,137
1986	6th	72	89	.447	23.5	Chuck Tanner	1,387,181
1987	5th	69	92	.429	20.5	Chuck Tanner	1,217,402
1988	6th	54	106	.338	39.5	Chuck Tanner, Russ Nixon	848,089
1989	6th	63	97	.394	28.0	Russ Nixon	984,930
1990	6th	65	97	.401	26.0	Russ Nixon, Bobby Cox	980,129
1991	1st (C,s)	94	68	.580	+1.0	Bobby Cox	2,140,217
1992	1st (C,s)	98	64	.605	+8.0	Bobby Cox	3,077,400
1993	1st (c)	104	58	.642	+1.0	Bobby Cox	3,884,725

EAST DIVISION

Year	Position	W	L	Pct.	GB	Manager	Attendance
1994	2nd...............68	46		.596	6.0	Bobby Cox	2,539,240
1995	1st (D,C,S)........90	54		.625	+21.0	Bobby Cox	2,561,831
1996	1st (D,C,s)........96	66		.593	+8.0	Bobby Cox	2,901,242
1997	1st (D,c)..........101	61		.623	+9.0	Bobby Cox	3,464,488
1998	1st (D,c)..........106	56		.654	+18.0	Bobby Cox	3,361,350
1999	1st(D,C,s)........103	59		.636	+6.5	Bobby Cox	3,284,897
2000	1st (d)............95	67		.586	+1.0	Bobby Cox	3,234,301
2001	1st (D,c)..........88	74		.543	+2.0	Bobby Cox	2,823,494
2002	1st (d)............101	59		.631	+19.0	Bobby Cox	2,603,482
2003	1st (d)............101	61		.623	+10.0	Bobby Cox	2,401,082
2004	1st (d)............96	66		.593	+10.0	Bobby Cox	2,322,565

(c) lost League Championship Series; *first half 25-29, second half 25-27; (C) won League Championship Series; (s) lost World Series; (D) won Division Series; (S) won World Series; (d) lost Division Series

INDIVIDUAL AND CLUB RECORDS
BATTING

	Individual		Career	Club
	Season			Season
Games	162—Felix Millan, 1969		1,926—Dale Murphy	163 (1966, 1968, 1974)
	Dale Murphy, 1982, 1983, 1984, 1985			
	Andruw Jones, 1999			
At-bats	671—Marquis Grissom, 158 g, 1996		7,098—Dale Murphy	5,670 (2003)
Runs	131—Dale Murphy, 162 g, 1983		1,103—Dale Murphy	907 (2003)
				Fewest—514 (1968)
Hits	219—Ralph Garr, 154 g, 1971		1,901—Dale Murphy	1,608 (2003)
				Fewest—1,281 (1989)
Hitting streak	31 g—Rico Carty, 1970			
Singles	180—Ralph Garr, 154 g, 1971		1,187—Dale Murphy	1,109 (1968)
Doubles	49—Marcus Giles, 145 g, 2003		325—Chipper Jones	321 (2003)
Triples	17—Ralph Garr, 143 g, 1974		40—Ralph Garr	48 (1992)

HOME RUNS

				235 (2003)
				Fewest—80 (1968)
Righthander	47—Hank Aaron, 139 g, 1971		371—Dale Murphy	
Lefthander	41—Darrell Evans, 161 g, 1973		160—David Justice	
Switch-hitter	45—Chipper Jones, 157 g, 1999		310—Chipper Jones	
Rookie	33—Earl Williams, 145 g, 1971			
Home	31—Hank Aaron, 1971		205—Dale Murphy	119 (1966)
Road	28—Andres Galarraga, 1998		166—Dale Murphy	124 (2003)
Month	14—Bob Horner, July 1980			55 (May 2003)
Pinch	4—Tommy Gregg, 1990		6—Tommy Gregg	9 (1992)
			Mike Lum	
Grand slams	3—Chipper Jones, 157 g, 1997		7—Hank Aaron	12 (1997)
			Javy Lopez	
Home runs at Atlanta-Fulton County Stadium, all teams				211 (1970)
Home runs at Turner Field, all teams				179 (2003)

	Individual		Career	Club
Total bases	359—Chipper Jones, 157 g, 1999		3,394—Dale Murphy	2,696 (2003)
Extra base hits	87—Chipper Jones, 157 g, 1999		714—Dale Murphy	587 (2003)
Sacrifice hits	20—Rod Gilbreath, 116 g, 1976		168—Tom Glavine	109 (1974)
	Glenn Hubbard, 145 g, 1982			
Sacrifice flies	10—Bob Horner, 141 g, 1986		64—Chipper Jones	52 (1997, 2001)
	Gerald Perry, 141 g, 1988			
	Chipper Jones, 156 g, 2000			
Bases on balls	127—Jimmy Wynn, 148 g, 1976		937—Chipper Jones	641 (1987)
	Fewest—414 (1968)			
Strikeouts	147—Andruw Jones, 154 g, 2004		1,581—Dale Murphy	1,160 (1997)
	Fewest—35—Felix Millan, 162 g, 1969			Fewest—665 (1969)
Hit by pitch	25—Andres Galarraga, 153 g, 1998		75—Jeff Blauser	61 (1998)
				Fewest—17 (1977, 1983)
Runs batted in	132—Gary Sheffield, 155 g, 2003		1,143—Dale Murphy	872 (2003)
				Fewest—480 (1968)
Grounded into double plays	24—Dale Murphy, 156 g, 1988		170—Dale Murphy	154 (1985)
	Andruw Jones, 154 g, 2004			Fewest—82 (1992)
	Fewest—1—Rafael Furcal, 156 g, 2003			

	Individual		Club
	Season	**Career**	**Season**
Left on base			1,213 (1974)
			Fewest—1,038 (1988)
Batting average	.366—Rico Carty, 136 g, 1970	.317—Ralph Garr	.284 (2003)
			Lowest—.234 (1989)
Most .300 hitters			4 (2003)
Slugging average	.669—Hank Aaron, 139 g, 1971	.567—Hank Aaron	.475 (2003)
			Lowest—.334 (1976)
On-base percentage	.454—Rico Carty, 136 g, 1970	.401—Chipper Jones	.349 (2003)
			Lowest—.298 (1989)

BASERUNNING

Stolen bases	72—Otis Nixon, 124 g, 1991	186—Otis Nixon	165 (1991)
Caught stealing	23—Brett Butler, 151 g, 1983	83—Jerry Royster	88 (1983)

PITCHING

Games	84—Chris Reitsma, 2004	689—Phil Niekro	
Games started	44—Phil Niekro, 1979	594—Phil Niekro	
Complete games	23—Phil Niekro, 1979	226—Phil Niekro	46 (1974)
Wins	24—John Smoltz, 1996	266—Phil Niekro	
Percentage	.905—Greg Maddux (19-2), 1995	.688—Greg Maddux	
Winning streak	14—John Smoltz, 1996		
20-win seasons		5—Tom Glavine	
Losses	20—Phil Niekro, 1977, 1979	227—Phil Niekro	
Losing streak	9—Tommy Boggs, 1981		
	Marty Clary, 1990		
Losing streak, two seasons	11—Jim Acker, 1986 (6), 1987 (5)		
Saves	55—John Smoltz, 2002	154—John Smoltz	57 (2002)
Innings	342—Phil Niekro, 1979	4,533—Phil Niekro	1,474.2 (1968, 1971)
Hits	315—Phil Niekro, 1977	4,136—Phil Niekro	1,581 (1977)
Runs	166—Phil Niekro, 1977	1,880—Phil Niekro	895 (1977)
Earned runs	148—Phil Niekro, 1977	1,613—Phil Niekro	779 (1977)
Bases on balls	164—Phil Niekro, 1977	1,425—Phil Niekro	701 (1977)
Strikeouts	276—John Smoltz, 1996	2,855—Phil Niekro	1,245 (1996)
Strikeouts, game	15—John Smoltz, May 24, 1992		
Hit batsmen	13—Phil Niekro, 1978	104—Phil Niekro	45 (1979)
Wild pitches	27—Tony Cloninger, 1966	190—Phil Niekro	83 (1966)
Home runs	41—Phil Niekro, 1979	386—Phil Niekro	185 (1970)
Sacrifice hits	22—Tom Glavine, 1999	193—Phil Niekro	107 (1975)
Sacrifice flies	12—Tony Cloninger, 1966	84—Tom Glavine	60 (1973)
	Carl Morton, 1974		
Earned run average	1.56—Greg Maddux, 202 inn, 1994	2.63—Greg Maddux	2.92 (1968)
Shutouts	6—Phil Niekro, 1974	43—Phil Niekro	24 (1992)
			Lost—24 (1978)
1-0 games won	2—Phil Niekro, 1969	6—Greg Maddux	7 (1974)
	Greg Maddux, 1995, 2001	Phil Niekro	Lost—4 (1988, 1989)

TEAM FIELDING

Putouts	4,424 (1971)	**Assists**	2,028 (1985)
	Fewest—4,223 (1979)		Fewest—1,635 (1969)
Chances accepted	6,400 (1985)	**Errors**	183 (1979)
	Fewest—5,970 (1969)		Fewest—91 (1998)
Double plays	197 (1985)	**Passed balls**	42 (1967)
	Fewest—114 (1969)		Fewest—6 (1983)
Errorless games	97 (1998)	**Fielding average**	.985 (1998)
	Consecutive—10 (2001, 2004)		Lowest—.970 (1979)

MISCELLANEOUS

Most players, season 47 (2000, 2001)
Fewest players, season 32 (1980)
Games won 106 (1998)
  Month 21 (May 1988, Aug 1999, Jun 2002)
  Consecutive 15 (2000)
Winning percentage .654 (1998), 106-56
  Lowest .338 (1988), 54-106
Number of league championships 5
  Most recent 1999
Runs, game 20 vs Colorado, Apr 18, 1999
                vs Florida, Oct 5, 2001
  Opponents' 23 by Cincinnati, Apr 25, 1977
                by San Francisco, Jun 8, 1990
Hits, game 25 vs Cincinnati, May 1, 1985
Home runs, game 7 vs Chicago, Aug 3, 1967
Runs, shutout 18 vs Florida, Oct 3, 1999
  Opponents' 19 by Montreal, Jul 30, 1978
Longest 1-0 win 13 inn, vs St. Louis, May 16, 1997

Most seasons, non-pitcher 15—Dale Murphy
Most seasons, pitcher 19—Phil Niekro
Games lost 106 (1988)
  Month 21 (May 1976)
  Consecutive 17 (1977)
Overall record 3,179-2,996 (39 seasons)
  Interleague play 79-57
Number of times worst record in league 4
  Most recent 1990
Runs, inning 13 vs Houston, Sept 20, 1972, 2nd

Total bases, game 46 vs Chicago, Apr 15, 1994
Consecutive games with one or more home runs 25 (45 hrs), 1998
Longest shutout 16 inn, 3-0 vs Chicago, Sept 22, 1975

Longest 1-0 loss 13 inn, vs Los Angeles, May 18, 1974
                13 inn, vs St. Louis, May 20, 1989

ATTENDANCE

Highest home attendance		Largest crowds	
Atlanta-Fulton County Stadium	3,884,725 (1993)	**Day**	51,638 vs Philadelphia, Apr 1, 2002
Turner Field	3,464,488 (1997)	**Night**	53,775 vs Los Angeles, Apr 8, 1974
		Doubleheader	50,597 vs Chicago, Jul 4, 1972
Highest road attendance	2,944,157 (1993)	**Home opener**	53,775 vs Los Angeles, Apr 8, 1974

BOSTON BRAVES
YEARLY FINISHES

(Original National League franchise moved to Milwaukee after the 1952 season)

Year	Position	W	L	Pct.	GB	Manager	Attendance
1876	4th	39	31	.557	15.0	Harry Wright	51,000
1877	1st	42	18	.700	+7.0	Harry Wright	55,240
1878	1st	41	19	.683	+4.0	Harry Wright	48,915
1879	2nd	54	30	.643	5.0	Harry Wright	36,501
1880	6th	40	44	.476	27.0	Harry Wright	34,000
1881	6th	38	45	.458	17.5	Harry Wright	34,343
1882	3rd (tied)	45	39	.536	10.0	John Morrill	50,971
1883	1st	63	35	.643	+4.0	Jack Burdock, John Morrill	128,968
1884	2nd	73	38	.658	10.5	John Morrill	146,777
1885	5th	46	66	.411	41.0	John Morrill	110,290
1886	5th	56	61	.479	30.5	John Morrill	133,683
1887	5th	61	06	.504	16.5	John Morrill	261,000
1888	4th	70	64	.522	15.5	John Morrill	265,015
1889	2nd	83	45	.648	1.0	Jim Hart	283,257
1890	5th	76	57	.571	12.0	Frank Selee	147,539
1891	1st	87	51	.630	+3.5	Frank Selee	184,472
1892	1st/2nd (C)	102	48	.680	**	Frank Selee	146,421
1893	1st	86	43	.667	+5.0	Frank Selee	193,300
1894	3rd	83	49	.629	8.0	Frank Selee	152,800
1895	5th (tied)	71	60	.542	16.5	Frank Selee	242,000
1896	4th	74	57	.565	17.0	Frank Selee	240,000
1897	1st (T)	93	39	.705	+2.0	Frank Selee	334,800
1898	1st	102	47	.685	+6.0	Frank Selee	229,275
1899	2nd	95	57	.625	8.0	Frank Selee	200,384
1900	4th	66	72	.478	17.0	Frank Selee	190,000
1901	5th	69	69	.500	20.5	Frank Selee	146,502
1902	3rd	73	64	.533	29.0	Al Buckenberger	116,960
1903	6th	58	80	.420	32.0	Al Buckenberger	143,155
1904	7th	55	98	.359	51.0	Al Buckenberger	140,694
1905	7th	51	103	.331	54.5	Fred Tenney	150,003
1906	8th	49	102	.325	66.5	Fred Tenney	143,280
1907	7th	58	90	.392	47.0	Fred Tenney	203,221
1908	6th	63	91	.409	36.0	Joe Kelley	253,750
1909	8th	45	108	.294	65.5	Frank Bowerman, Harry Smith	195,188
1910	8th	53	100	.346	50.5	Fred Lake	149,027
1911	8th	44	107	.291	54.0	Fred Tenney	116,000
1912	8th	52	101	.340	52.0	Johnny Kling	121,000
1913	5th	69	82	.457	31.5	George Stallings	208,000
1914	1st (S)	94	59	.614	+10.5	George Stallings	382,913

Year	Position	W	L	Pct.	GB	Manager	Attendance
1915	2nd	83	69	.546	7.0	George Stallings	376,283
1916	3rd	89	63	.586	4.0	George Stallings	313,495
1917	6th	72	81	.471	25.5	George Stallings	174,253
1918	7th	53	71	.427	28.5	George Stallings	84,938
1919	6th	57	82	.410	38.5	George Stallings	167,401
1920	7th	62	90	.408	30.0	George Stallings	162,483
1921	4th	79	74	.516	15.0	Fred Mitchell	318,627
1922	8th	53	100	.346	39.5	Fred Mitchell	167,965
1923	7th	54	100	.351	41.5	Fred Mitchell	227,802
1924	8th	53	100	.346	40.0	Dave Bancroft	117,478
1925	5th	70	83	.458	25.0	Dave Bancroft	313,528
1926	7th	66	86	.434	22.0	Dave Bancroft	303,598
1927	7th	60	94	.390	34.0	Dave Bancroft	288,685
1928	7th	50	103	.327	44.5	Jack Slattery, Rogers Hornsby	227,001
1929	8th	56	98	.364	43.0	Emil Fuchs	372,351
1930	6th	70	84	.455	22.0	Bill McKechnie	464,835
1931	7th	64	90	.416	37.0	Bill McKechnie	515,005
1932	5th	77	77	.500	13.0	Bill McKechnie	507,606
1933	4th	83	71	.539	9.0	Bill McKechnie	517,803
1934	4th	78	73	.517	16.0	Bill McKechnie	303,205
1935	8th	38	115	.248	61.5	Bill McKechnie	232,754
1936	6th	71	83	.461	21.0	Bill McKechnie	340,585
1937	5th	79	73	.520	16.0	Bill McKechnie	385,339
1938	5th	77	75	.507	12.0	Casey Stengel	341,149
1939	7th	63	88	.417	32.5	Casey Stengel	285,994
1940	7th	65	87	.428	34.5	Casey Stengel	241,616
1941	7th	62	92	.403	38.0	Casey Stengel	263,680
1942	7th	59	89	.399	44.0	Casey Stengel	285,332
1943	6th	68	85	.444	36.5	Casey Stengel	271,289
1944	6th	65	89	.422	40.0	Bob Coleman	208,691
1945	6th	67	85	.441	30.0	Bob Coleman, Del Bissonette	374,178
1946	4th	81	72	.529	15.5	Billy Southworth	969,673
1947	3rd	86	68	.558	8.0	Billy Southworth	1,277,361
1948	1st	91	62	.595	+6.5	Billy Southworth	1,455,439
1949	4th	75	79	.487	22.0	Billy Southworth	1,081,795
1950	4th	83	71	.539	8.0	Billy Southworth	944,391
1951	4th	76	78	.494	20.5	Billy Southworth, Tommy Holmes	487,475
1952	7th	64	89	.418	32.0	Tommy Holmes, Charlie Grimm	281,278

**first half 52-22; second half 50-26; (C) won championship series; (T) won Temple Cup; (S) won World Series

INDIVIDUAL AND CLUB RECORDS
BATTING

	Individual		Club
	Season	Career	Season
Games	158—Ed Konetchy, 1916	1,795—Rabbit Maranville	158 (1914, 1916)
At-bats	647—Herman Long, 151 g, 1892	6,764—Herman Long	5,506 (1932)
	*637—Gene Moore, 151 g, 1936	*6,724—Rabbit Maranville	
Runs	160—Hugh Duffy, 125 g, 1894	1,294—Herman Long	1,220 (1894)
	*125—Tommy Holmes, 154 g, 1945	*801—Rabbit Maranville	*785 (1950)
			Fewest—408 (1906)
Hits	236—Hugh Duffy, 125 g, 1894	2,002—Fred Tenney	1,567 (1925)
	*224—Tommy Holmes, 154 g, 1945	*1,696—Rabbit Maranville	Fewest—1,115 (1906)
Hitting streak	37 g—Tommy Holmes, 1945		
Singles	172—Fred Tenney, 150 g, 1899	1,661—Fred Tenney	1,196 (1925)
	*166—Lance Richbourg, 148 g, 1928	*1,326—Rabbit Maranville	
Doubles	50—Hugh Duffy, 125 g, 1894	295—Herman Long	272 (1948)
	*47—Tommy Holmes, 154 g, 1945	*291—Tommy Holmes	
Triples	20—Dick Johnston, 124 g, 1887	103—Rabbit Maranville	100 (1921)
	*18—Ray Powell, 149 g, 1921		

HOME RUNS

			148 (1950)
			Fewest—2 (1878)
			*14 (1902, 1909)
Righthander	38—Wally Berger, 151 g, 1930	199—Wally Berger	
Lefthander	28—Tommy Holmes, 154 g, 1945	88—Herman Long	
		Tommy Holmes	
Switch-hitter	18—Sam Jethroe, 141 g, 1950	49—Sam Jethroe	
	Sam Jethroe, 148 g, 1951		
Rookie	38—Wally Berger, 151 g, 1930		
Home	19—Chuck Workman, 1945	103—Wally Berger	77 (1894) *69 (1945)

	Individual		Club
	Season	**Career**	**Season**
Road	22—Sid Gordon, 1950	96—Wally Berger	89 (1950)
Month	11—Wally Berger, May 1930		33 (Jun 1950)
Pinch	5—Butch Nieman, 1945	5—Butch Nieman	6 (1945)
Grand slams	4—Sid Gordon, 134 g, 1950	6—Wally Berger	7 (1950)
Home runs at South End Grounds, all teams			147 (1894)
Home runs at Braves Field, all teams			131 (1945)
Total bases	374—Hugh Duffy, 125 g, 1894	2,629—Herman Long	2,173 (1950)
	*367—Tommy Holmes, 154 g, 1945	*2,215—Rabbit Maranville	
Extra base hits	81—Hugh Duffy, 125 g, 1894	499—Wally Berger	430 (1950)
	Tommy Holmes, 154 g, 1945		
Sacrifice hits	31—Freddie Maguire, 148 g, 1931	244—Fred Tenney	140 (1948)
		*220—Rabbit Maranville	
Bases on balls	131—Bob Elliott, 151 g, 1948	750—Fred Tenney	684 (1949)
		*561—Rabbit Maranville	Fewest—35 (1878)
			*302 (1905)
Strikeouts	134—Vince DiMaggio, 150 g, 1938	632—John Morrill	711 (1952)
	Fewest—9—Tommy Holmes, 154 g, 1945	*544—Wally Berger	Fewest—348 (1926)
Hit by pitch	11—Sam Jethroe, 148 g, 1951	150—Tommy Tucker	45 (1917)
		*45—Fred Tenney	Fewest—13 (1941)
Runs batted in	130—Wally Berger, 150 g, 1935	746—Wally Berger	1,043 (1894)
			*726 (1950)
			Fewest—330 (1906)
Grounded into double plays	28—Sid Gordon, 150 g, 1951	95—Tommy Holmes	146 (1936)
	Fewest—4—Vince DiMaggio, 150 g, 1938		Fewest—93 (1944)
Left on base			1,255 (1948)
			Fewest—1,003 (1933)
Batting average	.438—Hugh Duffy, 125 g, 1894	.338—Billy Hamilton	.292 (1925)
	*.387—Rogers Hornsby, 140 g, 1928	*.311—Lance Richbourg	Lowest—.223 (1909)
Most .300 hitters			8 (1931)
Slugging average	.694—Hugh Duffy, 125 g, 1894	.533—Wally Berger	.405 (1950)
	*.632—Rogers Hornsby, 140 g, 1928		Lowest—.274 (1909)
On-base percentage	.502—Hugh Duffy, 125 g, 1894	unknown	.401 (1894) *359 (1948)
	*.498—Rogers Hornsby, 140 g, 1928		Lowest—.253 (1878)
			*.284 (1905)

BASERUNNING

Stolen bases	93—Billy Hamilton, 131 g, 1896	431—Herman Long	189 (1902)
	*57—Hap Myers, 140 g, 1913	*194—Rabbit Maranville	
Caught stealing	20—Billy Southworth, 141 g, 1921	unknown	100 (1921)

PITCHING

Games	73—John Clarkson, 1889	557—Kid Nichols	
	*57—Johnny Hutchings, 1945	*349—Bob Smith	
Games started	72—John Clarkson, 1889	502—Kid Nichols	
	*46—Vic Willis, 1902	*239—Dick Rudolph	
Complete games	68—John Clarkson, 1889	477—Kid Nichols	142 (1892) *139 (1905)
	*45—Vic Willis, 1902	*204—Vic Willis	
Wins	49—John Clarkson, 1889	329—Kid Nichols	
	*27—Togie Pittinger, 1902	*122—Warren Spahn	
	Vic Willis, 1902		
Percentage	.842—Tom Hughes (16-3), 1916	.647—John Clarkson	
		*.573—Warren Spahn	
Winning streak	13—Charlie Buffinton, 1884		
	Fred Klobedanz, 1897		
	Ted Lewis, 1898		
	*11—Dick Rudolph, 1914		
Winning streak, two seasons	13—Charlie Buffinton, 1883 (5), 1884 (8)		
	Harry Staley, 1891 (5), 1892 (8)		
	Bill James, 1914 (10), 1915 (3)		

	Individual		Club
	Season	Career	Season
20-win seasons		4—Johnny Sain Warren Spahn	
Losses	33—Jim Whitney, 1881 *29—Vic Willis, 1905	180—Kid Nichols *129—Vic Willis	
Losing streak	18—Cliff Curtis, 1910		
Innings	620—John Clarkson, 1889 *410—Vic Willis, 1902	4,538—Kid Nichols *2,035—Dick Rudolph	1,424.2 (1917)
Hits	628—Hoss Radbourn, 1887 *396—Togie Pittinger, 1903	4,434—Kid Nichols *2,010—Bob Smith	1,662 (1923)
Runs	308—Kid Nichols, 1894 *205—Togie Pittinger, 1903	2,270—Kid Nichols *947—Bob Smith	1,021 (1911)
Earned runs	215—Hoss Radbourn, 1887 Kid Nichols, 1894 *136—Togie Pittinger, 1903	1,511—Kid Nichols *818—Bob Smith	776 (1911)
Bases on balls	203—John Clarkson, 1889 *149—Chick Fraser, 1905	1,159—Kid Nichols *678—Lefty Tyler	672 (1911)
Strikeouts	417—Charlie Buffinton, 1884 *225—Vic Willis, 1902	1,672—Kid Nichols *1,000—Warren Spahn	742 (1884) *687 (1952)
Strikeouts, game	13—Vic Willis, May 28, 1902 Warren Spahn, Sept 13, 1952 (18—Warren Spahn, Jun 14, 1952, 15 inn)		
Hit batsmen	30—Vic Willis, 1898, 1899 *17—Togie Pittinger, 1903	134—Vic Willis *74—Vic Willis	69 (1899) *68 (1907)
Wild pitches	63—Bill Stemmeyer, 1886 *14—Togie Pittinger, 1903	162—Jim Whitney *53—Vic Willis	95 (1886) *50 (1904)
Home runs	34—Johnny Sain, 1950	151—Kid Nichols *128—Warren Spahn	129 (1950)
Sacrifice hits	45—Bob Smith, 1927	227—Dick Rudolph	239 (1927)
Earned run average	1.90—Bill James, 332.1 inn, 1914	2.21—Tommy Bond *2.62—Dick Rudolph	2.15 (1877) *2.19 (1916)
Shutouts	11—Tommy Bond, 1879 *7—Togie Pittinger, 1902 Irv Young, 1905 Warren Spahn, 1947, 1951	44—Kid Nichols *27—Dick Rudolph Warren Spahn	23 (1916) Lost—28 (1906)
1-0 games won	4—Dick Rudolph, 1916 Joe Oeschger, 1920	10—Kid Nichols *10—Dick Rudolph	9 (1916) Lost—6 (1906, 1933)

TEAM FIELDING

Putouts	4,262 (1914) Fewest—3,975 (1906)	Assists	2,225 (1908) Fewest—1,665 (1946)
Chances accepted	6,424 (1914) Fewest—5,750 (1935)	Errors	353 (1904) Fewest—138 (1933)
Double plays	178 (1939) Fewest—101 (1935)	Passed balls	167 (1883) *42 (1905) Fewest—2 (1943)
Errorless games	91 (1989) Consecutive—5 (1933, twice)	Fielding average	.978 (1933) Lowest—.945 (1904)

MISCELLANEOUS

Most players, season 48 (1946)

Fewest players, season 23 (1905)

Games won 102 (1892, 1898)   *94 (1914)
Month 26 (Sept 1914)
Consecutive 18 (1891)   *9 (1902, 1914 twice, 1945)
Winning percentage .705 (1897), 93-39   *.614 (1914), 94-59
Lowest .248 (1935), 38-115
Number of league championships 10
Most recent 1948
Runs, game 30 vs Detroit, Jun 9, 1883
*20 vs Philadelphia, Jun 25, 1900
vs Philadelphia, Oct 6, 1910
vs St. Louis, Sept 18, 1915, 1st game
vs St. Louis, Aug 25, 1936, 1st game

Most seasons, non-pitcher 15—Fred Tenney
Rabbit Maranville
Johnny Cooney
Most seasons, pitcher 12—Kid Nichols
*11—Dick Rudolph
Games lost 115 (1935)
Month 25 (Sept 1928, Sept 1935)
Consecutive 19 (1906)
Overall record 5,118-5,598 (77 seasons)

Number of times worst record in league 9
Most recent 1935
Runs, inning 16 vs Baltimore, Jun 18, 1894, a.m. game, 1st
*13 vs St. Louis, Jul 25, 1900, 1st

Opponents' 27 by Pittsburgh, Jun 6, 1894
  *26 by Cincinnati, Jun 4, 1911
Hits, game 32 vs St. Louis, Sept 3, 1896, 1st game
  *25 vs St. Louis, Aug 25, 1936, 1st game

Home runs, game 5 vs Cincinnati, May 30, 1894, p.m. game
  vs Chicago, May 13, 1942
  vs Cincinnati, May 6, 1950
Runs, shutout 18 vs Buffalo, Oct 3, 1885
  *16 vs Brooklyn, May 7, 1918
  vs Pittsburgh, Sept 12, 1952, 2nd game
Opponents' 17 by Chicago, Sept 16, 1884
  *15, seven times, last time
  by St. Louis, May 7, 1950
Longest 1-0 win 13 inn, six times, last time
  vs Brooklyn, May 4, 1923

Total bases, game 46 vs Detroit, Jun 9, 1883
  vs Cleveland, Jul 5, 1984
  *37 vs Philadelphia, Jul 6, 1934
  vs Cincinnati, May 6, 1950
Consecutive games with one or more home runs unknown
  with one or more home runs

Longest shutout unknown

Longest 1-0 loss 17 inn vs Chicago, Sept 21, 1901

ATTENDANCE

Highest home attendance		**Largest crowds**	
South End Grounds	382,913 (1914)	Day	41,527 vs Chicago, Aug 8, 1948
Braves Field	1,455,439 (1948)	Night	39,549 vs Brooklyn, Aug 5, 1946
		Doubleheader	47,123 vs Philadelphia, May 22, 1932
Highest road attendance	1,308,175 (1947)	Home opener	25,000 vs New York, Apr 16, 1935

*records made since 1900 that do not exceed pre-1900 records

BROOKLYN DODGERS
YEARLY FINISHES

(American Association franchise moved to the National League after the 1889 season)

Year	Position	W	L	Pct.	GB	Manager	Attendance
1890	1st	86	43	.667	+6.0	Bill McGunnigle	121,412
1891	6th	71	76	.445	25.5	John Montgomery Ward	181,477
1892	2nd/3rd	95	59	.617	**	John Montgomery Ward	183,727
1893	6th (tied)	65	63	.508	20.5	Dave Foutz	235,000
1894	5th	70	61	.534	20.5	Dave Foutz	214,000
1895	5th (tied)	71	60	.542	16.5	Dave Foutz	230,000
1896	9th (tied)	58	73	.443	33.0	Dave Foutz	201,000
1897	6th (tied)	61	71	.462	32.0	Billy Barnie	220,831
1898	10th	54	91	.372	46.0	Billy Barnie, Mike Griffin, Charlie Ebbets	122,514
1899	1st	101	47	.682	+8.0	Ned Hanlon	269,641
1900	1st (C)	82	54	.603	+4.5	Ned Hanlon	170,000
1901	3rd	79	57	.581	9.5	Ned Hanlon	189,200
1902	2nd	75	63	.543	27.5	Ned Hanlon	199,868
1903	5th	70	66	.515	19.0	Ned Hanlon	224,670
1904	6th	56	97	.366	50.0	Ned Hanlon	214,600
1905	8th	48	104	.316	56.5	Ned Hanlon	227,924
1906	5th	66	86	.434	50.0	Patsy Donovan	227,400
1907	5th	65	83	.439	40.0	Patsy Donovan	312,500
1908	7th	53	101	.344	46.0	Patsy Donovan	275,600
1909	6th	55	98	.359	55.5	Harry Lumley	321,300
1910	6th	64	90	.416	40.0	Bill Dahlen	279,321
1911	7th	64	86	.427	33.5	Bill Dahlen	269,000
1912	7th	58	95	.379	46.0	Bill Dahlen	243,000
1913	6th	65	84	.436	34.5	Bill Dahlen	347,000
1914	5th	75	79	.487	19.5	Wilbert Robinson	122,671
1915	3rd	80	72	.526	10.0	Wilbert Robinson	297,766
1916	1st	94	60	.610	+2.5	Wilbert Robinson	447,747
1917	7th	70	81	.464	26.5	Wilbert Robinson	221,619
1918	5th	57	69	.452	25.5	Wilbert Robinson	83,831
1919	5th	69	71	.493	27.0	Wilbert Robinson	360,721
1920	1st (s)	93	61	.604	+7.0	Wilbert Robinson	808,722
1921	5th	77	75	.507	16.5	Wilbert Robinson	613,245
1922	6th	76	78	.494	17.0	Wilbert Robinson	498,856
1923	6th	76	78	.494	19.5	Wilbert Robinson	564,666
1924	2nd	92	62	.597	1.5	Wilbert Robinson	818,883
1925	6th (tied)	68	85	.444	27.0	Wilbert Robinson	659,435
1926	6th	71	82	.464	17.5	Wilbert Robinson	650,819
1927	6th	65	88	.425	28.5	Wilbert Robinson	637,230
1928	6th	77	76	.503	17.5	Wilbert Robinson	664,863
1929	6th	70	83	.458	28.5	Wilbert Robinson	731,886
1930	4th	86	68	.558	6.0	Wilbert Robinson	1,097,339
1931	4th	79	73	.520	21.0	Wilbert Robinson	753,133
1932	3rd	81	73	.526	9.0	Max Carey	681,827
1933	6th	65	88	.425	26.5	Max Carey	526,815

– 285 –

Year	Position	W	L	Pct.	GB	Manager	Attendance
1934	6th	71	81	.467	23.5	Casey Stengel	434,188
1935	5th	70	83	.458	29.5	Casey Stengel	470,517
1936	7th	67	87	.435	25.0	Casey Stengel	489,618
1937	6th	62	91	.405	33.5	Burleigh Grimes	482,481
1938	7th	69	80	.463	18.5	Burleigh Grimes	663,087
1939	3rd	84	69	.549	12.5	Leo Durocher	955,668
1940	2nd	88	65	.575	12.0	Leo Durocher	975,978
1941	1st (s)	100	54	.649	+2.5	Leo Durocher	1,214,910
1942	2nd	104	50	.675	2.0	Leo Durocher	1,037,765
1943	3rd	81	72	.529	23.5	Leo Durocher	661,739
1944	7th	63	91	.409	42.0	Leo Durocher	605,905
1945	3rd	87	67	.565	11.0	Leo Durocher	1,059,220
1946	2nd (I)	96	60	.615	2.0	Leo Durocher	1,796,824
1947	1st (s)	94	60	.610	+5.0	Clyde Sukeforth, Burt Shotton	1,807,526
1948	3rd	84	70	.545	7.5	Leo Durocher, Burt Shotton	1,398,967
1949	1st (s)	97	57	.630	+1.0	Burt Shotton	1,633,747
1950	2nd	89	65	.578	2.0	Burt Shotton	1,185,896
1951	2nd (I)	97	60	.618	1.0	Chuck Dressen	1,282,628
1952	1st (s)	96	57	.627	+4.5	Chuck Dressen	1,088,704
1953	1st (s)	105	49	.682	+13.0	Chuck Dressen	1,163,419
1954	2nd	92	62	.597	5.0	Walter Alston	1,020,531
1955	1st (S)	98	55	.641	+13.5	Walter Alston	1,033,589
1956	1st (s)	93	61	.604	+1.0	Walter Alston	1,213,562
1957	3rd	84	70	.545	11.0	Walter Alston	1,028,258

**first half 51-26, second half 44-33; (C) won Chronicle-Telegraph Cup; (s) lost World Series; (I) lost league playoff; (S) won World Series

INDIVIDUAL AND CLUB RECORDS
BATTING

	Individual		Club
	Season	Career	Season
Games	158—Carl Furillo, 1951 Gil Hodges, 1951	2,318—Zack Wheat	158 (1892, 1951)
At-bats	667—Carl Furillo, 158 g, 1951	8,859—Zack Wheat	5,574 (1936)
Runs	148—Hub Collins, 129 g, 1890 *143—Babe Herman, 153 g, 1930	1,317—Pee Wee Reese	1,021 (1894) *955 (1953) Fewest—375 (1908)
Hits	241—Babe Herman, 153 g, 1930	2,804—Zack Wheat	1,654 (1930) Fewest—1,044 (1908)
Hitting streak	29 g—Zack Wheat, 1916		
Singles	188—Willie Keeler, 141 g, 1899 *179—Willie Keeler, 137 g, 1900	2,038—Zack Wheat	1,223 (1925)
Doubles	52—Johnny Frederick, 148 g, 1929	464—Zack Wheat	303 (1930)
Triples	26—George Treadway, 124 g, 1894 *22—Hy Myers, 154 g, 1920	171—Zack Wheat	130 (1894) *99 (1920)

HOME RUNS

			208 (1953) Fewest—14 (1915)
Righthander	42—Gil Hodges, 154 g, 1954	298—Gil Hodges	
Lefthander	43—Duke Snider, 151 g, 1956	316—Duke Snider	
Switch-hitter	13—Jim Gilliam, 146 g, 1954	44—Tom Daly	
Rookie	25—Del Bissonette, 155 g, 1928		
Home	25—Gil Hodges, 1954 Duke Snider (inc. 2 at Jersey City), 1956	177—Duke Snider	119 (1955)
Road	24—Gil Hodges, 1951	139—Duke Snider	98 (1953)
Month	15—Duke Snider, Aug 1953		49 (Jul 1953, Aug 1953)
Pinch	6—Johnny Frederick, 1932	8—Johnny Frederick	7 (1932)
Grand slams	2—many players	13—Gil Hodges	8 (1952)
Home runs at Ebbets Field, all teams			206 (1950)

Total bases	416—Babe Herman, 153 g, 1930	4,003—Zack Wheat	2,545 (1953)
Extra base hits	94—Babe Herman, 153 g, 1930	766—Zack Wheat	541 (1953)
Sacrifice hits	39—Jake Daubert, 150 g, 1915	237—Jake Daubert	197 (1907)
Sacrifice flies	19—Gil Hodges, 154 g, 1954	37—Gil Hodges	59 (1954)
Bases on balls	148—Eddie Stanky, 153 g, 1945	1,184—Pee Wee Reese	732 (1947) Fewest—179 (1884) *312 (1901)
Strikeouts	115—Dolf Camilli, 149 g, 1941 Fewest—15—Jimmy Johnston, 151 g, 1923	875—Pee Wee Reese	848 (1957) Fewest—255 (1897) *272 (1900)

	Individual		Club
	Season	**Career**	**Season**
Hit by pitch	20—Hughie Jennings, 115 g, 1900	72—Jackie Robinson	125 (1899) *81 (1900)
			Fewest—14 (1942, 1944)
Runs batted in	142—Roy Campanella, 144 g, 1953	1,227—Zack Wheat	887 (1953)
			Fewest—306 (1908)
Grounded into double plays	27—Carl Furillo, 149 g, 1956	187—Carl Furillo	151 (1952)
	Fewest—5—Jackie Robinson, 151 g, 1947		Fewest—87 (1947)
	Pee Wee Reese, 155 g, 1949		
	Jim Gilliam, 153 g, 1956		
Left on base			1,278 (1947)
			Fewest—1,012 (1921)
Batting average	.393—Babe Herman, 153 g, 1930	.352—Willie Keeler	.313 (1894) *.304 (1930)
		*.339—Babe Herman	Lowest—.213 (1908)
Most .300 hitters			6 (1900, 1922, 1925, 1930, 1943, 1953)
Slugging average	.678—Babe Herman, 153 g, 1930	.560—Duke Snider	.474 (1953)
			Lowest—.277 (1908)
On-base percentage	.467—Mike Griffin, 107 g, 1894	.409—Jackie Robinson	.378 (1894) *.366 (1953)
	*.455—Babe Herman, 153 g, 1930		Lowest—.263 (1884)
			*.266 (1908)

BASERUNNING

Stolen bases	91—Darby O'Brien, 136 g, 1889	298—Tom Daly	409 (1882, 1987)
	*67—Jimmy Sheckard, 139 g, 1903	*231—Pee Wee Reese	*274 (1900)
Caught stealing	23—George Cutshaw, 154 g, 1915	83 Jimmy Johnston	126 (1915)

PITCHING

Games	62—Clem Labine, 1956	382—Brickyard Kennedy	
		*378—Dazzy Vance	
Games started	56—Adonis Terry, 1884	333—Brickyard Kennedy	
	*41—Oscar Jones, 1904	*328—Dazzy Vance	
Complete games	55—Adonis Terry, 1884	280—Brickyard Kennedy	138 (1886, 1888)
	*30—Oscar Jones, 1904	*212—Dazzy Vance	*135 (1904)
Wins	40—Bob Caruthers, 1889	190—Dazzy Vance	
	*28—Joe McGinnity, 1900		
Percentage	.889—Freddie Fitzsimmons (16-2), 1940	.677 Bob Caruthers	
		*672—Don Newcombe	
Winning streak	15—Dazzy Vance, 1924		
20-win seasons		4—Burleigh Grimes	
Losses	35—Adonis Terry, 1884	144—Brickyard Kennedy	
	*27—George Bell, 1910	*134—Nap Rucker	
Losing streak	14—Jim Pastorius, 1908		
Innings	485—Adonis Terry, 1884	2,857—Brickyard Kennedy	1,433 (1940)
	*377—Oscar Jones, 1904	*2,757.2—Dazzy Vance	
Hits	512—Henry Porter, 1887	3,102—Brickyard Kennedy	1,608 (1925)
	*387—Oscar Jones, 1904	*2,579—Dazzy Vance	
Runs	308—Adonis Terry, 1884	1,772—Brickyard Kennedy	1,007 (1894) *888 (1929)
	*188—Harry McIntire, 1905	*1,175—Burleigh Grimes	
Earned runs	197—Brickyard Kennedy, 1894	1,264—Brickyard Kennedy	743 (1929)
	*138—Burleigh Grimes, 1925	*972—Dazzy Vance	
Bases on balls	171—Ed Stein, 1894	1,128—Brickyard Kennedy	671 (1946)
	*152—Bill Donovan, 1901	*764—Dazzy Vance	
Strikeouts	262—Dazzy Vance, 1924	1,918—Dazzy Vance	891 (1957)
Strikeouts, game	17—Dazzy Vance, Jul 20, 1925, 10 inn		
	(16—Nap Rucker, Jul 24, 1909)		
Hit batsmen	41—Joe McGinnity, 1900	82—Harry McIntire	72 (1900)
Wild pitches	39—John Harkins, 1885	107—Adonis Terry	80 (1885) *42 (1956)
	*15—Larry Cheney, 1916	*62—Burleigh Grimes	
Home runs	35—Don Newcombe, 1955	180—Carl Erskine	171 (1956)

	Individual		Club
	Season	Career	Season
Sacrifice hits	54—Nap Rucker, 1908	272—Burleigh Grimes	216 (1926)
Sacrifice flies	8—Roger Craig, 1956	15—Carl Erskine	44 (1954)
	Clem Labine, 1957		
Earned run average	1.58—Rube Marquard, 205 inn, 1916	2.31—Jeff Pfeffer	2.12 (1916)
Shutouts	7—Bob Caruthers, 1889	38—Nap Rucker	22 (1906, 1916)
	Burleigh Grimes, 1918		Lost—26 (1907)
	Whit Wyatt, 1941		
1-0 games won	3—Nap Rucker, 1911	11—Nap Rucker	7 (1907, 1909)
			Lost—9 (1910, 1913)

TEAM FIELDING

Putouts	4,286 (1940)	Assists	2,132 (1921)
	Fewest—2,840 (1884) *3,636 (1901)		Fewest—1,340 (1884) *1,577 (1944)
Chances accepted	6,334 (1920)	Errors	610 (1886) *408 (1905)
	Fewest—5,672 (1944)		Fewest—106 (1952)
Double plays	192 (1951)	Passed balls	169 (1884) *31 (1901)
	Fewest—56 (1885) *73 (1906)		Fewest—4 (1933, 1951, 1953, 1954)
Errorless games	unknown	Fielding average	.993 (1952)
	Consecutive—10 (1942)		Lowest—.864 (1887) *.947 (1900)

MISCELLANEOUS

Most players, season 53 (1944)
Fewest players, season 23 (1905)
Games won 105 (1953)
   Month 25 (July 1947, Aug 1953)
   Consecutive 15 (1924)
Winning percentage .682 (1899), 101-47 and (1953), 105-49
   Lowest .316 (1905), 48-104
Number of league championships 13
   Most recent 1956
Runs, game 25 vs Pittsburgh, May 20, 1896
   *25 vs Cincinnati, Sept 23, 1901
   Opponents' 28 by Chicago, Aug 25, 1891
     *26 by New York, Apr 30, 1944, 1st game
Hits, game 28 vs Pittsburgh, Jun 23, 1930
Home runs, game 6 vs Milwaukee, Jun 1, 1955
Runs, shutout 15 vs Philadelphia, Aug 16, 1952, 6 inn
   Opponents' 17 by St. Louis, Aug 24, 1924, 2nd game
Longest 1-0 win 13 inn vs St. Louis, Aug 21, 1909
   vs Boston, May 29, 1938

Most seasons, non-pitcher 18—Zack Wheat
Most seasons, pitcher 12—Dazzy Vance
Games lost 104 (1905)
   Month 27 (Sept 1908)
   Consecutive 16 (1944)
Overall record 5,214-4,926 (68 seasons)

Number of times worst record in league 1
   Most recent 1905
Runs, inning 15 vs Cincinnati, May 21, 1952, 1st

Total bases, game 46 vs Philadelphia, Sept 23, 1939, 1st game
Consecutive games with one or more home runs 24 (39 hrs), 1953
Longest shutout unknown

Longest 1-0 loss 15 inn vs Cincinnati, Jun 11, 1915

ATTENDANCE

Highest home attendance		Largest crowds	
Washington Park I	181,477 (1891)	Day	37,512 vs New York, Aug 30, 1947
Eastern Park	235,000 (1893)	Night	35,583 vs Philadelphia, Sept 24, 1949
Washington Park II	321,300 (1909)	Doubleheader	41,209 vs New York, May 30, 1934
Ebbets Field	1,807,526 (1947)	Home opener	34,530 vs New York, Apr 19, 1949
Highest road attendance	1,863,542 (1947)		

*records made since 1900 that do not exceed pre-1900 records

CHICAGO CUBS
YEARLY FINISHES

(Original National League franchise)

Year	Position	W	L	Pct.	GB	Manager	Attendance
1876	1st	52	14	.788	+6.0	Albert Spalding	65,441
1877	5th	26	33	.441	15.5	Albert Spalding	46,454
1878	4th	30	30	.500	11.0	Bob Ferguson	58,691
1879	4th	46	33	.582	10.5	Cap Anson	67,687
1880	1st	67	17	.798	+15.0	Cap Anson	66,708
1881	1st	56	28	.667	+9.0	Cap Anson	82,000
1882	1st	55	29	.665	+3.0	Cap Anson	125,452
1883	2nd	59	39	.602	4.0	Cap Anson	124,880
1884	4th (tied)	62	50	.554	22.0	Cap Anson	87,667
1885	1st	87	25	.777	+2.0	Cap Anson	117,519
1886	1st	90	34	.726	+2.5	Cap Anson	142,438
1887	3rd	71	50	.587	6.5	Cap Anson	217,070
1888	2nd	77	58	.570	9.0	Cap Anson	228,906

Year	Position	W	L	Pct.	GB	Manager	Attendance
1889	3rd	67	65	.508	19.0	Cap Anson	149,175
1890	2nd	84	53	.613	6.0	Cap Anson	102,536
1891	2nd	82	53	.607	3.5	Cap Anson	201,188
1892	8th/7th	70	76	.479	**	Cap Anson	109,067
1893	9th	56	71	.441	29.0	Cap Anson	223,500
1894	8th	57	75	.432	34.0	Cap Anson	239,000
1895	4th	72	58	.554	15.0	Cap Anson	382,300
1896	5th	71	57	.555	18.5	Cap Anson	317,500
1897	9th	59	73	.447	34.0	Cap Anson	327,160
1898	4th	85	65	.567	17.5	Tom Burns	424,352
1899	8th	75	73	.507	26.0	Tom Burns	352,130
1900	5th (tied)	65	75	.464	19.0	Tom Loftus	248,577
1901	6th	53	86	.381	37.0	Tom Loftus	205,071
1902	5th	68	69	.496	34.0	Frank Selee	263,700
1903	3rd	82	56	.594	8.0	Frank Selee	386,205
1904	2nd	93	60	.608	13.0	Frank Selee	439,100
1905	3rd	92	61	.601	13.0	Frank Selee, Frank Chance	509,900
1906	1st (s)	116	36	.763	+20.0	Frank Chance	654,300
1907	1st (S)	107	45	.704	+17.0	Frank Chance	422,550
1908	1st (S)	99	55	.643	+1.0	Frank Chance	665,325
1909	2nd	104	49	.680	6.5	Frank Chance	633,480
1910	1st (s)	104	50	.675	+13.0	Frank Chance	526,152
1911	2nd	92	62	.597	7.5	Frank Chance	576,000
1912	3rd	91	59	.607	11.5	Frank Chance	514,000
1913	3rd	88	65	.575	13.5	Johnny Evers	419,000
1914	4th	78	76	.506	16.5	Hank O'Day	202,516
1915	4th	73	80	.477	17.5	Roger Bresnahan	217,058
1916	5th	67	86	.438	26.5	Joe Tinker	453,685
1917	5th	74	80	.481	24.0	Fred Mitchell	360,218
1918	1st (s)	84	45	.651	+10.5	Fred Mitchell	337,256
1919	3rd	75	65	.536	21.0	Fred Mitchell	424,430
1920	5th (tied)	75	79	.487	18.0	Fred Mitchell	480,783
1921	7th	64	89	.418	30.0	Johnny Evers, Bill Killefer	410,107
1922	5th	80	74	.519	13.0	Bill Killefer	542,283
1923	4th	83	71	.539	12.5	Bill Killefer	703,705
1924	5th	81	72	.529	12.0	Bill Killefer	716,922
1925	8th	68	86	.442	27.5	Bill Killefer, Rabbit Maranville, George Gibson	622,610
1926	4th	82	72	.532	7.0	Joe McCarthy	885,063
1927	4th	85	68	.556	8.5	Joe McCarthy	1,159,168
1928	3rd	91	63	.591	4.0	Joe McCarthy	1,143,740
1929	1st (s)	98	54	.645	+10.5	Joe McCarthy	1,485,166
1930	2nd	90	64	.584	2.0	Joe McCarthy, Rogers Hornsby	1,463,624
1931	3rd	84	70	.545	17.0	Rogers Hornsby	1,086,422
1932	1st (s)	90	64	.584	+4.0	Rogers Hornsby, Charlie Grimm	974,688
1933	3rd	86	68	.558	6.0	Charlie Grimm	594,112
1934	3rd	86	65	.570	8.0	Charlie Grimm	707,525
1935	1st (s)	100	54	.649	+4.0	Charlie Grimm	692,604
1936	2nd (tied)	87	67	.565	5.0	Charlie Grimm	699,370
1937	2nd	93	61	.604	3.0	Charlie Grimm	895,020
1938	1st	89	63	.586	+2.0	Charlie Grimm, Gabby Hartnett	951,640
1939	4th	84	70	.545	13.0	Gabby Hartnett	726,003
1940	5th	75	79	.487	25.5	Gabby Hartnett	534,878
1941	6th	70	84	.455	30.0	Jimmy Wilson	545,159
1942	6th	68	86	.442	38.0	Jimmy Wilson	590,872
1943	5th	74	79	.484	30.5	Jimmy Wilson	508,247
1944	4th	75	79	.487	30.0	Jimmy Wilson, Charlie Grimm	640,110
1945	1st (s)	98	56	.636	+3.0	Charlie Grimm	1,036,386
1946	3rd	82	71	.536	14.5	Charlie Grimm	1,342,970
1947	6th	69	85	.448	25.0	Charlie Grimm	1,364,039
1948	8th	64	90	.416	27.5	Charlie Grimm	1,237,792
1949	8th	61	93	.396	36.0	Charlie Grimm, Frankie Frisch	1,143,139
1950	7th	64	89	.418	26.5	Frankie Frisch	1,165,944
1951	8th	62	92	.403	34.5	Frankie Frisch, Phil Cavarretta	894,415
1952	5th	77	77	.500	19.5	Phil Cavarretta	1,024,826
1953	7th	65	89	.422	40.0	Phil Cavarretta	763,658
1954	7th	64	90	.416	33.0	Stan Hack	748,183
1955	6th	72	81	.471	26.0	Stan Hack	875,800
1956	8th	60	94	.390	33.0	Stan Hack	720,118
1957	7th (tied)	62	92	.403	33.0	Bob Scheffing	670,629
1958	5th (tied)	72	82	.468	20.0	Bob Scheffing	979,904
1959	5th (tied)	74	80	.481	13.0	Bob Scheffing	858,255
1960	7th	60	94	.390	35.0	Charlie Grimm, Lou Boudreau	809,770
1961	7th	64	90	.416	29.0	Vedie Himsl, Harry Craft, Elvin Tappe, Lou Klein	673,057
1962	9th	59	103	.364	42.5	Charlie Metro, Elvin Tappe, Lou Klein	609,802
1963	7th	82	80	.506	17.0	Bob Kennedy	979,551
1964	8th	76	86	.469	17.0	Bob Kennedy	751,647

Year	Position	W	L	Pct.	GB	Manager	Attendance
1965	8th	72	90	.444	25.0	Bob Kennedy, Lou Klein	641,361
1966	10th	59	103	.364	36.0	Leo Durocher	635,891
1967	3rd	87	74	.540	14.0	Leo Durocher	977,226
1968	3rd	84	78	.519	13.0	Leo Durocher	1,043,409

EAST DIVISION

Year	Position	W	L	Pct.	GB	Manager	Attendance
1969	2nd	92	70	.568	8.0	Leo Durocher	1,674,993
1970	2nd	84	78	.519	5.0	Leo Durocher	1,642,705
1971	3rd (tied)	83	79	.512	14.0	Leo Durocher	1,653,007
1972	2nd	85	70	.548	11.0	Leo Durocher, Whitey Lockman	1,299,163
1973	5th	77	84	.478	5.0	Whitey Lockman	1,351,705
1974	6th	66	96	.407	22.0	Whitey Lockman, Jim Marshall	1,015,378
1975	5th (tied)	75	87	.463	17.5	Jim Marshall	1,034,819
1976	4th	75	87	.463	26.0	Jim Marshall	1,026,217
1977	4th	81	81	.500	20.0	Herman Franks	1,439,834
1978	3rd	79	83	.488	11.0	Herman Franks	1,525,311
1979	5th	80	82	.494	18.0	Herman Franks, Joe Amalfitano	1,648,587
1980	6th	64	98	.395	27.0	Preston Gomez, Joe Amalfitano	1,206,776
1981	6th/5th	38	65	.369	*	Joe Amalfitano	565,637
1982	5th	73	89	.451	19.0	Lee Elia	1,249,278
1983	5th	71	91	.438	19.0	Lee Elia, Charlie Fox	1,479,717
1984	1st (c)	96	65	.596	+6.5	Jim Frey	2,104,219
1985	4th	77	84	.478	23.5	Jim Frey	2,161,534
1986	5th	70	90	.438	37.0	Jim Frey, John Vukovich, Gene Michael	1,859,102
1987	6th	76	85	.472	18.5	Gene Michael, Frank Lucchesi	2,035,130
1988	4th	77	85	.475	24.0	Don Zimmer	2,089,034
1989	1st (c)	93	69	.574	+6.0	Don Zimmer	2,491,942
1990	4th	77	85	.475	18.0	Don Zimmer	2,243,791
1991	4th	77	83	.481	20.0	Don Zimmer, Joe Altobelli, Jim Essian	2,314,250
1992	4th	78	84	.481	18.0	Jim Lefebvre	2,126,720
1993	4th	84	78	.519	13.0	Jim Lefebvre	2,653,763

CENTRAL DIVISION

Year	Position	W	L	Pct.	GB	Manager	Attendance
1994	5th	49	64	.434	16.5	Tom Trebelhorn	1,845,208
1995	3rd	73	71	.507	12.0	Jim Riggleman	1,918,265
1996	4th	76	86	.469	12.0	Jim Riggleman	2,219,110
1997	5th	68	94	.420	16.0	Jim Riggleman	2,190,308
1998	2nd (W,d)	90	73	.552	12.5	Jim Riggleman	2,623,000
1999	6th	67	95	.414	30.0	Jim Riggleman	2,813,854
2000	6th	65	97	.401	30.0	Don Baylor	2,789,511
2001	3rd	88	74	.543	5.0	Don Baylor	2,779,456
2002	5th	67	95	.414	30.0	Don Baylor, Bruce Kimm	2,693,071
2003	1st (D,c)	88	74	.543	+1.0	Dusty Baker	2,962,630
2004	3rd	89	73	.549	16.0	Dusty Baker	3,170,184

**first half 31-39, second half 39-37; (s) lost World Series; (S) won World Series; *first half 15-37, second half 23-28; (c) lost League Championship Series; (W) won wild card playoff; (d) lost Division Series; (D) won Division Series

INDIVIDUAL AND CLUB RECORDS

BATTING

	Individual		Club
	Season	**Career**	**Season**
Games	164—Ron Santo, 1965 Billy Williams, 1965	2,528—Ernie Banks	164 (1965)
At-bats	666—Billy Herman, 154 g, 1935	9,421—Ernie Banks	5,675 (1988)
Runs	156—Rogers Hornsby, 156 g, 1929 *1,316—Ryne Sandberg	1,445—Cap Anson	1,041 (1894) *998 (1930) Fewest—366 (1877) *520 (1916)
Hits	229—Rogers Hornsby, 156 g, 1929	2,589—Cap Anson *2,583—Ernie Banks	1,722 (1930) Fewest—633 (1877) *1,200 (1902)
Hitting streak	42 g—Bill Dahlen, 1894 *30 g—Jerome Walton, 1989		
Singles	165—Sparky Adams, 146 g, 1927	1,910—Cap Anson *1,692—Stan Hack	1,230 (1887) *1,226 (1921)
Doubles	57—Billy Herman, 154 g, 1935 Billy Herman, 153 g, 1936	476—Cap Anson *456—Mark Grace	340 (1931)
Triples	21—Wildfire Schulte, 154 g, 1911 Vic Saier, 149 g, 1913	142—Jimmy Ryan *2,583—Wildfire Schulte	101 (1911)

	Individual		Club
	Season	Career	Season
HOME RUNS			235 (2004)
			Fewest—127 (1997)
Righthander	66—Sammy Sosa, 159 g, 1998	545—Sammy Sosa	
Lefthander	42—Billy Williams, 161 g, 1970	392—Billy Williams	
Switch-hitter	27—Mark Bellhorn, 146 g, 2002	59—Augie Galan	
Rookie	25—Billy Williams, 146 g, 1961		
Home	35—Sammy Sosa, 1998	293—Sammy Sosa	131 (1884)
Road	31—Sammy Sosa, 1998	242—Sammy Sosa	101 (1998, 2002)
Month	20—Sammy Sosa, June 1998		47 (Aug 1987, Jun 1998)
Pinch	4—Glenallen Hill, 1999	9—Glenallen Hill	10 (1998)
Grand slams	5—Ernie Banks, 154 g, 1955	12—Ernie Banks	9 (1929)
Home runs at Wrigley Field, all teams			233 (2004)
Total bases	425—Sammy Sosa, 160 g, 2001	4,706—Ernie Banks	2,684 (1930)
Extra base hits	103—Sammy Sosa, 160 g, 2001	1,009—Ernie Banks	572 (1904)
Sacrifice hits	40—Jimmy Sheckard, 149 g, 1906	263—Wildfire Schulte	270 (1908)
Sacrifice flies	14—Ron Santo, 1969	96—Ernie Banks	66 (1975)
Bases on balls	147—Jimmy Sheckard, 156 g, 1911	1,092—Stan Hack	650 (1975)
			Fewest—57 (1877)
			*298 (1904)
Strikeouts	174—Sammy Sosa, 162 g, 1997	1,815—Sammy Sosa	1,269 (2002)
	Fewest—5—Charlie Hollocher, 152 g, 1922		Fewest—45 (1876)
			*374 (1921)
Hit by pitch	23—Bill Dahlen, 142 g, 1898	137—Frank Chance	66 (2001)
	*14—Scott Servais, 129 g, 1996	*70—Ernie Banks	Fewest—71 (1898)
			*13 (1956)
Runs batted in	191—Hack Wilson, 155 g, 1930	1,879—Cap Anson	940 (1930)
		*1,636—Ernie Banks	Fewest—248 (1877)
			*423 (1902)
Grounded into	27—Ron Santo, 149 g, 1973	240—Ron Santo	161 (1933)
double plays	Fewest—0—Augie Galan, 154 g, 1935		Fewest—87 (1991)
Left on base			1,262 (1975)
			Fewest—964 (1924)
Batting average	.421 Cap Anson, 122 g, 1887	.309—Billy Herman	.333 (1887) *.309 (1930)
	*.380—Rogers Hornsby, 156 g, 1929		Lowest—.235 (1892)
			*.238 (1963, 1965)
Most .300 hitters			8 (1921)
Slugging average	.737—Sammy Sosa, 160 g, 2001	.569—Sammy Sosa	.481 (1930)
			Lowest—.298 (1902)
On-base percentage	.483—King Kelly, 118 g, 1886	.398—Cap Anson	.388 (1887) *.378 (1930)
	*.459—Rogers Hornsby, 156 g, 1929	*.394—Stan Hack	Lowest—.276 (1879)
			*.295 (1904)

BASERUNNING

Stolen bases	100—Bill Lange, 123 g, 1896	404—Frank Chance	382 (1887) *283 (1906)
	*67—Frank Chance, 123 g, 1903		
Caught stealing	29—Charlie Hollocher, 152 g, 1922	385—Frank Chance	149 (1924)
		*107—Ryne Sandberg	

PITCHING

Games	84—Ted Abernathy, 1965	605—Charlie Root	
	Dick Tidrow, 1980		
Games started	70—John Clarkson, 1885	347—Ferguson Jenkins	
	Bill Hutchison, 1892		
	*42—Ferguson Jenkins, 1969		
Complete games	68—John Clarkson, 1885	317—Bill Hutchison	147 (1889) *139 (1904)
	*34—Jack Taylor, 1902	*206—Mordecai Brown	
Wins	53—John Clarkson, 1885	201—Charlie Root	
	*29—Mordecai Brown, 1908		
Percentage	.941—Rick Sutcliffe (16-1), 1984	.706—John Clarkson	
		*.686—Mordecai Brown	

	Individual		Club
	Season	Career	Season
Winning streak	17—John Luby, 1890 *14—Ed Reulbach, 1909 Rick Sutcliffe, 1984		
20-win seasons		6—Mordecai Brown Ferguson Jenkins Clark Griffith	
Losses	36—Bill Hutchison, 1892 *23—Tom Hughes, 1901	156—Charlie Root	
Losing streak	13—Dutch McCall, 1948		
Saves	53—Randy Myers, 1993	180—Lee Smith	56 (1993, 1998)
Innings	623—John Clarkson, 1885 *363.1—Grover Alexander, 1920	3,137.1—Charlie Root	1,479 (1980)
Hits	605—John Clarkson, 1887 *347—Nixey Callahan, 1900	3,184—Charlie Root	1,642 (1930)
Runs	316—Bill Hutchison, 1892 *195—Nixey Callahan, 1900	1,861—Bill Hutchison *1,422—Charlie Root	1,080 (1894) *920 (1999)
Earned runs	191—Bill Hutchison, 1892 *155—Guy Bush, 1930	1,236—Charlie Root	849 (2000)
Bases on balls	199—Bill Hutchison, 1890 *185—Sam Jones, 1955	1,109—Bill Hutchison *871—Charlie Root	658 (2000)
Strikeouts	314—Bill Hutchison, 1892 *274—Ferguson Jenkins, 1970	2,038—Ferguson Jenkins	1,404 (2001)
Strikeouts, game	20—Kerry Wood, May 6, 1998		
Hit batsmen	39—Danny Friend, 1896 *22—Nixey Callahan, 1900	116—Clark Griffith *85—Ed Reulbach	82 (1898, 1899) *81 (1900)
Wild pitches	41—Mark Baldwin, 1887 *26—Larry Cheney, 1914	120—Bill Hutchison *71—Larry Cheney	86 (1887) *68 (1992)
Home runs	38—Warren Hacker, 1955	271—Ferguson Jenkins	231 (2000)
Sacrifice hits	23—Bill Bonham, 1974	117—Rick Reuschel	107 (1990)
Sacrifice flies	14—Rick Reuschel, 1980 Steve Trachsel, 1999	73—Ferguson Jenkins	74 (1954)
Earned run average	1.04—Mordecai Brown, 277.1 inn, 1906	1.80—Mordecai Brown	1.73 (1907)
Shutouts	10—John Clarkson, 1885 *9—Mordecai Brown, 1906, 1908 Orval Overall, 1909 Grover Alexander, 1919 Bill Lee, 1938	48—Hippo Vaughn	32 (1907, 1909) Lost—22 (1915, 1968)
1-0 games won	3—many pitchers	10—Mordecai Brown Hippo Vaughn	9 (1906) Lost—10 (1916)

TEAM FIELDING

Putouts	4,437 (1980) Fewest—1,602 (1877) *3,693 (1903)	Assists	2,178 (1899) *2,155 (1916) Fewest—731 (1876) *1,493 (2001)
Chances accepted	6,508 (1977) Fewest—2,356 (1877) *5,468 (1903)	Errors	595 (1884) *418 (1900) Fewest—86 (2004)
Double plays	176 (1928) Fewest—33 (1876) *76 (1908)	Passed balls	144 (1886) *38 (1900) Fewest—4 (1967)
Errorless games	99 (2004) Consecutive—10 (1984, 1998)	Fielding average	.986 (2004) Lowest—.879 (1883) *.93 (1900)

MISCELLANEOUS

Most players, season 51 (2000)

Fewest players, season 20 (1905)
Games won 116 (1906)
  Month 26 (Aug 1906, Jul 1935, Jul 1945)
  Consecutive 21 (1880, 1935)
Winning percentage .798 (1880), 67-17
     *.763 (1906), 116-36
  Lowest .364 (1962, 1966), 59-103
Number of league championships 16
  Most recent 1945

Most seasons, non-pitcher 22—Cap Anson
     *20—Phil Cavarretta
Most seasons, pitcher 16—Charlie Root
Games lost 103 (1962, 1966)
  Month 24 (Jul 1957, Aug 1999)
  Consecutive 14 (1997)
Overall record 9,755-9,203 (129 seasons)
  Interleague play 60-55

Number of times worst record in league 11
  Most recent 2000

Runs, game 36 vs Louisville, Jun 29, 1897
    *26 vs Philadelphia, Aug 25, 1922
    vs Colorado, Aug 18, 1995
Opponents' 25 by Boston, Sept 10, 1894
    *23 five times, last by New York, Aug 16, 1987
Hits, game 32 vs Buffalo, Jul 3, 1883
    vs Louisville, Jun 29, 1897
    *28 vs Boston, Jul 3, 1945

Home runs, game 7 vs New York, Jun 11, 1967, 2nd game
    vs San Diego, Aug 19, 1970
    vs San Diego, May 17, 1977
Runs, shutout 20 vs Washington, May 28, 1886
    *19 vs New York, Jun 7, 1906
    vs San Diego, May 13, 1969
Opponents' 22 by Pittsburgh, Sept 16, 1975
Longest 1-0 win 17 inn, vs Boston, Apr 13, 1901

Runs, inning 18 vs Detroit, Sept 6, 1883, 7th
    *14 vs Philadelphia, Aug 25, 1922, 4th

Total bases, game 54 vs Brooklyn, Aug 25, 1891
    *45 vs New York, Jun 11, 1967, 2nd game
    vs Colorado, Aug 18, 1995
    (49 vs Philadelphia, May 17, 1979, 10 inn)
Consecutive games with one or more home runs 17 (28 hrs), 1998

Longest shutout 17 inn, vs. Boston, Sept 21, 1901

Longest 1-0 loss 17 inn, vs Houston, Aug 23, 1980

ATTENDANCE

Highest home attendance		**Largest crowds**	
23rd Street Grounds	65,441 (1876)	**Day**	51,556 vs Brooklyn, Jun 27, 1930
Lake Front Park	125,452 (1882)	**Night**	40,656 vs Milwaukee, Aug 20, 2001
West Side Park	228,906 (1888)	**Doubleheader**	46,965 vs Pittsburgh, May 31, 1948
West Side Grounds	665,325 (1908)	**Home opener**	45,777 vs Pittsburgh, Apr 14, 1978
Wrigley Field	3,170,184 (2004)		(Cubs drew 55,000 to their 2000 "home
			opener in Tokyo, Japan, March 30.)

Highest road attendance   2,900,959 (1998)
*records made since 1900 that do not exceed pre-1900 records

CINCINNATI REDS
YEARLY FINISHES

(American Association franchise moved to the National League after the 1889 season)

Year	Position	W	L	Pct.	GB	Manager	Attendance
1890	4th	77	55	.583	10.5	Tom Loftus	97,500
1891	7th	56	81	.409	30.5	Tom Loftus	196,473
1892	4th/8th	82	68	.547	**	Charlie Comiskey	194,250
1893	6th (tied)	65	63	.508	20.5	Charlie Comiskey	158,000
1894	10th	55	75	.423	35.0	Charlie Comiskey	281,000
1895	8th	66	64	.508	21.0	Buck Ewing	373,000
1896	3rd	77	50	.606	12.0	Buck Ewing	336,800
1897	4th	76	56	.576	17.0	Buck Ewing	336,800
1898	3rd	92	60	.605	11.5	Buck Ewing	336,378
1899	6th	83	67	.553	19.0	Buck Ewing	259,536
1900	7th	62	77	.446	21.5	Bob Allen	155,000
1901	8th	52	87	.374	38.0	Bid McPhee	205,728
1902	4th	70	70	.500	33.5	Bid McPhee, Frank Bancroft, Joe Kelley	217,300
1903	4th	74	65	.532	16.5	Joe Kelley	351,680
1904	3rd	88	65	.575	18.0	Joe Kelley	391,915
1905	5th	79	74	.516	26.0	Joe Kelley	313,927
1906	6th	64	87	.424	51.5	Ned Hanlon	330,056
1907	6th	66	87	.431	41.5	Ned Hanlon	317,500
1908	5th	73	81	.474	26.0	John Ganzel	399,200
1909	4th	77	76	.503	33.5	Clark Griffith	424,643
1910	5th	75	79	.487	29.0	Clark Griffith	380,622
1911	6th	70	83	.458	29.0	Clark Griffith	300,000
1912	4th	75	78	.490	29.0	Hank O'Day	344,000
1913	7th	64	89	.418	37.5	Joe Tinker	258,000
1914	8th	60	94	.390	34.5	Buck Herzog	100,791
1915	7th	71	83	.461	20.0	Buck Herzog	218,878
1916	7th (tied)	60	93	.392	33.5	Buck Herzog, Christy Mathewson	255,846
1917	4th	78	76	.506	20.0	Christy Mathewson	269,056
1918	3rd	68	60	.531	15.5	Christy Mathewson, Heinie Groh	163,009
1919	1st (S)	96	44	.686	+9.0	Pat Moran	532,501
1920	3rd	82	71	.536	10.5	Pat Moran	568,107
1921	6th	70	83	.458	24.0	Pat Moran	311,227
1922	2nd	86	68	.558	7.0	Pat Moran	493,754
1923	2nd	91	63	.591	4.5	Pat Moran	575,063
1924	4th	83	70	.542	10.0	Jack Hendricks	437,707
1925	3rd	80	73	.523	15.0	Jack Hendricks	464,920
1926	2nd	87	67	.565	2.0	Jack Hendricks	672,987
1927	5th	75	78	.490	18.5	Jack Hendricks	442,164
1928	5th	78	74	.513	16.0	Jack Hendricks	490,490
1929	7th	66	88	.429	33.0	Jack Hendricks	295,040
1930	7th	59	95	.383	33.0	Dan Howley	386,727

Year	Position	W	L	Pct.	GB	Manager	Attendance
1931	8th	58	96	.377	43.0	Dan Howley	263,316
1932	8th	60	94	.390	30.0	Dan Howley	356,950
1933	8th	58	94	.382	33.0	Donie Bush	218,281
1934	8th	52	99	.344	42.0	Bob O'Farrell, Chuck Dressen	206,773
1935	6th	68	85	.444	31.5	Chuck Dressen	448,247
1936	5th	74	80	.481	18.0	Chuck Dressen	466,245
1937	8th	56	98	.364	40.0	Chuck Dressen, Bobby Wallace	411,221
1938	4th	82	68	.547	6.0	Bill McKechnie	706,756
1939	1st (s)	97	57	.630	+4.5	Bill McKechnie	981,443
1940	1st (S)	100	53	.654	+12.0	Bill McKechnie	850,180
1941	3rd	88	66	.571	12.0	Bill McKechnie	643,513
1942	4th	76	76	.500	29.0	Bill McKechnie	427,031
1943	2nd	87	67	.565	18.0	Bill McKechnie	379,122
1944	3rd	89	65	.578	16.0	Bill McKechnie	409,567
1945	7th	61	93	.396	37.0	Bill McKechnie	290,070
1946	6th	67	87	.435	30.0	Bill McKechnie	715,751
1947	5th	73	81	.474	21.0	Johnny Neun	899,975
1948	7th	64	89	.418	27.0	Johnny Neun, Bucky Walters	823,386
1949	7th	62	92	.403	35.0	Bucky Walters	707,782
1950	6th	66	87	.431	24.5	Luke Sewell	538,794
1951	6th	68	86	.442	28.5	Luke Sewell	588,268
1952	6th	69	85	.448	27.5	Luke Sewell, Rogers Hornsby	604,197
1953	6th	68	86	.442	37.0	Rogers Hornsby, Buster Mills	548,086
1954	5th	74	80	.481	23.0	Birdie Tebbetts	704,167
1955	5th	75	79	.487	23.5	Birdie Tebbetts	693,662
1956	3rd	91	63	.591	2.0	Birdie Tebbetts	1,125,928
1957	4th	80	74	.519	15.0	Birdie Tebbetts	1,070,850
1958	4th	76	78	.494	16.0	Birdie Tebbetts, Jimmie Dykes	788,582
1959	5th (tied)	74	80	.481	13.0	Mayo Smith, Fred Hutchinson	801,289
1960	6th	67	87	.435	28.0	Fred Hutchinson	663,486
1961	1st (s)	93	61	.604	+4.0	Fred Hutchinson	1,117,603
1962	3rd	98	64	.605	3.5	Fred Hutchinson	982,085
1963	5th	86	76	.531	13.0	Fred Hutchinson	858,805
1964	2nd (tied)	92	70	.568	1.0	Fred Hutchinson, Dick Sisler	862,466
1965	4th	89	73	.549	8.0	Dick Sisler	1,047,824
1966	7th	76	84	.475	18.0	Don Heffner, Dave Bristol	742,958
1967	4th	87	75	.537	14.5	Dave Bristol	958,300
1968	4th	83	79	.512	14.0	Dave Bristol	733,354

WEST DIVISION

Year	Position	W	L	Pct.	GB	Manager	Attendance
1969	3rd	89	73	.549	4.0	Dave Bristol	987,991
1970	1st (C,s)	102	60	.630	+14.5	Sparky Anderson	1,803,568
1971	4th (tied)	79	83	.488	11.0	Sparky Anderson	1,501,122
1972	1st (C,s)	95	59	.617	+10.5	Sparky Anderson	1,611,459
1973	1st (c)	99	63	.611	+3.5	Sparky Anderson	2,017,601
1974	2nd	98	64	.605	4.0	Sparky Anderson	2,164,307
1975	1st (C,S)	108	54	.667	+20.0	Sparky Anderson	2,315,603
1976	1st (C,S)	102	60	.630	+10.0	Sparky Anderson	2,629,708
1977	2nd	88	74	.543	10.0	Sparky Anderson	2,519,670
1978	2nd	92	69	.571	2.5	Sparky Anderson	2,532,497
1979	1st (c)	90	71	.559	+1.5	John McNamara	2,356,933
1980	3rd	89	73	.549	3.5	John McNamara	2,022,450
1981	2nd/2nd	66	42	.611	*	John McNamara	1,093,730
1982	6th	61	101	.377	28.0	John McNamara, Russ Nixon	1,326,528
1983	6th	74	88	.457	17.0	Russ Nixon	1,190,419
1984	5th	70	92	.432	22.0	Vern Rapp, Pete Rose	1,275,887
1985	2nd	89	72	.553	5.5	Pete Rose	1,834,619
1986	2nd	86	76	.531	10.0	Pete Rose	1,692,432
1987	2nd	84	78	.519	6.0	Pete Rose	2,185,205
1988	2nd	87	74	.540	7.0	Pete Rose	2,072,528
1989	5th	75	87	.463	17.0	Pete Rose, Tommy Helms	1,979,320
1990	1st (C,S)	91	71	.562	+5.0	Lou Piniella	2,400,892
1991	5th	74	88	.457	20.0	Lou Piniella	2,372,377
1992	2nd	90	72	.556	8.0	Lou Piniella	2,315,946
1993	5th	73	89	.451	31.0	Tony Perez, Dave Johnson	2,453,232

CENTRAL DIVISION

Year	Position	W	L	Pct.	*GB	Manager	Attendance
1994	1st	66	48	.579	+0.5	Dave Johnson	1,897,681
1995	1st (D,c)	85	59	.590	+9.0	Dave Johnson	1,837,649
1996	3rd	81	81	.500	7.0	Ray Knight	1,861,428
1997	3rd	76	86	.469	8.0	Ray Knight, Jack McKeon	1,785,788
1998	4th	77	85	.475	25.0	Jack McKeon	1,793,649
1999	2nd (w)	96	67	.589	1.5	Jack McKeon	2,061,222
2000	2nd	85	77	.525	10.0	Jack McKeon	2,577,351
2001	5th	66	96	.407	27.0	Bob Boone	1,882,732
2002	3rd	78	84	.481	19.0	Bob Boone	1,855,973
2003	5th	69	93	.426	19.0	Bob Boone, Dave Miley	2,355,160
2004	4th	76	86	.469	29.0	Dave Miley	2,287,250

(S) won World Series; (s) lost World Series; (C) won League Championship Series; (c) lost League Championship Series; *first half 35-21, second half 31-21; (D) won Division Series; (w) lost wild card playoff

BATTING

	Individual	Career	Club
	Season	**Career**	**Season**
Games	163—Leo Cardenas, 1964 Pete Rose, 1974	2,722—Pete Rose	163 (1964, 1968, 1969, 1974, 1980, 1999, 2000)
At-bats	680—Pete Rose, 160 g, 1973	10,934—Pete Rose	5,767 (1968)
Runs	134—Frank Robinson, 162 g, 1962	1,741—Pete Rose	865 (1999) Fewest—488 (1908)
Hits	230—Pete Rose, 160 g, 1973	3,358—Pete Rose	1,599 (1976) Fewest—1,108 (1908)
Hitting streak	44 g—Pete Rose, 1978		
Singles	181—Pete Rose, 160 g, 1973	2,490—Pete Rose	1,191 (1922)
Doubles	51—Frank Robinson, 162 g, 1962 Pete Rose, 159 g, 1978	601—Pete Rose	312 (1999)
Triples	25—Bid McPhee, 132 g, 1890 *23—Sam Crawford, 140 g, 1902	152—Edd Roush	120 (1926)

HOME RUNS

221 (1956)
Fewest—14 (1908, 1916)

Righthander	52—George Foster, 158 g, 1977	389—Johnny Bench	
Lefthander	49—Ted Kluszewski, 149 g, 1954	251—Ted Kluszewski	
Switch-hitter	21—Dmitri Young, 142 g, 2001	152—Pete Rose	
Rookie	38—Frank Robinson, 152 g, 1956		
Home	34—Ted Kluszewski, 1954	195—Johnny Bench	128 (1956)
Road	31 George Foster, 1977	194—Johnny Bench	112 (1999)
Month	14—Frank Robinson, Aug 1962 Greg Vaughn, Sept 1999		51 (Sept 1999)
Pinch	5—Jerry Lynch, 1961	13—Jerry Lynch	12 (1957)
Grand slams	3—Frank Robinson, 162 g, 1962 Lee May, 153 g, 1970 Ray Knight, 162 g, 1980 Eric Davis, 129 g, 1987 Chris Sabo, 148 g, 1993	11—Johnny Bench	9 (2002)

Home runs at Crosley Field, all teams	219 (1957)
Home runs at Riverfront Stadium, all teams	213 (1999)
Home runs at Great American Ball Park, all teams	220 (2004)

Total bases	388—George Foster, 158 g, 1977	4,645—Pete Rose	2,549 (1999)
Extra base hits	92—Frank Robinson, 162 g, 1962	868—Pete Rose	558 (1999)
Sacrifice hits	33—Dummy Hoy, 1896 *31—Roy McMillan, 154 g, 1954	186—Edd Roush	195 (1907)
Sacrifice flies	13—Johnny Temple, 149 g, 1959	90—Johnny Bench	66 (1993)
Bases on balls	132—Joe Morgan, 146 g, 1975	1,210—Pete Rose	693 (1974) Fewest—297 (1902)
Strikeouts	195—Adam Dunn, 161 g, 2004 Fewest—13—Frank McCormick, 154 g, 1941	1,306—Tony Perez	1,335 (2004) Fewest—308 (1921)
Hit by pitch	24—Jason LaRue, 114 g, 2004	118—Frank Robinson	81 (2004) Fewest—11 (1951)
Runs batted in	149—George Foster, 158 g, 1977	1,376—Johnny Bench	820 (1999) Fewest—398 (1908)
Grounded into double plays	30—Ernie Lombardi, 129 g, 1938 Fewest—3—Billy Myers, 151 g, 1939	266—Dave Concepcion	161 (1933) Fewest—85 (1991)
Left on base			1,328 (1976) Fewest—984 (1920)
Batting average	.383—Bug Holliday, 122 g, year *.377—Cy Seymour, 149 g, 1905	.332—Cy Seymour	.296 (1922) Lowest—.227 (1968)
Most .300 hitters			8 (1926)
Slugging average	.642—Ted Kluszewski, 149 g, 1954	.554—Frank Robinson	.451 (1999) Lowest—.304 (1906)
On-base percentage	.466—Joe Morgan, 146 g, 1975	.415—Joe Morgan	.368 (1894) *.357 (1976) Lowest—.288 (1908)

BASERUNNING

	Individual		Club
	Season	**Career**	**Season**
Stolen bases	93—Arlie Latham, 135 g, 1891	406—Joe Morgan	310 (1910)
	*81—Bob Bescher, 153 g, 1911		
Caught stealing	28—Pat Duncan, 151 g, 1922	110—Pete Rose	136 (1922)

PITCHING

	Season	**Career**	**Season**
Games	90—Wayne Granger, 1969	531—Pedro Borbon Sr.	
Games started	42—Noodles Hahn, 1901	357—Eppa Rixey	
	Pete Schneider, 1917		
	Fred Toney, 1917		
Complete games	41—Noodles Hahn, 1901	195—Bucky Walters	142 (1904)
Wins	27—Dolf Luque, 1923	179—Eppa Rixley	
	Bucky Walters, 1939		
Percentage	.826—Elmer Riddle (19-4), 1941	.663—Will White	
		*.623—Jim Maloney	
Winning streak	16—Ewell Blackwell, 1947		
20-win seasons		4—Paul Derringer	
Losses	25—Paul Derringer, 1933	152—Dolf Luque	
Losing streak	12—Henry Thielman, 1902		
	Pete Schneider, 1914		
	Si Johnson, 1933		
Saves	44—Jeff Brantley, 1996	172—Danny Graves	60 (1970, 1972)
Innings	375—Noodles Hahn, 1901	2,890.2—Eppa Rixey	1,490 (1968)
Hits	370—Noodles Hahn, 1901	3,115—Eppa Rixey	1,650 (1930)
Runs	159—Noodles Hahn, 1901	1,442—Tony Mullane	907 (2004)
		*1,304—Eppa Rixey	
Earned runs	145—Herm Wehmeier, 1950	1,068—Eppa Rixey	832 (2004)
Bases on balls	162—Johnny Vander Meer, 1943	1,072—Johnny Vander Meer	659 (2000)
Strikeouts	274—Mario Soto, 1982	1,592—Jim Maloney	1,159 (1997)
Strikeouts, game	16—Noodles Hahn, May 22, 1901		
	Jim Maloney, May 1, 1963		
	Ron Villone, Sept 29, 2000		
	(18—Jim Maloney, Jun 14, 1965, 11 inn)		
Hit batsmen	23—Jake Weimer, 1907	139—Tony Mullane	77 (1997)
		*66—Rube Benton	
Wild pitches	21—Scott Williamson, 2000	184—Tony Mullane	96 (2000)
		*121—Jim Maloney	
Home runs	36—Tom Browning, 1988	234—Tom Browning	236 (2004)
Sacrifice hits	26—Si Johnson, 1933	354—Eppa Rixey	205 (1928)
Sacrifice flies	13—Bill Gullickson, 1986	62—Tom Browning	60 (1986)
Earned run average	1.57—Fred Toney, 223 inn, 1915	2.37—Bob Ewing	1.65 (1882) *2.23 (1919)
Shutouts	7—Jake Weimer, 1906	32—Bucky Walters	23 (1919)
	Fred Toney, 1917		Lost—24 (1908)
	Hod Eller, 1919		
	Jack Billingham, 1973		
1-0 games won	4—Jake Weimer, 1906	7—Johnny Vander Meer	7 (1910, 1943, 1963)
			Lost—7 (1907, 1916)

TEAM FIELDING

Putouts	4,471 (1968)	**Assists**	2,151 (1905)
	Fewest—4,006 (1930)		Fewest—1,534 (1966)
Chances accepted	6,399 (1915)	**Errors**	314 (1914)
	Fewest—5,655 (1950)		Fewest—95 (1977)
Double plays	194 (1928, 1931, 1954)	**Passed balls**	39 (1914)
	Fewest—108 (1989)		Fewest—3 (1975)
Errorless games	99 (1992)	**Fielding average**	.985 (1995)
	Consecutive—15 (1975)		Lowest—.952 (1914)

MISCELLANEOUS

Most players, season 57 (2003)

Fewest players, season 21 (1904)
Games won 108 (1975)
  Month 24 (Aug 1918, Jul 1973)
  Consecutive 14 (1899)
    *12 (1939, 1957)
Winning percentage .686 (1919), 96-44
  Lowest .344 (1934), 52-99
Number of league championships 9
  Most recent 1990
Runs, game 30 vs Louisville, Jun 18, 1893
  *26 vs Boston, Jun 4, 1911
  Opponents' 26 by Philadelphia, Jul 26, 1892
    *25 by New York, Jun 9, 1901
    by Brooklyn, Sept 23, 1901
Hits, game 32 vs Louisville, Jun 18, 1893
  *28 vs Philadelphia, May 13, 1902
  vs Colorado, May 19, 1999
  vs Boston, Jun 20, 1980
Home runs, game 9 vs Philadelphia, Sept 4, 1999
Runs, shutout 18 vs Los Angeles, Aug 8, 1965
  Opponents' 18 by Philadelphia, Aug 10, 1930, 1st game
  by Philadelphia, Jul 14, 1934, 1st game
  by St. Louis, Jun 10, 1944
Longest 1-0 win 15 inn vs New York, Jul 16, 1933, 1st game
  vs Brooklyn, Jun 11, 1915

Most seasons, non-pitcher 19—Dave Concepcion
    Barry Larkin
    Pete Rose
Most seasons, pitcher 15—Joe Nuxhall
Games lost 101 (1982)
  Month 26 (Sept 1914)
  Consecutive 19 (1914)

Overall record 8,898-8,719 (115 seasons)
  Interleague play 48-61
Number of times worst record in league 11 (tied in 1916)
  Most recent 1982
Runs, inning 14 vs Louisville, Jun 18, 1893, 1st
  *14 vs Houston, Aug 3, 1989, 1st

Total bases, game 55 vs Louisville, Jun 18, 1893
  *55 vs Colorado, May 19, 1999

Consecutive games with one or more home runs 21 (41 hrs), 1956
Longest shutout 16 inn 3-0 vs Chicago, Sept 22, 1975

Longest 1-0 loss 21 inn vs San Francisco, Sept 1, 1967

ATTENDANCE

Highest home attendance		Largest crowds	
League Park I	196,473 (1892)	Day	55,596 vs Milwaukee, Apr 3, 2000
League Park II	373,000 (1896)	Night	54,621 vs New York, Oct 4, 1999
Palace of the Fans	424,643 (1909)	Doubleheader	53,328 vs Pittsburgh, Jul 9, 1976
Crosley Field	1,125,928 (1956)	Home opener	55,596 vs Milwaukee, Apr 3, 2000
Cinergy Field	2,629,708 (1976)		
Great American Ballpark	2,355,160 (2003)		
Highest road attendance	3,016,074 (2000)		

*records made since 1900 that do not exceed pre-1900 records

COLORADO ROCKIES
YEARLY FINISHES

(National League expansion franchise)
WEST DIVISION

Year	Position	W	L	Pct.	GB	Manager	Attendance
1993	6th	67	95	.414	37.0	Don Baylor	4,483,350
1994	3rd	53	64	.453	6.5	Don Baylor	3,281,511
1995	2nd (d)	77	67	.535	1.0	Don Baylor	3,390,037
1996	3rd	83	79	.512	8.0	Don Baylor	3,891,014
1997	3rd	83	79	.512	7.0	Don Baylor	3,888,453
1998	4th	77	85	.475	21.0	Don Baylor	3,789,347
1999	5th	72	90	.444	28.0	Jim Leyland	3,481,065
2000	4th	82	80	.506	15.0	Buddy Bell	3,285,710
2001	5th	73	89	.451	19.0	Buddy Bell	3,159,385
2002	4th	73	89	.451	25.0	Buddy Bell, Clint Hurdle	2,737,918
2003	4th	74	88	.457	26.5	Clint Hurdle	2,334,085
2004	4th	68	94	.420	25.0	Clint Hurdle	2,338,069

(d) lost Division Series

INDIVIDUAL AND CLUB RECORDS
BATTING

	Individual		Club
	Season	Career	Season
Games	162—Vinny Castilla, 1998	1,170—Larry Walker	162 (1993, 1996-2004)
	Neifi Perez, 1998, 2000		
At-bats	690—Neifi Perez, 157 g, 1999	4,078—Vinny Castilla	5,717 (1999)

	Individual		Club
	Season	**Career**	**Season**
Runs	143—Larry Walker, 153 g, 1997	892—Larry Walker	968 (2000)
			Fewest—758 (1993)
Hits	219—Dante Bichette, 161 g, 1998	1,372—Todd Helton	1,664 (2000)
			Fewest—1,472 (2003)
Hitting streak	23 g—Dante Bichette, 1995		
Singles	163—Juan Pierre, 156 g, 2001	789—Dante Bichette	1,130 (2000)
Doubles	59—Todd Helton, 160 g, 2000	328—Todd Helton	333 (1998)
Triples	11—Neifi Perez, 157 g, 1999	49—Neifi Perez	61 (2001)
	Neifi Perez, 162 g, 2000		
	Juan Pierre, 156 g, 2001		
	Juan Uribe, 72 g, 2001		

HOME RUNS

			239 (1997)
			Fewest—142 (1993)
Righthander	47—Andres Galarraga, 159 g, 1996	238—Vinny Castilla	
Lefthander	49—Larry Walker, 153 g, 1997	258—Larry Walker	
	Todd Helton, 159 g, 2001		
Switch-hitter	13—Greg Norton, 117 g, 2001	43—Neifi Perez	
Rookie	25—Todd Helton, 152 g, 1998		
Home	32—Andres Galarraga, 1996	155—Todd Helton	149 (1996)
Road	29—Larry Walker, 1997	104—Larry Walker	115 (1997)
Month	12—Dante Bichette, Aug 1995		53 (Aug 1996)
	Vinny Castilla, Jun 1996		
	Andres Galarraga, Aug 1996		
	Vinny Castilla, Jul 1998		
Pinch	5—Mark Sweeney, 2004	12—John Vander Wal	11 (1995)
Grand slams	2—many players	6—Andres Galarraga	5 (1994, 1998, 2000, 2002)
		Dante Bichette	
Home runs at Mile High Stadium, all teams			184 (1993)
Home runs at Coors Field, all teams			303 (1999)

Total bases	409—Larry Walker, 153 g, 1997	2,520—Larry Walker	2,748 (2001)
Extra base hits	105—Todd Helton, 159 g, 2001	601—Todd Helton	598 (2001)
Sacrifice hits	24—Royce Clayton, 146 g, 2004	48—Neifi Perez	98 (1998)
Sacrifice flies	12—Jeff Cirillo, 157 g, 2000	48—Dante Bichette	75 (2000)
Bases on balls	127—Todd Helton, 154 g, 2004	667—Todd Helton	619 (2003)
			Fewest—388 (1993)
Strikeouts	157—Andres Galarraga, 159 g, 1996	659—Larry Walker	1,181 (2004)
	Fewest—29—Juan Pierre, 156 g, 2001		Fewest—863 (1999)
Hit by pitch	21—Eric Young, 141 g, 1996	98—Larry Walker	82 (1996)
			Fewest—37 (1998)
Runs batted in	150—Andres Galarraga, 159 g, 1996	848—Larry Walker	909 (1996)
			Fewest—703 (1993)
Grounded into	27—Todd Zeile, 144 g, 2002	126—Vinny Castilla	148 (1998)
double plays	Jay Payton, 157 g, 2003		Fewest—116 (2001)
	Fewest—4—Neifi Perez, 157 g, 1999		
Left on base			1,198 (2000)
			Fewest—978 (1993)
Batting average	.379—Larry Walker, 127 g, 1999	.339—Todd Helton	.294 (2000)
			Lowest—.267 (2003)
Most .300 hitters			5 (1996)
Slugging average	.720—Larry Walker, 153 g, 1997	.618—Larry Walker	.483 (2001)
			Lowest—.422 (1993)
On-base percentage	.469—Todd Helton, 154 g, 2004	.432—Todd Helton	.362 (2000)
			Lowest—.323 (1993)

BASERUNNING

Stolen bases	53—Eric Young, 141 g, 1996	180—Eric Young	201 (1996)
Caught stealing	19—Eric Young, 144 g, 1993	69—Eric Young	90 (1993)
	Eric Young, 141 g, 1996		

PITCHING

	Individual		Club
	Season	**Career**	**Season**
Games	79—Todd Jones, 2002	461—Steve Reed	
Games started	35—Kevin Ritz, 1996	129—Pedro Astacio	
	Darryl Kile, 1998		
Complete games	7—Pedro Astacio, 1999	14—Pedro Astacio	12 (1999)
Wins	17—Kevin Ritz, 1970	53—Pedro Astacio	
	Pedro Astacio, 1999		
Percentage	.667—Jason Jennings (16-8), 2002	none over 1500 inn	
Winning streak	9—Julian Tavarez, 2000		
20-win seasons		none	
Losses	17—Darryl Kile, 1998	48—Pedro Astacio	
Losing streak	8—Greg Harris, 1994		
	Darryl Kile, 1998		
Losing streak, two seasons	12—Jose Jimenez, 2002 (6), 2003 (6)		
Saves	41—Jose Jimenez, 2002	102—Jose Jimenez	43 (1995, 2002)
Innings	232.0—Pedro Astacio,1999	827.1—Pedro Astacio	1,435.1 (2004)
Hits	258—Pedro Astacio, 1998	920—Pedro Astacio	1,700 (1999)
Runs	160—Pedro Astacio, 1998	533—Pedro Astacio	1,028 (1999)
Earned runs	145—Pedro Astacio, 1998	499—Pedro Astacio	955 (1999)
Bases on balls	109—Darryl Kile, 1999	306—Jamey Wright	737 (1999)
Strikeouts	210—Pedro Astacio, 1999	749—Pedro Astacio	1,058 (2001)
Strikeouts, game	14—Darryl Kile, Aug 20, 1998		
Hit batsmen	17—Pedro Astacio, 1998	58—Pedro Astacio	84 (2003)
Wild pitches	13—Marvin Freeman, 1996	34—Curtis Leskanic	82 (1993)
	Darryl Kile, 1999		
Home runs	39—Pedro Astacio, 1998	139—Pedro Astacio	239 (2001)
	Ramon Ortiz, 2002		
Sacrifice hits	18—Brian Bohanon, 1999	32—John Thompson	82 (1993)
Sacrifice flies	10—Pedro Astacio, 1999	23—Pedro Astacio	78 (1993)
Earned run average	3.66—Joe Kennedy, 162.1 inn, 2004	none with 1,500 inn	4.97 (1995)
Shutouts	2—Roger Bailey, 1997	2—Roger Bailey	8 (2001, 2002)
		Brian Bohanon	Lost—13 (1993)
		John Thomson	
1-0 games won	none	none	2 (1994, 1998, 2002)
			Lost—2 (2003)

TEAM FIELDING

Putouts	4,306 (2004)	**Assists**	1,946 (1997)
	Fewest—4,260 (2003)		Fewest—1,694 (2001)
Chances accepted	6,244 (1997)	**Errors**	167 (1993)
	Fewest—5,981 (2002)		Fewest—89 (2004)
Double plays	202 (1997)	**Passed balls**	19 (1996)
	Fewest—149 (1993)		Fewest—5 (1997)
Errorless games	93 (2001)	**Fielding average**	.986 (2004)
	Consecutive—13 (1998)		Lowest—.973 (1993)

MISCELLANEOUS

Most players, season 53 (2001)	**Most seasons, non-pitcher** 10—Larry Walker
Fewest players, season 42 (1998)	**Most seasons, pitcher** 7—Curtis Leskanic
	Steve Reed
Games won 83 (1996, 1997)	**Games lost** 95 (1993)
Month 19 (May 2002)	**Month** 22 (July 2000)
Consecutive 9 (1997)	**Consecutive** 13 (1993)
Winning percentage .535 (1995, 1997), 77-67	**Overall record** 882-99 (12 seasons)
Lowest .414 (1993), 67-95	**Interleague play** 49-66
Number of league championships 0	**Number of times worst record in league** 0
Most recent ---	**Most recent** ---
Runs, game 20 vs Arizona, Sept 23, 2003	**Runs, inning** 11 vs San Diego, Jul 12, 1996, 7th
Opponents' 26 by Chicago, Aug 18, 1995	
Hits, game 24 vs Montreal, May 3, 2000	**Total bases, game** 43 vs Pittsburgh, Aug 3, 2003
vs Pittsburgh, Aug 3, 2003	

Home runs, game 7 vs Montreal, Apr 5, 1997

Consecutive games with one or more home runs 17 (24 hrs), 1993 (36 hrs), 1996

Runs, shutout 11 vs Florida, Aug 6, 1996
vs San Diego, Sept 13, 2000
Opponents' 17 by Florida, Sept 17, 1995
Longest 1-0 win 11 inn, vs San Diego, Sept 20, 1998

Longest shutout 11 inn, 1-0 vs San Diego, Sept 20, 1998

Longest 1-0 loss 11 inn, vs Los Angeles, Jul 24, 2003

ATTENDANCE

Highest home attendance		Largest crowds	
Mile High Stadium	4,483,350 (1993)	Day	80,227 vs Montreal, Apr 9, 1993
Coors Field	3,891,014 (1996)	Night	73,957 vs San Francisco, Jun 24, 1994
		Doubleheader	60,613 vs New York, Aug 21, 1993
Highest road attendance	2,695,071 (1993)	Home opener	80,227 vs Montreal, Apr 9, 1993

FLORIDA MARLINS
YEARLY FINISHES

(National League expansion franchise)
EAST DIVISION

Year	Position	W	L	Pct.	GB	Manager	Attendance
1993	6th	64	98	.395	33.0	Rene Lachemann	3,064,847
1994	5th	51	64	.443	23.5	Rene Lachemann	1,937,467
1995	4th	67	76	.469	22.5	Rene Lachemann	1,700,466
1996	3rd	80	82	.494	16.0	Rene Lachemann, John Boles	1,746,767
1997	2nd (D,C,S)	92	70	.568	9.0	Jim Leyland	2,364,387
1998	5th	54	108	.333	52.0	Jim Leyland	1,750,395
1999	5th	64	98	.395	39.0	John Boles	1,369,421
2000	3rd	79	82	.491	15.5	John Boles	1,218,326
2001	4th	76	86	.469	12.0	John Boles, Tony Perez	1,261,220
2002	4th	79	83	.488	23.0	Jeff Torborg	813,111
2003	2nd (D,C,S)	91	71	.562	10.0	Jeff Torborg, Jack McKeon	1,303,214
2004	3rd	83	79	.512	13.0	Jack McKeon	1,723,105

(D) won Division Series; (C) won League Championship Series; (S) won World Series

INDIVIDUAL AND CLUB RECORDS
BATTING

	Individual		Club
	Season	Career	Season
Games	162—Jeff Conine, 1993	1,006—Luis Castillo	162 (1993, 1996-1999, 2001-2004)
	Derrek Lee, 2002		
	Juan Pierre, 2003, 2004		
At-bats	678—Juan Pierre, 162 g, 2004	3,908—Luis Castillo	5,578 (1999)
Runs	123—Cliff Floyd, 149 g, 2001	603—Luis Castillo	751 (2003)
			Fewest—581 (1993)
Hits	221—Juan Pierre, 162 g, 2004	1,141—Luis Castillo	1,465 (1999)
			Fewest—1,356 (1993)
Hitting streak	35 g—Luis Castillo, 2002		
Singles	184—Juan Pierre, 162 g, 2004	969—Luis Castillo	1,034 (1993)
Doubles	45—Cliff Floyd, 153 g, 1998	205—Mike Lowell	325 (2001)
Triples	12—Juan Pierre, 162 g, 2004	38—Luis Castillo	44 (1999, 2003)

HOME RUNS

	Individual		Club
			166 (2001)
			Fewest—94 (1993)
Righthander	42—Gary Sheffield, 161 g, 1996	135—Mike Lowell	
Lefthander	31—Cliff Floyd, 149 g, 2001	110—Cliff Floyd	
Switch-hitter	20—Orestes Destrade, 153 g, 1993	25—Orestes Destrade	
Rookie	26—Preston Wilson, 149 g, 1999		
Home	19—Gary Sheffield, 1996	61—Gary Sheffield	84 (2001)
Road	23—Gary Sheffield, 1996	88—Derrek Lee	89 (2000)
Month	11—Gary Sheffield, Apr 1996		35 (Apr 2001)
Pinch	3—Preston Wilson, 1999	3—Preston Wilson	8 (1999)
Grand slams	3—Bobby Bonilla, 153 g, 1997	4—Derrek Lee	9 (1997)
Home runs at Pro Player Stadium, all teams			153 (2001)
Total bases	324—Gary Sheffield, 161 g, 1996	1,461—Mike Lowell	2,344 (2001)

	Individual		Club
	Season	Career	Season
Extra base hits	79—Cliff Floyd, 149 g, 2001	342—Mike Lowell	521 (2001)
Sacrifice hits	19—Edgar Renteria, 154 g, 1997	47—Luis Castillo	82 (2003)
Sacrifice flies	12—Jeff Conine, 133 g, 1995	46—Mike Lowell	56 (1999)
Bases on balls	142—Gary Sheffield, 161 g, 1996	468—Luis Castillo	686 (1997)
			Fewest—470 (2001)
Strikeouts	187—Preston Wilson, 161 g, 2000	734—Derrek Lee	1,184 (2000)
	Fewest—35—Juan Pierre, 162 g, 2003		Fewest—968 (2004)
	Juan Pierre, 162 g, 2004		
Hit by pitch	15—Gary Sheffield, 135 g, 1997	43—Alex Gonzalez	67 (2001)
		Gary Sheffield	Fewest—45 (1998)
Runs batted in	121—Preston Wilson, 161 g, 2000	520—Jeff Conine	713 (2001)
		Mike Lowell	Fewest—542 (1993)
Grounded into	22—Greg Colbrunn, 141 g, 1996	80—Jeff Conine	142 (2004)
double plays	Fewest—5—Walt Weiss, 158 g, 1993		Fewest—100 (2000)
Left on base			1,248 (1997)
			Fewest—1,114 (2003)
Batting average	.334—Luis Castillo, 136 g, 2000	.291—Luis Castillo	.266 (2003)
			Lowest—.248 (1993, 1998)
Most .300 hitters			2 (2003)
Slugging average	.624—Gary Sheffield, 161 g, 1996	.543—Gary Sheffield	.423 (2001)
			Lowest—.346 (1993)
On-base percentage	.465—Gary Sheffield, 161 g, 1996	.368—Luis Castillo	.346 (1997)
			Lowest—.314 (1993)

BASERUNNING

Stolen bases	65—Juan Pierre, 162 g, 2003	271—Luis Castillo	177 (2002)
Caught stealing	24—Juan Pierre, 162 g, 2004	105—Luis Castillo	74 (2003)

PITCHING

Games	78—Braden Looper, 2002	368—Braden Looper	
Games started	34—Charlie Hough, 1993	130—Brad Penny	
	Ryan Dempster, 2001		
Complete games	9—Livan Hernandez, 1998	11—Kevin Brown	12 (1995, 1997)
		Livan Hernandez	
Wins	18—Carl Pavano, 2004	48—Brad Penny	
Percentage	.692—Carl Pavano (18-8), 2004	none with 1,500 inn	
Winning streak	9—Pat Rapp, 1995		
	Livan Hernandez, 1997		
20-win seasons		none	
Losses	17—Jack Armstrong, 1993	43—Pat Rapp	
		Ryan Dempster	
Losing streak	8—Reid Cornelius, 2000		
	Brad Penny, 2001		
Saves	47—Armando Benitez, 2004	108—Robb Nen	53 (2004)
Innings	237.1—Kevin Brown, 1997	781.2—Brad Penny	1,456.1 (2002)
Hits	265—Livan Hernandez, 1998	772—Ryan Dempster	1,617 (1998)
Runs	133—Livan Hernandez, 1998	415—Ryan Dempster	923 (1998)
Earned runs	123—Livan Hernandez, 1998	392—Ryan Dempster	834 (1998)
Bases on balls	119—Al Leiter, 1996	395—Ryan Dempster	715 (1998)
Strikeouts	209—Ryan Dempster, 2000	628—Ryan Dempster	1,188 (1997)
Strikeouts, game	14—A.J. Burnett, Aug 29, 2004		
Hit batsmen	16—Kevin Brown, 1996	37—Ryan Dempster	70 (2001)
Wild pitches	15—Matt Clement, 2001	36—Pat Rapp	85 (1993)
Home runs	37—Livan Hernandez, 1998	90—Ryan Dempster	182 (1998)
Sacrifice hits	16—Brian Meadows, 1999	43—Pat Rapp	95 (1998)
Sacrifice flies	12—Jesus Sanchez, 2000	27—Ryan Dempster	69 (1999)
Earned run average	1.89—Kevin Brown, 233 inn, 1996	none with 1,500 inn	3.83 (1997)
Shutouts	5—A.J. Burnett, 2002	6—A.J. Burnett	14 (2004)
			Lost—14 (1993, 1996)

	Individual		Club	
	Season		**Career**	**Season**
1-0 games won	1—Alex Fernandez, 1997		1—Alex Fernandez	3 (2001, 2002)
	Brad Penny, 2002		Brad Penny	Lost—4 (1993)
	Dontrelle Willis, 2003		Dontrelle Willis	

TEAM FIELDING

Putouts	4,369 (2002)	**Assists**	1,796 (1996)
	Fewest—4,289 (2000)		Fewest—1,590 (2003)
Chances accepted	6,125 (1996)	**Errors**	129 (1998)
	Fewest—5,920 (2004)		Fewest—78 (2003)
Double plays	187 (1996)	**Passed balls**	29 (1993)
	Fewest—130 (1993)		Fewest—6 (2002)
Errorless games	100 (2003)	**Fielding average**	.987 (2003)
	Consecutive—9 (2003)		Lowest—.979 (1998, 1999)

MISCELLANEOUS

Most players, season 49 (1998)
Fewest players, season 40 (2000, 2003)
Games won 92 (1997)
  Month 19 (Aug 1997)
  Consecutive 9 (1996)
Winning percentage .568 (1997), 92-70
  Lowest .333 (1998), 54-108
Number of league championships 2
  Most recent 2003
Runs, game 20 vs Atlanta, Jul 1, 2003
  Opponents' 25 by Boston, Jun 27, 2003
Hits, game 25 vs Atlanta, Jul 1, 2003
Home runs, game 4, many times
Runs, shutout 17 vs Colorado, Sept 17, 1995
  Opponents' 18 by Atlanta, Oct 3, 1999
Longest 1-0 win 13 inn, vs Philadelphia, Sept 26, 1998

Most seasons, non-pitcher 9—Luis Castillo
Most seasons, pitcher 6—A. J. Burnett
Games lost 108 (1998)
  Month 20 (May 1995, May 1998, Aug 1998, Aug 2001)
  Consecutive 11 (1998)
Overall record 880-997 (12 seasons)
  Interleague play 77-58
Number of times worst record in league 2
  Most recent 1999
Runs, inning 8, many times

Total bases, game 43 vs Atlanta, Jul 1, 2003
Consecutive games with one or more home runs 11 (18 hrs), 1995
Longest shutout 16 inn, 3-0 vs Chicago, Sept 22, 1975

Longest 1-0 loss none over nine innings

ATTENDANCE

Highest home attendance	3,064,847 (1993)	**Largest crowds**	
		Day	55,315 vs Montreal, Apr 6, 2004
Highest road attendance	2,701,068 (1993)	**Night**	45,796 vs San Francisco, Aug 27, 1993
		Doubleheader	37,007 vs Philadelphia, Sept 27, 1998
		Home opener	55,315 vs Montreal, Apr 6, 2004

HOUSTON ASTROS
YEARLY FINISHES

(National League expansion franchise known as Houston Colt .45s through 1964)

Year	Position	W	L	Pct.	GB	Manager	Attendance
1962	8th	64	96	.400	36.5	Harry Craft	924,456
1963	9th	66	96	.407	33.0	Harry Craft	719,502
1964	9th	66	96	.407	27.0	Harry Craft, Luman Harris	725,773
1965	9th	65	97	.401	32.0	Luman Harris	2,151,470
1966	8th	72	90	.444	23.0	Grady Hatton	1,872,108
1967	9th	69	93	.426	32.5	Grady Hatton	1,348,303
1968	10th	72	90	.444	25.0	Grady Hatton, Harry Walker	1,312,887

WEST DIVISION

Year	Position	W	L	Pct.	GB	Manager	Attendance
1969	5th	81	81	.500	12.0	Harry Walker	1,442,995
1970	4th	79	83	.488	23.0	Harry Walker	1,253,444
1971	4th (tied)	79	83	.488	11.0	Harry Walker	1,261,589
1972	2nd	84	69	.549	10.5	Harry Walker, Salty Parker, Leo Durocher	1,469,247
1973	4th	82	80	.506	17.0	Leo Durocher, Preston Gomez	1,394,004
1974	4th	81	81	.500	21.0	Preston Gomez	1,090,728
1975	6th	64	97	.398	43.5	Preston Gomez, Bill Virdon	858,002
1976	3rd	80	82	.494	22.0	Bill Virdon	886,146
1977	3rd	81	81	.500	17.0	Bill Virdon	1,109,560
1978	5th	74	88	.457	21.0	Bill Virdon	1,126,145
1979	2nd	89	73	.549	1.5	Bill Virdon	1,900,312
1980	1st (P,c)	93	70	.571	+1.0	Bill Virdon	2,278,217
1981	3rd/1st (i)	61	49	.555	*	Bill Virdon	1,321,282
1982	5th	77	85	.475	12.0	Bill Virdon, Bob Lillis	1,558,555

Year	Position	W	L	Pct.	GB	Manager	Attendance
1983	3rd	85	77	.525	6.0	Bob Lillis	1,351,962
1984	2nd (tied)	80	82	.494	12.0	Bob Lillis	1,229,862
1985	3rd (tied)	83	79	.512	12.0	Bob Lillis	1,184,314
1986	1st (c)	96	66	.593	+10.0	Hal Lanier	1,734,276
1987	3rd	76	86	.469	14.0	Hal Lanier	1,909,902
1988	5th	82	80	.506	12.5	Hal Lanier	1,933,505
1989	3rd	86	76	.531	6.0	Art Howe	1,834,908
1990	4th (tied)	75	87	.463	16.0	Art Howe	1,310,927
1991	6th	65	97	.401	29.0	Art Howe	1,196,152
1992	4th	81	81	.500	17.0	Art Howe	1,211,412
1993	3rd	85	77	.525	19.0	Art Howe	2,084,546

CENTRAL DIVISION

Year	Position	W	L	Pct.	GB	Manager	Attendance
1994	2nd	66	49	.574	0.5	Terry Collins	1,561,136
1995	2nd	76	68	.528	9.0	Terry Collins	1,363,801
1996	2nd	82	80	.506	6.0	Terry Collins	1,975,888
1997	1st (d)	84	78	.519	+5.0	Larry Dierker	2,046,781
1998	1st (d)	102	60	.630	+12.5	Larry Dierker	2,450,451
1999	1st (d)	97	65	.599	+1.5	Larry Dierker	2,706,017
2000	4th	72	90	.444	23.0	Larry Dierker	3,056,139
2001	1st (tied) (d)	93	69	.574	0.0	Larry Dierker	2,904,280
2002	2nd	84	78	.519	13.0	Jimy Williams	2,517,407
2003	2nd	87	75	.537	1.0	Jimy Williams	2,454,038
2004	2nd (D,c)	92	70	.568	13.0	Jimy Williams, Phil Garner	3,087,872

(P) won division playoff; (c) lost League Championship Series; (i) lost intra-divisional playoff; *first half 28-29, second half 33-20; (d) lost Division Series; (D) won Division Series

INDIVIDUAL AND CLUB RECORDS

BATTING

	Individual		Club
	Season	**Career**	**Season**
Games	162—Enos Cabell, 1978 Bill Doran, 1987 Jeff Bagwell, 1992, 1996, 1997, 1999 Craig Biggio, 1992, 1996, 1997 Steve Finley, 1992	2,409—Craig Biggio	163 (1966, 1980)
At-bats	660—Enos Cabell, 162 g, 1978	9,221—Craig Biggio	5,641 (1998)
Runs	152—Jeff Bagwell, 159 g, 2000	1,603—Craig Biggio	938 (2000) Fewest—464 (1963)
Hits	210—Craig Biggio, 160 g, 1998	2,639—Craig Biggio	1,578 (1998) Fewest—1,184 (1963)
Hitting streak	25 g—Jeff Kent, 2004		
Singles	160—Sonny Jackson, 150 g, 1966	1,790—Craig Biggio	1,097 (1984)
Doubles	56—Craig Biggio, 160 g, 1999	564—Craig Biggio	326 (1998)
Triples	14—Roger Metzger, 154 g, 1973	80—Jose Cruz	67 (1980, 1984)

HOME RUNS

			249 (2000) Fewest—49 (1979)
Righthander	47—Jeff Bagwell, 159 g, 2000	446—Jeff Bagwell	
Lefthander	23—Franklin Stubbs, 146 g, 1990	138—Jose Cruz	
Switch-hitter	42—Lance Berkman, 158 g, 2002	156—Lance Berkman	
Rookie	21—Lance Berkman, 114 g, 2000		
Home	28—Jeff Bagwell, 2000	231—Jeff Bagwell	135 (2000)
Road	30—Jeff Bagwell, 1999	215—Jeff Bagwell	114 (2000)
Month	13—Jeff Bagwell, June 1994		49 (Jun 2001)
Pinch	5—Cliff Johnson, 1974	9—Cliff Johnson	9 (1995)
Grand slams	2—many players	6—Bob Aspromonte	7 (2001)
Home runs at Colt Stadium, all teams			85 (1962)
Home runs at Astrodome, all teams			153 (1998)
Home runs at Minute Maid Field, all teams			266 (2000)
Total bases	363—Jeff Bagwell, 159 g, 2000	4,175—Jeff Bagwell	2,655 (2000)
Extra base hits	94—Lance Berkman, 156 g, 2001	962—Jeff Bagwell	574 (2000)
Sacrifice hits	34—Craig Reynolds, 146 g, 1979	100—Joe Niekro	109 (1979)
Sacrifice flies	13—Ray Knight, 158 g, 1982 Jeff Bagwell, 162 g, 1999	98—Jeff Bagwell	61 (2000)

	Individual		Club
	Season	**Career**	**Season**
Bases on balls	149—Jeff Bagwell, 162 g, 1999	1,383—Jeff Bagwell	728 (1999)
			Fewest—381 (1964)
Strikeouts	145—Lee May, 148 g, 1972	1,537—Jeff Bagwell	1,138 (1999)
	Fewest—39—Greg Gross, 156 g, 1974		Fewest—719 (1976)
Hit by pitch	34—Craig Biggio, 162 g, 1997	256—Craig Biggio	100 (1997)
			Fewest—13 (1980)
Runs batted in	135—Jeff Bagwell, 162 g, 1997	1,510—Jeff Bagwell	900 (2000)
			Fewest—420 (1963)
Grounded into	30—Brad Ausmus, 130 g, 2002	219—Jeff Bagwell	154 (2000)
double plays	Fewest—0—Craig Biggio, 162 g, 1997		Fewest—76 (1983)
Left on base			1,252 (1999)
			Fewest—1,040 (1964)
Batting average	.355—Moises Alou, 126 g, 2000	.297—Jeff Bagwell	.280 (1998)
		Bob Watson	Lowest—.220 (1963)
Most .300 hitters			4 (1998)
Slugging average	.636—Richard Hidalgo, 153 g, 2000	.542—Jeff Bagwell	.477 (2000)
			Lowest—.301 (1963)
On-base percentage	.454—Jeff Bagwell, 162 g, 1999	.417—Lance Berkman	.361 (2000)
			Lowest—.283 (1963)

BASERUNNING

Stolen bases	65—Gerald Young, 149 g, 1988	487—Cesar Cedeno	198 (1988)
Caught stealing	27—Gerald Young, 149 g, 1988	149—Cesar Cedeno	95 (1979, 1983)

PITCHING

Games	83—Octavio Dotel, 2002	563—Dave Smith	
Games started	40—Jerry Reuss, 1973	320—Larry Dierker	
Complete games	20—Lary Dierker, 1969	106—Larry Dierker	55 (1979)
Wins	22—Mike Hampton, 1999	144—Joe Niekro	
Percentage	.846—Mike Hampton (22-4), 1999	.601—J.R. Richard	
Winning streak	12—Mark Portugal, 1993		
	Wade Miller, 2002		
20-win seasons		2—Joe Niekro	
Losses	20—Dick Farrell, 1962	117—Larry Dierker	
Losing streak	13—Jose Lima, 2000		
Saves	44—Billy Wagner, 2003	225—Billy Wagner	51 (1986)
Innings	305—Larry Dierker, 1969	2,294.1—Larry Dierker	1,482.2 (2000)
Hits	271—Jerry Reuss, 1973	2,090—Larry Dierker	1,596 (2000)
Runs	152—Jose Lima, 2000	934—Joe Niekro	944 (2000)
Earned runs	145—Jose Lima, 2000	837—Larry Dierker	864 (2000)
	Jerry Reuss, 1973		
Bases on balls	151—J.R. Richard, 1976	818—Joe Niekro	679 (1975)
Strikeouts	313—J.R. Richard, 1979	1,866—Nolan Ryan	1,228 (2001)
Strikeouts, game	18—Don Wilson, Jul 14, 1968, 2nd game		
Hit batsmen	16—Jack Billingham, 1971	72—Darryl Kile	74 (2003)
	Darryl Kile, 1996		
Wild pitches	21—Joe Niekro, 1985	128—Joe Niekro	91 (1970)
Home runs	48—Jose Lima, 2000	177—Larry Dierker	234 (2000)
Sacrifice hits	22—Bob Knepper, 1986	91—Bob Knepper	99 (1964)
Sacrifice flies	13—Mark Lemongello, 1978	78—Joe Niekro	64 (2000)
	Jim Deshaies, 1988		
Earned run average	2.21—Danny Darwin, 162.2 inn, 1990	3.13—Nolan Ryan	2.66 (1981)
Shutouts	6—Dave A. Roberts, 1973	25—Larry Dierker	19 (1979, 1981, 1986)
			Lost—23 (1963)
1-0 games won	3—Bob Bruce, 1964	5—Mike Scott	9 (1976)
	J.R. Richard, 1976		Lost—6 (1964, 1969)
	Bob Knepper, 1981		

TEAM FIELDING

Putouts	4,448 (1980)	**Assists**	1,880 (1975)
	Fewest—4,284 (1964)		Fewest—1,561 (2000)
Chances accepted	6,255 (1975)	**Errors**	174 (1966)
	Fewest—5,827 (1972)		Fewest—83 (2002)
Double plays	175 (1999)	**Passed balls**	38 (1984)
	Fewest—100 (1963)		Fewest—4 (2001, 2003, 2004)
Errorless games	96 (2002)	**Fielding average**	.986 (2002)
	Consecutive—11 (1973, 1994)		Lowest—.972 (1966)

MISCELLANEOUS

Most players, season 48 (1965)
Fewest players, season 32 (1972)
Games won 102 (1998)
  Month 22 (Aug 1998)
  Consecutive 12 (1999, 2004)
Winning percentage .630 (1998), 102-60
  Lowest .398 (1975), 64-97
Number of league championships 0
  Most recent ----
Runs, game 19 vs Chicago, Jun 25, 1995
  vs Pittsburgh, May 11, 1999
  Opponents' 22 by Chicago, June 3, 1987
Hits, game 25 vs Atlanta, May 30, 1976, 2nd game
  (25 vs Cincinnati, Jul 2, 1976, 1st game, 14 inn)
Home runs, game 7 vs Chicago, Sept 9, 2000
Runs, shutout 15 vs Montreal, Apr 26, 1998
  Opponents' 16 by Philadelphia, Sept 10, 1963
Longest 1-0 win 24 inn, vs New York, Apr 15, 1968

Most seasons, non-pitcher 17—Craig Biggio
Most seasons, pitcher 13—Larry Dierker
Games lost 97 (1965, 1975, 1991)
  Month 24 (July 1962)
  Consecutive 11 (1995)
Overall record 3,408-3,430 (43 seasons)
  Interleague play 64-52
Number of times worst record in league 3
  Most recent 1991
Runs, inning 12 vs Philadelphia, May 31, 1975, 8th
  vs Chicago, May 12, 1997, 7th

Total bases, game 44 vs Chicago, Sept 9, 2000

Consecutive games with one or more home runs 18 (33 hrs), 2000
Longest shutout 16 inn, 3-0 vs Chicago, Sept 22, 1975

Longest 1-0 loss 16 inn, vs Chicago, May 31, 2003

ATTENDANCE

Highest home attendance		**Largest crowds**	
Colt Stadium	924,456 (1962)	Day	52,199 vs Chicago, Aug 16, 1998
Astrodome	2,706,017 (1999)	Night	54,037 vs Cincinnati, Sept 28, 1999
Minute Maid Park	3,087,872 (2004)	Doubleheader	45,115 vs Atlanta, Aug 4, 1979
Highest road attendance	2,446,596 (2000)	Home opener	51,668 vs Chicago, Apr 6, 1999

LOS ANGELES DODGERS
YEARLY FINISHES

(American Association franchise moved to the National League after the 1889 season
and from Brooklyn to Los Angeles after the 1957 season)

Year	Position	W	L	Pct.	GB	Manager	Attendance
1958	7th	71	83	.461	21.0	Walter Alston	1,845,556
1959	1st (L,S)	88	68	.564	+2.0	Walter Alston	2,071,045
1960	4th	82	72	.532	13.0	Walter Alston	2,253,887
1961	2nd	89	65	.578	4.0	Walter Alston	1,804,250
1962	2nd (l)	102	63	.618	1.0	Walter Alston	2,755,184
1963	1st (S)	99	63	.611	+6.0	Walter Alston	2,538,602
1964	6th (tied)	80	82	.494	13.0	Walter Alston	2,228,751
1965	1st (S)	97	65	.599	+2.0	Walter Alston	2,553,577
1966	1st (s)	95	67	.586	+1.5	Walter Alston	2,617,029
1967	8th	73	89	.451	28.5	Walter Alston	1,664,362
1968	7th	76	86	.469	21.0	Walter Alston	1,581,093

WEST DIVISION

Year	Position	W	L	Pct.	GB	Manager	Attendance
1969	4th	85	77	.525	8.0	Walter Alston	1,784,527
1970	2nd	87	74	.540	14.5	Walter Alston	1,697,142
1971	2nd	89	73	.549	1.0	Walter Alston	2,064,594
1972	3rd	85	70	.548	10.5	Walter Alston	1,860,858
1973	2nd	95	66	.590	3.5	Walter Alston	2,136,192
1974	1st (C,s)	102	60	.630	+4.0	Walter Alston	2,632,474
1975	2nd	88	74	.543	20.0	Walter Alston	2,539,349
1976	2nd	92	70	.568	10.0	Walter Alston, Tommy Lasorda	2,386,301
1977	1st (C,s)	98	64	.605	+10.0	Tommy Lasorda	2,955,087
1978	1st (C,s)	95	67	.586	+2.5	Tommy Lasorda	3,347,845
1979	3rd	79	83	.488	11.5	Tommy Lasorda	2,860,954
1980	2nd (p)	92	71	.564	1.0	Tommy Lasorda	3,249,287
1981	1st/4th (M,C,S)	63	47	.573	*	Tommy Lasorda	2,381,292
1982	2nd	88	74	.543	1.0	Tommy Lasorda	3,608,881

Year	Position	W	L	Pct.	GB	Manager	Attendance
1983	1st (c)	91	71	.562	+3.0	Tommy Lasorda	3,510,313
1984	4th	79	83	.488	13.0	Tommy Lasorda	3,134,824
1985	1st (c)	95	67	.586	+5.5	Tommy Lasorda	3,264,593
1986	5th	73	89	.451	23.0	Tommy Lasorda	3,023,208
1987	4th	73	89	.451	17.0	Tommy Lasorda	2,797,409
1988	1st (C,S)	94	67	.584	+7.0	Tommy Lasorda	2,980,262
1989	4th	77	83	.481	14.0	Tommy Lasorda	2,944,653
1990	2nd	86	76	.531	5.0	Tommy Lasorda	3,002,396
1991	2nd	93	69	.574	1.0	Tommy Lasorda	3,348,170
1992	6th	63	99	.389	35.0	Tommy Lasorda	2,473,266
1993	4th	81	81	.500	23.0	Tommy Lasorda	3,170,392
1994	1st	58	56	.509	+3.5	Tommy Lasorda	2,279,355
1995	1st (d)	78	66	.542	+1.0	Tommy Lasorda	2,766,251
1996	2nd (d)	90	72	.556	1.0	Tommy Lasorda, Bill Russell	3,188,454
1997	2nd	88	74	.543	2.0	Bill Russell	3,319,504
1998	3rd	83	79	.512	15.0	Bill Russell, Glenn Hoffman	3,089,201
1999	3rd	77	85	.475	23.0	Dave Johnson	3,095,346
2000	2nd	86	76	.531	11.0	Dave Johnson	3,010,819
2001	3rd	86	76	.531	6.0	Jim Tracy	3,017,502
2002	3rd	92	70	.568	6.0	Jim Tracy	3,131,077
2003	2nd	85	77	.525	15.5	Jim Tracy	3,138,626
2004	1st (d)	93	69	.574	+2.0	Jim Tracy	3,448,283

(L) won league playoff; (S) won World Series; (I) lost league playoff; (s) lost World Series; (C) won League Championship Series; (p) lost division playoff; (M) won intra-divisional playoff; *first half 36-21, second half 27-26; (c) lost League Championship Series; (d) lost division series

INDIVIDUAL AND CLUB RECORDS

BATTING

	Individual		Club
	Season	**Career**	**Season**
Games	165—Maury Wills, 1962	2,181—Bill Russell	165 (1962)
At-bats	695—Maury Wills, 165 g, 1962	7,495—Willie Davis	5,642 (1982)
Runs	130—Maury Wills, 165 g, 1962	1,004—Willie Davis	842 (1962)
			Fewest—470 (1968)
Hits	230—Tommy Davis, 163 g, 1962	2,091—Willie Davis	1,515 (1970)
			Fewest—1,234 (1968)
Hitting streak	31 g—Willie Davis, 1969		
Singles	179—Maury Wills, 165 g, 1962	1,530—Bill Russell	1,128 (1970)
Doubles	49—Shawn Green, 160 g, 2003	333—Steve Garvey	286 (2002)
Triples	16—Willie Davis, 146 g, 1970	110—Willie Davis	67 (1970)

HOME RUNS

			211 (2000)
			Fewest—67 (1968)
Righthander	48—Adrian Beltre, 156 g, 2004	270—Eric Karros	
Lefthander	49—Shawn Green, 161 g, 2001	162—Shawn Green	
Switch-hitter	32—Reggie Smith, 148 g, 1977	97—Reggie Smith	
Rookie	35—Mike Piazza, 149 g, 1993		
Home	23—Gary Sheffield, 2000	130—Eric Karros	108 (2000)
	Adrian Beltre, 2004		
Road	30—Shawn Green, 2001	140—Eric Karros	112 (2001)
Month	15—Pedro Guerrero, June 1985		43 (May 1979)
Pinch	7—Dave Hansen, 2000	13—Dave Hansen	12 (2000)
Grand slams	3—Kal Daniels, 130 g, 1990	8—Mike Piazza	9 (2000)
	Mike Piazza, 37 g, 1998		
	Adrian Beltre, 156 g, 2004		
Home runs at Los Angeles Coliseum, all teams			193 (1958)
Home runs at Dodger Stadium, all teams			194 (1999)

Total bases	376—Adrian Beltre, 156 g, 2004	3,094—Willie Davis	2,362 (2000)
Extra base hits	84—Shawn Green, 161 g, 2001	585—Willie Davis	504 (2000)
Sacrifice hits	25—Jose Offerman, 158 g, 1993	132—Bill Russell	120 (1964)
Sacrifice flies	13—Reggie Smith, 128 g, 1978	74—Eric Karros	64 (1974)
Bases on balls	110—Jimmy Wynn, 130 g, 1975	765—Ron Cey	668 (2000)
			Fewest—407 (2003)
Strikeouts	149—Bill Grabarkewitz, 156 g, 1970	1,105—Eric Karros	1,190 (1996)
	Fewest—26—Bill Buckner, 154 g, 1976		Fewest—744 (1976)
Hit by pitch	18—Alex Cora, 138 g, 2004	52—Alex Cora	72 (2003)
			Fewest—14 (1984)

	Individual		Club
	Season	**Career**	**Season**
Runs batted in	153—Tommy Davis, 163 g, 1962	992—Steve Garvey	781 (1962)
			Fewest—434 (1968)
Grounded into	27—Eric Karros, 154 g, 1996	174—Bill Russell	145 (1979)
double plays	Fewest—2—Todd Hollandsworth, 149 g, 1996		Fewest—79 (1965)
Left on base			1,223 (1982)
			Fewest—1,012 (1958)
Batting average	.362—Mike Piazza, 152 g, 1997	.309—Pedro Guerrero	.272 (1974)
			Lowest—.230 (1968)
Most .300 hitters			4 (1970)
Slugging average	.643—Gary Sheffield, 141 g, 2000	.512—Pedro Guerrero	.431 (2000)
			Lowest—.319 (1968)
On-base percentage	.438—Gary Sheffield, 141 g, 2000	.381—Pedro Guerrero	.342 (1974)
			Lowest—.289 (1968)

BASERUNNING

Stolen bases	104—Maury Wills, 165 g, 1962	490—Maury Wills	198 (1962)
Caught stealing	31—Maury Wills, 158 g, 1965	171—Maury Wills	78 (1992)

PITCHING

Games	106—Mike G. Marshall, 1974	550—Don Sutton	
Games started	42—Don Drysdale, 1963, 1965	533—Don Sutton	
Complete games	27—Sandy Koufax, 1965, 1966	156—Don Drysdale	58 (1965)
		Don Sutton	
Wins	27—Sandy Koufax, 1966	233—Don Sutton	
Percentage	.864—Orel Hershiser (19-3), 1985	.670—Sandy Koufax	
Winning streak	13—Phil Regan, 1966		
Winning streak, two seasons	15—Phil Regan, 1966 (13), 1967 (2)		
20-win seasons		3—Sandy Koufax	
Losses	18—Claude Osteen, 1968	181—Don Sutton	
	Don Sutton, 1969		
Losing streak	11—Rick Honeycutt, 1987		
Saves	55—Eric Gagne, 2003	152—Eric Gagne	58 (2003)
Innings	336—Sandy Koufax, 1965	3,816.1—Don Sutton	1,491 (1973)
Hits	298—Claude Osteen, 1967	3,291—Don Sutton	1,438 (1999)
Runs	127—Don Sutton, 1970	1,450—Don Sutton	787 (1999)
Earned runs	118—Don Sutton, 1970	1,311—Don Sutton	718 (1999)
Bases on balls	124—Fernando Valenzuela, 1987	996—Don Sutton	614 (1959)
	Chan Ho Park, 2000		
Strikeouts	382—Sandy Koufax, 1965	2,696—Don Sutton	1,289 (2003)
Strikeouts, game	18—Sandy Koufax, Aug 31, 1959		
	Sandy Koufax, Apr 24, 1962		
	Ramon Martinez, Jun, 1990		
Hit batsmen	20—Don Drysdale, 1961	144—Don Drysdale	75 (2000)
	Chan Ho Park, 2001		
Wild pitches	19—Hideo Nomo, 1995	94—Fernando Valenzuela	70 (1958)
Home runs	38—Don Sutton, 1970	309—Don Sutton	192 (1999)
Sacrifice hits	27—Fernando Valenzuela, 1983	169—Don Sutton	109 (1992)
Sacrifice flies	11—Burt Hooton, 1979	85—Don Sutton	50 (1979)
Earned run average	1.73—Sandy Koufax, 323 inn, 1966	2.64—Sandy Koufax	2.62 (1966)
Shutouts	11—Sandy Koufax, 1963	52—Don Sutton	24 (1963, 1988)
			Lost—23 (1968)
1-0 games won	4—Don Drysdale, 1968	10—Sandy Koufax	7 (1963, 1984)
			Lost—7 (1989)

TEAM FIELDING

Putouts	4,473 (1973) Fewest—4,105 (1958)	**Assists**	1,946 (1982) Fewest—1,563 (1997)
Chances accepted	6,411 (1982) Fewest—5,708 (1961)	**Errors**	193 (1962) Fewest—73 (2004)
Double plays	198 (1958) Fewest—104 (1997)	**Passed balls**	24 (1973) Fewest—6 (1958)
Errorless games	102 (2004) Consecutive—11 (1979)	**Fielding average**	.988 (2004) Lowest—.970 (1962)

MISCELLANEOUS

Most players, season 53 (1998)
Fewest players, season 30 (1962)
Games won 102 (1962, 1974)
  Month 21 (May 1962, Jul 1963, Jun 1973, Jul 2004)
  Consecutive 13 (1962, 1965)
Winning percentage .630 (1974), 102-60
  Lowest .389 (1992), 63-99
Number of league championships 9
  Most recent 1988
Runs, game 22 vs Colorado, Jul 21, 2001
  Opponents' 20 by Chicago, May 20, 1967
    by Chicago, May 5, 2001
Hits, game 24 vs Chicago, Aug 20, 1974
  vs Arizona, Sept 2, 2002
Home runs, game 8 vs Milwaukee, May 23, 2002
Runs, shutout 19 vs San Diego, Jun 28, 1969
  Opponents' 18 by Cincinnati, Aug 8, 1965
Longest 1-0 win 22 inn, vs Montreal, Aug 23, 1989

Most seasons, non-pitcher 18—Bill Russell
Most seasons, pitcher 16—Don Sutton
Games lost 99 (1992)
  Month 20 (Jul 1968, Jun 1979)
  Consecutive 10 (1961, 1992)
Overall record 4,011-3,447 (47 seasons)
  Interleague play 70-58
Number of times worst record in league 1
  Most recent 1992
Runs, inning 10 vs San Diego, Jun 28, 1969, 3rd
    vs San Francisco, Jul 4, 1971, 8th
    vs San Diego, Sept 13, 1977, 2nd
Total bases, game 48 vs Chicago, Aug 20, 1974

Consecutive games with one or more home runs 15 (23 hrs), 1977
Longest shutout 16 inn, 3-0 vs Chicago, Sept 22, 1975

Longest 1-0 loss 16 inn, vs Houston, Apr 21, 1976

ATTENDANCE

Highest home attendance
  Los Angeles Coliseum   2,253,887 (1960)
  Dodger Stadium   3,608,881 (1982)

Highest road attendance   2,678,742 (2000)

Largest crowds
  Day   78,672 vs San Francisco, Apr 18, 1958
  Night   67,550 vs Chicago, Apr 12, 1960
  Doubleheader   72,140 vs Cincinnati, Aug 16, 1961
  Home opener   78,672 vs San Francisco, Apr 18, 1958

MILWAUKEE BRAVES
YEARLY FINISHES

*(Original National League franchise moved from Boston to Milwaukee after the 1952 season
and to Atlanta after the 1965 season)*

Year	Position	W	L	Pct.	GB	Manager	Attendance
1953	2nd	92	62	.597	13.0	Charlie Grimm	1,826,397
1954	3rd	89	65	.578	8.0	Charlie Grimm	2,131,388
1955	2nd	85	69	.552	13.5	Charlie Grimm	2,005,836
1956	2nd	92	62	.597	1.0	Charlie Grimm, Fred Haney	2,046,331
1957	1st (S)	95	59	.617	+8.0	Fred Haney	2,215,404
1958	1st (s)	92	62	.597	+8.0	Fred Haney	1,971,101
1959	2nd (I)	86	70	.551	2.0	Fred Haney	1,749,112
1960	2nd	88	66	.571	7.0	Chuck Dressen	1,497,799
1961	4th	83	71	.539	10.0	Chuck Dressen, Birdie Tebbetts	1,101,441
1962	5th	86	76	.531	15.5	Birdie Tebbetts	766,921
1963	6th	84	78	.519	15.0	Bobby Bragan	773,018
1964	5th	88	74	.543	5.0	Bobby Bragan	910,911
1965	5th	86	76	.531	11.0	Bobby Bragan	555,584

(S) won World Series; (s) lost World Series; (I) lost pennant playoff

INDIVIDUAL AND CLUB RECORDS
BATTING

	Individual		Club
	Season	**Career**	**Season**
Games	161—Hank Aaron, 1963	1,944—Eddie Mathews	163 (1963)
At-bats	636—Bill Bruton, 149 g, 1955	7,080—Hank Aaron	5,591 (1964)
Runs	127—Hank Aaron, 156 g, 1962	1,300—Eddie Mathews	803 (1964) Fewest—670 (1954)
Hits	223—Hank Aaron, 154 g, 1959	2,266—Hank Aaron	1,522 (1964) Fewest—1,345 (1963)

	Individual		Club
	Season	**Career**	**Season**
Hitting streak	25 g—Hank Aaron, 1956		
	Hank Aaron, 1962		
Singles	132—Joe Torre, 154 g, 1964	1,397—Hank Aaron	1,057 (1964)
Doubles	46—Hank Aaron, 154 g, 1959	391—Hank Aaron	274 (1964)
Triples	15—Bill Bruton, 147 g, 1956	80—Hank Aaron	62 (1957)

HOME RUNS

			181 (1962)
			Fewest—170 (1960)
Righthander	45—Hank Aaron, 156 g, 1962	398—Hank Aaron	
Lefthander	47—Eddie Mathews, 157 g, 1953	452—Eddie Mathews	
Switch-hitter	6—Red Schoendienst, 93 g, 1957	8—Red Schoendienst	
Rookie	22—Rico Carty, 133 g, 1964		
Home	23—Joe Adcock, 1956	211—Eddie Mathews	98 (1965)
	Eddie Mathews, 1960		
Road	30—Eddie Mathews, 1953	241—Eddie Mathews	124 (1957)
Month	15—Joe Adcock, July 1956		52 (Jun 1961)
Pinch	2—many players	7—Joe Adcock	7 (1965)
Grand slams	3—Del Crandall, 133 g, 1955	9—Hank Aaron	8 (1962)
	Hank Aaron, 156 g, 1962	Joe Adcock	
Home runs at County Stadium, all teams			173 (1965)

Total bases	400—Hank Aaron, 154 g, 1959	4,011—Hank Aaron	2,411 (1957)
Extra base hits	92—Hank Aaron, 154 g, 1959	869—Hank Aaron	482 (1957)
Sacrifice hits	31—Johnny Logan, 148 g, 1956	107—Johnny Logan	142 (1956)
Sacrifice flies	12—Hank Aaron, 153 g, 1960	72—Hank Aaron	60 (1960)
	Del Crandall, 142 g, 1960		
Bases on balls	124—Eddie Mathews, 158 g, 1963	1,254—Eddie Mathews	581 (1962)
			Fewest—408 (1965)
Strikeouts	122—Mack Jones, 122 g, 1965	1,190—Eddie Mathews	976 (1965)
	Fewest—33—Johnny Logan, 150 g, 1953		Fewest—619 (1954)
Hit by pitch	9—Frank Torre, 129 g, 1957	36—Johnny Logan	43 (1963)
	Mack Jones, 122 g, 1965		Fewest—20 (1956)
Runs batted in	135—Eddie Mathews, 157 g, 1953	1,305—Hank Aaron	755 (1964)
			Fewest—624 (1963)
Grounded into	26—Joe Torre, 154 g, 1964	193—Hank Aaron	134 (1964)
double plays	Fewest—4—Eddie Mathews, 151 g, 1956		Fewest—99 (1956)
	Bill Bruton, 161 g, 1960		
Left on base			1,138 (1962, 1963)
			Fewest—1,021 (1953)
Batting average	.355—Hank Aaron, 154 g, 1959	.320—Hank Aaron	.272 (1964)
			Lowest—.244 (1963)
Most .300 hitters			5 (1964)
Slugging average	.636—Hank Aaron, 154 g, 1959	.567—Hank Aaron	.442 (1957)
			Lowest—.370 (1963)
On-base percentage	.423—Eddie Mathews, 138 g, 1954	.385—Eddie Mathews	.333 (1964)
			Lowest—.310 (1965)

BASERUNNING

Stolen bases	34—Bill Bruton, 142 g, 1954	149—Hank Aaron	75 (1963)
Caught stealing	13—Bill Bruton, 142 g, 1954	64—Bill Bruton	52 (1963)
	Bill Bruton, 151 g, 1960		

PITCHING

Games	62—Billy O'Dell, 1965	452—Warren Spahn	
Games started	39—Lew Burdette, 1959	399—Warren Spahn	
Complete games	24—Warren Spahn, 1953	232—Warren Spahn	72 (1953, 1958)
Wins	24—Tony Cloninger, 1965	234—Warren Spahn	
Percentage	.767—Warren Spahn (23-7), 1953, 1963	.629—Warren Spahn	
Winning streak	11—Warren Spahn, 1954		
20-win seasons		9—Warren Spahn	
Losses	15—Lew Burdette, 1959	138—Warren Spahn	
	Warren Spahn, 1959		

	Individual		Club
	Season	Career	Season
Losing streak	unknown		
Innings	292—Warren Spahn, 1959	3,162—Warren Spahn	1,471.2 (1963)
Hits	312—Lew Burdette, 1959	2,934—Warren Spahn	1,443 (1962)
Runs	144—Lew Burdette, 1959	1,181—Warren Spahn	744 (1964)
Earned runs	131—Lew Burdette, 1959	1,073—Warren Spahn	656 (1964)
Bases on balls	121—Bob Buhl, 1957	791—Warren Spahn	591 (1955)
Strikeouts	211—Tony Cloninger, 1965	1,493—Warren Spahn	966 (1965)
Strikeouts, game	15—Warren Spahn, Sept 16, 1960		
Hit batsmen	12—Bob Shaw, 1962	37—Lew Burdette	35 (1960)
Wild pitches	22—Tony Cloninger, 1965	58—Tony Cloninger	71 (1964)
Home runs	38—Lew Burdette, 1959	280—Warren Spahn	160 (1964)
Sacrifice hits	20—Warren Spahn, 1961	134—Warren Spahn	87 (1961)
Sacrifice flies	11—Lew Burdette, 1957	67—Warren Spahn	43 (1957)
Earned run average	2.10—Warren Spahn, 266 inn, 1953	3.05—Warren Spahn	3.11 (1956)
Shutouts	7—Warren Spahn, 1963	36—Warren Spahn	18 (1959, 1963)
			Lost—13 (1963)
1-0 games won	2—Bob Buhl	6—Lew Burdette	4 (1963)
	Warren Spahn, 1961, 1963	Warren Spahn	Lost—unknown

TEAM FIELDING

Putouts	4,416 (1963)	Assists	1,848 (1961, 1963)
	Fewest—4,128 (1958)		Fewest—1,665 (1960)
Chances accepted	6,264 (1963)	Errors	152 (1955)
	Fewest—5,827 (1960)		Fewest—111 (1961)
Double plays	173 (1957)	Passed balls	28 (1965)
	Fewest—137 (1960)		Fewest—5 (1956, 1959
Errorless games	unknown	Fielding average	.982 (1961)
	Consecutive—7 (1954, 1956, 1964)		Lowest—.975 (1955)

MISCELLANEOUS

Most players, season 42 (1964)
Fewest players, season 31 (1953, 1954)
Games won 95 (1957)
  Month 23 (Aug 1953, Aug 1958)
  Consecutive 11 (1956)
Winning percentage .617 (1957), 95-59
  Lowest .519 (1963), 84-78
Number of league championships 2
  Most recent 1958
Runs, game 23 vs Chicago, Sept 2, 1957, 1st game
  Opponents' unknown
Hits, game 26 vs Chicago, Sept 2, 1957, 1st game
Home runs, game 8 vs Pittsburgh, Aug 30, 1953, 1st game
Runs, shutout 15 vs Cincinnati, May 13, 1956, 1st game
  Opponents' 10 by Philadelphia, Jul 21, 1953, 1st game
Longest 1-0 win 15 inn, vs Chicago, Apr 13, 1963

Most seasons, non-pitcher 13—Eddie Mathews
Most seasons, pitcher 12—Warren Spahn
Games lost 78 (1963)
  Month 18 (Jun 1954)
  Consecutive 8 (1961)
Overall record 1,146-890 (13 seasons)

Number of times worst record in league 0
  Most recent ---
Runs, inning 10 vs Pittsburgh, Jun 12, 1953, 2nd game, 1st

Total bases, game 47 vs Pittsburgh, Aug 30, 1953, 1st game
Consecutive games with one or more home runs 22 (39 hrs), 1956
Longest shutout unknown

Longest 1-0 loss 16 inn, vs San Francisco, Jul 2, 1963

ATTENDANCE

Highest home attendance	2,215,404 (1957)	Largest crowds	
		Day	48,642 vs Philadelphia, Sept 27, 1959
Highest road attendance	1,633,569 (1959)	Night	46,944 vs New York, Aug 27, 1954
		Doubleheader	47,604 vs Cincinnati, Sept 3, 1956
		Home opener	43,640 vs Cincinnati, Apr 12, 1955

MILWAUKEE BREWERS
YEARLY FINISHES

(American League expansion franchise moved from Seattle to Milwaukee after the 1969 season

and from the American League to the National League after the 1997 season)

AMERICAN LEAGUE WEST DIVISION

Year	Position	W	L	Pct.	GB	Manager	Attendance
1970	4th	65	97	.401	33.0	Dave Bristol	933,690
1971	6th	69	92	.429	32.0	Dave Bristol	731,531

AMERICAN LEAGUE EAST DIVISION

Year	Position	W	L	Pct.	GB	Manager	Attendance
1972	6th	65	91	.417	21.0	Dave Bristol, Del Crandall	600,440
1973	5th	74	88	.457	23.0	Del Crandall	1,092,158
1974	5th	76	86	.469	15.0	Del Crandall	955,741
1975	5th	68	94	.420	28.0	Del Crandall	1,213,357
1976	6th	66	95	.410	32.0	Alex Grammas	1,012,164
1977	6th	67	95	.414	33.0	Alex Grammas	1,114,938
1978	3rd	93	69	.574	6.5	George Bamberger	1,601,406
1979	2nd	95	66	.590	8.0	George Bamberger	1,918,343
1980	3rd	86	76	.531	17.0	George Bamberger, Buck Rodgers	1,857,408
1981	3rd/1st (i)	62	47	.569	*	Buck Rodgers	878,432
1982	1st (C,s)	95	67	.586	+1.0	Buck Rodgers, Harvey Kuenn	1,978,896
1983	5th	87	75	.537	11.0	Harvey Kuenn	2,397,131
1984	7th	67	94	.416	36.5	Rene Lachemann	1,608,509
1985	6th	71	90	.441	28.0	George Bamberger	1,360,265
1986	6th	77	84	.478	18.0	George Bamberger, Tom Trebelhorn	1,265,041
1987	3rd	91	71	.562	7.0	Tom Trebelhorn	1,909,244
1988	3rd (tied)	87	75	.537	2.0	Tom Trebelhorn	1,923,238
1989	4th	81	81	.500	8.0	Tom Trebelhorn	1,970,735
1990	6th	74	88	.457	14.0	Tom Trebelhorn	1,752,900
1991	4th	83	79	.512	8.0	Tom Trebelhorn	1,478,729
1992	2nd	92	70	.568	4.0	Phil Garner	1,857,314
1993	7th	69	93	.426	26.0	Phil Garner	1,688,080

AMERICAN LEAGUE CENTRAL DIVISION

Year	Position	W	L	Pct.	GB	Manager	Attendance
1994	5th	53	62	.461	15.0	Phil Garner	1,268,399
1995	4th	65	79	.451	35.0	Phil Garner	1,087,560
1996	3rd	80	82	.494	19.5	Phil Garner	1,327,155
1997	3rd	78	83	.484	8.0	Phil Garner	1,444,027

NATIONAL LEAGUE CENTRAL DIVISION

Year	Position	W	L	Pct.	GB	Manager	Attendance
1998	5th	74	88	.457	28.0	Phil Garner	1,811,548
1999	5th	74	87	.460	22.5	Phil Garner, Jim Lefebvre	1,701,796
2000	3rd	73	89	.451	22.0	Davey Lopes	1,573,621
2001	4th	68	94	.420	25.0	Davey Lopes	2,811,041
2002	6th	56	106	.346	41.0	Davey Lopes, Jerry Royster	1,969,693
2003	6th	68	94	.420	20.0	Ned Yost	1,685,049
2004	6th	67	94	.416	37.5	Ned Yost	2,062,382

(i) lost intra-divisional series; *first half 31-25, second half 31-22; (C) won League Championship Series; (s) lost World Series

INDIVIDUAL AND CLUB RECORDS

Note: All records prior to 1998 are as an American League club.

BATTING

	Individual		Club
	Season	**Career**	**Season**
Games	162—Gorman Thomas, 1980 Robin Yount, 1988 Richie Sexson, 2003	2,856—Robin Yount	163 (1970, 1982, 2000)
At-bats	666—Paul Molitor, 160 g, 1982	11,008—Robin Yount	5,733 (1982)
Runs	136—Paul Molitor, 160 g, 1982	1,632—Robin Yount	894 (1996) Fewest—534 (1971)
Hits	219—Cecil Cooper, 153 g, 1980	3,142—Robin Yount	1,599 (1982) Fewest—1,188 (1971)
Hitting streak	39 g—Paul Molitor, 1987		
Singles	157—Cecil Cooper, 153 g, 1980	2,182—Robin Yount	1,107 (1991)
Doubles	53—Lyle Overbay, 159 g, 2004	583—Robin Yount	304 (1996)
Triples	16—Paul Molitor, 140 g, 1979	126—Robin Yount	57 (1983)

HOME RUNS

			216 (1982) Fewest—82 (1992)
Righthander	45—Gorman Thomas, 156 g, 1979 Richie Sexson, 158 g, 2001 Richie Sexson, 162 g, 2003	251—Robin Yount	
Lefthander	41—Ben Oglivie, 156 g, 1980	201—Cecil Cooper	
Switch-hitter	25—Dale Sveum, 153 g, 1987	90—Jose Valentin	
Rookie	17—Greg Vaughn, 120 g, 1990 Danny Walton, 117 g, 1970		

	Individual			Club
	Season		**Career**	**Season**
Home	28—Richie Sexson, 2001		124—Robin Yount	108 (2003)
Road	26—Ben Oglivie, 1980		127—Robin Yount	127 (1982)
Month	12—Gorman Thomas, Aug 1979			47 (Jun 1982)
	Greg Vaughn, Jun 1996			
	Jeromy Burnitz, Jun 1999			
Pinch	4—Bob Hamelin, 1998		4—Bob Hamelin	8 (2002)
Grand slams	3—John Jaha, 88 g, 1995		5—Cecil Cooper	10 (1995)
	Devon White, 126 g, 2001		John Jaha	
	John Vander Wal, 117 g, 2003		Jeromy Burnitz	
Home runs at County Stadium, all teams				187 (1999)
Home runs at Miller Park, all teams				232 (2003)
Total bases	367—Robin Yount, 156 g, 1982		4,730—Robin Yount	2,606 (1982)
Extra base hits	87—Robin Yount, 156 g, 1982		960—Robin Yount	537 (1980)
Sacrifice hits	19—Ron Theobald, 126 g, 1971		106—Jim Gantner	115 (1970)
Sacrifice flies	14—Dave Parker, 157 g, 1990		123—Robin Yount	72 (1992)
Bases on balls	99—Jeromy Burnitz, 161 g, 2000		966—Robin Yount	658 (1999)
				Fewest—432 (1984)
Strikeouts	188—Jose Hernandez, 152 g, 2002		1,350—Robin Yount	1,399 (2001)
	Fewest—42—Cecil Cooper, 153 g, 1980			Fewest—665 (1983)
	Charlie Moore, 151 g, 1983			
Hit by pitch	25—Fernando Vina, 159 g, 1998		58—Fernando Vina	72 (2001)
				Fewest—18 (1982)
Runs batted in	126—Cecil Cooper, 160 g, 1983		1,406—Robin Yount	845 (1996)
				Fewest—496 (1971)
Grounded into double plays	26—George Scott, 158 g, 1975		217—Robin Yount	158 (2003)
	Jeff Cirillo, 156 g, 1998			Fewest—94 (1978)
	Fewest—2—Jose Valentin, 151 g, 1998			
Left on base				1,276 (1999)
				Fewest—1,031 (1972)
Batting average	.353—Paul Molitor, 118 g, 1987		.303—Paul Molitor	.280 (1979)
				Lowest—.229 (1971)
Most .300 hitters				3 (1979, 1980, 1982, 1983, 1986)
Slugging average	.588—Geoff Jenkins, 135 g, 2000		.470—Cecil Cooper	.455 (1982)
				Lowest—.329 (1971)
On-base percentage	.438—Paul Molitor, 118 g, 1987		.367—Paul Molitor	.353 (1996, 1999)
				Lowest—.302 (1972)

BASERUNNING

Stolen bases	70—Scott Podsednik, 154 g, 2004		412—Paul Molitor	256 (1992)
Caught stealing	18—Pat Listach, 149 g, 1992		115—Paul Molitor	115 (1992)

PITCHING

Games	83—Ken Sanders, 1971		365—Dan Plesac	
Games started	38—Jim Slaton, 1973, 1976		268—Jim Slaton	
Complete games	23—Mike Caldwell, 1978		81—Mike Caldwell	62 (1978)
Wins	22—Mike Caldwell, 1978		117—Jim Slaton	
Percentage	.750—Pete Vuckovich (18-6), 1982		.560—Mike Caldwell	
Winning streak	10—Chris Bosio, 1992			
	Cal Eldred, 1992			
20-win seasons			1—Jim Colborn	
			Mike Caldwell	
			Teddy Higuera	
Losses	20—Clyde Wright, 1974		121—Jim Slaton	
Losing streak	10—Danny Darwin, 1985			
Saves	39—Danny Kolb, 2004		133—Dan Plesac	51 (1988)
Innings	314—Jim Colborn, 1973		2,025.1—Jim Slaton	1,467.1 (1982)
Hits	297—Jim Colborn, 1973		2,054—Jim Slaton	1,618 (1999)
Runs	135—Jaime Navarro, 1993		971—Jim Slaton	899 (1996)

	Individual		Club
	Season	**Career**	**Season**
Earned runs	127—Jaime Navarro, 1993	869—Jim Slaton	826 (1996)
Bases on balls	106—Pete Broberg, 1975	760—Jim Slaton	728 (2000)
Strikeouts	264—Ben Sheets, 2004	1,081—Teddy Higuera	1,098 (2004)
Strikeouts, game	18—Ben Sheets, May 16, 2004		
Hit batsmen	20—Jamey Wright, 2001	49—Jamey Wright	72 (2001)
Wild pitches	14—Jim Slaton, 1974	71—Jim Slaton	65 (1975)
	Chris Bosio, 1987		
Home runs	36—Wayne Franklin, 2003	192—Jim Slaton	219 (2003)
Sacrifice hits	15—Jim Slaton, 1976	76—Jim Slaton	93 (2002)
Sacrifice flies	17—Jaime Navarro, 1993	74—Jim Slaton	76 (1993)
Earned run average	2.37—Mike Caldwell, 293 inn, 1978	3.74—Mike Caldwell	3.38 (1971)
Shutouts	6—Mike Caldwell, 1978	19—Jim Slaton	23 (1971)
			Lost—20 (1972)
1-0 games won	1—many pitchers	5—Teddy Higuera	5 (1971)
			Lost—5 (2001)

TEAM FIELDING

Putouts	4,402 (1982)	**Assists**	1,976 (1978)
	Fewest—4,175 (1972)		Fewest—1,521 (1986)
Chances accepted	6,284 (1978)	**Errors**	180 (1975)
	Fewest—5,784 (1972)		Fewest—89 (1992)
Double plays	192 (1998)	**Passed balls**	34 (1995)
	Fewest—132 (2004)		Fewest—4 (1978)
Errorless games	90 (1992)	**Fielding average**	.986 (1992)
	Consecutive—10 (1970, 1979)		Lowest—.971 (1975)

MISCELLANEOUS

Most players, season 49 (2002)
Fewest players, season 31 (1979)
Games won 95 (1979, 1982)
  Month 21 (Jun 1978)
  Consecutive 13 (1987)
Winning percentage .500 (1979), 95-66
  Lowest .346 (2002), 56-106
Number of league championships 1
  Most recent 1982
Runs, game 22 vs Toronto, Aug 28, 1992
  Opponents' 20 by Boston, Sept 6, 1975
    by Chicago, May 15, 1996
Hits, game 31 vs Toronto, Aug 28, 1992

Home runs, game 7 vs Cleveland, Apr 29, 1980
Runs, shutout 18 vs Boston, Apr 16, 1990
  Opponents' 17 by Cincinnati, Aug 7, 1998
Longest 1-0 win 17 inn, vs Anaheim A.L., Jun 8, 2004

Most seasons, non-pitcher 20—Robin Yount
Most seasons, pitcher 12—Jim Slaton
Games lost 106 (2002)
  Month 23 (Aug 1977)
  Consecutive 14 (1994)
  Overall record 2,010-2,921 (35 seasons)
  Interleague play 50-59
Number of times worst record in league 2
  Most recent 2002
Runs, inning 13 vs California, July 8, 1990, 5th

Total bases, game 38 vs Toronto, Aug 28, 1992
  vs New York, Apr 26, 2001
  (40 vs Philadelphia, May 15, 2001, 10 inn)
Consecutive games with one or more home runs 19 (35 hrs), 1996
Longest shutout unknown

Longest 1-0 loss 17 inn, vs Baltimore, Sept 27, 1974

ATTENDANCE

Highest home attendance		**Largest crowds**	
County Stadium	2,397,131 (1983)	Day	56,354 vs Cincinnati, Sept 28, 2000
Miller Park	2,811,041 (2001)	Night	55,716 vs Boston, July 3, 1982
		Doubleheader	54,630 vs Detroit, July 6, 1979
Highest road attendance	2,331,670 (1998)	Home opener	55,887 vs New York, Apr 15, 1988

MONTREAL EXPOS
YEARLY FINISHES

(National League expansion franchise moved from Montreal to Washington after the 2004 season)

EAST DIVISION

Year	Position	W	L	Pct.	GB	Manager	Attendance
1969	6th	52	110	.321	48.0	Gene Mauch	1,212,608
1970	6th	73	89	.451	16.0	Gene Mauch	1,424,683
1971	5th	71	90	.441	25.5	Gene Mauch	1,290,963

Year	Position	W	L	Pct.	GB	Manager	Attendance
1972	5th	70	86	.449	26.5	Gene Mauch	1,142,145
1973	4th	79	83	.488	3.5	Gene Mauch	1,246,863
1974	4th	79	82	.491	8.5	Gene Mauch	1,019,134
1975	5th (tied)	75	87	.463	17.5	Gene Mauch	908,292
1976	6th	55	107	.340	46.0	Karl Kuehl, Charlie Fox	646,704
1977	5th	75	87	.463	26.0	Dick Williams	1,433,757
1978	4th	76	86	.469	14.0	Dick Williams	1,427,007
1979	2nd	95	65	.594	2.0	Dick Williams	2,102,173
1980	2nd	90	72	.556	1.0	Dick Williams	2,208,175
1981	3rd/1st (l,c)	60	48	.556	*	Dick Williams, Jim Fanning	1,534,564
1982	3rd	86	76	.531	6.0	Jim Fanning	2,318,292
1983	3rd	82	80	.506	8.0	Bill Virdon	2,320,651
1984	5th	78	83	.484	18.0	Bill Virdon, Jim Fanning	1,606,531
1985	3rd	84	77	.522	16.5	Buck Rodgers	1,502,494
1986	4th	78	83	.484	29.5	Buck Rodgers	1,128,981
1987	3rd	91	71	.562	4.0	Buck Rodgers	1,850,324
1988	3rd	81	81	.500	20.0	Buck Rodgers	1,478,659
1989	4th	81	81	.500	12.0	Buck Rodgers	1,783,533
1990	3rd	85	77	.525	10.0	Buck Rodgers	1,373,087
1991	6th	71	90	.441	26.5	Buck Rodgers, Tom Runnells	934,742
1992	2nd	87	75	.537	9.0	Tom Runnells, Felipe Alou	1,669,077
1993	2nd	94	68	.580	3.0	Felipe Alou	1,641,437
1994	1st (n)	74	40	.649	+6.0	Felipe Alou	1,276,250
1995	5th	66	78	.458	24.0	Felipe Alou	1,309,618
1996	2nd	88	74	.543	8.0	Felipe Alou	1,616,709
1997	4th	78	84	.481	23.0	Felipe Alou	1,497,609
1998	4th	65	97	.401	41.0	Felipe Alou	914,717
1999	4th	68	94	.420	35.0	Felipe Alou	773,277
2000	4th	67	95	.414	28.0	Felipe Alou	926,263
2001	5th	68	94	.420	20.0	Felipe Alou, Jeff Torborg	609,473
2002	2nd	83	79	.512	19.0	Frank Robinson	732,901
2003	4th	83	79	.512	18.0	Frank Robinson	1,023,680
2004	5th	67	95	.414	29.0	Frank Robinson	748,550

(l) won intra-divisional playoff; (c) lost League Championship Series; *first half 30-25, second half 30-23; (n) no World Series

INDIVIDUAL AND CLUB RECORDS

BATTING

	Individual		Club
	Season	**Career**	**Season**
Games	162—Rusty Staub, 1971 Ken Singleton, 1973 Warren Cromartie, 1980 Orlando Cabrera, 2001, 2003	1,767—Tim Wallach	163 (1983, 1988, 1993)
At-bats	659—Warren Cromartie, 158 g, 1979	6,529—Tim Wallach	5,675 (1977)
Runs	133—Tim Raines Sr., 156 g, 1983	947—Tim Raines Sr.	741 (1987, 1996) Fewest—531 (1976)
Hits	206—Vlad Guerrero, 161 g, 2002	1,694—Tim Wallach	1,482 (1983) Fewest—1,275 (1976)
Hitting streak	31 g—Vlad Guerrero, 1999		
Singles	157—Mark Grudzielanek, 153 g, 1996	1,163—Tim Raines Sr.	1,042 (1983)
Doubles	54—Mark Grudzielanek, 156 g, 1997	360—Tim Wallach	339 (1997)
Triples	13—Rodney Scott, 154 g, 1980 Tim Raines Sr., 150 g, 1985 Mitch Webster, 151 g, 1986	82—Tim Raines Sr.	61 (1980)

HOME RUNS

			178 (2000) Fewest—86 (1974)
Righthander	44—Vlad Guerrero, 154 g, 2000	234—Vlad Guerrero	
Lefthander	36—Henry Rodriguez, 145 g, 1996	99—Larry Walker	
Switch-hitter	24—Jose Vidro, 153 g, 2000	101—Jose Vidro	
Rookie	20—Brad Wilkerson, 153 g, 2002		
Home	25—Vlad Guerrero, 2000	128—Vlad Guerrero	88 (2000)
Road	22—Andre Dawson, 1983	130—Andre Dawson	91 (1997)
Month	13—Vlad Guerrero, Sept 2000		48 (Aug 1999)
Pinch	4—Hal Breeden, 1973	5—Jose Morales	9 (1973, 2002)
Grand slams	2—many players	7—Gary Carter	9 (1996)
Home runs at Jarry Park, all teams			168 (1970)
Home runs at Olympic Stadium, all teams			190 (2000)
Total bases	379—Vlad Guerrero, 154 g, 2000	2,728—Tim Wallach	2,389 (2000)

	Individual		Club
	Season	**Career**	**Season**
Extra base hits	84—Vlad Guerrero, 160 g, 1999	595—Tim Wallach	545 (1997)
Sacrifice hits	23—Larry Lintz, 113 g, 1974	101—Steve Rogers	115 (1973)
Sacrifice flies	18—Andre Dawson, 159 g, 1983	71—Andre Dawson	57 (1983)
Bases on balls	123—Ken Singleton, 162 g, 1973	793—Tim Raines Sr.	695 (1973)
			Fewest—396 (1978)
Strikeouts	169—Andres Galarraga, 155 g, 1990	1,009—Tim Wallach	1,104 (2002)
	Fewest—29—Dave Cash, 159 g, 1978		Fewest—733 (1983)
Hit by pitch	50—Ron Hunt, 152 g, 1971	114—Ron Hunt	78 (1971)
			Fewest—16 (1976)
Runs batted in	131—Vlad Guerrero, 160 g, 1999	905—Tim Wallach	705 (2000)
			Fewest—507 (1976)
Grounded into	27—John Bateman, 139 g, 1971	152—Tim Wallach	151 (2001)
double plays	Ken Singleton, 162 g, 1973		Fewest—95 (1993, 1997)
	Fewest—1—Ron Hunt, 152 g, 1971		
Left on base			1,232 (1973)
			Fewest—1,024 (2001)
Batting average	.345—Vlad Guerrero, 154 g, 2000	.323—Vlad Guerrero	.278 (1994)
			Lowest—.235 (1976)
Most .300 hitters			3 (1999)
Slugging average	.664—Vlad Guerrero, 154 g, 2000	.588—Vlad Guerrero	.435 (1994)
			Lowest—.340 (1976)
On-base percentage	.429—Tim Raines Sr., 139 g, 1987	.391—Tim Raines Sr.	.343 (1994)
			Lowest—.291 (1976)

BASERUNNING

	Season	Career	Season
Stolen bases	97—Ron LeFlore, 139 g, 1980	635—Tim Raines Sr.	237 (1980)
Caught stealing	23—Delino DeShields, 151 g, 1991	106—Tim Raines Sr.	100 (1991)

PITCHING

	Season	Career	Season
Games	92—Mike Marshall, 1973	425—Tim Burke	
Games started	40—Steve Rogers, 1977	393—Steve Rogers	
Complete games	20—Bill Stoneman, 1971	129—Steve Rogers	49 (1971)
Wins	20—Ross Grimsley, 1978	158—Steve Rogers	
Percentage	.783—Bryn Smith (18 5), 1985	.581—Dennis Martinez	
Winning streak	11—Dennis Martinez, 1989		
20-win seasons		1—Ross Grimsley	
Losses	22—Steve Rogers, 1974	152—Steve Rogers	
Losing streak	10—Steve Renko, 1972		
Saves	43—John Wetteland, 1993	152—Jeff Reardon	61 (1993)
Innings	302—Steve Rogers, 1977	2,837.2—Steve Rogers	1,482.2 (1988)
Hits	281—Carl Morton, 1970	2,619—Steve Rogers	1,575 (2000)
Runs	139—Steve Rogers, 1974	1,122—Steve Rogers	902 (2000)
Earned runs	126—Steve Rogers, 1974	1,001—Steve Rogers	812 (2000)
Bases on balls	146—Bill Stoneman, 1971	876—Steve Rogers	716 (1970)
Strikeouts	305—Pedro Martinez, 1997	1,621—Steve Rogers	1,206 (1996)
Strikeouts, game	18—Bill Gullickson, Sept 10, 1980		
Hit batsmen	14—Bill Stoneman, 1970	52—Dennis Martinez	79 (2004)
Wild pitches	19—Steve Renko, 1974	87—Steve Rogers	71 (2003)
Home runs	31—Javier Vazquez, 1998	155—Javier Vasquez	191 (2004)
Sacrifice hits	21—Steve Rogers, 1979	153—Steve Rogers	106 (1976)
Sacrifice flies	11—Woodie Fryman, 1976	70—Steve Rogers	58 (2000)
	Miguel Batista, 1999		
Earned run average	1.90—Pedro Martinez, 241.1 inn, 1997	3.06—Dennis Martinez	3.08 (1988)
Shutouts	5—Bill Stoneman, 1969	37—Steve Rogers	18 (1979)
	Steve Rogers, 1979, 1983		Lost—20 (1972)
	Dennis Martinez, 1991		
	Carlos Perez, 1997		
1-0 games won	2—Carl Morton, 1970	3—Woodie Fryman	4 (1972, 1991)
	Bill Stoneman, 1972	Carl Morton	Lost—5 (1982, 1986)
	Woodie Fryman, 1976	Scott Sanderson	
	Scott Sanderson, 1980	Bill Stoneman	
	Pascual Perez, 1988		
	Carlos Perez, 1997		

TEAM FIELDING

Putouts	4,448 (1988)	**Assists**	1,956 (1976)
	Fewest—4,204 (1972)		Fewest—1,618 (1999)
Chances accepted	6,393 (1975)	**Errors**	184 (1969)
	Fewest—5,915 (2001)		Fewest—99 (2004)
Double plays	193 (1970)	**Passed balls**	24 (1973)
	Fewest—113 (1992)		Fewest—3 (1978)
Errorless games	93 (2003)	**Fielding average**	.984 (2004)
	Consecutive—10 (1977, 2004)		Lowest—.971 (1969)

MISCELLANEOUS

Most players, season 49 (2000)

Fewest players, season 30 (1972)
Games won 95 (1979)
  Month 23 (Sept 1979)
  Consecutive 10 (1979, 1980, 1997)
Winning percentage .649 (1994), 74-40
  Lowest .321 (1969), 52-110
Number of league championships 0
  Most recent ----
Runs, game 21 vs Colorado, Apr 28, 1996
  Opponents' 20 by San Diego, May 19, 2001
Hits, game 28 vs Atlanta, Jul 30, 1978
Home runs, game 8 vs Atlanta, Jul 30, 1978
Runs, shutout 19 vs Atlanta, Jul 30, 1978
  Opponents' 18 by San Francisco, May 24, 2000
Longest 1-0 win 17 inn, vs Philadelphia, Sept 21, 1981

Most seasons, non-pitcher 13—Tim Wallach
  Tim Raines Sr.
Most seasons, pitcher 13—Steve Rogers
Games lost 110 (1969)
  Month 23 (Aug 1969, Sept 1976)
  Consecutive 20 (1969)
Overall record 2,755-2,943 (36 seasons)
  Interleague play 69-70
Number of times worst record in league 3 (inc. 1 tie)
  Most recent 2001
Runs, inning 13 vs San Francisco, May 7, 1997, 6th

Total bases, game 58 vs Atlanta, Jul 30, 1978
Consecutive games with one or more home runs 16 (29 hrs), 1999
Longest shutout 16 inn, 3-0 vs Chicago, Sept 22, 1975

Longest 1-0 loss 22 inn, vs Los Angeles, Aug 23, 1989

ATTENDANCE

Highest home attendance		**Largest crowds**	
Jarry Park	1,424,683 (1970)	**Day**	57,694 vs Philadelphia, Aug 15, 1982
Olympic Stadium	2,320,651 (1983)	**Night**	57,121 vs Philadelphia, Oct 3, 1980
		Doubleheader	59,282 vs St. Louis, Sept 16, 1979
Highest road attendance	2,620,064 (1993)	**Home opener**	57,592 vs Philadelphia, Apr 15, 1977

NEW YORK GIANTS
YEARLY FINISHES

(National League franchise established in 1883 moved from New York to San Francisco after the 1957 season)

Year	Position	W	L	Pct.	GB	Manager	Attendance
1883	6th	46	50	.479	16.0	John Clapp	75,000
1884	4th (tied)	62	50	.554	22.0	Jim Pierce, John Montgomery Ward	105,000
1885	2nd	85	27	.759	2.0	Jim Mutrie	185,000
1886	3rd	75	44	.630	12.5	Jim Mutrie	189,000
1887	4th	68	55	.553	10.5	Jim Mutrie	270,945
1888	1st	84	47	.641	+9.0	Jim Mutrie	305,455
1889	1st	83	43	.659	+1.0	Jim Mutrie	201,989
1890	6th	63	68	.481	24.0	Jim Mutrie	60,667
1891	3rd	71	61	.538	13.0	Jim Mutrie	210,568
1892	10th/6th	71	80		**	Pat Powers	130,566
1893	5th	68	64	.515	19.5	John Montgomery Ward	290,000
1894	2nd (t)	88	44	.667	3.0	John Montgomery Ward	387,000
1895	9th	6	65	.504	21.5	George Davis, Jack Doyle, Harvey Watkins	240,000
1896	7th	64	67	.489	27.0	Art Irwin, Bill Joyce	274,000
1897	3rd	83	48	.634	9.5	Bill Joyce	390,340
1898	7th	77	73	.513	25.5	Bill Joyce, Cap Anson, Bill Joyce	206,700
1899	10th	60	90	.400	42.0	John Day, Fred Hoey	121,384
1900	8th	60	78	.435	23.0	Buck Ewing, George Davis	175,000
1901	7th	52	85	.380	37.0	George Davis	297,650
1902	8th	48	88	.353	53.5	Horace Fogel, Heinie Smith, John McGraw	302,875
1903	2nd	84	55	.604	6.5	John McGraw	579,530
1904	1st (n)	106	47	.693	+13.0	John McGraw	609,826
1905	1st (S)	105	48	.686	+9.0	John McGraw	552,700
1906	2nd	96	56	.632	20.0	John McGraw	402,850
1907	4th	82	71	.536	25.5	John McGraw	538,350
1908	2nd (tied)	98	56	.636	1.0	John McGraw	910,000
1909	3rd	92	61	.601	18.5	John McGraw	783,700
1910	2nd	91	63	.591	13.0	John McGraw	511,785
1911	1st (s)	99	54	.647	+7.5	John McGraw	675,000
1912	1st (s)	103	48	.682	+10.0	John McGraw	638,000

Year	Position	W	L	Pct.	GB	Manager	Attendance
1913	1st (s)	101	51	.664	+12.5	John McGraw	630,000
1914	2nd	84	70	.545	10.5	John McGraw	364,313
1915	8th	69	83	.454	21.0	John McGraw	391,850
1916	4th	86	66	.566	7.0	John McGraw	552,056
1917	1st (s)	98	56	.636	+10.0	John McGraw	500,264
1918	2nd	71	53	.573	10.5	John McGraw	256,618
1919	2nd	87	53	.621	9.0	John McGraw	708,857
1920	2nd	86	68	.558	7.0	John McGraw	929,609
1921	1st (S)	94	59	.614	+4.0	John McGraw	773,477
1922	1st (S)	93	61	.604	+7.0	John McGraw	945,809
1923	1st (s)	95	58	.621	+4.5	John McGraw	820,780
1924	1st (s)	93	60	.608	+1.5	John McGraw	844,068
1925	2nd	86	66	.566	8.5	John McGraw	778,993
1926	5th	74	77	.490	13.5	John McGraw	700,362
1927	3rd	92	62	.597	2.0	John McGraw, Rogers Hornsby	858,190
1928	2nd	93	61	.604	2.0	John McGraw	916,191
1929	3rd	84	67	.556	13.5	John McGraw	868,806
1930	3rd	87	67	.565	5.0	John McGraw	868,714
1931	2nd	87	65	.572	13.0	John McGraw	812,163
1932	6th (tied)	72	82	.468	18.0	John McGraw, Bill Terry	484,868
1933	1st (S)	91	61	.599	+5.0	Bill Terry	604,471
1934	2nd	93	60	.608	2.0	Bill Terry	730,851
1935	3rd	91	62	.595	8.5	Bill Terry	748,748
1936	1st (s)	92	62	.597	+5.0	Bill Terry	837,952
1937	1st (s)	95	57	.625	+3.0	Bill Terry	926,887
1938	3rd	83	67	.553	5.0	Bill Terry	799,633
1939	5th	77	74	.510	18.5	Bill Terry	702,457
1940	6th	72	80	.474	27.5	Bill Terry	747,852
1941	5th	74	79	.484	25.5	Bill Terry	763,098
1942	3rd	85	67	.559	20.0	Mel Ott	779,621
1943	8th	55	98	.359	49.5	Mel Ott	466,095
1944	5th	67	87	.435	38.0	Mel Ott	674,083
1945	5th	78	74	.513	19.0	Mel Ott	1,016,468
1946	8th	61	93	.396	36.0	Mel Ott	1,219,873
1947	4th	81	73	.526	13.0	Mel Ott	1,600,793
1948	5th	78	76	.506	13.5	Mel Ott, Leo Durocher	1,459,269
1949	5th	73	81	.474	24.0	Leo Durocher	1,218,446
1950	3rd	86	68	.558	5.0	Leo Durocher	1,008,876
1951	1st (L,s)	98	59	.624	+1.0	Leo Durocher	1,059,539
1952	2nd	92	62	.597	4.5	Leo Durocher	984,940
1953	5th	70	84	.455	35.0	Leo Durocher	811,518
1954	1st (S)	97	57	.630	+5.0	Leo Durocher	1,155,067
1955	3rd	80	74	.519	18.5	Leo Durocher	824,112
1956	6th	67	87	.435	26.0	Bill Rigney	629,179
1957	6th	69	85	.448	26.0	Bill Rigney	653,923

**first half 31-43, second half 40-37; (t) lost Temple Cup; (S) won World Series; (s) lost World Series; (L) won league playoff

INDIVIDUAL AND CLUB RECORDS
BATTING

	Individual		Club
	Season	Career	Season
Games	157—Art Devlin, 1908	2,730—Mel Ott	158 (1904, 1909, 1917)
At-bats	681—Joe Moore, 155 g, 1935	9,456—Mel Ott	5,623 (1935)
Runs	147—Mike Tiernan, 122 g, 1889	1,859—Mel Ott	959 (1930)
	*139—Bill Terry, 154 g, 1930		Fewest—540 (1956)
Hits	254—Bill Terry, 154 g, 1930	2,876—Mel Ott	1,769 (1930)
			Fewest—1,217 (1906)
Hitting streak	33 g—George Davis, 1893		
	*24—Freddie Lindstrom, 1930		
	Don Mueller, 1955		
Singles	177—Bill Terry, 154 g, 1930	1,805—Mel Ott	1,279 (1930)
Doubles	43—Bill Terry, 153 g, 1931	488—Mel Ott	276 (1928)
Triples	27—George Davis, 133 g, 1893	162—Mike Tiernan	103 (1911)
	*25—Larry Doyle, 141 g, 1911	*117—Larry Doyle	

HOME RUNS

			179 (1951)
			Fewest—145 (1956)
Righthander	51—Willie Mays, 152 g, 1955	189—Bobby Thomson	
Lefthander	51—Johnny Mize, 154 g, 1947	511—Mel Ott	
Switch-hitter	12—Frankie Frisch, 151 g, 1923	54—Frankie Frisch	
Rookie	29—Bobby Thomson, 138 g, 1947		
Home	29—Johnny Mize, 1947	323—Mel Ott	131 (1947)

	Individual		Club
	Season	**Career**	**Season**
Road	29—Willie Mays, 1955	188—Mel Ott	90 (1947)
Month	13—Walker Cooper, Jun 1947		55 (Jul 1947)
	Johnny Mize, Aug 1947		
	Willie Mays, Jul 1955		
Pinch	4—Ernie Lombardi, 1946	9—Bobby Hofman	10 (1954)
	Bill Taylor, 1955		
Grand slams	3—George Kelly, 149 g, 1921	7—George Kelly	8 (1951)
	Sid Gordon, 142 g, 1948	Mel Ott	
	Wes Westrum, 124 g, 1951		
Home runs at Polo Grounds V, all teams			206 (1947)
Total bases	392—Bill Terry, 154 g, 1930	5,041—Mel Ott	2,628 (1930)
Extra base hits	87—Willie Mays, 151 g, 1954	1,071—Mel Ott	490 (1930)
Sacrifice hits	36—Art Devlin, 143 g, 1907	171—Travis Jackson	250 (1908)
Sacrifice flies	8—Don Mueller, 153 g, 1954	23—Willie Mays	52 (1954)
	Hank Thompson, 135 g, 1955		
	Ray Jablonski, 107 g, 1957		
Bases on balls	144—Eddie Stanky, 152 g, 1950	1,708—Mel Ott	671 (1951)
			Fewest—127 (1883)
			*252 (1902)
Strikeouts	93—Wes Westrum, 124 g, 1951	896—Mel Ott	672 (1952)
	Fewest—12—Frankie Frisch, 151 g, 1917		Fewest—376 (1928)
Hit by pitch	25—Eddie Burke, 135 g, 1893	132—Art Fletcher	91 (1903)
	*22—Charlie Bass, 121 g, 1903		Fewest—15 (1933)
Runs batted in	151—Mel Ott, 150 g, 1929	1,860—Mel Ott	880 (1930)
			Fewest—336 (1902)
Grounded into	26—Bill Jurges, 138 g, 1939	106—Bobby Thomson	153 (1939)
double plays	Sid Gordon, 131 g, 1943		Fewest—96 (1952)
	Fewest—3—Joe Moore, 152 g, 1936		
Left on base			1,214 (1935)
			Fewest—975 (1926)
Batting average	.401—Bill Terry, 154 g, 1930	.341—Bill Terry	.319 (1930)
			Lowest—.238 (1902)
Most .300 hitters			8 (1921, 1922, 1924, 1930, 1931)
Slugging average	.667—Willie Mays, 151 g, 1954	.593—Willie Mays	.473 (1930)
			Lowest—.290 (1902)
On-base percentage	.464—Roger Connor, 127 g, 1887	.414—Mel Ott	.384 (1887) *.369 (1930)
	*.460—Eddie Stanky, 152 g, 1950		Lowest—.281 (1883)
			*.283 (1902)

BASERUNNING

	Individual		Club
Stolen bases	111—Monte Ward, 129 g, 1887	428—Mike Tiernan	347 (1911)
	*62—George J. Burns, 154 g, 1914	*334—George J. Burns	
Caught stealing	35—George J. Burns, 150 g, 1913	123—George J. Burns	114 (1915)

PITCHING

	Individual		Club
Games	71—Hoyt Wilhelm, 1952	634—Christy Mathewson	
Games started	48—Joe McGinnity, 1903	550—Christy Mathewson	
Complete games	44—Joe McGinnity, 1903	433—Christy Mathewson	140 (1898) *127 (1904)
Wins	37—Christy Mathewson, 1908	372—Christy Mathewson	
Percentage	.833—Hoyt Wilhelm (15-3), 1952	.682—Tim Keefe	
		*.664—Christy Mathewson	
Winning streak	19—Rube Marquard, 1912		
Winning streak, two seasons	24—Carl Hubbell, 1936 (16), 1937 (8)		
20-win seasons		13—Christy Mathewson	
Losses	27—Dummy Taylor, 1901	188—Christy Mathewson	
Losing streak	12—Rube Marquard, 1914		

	Individual		Club
	Season	**Career**	**Season**
Innings	434—Joe McGinnity, 1903	4,771.2—Christy Mathewson	1,440.2 (1909)
Hits	415—Bill Carrick, 1900	4,203—Christy Mathewson	1,546 (1930)
Runs	224—Bill Carrick, 1900	1,860—Amos Rusie	814 (1930)
		*1,609—Christy Mathewson	
Earned runs	117—Freddie Fitzsimmons, 1932	1,188— Carl Hubbell	699 (1930)
Bases on balls	128—Jeff Tesreau, 1914	902—Hal Schumacher	660 (1946)
Strikeouts	267—Christy Mathewson, 1903	2,504—Christy Mathewson	771 (1911)
Strikeouts, game	16—Christy Mathewson, Oct 3, 1904		
Hit batsmen	36—Ed Doheny, 1889	93—Ed Doheny	100 (1899) *94 (1900)
	*22—Ed Doheny, 1990	*84—Joe McGinnity	
Wild pitches	30—Red Ames, 1905	222—Mickey Welch	101 (1884) *58 (1905)
		*113—Christy Mathewson	
Home runs	36—Larry Jensen, 1949	227—Carl Hubbell	155 (1955)
Sacrifice hits	45—Jesse Barnes, 1920	396—Christy Mathewson	185 (1921)
Sacrifice flies	9—Ruben Gomez, 1957	26—Ruben Gomez	47 (1957)
Earned run average	1.66—Carl Hubbell, 309 inn, 1933	2.12—Christy Mathewson	1,72 (1885) *2.14 (1908)
Shutouts	11—Christy Mathewson, 1908	79—Christy Mathewson	25 (1908)
			Lost—20 (1915)
1-0 games won	5—Carl Hubbell, 1933	14—Christy Mathewson	6 (1907, 1933)
			Lost—8 (1907)

TEAM FIELDING

Putouts	4,306 (1909)	**Assists**	2,240 (1920)
	Fewest—3,964 (1939)		Fewest—1,660 (1956)
Chances accepted	6,472 (1920)	**Errors**	307 (1909)
	Fewest—5,794 (1956)		Fewest—137 (1942, 1950)
Double plays	181 (1950)	**Passed balls**	26 (1906)
	Fewest—75 (1907)		Fewest—4 (1928)
Errorless games	91 (1989)	**Fielding average**	.977 (1940, 1942, 1950)
	Consecutive—8 (1950)		Lowest—.954 (1909)

MISCELLANEOUS

Most players, season 49 (1946)
Fewest players, season 21 (1905)
Games won 106 (1904)
  Month 29 (Sept 1916)
  Consecutive 20 (1916)
Winning percentage .759 (1885), 85-27
        *.693 (1904), 106-47
  Lowest .353 (1902), 48-88
Number of league championships 17
  Most recent 1954
Runs, game 29 vs Philadelphia, Jun 15, 1887
    *26 vs Brooklyn, Apr 30, 1944, 1st game
  Opponents' 28 by Hartford, May 13, 1876
      vs St. Louis, May 13, 1911, 1st
      *16 vs Brooklyn, Aug 2, 1948
Hits, game 31 vs Cincinnati, Jun 9, 1901
Home runs, game 7 vs Indianapolis, May 9, 1888
      vs Cincinnati, Jun 6, 1939
      vs Philadelphia, Aug 13, 1939, 1st game
      vs Cincinnati, Jun 24, 1950
      vs Pittsburgh, Jul 8, 1956, 1st game
Runs, shutout 24 vs Buffalo, May 27, 1885
    *16 vs Brooklyn, Jul 3, 1949
  Opponents' 19 by Chicago, Jun 7, 1906
Longest 1-0 win 18 inn vs St. Louis, Jul 2, 1933, 1st game

Most seasons, non-pitcher 22—Mel Ott
Most seasons, pitcher 17—Christy Mathewson
Games lost 98 (1943)
  Month 25 (Aug 1953)
  Consecutive 13 (1902, 1944)
Overall record 6,067-4,890 (75 seasons)

Number of times worst record in league 5
  Most recent 1946
Runs, inning 13 vs Philadelphia, Sept 8, 1883, 3rd
        vs Cleveland, Jul 19, 1890, 1st game, 2nd

Total bases, game 47 vs Philadelphia, Jul 11, 1931, 1st game
Consecutive games with one or more home runs 19 (33 hrs), 1947

Longest shutout 16 inn 3-0 vs Chicago, Sept 22, 1975

Longest 1-0 loss 15 inn vs Cincinnati, Jul 16, 1933, 1st game

ATTENDANCE

Highest home attendance	1,600,793 (1947)	**Largest crowds**	
		Day	54,922 vs Brooklyn, Apr 20, 1941
		Night	51,790 vs Brooklyn, May 27, 1947
		Doubleheader	60,747 vs Brooklyn, May 31, 1937
		Home opener	54,392 vs Brooklyn, Apr 14, 1936

*records made since 1900 that do not exceed pre-1900 records

NEW YORK METS
YEARLY FINISHES

(National League expansion franchise)

Year	Position	W	L	Pct.	GB	Manager	Attendance
1962	10th	40	120	.250	60.5	Casey Stengel	922,530
1963	10th	51	111	.315	48.0	Casey Stengel	1,080,108
1964	10th	53	109	.327	40.0	Casey Stengel	1,732,597
1965	10th	50	112	.309	47.0	Casey Stengel, Wes Westrum	1,768,389
1966	9th	66	95	.410	28.5	Wes Westrum	1,932,693
1967	10th	61	101	.377	40.5	Wes Westrum, Salty Parker	1,565,492
1968	9th	73	89	.451	24.0	Gil Hodges	1,781,657

EAST DIVISION

Year	Position	W	L	Pct.	GB	Manager	Attendance
1969	1st (C,S)	100	62	.617	+8.0	Gil Hodges	2,175,373
1970	3rd	83	79	.512	6.0	Gil Hodges	2,697,479
1971	3rd (tied)	83	79	.512	14.0	Gil Hodges	2,266,680
1972	3rd	83	73	.532	13.5	Yogi Berra	2,134,185
1973	1st (C,s)	82	79	.509	+1.5	Yogi Berra	1,912,390
1974	5th	71	91	.438	17.0	Yogi Berra	1,722,209
1975	3rd (tied)	82	80	.506	10.5	Yogi Berra, Roy McMillan	1,730,566
1976	3rd	86	76	.531	15.0	Joe Frazier	1,468,754
1977	6th	64	98	.395	37.0	Joe Frazier, Joe Torre	1,066,825
1978	6th	66	96	.407	24.0	Joe Torre	1,007,328
1979	6th	63	99	.389	35.0	Joe Torre	788,905
1980	5th	67	95	.414	24.0	Joe Torre	1,192,073
1981	5th/4th	41	62	.398	*	Joe Torre	704,244
1982	6th	65	97	.401	27.0	George Bamberger	1,323,036
1983	6th	68	94	.420	22.0	George Bamberger, Frank Howard	1,112,774
1984	2nd	90	72	.556	6.5	Dave Johnson	1,842,695
1985	2nd	98	64	.605	3.0	Dave Johnson	2,761,601
1986	1st (C,S)	108	54	.667	+21.5	Dave Johnson	2,767,601
1987	2nd	92	70	.568	3.0	Dave Johnson	3,034,129
1988	1st (c)	100	60	.625	+15.0	Dave Johnson	3,055,445
1989	2nd	87	75	.537	6.0	Dave Johnson	2,918,710
1990	2nd	91	71	.562	4.0	Dave Johnson, Bud Harrelson	2,732,745
1991	5th	77	84	.478	20.5	Bud Harrelson, Mike Cubbage	2,284,484
1992	5th	72	90	.444	24.0	Jeff Torborg	1,779,534
1993	7th	59	103	.364	38.0	Jeff Torborg, Dallas Green	1,873,183
1994	3rd	55	58	.487	18.5	Dallas Green	1,151,471
1995	2nd (tied)	69	75	.479	21.0	Dallas Green	1,273,183
1996	4th	71	91	.438	25.0	Dallas Green, Bobby Valentine	1,588,323
1997	3rd	88	74	.543	13.0	Bobby Valentine	1,766,174
1998	2nd	88	74	.543	18.0	Bobby Valentine	2,287,942
1999	2nd (W,D,c)	97	66	.595	6.5	Bobby Valentine	2,725,668
2000	2nd (D,C,s)	94	68	.580	1.0	Bobby Valentine	2,800,221
2001	3rd	82	80	.506	6.0	Bobby Valentine	2,658,279
2002	5th	75	86	.466	26.5	Bobby Valentine	2,804,838
2003	5th	66	95	.410	34.5	Art Howe	2,132,341
2004	4th	71	91	.438	29.0	Art Howe	2,318,321

(C) won League Championship Series; (S) won World Series; (s) lost World Series; *first half 17-34, second half 24-28; (c) lost League Championship Series; (W) won wild card playoff; (D) won Division Series

INDIVIDUAL AND CLUB RECORDS
BATTING

	Individual		Club
	Season	**Career**	**Season**
Games	162—Felix Millan, 1975 John Olerud, 1999	1,853—Ed Kranepool	164 (1965)
At-bats	682—Lance Johnson, 160 g, 1996	5,436—Ed Kranepool	5,618 (1996)
Runs	123—Edgardo Alfonso, 158 g, 1999	662—Darryl Strawberry	853 (1999) Fewest—473 (1968)
Hits	227—Lance Johnson, 160 g, 1996	1,418—Ed Kranepool	1,553 (1999) Fewest—1,168 (1963)
Hitting streak	24 g—Hubie Brooks, 1984 Mike Piazza, 1999		
Singles	166—Lance Johnson, 160 g, 1996	1,050—Ed Kranepool	1,087 (1980)
Doubles	44—Bernard Gilkey, 153 g, 1996	225—Ed Kranepool	297 (1999)
Triples	21—Lance Johnson, 160 g, 1996	21—Mookie Wilson	47 (1978, 1996)

	Individual		Club
HOME RUNS	**Season**	**Career**	**Season**
			198 (2000)
			Fewest—61 (1980)
Righthander	40—Mike Piazza, 141 g, 1999	201—Mike Piazza	
Lefthander	39—Darryl Strawberry, 154 g, 1987	252—Darryl Strawberry	
	Darryl Strawberry, 153 g, 1988		
Switch-hitter	41—Todd Hundley, 153 g, 1996	192—Howard Johnson	
Rookie	26—Darryl Strawberry, 122 g, 1983		
Home	24—Darryl Strawberry, 1990	123—Darryl Strawberry	93 (1962, 1987, 2000)
Road	23—Howard Johnson, 1987	129—Darryl Strawberry	105 (2000)
Month	13—Dave Kingman, July 1975		39 (Jun 1990, May 1999,
			Sept 2002)
	Gary Carter, Sep 1985		
Pinch	4—Mark Carreon, 1989	8—Mark Carreon	12 (1983)
	Danny Heep, 1983		
Grand slams	3—John Milner, 127 g, 1976	6—Mike Piazza	8 (1999, 2000)
	Robin Ventura, 161 g, 1999		
	Mike Piazza, 136 g, 2000		
Home runs at Polo Grounds, all teams			213 (1962)
Home runs at Shea Stadium, all teams			165 (2000)
			(inc. 3 at Tokyo)
Total bases	327—Lance Johnson, 160 g, 1996	2,047—Ed Kranepool	2,430 (1987)
Extra base hits	80—Howard Johnson, 153 g, 1989	469—Darryl Strawberry	513 (1987)
Sacrifice hits	24—Feliz Millan, 136 g, 1974	85—Dwight Gooden	108 (1973)
Sacrifice flies	15—Gary Carter, 132 g, 1986	58—Ed Kranepool	59 (1997)
	Howard Johnson, 156 g, 1991		
Bases on balls	125—John Olerud, 162 g, 1999	580—Darryl Strawberry	717 (1999)
			Fewest—353 (1964)
Strikeouts	156—Tommie Agee, 153 g, 1970	960—Darryl Strawberry	1,203 (1968)
	Dave Kingman, 149 g, 1982		Fewest—735 (1974)
	Fewest—22—Felix Millan, 153 g, 1973		
Hit by pitch	13—Ron Hunt, 143 g, 1963	41—Ron Hunt	65 (2001)
	John Olerud, 154 g, 1997		Fewest—20 (1984, 1985)
Runs batted in	124—Mike Piazza, 141 g, 1999	733—Darryl Strawberry	814 (1999)
			Fewest—434 (1968)
Grounded into	27—Mike Piazza, 141 g, 1999	138—Ed Kranepool	149 (1999)
double plays	Fewest—3—Wally Backman, 145 g, 1985		Fewest—87 (1989)
	Kaz Matsui, 114 g, 2004		
Left on base			1,267 (1999)
			Fewest—1,011 (1993)
Batting average	.354—John Olerud, 160 g, 1998	.307—Mike Piazza	.279 (1999)
			Lowest—.219 (963)
Most .300 hitters			5 (1999)
Slugging average	.614—Mike Piazza, 136 g, 2000	.573—Mike Piazza	.434 (1987, 1999)
			Lowest—.315 (1963, 1968)
On-base percentage	.447—John Olerud, 160 g, 1998	.387—Keith Hernandez	.363 (1999)
			Lowest—.277 (1965)

BASERUNNING

	Individual		Club
Stolen bases	66—Roger Cedeno, 155 g, 1999	281—Mookie Wilson	159 (1987)
Caught stealing	21—Lenny Randle, 136 g, 1977	90—Mookie Wilson	99 (1980)

PITCHING

	Individual		Club
Games	83—Mike Stanton, 2004	695—John Franco	
Games started	36—Jack Fisher, 1965	395—Tom Seaver	
	Tom Seaver, 1970, 1973, 1975		
Complete games	21—Tom Seaver, 1971	171—Tom Seaver	53 (1976)
Wins	25—Tom Seaver, 1969	198—Tom Seaver	
Percentage	.870—David Cone (20-3), 1988	.649—Dwight Gooden	

	Individual		Club
	Season	Career	Season
Winning streak	14—Dwight Gooden, 1985		
20-win seasons		4—Tom Seaver	
Losses	24—Roger Craig, 1962	137—Jerry Koosman	
	Jack Fisher, 1965		
Losing streak	18—Roger Craig, 1963		
Losing streak, two seasons	27—Anthony Young, 1992 (14), 1993 (13)		
Saves	43—Armando Benitez, 2001	276—John Franco	51 (1987)
Innings	291—Tom Seaver, 1970	3,045.1—Tom Seaver	1,488 (1985)
Hits	261—Roger Craig, 1962	2,431—Tom Seaver	1,577 (1962)
Runs	137—Jay Hook, 1962	994—Jerry Koosman	948 (1962)
Earned runs	117—Roger Craig, 1962	875—Jerry Koosman	801 (1962)
Bases on balls	116—Nolan Ryan, 1971	847—Tom Seaver	617 (1999)
Strikeouts	289—Tom Seaver, 1971	2,541—Tom Seaver	1,217 (1990)
Strikeouts, game	19—Tom Seaver, Apr 22, 1970		
	David Cone, Oct 6, 1991		
Hit batsmen	16—Pedro Astacio, 2002	63—Al Leiter	68 (1998)
Wild pitches	18—Jack Hamilton, 1966	81—Tom Seaver	76 (1966)
Home runs	35—Roger Craig, 1962	212—Tom Seaver	192 (1962)
Sacrifice hits	21—Mike Scott, 1982	130—Jerry Koosman	96 (1980)
Sacrifice flies	13—Ron Darling, 1989	75—Jerry Koosman	59 (1978)
Earned run average	1.53—Dwight Gooden, 276.2 inn, 1985	2.57—Tom Seaver	2.72 (1968)
Shutouts	8—Dwight Gooden, 1985	44—Tom Seaver	28 (1969)
			Lost—30 (1963)
1-0 games won	3—Bob Ojeda, 1988	8—Jerry Koosman	9 (1969)
			Lost—8 (1963)

TEAM FIELDING

Putouts	4,464 (1985)	Assists	1,995 (1966)
	Fewest—4,240 (2003)		Fewest—1,462 (1989)
Chances accepted	6,309 (1965)	Errors	210 (1962, 1963)
	Fewest—5,825 (1989)		Fewest—68 (1999)
Double plays	171 (1966, 1983)	Passed balls	32 (1964)
	Fewest—107 (1990)		Fewest—2 (1980)
Errorless games	104 (1999)	Fielding average	.989 (1999)
	Consecutive—12 (1999)		Lowest—.967 (1962, 1963)

MISCELLANEOUS

Most players, season 54 (1967)
Fewest players, season 32 (1988)
Games won 108 (1986)
  Month 23 (Sept 1969)
  Consecutive 11 (1969, 1972, 1986, 1990)
Winning percentage .667 (1986), 108-54
  Lowest .250 (1962), 40-120
Number of league championships 4
  Most recent 2000
Runs, game 23 vs Chicago, Aug 16, 1987
  Opponents' 26 by Philadelphia, Jun 11, 1985
Hits, game 23 vs Chicago, May 26, 1964
  vs Colorado, Apr 29, 2000
  (28 vs Atlanta, Jul 4, 1985, 19 inn)
Home runs, game 6 vs Montreal, April 4, 1988
  vs Cincinnati, Jun 15, 1999
Runs, shutout 14 vs Chicago, Jul 29, 1965, 1st game
  vs Cincinnati, Apr 19, 1998
  Opponents' 16 by Atlanta, Jul 2, 1999
Longest 1-0 win 15 inn, vs Los Angeles, Jul 4, 1969

Most seasons, non-pitcher 18—Ed Kranepool
Most seasons, pitcher 14—John Franco
Games lost 120 (1962)
  Month 26 (Aug 1962)
  Consecutive 17 (1962)
Overall record 3,228-3,598 (43 seasons)
  Interleague play 72-64
Number of times worst record in league 9
  Most recent 1993
Runs, inning 10 vs Cincinnati, Jun 12, 1979, 6th
  vs Atlanta, June 30, 2000, 8th
Total bases, game 38 vs Atlanta, Jul 4, 1985, 19 inn
  vs Houston, Aug 30, 1999

Consecutive games with one or more home runs 21 (29 hrs), 1996

Longest shutout 16 inn, 3-0 vs Chicago, Sept 22, 1975

Longest 1-0 loss 24 inn, vs Houston, Apr 15, 1968

ATTENDANCE

Highest home attendance	3,055,445 (1988)	**Largest crowds**	
Polo Grounds	1,080,108 (1963)	**Day**	56,738 vs Los Angeles, Jun 23, 1968
Shea Stadium	3,055,445 (1988)	**Night**	56,658 vs San Francisco, May 13, 1966
		Doubleheader	57,175 vs Los Angeles, June 13, 1965
Highest road attendance	2,660,426 (1993)	**Home opener**	53,734 vs Pittsburgh, Apr 1, 2002
			(Mets drew 55,000 to their "home
			opener" in Tokyo, Mar 29, 2000.)

PHILADELPHIA PHILLIES
YEARLY FINISHES

(National League franchise established in 1883)

Year	Position	W	L	Pct.	GB	Manager	Attendance
1883	8th	17	81	.173	46.0	Bob Ferguson, Blondie Purcell	55,992
1884	6th	39	73	.348	45.0	Harry Wright	100,475
1885	3rd	56	54	.509	30.0	Harry Wright	150,698
1886	4th	71	43	.623	14.0	Harry Wright	175,623
1887	2nd	75	48	.610	3.5	Harry Wright	253,671
1888	3rd	69	61	.531	14.5	Harry Wright	151,804
1889	4th	63	64	.496	20.5	Harry Wright	281,869
1890	3rd	78	54	.591	9.5	Harry Wright	148,366
1891	4th	68	69	.496	18.5	Harry Wright	217,282
1892	3rd/4th	87	66	.569	**	Harry Wright	193,731
1893	4th	72	57	.558	14.0	Harry Wright	293,019
1894	4th	71	57	.555	18.0	Art Irwin	352,773
1895	3rd	78	53	.595	9.5	Art Irwin	474,971
1896	8th	62	68	.477	28.5	Billy Nash	357,025
1897	10th	55	77	.417	38.0	George Stallings	288,816
1898	6th	78	71	.523	24.0	George Stallings, Bill Shettsline	265,414
1899	3rd	94	58	.618	9.0	Bill Shettsline	388,933
1900	3rd	75	63	.543	8.0	Bill Shettsline	301,913
1901	2nd	83	57	.593	7.5	Bill Shettsline	234,937
1902	7th	56	81	.409	46.0	Bill Shettsline	112,066
1903	7th	49	86	.363	39.5	Chief Zimmer	151,729
1904	8th	52	100	.342	53.5	Hugh Duffy	140,771
1905	4th	83	69	.546	21.5	Hugh Duffy	317,932
1906	4th	71	82	.464	45.5	Hugh Duffy	294,680
1907	3rd	83	64	.565	21.5	Bill Murray	341,216
1908	4th	83	71	.539	16.0	Bill Murray	420,660
1909	5th	74	79	.484	36.5	Bill Murray	303,177
1910	4th	78	75	.510	25.5	Red Dooin	296,597
1911	4th	79	73	.520	19.5	Red Dooin	416,000
1912	5th	73	79	.480	30.5	Red Dooin	250,000
1913	2nd	88	63	.583	12.5	Red Dooin	470,000
1914	6th	74	80	.481	20.5	Red Dooin	138,474
1915	1st (s)	90	62	.592	+7.0	Pat Moran	449,898
1916	2nd	91	62	.595	2.5	Pat Moran	515,365
1917	2nd	87	65	.572	10.0	Pat Moran	354,428
1918	6th	55	68	.447	26.0	Pat Moran	122,266
1919	8th	47	90	.343	47.5	Jack Coombs, Gavvy Cravath	240,424
1920	8th	62	91	.405	30.5	Gavvy Cravath	330,998
1921	8th	51	103	.331	43.5	Bill Donovan, Kaiser Wilhelm	273,961
1922	7th	57	96	.373	35.5	Kaiser Wilhelm	232,471
1923	8th	50	104	.325	45.5	Art Fletcher	228,168
1924	7th	55	96	.364	37.0	Art Fletcher	299,818
1925	6th (tied)	68	85	.444	27.0	Art Fletcher	304,905
1926	8th	58	93	.384	29.5	Art Fletcher	240,600
1927	8th	51	103	.331	43.0	Stuffy McInnis	305,420
1928	8th	43	109	.283	51.0	Burt Shotton	182,168
1929	5th	71	82	.464	27.5	Burt Shotton	281,200
1930	8th	52	102	.338	40.0	Burt Shotton	299,007
1931	6th	66	88	.429	35.0	Burt Shotton	284,849
1932	4th	78	76	.506	12.0	Burt Shotton	268,914
1933	7th	60	92	.395	31.0	Burt Shotton	156,421
1934	7th	56	93	.376	37.0	Jimmy Wilson	169,885
1935	7th	64	89	.418	35.5	Jimmy Wilson	205,470
1936	8th	54	100	.351	38.0	Jimmy Wilson	249,219
1937	7th	61	92	.399	34.5	Jimmy Wilson	212,790
1938	8th	45	105	.300	43.0	Jimmy Wilson, Hans Lobert	166,111
1939	8th	45	106	.298	50.5	Doc Prothro	277,973
1940	8th	50	103	.327	50.0	Doc Prothro	207,177
1941	8th	43	111	.279	57.0	Doc Prothro	231,401
1942	8th	42	109	.278	62.5	Hans Lobert	230,183
1943	7th	64	90	.416	41.0	Bucky Harris, Fred Fitzsimmons	466,975
1944	8th	61	92	.399	43.5	Fred Fitzsimmons	369,586
1945	8th	46	108	.299	52.0	Fred Fitzsimmons, Ben Chapman	285,057
1946	5th	69	85	.448	28.0	Ben Chapman	1,045,247
1947	7th (tied)	62	92	.403	32.0	Ben Chapman	907,332

Year	Position	W	L	Pct.	GB	Manager	Attendance
1948	6th	66	88	.429	25.5	Ben Chapman, Dusty Cooke, Eddie Sawyer	767,429
1949	3rd	81	73	.526	16.0	Eddie Sawyer	819,698
1950	1st (s)	91	63	.591	+2.0	Eddie Sawyer	1,217,035
1951	5th	73	81	.474	23.5	Eddie Sawyer	937,658
1952	4th	87	67	.565	9.5	Eddie Sawyer, Steve O'Neill	775,417
1953	3rd (tied)	83	71	.539	22.0	Steve O'Neill	853,644
1954	4th	75	79	.487	22.0	Steve O'Neill, Terry Moore	738,991
1955	4th	77	77	.500	21.5	Mayo Smith	922,886
1956	5th	71	83	.461	22.0	Mayo Smith	934,798
1957	5th	77	77	.500	19.0	Mayo Smith	1,146,230
1958	8th	69	85	.448	23.0	Mayo Smith, Eddie Sawyer	931,110
1959	8th	64	90	.416	23.0	Eddie Sawyer	802,815
1960	8th	59	95	.383	36.0	Eddie Sawyer, Andy Cohen, Gene Mauch	862,205
1961	8th	47	107	.305	46.0	Gene Mauch	590,039
1962	7th	81	80	.503	20.0	Gene Mauch	762,034
1963	4th	87	75	.537	12.0	Gene Mauch	907,141
1964	2nd (tied)	92	70	.568	1.0	Gene Mauch	1,425,891
1965	6th	85	76	.528	11.5	Gene Mauch	1,166,376
1966	4th	87	75	.537	8.0	Gene Mauch	1,108,201
1967	5th	82	80	.506	19.5	Gene Mauch	828,888
1968	7th (tied)	76	86	.469	21.0	Gene Mauch, George Myatt, Bob Skinner	664,546

EAST DIVISION

Year	Position	W	L	Pct.	GB	Manager	Attendance
1969	5th	63	99	.389	37.0	Bob Skinner, George Myatt	519,414
1970	5th	73	88	.453	15.5	Frank Lucchesi	708,247
1971	6th	67	95	.414	30.0	Frank Lucchesi	1,511,223
1972	6th	59	97	.378	37.5	Frank Lucchesi, Paul Owens	1,343,329
1973	6th	71	91	.438	11.5	Danny Ozark	1,475,934
1974	3rd	80	82	.494	8.0	Danny Ozark	1,808,648
1975	2nd	86	76	.531	6.5	Danny Ozark	1,909,233
1976	1st (c)	101	61	.623	+9.0	Danny Ozark	2,480,150
1977	1st (c)	101	61	.623	+5.0	Danny Ozark	2,700,070
1978	1st (c)	90	72	.556	+1.5	Danny Ozark	2,583,389
1979	4th	84	78	.519	14.0	Danny Ozark, Dallas Green	2,775,011
1980	1st (C,S)	91	71	.562	+1.0	Dallas Green	2,651,650
1981	1st/3rd (i)	59	48	.551	*	Dallas Green	1,638,752
1982	2nd	89	73	.549	3.0	Pat Corrales	2,376,394
1983	1st (C,s)	90	72	.556	+6.0	Pat Corrales, Paul Owens	2,128,339
1984	4th	81	81	.500	15.5	Paul Owens	2,062,693
1985	5th	75	87	.463	26.0	John Felske	1,830,350
1986	2nd	86	75	.534	21.5	John Felske	1,933,335
1987	4th (tied)	80	82	.494	15.0	John Felske, Lee Elia	2,100,110
1988	6th	65	96	.404	35.5	Lee Elia, John Vukovich	1,990,041
1989	6th	67	95	.414	26.0	Nick Leyva	1,861,985
1990	4th (tied)	77	85	.475	18.0	Nick Leyva	1,992,484
1991	3rd	78	84	.481	20.0	Nick Leyva, Jim Fregosi	2,050,012
1992	6th	70	92	.432	26.0	Jim Fregosi	1,927,448
1993	1st (C,s)	97	65	.599	+3.0	Jim Fregosi	3,137,674
1994	4th	54	61	.470	20.5	Jim Fregosi	2,290,971
1995	2nd (tied)	69	75	.479	21.0	Jim Fregosi	2,043,598
1996	5th	67	95	.414	29.0	Jim Fregosi	1,801,677
1997	5th	68	94	.420	33.0	Terry Francona	1,490,638
1998	3rd	75	87	.463	31.0	Terry Francona	1,715,702
1999	3rd	77	85	.475	26.0	Terry Francona	1,825,337
2000	5th	65	97	.401	30.0	Terry Francona	1,612,769
2001	2nd	86	76	.531	2.0	Larry Bowa	1,782,460
2002	3rd	80	81	.497	21.5	Larry Bowa	1,618,141
2003	3rd	86	76	.531	15.0	Larry Bowa	2,223,353
2004	2nd	86	76	.531	10.0	Larry Bowa, Gary Varsho	3,206,532

(s) lost World Series; (c) lost League Championship Series; (C) won League Championship Series; (S) won World Series; (i) lost intra-divisional playoff; *first half 34-21, second half 25-27

INDIVIDUAL AND CLUB RECORDS

BATTING

	Individual		Club
	Season	Career	Season
Games	163—Pete Rose, 1979	2,404—Mike Schmidt	163 (1979, 1983, 1989)
At-bats	701—Juan Samuel, 160 g, 1984	8,352—Mike Schmidt	5,685 (1993)
Runs	196—Billy Hamilton, 131 g, 1894	1,506—Mike Schmidt	944 (1930)
	*158—Chuck Klein, 156 g, 1930		Fewest—394 (1942)
Hits	254—Lefty O'Doul, 154 g, 1929	2,234—Mike Schmidt	1,783 (1930)
			Fewest—1,113 (1907)
Hitting streak	36 g—Billy Hamilton, 1894		
	*26 g—Chuck Klein, 1930 (twice)		
Singles	183—Billy Hamilton, 1894	1,811—Richie Ashburn	1,338 (1894) *1,268 (1930)
	*181—Lefty O'Doul, 154 g, 1929		
	Richie Ashburn, 154 g, 1951		

	Individual		**Club**
	Season	**Career**	**Season**
Doubles	59—Chuck Klein, 156 g, 1930	442—Ed Delahanty	345 (1930)
		*408—Mike Schmidt	
Triples	26—Sam Thompson, 102 g, 1894	158—Ed Delahanty	148 (1894) *82 (1905)
	*19—Juan Samuel, 160 g, 1984	*127—Sherry Magee	

HOME RUNS

			215 (2004)
			Fewest—11 (1908)
Righthander	48—Mike Schmidt, 150 g, 1980	548—Mike Schmidt	
Lefthander	47—Jim Thome, 159 g, 2003	243—Chuck Klein	
Switch-hitter	27—Dave Hollins, 156 g, 1992	67—Dave Hollins	
Rookie	30—Willie Montanez, 158 g, 1971		
Home	29—Chuck Klein, 1932	265—Mike Schmidt	101 (1977)
Road	29—Mike Schmidt, 1979	283—Mike Schmidt	89 (1987)
Month	15—Cy Williams, May 1923		42 (Jun 1977)
	Jim Thome, Jun 2004		
Pinch	5—Gene Freese, 1959	9—Cy Williams	11 (1958)
Grand slams	4—Vince DiMaggio, 127 g, 1945	7—Mike Schmidt	8 (1993)
Home runs at Baker Bowl, all teams			160 (1929)
Home runs at Connie Mack Stadium, all teams			154 (1955)
Home runs at Veterans Stadium, all teams			185 (1999)
Home runs at Citizens Bank Park, all teams			228 (2004)
Total bases	445—Chuck Klein, 156 g, 1930	4,404—Mike Schmidt	2,594 (1930)
Extra base hits	107—Chuck Klein, 156 g, 1930	1,015—Mike Schmidt	541 (2004)
Sacrifice hits	43—Kid Gleason, 155 g, 1905	216—Otto Knabe	174 (1905)
Sacrifice flies	13—Willie Montanez, 158 g, 1971	108—Mike Schmidt	74 (1977)
	Mike Schmidt, 150 g, 1980		
Bases on balls	129—Lenny Dykstra, 161 g, 1993	1,507—Mike Schmidt	665 (1993)
Strikeouts	182—Jim Thome, 159 g, 2003	1,883—Mike Schmidt	1,155 (2003)
	Fewest—8—Emil Verban, 155 g, 1947		Fewest—452 (1924)
Hit by pitch	19—Dave Hollins, 156 g, 1992	80—Ed Delahanty	58 (2004)
		*79—Mike Schmidt	Fewest—9 (1939)
Runs batted in	170—Chuck Klein, 154 g, 1930	1,595—Mike Schmidt	884 (1930)
			Fewest—298 (1883)
			*356 (1942)
Grounded into	25—Del Ennis, 153 g, 1950	171—Del Ennis	144 (1950)
double plays	Ted Sizemore, 152 g, 1977	Granny Hamner	Fewest—91 (1935, 1973)
	Fewest—1—Richie Ashburn, 117 g, 1948		
Left on base			1,281 (1993)
			Fewest—991 (1920)
Batting average	.408—Ed Delahanty, 145 g, 1899	.362—Billy Hamilton	.343 (1894) *.315 (1930)
	*.398—Lefty O'Doul, 154 g, 1929	*.326—Chuck Klein	Lowest—.225 (1888)
			*.232 (1942)
Most .300 hitters			10 (1925)
Slugging average	.687—Chuck Klein, 156 g, 1930	.553—Chuck Klein	.467 (1929)
			Lowest—.305 (1907)
On-base percentage	.523—Billy Hamilton, 1894	.468—Billy Hamilton	.414 (1894) *.377 (1929)
	*.465—Lefty O'Doul, 1929	*.460—Lefty O'Doul	Lowest—.269 (1883)
			*.289 (1942)

BASERUNNING

Stolen bases	115—Billy Hamilton, 133 g, 1891	508—Billy Hamilton	200 (1908)
	*72—Juan Samuel, 160 g, 1984	*387—Sherry Magee	
Caught stealing	19—Juan Samuel, 161 g, 1985	94—Larry Bowa	83 (1920)

PITCHING

Games	90—Kent Tekulve, 1987	529—Robin Roberts	
Games started	45—Grover Alexander, 1916	499—Steve Carlton	
Complete games	38—Grover Alexander, 1916	272—Robin Roberts	131 (1904)
Wins	33—Grover Alexander, 1916	241—Steve Carlton	

	Individual		**Club**
	Season	**Career**	**Season**
Percentage	.800—Robin Roberts (28-7), 1952 Tommy Greene (16-4), 1993	.676—Grover Alexander	
Winning streak	15—Steve Carlton, 1972		
20-win seasons		6—Grover Alexander Robin Roberts	
Losses	24—Chick Fraser, 1904	199—Robin Roberts	
Losing streak	12—Russ Miller, 1928 Hugh Mulcahy, 1940 Ken Reynolds, 1972		
Saves	45—Jose Mesa, 2002	111—Jose Mesa	48 (1987)
Innings	389—Grover Alexander, 1916	3,739.1—Robin Roberts	1,480 (1980)
Hits	348—Claude Passeau, 1937	3,661—Robin Roberts	1,993 (1930)
Runs	178—Ray Benge, 1930	1,501—Robin Roberts	1,199 (1930)
Earned runs	147—Robin Roberts, 1956	1,437—Robin Roberts	1,024 (1930)
Bases on balls	164—Earl Moore, 1911	1,252—Steve Carlton	682 (1974)
Strikeouts	319—Curt Schilling, 1997	3,031—Steve Carlton	1,209 (1997)
Strikeouts, game	17—Art Mahaffey, Apr 23, 1961, second game		
	(18—Chris Short, Oct 2, 1965, 2nd game, pitched first 15 inn of 18-inn game)		
Hit batsmen	19—Fred Mitchell, 1903 Jim Bunning, 1966	82—Bill Duggleby	77 (2003)
Wild pitches	22—Jack Hamilton, 1962	120—Steve Carlton	91 (1989)
Home runs	46—Robin Roberts, 1956	402—Robin Roberts	212 (1999)
Sacrifice hits	27—Tommy Hughes, 1942	221—Grover Alexander	221 (1928)
Sacrifice flies	15—Randy Lerch, 1979	82—Steve Carlton	63 (1960, 1997)
Earned run average	1.22—Grover Alexander, 376 inn, 1915	1.79—George McQuillan	2.18 (1915)
Shutouts	16—Grover Alexander, 1916	61—Grover Alexander	24 (1916) Lost—23 (1908, 1909)
1-0 games won	4—Grover Alexander, 1916	13—Grover Alexander	7 (1913) Lost—10 (1967)

TEAM FIELDING

Putouts	4,440 (1980) Fewest—3,887 (1907)	**Assists**	2,176 (1921) Fewest—1,437 (1957)
Chances accepted	6,440 (1913) Fewest—5,545 (1955)	**Errors**	403 (1904) Fewest—81 (2004)
Double plays	179 (1961, 1973) Fewest—111 (1991)	**Passed balls**	27 (1947, 1971) Fewest—3 (1952, 1956)
Errorless games	103 (2004) Consecutive—11 (1967, 1998)	**Fielding average**	.987 (2004) Lowest—.936 (1904)

MISCELLANEOUS

Most players, season 54 (1996)
Fewest players, season 23 (1915)
Games won 101 (1976, 1977)
  Month 22 (Sept 1916, Jul 1950, Jul 1952,
    May 1976, Aug 1977, Sep 1983)
  Consecutive 16 (1887, 1890, 1892)
    *13 (1977, 1991)
Winning percentage .623 (1886), 71-43
    *.623 (1976, 1977), 101-61
  Lowest .173 (1883), 17-81
    *.279 (1941) 43-111
Number of league championships 5
  Most recent 1993
Runs, game 29 vs Louisville, Aug 17, 1894
    *26 vs New York, Jun 11, 1985
  Opponents' 29 by Boston, Jun 20, 1883
    by New York, Jun 15, 1887
    *28 by St. Louis, Jul 6, 1929, 2nd game
Hits, game 36 vs Louisville, Aug 17, 1894
    *27 vs New York, Jun 11, 1985

Home runs, game 7 vs New York, Sept 8, 1998

Most seasons, non-pitcher 18—Mike Schmidt
Most seasons, pitcher 15—Steve Carlton
Games lost 111 (1941)
  Month 27 (Sept 1939)

  Consecutive 23 (1961)

Overall record 8,591-9,805 (122 seasons)
  Interleague play 66-69

Number of times worst record in league 27 (tied in 1947, 1997, 2000)
  Most recent 2000
Runs, inning 13 vs Cincinnati, Apr 13, 2003, 4th

Total bases, game 49 vs Louisville, Aug 17, 1894
    *47 vs. New York, Jun 11, 1985
    (48 vs Pittsburgh, Jul 23, 1930, 2nd game, 13 inn
    vs Chicago, May 17, 1979, 10 inn)
Consecutive games with one or more home runs 16 (24 hrs), 2002

Runs, shutout 24 vs Indianapolis, Jun 28, 1887
*18 vs Pittsburgh, Jul 11, 1910
vs Cincinnati, Aug 10, 1930, 1st game
vs Cincinnati, Jul 14, 1934, 1st game
Opponents' 28 by Providence, Aug 21, 1883
*16 by Chicago, May 4, 1929, 1st game

Longest shutout 16 inn 3-0 vs Chicago, Sept 22, 1975

Longest 1-0 win 16 inn vs Chicago, May 17, 1991

Longest 1-0 loss 17 inn vs Montreal, Sept 21, 1981

ATTENDANCE

Highest home attendance		**Largest crowds**	
Baker Bowl	449,898 (1915)	Day	61,068 vs Boston, Sept 1, 2003
Connie Mack Stadium	1,425,891 (1964)	Night	63,816 vs Cincinnati, Jul 3, 1984
Veterans Stadium	3,137,674 (1993)	Doubleheader	63,346 vs Pittsburgh, Aug 10, 1979
Citizens Bank Park	3,250,092 (2004)	Home opener	60,985 vs Chicago, Apr 9, 1993
Highest road attendance	2,666,219 (1993)		

*records made since 1900 that do not exceed pre-1900 records

PITTSBURGH PIRATES
YEARLY FINISHES

(American Association franchise moved to the National League after the 1886 season)

Year	Position	W	L	Pct.	GB	Manager	Attendance
1887	6th	55	69	.444	24.0	Horace Phillips	140,000
1888	6th	66	68	.493	19.5	Horace Phillips	112,000
1889	5th	61	71	.462	25.0	Horace Phillips, Fred Dunlap, Ned Hanlon	117,338
1890	8th	23	113	.169	66.5	Guy Hecker	16,064
1891	8th	55	80	.407	30.5	Ned Hanlon, Bill McGunnigle	128,000
1892	6th/4th	80	73	.523	**	Al Buckenberger, Tom Burns, Al Buckenberger	177,205
1893	2nd	81	48	.628	5.0	Al Buckenberger	184,000
1894	7th	65	65	.500	25.0	Al Buckenberger, Connie Mack	159,000
1895	7th	71	61	.538	17.0	Connie Mack	188,000
1896	6th	66	63	.512	24.0	Connie Mack	197,000
1897	8th	60	71	.458	32.5	Patsy Donovan	165,950
1898	8th	72	76	.486	29.5	Bill Watkins	150,900
1899	7th	76	73	.510	25.5	Bill Watkins, Patsy Donovan	251,834
1900	2nd (t)	79	60	.568	4.5	Fred Clarke	250,000
1901	1st	90	49	.647	+7.5	Fred Clarke	251,955
1902	1st	103	36	.741	+27.5	Fred Clarke	243,026
1903	1st (s)	91	49	.650	+6.5	Fred Clarke	326,855
1904	4th	87	66	.569	19.0	Fred Clarke	340,615
1905	2nd	96	57	.627	9.0	Fred Clarke	369,124
1906	3rd	93	60	.608	23.5	Fred Clarke	394,877
1907	2nd	91	63	.591	17.0	Fred Clarke	319,506
1908	2nd	98	56	.636	1.0	Fred Clarke	382,444
1909	1st (S)	110	42	.724	+6.5	Fred Clarke	534,950
1910	3rd	86	67	.562	17.5	Fred Clarke	436,586
1911	3rd	85	69	.552	14.5	Fred Clarke	432,000
1912	2nd	93	58	.616	10.0	Fred Clarke	384,000
1913	4th	78	71	.523	21.5	Fred Clarke	296,000
1914	7th	69	85	.448	25.5	Fred Clarke	139,620
1915	5th	73	81	.474	18.0	Fred Clarke	225,743
1916	6th	65	89	.422	29.0	Jimmy Callahan	289,132
1917	8th	51	103	.331	47.0	Jimmy Callahan, Honus Wagner, Hugo Bezdek	192,807
1918	4th	65	60	.520	17.0	Hugo Bezdek	213,610
1919	4th	71	68	.511	24.5	Hugo Bezdek	276,810
1920	4th	79	75	.513	14.0	George Gibson	429,037
1921	2nd	90	63	.588	4.0	George Gibson	701,567
1922	3rd (tied)	85	69	.552	8.0	George Gibson, Bill McKechnie	523,675
1923	3rd	87	67	.565	8.5	Bill McKechnie	611,082
1924	3rd	90	63	.588	3.0	Bill McKechnie	736,883
1925	1st (S)	95	58	.621	+8.5	Bill McKechnie	804,354
1926	3rd	84	69	.549	4.5	Bill McKechnie	798,542
1927	1st (s)	94	60	.610	+1.5	Donie Bush	869,720
1928	4th	85	67	.559	9.0	Donie Bush	495,070
1929	2nd	88	65	.575	10.5	Donie Bush, Jewel Ens	491,377
1930	5th	80	74	.519	12.0	Jewel Ens	357,795
1931	5th	75	79	.487	26.0	Jewel Ens	260,392
1932	2nd	86	68	.558	4.0	George Gibson	287,262
1933	2nd	87	67	.565	5.0	George Gibson	288,747
1934	5th	74	76	.493	19.5	George Gibson, Pie Traynor	322,622
1935	4th	86	67	.562	13.5	Pie Traynor	352,885
1936	4th	84	70	.545	8.0	Pie Traynor	372,524
1937	3rd	86	68	.558	10.0	Pie Traynor	459,679
1938	2nd	86	64	.573	2.0	Pie Traynor	641,033

Year	Position	W	L	Pct.	GB	Manager	Attendance
1939	6th	68	85	.444	28.5	Pie Traynor	376,734
1940	4th	78	76	.506	22.5	Frankie Frisch	507,934
1941	4th	81	73	.526	19.0	Frankie Frisch	482,241
1942	5th	66	81	.449	36.5	Frankie Frisch	448,897
1943	4th	80	74	.519	25.0	Frankie Frisch	604,278
1944	2nd	90	63	.588	14.5	Frankie Frisch	498,740
1945	4th	82	72	.532	16.0	Frankie Frisch	604,694
1946	7th	63	91	.409	34.0	Frankie Frisch, Spud Davis	749,962
1947	7th (tied)	62	92	.403	32.0	Billy Herman, Bill Burwell	1,283,531
1948	4th	83	71	.539	8.5	Billy Meyer	1,517,021
1949	6th	71	83	.461	26.0	Billy Meyer	1,499,435
1950	8th	57	96	.373	33.5	Billy Meyer	1,166,267
1951	7th	64	90	.416	32.5	Billy Meyer	980,590
1952	8th	42	112	.273	54.5	Billy Meyer	686,673
1953	8th	50	104	.325	55.0	Fred Haney	572,757
1954	8th	53	101	.344	44.0	Fred Haney	475,494
1955	8th	60	94	.390	38.5	Fred Haney	469,397
1956	7th	66	88	.429	27.0	Bobby Bragan	949,878
1957	7th (tied)	62	92	.403	33.0	Bobby Bragan, Danny Murtaugh	850,732
1958	2nd	84	70	.545	8.0	Danny Murtaugh	1,311,988
1959	4th	78	76	.506	9.0	Danny Murtaugh	1,359,917
1960	1st (S)	95	59	.617	+7.0	Danny Murtaugh	1,705,828
1961	6th	75	79	.487	18.0	Danny Murtaugh	1,199,128
1962	4th	93	68	.578	8.0	Danny Murtaugh	1,090,648
1963	8th	74	88	.457	25.0	Danny Murtaugh	783,648
1964	6th (tied)	80	82	.494	13.0	Danny Murtaugh	759,496
1965	3rd	90	72	.556	7.0	Harry Walker	909,279
1966	3rd	92	70	.568	3.0	Harry Walker	1,196,618
1967	6th	81	81	.500	20.5	Harry Walker, Danny Murtaugh	907,012
1968	6th	80	82	.494	17.0	Larry Shepard	693,485

EAST DIVISION

Year	Position	W	L	Pct.	GB	Manager	Attendance
1969	3rd	88	74	.543	12.0	Larry Shepard, Alex Grammas	769,369
1970	1st (c)	89	73	.549	+5.0	Danny Murtaugh	1,341,947
1971	1st (C,S)	97	65	.599	+7.0	Danny Murtaugh	1,501,132
1972	1st (c)	96	59	.619	+11.0	Bill Virdon	1,427,460
1973	3rd	80	82	.494	2.5	Bill Virdon, Danny Murtaugh	1,319,913
1974	1st (c)	88	74	.543	+1.5	Danny Murtaugh	1,110,552
1975	1st (c)	92	69	.571	+6.5	Danny Murtaugh	1,270,018
1976	2nd	92	70	.568	9.0	Danny Murtaugh	1,025,945
1977	2nd	96	66	.593	5.0	Chuck Tanner	1,237,349
1978	2nd	88	73	.547	1.5	Chuck Tanner	964,106
1979	1st (C,S)	98	64	.605	+2.0	Chuck Tanner	1,435,454
1980	3rd	83	79	.512	8.0	Chuck Tanner	1,646,757
1981	4th/6th	46	56	.451	*	Chuck Tanner	541,789
1982	4th	84	78	.519	8.0	Chuck Tanner	1,024,106
1983	2nd	84	78	.519	6.0	Chuck Tanner	1,225,916
1984	6th	75	87	.463	21.5	Chuck Tanner	773,500
1985	6th	57	104	.354	43.5	Chuck Tanner	735,900
1986	6th	64	98	.395	44.0	Jim Leyland	1,000,917
1987	4th (tied)	80	82	.494	15.0	Jim Leyland	1,161,193
1988	2nd	85	75	.531	15.0	Jim Leyland	1,866,713
1989	5th	74	88	.457	19.0	Jim Leyland	1,374,141
1990	1st (c)	95	67	.586	+4.0	Jim Leyland	2,049,908
1991	1st (c)	98	64	.605	+14.0	Jim Leyland	2,065,302
1992	1st (c)	96	66	.593	+9.0	Jim Leyland	1,829,395
1993	5th	75	87	.463	22.0	Jim Leyland	1,650,593

CENTRAL DIVISION

Year	Position	W	L	Pct.	GB	Manager	Attendance
1994	3rd (tied)	53	61	.465	13.0	Jim Leyland	1,222,520
1995	5th	58	86	.403	27.0	Jim Leyland	905,517
1996	5th	73	89	.451	15.0	Jim Leyland	1,332,150
1997	2nd	79	83	.488	5.0	Gene Lamont	1,657,022
1998	6th	69	93	.426	33.0	Gene Lamont	1,560,950
1999	3rd	78	83	.484	18.5	Gene Lamont	1,638,023
2000	5th	69	93	.426	26.0	Gene Lamont	1,748,908
2001	6th	62	100	.383	31.0	Lloyd McClendon	2,436,126
2002	4th	72	89	.447	24.5	Lloyd McClendon	1,784,993
2003	4th	75	87	.463	13.0	Lloyd McClendon	1,636,761
2004	5th	72	89	.447	32.5	Lloyd McClendon	1,583,031

**first half 37-39, second half 43-34; (t) lost Chronicle-Telegraph Cup; (s) lost World Series; (S) won World Series; (c) lost League Championship Series; (C) won League Championship Series; *first half 25-23, second half 21-33

INDIVIDUAL AND CLUB RECORDS

BATTING

	Individual		Club
	Season	**Career**	**Season**
Games	163—Bill Mazeroski, 1967 Bobby Bonilla, 1989	2,433—Roberto Clemente	164 (1989)
At-bats	698—Matty Alou, 162 g, 1969	9,454—Roberto Clemente	5,724 (1967)
Runs	148—Jake Stenzel, 131 g, 1894 *144—Kiki Cuyler, 153 g, 1925	1,521—Honus Wagner	912 (1925) Fewest—464 (1917)
Hits	237—Paul Waner, 155 g, 1927	3,000—Roberto Clemente	1,698 (1922) Fewest—1,197 (1914)
Hitting streak	27 g—Jimmy Williams, 1899 *26 g—Danny O'Connell, 1953		
Hitting streak, two seasons	30 g—Charlie Grimm, 1922 (5), 1923 (25)		
Singles	198—Lloyd Waner, 150 g, 1927	2,154—Roberto Clemente	1,297 (1922)
Doubles	62—Paul Waner, 154 g, 1932	558—Paul Waner	320 (2000)
Triples	36—Owen Wilson, 152 g, 1912	232—Honus Wagner	129 (1912)

HOME RUNS

			171 (1999) Fewest—9 (1917)
Righthander	54—Ralph Kiner, 152 g, 1949	301—Ralph Kiner	
Lefthander	48—Willie Stargell, 141 g, 1971	475—Willie Stargell	
Switch-hitter	32—Bobby Bonilla, 160 g, 1990	114—Bobby Bonilla	
Rookie	26—Jason Bay, 120 g, 2004		
Home	31—Ralph Kiner, 1948	221—Willie Stargell	95 (1947)
Road	27—Willie Stargell, 1971	254—Willie Stargell	110 (1966)
Month	16—Ralph Kiner, Sep 1949		43 (Aug 1947)
Pinch	7—Craig Wilson, 2001	9—Craig Wilson	10 (1996, 2001)
Grand slams	4—Ralph Kiner, 152 g, 1949	11—Ralph Kiner Willie Stargell	7 (1978, 1996)
Home runs at Forbes Field, all teams			182 (1947)
Home runs at Three Rivers Stadium, all teams			172 (2000)
Home runs at PNC Park, all teams			161 (2003)

Total bases	369—Kiki Cuyler, 153 g, 1925	4,492—Roberto Clemente	2,430 (1966)
Extra base hits	90—Willie Stargell, 148 g, 1973	953—Willie Stargell	519 (2000)
Sacrifice hits	39—Jay Bell, 159 g, 1990	257—Max Carey	190 (1906)
Sacrifice flies	15—Bobby Bonilla, 160 g, 1990	75—Willie Stargell	67 (1982)
Bases on balls	137—Ralph Kiner, 151 g, 1951 Fewest—194 (1888) *327 (1900)	937—Willie Stargell	620 (1991)
Strikeouts	169—Craig Wilson, 155 g, 2004 Fewest—13—Carson Bigbee, 150 g, 1922 Lloyd Waner, 152 g, 1928	1,936—Willie Stargell	1,197 (1999) Fewest—326 (1922)
Hit by pitch	31—Jason Kendall, 144 g, 1997 Jason Kendall, 149 g, 1998	177—Jason Kendall	95 (2004) Fewest—11 (1937)
Runs batted in	131—Paul Waner, 155 g, 1927	1,540—Willie Stargell	844 (1930) Fewest—392 (1888) *396 (1917)
Grounded into double plays	25—Al Todd, 133 g, 1938 Fewest—3—Rob Mackowiak, 155 g, 2004	275—Roberto Clemente	142 (1950) Fewest—95 (1978)
Left on base			1,241 (1936) Fewest—992 (1924)
Batting average	.385—Arky Vaughan, 137 g, 1935	.340—Paul Waner	.309 (1928) Lowest—.231 (1952)
Most .300 hitters			9 (1928)
Slugging average	.658—Ralph Kiner, 152 g, 1949	.591—Brian Giles	.449 (1930) Lowest—.298 (1917)
On-base percentage	.491—Arky Vaughan, 137 g, 1935	.415—Arky Vaughan	.379 (1894) *.369 (1925) Lowest—.264 (1888) *.295 (1914)

BASERUNNING

	Individual		Club
	Season	**Career**	**Season**
Stolen bases	96—Omar Moreno, 162 g, 1980	688—Max Carey	264 (1907)
Caught stealing	33—Omar Moreno, 162 g, 1980	137—Omar Moreno	120 (1977)

PITCHING

Games	94—Kent Tekulve, 1979	802—Roy Face	
Games started	42—Bob Friend, 1956	477—Bob Friend	
Complete games	32—Vic Willis, 1906	263—Wilbur Cooper	133 (1904)
Wins	28—Jack Chesbro, 1902	202—Wilbur Cooper	
Percentage	.947—Roy Face (18-1), 1959	.661—Sam Leever	
Winning streak	17—Roy Face, 1959		
Winning streak, two seasons	22—Roy Face, 1958 (5), 1959 (17)		
20-win seasons		4—Deacon Phillipe Vic Willis Wilbur Cooper	
Losses	21—Murry Dickson, 1952	218—Bob Friend	
Losing streak	13—Burleigh Grimes, 1917		
Saves	46—Mike Williams, 2002	158—Kent Tekulve	52 (1979)
Innings	331—Burleigh Grimes, 1928	3,480.1—Bob Friend	1,493 (1979)
Hits	366—Ray Kremer, 1930	3,610—Bob Friend	1,730 (1930)
Runs	181—Ray Kremer, 1930	1,575—Bob Friend	928 (1930)
Earned runs	154—Ray Kremer, 1930	1,372—Bob Friend	792 (1930)
Bases on balls	159—Marty O'Toole, 1912	869—Bob Friend	711 (2000)
Strikeouts	276—Bob Veale, 1965	1,682—Bob Friend	1,124 (1969)
Strikeouts, game	16—Bob Veale, Jun 1, 1965		
Hit batsmen	21—Jack Chesbro, 1902	93—Wilbur Cooper	80 (2001)
Wild pitches	18—Bob Veale, 1964	90—Bob Veale	67 (2000)
Home runs	32—Murry Dickson, 1951 Ramon Ortiz, 2002	273—Bob Friend	183 (1996)
Sacrifice hits	24—Cy Blanton, 1935	354—Wilbur Cooper	207 (1917)
Sacrifice flies	12—Vern Law, 1954 George O'Donnell, 1954 John Candelaria, 1974	73—Vernon Law	79 (1954)
Earned run average	1.87—Wilbur Cooper, 246 inn, 1916	2.38—Lefty Leifield	2.07 (1909)
Shutouts	8—Jack Chesbro, 1902 Lefty Leifield, 1906 Al Mamaux, 1915 Babe Adams, 1920	44—Babe Adams	26 (1906) Lost—27 (1916)
1-0 games won	3—Vic Willis, 1908 Claude Hendrix, 1912 Wilbur Cooper, 1917	8—Babe Adams Wilbur Cooper	10 (1908) Lost—10 (1914)

TEAM FIELDING

Putouts	4,480 (1979) Fewest—3,983 (1934)	**Assists**	2,089 (1905) Fewest—1,584 (1934)
Chances accepted	6,462 (1968) Fewest—5,567 (1934)	**Errors**	291 (1904) Fewest—101 (1992)
Double plays	215 (1966) Fewest—94 (1935)	**Passed balls**	32 (1953) Fewest—2 (2004)
Errorless games	87 (1992) Consecutive—10 (2001, 2004)	**Fielding average**	.984 (1992) Lowest—.955 (1904)

MISCELLANEOUS

Most players, season 49 (1987, 2001)
Fewest players, season 25 (1938)
Games won 110 (1909)
  Month 25 (Sept 1901, Sept 1908, Jul 1932)
  Consecutive 16 (1909)
Winning percentage .741 (1902), 103-36
  Lowest .169 (1890), 23-113
    *.273 (1952), 42-112

Most seasons, non-pitcher 21—Willie Stargell
Most seasons, pitcher 18—Babe Adams
Games lost 113 (1890) *112 (1952)
  Month 24 (Sept 1916)
  Consecutive 23 (1890) *12 (1939)
Overall record 9,186-8,805 (118 seasons)
  Interleague play 44-65

Number of league championships 9
  Most recent 1979
Runs, game 27 vs Boston, Jun 6, 1894
  *24 vs St. Louis, Jun 22, 1925
  Opponents' 28 by Boston, Aug 27, 1887
    *23 by Philadelphia, Jul 13, 1900, 8 inn
    by Brooklyn, Jul 10, 1943
Hits, game 27 vs Philadelphia, Aug 8, 1922, 1st game
    vs Boston, Jun 20, 1980
Home runs, game 7 vs Boston, Jun 8, 1894
    vs St. Louis, Aug 16, 1947
    vs St. Louis, Aug 20, 2003
Runs, shutout 22 vs Chicago, Sept 16, 1975
  Opponents' 18 by Philadelphia, Jul 11, 1910
Longest 1-0 win 18 inn vs San Diego, Jun 7, 1972, 2nd game

Number of times worst record in league 11 (tied in 1947, 1957)
  Most recent 1995
Runs, inning 12 vs St. Louis, Apr 22, 1892, 1st
    vs Boston, Jun 6, 1894, 3rd
    *11 vs St. Louis, Sept 7, 1942, 1st game, 6th inn
    vs Cincinnati, May 4, 1992, 6th

Total bases, game 47 vs Atlanta, Aug 1, 1970

Consecutive games with one or more home runs 13 (21 hrs), 1994

Longest shutout 16 inn 3-0 vs Chicago, Sept 22, 1975

Longest 1-0 loss 14 inn vs Cincinnati, Jun 18, 1943

ATTENDANCE

Highest home attendance		Largest crowds	
Exposition Park	394,877 (1906)	Day	55,351 vs Chicago, Oct 1, 2000
Forbes Field	1,705,828 (1960)	Night	54,274 vs Montreal, Apr 8, 1991
Three Rivers Stadium	2,065,302 (1991)	Doubleheader	49,886 vs New York, Jul 27, 1972
PNC Park	2,436,139 (2001)	Home opener	54,274 vs Montreal, Apr 8, 1991
Highest road attendance	2,507,346 (1993)		

*records made since 1900 that do not exceed pre-1900 records

ST. LOUIS CARDINALS
YEARLY FINISHES

(American Association franchise moved to the National League after the 1891 season)

Year	Position	W	L	Pct.	GB	Manager	Attendance
1892	9th/11th	56	94	.373	**	Chris von der Ahe	192,442
1893	10th	57	75	.432	30.5	Bill Watkins	195,000
1894	9th	56	76	.424	35.0	George Miller	155,000
1895	11th	39	92	.298	48.5	Al Buckenberger, Chris von der Ahe, Joe Quinn, Lew Phelan	170,000
1896	11th	40	90	.308	50.5	Harry Diddlebock, Arlie Latham, Chris von der Ahe, Roger Connor, Tommy Dowd	184,000
1897	12th	29	102	.221	63.5	Tommy Dowd, Hugh Nicol, Bill Hallman, Chris von der Ahe	136,400
1898	12th	39	111	.260	63.5	Tim Hurst	151,700
1899	5th	84	67	.556	18.5	Patsy Tebeau	373,909
1900	5th (tied)	65	75	.464	19.0	Patsy Tebeau, Louis Heilbroner	255,000
1901	4th	76	64	.543	14.5	Patsy Donovan	379,988
1902	6th	56	78	.418	44.5	Patsy Donovan	226,417
1903	8th	43	94	.314	46.5	Patsy Donovan	226,538
1904	5th	75	79	.487	31.5	Kid Nichols	386,750
1905	6th	58	96	.377	47.5	Kid Nichols, Jimmy Burke, Matt Robison	292,800
1906	7th	52	98	.347	63.0	John McCloskey	283,770
1907	8th	52	101	.340	55.5	John McCloskey	185,377
1908	8th	49	105	.318	50.0	John McCloskey	205,129
1909	7th	54	98	.355	56.0	Roger Bresnahan	299,982
1910	7th	63	90	.412	40.5	Roger Bresnahan	355,668
1911	5th	75	74	.503	22.0	Roger Bresnahan	447,768
1912	6th	63	90	.412	41.0	Roger Bresnahan	241,759
1913	8th	51	99	.340	49.0	Miller Huggins	203,531
1914	3rd	81	72	.529	13.0	Miller Huggins	256,099
1915	6th	72	81	.471	18.5	Miller Huggins	252,666
1916	7th (tied)	60	93	.392	33.5	Miller Huggins	224,308
1917	3rd	82	70	.539	15.0	Miller Huggins	288,491
1918	8th	51	78	.395	33.0	Jack Hendricks	110,599
1919	7th	54	83	.394	40.5	Branch Rickey	167,059
1920	5th (tied)	75	79	.487	18.0	Branch Rickey	326,836
1921	3rd	87	66	.569	7.0	Branch Rickey	384,773
1922	3rd (tied)	85	69	.552	8.0	Branch Rickey	536,998
1923	5th	79	74	.516	16.0	Branch Rickey	338,551
1924	6th	65	89	.422	28.5	Branch Rickey	272,885
1925	4th	77	76	.503	18.0	Branch Rickey, Rogers Hornsby	404,959
1926	1st (S)	89	65	.578	+2.0	Rogers Hornsby	668,428
1927	2nd	92	61	.601	1.5	Bob O'Farrell	749,340
1928	1st (s)	95	59	.617	+2.0	Bill McKechnie	761,574
1929	4th	78	74	.513	20.0	Bill McKechnie, Billy Southworth	399,887
1930	1st (s)	92	62	.597	+2.0	Gabby Street	508,501
1931	1st (S)	101	53	.656	+13.0	Gabby Street	608,535
1932	6th (tied)	72	82	.468	18.0	Gabby Street	279,219
1933	5th	82	71	.536	9.5	Gabby Street, Frankie Frisch	256,171

Year	Position	W	L	Pct.	GB	Manager	Attendance
1934	1st (S)	95	58	.621	+2.0	Frankie Frisch	325,056
1935	2nd	96	58	.623	4.0	Frankie Frisch	506,084
1936	2nd (tied)	87	67	.565	5.0	Frankie Frisch	448,078
1937	4th	81	73	.526	15.0	Frankie Frisch	430,811
1938	6th	71	80	.470	17.5	Frankie Frisch, Mike Gonzalez	291,418
1939	2nd	92	61	.601	4.5	Ray Blades	400,245
1940	3rd	84	69	.549	16.0	Ray Blades, Mike Gonzalez, Billy Southworth	324,078
1941	2nd	97	56	.634	2.5	Billy Southworth	633,645
1942	1st (S)	106	48	.688	+2.0	Billy Southworth	553,552
1943	1st (s)	105	49	.682	+18.0	Billy Southworth	517,135
1944	1st (S)	105	49	.682	+14.5	Billy Southworth	461,968
1945	2nd	95	59	.617	3.0	Billy Southworth	594,630
1946	1st (L,S)	98	58	.628	+2.0	Eddie Dyer	1,061,807
1947	2nd	89	65	.578	5.0	Eddie Dyer	1,247,913
1948	2nd	85	69	.552	6.5	Eddie Dyer	1,111,440
1949	2nd	96	58	.623	1.0	Eddie Dyer	1,430,676
1950	5th	78	75	.510	12.5	Eddie Dyer	1,093,411
1951	3rd	81	73	.526	15.5	Marty Marion	1,013,429
1952	3rd	88	66	.571	8.5	Eddie Stanky	913,113
1953	3rd (tied)	83	71	.539	22.0	Eddie Stanky	880,242
1954	6th	72	82	.468	25.0	Eddie Stanky	1,039,698
1955	7th	68	86	.442	30.5	Eddie Stanky, Harry Walker	849,130
1956	4th	76	78	.494	17.0	Fred Hutchinson	1,029,773
1957	2nd	87	67	.565	8.0	Fred Hutchinson	1,183,575
1958	5th (tied)	72	82	.468	20.0	Fred Hutchinson, Stan Hack	1,063,730
1959	7th	71	83	.461	16.0	Solly Hemus	929,953
1960	3rd	86	68	.558	9.0	Solly Hemus	1,096,632
1961	5th	80	74	.519	13.0	Solly Hemus, Johnny Keane	855,305
1962	6th	84	78	.519	17.5	Johnny Keane	953,895
1963	2nd	93	69	.574	6.0	Johnny Keane	1,170,546
1964	1st (S)	93	69	.574	+1.0	Johnny Keane	1,143,294
1965	7th	80	81	.497	16.5	Red Schoendienst	1,241,201
1966	6th	83	79	.512	12.0	Red Schoendienst	1,712,980
1967	1st (S)	101	60	.627	+10.5	Red Schoendienst	2,090,145
1968	1st (s)	97	65	.599	+9.0	Red Schoendienst	2,011,167

EAST DIVISION

Year	Position	W	L	Pct.	GB	Manager	Attendance
1969	4th	87	75	.537	13.0	Red Schoendienst	1,682,783
1970	4th	76	86	.469	13.0	Red Schoendienst	1,629,736
1971	2nd	90	72	.556	7.0	Red Schoendienst	1,604,671
1972	4th	75	81	.481	21.5	Red Schoendienst	1,196,894
1973	2nd	81	81	.500	1.5	Red Schoendienst	1,574,046
1974	2nd	86	75	.534	1.5	Red Schoendienst	1,838,413
1975	3rd (tied)	82	80	.506	10.5	Red Schoendienst	1,695,270
1976	5th	72	90	.444	29.0	Red Schoendienst	1,207,079
1977	3rd	83	79	.512	18.0	Vern Rapp	1,659,287
1978	5th	69	93	.426	21.0	Vern Rapp, Jack Krol, Ken Boyer	1,278,215
1979	3rd	86	76	.531	12.0	Ken Boyer	1,627,256
1980	4th	74	88	.457	17.0	Ken Boyer, Jack Krol, Whitey Herzog, Red Schoendienst	1,385,147
1981	2nd/2nd	59	43	.578	*	Whitey Herzog	1,010,247
1982	1st (L,S)	92	70	.568	+3.0	Whitey Herzog	2,111,906
1983	4th	79	83	.488	11.0	Whitey Herzog	2,317,914
1984	3rd	84	78	.519	12.5	Whitey Herzog	2,037,448
1985	1st (L,s)	101	61	.623	+3.0	Whitey Herzog	2,637,563
1986	3rd	79	82	.491	28.5	Whitey Herzog	2,471,974
1987	1st (L,s)	95	67	.586	+3.0	Whitey Herzog	3,072,122
1988	5th	76	86	.469	25.0	Whitey Herzog	2,892,799
1989	3rd	86	76	.531	7.0	Whitey Herzog	3,080,980
1990	6th	70	92	.432	25.0	Whitey Herzog, Red Schoendienst, Joe Torre	2,573,225
1991	2nd	84	78	.519	14.0	Joe Torre	2,448,699
1992	3rd	83	79	.512	13.0	Joe Torre	2,418,483
1993	3rd	87	75	.537	10.0	Joe Torre	2,844,328

CENTRAL DIVISION

Year	Position	W	L	Pct.	GB	Manager	Attendance
1994	3rd (tied)	53	61	.465	13.0	Joe Torre	1,866,544
1995	4th	62	81	.434	22.5	Joe Torre, Mike Jorgensen	1,756,727
1996	1st (D,c)	88	74	.543	+6.0	Tony La Russa	2,654,718
1997	4th	73	89	.451	11.0	Tony La Russa	2,634,014
1998	3rd	83	79	.512	19.0	Tony La Russa	3,194,092
1999	4th	75	86	.466	21.5	Tony La Russa	3,225,334
2000	1st (D,c)	95	67	.586	+10.0	Tony La Russa	3,336,493
2001	1st (tied) (d)	93	69	.574	0.0	Tony La Russa	3,113,091
2002	1st (D,c)	97	65	.599	+13.0	Tony La Russa	3,011,756
2003	3rd	85	77	.525	3.0	Tony La Russa	2,910,371
2004	1st (D,C,s)	105	57	.648	+13.0	Tony La Russa	3,048,427

**first half 31-42, second half 25-52; (S) won World Series; (s) lost World Sereies; (L) won league playoff; *first half 30-20, second half 29-23; (L) won League Championship Series; (D) won Division Series; (c) lost League Championship Series; (d) lost Division Series

INDIVIDUAL AND CLUB RECORDS
BATTING

	Individual		Club
	Season	**Career**	**Season**
Games	163—Jose Oquendo, 1989	3,026—Stan Musial	164 (1989)
At-bats	689—Lou Brock, 159 g, 1967	10,972—Stan Musial	5,734 (1979)
Runs	141—Rogers Hornsby, 154 g, 1922	1,949—Stan Musial	1,004 (1930)
			Fewest—372 (1908)
Hits	250—Rogers Hornsby, 154 g, 1922	3,630—Stan Musial	1,732 (1930)
			Fewest—1,105 (1908)
Hitting streak	33 g—Rogers Hornsby, 1922		
Singles	194—Jesse Burkett, 141 g, 1901	2,253—Stan Musial	1,223 (1920)
Doubles	64—Joe Medwick, 155 g, 1936	725—Stan Musial	373 (1939)
Triples	33—Perry Werden, 124 g, 1893	177—Stan Musial	96 (1920)
	*25—Tommy Long, 140 g, 1915		

HOME RUNS

			235 (2000)
			Fewest—10 (1906)
Righthander	70—Mark McGwire,155 g, 1998	255—Ken Boyer	
Lefthander	43—Johnny Mize, 155 g, 1940	475—Stan Musial	
Switch-hitter	35—Rip Collins, 154 g, 1934	172—Ted Simmons	
Rookie	37—Albert Pujols, 161 g, 2001		
Home	38—Mark McGwire, 1998	252—Stan Musial	124 (2000)
Road	32—Mark McGwire, 1998	223—Stan Musial	111 (2000, 2003)
Month	16—Mark McGwire, May 1998		55 (Apr 2000)
	Mark McGwire, Jul 1999		
Pinch	4—George Crowe, 1959	8—George Crowe	10 (1998)
	George Crowe, 1960		
	Carl Sawatski, 1961		
Grand slams	3—Jim Bottomley, 153 g, 1925	9—Stan Musial	12 (2000)
	Keith Hernandez, 161 g, 1977		
	Fernando Tatis, 149 g, 1999		
Home runs at Sportsman's Park, all teams			176 (1955)
Home runs at Busch Stadium, all teams			229 (2000)

Total bases	450—Rogers Hornsby, 154 g, 1922	6,134—Stan Musial	2,595 (1930)
Extra base hits	103—Stan Musial, 155 g, 1948	1,377—Stan Musial	570 (2003)
Sacrifice hits	36—Harry Walker, 148 g, 1943	154—Jim Bottomley	172 (1943)
Sacrifice flies	14—George Hendrick, 136 g, 1982	67—Ted Simmons	70 (2004)
Bases on balls	162—Mark McGwire, 155 g, 1998	1,599—Stan Musial	676 (1998)
			Fewest—273 (1902)
Strikeouts	167—Jim Edmonds, 152 g, 2000	1,469—Lou Brock	1,253 (2000)
	Fewest—10—Frankie Frisch, 153 g, 1927		Fewest—414 (1925)
Hit by pitch	31—Steve Evans, 151 g, 1910	87—Steve Evans	84 (2000)
			Fewest—15 (1925)
Runs batted in	154—Joe Medwick, 156 g, 1937	1,951—Stan Musial	942 (1930)
			Fewest—301 (1908)

Grounded into	29—Ted Simmons, 161 g, 1973	243—Stan Musial	166 (1958)
double plays	Fewest—2—Lou Brock, 155 g, 1965		Fewest—75 (1945)
	Lou Brock, 157 g, 1969		

Left on base			1,251 (1939)
			Fewest—968 (1924)
Batting average	.424—Rogers Hornsby, 143 g, 1924	.359—Rogers Hornsby	.314 (1930)
			Lowest—.223 (1908)
Most .300 hitters			11 (1930)
Slugging average	.756—Rogers Hornsby, 138 g, 1925	.683—Mark McGwire	.471 (1930)
			Lowest—.288 (1908)
On-base percentage	.507—Rogers Hornsby, 143 g, 1924	.427—Mark McGwire	.372 (1930)
			Lowest—.271 (1908)

BASERUNNING

Stolen bases	118—Lou Brock, 153 g, 1974	888—Lou Brock	314 (1985)
Caught stealing	36—Miller Huggins, 148 g, 1914	285—Lou Brock	118 (1992)

PITCHING

	Individual		Club
	Season	**Career**	**Season**
Games	89—Steve Kline, 2001	554—Jesse Haines	
Games started	41—Bob Harmon, 1911	482—Bob Gibson	
Complete games	39—Jack W. Taylor, 1904	255—Bob Gibson	146 (1904)
Wins	30—Dizzy Dean, 1934	251—Bob Gibson	
Percentage	.811—Dizzy Dean (30-7), 1934	.705—John Tudor	
Winning streak	15—Bob Gibson, 1968		
20-win seasons		5—Bob Gibson	
Losses	25—Stoney McGlynn, 1907	174—Bob Gibson	
	Bugs Raymond, 1908		
Losing streak	12—Bill Hart, 1897		
	*9—Bill McGee, 1938		
	Tom Poholsky, 1951		
	Bob Forsch, 1978		
	Danny Jackson, 1995		
Saves	47—Lee Smith, 1991	160—Lee Smith	57 (2004)
	Jason Isringhausen, 2004		
Innings	352—Jack Taylor, 1904	3,884.1—Bob Gibson	1,486 (1979)
	Stoney McGlynn, 1907		
Hits	353—Jack Powell, 1901	3,455—Jesse Haines	1,553 (1993)
Runs	194—Jack Powell, 1900	1,555—Jesse Haines	838 (1999)
Earned runs	129—Bill Sherdel, 1929	1,297—Jesse Haines	778 (1897) *761 (1999)
Bases on balls	181—Bob Harmon, 1911	1,336—Bob Gibson	667 (1999)
Strikeouts	274—Bob Gibson, 1970	3,117—Bob Gibson	1,130 (1997)
Strikeouts, game	19—Steve Carlton, Sept 15, 1969		
Hit batsmen	17—Gerry Staley, 1953	102—Bob Gibson	86 (1898) *72 (2001)
Wild pitches	15—Fred Beebe, 1907, 1909	108—Bob Gibson	66 (1970)
	Dave LaPoint, 1984		
Home runs	39—Murry Dickson, 1948	257—Bob Gibson	210 (2003)
Sacrifice hits	21—Bill Hallahan, 1933	337—Jesse Haines	221 (1914)
Sacrifice flies	13—Bob Forsch, 1979	95—Bob Gibson	64 (1990)
Earned run average	1.12—Bob Gibson, 305 inn, 1968	2,67—Slim Sallee	2.49 (1968)
Shutouts	13—Bob Gibson, 1968	56—Bob Gibson	30 (1968)
			Lost—33 (1908)
1-0 games won	4—Bob Gibson, 1968	9—Bob Gibson	8 (1907, 1968)
			Lost—8 (1918)

TEAM FIELDING

Putouts	4,460 (1979)	**Assists**	2,293 (1917)
	Fewest—3,952 (1906)		Fewest—1,524 (2000)
Chances accepted	6,459 (1917)	**Errors**	348 (1908)
	Fewest—5,742 (1960)		Fewest—77 (2003)
Double plays	192 (1974)	**Passed balls**	38 (1906)
	Fewest—114 (1990)		Fewest—4 (1925)
Errorless games	105 (2003)	**Fielding average**	.987 (2003)
	Consecutive—16 (1992)		Lowest—.946 (1908)

MISCELLANEOUS

Most players, season 51 (1997)
Fewest players, season 25 (1904)
Games won 106 (1942)
  Month 26 (Jul 1944)
  Consecutive 14 (1935)
Winning percentage .688 (1942), 106-48
  Lowest .221 (1897), 29-102
  *.314 (1903), 43-94
Number of league championships 16
  Most recent 2004
Runs, game 28 vs Philadelphia, Jul 6, 1929, 2nd game
  Opponents' 28 by Boston, Sept 3, 1896, 1st game
  *24 by Pittsburgh, Jun 22, 1925
Hits, game 30 vs New York, Jun 1, 1895

Most seasons, non-pitcher 22—Stan Musial
Most seasons, pitcher 18—Jesse Haines
Games lost 111 (1898) *105 (1908)
  Month 27 (Sept 1908)
  Consecutive 18 (1897) *15 (1909)
Overall record 8,801-8,539 (113 seasons)
  Interleague play 63-52

Number of times worst record in league 8 (tied in 1916)
  Most recent 1918
  Runs, inning 12 vs Philadelphia, Sept 16, 1926, 1st game, 3rd

Total bases, game 49 vs Brooklyn, May 7, 1940
  *28 vs Philadelphia, Jul 6, 1929, 2nd game

Home runs, game 7 vs Brooklyn, May 7, 1940
                vs Chicago, Jul 12, 1996
Runs, shutout 18 vs Cincinnati, Jun 10, 1944
  Opponents' 19 by Pittsburgh, Aug 3, 1961
Longest 1-0 win 14 inn vs Boston, Jun 15, 1939

Consecutive games with one or more home runs 17 (34 hrs), 1998

Longest shutout 16 inn 3-0 vs Chicago, Sept 22, 1975

Longest 1-0 loss 18 inn vs New York, Jul 2, 1933, 1st game

ATTENDANCE

Highest home attendance		**Largest crowds**	
Robison Field	447,768 (1911)	Day	52,876 vs Cincinnati, Sept 28, 1996
Sportsman's Park	1,247,913 (1947)	Night	53,415 vs Chicago, Jul 30, 1994
Busch Stadium	3,336,493 (2000)	Doubleheader	52,657 vs Atlanta, Jul 22, 1994
		Home opener	52,841 vs Montreal, Apr 8, 1996
Highest road attendance	2,820,564 (1999)		

*records made since 1900 that do not exceed pre-1900 records

SAN DIEGO PADRES
YEARLY FINISHES

(National League expansion franchise)

WEST DIVISION

Year	Position	W	L	Pct.	GB	Manager	Attendance
1969	6th	52	110	.321	41.0	Preston Gomez	512,970
1970	6th	63	99	.389	39.0	Preston Gomez	643,679
1971	6th	61	100	.379	28.5	Preston Gomez	557,513
1972	6th	58	95	.379	36.5	Preston Gomez, Don Zimmer	644,273
1973	6th	60	102	.370	39.0	Don Zimmer	611,826
1974	6th	60	102	.370	42.0	John McNamara	1,075,399
1975	4th	71	91	.438	37.0	John McNamara	1,281,747
1976	5th	73	89	.451	29.0	John McNamara	1,458,478
1977	5th	69	93	.426	29.0	John McNamara, Bob Skinner, Alvin Dark	1,376,269
1978	4th	84	78	.519	11.0	Roger Craig	1,670,107
1979	5th	68	93	.422	22.0	Roger Craig	1,456,967
1980	6th	73	89	.451	19.5	Jerry Coleman	1,139,026
1981	6th/6th	41	69	.373	*	Frank Howard	519,161
1982	4th	81	81	.500	8.0	Dick Williams	1,607,516
1983	4th	81	81	.500	10.0	Dick Williams	1,539,815
1984	1st (C,s)	92	70	.568	+12.0	Dick Williams	1,983,904
1985	3rd (tied)	83	79	.512	12.0	Dick Williams	2,210,352
1986	4th	74	88	.457	22.0	Steve Boros	1,805,716
1987	6th	65	97	.401	25.0	Larry Bowa	1,454,061
1988	3rd	83	78	.516	11.0	Larry Bowa, Jack McKeon	1,506,896
1989	2nd	89	73	.549	3.0	Jack McKeon	2,009,031
1990	4th (tied)	75	87	.463	16.0	Jack McKeon, Greg Riddoch	1,856,396
1991	3rd	84	78	.519	10.0	Greg Riddoch	1,804,289
1992	3rd	82	80	.506	16.0	Greg Riddoch, Jim Riggleman	1,722,102
1993	7th	61	101	.377	43.0	Jim Riggleman	1,375,432
1994	4th	47	70	.402	12.5	Jim Riggleman	953,857
1995	3rd	70	74	.486	8.0	Bruce Bochy	1,041,805
1996	1st (d)	91	71	.562	+1.0	Bruce Bochy	2,187,886
1997	4th	76	86	.469	14.0	Bruce Bochy	2,089,333
1998	1st (D,C,s)	98	64	.605	+9.5	Bruce Bochy	2,555,901
1999	4th	74	88	.457	26.0	Bruce Bochy	2,523,538
2000	5th	76	86	.469	21.0	Bruce Bochy	2,423,149
2001	4th	79	83	.488	13.0	Bruce Bochy	2,377,969
2002	5th	66	96	.407	32.0	Bruce Bochy	2,220,416
2003	5th	64	98	.395	36.5	Bruce Bochy	2,030,064
2004	3rd	87	75	.537	6.0	Bruce Bochy	3,040,046

*first half 23-33, second half 18-36; (C) won League Championship Series; (s) lost World Series; (d) lost Division Series; (D) won Division Series

INDIVIDUAL AND CLUB RECORDS
BATTING

	Individual		Club
	Season	Career	Season
Games	162—Dave Winfield, 1980 Steve Garvey, 1985 Joe Carter, 1990	2,440—Tony Gwynn	163 (1980, 1983)
At-bats	655—Steve Finley, 161 g, 1996	9,288—Tony Gwynn	5,655 (1996)
Runs	126—Steve Finley, 161 g, 1996	1,383—Tony Gwynn	795 (1997) Fewest—468 (1969)

	Individual		Club
	Season	**Career**	**Season**
Hits	220—Tony Gwynn, 149 g, 1997	3,141—Tony Gwynn	1,521 (2004)
			Fewest—1,203 (1969)
Hitting streak	34 g—Benito Santiago, 1987		
Singles	177—Tony Gwynn, 158 g, 1984	2,378—Tony Gwynn	1,105 (1980)
Doubles	49—Tony Gwynn, 149 g, 1997	543—Tony Gwynn	304 (2004)
Triples	13—Tony Gwynn, 157 g, 1987	85—Tony Gwynn	53 (1979)

HOME RUNS

			172 (1970)
			Fewest—64 (1976)
Righthander	50—Greg Vaughn, 158 g, 1998	163—Nate Colbert	
Lefthander	35—Fred McGriff, 152 g, 1992	135—Tony Gwynn	
Switch-hitter	40—Ken Caminiti, 146 g, 1996	121—Ken Caminiti	
Rookie	24—Nate Colbert, 139 g, 1969		
Home	23—Greg Vaughn, 1998	72—Nate Colbert	87 (1992, 1993)
	Gary Sheffield, 1992		
Road	27—Greg Vaughn, 1998	91—Nate Colbert	104 (1970)
Month	14—Ken Caminiti, Aug 1996		47 (May 1970)
Pinch	5—Jerry Turner, 1978	9—Jerry Turner	10 (1995)
Grand slams	4—Phil Nevin, 149 g, 2001	6—Phil Nevin	10 (2001)
Home runs at Qualcomm Stadium, all teams			178 (2001)
Home runs at Petco Park, all teams			132 (2004)

Total bases	348—Steve Finley, 161 g, 1996	4,259—Tony Gwynn	2,306 (2004)
Extra base hits	84—Steve Finley, 161 g, 1996	763—Tony Gwynn	489 (1998)
Sacrifice hits	28—Ozzie Smith, 159 g, 1978	83—Enzo Hernandez	133 (1975)
		Ozzie Smith	
Sacrifice flies	16—Mark Loretta, 154 g, 2004	85—Tony Gwynn	66 (2004)
Bases on balls	132—Jack Clark, 142 g, 1989	790—Tony Gwynn	678 (2001)
			Fewest—401 (1973)
Strikeouts	150—Nate Colbert, 156 g, 1970	773—Nate Colbert	1,273 (2001)
	Fewest—23—Tony Gwynn, 158 g, 1984		Fewest—716 (1976)
Hit by pitch	13—Gene Tenace, 147 g, 1977	35—Gene Tenace	59 (1993)
			Fewest—9 (1989)
Runs batted in	130—Ken Caminiti, 146 g, 1996	1,138—Tony Gwynn	761 (1997)
			Fewest—431 (1969)

Grounded into	25—Steve Garvey, 161 g, 1984	260—Tony Gwynn	146 (1996)
double plays	Steve Garvey, 162 g, 1985		Fewest—81 (1978)
	Fewest—2—Alan Wiggins, 158 g, 1984		
Left on base			1,239 (1980)
			Fewest—1,006 (1972)
Batting average	.372—Tony Gwynn, 149 g, 1997	.338—Tony Gwynn	.275 (1994)
			Lowest—.225 (1969)
Most .300 hitters			3 (1987)
Slugging average	.621—Ken Caminiti, 146 g, 1996	.540—Ken Caminiti	.414 (2004)
			Lowest—.329 (1969)
On-base percentage	.454—Tony Gwynn, 110 g, 1994	.388—Tony Gwynn	.343 (2004)
			Lowest—.283 (1972)

BASERUNNING

Stolen bases	70—Alan Wiggins, 158 g, 1984	319—Tony Gwynn	239 (1980)
Caught stealing	21—Alan Wiggins, 158 g, 1984	125—Tony Gwynn	91 (1987)

PITCHING

Games	83—Craig Lefferts, 1986	668—Trevor Hoffman	
Games started	40—Randy Jones, 1976	253—Randy Jones	
Complete games	25—Randy Jones, 1976	71—Randy Jones	47 (1971, 1976)
Wins	22—Randy Jones, 1976	100—Eric Show	
Percentage	.778—Gaylord Perry (21-6), 1978	.535—Eric Show	
Winning streak	11—Andy Hawkins, 1985		
	LaMarr Hoyt, 1985		
	Kevin Brown, 1998		

	Individual		Club
	Season	**Career**	**Season**
20-win seasons		2—Randy Jones	
Losses	22—Randy Jones, 1974	105—Randy Jones	
Losing streak	11—Gary Ross, 1969		
Saves	53—Trevor Hoffman, 1998	391—Trevor Hoffman	59 (1998)
Innings	315—Randy Jones, 1976	1,766—Randy Jones	1,489 (1996)
Hits	274—Randy Jones, 1986	1,720—Randy Jones	1,581 (1997)
Runs	137—Bobby J. Jones, 2001	759—Randy Jones	891 (1997)
Earned runs	117—Bill Greif, 1974 Matt Clement, 2000	648—Randy Jones	802 (1997)
Bases on balls	125—Matt Clement, 2000	593—Eric Show	715 (1974)
Strikeouts	257—Kevin Brown, 1998	1,036—Andy Benes	1,217 (1998)
Strikeouts, game	15—Fred Norman, Sept 15, 1972 Sterling Hitchcock, Aug 29, 1998 (pitched first 13 inn of 15-inn game)		
Hit batsmen	16—Matt Clement, 2000	46—Joey Hamilton Eric Show	68 (2000)
Wild pitches	23—Matt Clement, 2000	48—Clay Kirby	73 (1999)
Home runs	37—Kevin Jarvis, 2001 Bobby J. Jones, 2001	166—Eric Show	219 (2001)
Sacrifice hits	23—Randy Jones, 1979	109—Randy Jones	112 (1975)
Sacrifice flies	12—Dave A. Roberts, 1971 Andy Hawkins, 1985	48—Randy Jones	62 (1993)
Earned run average	2.10—David Roberts, 270 inn, 1971	3.30—Randy Jones	3.22 (1971)
Shutouts	6—Fred Norman, 1972 Randy Jones, 1975	18—Randy Jones	19 (1985) Lost—23 (1969, 1976)
1-0 games won	2—Joe Niekro, 1969 Randy Jones, 1975, 1978 Greg W. Harris, 1991	5—Randy Jones	6 (1985) Lost—5 (1976, 1996)

TEAM FIELDING

Putouts	4,467 (1996) Fewest—4,211 (1972)	**Assists**	2,012 (1980) Fewest—1,607 (2001)
Chances accepted	6,411 (1980) Fewest—5,832 (1972)	**Errors**	189 (1977) Fewest—102 (2003)
Double plays	171 (1978) Fewest—126 (1974)	**Passed balls**	22 (1987) Fewest—2 (1992)
Errorless games	89 (2003) Consecutive—9 (1979)	**Fielding average**	.983 (1998, 2003) Lowest .971 (1975, 1977)

MISCELLANEOUS

Most players, season 59 (2002)
Fewest players, season 31 (1984)
Games won 98 (1998)
  Month 19 (Jun 1984, Jul 1984, Sept 1989)
  Consecutive 14 (1999)
Winning percentage .605 (1998), 98-64
  Lowest .321 (1969), 52-110
Number of league championships 2
  Most recent 1998
Runs, game 20 vs Florida, Jul 27, 1996
             vs Montreal, May 19, 2001
  Opponents' 23 by Chicago, May 17, 1977
Hits, game 24 vs San Francisco, Apr 19, 1982
          vs Atlanta, Aug 12, 2003
Home runs, game 6 vs Cincinnati, Jul 17, 1998
Runs, shutout 13 vs Cincinnati, Aug 11, 1991
  Opponents' 19 by Chicago, May 13, 1969
           by Los Angeles, Jun 28, 1969
Longest 1-0 win 14 inn, vs Cincinnati, Aug 4, 1974, 2nd game

Most seasons, non-pitcher 20—Tony Gwynn
Most seasons, pitcher 12—Trevor Hoffman
Games lost 110 (1969)
  Month 23 (May 2003)
  Consecutive 13 (1994)
Overall record 2,611-3,094 (36 seasons)
  Interleague play 60-68
Number of times worst record in league 9 (inc. one tie)
  Most recent 2003
Runs, inning 13 vs St. Louis, Aug 24, 1993, 1st
            vs Pittsburgh, May 31, 1994, 2nd

Total bases, game 38 vs Philadelphia, Aug 10, 2000
           (39 vs San Francisco, May 23, 1970, 15 inn)
Consecutive games with one or more home runs 14 (23 hrs), 1998
Longest shutout unknown

Longest 1-0 loss 18 inn, vs Pittsburgh, Jun 7, 1972, 2nd game

ATTENDANCE

Highest home attendance	2,555,901	**Largest crowds**	
Qualcomm Stadium	2,555,901 (1998)	**Day**	61,707 vs San Francisco, Mar 31, 2003
Petco Park	3,040,046 (2004)	**Night**	61,674 vs Arizona, Apr 24, 1999
		Doubleheader	43,473 vs Philadelphia, Jun 13, 1976
Highest road attendance	2,534,072 (1993)	**Home opener**	61,707 vs San Francisco, Mar 31, 2003

SAN FRANCISCO GIANTS
YEARLY FINISHES

(National League franchise established in 1883 moved from New York to San Francisco after the 1957 season)

Year	Position	W	L	Pct.	GB	Manager	Attendance
1958	3rd	80	74	.519	12.0	Bill Rigney	1,272,625
1959	3rd	83	71	.539	4.0	Bill Rigney	1,422,130
1960	5th	79	75	.513	16.0	Bill Rigney, Tom Sheehan	1,795,356
1961	3rd	85	69	.552	8.0	Alvin Dark	1,390,679
1962	1st (L,s)	103	62	.624	+1.0	Alvin Dark	1,592,594
1963	3rd	88	74	.543	11.0	Alvin Dark	1,571,306
1964	4th	90	72	.556	3.0	Alvin Dark	1,504,364
1965	2nd	95	67	.586	2.0	Herman Franks	1,546,075
1966	2nd	93	68	.578	1.5	Herman Franks	1,657,192
1967	2nd	91	71	.562	10.5	Herman Franks	1,242,480
1968	2nd	88	74	.543	9.0	Herman Franks	837,220

WEST DIVISION

Year	Position	W	L	Pct.	GB	Manager	Attendance
1969	2nd	90	72	.556	3.0	Clyde King	873,603
1970	3rd	86	76	.531	16.0	Clyde King, Charlie Fox	740,720
1971	1st (c)	90	72	.556	+1.0	Charlie Fox	1,106,043
1972	5th	69	86	.445	26.5	Charlie Fox	647,744
1973	3rd	88	74	.543	11.0	Charlie Fox	834,193
1974	5th	72	90	.444	30.0	Charlie Fox, Wes Westrum	519,987
1975	3rd	80	81	.497	27.5	Wes Westrum	522,919
1976	4th	74	88	.457	28.0	Bill Rigney	626,868
1977	4th	75	87	.463	23.0	Joe Altobelli	700,056
1978	3rd	89	73	.549	6.0	Joe Altobelli	1,740,477
1979	4th	71	91	.438	19.5	Joe Altobelli, Dave Bristol	1,456,402
1980	5th	75	86	.466	17.0	Dave Bristol	1,096,115
1981	5th/3rd	56	55	.505	*	Frank Robinson	632,274
1982	3rd	87	75	.537	2.0	Frank Robinson	1,200,948
1983	5th	79	83	.488	12.0	Frank Robinson	1,251,530
1984	6th	66	96	.407	26.0	Frank Robinson, Danny Ozark	1,001,545
1985	6th	62	100	.383	33.0	Jim Davenport, Roger Craig	818,697
1986	3rd	83	79	.512	13.0	Roger Craig	1,528,748
1987	1st (c)	90	72	.556	+6.0	Roger Craig	1,917,168
1988	4th	83	79	.512	11.5	Roger Craig	1,785,297
1989	1st (C,s)	92	70	.568	+3.0	Roger Craig	2,059,701
1990	3rd	85	77	.525	6.0	Roger Craig	1,975,528
1991	4th	75	87	.463	19.0	Roger Craig	1,737,478
1992	5th	72	90	.444	26.0	Roger Craig	1,561,987
1993	2nd	103	59	.636	1.0	Dusty Baker	2,606,354
1994	2nd	55	60	.478	3.5	Dusty Baker	1,704,608
1995	4th	67	77	.465	11.0	Dusty Baker	1,241,500
1996	4th	68	94	.420	23.0	Dusty Baker	1,413,922
1997	1st (d)	90	72	.556	+2.0	Dusty Baker	1,690,869
1998	2nd (w)	89	74	.546	9.5	Dusty Baker	1,925,634
1999	2nd	86	76	.531	14.0	Dusty Baker	2,078,399
2000	1st (d)	97	65	.599	+11.0	Dusty Baker	3,315,330
2001	2nd	90	72	.556	2.0	Dusty Baker	3,277,244
2002	2nd (D,C,s)	95	66	.590	2.5	Dusty Baker	3,253,205
2003	1st (d)	100	61	.621	+15.5	Felipe Alou	3,264,903
2004	2nd	91	71	.562	2.0	Felipe Alou	3,258,864

(L) won league playoff; (s) lost World Series; (c) lost League Championship Series; *first half 27-32, second half 29-23; (C) won League Championship Series; (d) lost Division Series; (w) lost wild card playoff; (D) won Division Series

INDIVIDUAL AND CLUB RECORDS
BATTING

	Individual		Club
	Season	Career	Season
Games	164—Jose Pagan, 1962	2,256—Willie McCovey	165 (1962)
At-bats	663—Bobby Bonds, 157 g, 1970	7,578—Willie Mays	5,650 (1984)
Runs	134—Bobby Bonds, 157 g, 1970	1,480—Willie Mays	925 (2000)
			Fewest—556 (1985)
Hits	208—Willie Mays, 152 g, 1958	2,284—Willie Mays	1,552 (1962)
			Fewest—1,263 (1985)
Hitting streak	26 g—Jack Clark, 1978		
Singles	160—Brett Butler, 160 g, 1990	1,373—Willie Mays	1,132 (1984)

– 338 –

	Individual		**Club**
	Season	**Career**	**Season**
Doubles	49—Jeff Kent, 159 g, 2001	376—Willie Mays	314 (2004)
Triples	12—Willie Mays, 153 g, 1960	76—Willie Mays	62 (1960)

HOME RUNS

235 (2001)
Fewest—80 (1980)

	Season	**Career**	**Season**
Righthander	52—Willie Mays, 157 g, 1965	459—Willie Mays	
Lefthander	73—Barry Bonds, 153 g, 2001	527—Barry Bonds	
Switch-hitter	28—J.T. Snow, 157 g, 1997	120—J.T. Snow	
Rookie	31—Jim Hart, 153 g, 1964		
Home	37—Barry Bonds, 2001	266—Barry Bonds	118 (1987)
Road	36—Barry Bonds, 2001	261—Barry Bonds	138 (2001)
Month	17—Willie Mays, Aug 1965		45 (Aug 1999, May 2001)
	Barry Bonds, May 2001		
Pinch	4—Mike Ivie, 1978	13—Willie McCovey	14 (2001)
	Candy Maldonado, 1986		
	Ernest Riles, 1990		
Grand slams	3—Willie McCovey, 135 g, 1967	16—Willie McCovey	7 (1970, 1998, 2000)
	Jeff Kent, 155 g, 1997		
Home runs at Seals Stadium, all teams			173 (1958)
Home runs at Candlestick Park, all teams			190 (1987)
Home runs at SBC Park, all teams			171 (2000)
Total bases	411—Barry Bonds, 153 g, 2001	4,189—Willie Mays	2,605 (2000)
Extra base hits	107—Barry Bonds, 153 g, 2001	911—Willie Mays	579 (2001)
		Barry Bonds	
Sacrifice hits	19—Rick Reuschel, 36 g, 1988	111—Jim Davenport	127 (1978)
Sacrifice flies	14—J.T. Snow, 155 g, 2000	67—Willie Mays	66 (2000)
		Willie McCovey	
Bases on balls	232—Barry Bonds, 147 g, 2004	1,691—Barry Bonds	729 (1970)
			Fewest—414 (1966)
Strikeouts	189—Bobby Bonds, 157 g, 1970	1,351—Willie McCovey	1,189 (1996)
	Fewest—22—Dave Rader, 148 g, 1973		Fewest—764 (1961)
Hit by pitch	26—Ron Hunt, 117 g, 1970	76—Ron Hunt	72 (2004)
			Fewest—14 (1980)
Runs batted in	142—Orlando Cepeda, 152 g, 1961	1,388—Willie McCovey	889 (2000)
			Fewest—517 (1985)
Grounded into	27—A.J. Pierzynski, 131 g, 2004	172—Willie Mays	149 (1961)
double plays	Fewest—2—Jose Uribe, 157 g, 1986		Fewest—83 (1986, 1990)
	Will Clark, 150 g, 1987		
	Brett Butler, 157 g, 1988		
Left on base			1,289 (2004)
			Fewest—983 (1961)
Batting average	.370—Barry Bonds, 143 g, 2002	.317—Barry Bonds	.278 (1962, 2000)
			Lowest—.233 (1985)
Most .300 hitters			4 (1962)
Slugging average	.863—Barry Bonds, 153 g, 2001	.680—Barry Bonds	.472 (2000)
			Lowest—.341 (1968)
On-base percentage	.609—Barry Bonds, 147 g, 2004	.479—Barry Bonds	.362 (2000)
			Lowest—.299 (1985)

BASERUNNING

	Season	**Career**	**Season**
Stolen bases	58—Bill North, 142 g, 1979	263—Bobby Bonds	148 (1986)
Caught stealing	24—Bill North, 142 g, 1979	69—Barry Bonds	97 (1987)

PITCHING

	Season	**Career**	**Season**
Games	89—Julian Tavarez, 1997	647—Gary Lavelle	
	Jim Brower, 2004		
Games started	42—Jack Sanford, 1963	446—Juan Marichal	
Complete games	30—Juan Marichal, 1968	244—Juan Marichal	77 (1968)
Wins	26—Juan Marichal, 1968	238—Juan Marichal	
Percentage	.806—Juan Marichal (25-6), 1966	.630—Juan Marichal	
Winning streak	16—Jack Sanford, 1962		

	Individual		Club
	Season	**Career**	**Season**
20-win seasons		6—Juan Marichal	
Losses	18—Ray Sadecki, 1968	140—Juan Marichal	
Losing streak	9—Mark Davis, 1984		
	Terry Mulholland, 1995		
	Rod Beck, 1996		
Saves	48—Rod Beck, 1993	206—Robb Nen	50 (1993)
Innings	328.2—Gaylord Perry, 1970	3,444—Juan Marichal	1,477 (1998)
Hits	295—Juan Marichal, 1968	3,081—Juan Marichal	1,589 (1984)
Runs	143—Vida Blue, 1979	1,288—Juan Marichal	862 (1996)
	Livan Hernandez, 2001		
Earned runs	132—Vida Blue, 1979	1,086—Juan Marichal	762 (1999)
	Livan Hernandez, 2001		
Bases on balls	125—Russ Ortiz, 1999	690—Juan Marichal	655 (1999)
Strikeouts	251—Jason Schmidt, 2004	2,281—Juan Marichal	1,089 (1998)
Strikeouts, game	15—Gaylord Perry, Jul 22, 1966		
Hit batsmen	17—Mark Leiter, 1995	53—Bobby Bolin	67 (1996)
	Jerome Williams, 2004		
Wild pitches	18—Rich Robertson, 1970	81—Gaylord Perry	76 (1970)
Home runs	34—Juan Marichal, 1962	315—Juan Marichal	194 (1996, 1999)
Sacrifice hits	19—Kirk Rueter, 2000	122—Juan Marichal	99 (1975, 1976)
Sacrifice flies	14—Rick Reuschel, 1988	64—Jim Barr	64 (1984)
		Juan Marichal	
Earned run average	1.98—Bobby Bolin, 177 inn, 1968	2,84—Juan Marichal	2.71 (1968)
Shutouts	10—Juan Marichal, 1965	52—Juan Marichal	20 (1968)
			Lost—18 (1992)
1-0 games won	2—many pitchers	7—Juan Marichal	6 (1968)
			Lost—4 (1972, 1976, 1978, 1985, 1989, 1996)

TEAM FIELDING

Putouts	4,431 (1998)	**Assists**	1,940 (1976)
	Fewest—4,129 (1959)		Fewest—1,513 (1961)
Chances accepted	6,349 (1969)	**Errors**	186 (1976)
	Fewest—5,677 (1961)		Fewest—80 (2003)
Double plays	183 (1987)	**Passed balls**	30 (1970)
	Fewest—109 (1983)		Fewest—6 (1978, 1994)
Errorless games	96 (2000)	**Fielding average**	.987 (2003)
	Consecutive—11 (1999, 2000)		Lowest—.971 (1976)

MISCELLANEOUS

Most players, season 51 (1990)
Fewest players, season 31 (1962, 1968)
Games won 103 (1962, 1993)
  Month 21 (Sept 1965, Aug 1968)
  Consecutive 14 (1965)
Winning percentage .636 (1993), 103-59
  Lowest .383 (1985), 62-100
Number of league championships 3
  Most recent 2002
Runs, game 23 vs Atlanta, Jun 8, 1990
  Opponents' 20 by Chicago, Aug 13, 1959
Hits, game 27 vs Atlanta, Jun 8, 1990
Home runs, game 8 vs Milwaukee Apr 30, 1961

Runs, shutout 18 vs Montreal, May 24, 2000
  Opponents' 15 by Chicago, Aug 22, 1970
Longest 1-0 win 21 inn, vs Cincinnati, Sept 1, 1967

Most seasons, non-pitcher 19—Willie McCovey
Most seasons, pitcher 14—Juan Marichal
Games lost 100 (1985)
  Month 21 (May 1972)
  Consecutive 10 (1985, 1996)
Overall record 3,895-3,563 (47 seasons)
  Interleague play 72-56
Number of times worst record in league 1
  Most recent 1984
Runs, inning 13 vs St. Louis, May 7, 1966, 3rd
  vs San Diego, July 15, 1997, 7th
Total bases, game 50 vs Los Angeles, May 13, 1958
Consecutive games with one or more home runs 16 (22 hrs), 1962
  (30 hrs), 1963
Longest shutout 21 inn, 1-0 vs Cincinnati, Sept 1, 1967

Longest 1-0 loss 18 inn, vs Arizona, May 29, 2001

ATTENDANCE

Highest home attendance		**Largest crowds**	
Seals Stadium	1,442,130 (1959)	Day	61,389 vs Los Angeles, Sept 30, 1999
Candlestick Park	2,606,354 (1963)	Night	55,920 vs Cincinnati, Jun 20, 1978
SBC Park	3,315,330 (2000)	Doubleheader	53,178 vs Los Angeles, Jul 31, 1983
Highest road attendance	2,856,363 (2001)	Home opener	58,077 vs Pittsburgh, Apr 4, 1994

DIVISION SERIES

SERIES WINNERS

AMERICAN LEAGUE

Year	Winner	Loser	Games
1995	Cleveland (Central)	Boston (East)	3-0
	Seattle (West)	New York (East)*	3-2
1996	Baltimore (East)*	Cleveland (Central)	3-1
	New York (East)	Texas (West)	3-1
1997	Baltimore (East)	Seattle (West)	3-1
	Cleveland (Central)	New York (East)*	3-2
1998	Cleveland (Central)	Boston (East)*	3-1
	New York (East)	Texas (West)	3-0
1999	Boston (East)*	Cleveland (Central)	3-2
	New York (East)	Texas (West)	3-0
2000	Seattle (West)*	Chicago (Central)	3-0
	New York (East)	Oakland (West)	3-2
2001	Seattle (West)	Cleveland (Central)	3-2
	New York (East)	Oakland (West)*	3-2
2002	Anaheim (West)*	New York (East)	3-1
	Minnesota (Central)	Oakland (West)	3-2
2003	New York (East)	Minnesota (Central)	3-1
	Boston (East)*	Oakland (West)	3-2
2004	New York (East)	Minnesota (Central)	3-1
	Boston (East)*	Anaheim (West)	3-0

*wild-card team

NATIONAL LEAGUE

Year	Winner	Loser	Games
1995	Atlanta (East)	Colorado (West)*	3-1
	Cincinnati (Central)	Los Angeles (West)	3-0
1996	Atlanta (East)	Los Angeles (West)*	3-0
	St. Louis (Central)	San Diego (West)	3-0
1997	Atlanta (East)	Houston (Central)	3-0
	Florida (East)*	San Francisco (West)	3-0
1998	San Diego (West)	Houston (Central)	3-1
	Atlanta (East)	Chicago (Central)*	3-0
1999	Atlanta (East)	Houston (Central)	3-1
	New York (East)*	Arizona (West)	3-1
2000	St. Louis (Central)	Atlanta (East)	3-0
	New York (East)*	San Francisco (West)	3-1
2001	Arizona (West)	St. Louis (Central)*	3-2
	Atlanta (East)	Houston (Central)	3-0
2002	St. Louis (Central)	Arizona (West)	3-0
	San Francisco (West)*	Atlanta (East)	3-2
2003	Chicago (Central)	Atlanta (East)	3-2
	Florida (East)*	San Francisco (West)	3-1
2004	St. Louis (Central)	Los Angeles (West)	3-1
	Houston (Central)*	Atlanta (East)	3-2

*wild-card team

INDIVIDUAL SERVICE

ALL PLAYERS
SERIES AND CLUBS

Most series played
A.L.—10—Bernie Williams, New York, 1995 through 2004
   Mariano Rivera, New York, 1995 through 2004
N.L.—10—Chipper Jones, Atlanta, 1995 through 2004

Most clubs, career
Both leagues—5—Kenny Lofton, Cleveland A.L., 1995, 1996, 1998 through 2001; Atlanta N.L., 1997; San Francisco N.L., 2002; Chicago N.L., 2003; New York A.L., 2004
N.L.—5—Reggie Sanders, Cincinnati, 1995; Atlanta, 2000; Arizona, 2001; San Francisco, 2002; St. Louis, 2004
A.L.—3—Harold Baines, Baltimore, 1997; Cleveland, 1999; Chicago, 2000
   Keith Foulke, Chicago, 2000; Oakland, 2003; Boston, 2004
   Mike Stanton, Boston, 1995; Texas, 1996; New York, 1997, 2001, 2002

BY POSITION (EXCEPT PITCHERS)

Most series by first baseman
Both leagues—8—Tino Martinez, Seattle A.L., 1995; New York A.L., 1996 through 2001; St. Louis, 2002; 33 G
A.L.—7—Tino Martinez, Seattle, 1995; New York, 1996 through 2001; 30 G
N.L.—5—Jeff Bagwell, Houston, 1997 through 1999, 2001, 2004; 19 G

Most series by second baseman
N.L.—6—Keith Lockhart, Atlanta, 1997 through 2002; 15 G
A.L.—4—Mark McLemore, Texas, 1996, 1998, 1999; Seattle, 2000; 13 G
   Roberto Alomar, Baltimore, 1996, 1997; Cleveland, 1999, 2001; 18 G

Most series by third baseman
N.L.—8—Chipper Jones, Atlanta, 1995 through 2001, 2004; 28 G
A.L.—4—Scott Brosius, New York, 1998 through 2001; 16 G
   Eric Chavez, Oakland, 2000 through 2003; 20 g

Most series by shortstop
A.L.—9—Derek Jeter, New York, 1996 through 2004; 37 G
N.L.—5—Edgar Renteria, Florida, 1997; St. Louis, 2000 through 2002, 2004; 18 G

Most series by outfielder
A.L.—10—Bernie Williams, New York, 1995 through 2004; 42 G
N.L.—9—Andruw Jones, Atlanta, 1996 through 2004; 34 G

Most series by catcher
A.L.—8—Jorge Posada, New York, 1997 through 2004; 26 G
N.L.—7—Javy Lopez, Atlanta, 1995 through 1998, 2000, 2003; 21 G

YOUNGEST AND OLDEST NON-PITCHERS

Youngest division series non-pitcher
N.L.—19 years, 5 months, 9 days—Andruw Jones, Atlanta, October 2, 1996
A.L.—20 years, 2 months, 11 days—Alex Rodriguez, Seattle, October 8, 1995

Oldest division series non-pitcher
N.L.—46 years, 1 month, 16 days—Julio Franco, Atlanta, October 9, 2004
A.L.—41 years, 10 months, 12 days—Rickey Henderson, Seattle, October 6, 2000

YEARS BETWEEN SERIES (INCLUDES PITCHERS)

Most years between first and second series
A.L.—9—Ruben Sierra, New York, 1995; New York, 2004
N.L.—9—Larry Walker, Colorado, 1995; St. Louis, 2004

Most years between first and last series
A.L.—9—Mariano Rivera, New York, 1995; New York, 2004
   Ruben Sierra, New York, 1995; New York, 2004
   Bernie Williams, New York, 1995; New York, 2004
N.L.—9—Chipper Jones, Atlanta, 1995; Atlanta, 2004
   Larry Walker, Colorado, 1995; St. Louis, 2004

POSITIONS

Most positions played, career
A.L.—4—Randy Velarde, New York, 1995; Oakland, 2000, 2002 (2B, 3B, LF, 1B)
N.L.—3—many players

Most positions played, series
A.L.—3—Randy Velarde, New York, 1995 (2B, 3B, LF)
   Jeff Kent, Cleveland, 1996 (2B, 1B, 3B)
N.L.—3—Craig Paquette, St. Louis, 2001 (RF, LF, 3B)
   Albert Pujols, St. Louis, 2002 (LF, 3B, 1B)

PITCHERS
SERIES

Most series pitched
A.L.—10—Mariano Rivera, New York, 1995 through 2004; 25 G
N.L.—9—Greg Maddux, Atlanta, 1995 through 2003; 12 G

Most series pitched by relief pitcher
A.L.—10—Mariano Rivera, New York, 1995 through 2004; 25 G
N.L.—5—Mike Remlinger, Atlanta, 1999 through 2002;
Chicago, 2003; 11 g

YOUNGEST AND OLDEST PITCHERS

Youngest division series pitcher
N.L.—21 years, 2 months, 15 days—Rick Ankiel, St. Louis,
October 3, 2000
A.L.—20 years, 8 months, 25 days—Francisco Rodriguez,
Anaheim, October 2, 2002

Oldest division series pitcher
A.L.—43 years, 11 months, 29 days—Dennis Eckersley,
Boston, October 2, 1998
N.L.—42 years, 3 months, 6 days—Rick Honeycutt, St. Louis,
October 5, 1996

CLUB SERVICE

PLAYERS USED

Most players, series
A.L.-N.L.—25—many clubs

**For a list of players and pitchers used each
series, see page 385.**

Most players used by both clubs, series
A.L.—50—Boston 25, Cleveland 25, 1999 (5-game series)
Minnesota 25, Oakland 25, 2002 (5-game series)
N.L.—49—San Francisco 25, New York 24, 2000 (4-game
series)
Atlanta 25, Houston 24, 2004 (5-game series)

Fewest players, series
A.L.—17—Texas vs. New York, 1998 (3-game series)
N.L.—18—Cincinnati vs. Los Angeles, 1995 (3-game series)
Atlanta vs. Houston, 1997 (3-game series)

Fewest players used by both clubs, series
A.L.—36—New York 19, Texas 17, 1998 (3-game series)
N.L.—40—Los Angeles 22, Cincinnati 18, 1995 (3-game series)
San Francisco 21, Florida 19, 1997 (3-game series)

Most times one club using only nine players in game, series
N.L.—1—Arizona vs. St. Louis, 2001 (5-game series)
Los Angeles vs. St. Louis, 2004 (4-game series)
A.L.—none

Most players, game
N.L.—20—Colorado vs. Atlanta, October 3, 1995
(20—Atlanta vs. Houston, October 8, 1999, 12 Inn)
A.L.—20—Texas vs. New York, October 5, 1996
(20—New York vs. Texas, October 2, 1996, 12 inn)

Most players used by both clubs, game
A.L.—39—Texas 20, New York 19, October 5, 1996
N.L.—37—Colorado 20, Atlanta 17, October 3, 1995
Florida 19, San Francisco 18, October 1, 2003
(38—San Francisco 19, New York 19, October 7, 2000, 10 inn)

PINCH-HITTERS

Most pinch-hitters, series
N.L.—14—Atlanta vs. San Francisco, 2002 (5-game series)
A.L.—10—Oakland vs. New York, 2001 (5-game series)

Most pinch-hitters used by both clubs, series
N.L.—22—Atlanta 12, Colorado 10, 1995 (4-game series)
A.L.—14—Oakland 8, Minnesota 6, 2002 (5-game series)

Fewest pinch-hitters, series
A.L.—0—Texas vs. New York, 1999 (3-game series)
Boston vs. Anaheim, 2004 (3-game series)
New York vs. Minnesota, 2004 (4-game series)
N.L.—1—Atlanta vs. Houston, 1997 (3-game series)

Fewest pinch-hitters used by both clubs, series
A.L.—2—Texas 1, New York 1, 1998 (3-game series)
New York 2, Texas 0, 1999 (3-game series)
N.L.—8—Houston 7, Atlanta 1, 1997 (3-game series)

Most pinch-hitters, game
A.L.-N.L.—4—many clubs

Most pinch-hitters used by both clubs, game
N.L.—7—Atlanta 4, Colorado 3, October 4, 1995
Atlanta 4, San Francisco 3, October 7, 2002
(7—Atlanta 4, Houston 3, October 8, 1999, 12 inn)
A.L.—5—Seattle 4, Cleveland 1, October 13, 2001
Oakland 4, New York 1, October 14, 2001
(5—Boston 3, Oakland 2, October 1, 2003, 12 inn)

Most pinch-hitters, inning
N.L.—4—Arizona vs. St. Louis, October 10, 2001, 8th
A.L.—4—Anaheim vs. Boston, October 8, 2004, 7th

PINCH-RUNNERS

Most pinch-runners, series
A.L.—7—Baltimore vs. Cleveland, 1996 (4-game series)
N.L.—3—San Diego vs. Houston, 1998 (4-game series)
New York vs. San Francisco, 2000 (4-game series)
Arizona vs. St. Louis, 2001 (5-game series)
Atlanta vs. Houston, 2004 (5-game series)

Most pinch-runners used by both clubs, series
A.L.—9—Baltimore 7, Cleveland 2, 1996 (4-game series)
N.L.—4—Atlanta 3, Houston 1, 2004 (5-game series)

Fewest pinch-runners used, series
A.L.-N.L.—0—many clubs

Fewest pinch-runners used by both clubs, series
N.L.—0—Houston 0, Atlanta 0, 1997 (3-game series)
Atlanta 0, Chicago 0, 1998 (3-game series)
Atlanta 0, Houston 0, 2001 (3-game series)
Atlanta 0, San Francisco 0, 2002 (5-game series)
Los Angeles 0, St. Louis 0, 2004 (4-game series)
A.L.—0—Minnesota 0, Oakland 0, 2002 (5-game series)

Most pinch-runners, game
A.L.—3—Baltimore vs. Cleveland, October 2, 1996
N.L.—2—Arizona vs. St. Louis, October 14, 2001
Atlanta vs. Chicago, October 1, 2003
(2—Atlanta vs. Houston, October 7, 2004, 11 inn)

Most pinch-runners used by both clubs, game
A.L.—4—Baltimore 3, Cleveland 1, October 2, 1996
N.L.—3—Atlanta 2, Chicago 1, October 1, 2003

Most pinch-runners, inning
A.L.—3—Baltimore vs. Cleveland, October 2, 1996, 8th
N.L.—2—Arizona vs. St. Louis, October 14, 2001, 9th
Atlanta vs. Houston, October 7, 2004, 8th

NUMBER OF PLAYERS USED BY POSITION
FIRST BASEMEN

Most first basemen, series
A.L.—4—Oakland vs. Minnesota, 2002 (5-game series)
N.L.—3—Arizona vs. St. Louis, 2002 (3-game series)

Most first basemen used by both clubs, series
A.L.—5—Oakland 4, Minnesota 1, 2002 (5-game series)

Minnesota 3, New York 2, 2004 (4-game series)
N.L.—5—Arizona 3, St. Louis 2, 2002 (3-game series)

Most first basemen, game
A.L.—3—Oakland vs. Minnesota, October 1, 2002
 (3—Minnesota vs. New York, October 6, 2004, 12 inn)
N.L.—2—many games

Most first basemen used by both clubs, game
N.L.—4—Chicago 2, Atlanta 2, October 1, 2003
A.L.—3—many games
 (4—Minnesota 3, New York 1, October 6, 2004, 12 inn)

SECOND BASEMEN

Most second basemen, series
A.L.—3—New York vs. Cleveland, 1997 (5-game series)
 Minnesota vs. New York, 2003 (4-game series)
N.L.—3—Atlanta vs. Chicago, 2003 (5-game series)

Most second basemen used by both clubs, series
A.L.—5—New York 3, Cleveland 2, 1997 (5-game series)
N.L.—4—Florida 2, San Francisco 2, 1997 (3-game series)
 Atlanta 3, Chicago 1, 2003 (5-games series)

Most second basemen, game
A.L.—3—New York vs. Cleveland, October 6, 1997
 Minnesota vs. New York, October 4, 2003
N.L.—3—Atlanta vs. Chicago, September 30, 2003

Most second basemen used by both clubs, game
A.L.—4—New York 3, Cleveland 1, October 6, 1997
 Minnesota 3, New York 1, October 4, 2003
 Oakland 2, Boston 2, October 6, 2003
 Anaheim 2, Boston 2, October 5, 2004
 (4—New York 2, Seattle 2, October 4, 1995, 15 inn)
N.L.—4—Atlanta 3, Chicago 1, September 30, 2003

THIRD BASEMEN

Most third basemen, series
A.L.—3—Seattle vs. Baltimore, 1997 (4-game series)
N.L.—3—St. Louis vs. Arizona, 2002 (3-game series)

Most third basemen used by both clubs, series
N.L.—5—St. Louis 3, Arizona 2, 2002 (3-game series)
A.L.—4—New York 2, Seattle 2, 1995 (5-game series)
 Seattle 3, Baltimore 1, 1997 (4-game series)
 Anaheim 2, Boston 2, 2004 (3-game series)

Most third basemen, game
N.L.—3—St. Louis vs. Arizona, October 3, 2002
A.L.—2—many clubs

Most third basemen used by both clubs, game
N.L.—4—St. Louis 3, Arizona 1, October 3, 2002
A.L.—3—many games

SHORTSTOPS

Most shortstops, series
A.L.—3—Seattle vs. New York, 1995 (5-game series)
N.L.—3—Atlanta vs. Colorado, 1995 (3-game series)
 Houston vs. Atlanta, 2004 (5-game series)

Most shortstops used by both clubs, series
A.L.—4—Seattle 3, New York 1, 1995 (5-game series)
N.L.—4—Atlanta 3, Colorado 1, 1995 (4-game series)
 Atlanta 2, Houston 2, 1999 (4-game series)
 San Francisco 2, New York 2, 2000 (4-game series)
 Atlanta 2, Houston 2, 2001 (3-game series)
 Houston 3, Atlanta 1, 2004 (5-game series)

Most shortstops, game
N.L.—2—many clubs
 (3—Atlanta vs. Colorado, October 6, 1995, 10 inn)
A.L.—2—many clubs

Most shortstops used by both clubs, game
N.L.—4—Atlanta 2, Houston 2, October 9, 2001
 (4—Atlanta 3, Colorado 1, October 6, 1995, 10 inn
 New York 2, San Francisco 2, October 7, 2000, 13 inn)
A.L.—3—many games

LEFT FIELDERS

Most left fielders, series
A.L.—4—Cleveland vs. Seattle, 2001 (5-game series)
 Oakland vs. Boston, 2003 (5-game series)
N.L.—4—Houston vs. Atlanta, 1999 (4-game series)
 St. Louis vs. Arizona, 2001 (5-game series)

Most left fielders used by both clubs, series
A.L.—7—Cleveland 4, Seattle 3, 2001 (5-game series)
N.L.—6—Houston 4, Atlanta 2, 1999 (4-game series)
 Atlanta 3, Houston 3, 2004 (5-game series)

Most left fielders, game
A.L.—3—Seattle vs. Chicago, October 4, 2000
 (3—New York vs. Seattle, October 4, 1995, 15 inn
 Oakland vs. Boston, October 1, 2003, 12 inn)
N.L.—3—New York vs. San Francisco, October 4, 2000
 St. Louis vs. Arizona, October 10, 2001
 (3—Houston vs. Atlanta, October 8, 1999, 12 inn
 New York vs. San Francisco, October 5, 2000, 10 inn)

Most left fielders used by both clubs, game
A.L.—4—many games
 (5—New York 3, Seattle 2, October 4, 1995, 15 inn)
N.L.—4—many games
 (5—Houston 3, Atlanta 2, October 8, 1999, 12 inn)

CENTER FIELDERS

Most center fielders, series
N.L.—4—New York vs. Arizona, 1999 (4-game series)
A.L.—3—Boston vs. Cleveland, 1995 (3-game series)

Most center fielders used by both clubs, series
N.L.—5—New York 4, Arizona 1, 1999 (4-game series)
A.L.—4—Boston 3, Cleveland 1, 1995 (3-game series)
 Boston 2, Cleveland 2, 1999 (5-game series)
 Boston 2, Oakland 2, 2003 (5-games series)

Most center fielders, game
N.L.—3—New York vs. Arizona, October 5, 1999
A.L.—2—many clubs

Most center fielders used by both clubs, game
N.L.—4—New York 3, Arizona 1, October 5, 1999
A.L.—3—many games

RIGHT FIELDERS

Most right fielders, series
A.L.—5—Oakland vs. New York, 2000 (5-game series)
N.L.—4—Houston vs. Atlanta, 1999 (4-game series)

Most right fielders used by both clubs, series
N.L.—5—Houston 4, Atlanta 1, 1999 (4-game series)
 New York 3, San Francisco 2, 2000 (4-game series)
A.L.—6—Oakland 5, New York 1, 2000 (5-game series)

Most right fielders, game
A.L.—3—Baltimore vs. Seattle, October 2, 1997
 Oakland vs. New York, October 7, 2000
 Minnesota vs. Oakland, October 2, 2002
 Minnesota vs. Oakland, October 5, 2002
 (3—Boston vs. Oakland, October 1, 2003, 12 inn)
N.L.—2—many clubs

Most right fielders used by both clubs, game
A.L.—4—Baltimore 3, Seattle 1, October 2, 1997
 Oakland 3, New York 1, October 7, 2000
 Minnesota 3, Oakland 1, October 2, 2002
 Minnesota 3, Oakland 1, October 5, 2002
 (5—Boston 3, Oakland 2, October 1, 2003, 12 inn)
N.L.—4—many games

CATCHERS

Most catchers, series
A.L.—3—Minnesota vs. New York, 2004 (4-game series)
N.L.—3—Chicago vs. Atlanta, 1998 (3-game series)
 Arizona vs. St. Louis, 2002 (3-game series)

Los Angeles vs. St. Louis, 2004* (4-game series)

Most catchers used by both clubs, series
N.L.—5—Houston 3, Atlanta 2, 1997 (3-game series)
Chicago 3, Atlanta 2, 1998 (3-game series)
A.L.—4—many series

Most catchers, game
N.L.—3—Los Angeles vs. St. Louis, October 10, 2004
A.L.—2—many clubs

Most catchers used by both clubs, game
A.L.-N.L.—4—many games

PITCHERS

Most pitchers, series
3-game series
A.L.—10—Boston vs. Cleveland, 1995
Chicago vs. Seattle, 2000
N.L.—10—Los Angeles vs. Atlanta, 1996
Arizona vs. St. Louis, 2002
4-game series
N.L.—12—San Francisco vs. Florida, 2003
A.L.—11—Texas vs. New York, 1996
Cleveland vs. Boston, 1998
5-game series
A.L.—11—Boston vs. Cleveland, 1999
Cleveland vs. Boston, 1999
Oakland vs. New York, 2001
Minnesota vs. Oakland, 2002
N.L.—11—San Francisco vs. Atlanta, 2002
Chicago vs. Atlanta, 2003
Atlanta vs. Houston, 2004

For a list of players and pitchers used each series, see page 385.

Most pitchers used by both clubs, series
3-game series
A.L.—19—Boston 10, Cleveland 9, 1995
N.L.—18—St. Louis 9, Atlanta 9, 2000
Arizona 10, St. Louis 8, 2002
4-game series
N.L.—21—Colorado 11, Atlanta 10, 1995
New York 11, Arizona 10, 1999
San Francisco 11, New York 10, 2000
San Francisco 12, Florida 9, 2003
St. Louis 11, Los Angeles 10, 2004
A.L.—21—Texas 11, New York 10, 1996
Cleveland 11, Boston 10, 1998

5-game series
A.L.—22—Boston 11, Cleveland 11, 1999.
N.L.—21—San Francisco 11, Atlanta 10, 2002
Chicago 11, Atlanta 10, 2003
Atlanta 11, Houston 10, 2004

Fewest pitchers, series
N.L.—5—Atlanta vs. Houston, 1997 (3-game series)
A.L.—5—Texas vs. New York, 1998 (3-game series)
New York vs. Texas, 1999 (3-game series)

Fewest pitchers used by both clubs, series
A.L.—11—New York 6, Texas 5, 1998 (3-game series)
N.L.—14—Los Angeles 8, Cincinnati 6, 1995 (3-game series)
Houston 9, Atlanta 5, 1997 (3-game series)
San Francisco 8, Florida 6, 1997 (3-game series)

Most pitchers used by winning club, game
A.L.—6—Seattle vs. New York, October 7, 1995
Cleveland vs. Baltimore, October 4, 1996
Cleveland vs. Boston, October 3, 1998
Boston vs. Cleveland, October 10, 1999
(7—Cleveland vs. Boston, October 3, 1995, 13 inn
New York vs. Texas, October 2, 1996, 12 inn)
N.L.—5—many clubs
(7—Colorado vs. Atlanta, October 6, 1995, 10 inn
Atlanta vs. Houston, October 8, 1999, 12 inn)

Most pitchers used by losing club, game
A.L.—8—Texas vs. New York, October 5, 1996
N.L.—8—San Francisco vs. Atlanta, October 5, 2002

Most pitchers used by both clubs, game
N.L.—14—San Francisco 7, Florida 7, October 1, 2003
A.L.—13—Texas 8, New York 5, October 5, 1996
(14—Boston 7, Cleveland 7, October 3, 1995, 13 inn)

Most pitchers, inning
N.L.—4—Los Angeles vs. Cincinnati, October 6, 1995, 6th
Colorado vs. Atlanta, October 6, 1995, 7th
Atlanta vs. Houston, October 9, 1999, 8th
San Francisco vs. Atlanta, October 5, 2002, 9th
A.L.—4—New York vs. Texas, October 2, 1996, 12th
Boston vs. Cleveland, October 10, 1999, 5th
Boston vs. Anaheim, October 8, 2004, 7th

SERIES

Most series played
A.L.—10—New York, 1995 through 2004; won 7, lost 3
N.L.—10—Atlanta, 1995 through 2004; won 6, lost 4

For a complete list of series won and lost by teams, see page 381.

DIVISION SERIES   Individual batting

INDIVIDUAL BATTING

GAMES

Most games, career
A.L.—42—Bernie Williams, New York, 1995 through 2004; 10 series
N.L.—38—Chipper Jones, Atlanta, 1995 through 2004; 10 series

Most games with one club, career
A.L.—42—Bernie Williams, New York, 1995 through 2004; 10 series
N.L.—38—Chipper Jones, Atlanta, 1995 through 2004; 10 series

Most games by pinch-hitter, career
Both leagues—9—John Vander Wal, Colorado N.L., 1995; San Diego N.L., 1998; New York A.L., 2002 (9 PA, 9 AB)
N.L.—7—John Vander Wal, Colorado, 1995; San Diego, 1998 (7 PA, 7 AB)
A.L.—4—Olmedo Saenz, Oakland, 2000, 2001 (4 PA, 4 AB)

Most games by pinch-hitter, series
N.L.—5—Orlando Palmeiro, Houston, 2004 (5-game series)
Dewayne Wise, Atlanta, 2004 (5-game series)
A.L.—3—Midre Cummings, Boston, 1998 (4-game series)

Olmedo Saenz, Oakland, 2001 (5-game series)
Randy Velarde, Oakland, 2002 (5-game series)
Matthew LeCroy, Minnesota, 2004 (4-game series)
Jose Offerman, Minnesota, 2004 (4-game series)

Most games by pinch-runner, career
A.L.—4—Andy Fox, New York, 1996, 1997; 2 series
Damon Buford, Texas, 1996; Boston, 1998; 2 series
N.L.—3—Joe McEwing, New York, 2000; 1 series

Most games by pinch-runner, series
N.L.—4—Mike Lamb, Houston, 2004 (5-game series)
A.L.—3—Pat Kelly, New York, 1995 (5-game series)
Manny Alexander, Baltimore, 1996 (4-game series)
Mike Devereaux, Baltimore, 1996 (4-game series)
Jose Offerman, Minnesota, 2004 (4-game series)

BATTING AVERAGE

Highest batting average, career (50 or more PA)
A.L.—.400—Mike Stanley, New York, 1995, 1997; Boston, 1998, 1999; 4 series, 15 G, 55 AB, 22 H
N.L.—.404—Fernando Vina, St. Louis, 2000 through 2002; 3 series, 11 G, 47 AB, 19 H

For a list of batting leaders each series and a complete list of .500 hitters, see page 382.

Highest batting average, series (10 or more PA)
3-game series
A.L.—.600—Luis Alicea, Boston, 1995
N.L.—.600—Fernando Vina, St. Louis, 2002
4-game series
N.L.—.588—Dante Bichette, Colorado, 1995
A.L.—.500—Derek Jeter, New York, 2002
5-game series
A.L.—.600—Ichiro Suzuki, Seattle, 2001
N.L.—.526—Andruw Jones, Atlanta, 2004

ON-BASE PERCENTAGE

Highest on-base percentage, career (50 or more PA)
A.L.—.481—Edgar Martinez, Seattle, 1995, 1997, 2000, 2001; 4 series, 17 G, 64 AB, 24 H, 2 BB
N.L.—.451—Fernando Vina, St. Louis, 2000-2002; 3 series, 11 G, 47 AB, 19 H, 2 BB, 2 HP, 1 SH

Highest on-base percentage, series (10 or more PA)
3-game series
N.L.—.714—Gary Sheffield, Florida, 1997
A.L.—.688—David Ortiz, Boston, 2004
4-game series
N.L.—.611—Dante Bichette, Colorado, 1995
A.L.—.571—Mike Bordick, Baltimore, 1997
5-game series
A.L.—.667—Edgar Martinez, Seattle, 1995
N.L.—.571—Andruw Jones, Atlanta, 2004

SLUGGING AVERAGE

Highest slugging average, career (50 or more PA)
A.L.—.781—Edgar Martinez, Seattle, 1995, 1997, 2000, 2001; 4 series, 17 G, 64 AB, 24 H, 5 doubles, 7 HR, 50 TB
N.L.—.737—Jim Edmonds, St. Louis, 1999, 2000-2001, 2004; 4 series, 15 G, 57 AB, 19 H, 5 doubles, 6 HR, 42 TB

Highest slugging average, series (10 or more PA)
3-game series
N.L.—1.286—Jim Edmonds, St. Louis, 2000
A.L.—1.091—Troy Glaus, Anaheim, 2004
4-game series
A.L.—1.375—Juan Gonzalez, Texas, 1996
N.L.—1.300—Jim Leyritz, San Diego, 1998
5-game series
N.L.—1.091—Carlos Beltran, Houston, 2004
A.L.—1.083—Nomar Garciaparra, Boston, 1999

AT-BATS AND PLATE APPEARANCES

Most at-bats, career
A.L.—161—Bernie Williams, New York, 1995 through 2004; 10 series, 42 G
N.L.—134—Chipper Jones, Atlanta, 1995 through 2004; 10 series, 38 G

Most at-bats by pinch-hitter, career
Both leagues—9—John Vander Wal, Colorado N.L., 1995; San Diego N.L., 1998; New York A.L., 2002; 3 series, 9 G
N.L.—7—John Vander Wal, Colorado, 1995; San Diego, 1998; 2 series, 7 G
A.L.—4—Olmedo Saenz, Oakland, 2000, 2001; 2 series, 4 G

Most plate appearances by pinch-hitter, career
Both leagues—9—John Vander Wal, Colorado N.L., 1995; San Diego N.L., 1998; New York A.L., 2002; 3 series, 9 G
N.L.—7—John Vander Wal, Colorado, 1995; San Diego, 1998; 2 series, 7 G
A.L.—4—Olmedo Saenz, Oakland, 2000, 2001; 2 series, 4 G

Most consecutive hitless times at bat, career
A.L.—19—Joey Cora, Seattle, 1997 (last 9 AB); Cleveland, 1998 (all 10 AB)

N.L.—17—Tim Wallach, Los Angeles, 1995 (last 6 AB), 1996 (all 11 AB)

Most at-bats, series
3-game series
A.L.—15—Mike Greenwell, Boston, 1995
Johnny Damon, Boston, 2004
N.L.—15—Brett Butler, Los Angeles, 1995
Fernando Vina, St. Louis, 2002
4-game series
N.L.—21—Marquis Grissom, Atlanta, 1995
A.L.—20—Jacque Jones, Minnesota, 2004
Shannon Stewart, Minnesota, 2004
5-game series
A.L.—24—Jay Buhner, Seattle, 1995
Don Mattingly, New York, 1995
N.L.—24—Rafael Furcal, Atlanta, 2002
Marcus Giles, Atlanta, 2004

Most at-bats by pinch-hitter, series
N.L.—5—Dewayne Wise, Atlanta, 2004 (5-game series)
A.L.—3—Midre Cummings, Boston, 1998 (4-game series)
Jose Offerman, Minnesota, 2004 (4-game series)
Olmedo Saenz, Oakland, 2001 (5-game series)
Bobby Kielty, Minnesota, 2002 (5-game series)
Randy Velarde, Oakland, 2002 (5-game series)

Most at-bats by player with no hits, career
A.L.—13—Jose Canseco, Boston, 1995
N.L.—11—Tino Martinez, 2003
Jose Cruz, 2003
Robert Fick, 2003

Most at-bats, game
N.L.—6—Marquis Grissom, Atlanta, October 4, 1995
Fernando Vina, St. Louis, October 1, 2002
(6—many players in extra innings)
A.L.—6—Brian Daubach, Boston, October 10, 1999
Mike Stanley, Boston, October 10, 1999
Juan Gonzalez, Cleveland, October 13, 2001
Jim Thome, Cleveland, October 13, 2001
Omar Vizquel, Cleveland, October 13, 2001.
(7—Luis Sojo, Seattle, October 4, 1995, 15 inn
Tino Martinez, Seattle, October 4, 1995, 15 inn
Ruben Sierra, New York, October 4, 1995, 15 inn)

Most at-bats by player with no hits, game
A.L.—6—Brian Daubach, Boston, October 10, 1999
N.L.—5—many players

Most at-bats, inning
A.L.-N.L.—2—many players

Most times faced pitcher, inning
A.L.-N.L.—2—many players

RUNS

Most runs, career
A.L.—34—Bernie Williams, New York, 1995 through 2004; 10 series, 42 G
N.L.—27—Chipper Jones, Atlanta, 1995 through 2004; 10 series, 38 G

Most runs by pinch-hitter, career
N.L.—2—Turner Ward, Arizona, 1999; 1 series, 2 G
A.L.—1—many players

Most runs by pinch-runner, career
A.L.—2—Pat Kelly, New York, 1995; 1 series, 3 G
N.L.—1—many players

Most runs, series
3-game series
N.L.—5—Hal Morris, Cincinnati, 1995
Charles Johnson, Florida, 1997
Jim Edmonds, St. Louis, 2000
Edgar Renteria, St. Louis, 2000
A.L.—4—Dwayne Murphy, Oakland, 1995
Johnny Damon, Boston, 2004
David Ortiz, Boston, 2004

4-game series
N.L.—6—Dante Bichette, Colorado, 1995
Edgardo Alfonzo, New York, 1999
Larry Walker, St. Louis, 2004
A.L.—6—Derek Jeter, New York, 2002
5-game series
A.L.—9—Ken Griffey Jr., Seattle, 1995
N.L.—9—Carlos Beltran, Houston, 2004

Most runs by pinch-hitter, series
A.L.-N.L.—1—many players

Most runs by pinch-runner, series
A.L.—2—Pat Kelly, New York, 1995 (5-game series)
N.L.—1—many players

Most runs, game
A.L.—5—Jason Varitek, Boston, October 10, 1999
N.L.—3—many players

Most runs, inning
A.L.—2—Shawn Wooten, Anaheim, October 5, 2002, 5th
N.L.—1—many players

HITS
CAREER AND SERIES

Most hits, career
A.L.—52—Derek Jeter, New York, 1996 through 2004; 9 series, 37 G
N.L.—38—Chipper Jones, Atlanta, 1995 through 2004; 10 series, 38 G

Most hits by pinch-hitter, career
N.L.—3—Greg Colbrunn, Atlanta, 1997, 1998; Arizona, 2001; 3 series, 6 G
A.L.—2—Randy Velarde, Oakland, 2002; 1 series, 3 G

Most hits, series
3-game series
N.L.—9—Fernando Vina, St. Louis, 2002
A.L.—7—Johnny Damon, Boston, 2004
4-game series
N.L.—11—Marquis Grissom, Atlanta, 1995
A.L.—8—Cal Ripken, Baltimore, 1996
Darin Erstad, Anaheim, 2002
Derek Jeter, New York, 2002, 2004
5-game series
A.L.—12—Edgar Martinez, Seattle, 1995
Ichiro Suzuki, Seattle, 2001
N.L.—10—Moises Alou, Chicago, 2003
Carlos Beltran, Houston, 2004
Andruw Jones, Atlanta, 2004

Most hits by pinch-hitter, series
N.L.—2—many players
A.L.—2—Randy Velarde, Oakland, 2002

Most hits, two consecutive series
A.L.—16—Bernie Williams, New York, 1995 (9), 1996 (7)
Derek Jeter, New York, 2001 (8), 2002 (8)
N.L.—15—Fernando Vina, St. Louis, 2001 (6), 2002 (9)

Most series with one or more hits
N.L.—8—Chipper Jones, Atlanta, 1995 through 2002
A.L.—7—Tino Martinez, Seattle, 1995; New York, 1996 through 2001
Paul O'Neill, New York, 1995 through 2001
Bernie Williams, New York, 1995 through 2002, except 1998
Derek Jeter, New York, 1996 through 2002

Most consecutive hits, career
A.L.—5—Derek Jeter, New York, October 1 (2), 2 (3), 2002 (2 BB during streak)
N.L.—5—Marquis Grissom, Atlanta, October 7 (5), 1995
Chad Fonville, Los Angeles, October 3 (1), 4 (4), 1995 (1 SH during streak)
Andruw Jones, Atlanta, October 9 (2), 10 (3), 2001
Moises Alou, Chicago, October 3 (2), 4 (3), 2003

Most consecutive hits by pinch-hitter, career
N.L.—2—Chris Gwynn, San Diego, October 1, 3, 1996
Darryl Hamilton, New York, October 5, 7, 2000
Greg Colbrunn, Arizona, October 10, 12, 2001

A.L.—2—Randy Velarde, Oakland, October 1, 4, 2002

Most consecutive hits, series
A.L.—5—Derek Jeter, New York, October 1 (2), 2 (3), 2002 (2 BB during streak)
N.L.—5—Marquis Grissom, Atlanta, October 7 (5), 1995
Chad Fonville, Los Angeles, October 3 (1), 4 (4), 1995 (1 SH during streak)
Andruw Jones, Atlanta, October 9 (2), 10 (3), 2001
Moises Alou, Chicago, October 3 (2), 4 (3), 2003

GAME AND INNING

Most hits, game
N.L.—5—Marquis Grissom, Atlanta, October 7, 1995
A.L.—5—Mike Stanley, Boston, October 10, 1999

Most times reached base safely, game (batting 1.000)
N.L.—5—Marquis Grissom, Atlanta, October 7, 1995 (4 singles, 1 double)
A.L.—5—Johnny Damon, Oakland, October 10, 2001 (4 singles, 1 BB)

Most hits accounting for all club's hits, game
A.L.—2—Ivan Rodriguez, Texas, October 5, 1999
N.L.—1—Ken Caminiti, Houston, October 6, 1999
Jeff Kent, San Francisco, October 8, 2000

Most consecutive games with one or more hits, career
A.L.—12—Derek Jeter, New York, 2002 (all 4), 2003 (all 4), 2004 (all 4)
N.L.—10—Edgardo Alfonzo, New York, 1999 (last 2), 2000 (all 4); San Francisco, 2003 (all 4)

Most hits in two consecutive games, series (18 inn)
N.L.—7—Fernando Vina, St. Louis, October 1 (3), 2 (4), 2002
A.L.—6—John Valentin, Boston, October 9 (2), 10 (4), 1999
Johnny Damon, Oakland, October 10 (4), 11 (2), 2001
Juan Gonzalez, Cleveland, October 13 (4), 14 (2), 2001
Omar Vizquel, Cleveland, October 13 (4), 14 (2), 2001
Ichiro Suzuki, Seattle, October 14 (3), 15 (3), 2001

Most hits in two consecutive games, series (more than 18 inn)
N.L.—7—Marquis Grissom, Atlanta, October 6, 10 inn (2), 7 (5), 1995
A.L.—6—Edgar Martinez, Seattle, October 3 (3), 4, 15 inn (3), 1995
Edgar Martinez, Seattle, October 7 (3), 8, 11 inn (3), 1995
Jay Buhner, Seattle, October 7 (3), 8, 11 inn (3), 1995
Alex Rodriguez, New York, October 5 (2), 6, 12 inn (4), 2004

Most hits, inning
A.L.—2—Chuck Knoblauch, New York, October 8, 2000, 1st
Doug Mientkiewicz, Minnesota, October 5, 2002, 4th
Shawn Wooten, Anaheim, October 5, 2002, 5th
Benji Gil, Anaheim, October 5, 2002, 5th
N.L.—1—many players

SINGLES

Most singles, career
A.L.—40—Derek Jeter, New York, 1996 through 2004; 9 series, 37 G
N.L.—27—Chipper Jones, Atlanta, 1995 through 2004; 10 series, 38 G

Most singles by pinch-hitter, career
N.L.—3—Greg Colbrunn, Atlanta, 1997, 1998; Arizona, 2001; 3 series, 6 G
A.L.—1—many players

Most singles, series
3-game series
N.L.—9—Fernando Vina, St. Louis, 2002
A.L.—6—Johnny Damon, Boston, 2004
4-game series
A.L.—7—Michael Cuddyer, Minnesota, 2004
N.L.—6—Dante Bichette, Colorado, 1995
Marquis Grissom, Atlanta, 1995
Ryan Klesko, Atlanta, 1995

5-game series
A.L.—11—Ichiro Suzuki, Seattle, 2001
N.L.—9—Moises Alou, Chicago, 2003

Most singles by pinch-hitter, series
N.L.—2—Dave Hansen, Los Angeles, 1995 (3-game series)
Chris Gwynn, San Diego, 1996 (3-game series)
Greg Colbrunn, Arizona, 2001 (5-game series)
A.L.—1—many players

Most singles, game
N.L.—4—Chad Fonville, Los Angeles, October 4, 1995
Marquis Grissom, Atlanta, October 7, 1995
Fernando Vina, St. Louis, October 3, 2002
A.L.—4—Johnny Damon, Oakland, October 10, 2001
Jason Giambi, Oakland, October 15, 2001

Most singles, inning
A.L.—2—Chuck Knoblauch, New York, October 8, 2000, 1st
Doug Mientkiewicz, Minnesota, October 5, 2002, 4th
Benji Gil, Anaheim, October 5, 2002, 5th
N.L.—1—many players

DOUBLES

Most doubles, career
A.L.—14—Bernie Williams, New York, 1995 through 2004; 10 series, 42 G
N.L.—7—Edgardo Alfonzo, New York, 1999, 2000; San Francisco, 2003; 3 series, 12 G

Most doubles by pinch-hitter, career
N.L.-A.L.—1—many players

Most doubles, series
3-game series
N.L.—4—Jim Edmonds, St. Louis, 2000
A.L.—2—many players
4-game series
A.L.—4—David Justice, Cleveland, 1998
N.L.—4—Edgardo Alfonzo, San Francisco, 2003
5-game series
A.L.—4—Don Mattingly, New York, 1995
Roberto Alomar, Cleveland, 1999
Torii Hunter, Minnesota, 2002
N.L.—3—Jeff Kent, Houston, 2004

Most doubles, game
N.L.—3—Jim Edmonds, St. Louis, October 5, 2000
A.L.—2—many players

Most doubles, inning
A.L.-N.L.—1—many players

TRIPLES

Most triples, career
A.L.—2—Omar Vizquel, Cleveland, 1995 through 1999, 2001; 6 series, 26 G
David Justice, Cleveland, 1997 through 1999; New York, 2000, 2001; Oakland, 2002; 6 series, 26 G
N.L.—2—Rafael Furcal, Atlanta, 2000, 2002 through 2004; 4 series, 18 G
Tony Womack, Arizona, 1999, 2001, 2002; St. Louis, 2004; 4 series, 16 G

Most triples by pinch-hitter, career
N.L.—1—John Vander Wal, Colorado, 1995; San Diego, 1998; 2 series, 7 G
A.L.—none

Most triples, series and game
A.L.-N.L.—1—many players

Most bases-loaded triples, game
A.L.—1—David Justice, Oakland, October 2, 2002, 4th inn
N.L.—none

HOME RUNS
CAREER AND SERIES

Most home runs, career
A.L.—8—Juan Gonzalez, Texas, 1996, 1998, 1999; Cleveland, 2001; 4 series, 15 G

Jim Thome, Cleveland, 1995 through 1999, 2001; 6 series, 25 G
Bernie Williams, New York, 1995 through 2004; 10 series, 42 G
N.L.—8—Chipper Jones, Atlanta, 1995 through 2004; 10 series, 38 G

For a list of all home runs each series, and a complete list of players with four or more career home runs, see page 382.

Most home runs, series
3-game series
N.L.—3—Ken Caminiti, San Diego, 1996
A.L.—2—Shane Spencer, New York, 1998
Troy Glaus, Anaheim, 2004
4-game series
A.L.—5—Juan Gonzalez, Texas, 1995
N.L.—3—many players
5-game series
A.L.—5—Ken Griffey Jr., Seattle, 1995
N.L.—4—Carlos Beltran, Houston, 2004

Most series with one or more home runs
N.L.—5—Chipper Jones, Atlanta, 1995 (2), 1996 (1), 1997 (1), 2001 (2), 2003 (2)
A.L.—5—Bernie Williams, New York, 1995 (2), 1996 (3), 1999 (1), 2002 (1), 2004 (1)

Most series with two or more home runs
A.L.—3—Edgar Martinez, Seattle, 1995 (2), 1997 (2), 2001 (2)
N.L.—3—Chipper Jones, Atlanta, 1995 (2), 2001 (2), 2003 (2)

GAME AND INNING

Most home runs, game
N.L.—2—Chipper Jones, Atlanta, October 3, 1995
Eric Karros, Los Angeles, October 4, 1995
Marquis Grissom, Atlanta, October 4, 1995
Fred McGriff, Atlanta, October 7, 1995
Ken Caminiti, San Diego, October 5, 1996
Jeff Kent, San Francisco, October 3, 1997
Edgardo Alfonzo, New York, October 5, 1999
Chipper Jones, Atlanta, October 4, 2003
Eric Karros, Chicago, October 4, 2003
Larry Walker, St. Louis, October 5, 2004
Shawn Green, Los Angeles, October 9, 2004
Carlos Beltran, Houston, October 11, 2004
A.L.—2—Ken Griffey Jr., Seattle, October 3, 1995
Bernie Williams, New York, October 6, 1995
Edgar Martinez, Seattle, October 7, 1995
B.J. Surhoff, Baltimore, October 1, 1996
Juan Gonzalez, Texas, October 2, 1996
Bernie Williams, New York, October 5, 1996
Mo Vaughn, Boston, September 29, 1998
Manny Ramirez, Cleveland, October 2, 1998
John Valentin, Boston, October 10, 1999
Jim Thome, Cleveland, October 11, 1999
Troy O'Leary, Boston, October 11, 1999
Terrence Long, Oakland, October 10, 2001
Troy Glaus, Anaheim, October 1, 2002
Todd Walker, Boston, October 1, 2003

Most grand slams, game
A.L.—1—Edgar Martinez, Seattle, October 7, 1995, 8th inn
Bobby Bonilla, Baltimore, October 1, 1996, 6th inn
Albert Belle, Cleveland, October 4, 1996, 7th inn
Paul O'Neill, New York, October 4, 1997, 4th inn
Jim Thome, Cleveland, October 7, 1999, 4th inn
Troy O'Leary, Boston, October 11, 1999, 3rd inn
Vlad Guerrero, Anaheim, October 9, 2004, 7th inn
N.L.—1—Mark Lewis, Cincinnati, October 6, 1995, 6th inn
Devon White, Florida, October 3, 1997, 6th inn
Ryan Klesko, Atlanta, September 30, 1998, 7th inn
Eddie Perez, Atlanta, October 3, 1998, 8th inn
Edgardo Alfonzo, New York, October 5, 1999, 9th inn

Inside-the-park home runs
A.L.—Ray Durham, Oakland, October 4, 2002, 1st inn
N.L.—none

Home runs by pinch-hitter, game
N.L.—Mark Lewis, Cincinnati, October 6, 1995, 6th inn
  Jim Leyritz, San Diego, October 1, 1998, 9th inn
  Turner Ward, Arizona, October 8, 1999, 5th inn
  Mark McGwire, St. Louis, October 5, 2000, 8th inn
  J.T. Snow, San Francisco, October 5, 2000, 9th inn
  Daryle Ward, Houston, October 12, 2001, 7th inn
A.L.—David Justice, New York, October 15, 2001, 6th inn

Home runs by leadoff batter, start of game
N.L.—Marquis Grissom, Atlanta, October 4, 1995 (at Colorado)
  Fernando Vina, St. Louis, October 7, 2000 (at Atlanta)
A.L.—Brady Anderson, Baltimore, October 1, 1996 (at Baltimore)
  Ray Durham, Oakland, October 4, 2002 (at Minnesota)
  Derek Jeter, New York, October 6, 2004 (at New York)

Home runs winning 1-0 games
A.L.—Jorge Posada, New York, October 13, 2001, 5th inn
N.L.—none

Most home runs by pitcher, game
A.L.-N.L.—none

Most home runs by rookie, game
N.L.—2—Chipper Jones, Atlanta, October 3, 1995

Hitting home runs from both sides of plate, game
A.L.—Bernie Williams, New York, October 6, 1995
  Bernie Williams, New York, October 5, 1996
N.L.—none

Most consecutive games hitting one or more home runs, career
A.L.—4—Juan Gonzalez, Texas, October 1, 2 (2 in 12 inn), 4, 5, 1996
N.L.—3—Jim Leyritz, San Diego, October 1, 3, 4, 1998
  Vinny Castilla, Colorado, October 6, 7, 1995; Atlanta, October 9, 2001

Most consecutive games hitting one or more home runs, series
A.L.—4—Juan Gonzalez, Texas, October 1, 2 (2 in 12 inn), 4, 5, 1996
N.L.—3—Jim Leyritz, San Diego, October 1, 3, 4, 1998

Most home runs in two consecutive games, series (homering each game)
A.L.—3—Ken Griffey, Jr., Seattle, October 3 (2), 4, (1 in 15 inn), 1995
  Juan Gonzalez, Texas, October 1 (1), 2, (2 in 12 inn), 1996
  Juan Gonzalez, Texas, October 2, (2 in 12 inn), 4 (1), 1996
  Bernie Williams, New York, October 4 (1), 5 (2), 1996
  John Valentin, Boston, October 9 (1), 10 (2), 1999
  Troy Glaus, Anaheim, October 1 (2), 2 (1), 2002
N.L.—3—Marquis Grissom, Atlanta, October 3 (1), 4 (2), 1995
  Ken Caminiti, San Diego, October 3 (1), 5 (2), 1996
  Shawn Green, Los Angeles, October 7 (1), 9 (2), 2004

Most home runs in three consecutive games, series (homering each game)
A.L.—4—Juan Gonzalez, Texas, October 1 (1), 2 (2 in 12 inn), 4 (1), 1996
N.L.—3—Jim Leyritz, San Diego, October 1, 3, 4, 1998

Most home runs in four consecutive games, series (homering each game)
A.L.—5—Juan Gonzalez, Texas, October 1 (1), 2 (2 in 12 inn), 4 (1), 5 (1), 1996
N.L.—none

Hitting home run in first division series at-bat (*not first plate appearance)
N.L.—Benito Santiago, Cincinnati, October 3, 1995, 1st inn
  Edgardo Alfonzo, New York, October 5, 1999, 1st inn
  Mark McGwire, St. Louis, October 5, 2000, 8th inn*
A.L.—Brady Anderson, Baltimore, October 1, 1996, 1st inn
  Harold Baines, Baltimore, October 2, 1997, 2nd inn
  Shane Spencer, New York, September 30, 1998, 2nd inn
  Todd Walker, Boston, October 1, 2003, 1st inn

Hitting home runs in first two division series at-bats
A.L.-N.L.—none

Most home runs, inning
A.L.-N.L.—1—many players

Most home runs, two consecutive innings
A.L.—2—Juan Gonzalez, Texas, October 2, 1996, 2nd and 3rd

N.L.—none

Most total bases, career
A.L.—85—Bernie Williams, New York, 1995 through 2004; 10 series, 42 G
N.L.—65—Chipper Jones, Atlanta, 1995 through 2004; 10 series, 38 G

Most total bases by pinch-hitter, career
N.L.—4—many players
A.L.—4—David Justice, New York, 2001; 1 series, 1 G
  Trot Nixon, Boston, 2003; 1 series, 1 G

Most total bases, series
3-game series
  N.L.—18—Jim Edmonds, St. Louis, 2000
  A.L.—12—Troy Glaus, Anaheim, 2004
4-game series
  A.L.—22—Juan Gonzalez, Texas, 1996
  N.L.—22—Marquis Grissom, Atlanta, 1995
5-game series
  A.L.—24—Ken Griffey Jr., Seattle, 1995
  N.L.—24—Carlos Beltran, 2004

Most total bases by pinch-hitter, series
N.L.—6—many players
A.L.—4—David Justice, New York, 2001; 1 G
  Trot Nixon, Boston, 2003, 1G

Most total bases, game
A.L.—11—John Valentin, Boston, October 10, 1999 (1 single, 1 double, 2 HR)
N.L.—10—Eric Karros, Los Angeles, October 4, 1995 (1 double, 2 HR)
  Carlos Beltran, Houston, October 11, 2004 (2 singles, 2 HR)

Most total bases, inning
A.L.—5—Shawn Wooten, Anaheim, October 5, 2002, 5th inn (1 single, 1 HR)
N.L.—4—many players

Most extra base hits, career
A.L.—22—Bernie Williams, New York, 1995 through 2004; 10 series, 42 G
N.L.—11—Chipper Jones, Atlanta, 1995 through 2004; 10 series, 38 G
  Edgardo Alfonzo, New York, 1999, 2000; San Francisco, 2003; 3 series, 12 G
  Jim Edmonds, St. Louis, 2000 through 2002, 2004; 4 series, 15 G

Most extra base hits, series
3-game series
  N.L.—6—Jim Edmonds, St. Louis, 2000
  A.L.—4—Troy Glaus, Anaheim, 2004
4-game series
  A.L.—5—Juan Gonzalez, Texas, 1996
    David Justice, Cleveland, 1998
  N.L.—5—Marquis Grissom, Atlanta, 1995
5-game series
  A.L.—5—many players
  N.L.—6—Carlos Beltran, Houston, 2004

Most extra base hits, game
N.L.—3—Eric Karros, Los Angeles, October 4, 1995 (1 double, 2 HR)
  Jim Edmonds, St. Louis, October 5, 2000 (3 doubles)
A.L.—3—Mo Vaughn, Boston, September 29, 1998 (1 double, 2 HR)
  John Valentin, Boston, October 10, 1999 (1 double, 2 HR)
  Jason Varitek, Boston, October 10, 1999 (2 doubles, 1 HR)
  Juan Gonzalez, Cleveland, October 13, 2001 (2 doubles, 1 HR)

DIVISION SERIES Individual batting

Troy Glaus, Anaheim, October 5, 2004 (2 doubles, 1 HR)
David Ortiz, Boston, October 8, 2004 (2 doubles, 1 HR)

Most extra base hits in two consecutive games, series
A.L.—5—John Valentin, Boston, October 9 (double and HR),
October 10 (double and 2 HR), 1999
Juan Gonzalez, Cleveland, October 13 (2 doubles and 1 HR),
October 14 (double and HR), 2001
N.L.—5—Jim Edmonds, St. Louis, October 5 (3 doubles),
October 7 (double and HR), 2000

Most extra base hits, inning
A.L.-N.L.—1—many players

RUNS BATTED IN

Most runs batted in, career
A.L.—32—Bernie Williams, New York, 1995 through 2004; 10
series, 42 G
N.L.—24—Chipper Jones, Atlanta, 1995 through 2004; 10
series, 38 G

Most runs batted in by pinch-hitter, career
N.L.—5—Mark Lewis, Cincinnati, 1995; 1 series, 2 G
A.L.—2—B.J. Surhoff, Baltimore, 1996, 1997; 2 series, 2 G

Most runs batted in, series
3-game series
N.L.—7—Jim Edmonds, St. Louis, 2000
A.L.—7—Manny Ramirez, Boston, 2004
4-game series
A.L.—9—Juan Gonzalez, Texas, 1996
N.L.—8—Ken Caminiti, Houston, 1999
5-game series
A.L.—12—John Valentin, Boston, 1999
N.L.—9—Carlos Beltran, Houston, 2004

Most runs batted in by pinch-hitter, series
N.L.—5—Mark Lewis, Cincinnati, 1995; 2 G
A.L.—2—B.J.Surhoff, Baltimore, 1997; 1 G

Most runs batted in, game
A.L.—7—Edgar Martinez, Seattle, October 7, 1995
Mo Vaughn, Boston, September 29, 1998
John Valentin, Boston, October 10, 1999
Troy O'Leary, Boston, October 11, 1999
N.L.—5—Fred McGriff, Atlanta, October 7, 1995
Edgardo Alfonzo, New York, October 5, 1999
Steve Finley, Arizona, October 6, 1999
Carlos Beltran, Houston, October 11, 2004
(5—Brian Jordan, Atlanta, October 8, 1999, 12 inn)

Most runs batted in by pinch-hitter, game
N.L.—4—Mark Lewis, Cincinnati, October 6, 1995
A.L.—2—B.J. Surhoff, Baltimore, October 1, 1997

Most consecutive games with one or more runs batted in, career
N.L.—7—Edgardo Alfonzo, October 5, 2000 through October 4,
2003
A.L.—5—Nomar Garciaparra, Boston, September 29, 1998
through October 6, 1999

Most runs batted in accounting for all club's runs, game
N.L.—5—Brian Jordan, October 8, 1999, 12 inn
A.L.—4—Juan Gonzalez, Texas, October 2, 1996, 12 inn

Most runs batted in, inning
A.L.—4—many players
N.L.—4—Mark Lewis, Cincinnati, October 6, 1995, 6th
Devon White, Florida, October 3, 1997, 6th
Ryan Klesko, Atlanta, September 30, 1998, 7th
Eddie Perez, Atlanta, October 3, 1998, 8th
Edgardo Alfonzo, New York, October 5, 1999, 9th

BASES ON BALLS

Most bases on balls, career
N.L.—32—Chipper Jones, Atlanta, 1995 through 2004; 10
series, 38 G
A.L.—25—Bernie Williams, New York, 1995 through 2004; 10
series, 42 G

Most bases on balls, series
3-game series
N.L.—5—Gary Sheffield, Florida, 1997

Jeff Bagwell, Houston, 2001
A.L.—5—Mark Bellhorn, Boston, 2004
David Ortiz, Boston, 2004
4-game series
N.L.—8—Barry Bonds, San Francisco, 2003
A.L.—5—Mickey Tettleton, Texas, 1996
5-game series
A.L.—7—Bernie Williams, New York, 1995
Jose Offerman, Boston, 1999
Jason Giambi, Oakland, 2000
N.L.—7—Gary Sheffield, Atlanta, 2002

Most consecutive bases on balls, series
A.L.—4—Edgar Martinez, Seattle, October 6, 1995 (3), October
7 (1), 1995
N.L.—3—Chipper Jones, Atlanta, October 1, 1997
Richard Hidalgo, Houston, October 9, 2001
Gary Sheffield, Atlanta, October 5, 2002
(Jeff Bagwell, Houston, October 8, 1999, 12 inn)

Most bases on balls, game
A.L.—3—many players
(4—Bernie Williams, New York, October 8, 1995, 11 inn)
N.L.—3—many players
(3—Jeff Bagwell, Houston, October 8, 1999, 12 inn)

Most bases on balls with bases filled, game
A.L.-N.L.—1—many players

Bases on balls with bases filled by pinch-hitters, game
A.L.—Jim Leyritz, New York, October 7, 1999, 8th inn
N.L.—none

Most bases on balls, two consecutive games
A.L.—5—Jason Giambi, Oakland, October 6 (2), 7 (3), 2000
Bernie Williams, New York, October 7 (1), 8 (4 in 11 inn),
1995
David Ortiz, Boston, October 5 (2), 6 (3), 2004
N.L.—5—Barry Bonds, San Francisco, September 30 (3),
October 1 (2), 2003

Most bases on balls, inning
A.L.-N.L.—1—many players

STRIKEOUTS

Most strikeouts, career
A.L.—34—Jim Thome, Cleveland, 1995 through 1999, 2001; 6
series, 25 G
N.L.—26—Chipper Jones, Atlanta, 1995 through 2004; 10
series, 38 G

Most strikeouts, series
3-game series
N.L.—9—Reggie Sanders, Cincinnati, 1995
A.L.—7—Mo Vaughn, Boston, 1995
4-game series
A.L.—9—Dan Wilson, Seattle, 1997
N.L.—9—Jim Edmonds, St. Louis, 2004
5-game series
A.L.—11—Bret Boone, Seattle, 2001
N.L.—7—Jeff Kent, San Francisco, 2002
Andruw Jones, Atlanta, 2003
J.D. Drew, Atlanta, 2004

Most strikeouts by pinch-hitter, series
N.L.—2—John Vander Wal, Colorado, 1995; 4 G
Dave Clark, Los Angeles, 1996; 2 G
Billy Ashley, Los Angeles, 1996; 2 G
Bob Abreu, Houston, 1997; 2 G
Tom Goodwin, San Francisco, 2002; 2 G
A.L.—1—many players

Most consecutive strikeouts, series (consecutive at-bats)
A.L.—6—Dan Wilson, Seattle, October 1 (1), October 2 (4),
October 4 (1), 1997
N.L.—5—Reggie Sanders, Cincinnati, October 6 (5), 1995

Most strikeouts, game
N.L.—5—Reggie Sanders, Cincinnati, October 6, 1995
A.L.—4—Dan Wilson, Seattle, October 2, 1997
Brady Anderson, Baltimore, October 5, 1997

Ben Grieve, Oakland, October 8, 2000
Bret Boone, Seattle, October 13, 2001
(4—Rafael Palmeiro, Baltimore, October 5, 1996, 12 inn
Bobby Bonilla, Baltimore, October 5, 1996, 12 inn
Pete Incaviglia, Baltimore, October 5, 1996, 12 inn
Derek Jeter, New York, October 9, 2004, 11 inn)

Most strikeouts, inning
A.L.-N.L.—1—many players

SACRIFICE HITS

Most sacrifice hits, career
A.L.—4—Omar Vizquel, Cleveland, 1995 through 1999, 2001; 6
series, 26 G
N.L.—3—Placido Polanco, St. Louis, 2000, 2001; 2 series, 8 G
  Mike Matheny, St. Louis, 2000 through 2002, 2004; 4 series,
  11 G
  John Smoltz, Atlanta, 1995 through 1999, 2001 through
  2004; 9 series, 14 G

Most sacrifice hits, series
A.L.—3—Joey Cora, Seattle, 1995; 5 G
N.L.—3—Placido Polanco, St. Louis, 2001; 5 G

Most sacrifice hits, game
N.L.—3—Placido Polanco, St. Louis, October 13, 2001
A.L.—2—Stan Javier, Seattle, October 15, 2001

SACRIFICE FLIES

Most sacrifice flies, career
A.L.—3—Luis Sojo, Seattle, 1995; New York, 1996, 2000; 3
series, 12 G
  Bernie Williams, New York, 1995 through 2004; 10 series, 42 G
N.L.—3—Barry Bonds, San Francisco, 1997, 2000, 2002, 2003;
  4 series, 16 G

Most sacrifice flies, series
A.L.—2—Luis Sojo, Seattle, 1995; 5 G
  Nomar Garciaparra, Boston, 1998; 4 G
  Trot Nixon, Boston, 1999; 5 G
  Adam Kennedy, Anaheim, 2002, 4 G
  Manny Ramirez, Boston, 2004, 3 G
N.L.—1—many players

Most sacrifice flies, game
A.L.-N.L. 1—many players

HIT BY PITCH

Most hit by pitch, career
A.L.—4—Manny Ramirez, Cleveland, 1995 through 1999;

Boston, 2003, 2004; 7 series, 29 G
N.L.—2—Jeff Bagwell, Houston, 1997 through 1999, 2001,
2004; 5 series, 19 G
  Mike Bordick, New York, 2000; 1 series, 4 G

Most hit by pitch, series
A.L.—2—Manny Ramirez, Cleveland, 1998, 4 G
  Tino Martinez, New York, 2001; 5 G
  Raul Mondesi, New York, 2002; 4 G
  Lew Ford, Minnesota, 2004, 3 G
  Cory Koskie, Minnesota, 2004, 4 G
N.L.—2—Craig Biggio, Houston, 1998, 4 G
  Mike Bordick, New York, 2000, 4 G
  Derrek Lee, Florida, 2003; 4 G

Most hit by pitch, game
A.L.—2—Manny Ramirez, Cleveland, September 30, 1998
N.L.—1—many players

GROUNDING INTO DOUBLE PLAYS

Most grounding into double plays, career
A.L.—11—Bernie Williams, New York, 1995 through 2004; 10
series, 42 G
N.L.—6—Chipper Jones, Atlanta, 1995 through 2004; 10
series, 38 G

Most grounding into double plays, series
A.L.—4—Bernie Williams, New York, 2004 (4-game series)
N.L.—2—Chipper Jones, Atlanta, 1995 (4-game series)
  Joe Girardi, Colorado, 1995 (4-game series)
  Ken Caminiti, Houston, 1999 (4-game series)
  Lance Berkman, Houston, 2001 (3-game series)
  Alex Cora, Los Angeles, 2004 (4-game series)

Most grounding into double plays, game
N.L.—2—Chipper Jones, Atlanta, October 3, 1995
  Lance Berkman, Houston, October 10, 2001
  Jeff Kent, Houston, October 10, 2004
A.L.—2—Paul O'Neill, New York, October 4, 1996
  Sandy Alomar Jr., Cleveland, September 30, 1998
  Roberto Alomar, Cleveland, October 15, 2001
  Darin Erstad, Anaheim, October 5, 2002
  Bernie Williams, New York, October 8, 2004

REACHING BASE ON INTERFERENCE

Most times awarded first base on catcher's interference, game
A.L.-N.L.—none

CLUB BATTING

GAMES

Most games, total series
A.L.—42—New York; 10 series, won 26, lost 16
N.L.—38—Atlanta; 10 series, won 24, lost 14

For summaries of series won and lost,
games won and lost, and home and road
games, see page 381. For a yearly list of
batting statistics by teams, see page 384.

BATTING AVERAGE

Highest batting average, series
3-game series
  N.L.—.314—St. Louis vs. Arizona, 2002
  A.L.—.302—Boston vs. Anaheim, 2004
4-game series
  A.L.—.376—Anaheim vs. New York, 2002
  N.L.—.331—Atlanta vs. Colorado, 1995

5-game series
  A.L.—.318—Boston vs. Cleveland, 1999
  N.L.—.322—Houston vs. Atlanta, 2004

Highest batting average by both clubs, series
3-game series
  N.L.—.279—Cincinnati .279, Los Angeles .279, 1995
  A.L.—.266—Boston .302, Anaheim .226, 2004
4-game series
  A.L.—.331—Anaheim .376, New York .281, 2002
  N.L.—.310—Atlanta .331, Colorado .287, 1995
5-game series
  A.L.—.289—Minnesota .291, Oakland .288, 2002
  N.L.—.253—Atlanta .259, San Francisco .247, 2002

Highest batting average by losing club, series
N.L.—.287—Colorado vs. Atlanta, 1995 (4-game series)
A.L.—.281—New York vs. Anaheim, 2002 (4-game series)

Lowest batting average, series
3-game series
  A.L.—.141—Texas vs. New York, 1998
  N.L.—.147—Los Angeles vs. Atlanta, 1996
4-game series
  N.L.—.182—Houston vs. San Diego, 1998

A.L.—.198—Minnesota vs. New York, 2003
5-game series
  N.L.—.191—St. Louis vs. Arizona, 2001
  A.L.—.211—Boston vs. Oakland, 2003

Lowest batting average by both clubs, series
3-game series
  N.L.—.163—Atlanta .180, Los Angeles .147, 1996
  A.L.—.195—New York .235, Texas .152, 1999
4-game series
  N.L.—.199—San Diego .216, Houston .182, 1998
  A.L.—.230—Boston .252, Cleveland .206, 1998
5-game series
  A.L.—.212—Oakland .213, Boston .211, 2003
  N.L.—.214—St. Louis .191, Arizona .237, 2001

Lowest batting average by winning club, series
N.L.—.180—Atlanta vs. Los Angeles, 1996 (3-game series)
A.L.—.206—Cleveland vs. Boston, 1998 (4-game series)

ON-BASE PERCENTAGE

Highest on-base percentage, series
3-game series
  A.L.—.403—Boston vs. Anaheim, 2004
  N.L.—.395—Florida vs. San Francisco, 1997
4-game series
  A.L.—.406—Anaheim vs. New York, 2002
  N.L.—.381—Atlanta vs. Colorado, 1995
5-game series
  A.L.—.391—Seattle vs. New York, 1995
  N.L.—.390—Houston vs. Atlanta, 2004

Highest on-base percentage by both clubs, series
3-game series
  A.L.—.360—Boston .403, Anaheim .311, 2004
  N.L.—.342—St. Louis .370, Atlanta .313, 2000
4-game series
  A.L.—.387—Anaheim .406, New York .367, 2002
  N.L.—.360—Atlanta .381, Colorado .338, 1995
5-game series
  A.L.—.378—Seattle .391, New York .365, 1995
  N.L.—.366—Houston .390, Atlanta .342, 2004

Lowest on-base percentage, series
3-game series
  A.L.—.177—Texas vs. New York, 1998
  N.L.—.204—Los Angeles vs. Atlanta, 1996
4-game series
  A.L.—.248—Minnesota vs. New York, 2003
  N.L.—.277—Houston vs. San Diego, 1998
5-game series
  N.L.—.253—St. Louis vs. Arizona, 2001
  A.L.—.290—Boston vs. Oakland, 2003

Lowest on-base percentage by both clubs, series
3-game series
  N.L.—.242—Atlanta .282, Los Angeles .204, 1996
  A.L.—.246—New York .313, Texas .177, 1998
4-game series
  N.L.—.277—Houston .277, San Diego .277, 1998
  A.L.—.298—New York .344, Minnesota .248, 2003
5-game series
  N.L.—.287—Arizona .320, St. Louis .253, 2001
  A.L.—.300—Oakland .310, Boston .290, 2003

SLUGGING AVERAGE

Highest slugging average, series
3-game series
  N.L.—.545—Atlanta vs. Houston, 2001
  A.L.—.457—Boston vs. Anaheim, 2004
4-game series
  A.L.—.624—Anaheim vs. New York, 2002
  N.L.—.519—Atlanta vs. Colorado, 1995
5-game series
  A.L.—.597—Boston vs. Cleveland, 1999
  N.L.—.572—Houston vs. Atlanta, 2004

Highest slugging average by both clubs, series
3-game series
  N.L.—.432—Atlanta .545, Houston .316, 2001
  A.L.—.414—Boston .457, Anaheim .368, 2004
4-game series
  N.L.—.492—Atlanta .519, Colorado .462, 1995
  A.L.—.549—Anaheim .624, New York .467, 2002
5-game series
  A.L.—.510—Boston .597, Cleveland .417, 1999
  N.L.—.494—Houston .572, Atlanta .417, 2004

Lowest slugging average, series
3-game series
  A.L.—.174—Texas vs. New York, 1998
  N.L.—.208—Houston vs. Atlanta, 1997
4-game series
  N.L.—.248—Houston vs. San Diego, 1998
  A.L.—.282—Minnesota vs. New York, 2003
5-game series
  N.L.—.301—Atlanta vs. Chicago, 2003
  A.L.—.287—Oakland vs. Boston, 2003

Lowest slugging average by both clubs, series
3-game series
  N.L.—.282—Atlanta .359, Houston .208, 1997
  A.L.—.295—New York .378, Texas .207, 1999
4-game series
  A.L.—.335—New York .384, Minnesota .282, 2003
  N.L.—.317—San Diego .384, Houston .248, 1998
5-game series
  N.L.—.328—St. Louis .329, Arizona .327, 2001
  A.L.—.332—Boston .378, Oakland .287, 2003

AT-BATS AND PLATE APPEARANCES

Most at-bats, total series
A.L.—1,439—New York; 10 series, 42 G
N.L.—1,291—Atlanta; 10 series, 38 G

Most at-bats, series
3-game series
  A.L.—116—Boston vs. Anaheim, 2004
  N.L.—111—Los Angeles vs. Cincinnati, 1995
4-game series
  N.L.—154—Atlanta vs. Colorado, 1995
  A.L.—154—New York vs. Minnesota, 2004
5-game series
  A.L.—200—Seattle vs. New York, 1995
  N.L.—180—Atlanta vs. Houston, 2004
               Houston vs. Atlanta, 2004

Most at-bats by both clubs, series
3-game series
  A.L.—228—Boston 114, Cleveland 114, 1995
  N.L.—215—Los Angeles 111, Cincinnati 104, 1995
4-game series
  A.L.—306—New York 154, Minnesota 152, 2004
  N.L.—297—Atlanta 154, Colorado 143, 1995
5-game series
  A.L.—393—Seattle 200, New York 193, 1995
  N.L.—360—Atlanta 180, Houston 180, 2004

Most at-bats by pinch-hitters, series
N.L.—11—Atlanta vs. Colorado, 1995 (4-game series)
  Atlanta vs. San Francisco, 2002 (5-game series)
A.L.—9—Oakland vs. New York, 2001 (5-game series)

Most at-bats by pinch-hitters on both clubs, series
N.L.—20—Atlanta 11, Colorado 9, 1995 (4-game series)
A.L.—13—Oakland 7, Minnesota 6, 2002 (5-game series)

Most plate appearances by pinch-hitters, series
N.L.—11—Atlanta vs. Colorado, 1995 (4-game series)
A.L.—9—Oakland vs. New York, 2001 (5-game series)

Most plate appearances by pinch-hitters on both clubs, series
N.L.—21—Atlanta 11, Colorado 10, 1995 (4-game series)
A.L.—14—Oakland 8, Minnesota 6, 2002 (5-game series)

Fewest at-bats, series
3-game series
  N.L.—89—Atlanta vs. Los Angeles, 1996

A.L.—91—New York vs. Texas, 1998
4-game series
  N.L.—121—Houston vs. San Diego, 1998
  A.L.—126—Cleveland vs. Boston, 1998
5-game series
  N.L.—152—St. Louis vs. Arizona, 2001
  A.L.—158—Seattle vs. Cleveland, 2001

Fewest at-bats by both clubs, series
3-game series
  A.L.—183—Texas 92, New York 91, 1998
  N.L.—184—Los Angeles 95, Atlanta 89, 1996
4-game series
  N.L.—246—San Diego 125, Houston 121, 1998
  A.L.—261—Boston 135, Cleveland 126, 1998
5-game series
  N.L.—308—Arizona 156, St. Louis 152, 2001
  A.L.—331—Cleveland 173, Seattle 158, 2001

Most at-bats by club, game
A.L.—48—Boston vs. Cleveland, October 10, 1999
  (56—Seattle vs. New York, October 4, 1995, 15 inn)
N.L.—42—Florida vs. San Francisco, October 1, 2003
  (49—San Francisco vs. New York, October 7, 2000, 13 inn)

Most at-bats by both clubs, game
A.L.—79—Boston 48, Cleveland 31, October 10, 1999
  (107—Seattle 56, New York 51, October 4, 1995, 15 inn)
N.L.—77—Atlanta 41, Colorado 36, October 4, 1995
  (92—San Francisco 49, New York 43, October 7, 2000, 13 inn)

Most at-bats by pinch-hitters, game
N.L.—4—Atlanta vs. Colorado, October 4, 1995
  Los Angeles vs. Cincinnati, October 6, 1995
  San Diego vs. Houston, October 1, 1998
  New York vs. Arizona, October 6, 1999
  Atlanta vs. St. Louis, October 3, 2000
  San Francisco vs. Florida, October 4, 2003
  (4—Atlanta vs. Houston, October 8, 1999, 12 inn)
A.L.—4—Seattle vs. Cleveland, October 13, 2001
  Oakland vs. New York, October 14, 2001

Most at-bats by pinch-hitters on both clubs, game
N.L.—7—Atlanta 4, Colorado 3, October 4, 1995
A.L.—5—Seattle 4, Cleveland 1, October 13, 2001

Most plate appearances by pinch hitters, game
N.L.—4—Atlanta vs. Colorado, October 4, 1995
  Los Angeles vs. Cincinnati, October 6, 1995
  San Diego vs. Houston, October 1, 1998
  New York vs. Arizona, October 6, 1999
  Atlanta vs. St. Louis, October 3, 2000
  San Francisco vs. Florida, October 4, 2003
  Los Angeles vs. St. Louis, October 5, 2004
  (4—Atlanta vs. Houston, October 8, 1999, 12 inn
  San Francisco vs. New York, October 5, 2000, 10 inn)
A.L.—4—Seattle vs. Cleveland, October 13, 2001
  Oakland vs. New York, October 14, 2001

Most plate appearances by pinch-hitters on both clubs, game
N.L.—7—Atlanta 4, Colorado 3, October 4, 1995
  (7—Atlanta 4, Houston 3, October 8, 1999, 12 inn)
A.L.—5—Seattle 4, Cleveland 1, October 13, 2001
  Oakland 4, New York 1, October 14, 2001

Fewest at-bats, game
N.L.—24—San Diego vs. Houston, October 3, 1998 (batted 8 inn)
A.L.—25—New York vs. Texas, September 29, 1998 (batted 8 inn)
  Chicago vs. Seattle, October 6, 2000

Fewest at-bats by both clubs, game
N.L.—52—Houston 28, San Diego 24, October 3, 1998 (San Diego batted 8 inn)
A.L.—53—Seattle 28, Chicago 25, October 6, 2000

Most at-bats, inning
A.L.—13—Anaheim vs. New York, October 5, 2002, 5th
N.L.—9—Atlanta vs. Houston, October 9, 1999, 6th

Most at-bats by both clubs, inning
A.L.—17—Anaheim 13, New York 4, October 5, 2002, 5th
N.L.—13—Atlanta 7, Colorado 6, October 7, 1995, 3rd

Atlanta 7, Chicago 6, October 3, 1998, 8th
San Francisco 7, Atlanta 6, October 2, 2002, 2nd
Houston 7, Atlanta 6, October 10, 2004, 2nd

Most batters facing pitcher, inning
A.L.—13—Anaheim vs. New York, October 5, 2002, 5th
N.L.—11—St. Louis vs. Arizona, October 1, 2002, 7th

Most batters facing pitcher by both clubs, inning
A.L.—18—Anaheim 13, New York 5, October 5, 2002, 5th
  New York, 12, Minnesota 6, October 5, 2003, 4th
N.L.—16—Atlanta 9, Chicago 7, October 3, 1998, 8th

RUNS
SERIES AND GAMES

Most runs, total series
A.L.—195—New York; 10 series, 42 G
N.L.—175—Atlanta; 10 series, 38 G

Most runs, series
3-game series
  A.L.—25—Boston vs. Anaheim, 2004
  N.L.—24—St. Louis vs. Atlanta, 2000
4-game series
  A.L.—31—Anaheim vs. New York, 2002
  N.L.—27—Atlanta vs. Colorado, 1995
5-game series
  A.L.—47—Boston vs. Cleveland, 1999
  N.L.—36—Houston vs. Atlanta, 2004

Most runs by both clubs, series
3 game series
  A.L.—37—Boston 25, Anaheim 12, 2004
  N.L.—34—St. Louis 24, Atlanta 10, 2000
4-game series
  A.L.—56—Anaheim 31, New York 25, 2002
  N.L.—46—Atlanta 27, Colorado 19, 1995
5-game series
  A.L.—79—Boston 47, Cleveland 32, 1999
  N.L.—57—Houston 36, Atlanta 21, 2004

Most runs by losing club, series
A.L.—33—New York vs. Seattle, 1995 (5-game series)
N.L.—26—Atlanta vs. San Francisco, 2002 (5-game series)

Fewest runs, series
3-game series
  A.L.—1—Texas vs. New York, 1998
        Texas vs. New York, 1999
  N.L.—4—Chicago vs. Atlanta, 1998
4-game series
  A.L.—6—Minnesota vs. New York, 2003
  N.L.—8—Houston vs. San Diego, 1998
5-game series
  N.L.—10—Arizona vs. St. Louis, 2001
  A.L.—12—Oakland vs. New York, 2001

Fewest runs by both clubs, series
3-game series
  A.L.—10—New York 9, Texas 1, 1998
  N.L.—15—Atlanta 10, Los Angeles 5, 1996
4-game series
  N.L.—22—San Diego 14, Houston 8, 1998
  A.L.—22—New York 16, Minnesota 6, 2003
5-game series
  N.L.—22—St. Louis 12, Arizona 10, 2001
  A.L.—30—New York 18, Oakland 12, 2001

Most runs, game
A.L.—23—Boston vs. Cleveland, October 10, 1999
N.L.—13—Atlanta vs. Houston, October 1, 1997

Most earned runs, game
A.L.—23—Boston vs. Cleveland, October 10, 1999
N.L.—12—Houston vs. Atlanta, October 11, 2004

Most runs by both clubs, game
A.L.—30—Boston 23, Cleveland 7, October 10, 1999
N.L.—15—Houston 12, Atlanta 3, October 11, 2004

Largest score, shutout game
A.L.—New York 8, Texas 0, October 5, 1999
N.L.—New York 4, San Francisco 0, October 8, 2000
    Los Angeles 4, St. Louis 0, October 9, 2004

Most players scoring one or more runs, game
A.L.—10—Cleveland vs. Seattle, October 13, 2001
N.L.—8—St. Louis vs. Arizona, October 1, 2002
    San Francisco vs. Atlanta, October 2, 2002
    Houston vs. Atlanta, October 11, 2004

Most players from both clubs scoring one or more runs, game
A.L.—15—Boston 9, Cleveland 6, October 10, 1999
N.L.—12—San Francisco 8, Atlanta 4, October 2, 2002

INNING

Most runs, inning
A.L.—8—Anaheim vs. New York, October 5, 2002, 5th
N.L.—6—New York vs. Arizona, October 8, 1999, 6th
    St. Louis vs. Atlanta, October 3, 2000, 1st
    St. Louis vs. Arizona, October 1, 2001, 7th

Most runs by both clubs, inning
A.L.—9—Anaheim 8, New York 1, October 5, 2002, 5th
N.L.—7—Atlanta 4, Colorado 3, October 7, 1995, 3rd
    Atlanta 5, Chicago 2, October 3, 1998, 8th
    Houston 5, Atlanta 2, October 10, 2004, 2nd

Most runs, extra inning
A.L.—3—Seattle vs. Chicago, October 3, 2000, 10th
N.L.—2—Colorado vs. Atlanta, October 6, 1995, 10th
    Atlanta vs. Houston, October 8, 1999, 12th
    Florida vs. San Francisco, October 3, 2003 11th
    Atlanta vs. Houston, October 7, 2004, 11th

Most runs by both clubs, extra inning
A.L.—3—Seattle 2, New York 1, October 8, 1995, 11th
    Seattle 3, Chicago 0, October 3, 2000, 10th
    New York 2, Minnesota 1, October 6, 2004, 12th
N.L.—3—Florida 2, San Francisco 1, October 3, 2003, 11th

Most innings scored, game
A.L.—7—Boston vs. Cleveland, October 10, 1999
N.L.—6—San Francisco vs. Florida, October 1, 1997
    St. Louis vs. Atlanta, October 5, 2000

Most innings scored by both clubs, game
N.L.—11—San Francisco 6, Florida 5, October 1, 1997
A.L.—11—Boston 7, Cleveland 4, October 10, 1999

Most runs, 1st inning
A.L.—6—New York vs. Oakland, October 8, 2000
N.L.—6—St. Louis vs. Atlanta, October 3, 2000

Most runs, 2nd inning
A.L.—5—Cleveland vs. Boston, September 30, 1998
    Boston vs. Cleveland, October 10, 1999
    Oakland vs. Boston, October 2, 2003
N.L.—5—Houston vs. Atlanta, October 10, 2004

Most runs, 3rd inning
A.L.—6—Cleveland vs. Boston, October 7, 1999
N.L.—5—St. Louis vs. Los Angeles, October 6, 2004

Most runs, 4th inning
A.L.—7—Minnesota vs. Oakland, October 5, 2002
    Boston vs. Anaheim, October 5, 2004
N.L.—4—Atlanta vs. Los Angeles, October 5, 1996

Most runs, 5th inning
A.L.—8—Anaheim vs. New York, October 5, 2002
N.L.—3—many clubs

Most runs, 6th inning
N.L.—6—New York vs. Arizona, October 8, 1999
    Atlanta vs. San Francisco, October 5, 2002
A.L.—5—Cleveland vs. Boston, October 6, 1995
    Baltimore vs. Cleveland, October 1, 1996
    New York vs. Cleveland, September 30, 1997

Most runs, 7th inning
A.L.—6—Boston vs. Cleveland, October 9, 1999

N.L.—6—St. Louis vs. Arizona, October 1, 2002

Most runs, 8th inning
A.L.—5—Seattle vs. New York, October 7, 1995
    Cleveland vs. Seattle, October 13, 2001
N.L.—5—Atlanta vs. Chicago, October 3, 1998

Most runs, 9th inning
N.L.—4—Atlanta vs. Colorado, October 4, 1995
    New York vs. Arizona, October 5, 1999
    Houston vs. Atlanta, October 5, 1999
    Atlanta vs. San Francisco, October 5, 2002
A.L.—4—Oakland vs. New York, October 7, 2000
    Boston vs. Anaheim, October 6, 2004

Most runs, 10th inning
A.L.—3—Seattle vs. Chicago, October 3, 2000
N.L.—2—Colorado vs. Atlanta, October 6, 1995

Most runs, 11th inning
A.L.—2—Seattle vs. New York, October 8, 1995
    Boston vs. Oakland, October 4, 2003
N.L.—2—Florida vs. San Francisco, October 3, 2003
    Atlanta vs. Houston, October 7, 2004

Most runs, 12th inning
N.L.—2—Atlanta vs. Houston, October 8, 1999
A.L.—2—New York vs. Minnesota, October 6, 2004

Most runs, 13th inning
A.L.—1—Cleveland vs. Boston, October 3, 1995
N.L.—1—New York vs. San Francisco, October 7, 2000

Most runs, 14th inning
A.L.-N.L.—none

Most runs, 15th inning
A.L.—2—New York vs. Seattle, October 4, 1995
N.L.—none

GAMES BEING SHUT OUT

Most times being shut out, total series
A.L.—4—Texas; 3 series, 10 G
N.L.—1—many times

Most consecutive games without being shut out, total series
N.L.—38—Atlanta, October 3, 1995 through October 11, 2004
A.L.—26—New York, October 3, 1995 through October 10, 2001
    Cleveland, October 3, 1995 through October 15, 2001

HITS
SERIES

Most hits, total series
A.L.—376—New York; 10 series, 42 G
N.L.—330—Atlanta; 10 series, 38 G

Most hits, series
3-game series
    A.L.—35—Boston vs. Anaheim, 2004
    N.L.—33—St. Louis vs. Arizona, 2002
4-game series
    A.L.—56—Anaheim vs. New York, 2002
    N.L.—51—Atlanta vs. Colorado, 1995
5-game series
    A.L.—63—Seattle vs. New York, 1995
    N.L.—58—Houston vs. Atlanta, 2004

Most hits by both clubs, series
3-game series
    N.L.—60—Los Angeles 31, Cincinnati 29, 1995
    A.L.—59—Boston 35, Anaheim 24, 2004
4-game series
    A.L.—94—Anaheim 56, New York 38, 2002
    N.L.—92—Atlanta 51, Colorado 41, 1995
5-game series
    A.L.—113—Seattle 63, New York 50, 1995
    N.L.—106—Houston 58, Atlanta 48, 2004

Fewest hits, series
3-game series
    A.L.—13—Texas vs. New York, 1998

N.L.—14—Los Angeles vs. Atlanta, 1996
4-game series
  N.L.—22—Houston vs. San Diego, 1998
  A.L.—26—Cleveland vs. Boston, 1998
           Minnesota vs. New York, 2003
5-game series
  N.L.—29—St. Louis vs. Arizona, 2001
  A.L.—38—Boston vs. Oakland, 2003
           Oakland vs. Boston, 2003

Fewest hits by both clubs, series
3-game series
  N.L.—30—Atlanta 16, Los Angeles 14, 1996
  A.L.—37—New York 23, Texas 14, 1999
4-game series
  N.L.—49—San Diego 27, Houston 22, 1998
  A.L.—60—Boston 34, Cleveland 26, 1998
5-game series
  N.L.—66—Arizona 37, St. Louis 29, 2001
  A.L.—76—Boston 38, Oakland 38, 2003

Most hits by pinch-hitters, series
N.L.—5—Atlanta vs. Colorado, 1995 (4-game series)
A.L.—2—Oakland vs. Minnesota, 2002 (5-game series)

Most hits by pinch-hitters on both clubs, series
N.L.—6—Atlanta 5, Colorado 1, 1995 (4-game series)
A.L.—2—many games

GAME AND INNING

Most hits, game
A.L.—24—Boston vs. Cleveland, October 10, 1999
N.L.—17—Houston vs. Atlanta, October 11, 2004

Most hits by both clubs, game
A.L.—32—Boston 24, Cleveland 8, October 10, 1999
N.L.—26—Atlanta 15, Colorado 11, October 7, 1995
  Houston 17, Atlanta 9, October 11, 2004

Most hits by pinch-hitters, game
N.L.—2—Atlanta vs. Colorado, October 4, 1995
  Arizona vs. St. Louis, October 10, 2001
  St. Louis vs. Arizona, October 12, 2001
  (2—Atlanta vs. Colorado, October 6, 1995, 10 inn
  Houston vs. Atlanta, October 8, 1999, 12 inn
  San Francisco vs. New York, October 5, 2000, 10 inn)
A.L.—1—many clubs

Most hits by pinch-hitters on both clubs, game
N.L.—3—Atlanta 2, Colorado 1, October 4, 1995
  (3—San Francisco 2, New York 1, October 5, 2000, 10 inn)
A.L.—1—many games

Fewest hits, game
N.L.—1—Houston vs. Atlanta, October 6, 1999
  San Francisco vs. New York, October 8, 2000
A.L.—2—Seattle vs. Baltimore, October 5, 1997
  Texas vs. New York, October 5, 1999
  New York vs. Oakland, October 13, 2001

Fewest hits by both clubs, game
A.L.—7—Cleveland 4, Boston 3, October 4, 1995
N.L.—6—Florida 3, San Francisco 3, September 30, 2003

Most players with one or more hits, game
N.L.—10—Atlanta vs. Colorado, October 4, 1995
  Florida vs. San Francisco, October 1, 2003
  (10—Atlanta vs. Houston, October 7, 2004, 11 inn)
A.L.—10—Boston vs. Anaheim, October 6, 2004

Most players with one or more hits by both clubs, game
A.L.—17—Anaheim 9, New York 8, October 2, 2002
N.L.—17—San Francisco 9, Atlanta 8, October 2, 2002
  Florida 10, San Francisco 7, October 1, 2003

Most hits, inning
A.L.—10—Anaheim vs. New York, October 5, 2002, 5th
N.L.—7—Atlanta vs. Houston, October 9, 1999, 6th

Most hits by pinch-hitters, inning
N.L.—2—Houston vs. Atlanta, October 8, 1999, 7th

Arizona vs. St. Louis, October 10, 2001, 8th
A.L.—1—many clubs

Most hits by both clubs, inning
A.L.—11—Anaheim 10, New York 1, October 5, 2002, 5th
N.L.—9—Houston 5, Atlanta 4, October 10, 2004, 8th

Most consecutive hits, inning (consecutive at-bats)
A.L.—6—Boston vs. Cleveland, October 10, 1999, 2nd
N.L.—6—Atlanta vs. Houston, October 9, 1999, 6th (1 SH during streak)

Most consecutive hits, inning (consecutive plate appearances)
A.L.—6—Boston vs. Cleveland, October 10, 1999, 2nd
N.L.—5—Atlanta vs. Houston, October 9, 1999, 6th
  Houston vs. Atlanta, October 11, 2004, 7th

SINGLES

Most singles, total series
A.L.—250—New York; 10 series, 42 G
N.L.—239—Atlanta; 10 series, 38 G

Most singles, series
3-game series
  N.L.—27—St. Louis vs. Arizona, 2002
  A.L.—25—Boston vs. Anaheim, 2004
4-game series
  A.L.—37—Anaheim vs. New York, 2002
  N.L.—36—Atlanta vs. Colorado, 1995
5-game series
  A.L.—45—Seattle vs. New York, 1995
  N.L.—36—Houston vs. Atlanta, 2004

Most singles by both clubs, series
3-game series
  N.L.—44—Los Angeles 26, Cincinnati 18, 1995
  A.L.—42—Boston 25, Anaheim 17, 2004
4-game series
  N.L.—64—Atlanta 36, Colorado 28, 1995
  A.L.—64—Anaheim 37, New York 27, 2002
5-game series
  A.L.—72—Seattle 45, New York 27, 1995
  N.L.—71—Atlanta 36, Houston 35, 2004

Fewest singles, series
3-game series
  N.L.—7—Los Angeles vs. Atlanta, 1996
  A.L.—8—Chicago vs. Seattle, 2000
4-game series
  A.L.—7—Cleveland vs. Boston, 1998
  N.L.—13—Los Angeles vs. St. Louis, 2004
5-game series
  N.L.—20—St. Louis vs. Arizona, 2001
  A.L.—23—Cleveland vs. Boston, 1999

Fewest singles by both clubs, series
3-game series
  N.L.—15—Atlanta 8, Los Angeles 7, 1996
  A.L.—23—New York 13, Texas 10, 1998
4-game series
  A.L.—30—Boston 23, Cleveland 7, 1998
  N.L.—33—San Diego 17, Houston 16, 1998
5-game series
  N.L.—49—Arizona 29, St. Louis 20, 2001
  A.L.—51—Boston 28, Cleveland 23, 1999

Most singles by pinch-hitters, series
N.L.—3—Atlanta vs. Colorado, 1995 (4-game series)
  San Diego vs. St. Louis, 1996 (3-game series)
  Arizona vs. St. Louis, 2001 (5-game series)
A.L.—1—many clubs

Most singles by pinch-hitters on both clubs, series
N.L.—5—Arizona 3, St. Louis 2, 2001 (5-game series)
A.L.—1—many times

Most singles, game
N.L.—13—Atlanta vs. Houston, October 9, 1999
A.L.—12—Seattle vs. New York, October 7, 1995

Boston vs. Cleveland, October 10, 1999
Anaheim vs. New York, October 2, 2002
Anaheim vs. New York, October 5, 2002

Most singles by both clubs, game
A.L.—22—Anaheim 12, New York 10, October 2, 2002
N.L.—19—Atlanta 10, Colorado 9, October 7, 1995

Fewest singles, game
N.L.—0—Atlanta vs. Houston, September 30, 1997
Houston vs. Atlanta, October 6, 1999
San Francisco vs. New York, October 8, 2000
A.L.—0—New York vs. Oakland, October 13, 2001

Fewest singles by both clubs, game
N.L.—2—New York 2, San Francisco 0, October 8, 2000
A.L.—4—Boston 3, Cleveland 1, October 4, 1995
Boston 2, Cleveland 2, October 3, 1998
Boston 3, Cleveland 1, October 11, 1999
Oakland 4, New York 0, October 13, 2001

Most singles, inning
A.L.—8—Anaheim vs. New York, October 5, 2002, 5th
N.L.—7—Atlanta vs. Houston, October 9, 1999, 6th

Most singles by both clubs, inning
A.L.—8—Anaheim 8, New York 0, October 5, 2002, 5th
N.L.—7—Atlanta 7, Houston 0, October 9, 1999, 6th
Atlanta vs. Houston, October 10, 2004, 2nd

DOUBLES

Most doubles, total series
A.L.—78—New York; 10 series, 42 G
N.L.—46—Atlanta; 10 series, 38 G

Most doubles, series
3-game series
N.L.—7—Los Angeles vs. Atlanta, 1996
A.L.—6—New York vs. Texas, 1998
New York vs. Texas, 1999
Chicago vs. Seattle, 2000
Boston vs. Anaheim, 2004
4-game series
A.L.—12—Boston vs. Cleveland, 1998
N.L.—8—Atlanta vs. Colorado, 1995
Florida vs. San Francisco, 2003
5-game series
A.L.—17—Boston vs. Cleveland, 1999
N.L.—12—Houston vs. Atlanta, 2004

Most doubles by both clubs, series
3-game series
N.L.—10—Los Angeles 7, Atlanta 3, 1996
St. Louis 5, Atlanta 5, 2000
A.L.—9—New York 6, Texas 3, 1998
Boston 6, Anaheim 3, 2004
4-game series
A.L.—18—Cleveland 12, Boston 6, 1998
N.L.—15—Atlanta 8, Colorado 7, 1995
Florida 8, San Francisco 7, 2003
5-game series
A.L.—28—Minnesota 15, Oakland 13, 2002
N.L.—16—Houston 12, Atlanta 4, 2004

Fewest doubles, series
3-game series
A.L.—2—Texas vs. New York, 1999
N.L.—1—Houston vs. Atlanta, 1997
4-game series
N.L.—2—Houston vs. Atlanta, 1999
A.L.—3—Minnesota vs. New York, 2003
5-game series
N.L.—3—St. Louis vs. Arizona, 2001
A.L.—6—Seattle vs. New York, 1995
Cleveland vs. New York, 1997
Boston vs. Oakland, 2003

Fewest doubles by both clubs, series
3-game series
N.L.—4—Atlanta 2, Chicago 2, 1998
St. Louis 2, Arizona 2, 2002

A.L.—6—Cleveland 4, Boston 2, 1995
4-game series
N.L.—7—Atlanta 5, Houston 2, 1999
Los Angeles 4, St. Louis 3, 2004
A.L.—8—New York 4, Texas 4, 1996
5-game series
N.L.—8—Arizona 5, St. Louis 3, 2001
A.L.—13—New York 7, Cleveland 6, 1997

Most doubles by pinch-hitters, series
N.L.—2—Atlanta vs. Colorado, 1995 (4-game series)
A.L.—1—Baltimore vs. Seattle, 1997 (4-game series)
Boston vs. Cleveland, 1999 (5-game series)
Oakland vs. New York, 2000 (5-game series)
Oakland vs. Minnesota, 2002 (5-game series)

Most doubles by pinch-hitters on both clubs, series
N.L.—2—Atlanta 2, Colorado 0, 1995 (4-game series)
Atlanta 1, Chicago 1, 2003 (5-game series)
A.L.—1—Baltimore 1, Seattle 0, 1997 (4-game series)
Boston 1, Cleveland 0, 1999 (5-game series)
Oakland 1, New York 0, 2000 (5-game series)
Oakland 1, Minnesota 0, 2002 (5-game series)

Most doubles, game
A.L.—7—Boston vs. Cleveland, October 10, 1999
N.L.—5—Cincinnati vs. Los Angeles, October 3, 1995

Most doubles by both clubs, game
A.L.—9—Cleveland 5, Seattle 4, October 13, 2001
N.L.—7—Los Angeles 4, Atlanta 3, October 5, 1996
Florida 4, San Francisco 3, October 4, 2003

Most doubles, inning
N.L.—3—Cincinnati vs. Los Angeles, October 3, 1995, 5th
A.L.—4—New York vs. Minnesota, October 5, 2003, 4th

TRIPLES

Most triples, total series
A.L.—4—Cleveland; 6 series, 26 G
N.L.—3—St. Louis; 5 series, 18 G
Atlanta; 10 series, 38 G

Most triples, series
A.L.—2—Chicago vs. Seattle, 2000 (3-game series)
N.L.—2—Atlanta vs. San Francisco, 2002 (5-game series)

Most triples by both clubs, series
3-game series
A.L.—2—Chicago 2, Seattle 0, 2000
N.L.—1—St. Louis 1, San Diego 0, 1996
St. Louis 1, Arizona 0, 2002
4-game series
N.L.—2—Florida 1, San Francisco 1, 2003
Los Angeles 1, St. Louis 1, 2004
A.L.—none
5-game series
A.L.—3—Minnesota 2, Oakland 1, 2002
N.L.—2—Atlanta 2, San Francisco 0, 2002

Fewest triples, series
A.L.-N.L.—0—many clubs

Fewest triples by both clubs, series
A.L.-N.L.—0—many series

Most triples by pinch-hitters, series
N.L.—1—San Diego vs. Houston, 1998 (4-game series)
San Francisco vs. Florida, 2003 (4-game series)
A.L.—none

Most triples, game
A.L.—1—many clubs
(2—Chicago vs. Seattle, October 3, 2000, 10 inn)
N.L.—1—many clubs
(1—many clubs in extra innings)

Most triples by both clubs, game
N.L.—1—many games
A.L.—1—many games
(2—Chicago 2, Seattle 0, October 3, 2000, 10 inn)

Most triples, inning
A.L.-N.L.—1—many clubs

HOME RUNS
SERIES

Most home runs, total series
A.L.—46—New York; 10 series, 42 G
N.L.—42—Atlanta; 10 series, 38 G

Most grand slams, total series
N.L.—2—Atlanta; 10 series, 38 G
A.L.—2—Cleveland; 6 series; 26 G

Most home runs, series
3-game series
    N.L.—6—St. Louis vs. Atlanta, 2000
        Atlanta vs. Houston, 2001
    A.L.—4—Cleveland vs. Boston, 1995
        New York vs. Texas, 1998
        Seattle vs. Chicago, 2000
        Anaheim vs. Boston, 2004
        Boston vs. Anaheim, 2004
4-game series
    A.L.—9—Baltimore vs. Cleveland, 1996
        Anaheim vs. New York, 2002
    N.L.—7—Atlanta vs. Colorado, 1995
        Los Angeles vs. St. Louis, 2004
        St. Louis vs. Los Angeles, 2004
5-game series
    A.L.—11—New York vs. Seattle, 1995
        Seattle vs. New York, 1995
    N.L.—11—Houston vs. Atlanta, 2004

Most home runs by both clubs, series
3-game series
    N.L.—9—Atlanta 6, Houston 3, 2001
    A.L.—8—Anaheim 4, Boston 4, 2004
4-game series
    A.L.—16—Anaheim 9, New York 7, 2002
    N.L.—14—Los Angeles 7, St. Louis 7, 2004
5-game series
    A.L.—22—New York 11, Seattle 11, 1995
    N.L.—18—Houston 11, Atlanta 7, 2004

Fewest home runs, series
3-game series
    A.L.—0—Texas vs. New York, 1998
    N.L.—0—Los Angeles vs. Atlanta, 1996
4-game series
    N.L.—0—San Francisco vs. Florida, 2003
    A.L.—2—Minnesota vs. New York, 2003
        New York vs. Minnesota, 2003
5-game series
    A.L.—1—New York vs. Oakland, 2000
        Oakland vs. Boston, 2003
    N.L.—3—Arizona vs. St. Louis, 2001
        Atlanta vs. Chicago, 2003

Fewest home runs by both clubs, series
3-game series
    A.L.—3—New York 2, Texas 1, 1999
    N.L.—5—Atlanta 5, Los Angeles 0, 1996
        Atlanta 4, Chicago 1, 1998
        St. Louis 3, Arizona 2, 2002
4-game series
    N.L.—2—Florida 2, San Francisco 0, 2003
    A.L. 4—Minnesota 2, New York 2, 2003
5-game series
    A.L.—3—Oakland 2, New York 1, 2000
    N.L.—7—Chicago 4, Atlanta 3, 2003

Most grand slams, series
N.L.—2—Atlanta vs. Chicago, 1998
A.L.—1—many clubs

Most home runs by pinch-hitters, series
A.L.—1—New York vs. Oakland, 2001 (5-game series)
    Boston vs. Oakland, 2003 (5-game series)
N.L.—1—Cincinnati vs. Los Angeles, 1995 (3-game series)
    San Diego vs. Houston, 1998 (4-game series)
    Arizona vs. New York, 1999 (4-game series)
    St. Louis vs. Atlanta, 2000 (3-game series)

San Francisco vs. New York, 2000 (4-game series)
Houston vs. Atlanta, 2001 (3-game series)

GAME AND INNING

Most home runs, game
A.L.—4—Seattle vs. New York, October 7, 1995
    Baltimore vs. Cleveland, October 1, 1996
    New York vs. Cleveland, September 30, 1997
    Cleveland vs. Boston, October 2, 1998
    Boston vs. Cleveland, October 10, 1999
    New York vs. Anaheim, October 1, 2002
    Anaheim vs. New York, October 2, 2002
    Oakland vs. Minnesota, October 4, 2002
    (4—New York vs. Seattle, October 4, 1995, 15 inn)
N.L.—5—St. Louis vs. Los Angeles, October 5, 2004

Most home runs by both clubs, game
A.L.—6—New York 4, Anaheim 2, October 1, 2002
    Anaheim 4, New York 2, October 2, 2002
    (6—New York 4, Seattle 2, October 4, 1995, 15 inn)
N.L.—7—St. Louis 5, Los Angeles 2, October 5, 2004

Most consecutive games with one or more home runs, total series
N.L.—10—Atlanta, last G vs. Colorado, 1995 (2 HR), all 3 G vs. Los Angeles, 1996 (5 HR), all 3 G vs. Houston, 1997 (3 HR), all 3 G vs. Chicago, 1998 (4 HR)
A.L.—6—Cleveland, all 3 G vs. Boston, 1995 (4 HR), first 3 G vs. Baltimore, 1996 (4 HR)
    New York, last 3 G vs. Texas, 1996 (4 HR), first 3 G vs. Cleveland, 1997 (6 HR)

Most consecutive games with one or more home runs, series
A.L.—5—New York vs. Seattle, October 3, 4, 6, 7, 8, 1995 (11 HR)
    Seattle vs. New York, October 3, 4, 6, 7, 8, 1995 (11 HR)
N.L.—4—Colorado vs. Atlanta, October 3, 4, 6, 7, 1995 (6 HR)
    San Diego vs. Houston, September 29, October 1, 3, 4, 1998 (5 HR)
    St. Louis vs. Arizona, October 10, 12, 13, 14, 2001 (6 HR)
    San Francisco vs. Atlanta, October 3, 5, 6, 7, 2002 (6 HR)

Most home runs, inning
A.L.—3—New York vs. Cleveland, September 30, 1997, 6th inn (consecutive)
N.L.—2—many clubs

Most home runs by both clubs, inning
A.L.—3—New York 3, Cleveland 0, September 30, 1997, 6th
    Boston 2, Anaheim 1, October 5, 2004, 4th
N.L.—3—Atlanta 2, San Francisco 1, October 3, 2002, 2nd

Most consecutive home runs, inning
A.L.—3—New York (Raines Sr., Jeter, O'Neill) vs. Cleveland, September 30, 1997, 6th
N.L.—2—Atlanta (Lopez, Castilla) vs. San Francisco, October 3, 2002, 2nd
    Los Angeles (Green, Bradley) vs. St. Louis, October 7, 2004, 4th

TOTAL BASES

Most total bases, total series
A.L.—596—New York; 10 series, 42 G
N.L.—508—Atlanta; 10 series, 38 G

Most total bases, series
3-game series
    N.L.—54—Atlanta vs. Houston, 2001
    A.L.—53—Boston vs. Anaheim, 2004
4-game series
    A.L.—93—Anaheim vs. New York, 2002
    N.L.—80—Atlanta vs. Colorado, 1995
5-game series
    A.L.—105—Boston vs. Cleveland, 1999
    N.L.—103—Houston vs. Atlanta, 2004

Most total bases by both clubs, series
3-game series
    N.L.—92—Cincinnati 50, Los Angeles 42, 1995

DIVISION SERIES Club batting

A.L.—92—Boston 53, Anaheim 39, 2004
4-game series
  A.L.—156—Anaheim 93, New York 63, 2002
  N.L.—146—Atlanta 80, Colorado 66, 1995
5-game series
  A.L.—199—Seattle 104, New York 95, 1995
  N.L.—178—Houston 103, Atlanta 75, 2004

Fewest total bases, series
3-game series
  A.L.—16—Texas vs. New York, 1998
  N.L.—20—Houston vs. Atlanta, 1997
4-game series
  N.L.—30—Houston vs. San Diego, 1998
  A.L.—37—Minnesota vs. New York, 2003
5-game series
  N.L.—49—Atlanta vs. Chicago, 2003
  A.L.—51—Oakland vs. Boston, 2003

Fewest total bases by both clubs, series
3-game series
  N.L.—53—Atlanta 33, Houston 20, 1997
  A.L.—56—New York 37, Texas 19, 1999
4-game series
  N.L.—78—San Diego 48, Houston 30, 1998
  A.L.—90—New York 53, Minnesota 37, 2003
5-game series
  N.L.—101—Arizona 51, St. Louis 50, 2001
  A.L.—115—Oakland 59, New York 56, 2000

Most total bases, game
A.L.—45—Boston vs. Cleveland, October 10, 1999
N.L.—30—Houston vs. Atlanta, October 11, 2004

Most total bases by both clubs, game
A.L.—57—Boston 45, Cleveland 12, October 10, 1999
N.L.—45—Houston 30, Atlanta 15, October 11, 2004

Fewest total bases, game
N.L.—2—San Francisco vs. New York, October 8, 2000
A.L.—3—Boston vs. Cleveland, October 4, 1995
  Texas vs. New York, October 2, 1998
  Texas vs. New York, October 5, 1999

Fewest total bases by both clubs, game
N.L.—7—San Francisco 4, Florida 3, September 30, 2003
A.L.—10—Seattle 6, Chicago 4, October 6, 2000

Most total bases, inning
A.L.—14—New York vs. Cleveland, September 30, 1997, 6th
  Anaheim vs. New York, October 5, 2002, 5th
N.L.—11—St. Louis vs. Los Angeles, October 5, 2004, 3rd
  Houston vs. Atlanta, October 6, 2004, 3rd

Most total bases by both clubs, inning
A.L.—16—Anaheim 14, New York 2, October 5, 2002, 5th
N.L.—14—Atlanta 8, Colorado 6, October 7, 1995, 3rd

EXTRA BASE HITS

Most extra base hits, total series
A.L.—126—New York; 10 series, 42 G
N.L.—91—Atlanta; 10 series, 38 G

Most extra base hits, series
3-game series
  N.L.—12—Atlanta vs. Houston, 2001
  A.L.—10—New York vs. Texas, 1998
        Boston vs. Anaheim, 2004
4-game series
  A.L.—19—Cleveland vs. Boston, 1998
        Anaheim vs. New York, 2002
  N.L.—15—Atlanta vs. Colorado, 1995
5-game series
  A.L.—28—Boston vs. Cleveland, 1999
  N.L.—23—Houston vs. Atlanta, 2004

Most extra base hits by both clubs, series
3-game series
  N.L.—17—Florida 9, San Francisco 8, 1997
        St. Louis 11, Atlanta 6, 2000
        Atlanta 12, Houston 5, 2001
  A.L.—17—Boston 10, Anaheim 7, 2004

4-game series
  A.L.—30—Cleveland 19, Boston 11, 1998
        Oakland 18, New York 12, 2001
        Anaheim 19, New York 11, 2002
  N.L.—28—Atlanta 15, Colorado 13, 1995
5-game series
  A.L.—43—Boston 28, Cleveland 15, 1999
  N.L.—35—Houston 23, Atlanta 12, 2004

Fewest extra base hits, series
3-game series
  A.L.—3—Texas vs. New York, 1998
       Texas vs. New York, 1999
  N.L.—2—Houston vs. Atlanta, 1997
4-game series
  N.L.—6—Houston vs. San Diego, 1998
       Atlanta vs. Houston, 1999
  A.L.—6—Minnesota vs. New York, 2003
5-game series
  N.L.—8—Arizona vs. St. Louis, 2001
       Atlanta vs. Chicago, 2003
  A.L.—10—Oakland vs. Boston, 2003

Fewest extra base hits by both clubs, series
3-game series
  N.L.—9—Atlanta 7, Houston 2, 1997
      Atlanta 6, Chicago 3, 1998
  A.L.—12—New York 9, Texas 3, 1999
4-game series
  N.L.—13—Houston 7, Atlanta 6, 1999
  A.L.—17—New York 11, Minnesota 6, 2003
5-game series
  N.L.—17—St. Louis 9, Arizona 8, 2001
  A.L.—24—New York 13, Cleveland 11, 1997
        New York 13, Oakland 11, 2000
        Boston 14, Oakland 10, 2003

Most extra base hits, game
A.L.—12—Boston vs. Cleveland, October 10, 1999 (7 doubles, 1 triple, 4 HR)
N.L.—7—St. Louis vs. Atlanta, October 5, 2000 (4 doubles, 3 HR)
  Houston vs. Atlanta, October 11, 2004 (4 doubles, 3 HR)

Most extra base hits by both clubs, game
A.L.—14—Boston 12 (7 doubles, 1 triple, 4 HR), Cleveland 2 (1 double, 1 HR), October 10, 1999
N.L.—10—St. Louis 7 (4 doubles, 3 HR), Atlanta 3 (2 doubles, 1 HR), October 5, 2000
  St. Louis 6 (1 double, 5 HR), Los Angeles 4 (2 doubles, 1 triple, 1 HR), October 5, 2004

RUNS BATTED IN

Most runs batted in, total series
A.L.—186—New York; 10 series, 42 G
N.L.—163—Atlanta; 10 series, 38 G

Most runs batted in, series
3-game series
  N.L.—23—St. Louis vs. Atlanta, 2000
  A.L.—23—Boston vs. Anaheim, 2004
4-game series
  A.L.—31—Anaheim vs. New York, 2002
  N.L.—24—Atlanta vs. Colorado, 1995
5-game series
  A.L.—47—Boston vs. Cleveland, 1999
  N.L.—36—Houston vs. Atlanta, 2004

Most runs batted in by both clubs, series
3-game series
  A.L.—35—Boston 23, Anaheim 12, 2004
  N.L.—32—St. Louis 23, Atlanta 9, 2000
4-game series
  A.L.—55—Anaheim 31, New York 24, 2002
  N.L.—42—Atlanta 24, Colorado 18, 1995
5-game series
  A.L.—78—Boston 47, Cleveland 31, 1999
  N.L.—56—Houston 36, Atlanta 20, 2004

Fewest runs batted in, series
3-game series
  A.L.—1—Texas vs. New York, 1998

Texas vs. New York, 1999
N.L.—4—Chicago vs. Atlanta, 1998
4-game series
  N.L.—7—Houston vs. San Diego, 1998
  A.L.—5—Minnesota vs. New York, 2003
5-game series
  N.L.—10—Arizona vs. St. Louis, 2001
  A.L.—13—Milwaukee vs. New York, 1995

Fewest runs batted in by both clubs, series
3-game series
  A.L.—9—New York 8, Texas 1, 1998
  N.L.—15—Atlanta 10, Los Angeles 5, 1996
4-game series
  N.L.—20—San Diego 13, Houston 7, 1998
  A.L.—20—New York 15, Minnesota 5, 2003
5-game series
  N.L.—22—St. Louis 12, Arizona 10, 2001
  A.L.—27—New York 16, Oakland 11, 2001

Most runs batted in by pinch-hitters, series
N.L.—5—Cincinnati vs. Los Angeles, 1995 (3-game series)
A.L.—2—Baltimore vs. Seattle, 1997 (4-game series)
  Boston vs. Oakland, 2003 (5-game series)

Most runs batted in by pinch-hitters on both clubs, series
N.L.—5—Cincinnati 5, Los Angeles 0, 1995 (3-game series)
A.L.—3—Baltimore 2, Seattle 1, 1997 (4-game series)
  Boston 2, Oakland 1, 2003 (5-game series)

Most runs batted in, game
A.L.—23—Boston vs. Cleveland, October 10, 1999
N.L.—12—Houston vs. Atlanta, October 11, 2004

Most runs batted in by both clubs, game
A.L.—30—Boston 23, Cleveland 7, October 10, 1999
N.L.—15—Houston 12, Atlanta 3, October 11, 2004

Fewest runs batted in by both clubs, game
N.L.—0—Atlanta 0, Houston 0, October 10, 2001
A.L.—1—New York 1, Texas 0, September 29, 1998
  Oakland 1, New York 0, October 11, 2001
  New York 1, Oakland 0, October 13, 2001

Most runs batted in, inning
A.L.—8—Anaheim vs. New York, October 5, 2002, 5th
N.L.—6—New York vs. Arizona, October 8, 1999, 6th

Most runs batted in by both clubs, inning
A.L.—9—Anaheim 8, New York 1, October 5, 2002, 5th
N.L.—7—Atlanta 4, Colorado 3, October 7, 1995, 3rd

Most runs batted in by pinch-hitters, inning
N.L.—4—Cincinnati vs. Los Angeles, October 6, 1995, 6th
A.L.—2—Baltimore vs. Seattle, October 1, 1997, 6th

BASES ON BALLS

Most bases on balls, total series
A.L.—154—New York; 10 series, 42 G
N.L.—146—Atlanta; 10 series, 38 G

Most bases on balls, series
3-game series
  A.L.—20—Boston vs. Anaheim, 2004
  N.L.—19—Florida vs. San Francisco, 1997
4-game series
  N.L.—21—New York vs. Arizona, 1999
  A.L.—20—Texas vs. New York, 1996
5-game series
  A.L.—32—New York vs. Seattle, 1995
  N.L.—22—Atlanta vs. San Francisco, 2002

Most bases on balls by both clubs, series
3-game series
  A.L.—31—Boston 20, Anaheim 11, 2004
  N.L.—25—Florida 19, San Francisco 6, 1997
4-game series
  N.L.—40—Florida 20, San Francisco 20, 2003
  A.L.—33—Texas 20, New York 13, 1996
5-game series
  A.L.—57—New York 32, Seattle 25, 1995
  N.L.—41—Atlanta 21, Chicago 20, 2003

Fewest bases on balls, series
3-game series
  N.L.—4—San Diego vs. St. Louis, 1996
    Atlanta vs. Houston, 2001
  A.L.—4—Texas vs. New York, 1998
4-game series
  A.L.—7—Seattle vs. Baltimore, 1997
    Anaheim vs. New York, 2002
    Minnesota vs. New York, 2004
  N.L.—9—Colorado vs. Atlanta, 1995
    San Diego vs. Houston, 1998
5-game series
  A.L.—10—Cleveland vs. New York, 1997
  N.L.—12—St. Louis vs. Arizona, 2001

Fewest bases on balls by both clubs, series
3-game series
  A.L.—11—New York 7, Texas 4, 1998
  N.L.—12—Houston 8, Atlanta 4, 2001
4-game series
  N.L.—20—Houston 11, San Diego 9, 1998
  A.L.—22—New York 15, Minnesota 7, 2004
5-game series
  A.L.—22—Milwaukee 13, New York 9, 1995
  N.L.—26—Los Angeles 13, Houston 13, 1995

Most bases on balls by pinch-hitters, series
N.L.—3—Houston vs. Atlanta, 1999 (4-game series)
A.L.—2—Seattle vs. New York, 1995 (5-game series)

Most bases on balls by pinch-hitters on both clubs, series
A.L.—2—Seattle 2, New York 0, 1995 (5-game series)
  Baltimore 1, Cleveland 1, 1996 (4-game series)
  Baltimore 1, Seattle 1, 1997 (4-game series)
N.L.—3—Houston 2, San Diego 1, 1998 (4-game series)
  New York 2, Arizona 1, 1999 (4-game series)
  Houston 3, Atlanta 0, 1999 (4-game series)

Most bases on balls, game
N.L.—10—Atlanta vs. Houston, October 1, 1997
A.L.—8—New York vs. Seattle, October 7, 1995
  (10—New York vs. Seattle, October 8, 1995, 11 inn)

Most bases on balls by both clubs, game
N.L.—16—Atlanta 10, Houston 6, October 1, 1997
A.L.—14—Cleveland 9, Boston 5, October 10, 1999
  (17—Oakland 10, Boston 7, October 1, 2003, 12 inn)

Fewest bases on balls, game
A.L.-N.L.—0—many clubs

Fewest bases on balls by both clubs, game
N.L.—1—Atlanta 1, Los Angeles 0, October 3, 1996
A.L.—1—New York 1, Texas 0, September 30, 1998
  Minnesota 1, New York, 1, October 8, 2004

Most bases on balls by pinch-hitters, game
A.L.—1—many clubs
  (2—Seattle vs. New York, October 8, 1995, 11 inn)
N.L.—1—many clubs
  (1—many clubs in extra innings)

Most bases on balls by pinch-hitters on both clubs, game
N.L.—2—San Diego 1, Houston 1, October 3, 1998
A.L.—1—many clubs
  (2—Seattle 2, New York 0, October 8, 1995, 11 inn)

Most bases on balls, inning
N.L.—5—Florida vs. San Francisco, October 1, 1997, 4th
A.L.—5—Cleveland vs. Boston, October 10, 1999, 5th

Most bases on balls by both clubs, inning
N.L.—6—Florida 5, San Francisco 1, October 1, 1997, 4th
A.L.—5—Baltimore 4, Cleveland 1, October 2, 1996, 8th
  Cleveland 3, Baltimore 2, October 4, 1996, 7th
  Cleveland 5, Boston 0, October 10, 1999, 5th
  Oakland 3, Boston 2, October 1, 2003, 12th

Most bases on balls by pinch-hitters, inning
A.L.—2—Seattle vs. New York, October 8, 1995, 8th
N.L.—1—many clubs

STRIKEOUTS

Most strikeouts, total series
A.L.—281—New York; 10 series, 42 G
N.L.—280—Atlanta; 10 series, 38 G

Most strikeouts, series
3-game series
 N.L.—29—Los Angeles vs. Atlanta, 1996
 A.L.—28—Anaheim vs. Boston, 2004
4-game series
 N.L.—49—Houston vs. San Diego, 1998
 A.L.—42—Seattle vs. Baltimore, 1997
5-game series
 A.L.—48—Seattle vs. Cleveland, 2001
 N.L.—45—San Francisco vs. Atlanta, 2002
  Atlanta vs. Houston, 2004

Most strikeouts by both clubs, series
3-game series
 N.L.—53—Los Angeles 29, Atlanta 24, 1996
 A.L.—51—Texas 27, New York 24, 1998
  Anaheim 28, Boston 23, 2004
4-game series
 N.L.—81—Houston 49, San Diego 32, 1998
 A.L.—72—Baltimore 40, Cleveland 32, 1996
5-game series
 A.L.—91—Seattle 48, Cleveland 43, 2001
 N.L.—80—Atlanta 42, Chicago 38, 2003

Fewest strikeouts, series
3-game series
 A.L.—13—Seattle vs. Chicago, 2000
 N.L.—16—Florida vs. San Francisco, 1997
  Houston vs. Atlanta, 2001
4-game series
 A.L.—18—Anaheim vs. New York, 2002
 N.L.—20—Los Angeles vs. St. Louis, 2004
5-game series
 A.L.—22—Cleveland vs. New York, 1997
 N.L.—29—Arizona vs. St. Louis, 2001

Fewest strikeouts by both clubs, series
3-game series
 A.L.—29—Chicago 16, Seattle 13, 2000
 N.L.—34—Atlanta 18, Houston 16, 2001
4-game series
 A.L.—43—New York 25, Anaheim 18, 2002
 N.L.—46—St. Louis 26, Los Angeles 20, 2004
5-game series
 A.L.—48—New York 26, Cleveland 22, 1997
 N.L.—67—St. Louis 38, Arizona 29, 2002

Most strikeouts by pinch-hitters, series
N.L.—4—Los Angeles vs. Atlanta, 1996 (3-game series)
 Houston vs. Atlanta, 1997 (3-game series)
 San Francisco vs. Atlanta, 2002 (5-game series)
A.L.—3—New York vs. Seattle, 1995 (5-game series)
 Seattle vs. Baltimore, 1997 (4-game series)
 Oakland vs. Minnesota, 2002 (5-game series)
 Oakland vs. Boston, 2003 (5-game series)

Most strikeouts by pinch-hitters on both clubs, series
N.L.—6—Los Angeles 4, Atlanta 2, 1996 (3-game series)
A.L.—5—Oakland 3, Minnesota 2, 2002 (5-game series)
 Oakland 3, Boston 2, 2003 (5-games series)

Most strikeouts, game
N.L.—17—Houston vs. San Diego, September 29, 1998
 (18—Atlanta vs. Houston, October 8, 1999, 12 inn)
A.L.—13—Baltimore vs. Seattle, October 4, 1997
 Cleveland vs. Seattle, October 9, 2001
 Cleveland vs. Seattle, October 15, 2001
 (23—Baltimore vs. Cleveland, October 5, 1996, 12 inn)

Most strikeouts by pinch-hitters, game
N.L.—3—Houston vs. Atlanta, October 3, 1997

A.L.—2—Minnesota vs. Oakland, October 5, 2002

Most strikeouts by both clubs, game
N.L.—28—Houston 17, San Diego 11, September 29, 1998
 (30—Atlanta 18, Houston 12, October 8, 1999, 12 inn)
A.L.—25—Cleveland 13, Seattle 12, October 9, 2001
 (33—Baltimore 23, Cleveland 10, October 5, 1996, 12 inn)

Fewest strikeouts, game
N.L.—2—Atlanta vs. Houston, October 5, 1999
 Arizona vs. New York, October 8, 1999
 Arizona vs. St. Louis, October 13, 2001
 Houston vs. Atlanta, October 11, 2004
A.L.—1—Cleveland vs. New York, October 4, 1997

Fewest strikeouts by both clubs, game
A.L.—3—New York 2, Cleveland 1, October 4, 1997
N.L.—7—New York 5, Arizona 2, October 8, 1999
 St. Louis 5, Arizona 2, October 13, 2001

Most consecutive strikeouts, game
A.L.—5—Seattle vs. New York, October 8, 1995 (3 in 6th inn, 2 in 7th inn)
 Chicago vs. Seattle, October 4, 2000 (2 in 8th inn, 3 in 9th inn)
 Boston vs. Oakland, October 2, 2003 (3 in 4th inn, 2 in 5th inn)
N.L.—6—Chicago vs. Atlanta, October 1, 2003 (3 in 1st inn, 3 in 2nd inn)

Most strikeouts, inning
A.L.-N.L.—3—many clubs

Most strikeouts by both clubs, inning
A.L.—6—Seattle 3, Chicago 3, October 4, 2000, 9th
N.L.—5—Atlanta 3, Houston 2, October 3, 1997, 2nd
 San Francisco 3, Florida 2, September 30, 2003, 3rd
 Chicago 3, Atlanta 2, September 30, 2003, 7th

Most strikeouts by pinch-hitters, inning
N.L.—2—Houston vs. Atlanta, October 3, 1997, 8th
A.L.—1—many clubs

SACRIFICE HITS

Most sacrifice hits, total series
N.L.—16—St. Louis; 5 series, 18 G
A.L.—16—New York; 10 series, 42 G

Most sacrifice hits, series
N.L.—8—St. Louis vs. Arizona, 2001 (5-game series)
A.L.—4—Seattle vs. New York, 1995 (5-game series)
 Texas vs. New York, 1996 (4-game series)
 Cleveland vs. New York, 1997 (5-game series)
 Seattle vs. Chicago, 2000 (3-game series)
 Anaheim vs. New York, 2002 (4-game series)

Most sacrifice hits by both clubs, series
N.L.—14—St. Louis 8, Arizona 6, 2001 (5-game series)
A.L.—7—Texas 4, New York 3, 1996 (4-game series)

Fewest sacrifice hits, series
A.L.-N.L.—0—many clubs

Fewest sacrifice hits by both clubs, series
N.L.—0—Atlanta 0, Houston 0, 1997 (3-game series)
A.L.—1—Boston 1, Cleveland 0, 1998 (4-game series)
 New York 1, Texas 0, 1999 (3-game series)
 Cleveland 1, Boston 0, 1999 (5-game series)
 Oakland 1, Boston 1, 2003 (5-game series)
 Anaheim 1, Boston 0, 2004 (3-game series)

Most sacrifice hits, game
A.L.—3—Seattle vs. Chicago, October 6, 2000
N.L.—3—St. Louis vs. Arizona, October 13, 2001
 (3—Chicago vs. Atlanta, October 1, 1998, 10 inn)

Most sacrifice hits by both clubs, game
A.L.—4—Seattle 3, Chicago 1, October 6, 2000
 (4—Texas 2, New York 2, October 2, 1996, 12 inn)
N.L.—3—Atlanta 2, Houston 1, October 9, 1999

St. Louis 2, Arizona 1, October 10, 2001
Arizona 2, St. Louis 1, October 12, 2001
St. Louis 3, Arizona 0, October 13, 2001
Arizona 2, St. Louis 1, October 14, 2001
(5—Chicago 3, Atlanta 2, October 1, 1998, 10 inn)

Most sacrifice hits, inning
A.L.-N.L.—1—many clubs

SACRIFICE FLIES

Most sacrifice flies, total series
A.L.—16—New York; 10 series, 42 G
N.L.—10—Atlanta; 10 series, 38 G

Most sacrifice flies, series
A.L.—4—Cleveland vs. Boston, 1999 (5-game series)
 Minnesota vs. New York, 2004 (4-game series)
N.L.—3—Atlanta vs. Houston, 1999 (4-game series)
 Houston vs. Atlanta, 2004 (5-game series)

Most sacrifice flies by both clubs, series
A.L.—7—Cleveland 4, Boston 3, 1999 (5-game series)
N.L.—4—Atlanta 3, Houston 1, 1999 (4-game series)
 Houston 3, Atlanta 1, 2004 (5-game series)

Most sacrifice flies, game
A.L.—2—Cleveland vs. Boston, October 10, 1999
 New York vs. Oakland, October 8, 2000
 Oakland vs. New York, October 8, 2000
 Oakland vs. New York, October 10, 2001
 New York vs. Anaheim, October 4, 2002
N.L.—2—Atlanta vs. Houston, October 6, 1999
 San Francisco vs. Florida, October 4, 2003

Most sacrifice flies by both clubs, game
A.L.—4—New York 2, Oakland 2, October 8, 2000

N.L.—2—Atlanta 2, Houston 0, October 6, 1999

Most sacrifice flies, inning
A.L.—2—New York vs. Oakland, October 8, 2000, 1st
 Oakland vs. New York, October 8, 2000, 4th
N.L.—1—many clubs

HIT BY PITCH

Most hit by pitch, total series
A.L.—20—New York; 10 series, 42 G
N.L.—9—St. Louis; 5 series; 148 G

Most hit by pitch, series
A.L.—4—Cleveland vs. Boston, 1995 (3-game series)
 Baltimore vs. Cleveland, 1996 (4-game series)
 New York vs. Oakland, 2001 (5-game series)
 New York vs. Anaheim, 2002 (4-game series)
 Minnesota vs. New York, 2004 (4-game series)
N.L.—4—Houston vs. San Diego, 1998 (4-game series)

Most hit by pitch by both clubs, series
A.L.—7—New York 4, Oakland 3, 2001 (5-game series)
N.L.—6—Houston 4, San Diego 2, 1998 (4-game series)

Most hit by pitch, game
A.L.-N.L.—2—many clubs

Most hit by pitch by both clubs, game
A.L.—3—Baltimore 2, Cleveland 1, October 1, 1996
 New York 2, Oakland 1, October 15, 2001
 Anaheim 2, New York 1, October 4, 2002
N.L.—3—Florida 2, San Francisco 1, October 4, 2003

Most hit by pitch, inning
A.L.—2—Minnesota vs. New York, October 8, 2004, 9th
N.L.—2—St. Louis vs. Los Angeles, October 7, 2004, 5th

INDIVIDUAL BASERUNNING

STOLEN BASES

Most stolen bases, career
Both leagues—13—Kenny Lofton, Cleveland A.L., 1995, 1996;
Atlanta N.L., 1997; Cleveland A.L., 1998, 1999, 2001; San
Francisco N.L., 2002; Chicago N.L., 2003; New York A.L.,
2004; 9 series, 35 G
A.L.—10—Omar Vizquel, Cleveland, 1995 through 1999, 2001;
 6 series, 26 G
N.L.—6—Rickey Henderson, San Diego, 1996; New York, 1999;
 2 series, 7 G

Most stolen bases, series
3-game series
 N.L.—4—Barry Larkin, Cincinnati, 1995
 A.L.—3—Jose Valentin, Chicago, 2000
 Johnny Damon, Boston, 2004
4-game series
 N.L.—6—Rickey Henderson, New York, 1999
 A.L.—5—Kenny Lofton, Cleveland, 1996
5-game series
 N.L.—3—Kenny Lofton, Chicago, 2003
 Rafael Furcal, Atlanta, 2004
 A.L.—2—Ken Griffey Jr., Seattle, 1997
 Johnny Damon, Oakland, 2001
 Cristian Guzman, Minnesota, 2002
 Alfonso Soriano, New York, 2003

Most stolen bases, game
A.L.—3—Kenny Lofton, Cleveland, October 4, 1995
N.L.—3—Rickey Henderson, New York, October 6, 1999

Most stolen bases by pinch-runner, game
A.L.—1—Chone Figgins, Anaheim, October 2, 2002, 8th inn
N.L.—none

Most times stealing home, game
A.L.-N.L.—none

Most stolen bases, inning
A.L.—2—Kenny Lofton, Cleveland, October 2, 1996, 6th
N.L.—2—Barry Larkin, Cincinnati, October 3, 1995, 9th
 Reggie Sanders, Cincinnati, October 4, 1995, 9th
 Barry Larkin, Cincinnati, October 6, 1995, 1st

CAUGHT STEALING

Most caught stealing, career
Both leagues—3—Marquis Grissom, Atlanta N.L., 1995;
 Cleveland A.L., 1997; San Francisco N.L., 2003; 4 series, 16 G
 Kenny Lofton, Cleveland A.L, 1995, 1996; Atlanta N.L., 1997;
 Cleveland 1998, 1999, 2001; San Francisco N.L., 2002;
 Chicago N.L., 2003; New York A.L., 2004; 9 series, 35 G
A.L.—3—Bernie Williams, New York, 1995 through 2004; 10
 series, 42 G
N.L.—2—many players

Most caught stealing, series
N.L.—2—Luis Alicea, St. Louis, 1996; 0 SB (3-game series)
 Sammy Sosa, Chicago, 1998; 0 SB (3-game series)
A.L.—2—Omar Vizquel, Cleveland, 1996; 4 SB (4-game series)
 Ichiro Suzuki, Seattle, 2001; 1 SB (5-game series)

Most caught stealing, game
A.L.-N.L.—1—many players

Most caught stealing by pinch-runner, game
A.L.-N.L.—none

Most caught stealing, inning
A.L.-N.L.—1—none

CLUB BASERUNNING

STOLEN BASES

Most stolen bases, total series
N.L.—28—Atlanta; 10 series, 38 G
A.L.—27—Cleveland; 6 series, 26 G

Most stolen bases, series
3-game series
   N.L.—9—Cincinnati vs. Los Angeles, 1995
   A.L.—4—Chicago vs. Seattle, 2000
4-game series
   A.L.—11—Cleveland vs. Baltimore, 1996
   N.L.—8—New York vs. Arizona, 1999
5-game series
   N.L.—7—Atlanta vs. Houston, 2004
   A.L.—6—Cleveland vs. New York, 1997

Most stolen bases by both clubs, series
3-game series
   N.L.—9—Cincinnati 9, Los Angeles 0, 1995
   A.L.—6—Chicago 4, Seattle 2, 2000
4-game series
   A.L.—12—Cleveland 11, Baltimore 1, 1996
   N.L.—8—New York 8, Arizona 0, 1999
5-game series
   N.L.—10—Atlanta 7, Houston 3, 2004
   A.L.—9—Cleveland 6, New York 3, 1997

Fewest stolen bases, series
A.L.-N.L.—0—many clubs

Fewest stolen bases by both clubs, series
3-game series
   A.L.—1—Texas 1, New York 0, 1999
   N.L.—1—Atlanta 1, Houston 0, 2001
4-game series
   A.L.—2—New York 1, Texas 1, 1996
   N.L.—1—Houston 1, San Diego 0, 1998
5-game series
   A.L.—3—Minnesota 2, Oakland 1, 2002
   N.L.—3—Atlanta 2, San Francisco 1, 2002

Most stolen bases, game
A.L.—5—Cleveland vs. Baltimore, October 4, 1996
N.L.—4—Cincinnati vs. Los Angeles, October 4, 1995
   New York vs. Arizona, October 6, 1999
   Atlanta vs. Houston, October 10, 2004

Most stolen bases by both clubs, game
A.L.—6—Cleveland 5, Baltimore 1, October 4, 1996
N.L.—4—Cincinnati 4, Los Angeles 0, October 4, 1995
   St. Louis 2, San Diego 2, October 1, 1996
   New York 4, Arizona 0, October 6, 1999
   St. Louis 3, Atlanta 1, October 7, 2000
   Atlanta 4, Houston 0, October 10, 2004

Longest game with no stolen bases, one club
A.L.—15 inn—New York vs. Seattle, October 4, 1995
   Seattle vs. New York, October 4, 1995
N.L.—13 inn—San Francisco vs. New York, October 7, 2000

Longest game with no stolen bases, both clubs
A.L.—15 inn—New York 0, Seattle 0, October 4, 1995
N.L.—10 inn—Arizona 0, New York 0, October 9, 1999

Most stolen bases, inning
N.L.—3—Cincinnati vs. Los Angeles, October 4, 1995, 9th
A.L.—2—Seattle vs. New York, October 6, 1995, 7th
   Cleveland vs. Baltimore, October 2, 1996, 6th
   Cleveland vs. Baltimore, October 4, 1996, 1st
   Cleveland vs. Baltimore, October 4, 1996, 8th
   Chicago vs. Seattle, October 4, 2000, 3rd

CAUGHT STEALING

Most caught stealing, series
3-game series
   N.L.—3—Atlanta vs. Los Angeles, 1996

   San Francisco vs. Florida, 1997
   Chicago vs. Atlanta, 1998
   Atlanta vs. St. Louis, 2000
   Atlanta vs. Houston, 2001
   St. Louis vs. Arizona, 2002
   A.L.—2—New York vs. Texas, 1998
4-game series
   A.L.—4—Minnesota vs. New York, 2004
   N.L.—2—Atlanta vs. Colorado, 1995
   New York vs. San Francisco, 2000
   St. Louis vs. Los Angeles, 2004
5-game series
   A.L.—4—New York vs. Oakland, 2001
   N.L.—2—Arizona vs. St. Louis, 2001
   Chicago vs. Atlanta, 2003
   Houston vs. Atlanta, 2004

Most caught stealing by both clubs, series
3-game series
   N.L.—4—Atlanta 3, Los Angeles 1, 1996
   Atlanta 3, St. Louis 1, 2000
   Atlanta 3, Houston 1, 2001
   A.L.—3—New York 2, Texas 1, 1998
4-game series
   A.L.—6—Minnesota 4, New York 2, 2004
   N.L.—4—Los Angeles 2, St. Louis 2, 2004
5-game series
   A.L.—4—New York 4, Oakland 0, 2001
   N.L.—3—Houston 2, Atlanta 1, 2004

Fewest caught stealing, series
A.L.-N.L.—0—many clubs

Fewest caught stealing by both clubs, series
3-game series
   N.L.—0—Cincinnati 0, Los Angeles 0, 1995
   A.L.—0—New York 0, Texas 0, 1999
4-game series
   A.L.—0—Anaheim 0, New York 0, 2002
   N.L.—1—Arizona 1, New York 0, 1999
   San Francisco 1, Florida 0, 2003
5-game series
   A.L.—0—Minnesota 0, Oakland 0, 2002
   N.L.—2—Arizona 2, St. Louis 0, 2001
   San Francisco 1, Atlanta 1, 2002
   Chicago 2, Atlanta 0, 2003

Most caught stealing, game
A.L.—3—New York vs. Texas, October 4, 1996
   (3—Minnesota vs. New York, October 9, 2004, 11 inn)
N.L.—2—Atlanta vs. St. Louis, October 3, 2000
   Atlanta vs. Houston, October 9, 2001
   (3—Atlanta vs. Los Angeles, October 2, 1996, 10 inn)

Most caught stealing by both clubs, game
A.L.—2—many games
   (3—Minnesota 3, New York 0, October 9, 2004, 11 inn)
N.L.—2—St. Louis 2, San Diego 0, October 1, 1996
   Atlanta 2, St. Louis 0, October 3, 2000
   Atlanta 2, Houston 0, October 9, 2001
   (4—Atlanta 3, Los Angeles 1, October 2, 1996, 10 inn)

Most caught stealing, inning
A.L.—2—New York vs. Texas, October 4, 1996, 4th
N.L.—1—many clubs

LEFT ON BASE

Most left on base, total series
A.L.—324—New York; 10 series, 42 G
N.L.—273—Atlanta; 10 series, 38 G

Most left on base, series
3-game series
   N.L.—30—Los Angeles vs. Cincinnati, 1995
   A.L.—31—Boston vs. Anaheim, 2004

4-game series
  A.L.—45—Baltimore vs. Cleveland, 1996
  N.L.—36—New York vs. San Francisco, 2000
           San Francisco vs. Florida, 2003
5-game series
  A.L.—49—Seattle vs. New York, 1995
  N.L.—43—Atlanta vs. Houston, 2004

Most left on base by both clubs, series
3-game series
  A.L.—55—Boston 28, Cleveland 27, 1995
           Boston 31, Anaheim 24, 2004
  N.L.—49—Los Angeles 30, Cincinnati 19, 1995
4-game series
  N.L.—71—San Francisco 36, Florida 35, 2003
  A.L.—65—Baltimore 36, Cleveland 29, 1996
5-game series
  A.L.—94—Seattle 49, New York 45, 1995
  N.L.—78—Atlanta 41, Chicago 37, 2003

Fewest left on base, series
3-game series
  N.L.—14—Atlanta vs. Los Angeles, 1996
           Los Angeles vs. Atlanta, 1996
           Atlanta vs. Houston, 1997
           Atlanta vs. Houston, 2001
  A.L.—15—Texas vs. New York, 1998
4-game series
  N.L.—20—Arizona vs. New York, 1999
  A.L.—21—Seattle vs. Baltimore, 1997
5-game series
  A.L.—25—Boston vs. Cleveland, 1999
  N.L.—30—St. Louis vs. Arizona, 2001

Fewest left on base by both clubs, series
3-game series
  N.L.—28—Atlanta 14, Los Angeles 14, 1996
  A.L.—31—New York 16, Texas 15, 1998
4-game series

A.L.—46—Baltimore 25, Seattle 21, 1997
N.L.—48—Houston 25, San Diego 23, 1998
5-game series
  A.L.—61—Cleveland 36, Boston 25, 1999
  N.L.—69—Atlanta 36, San Francisco 33, 2002

Most left on bases, game
N.L.—12—Atlanta vs. Colorado, October 4, 1995
         Atlanta vs. San Francisco, October 7, 2002
         Atlanta vs. Chicago, October 4, 2003
         Atlanta vs. Houston, October 6, 2004
         (18—San Francisco vs. Florida, October 3, 2003, 11 inn)
A.L.—12—Boston vs. Cleveland, October 6, 1995
         New York vs. Seattle, October 7, 1995
         Oakland vs. Minnesota, October 1, 2002
         (13—Seattle vs. New York, October 8, 1995, 11 inn
         Baltimore vs. Cleveland, October 5, 1996, 12 inn
         Boston vs. Oakland, October 1, 2003, 12 inn)

Most left on base by both clubs, game
A.L.—22—Boston 12, Cleveland 10, October 6, 1995
         New York 12, Seattle 10, October 7, 1995
         (25—Boston 13, Oakland 12, October 1, 2003, 12 inn)
N.L.—22—Atlanta 11, St. Louis 11, October 3, 2000
         (30—San Francisco 18, Florida 12, October 3, 2003, 11 inn)

Fewest left on base, game
A.L.—0—New York vs. Anaheim, October 1, 2002
N.L.—1—Los Angeles vs. Atlanta, October 3, 1996
        Houston vs. Atlanta, October 6, 1999

Fewest left on base by both clubs, game
N.L.—3—Atlanta 2, Los Angeles 1, October 3, 1996
A.L.—6—Cleveland 3, Boston 3, October 2, 1998

Most left on base, shutout defeat
A.L.—8—New York vs. Oakland, October 11, 2001 (lost 2-0)
N.L.—5—St. Louis vs. Arizona, October 9, 2001 (lost 1-0)
        Houston vs. Atlanta, October 10, 2001 (lost 1-0)

INDIVIDUAL PITCHING

GAMES

Most games, career
A.L.—25—Mariano Rivera, New York, 1995 through 2004; 10 series
N.L.—14—John Smoltz, Atlanta, 1995 through 2004, except 2000; 9 series

Most games, series
3-game series
  A.L.-N.L.—3—many pitchers
4-game series
  A.L.—4—Jesse Orosco, Baltimore, 1996
          Steve Karsay, New York, 2002
          Mariano Rivera, New York, 2004
  N.L.—4—Mike Munoz, Colorado, 1995
          Bruce Ruffin, Colorado, 1995
          Trevor Hoffman, San Diego, 1998
5-game series
  A.L.—5—Scott Williamson, Boston, 2003
  N.L.—5—Kevin Gryboski, Atlanta, 2003, 2004

Most consecutive games, series
A.L.—5—Scott Williamson, Boston, 2003
N.L.—5— Kevin Gryboski, Atlanta, 2003, 2004

GAMES STARTED

Most games started, career
A.L.—11—Andy Pettitte, New York, 1995 through 2003; 9 series, 11 G
N.L.—10—Greg Maddux, Atlanta, 1995 through 2003; 9 series, 11 G

Most opening games started, career
N.L.—5—Greg Maddux, Atlanta, 1995, 1997, 1999, 2000, 2001

A.L.—3—David Cone, New York, 1995, 1996, 1997
        Roger Clemens, Boston, 1995; New York, 2000, 2001
        Pedro Martinez, Boston, 1998, 1999, 2003

Most games started, series
A.L.-N.L.—2—many pitchers

GAMES RELIEVED

Most games by relief pitcher, career
A.L.—25—Mariano Rivera, New York, 1995 through 2004; 10 series
N.L.—13—Kevin Gryboski, Atlanta, 2002 through 2004; 3 series

Most games by relief pitcher, series
A.L.—5—Scott Williamson, Boston, 2003
N.L.—5—Kevin Gryboski, Atlanta, 2003, 2004

COMPLETE GAMES

Most complete games pitched, career
N.L.—2—Curt Schilling, Arizona, 2001, 2002; 2 series, 3 G
A.L.—1—many pitchers

Most complete games, series
N.L.—2—Curt Schilling, Arizona, 2001 (5-game series)
A.L.—1—many pitchers

INNINGS

Most innings pitched, career
A.L.—67.0—Andy Pettitte, New York, 1995 through 2003; 9 series, 11 G
N.L.—66.0—Greg Maddux, Atlanta, 1995 through 2003; 9 series, 11 G

Most innings pitched, series
3-game series
 A.L.—8.0—Erik Hanson, Boston, 1995
  Orlando Hernandez, New York, 1999
  Todd Stottlemyre, Texas, 1998
  David Wells, New York, 1998
 N.L.—9.0—John Smoltz, Atlanta, 1996, 1997
  Greg Maddux, Atlanta, 1997
4-game series
 N.L.—14.2—Kevin Brown, San Diego, 1998
 A.L.—14.0—Mike Mussina, Baltimore, 1997
5-game series
 N.L.—18.0—Curt Schilling, Arizona, 2001
 A.L.—15.2—David Cone, New York, 1995

Most innings pitched, game
A.L.-N.L.—9.0—many pitchers

GAMES WON

Most games won, career
N.L.—6—John Smoltz, Atlanta, 1995 through 2004, except
 2000; 9 series, 14 G
A.L.—4—David Wells, Baltimore, 1996; New York, 1997, 1998,
 2002, 2003; 5 series, 6 G
 Andy Pettitte, New York, 1995 through 2003; 9 series, 11 G
 Pedro Martinez, Boston, 1998, 1999, 2000, 2003; 4 series, 6 G

For a complete list of pitchers with three or
more victories, see page 383.

Most games won by undefeated pitcher, career
N.L.—6—John Smoltz, Atlanta, 1995 through 2004, except
 2000; 9 series, 14 G
A.L.—4—Pedro Martinez, Boston, 1998, 1999, 2003, 2004; 4
 series, 6 G

Most opening games won, career
A.L.—2—David Wells, Baltimore, 1996; New York, 1998
N.L.—2—John Smoltz, Atlanta, 1996, 1998

Most consecutive games won, career
Both leagues—4—David Wells, Cincinnati N.L., October 6,
 1995; Baltimore A.L., October 1, 1996; New York A.L.,
 October 4, 1997; September 29, 1998
N.L.—4—Greg Maddux, Atlanta, October 7, 1995; October 3,
 1996; September 30, 1997; October 3, 1998
 John Smoltz, Atlanta, October 2, 1996; October 3, 1997;
 September 30, 1998; October 9, 1999
A.L.—3—David Wells, Baltimore, October 1, 1996; New York,
 October 4, 1997; September 29, 1998
 Mike Mussina, Baltimore, October 1, 5, 1997; New York,
 October 13, 2001

Most consecutive complete games won, career
N.L.—2—Curt Schilling, Arizona, October 9, 14, 2001
A.L.—none with more than 1

Most games won, series
A.L-N.L.—2—many pitchers

Most games won by relief pitcher, series
N.L.—2—Alejandro Pena, Atlanta, 1995 (4-game series)
 Jeff Fassero, St. Louis, 2002 (3-game series)
A.L.—2—Armando Benitez, Baltimore, 1996 (4-game series)
 Francisco Rodriguez, Anaheim, 2002 (4-game series)

SAVES

Most saves, career
A.L.—13—Mariano Rivera, New York, 1995 through 2004; 10
 series, 25 G
N.L.—5—Mark Wohlers, Atlanta, 1995, 1996, 1997; 3 series, 7
 G

Most saves, series
3-game series
 N.L.—3—Dennis Eckersley, St. Louis, 1996
  Mark Wohlers, Atlanta, 1996
 A.L.—2—Mariano Rivera, New York, 1998
  Kazuhiro Sasaki, Seattle, 2000

4-game series
 A.L.—3—Mike Jackson, Cleveland, 1998
 N.L.—2—Mark Wohlers, Atlanta, 1995
  Trevor Hoffman, San Diego, 1998
5-game series
 A.L.—3—Mariano Rivera, New York, 2000
 N.L.—2—John Smoltz, Atlanta, 2001
  Steve Kline, St. Louis, 2001
  Robb Nen, San Francisco, 2002

GAMES LOST

Most games lost, career
Both leagues—7—Randy Johnson, Seattle A.L., 1995, 1997;
 Houston N.L., 1998; Arizona N.L., 1999, 2001, 2002 (2 in
 A.L., 5 in N.L.); 6 series, 9 G
N.L.—5—Randy Johnson, Houston, 1998; Arizona, 1999, 2001,
 2002; 4 series, 5 G
A.L.—3—Andy Pettitte, New York, 1995 through 2003; 9 series,
 11 G
 Roger Clemens, Boston, 1995; New York, 1999 through 2003;
 6 series, 8 G
 Aaron Sele, Texas, 1998, 1999; Seattle, 2000, 2001; 4 series,
 4 G
 Tim Wakefield, Boston, 1995, 1998, 1999, 2003, 4 series, 6 G

Most games lost by winless pitcher, career
Both leagues—3—Bret Saberhagen, Colorado N.L., 1995;
 Boston, 1998, 1999 (2 in A.L., 1 in N.L.); 3 series, 4 G
A.L.—3—Tim Wakefield, Boston, 1995, 1998, 2003, 2004; 4
 series, 6 G
N.L.—3—Mike Hampton, Houston, 1997, 1998, 1999; New
 York, 2000; Atlanta, 2003; 5 series, 6 G

Most opening games lost, career
Both leagues—4—Randy Johnson, Seattle A.L., 1997; Houston
 N.L., 1998; Arizona N.L., 1999, 2002
N.L.—3—Randy Johnson, Houston, 1998; Arizona, 1999, 2002
A.L.—2—Roger Clemens, New York, 2000, 2002

Most consecutive games lost, career
Both leagues—7—Randy Johnson, Seattle A.L., October 1, 5,
 1997; Houston N.L., September 29, October 5; Arizona N.L.,
 October 5, 2000, October 10, 2001, October 1, 2002
A.L.—3—Roger Clemens, New York, October 3, 7, 2000,
 October 10, 2001
 Aaron Sele, Texas, October 2, 1998, October 5, 1999; Seattle,
 October 13, 2001
N.L.—2—many pitchers

Most games lost, series
N.L.—2—Randy Johnson, Houston, 1998 (4-game series)
 Tom Glavine, Atlanta, 2002 (5-game series)
 Jaret Wright, Atlanta, 2004 (5-game series
A.L.—2—many pitchers

RUNS

Most runs allowed, career
A.L.—32—Andy Pettitte, New York, 1995 through 2003; 9
 series, 11 G
N.L.—30—Tom Glavine, Atlanta, 1995 through 2002; 8 series, 9
 G

Most runs allowed, series
3-game series
 A.L.—8—Jarrod Washburn, Anaheim, 2004
 N.L.—7—Ramon Martinez, Los Angeles, 1995
  Tom Glavine, Atlanta, 2000
  Greg Maddux, Atlanta, 2000
4-game series
 A.L.—9—Charles Nagy, Cleveland, 1996
 N.L.—8—Odalis Perez, Los Angeles, 2004
5-game series
 N.L.—13—Tom Glavine, Atlanta, 2002
 A.L.—11—Andy Pettitte, New York, 1997
  Bret Saberhagen, Boston, 1999
  Tim Hudson, Oakland, 2002

Most runs allowed, game
A.L.—8—Steve Reed, Cleveland, October 10, 1999
 Charles Nagy, Cleveland, October 11, 1999

Paul Abbott, Seattle, October 13, 2001
David Wells, New York, October 5, 2002
N.L.—7—many pitchers

Most runs allowed, inning
A.L.—7—David Wells, New York, October 5, 2002, 5th
N.L.—6—Greg Maddux, Atlanta, October 3, 2000, 1st

EARNED RUNS

Most earned runs allowed, career
A.L.—32—Andy Pettitte, New York, 1995 through 2003; 9 series, 11 G
N.L.—29—Tom Glavine, Atlanta, 1995 through 2002; 8 series, 9 G

Most earned runs allowed, series
3-game series
A.L.—7—Tim Wakefield, Boston, 1995
N.L.—7—Ramon Martinez, Los Angeles, 1995
    Tom Glavine, Atlanta, 2000
4-game series
A.L.—9—Charles Nagy, Cleveland, 1996
N.L.—8—Odalis Perez, Los Angeles, 2004
5-game series
N.L.—13—Tom Glavine, Atlanta, 2002
A.L.—11—Andy Pettitte, New York, 1997
    Bret Saberhagen, Boston, 1999

Most earned runs allowed, game
A.L.—8—Steve Reed, Cleveland, October 10, 1999
  Paul Abbott, Seattle, October 13, 2001
  David Wells, New York, October 5, 2002
N.L.—7—Ramon Martinez, Los Angeles, October 3, 1995
  Randy Johnson, Arizona, October 5, 1999
  Tom Glavine, Atlanta, October 5, 2000
  Tom Glavine, Atlanta, October 6, 2002

Most earned runs allowed, inning
A.L.—7—David Wells, New York, October 5, 2002, 5th
N.L.—5—Odalis Perez, Los Angeles, October 5, 2004, 3rd
  Russ Ortiz, Atlanta, October 10, 2004, 2nd

EARNED-RUN AVERAGE

Lowest earned-run average, career (30 or more innings)
A.L.—0.23—Mariano Rivera, New York, 1995 through 2004; 10 series, 25 G (39 IP)
N.L.—2.03—Matt Morris, St. Louis, 2000, 2001, 2002, 2004; 4 series, 6 G (31 IP)

SHUTOUTS AND SCORELESS INNINGS

Most shutouts, series
N.L.—1—Bobby J. Jones, New York, 2000
  Curt Schilling, Arizona, 2001
  Jason Schmidt, San Francisco, 2003
A.L.—none

For a complete list of shutouts, see page 381.

Most consecutive scoreless innings, career
A.L.—17—David Wells, New York, October 4 (7), 1997; September 29 (8), 1998; October 5 (2), 2002
N.L.—16—Curt Schilling, Arizona, October 9 (9), October 14 (7), 2001

Most consecutive scoreless innings, series
N.L.—16—Curt Schilling, Arizona, October 9 (9), October 14 (7), 2001
A.L.—14—Bartolo Colon, Cleveland, October 9 (8), October 14 (6), 2001

HITS

Most hits allowed, career
A.L.—72—Andy Pettitte, New York, 1995 through 2003; 9 series, 11 G
N.L.—70—Greg Maddux, Atlanta, 1995 through 2003; 9 series, 11 G

Most consecutive hitless innings, career

A.L.—8—Mike Mussina, Baltimore, October 5, 1997 (5 inn); New York, October 13, 2001 (3 inn)
  Pedro Martinez, October 6 (1), October 11 (6), 1999; October 1 (1), 2003
N.L.—7—Kevin Millwood, Atlanta, October 6, 1999

Most hits allowed, series
3-game series
A.L.—9—Curt Schilling, Boston, 2004
N.L.—10—Ramon Martinez, Los Angeles, 1995
    Randy Johnson, Arizona, 2002
4-game series
N.L.—19—Greg Maddux, Atlanta, 1995
A.L.—15—David Wells, Baltimore, 1996
    Charles Nagy, Cleveland, 1996
5-game series
N.L.—17—Tom Glavine, Atlanta, 2002
A.L.—15—David Cone, New York, 1995
    Andy Pettitte, New York, 1997
    Andy Pettitte, New York, 2000

Most hits allowed, game
A.L.—10—John Burkett, Texas, October 1, 1996
  Andy Pettitte, New York, October 8, 2000
  David Wells, New York, October 5, 2002
  Tim Hudson, Oakland, October 1, 2003
  Carlos Silva, Minnesota, October 8, 2004
N.L.—11—Carlos Zambrano, Chicago, October 1, 2003

Most consecutive hitless innings, game
N.L.—7—Kevin Millwood, Atlanta, October 6, 1999 (3rd-9th inn)
A.L.—6—Pedro Martinez, Boston, October 11, 1999 (4th-9th inn)

Fewest hits allowed, game
N.L.—1—Kevin Millwood, Atlanta, October 6, 1999
  Bobby J. Jones, New York, October 8, 2000
A.L.—4—Erik Hanson, Boston, October 4, 1995

Most hits allowed, inning
A.L.—7—David Wells, New York, October 5, 2002, 5th
N.L.—5—Greg Maddux, Atlanta, October 3, 2000, 1st
  Randy Johnson, Arizona, October 1, 2002, 4th
  Russ Ortiz, Atlanta, October 10, 2004, 2nd

Most consecutive hits allowed, inning (consecutive at-bats)
A.L.—5—Bartolo Colon, Cleveland, October 10, 1999, 2nd
  Freddy Garcia, Seattle, October 9, 2001, 4th
  David Wells, New York, October 5, 2002, 5th
N.L.—4—Bret Saberhagen, Colorado, October 7, 1995, 3rd
  Greg Maddux, Atlanta, October 3, 2000, 1st
  Tom Glavine, Atlanta, October 2, 2002, 2nd
  Tom Glavine, Atlanta, October 2, 2002, 4th
  Kirk Rueter, San Francisco, October 3, 2002, 2nd (1 SH during streak)

Most consecutive hits allowed, inning (consecutive plate appearances)
A.L.—5—Bartolo Colon, Cleveland, October 10, 1999, 2nd
  David Wells, New York, October 5, 2002, 5th
N.L.—4—Bret Saberhagen, Colorado, October 7, 1995, 3rd
  Greg Maddux, Atlanta, October 3, 2000, 1st
  Tom Glavine, Atlanta, October 2, 2002, 2nd
  Tom Glavine, Atlanta, October 2, 2002, 4th

DOUBLES, TRIPLES AND HOME RUNS

Most doubles allowed, game
N.L.—4—Ramon Martinez, Los Angeles, October 3, 1995
A.L.—4—Andy Pettitte, New York, October 11, 2001
  Mark Mulder, Oakland, October 6, 2002
  Johan Santana, Minnesota, October 5, 2003
  Pedro Martinez, Boston, October 6, 2003

Most triples allowed, game
A.L.—2—Freddie Garcia, Seattle, October 3, 2000 (pitched 3.1 inn of 10-inn game
N.L.—1—many pitchers

Most home runs allowed, career
Both leagues—11—Randy Johnson, Seattle A.L., 1995, 1997; Houston N.L., 1998; Arizona N.L., 1999, 2001, 2002 (4 in A.L., 7 in N.L.); 6 series, 9 G
A.L.—9—Andy Pettitte, New York, 1995 through 2003; 9 series, 11 G

N.L.—8—John Smoltz, Atlanta, 1995 through 2004, except 2000; 9 series, 14 G

Most home runs allowed, series

3-game series
 N.L.—3—Ismael Valdes, Los Angeles, 1996
 A.L.—2—many pitchers
4-game series
 A.L.—4—Charles Nagy, Cleveland, 1996
 N.L.—4—Odalis Perez, Los Angeles, 2004
5-game series
 N.L.—5—Jaret Wright, Atlanta, 2004
 A.L.—4—David Cone, New York, 1995
  Rick Reed, Minnesota, 2002

Most home runs allowed, game

A.L.—4—Rick Reed, Minnesota, October 4, 2002
N.L.—3—Ismael Valdes, Los Angeles, October 3, 1996
 Odalis Perez, Los Angeles, October 5, 2004
 Jaret Wright, Atlanta, October 6, 2004
 Jason Marquis, St. Louis, October 7, 2004

Most grand slams allowed, game

N.L.—1—Mark Guthrie, Los Angeles, October 6, 1995, 6th inn
 Wilson Alvarez, San Francisco, October 3, 1997, 6th inn
 Matt Karchner, Chicago, September 30, 1998, 7th inn
 Rod Beck, Chicago, October 3, 1998, 8th inn
 Bobby Chouinard, Arizona, October 5, 1999, 9th inn
A.L.—1—John Wetteland, New York, October 7, 1995, 8th inn
 Paul Shuey, Cleveland, October 1, 1996, 6th inn
 Armando Benitez, Baltimore, October 4, 1996, 7th inn
 Chad Ogea, Cleveland, October 4, 1997, 4th inn
 John Wasdin, Boston, October 7, 1999, 4th inn
 Charles Nagy, Cleveland, October 11, 1999, 3rd inn

Most home runs allowed, inning

A.L.-N.L.—2—many pitchers

TOTAL BASES

Most total bases allowed, career

A.L.—114—Andy Pettitte, New York, 1995 through 2003; 9 series, 11 G
N.L.—97—Greg Maddux, Atlanta, 1995 through 2003; 9 series, 11 G

Most total bases allowed, game

A.L.—19—Paul Abbott, Seattle, October 13, 2001
 Brad Radke, Minnesota, October 6, 2004
N.L.—19—Randy Johnson, Arizona, October 1, 2002

BASES ON BALLS

Most bases on balls, career

Both leagues—27—Roger Clemens, Boston, A.L., 1995; New York A.L., 1999 through 2003; Houston N.L., 2004; 7 series, 10 G
N.L.—23—Tom Glavine, Atlanta, 1995 through 2002; 8 series, 9 G
 Mike Hampton, Houston, 1997 through 1999; New York, 2000; Atlanta, 2003, 2004; 6 series, 8 G
A.L.—19—Roger Clemens, Boston, 1995; New York, 1999 through 2003; 6 series, 8 G

Most bases on balls, series

3-game series
 N.L.—8—Mike Hampton, Houston, 1997
 A.L.—6—Orlando Hernandez, New York, 1999
4-game series
 N.L.—7—Kevin Brown, San Diego, 1998
  Odalis Perez, Los Angeles, 2004
 A.L.—6—Andy Pettitte, New York, 1996
  Randy Johnson, Seattle, 1997
5-game series
 A.L.—9—Andy Benes, Seattle, 1995
  David Cone, New York, 1995
 N.L.—8—Russ Ortiz, San Francisco, 2002
  Roger Clemens, Houston, 2004

Most bases on balls, game

N.L.—8—Mike Hampton, Houston, October 1, 1997

A.L.—6—David Cone, New York, October 3, 1995
 Andy Benes, Seattle, October 8, 1995
 Andy Pettitte, New York, October 2, 1996
 Charles Nagy, Cleveland, October 4, 1997
 Orlando Hernandez, New York, October 5, 1999

Most bases on balls, inning

A.L.—4—Andy Benes, Seattle, October 8, 1995, 6th
N.L.—4—Mike Hampton, Houston, October 1, 1997, 5th (consecutive)
 Rick Ankiel, St. Louis, October 3, 2000, 3rd

Most consecutive bases on balls, inning

N.L.—4—Mike Hampton, Houston, October 1, 1997, 5th
A.L.—3—Tim Wakefield, Boston, October 6, 1995, 3rd
 Andy Benes, Seattle, October 8, 1995, 6th

STRIKEOUTS

Most strikeouts, career

Both leagues—73—Randy Johnson, Seattle A.L., 1995, 1997; Houston N.L., 1998; Arizona, 1999, 2001, 2002 (32 in A.L., 41 in N.L.); 6 series, 9 G
N.L.—48—John Smoltz, Atlanta, 1995 through 2004, except 2000; 9 series, 14 G
A.L.—43—Andy Pettitte, New York, 1995 through 2003; 9 series, 11 G

Most strikeouts, series

3-game series
 N.L.—11—John Smoltz, Atlanta, 1997
 A.L.—9—Rick Helling, Texas, 1998
  David Wells, New York, 1998
4-game series
 N.L.—21—Kevin Brown, San Diego, 1998
 A.L.—16—Randy Johnson, Seattle, 1997
  Mike Mussina, Baltimore, 1997
5-game series
 N.L.—18—Curt Schilling, Arizona, 2001
  Kerry Wood, Chicago, 2003
 A.L.—16—Randy Johnson, Seattle, 1995

Most strikeouts, game

N.L.—16—Kevin Brown, San Diego, September 29, 1998
A.L.—13—Randy Johnson, Seattle, October 5, 1997

For a complete list of pitchers with 10 or more strikeouts in a game, see page 384.

Most strikeouts, game, relief pitcher

A.L.—8—Pedro Martinez, Boston, October 11, 1999; 6 IP
N.L.—6—Jose Cabrera, Houston, October 8, 1999; 2 IP

Most consecutive strikeouts, game

A.L.—5—David Cone, New York, October 8, 1995 (3 in 6th inn, 2 in 7th inn)
 Barry Zito, Oakland, October 2, 2003 (3 in 4th inn, 2 in 5th inn)
N.L.—6—Mike Hampton, Atlanta, October 1, 2003, (3 in 1st inn, but not first batter, 3 in 2nd inn)

Most consecutive strikeouts from start of game

N.L.—2—Hideo Nomo, Los Angeles, October 5, 1996
  Livan Hernandez, San Francisco, October 4, 2002
A.L.—2—Andy Benes, Seattle, October 8, 1995

Most strikeouts, inning

A.L.-N.L.—3—many pitchers

HIT BATSMEN, WILD PITCHES AND BALKS

Most hit batsmen, career

Both leagues—4—Steve Reed, Colorado N.L., 1995; Cleveland, 1998, 1999; Atlanta, 2001; 4 series, 8 G
A.L.—4—Tim Wakefield, Boston, 1995, 1998, 1999, 2003; 4 series, 6 G
N.L.—3—Kevin Brown, Florida, 1997; San Diego, 1998; 2 series, 3 G

Most hit batsmen, series
N.L.—3—Kevin Brown, San Diego, 1998
A.L.—2—many pitchers

Most hit batsmen, game
N.L.—2—Kevin Brown, San Diego, October 3, 1998
  Jeff Weaver, Los Angeles, October 7, 2004
A.L.—2—many pitchers

Most hit batsmen, inning
A.L.—2—Felix Heredia, New York, October 8, 2004, 9th
N.L.—2—Jeff Weaver, Los Angeles, October 7, 2004, 5th

Most wild pitches, career
Both leagues—5—Roger Clemens, Boston A.L., 1995; New
  York A.L., 1999 through 2003; Houston N.L., 2004; 7 series,
  10 G
N.L.—5—Rick Ankiel, St. Louis, 2000; 1 series, 1 G
A.L.—3—David Cone, New York, 1995, 1996, 1997, 1998; 4
  series, 5 G
  Francisco Rodriguez, Anaheim, 2002, 2004; 2 series, 5 G

Most wild pitches, series
N.L.—5—Rick Ankiel, St. Louis, 2000 (3-game series)

A.L.—2—David Cone, New York, 1995 (5-game series)
  Steve Karsay, Cleveland, 1999 (5-game series)
  Francisco Rodriguez, Anaheim, 2004 (3-game series)

Most wild pitches, game
N.L.—5—Rick Ankiel, St. Louis, October 3, 2000, 2.2 IP
A.L.—2—David Cone, New York, October 8, 1995 (pitched 7.2
  inn of 11-inn game)
  Steve Karsay, Cleveland, October 10, 1999, 2 IP
  Francisco Rodriguez, Anaheim, October 6, 2004, 2 IP

Most wild pitches, inning
N.L.—5—Rick Ankiel, St. Louis, October 3, 2000, 3rd
A.L.—1—many pitchers

Most balks, nine-inning game
N.L.—1—Kevin Millwood, Atlanta, October 7, 2000
  Andy Benes, St. Louis, October 5, 2002
  (1—Kevin Tapani, Chicago, October 1, 1998, pitched 9 inn of
  10-inn game)
A.L.—none

CLUB PITCHING

APPEARANCES

Most appearances by pitchers, series
3-game series
  N.L.—16—Los Angeles vs. Cincinnati, 1995
        Atlanta vs. St. Louis, 2000
  A.L.—15—Chicago vs. Seattle, 2000
4-game series
  N.L.—24—Colorado vs. Atlanta, 1995
  A.L.—21—Cleveland vs. Baltimore, 1996
5-game series
  N.L.—27—Atlanta vs. Houston, 2004
  A.L.—22—Seattle vs. New York, 1995

Most appearances by pitchers of both clubs, series
3-game series
  N.L.—30—Atlanta 16, St. Louis 14, 2000
  A.L.—28—Chicago 15, Seattle 13, 2000
4-game series
  A.L.—40—Cleveland 21, Baltimore 19, 1996
  N.L.—40—Colorado 24, Atlanta 16, 1995
5-game series
  N.L.—49—Atlanta 27, Houston 22, 2004
  A.L.—41—Seattle 22, New York 19, 1995
        Boston 21, Cleveland 20, 1999
        Oakland 21, Boston 20, 2003

COMPLETE GAMES

Most complete games, series
N.L.—2—Atlanta vs. Houston, 1997 (3-game series)
  Arizona vs. St. Louis, 2001 (5-game series)
A.L.—1—many teams

Most complete games by both clubs, series
N.L.—2—Atlanta 2, Houston 0, 1997 (3-game series)
  Arizona 2, St. Louis 0, 2001 (5-game series)
A.L.—1—many series

SAVES

Most saves, series
3-game series
  N.L.—3—St. Louis vs. San Diego, 1996
        Atlanta vs. Los Angeles, 1996
  A.L.—2—New York vs. Texas, 1998
        New York vs. Texas, 1999
        Seattle vs. Chicago, 2000
4-game series
  A.L.—3—Cleveland vs. Boston, 1998
  N.L.—2—Atlanta vs. Colorado, 1995
        San Diego vs. Houston, 1998
        Atlanta vs. Houston, 1999

5-game series
  A.L.—3—New York vs. Oakland, 2000
  N.L.—2—St. Louis vs. Arizona, 2001
        San Francisco vs. Atlanta, 2002

Most saves by both clubs, series
3-game series
  N.L.—3—St. Louis 3, San Diego 0, 1996
        Atlanta 3, Los Angeles 0, 1996
  A.L.—2—New York 2, Texas 0, 1998
        New York 2, Texas 0, 1999
        Seattle 2, Chicago 0, 2000
4-game series
  N.L.—3—Atlanta 2, Colorado 1, 1995
  A.L.—3—Cleveland 3, Boston 0, 1998
        Anaheim 2, New York 1, 2002
        New York 2, Minnesota 1, 2003
5-game series
  A.L.—4—New York 3, Oakland 1, 2000
        Oakland 2, New York 2, 2001
  N.L.—3—St. Louis 2, Arizona 1, 2001

Fewest saves by one and both clubs, series
A.L.-N.L.—0—many clubs

RUNS AND SHUTOUTS

Most runs allowed, total series
A.L.—163—New York; 10 series, 42 G
N.L.—157—Atlanta; 10 series, 38 G

Most shutouts won, total series
A.L.—7—New York; 10 series, 42 G
N.L.—1—many clubs

For a complete list of shutouts, see page 381.

Most shutouts won, series
A.L.—2—New York vs. Texas, 1998 (3-game series)
  New York vs. Texas, 1999 (3-game series)
N.L.—1—New York vs. San Francisco, 2000 (4-game series)
  Atlanta vs. Houston, 2001 (3-game series)
  Arizona vs St. Louis, 2001 (5-game series)
  San Francisco vs. Florida, 2003 (4-game series)
  Los Angeles vs. St. Louis, 2004 (4-game series)

Most consecutive shutouts won, series
A.L.-N.L.—1—many clubs

Most shutouts by both clubs, series
A.L.—2—New York 2, Texas 0, 1998 (3-game series)
  New York 2, Texas 0, 1999 (3-game series)
  Oakland 1, New York 1, 2001 (5-game series)

N.L.—1—New York 1, San Francisco 0, 2000 (4-game series)
　Atlanta 1, Houston 0, 2001 (3-game series)
　Arizona 1, St. Louis 0, 2001 (5-game series)
　San Francisco 1, Florida 0, 2003 (4-game series)
　Los Angeles 1, St. Louis 0, 2004 (4-game series)

Largest score, shutout game
A.L.—8-0—New York 8, Texas 0, October 5, 1999
N.L.—4-0—New York 4, San Francisco 0, October 8, 2000
　　　　　Los Angeles 4, St. Louis 0, October 9, 2004

Longest shutout game
A.L.-N.L.—none more than 9 inn

Most consecutive innings shutting out opponent, total series
A.L.—25—New York vs. Texas, September 30 (6th), 1998
　through October 7 (3rd), 1999
N.L.—18—New York vs. San Francisco, October 7 (5th inn of
　13-inn game) through October 8 (9th), 2000

Most consecutive innings shutting out opponent, series
A.L.—14—Boston vs. Cleveland, October 3 (12th inn of 13-inn
　game) through October 6 (3rd), 1995
　New York vs. Texas, October 7 (5th) through October 9,
　(9th), 1999

Oakland vs New York, October 10 (9th) through October 13
　(4th), 2001
N.L.—18—New York vs. San Francisco, October 7 (5th inn of
　13-inn game) through October 8 (9th), 2000

WILD PITCHES AND BALKS

Most wild pitches, series
N.L.—5—St. Louis vs. Atlanta, 2000 (3-game series)
A.L.—4—Oakland vs. Minnesota, 2002 (5-game series)
　　　　Anaheim vs. Boston, 2004 (3-game series)

Most wild pitches by both clubs, series
N.L.—6—St. Louis 5, Atlanta 1, 2000 (3-game series)
　　　　Chicago 4, Atlanta 2, 2003 (5-games series)
A.L.—5—Oakland 4, Minnesota 1, 2002 (5-game series)

Most balks, series
N.L.—1—Chicago vs. Atlanta, 1998 (3-game series)
　Atlanta vs. St. Louis, 2000 (3-game series)
　St. Louis vs. Arizona, 2002 (3-game series)
A.L.—none

INDIVIDUAL FIELDING

FIRST BASEMEN
GAMES

Most games, career
M.L.—33—Tino Martinez, Seattle A.L., 1995; New York A.L., 1996
　through 2001; St. Louis N.L., 2002; 8 series
A.L.—30—Tino Martinez, Seattle, 1995; New York, 1996 through
　2001; 7 series
N.L.—19—Jeff Bagwell, Houston, 1997, 1998, 1999, 2001, 2003;
　5 series

PUTOUTS, ASSISTS AND CHANCES ACCEPTED

Most putouts, career
M.L.—290—Tino Martinez, Seattle A.L., 1995; New York A.L.,
　1996 through 2001; St. Louis N.L., 2002; 8 series, 33 G
A.L.—268—Tino Martinez, Seattle, 1995; New York, 1996
　through 2001; 7 series, 30 G
N.L.—153—Jeff Bagwell, Houston, 1997, 1998, 1999, 2001,
　2004; 5 series, 19 G

Most putouts, series
3-game series
　A.L.—29—Tino Martinez, New York, 1999
　N.L.—28—Eric Karros, Los Angeles, 1996
4-game series
　N.L.—43—Albert Pujols, St. Louis, 2004
　A.L.—42—Nick Johnson, New York, 2003

5-game series
　A.L.—53—Jason Giambi, Oakland, 2001
　N.L.—48—Jeff Bagwell, Houston, 2004

Most putouts, game
A.L.—16—Tino Martinez, New York, October 4, 2000
N.L.—14—Fred McGriff, Atlanta, October 3, 1995
　Jeff Kent, San Francisco, October 1, 1997
　Jeff Bagwell, Houston, October 5, 1999

Most putouts, inning
A.L.-N.L.—3—many first basemen

Most assists, career
M.L.—26—Tino Martinez, Seattle A.L., 1995; New York A.L.,
　1996 through 2001; St. Louis N.L., 2002; 8 series, 33 G
A.L.—25—Tino Martinez, Seattle, 1995; New York, 1996
　through 2001; 7 series, 30 G
N.L.—18—Jeff Bagwell, Houston, 1997, 1998, 1999, 2001,
　2004; 5 series, 19 G

Most assists, series
3-game series
　N.L.—6—Jeff Bagwell, Houston, 1997
　A.L.—5—Paul Sorrento, Cleveland, 1995
4-game series
　A.L.—6—John Olerud, New York, 2004
　N.L.—4—Jeff Bagwell, Houston, 1998
　　　　　John Olerud, New York, 1999
　　　　　Todd Zeile, New York, 2000
5-game series
　A.L.—10—Kevin Millar, Boston, 2003
　N.L.—7—J.T. Snow, San Francisco, 2002

Most assists, game
N.L.—3—Jeff Bagwell, Houston, October 1, 1997
　　　　Andres Galarraga, Atlanta, October 3, 1998
　　　　John Olerud, New York, October 8, 1999
A.L.—4—Jim Thome, Cleveland, October 7, 1999
　(5—Kevin Millar, Boston, October 4, 2003, 11 inn)

Most assists, inning
A.L.-N.L.—2—many first basemen

Most chances accepted, career
M.L.—316—Tino Martinez, Seattle A.L., 1995; New York A.L.,
　1996 through 2001; St. Louis N.L., 2002; 8 series, 33 G
A.L.—293—Tino Martinez, Seattle, 1995; New York, 1996
　through 2001; 7 series, 30 G
N.L.—171—Jeff Bagwell, Houston, 1997, 1998, 1999, 2001,
　2003; 5 series, 19 G

Most chances accepted, series
3-game series
　A.L.—32—Paul Sorrento, Cleveland, 1995
　N.L.—30—Eric Karros, Los Angeles, 1996
　　　　　Fred McGriff, Atlanta, 1997
4-game series
　N.L.—44—Albert Pujols, St. Louis, 2004
　A.L.—43—Nick Johnson, New York, 2003
5-game series
　A.L.—55—Jason Giambi, Oakland, 2001
　N.L.—51—Jeff Bagwell, Houston, 2004

Most chances accepted, game
A.L.—17—Tino Martinez, New York, October 4, 2000 (16 PO, 1 A)
N.L.—15—Fred McGriff, Atlanta, October 3, 1995 (14 PO, 1 A)
　Jeff Kent, San Francisco, October 1, 1997 (14 PO, 1 A)
　Jeff Bagwell, Houston, October 5, 1999 (14 PO, 1 A)

Fewest chances offered, game
N.L.—3—Eric Karros, Los Angeles, October 6, 1995 (3 PO)
　J.T. Snow, San Francisco, September 30, 1997 (3 PO)
A.L.—3—Mike Stanley, Boston, October 7, 1999 (2 PO, 1 A)

Most chances accepted, inning
A.L.-N.L.—3—many first basemen

ERRORS AND DOUBLE PLAYS

Most errors, career
A.L.—3—Paul Sorrento, Cleveland, 1995; Seattle, 1997; 2 series, 7 G
N.L.—3—Jeff Bagwell, Houston, 1997, 1998, 1999, 2001, 2004; 5 series, 19 G

Most consecutive errorless games, career
A.L.—18—Tino Martinez, Seattle, New York, October 3, 1995 through October 5, 1999
N.L.—15—Jeff Bagwell, Houston, September 29, 1998 through October 10, 2004

Most errors, series
A.L.—2—Paul Sorrento, Cleveland, 1995 (3-game series)
N.L.—2—Jeff Bagwell, Houston, 1997 (3-game series)
J.T. Snow, San Francisco, 2003 (4-game series)

Most chances accepted, errorless series
A.L.—54—Tino Martinez, New York, 1997 (5-game series)
N.L.—49—J.T. Snow, San Francisco, 2002 (5-game series)

Most errors, game
A.L.-N.L.—1—many first basemen

Most errors, inning
A.L.-N.L.—1—many first basemen

Most double plays, career
A.L.—25—Tino Martinez, Seattle, 1995; New York, 1996 through 2001; 7 series, 30 G
N.L.—16—Jeff Bagwell, Houston, 1997, 1998, 1999, 2001, 2004; 5 series, 19 G

Most double plays, series
A.L.—7—Justin Morneau, Minnesota, 2004 (4-game series)
N.L.—6—J.T. Snow, San Francisco, 2002 (5-game series)
Adam LaRoche, Atlanta, 2004 (5-game series)

Most double plays started, series
A.L.—3—Tino Martinez, New York, 2001 (5-game series)
N.L.—2—J.T. Snow, San Francisco, 2002 (5-game series)

Most double plays, game
N.L.—4—Fred McGriff, Atlanta, October 3, 1995
A.L.—4—Scott Spiezio, Anaheim, October 1, 2002

Most double plays started, game
A.L.-N.L.—1—many first basemen

Most unassisted double plays, game
A.L.—1—Tino Martinez, New York, October 5, 1999, 6th inn
Tino Martinez, New York, October 10, 2001, 7th inn
Kevin Millar, Boston, October 5, 2003, 6th inn
Kevin Millar, Boston, October 6, 2004, 3rd inn
N.L.—none

SECOND BASEMEN
GAMES

Most games, career
M.L.—18—Jeff Kent, Cleveland A.L., 1996; San Francisco N.L., 1997, 2000, 2002; Houston N.L., 2004; 5 series
A.L.—18—Roberto Alomar, Baltimore, 1996, 1997; Cleveland, 1999, 2001; 4 series
N.L.—17—Jeff Kent, San Francisco, 1997, 2000, 2002, Houston, 2004; 4 series

PUTOUTS, ASSISTS AND CHANCES ACCEPTED

Most putouts, career
A.L.—35—Roberto Alomar, Baltimore, 1996, 1997; Cleveland, 1999, 2001; 4 series, 18 G
N.L.—29—Jeff Kent, San Francisco, 1997, 2000, 2002, Houston, 2004; 17 G

Most putouts, series
3-game series
A.L.—10—Ray Durham, Chicago, 2000

N.L.—9—Keith Lockhart, Atlanta, 1998
4-game series
N.L.—14—Craig Biggio, Houston, 1999
A.L.—12—Mike Benjamin, Boston, 1998
5-game series
N.L.—17—Marcus Giles, Atlanta, 2004
A.L.—15—Rey Sanchez, New York, 1997

Most putouts, game
A.L.—8—Rey Sanchez, New York, October 4, 1997
N.L.—6—Craig Biggio, Houston, October 3, 1998
Jeff Kent, San Francisco, October 2, 2002
(6—Luis Castillo, Florida, October 3, 2003, 11 inn)

Most putouts, inning
A.L.-N.L.—2—many second basemen

Most assists, career
M.L.—53—Jeff Kent, Cleveland A.L., 1996; San Francisco N.L., 1997, 2000, 2002; Houston N.L., 2004; 5 series, 18 G
N.L.—52—Jeff Kent, San Francisco, 1997, 2000, 2002, Houston, 2004; 17 G
A.L.—46—Mark McLemore, Texas, 1996, 1998, 1999; Seattle, 2000; 4 series, 13 G

Most assists, series
3-games series
N.L.—13—Fernando Vina, St. Louis, 2000
A.L.—12—Mark McLemore, Texas, 1998
4-game series
A.L.—16—Mark McLemore, Texas, 1996
N.L.—16—Mark Lemke, Atlanta, 1995
5-game series
N.L.—25—Marcus Giles, Atlanta, 2004
A.L.—22—Luis Sojo, New York, 2000

Most assists, game
N.L.—8—Mark Lemke, Atlanta, October 3, 1995
A.L.—7—Bip Roberts, Cleveland, September 30, 1997

Most assists, inning
N.L.—3—Tony Womack, St. Louis, October 9, 2004, 8th
A.L.—2—many second basemen

Most chances accepted, career
M.L.—84—Jeff Kent, Cleveland A.L., 1996; San Francisco N.L., 1997, 2000, 2002; Houston N.L., 2004; 5 series, 18 G
A.L.—70—Roberto Alomar, Baltimore, 1996, 1997; Cleveland, 1999, 2001; 4 series, 18 G
N.L.—81—Jeff Kent, San Francisco, 1997, 2000, 2002; Houston, 2004; 17 G

Most chances accepted, series
3-game series
N.L.—20—Fernando Vina, St. Louis, 2000
Junior Spivey, Arizona, 2002
A.L.—17—Luis Alicea, Boston, 1995
4-game series
A.L.—26—Mark McLemore, Texas, 1996
N.L.—26—Bret Boone, Atlanta, 1999
5-game series
N.L.—42—Marcus Giles, Atlanta, 2004
A.L.—31—Luis Sojo, New York, 2000

Most chances accepted, game
N.L.—11—Mark Lemke, Atlanta, October 3, 1995 (3 PO, 8 A)
Jeff Kent, San Francisco, October 2, 2002 (6 PO, 5 A)
A.L.—11—Luis Sojo, New York, October 7, 2000 (4 PO, 7 A)
(11—Randy Velarde, New York, October 4, 1995 (6 PO, 5 A), 15 inn)

Fewest chances offered, game
A.L.—0—Mark McLemore, Texas, October 7, 1999
N.L.—1—Fernando Vina, St. Louis, October 9, 2001
Marcus Giles, Atlanta, October 12, 2001

Most chances accepted, inning
A.L.-N.L.—3—many second basemen

ERRORS AND DOUBLE PLAYS

Most errors, career
N.L.—3—Eric Young, Colorado, 1995; 1 series, 4 G

A.L.—2—Chuck Knoblauch, New York, 1998, 1999; 2 series, 6 G
Randy Velarde, New York, 1995; Oakland, 2000; 2 series, 9 G
Alfonso Soriano, New York, 2001, 2002, 2003; 3 series, 13 G
Mark Ellis, Oakland, 2002, 2003; 2 series, 10 G
Todd Walker, Boston, 2003; 1 series, 5 G

Most consecutive errorless games, career
A.L.—13—Mark McLemore, Texas, Seattle, October 1, 1996 through October 6, 2000
N.L.—13—Keith Lockhart, Atlanta, September 30, 1998 through October 7, 2002

Most errors, series
N.L.—3—Eric Young, Colorado, 1995 (4-game series)
A.L.—2—Randy Velarde, Oakland, 2000 (5-game series)
Todd Walker, Boston, 2003 (5-game series)

Most chances accepted, errorless series
N.L.—42—Marcus Giles, Atlanta, 2004 (5-game series)
A.L.—29—Rey Sanchez, New York, 1997 (5-game series)

Most errors, game
N.L.—2—Eric Young, Colorado, October 4, 1995
A.L.—1—many second basemen
Most errors, inning
A.L.-N.L.—1—many second basemen

Most double plays, career
A.L.—11—Mark McLemore, Texas, 1996, 1998, 1999; New York, 2000; 4 series, 13 G
N.L.—13—N.L.—42—Marcus Giles, Atlanta, 2001, 2003, 2004; 3 series, 12 G

Most double plays, series
A.L.—6—Luis Sojo, New York, 2000 (5-game series)
N.L.—6—Marcus Giles, Atlanta, 2004 (5-game series)

Most double plays started, series
N.L.—4—Quilvio Veras, San Diego, 1998 (4-game series)
A.L.—3—Mark McLemore, Seattle, 2000 (3-game series)
Luis Sojo, New York, 2000 (5-game series)

Most double plays, game
N.L.—3—Mark Lemke, Atlanta, October 3, 1995
Jeff Kent, San Francisco, October 2, 2002
A.L.—3—Bip Roberts, Cleveland, September 30, 1997
Adam Kennedy, Anaheim, October 1, 2002

Most double plays started, game
N.L.—2—Mark Lemke, Atlanta, October 3, 1995
Quilvio Veras, San Diego, October 3, 1998
(2—Bret Boone, Atlanta, October 8, 1999, 12 inn)
A.L.—2—Mark McLemore, Seattle, October 6, 2000
(2—Ray Durham, Chicago, October 3, 2000, 10 inn)

Most unassisted double plays, game
A.L.-N.L.—none

THIRD BASEMEN
GAMES

Most games, career
N.L.—28—Chipper Jones, Atlanta, 1995 through 2001, 2004; 8 series
A.L.—20—Eric Chavez, Oakland, 2000 through 2003; 4 series

PUTOUTS, ASSISTS AND CHANCES ACCEPTED

Most putouts, career
A.L.—22—Eric Chavez, Oakland, 2000 through 2003; 4 series, 20 G
N.L.—17—Chipper Jones, Atlanta, 1995 through 2001, 2004; 8 series, 28 G

Most putouts, series
3-game series
A.L.—6—Jim Thome, Cleveland, 1995
N.L.—5—Vinny Castilla, Houston, 2001
4-game series
N.L.—7—Robin Ventura, New York, 2000
A.L.—5—John Valentin, Boston, 1998
Travis Fryman, Cleveland, 1998
Alex Rodriguez, New York, 2004

5-game series
A.L.—9—Bill Mueller, Boston, 2003
N.L.—4—Aramis Ramirez, Chicago, 2003

Most putouts, game
N.L.—4—Vinny Castilla, Houston, October 10, 2001
(5—Robin Ventura, New York, October 5, 2000, 10 inn)
A.L.—5—Bill Mueller, Boston, October 5, 2003
(5—Eric Chavez, Oakland, October 4, 2003, 11 inn)

Most putouts, inning
A.L.-N.L.—2—many third basemen

Most assists, career
N.L.—46—Vinny Castilla, Colorado, 1995; Houston, 2001; Atlanta, 2002, 2003; 4 series, 17 G
A.L.—34—Eric Chavez, Oakland, 2000 through 2003; 4 series, 20 G

Most assists, series
3-game series
N.L.—9—Bill Mueller, San Francisco, 1997
A.L.—7—Herbert Perry, Chicago, 2000
4-game series
N.L.—13—Vinny Castilla, Colorado, 1995
A.L.—11—Troy Glaus, Anaheim, 2002
Alex Rodriguez, New York, 2004
5-game series
N.L.—15—Placido Polanco, St. Louis, 2001
Matt Williams, Arizona, 2001
A.L.—11—John Valentin, Boston, 1999
Eric Chavez, Oakland, 2001

Most assists, game
N.L.—7—Matt Williams, Arizona, October 12, 2001
David Bell, San Francisco, October 3, 2002
Vinny Castilla, Atlanta, October 5, 2003
A.L.—5—Scott Brosius, New York, October 4, 2000
(6—Todd Zeile, Baltimore, October 5, 1996, 12 inn)

Most assists, inning
N.L.—3—Vinny Castilla, Colorado, October 4, 1995, 4th
A.L.—3—Travis Fryman, Cleveland, October 11, 2001, 3rd

Most chances accepted, career
N.L.—59—Vinny Castilla, Colorado, 1995; Houston, 2001; Atlanta, 2002, 2003; 4 series, 17 G
A.L.—56—Eric Chavez, Oakland, 2000 through 2003; 4 series, 20 G

Most chances accepted, series
3-game series
A.L.—12—Jim Thome, Cleveland, 1995
Herbert Perry, Chicago, 2000
N.L.—12—Vinny Castilla, Houston, 2001
4-game series
N.L.—16—Vinny Castilla, Colorado, 1995
A.L.—16—Alex Rodriguez, New York, 2004
5-game series
A.L.—19—Bill Mueller, Boston, 2003.
N.L.—17—Matt Williams, Arizona, 2001
David Bell, San Francisco, 2002
Vinny Castilla, Atlanta, 2003

Most chances accepted, game
N.L.—9—Vinny Castilla, Houston, October 10, 2001 (4 PO, 5 A)
A.L.—7—Eric Chavez, Oakland, October 4, 2002 (4 PO, 3 A)
Bill Mueller, Boston, October 5, 2003 (5 PO, 2 A)
(7—Todd Zeile, Baltimore, October 5, 1996 (1 PO, 6 A),12 inn)

Fewest chances offered, game
A.L.-N.L.—0—many third basemen

Most chances accepted, inning
A.L.-N.L.—3—many third basemen

ERRORS AND DOUBLE PLAYS

Most errors, career
A.L.—4—Todd Zeile, Texas, 1996, 1998, 1999; 3 series, 10 G
N.L.—4—Ken Caminiti, San Diego, 1996, 1998, 1999; 3 series, 11 G
Chipper Jones, Atlanta, 1995 through 2001, 2004; 8 series, 28 G

Most consecutive errorless games, career
M.L.—15 Bill Mueller, San Francisco N.L., Boston A.L., September 30, 1997 through October 8, 2004
A.L.—14—Travis Fryman, Cleveland, September 29, 1998 through October 15, 2001
N.L.—13—Vinny Castilla, Colorado, Houston, Atlanta, October 4, 1995 through October 1, 2003

Most errors, series
N.L.—3—Ken Caminiti, San Diego, 1996 (3-game series)
A.L.—3—Charlie Hayes, New York, 1997 (5-game series)
Scott Brosius, New York, 2001 (5-game series)

Most chances accepted, errorless series
A.L.—19—Bill Mueller, Boston, 2003 (5-game series)
N.L.—14—Vinny Castilla, Atlanta, 2002 (5-game series)
Aramis Ramirez, Chicago, 2003 (5-games series)

Most errors, game
N.L.—2—Ken Caminiti, San Diego, October 5, 1996
A.L.—1—many third basemen
(2—Eric Chavez, Oakland, October 4, 2003, 11 inn)

Most errors, inning
A.L.-N.L.—1—many third basemen

Most double plays, career
N.L.—8—Vinny Castilla, Colorado, 1995; Houston, 2001; Atlanta, 2002, 2003; 4 series, 17 G
A.L.—6—Eric Chavez, Oakland, 2000 through 2003; 4 series, 20 G

Most double plays, series
A.L.—3—John Valentin, Boston, 1998 (4-game series)
Scott Brosius, New York, 2000 (5-game series)
Eric Chavez, Oakland, 2003 (5 game series)
N.L.—3—Vinny Castilla, Houston, 2001 (3-game series)
Matt Williams, Arizona, 2001 (5-game series)
Vinny Castilla, Atlanta, 2003 (5-game series)
Chipper Jones, Atlanta, 2004 (5-game series)

Most double plays started, series
A.L.—3—John Valentin, Boston, 1998 (4-game series)
Scott Brosius, New York, 2000 (5-game series)
Eric Chavez, Oakland, 2003 (5-game series)
N.L.—3—Vinny Castilla, Houston, 2001 (3-game series)
Matt Williams, Arizona, 2001 (5-game series)
Chipper Jones, Atlanta, 2004 (5-game series)

Most double plays, game
N.L.—3—Vinny Castilla, Houston, October 10, 2001
A.L.—2—Scott Brosius, New York, October 4, 2000
Troy Glaus, Anaheim, October 1, 2002

Most double plays started, game
N.L.—3—Vinny Castilla, Houston, October 10, 2001
A.L.—2—Scott Brosius, New York, October 4, 2000
(2—Eric Chavez, Oakland, October 4, 2003, 11 inn)

Most unassisted double plays, game
A.L.—1—Scott Brosius, New York, October 3, 2000
N.L.—none

SHORTSTOPS
GAMES

Most games, career
A.L.—37—Derek Jeter, New York, 1996 through 2004; 9 series
N.L.—18—Edgar Renteria, Florida, 1997; St. Louis, 2000 through 2002, 2004; 5 series
Rafael Furcal, Atlanta, 2000, 2002, 2003, 2004; 4 series

PUTOUTS, ASSISTS AND CHANCES ACCEPTED

Most putouts, career
A.L.—65—Derek Jeter, New York, 1996 through 2004; 9 series, 37 G
N.L.—38—Edgar Renteria, Florida, 1997; St. Louis, 2000 through 2002, 2004; 5 series, 18 G

Most putouts, series
3-game series
A.L.—10—Jose Valentin, Chicago, 2000
N.L.—9—Edgar Renteria, Florida, 1997
4-game series
A.L.—15—Derek Jeter, New York, 2004
N.L.—10—Rich Aurilia, San Francisco, 2000
Edgar Renteria, St. Louis, 2004
5-game series
A.L.—12—Derek Jeter, New York, 1997
Omar Vizquel, Cleveland, 1997
N.L.—9—Rafael Furcal, Atlanta, 2004

Most putouts, game
N.L.—6—Rey Sanchez, Atlanta, October 10, 2001
A.L.—5—Alex Rodriguez, Seattle, October 2, 1997
Omar Vizquel, Cleveland, October 6, 1997
(7—Derek Jeter, New York, October 9, 2004, 11 inn)

Most putouts, inning
A.L.-N.L.—2—many shortstops

Most assists, career
A.L.—97—Derek Jeter, New York, 1996 through 2004; 9 series, 37 G
N.L.—64—Rafael Furcal, Atlanta, 2000, 2002, 2003, 2004; 4 series, 18 G

Most assists, series
3-game series
A.L.—17—Jose Valentin, Chicago, 2000
N.L.—11—Edgar Renteria, Florida, 1997
4-game series
N.L.—17—Rich Aurilia, San Francisco, 2003
A.L.—21—Cristian Guzman, Minnesota, 2004
5-game series
N.L.—22—Rafael Furcal, Atlanta, 2003
A.L.—21—Omar Vizquel, Cleveland, 2001

Most assists, game
A.L.—9—Nomar Garciaparra, Boston, October 6, 2003
N.L.—7—Ricky Gutierrez, Houston, October 3, 1998
Alex S. Gonzalez, Chicago, October 3, 2003
Rafael Furcal, Atlanta, October 9, 2004

Most assists, inning
N.L.—3—Jeff Blauser, Atlanta, October 4, 1995, 7th
A.L.—3—Derek Jeter, New York, October 2, 2002, 4th

Most chances accepted, career
A.L.—162—Derek Jeter, New York, 1996 through 2004; 9 series, 37 G
N.L.—89—Rafael Furcal, Atlanta, 2000, 2002, 2003, 2004; 4 series, 18 G

Most chances accepted, series
3-game series
A.L.—27—Jose Valentin, Chicago, 2000
N.L.—20—Edgar Renteria, Florida, 1997
4-game series
A.L.—27—Cristian Guzman, Minnesota, 2004
N.L.—25—Rich Aurilia, San Francisco, 2003
5-game series
N.L.—30—Rafael Furcal, Atlanta, 2003
A.L.—27—Derek Jeter, New York, 1997
Omar Vizquel, Cleveland, 2001

Most chances accepted, game
A.L.—11—Jose Valentin, Chicago, October 4, 2000 (4 PO, 7 A)
Cristian Guzman, Minnesota, October 8, 2004 (4 PO, 7 A)
(11—Luis Sojo, Seattle, October 4, 1995 (3 PO, 8 A), 15 inn
Jose Valentin, Chicago, October 3, 2000 (5 PO, 6 A), 10 inn)
N.L.—9—Ricky Gutierrez, Houston, October 3, 1998 (2 PO, 7 A)
Rey Sanchez, Atlanta, October 10, 2001 (6 PO, 3 A)
Alex S. Gonzalez, Chicago, October 3, 2003 (2 PO, 7 A)
Rafael Furcal, Atlanta, October 9, 2004 (2 PO, 7 A)

Fewest chances offered, game

N.L.—0—Chris Gomez, San Diego, October 3, 1996
　　Jose Vizcaino, San Francisco, September 30, 1997
　　Hanley Frias, Arizona, October 5, 1999
A.L.—1—Alex Rodriguez, Seattle, October 5, 1997
　　Derek Jeter, New York, September 30, 1998
　　Nomar Garciaparra, Boston, October 6, 1999
　　Derek Jeter, New York, October 4, 2002

Most chances accepted, inning

A.L.-N.L.—3—many shortstops

ERRORS AND DOUBLE PLAYS

Most errors, career

N.L.—5—Edgar Renteria, Florida, 1997; St. Louis, 2000 through
　　2002, 2004; 5 series, 18 G
A.L.—5—Derek Jeter, New York, 1996 through 2004; 9 series,
　　37 G

Most consecutive errorless games, career

A.L.—24—Omar Vizquel, Cleveland, October 3, 1995 through
　　October 13, 2001
N.L.—11—Walt Weiss, Colorado, Atlanta, October 3, 1995
　　through October 3, 2000

Most errors, series

N.L.—3—Julio Lugo, Houston, 2001 (3-game series)
A.L.—1—many shortstops

Most chances accepted, errorless series

A.L.—27—Derek Jeter, New York, 1997 (5-game series)
　　Derek Jeter, New York, 2003 (4-game series)
N.L.—29—Rafael Furcal, Atlanta, 2004 (5-game series)

Most errors, game

N.L.—2—Edgar Renteria, Florida, October 3, 1997
　　Julio Lugo, Houston, October 10, 2001
A.L.—1—many shortstops

Most errors, inning

A.L.-N.L.—1—many shortstops

Most double plays, career

A.L.—25—Derek Jeter, New York, 1996 through 2004; 9 series,
　　37 G
N.L.—10—Rich Aurilia, San Francisco, 2000, 2002, 2003; 3
　　series, 13 G

Most double plays, series

A.L.—6—Cristian Guzman, Minnesota, 2004 (4-game series)
N.L.—5—Rey Sanchez, Atlanta, 2001 (3-game series)
　　Rich Aurilia, San Francisco, 2002 (5-game series)
　　Rafael Furcal, Atlanta, 2003 (5-game series)

Most double plays started, series

A.L.—5—Christian Guzman, Minnesota, 2004 (4-game series)
N.L.—4—Rafael Furcal, Atlanta, 2003 (5-game series)

Most double plays, game

N.L.—3—Jeff Blauser, Atlanta, October 3, 1995
　　Rey Sanchez, Atlanta, October 10, 2001
A.L.—3—Kevin Elster, Texas, October 4, 1996
　　Jose Valentin, Chicago, October 4, 2000
　　Cristian Guzman, Minnesota, October 5, 2004

Most double plays started, game

A.L.—3—Cristian Guzman, Minnesota, October 5, 2004
N.L.—2—Rey Sanchez, Atlanta, October 9, 2001
　　Rich Aurilia, San Francisco, October 2, 2002
　　Rafael Furcal, Atlanta, September 30, 2003
　　Rafael Furcal, Atlanta, October 4, 2003

Most unassisted double plays, game

A.L.-N.L.—none

OUTFIELDERS
GAMES

Most games, career

A.L.—42—Bernie Williams, New York, 1995 through 2004; 10
　　series
N.L.—34—Andruw Jones, Atlanta, 1996 through 2004; 9 series

PUTOUTS, ASSISTS AND CHANCES ACCEPTED

Most putouts, career

A.L.—105—Bernie Williams, New York, 1995 through 2004; 10
　　series, 42 G
N.L.—80—Andruw Jones, Atlanta, 1996 through 2004; 9
　　series, 34 G

Most putouts, series

3-game series
　　A.L.—15—Bernie Williams, New York, 1999
　　N.L.—13—Luis Gonzalez, Houston, 1997
4-game series
　　A.L.—16—Darryl Hamilton, Texas, 1996
　　N.L.—15—Jose Cruz, Jr., San Francisco, 2003
5-game series
　　A.L.—20—Jacque Jones, Minnesota, 2002
　　N.L.—13—Andruw Jones, Atlanta, 2003
　　　　　　 Carlos Beltran, Houston, 2004

Most putouts by left fielder, game

N.L.—6—Luis Gonzalez, Houston, September 30, 1997
A.L.—5—Albert Belle, Cleveland, October 4, 1995
　　Jacque Jones, Minnesota, October 1, 2002
　　Jacque Jones, Minnesota, October 4, 2002
　　(6—Vince Coleman, Seattle, October 8, 1995, 11 inn)

Most putouts by center fielder, game

A.L.—7—Bernie Williams, New York, October 5, 1999
　　Johnny Damon, Oakland, October 13, 2001
N.L.—6—Willie McGee, St. Louis, October 1, 1996
　　Andruw Jones, Atlanta, October 9, 1999

Most putouts by right fielder, game

N.L.—8—Jose Cruz, Jr., September 20, 2003
A.L.—6—Ichiro Suzuki, Seattle, October 11, 2001
　　(6—Paul O'Neill, New York, October 2, 1996, 12 inn)

Most consecutive putouts, game

A.L.—3—Johnny Damon, Oakland, October 13, 2001; 2 in 5th
　　inn, 1 in 6th inn
N.L.—2—many outfielders

Most putouts, inning

N.L.—2—many outfielders
A.L.—3—Bernie Williams, New York, October 5, 1999, 3rd (CF)
　　Adam Piatt, Oakland, October 4, 2000, 1st (RF)
　　Mike Cameron, Seattle, October 6, 2000, 2nd (CF)
　　Johnny Damon, Oakland, October 13, 2001, 5th (CF)

Most assists, career

A.L.—4—David Justice, Cleveland, 1998, 1999; New York,
　　2000, 2001; Oakland, 2002; 5 series, 17 G
　　Manny Ramirez, Cleveland, 1995 through 1999; Boston,
　　2003, 2004; 7 series, 29 G
N.L.—2—Albert Pujols, St. Louis, 2001, 2002, 2004; 3 series, 10 G
　　Kenny Lofton, Atlanta, 1997; San Francisco, 2002; Chicago,
　　2003; 3 series, 18G
　　Andruw Jones, Atlanta, 1996 through 2004; 9 series, 34 G

Most assists, series

A.L.—2—Manny Ramirez, Cleveland, 1996 (4-game series)
　　David Justice, Cleveland, 1999 (5-game series)
　　Johnny Damon, Boston, 2003 (5-game series)
N.L.—2—Albert Pujols, St. Louis, 2002 (3-game series)

Most assists, game

A.L.-N.L.—1—many outfielders

Most assists, inning

A.L.-N.L.—1—many outfielders

Most chances accepted, career

A.L.—106—Bernie Williams, New York, 1995 through 2004; 10
　　series, 42 G
N.L.—82—Andruw Jones, Atlanta, 1996 through 2004; 9
　　series, 34 G

Most chances accepted, series

3-game series
　　A.L.—15—Bernie Williams, New York, 1999
　　N.L.—14—Luis Gonzalez, Houston, 1997

4-game series
 A.L.—17—Darryl Hamilton, Texas, 1996
 N.L.—15—Jose Cruz, Jr, San Francisco, 2003
5-game series
 A.L.—20—Jacque Jones, Minnesota, 2002
 N.L.—13—Andruw Jones, Atlanta, 2002
   Carlos Beltran, Houston, 2004

Most chances accepted by left fielder, game
N.L.—6—Luis Gonzalez, Houston, September 30, 1997 (6 PO)
A.L.—5—Albert Belle, Cleveland, October 4, 1995 (5 PO)
 Jacque Jones, Minnesota, October 1, 2002 (5 PO)
 Jacque Jones, Minnesota, October 4, 2002 (5 PO)
 (6—Vince Coleman, Seattle, October 8, 1995 (6 PO), 11 inn)

Most chances accepted by center fielder, game
A.L.—7—Bernie Williams, New York, October 5, 1999 (7 PO)
 Johnny Damon, Oakland, October 13, 2001 (7 PO)
 (7—Darryl Hamilton, Texas, October 2, 1996 (6 PO, 1 A), 12 inn)
N.L.—6—Willie McGee, St. Louis, October 1, 1996 (6 PO)
 Andruw Jones, Atlanta, October 9, 1999 (6 PO)

Most chances accepted by right fielder, game
N.L.—8—Jose Cruz, Jr., San Francisco, September 20, 2003 (8 PO)
A.L.—6—Ichiro Suzuki, Seattle, October 11, 2001 (6 PO)
 (6—Paul O'Neill, New York, October 2, 1996 (6 PO), 12 inn)

Longest game with no chances offered to outfielder
A.L.—13 inn—Albert Belle, Cleveland, October 3, 1995
N.L.—12 inn—Carl Everett, Houston, October 8, 1999

Most chances accepted, inning
A.L.-N.L.—3—many outfielders

ERRORS AND DOUBLE PLAYS

Most errors, career
A.L.—3—Kenny Lofton, Cleveland, 1995, 1996, 1998, 1999, 2001; 5 series, 21 G
N.L.—2—Ryan Klesko, Atlanta, 1995, 1996, 1997, 1998; 4 series, 13 G
 Tony Womack, Arizona, 1999; 1 series, 4 G
 Marquis Grissom, Atlanta, 1995, 1996; San Francisco, 2003; 3 series, 11 G

Most consecutive errorless games, career
A.L.—36—Bernie Williams, New York, October 3, 1995 through October 2, 2003
N.L.—26—Andruw Jones, Atlanta, October 2, 1996 through October 1, 2003

Most errors, series
A.L.—2—Kenny Lofton, Cleveland, 1995 (3-game series)
N.L.—2—Tony Womack, Arizona, 1999 (4-game series)

Most chances accepted, errorless series
A.L.—18—Johnny Damon, Boston, 2003 (5-game series)
N.L.—13—Andruw Jones, Atlanta, 2002 (5-game series)

Most errors, game
A.L.-N.L.—1—many outfielders

Most errors, inning
A.L.-N.L.—1—many outfielders

Most double plays, career
A.L.-N.L.—1—many outfielders

Most double plays, game
A.L.-N.L.—1—many outfielders

Most double plays started, game
A.L.-N.L.—1—many outfielders

Most unassisted double plays, game
A.L.-N.L.—none

Most games, career
A.L.—26—Jorge Posada, New York, 1997 through 2004; 8 series
N.L.—21—Javy Lopez, Atlanta, 1995 through 1998, 2000, 2002, 2003; 7 series

PUTOUTS, ASSISTS AND CHANCES ACCEPTED

Most putouts, career
N.L.—171—Javy Lopez, Atlanta, 1995 through 1998, 2000, 2002, 2003; 7 series, 21 G
A.L.—162—Jorge Posada, New York, 1997 through 2004; 8 series, 26 G

Most putouts, series
3-game series
 N.L.—31—Mike Piazza, Los Angeles, 1995
 A.L.—29—Jason Varitek, Boston, 2004
4-game series
 A.L.—40—Sandy Alomar Jr., Cleveland, 1995
 N.L.—35—Eddie Perez, Atlanta, 1999
5-game series
 A.L.—51—Einar Diaz, Cleveland, 2001
 N.L.—39—Damian Miller, Arizona, 2001
   Javy Lopez, Atlanta, 2003

Most putouts, game
A.L.—13—Einar Diaz, Cleveland, October 9, 2001
 (22—Sandy Alomar Jr., Cleveland, October 5, 1996, 12 inn)
N.L.—15—Carlos Hernandez, San Diego, September 29, 1998
 (16—Tony Eusebio, Houston, October 8, 1999, 12 inn)

Most putouts, inning
A.L.-N.L.—3—many catchers

Most assists, career
N.L.—14—Javy Lopez, Atlanta, 1995 through 1998, 2000, 2002, 2003; 7 series, 21 G
A.L.—11—Jorge Posada, New York, 1995 through 2004; 8 series, 26 G

Most assists, series
3-game series
 N.L.—4—Mike Piazza, Los Angeles, 1996
   Carlos Hernandez, St. Louis, 2000
 A.L.—3—Ivan Rodriguez, Texas, 1998
4-game series
 N.L.—6—Carlos Hernandez, San Diego, 1998
 A.L.—5—Jorge Posada, New York, 2004
5-game series
 N.L.—4—Javy Lopez, Atlanta, 2003
   Raul Chavez, Houston, 2004
 A.L.—4—Greg Myers, Oakland, 2001
   Einar Diaz, Cleveland, 2001

Most assists, game
N.L.—4—Raul Chavez, Houston, October 7, 2004
A.L.—2—many catchers
 (3—Jorge Posada, New York, October 9, 2004, 11 inn)

Most assists, inning
A.L.-N.L.—1—many catchers

Most chances accepted, career
N.L.—185—Javy Lopez, Atlanta, 1995 through 1998, 2000, 2002, 2003; 7 series, 21 G
A.L.—176—Jorge Posada, New York, 1997 through 2004; 8 series, 26 G

Most chances accepted, series
3-game series
 N.L.—31—Mike Piazza, Los Angeles, 1995
 A.L.—31—Jason Varitek, Boston, 2004
4-game series
 A.L.—44—Sandy Alomar Jr., Cleveland, 1996
 N.L.—40—Carlos Hernandez, San Diego, 1998

DIVISION SERIES Individual fielding

5-game series
A.L.—55—Einar Diaz, Cleveland, 2001
N.L.—43—Javy Lopez, Atlanta, 2003

Most chances accepted, game
N.L.—17—Carlos Hernandez, San Diego, September 29, 1998
(15 PO, 2 A)
(18—Tony Eusebio, Houston, October 8, 1999 (16 PO, 2 A),
12 inn)
A.L.—16—Einar Diaz, Cleveland, October 15, 2001 (14 PO, 2 A)
(24—Sandy Alomar, Jr., Cleveland, October 5, 1996 (22 PO, 2
A), 12 inn)

Fewest chances offered, game
A.L.—1—Joe Girardi, New York, October 4, 1997
N.L.—2—Eli Marrero, St. Louis, October 13, 2001

Most chances accepted, inning
A.L.-N.L.—3—many catchers

ERRORS AND PASSED BALLS

Most errors, career
A.L.—4—Sandy Alomar Jr., Cleveland, 1995, 1996, 1997, 1998,
1999; 5 series, 21 G
N.L.—2—Javy Lopez, Atlanta, 1995 through 1998, 2000, 2002,
2003; 7 series, 21 G

Most consecutive errorless games, career
M.L.—14—Ivan Rodriguez, Texas A.L., Florida N.L., October 1,
1996 through October 4, 2003
A.L.—14—Jorge Posada, New York, October 2, 1997 through
October 15, 2001
Ramon Hernandez, Oakland, October 7, 2000 through October
2, 2003
N.L.—14—Javy Lopez, Atlanta, October 5, 1996 through
October 1, 2003

Most errors, series
A.L.—2—Mike Macfarlane, Boston, 1995 (3-game series)
N.L.—1—many catchers

Most chances accepted, errorless series
N.L.—42—Damian Miller, Arizona, 2001 (5-game series)
A.L.—41—Dan Wilson, Seattle, 2001 (5-game series)

Most errors, game
A.L.-N.L.—1—many catchers

Most errors, inning
A.L.-N.L.—1—many catchers

Most passed balls, career
A.L.—5—Jason Varitek, Boston, 1998, 1999, 2003, 2004; 4 series,
13 G
N.L.—2—Carlos Hernandez, San Diego, 1998; St. Louis, 2000; 2
series, 7 G

Most passed balls, series
A.L.—3—Jason Varitek, Boston, 1999 (5-game series)
N.L.—2—Carlos Hernandez, San Diego, 1998 (4-game series)

Most passed balls, game
N.L.—2—Carlos Hernandez, San Diego, September 29, 1998
A.L.—2—Jason Varitek, Boston, September 30, 1998
Jason Varitek, Boston, October 10, 1999

Most passed balls, inning
N.L.—2—Carlos Hernandez, San Diego, September 29, 1998, 3rd
A.L.—2—Jason Varitek, Boston, September 30, 1998, 1st

DOUBLE PLAYS AND RUNNERS CAUGHT STEALING

Most double plays, career
M.L.—4—Joe Girardi, Colorado N.L., 1995; New York A.L.,
1996, 1997, 1998, 1999; 5 series, 17 G (2 in A.L., 2 in N.L.)
N.L.—3—Javy Lopez, Atlanta, 1995 through 1998, 2000, 2002,
2003; 7 series, 21 G

A.L.—2—Ivan Rodriguez, Texas, 1996, 1998, 1999; 3 series, 10
G
Jorge Posada, New York, 1997 through 2004; 8 series, 26 G
Jason Varitek, Boston, 1998, 1999, 2003, 2004; 4 series, 13
G
Henry Blanco, Minnesota, 2004; 1 series, 4 G

Most double plays, series
N.L.—2—Joe Girardi, Colorado, 1995 (4-game series)
Brian Johnson, San Diego, 1996 (3-game series)
Mike Piazza, Los Angeles, 1996 (3-game series)
Javy Lopez, Atlanta, 1998 (3-game series)
Bobby Estalella, San Francisco, 2000 (4-game series)
A.L.—2—Henry Blanco, Minnesota, 2004 (4-game series)

Most double plays started, series
N.L.—2—Joe Girardi, Colorado, 1995 (4-game series)
Mike Piazza, Los Angeles, 1996 (3-game series)
Javy Lopez, Atlanta, 1998 (3-game series)
Bobby Estalella, San Francisco, 2000 (4-game series)
A.L.—1—many catchers

Most double plays, game
N.L.—2—Mike Piazza, Los Angeles, October 5, 1996
(2—Joe Girardi, Colorado, October 6, 1995, 10 inn
Javy Lopez, Atlanta, October 1, 1998, 10 inn)
A.L.—2—Henry Blanco, Minnesota, October 5, 2004

Most double plays started, game
N.L.—2—Mike Piazza, Los Angeles, October 5, 1996
(2—Joe Girardi, Colorado, October 6, 1995, 10 inn
Javy Lopez, Atlanta, October 1, 1998, 10 inn)
A.L.—1—many catchers

Most unassisted double plays, game
A.L.—1—Jason Varitek, Boston, October 1, 2003, 2nd inn
N.L.—none

Most runners caught stealing, career
N.L.—7—Javy Lopez, Atlanta, 1995 through 1998, 2000, 2002,
2003; 7 series, 21 G
A.L.—6—Jorge Posada, New York, 1997 through 2004; 8
series, 26 G

Most runners caught stealing, series
A.L.—3—Chris Hoiles, Baltimore, 1996 (4-game series)
Jorge Posada, New York, 2004 (4-game series)
N.L.—3—Mike Piazza, Los Angeles, 1996 (3-game series)
Javy Lopez, Atlanta, 1998 (3-game series)
Carlos Hernandez, St. Louis, 2000 (3-game series)

Most runners caught stealing, game
A.L.—2—Ivan Rodriguez, Texas, September 29, 1998
Jorge Posada, New York, October 9, 2004
(2—Chris Hoiles, Baltimore, October 5, 1996, 12 inn)
N.L.—2—Brian Johnson, San Diego, October 1, 1996
Carlos Hernandez, St. Louis, October 3, 2000
Brad Ausmus, Houston, October 9, 2001
(3—Mike Piazza, Los Angeles, October 2, 1996, 10 inn)

Most runners caught stealing, inning
A.L.-N.L.—1—many catchers

PITCHERS
GAMES

Most games, career
A.L.—25—Mariano Rivera, New York, 1995 through 2004; 10
series
N.L.—14—John Smoltz, Atlanta, 1995 through 2004, except
2000; 9 series

Most games, series
3-game series
A.L.-N.L.—3—many pitchers
4-game series
A.L.—4—Jesse Orosco, Baltimore, 1996

Steve Karsay, New York, 2002
Mariano Rivera, New York, 2004
N.L.—4—Mike Munoz, Colorado, 1995
Bruce Ruffin, Colorado, 1995
Trevor Hoffman, San Diego, 1998
5-game series
N.L.—4—Steve Kline, St. Louis, 2001
Robb Nen, San Francisco, 2002
Chad Qualls, Houston, 2004
A.L.—4—Norm Charlton, Seattle, 1995
Bill Risley, Seattle, 1995
Paul Assenmacher, Cleveland, 1997
Mike Jackson, Cleveland, 1997
Jeff Nelson, New York, 1997

PUTOUTS, ASSISTS AND CHANCES ACCEPTED

Most putouts, career
N.L.—7—Mike Hampton, Houston, 1997 through 1999; New York, 2000; Atlanta, 2003, 2004; 6 series, 8 G
A.L.—6—Derek Lowe, Boston, 1998, 1999, 2003, 2004; 4 series, 9 G
Mariano Rivera, New York, 1995 thrugh 2004; 10 series, 25 G

Most putouts, series
3-game series
N.L.—3—Mike Hampton, Houston, 1997
A.L.—2—Charles Nagy, Cleveland, 1995
Pedro Martinez, Boston, 2004
Curt Schilling, Boston, 2004
4-game series
A.L.—2—Jamie Moyer, Seattle, 1997
Mike Mussina, Baltimore, 1997
Pete Schourek, Boston, 1998
Mariano Rivera, New York, 2003, 2004
Jon Lieber, New York, 2004
N.L.—2—Mike Hampton, New York, 2000
5-game series
A.L.—6—Derek Lowe, Boston, 2003
N.L.—2—Woody Williams, St. Louis, 2001
Livan Hernandez, San Francisco, 2002
John Smoltz, Atlanta, 2004

Most putouts, game
N.L.—3—Mike Hampton, Houston, October 1, 1997
Mike Hampton, New York, October 4, 2000
A.L.—3—Charles Nagy, Cleveland, October 7, 1999
(6—Derek Lowe, Boston, October 4, 2003, pitched 7 inn of 11-inn game)

Most putouts, inning
A.L.—2—Charles Nagy, Cleveland, October 6, 1995, 4th
N.L.—2—Jay Powell, Houston, October 1, 1998, 8th

Most assists, career
A.L.—16—Andy Pettitte, New York, 1995 through 2003; 9 series, 11 G
N.L.—12—Greg Maddux, Atlanta, 1995 through 2003; 9 series, 11 G

Most assists, series
3-game series
A.L.—3—Roger Clemens, New York, 1999
N.L.—3—Tom Glavine, Atlanta, 2001
Shane Reynolds, Houston, 2001
4-game series
N.L.—5—Greg Maddux, Atlanta, 1995
A.L.—4—Charles Nagy, Cleveland, 1996
Jeff Fassero, Seattle, 1997
Mike Mussina, Baltimore, 1997
5-game series
A.L.—5—Andy Pettitte, New York, 1997
N.L.—4—Mike Hampton, Atlanta, 2003

Most assists, game
A.L.—4—Charles Nagy, Cleveland, October 1, 1996
Jeff Fassero, Seattle, October 4, 1997
Andy Pettitte, New York, October 6, 1997
Tim Hudson, Oakland, October 11, 2001
Mark Mulder, Oakland, October 2, 2002
N.L.—4—Greg Maddux, Atlanta, October 3, 1995

Kevin Millwood, Atlanta, October 6, 1999

Most assists, inning
A.L.—2—Ken Hill, Cleveland, October 3, 1995, 13th
Jeff Fassero, Seattle, October 4, 1997, 1st
Mike Mussina, Baltimore, October 5, 1997, 7th
Roger Clemens, New York, October 7, 2000, 4th
Roger Clemens, New York, October 1, 2002, 2nd
N.L.—2—Kevin Millwood, Atlanta, October 6, 1999, 3rd

Most chances accepted, career
A.L.—18—Andy Pettitte, New York, 1995 through 2003; 9 series, 11 G
N.L.—17—Greg Maddux, Atlanta, 1995 through 2003; 9 series, 11 G

Most chances accepted, series
3-game series
A.L.—4—Erik Hanson, Boston, 1995
Roger Clemens, New York, 1999
N.L.—4—Greg Maddux, Atlanta, 1996
Tom Glavine, Atlanta, 2001
4-game series
N.L.—6—Greg Maddux, Atlanta, 1995
A.L.—6—Mike Mussina, Baltimore, 1997
5-game series
A.L.—8—Derek Lowe, Boston, 2003
N.L.—5—Mike Hampton, Atlanta, 2003

Most chances accepted, game
N.L.—5—Greg Maddux, Atlanta, October 3, 1995
Kevin Millwood, Atlanta, October 6, 1999
A.L.—5—Jeff Fassero, Seattle, October 4, 1997
Andy Pettitte, New York, October 6, 1997
Tim Hudson, Oakland, October 11, 2001
(8—Derek Lowe, Boston, October 4, 2003, pitched 7 inn of 11-inn game)

Most chances accepted, inning
A.L.-N.L.—2—many pitchers

ERRORS AND DOUBLE PLAYS

Most errors, career
A.L.—2—LaTroy Hawkins, Minnesota, 2002, 2003; 2 series, 6 G
N.L.—1—many pitchers

Most consecutive errorless games, career
A.L.—25—Mariano Rivera, New York, October 4, 1995 through October 9, 2004
N.L.—14—John Smoltz, Atlanta, October 6, 1995 through October 10, 2004

Most errors, series
A.L.—2—LaTroy Hawkins, Minnesota, 2003 (4-game series)
N.L.—1—many pitchers

Most chances accepted, errorless series
N.L.—6—Greg Maddux, Atlanta, 1995 (4-game series)
A.L.—6—Mike Mussina, Baltimore, 1997 (4-game series)
Andy Pettitte, New York, 1997 (5-game series)

Most errors, game
A.L.-N.L.—1—many pitchers

Most double plays, career
A.L.—2—Darren Oliver, Texas, 1996; 1 series, 1 G
N.L.—1—many pitchers

Most double plays, series
A.L.—2—Darren Oliver, Texas, 1996 (4-game series)
N.L.—1—many pitchers

Most double plays started, series
A.L.-N.L.—1—many pitchers

Most double plays, game
A.L.—2—Darren Oliver, Texas, October 4, 1996
N.L.—1—many pitchers

Most double plays started, game
A.L.-N.L.—1—many pitchers

Most unassisted double plays, game
A.L.-N.L.—none

CLUB FIELDING

AVERAGE

Highest fielding average, series
3-game series
N.L.—1.000—San Francisco vs. Florida, 1997
　　　　　　Atlanta vs. Chicago, 1998
A.L.—.991—New York vs. Texas, 1998
　　　　　Texas vs. New York, 1998
　　　　　Seattle vs. Chicago, 2000
　　　　　Boston vs. Anaheim, 2004
4-game series
A.L.—1.000—Baltimore vs. Seattle, 1997
　　　　　　Boston vs. Cleveland, 1998
N.L.—1.000—New York vs. Arizona, 1999
　　　　　　New York vs. San Francisco, 2000
　　　　　　St. Louis vs. Los Angeles, 2004
5-game series
N.L.—1.000—Atlanta vs. San Francisco, 2002
　　　　　　Chicago vs. Atlanta, 2003
A.L.—.990—Seattle vs. New York, 1995

For a list of fielding statistics by teams each series, see page 385.

Highest fielding average by both clubs, series
3-game series
A.L.—.991—New York .991, Texas .991, 1998
N.L.—.983—Los Angeles .991, Atlanta .974, 1996
4-game series
A.L.—.997—Baltimore 1.000, Seattle .993, 1997
　　　　　Boston 1.000, Cleveland .993, 1998
N.L.—.997—New York 1.000, San Francisco .994, 2000
5-game series
N.L.—.989—Atlanta 1.000, San Francisco .979, 2002
A.L.—.988—Seattle .990, New York .985, 1995

Lowest fielding average, series
3-game series
N.L.—.954—Atlanta vs. St. Louis, 2000
A.L.—.955—Cleveland vs. Boston, 1995
4-game series
N.L.—.955—San Francisco vs. Florida, 2003
A.L.—.972—New York vs. Anaheim, 2002
5-game series
N.L.—.945—San Francisco vs. Atlanta, 2002
A.L.—.970—Oakland vs. New York, 2001

Lowest fielding average by both clubs, series
3-game series
A.L.—.961—Boston .967, Cleveland .955, 1995
N.L.—.969—Atlanta .974, Houston .962, 1997
4-game series
N.L.—.970—Florida .986, San Francisco .955, 2003
A.L.—.975—Cleveland .980, Baltimore .975, 1996
5-game series
A.L.—.974—New York .978, Oakland .970, 2001
N.L.—.981—St. Louis .984, Arizona .979, 2001

PUTOUTS

Most putouts, total series
A.L.—1,159—New York; 10 series, 42 G
N.L.—1,035—Atlanta; 10 series, 38 G

Most putouts, series
3-game series
A.L.—93—Cleveland vs. Boston, 1995
N.L.—84—Atlanta vs. Los Angeles, 1996
　　　　Atlanta vs. Chicago, 1998
4-game series
A.L.—123—New York vs. Minnesota, 2004
N.L.—120—New York vs. San Francisco, 2000

5-game series
A.L.—154—Seattle vs. New York, 1995
N.L.—140—Houston vs. Atlanta, 2004

Most putouts by both clubs, series
3-game series
A.L.—182—Cleveland 93, Boston 89, 1995
N.L.—165—Atlanta 84, Los Angeles 81, 1996
4-game series
A.L.—245—New York 123, Minnesota 122, 2004
N.L.—238—New York 120, San Francisco 118, 2000
5-game series
A.L.—304—Seattle 154, New York 150, 1995
N.L.—278—Houston 140, Atlanta 138, 2004

Fewest putouts, series
3-game series
N.L.—75—San Diego vs. St. Louis, 1996
　　　　Houston vs. Atlanta, 1997
　　　　Atlanta vs. St. Louis, 2000
A.L.—75—Texas vs. New York, 1998
　　　　Texas vs. New York, 1999
4-game series
N.L.—102—Houston vs. San Diego, 1998
　　　　　Los Angeles vs. St. Louis, 2004
A.L.—102—New York vs. Anaheim, 2002
5-game series
A.L.—129—Cleveland vs. Boston, 1999
　　　　　Cleveland vs. Seattle, 2001
N.L.—131—St. Louis vs. Arizona, 2001

Fewest putouts by both clubs, series
3-game series
N.L.—156—St. Louis 81, San Diego 75, 1996
　　　　　Atlanta 81, Houston 75, 1997
　　　　　St. Louis 81, Atlanta 75, 2000
A.L.—156—New York 81, Texas 75, 1998
　　　　　New York 81, Texas 75, 1999
4-game series
A.L.—207—Anaheim 105, New York 102, 2002
N.L.—207—St. Louis 105, Los Angeles 102, 2004
5-game series
A.L.—259—Boston 130, Cleveland 129, 1999
N.L.—263—Arizona 132, St. Louis 131, 2001

Most putouts by outfield, game
A.L.—13—New York vs. Texas, October 5, 1999
N.L.—12—San Francisco vs. Florida, September 30, 1997
　　　(13—New York vs. San Francisco, October 7, 2000, 13 inn)

Most putouts by outfield of both clubs, game
A.L.—22—New York 12, Seattle 10, October 3, 1995
N.L.—19—Cincinnati 11, Los Angeles 8, October 4, 1995
Los Angeles 10, St. Louis 9, October 7, 2004
　　　(24—San Francisco 13, New York 11, October 7, 2000, 13 inn)

Fewest putouts by outfield, game
N.L.—2—Houston vs. San Diego, October 3, 1998 (fielded 8 inn)
Atlanta vs. Chicago, September 30, 2003
Atlanta vs. Chicago, October 5, 2003
Los Angeles vs. St. Louis, October 5, 2004 (fielded 8 inn)
　　　(3—Los Angeles vs. Atlanta, October 2, 1996, 10 inn)
A.L.—2—many teams
　　　(4—Oakland vs. Boston, October 4, 2003, 11 inn
Anaheim vs. Boston, October 8, 2004, 10 inn
New York vs. Minnesota, October 6, 2004, 12 inn)

Fewest putouts by outfield of both clubs, game
N.L.—7—many games
　　　(8—Atlanta 4, Houston 4, October 7, 2004, 10 inn)
A.L.—5—Seattle 3, Cleveland 2, October 15, 2001 (Cleveland fielded 8 inn)
　　　(9—Boston 5, Oakland 4, October 4, 2003, 11 inn)

Most putouts by outfield, inning
A.L.-N.L.—3—many clubs

Most putouts by outfield of both clubs, inning
A.L.-N.L.—5—many times

Most putouts by catchers of both clubs, inning
A.L.—6—Chicago 3, Seattle 3, October 4, 2000, 9th
N.L.—5—Houston 3, Atlanta 2, October 3, 1997, 2nd

ASSISTS

Most assists, total series
A.L.—435—New York; 10 series, 42 G
N.L.—413—Atlanta; 10 series, 38 G

Most assists, series
3-game series
  A.L.—38—Chicago vs. Seattle, 2000
  N.L.—34—Arizona vs. St. Louis, 2002
4-game series
  A.L.—55—New York vs. Minnesota, 2004
  N.L.—50—Colorado vs. Atlanta, 1995
         Houston vs. Atlanta, 1999
5-game series
  N.L.—68—Atlanta vs. Chicago, 2003
  A.L.—60—Oakland vs. New York, 2001

Most assists by both clubs, series
3-game series
  A.L.—66—Chicago 38, Seattle 28, 2000
  N.L.—64—Florida 33, San Francisco 31, 1997
4-game series
  A.L.—105—New York 55, Minnesota 50, 2004
  N.L.—99—Colorado 50, Atlanta 49, 1995
5-game series
  N.L.—122—Atlanta 64, Houston 58, 2004
  A.L.—113—Cleveland 58, New York 55, 1997

Fewest assists, series
3-game series
  N.L.—18—St. Louis vs. San Diego, 1996
  A.L.—25—Anaheim vs. Boston, 2004
          Boston vs. Anaheim, 2004
4-game series
  N.L.—31—Los Angeles vs. St. Louis, 2004
  A.L.—33—Boston vs. Cleveland, 1998
          Anaheim vs. New York, 2002
5-game series
  A.L.—36—Minnesota vs. Oakland, 2002
  N.L.—40—Atlanta vs. San Francisco, 2002

Fewest assists by both clubs, series
3-game series
  N.L.—45—Atlanta 25, Chicago 20, 1998
  A.L.—50—Anaheim 25, Boston 25, 2004
4-game series
  N.L.—65—St. Louis 34, Los Angeles 31, 2004
  A.L.—72—New York 39, Anaheim 33, 2002
5-game series
  A.L.—84—Oakland 48, Minnesota 36, 2002
  N.L.—96—San Francisco 56, Atlanta 40, 2002

Most assists, game
N.L.—21—Atlanta vs. Colorado, October 3, 1995
A.L.—17—New York vs. Cleveland, October 6, 1997
  New York vs. Oakland, October 4, 2000
  (21—New York vs. Seattle, October 4, 1995, 15 inn)

Most assists by both clubs, game
N.L.—35—Atlanta 21, Colorado 14, October 3, 1995
A.L.—32—New York 17, Cleveland 15, October 6, 1997
  (38—New York 21, Seattle 17, October 4, 1995, 15 inn)

Fewest assists, game
A.L.—4—Boston vs. Cleveland, October 2, 1998 (fielded 8 inn)
  Minnesota vs. Oakland, October 5, 2002
  (4—Cleveland vs. Baltimore, October 5, 1996, 12 inn)
N.L.—2—Los Angeles vs. St. Louis, October 7, 2004 (fielded 8 inn)

Fewest assists by both clubs, game
A.L.—15—Baltimore 10, Cleveland 5, October 4, 1996
  (10—New York 5, Seattle 5, October 8, 1995, 11 inn)
N.L.—10—St. Louis 8, Los Angeles 2, October 7, 2004

Most assists by outfield, game
A.L.—2—Cleveland vs. Baltimore, October 2, 1996
  Seattle vs. Baltimore, October 2, 1997
  New York vs. Minnesota, October 8, 2004
  (2—Seattle vs. New York, October 4, 1995, 15 inn)
N.L.—1—many clubs

Most assists by outfield of both clubs, game
A.L.—3—Seattle 2, Baltimore 1, October 2, 1997
  (3—Seattle 2, New York 1, October 4, 1995, 15 inn)
N.L.—1—many games

Most assists by outfield, inning
A.L.-N.L.—1—many clubs

CHANCES OFFERED

Fewest chances offered to outfield, game
N.L.—2—Houston vs. San Diego, October 3, 1998 (fielded 8 inn)
  Atlanta vs. Chicago, October 5, 2003
  Los Angeles vs. St. Louis, October 5, 2004 (fielded 8 inn)
  (3—Los Angeles vs. Atlanta, October 2, 1996, 10 inn)
A.L.—2—Boston vs. Cleveland, October 11, 1999
  (4—Anaheim vs. Boston, October 8, 2004, 10 inn)

Fewest chances offered to outfield of both clubs, game
N.L.—7—Florida 4, San Francisco 3, October 1, 1997
  Houston 4, San Diego 3, October 4, 1998
  New York 4, Arizona 3, October 6, 1999
  St. Louis 5, Los Angeles 2, October 5, 2004 (Los Angeles fielded 8 inn)
  (8—Atlanta 4, Houston 4, October 7, 2004, 11 inn)
A.L.—7—Boston 4, Cleveland 3, September 30, 1998 (Boston fielded 8 inn)
  (11—Minnesota 6, New York 5, October 9, 2004, 11 inn)

ERRORS

Most errors, total series
A.L.—26—New York; 10 series, 42 G
N.L.—23—Atlanta; 10 series, 38 G

Most errors, series
3-game series
  A.L.—6—Cleveland vs. Boston, 1995
  N.L.—5—Atlanta vs. St. Louis, 2000
4-game series
  N.L.—7—Colorado vs. Atlanta, 1995
         San Francisco vs. Florida, 2003
  A.L.—4—Baltimore vs. Cleveland, 1996
         New York vs. Anaheim, 2002
5-game series
  N.L.—6—Atlanta vs. Chicago, 2003
  A.L.—6—Oakland vs. New York, 2001

Most errors by both clubs, series
3-game series
  A.L.—10—Cleveland 6, Boston 4, 1995
  N.L.—7—Houston 4, Atlanta 3, 1997
4-game series
  N.L.—9—Colorado 7, Atlanta 2, 1995
         San Francisco 7, Florida 2, 2003
  A.L.—7—Baltimore 4, Cleveland 3, 1996
5-game series
  A.L.—10—Oakland 6, New York 4, 2001
          Boston 5, Oakland 5, 2003
  N.L.—7—Arizona 4, St. Louis 3, 2001

Fewest errors, series
3-game series
  N.L.—0—San Francisco vs. Florida, 1997
         Atlanta vs. Chicago, 1998
  A.L.—1—New York vs. Texas, 1998
         Texas vs. New York, 1998
         Seattle vs. Chicago, 1998
         Boston vs. Anaheim, 2004
4-game series
  A.L.—0—Baltimore vs. Seattle, 1997
         Boston vs. Cleveland, 1998
  N.L.—0—New York vs. Arizona, 1999

New York vs. San Francisco, 2000
St. Louis vs. Los Angeles, 2004
5-game series
N.L.—0—Atlanta vs. San Francisco, 2002
Chicago vs. Atlanta, 2003
A.L.—2—Seattle vs. New York, 1995
New York vs. Oakland, 2000

Fewest errors by both clubs, series
3-game series
A.L.—1—Cleveland 1, Boston 0, 1998
N.L.—4—Atlanta 3, Los Angeles 1, 1996
Florida 4, San Francisco 0, 1997
Chicago 4, Atlanta 0, 1998
Houston 3, Atlanta 1, 2001
St. Louis 2, Arizona 2, 2002
4-game series
A.L.—1—Seattle 1, Baltimore 0, 1997
N.L.—1—San Francisco 1, New York 0, 2000
5-game series
N.L.—4—San Francisco 4, Atlanta 0, 2002
Houston 3, Atlanta 1, 2004
A.L.—5—New York 3, Seattle 2, 1995

Most errors, game
N.L.—4—Colorado vs. Atlanta, October 3, 1995
Atlanta vs. Chicago, October 3, 2003
A.L.—3—Oakland vs. New York, October 15, 2001
Seattle vs. Cleveland, October 13, 2001
Minnesota vs. Oakland, October 1, 2003
(4—Oakland vs. Boston, October 4, 2003, 11 inn)

Most errors by both clubs, game
A.L.—4—Oakland 3, New York 1, October 15, 2001
(6—Oakland 4, Boston 2, October 4, 2003, 11 inn)
N.L.—5—Colorado 4, Atlanta 1, October 3, 1995

Most errors by infield, game
N.L.—3—many teams
A.L.—2—many clubs
(3—Oakland vs. Boston, October 4, 2003, 11 inn)

Most errors by infields of both clubs, game
N.L.—3—Colorado 2, Atlanta 1, October 4, 1995
Atlanta 2, Houston 1, October 3, 1997
San Francisco 2, Florida 1, September 30, 2003
A.L.—3—Oakland 2, New York 1, October 15, 2001
(4—Oakland 3, Boston 1, October 4, 2003, 11 inn)

Most errors by outfield, game
N.L.—2—Atlanta vs. Los Angeles, October 3, 1996
A.L.—2—Seattle vs. Cleveland, October 13, 2001

Most errors by outfields of both clubs, game
N.L.—2—Atlanta 1, Colorado 1, October 3, 1995
Cincinnati 1, Los Angeles 1, October 6, 1995
Houston 1, Atlanta 1, October 1, 1997
Atlanta 2, Los Angeles 0, October 3, 1996
A.L.—2—Seattle 2, Cleveland 0, October 13, 2001

Longest errorless game
A.L.—15 inn—New York vs. Seattle, October 4, 1995
N.L.—13 inn—New York vs. San Francisco, October 7, 2000
San Francisco vs. New York, October 7, 2000

Longest errorless game by both clubs
A.L.—11 inn—New York 0, Seattle 0, October 8, 1995
N.L.—13 inn—New York 0, San Francisco 0, October 7, 2000

Most errors, inning
A.L.—3—Oakland vs. Boston, October 4, 2003, 2nd
N.L.—2—Colorado vs. Atlanta, October 3, 1995, 6th
Florida vs. San Francisco, October 1, 1997, 9th
Atlanta vs. St. Louis, October 3, 2000, 1st
Atlanta vs. Chicago, October 6, 2003, 5th

PASSED BALLS

Most passed balls, total series
A.L.—8—Boston; 5 series, 20 G
N.L.—2—San Diego; 2 series, 7 G

Most passed balls, series
A.L.—3—Boston vs. Cleveland, 1999 (5-game series)
N.L.—2—San Diego vs. Houston, 1998 (4-game series)

Most passed balls by both clubs, series
A.L.—3—Boston 3, Cleveland 0, 1999 (5-game series)
N.L.—2—San Diego 2, Houston 0, 1998 (4-game series)

Most passed balls, game
N.L.—2—San Diego vs. Houston, September 29, 1998
A.L.—2—Boston vs. Cleveland, September 30, 1998
Boston vs. Cleveland, October 10, 1999

DOUBLE AND TRIPLE PLAYS

Most double plays, total series
A.L.—38—New York; 10 series, 42 G
N.L.—36—Atlanta; 10 series, 38 G

Most double plays, series
3-game series
N.L.—7—Houston vs. Atlanta, 2001
A.L.—5—New York vs. Texas, 1999
Seattle vs. Chicago, 2000
Chicago vs. Seattle, 2000
4-game series
A.L.—9—Minnesota vs. New York, 2004
N.L.—5—Atlanta vs. Colorado, 1995
Colorado vs. Atlanta, 1995
San Diego vs. Houston, 1998
New York vs. Arizona, 1999
5-game series
N.L.—8—Atlanta vs. Chicago, 2003
A.L.—7—New York vs. Oakland, 2000

Most double plays by both clubs, series
3-game series
N.L.—12—Houston 7, Atlanta 5, 2001
A.L.—10—Seattle 5, Chicago 5, 2000
4-game series
A.L.—13—Minnesota 9, New York 4, 2004
N.L.—10—Atlanta 5, Colorado 5, 1995
5-game series
N.L.—11—Atlanta 7, Houston 4, 2004
A.L.—10—New York 7, Oakland 3, 2000

Fewest double plays, series
3-game series
A.L.—0—Boston vs. Cleveland, 1995
N.L.—0—St. Louis vs. San Diego, 1996
Atlanta vs. St. Louis, 2000
St. Louis vs. Arizona, 2002
4-game series
A.L.—1—Cleveland vs. Baltimore, 1996
Baltimore vs. Seattle, 1997
N.L.—1—Houston vs. San Diego, 1998
New York vs. San Francisco, 2000
5-game series
A.L.—2—New York vs. Cleveland, 1997
Oakland vs. Minnesota, 2002
Boston vs. Oakland, 2003
N.L.—2—Atlanta vs. San Francisco, 2002
Chicago vs. Atlanta, 2003

Fewest double plays by both clubs, series
3-game series
A.L.—1—Cleveland 1, Boston 0, 1995
N.L.—1—Arizona 1, St. Louis 0, 2002
4-game series
A.L.—3—Baltimore 2, Cleveland 1, 1996
N.L.—3—San Francisco 3, Florida 0, 2003
5-game series
N.L.—8—Arizona 4, St. Louis 4, 2001
San Francisco 6, Atlanta 2, 2002
A.L.—6—Oakland 4, Minnesota 2, 2002
Oakland 4, Boston 2, 2003

Most double plays, game
A.L.—5—Minnesota vs. New York, October 5, 2004
N.L.—4—Atlanta vs. Colorado, October 3, 1995
Houston vs. Atlanta, October 10, 2001

Most double plays by both clubs, game
N.L.—7—Houston 4, Atlanta 3, October 10, 2001
A.L.—6—Anaheim 4, New York 2, October 1, 2002

Most triple plays, series
A.L.-N.L.—none

MISCELLANEOUS

CLUB AND DIVISION
ONE-RUN DECISIONS

Most one-run games won, series
A.L.—2—New York vs. Texas, 1996 (4-game series)
  Cleveland vs. New York, 1997 (5-game series)
  Cleveland vs. Boston, 1998 (4-game series)
  Boston vs. Oakland, 2003 (5-game series)
  New York vs. Minnesota, 2004 (4-game series)
N.L.—2—Atlanta vs. Los Angeles, 1996 (3-game series)
  Florida vs. San Francisco, 1997 (3-game series)
  San Diego vs. Houston, 1998 (4-game series)
  New York vs. San Francisco, 2000 (4-game series)
  Arizona vs. St. Louis, 2001 (5-game series)
  Florida vs. San Francisco, 2003 (5-game series)

Most one-run games by both clubs, series
N.L.—3—San Diego (won 2) vs. Houston (won 1), 1998 (4-game series)
A.L.—3—Boston (won 2) vs. Oakland (won 1), 2003 (5-game series)

LENGTH OF GAMES
BY INNINGS

Longest game
A.L.—15 inn—Seattle 5 at New York 7, October 4, 1995
N.L.—13 inn—San Francisco 2 at New York 3, October 7, 2000

For a complete list of extra-inning games, see page 381.

Most extra-inning games, total series
A.L.—5—New York; 10 series, 42 G; won 4, lost 1
N.L.—4—Atlanta; 10 series, 38 G; won 3, lost 1

Most extra-inning games won, total series
A.L.—4—New York; 10 series, 42 G; lost 1
N.L.—3—Atlanta; 10 series, 38 G; lost 1

Most extra-inning games lost, total series
N.L.—2—San Francisco; 3 series, 12 G; won 0
A.L.—2—Boston; 4 series, 20 G; won 2
  Minnesota, 3 series, 13 G; won 0

Most extra-inning games, series
A.L.—2—New York vs. Seattle, 1995 (5-game series)
  Oakland vs. Boston, 2003 (5-game series)
  New York vs. Minnesota, 2004 (4-game series)
N.L.—2—New York vs. San Francisco, 2000 (4-game series)

BY TIME

Longest 9-inning game
A.L.—4 hours, 13 minutes—New York 9 at Oakland 2, October 14, 2001
N.L.—3 hours, 47 minutes—San Francisco 3 at Atlanta 1, October 7, 2002

Longest extra-inning game
N.L.—5 hours, 22 minutes—San Francisco 2 at New York 3, October 7, 2000, 13 inn
A.L.—5 hours, 13 minutes—Seattle 5 at New York 7, October 4, 1995, 15 inn

Shortest game
N.L.—2 hours, 8 minutes—Atlanta 3 at Los Angeles 2, October 3, 1996
A.L.—2 hours, 27 minutes—Cleveland 4 at Boston 3, October 2, 1998

SERIES STARTING AND FINISHING DATES

Earliest date for series game
N.L.—September 29, 1998—San Diego at Houston
A.L.—September 29, 1998—Texas at New York
  September 29, 1998—Boston at Cleveland

Earliest date for series final game
A.L.—October 2, 1998—New York at Texas (3-game series)
N.L.—October 3, 1997—Florida at San Francisco (3-game series)
  October 3, 1997—Atlanta at Houston (3-game series)
  October 3, 1998—Atlanta at Chicago (3-game series)

Latest date for series start
A.L.—October 10, 2001—Oakland at New York
N.L.—October 9, 2001—Atlanta at Houston
  October 9, 2001—St. Louis at Arizona

Latest date for series finish
A.L.—October 15, 2001—Oakland at New York (5-game series)
  October 15, 2001—Cleveland at Seattle (5-game series)
N.L.—October 14, 2001—St. Louis at Arizona (5-game series)

SERIES AND GAMES WON

Most series won
N.L.—6—Atlanta, 1995, 1996, 1997, 1998, 1999, 2001 (lost 4)
A.L.—7—New York, 1996, 1998, 1999, 2000, 2001, 2003, 2004 (lost 3)

For complete lists of results, and series played by all teams, see page 340.

Most times winning series in three consecutive games
N.L.—4—Atlanta, 1996, 1997, 1998, 2001
A.L.—2—New York, 1998, 1999

Winning series after winning first game
N.L.—accomplished 17 times
A.L.—accomplished 8 times

Winning series after losing first game
A.L.—accomplished 12 times
N.L.—accomplished 3 times

Winning series after trailing two games to one
N.L.—San Francisco vs. Atlanta, 2002
A.L.—Seattle vs. New York, 1995
  Cleveland vs. New York, 1997
  Boston vs. Cleveland, 1999
  New York vs. Oakland, 2001
  Seattle vs. Cleveland, 2001
  Minnesota vs. Oakland, 2002
  Boston vs. Oakland, 2003

Winning series after losing first two games
A.L.—Seattle vs. New York, 1995
  Boston vs. Cleveland, 1999
  New York vs. Oakland, 2001
  Boston vs. Oakland, 2003
N.L.—none

Most games won, total series
A.L.—26—New York; 10 series; won 26, lost 16
N.L.—24—Atlanta; 10 series; won 24, lost 14

For complete lists of results, and games played by all teams, see page 340.

Most consecutive games won, total series
N.L.—10—Atlanta, 1995 (last 1), 1996 (all 3), 1997 (all 3), 1998 (all 3)
A.L.—6—New York, 1998 (all 3), 1999 (all 3)

SERIES AND GAMES LOST

Most series lost
N.L.—4—Houston, 1997, 1998, 1999, 2001 (won 1)
      Atlanta, 2000, 2002, 2003, 2004 (won 6)
A.L.—4—Oakland, 2000, 2001, 2002, 2003 (won 0)

**For complete lists of results, and games
played by all teams, see page 340.**

Most games lost, total series
A.L.—16—New York; 10 series; won 26, lost 16
N.L.—14—Atlanta; 10 series; won 24, lost 14
      Houston; 5 series; won 5, lost 14

Most consecutive games lost, total series
A.L.—9—Texas, 1996 (last 3), 1998 (all 3), 1999 (all 3)
N.L.—8—Los Angeles, 1995 (all 3), 1996 (all 3), 2004 (first 2)

ATTENDANCE

Largest attendance, series
3-game series
   A.L.—164,853—New York vs. Texas, 1999
   N.L.—164,844—St. Louis vs. San Diego, 1996
4-game series
   N.L.—225,763—San Diego vs. Houston, 1998
   A.L.—224,561—New York vs. Minnesota, 2003
5-game series
   A.L.—286,839—New York vs. Seattle, 1995
   N.L.—239,108—Chicago vs. Atlanta, 2003

**For a list of attendance each series, see
page 382.**

Smallest attendance, series
3-game series
   N.L.—111,180—Atlanta vs. Houston, 2001
   A.L.—122,693—Boston vs. Cleveland, 1995
4-game series
   A.L.—157,065—Cleveland vs. Boston, 1998
   N.L.—178,210—Atlanta vs. Houston, 1999
5-game series
   A.L.—202,917—Boston vs. Cleveland, 1999
   N.L.—220,386—San Francisco vs. Atlanta, 2002

Largest attendance, game
N.L.—65,464—At Florida, October 4, 2003 (Florida 7, San
   Francisco 6)
A.L.—59,579—At Seattle, October 1, 1997 (Baltimore 9, Seattle 3)

Smallest attendance, game
A.L.—31,953—At Oakland, October 2, 2002 (Oakland 9,
   Minnesota 1)
N.L.—35,553—At Houston, October 9, 2001 (Atlanta 7,
   Houston 4)

Largest attendance by each club, game

AMERICAN LEAGUE

Club	Attendance	Date
Anaheim	45,118	Oct. 6, 2004
Baltimore	49,137	Oct. 4, 1997
Boston	35,547	Oct. 8, 2004
Chicago	45,383	Oct. 4, 2000
Cleveland	45,274	Oct. 4, 1997
Minnesota	55,960	Oct. 5, 2002
New York	57,485	Oct. 7, 1999
Oakland	55,861	Oct. 13, 2001
Seattle	59,579	Oct. 1, 1997
Texas	50,860	Oct. 4, 1996

NATIONAL LEAGUE

Club	Attendance	Date
Arizona	49,584	Oct. 5, 1999
Atlanta	54,357	Oct. 5, 2003
Chicago	39,983	Oct. 4, 2003
Cincinnati	53,276	Oct. 6, 1995
Colorado	50,063	Oct. 4, 1995
Florida	65,464	Oct. 4, 2003
Houston	53,688	Oct. 3, 1997
Los Angeles	56,286	Oct. 10, 2004
New York	56,270	Oct. 7, 2000
St. Louis	56,752	Oct. 3, 1996
San Diego	65,235	Oct. 3, 1998
San Francisco	57,188	Oct. 3, 1997

Smallest attendance by each club, game

AMERICAN LEAGUE

Club	Attendance	Date
Anaheim	44,608	Oct. 5, 2004
Baltimore	47,644	Oct. 1, 1996
Boston	33,114	Oct. 2, 1998
Chicago	45,290	Oct. 3, 2000
Cleveland	44,218	Oct. 3, 1995
Minnesota	52,495	Oct. 9, 2004
New York	55,749	Oct. 5, 2004
Oakland	31,953	Oct. 2, 2002
Seattle	47,867	Oct. 15, 2001
Texas	49,950	Oct. 2, 1998

NATIONAL LEAGUE

Club	Attendance	Date
Arizona	41,793	Oct. 10, 2001
Atlanta	39,119	Oct. 5, 1999
Chicago	39,597	Oct. 3, 1998
Cincinnati	53,276	Oct. 6, 1995
Colorado	50,040	Oct. 3, 1995
Florida	41,283	Oct. 1, 1997
Houston	35,553	Oct. 9, 2001
Los Angeles	44,199	Oct. 3, 1995
New York	52,888	Oct. 8, 2000
St. Louis	52,127	Oct. 5, 2004
San Diego	53,899	Oct. 5, 1996
San Francisco	40,430	Oct. 4, 2000
San Francisco	40,430	Oct. 5, 2000

NON-PLAYING PERSONNEL

MANAGERS

Most series by manager
N.L.—10—Bobby Cox, Atlanta, 1995 through 2004; won 6, lost 4
A.L.—9—Joe Torre, New York, 1996 through 2004; won 7, lost 2

**For a complete list of managers and their
records, see page 386.**

Most division series winners managed
N.L.—6—Bobby Cox, Atlanta, 1995, 1996, 1997, 1998, 1999,
   2001; lost 4
A.L.—7—Joe Torre, New York, 1996, 1998, 1999, 2000, 2001,
   2003, 2004; lost 2

Most division series losers managed
N.L.—4—Larry Dierker, Houston, 1997, 1998, 1999, 2001; won 0
   Bobby Cox, Atlanta, 2000, 2002, 2003, 2004; won 6
A.L.—3—Johnny Oates, Texas, 1996, 1998, 1999; won 0

Art Howe, Oakland, 2000, 2001, 2002; won 0

Most different clubs managed, major leagues
2—Dave Johnson, Cincinnati N.L., 1995; Baltimore A.L., 1996, 1997
   Buck Showalter, New York A.L., 1995; Arizona N.L., 1999
   Dusty Baker, San Francisco N.L., 1997, 2000, 2002; Chicago
   N.L., 2003

Most different clubs managed, league
N.L.—2—Dusty Baker, San Francisco, 1997, 2000, 2002;
   Chicago, 2003
A.L.—1—many managers

UMPIRES

Most years umpired
7—Bruce Froemming, 1995, 1996, 1998, 1999, 2001, 2002,
   2003; 28 G

Most games umpired
28—Bruce Froemming, 7 years

GENERAL REFERENCE

SERIES WON AND LOST BY TEAMS
AMERICAN LEAGUE

	W	L	Pct.
Baltimore	2	0	1.000
Seattle	3	1	.750
New York	7	3	.700
Boston	3	2	.600
Cleveland	3	3	.500
Anaheim	1	1	.500
Minnesota	1	2	.333
Oakland	0	4	.000
Chicago	0	1	.000
Texas	0	3	.000

Total Series: 20

NATIONAL LEAGUE

	W	L	Pct.
Florida	2	0	1.000
New York	2	0	1.000
Cincinnati	1	0	1.000
St. Louis	4	1	.800
Atlanta	6	4	.600
Chicago	1	1	.500
San Diego	1	1	.500
Arizona	1	2	.333
San Francisco	1	3	.250
Houston	1	4	.200
Colorado	0	1	.000
Los Angeles	0	3	.000

Total Series: 20

GAMES WON AND LOST BY TEAMS
AMERICAN LEAGUE

	W	L	Pct.
Baltimore	6	2	.750
New York	26	16	.619
Seattle	10	7	.588
Cleveland	14	12	.538
Boston	10	10	.500
Anaheim	3	4	.429
Oakland	8	12	.400
Minnesota	5	8	.385
Texas	1	9	.100
Chicago	0	3	.000

Total Games: 83

NATIONAL LEAGUE

	W	L	Pct.
Cincinnati	3	0	1.000
Florida	6	1	.857
St. Louis	14	4	.778
New York	6	2	.750
Atlanta	24	14	.632
San Diego	3	4	.429
Chicago	3	5	.375
Arizona	4	8	.333
San Francisco	5	11	.313
Houston	5	14	.263
Colorado	1	3	.250
Los Angeles	1	9	.100

Total Games: 75

HOME AND ROAD GAMES BY TEAMS
AMERICAN LEAGUE

	Series	Games	Home	Away
New York	10	42	21	21
Cleveland	6	26	14	12
Boston	5	20	8	12
Oakland	4	20	11	9
Seattle	4	17	9	8
Minnesota	3	13	6	7
Texas	3	10	4	6
Baltimore	2	8	4	4
Anaheim	2	7	4	3

	Series	Games	Home	Away
Chicago	1	3	2	1
Totals	**10**	**166**	**83**	**83**

NATIONAL LEAGUE

	Series	Games	Home	Away
Atlanta	10	38	20	18
Houston	5	19	9	10
St. Louis	5	18	9	9
San Francisco	4	16	7	9
Arizona	3	12	7	5
Los Angeles	3	10	6	4
New York	2	8	4	4
Chicago	2	8	3	5
Florida	2	7	4	3
San Diego	2	7	3	4
Colorado	1	4	2	2
Cincinnati	1	3	1	2
Totals	**10**	**150**	**75**	**75**

SHUTOUTS
AMERICAN LEAGUE

Oct. 4, 1995 Orel Hershiser, Julian Tavarez, Paul Assenmacher and Jose Mesa, Cleveland 4, Boston 0 (three hits).
Sept. 29, 1998 David Wells and Mariano Rivera, New York 2, Texas 0 (five hits).
Oct. 2, 1998 David Cone, Graeme Lloyd, Jeff Nelson and Mariano Rivera, New York 4, Texas 0 (three hits).
Oct. 5, 1999 Orlando Hernandez and Jeff Nelson, New York 8, Texas 0 (two hits).
Oct. 9, 1999 Roger Clemens, Jeff Nelson and Mariano Rivera, New York 3, Texas 0 (five hits).
Oct. 4, 2000 Andy Pettitte and Mariano Rivera, New York 4, Oakland 0 (six hits).
Oct. 9, 2001 Bartolo Colon and Bob Wickman, Cleveland 5, Seattle 0 (six hits).
Oct. 11, 2001 Tim Hudson and Jason Isringhausen, Oakland 2, New York 0 (seven hits).
Oct. 13, 2001 Mike Mussina and Mariano Rivera, New York 1, Oakland 0 (six hits).
Oct. 5, 2004 Mike Mussina, Tom Gordon, Mariano Rivera, New York 2, Minnesota 0 (seven hits)
Total number of shutouts: 10

NATIONAL LEAGUE

Oct. 8, 2000 Bobby J. Jones, New York 4, San Francisco 0 (one hit).
Oct. 9, 2001 Curt Schilling, Arizona 1, St. Louis 0 (three hits).
Oct. 10, 2001 Tom Glavine and John Smoltz, Atlanta 1, Houston 0 (seven hits).
Sept. 30, 2003 Jason Schmidt, San Francisco 2, Florida 0 (three hits).
Oct. 9, 2004 Jose Lima, Los Angeles 4, St. Louis 0 (five hits).
Total number of shutouts: 5

EXTRA-INNING GAMES
AMERICAN LEAGUE

Oct. 3, 1995 13 inn, Cleveland 5, Boston 4
Oct. 4, 1995 15 inn, New York 7, Seattle 5
Oct. 8, 1995 11 inn, Seattle 6, New York 5
Oct. 2, 1996 12 inn, New York 5, Texas 4
Oct. 5, 1996 12 inn, Baltimore 4, Cleveland 3
Oct. 3, 2000 10 inn, Seattle 7, Chicago 4
Oct. 1, 2003 12 inn, Oakland 5, Boston 4
Oct. 4, 2003 11 inn, Boston 3, Oakland 1
Oct. 6, 2004 12 inn, New York 7, Minnesota 6
Oct. 8, 2004 10 inn, Boston 8, Anaheim 6
Oct. 9, 2004 11 inn, New York 6, Minnesota 5
Total number of extra-inning games: 11

NATIONAL LEAGUE

Oct. 6, 1995 10 inn, Colorado 7, Atlanta 5
Oct. 2, 1996 10 inn, Atlanta 2, Los Angeles 1

Oct. 1, 1998   10 inn, Atlanta 2, Chicago 1
Oct. 8, 1999   12 inn, Atlanta 5, Houston 3
Oct. 9, 1999   10 inn, New York 4, Arizona 3
Oct. 5, 2000   10 inn, New York 5, San Francisco 4
Oct. 7, 2000   13 inn, New York 3, San Francisco 2
Oct. 3, 2003   11 inn, Florida 4, San Francisco 3
Oct 7, 2004   11 inn, Atlanta 4, Houston 2
Total number of extra-inning games: 9

ATTENDANCE

AMERICAN LEAGUE

Year	Series	Games	Total	Series	Games	Total
1995	Cle.-Bos.	3	122,693	Sea.-N.Y.	5	286,839
1996	Bal.-Cle.	4	185,144	N.Y.-Tex.	4	215,287
1997	Bal.-Sea.	4	216,791	Cle.-N.Y.	5	250,466
1998	Cle.-Bos.	4	157,065	N.Y.-Tex.	3	164,672
1999	Bos.-Cle.	5	202,917	N.Y.-Tex.	3	164,853
2000	Sea.-Chi.	3	138,683	N.Y.-Oak.	5	249,911
2001	Sea.-Cle.	5	234,046	N.Y.-Oak.	5	269,565
2002	Min.-Oak.	5	210,844	Ana.-N.Y.	4	203,544
2003	N.Y.-Min.	4	224,561	Oak.-Bos.	5	206,816
2004	N.Y.-Min.	4	219,404	Bos.-Ana.	3	125,273

NATIONAL LEAGUE

Year	Series	Games	Total	Series	Games	Total
1995	Cin.-L.A.	3	143,526	Atl.-Col.	4	201,430
1996	Atl.-L.A.	3	151,873	St.L.-S.D.	3	164,844
1997	Fla.-S.F.	3	140,638	Atl.-Hou.	3	149,355
1998	S.D.-Hou.	4	225,763	Atl.-Chi.	3	136,908
1999	N.Y.-Ari.	4	211,269	Atl.-Hou.	4	178,210
2000	N.Y.-S.F.	4	190,018	St.L.-Atl.	3	154,665
2001	Atl.-Hou.	3	111,180	Ari.-St.L.	5	231,321
2002	St.L.-Ari.	3	150,199	S.F.-Atl.	5	220,386
2003	Atl.-Chi.	5	239,108	S.F.-Fla.	4	214,422
2004	St.L-L.A.	4	216,615	Atl.-Hou.	5	222,490

INDIVIDUAL BATTING

LEADING BATTERS

(Playing in all games, each series, with four or more hits)

AMERICAN LEAGUE

Year	Player, Club	AB	H	TB	Avg.
1995	Luis Alicea, Boston	10	6	10	.600
1996	Bernie Williams, New York	15	7	16	.467
1997	Omar Vizquel, Cleveland	18	9	9	.500
1998	John Valentin, Boston	15	7	8	.467
1999	Mike Stanley, Boston	20	10	14	.500
2000	Herbert Perry, Chicago	9	4	5	.444
2001	Ichiro Suzuki, Seattle	20	12	13	.600
2002	Benji Gil, Anaheim	5	4	4	.800
2003	Eric Byrnes, Oakland	13	6	7	.462
2004	David Ortiz, Boston	11	6	11	.545

NATIONAL LEAGUE

Year	Player, Club	AB	H	TB	Avg.
1995	Dante Bichette, Colorado	17	10	16	.588
1996	Ron Gant, St. Louis	10	4	8	.400
1997	Gary Sheffield, Florida	9	5	9	.556
1998	Carlos Hernandez, San Diego	12	5	5	.417
1999	Bret Boone, Atlanta	19	9	10	.474
2000	Jim Edmonds, St. Louis	14	8	18	.571
2001	Andruw Jones, Atlanta	12	6	9	.500
2002	Miguel Cairo, St. Louis	4	4	5	1.000
2003	Edgardo Alfonzo, San Francisco	17	9	13	.529
2004	Andruw Jones, Atlanta	19	10	18	.526

.500 HITTERS

(Playing in all games and having nine or more at-bats)

AMERICAN LEAGUE

Player, Club	Year	AB	H	TB	Avg.
Shawn Wooten, Anaheim	2002	9	6	9	.667
Luis Alicea, Boston	1995	10	6	10	.600
Ichiro Suzuki, Seattle	2001	20	12	13	.600
Edgar Martinez, Seattle	1995	21	12	21	.571
David Ortiz, Boston	2004	11	6	11	.545
Omar Vizquel, Cleveland	1997	18	9	9	.500
Mike Stanley, Boston	1999	20	10	14	.500
Derek Jeter, New York	2002	16	8	14	.500
Scott Hatteberg, Oakland	2002	14	7	12	.500
Darin Erstad, Anaheim	2004	10	5	9	.500

Total number of occurrences: 10

NATIONAL LEAGUE

Player, Club	Year	AB	H	TB	Avg.
Fernando Vina, St. Louis	2002	15	9	9	.600
Dante Bichette, Colorado	1995	17	10	16	.588
Jim Edmonds, St. Louis	2000	14	8	18	.571
Gary Sheffield, Florida	1997	9	5	9	.556
Edgardo Alfonzo, San Francisco	2003	17	9	13	.529
Andruw Jones, Atlanta	2004	19	10	18	.526
Marquis Grissom, Atlanta	1995	21	11	22	.524
Chad Fonville, Los Angeles	1995	12	6	6	.500
Eric Karros, Los Angeles	1995	12	6	13	.500
Hal Morris, Cincinnati	1995	10	5	6	.500
Andruw Jones, Atlanta	2001	12	6	9	.500
Moises Alou, Chicago	2003	20	10	20	.500

Total number of occurrences: 12

HOME RUNS

AMERICAN LEAGUE

1995—11—Seattle (West), Ken Griffey Jr. 5, Edgar Martinez 2, Jay Buhner, Vince Coleman, Joey Cora, Tino Martinez.
    11—New York (East), Paul O'Neill 3, Ruben Sierra 2, Bernie Williams 2, Wade Boggs, Jim Leyritz, Don Mattingly, Mike Stanley.
    4—Cleveland (Central), Albert Belle, Eddie Murray, Tony Pena, Jim Thome.
    3—Boston (East), Luis Alicea, Tim Naehring, John Valentin.
1996—9—Baltimore (East), B.J. Surhoff 3, Brady Anderson 2, Bobby Bonilla 2, Roberto Alomar, Rafael Palmeiro.
    4—Cleveland (Central), Albert Belle 2, Manny Ramirez 2.
    6—Texas (West), Juan Gonzalez 5, Dean Palmer.
    4—New York (East), Bernie Williams 3, Cecil Fielder.
1997—4—Cleveland (Central), Sandy Alomar, David Justice, Matt Williams.
    6—New York (East), Derek Jeter 2, Paul O'Neill 2, Tino Martinez, Tim Raines Sr.
    6—Baltimore (East), German Berroa 2, Brady Anderson, Harold Baines, Chris Hoiles, Jeff Reboulet.
    6—Seattle (West), Jay Buhner 2, Edgar Martinez 2, Alex Rodriguez, Paul Sorrento.
1998—4—New York (East), Shane Spencer 2, Scott Brosius, Paul O'Neill.
    0—Texas (West), None.
    7—Cleveland (Central), Kenny Lofton 2, Manny Ramirez 2, Jim Thome 2, David Justice.
    5—Boston (East), Nomar Garciaparra 3, Mo Vaughn 2.
1999—2—New York (East), Darryl Strawberry, Bernie Williams.
    1—Texas (West), Juan Gonzalez.
    10—Boston (East), John Valentin 3, Nomar Garciaparra 2, Troy O'Leary 2, Brian Daubach, Jose Offerman, Jason Varitek.
    7—Cleveland (Central), Jim Thome 4, Harold Baines, Wil Cordero, Travis Fryman.
2000—1—New York (East), David Justice.
    2—Oakland (West), Terrence Long, Olmedo Saenz.
    4—Seattle (West), Jay Buhner, Edgar Martinez, John Olerud, Joe Oliver.
    1—Chicago (Central), Ray Durham.
2001—4—Seattle (West), Edgar Martinez 2, David Bell, Mike Cameron.
    5—Cleveland (Central), Juan Gonzalez 2, Ellis Burks, Kenny Lofton, Jim Thome.
    3—New York (East), David Justice, Tino Martinez, Jorge Posada.
    4—Oakland (West), Terrence Long 2, Ron Gant, Jason Giambi.
2002—9—Anaheim (West), Troy Glaus 3, Tim Salmon 2, Garret Anderson, Adam Kennedy, Scott Spiezio, Shawn Wooten.
    7—New York (East), Derek Jeter 2, Jason Giambi, Jorge Posada, Alfonso Soriano, Rondell White, Bernie Williams.

5—Minnesota (Central), Doug Mientkiewicz 2, Cristian Guzman, Corey Koskie, A.J. Pierzynski.

8—Oakland (West), Ray Durham 2, Eric Chavez, Jermaine Dye, Mark Ellis, Scott Hatteberg, Terrence Long, Miguel Tejada.

2003—8—Boston (East), Todd Walker 3, Jason Varitek 2, Johnny Damon, Trot Nixon, Manny Ramirez.

2—New York (East), Derek Jeter, Hideki Matsui.

2—Minnesota (Central), Torii Hunter, A.J. Pierzynski.

1—Oakland (West), Jermaine Dye.

2004—4—Anaheim (West), Troy Glaus 2, Darin Erstad, Vlad Guerrero.

4—Boston (East), Kevin Millar, David Ortiz, Manny Ramirez, Jason Varitek.

4—Minnesota, (Central), Jacque Jones 2, Henry Blanco, Torii Hunter.

6—New York (East), Derek Jeter, Hideki Matsui, Alex Rodriguez, Gary Sheffield, Ruben Sierra, Bernie Williams.

Total number of home runs: 194

NATIONAL LEAGUE

1995—7—Atlanta (East), Marquis Grissom 3, Chipper Jones 2, Fred McGriff 2.

6—Colorado (West), Vinny Castilla 3, Dante Bichette, Larry Walker, Eric Young.

5—Cincinnati (Central), Bret Boone, Ron Gant, Mark Lewis, Reggie Sanders, Benito Santiago.

3—Los Angeles (West), Eric Karros 2, Mike Piazza.

1996—5—Atlanta (East), Jermaine Dye, Chipper Jones, Ryan Klesko, Javy Lopez, Fred McGriff.

0—Los Angeles (West), None.

4—San Diego (West), Ken Caminiti 3, Rickey Henderson.

3—St. Louis (Central), Gary Gaetti, Ron Gant, Brian Jordan.

1997—3—Atlanta (East), Jeff Blauser, Chipper Jones, Ryan Klesko.

1—Houston (Central), Chuck Carr.

4—Florida (East), Bobby Bonilla, Charles Johnson, Gary Sheffield, Devon White.

4—San Francisco (West), Jeff Kent 2, Brian Johnson, Bill Mueller.

1998—5—San Diego (West), Jim Leyritz 3, Wally Joyner, Greg Vaughn.

1—Houston (Central), Derek Bell.

4—Atlanta (East), Ryan Klesko, Javy Lopez, Eddie Perez, Michael Tucker.

1—Chicago (Central), Tyler Houston.

1999—1—Atlanta (East), Brian Jordan.

5—Houston (Central), Ken Caminiti 3, Tony Eusebio, Daryle Ward.

5—New York (East), Edgardo Alfonzo 3, John Olerud, Todd Pratt.

4—Arizona (West), Greg Colbrunn, Erubiel Durazo, Luis Gonzalez, Turner Ward.

2000—3—New York (East), Benny Agbayani, Edgardo Alfonzo, Robin Ventura.

2—San Francisco (West), Ellis Burks, J.T. Snow.

6—St. Louis (Central), Jim Edmonds 2, Will Clark, Carlos Hernandez, Mark McGwire, Fernando Vina.

1—Atlanta (East), Andruw Jones.

2001—6—Atlanta (East), Chipper Jones 2, Paul Bako, Julio Franco, Andruw Jones, Brian Jordan.

3—Houston (Central), Brad Ausmus, Vinny Castilla, Daryle Ward.

3—Arizona (West), Craig Counsell, Luis Gonzalez, Reggie Sanders.

6—St. Louis (Central), Jim Edmonds 2, J.D. Drew, Albert Pujols, Edgar Renteria, Fernando Vina.

2002—3—St. Louis (Central), J.D. Drew, Jim Edmonds, Scott Rolen.

2—Arizona (West), Rod Barajas, David Dellucci.

6—San Francisco (West), Barry Bonds 3, Rich Aurilia 2, J.T. Snow.

5—Atlanta (East), Javy Lopez 2, Vinny Castilla, Keith Lockhart, Gary Sheffield.

2003—4—Chicago (Central), Eric Karros 2, Alex S. Gonzalez, Aramis Ramirez.

3—Atlanta (East), Chipper Jones 2, Marcus Giles.

2—Florida (East), Juan Encarnacion, Ivan Rodriguez.

0—San Francisco (West), none.

2004—7—Atlanta (East), Johnny Estrada 2, Rafael Furcal 2, Andruw Jones 2, Adam LaRoche.

11—Houston (Central), Carlos Beltran 4, Jeff Bagwell 2, Brad Ausmus, Lance Berkman, Craig Biggio, Raul Chavez, Jason Lane.

7—Los Angeles (West), Shawn Green 3, Jayson Werth 2,

Milton Bradley, Tom Wilson.

7—St. Louis (Central), Albert Pujols 2, Larry Walker 2, Jim Edmonds, Mike Matheny, Reggie Sanders.

Total number of home runs: 158

PLAYERS WITH FOUR HOME RUNS

BOTH LEAGUES

Player	Series	No.
Jim Leyritz	4	4

Total number of players: 1

AMERICAN LEAGUE

Player	Series	No.
Juan Gonzalez	4	8
Jim Thome	6	8
Bernie Williams	10	8
Edgar Martinez	4	7
Paul O'Neill	7	6
Manny Ramirez	7	6
Derek Jeter	9	6
Ken Griffey Jr.	2	5
Nomar Garciaparra	3	5
Troy Glaus	2	4
John Valentin	3	4
Jay Buhner	4	4
Terrence Long	4	4
Jason Varitek	4	4
David Justice	7	4

Total number of players: 15

NATIONAL LEAGUE

Player	Series	No.
Chipper Jones	10	8
Ken Caminiti	4	6
Jim Edmonds	4	6
Vinny Castilla	1	5
Carlos Beltran	1	4
Edgardo Alfonzo	3	4
Eric Karros	3	4
Javy Lopez	7	4
Andruw Jones	9	4

Total number of players: 9

INDIVIDUAL PITCHING

PITCHERS WITH THREE VICTORIES

BOTH LEAGUES

Pitcher, Club	Yrs.	W	L
David Wells, Cincinnati N.L., Baltimore A.L., New York A.L.	6	5	1
Jeff Fassero, Seattle A.L., Texas A.L., St. Louis N.L.	3	3	0
Curt Schilling, Arizona N.L., Boston A.L.	2	3	0
Armando Benitez, Baltimore A.L., New York N.L.	4	3	0
Roger Clemens, New York A.L., Houston N.L.	5	3	3

Total number of pitchers: 5

AMERICAN LEAGUE

Pitcher, Club	Yrs.	W	L
Pedro Martinez, Boston	4	4	0
David Wells, Baltimore, New York	4	4	1
Andy Pettitte, New York	9	4	3
Orlando Hernandez, New York	4	3	1
Barry Zito, Oakland	4	3	2
Charles Nagy, Cleveland	5	3	2
Mike Mussina, Baltimore, New York	6	3	2

Total number of pitchers: 7

DIVISION SERIES *General reference*

NATIONAL LEAGUE

Pitcher, Club	Yrs.	W	L
John Smoltz, Atlanta	9	6	0
Greg Maddux, Atlanta	9	5	3
Russ Ortiz, San Francisco, Atlanta	4	3	1
Tom Glavine, Atlanta	8	3	3

Total number of pitchers: 4

10-STRIKEOUT GAMES BY PITCHERS

AMERICAN LEAGUE

Date	Pitcher, Club	No.
Oct. 6, 1995	Randy Johnson, Sea. vs. N.Y.	10

Date	Pitcher, Club	No.
Oct. 5, 1996	Charles Nagy, Cle. vs. Bal.	12
Oct. 5, 1997	Randy Johnson, Sea. vs. Bal.	13
Oct. 6, 1999	Bartolo Colon, Cle. vs. Bos.	11
Oct. 9, 2001	Bartolo Colon, Cle. vs. Sea.	10
Oct. 2, 2003	Andy Pettitte, N.Y. vs. Min.	10

Total number of occurrences: 6

NATIONAL LEAGUE

Date	Pitcher, Club	No.
Sept. 29, 1998	Kevin Brown, S.D. vs. Hou.	16
Oct. 4, 1998	Sterling Hitchcock, S.D. vs. Hou.	11
Oct. 5, 1999	Randy Johnson, Ari. vs. N.Y.	11
Sept. 30, 2003	Kerry Wood, Chi. vs. Atl.	11

Total number of occurrences: 4

CLUB BATTING

AMERICAN LEAGUE

Year	Team, Division	G	AB	R	H	TB	2B	3B	HR	SH	SF	SB	BB	SO	RBI	Avg.	LOB
1995	Boston, East	3	114	6	21	32	2	0	3	1	1	2	11	26	6	.184	28
	Cleveland, Central	3	114	17	25	43	4	1	4	2	0	1	13	22	17	.219	27
	New York, East*	5	193	33	50	95	12	0	11	2	3	1	32	43	32	.259	45
	Seattle, West	5	200	35	63	104	6	1	11	4	3	3	25	41	33	.315	49
1996	Baltimore, East*	4	149	25	43	76	6	0	9	0	2	1	17	40	23	.289	36
	Cleveland, Central	4	143	20	35	54	7	0	4	2	2	11	15	32	20	.245	29
	New York, East	4	140	16	37	53	4	0	4	3	2	1	13	20	15	.264	30
	Texas, West	4	142	16	31	53	4	0	6	4	0	1	20	30	16	.218	33
1997	Baltimore, East*	4	135	23	39	68	11	0	6	2	0	2	16	27	23	.289	25
	Seattle, West	4	133	11	29	52	5	0	6	0	0	2	7	42	11	.218	21
	Cleveland, Central	5	167	21	43	63	6	1	4	4	1	6	10	22	20	.257	32
	New York, East*	5	166	24	43	68	7	0	6	2	2	3	20	26	23	.259	37
1998	Cleveland, Central	4	126	18	26	59	12	0	7	0	1	3	15	26	17	.206	22
	Boston, East*	4	135	20	34	55	6	0	5	1	2	1	14	28	19	.252	26
	New York, East	3	91	9	23	41	6	0	4	1	0	2	7	24	8	.253	16
	Texas, West	3	92	1	13	16	3	0	0	1	0	0	4	27	1	.141	15
1999	Boston, East*	5	176	47	56	105	17	1	10	0	3	1	19	35	47	.318	25
	Cleveland, Central	5	163	32	38	68	7	1	7	1	4	5	28	43	31	.233	36
	New York, East	3	98	14	23	37	6	1	2	1	0	0	10	19	13	.235	21
	Texas, West	3	92	1	14	19	2	0	1	0	0	1	9	17	1	.152	19
2000	New York, East	5	168	19	41	56	12	0	1	1	3	1	16	35	19	.244	38
	Oakland, West	5	167	23	44	59	9	0	2	1	2	3	19	31	22	.263	36
	Seattle, West*	3	99	14	28	42	2	0	4	4	1	2	12	13	14	.283	22
	Chicago, Central	3	92	7	17	30	6	2	1	2	2	4	15	16	6	.185	21
2001	New York, East	5	166	18	40	59	8	1	3	2	1	4	11	29	16	.241	34
	Oakland, West*	5	174	12	43	70	13	1	4	0	2	3	11	31	11	.247	43
	Seattle, West	5	158	16	39	59	6	0	4	2	1	3	18	48	16	.247	35
	Cleveland, Central	5	173	26	45	71	9	1	5	0	1	1	13	43	25	.260	30
2002	Anaheim, West*	4	149	31	56	93	10	0	9	4	2	4	7	18	31	.376	31
	New York, East	4	135	25	38	63	4	0	7	0	3	1	16	25	24	.281	28
	Minnesota, Central	5	179	27	52	86	15	2	5	2	0	2	14	42	23	.291	38
	Oakland, West	5	184	26	53	92	13	1	8	0	1	1	12	34	25	.288	40
2003	New York, East	4	138	16	38	53	9	0	2	2	1	4	14	29	15	.275	35
	Minnesota, Central	4	131	6	26	37	3	1	2	1	1	1	9	33	5	.198	28
	Boston, East*	5	180	17	38	68	6	0	8	0	0	3	18	39	16	.211	38
	Oakland, West*	5	178	18	38	51	8	1	1	1	0	3	21	37	15	.213	40
2004	Boston, East*	3	116	25	35	53	6	0	4	0	2	3	20	23	23	.302	31
	Anaheim, West	3	106	12	24	39	3	0	4	1	0	1	11	28	12	.226	24
	New York, East	4	154	21	43	71	10	0	6	2	1	4	15	30	20	.279	30
	Minnesota, Central	4	152	12	43	62	7	0	4	1	4	4	7	28	17	.283	28

*wild card team

NATIONAL LEAGUE

Year	Team, Division	G	AB	R	H	TB	2B	3B	HR	SH	SF	SB	BB	SO	RBI	Avg.	LOB
1995	Cincinnati, Central	3	104	22	29	50	6	0	5	1	1	9	13	28	22	.279	19
	Los Angeles, West	3	111	7	31	42	2	0	3	1	0	0	5	17	7	.279	30
	Atlanta, East	4	154	27	51	80	8	0	7	0	1	3	12	27	24	.331	33
	Colorado, West*	4	143	19	41	66	7	0	6	3	1	3	9	29	18	.287	29
1996	Atlanta, East	3	89	10	16	34	3	0	5	2	1	5	12	24	10	.180	14
	Los Angeles, West*	3	95	5	14	21	7	0	0	0	1	0	7	29	5	.147	14
	St. Louis, Central	3	94	15	24	38	3	1	3	2	0	3	13	23	14	.255	20

Year	Team, Division	G	AB	R	H	TB	2B	3B	HR	SH	SF	SB	BB	SO	RBI	Avg.	LOB
	San Diego, West	3	105	10	25	40	3	0	4	2	0	2	4	28	9	.238	21
1997	Florida, East*	3	99	15	27	44	5	0	4	1	0	1	19	16	14	.273	27
	San Fran., West	3	98	9	22	38	4	0	4	2	1	2	6	21	8	.224	17
	Atlanta, East	3	92	19	20	33	4	0	3	0	1	1	15	20	15	.217	14
	Houston, Central	3	96	5	16	20	1	0	1	0	0	2	8	24	5	.167	18
1998	San Diego, West	4	125	14	27	48	4	1	5	2	1	0	9	32	13	.216	23
	Houston, Central	4	121	8	22	30	5	0	1	2	0	1	11	49	7	.182	25
	Atlanta, East	3	101	15	23	37	2	0	4	2	1	3	14	20	14	.228	24
	Chicago, Central*	3	94	4	17	22	2	0	1	3	1	1	5	24	4	.181	15
1999	New York, East*	4	134	22	34	54	5	0	5	4	1	8	21	28	22	.254	32
	Arizona, West	4	126	16	26	47	7	1	4	0	1	0	14	22	16	.206	20
	Atlanta, East	4	148	18	45	53	5	0	1	3	3	4	11	35	18	.304	33
	Houston, Central	4	141	15	31	48	2	0	5	2	1	3	17	33	15	.220	31
2000	New York, East*	4	143	13	30	46	7	0	3	0	1	3	20	30	13	.210	36
	San Fran., West	4	146	11	30	44	6	1	2	2	0	2	16	36	11	.205	33
	St. Louis, Central	3	102	24	28	51	5	0	6	2	1	6	14	19	23	.275	22
	Atlanta, East	3	95	10	18	26	5	0	1	0	0	1	16	20	9	.189	21
2001	Atlanta, East	3	99	14	30	54	6	0	6	1	1	1	4	18	13	.303	14
	Houston, Central	3	95	6	19	30	2	0	3	0	0	0	8	16	6	.200	16
	Arizona, West	5	156	10	37	51	5	0	3	6	0	1	18	29	10	.237	40
	St. Louis, Central*	5	152	12	29	50	3	0	6	8	1	3	12	38	12	.191	30
2002	St. Louis, Central	3	105	20	33	46	2	1	3	3	1	2	12	17	19	.314	25
	Arizona, West	3	98	6	18	26	2	0	2	0	1	1	11	21	6	.184	23
	San Fran., West*	5	166	24	41	68	9	0	6	2	2	1	18	45	24	.247	33
	Atlanta, East	5	170	26	44	67	4	2	5	1	0	2	22	30	25	.259	36
2003	Florida, East*	4	146	20	37	53	8	1	2	3	0	2	14	25	18	.253	35
	San Fran., West	4	136	16	32	41	7	1	0	3	2	1	20	28	15	.235	36
	Chicago, Central	5	167	19	43	63	8	0	4	0	1	5	20	38	19	.257	37
	Atlanta, East	5	163	15	35	49	5	0	3	2	1	1	21	42	15	.215	41
2004	St. Louis, Central	4	130	22	33	59	3	1	7	1	0	4	15	26	21	.254	25
	Los Angeles, West	4	126	12	25	52	4	1	7	1	1	2	15	20	12	.198	26
	Houston, Central*	5	180	36	58	103	12	0	11	3	3	3	21	30	36	.322	34
	Atlanta, East	5	180	21	48	75	4	1	7	2	1	7	19	45	20	.267	43

*Wild-card team

CLUB FIELDING AND PLAYERS USED

AMERICAN LEAGUE

Year	Team, Division	G	PO	A	E	DP	PB	Fielding Avg.	Players Used	Pitchers Used
1995	Boston, East	3	80	29	4	0	2	.967	23	10
	Cleveland, Central	3	93	34	6	1	0	.955	22	9
	New York, East*	5	150	49	3	4	0	.985	24	9
	Seattle, West	5	154	47	2	5	0	.990	24	9
1996	Baltimore, East*	4	114	43	4	2	0	.975	21	8
	Cleveland, Central	4	111	34	3	1	0	.980	24	10
	New York, East	4	117	38	2	3	0	.987	25	10
1997	Baltimore, East	4	108	38	0	1	1	1.000	23	9
	Seattle, West	4	105	42	1	3	0	.993	23	9
	Cleveland, Central	5	132	58	4	6	0	.979	20	9
	New York, East*	5	130	55	4	2	0	.979	25	10
1998	Cleveland, Central	4	108	43	1	3	0	.993	22	11
	Boston, East*	4	105	33	0	4	2	1.000	24	10
	New York, East	3	81	28	1	2	0	.991	19	6
	Texas, West	3	75	31	1	4	1	.991	17	5
1999	Boston, East*	5	130	45	3	3	3	.983	25	11
	Cleveland, Central	5	129	48	2	4	0	.983	25	11
	New York, East	3	81	29	2	5	0	.982	19	5
	Texas, West	3	75	27	3	1	0	.981	19	9
2000	New York, East	5	132	56	2	7	0	.989	21	8
	Oakland, West	5	132	42	5	3	0	.972	24	9
	Seattle, West*	3	84	28	1	5	0	.991	22	8
	Chicago, Central	3	82	38	2	5	0	.984	24	10
2001	New York, East	5	135	42	4	4	0	.978	21	9
	Oakland, West*	5	132	60	6	4	0	.970	25	11
	Seattle, West	5	132	43	5	5	1	.972	25	10
	Cleveland, Central	5	129	53	3	4	0	.984	22	10
2002	Anaheim, West*	4	105	33	2	6	0	.986	22	9
	New York, East	4	102	39	4	5	0	.972	24	10

Year	Team, Division	G	PO	A	E	DP	PB	Fielding Avg.	Players Used	Pitchers Used
	Minnesota, Central	5	132	36	4	2	0	.977	25	11
	Oakland, West	5	132	48	3	4	0	.963	25	10
	Texas, West	4	114	47	2	5	0	.988	23	11
2003	New York, East	4	108	44	3	2	0	.981	19	8
	Minnesota, Central	4	105	40	2	3	1	.986	24	10
	Boston, East*	5	146	56	5	2	1	.976	22	8
	Oakland, West	5	145	44	5	4	0	.974	23	9
2004	Boston, East*	3	84	25	1	2	0	.991	22	8
	Anaheim, West	3	83	25	3	2	0	.973	14	8
	New York, East	4	123	55	1	4	1	.994	22	10
	Minnesota, Central	4	122	50	2	9	1	.989	24	10

*wild card team

NATIONAL LEAGUE

Year	Team, Division	G	PO	A	E	DP	PB	Fielding Avg.	Players Used	Pitchers Used
1995	Cincinnati, Central	3	81	30	2	1	0	.982	18	6
	Los Angeles, West	3	78	19	3	2	0	.970	22	8
	Atlanta, East	4	111	49	2	5	0	.988	24	10
	Colorado, West*	4	108	50	7	5	0	.958	24	11
1996	Atlanta, East	3	84	28	3	1	0	.974	19	6
	Los Angeles, West*	3	81	32	1	4	0	.991	23	10
	St. Louis, Central	3	81	18	2	0	0	.980	20	7
	San Diego, West	3	75	28	2	3	0	.972	23	9
1997	Florida, East*	3	81	33	4	3	0	.966	19	6
	San Francisco, West	3	77	31	0	4	0	1.000	21	8
	Atlanta, East	3	81	33	3	2	0	.974	18	5
	Houston, Central	3	75	27	4	2	1	.962	24	9
1998	San Diego, West	4	104	37	3	5	2	.979	22	7
	Houston, Central	4	102	41	2	1	0	.986	21	8
	Atlanta, East	3	84	25	0	2	0	1.000	21	7
	Chicago, Central*	3	79	20	4	1	1	.961	22	8
1999	New York, East*	4	108	41	0	5	0	1.000	25	11
	Arizona, West	4	106	37	5	2	0	.966	23	10
	Atlanta, East	4	117	46	2	4	0	.988	23	9
	Houston, Central	4	114	50	4	4	0	.976	24	10
2000	New York, East*	4	120	33	0	1	0	1.000	24	10
	San Francisco, West	4	118	40	1	4	0	.994	25	11
	St. Louis, Central	3	81	29	1	2	0	.991	21	9
	Atlanta, East	3	75	28	5	0	0	.954	22	9
2001	Atlanta, East	3	81	32	1	5	0	.991	21	8
	Houston, Central	3	78	30	3	7	0	.973	22	9
	Arizona, West	5	132	54	4	4	0	.979	23	8
	St. Louis, Central*	5	131	50	3	4	0	.984	22	10
2002	St. Louis, Central	3	81	26	2	0	0	.982	20	8
	Arizona, West	3	78	34	2	1	0	.982	25	10
	San Francisco, West*	5	132	56	4	6	1	.945	23	11
	Atlanta, East	5	132	40	0	2	0	1.000	24	10
2003	Florida, East*	4	111	33	2	0	0	.986	21	9
	San Francisco, West	4	110	40	7	3	0	.955	25	12
	Chicago, Central	5	132	52	0	2	0	1.000	25	11
	Atlanta	5	132	68	6	8	0	.971	23	10
2004	St. Louis	4	105	34	0	3	0	1.000	23	11
	Los Angeles	4	102	31	3	3	1	.978	24	10
	Houston	5	140	58	3	4	0	.985	24	10
	Atlanta	5	138	64	1	7	0	.995	25	11

*wild card team

MANAGERIAL RECORDS

AMERICAN LEAGUE

	Series W	L	Games W	L
Terry Francona, Boston	1	0	3	0
Ron Gardenhire, Minnesota	1	2	5	8
Mike Hargrove, Cleveland	3	2	12	9
Art Howe, Oakland	0	3	6	9
Dave Johnson, Baltimore	2	0	6	2
Kevin Kennedy, Boston	0	1	0	3
Grady Little, Boston	1	0	3	2
Ken Macha, Oakland	0	1	2	3
Charlie Manuel, Cleveland	0	1	2	3
Jerry Manuel, Chicago	0	1	0	3

DIVISION SERIES General reference

	Series		Games	
	W	L	W	L
John Oates, Texas	0	3	1	9
Lou Piniella, Seattle	3	1	10	7
Mike Scioscia, Anaheim	1	1	3	4
Buck Showalter, New York	0	1	2	3
Joe Torre, New York	7	2	24	13
Jimy Williams, Boston	1	1	4	5

Total number of managers: 16

NATIONAL LEAGUE

	Series		Games	
	W	L	W	L
Felipe Alou, San Francisco	0	1	1	3
Dusty Baker, San Francisco, Chicago	2	2	7	10
Don Baylor, Colorado	0	1	1	3
Bruce Bochy, San Diego	1	1	3	4
Bob Brenly, Arizona	1	1	3	5
Bobby Cox, Atlanta	6	4	24	14
Larry Dierker, Houston	0	4	2	12
Phil Garner, Houston	1	0	3	1
Dave Johnson, Cincinnati	1	0	3	0

	Series		Games	
	W	L	W	L
Tony LaRussa, St. Louis	4	1	14	4
Tom Lasorda, Los Angeles	0	1	0	3
Jim Leyland, Florida	1	0	3	0
Jack McKeon, Florida	1	0	3	1
Jim Riggleman, Chicago	0	1	0	3
Bill Russell, Los Angeles	0	1	0	3
Buck Showalter, Arizona	0	1	1	3
Jim Tracy, Los Angeles	0	1	1	3
Bobby Valentine, New York	2	0	6	2

Total number of managers: 18

COMBINED RECORDS FOR BOTH LEAGUES

	Series		Games	
	W	L	W	L
Dave Johnson, Cincinnati N.L., Baltimore A.L.	3	0	9	2
Buck Showalter, New York A.L., Arizona N.L.	0	2	3	6

Total number of managers: 2

ADDENDUM - 1981

Major league baseball played a split season in 1981 because of a mid-season strike by the Major League Baseball Players Association. Following the regular season, the teams that finished first in each division during the first half of the season played the teams that finished first during the second half of the season for the right to advance to the League Championship Series. These four intra-divisional playoffs (New York vs. Milwaukee in the A.L. East; Oakland vs. Kansas City in the A.L. West; Philadelphia vs. Montreal in the N.L. East; and Los Angeles vs. Houston in the N.L. West) were called, at the time, division series. But they are not the same as the Division Series played since 1995.

The 1997 edition of the Complete Baseball Record Book added a section for the Division Series. Included in this section were records set in 1981. Beginning with the 2004 edition, we removed the 1981 records from the Division Series section. We will continue to list Service, Batting, Baserunning, Pitching and Fielding records in this addendum so long as they have not been surpassed in Division Series play since 1995.

CLUB SERVICE

Fewest players, series
A.L.—16—Kansas City vs. Oakland (3-game series)

Fewest players used by both clubs, series
A.L.—36—Oakland 20, Kansas City 16 (3-game series)

Fewest pinch-hitters, series
A.L.—0—Kansas City vs. Oakland (3-game series)

Fewest pinch-hitters used by both clubs, series
A.L.—1—Oakland 1, Kansas City 0 (3-game series)

Most second basemen, series
A.L.—3—Milwaukee vs. New York (5-game series)

Most shortstops, series
N.L.—3—Houston vs. Los Angeles (5-game series)

Most shortstops used by both clubs, series
N.L.—4—Houston 3, Los Angeles 1 (5-game series)

Most right fielders, series
N.L.—4—Philadelphia vs. Montreal (5-games series)

Most right fielders used by both clubs, series
N.L.—6—Philadelphia 4, Montreal 2 (5-game series)

Fewest pitchers, series
A.L.—5—Kansas City vs. Oakland (3-game series)

Oakland vs. Kansas City (3-game series)

Fewest pitchers used by both clubs, series
A.L.—10—Kansas City 5, Oakland 5 (3-game series)

INDIVIDUAL BATTING

Most games by pinch-hitter, series
N.L.—4—George Vukovich, Philadelphia (5 game series)
A.L.—3—Roy Howell, Milwaukee (5-game series))

Highest slugging average, series (10 or more PA)s
A.L.—1.333—Oscar Gamble, New York (5-game series)

Most hits by pinch-hitter, career
N.L.—3—George Vukovich, Philadelphia; 4 G

Most hits by pinch-hitter, series
N.L.—3—George Vukovich, Philadelphia; 4 G

Most consecutive hits, career
A.L.—5—Tony Armas, Oakland, October 7 (4), 9 (1)

Most consecutive hits by pinch-hitter, career
N.L.—2—George Vukovich, Philadelphia, October 9, 10

Most consecutive hits, series
A.L.—5—Tony Armas, Oakland, October 7 (4), 9 (1)

Most singles by pinch-hitter, series
N.L.—2—George Vukovich, Philadelphia (5-game series)

Most doubles, series
N.L.—3—Gary Carter, Montreal (5-game series)

Home runs by pinch-hitter
N.L.—1—George Vukovich, Philadelphia, October 16, 10th inn

Hitting home run in first series at-bat
N.L.—Keith Moreland, Philadelphia, October 7, 2nd inn

Most total bases by pinch-hitter, career
N.L.—6—George Vukovich, Philadelphia; 4 G

Most total bases by pinch-hitter, series
N.L.—6—George Vuckovich, Philadelphia; 4 G

Most game-winning RBIs, career and series
A.L.—2—Tony Armas, Oakland (3-game series)
N.L.—2—Chris Speier, Montreal (5-game series)

Most consecutive bases on balls, series
N.L.—3—Chris Speier, Montreal, October 7

Most bases on balls, game
N.L.—3—Bill Russell, Los Angeles, October 7, 11 inn

Most strikeouts, series
N.L.—9—Warren Cromartie, Montreal (5-game series)

Most consecutive strikeouts, series (consecutive at-bats)
N.L.—8—Jerry Reuss, Los Angeles, October 7 (4 in 11 inn), October 11 (4)

Most sacrifice flies, series
A.L.—2—Cecil Cooper, Milwaukee (5-game series)

CLUB BATTING

Highest batting average by both clubs, series
N.L.—.260—Philadelphia .265, Montreal .255 (5-game series)

Lowest batting average, series
N.L.—.179—Houston vs. Los Angeles (5-game series)

Lowest batting average by both clubs, series
N.L.—.188—Los Angeles .198, Houston .179 (5-game series)

Lowest slugging average, series
N.L.—.235—Houston vs. Los Angeles (5-game series)

Lowest slugging average by both clubs, series
N.L.—.269—Los Angeles .302, Houston .235 (5-game series)

Fewest runs, series
N.L.—6—Houston vs. Los Angeles (5-game series)

Fewest runs by both clubs, series
N.L.—19—Los Angeles 13, Houston 6 (5-game series)

Largest score, shutout game
N.L.—Los Angeles 4, Houston 0, October 11

Fewest hits, series
N.L.—29—Houston vs. Los Angeles (5-game series)
A.L.—36—Milwaukee vs. New York (5-game series)

Fewest hits by both clubs, series
N.L.—61—Los Angeles 32, Houston 29 (5-game series)

Most hits by pinch-hitters, game
N.L.—2—Montreal vs. Philadelphia, October 10, 10 inn

Most hits by pinch-hitters on both clubs, game
N.L.—3—Montreal 2, Philadelphia 1, October 10, 10 inn

Most hits by pinch-hitters, inning
N.L.—2—Montreal vs. Philadelphia, October 10, 6th

Fewest singles by both clubs, series
N.L.—46—Houston 24, Los Angeles 22 (5-game series)

Most doubles, series
N.L.—10—Montreal vs. Philadelphia (5-game series)

Fewest doubles, series
3-game series
    A.L.—1—Kansas City vs. Oakland
5-game series
    N.L.—3—Houston vs. Los Angeles
    A.L.—6—Milwaukee vs. New York

Fewest doubles by both clubs, series
A.L.—6—Oakland 5, Kansas City 1 (3-game series)

Most triples by both clubs, series
N.L.—2—Montreal 1, Philadelphia 1 (5-game series)

Most triples by both clubs, game
N.L.—2—Montreal 1, Philadelphia 1, October 7

Fewest home runs, series
3-game series
    A.L.—0—Kansas City vs. Oakland
5-game series
N.L.—2—Houston vs. Los Angeles
        Montreal vs. Philadelphia

Fewest home runs by both clubs, series
A.L.—3—Oakland 3, Kansas City 0 (3-game series)
N.L.—5—Los Angeles 3, Houston 2 (5-game series)

Most home runs by pinch-hitters, series
N.L.—1—Philadelphia vs. Montreal (5-game series)

Most home runs, game
N.L.—3—Philadelphia vs. Montreal, October 10, 10 inn

Fewest total bases, series
N.L.—38—Houston vs. Los Angeles (5-game series)

Fewest total bases by both clubs, series
N.L.—87—Los Angeles 49, Houston 38 (5-game series)

Fewest extra base hits, series
3-game series
    A.L.—1—Kansas City vs. Oakland
5-game series
    N.L.—5—Houston vs. Los Angeles
    A.L.—10—Milwaukee vs. New York

Fewest extra base hits by both clubs, series
3-game series
    A.L.—9—Oakland 8, Kansas City 1
5-game series
    N.L.—15—Los Angeles 10, Houston 5
    A.L.—24—New York 14, Milwaukee 10

Fewest runs batted in, series
N.L.—6—Houston vs. Los Angeles (5-game series)

Fewest runs batted in by both clubs, series
N.L.—18—Los Angeles 12, Houston 6 (5-game series)

Fewest bases on balls, series
A.L.—9—New York vs. Milwaukee (5-game series)

Most bases on balls by pinch-hitters, series
A.L.—2—Milwaukee vs. New York (5-game series)

Most bases on balls by pinch-hitters on both clubs, series
A.L.—3—Milwaukee 2, New York 1 (5-game series)

Fewest strikeouts, series
3-game series
    A.L.—10—Oakland vs. Kansas City
5-game series
    N.L.—19—Phildelphia vs. Montreal
    A.L.—22—New York vs. Milwaukee

Fewest strikeouts by both clubs, series
A.L.—21—Kansas City 11, Oakland 10 (3-game series)
N.L.—55—Montreal 36, Philadelphia 19 (5-game series)

Most strikeouts, game
A.L.—14—Milwaukee vs. New York, October 8
Fewest strikeouts, game
N.L.—1—Los Angeles vs. Houston, October 10
A.L.—1—Milwaukee vs. New York, October 9
    New York vs. Milwaukee, October 11

Fewest strikeouts by both clubs, game
N.L.—5—Houston 4, Los Angeles 1, October 10

Most sacrifice hits, game
A.L.—3—Oakland vs. Kansas City, October 7

Most sacrifice hits by both clubs, game
N.L.—3—Los Angeles 2, Houston 1, October 10

INDIVIDUAL BASERUNNING

Most stolen bases, series
N.L.—3—Jerry White, Montreal (5-game series)

Most caught stealing, career
N.L.—2—Cesar Cedeno, Houston; 4 G

Most caught stealing, series
N.L.—2—Cesar Cedeno, Houston; 2 SB (5-game series)

CLUB BASERUNNING

Most stolen bases, series
N.L.—7—Montreal vs. Philadelphia (5-game series)

Fewest stolen bases by both clubs, series
A.L.—2—Milwaukee 1, New York 1 (5-game series)

Most stolen bases, game
N.L.—4—Montreal vs. Philadelphia, October 7

Most caught stealing, series
A.L.—3—Oakland vs. Kansas City (3-game series)
N.L.—5—Montreal vs Philadelphia (5-game series)

Most caught stealing by both clubs, series
A.L.—4—Milwaukee 2, New York 2 (5-game series)

Most caught stealing, game
N.L.—2—Montreal vs. Philadelphia, October 6
　　　　Montreal vs. Philadelphia, October 7

Most caught stealing by both clubs, game
N.L.—3—Montreal 2, Philadelphia 1, October 6

Most caught stealing, inning
A.L.—2—Oakland vs. Kansas City, October 9, 3rd

Fewest left on base by both clubs, series
N.L.—67—Los Angeles 35, Houston 32 (5-game series)

Fewest left on base, game
N.L.—1—Los Angeles vs. Houston, October 6

Most left on base, shutout defeat
A.L.—11—Milwaukee vs. New York, October 8 (lost 3-0)
N.L.—9—Houston vs. Los Angeles, October 11 (lost 4-0)
　　(13—Los Angeles vs. Houston, October 7 (lost 1-0), 11 inn

INDIVIDUAL PITCHING

Most innings pitched, series
3-game series
　　A.L.—9.0—Steve McCatty, Oakland
　　　　　　Mike Norris, Oakland
5-game series
　　N.L.—18.0—Jerry Reuss, Los Angeles

Most saves, series
A.L.—3—Rich Gossage, New York (5-game series)
N.L.—2—Jeff Reardon, Montreal (5-game series)

Most games lost, series
N.L.—2—Dave Stewart, Los Angeles (5-game series)
　　　　Steve Carlton, Philadelphia (5-game series)
A.L.—2—Moose Haas, Milwaukee (5-game series)

Most shutouts, series
A.L.—1—Mike Norris, Oakland
N.L.—1—Jerry Reuss, Los Angeles
　　　　Steve Rogers, Montreal

Most consecutive scoreless innings, career
N.L.—18—Jerry Reuss, Los Angeles, October 7 (9), 11 (9)

Most consecutive scoreless innings, series
N.L.—18—Jerry Reuss, Los Angeles, October 7 (9), 11 (9)

Most hits allowed, series
A.L.—10—Rick Langford, Oakland (3-game series)

Most hits allowed, game
A.L.—10—Rick Langford, Oakland, October 9

Fewest hits allowed, game
A.L.—4—Mike Norris, Oakland, October 6

Most doubles allowed, game
N.L.—4—Steve Carlton, Philadelphia, October 7

Most home runs allowed, inning
A.L.—2—Moose Haas, Milwaukee, October 11, 4th
　　(consecutive)

Most bases on balls, series
N.L.—8—Steve Carlton, Philadelphia (5-game series)

Most consecutive strikeouts from start of game
N.L.—3—Steve Carlton, Philadelphia, October 11
A.L.—2—Dave Righetti, New York, October 8

CLUB PITCHING

Most complete games, series
3-game series
　　A.L.—2—Oakland vs. Kansas City
5-game series
　　N.L.—2—Houston vs. Los Angeles
　　　　　Los Angeles vs. Houston

Most complete games by both clubs, series
N.L.—4—Houston 2, Los Angeles 2
A.L.—2—Oakland 2, Kansas City 0

Most saves, series
A.L.—3—New York vs. Milwaukee (5-game series)
N.L.—2—Montreal vs. Philadelphia (5-game series)

Most saves by both clubs, series
A.L.—4—New York 3, Milwaukee 1 (5-game series)

Most shutouts by both clubs, series
N.L.—2—Houston 1, Los Angeles 1 (5-game series)

Longest shutout game
N.L.—11 inn—Houston 1, Los Angeles 0, October 7

INDIVIDUAL FIELDING

Most putouts, series, first basemen
N.L.—49—Steve Garvey, Los Angeles (5-game series)

Most putouts, game, first basemen
N.L.—15—Steve Garvey, Los Angeles, October 7, 11 inn

Most assists, series, first basemen
N.L.—8—Pete Rose, Phildelphia (5-game series)

Most assists, game, first basemen
N.L.—4—Pete Rose, Phildelphia, October 7

Most chances accepted, series, first basemen
N.L.—54—Steve Garvey, Los Angeles (5-game series)

Most chances accepted, game, first basemen
N.L.—16—Steve Garvey, Los Angeles, October 7, 11 inn (15
　　PO, 1 A)

Fewest chances offered, game, first basemen
A.L.—3—Bob Watson, New York, October 7 (3 PO)

Most chances accepted, errorless series, first basemen
N.L.—54—Steve Garvey (5-game series)

Most assists, game, second basemen
N.L.—8—Jerry Manuel, Montreal, October 7

Fewest chances offered, game, second basemen
N.L.—0—Phil Garner, Houston, October 7, 11 inn

Most errors, career, second basemen
N.L.—3—Jerry Manuel, Montreal; 1 series, 5 G
A.L.—2—Jim Gantner, Milwaukee; 1 series, 4 G

Most errors, series, second basemen
N.L.—3—Jerry Manuel, Montreal (5-game series)
A.L.—2—Jim Gantner, Milwaukee (5-game series)

Most putouts, series, third basemen
N.L.—8—Larry Parrish, Montreal (5-game series)

Most assists, series, third basemen
N.L.—15—Pedro Guerrrero, Los Angeles (5-game series)

Most chances accepted, series, third basemen
N.L.—18—Pedro Guerrrero, Los Angeles (5-game series)

Most chances accepted, errorless series, third basemen
N.L.—14—Larry Parrish, Montreal (5-game series)

Most double plays, game, third basemen
A.L.—2—Wayne Gross, Oakland, October 6

Most double plays started, game, third basemen
A.L.—2—Wayne Gross, Oakland, October 6

Most putouts, series, shortstops
N.L.—17—Chris Speier, Montreal (5-game series)

Most putouts, game, shortstops
N.L.—7—Larry Bowa, Philadelphia, October 7
A.L.—5—Fred Stanley, Oakland, October 9

Most assists, series, shortstops
A.L.—23—Robin Yount, Milwaukee (5-game series)

Most chances accepted, series, shortstops
N.L.—32—Chris Speier, Montreal (5-game series)
A.L.—30—Robin Yount, Milwaukee (5-game series)

Most chances accepted, game, shortstops
N.L.—9—Dickie Thon, Houston, October 7, 11 inn (3 PO, 6 A)

Most chances accepted, errorless series, shortstops
N.L.—32—Chris Speier, Montreal (5-game series)

Most putouts, series, outfielders
N.L.—16—Ken Landreaux, Los Angeles (5-game series)

Most putouts by left fielder, game
A.L.—5—Dave Winfield, New York, October 11

Most putouts by center fielder, game
A.L.—7—Dwayne Murphy, Oakland, October 6
Amos Otis, Kansas City, October 7

Most putouts, inning, outfielders
N.L.—3—Jerry White, Montreal, October 8, 2nd (RF)

Most chances accepted, series, outfielders
N.L.—16—Ken Landreaux, Los Angeles (5-game series)

Most chances accepted by left fielder, game
A.L.—5—Dave Winfield, New York, October 11 (5 PO)

Most chances accepted by center fielder, game
A.L.—7—Dwayne Murphy, Oakland, October 6 (7 PO)
Amos Otis, Kansas City, October 7 (7 PO)

Most chances accepted, errorless series, outfielders
N.L.—16—Ken Landreaux, Los Angeles (5-game series)

Most putouts, game, catchers
A.L.—15—Rick Cerone, New York, October 8

Most assists, series, catchers
3-game series
  A.L.—3—John Wathan, Kansas City
5-game series
  N.L.—4—Gary Carter, Montreal
           Mike Scioscia, Los Angeles

Fewest chances offered, game, catchers
A.L.—1—Rick Cerone, New York, October 9

Most runners caught stealing, game, catchers
A.L.—2—John Wathan, Kansas City, October 9

Most runners caught stealing, inning, catchers
A.L.—2—John Wathan, Kansas City, October 9, 3rd

Most games, series, pitchers
A.L.—4—Jim Slaton, Milwaukee (5-game series)
N.L.—4—Ron Reed, Philadelphia (5-game series)

Most putouts, series, pitchers
A.L.—3—Rick Langford, Oakland (3-game series)
  Mike Norris, Oakland (3-game series)

Most putouts, inning, pitchers
A.L.—2—Rick Langford, Oakland, October 9, 1st
          Moose Haas, Milwaukee, October 11, 1st

Most assists, series, pitchers
A.L.—4—Steve McCatty, Oakland (3-game series)
N.L.—5—Fernando Valenzuela, Los Angeles (5-game series)

Most assists, game, pitchers
A.L.—4—Steve McCatty, Oakland, October 7
N.L.—4—Nolan Ryan, Houston, October 6

Most assists, inning, pitchers
A.L.—2—Steve McCatty, Oakland, October 7, 1st
          Tommy John, New York, October 9, 7th

Most chances accepted, series, pitchers
A.L.—4—Steve McCatty, Oakland (3-game series)

Most chances accepted, game, pitchers
N.L.—5—Verne Ruhle, Houston, October 10

CLUB FIELDING

Lowest fielding average by both clubs, series
N.L.—.976—Philadelphia .984, Montreal .969 (5-game series)

Most putouts by outfield of both clubs, game
N.L.—19—Philadelphia 11, Montreal 8, October 9

Fewest putouts by outfield, game
N.L.—0—Philadelphia vs. Montreal, October 8 (fielded 8 inn)

Fewest putouts by outfield of both clubs, game
N.L.—6—Montreal 4, Philadelphia 2, October 7 (Montreal fielded 8 inn)

Most assists, game
A.L.—18—New York vs. Milwaukee, October 9

Fewest assists, game
A.L.—4—New York vs. Milwaukee, October 7
  New York vs. Milwaukee, October 11

Fewest chances offered to outfield, game
N.L.—0—Philadelphia vs. Montreal, October 8 (fielded 8 inn)

Most errors, series
N.L.—6—Montreal vs. Philadelphia (5-game series)

Most errors by both clubs, series
N.L.—9—Montreal 6, Philadelphia 3 (5-game series)

Most errors, game
N.L.—4—Montreal vs. Philadelphia, October 9

Most errors by infield, game
N.L.—3—Houston vs. Los Angeles, October 11

Most errors by infields of both clubs, game
N.L.—5—Houston 3, Los Angeles 2, October 11

Most errors, inning
A.L.—3—Kansas City vs. Oakland, October 9, 3rd
N.L.—2—Montreal vs. Philadelphia, October 9, 8th

Fewest double plays, series
A.L.—1—New York vs. Milwaukee (5-game series)
N.L.—1—Houston vs. Los Angeles (5-game series)

Fewest double plays by both clubs, series
N.L.—3—Los Angeles 2, Houston 1 (5-game series)

CHAMPIONSHIP SERIES

Results: Series Winners

Service (Individual, Club)

Batting (Individual, Club)

Baserunning (Individual, Club)

Pitching (Individual, Club)

Fielding (Individual, Club)

Miscellaneous

Non-Playing Personnel

General Reference

SERIES WINNERS

AMERICAN LEAGUE

Year	Winner	Loser	Games
1969	Baltimore (East)	Minnesota (West)	3-0
1970	Baltimore (East)	Minnesota (West)	3-0
1971	Baltimore (East)	Oakland (West)	3-0
1972	Oakland (West)	Detroit (East)	3-2
1973	Oakland (West)	Baltimore (East)	3-2
1974	Oakland (West)	Baltimore (East)	3-1
1975	Boston (East)	Oakland (West)	3-0
1976	New York (East)	Kansas City (West)	3-2
1977	New York (East)	Kansas City (West)	3-2
1978	New York (East)	Kansas City (West)	3-1
1979	Baltimore (East)	California (West)	3-1
1980	Kansas City (West)	New York (East)	3-0
1981	New York (East)	Oakland (West)	3-0
1982	Milwaukee (East)	California (West)	3-2
1983	Baltimore (East)	Chicago (West)	3-1
1984	Detroit (East)	Kansas City (West)	3-0
1985	Kansas City (West)	Toronto (East)	4-3
1986	Boston (East)	California (West)	4-3
1987	Minnesota (West)	Detroit (East)	4-1
1988	Oakland (West)	Boston (East)	4-0
1989	Oakland (West)	Toronto (East)	4-1
1990	Oakland (West)	Boston (East)	4-0
1991	Minnesota (West)	Toronto (East)	4-1
1992	Toronto (East)	Oakland (West)	4-2
1993	Toronto (East)	Chicago (West)	4-2
1994	no series played		
1995	Cleveland (Central)	Seattle (West)	4-2
1996	New York (East)	Baltimore (East)*	4-1
1997	Cleveland (Central)	Baltimore (East)	4-2
1998	New York (East)	Cleveland (Central)	4-2
1999	New York (East)	Boston (East)*	4-1
2000	New York (East)	Seattle (West)*	4-2
2001	New York (East)	Seattle (West)	4-1
2002	Anaheim (West)*	Minnesota (Central)	4-1
2003	New York (East)	Boston (East)*	4-3
2004	Boston (East)*	New York (East)	4-3

NATIONAL LEAGUE

Year	Winner	Loser	Games
1969	New York (East)	Atlanta (West)	3-0
1970	Cincinnati (West)	Pittsburgh (East)	3-0
1971	Pittsburgh (East)	San Francisco (West)	3-1
1972	Cincinnati (West)	Pittsburgh (East)	3-2
1973	New York (East)	Cincinnati (West)	3-2
1974	Los Angeles (West)	Pittsburgh (East)	3-1
1975	Cincinnati (West)	Pittsburgh (East)	3-0
1976	Cincinnati (West)	Philadelphia (East)	3-0
1977	Los Angeles (West)	Philadelphia (East)	3-1
1978	Los Angeles (West)	Philadelphia (East)	3-1
1979	Pittsburgh (East)	Cincinnati (West)	3-0
1980	Philadelphia (East)	Houston (West)	3-2
1981	Los Angeles (West)	Montreal (East)	3-2
1982	St. Louis (East)	Atlanta (West)	3-0
1983	Philadelphia (East)	Los Angeles (West)	3-1
1984	San Diego (West)	Chicago (East)	3-2
1985	St. Louis (East)	Los Angeles (West)	4-2
1986	New York (East)	Houston (West)	4-2
1987	St. Louis (East)	San Francisco (West)	4-3
1988	Los Angeles (West)	New York (East)	4-3
1989	San Francisco (West)	Chicago (East)	4-1
1990	Cincinnati (West)	Pittsburgh (East)	4-2
1991	Atlanta (West)	Pittsburgh (East)	4-3
1992	Atlanta (West)	Pittsburgh (East)	4-3
1993	Philadelphia (East)	Atlanta (West)	4-2
1994	no series played		
1995	Atlanta (East)	Cincinnati (Central)	4-0
1996	Atlanta (East)	St. Louis (Central)	4-3
1997	Florida (East)*	Atlanta (East)	4-2
1998	San Diego (West)	Atlanta (East)	4-2
1999	Atlanta (East)	New York (East)*	4-2
2000	New York (East)*	St. Louis (Central)	4-1
2001	Arizona (West)	Atlanta (East)	4-1
2002	San Francisco (West)*	St. Louis (Central)	4-1
2003	Florida (East)*	Chicago (Central)	4-3
2004	St. Louis (Central)	Houston (Central)*	4-3

*wild-card team

INDIVIDUAL SERVICE

ALL PLAYERS
SERIES AND CLUBS

Most series played
A.L.—11—Reggie Jackson, Oakland, 1971 through 1975; New York, 1977, 1978, 1980, 1981; California, 1982, 1986.
N.L.—9—Tom Glavine, Atlanta, 1991 through 2001, except 1994 and 2000.
John Smoltz, Atlanta, 1991 through 2001, except 1994 and 2000.

Most consecutive years played in series
Both leagues—5—Tino Martinez, New York A.L., 1998 through 2001; St. Louis N.L., 2002.
A.L.—5—Sal Bando, Vida Blue, Bert Campaneris, Rollie Fingers, Reggie Jackson, Joe Rudi, Gene Tenace, Oakland, 1971 through 1975.
N.L.—5—Tom Glavine, Chipper Jones, Ryan Klesko, Greg Maddux and John Smoltz, Atlanta, 1995 through 1999.

Most series playing in all games
A.L.—9—Reggie Jackson, Oakland, 1971 through 1975; New York, 1977, 1978, 1980; California, 1982; 37 games.
N.L.—7—Pete Rose, Cincinnati, 1970, 1972, 1973, 1975, 1976; Philadelphia, 1980, 1983; 28 games.

Most series played with one club
N.L.—9—Tom Glavine, Atlanta, 1991 through 2001, except 1994 and 2000.
John Smoltz, Atlanta, 1991 through 2001, except 1994 and 2000.

A.L.—7—Jim Palmer, Baltimore, 1969, 1970, 1971, 1973, 1974, 1979, 1983.
Derek Jeter, New York, 1996, 1998 through 2001, 2003, 2004.
Bernie Williams, New York, 1996, 1998 through 2001, 2003, 2004.

Most series appeared in as pinch-hitter
Both leagues—4—Vic Davalillo, Pittsburgh N.L., 1971, 1972; Oakland A.L., 1973; Los Angeles N.L., 1977; five games.
Danny Heep, Houston N.L., 1980; New York N.L., 1986; Los Angeles N.L., 1988; Boston A.L., 1990; 10 games.
N.L.—4—Rick Monday, Los Angeles, 1977, 1978, 1981, 1983; four games.
Richie Hebner, Pittsburgh, 1971; Philadelphia, 1977, 1978; Chicago, 1984; five games.
Keith Lockhart, Atlanta, 1997, 1998, 1999, 2001; six games.
A.L.—3—Curt Motton, Baltimore, 1969, 1971, 1974; four games.
Jim Holt, Minnesota, 1970; Oakland, 1974; four games.
Cliff Johnson, New York, 1977; Toronto, 1985; five games.
Jamie Quirk, Kansas City, 1976, 1985; Oakland, 1990; four games.

Most times on series-winning club (playing one or more game each series)
Both leagues—6—David Justice, Atlanta N.L., 1991, 1992, 1995; Cleveland A.L., 1997; New York A.L., 2000, 2001.
Paul O'Neill, Cincinnati N.L., 1990; New York A.L., 1996, 1998 through 2001.
Mike Stanton, Atlanta N.L., 1991, 1992; New York A.L., 1998 through 2001.

CHAMPIONSHIP SERIES Series winners / Individual Service

A.L.—6—Reggie Jackson, Oakland, 1972, 1973, 1974; New York, 1977, 1978, 1981.

N.L.—6—Pete Rose, Cincinnati, 1970, 1972, 1975, 1976; Philadelphia, 1980, 1983.

Most times on series-losing club (playing one or more game each series)

N.L.—7—Richie Hebner, Pittsburgh, 1970, 1972, 1974, 1975; Philadelphia, 1977, 1978; Chicago, 1984.

A.L.—5—Bobby Grich, Baltimore, 1973, 1974; California, 1979, 1982, 1986.

Reggie Jackson, Oakland, 1971, 1975; New York, 1980; California, 1982, 1986.

Most clubs, career

A.L.—5—Don Baylor, Baltimore, 1973, 1974; California, 1979, 1982; Boston, 1986; Minnesota, 1987; Oakland, 1988.

N.L.—4—Shawon Dunston, Chicago, 1989; New York, 1999; St. Louis, 2000; San Francisco, 2002.

BY POSITION (EXCEPT PITCHERS)

Most series by first baseman

Both leagues—7—Tino Martinez, Seattle A.L., 1995; New York A.L., 1996, 1998 through 2001; St. Louis N.L., 2002; 37 games.

John Olerud, Toronto A.L., 1991, 1992, 1993; New York N.L., 1999; Seattle A.L., 2000, 2001; New York A.L., 2004; 38 games.

A.L.—6—Tino Martinez, Seattle, 1995; New York, 1996, 1998 through 2001; 33 games.

John Olerud, Toronto, 1991, 1992, 1993; Seattle, 2000, 2001; New York, 2004; 32 games.

N.L.—5—Tony Perez, Cincinnati, 1970, 1972, 1973, 1975, 1976; 17 games.

Bob Robertson, Pittsburgh, 1970, 1971, 1972, 1974, 1975; 11 games.

Steve Garvey, Los Angeles, 1974, 1977, 1978, 1981; San Diego, 1984; 22 games.

Most series by second baseman

N.L.—7—Joe Morgan, Cincinnati, 1972, 1973, 1975, 1976, 1979; Houston, 1980; Philadelphia, 1983; 27 games.

A.L.—6—Frank White, Kansas City, 1976, 1977, 1978, 1980, 1984, 1985; 26 games.

Most series by third baseman

Both leagues—6—Graig Nettles, New York A.L., 1976, 1977, 1978, 1980, 1981; San Diego N.L., 1984; 23 games.

A.L.—6—George Brett, Kansas City, 1976, 1977, 1978, 1980, 1984, 1985; 27 games.

N.L.—6—Terry Pendleton, St. Louis, 1985, 1987; Atlanta, 1991, 1992, 1993, 1996; 34 games.

Chipper Jones, Atlanta, 1995 through 2001, except 2000; 34 games.

Most series by shortstop

Both leagues—6—Walt Weiss, Oakland A.L., 1988, 1989, 1990, 1992; Atlanta N.L., 1998, 1999.

A.L.—7—Derek Jeter, New York, 1996, 1998 through 2001, 2003, 2004; 41 games.

N.L.—6—Jeff Blauser, Atlanta, 1991, 1992, 1993, 1995, 1996, 1997; 29 games.

Most series by outfielder

A.L.—10—Reggie Jackson, Oakland, 1971, 1972, 1973, 1974, 1975; New York, 1977, 1978, 1980, 1981; California, 1982; 32 games.

N.L.—5—Cesar Geronimo, Cincinnati, 1972, 1973, 1975, 1976, 1979; 17 games.

Garry Maddox, Philadelphia, 1976, 1977, 1978, 1980, 1983; 17 games.

Ron Gant, Atlanta, 1991, 1992, 1993; Cincinnati, 1995; St. Louis, 1996; 31 games.

Andruw Jones, Atlanta, 1996 through 2001, except 2000; 27 games.

Most series by catcher

Both leagues—6—Bob Boone, Philadelphia N.L., 1976, 1977, 1978, 1980; California A.L., 1982, 1986; 27 games.

N.L.—6—Johnny Bench, Cincinnati, 1970, 1972, 1973, 1975, 1976, 1979; 22 games.

Steve Yeager, Los Angeles, 1974, 1977, 1978, 1981, 1983, 1985; 15 games.

Javy Lopez, Atlanta, 1992, 1995 through 1998, 2001; 27 games.

A.L.—6—Jorge Posada, New York, 1998 through 2001, 2003, 2004; 33 games.

YOUNGEST AND OLDEST NON-PITCHERS

Youngest championship series non-pitcher

N.L.—19 years, 5 months, 16 days—Andruw Jones, Atlanta, October 9, 1996.

A.L.—20 years, 1 month, 5 days—Claudell Washington, Oakland, October 5, 1974.

Oldest championship series non-pitcher

N.L.—42 years, 5 months, 24 days—Pete Rose, Philadelphia, October 8, 1983.

A.L.—41 years, 10 months, 21 days—Rickey Henderson, Seattle, October 15, 2000.

YEARS BETWEEN SERIES (INCLUDES PITCHERS)

Most years between first and second series

Both leagues—16—Chuck Finley, California A.L., 1986, St. Louis N.L., 2002.

N.L.—14—Tony Gwynn, San Diego, 1984, 1998.

A.L.—12—Doyle Alexander, Baltimore, 1973; Toronto, 1985. (Bert Blyleven went 17 years between ALCS appearances with Minnesota in 1970 and 1987, but that span was interrupted by a 1979 NLCS appearance with Pittsburgh.)

Most years between first and last series

Both leagues—19—Dennis Martinez, Baltimore A.L., 1979; Atlanta N.L., 1998.

A.L.—19—Rickey Henderson, Oakland, 1981, Seattle, 2000.

N.L.—17—Nolan Ryan, New York, 1969; Houston, 1986.

POSITIONS

Most positions played, career

N.L.—4—Pete Rose, Cincinnati, 1970, 1972, 1973, 1975, 1976; Philadelphia, 1980; right field, left field, third base, first base; 24 games.

Pedro Guerrero, Los Angeles, 1981, 1983, 1985; right field, center field, third base, left field; 15 games.

Lloyd McClendon, Chicago, 1989; Pittsburgh, 1991, 1992; catcher, left field, first base, right field; 11 games.

A.L.—3—Held by many players.

Most positions played, series

A.L.—3—Cesar Tovar, Minnesota, 1970; center field, second base, left field; 3-game series, three games.

Stan Javier, Seattle, 2000; right field, center field, left field; 6-game series, four games.

Mark McLemore, Seattle, 2001; shortstop, left field, second base; 5-game series; five games.

N.L.—3—Melvin Mora, New York, 1999; left field, center field, right field; 6-game series, six games.

Joe McEwing, New York, 2000; left field, third base, right field; 5-game series, four games.

Craig Paquette, St. Louis, 2000; third base, left field, right field; 5-game series, four games.

Albert Pujols, St. Louis, 2002; left field, third base, first base; 5-game series, five games.

Miguel Cabrera, Florida, 2003; right field, third base, shortstop; 7-game series, seven games.

PITCHERS
SERIES

Most series pitched

N.L.—9—Tom Glavine, Atlanta, 1991 through 2001, except 1994 and 2000; 15 games.
John Smoltz, Atlanta, 1991 through 2001, except 1994 and 2000; 17 games.

A.L.—7—Roger Clemens, Boston, 1986, 1988, 1990; New York, 1999 through 2001, 2003; 11 games.
Jeff Nelson, Seattle, 1995, 2001; New York, 1996, 1998, 1999, 2000, 2003; 19 games.

Most series pitched by relief pitcher

Both leagues—7—Rick Honeycutt, Los Angeles N.L., 1983, 1985; Oakland A.L., 1988, 1989, 1990, 1992; St. Louis, 1996; 20 games as a relief pitcher.
Mark Wohlers, Atlanta N.L., 1991 through 1997, except 1994; New York A.L., 2001; 19 games as a relief pitcher.

N.L.—6—Tug McGraw, New York, 1969, 1973; Philadelphia, 1976, 1977, 1978, 1980; 15 games as a relief pitcher.
Mark Wohlers, Atlanta, 1991, 1992, 1993, 1995, 1996, 1997; 18 games as a relief pitcher.

A.L.—7—Jeff Nelson, Seattle, 1995, 2001; New York, 1996, 1998, 1999, 2000, 2003; 15 games as a relief pitcher.

YOUNGEST AND OLDEST PITCHERS

Youngest championship series pitcher

A.L.—19 years, 5 months, 29 days—Bert Blyleven, Minnesota, October 5, 1970.

N.L.—19 years, 8 months, 28 days—Don Gullett, Cincinnati, October 4, 1970.

Oldest championship series pitcher

N.L.—43 years, 6 months, 8 days—Phil Niekro, Atlanta, October 9, 1982.

A.L.—41 years, 6 months, 13 days—Don Sutton, California, October 15, 1986.

CLUB SERVICE

PLAYERS USED

Most players, series

A.L.-N.L.—25—Held by many clubs.

For a list of players and pitchers used each series, see page 451.

Most players used by both clubs, series

3-game series
  A.L.—46—Oakland 24, New York 22, 1981.
  N.L.—42—Pittsburgh 24, Cincinnati 18, 1975.
4-game series
  N.L.—46—Cincinnati 24, Atlanta 22, 1995.
  A.L.—45—Chicago 23, Baltimore 22, 1983.
5-game series
  A.L.—49—Oakland 25, Detroit 24, 1972.
      New York 25, Boston 24, 1999.
      Seattle 25, New York 24, 2001.
      Minnesota 25, Anaheim 24, 2002.
  N.L.—49—St. Louis 25, New York 24, 2000.
6-game series
  A.L.—50—Cleveland 25, Seattle 25, 1995.
  N.L.—50—Atlanta 25, New York 25, 1999.
7-game series
  N.L.—50—Pittsburgh 25, Atlanta 25, 1992.
  A.L.—46—Toronto 24, Kansas City 22, 1985.

Fewest players, series

3-game series
  A.L.—14—Baltimore vs. Minnesota, 1970.
      Boston vs. Oakland, 1975.
  N.L.—15—St. Louis vs. Atlanta, 1982.
4-game series
  A.L.—20—Oakland vs. Baltimore, 1974.
      Kansas City vs. New York, 1978.
      Baltimore vs. California, 1979.
      Boston vs. Oakland, 1988.
  N.L.—20—Philadelphia vs. Los Angeles, 1983.
5-game series
  N.L.—17—New York vs. Cincinnati, 1973.
  A.L.—18—New York vs. Kansas City, 1977.
6-game series
  A.L.—19—Toronto vs. Chicago, 1993.
  N.L.—21—Houston vs. New York, 1986.
      Pittsburgh vs. Cincinnati, 1990.
7-game series
  A.L.—20—Boston vs. California, 1986.
  N.L.—22—New York vs. Los Angeles, 1988.

Fewest players used by both clubs, series

3-game series

A.L.—35—Oakland 20, Baltimore 15, 1971.
      New York 20, Kansas City 15, 1980.
N.L.—35—Atlanta 20, St. Louis 15, 1982.
4-game series
  A.L.—41—New York 21, Kansas City 20, 1978.
  N.L.—42—Los Angeles 22, Philadelphia 20, 1983.
5-game series
  A.L.—40—Kansas City 22, New York 18, 1977.
      Milwaukee 20, California 20, 1982.
  N.L.—41—Cincinnati 24, New York 17, 1973.
6-game series
  A.L.—41—Chicago 22, Toronto 19, 1993.
  N.L.—43—New York 22, Houston 21, 1986.
7-game series
  A.L.—44—California 24, Boston 20, 1986.
  N.L.—46—St. Louis 23, San Francisco 23, 1987.
      Los Angeles 24, New York 22, 1988.

Most times one club using only nine players in game, series

N.L.—3—New York vs. Cincinnati, 1973 (5-game series).
A.L.—2—Baltimore vs. Minnesota, 1970 (3-game series).

Most players, game

N.L.—21—St. Louis vs. New York, October 16, 2000.
  (23—New York vs. Atlanta, October 17, 1999, 15 innings.)
A.L.—20—Oakland vs. Detroit, October 10, 1972.
  (20—Oakland vs. Detroit, October 11, 1972, 10 innings.)

Most players used by both clubs, game

N.L.—37—Pittsburgh 20, Atlanta 17, October 7, 1992.
  St. Louis 19, Atlanta 18, October 14, 1996.
  (45—New York 23, Atlanta 22, October 17, 1999, 15 innings.)
A.L.—37—Minnesota 19, Anaheim 18, October 13, 2002.
  (37—Baltimore 19, Cleveland 18, October 11, 1997, 12 innings.)

PINCH-HITTERS

Most pinch-hitters, series

N.L.—20—New York vs. Atlanta, 1999 (6-game series).
A.L.—14—Oakland vs. Detroit, 1972 (5-game series).

Most pinch-hitters used by both clubs, series

N.L.—32—New York 20, Atlanta 12, 1999 (6-game series).
A.L.—22—Oakland 14, Detroit 8, 1972 (5-game series).

Fewest pinch-hitters, series

A.L.-N.L.—0—Held by many clubs.

Fewest pinch-hitters used by both clubs, series

A.L.—2—California 2, Milwaukee 0, 1982 (5-game series).
  Chicago 2, Toronto 0, 1993 (6-game series).

Most pinch-hitters, game

A.L.—6—Oakland vs. Detroit, October 10, 1972.
N.L.—5—Held by many clubs.

(6—Los Angeles vs. New York, October 9, 1988, 12 innings.
Atlanta vs. New York, October 19, 1999, 11 innings.)

Most pinch-hitters used by both clubs, game
A.L.—7—Oakland 6, Detroit 1, October 10, 1972.
N.L.—7—Chicago 4, San Francisco 3, October 4, 1989.
Florida 4, Chicago 3, October 8, 2003.
(11—Atlanta 6, New York 5, October 19, 1999, 11 innings.)

Most pinch-hitters, inning
A.L.—4—Baltimore vs. Chicago, October 7, 1983, ninth inning.
N.L.—4—Philadelphia vs. Los Angeles, October 5, 1983,
ninth inning.

PINCH-RUNNERS

Most pinch-runners, series
A.L.—5—Oakland vs. Baltimore, 1974 (4-game series).
Oakland vs. Boston, 1990 (4-game series).
N.L.—4—New York vs. St. Louis, 2000 (5-game series).

Most pinch-runners used by both clubs, series
A.L.—8—Oakland 5, Baltimore 3, 1974 (4-game series).
N.L.—7—New York 4, St. Louis 3, 2000 (5-game series).

Fewest pinch-runners used, series
A.L.-N.L.—0—Held by many clubs.

Fewest pinch-runners used by both clubs, series
N.L.—0—Philadelphia 0, Los Angeles 0, 1978 (4-game series).
Florida 0, Atlanta 0, 1997 (6-game series).
San Francisco 0, St. Louis 0, 2002 (5-game series).
A.L.—0—Baltimore 0, Minnesota 0, 1969 (3-game series).
Kansas City 0, New York 0, 1980 (3-game series).

Most pinch-runners, game
A.L.—2—Held by many clubs.
(3—Kansas City vs. Detroit, October 3, 1984, 11 innings.)
N.L.—2—Held by many clubs.
(2—Held by many clubs in extra innings.)

Most pinch-runners used by both clubs, game
A.L.—3—Made in many games.
(4—Boston 2, California 2, October 12, 1986, 11 innings.)
N.L.—3—Made in many games.
(3—Philadelphia 2, Houston 1, October 12, 1980, 10 innings.
Atlanta 2, New York 1, October 17, 1999, 15 innings.)

Most pinch-runners, inning
A.L.—2—Oakland vs. Detroit, October 7, 1972, 11th inning.
Baltimore vs. Oakland, October 9, 1974, ninth inning.
New York vs. Seattle, October 13, 2000, ninth inning.
N.L.—2—New York vs. St. Louis, October 11, 2000, ninth
inning.

NUMBER OF PLAYERS USED BY POSITION
FIRST BASEMEN

Most first basemen, series
A.L.-N.L.—3—many clubs.

Most first basemen used by both clubs, series
A.L.—5—Oakland 3, Baltimore 2, 1973 (5-game series).
California 3, Boston 2, 1986 (7-game series).
N.L.—5—Pittsburgh 3, Cincinnati 2, 1990 (6-game series).
Pittsburgh 3, Atlanta 2, 1991 (7-game series).

Most first basemen, game
N.L.—3—Los Angeles vs. St. Louis, October 14, 1985.
Atlanta vs. New York, October 12, 1999.
A.L.—2—many games.

Most first basemen used by both clubs, game
N.L.—4—Los Angeles 3, St. Louis 1, October 14, 1985.
Atlanta 2, Pittsburgh 2, October 7, 1992.
Atlanta 2, Pittsburgh 2, October 10, 1992.
Atlanta 3, New York 1, October 12, 1999.
A.L.—4—Boston 2, New York 2, October 20, 2004.

SECOND BASEMEN

Most second basemen, series
A.L.—4—Oakland vs. Detroit, 1972 (5-game series).
N.L.—3—Atlanta vs. Pittsburgh, 1992 (7-game series).
Atlanta vs. San Diego, 1998 (6-game series.)
St. Louis vs. Houston, 2004 (7-game series.)

Most second basemen used by both clubs, series
A.L.—6—Oakland 4, Detroit 2, 1972 (5-game series).
N.L.—5—Atlanta 3, Pittsburgh 2, 1992 (7-game series).
Atlanta 3, St. Louis 2, 1996 (7-game series).
St. Louis 3, Houston 2, 2004 (7-game series).

Most second basemen, game
A.L.—3—Minnesota vs. Baltimore, October 3, 1970.
Oakland vs. Detroit, October 10, 1972.
Oakland vs. Boston, October 7, 1975.
New York vs. Kansas City, October 4, 1978.
(3—Oakland vs. Detroit, October 7, 1972, 11 innings.)
N.L.—2—many games.
(3—St. Louis vs. Houston, October 20, 2004, 12 innings.)

Most second basemen used by both clubs, game
A.L.—4—Minnesota 3, Baltimore 1, October 3, 1970.
Oakland 3, Detroit 1, October 10, 1972.
Oakland 3, Boston 1, October 7, 1975.
New York 3, Kansas City 1, October 4, 1978.
(4—Oakland 3, Detroit 1, October 7, 1972, 11 innings.)
N.L.—3—many games.
(4—St. Louis 3, Houston 1, October 20, 2004, 12 innings.)

THIRD BASEMEN

Most third basemen, series
A.L.-N.L.—3—Held by many clubs.

Most third basemen used by both clubs, series
N.L.—6—San Francisco 3, Chicago 3, 1989 (5-game series).
A.L.—5—Detroit 3, Kansas City 2, 1984 (3-game series).

Most third basemen, game
A.L.—3—Minnesota vs. Toronto, October 8, 1991.
(3—Detroit vs. Kansas City, October 3, 1984, 11 innings.)
N.L.—2—Held by many clubs.

Most third basemen used by both clubs, game
A.L.—4—New York 2, Oakland 2, October 14, 1981.
Minnesota 3, Toronto 1, October 8, 1991.
Cleveland 2, Seattle 2, October 15, 1995.
(5—Detroit 3, Kansas City 2, October 3, 1984, 11 innings.)
N.L.—4—Atlanta 2, St. Louis 2, October 14, 1996.

SHORTSTOPS

Most shortstops, series
A.L.—4—Oakland vs. Detroit, 1972 (5-game series).
N.L.—3—Cincinnati vs. New York, 1973 (5-game series).
Pittsburgh vs. Los Angeles, 1974 (4-game series).
Pittsburgh vs. Cincinnati, 1975 (3-game series).
Florida vs. Chicago, 2003 (7-game series).
Houston vs. St. Louis, 2004 (7-game series).

Most shortstops used by both clubs, series
A.L.—6—Oakland 4, Detroit 2, 1972 (5-game series).
N.L.—5—Florida 3, Chicago 2, 2003 (7-game series).
Houston 3, St. Louis 2, 2004 (7-game series).

Most shortstops, game
N.L.—3—Pittsburgh vs. Los Angeles, October 6, 1974.
(3—Cincinnati vs. New York, October 9, 1973, 12 innings.
Pittsburgh vs. Cincinnati, October 7, 1975, 10 innings.)
A.L.—2—many clubs.
(3—Oakland vs. Detroit, October 11, 1972, 10 innings.)

Most shortstops used by both clubs, game
A.L.-N.L.—4—many games.

LEFT FIELDERS

Most left fielders, series
N.L.—5—Philadelphia vs. Houston, 1980 (5-game series).
A.L.—5—Seattle vs. New York, 2000 (6-game series).
  Seattle vs. New York, 2001 (5-game series).

Most left fielders used by both clubs, series
A.L.—7—Seattle 5, New York 2, 2000 (6-game series).
  Seattle 5, New York 2, 2001 (5-game series).
N.L.—7—St. Louis 4, Houston 3, 2004 (7-game series).

Most left fielders, game
A.L.-N.L.—3—many clubs.

Most left fielders used by both clubs, game
N.L.—5—Atlanta 3, San Diego 2, October 12, 1998.
  St. Louis 3, Houston 2, October 17, 2004.
A.L.—4—many games.

CENTER FIELDERS

Most center fielders, series
N.L.—4—St. Louis vs. Atlanta, 1996 (7-game series).
A.L.—3—Oakland vs. Baltimore, 1973 (5-game series).
  New York vs. Kansas City, 1978 (4-game series).

Most center fielders used by both clubs, series
A.L.—5—Oakland 3, Baltimore 2, 1973 (5-game series).
N.L.—5—St. Louis 4, Atlanta 1, 1996 (7-game series).

Most center fielders, game
N.L.—3—New York vs. Atlanta, October 17, 1999.
A.L.—2—Held by many clubs.

Most center fielders used by both clubs, game
A.L.-N.L.—3—Made in many games.

RIGHT FIELDERS

Most right fielders, series
N.L.—5—St. Louis vs. San Francisco, 1987 (7-game series).
A.L.—4—New York vs. Oakland, 1981 (3-game series).
  Seattle vs. New York, 2000 (6-game series).
  New York vs. Boston, 2003 (7-game series).

Most right fielders used by both clubs, series
N.L.—7—St. Louis 5, San Francisco 2, 1987 (7-game series).
A.L.—6—Seattle 4, New York 2, 2000 (6-game series).
  Anaheim 3, Minnesota 3, 2002 (5-game series).

Most right fielders, game
N.L.—4—St. Louis vs. San Francisco, October 11, 1987.
A.L.—3—New York vs. Oakland, October 14, 1981.
  Seattle vs. New York, October 20, 2001.
  Anaheim vs. Minnesota, October 9, 2002.

Most right fielders used by both clubs, game
N.L.—5—St. Louis 4, San Francisco 1, October 11, 1987.
  St. Louis 3, San Francisco 2, October 13, 1987.
A.L.—5—Seattle 3, New York 2, October 20, 2001.
  Anaheim 3, Minnesota 2, October 9, 2002.

CATCHERS

Most catchers, series
A.L.—3—Kansas City vs. New York, 1976 (5-game series).
N.L.—3—Philadelphia vs. Cincinnati, 1976 (3-game series).
  Houston vs. Philadelphia, 1980 (5-game series).
  Chicago vs. San Francisco, 1989 (5-game series).
  Atlanta vs. Philadelphia, 1993 (6-game series).

Most catchers used by both clubs, series
N.L.—5—Houston 3, Philadelphia 2, 1980 (5-game series).
  Chicago 3, San Francisco 2, 1989 (5-game series).
  Atlanta 3, Philadelphia 2, 1993 (6-game series).
A.L.—4—many series.

Most catchers, game
A.L.-N.L.—2—many clubs.

Most catchers used by both clubs, game
N.L.—4—Chicago 2, San Francisco 2, October 8, 1989.
  Atlanta 2, St. Louis 2, October 14, 1996.
  Atlanta 2, San Diego 2, October 10, 1998.
  Houston 2, St. Louis 2, October 14, 2004.
  (4—New York 2, Los Angeles 2, October 9, 1988, 12 innings.
  Atlanta 2, New York 2, October 17, 1999, 15 innings.
  Atlanta 2, New York 2, October 19, 1999, 11 innings.)
A.L.—4—New York 2, Boston 2, October 16, 1999.
  Seattle 2, New York 2, October 20, 2001.
  Anaheim 2, Minnesota 2, October 13, 2002.
  (4—Baltimore 2, Minnesota 2, October 4, 1969, 12 innings.)

PITCHERS

Most pitchers, series
3-game series
  N.L.—10—Pittsburgh vs. Cincinnati, 1975.
  A.L.—9—Minnesota vs. Baltimore, 1969, 1970.
4-game series
  A.L.—10—Boston vs. Oakland, 1990.
  N.L.—9—San Francisco vs. Pittsburgh, 1971.
    Los Angeles vs. Philadelphia, 1977, 1978.
    Cincinnati vs. Atlanta, 1995.
5-game series
  A.L.—11—Seattle vs. New York, 2001.
    Minnesota vs. Anaheim, 2002.
  N.L.—10—Pittsburgh vs. Cincinnati, 1972.
    San Diego vs. Chicago, 1984.
    St. Louis vs. New York, 2000.
    New York vs. St. Louis, 2000.
    Atlanta vs. Arizona, 2001.
    San Francisco vs. St. Louis, 2002.
6-game series
  A.L.—11—Oakland vs. Toronto, 1992.
    Cleveland vs. Seattle, 1995.
    Cleveland vs. Baltimore, 1997.
    Cleveland vs. New York, 1998.
  N.L.—11—New York vs. Atlanta, 1999.
7-game series
  N.L.—11—Pittsburgh vs. Atlanta, 1991.
    Florida vs. Chicago, 2003.
    St. Louis vs. Houston, 2004.
  A.L.—11—Boston vs. New York, 2004.
    New York vs. Boston, 2004.

For a list of players and pitchers used each series, see page 451.

Most pitchers used by both clubs, series
3-game series
  N.L.—17—Pittsburgh 10, Cincinnati 7, 1975.
    Cincinnati 9, Pittsburgh 8, 1979.
  A.L.—16—Minnesota 9, Baltimore 7, 1969.
4-game series
  N.L.—17—Los Angeles 9, Philadelphia 8, 1978.
    Cincinnati 9, Atlanta 8, 1995.
  A.L.—16—Oakland 9, Boston 7, 1988.
    Boston 10, Oakland 6, 1990.
5-game series
  N.L.—20—New York 10, Atlanta 10, 1999.
    St. Louis 10, New York 10, 2000.
    San Francisco 10, St. Louis 10, 2002.
  A.L.—20—Seattle 11, New York 9, 2001.
    Minnesota 11, Anaheim 9, 2002.
6-game series
  A.L.—21—Cleveland 11, Seattle 10, 1995.
  N.L.—19—San Diego 10, Atlanta 9, 1998.
7-game series
  A.L.—22—Boston 11, New York 11, 2004.
  N.L.—21—Florida 11, Chicago 10, 2003.

Fewest pitchers, series
A.L.—4—Baltimore vs. Minnesota, 1970 (3-game series).

Baltimore vs. Oakland, 1971 (3-game series).
Kansas City vs. New York, 1980 (3-game series).
N.L.—5—Pittsburgh vs. Cincinnati, 1970 (3-game series).
St. Louis vs. Atlanta, 1982 (3-game series).
Philadelphia vs. Los Angeles, 1983 (4-game series).

Fewest pitchers used by both clubs, series
A.L.—10—New York 6, Kansas City 4, 1980 (3-game series).
N.L.—12—Cincinnati 7, Pittsburgh 5, 1970 (3-game series).

Most pitchers, game
A.L.—7—Minnesota vs. Baltimore, October 6, 1969.
Boston vs. New York, October 12, 2004.
(7—Cleveland vs. Baltimore, October 11, 1997, 12 innings.
Cleveland vs. New York, October 7, 1998, 12 innings.
Boston vs. New York, October 18, 2004, 14 innings.
New York vs. Boston, October 18, 2004, 14 innings.)
N.L.—7—San Francisco vs. St. Louis, October 14, 1987.
Pittsburgh vs. Atlanta, October 7, 1992.
Atlanta vs. Arizona, October 19, 2001.
(9—New York vs. Atlanta, October 17, 1999, 15 innings.)

Most pitchers used by winning club, game
N.L.—6—Los Angeles vs. Philadelphia, October 7, 1977.
St. Louis vs. Atlanta, October 13, 1996.
Arizona vs. Atlanta, October 20, 2001.
(9—New York vs. Atlanta, October 17, 1999, 15 innings.)
A.L.—6—Oakland vs. Boston, October 8, 1988.
Cleveland vs. Baltimore, October 12, 1997.
New York vs. Boston, October 14, 1999.
(7—Cleveland vs. Baltimore, October 11, 1997, 12 innings.
Cleveland vs. New York, October 7, 1998, 12 innings.

Boston vs. New York, October 18,. 2004, 14 innings.)

Most pitchers used by losing club, game
A.L.—7—Minnesota vs. Baltimore, October 6, 1969.
N.L.—7—San Francisco vs. St. Louis, October 14, 1987.
Pittsburgh vs. Atlanta, October 7, 1992.
Atlanta vs. Arizona, October 19, 2001.
(8—New York vs. Atlanta, October 19, 1999, 11 innings.)

Most pitchers used by both clubs, game
N.L.—12—Pittsburgh 7, Atlanta 5, October 7, 1992.
Arizona 6, Atlanta 6, October 20, 2001.
(15—New York 9, Atlanta 6, October 17, 1999, 15 innings.)
A.L.—11—Baltimore 6, New York 5, October 12, 1996.
Cleveland 6, Baltimore 5, October 12, 1997.
Minnesota 6, Anaheim 5, October 13, 2002.
Boston 6, New York 8, 1988, 8th inning.
New York vs. Atlanta, October 17, 1999, 7th inning.

SERIES

Most series played
A.L.—12—New York, 1976 through 1978, 1980, 1981, 1996,
1998 through 2001, 2003, 2004 (won ten, lost two).
N.L.—11—Atlanta, 1969, 1982, 1991, 1992, 1993, 1995
through 1999, 2001 (won five, lost six).

For a complete list of results and a complete
list of series won and lost by teams, see
page 442.

INDIVIDUAL BATTING

GAMES

Most games, career
Both leagues—46—David Justice, Atlanta N.L., 1991 through
1993, 1995; Cleveland A.L., 1997, 1998; New York A.L., 2000,
2001; eight series (23 in N.L., 23 in A.L.).
A.L.—45—Reggie Jackson, Oakland, 1971, 1972, 1973, 1974,
1975; New York, 1977, 1978, 1980, 1981; California, 1982,
1986; 11 series.
N.L.—38—Terry Pendleton, St. Louis, 1985, 1987; Atlanta,
1991, 1992, 1993, 1996; six series.

Most games with one club, career
N.L.—34—Chipper Jones, Atlanta, 1995 through 1999, 2001;
six series.
A.L.—41—Derek Jeter, New York, 1996, 1998 through 2001,
2003, 2004; seven series.
Bernie Williams, New York, 1996, 1998 through 2001, 2003,
2004; seven series.

Most games by pinch-hitter, career
N.L.—10—Greg Colbrunn, Atlanta, 1997 (3), 1998 (6), Arizona,
2001 (1) (ten plate appearances, ten at-bats).
A.L.—6—Dane Iorg, Kansas City, 1984 (2), 1985 (4) (six plate
appearances, four at-bats).

Most games by pinch-hitter, series
N.L.—6—Lonnie Smith, Atlanta, 1992 (7-game series).
Greg Colbrunn, Atlanta, 1998 (6-game series).
A.L.—4—George Hendrick, Oakland, 1972 (5-game series).
Dane Iorg, Kansas City, 1985 (7-game series).
Bobby Kielty, Minnesota, 2002 (5-game series).

Most games by pinch-runner, career
A.L.—4—Lance Blankenship, Oakland, 1990, 1992; two series.
N.L.—3—Dave Concepcion, Cincinnati, 1970, 1972; two series.

Most games by pinch-runner, series
A.L.—3—Dave Stapleton, Boston, 1986.
Lance Blankenship, Oakland, 1990.
Eric Fox, Oakland, 1992.
Ruben Amaro Jr., Cleveland, 1995.
Jose Vizcaino, New York, 2000.
Chone Figgins, Anaheim, 2002.
N.L.—3—Marty Malloy, Atlanta, 1998.
Joe McEwing, New York, 2000.

BATTING AVERAGE

Highest batting average, career (50 or more PA)
N.L.—.468—Will Clark, San Francisco, 1987, 1989; St. Louis,
2000; three series, 17 games, 62 at-bats, 29 hits.
A.L.—.392—Devon White, California, 1986; Toronto, 1991,
1992, 1993, four series, 21 games, 74 at-bats, 29 hits.

For a list of batting leaders each series and a
complete list of .500 hitters, see page 444.

Highest batting average, series (10 or more PA)
3-game series
N.L.—.778—Jay Johnstone, Philadelphia, 1976.
A.L.—.583—Brooks Robinson, Baltimore, 1970.
4-game series
N.L.—.467—Dusty Baker, Los Angeles, 1978.
Mike Schmidt, Philadelphia, 1983.
A.L.—.462—Reggie Jackson, New York, 1978.
5-game series
N.L.—.650—Will Clark, San Francisco, 1989.
A.L.—.611—Fred Lynn, California, 1982.
6-game series
N.L.—.500—Keith Lockhart, Atlanta, 1997.
Roger Cedeno, New York, 1999.
Eddie Perez, Atlanta, 1999.
A.L.—.458—Kenny Lofton, Cleveland, 1995.
7-game series
N.L.—.542—Javy Lopez, Atlanta, 1996.
A.L.—.455—Bob Boone, California, 1986.

ON-BASE PERCENTAGE

Highest on-base percentage, career (50 or more PA)
N.L.—.529—Will Clark, San Francisco, 1987, 1989; St. Louis,
2000; three series, 17 games, 62 at-bats, 29 hits, seven
walks, one hit by pitch.
A.L.—.446—Devon White, California, 1986; Toronto, 1991,
1992, 1993; four series, 21 games, 74 at-bats, 29 hits, eight
walks, one sacrifice fly.

CHAMPIONSHIP SERIES   Individual batting

Highest on-base percentage, series (10 or more PA)
3-game series
N.L.—.800—Jay Johnstone, Philadelphia, 1976.
A.L.—.600—Jerry Mumphrey, New York, 1981.
4-game series
A.L.—.588—Eddie Murray, Baltimore, 1979.
N.L.—.579—Jimmy Wynn, Los Angeles, 1974.
5-game series
N.L.—.682—Will Clark, San Francisco, 1989.
A.L.—.650—Fred Lynn, California, 1982.
6-game series
N.L.—.600—Sid Bream, Pittsburgh, 1990.
A.L.—.593—Frank Thomas, Chicago, 1993.
7-game series
N.L.—.750—Lloyd McClendon, Pittsburgh, 1992.
A.L.—.500—George Brett, Kansas City, 1985.
     Bob Boone, California, 1986.

SLUGGING AVERAGE

Highest slugging average, career (50 or more PA)
N.L.—.806—Will Clark, San Francisco, 1987, 1989; St. Louis, 2000; three series, 17 games, 62 at-bats, 29 hits, seven doubles, one triple, four home runs, 50 total bases.
A.L.—.728—George Brett, Kansas City, 1976, 1977, 1978, 1980, 1984, 1985; six series, 27 games, 103 at-bats, 35 hits, five doubles, four triples, nine home runs, 75 total bases).

Highest slugging average, series (10 or more PA)
3-game series
N.L.—1.182—Willie Stargell, Pittsburgh, 1979.
A.L.—.917—Tony Oliva, Minnesota, 1970.
     Reggie Jackson, Oakland, 1971.
     Bob Watson, New York, 1980.
4-game series
N.L.—1.250—Bob Robertson, Pittsburgh, 1971.
A.L.—1.056—George Brett, Kansas City, 1978.
5-game series
N.L.—1.200—Will Clark, San Francisco, 1989.
A.L.—1.167—Darryl Strawberry, New York, 1996.
6-game series
N.L.—.900—Eddie Perez, Atlanta, 1999.
A.L.—.826—Jim Thome, Cleveland, 1998.
7-game series
N.L.—1.182—Lloyd McClendon, Pittsburgh, 1992.
A.L.—.826—George Brett, Kansas City, 1985.

AT-BATS AND PLATE APPEARANCES

Most at-bats, career
A.L.—168—Derek Jeter, New York, 1996, 1998 through 2001, 2003, 2004; seven series, 41 games.
N.L.—135—Terry Pendleton, St. Louis, 1985, 1987; Atlanta, 1991, 1992, 1993, 1996; six series, 38 games.

Most at-bats by pinch-hitter, career
N.L.—10—Greg Colbrunn, Atlanta, 1997 (3), 1998 (6), Arizona, 2001 (1).
A.L.—5—Cliff Johnson, New York, 1977 (1), 1978 (1), Toronto, 1985 (3).

Most plate appearances by pinch-hitter, career
N.L.—10—Greg Colbrunn, Atlanta, 1997 (3), 1998 (6), Arizona, 2001 (1).
A.L.—6—Dane Iorg, Kansas City, 1984 (2), 1985 (4).

Most consecutive hitless times at bat, career
Both leagues—31—Billy North, Oakland A.L., 1974 (last 13 times at bat), 1975 (all 10 times at bat); Los Angeles N.L., 1978 (all eight times at bat).
N.L.—30—Cesar Geronimo, Cincinnati, 1973 (last 13 times at bat), 1975 (all 10 times at bat), 1976 (first seven times at bat).
A.L.—24—Bert Campaneris, Oakland, 1974 (last 13 times at bat), 1975 (all 11 times at bat); California, 1979 (no times at bat).

Most at-bats, series
3-game series
A.L.—15—Mark Belanger, Baltimore, 1969.
     Paul Blair, Baltimore, 1969.
N.L.—15—Ken Oberkfell, St. Louis, 1982.
4-game series
N.L.—19—Dave Cash, Pittsburgh, 1971.
     Garry Maddox, Philadelphia, 1978.
     Marquis Grissom, Atlanta, 1995.

A.L.—18—George Brett, Kansas City, 1978.
     Thurman Munson, New York, 1978.
     Rudy Law, Chicago, 1983.
5-game series
N.L.—24—Mike Schmidt, Philadelphia, 1980.
A.L.—24—Kirby Puckett, Minnesota, 1987.
     Derek Jeter, New York, 1996.
     Jose Offerman, Boston, 1999.
6-game series
N.L.—28—Gerald Williams, Atlanta, 1999.
A.L.—27—Joe Carter, Toronto, 1993.
     Tim Raines Sr., Chicago, 1993.
     Devon White, Toronto, 1993.
     Kenny Lofton, Cleveland, 1998.
7-game series
N.L.—35—Marquis Grissom, Atlanta, 1996.
A.L.—32—Doug DeCinces, California, 1986.

Most at-bats by pinch-hitter, series
N.L.—6—Lonnie Smith, Atlanta, 1992.
     Greg Colbrunn, Atlanta, 1998.
A.L.—4—George Hendrick, Oakland, 1972.

Most at-bats by player with no hits, career
A.L.—15—Tom Brookens, Detroit, 1984 (2), 1987 (15).
     Ron Karkovice, Chicago, 1993.
N.L.—13—Ray Lankford, St. Louis, 1996.

Most at-bats, game
A.L.—6—many players.
     (7—Tony Clark, New York, October 18, 2004, 14 innings.
     Derek Jeter, New York, October 18, 2004, 14 innings.
     Hideki Matsui, New York, October 18, 2004, 14 innings.
     Bernie Williams, New York, October 18, 2004, 14 innings.)
N.L.—6—many players.
     (7—many players in extra innings.)

Most at-bats by player with no hits, game
A.L.—6—Rickey Henderson, Toronto, October 5, 1993.
     (6—Don Buford, Baltimore, October 4, 1969, 12 innings.
     Chuck Knoblauch, New York, October 7, 1998, 12 innings.)
N.L.—5—many players.
     (6—Alan Ashby, Houston, October 15, 1986, 16 innings.)

Most at-bats, inning
A.L.-N.L.—2—many players.

Most times faced pitcher, inning
A.L.-N.L.—2—many players.

RUNS

Most runs, career
A.L.—31—Bernie Williams, New York, 1996, 1998 through 2001, 2003, 2004; seven series, 41 games.
N.L.—20—Chipper Jones, Atlanta, 1995 through 1999, 2001; six series, 34 games.

Most runs by pinch-hitter, career
N.L.—2—Held by many players.
A.L.—1—Held by many players.

Most runs by pinch-runner, career
A.L.—2—Marshall Edwards, Milwaukee, 1982; one series, two games.
     Devon White, California, 1986; one series, two games.
N.L.—2—Gene Clines, Pittsburgh, 1972, 1974; two series, two games.
     Rafael Landestoy, Houston, 1980; one series, two games.
     Jose Gonzalez, Los Angeles, 1988; one series, two games.
     Joe McEwing, New York, 2000; one series, three games.

Most runs, series
3-game series
A.L.—5—Mark Belanger, Baltimore, 1970.
N.L.—4—Held by many players.
4-game series
A.L.—7—George Brett, Kansas City, 1978.
N.L.—6—Steve Garvey, Los Angeles, 1978.
5-game series
A.L.—8—Rickey Henderson, Oakland, 1989.

N.L.—8—Will Clark, San Francisco, 1989.
      Timo Perez, New York, 2000.
6-game series
  A.L.—7—Dave Winfield, Toronto, 1992.
      Paul Molitor, Toronto, 1993.
  N.L.—6—Willie McGee, St. Louis, 1985.
      Fred McGriff, Atlanta, 1993.
      Gary Sheffield, Florida, 1997.
7-game series
  N.L.—12—Carlos Beltran, Houston, 2004.
  A.L.—9—Hideki Matsui, New York, 2004.

Most runs by pinch-hitter, series
N.L.—2—Ty Cline, Cincinnati, 1970; two games.
  Tim Flannery, San Diego, 1984, three games.
  Todd Hollandsworth, Florida, 2003, four games.
A.L.—1—Held by many players.

Most runs by pinch-runner, series
N.L.—2—Rafael Landestoy, Houston, 1980; two games.
  Jose Gonzalez, Los Angeles, 1988; two games.
  Joe McEwing, New York, 2000; three games.
A.L.—2—Marshall Edwards, Milwaukee, 1982; two games.
  Devon White, California, 1986; two games.

Most runs, game
N.L.—4—Bob Robertson, Pittsburgh, October 3, 1971.
  Steve Garvey, Los Angeles, October 9, 1974.
  Will Clark, San Francisco, October 4, 1989.
  Javy Lopez, Atlanta, October 14, 1996.
  Fred McGriff, Atlanta, October 17, 1996.
A.L.—5—Alex Rodriguez, New York, October 16, 2004.

Most runs, inning
A.L.—2—Scott Spiezio, Anaheim, October 13, 2002, seventh inning.
  Chone Figgins, Anaheim, October 13, 2002, seventh inning.
N.L.—2—Cesar Cedeno, St. Louis, October 13, 1985, second inning.
  Jack Clark, St. Louis, October 13, 1985, second inning.

HITS
CAREER AND SERIES

Most hits, career
N.L.—45—Pete Rose, Cincinnati, 1970, 1972, 1973, 1975, 1976; Philadelphia, 1980, 1983; seven series, 28 games.
A.L.—52—Bernie Williams, New York, 1996, 1998 through 2001, 2003, 2004; seven series, 41 games.

Most hits by pinch-hitter, career
N.L.—4—Greg Colbrunn, Atlanta, 1997, 1998; Arizona, 2001 (three series, ten games).
A.L.—2—Held by many players.

Most hits, series
3-game series
  A.L.—7—Brooks Robinson, Baltimore, 1969, 1970.
  N.L.—7—Art Shamsky, New York, 1969.
      Jay Johnstone, Philadelphia, 1976.
4-game series
  N.L.—8—Dave Cash, Pittsburgh, 1971.
  A.L.—7—George Brett, Kansas City, 1978.
      Rod Carew, California, 1979.
      Rudy Law, Chicago, 1983.
      Wade Boggs, Boston, 1990.
      Carney Lansford, Oakland, 1990.
5-game series
  N.L.—13—Will Clark, San Francisco, 1989.
  A.L.—11—Chris Chambliss, New York, 1976.
      Fred Lynn, California, 1982.
      Jose Offerman, Boston, 1999.
6-game series
  A.L.—12—Tim Raines Sr., Chicago, 1993.
      Devon White, Toronto, 1993.
  N.L.—10—Ozzie Smith, St. Louis, 1985.
      Fred McGriff, Atlanta, 1993.
      Eddie Perez, Atlanta, 1999.
7-game series
  N.L.—14—Albert Pujols, St. Louis, 2004.
  A.L.—14—Hideki Matsui, New York, 2004.

Most hits by pinch-hitter, series
N.L.—3—Paul Popovich, Pittsburgh, 1974 (three games).
  Todd Hollandsworth, Florida, 2003 (four games).
A.L.—2—Held by many players.

Most series with one or more hits
A.L.—10—Reggie Jackson, Oakland, 1971, 1972, 1973, 1974, 1975; New York, 1977, 1978, 1980; California, 1982, 1986.
N.L.—7—Richie Hebner, Pittsburgh, 1970, 1971, 1972, 1974, 1975; Philadelphia, 1977, 1978.
  Pete Rose, Cincinnati, 1970, 1972, 1973, 1975, 1976; Philadelphia, 1980, 1983.

Most consecutive hits, career
N.L.—6—Steve Garvey, Los Angeles, October 9, 1974 (4), October 4, 1977 (2).
  Kenny Lofton, Chicago, October 9 (4), 10 (2), 2003.
A.L.—6—Paul Molitor, Toronto, October 5 (4), 6 (2), 1993.

Most consecutive hits by pinch-hitter, career
N.L.—3—Paul Popovich, Pittsburgh, October 5, 6, 9, 1974.
A.L.—2—Held by many players.

Most consecutive hits, series
A.L.—6—Paul Molitor, Toronto, October 5 (4), 6 (2), 1993.
N.L.—6—Kenny Lofton, Chicago, October 9 (4), 10 (2), 2003.

GAME AND INNING

Most hits, game
A.L.—5—Paul Blair, Baltimore, October 6, 1969
  Hideki Matsui, New York, October 16, 2004
N.L.—4—many players

Most times reached base safely, game (batting 1.000)
A.L.—5—many players
N.L.—5—Felix Millan, Atlanta, October 5, 1969 (3 bases on balls, 2 singles).
  Will Clark, San Francisco, October 4, 1989 (1 base on balls, 1 single, 1 double, 2 home runs).

Most hits accounting for all club's hits, game
N.L.—2—Roberto Clemente, Pittsburgh, October 10, 1972.
  Andy Kosco, Cincinnati, October 7, 1973.
A.L.—2—Willie Wilson, Kansas City, October 12, 1985.

Most consecutive games with one or more hits, career
N.L.—15—Pete Rose, Cincinnati, 1973 (last 3), 1975 (3), 1976 (3); Philadelphia, 1980 (5), 1983 (first 1).
A.L.—12—Don Baylor, California, 1982 (last 3); Boston, 1986 (7); Minnesota, 1987 (2).

Most hits in two consecutive games, series
A.L.—7—Tim Raines Sr., Chicago, October 8 (4), 9 (3), 1993.
  Nomar Garciaparra, Boston, October 14 (3), 16 (4), 1999.
  Hideki Matsui, New York, October 16 (5), 17 (2 in 12 inn), 2004.
N.L.—7—Kenny Lofton, Chicago, October 8 (4), 10 (3 in 11 innings), 2003.

Most hits, inning
A.L.—2—Graig Nettles, New York, October 14, 1981, fourth inning.
  Rickey Henderson, Oakland, October 6, 1990, ninth inning.
  Scott Spiezio, Anaheim, October 13, 2002, seventh inning.
  Adam Kennedy, Anaheim, October 13, 2002, seventh inning.
N.L.—2—Jack Clark, St. Louis, October 13, 1985, second inning.
  Tito Landrum, St. Louis, October 13, 1985, second inning.
  Jerome Walton, Chicago, October 5, 1989, first inning.
  Barry Bonds, Pittsburgh, October 13, 1992, second inning.
  Lloyd McClendon, Pittsburgh, October 13, 1992, second inning.

SINGLES

Most singles, career
N.L.—34—Pete Rose, Cincinnati, 1970, 1972, 1973, 1975, 1976; Philadelphia, 1980, 1983; seven series, 28 games.
A.L.—33—Bernie Williams, 1996, 1998 through 2001, 2003, 2004; seven series, 41 games.

Most singles by pinch-hitter, career
N.L.—4—Greg Colbrunn, Atlanta, 1997, 1998; Arizona, 2001; three series, ten games.
A.L.—2—Held by many players.

Most singles, series
3-game series
  N.L.—7—Art Shamsky, New York, 1969.
  A.L.—6—Brooks Robinson, Baltimore, 1969.
4-game series
  N.L.—7—Bill Russell, Los Angeles, 1974.
  A.L.—6—Chris Chambliss, New York, 1978.
      Rudy Law, Chicago, 1983.
      Carney Lansford, Oakland, 1990.
5-game series
  A.L.—10—Jose Offerman, Boston, 1999.
  N.L.—8—Pete Rose, Philadelphia, 1980.
      Terry Puhl, Houston, 1980.
      Jerome Walton, Chicago, 1989.
6-game series
  A.L.—10—Tim Raines Sr., Chicago, 1993.
      Omar Vizquel, Cleveland, 1998.
  N.L.—7—Jack Clark, St. Louis, 1985.
      Ozzie Smith, St. Louis, 1985.
      Terry Pendleton, Atlanta, 1993.
      Fred McGriff, Atlanta, 1993.
7-game series
  A.L.—9—Marty Barrett, Boston, 1986.
      Bob Boone, California, 1986.
  N.L.—9—Jay Bell, Pittsburgh, 1991.
      Mark Lemke, Atlanta, 1996.
      Chipper Jones, Atlanta, 1996.
      Kenny Lofton, Chicago, 2003.

Most singles by pinch-hitter, series
N.L.—3—Paul Popovich, Pittsburgh, 1974 (three games).
A.L.—2—Held by many players.

Most singles, game
A.L.—4—Brooks Robinson, Baltimore, October 4, 1969, 12 innings.
  Chris Chambliss, New York, October 4, 1978.
  Kelly Gruber, Toronto, October 7, 1989.
  Jerry Browne, Oakland, October 12, 1992.
N.L.—4—Terry Puhl, Houston, October 12, 1980, 10 innings.
  Tito Landrum, St. Louis, October 13, 1985.
  Chipper Jones, Atlanta, October 9, 1996.
  Keith Lockhart, Atlanta, October 14, 1997.
  Kenny Lofton, Chicago, October 8, 2003.

Most singles, inning
A.L.—2—Graig Nettles, New York, October 14, 1981, fourth inning.
  Rickey Henderson, Oakland, October 6, 1990, ninth inning.
  Scott Spiezio, Anaheim, October 13, 2002, seventh inning.
N.L.—2—Jack Clark, St. Louis, October 13, 1985, second inning.
  Tito Landrum, St. Louis, October 13, 1985, second inning.
  Jerome Walton, Chicago, October 5, 1989, first inning.
  Lloyd McClendon, Pittsburgh, October 13, 1992, second inning.

DOUBLES

Most doubles, career
A.L.—10—Bernie Williams, New York, 1996, 1998 through 2001, 2003, 2004; seven series, 41 games.
N.L.—7—Pete Rose, Cincinnati, 1970, 1972, 1973, 1975, 1976; Philadelphia, 1980, 1983; seven series, 28 games.
  Richie Hebner, Pittsburgh, 1970, 1971, 1972, 1974, 1975; Philadelphia, 1977, 1978; Chicago, 1984; eight series, 27 games.
  Mike Schmidt, Philadelphia, 1976, 1977, 1978, 1980, 1983; five series, 20 games.
  Ron Cey, Los Angeles, 1974, 1977, 1978, 1981; Chicago, 1984; five series, 22 games.
  Fred McGriff, Atlanta, 1993, 1995, 1996, 1997; four series, 23 games.
  Javy Lopez, Atlanta, 1992, 1995, 1996, 1997, 1998; five series, 22 games.
  Will Clark, San Francisco, 1987, 1989; St. Louis, 2000; three series, 17 games.
  Chipper Jones, Atlanta, 1995 through 2001, except 2000; six series, 34 games.

Most doubles by pinch-hitter, career
N.L.—2—Manny Mota, Los Angeles, 1974, 1977, 1978; three series, six games.
A.L.—1—Held by many players.

Most doubles, series
3-game series
  N.L.—3—Joe Morgan, Cincinnati, 1975.
      Darrell Porter, St. Louis, 1982.
  A.L.—3—Bob Watson, New York, 1980.
4-game series
  N.L.—4—Fred McGriff, Atlanta, 1995.
  A.L.—3—Rod Carew, California, 1979.
5-game series
  A.L.—4—Matty Alou, Oakland, 1972.
      Tom Brunansky, Minnesota, 1987.
  N.L.—4—Pete Rose, Cincinnati, 1972.
6-game series
  N.L.—4—Tom Herr, St. Louis, 1985.
      Edgardo Alfonzo, New York, 1999.
  A.L.—3—Brian Giles, Cleveland, 1997.
      Mark McLemore, Seattle, 2000.
      John Olerud, Seattle, 2000.
7-game series
  A.L.—6—Hideki Matsui, New York, 2004.
  N.L.—5—Javy Lopez, Atlanta, 1996.

Most doubles, game
N.L.—2—Held by many players.
  (3—Fred McGriff, Atlanta, October 11, 1995, 10 innings.)
A.L.—2—Held by many players.

Most doubles, inning
A.L.-N.L.—1—Held by many players.

TRIPLES

Most triples, career
A.L.—4—George Brett, Kansas City, 1976, 1977, 1978, 1980, 1984, 1985; six series, 27 games.
N.L.—3—Willie McGee, St. Louis, 1982, 1985, 1987, 1996; four series, 22 games.
  Mariano Duncan, Los Angeles, Cincinnati, Philadelphia, 1985, 1990, 1993, 1995; four series, 17 games.

Most triples by pinch-hitter, career
N.L.—1—Ty Cline, Cincinnati, 1970; one series, two games.
  Lenny Dykstra, New York, 1986; one series, two games.
  Lonnie Smith, Atlanta, 1992; one series, six games.
  Dmitri Young, St. Louis, 1996; one series, three games.
  Doug Glanville, Chicago, 2003; one series, one game.
A.L.—1—Al Martin, Seattle, 2001; one series, two games.

Most triples, series
A.L.—2—George Brett, Kansas City, 1977 (5-game series).
  Kenny Lofton, Cleveland, 1995 (6-game series).
N.L.—2—Willie McGee, St. Louis, 1982 (3-game series).
  Mariano Duncan, Philadelphia, 1993 (6-game series).
  Juan Pierre, Florida, 2003 (7-game series).

Most triples, game
N.L.—2—Mariano Duncan, October 9, 1993.
A.L.—1—Held by many players.

Most bases-loaded triples, game
A.L.—1—Jim Sundberg, Kansas City, October 16, 1985.
  Mark McLemore, Seattle, October 20, 2001.
N.L.—1—Tom Glavine, Atlanta, October 17, 1996.

HOME RUNS
CAREER AND SERIES

Most home runs, career
A.L.—9—George Brett, Kansas City, 1976, 1977, 1978, 1980, 1984, 1985; six series, 27 games.
  Bernie Williams, New York, 1996, 1998 through 2001, 2003, 2004; seven series, 41 games.

N.L.—8—Steve Garvey, Los Angeles, 1974, 1977, 1978, 1981; San Diego, 1984; five series, 22 games.

For a list of all home runs each series and a complete list of players with four or more career home runs, see page 445.

Most home runs, series

3-game series
- N.L.—3—Hank Aaron, Atlanta, 1969.
- A.L.—2—Held by many players.

4-game series
- N.L.—4—Bob Robertson, Pittsburgh, 1971.
  - Steve Garvey, Los Angeles, 1978.
- A.L.—3—George Brett, Kansas City, 1978.
  - Jose Canseco, Oakland, 1988.

5-game series
- N.L.—3—Rusty Staub, New York, 1973.
- A.L.—3—Darryl Strawberry, New York, 1996.
  - Todd Zeile, Baltimore, 1996.
  - Bernie Williams, New York, 2001.
  - Adam Kennedy, Anaheim, 2002.

6-game series
- A.L.—4—Jim Thome, Cleveland, 1998.
- N.L.—3—Bill Madlock, Los Angeles, 1985.

7-game series
- N.L.—4—Jeffrey Leonard, San Francisco, 1987.
  - Carlos Beltran, Houston, 2004.
  - Albert Pujols, St. Louis, 2004.
- A.L.—3—George Brett, Kansas City, 1985.
  - Jason Giambi, New York, 2003.
  - Trot Nixon, Boston, 2003.
  - David Ortiz, Boston, 2004.

Most series with one or more home runs

N.L.—5—Johnny Bench, Cincinnati, 1970 (1), 1972 (1), 1973 (1), 1976 (1), 1979 (1).
A.L.—4—Graig Nettles, New York, 1976 (2), 1978 (1), 1980 (1), 1981 (1).
Reggie Jackson, Oakland, 1971 (2), 1975 (1); New York, 1978 (2); California, 1982 (1).
George Brett, Kansas City, 1976 (1), 1978 (3), 1980 (2), 1985 (3).
Eddie Murray, Baltimore, 1979, 1983, 1996; Cleveland, 1995.
Bernie Williams, New York, 1996 (2), 1999 (1), 2000 (1), 2001 (3).

Most series with two or more home runs

A.L.—3—George Brett, Kansas City, 1978 (3), 1980 (2), 1985 (3).
Manny Ramirez, Cleveland, 1995 (2), 1996 (2), 1998 (2).
N.L.—2—Steve Garvey, Los Angeles, 1974 (2), 1978 (4).
Willie Stargell, Pittsburgh, 1974 (2), 1979 (2).
Gary Matthews, Philadelphia, 1983 (3); Chicago, 1984 (2).
Ron Gant, Atlanta, 1992 (2); St. Louis, 1996.

GAME AND INNING

Most home runs, game
N.L.—3—Bob Robertson, Pittsburgh, October 3, 1971
A.L.—3—George Brett, Kansas City, October 6, 1978
Adam Kennedy, Anaheim, October 13, 2002

Most grand slams, game
A.L.—1—Mike Cuellar, Baltimore, October 3, 1970, 4th inning.
Don Baylor, California, October 9, 1982, 8th inning.
Jim Thome, Cleveland, October 13, 1998, 5th inning.
Ricky Ledee, New York, October 17, 1999, 9th inning.
Johnny Damon, Boston, October 20, 2004, 2nd inning.
N.L.—1—Ron Cey, Los Angeles, October 4, 1977, 7th inning.
Dusty Baker, Los Angeles, October 5, 1977, 4th inning.
Will Clark, San Francisco, October 4, 1989, 4th inning.
Ron Gant, Atlanta, October 7, 1992, 5th inning.
Gary Gaetti, St. Louis, October 10, 1996, 7th inning.
Andres Galarraga, Atlanta, October 11, 1998, 7th inning.
Aramis Ramirez, Chicago, October 11, 2003, 1st inning.

Inside-the-park home runs
A.L.—Graig Nettles, New York, October 9, 1980, 5th inning.

(none on base).
Paul Molitor, Milwaukee, October 6, 1982, 5th inning. (one on base).
N.L.—none

Most home runs by pinch-hitter, game
N.L.—1—Jerry Martin, Philadelphia, October 4, 1978, ninth inning.
Bake McBride, Philadelphia, October 7, 1978, seventh inning.
Harry Spilman, San Francisco, October 9, 1987, ninth inning.
Greg Myers, San Diego, October 12, 1998, ninth inning.
Erubiel Durazo, Arizona, October 21, 2001, fifth inning.
J.D. Drew, St. Louis, October 9, 2002, eighth inning.
Eduardo Perez, St. Louis, October 10, 2002, eighth inning.
A.L.—1—John Lowenstein, Baltimore, October 3, 1979, 10th inning.
Pat Sheridan, Kansas City, October 9, 1985, ninth inning.
Mike Pagliarulo, Minnesota, October 11, 1991, 10th inning.
Eric Davis, Baltimore, October 13, 1997, ninth inning.
Ricky Ledee, New York, October 17, 1999, ninth inning.
Jay Buhner, Seattle, October 20, 2001, ninth inning.

Home runs by leadoff batter, start of game
A.L.—Bert Campaneris, Oakland, October 7, 1973 (at Baltimore).
George Brett, Kansas City, October 6, 1978 (at New York).
Brady Anderson, Baltimore, October 8, 1997 (at Baltimore).
Kenny Lofton, Cleveland, October 11, 1998 (at Cleveland).
N.L.—Bob Dernier, Chicago, October 2, 1984 (at Chicago).
Orlando Merced, Pittsburgh, October 12, 1991 (at Atlanta).
Marcus Giles, Atlanta, October 17, 2001 (at Arizona).

Home runs winning 1-0 games
A.L.—Sal Bando, Oakland, October 8, 1974, fourth inning.
Tony Fernandez, Cleveland, October 15, 1997, 11th inning.
N.L.—Mike Schmidt, Philadelphia, October 4, 1983, first inning.
Glenn Davis, Houston, October 8, 1986, second inning.

Most home runs by pitcher, game
A.L.—1—Mike Cuellar, Baltimore, October 3, 1970 (three on base).
N.L.—1—Don Gullett, Cincinnati, October 4, 1975 (one on base).
Steve Carlton, Philadelphia, October 6, 1978 (two on base).
Rick Sutcliffe, Chicago, October 2, 1984 (none on base).

Most home runs by rookie, game
A.L.-N.L.—1—many players

Most consecutive games hitting one or more home runs, career
N.L.—4—Garry Mathews, Philadelphia, October 5, 7, 8, 1983; Chicago, October 2, 1984
Jeffrey Leonard, San Francisco, October 6, 7, 9, 10, 1987
Carlos Beltran, Houston, October 13, 14, 16, 17, 2004
A.L.—3—Bernie Williams, New York, October 20, 21, 22, 2001

Most consecutive games hitting one or more home runs, series
N.L.—4—Jeffrey Leonard, San Francisco, October 6, 7, 9, 10, 1987
Carlos Beltran, Houston, October 13, 14, 16, 17, 2004
A.L.—3—Bernie Williams, New York, October 20, 21, 22, 2001

Most home runs in two consecutive games, series (homering each game)
N.L.—4—Bob Robertson, Pittsburgh, October 3 (3), October 5 (1), 1971.
A.L.—3—Jay Buhner, Seattle, October 11 (1), October 13 (2 in 11 innings), 1995.
Darryl Strawberry, New York, October 12 (2), October 13 (1), 1996.
Jason Giambi, New York, October 15 (1), October 16 (2), 2003.

Hitting home run in first championship series at-bat
A.L.—Frank Robinson, Baltimore, October 4, 1969, fourth inning (received base on balls in first inning).
Norm Cash, Detroit, October 7, 1972, second inning.
Dan Ford, California, October 3, 1979, first inning.
John Lowenstein, Baltimore, October 3, 1979, 10th inning (pinch-hit).
Rich Cerone, New York, October 8, 1980, first inning.

Gorman Thomas, Milwaukee, October 5, 1982, second inning.
Gary Gaetti, Minnesota, October 7, 1987, second inning.
Mike Blowers, Seattle, October 10, 1995, second inning.
Rafael Palmeiro, Baltimore, October 9, 1996, fourth inning (received base on balls in second inning).
N.L.—Joe Morgan, Cincinnati, October 7, 1972, first inning.
Bob Dernier, Chicago, October 2, 1984, first inning.
Rick Sutcliffe, Chicago, October 2, 1984, third inning.
Glenn Davis, Houston, October 8, 1986, second inning.
Mark Grace, Chicago, October 4, 1989, first inning.
Orlando Merced, Pittsburgh, October 12, 1991, first inning.
Mike Lowell, Florida, October 7, 2003, 11th inning.

Hitting home runs in first two championship series at-bats
A.L.—Gary Gaetti, Minnesota, October 7, 1987, second and fifth innings.
N.L.—Never accomplished.

Most home runs, inning
A.L.-N.L.—1—Held by many players.

Most home runs, two consecutive innings
N.L.—2—Rusty Staub, New York, October 8, 1973, first and second innings.
Will Clark, San Francisco, October 4, 1989, third and fourth innings.
A.L.—Never accomplished.

TOTAL BASES

Most total bases, career
A.L.—89—Bernie Williams, 1996, 1998 through 2001, 2003, 2004; seven series, 41 games.
N.L.—63—Pete Rose, Cincinnati, 1970, 1972, 1973, 1975, 1976; Philadelphia, 1980, 1983; seven series, 28 games.

Most total bases by pinch-hitter, career
N.L.—6—Jerry Martin, Philadelphia, 1977, 1978; two series, three games.
J.D. Drew, St. Louis, 2000, 2002; two series, two games.
A.L.—4—John Lowenstein, Baltimore, 1979; one series, two games.
Pat Sheridan, Kansas City, 1985; one series, two games.
Mike Pagliarulo, Minnesota, 1991; one series, one game.
Eric Davis, Baltimore, 1997; one series, three games.
Ricky Ledee, New York, 1998, 1999; two series, two games.
Jay Buhner, Seattle, 2000, 2001; two series, two games.

Most total bases, series
3-game series
  N.L.—16—Hank Aaron, Atlanta, 1969.
  A.L.—11—Held by many players.
4-game series
  N.L.—22—Steve Garvey, Los Angeles, 1978.
  A.L.—19—George Brett, Kansas City, 1978.
5-game series
  N.L.—24—Will Clark, San Francisco, 1989.
  A.L.—20—Chris Chambliss, New York, 1976.
6-game series
  A.L.—19—Jim Thome, Cleveland, 1998.
  N.L.—18—Bill Madlock, Los Angeles, 1985.
7-game series
  N.L.—28—Albert Pujols, St. Louis, 2004.
  A.L.—28—Hideki Matsui, New York, 2004.

Most total bases by pinch-hitter, series
N.L.—6—Jerry Martin, Philadelphia, 1978; two games.
A.L.—4—John Lowenstein, Baltimore, 1979; two games.
Pat Sheridan, Kansas City, 1985; two games.
Mike Pagliarulo, Minnesota, 1991; two games.
Eric Davis, Baltimore, 1997; three games.
Ricky Ledee, New York, 1999; one game.
Jay Buhner, Seattle, 2001; one game.

Most total bases, game
N.L.—14—Bob Robertson, Pittsburgh, October 3, 1971 (1 double, 3 HR).
A.L.—13—Adam Kennedy, Anaheim, October 13, 2002 (1 single, 3 HR).
Hideki Matsui, New York, October 16, 2004 (1 single, 2 doubles, 2 HR).

Most total bases, inning
A.L.—5—Adam Kennedy, Anaheim, October 13, 2002, seventh inning (HR and single).

N.L.—5—Barry Bonds, Pittsburgh, October 13, 1992, second inning (HR and single).

EXTRA BASE HITS

Most extra base hits, career
A.L.—19—Bernie Williams, New York, 1996, 1998 through 2001, 2003, 2004; seven series, 41 games.
N.L.—12—Steve Garvey, Los Angeles, 1974, 1977, 1978, 1981; San Diego, 1984; five series, 22 games.
Will Clark, San Francisco, 1987, 1989; St. Louis, 2000; three series, 17 games.
Javy Lopez, Atlanta, 1992, 1995 through 1998, 2001; six series, 27 games.

Most extra base hits, series
3-game series
  N.L.—5—Hank Aaron, Atlanta, 1969
  A.L.—4—Bob Watson, New York, 1980
4-game series
  N.L.—6—Steve Garvey, Los Angeles, 1978
  A.L.—5—George Brett, Kansas City, 1978
5-game series
  A.L.—6—Tom Brunansky, Minnesota, 1987
  N.L.—6—Will Clark, San Francisco, 1989
6-game series
  N.L.—5—Tom Herr, St. Louis, 1985
  A.L.—5—Jay Buhner, Seattle, 1995
7-game series
  A.L.—9—Hideki Matsui, New York, 2004
  N.L.—7—Javy Lopez, Atlanta, 1996

Most extra base hits, game
N.L.—4—Bob Robertson, Pittsburgh, October 3, 1971 (1 double, 3 hrs)
A.L.—4—Hideki Matsui, New York, October 16, 2004 (2 doubles, 2 hrs)

Most extra base hits, inning
A.L.-N.L.—1—many players

RUNS BATTED IN

Most runs batted in, career
Both leagues—27—David Justice, Atlanta N.L., 1991 through 1993, 1995; Cleveland A.L., 1997, 1998; New York A.L., 2000, 2001; eight series (13 in N.L., 14 in A.L.).
N.L.—21—Steve Garvey, Los Angeles, 1974, 1977, 1978, 1981; San Diego, 1984; five series, 22 games.
A.L.—33—Bernie Williams, New York, 1996, 1998 through 2001, 2003, 2004; seven series, 41 games.

Most runs batted in by pinch-hitter, career
A.L.—4—Ricky Ledee, New York, 1998, 1999; two series, two games.
N.L.—2—J.C. Martin, New York, 1969; one series, two games.
Jerry Martin, Philadelphia, 1977, 1978; two series, three games.
Luis Quinones, Cincinnati, 1990; one series, three games.
Francisco Cabrera, Atlanta, 1992, 1993; two series, five games.
Dmitri Young, St. Louis, 1996; one series, three games.
Greg Myers, San Diego, 1998; one series, two games.
Erubiel Durazo, Arizona, 2001; one series, two games.

Most runs batted in, series
3-game series
  A.L.—9—Graig Nettles, New York, 1981.
  N.L.—7—Hank Aaron, Atlanta, 1969.
4-game series
  N.L.—8—Dusty Baker, Los Angeles, 1977.
    Gary Matthews, Philadelphia, 1983.
  A.L.—6—Reggie Jackson, New York, 1978.
5-game series
  A.L.—10—Don Baylor, California, 1982.
  N.L.—9—Matt Williams, San Francisco, 1989.
6-game series
  A.L.—8—Jim Thome, Cleveland, 1998.
    David Justice, New York, 2000.
  N.L.—7—Bill Madlock, Los Angeles, 1985.
7-game series
  A.L.—11—David Ortiz, Boston, 2004.
  N.L.—10—Ivan Rodriguez, Florida, 2003.

Most runs batted in by pinch-hitter, series
A.L.—4—Ricky Ledee, New York, 1999; one game.
N.L.—2—J.C. Martin, New York, 1969; two games.
  Jerry Martin, Philadelphia, 1978; two games.
  Luis Quinones, Cincinnati, 1990; three games.
  Dmitri Young, St. Louis, 1996; three games.
  Greg Myers, San Diego, 1998; two games.
  Jose Hernandez, Atlanta, 1999; two games.
  Erubiel Durazo, Arizona, 2001; two games.
  Todd Hollandsworth, Florida, 2003; four games.

Most runs batted in, game
N.L.—6—Will Clark, San Francisco, October 4, 1989.
  Aramis Ramirez, Chicago, October 11, 2003.
A.L.—6—Johnny Damon, Boston, October 20, 2004.

Most runs batted in by pinch-hitter, game
A.L.—4—Ricky Ledee, New York, October 17, 1999, ninth inning.
N.L.—2—J.C. Martin, New York, October 4, 1969, eighth inning.
  Dmitri Young, St. Louis, October 13, 1996, seventh inning.
  Greg Myers, San Diego, October 12, 1998, ninth inning.
  Jose Hernandez, Atlanta, October 19, 1999, sixth inning.
  Erubiel Durazo, Arizona, October 21, 2001, fifth inning.

Most consecutive games with one or more runs batted in, career
A.L.—6—Mark McGwire, Oakland, October 6, 8, 9, 1988; October 3, 4, 6, 1989.
N.L.—5—Gary Matthews, Philadelphia, October 5, 7, 8, 1983; Chicago, October 2, 3, 1984.
  Ivan Rodriguez, Florida, October 10, 11, 12, 14, 15, 2003.

Most runs batted in accounting for all club's runs, game
A.L.—3—Bert Campaneris, Oakland, October 5, 1974.
  Graig Nettles, New York, October 13, 1981.
N.L.—3—Keith Hernandez, New York, October 5, 1988.
  Jeff Blauser, Atlanta, October 13, 1993.
  Ron Gant, St. Louis, October 12, 1996.
  John Olerud, New York, October 16, 1999.
  Steve Finley, Arizona, October 19, 2001.

Most runs batted in, inning
A.L.—4—Mike Cuellar, Baltimore, October 3, 1970, 4th inning.
  Don Baylor, California, October 9, 1982, 8th inning.
  Jim Thome, Cleveland, October 13, 1998, 5th inning.
  Ricky Ledee, New York, October 17, 1999, 9th inning.
  Johnny Damon, Boston, October 20, 2004, 2nd inning.
N.L.—4—Ron Cey, Los Angeles, October 4, 1977, 7th inning.
  Dusty Baker, Los Angeles, October 5, 1977, 4th inning.
  Will Clark, San Francisco, October 4, 1989, 4th inning.
  Ron Gant, Atlanta, October 7, 1992, 5th inning.
  Gary Gaetti, St. Louis, October 10, 1996, 7th inning.
  Andres Galarraga, Atlanta, October 11, 1998, 7th inning.

Most game-winning RBIs, career (1980-88)
A.L.—3—George Brett, Kansas City, 1980, 1985 (2).
N.L.—3—Gary Carter, Montreal, 1981; New York, 1986, 1988.

Most game-winning RBIs, series (1980-88)
N.L.—2—Greg Luzinski, Philadelphia, 1980.
  Gary Carter, New York, 1986.
  Kirk Gibson, Los Angeles, 1988.
A.L.—2—Cecil Cooper, Milwaukee, 1982.
  Al Oliver, Toronto, 1985.
  George Brett, Kansas City, 1985.

BASES ON BALLS

Most bases on balls, career
A.L.—26—Jorge Posada, New York, 1998 through 2001, 2003, 2004; six series, 33 games.
N.L.—24—Chipper Jones, Atlanta, 1995 through 1999, 2001; six series, 34 games.
  Barry Bonds, Pittsburgh, 1990 through 1992; San Francisco, 2002; four series, 25 games.

Most bases on balls, series
3-game series
  A.L.—6—Harmon Killebrew, Minnesota, 1969.
  N.L.—6—Joe Morgan, Cincinnati, 1976.
4-game series
  N.L.—9—Jim Wynn, Los Angeles, 1974.
  A.L.—5—Reggie Jackson, Oakland, 1974.

  Eddie Murray, Baltimore, 1979.
  Gary Roenicke, Baltimore 1983.
  Jose Canseco, Oakland, 1990.
5-game series
  N.L.—10—Barry Bonds, San Francisco, 2002.
  A.L.—7—Lou Whitaker, Detroit, 1987.
    Rickey Henderson, Oakland, 1989.
6-game series
  A.L.—10—Frank Thomas, Chicago, 1993.
  N.L.—9—Chipper Jones, Atlanta, 1999.
7-game series
  N.L.—8—Carlos Beltran, Houston, 2004.
  A.L.—7—George Brett, Kansas City, 1985.
    Jorge Posada, New York, 2004.

Most consecutive bases on balls, series
A.L.—4—Harmon Killebrew, Minnesota, October 4 (3), 5 (1), 1969.
  Gary Roenicke, Baltimore, October 6 (1), 7 (1), 8 (2), 1983.
  Bernie Williams, New York, October 10 (3), 11 (1), 1998.
N.L.—4—Darren Daulton, Philadelphia, October 10 (3), 11 (1), 1993.

Most bases on balls, game
N.L.—4—Darren Daulton, Philadelphia, October 10, 1993.
  Ken Caminiti, San Diego, October 8, 1998.
A.L.—4—Ruppert Jones, California, October 11, 1986, 11 innings.
  Frank Thomas, Chicago, October 5, 1993.

Most bases on balls with bases filled, game
A.L.-N.L.—1—Held by many players.

Bases on balls with bases filled by pinch-hitters, game
N.L.—Duffy Dyer, Pittsburgh, October 7, 1975, ninth inning.
  Mike Sharperson, Los Angeles, October 8, 1988, eighth inning.
A.L.—Bobby Kielty, Minnesota, October 13, 2002, seventh inning.

Most bases on balls, inning
A.L.-N.L.—1—Held by many players.

STRIKEOUTS

Most strikeouts, career
A.L.—41—Reggie Jackson, Oakland, 1971, 1972, 1973, 1974, 1975; New York, 1977, 1978, 1980, 1981; California, 1982, 1986; 11 series, 45 games.
N.L.—26—Ron Gant, Atlanta, 1991, 1992, 1993; Cincinnati, 1995; St. Louis, 1996; five series, 31 games.

Most strikeouts, series
3-game series
  A.L.—7—Leo Cardenas, Minnesota, 1969.
  N.L.—7—Cesar Geronimo, Cincinnati, 1975.
4-game series
  N.L.—10—Reggie Sanders, Cincinnati, 1995.
  A.L.—7—Dave Henderson, Oakland, 1988.
5-game series
  N.L.—9—Jim Edmonds, St. Louis, 2000.
  A.L.—8—Kirk Gibson, Detroit, 1987.
    Chili Davis, Minnesota, 1991.
    Corey Koskie, Minnesota, 2002.
6-game series
  N.L.—12—Darryl Strawberry, New York, 1986.
  A.L.—10—Omar Vizquel, Cleveland, 1997.
    Rafael Palmeiro, Baltimore, 1997.
7-game series
  N.L.—12—John Shelby, Los Angeles, 1988.
  A.L.—11—Alfonso Soriano, New York, 2003.
    Mark Bellhorn, Boston, 2004.

Most strikeouts by pinch-hitter, series
N.L.—3—Lee Mazzilli, New York, 1986; five games.
  Curtis Wilkerson, Pittsburgh, 1991; four games.
  Tom Goodwin, Chicago, 2003; four games.
A.L.—2—Matt Nokes, Detroit, 1987; two games.
  Larry Parrish, Boston, 1988; three games.
  Glenallen Hill, New York, 2000; two games.

Individual batting

CHAMPIONSHIP SERIES

Bobby Kielty, Minnesota, 2002; four games.
Shawn Wooten, Anaheim, 2002; two games.

Most consecutive strikeouts, series (consecutive at-bats)
N.L.—7—Cesar Geronimo, Cincinnati, October 4 (1), 5 (3), 7 (3), 1975, first game 10 innings (one base on balls during streak).
A.L.—6—Corey Koskie, Minnesota, October 9 (1), 11 (4), 12 (1), 2002.

Most consecutive strikeouts, series (consecutive plate appearances)
A.L.—6—Corey Koskie, Minnesota, October 9 (1), 11 (4), 12 (1), 2002.
N.L.—5—Cesar Geronimo, Cincinnati, October 6 (1), 7 (3), 9 (1), 1973, third game 12 innings.
Reggie Sanders, Cincinnati, October 11 (2), 13 (3), 1995, first game 10 innings.

Most strikeouts, game
A.L.—4—Bobby Bonilla, Baltimore, October 10, 1996 (consec).
Corey Koskie, Minnesota, October 11, 2002 (consec).
Johnny Damon, Boston, October 12, 2004 (consec).
Mark Bellhorn, Boston, October 16, 2004 (consec).
(4—many players in extra innings.)
N.L.—4—John Kruk, Philadelphia, October 10, 1993.
Gerald Williams, Atlanta, October 10, 1998 (consecutive).
(4—Reggie Sanders, Cincinnati, October 11, 1995, 10 innings.)

Most strikeouts, inning
A.L.—2—Ron Karkovice, Chicago, October 8, 1993, third inning.
N.L.—1—Held by many players.

SACRIFICE HITS

Most sacrifice hits, career
N.L.—6—Greg Maddux, Chicago, 1989; Atlanta, 1993, 1995, 1996, 1997, 1998, 1999, 2001; eight series; 15 games.
A.L.—5—Derek Jeter, New York, 1996, 1998 through 2001, 2003, 2004; six series, 41 games.

Most sacrifice hits, series
A.L.—3—Enos Cabell, Houston, 1980 (5-game series).
N.L.—3—Rich Aurilia, San Francisco, 2002 (5-game series).
Mark Prior, Chicago, 2003 (7-game series).
Most sacrifice hits, game
A.L.-N.L.—2—Held by many players.

SACRIFICE FLIES

Most sacrifice flies, career
Both leagues—3—Robin Ventura, Chicago A.L., 1993; New York N.L., 1999, 2000; three series, 17 games.
A.L.-N.L.—2—Held by many players.

Most sacrifice flies, series
A.L.-N.L.—2—Held by many players.

Most sacrifice flies, game
A.L.-N.L.—1—Held by many players.

HIT BY PITCH

Most hit by pitch, career
N.L.—4—Richie Hebner, Pittsburgh, 1971 (1), 1972 (1), 1974 (1); Chicago, 1984 (1).
A.L.—4—Miguel Cairo, New York, 2004.

Most hit by pitch, series
N.L.—2—Lenny Dykstra, New York, 1988.
Jeff Blauser, Atlanta, 1996.
Morgan Ensberg, Houston, 2004.
Jeff Kent, Houston, 2004.
A.L.—4—Miguel Cairo, New York, 2004.

Most hit by pitch, game
A.L.—2—Dan Gladden, Minnesota, October 11, 1987.
Pat Sheridan, Detroit, October 12, 1987.
N.L.—1—Held by many players.

GROUNDING INTO DOUBLE PLAYS

Most grounding into double plays, career
A.L.—6—Manny Ramirez, Cleveland, 1995 through 1999; Boston, 2003, 2004; seven series, 35 games.
N.L.—5—Pedro Guerrero, Los Angeles, 1981, 1983, 1985; three series, 15 games.

Most grounding into double plays, series
N.L.—4—Pedro Guerrero, Los Angeles, 1981 (5-game series).
A.L.—3—Tony Taylor, Detroit, 1972 (5-game series).
Doug DeCinces, California, 1986 (7-game series).
Paul Sorrento, Cleveland, 1995 (6-game series).
German Berroa, Baltimore, 1997 (6-game series).

Most grounding into double plays, game
A.L.—3—Tony Taylor, Detroit, October 10, 1972.
N.L.—2—Cleon Jones, New York, October 4, 1969.
Pedro Guerrero, Los Angeles, October 16, 1981.
Jerry Royster, Atlanta, October 10, 1982.
Chris Gomez, San Diego, October 7, 1998.
Gerald Williams, Atlanta, October 13, 1999.
Damian Miller, Arizona, October 20, 2001.
(2—Bret Boone, Cincinnati, October 10, 1995, 11 innings.
Garry Maddox, Philadelphia, October 12, 1980, ten innings.)

REACHING BASE ON INTERFERENCE

Most times awarded first base on catcher's interference, game
N.L.—1—Richie Hebner, Pittsburgh, October 8, 1974, fifth inning.
Mike Scioscia, Los Angeles, October 14, 1985, fourth inning.
A.L.—Never accomplished.

CLUB BATTING

GAMES

Most games played, total series
A.L.—61—New York; 12 series; won 39, lost 22.
N.L.—60—Atlanta; 11 series; won 27, lost 33.

For summaries of series won and lost, games won and lost, and home and road games played, see page 442. For a list of batting statistics by teams each series, see page 448.

BATTING AVERAGE

Highest batting average, series
3-game series
A.L.—.336—New York vs. Oakland, 1981.
N.L.—.330—St. Louis vs. Atlanta, 1982.
4-game series
A.L.—.300—New York vs. Kansas City, 1978.
N.L.—.286—Los Angeles vs. Philadelphia, 1978.
5-game series
A.L.—.316—New York vs. Kansas City, 1976.
N.L.—.303—Chicago vs. San Francisco, 1989.
6-game series
A.L.—.301—Toronto vs. Chicago, 1993.
N.L.—.279—St. Louis vs. Los Angeles, 1985.
7-game series
N.L.—.309—Atlanta vs. St. Louis, 1996.
A.L.—.282—New York vs. Boston, 2004.

Highest batting average by both clubs, series
3-game series
N.L.—.292—New York .327, Atlanta .255, 1969.
A.L.—.286—Baltimore .330, Minnesota .238, 1970.

4-game series
    A.L.—.282—New York .300, Kansas City .263, 1978.
    N.L.—.268—Los Angeles .286, Philadelphia .250, 1978.
5-game series
    N.L.—.285—Chicago .303, San Francisco .267, 1989.
    A.L.—.283—New York .316, Kansas City .247, 1976.
6-game series
    A.L.—.271—Toronto .301, Chicago .237, 1993.
    N.L.—.256—St. Louis .279, Los Angeles .234, 1985.
7-game series
    A.L.—.279—New York, 282, Boston .277, 2004.
    N.L.—.262—Florida .266, Chicago .258, 2003.

Highest batting average by losing club, series
N.L.—.303—Chicago vs. San Francisco, 1989 (5-game series).
A.L.—.293—Boston vs. New York, 1999 (5-game series).

Lowest batting average, series
3-game series
    A.L.—.155—Minnesota vs. Baltimore, 1969.
    N.L.—.169—Atlanta vs. St. Louis, 1982.
4-game series
    A.L.—.177—Baltimore vs. Oakland, 1974.
    N.L.—.194—Pittsburgh vs. Los Angeles, 1974.
5-game series
    N.L.—.186—Cincinnati vs. New York, 1973.
    A.L.—.198—Detroit vs. Oakland, 1972.
6-game series
    A.L.—.184—Seattle vs. Cleveland, 1995.
    N.L.—.189—New York vs. Houston, 1986.
7-game series
    N.L.—.204—St. Louis vs. Atlanta, 1996.
    A.L.—.225—Kansas City vs. Toronto, 1985.

Lowest batting average by both clubs, series
3-game series
    A.L.—.202—Detroit .234, Kansas City .170, 1984.
    N.L.—.223—Pittsburgh .225, Cincinnati .220, 1970.
4-game series
    A.L.—.180—Oakland .183, Baltimore .177, 1974.
    N.L.—.232—Los Angeles .260, Pittsburgh .194, 1974.
5-game series
    N.L.—.203—New York .220, Cincinnati .186, 1973.
    A.L.—.205—Baltimore .211, Oakland .200, 1973.
6-game series
    N.L.—.204—Houston .218, New York .189, 1986.
    A.L.—.219—Cleveland .220, New York .218, 1998.
7-game series
    N.L.—.228—New York .242, Los Angeles .214, 1988.
                Atlanta .231, Pittsburgh .224, 1991.
    A.L.—.247—Toronto .269, Kansas City .225, 1985.

Lowest batting average by winning club, series
A.L.—.183—Oakland vs. Baltimore, 1974 (4-game series).
N.L.—.189—New York vs. Houston, 1986 (6-game series).

ON-BASE PERCENTAGE

Highest on-base percentage, series
3-game series
    A.L.—.415—New York vs. Oakland, 1981.
    N.L.—.395—St. Louis vs. Atlanta, 1982.
4-game series
    N.L.—.399—Los Angeles vs. Pittsburgh, 1974.
    A.L.—.399—Oakland vs. Boston, 1990
5-game series
    A.L.—.372—New York vs. Kansas City, 1976.
    N.L.—.371—New York vs. St. Louis, 2000.
6-game series
    A.L.—.371—St. Louis vs. Los Angeles, 1985.
    N.L.—.367—Toronto vs. Chicago, 1993.
7-game series
    N.L.—.375—Atlanta vs. St. Louis, 1996.
    A.L.—.371—New York vs. Boston, 2004.

Highest on-base percentage by both clubs, series
3-game series
    N.L.—.355—New York .382, Atlanta .328, 1969.
    A.L.—.350—Baltimore .395, Minnesota .300, 1970.
4-game series
    N.L.—.332—Los Angeles .399, Pittsburgh .252, 1974.

A.L.—.330—New York .331, Kansas City .329, 1978.
5-game series
    N.L.—.349—Chicago .361, San Francisco .337, 1989.
    A.L.—.340—Minnesota .359, Detroit .321, 1987.
6-game series
    A.L.—.360—Toronto .367, Chicago .352, 1993.
    N.L.—.336—St. Louis .371, Los Angeles .300, 1985.
7-game series
    A.L.—.358—New York, .371, Boston .344, 2004.
    N.L.—.332—Florida .340, Chicago .324, 2003.

Lowest on-base percentage, series
3-game series
    A.L.—.214—Kansas City vs. Detroit, 1984.
    N.L.—.219—Atlanta vs. St. Louis, 1982.
4-game series
    A.L.—.209—Baltimore vs. Oakland, 1974.
    N.L.—.252—Pittsburgh vs. Los Angeles, 1974.
5-game series
    N.L.—.243—Pittsburgh vs. Cincinnati, 1972.
    A.L.—.257—Detroit vs. Oakland, 1972.
6-game series
    N.L.—.234—New York vs. Houston, 1986.
    A.L.—.251—Seattle vs. Cleveland, 1995.
7-game series
    N.L.—.244—St. Louis vs. Atlanta, 1996.
    A.L.—.294—Kansas City vs. Toronto, 1985.

Lowest on-base percentage by both clubs, series
3-game series
    A.L.—.250—Detroit .284, Kansas City .214, 1984.
    N.L.—.293—Pittsburgh .307, Cincinnati .278, 1970.
4-game series
    A.L.—.264—Oakland .313, Baltimore .209, 1974.
    N.L.—.309—Philadelphia .336, Los Angeles .282, 1983.
5-game series
    N.L.—.269—Cincinnati .294, Pittsburgh .243, 1972.
    A.L.—.271—Oakland .285, Detroit .257, 1972.
6-game series
    N.L.—.255—Houston .276, New York .234, 1986.
    A.L.—.296—Cleveland .338, Seattle .251, 1995.
7-game series
    N.L.—.297—Atlanta .303, Pittsburgh .291, 1991.
    A.L.—.307—Toronto .319, Kansas City .294, 1985.

SLUGGING AVERAGE

Highest slugging average, series
3-game series
    N.L.—.575—New York vs. Atlanta, 1969.
    A.L.—.560—Baltimore vs. Minnesota, 1970.
4-game series
    N.L.—.544—Los Angeles vs. Philadelphia, 1978.
    A.L.—.511—Oakland vs. Boston, 1988.
5-game series
    A.L.—.497—Minnesota vs. Detroit, 1987.
                New York vs. Baltimore, 1996.
    N.L.—.494—Chicago vs. San Diego, 1984.
6-game series
    A.L.—.471—Toronto vs. Oakland, 1992.
    N.L.—.420—Philadelphia vs. Atlanta, 1993.
7-game series
    N.L.—.484—Chicago vs. Florida, 2003.
    A.L.—.469—New York vs. Boston, 2004.

Highest slugging average by both clubs, series
3-game series
    N.L.—.530—New York .575, Atlanta .481, 1969.
    A.L.—.476—Baltimore .560, Minnesota .386, 1970.
4-game series
    N.L.—.477—Los Angeles .544, Philadelphia .407, 1978.
    A.L.—.443—Kansas City .4436, New York .4428, 1978.
5-game series
    N.L.—.456—San Francisco .473, Chicago .440, 1989.
    A.L.—.448—New York .497, Baltimore .398, 1996.
6-game series
    N.L.—.415—Philadelphia .420, Atlanta .409, 1993.
    A.L.—.408—Toronto .471, Oakland .343, 1992.
7-game series
    N.L.—.469—Chicago .484, Florida .453, 2003.

A.L.—.454—New York, .469, Boston .439, 2004.

Lowest slugging average, series

3-game series
 N.L.—.180—Atlanta vs. St. Louis, 1982.
 A.L.—.198—Kansas City vs. Detroit, 1984.
4-game series
 A.L.—.241—Chicago vs. Baltimore, 1983.
 N.L.—.261—Cincinnati vs. Atlanta, 1995.
5-game series
 A.L.—.288—Oakland vs. Detroit, 1972.
      Minnesota vs. Anaheim, 2002.
 N.L.—.278—Montreal vs. Los Angeles, 1981.
6-game series
 N.L.—.260—Florida vs. Atlanta, 1997.
 A.L.—.299—Seattle vs. Cleveland, 1995.
7-game series
 N.L.—.288—Los Angeles vs. New York, 1988.
 A.L.—.366—Kansas City vs. Toronto, 1985.

Lowest slugging average by both clubs, series

3-game series
 A.L.—.300—Detroit .402, Kansas City .198, 1984.
 N.L.—.318—St. Louis .437, Atlanta .180, 1982.
4-game series
 A.L.—.283—Oakland .308, Baltimore .258, 1974.
 N.L.—.339—Los Angeles .391, Philadelphia .290, 1977.
5-game series
 A.L.—.304—Detroit .321, Oakland .288, 1972.
 N.L.—.307—Cincinnati .311, New York .304, 1973.
6-game series
 N.L.—.288—Houston .311, New York .264, 1986.
 A.L.—.351—Baltimore .394, Cleveland .304, 1997.
7-game series
 N.L.—.325—New York .363, Los Angeles .288, 1988.
 A.L.—.369—Toronto .372, Kansas City .366, 1985.

AT-BATS AND PLATE APPEARANCES

Most at-bats, total series

A.L.—2,132—New York; 12 series, 61 games.
N.L.—2,040—Atlanta; 11 series, 60 games.

Most at-bats, series

3-game series
 A.L.—123—Baltimore vs. Minnesota, 1969.
 N.L.—113—New York vs. Atlanta, 1969.
4-game series
 N.L.—149—Atlanta vs. Cincinnati, 1995.
 A.L.—140—New York vs. Kansas City, 1978.
5-game series
 N.L.—190—Philadelphia vs. Houston, 1980.
 A.L.—184—Boston vs. New York, 1999.
6-game series
 N.L.—227—New York vs. Houston, 1986.
 A.L.—218—Baltimore vs. Cleveland, 1997.
7-game series
 A.L.—277—New York vs. Boston, 2004.
 N.L.—256—Florida vs. Chicago, 2003.

Most at-bats by both clubs, series

3-game series
 A.L.—233—Baltimore 123, Minnesota 110, 1969.
 N.L.—219—New York 113, Atlanta 106, 1969.
4-game series
 N.L.—287—Los Angeles 147, Philadelphia 140, 1978.
 A.L.—273—New York 140, Kansas City 133, 1978.
5-game series
 N.L.—362—Philadelphia 190, Houston 172, 1980.
 A.L.—360—Boston 184, New York 176, 1999.
6-game series
 N.L.—452—New York 227, Houston 225, 1986.
 A.L.—425—Baltimore 218, Cleveland 207, 1997.
7-game series
 A.L.—548—Boston 277, New York 271, 2004.
 N.L.—508—Florida 256, Chicago 252, 2003.

Most at-bats by pinch-hitters, series

N.L.—15—Atlanta vs. Pittsburgh, 1992 (7-game series).
 New York vs. Atlanta, 1999 (6-game series).

St. Louis vs. New York, 2000 (5-game series).
A.L.—13—Oakland vs. Detroit, 1972 (5-game series).
 Toronto vs. Kansas City, 1985 (7-game series).

Most at-bats by pinch-hitters on both clubs, series

N.L.—25—Atlanta 15, Pittsburgh 10, 1992 (7-game series).
A.L.—20—Oakland 13, Detroit 7, 1972 (5-game series).

Most plate appearances by pinch-hitters, series

N.L.—18—New York vs. Atlanta, 1999 (6-game series).
A.L.—14—Oakland vs. Detroit, 1972.

Most plate appearances by pinch-hitters on both clubs, series

N.L.—29—New York 18, Atlanta 11, 1999 (6-game series).
A.L.—22—Oakland 14, Detroit 8, 1972 (5-game series).

Fewest at-bats, series

3-game series
 N.L.—89—Atlanta vs. St. Louis, 1982.
 A.L.—95—Baltimore vs. Oakland, 1971.
4-game series
 A.L.—120—Oakland vs. Baltimore, 1974.
 N.L.—129—Pittsburgh vs. Los Angeles, 1974.
      Los Angeles vs. Philadelphia, 1983.
5-game series
 A.L.—151—Milwaukee vs. California, 1982.
 N.L.—155—San Diego vs. Chicago, 1984.
6-game series
 N.L.—181—Florida vs. Atlanta, 1997.
 A.L.—191—Seattle vs. New York, 2000.
7-game series
 N.L.—215—St. Louis vs. San Francisco, 1987.
 A.L.—227—Kansas City vs. Toronto, 1985.

Fewest at-bats by both clubs, series

3-game series
 A.L.—191—Oakland 96, Baltimore 95, 1971.
 N.L.—192—St. Louis 103, Atlanta 89, 1982.
4-game series
 A.L.—244—Baltimore 124, Oakland 120, 1974.
 N.L.—259—Philadelphia 130, Los Angeles 129, 1983.
5-game series
 A.L.—308—California 157, Milwaukee 151, 1982.
 N.L.—317—Chicago 162, San Diego 155, 1984.
6-game series
 N.L.—375—Atlanta 194, Florida 181, 1997.
 A.L.—395—New York 204, Seattle 191, 2000.
7-game series
 N.L.—441—San Francisco 226, St. Louis 215, 1987.
 A.L.—469—Toronto 242, Kansas City 227, 1985.

Most at-bats by club, game

N.L.—47—Atlanta vs. St. Louis, October 14, 1996.
 (56—Houston vs. New York, October 15, 1986, 16 innings.)
A.L.—47—New York vs. Boston, October 16, 2004.
 (49—Toronto vs. Oakland, October 11, 1992, 11 innings.)

Most at-bats by both clubs, game

A.L.—87—New York 47, Boston 40, October 16, 2004
 (91—Toronto 49, Oakland 42, October 11, 1992, 11 innings.)
N.L.—80—Atlanta 47, St. Louis 33, October 14, 1996.
 Arizona 42, Atlanta 38, October 20, 2001.
 (110—Houston 56, New York 54, October 15, 1986, 16 innings.)

Most at-bats by pinch-hitters, game

A.L.—6—Oakland vs. Detroit, October 10, 1972.
N.L.—5—Atlanta vs. Pittsburgh, October 14, 1992.
 St. Louis vs. New York, October 16, 2000.

Most at-bats by pinch-hitters on both clubs, game

A.L.—7—Oakland 6, Detroit 1, October 10, 1972.
N.L.—6—Pittsburgh 3, Cincinnati 3, October 4, 1990.
 Atlanta 3, St. Louis 3, October 14, 1996.
 New York 4, St. Louis 2, October 14, 2000.
 (8—New York 4, Houston 4, October 15, 1986, 16 innings.
 New York 4, Atlanta 4, October 19, 1999, 11 innings.)

Most plate appearances by pinch-hitters, game

A.L.—6—Oakland vs. Detroit, October 10, 1972.
N.L.—6—Pittsburgh vs. Cincinnati, October 4, 1990.

Most plate appearances by pinch-hitters on both clubs, game

A.L.—7—Oakland 6, Detroit 1, October 10, 1972.

N.L.—6—Made in many games.
(10—New York 5, Houston 5, October 15, 1986, 16 innings.
New York 5, Atlanta 5, October 19, 1999, 11 innings.)

Fewest at-bats, game
N.L.—26—St. Louis vs. San Francisco, October 7, 1987.
Florida vs. Atlanta, October 12, 1997; batted eight innings.
A.L.—25—California vs. Milwaukee, October 6, 1982; batted
eight innings.
Toronto vs. Oakland, October 8, 1992; batted eight innings.
New York vs. Seattle, October 21, 2001.

Fewest at-bats by both clubs, game
A.L.—54—Seattle 29, New York 25, October 21, 2001.
N.L.—58—Cincinnati 30, New York 28, October 6, 1973.
New York 31, Cincinnati 27, October 7, 1973.
Chicago 29, San Diego 29, October 3, 1984.
St. Louis 30, San Francisco 28, October 11, 1987.
Atlanta 29, New York 29, October 16, 1999.

Most at-bats, inning
A.L.—13—Anaheim vs. Minnesota, October 13, 2002, seventh
inning.
N.L.—12—St. Louis vs. Los Angeles, October 13, 1985,
second inning.

Most at-bats by both clubs, inning
A.L.—18—Anaheim 13, Minnesota 5, October 13, 2002, sev-
enth inning.
N.L.—15—Philadelphia 8, Houston 7, October 12, 1980, eighth
inning.
St. Louis 12, Los Angeles 3, October 13, 1985, second inning.
Pittsburgh 8, Atlanta 7, October 7, 1992, seventh inning.

Most batters facing pitcher, inning
A.L.—15—Anaheim vs. Minnesota, October 13, 2002, seventh
inning.
N.L.—14—St. Louis vs. Los Angeles, October 13, 1985,
second inning.

Most batters facing pitcher by both clubs, inning
A.L.—22—Anaheim 15, Minnesota 7, October 13, 2002, seventh inning.
N.L.—19—Atlanta 10, Pittsburgh 9, October 7, 1992,
seventh inning.

RUNS
SERIES AND GAMES

Most runs, total series
A.L.—297—New York; 12 series, 61 games.
N.L.—247—Atlanta; 11 series, 60 games.

Most runs, series
3-game series
A.L.—27—Baltimore vs. Minnesota, 1970.
N.L.—27—New York vs. Atlanta, 1969.
4-game series
A.L.—26—Baltimore vs. California, 1979.
N.L.—24—Pittsburgh vs. San Francisco, 1971.
5-game series
A.L.—34—Minnesota vs. Detroit, 1987.
N.L.—31—New York vs. St. Louis, 2000.
6-game series
N.L.—33—Atlanta vs. Philadelphia, 1993.
A.L.—31—Toronto vs. Oakland, 1992.
New York vs. Seattle, 2000.
7-game series
A.L.—45—New York vs. Boston, 2004.
N.L.—44—Atlanta vs. St. Louis, 1996.

Most runs by both clubs, series
3-game series
N.L.—42—New York 27, Atlanta 15, 1969.
A.L.—37—Baltimore 27, Minnesota 10, 1970.
4-game series
A.L.—41—Baltimore 26, California 15, 1979.
N.L.—39—Pittsburgh 24, San Francisco 15, 1971.
5-game series
A.L.—57—Minnesota 34, Detroit 23, 1987.

N.L.—52—San Francisco 30, Chicago 22, 1989.
New York 31, St. Louis 21, 2000.
6-game series
N.L.—56—Atlanta 33, Philadelphia 23, 1993.
A.L.—55—Toronto 31, Oakland 24, 1992.
7-game series
A.L.—86—New York 45, Boston 41, 2004.
N.L.—82—Chicago 42, Florida 40, 2003.

Most runs by losing club, series
A.L.—45—New York vs. Boston, 2004 (7-game series).
N.L.—42—Chicago vs. Florida, 2003 (7-game series).

Fewest runs, series
3-game series
N.L.—3—Pittsburgh vs. Cincinnati, 1970.
A.L.—4—Oakland vs. New York, 1981.
Kansas City vs. Detroit, 1984.
4-game series
A.L.—3—Chicago vs. Baltimore, 1983.
N.L.—5—Cincinnati vs. Atlanta, 1995.
5-game series
N.L.—8—Cincinnati vs. New York, 1973.
A.L.—10—Detroit vs. Oakland, 1972.
6-game series
A.L.—12—Seattle vs. Cleveland, 1995.
N.L.—15—Pittsburgh vs. Cincinnati, 1990.
7-game series
N.L.—12—Pittsburgh vs. Atlanta, 1991.
A.L.—25—Toronto vs. Kansas Ctiy, 1985.

Fewest runs by both clubs, series
3-game series
N.L.—12—Cincinnati 9, Pittsburgh 3, 1970.
A.L.—18—Detroit 14, Kansas City 4, 1984.
4-game series
A.L.—18—Oakland 11, Baltimore 7, 1974.
N.L.—24—Atlanta 19, Cincinnati 5, 1995.
5-game series
A.L.—23—Oakland 13, Detroit 10, 1972.
N.L.—25—Los Angeles 15, Montreal 10, 1981.
6-game series
N.L.—35—Cincinnati 20, Pittsburgh 15, 1990.
A.L.—35—Cleveland 23, Seattle 12, 1995.
7-game series
N.L.—31—Atlanta 19, Pittsburgh 12, 1991.
A.L.—51—Kansas City 26, Toronto 25, 1985.

Most runs, game
A.L.—19—New York vs. Boston, October 16, 2004.
N.L.—15—Atlanta vs. St. Louis, October 17, 1996.

Most earned runs, game
A.L.—19—New York vs. Boston, October 16, 2004.
N.L.—15—Atlanta vs. St. Louis, October 17, 1996.

Most runs by both clubs, game
A.L.—27—New York 19, Boston 8, October 16, 2004.
N.L.—18—Atlanta 13, Pittsburgh 5, October 7, 1992.
(19—Atlanta 10, New York 9, October 19, 1999, 11 innings.)

Largest score, shutout game
N.L.—Atlanta 15, St. Louis 0, October 17, 1996.
A.L.—Baltimore 8, California 0, October 6, 1979.

Most players scoring one or more runs, game
N.L.—11—Atlanta vs. Philadelphia, October 7, 1993.
A.L.—11—Seattle vs. New York, October 20, 2001.

Most players from both clubs scoring one or more runs, game
A.L.—14—Baltimore 9, Minnesota 5, October 3, 1970.
Baltimore 7, California 7, October 4, 1979.
Seattle 11, New York 3, October 20, 2001.
New York 8, Boston 6, October 16, 2004.
N.L.—14—Atlanta 10, Pittsburgh 4, October 7, 1992.
Atlanta 11, Philadelphia 3, October 7, 1993.
(14—New York 7, Atlanta 7, October 19, 1999, 11 innings.
Chicago 7, Florida 7, October 7, 2003, 11 innings.)

INNING

Most runs, inning
A.L.—10—Anaheim vs. Minnesota, October 13, 2002, seventh inning.
N.L.—9—St. Louis vs. Los Angeles, October 13, 1985, second inning.

Most runs by both clubs, inning
A.L.—13—Anaheim 10, Minnesota 3, October 13, 2002, seventh inning.
N.L.—9—St. Louis 9, Los Angeles 0, October 13, 1985, second inning.
Atlanta 5, Pittsburgh 4, October 7, 1992, seventh inning.

Most runs, extra inning
N.L.—4—Houston vs. Philadelphia, October 8, 1980, 10th inning.
Atlanta vs. Cincinnati, October 11, 1995, 10th inning.
A.L.—3—Detroit vs. Oakland, October 11, 1972, 10th inning.
Baltimore vs. California, October 3, 1979, 10th inning.
Baltimore vs. Chicago, October 8, 1983, 10th inning.
Seattle vs. Cleveland, October 13, 1995, 11th inning.
Cleveland vs. New York, October 7, 1998, 12th inning.

Most runs by both clubs, extra inning
A.L.—5—Detroit 3, Oakland 2, October 11, 1972, 10th inning.
N.L.—5—Houston 4, Philadelphia 1, October 8, 1980, 10th inning.
New York 3, Houston 2, October 15, 1986, 16th inning.

Most innings scored, game
N.L.—6—New York vs. Atlanta, October 5, 1969.
Los Angeles vs. Pittsburgh, October 9, 1974.
Atlanta vs. St. Louis, October 14, 1996.
A.L.—6—Detroit vs. Kansas City, October 2, 1984.
Boston vs. New York, October 16, 1999.
New York vs. Boston, October 16, 2004.

Most innings scored by both clubs, game
N.L.—9—San Francisco 5, St. Louis 4, October 9, 2002.
(9—Atlanta 5, New York 4, October 19, 1999, 11 innings.)
A.L.—9—New York 6, Boston 3, October 16, 2004.
(9—New York 5, Baltimore 4, October 9, 1996, 11 innings.)

Most runs, 1st inning
N.L.—6—Chicago vs. San Francisco, October 5, 1989.
Atlanta vs. St. Louis, October 17, 1996.
A.L.—5—New York vs. Cleveland, October 6, 1998.

Most runs, 2nd inning
N.L.—9—St. Louis vs. Los Angeles, October 13, 1985.
A.L.—4—many clubs.

Most runs, 3rd inning
N.L.—6—Atlanta vs. Philadelphia, October 7, 1993.
A.L.—6—New York vs. Baltimore, October 13, 1996.

Most runs, 4th inning
A.L.—7—Baltimore vs. Minnesota, October 3, 1970.
New York vs. Oakland, October 14, 1981.
N.L.—4—Los Angeles vs. Philadelphia, October 5, 1977.
San Francisco vs. St. Louis, October 11, 1987.
San Francisco vs. Chicago, October 4, 1989.
Atlanta vs. St. Louis, October 17, 1996.

Most runs, 5th inning
N.L.—6—Chicago vs. San Diego, October 2, 1984.
A.L.—5—Toronto vs. Kansas City, October 11, 1985
Cleveland vs. New York, October 13, 1998.
Seattle vs. New York, October 15, 2000.

Most runs, 6th inning
A.L.—7—Seattle vs. New York, October 20, 2001.
N.L.—6—St. Louis vs. Houston, October 13, 2004.

Most runs, 7th inning
A.L.—10—Anaheim vs. Minnesota, October 13, 2002.
N.L.—6—Atlanta vs. San Diego, October 11, 1998.

Most runs, 8th inning
A.L.—7—New York vs. Seattle, October 11, 2000.

N.L.—8—Florida vs. Chicago, October 14, 2003.

Most runs, 9th inning
A.L.—7—Baltimore vs. Minnesota, October 4, 1970.
Oakland vs. Boston, October 6, 1990.
N.L.—4—New York vs. Cincinnati, October 7, 1973.
Los Angeles vs. Montreal, October 17, 1981.
Arizona vs. Atlanta, October 20, 2001.

Most runs, 10th inning
N.L.—4—Houston vs. Philadelphia, October 8, 1980.
Atlanta vs. Cincinnati, October 11, 1995.
A.L.—3—Detroit vs. Oakland, October 11, 1972.
Baltimore vs. California, October 3, 1979.
Baltimore vs. Chicago, October 8, 1983.

Most runs, 11th inning
N.L.—3—Pittsburgh vs. Cincinnati, October 2, 1979.
A.L.—3—Seattle vs. Cleveland, October 13, 1995.

Most runs, 12th inning
A.L.—3—Cleveland vs. New York, October 7, 1998.
N.L.—2—St. Louis vs. Houston, October 20, 2004.

Most runs, 14th inning
N.L.—1—Houston vs. New York, October 15, 1986.
New York vs. Houston, October 15, 1986.
A.L.—1—Boston vs. New York, October 18, 2004.

Most runs, 15th inning
N.L.—2—New York vs. Atlanta, October 17, 1999.
A.L.—none.

Most runs, 16th inning
N.L.—3—New York vs. Houston, October 15, 1986.
A.L.—none

GAMES BEING SHUT OUT

Most times being shut out, total series
N.L.—5—Pittsburgh, 1970, 1974, 1991 (3).
Atlanta, 1982, 1991, 1998 (2), 2001.
A.L.—4—Baltimore, 1973, 1974 (2), 1997.

Most consecutive games without being shut out, total series
N.L.—33—Atlanta, October 16, 1991 through October 7, 1998.
A.L.—36—New York, October 9, 1976 through October 18, 1999.

HITS
SERIES

Most hits, total series
A.L.—571—New York; 12 series, 61 games.
N.L.—507—Atlanta; 11 series, 60 games.

Most hits, series
3-game series
N.L.—37—New York vs. Atlanta, 1969.
A.L.—36—Baltimore vs. Minnesota, 1969, 1970.
New York vs. Oakland, 1981.
4-game series
N.L.—42—Los Angeles vs. Philadelphia, 1978.
Atlanta vs. Cincinnati, 1995.
A.L.—42—New York vs. Kansas City, 1978.
5-game series
A.L.—55—New York vs. Kansas City, 1976.
N.L.—55—Philadelphia vs. Houston, 1980.
6-game series
A.L.—65—Toronto vs. Chicago, 1993.
N.L.—59—Atlanta vs. Philadelphia, 1993.
7-game series
A.L.—78—New York vs. Boston, 2004.
N.L.—77—Atlanta vs. St. Louis, 1996.

Most hits by both clubs, series
3-game series
N.L.—64—New York 37, Atlanta 27, 1969.
A.L.—60—Baltimore 36, Minnesota 24, 1970.
4-game series
N.L.—77—Los Angeles 42, Philadelphia 35, 1978.
A.L.—77—New York 42, Kansas City 35, 1978.

5-game series
  N.L.—97—Chicago 53, San Francisco 44, 1989.
  A.L.—96—Boston 54, New York 42, 1999.
6-game series
  A.L.—111—Toronto 59, Oakland 52, 1992.
          Toronto 65, Chicago 46, 1993.
  N.L.—106—Atlanta 59, Philadelphia 47, 1993.
7-game series
  A.L.—153—New York 78, Boston 75, 2004.
  N.L.—133—Florida 68, Chicago 65, 2003.

Fewest hits, series
3-game series
  N.L.—15—Atlanta vs. St. Louis, 1982.
  A.L.—17—Minnesota vs. Baltimore, 1969.
4-game series
  A.L.—22—Baltimore vs. Oakland, 1974.
          Oakland vs. Baltimore, 1974.
  N.L.—25—Pittsburgh vs. Los Angeles, 1974.
5-game series
  N.L.—30—Pittsburgh vs. Cincinnati, 1972.
  A.L.—32—Detroit vs. Oakland, 1972.
          Oakland vs. Baltimore, 1973.
6-game series
  N.L.—36—Florida vs. Atlanta, 1997.
  A.L.—37—Seattle vs. Cleveland, 1995.
7-game series
  N.L.—45—St. Louis vs. Atlanta, 1996.
  A.L.—51—Kansas City vs. Toronto, 1985.

Fewest hits by both clubs, series
3-game series
  A.L.—43—Detroit 25, Kansas City 18, 1984.
  N.L.—45—Pittsburgh 23, Cincinnati 22, 1970.
4-game series
  A.L.—44—Baltimore 22, Oakland 22, 1974.
  N.L.—62—Los Angeles 37, Pittsburgh 25, 1974.
5-game series
  A.L.—68—Baltimore 36, Oakland 32, 1973.
  N.L.—68—New York 37, Cincinnati 31, 1973.
6-game series
  N.L.—85—Atlanta 49, Florida 36, 1997.
  A.L.—88—Cleveland 45, New York 43, 1998.
7-game series
  N.L.—104—Atlanta 53, Pittsburgh 51, 1991.
  A.L.—116—Toronto 65, Kansas City 51, 1985.

Most hits by pinch-hitters, series
A.L.—6—Toronto vs. Kansas City, 1985 (7-game series).
N.L.—4—Occurred in many series.

Most hits by pinch-hitters on both clubs, series
N.L.—8—Pittsburgh 4, Los Angeles 4, 1974 (4-game series).
  Chicago 4, Florida 4, 2003 (7-game series).
A.L.—8—Toronto 6, Kansas City 2, 1985 (7-game series).

GAME AND INNING

Most hits, game
N.L.—22—Atlanta vs. St. Louis, October 14, 1996.
A.L.—22—New York vs. Boston, October 16, 2004.

Most hits by both clubs, game
A.L.—37—New York 22, Boston 15, October 16, 2004.
N.L.—29—Atlanta 22, St. Louis 7, October 14, 1996.

Most hits by pinch-hitters, game
A.L.—2—Held by many teams.
  (3—Kansas City vs. Detroit, October 3, 1984, 11 innings.)
N.L.—2—Held by many teams.
  (3—New York vs. Atlanta, October 19, 1999, 11 innings.)

Most hits by pinch-hitters on both clubs, game
N.L.—4—Los Angeles 2, Pittsburgh 2, October 6, 1974.
  (5—New York 3, Atlanta 2, October 19, 1999, 11 innings.)
A.L.—3—Detroit 2, Minnesota 1, October 11, 1987.
  (3—Kansas City 3, Detroit 0, October 3, 1984, 11 innings.)

Fewest hits, game
A.L.—1—Oakland vs. Baltimore, October 9, 1974.
  Seattle vs. New York, October 14, 2000.
N.L.—1—Pittsburgh vs. Cincinnati, October 12, 1990.

St. Louis vs. Houston, October 18, 2004.

Fewest hits by both clubs, game
A.L.—6—Oakland 4, Baltimore 2, October 8, 1974.
  Baltimore 5, Oakland 1, October 9, 1974.
  Detroit 3, Kansas City 3, October 5, 1984.
  New York 5, Seattle 1, October 14, 2000.
  New York 4, Seattle 2, October 21, 2001.
N.L.—4—Houston 3, St. Louis 1, October 18, 2004.

Most players with one or more hits, game
N.L.—11—Chicago vs. San Diego, October 2, 1984.
  Atlanta vs. St. Louis, October 14, 1996.
A.L.—10—New York vs. Oakland, October 14, 1981.
  Toronto vs. Kansas City, October 11, 1985.
  Seattle vs. New York, October 20, 2001.
  Boston vs. New York, October 20, 2004.

Most players with one or more hits by both clubs, game
A.L.—18—New York 10, Oakland 8, October 14, 1981.
  (18—Boston 9, California 9, October 12, 1986, 11 innings.)
N.L.—17—Atlanta 11, St. Louis 6, October 14, 1996.
  Atlanta 9, Arizona 8, October 20, 2001.
  (18—New York 10, Atlanta 8, October 19, 1999, 11 innings.)

Most hits, inning
A.L.—10—Anaheim vs. Minnesota, October 13, 2002, seventh inning.
N.L.—8—St. Louis vs. Los Angeles, October 13, 1985, second inning.
  Pittsburgh vs. Atlanta, October 13, 1992, second inning.

Most hits by pinch-hitters, inning
A.L.-N.L.—2—Occurred many times.

Most hits by both clubs, inning
A.L.—13—Anaheim 10, Minnesota 3, October 13, 2002, seventh inning.
N.L.—9—Philadelphia 5, Houston 4, October 12, 1980, eighth inning.

Most consecutive hits, inning (consecutive at-bats)
A.L.—7—Baltimore vs. Minnesota, October 3, 1970, fourth inning (one sacrifice fly during streak).
N.L.—6—Atlanta vs. Arizona, October 17, 2001, eighth inning (one base on balls during streak).
  San Francisco vs. St. Louis, October 9, 2002, second inning.

Most consecutive hits, inning (consecutive plate appearances)
N.L.—6—San Francisco vs. St. Louis, October 9, 2002, second inning.
A.L.—6—Anaheim vs. Minnesota, October 13, 2002, seventh inning.

SINGLES

Most singles, total series
A.L.—383—New York; 12 series, 61 games.
N.L.—357—Atlanta; 11 series, 60 games.

Most singles, series
3-game series
  A.L.—29—New York vs. Oakland, 1981.
  N.L.—27—St. Louis vs. Atlanta, 1982.
4-game series
  A.L.—34—Oakland vs. Boston, 1990.
  N.L.—31—Atlanta vs. Cincinnati, 1995.
5-game series
  N.L.—45—Philadelphia vs. Houston, 1980.
  A.L.—37—Minnesota vs. Toronto, 1991.
6-game series
  A.L.—52—Toronto vs. Chicago, 1993.
  N.L.—42—St. Louis vs. Los Angeles, 1985.
7-game series
  N.L.—55—Atlanta vs. St. Louis, 1996.
  A.L.—53—California vs. Boston, 1986.

Most singles by both clubs, series
3-game series
  A.L.—46—New York 29, Oakland 17, 1981.
  N.L.—41—St. Louis 27, Atlanta 14, 1982.

4-game series
A.L.—55—New York 33, Kansas City 22, 1978.
N.L.—53—Atlanta 31, Cincinnati 22, 1995.
5-game series
N.L.—73—Philadelphia 45, Houston 28, 1980.
A.L.—73—Minnesota 37, Toronto 36, 1991.
6-game series
A.L.—87—Toronto 52, Chicago 35, 1993.
N.L.—79—San Diego 41, Atlanta 38, 1998.
7-game series
A.L.—103—California 53, Boston 50, 1986.
N.L.—90—Atlanta 55, St. Louis 35, 1996.

Fewest singles, series
3-game series
A.L.—10—Oakland vs. Baltimore, 1971.
N.L.—13—Atlanta vs. New York, 1969.
4-game series
A.L.—14—Oakland vs. Baltimore, 1974.
N.L.—19—Los Angeles vs. Philadelphia, 1983.
5-game series
N.L.—20—Pittsburgh vs. Cincinnati, 1972.
Cincinnati vs. New York, 1973.
A.L.—21—Detroit vs. Oakland, 1972.
Oakland vs. Baltimore, 1973.
6-game series
A.L.—24—Seattle vs. Cleveland, 1995.
Seattle vs. New York, 2000.
N.L.—25—Philadelphia vs. Atlanta, 1993.
7-game series
N.L.—29—Houston vs. St. Louis, 2004.
A.L.—34—Kansas City vs. Toronto, 1985.
New York vs. Boston, 2003.

Fewest singles by both clubs, series
3-game series
A.L.—24—Baltimore 14, Oakland 10, 1971.
N.L.—31—Philadelphia 17, Cincinnati 14, 1976.
4-game series
A.L.—32—Baltimore 18, Oakland 14, 1974.
N.L.—44—Philadelphia 25, Los Angeles 19, 1983.
5-game series
A.L.—47—Baltimore 26, Oakland 21, 1973.
N.L.—47—Cincinnati 27, Pittsburgh 20, 1972.
6-game series
A.L.—61—Cleveland 37, Seattle 24, 1995.
N.L.—63—Atlanta 36, Florida 27, 1997.
7-game series
N.L.—65—St. Louis 36, Houston 29, 2004.
A.L.—78—Toronto 44, Kansas City 34, 1985.

Most singles by pinch-hitters, series
N.L.—4—Pittsburgh vs. Los Angeles, 1974 (4-game series).
Cincinnati vs. Pittsburgh, 1990 (6-game series).
Atlanta vs. Philadelphia, 1993 (6-game series).
A.L.—4—Toronto vs. Kansas City, 1985 (7-game series).

Most singles by pinch-hitters on both clubs, series
N.L.—7—Pittsburgh 4, Los Angeles 3, 1974 (4-game series).
A.L.—4—Oakland 3, Detroit 1, 1972 (5-game series).
Toronto 4, Kansas City 0, 1985 (7-game series).
Detroit 3, Minnesota 1, 1987 (5-game series).

Most singles, game
A.L.—15—New York vs. Oakland, October 14, 1981.
N.L.—15—Atlanta vs. St. Louis, October 14, 1996.

Most singles by both clubs, game
A.L.—25—Kansas City 13, New York 12, October 4, 1978.
N.L.—22—Atlanta 15, St. Louis 7, October 14, 1996.

Fewest singles, game
A.L.—0—Oakland vs. Baltimore, October 9, 1974.
Seattle vs. New York, October 14, 2000.
N.L.—0—Pittsburgh vs. Cincinnati, October 12, 1990.

Fewest singles by both clubs, game
A.L.—2—Seattle 1, New York 1, October 21, 2001.
N.L.—3—Houston 2, St. Louis 1, October 18, 2004.

Most singles, inning
A.L.—9—Anaheim vs. Minnesota, October 13, 2002, seventh

inning.
N.L.—8—St. Louis vs. Los Angeles, October 13, 1985, second inning.

Most singles by both clubs, inning
A.L.—12—Anaheim 9, Minnesota 3, October 13, 2002, seventh inning.
N.L.—8—Philadelphia 4, Houston 4, October 12, 1980, eighth inning.
St. Louis 8, Los Angeles 0, October 13, 1985, second inning.

DOUBLES

Most doubles, total series
A.L.—110—New York; 12 series, 61 games.
N.L.—86—Atlanta; 11 series, 60 games.

Most doubles, series
3-game series
N.L.—9—Atlanta vs. New York, 1969.
A.L.—8—Baltimore vs. Minnesota, 1969.
Oakland vs. Baltimore, 1971.
Boston vs. Oakland, 1975.
4-game series
A.L.—9—Baltimore vs. Chicago, 1983.
N.L.—8—Los Angeles vs. Pittsburgh, 1974.
Los Angeles vs. Philadelphia, 1978.
5-game series
A.L.—13—New York vs. Kansas City, 1976.
Minnesota vs. Detroit, 1987.
Boston vs. New York, 1999.
N.L.—12—New York vs. St. Louis, 2000..
6-game series
N.L.—14—Atlanta vs. Philadelphia, 1993.
A.L.—12—Seattle vs. New York, 2000.
7-game series
A.L.—21—New York vs. Boston, 2004.
N.L.—20—Pittsburgh vs. Atlanta, 1992.

Most doubles by both clubs, series
3-game series
N.L.—17—Atlanta 9, New York 8, 1969.
A.L.—15—Oakland 8, Baltimore 7, 1971.
4-game series
A.L.—13—Baltimore 9, Chicago 4, 1983.
N.L.—11—Los Angeles 8, Philadelphia 3, 1978.
Atlanta 6, Cincinnati 5, 1995.
5-game series
N.L.—23—New York 12, St. Louis 11, 2000.
A.L.—21—New York 12, Kansas City 9, 1977.
6-game series
N.L.—25—Atlanta 14, Philadelphia 11, 1993.
A.L.—22—Seattle 12, New York 10, 2000.
7-game series
A.L.—33—New York 21, Boston 12, 2004.
N.L.—31—Pittsburgh 20, Atlanta 11, 1992.

Fewest doubles, series
3-game series
N.L.—1—Atlanta vs. St. Louis, 1982.
A.L.—1—Kansas City vs. Detroit, 1984.
4-game series
A.L.—1—Baltimore vs. Oakland, 1974.
N.L.—1—Pittsburgh vs. Los Angeles, 1974.
5-game series
N.L.—3—Los Angeles vs. Montreal, 1981.
San Francisco vs. St. Louis, 2002.
A.L.—4—Milwaukee vs. California, 1982.
Detroit vs. Minnesota, 1987.
Baltimore vs. New York, 1996.
New York vs. Boston, 1999.
Seattle vs. New York, 2001.
6-game series
A.L.—3—Cleveland vs. New York, 1998.
N.L.—4—New York vs. Houston, 1986.
Atlanta vs. San Diego, 1998.

7-game series
  N.L.—4—St. Louis vs. San Francisco, 1987.
        St. Louis vs. Atlanta, 1996.
  A.L.—9—Kansas City vs. Toronto, 1985.
        Boston vs. New York, 2003.

Fewest doubles by both clubs, series
3-game series
  N.L.—5—St. Louis 4, Atlanta 1, 1982.
  A.L.—5—Detroit 4, Kansas City 1, 1984.
4-game series
  A.L.—5—Oakland 4, Baltimore 1, 1974.
  N.L.—9—San Francisco 5, Pittsburgh 4, 1971.
        Los Angeles 8, Pittsburgh 1, 1974.
        Los Angeles 6, Philadelphia 3, 1977.
        Los Angeles 5, Philadelphia 4, 1983.
5-game series
  N.L.—10—Montreal 7, Los Angeles 3, 1981.
  A.L.—11—New York 7, Seattle 4, 2001.
6-game series
  N.L.—10—Houston 6, New York 4, 1986.
  A.L.—11—New York 8, Cleveland 3, 1998.
7-game series
  N.L.—11—San Francisco 7, St. Louis 4, 1987.
  A.L.—21—New York 12, Boston 9, 2003.

Most doubles by pinch-hitters, series
N.L.—3—St. Louis vs. New York, 2000 (5-game series).
A.L.—2—Toronto vs. Kansas City, 1985 (7-game series).

Most doubles by pinch-hitters on both clubs, series
A.L.—3—Toronto 2, Kansas City 1, 1985 (7-game series).
N.L.—3—St. Louis 3, New York 0, 2000 (5-game series).

Most doubles, game
A.L.—8—New York vs. Boston, October 16, 2004.
N.L.—6—Philadelphia vs. Cincinnati, October 12, 1976.
  New York vs. St. Louis, October 15, 2000.

Most doubles by both clubs, game
A.L.—13—New York 8, Boston 5, October 16, 2004.
N.L. 8—Los Angeles 5, St. Louis 3, October 12, 1985.
  Atlanta 5, Philadelphia 3, October 9, 1993.
  New York 6, St. Louis 2, October 15, 2000.
  (8—Philadelphia 5, Atlanta 3, October 6, 1993, 10 innings.)

Most doubles, inning
N.L.—5—New York vs. St. Louis, October 15, 2000, first inning.
A.L.—3—Oakland vs. Baltimore, October 10, 1973, second inning.
  Boston vs. Oakland, October 4, 1975, seventh inning.
  Minnesota vs. Detroit, October 8, 1987, second inning.
  New York vs. Boston, October 16, 2003, eighth inning.

TRIPLES

Most triples, total series
A.L.—13—Kansas City; six series, 27 games.
N.L.—11—Atlanta; 11 series, 60 games.

Most triples, series
3-game series
  N.L.—3—Cincinnati vs. Philadelphia, 1976.
  A.L.—1—Held by many clubs.
4-game series
  A.L.—3—Kansas City vs. New York, 1978.
  N.L.—3—Los Angeles vs. Philadelphia, 1978.
5-game series
  N.L.—5—Houston vs. Philadelphia, 1980.
  A.L.—4—Kansas City vs. New York, 1976.
6-game series
  N.L.—4—Philadelphia vs. Atlanta, 1993.
  A.L.—3—Toronto vs. Chicago, 1993.
        Cleveland 3, Seattle 0, 1995.
7-game series
  N.L.—4—St. Louis vs. San Francisco, 1987.
        Chicago vs. Florida, 2003.
  A.L.—2—Boston vs. California, 1986.

Boston vs. New York, 2003.
New York vs. Boston, 2004.

Most triples by both clubs, series
3-game series
  N.L.—4—Cincinnati 3, Philadelphia 1, 1976.
  A.L.—2—Baltimore 1, Minnesota 1, 1969.
        Baltimore 1, Oakland 1, 1971.
        Kansas City 1, New York 1, 1980.
4-game series
  N.L.—5—Los Angeles 3, Philadelphia 2, 1978.
  A.L.—4—Kansas City 3, New York 1, 1978.
5-game series
  A.L.—6—Kansas City 4, New York 2, 1976.
  N.L.—6—Houston 5, Philadelphia 1, 1980.
6-game series
  N.L.—4—Philadelphia 4, Atlanta 0, 1993.
  A.L.—4—Toronto 3, Chicago 1, 1993.
7-game series
  N.L.—7—Chicago 4, Florida 3, 2003.
  A.L.—3—Boston 2, New York 1, 2004.

Fewest triples, series
A.L.-N.L.—0—Held by many clubs.

Fewest triples by both clubs, series
A.L.-N.L.—0—Occurred many times.

Most triples by pinch-hitters, series
N.L.—1—Cincinnati vs. Pittsburgh, 1970 (3-game series).
  New York vs. Houston, 1986 (6-game series).
  Atlanta vs. Pittsburgh, 1992 (7-game series).
  St. Louis vs. Atlanta, 1996 (7-game series).
A.L.—1—Seattle vs. New York, 2001 (5-game series).

Most triples, game
N.L.—3—Philadelphia vs. Atlanta, October 9, 1993.
A.L.—2—Kansas City vs. New York, October 13, 1976.
  Kansas City vs. New York, October 8, 1977.
  Seattle vs. New York, October 20, 2001.

Most triples by both clubs, game
N.L.—3—Los Angeles 2, Philadelphia 1, October 4, 1978.
  Philadelphia 3, Atlanta 0, October 9, 1993.
A.L.—2—Baltimore 1, Minnesota 1, October 6, 1969.
  Kansas City 1, New York 1, October 9, 1976.
  Kansas City 2, New York 0, October 13, 1976.
  Kansas City 2, New York 0, October 8, 1977.
  Detroit 1, Kansas City 1, October 2, 1984.
  Toronto 1, Chicago 1, October 9, 1993.
  Seattle 2, New York 0, October 20, 2001.

Most triples, inning
A.L.—2—Kansas City vs. New York, October 8, 1977, third inning.
N.L.—2—Philadelphia vs. Atlanta, October 9, 1993, fourth inning.
  Chicago vs. Florida, October 7, 2003, first inning.

HOME RUNS
SERIES

Most home runs, total series
A.L.—69—New York; 12 series, 61 games.
N.L.—53—Atlanta; 11 series, 60 games.

Most grand slams, total series
N.L.—2—Los Angeles, 1977 (2).
  Atlanta, 1992, 1997.
A.L.—1—Baltimore, 1970.
  California, 1982.
  Cleveland, 1998.
  New York, 1999.
  Boston, 2004.

Most home runs, series
3-game series
  N.L.—6—New York vs. Atlanta, 1969.
  A.L.—6—Baltimore vs. Minnesota, 1970.
4-game series
  N.L.—8—Pittsburgh vs. San Francisco, 1971.

Los Angeles vs. Philadelphia, 1978.
A.L.—7—Oakland vs. Boston, 1988.
5-game series
  A.L.—10—New York vs. Baltimore, 1996.
  N.L.—9—Chicago vs. San Diego, 1984.
6-game series
  A.L.—10—Toronto vs. Oakland, 1992.
  N.L.—7—Philadelphia vs. Atlanta, 1993.
7-game series
  N.L.—14—Houston vs. St. Louis, 2004.
  A.L.—12—Boston vs. New York, 2003.

Most home runs by both clubs, series
3-game series
  N.L.—11—New York 6, Atlanta 5, 1969.
  A.L.—9—Baltimore 6, Minnesota 3, 1970.
4-game series
  N.L.—13—Pittsburgh 8, San Francisco 5, 1971.
    Los Angeles 8, Philadelphia 5, 1978.
  A.L.—9—New York 5, Kansas City 4, 1978.
    Oakland 7, Boston 2, 1988.
5-game series
  A.L.—19—New York 10, Baltimore 9, 1996.
  N.L.—14—San Francisco 7, St. Louis 7, 2002.
6-game series
  A.L.—14—Toronto 10, Oakland 4, 1992.
  N.L.—12—Philadelphia 7, Atlanta 5, 1993.
7-game series
  N.L.—25—Houston 14, St. Louis 11, 2004.
  A.L.—20—Boston 12, New York 8, 2003.

Fewest home runs, series
3-game series
  N.L.—0—Pittsburgh vs. Cincinnati, 1970.
    Atlanta vs. St. Louis, 1982.
  A.L.—0—Oakland vs. New York, 1981.
    Kansas City vs. Detroit, 1984.
4-game series
  N.L.—0—Cincinnati vs. Atlanta, 1995.
  A.L.—0—Chicago vs. Baltimore, 1983.
    Oakland vs. Boston, 1990.
5-game series
  N.L.—0—Houston vs. Philadelphia, 1980.
  A.L.—0—Minnesota vs. Anaheim, 2002.
6-game series
  N.L.—1—Florida vs. Atlanta, 1997.
  A.L.—2—Toronto vs. Chicago, 1993.
7-game series
  A.L.—2—Toronto vs. Kansas City, 1985.
  N.L.—2—St. Louis vs. San Francisco, 1987.

Fewest home runs by both clubs, series
3-game series
  N.L.—1—St. Louis 1, Atlanta 0, 1982.
  A.L.—2—New York 2, Oakland 0, 1981.
4-game series
  A.L.—1—Boston 1, Oakland 0, 1990.
  N.L.—4—Atlanta 4, Cincinnati 0, 1995.
5-game series
  N.L.—1—Philadelphia 1, Houston 0, 1980.
  A.L.—4—Minnesota 3, Toronto 1, 1991.
6-game series
  A.L.—7—Chicago 5, Toronto 2, 1993.
  N.L.—7—Atlanta 6, Florida 1, 1997.
7-game series
  N.L.—8—New York 5, Los Angeles 3, 1988.
    Atlanta 5, Pittsburgh 3, 1991.
  A.L.—9—Kansas City 7, Toronto 2, 1985.

Most grand slams, series
N.L.—2—Los Angeles vs. Philadelphia, 1977.
A.L.—1—Baltimore vs. Minnesota, 1970.
California vs. Milwaukee, 1982.
  Cleveland vs. New York, 1998.
  New York vs. Boston, 1999.
  Boston vs. New York, 2004.

Most home runs by pinch-hitters, series
N.L.—2—Philadelphia vs. Los Angeles, 1978 (4-game series).

St. Louis vs. San Francisco, 2002 (5-game series).
A.L.—1—Baltimore vs. California, 1979 (4-game series).
  Kansas City vs. Toronto, 1985 (7-game series).
  Minnesota vs. Toronto, 1991 (5-game series).
  New York vs. Boston, 1999 (5-game series).
  Seattle vs. New York, 2001 (5-game series).
  New York vs. Boston, 2003 (7-game series).

GAME AND INNING

Most home runs, game
N.L.—5—Chicago vs. San Diego, October 2, 1984.
A.L.—4—Baltimore vs. Oakland, October 4, 1971.
  Oakland vs. Baltimore, October 7, 1973.
  Oakland vs. Boston, October 8, 1988.
  New York vs. Baltimore, October 12, 1996.
  Cleveland vs. New York, October 9, 1998.
  Anaheim vs. Minnesota, October 13, 2002.

Most home runs by both clubs, game
N.L.—7—Florida 4, Chicago 3, October 7, 2003.
A.L.—6—New York 3, Baltimore 3, October 13, 1996.
  New York 4, Boston 2, October 16, 2004.

Most consecutive games with one or more home runs, total series
A.L.—10—Baltimore, last three games vs. Chicago, 1983 (three home runs), all five games vs. New York, 1996 (nine home runs), first two games vs. Cleveland, 1997 (three home runs).
N.L.—7—Philadelphia, all four games vs. Los Angeles, 1983 (five home runs), first three games vs. Atlanta, 1993 (four home runs).

Most consecutive games with one or more home runs, series
A.L.—6—Toronto vs. Oakland, October 7, 8, 10, 11, 12, 14, 1992 (10 home runs).
N.L.—5—San Francisco vs. St. Louis, October 6, 7, 9, 10, 11, 1987 (nine home runs).

Most home runs, inning
A.L.—3—Baltimore vs. Minnesota, October 3, 1970, fourth inning (first two consecutive).
  New York vs. Baltimore, October 13, 1996, third inning (first two consecutive).
  Baltimore vs. Cleveland, October 12, 1997, third inning (last two consecutive).
  Cleveland vs. New York, October 9, 1998, fifth inning (last two consecutive).
N.L.—3—Florida vs. Chicago, October 7, 2003, third inning (last two consecutive).

Most home runs by both clubs, inning
A.L.—3—Baltimore 3, Minnesota 0, October 3, 1970, fourth inning.
  Toronto 2, Kansas City 1, October 11, 1985, fifth inning.
  Oakland 2, Boston 1, October 8, 1988, second inning.
  New York 3, Baltimore 0, October 13, 1996, third inning.
  Baltimore 3, Cleveland 0, October 12, 1997, third inning.
  Cleveland 3, New York 0, October 9, 1998, fifth inning.
N.L.—3—San Francisco 2, Pittsburgh 1, October 6, 1971, second inning.
  Florida 3, Chicago 0, October 7, 2003, third inning.
  Florida 2, Chicago 1, October 9, 2003, sixth inning.

Most consecutive home runs, inning
A.L.—2—Baltimore (Cuellar and Buford) vs. Minnesota, October 3, 1970, 4th inn
  Minnesota (Killebrew and Oliva) vs. Baltimore, October 4, 1970, 4th inn
  Oakland (Rudi and Bando) vs. Baltimore, October 7, 1973, 6th inn
  New York (Cerone and Piniella) vs. Kansas City, October 8, 1980, 2nd inn
  Oakland (McGwire and Steinbach) vs. Toronto, October 7, 1992, 2nd inn
  New York (Fielder and Strawberry) vs. Baltimore, October 13, 1996, 3rd inn
  Baltimore (Baines and Palmeiro) vs. Cleveland, October 12, 1997, 3rd inn
  Cleveland (Thome and Whiten) vs. New York, October 9,

1998, 5th inn

New York (Williams, T. Martinez) vs. Seattle, October 13, 2000, 2nd inn

Seattle (E. Martinez, Olerud) vs. New York, October 15, 2000, 5th inn

N.L.—2—Cincinnati (Perez and Bench) vs. Pittsburgh, October 5, 1970, 1st inn

Cincinnati (Foster and Bench) vs. Philadelphia, October 12, 1976, 9th inn

Los Angeles (Guerrero and Scioscia) vs. Montreal, October 13, 1981, 8th inn

Chicago (Davis and Durham) vs. San Diego, October 6, 1984, 4th inn

New York (Strawberry and McReynolds) vs. Los Angeles, October 9, 1988, 4th inn

Atlanta (Jordan and Klesko) vs. New York, October 16, 1999, 8th inn

Florida (Cabrera and Encarnacion) vs. Chicago, October 7, 2003, 3rd inn

Florida (Lee and Cabrera) vs. Chicago, October 8, 2003, 6th inn

St. Louis (Pujols and Rolen) vs. Houston, October 14, 2004, 8th inn

TOTAL BASES

Most total bases, total series
A.L.—906—New York; 12 series, 61 games.
N.L.—774—Atlanta; 11 series, 60 games.

Most total bases, series
3-game series
  N.L.—65—New York vs. Atlanta, 1969.
  A.L.—61—Baltimore vs. Minnesota, 1970.
4-game series
  N.L.—80—Los Angeles vs. Philadelphia, 1978.
  A.L.—70—Oakland vs. Boston, 1988.
5-game series
  A.L.—91—New York vs. Baltimore, 1996.
  N.L.—80—Chicago vs. San Diego, 1984.
6-game series
  A.L.—99—Toronto vs. Oakland, 1992.
  N.L.—88—Atlanta vs. Philadelphia, 1993.
7-game series
  A.L.—130—New York vs. Boston, 2004.
  N.L.—122—Chicago vs. Florida, 2003.

Most total bases by both clubs, series
3-game series
  N.L.—116—New York 65, Atlanta 51, 1969.
  A.L.—100—Baltimore 61, Minnesota 39, 1970.
4-game series
  N.L.—137—Los Angeles 80, Philadelphia 57, 1978.
  A.L.—121—New York 62, Kansas City 59, 1978.
5-game series
  A.L.—161—New York 91, Baltimore 70, 1996.
  N.L.—155—San Francisco 78, Chicago 77, 1989.
6-game series
  N.L.—175—Atlanta 88, Philadelphia 87, 1993.
  A.L.—170—Toronto 99, Oakland 71, 1992.
7-game series
  N.L.—238—Chicago 122, Florida 116, 2003.
  A.L.—249—New York 130, Boston 119, 2004.

Fewest total bases, series
3-game series
  N.L.—16—Atlanta vs. St. Louis, 1982.
  A.L.—21—Kansas City vs. Detroit, 1984.
4-game series
  A.L.—31—Boston vs. Oakland, 1990.
  N.L.—35—Pittsburgh vs. Los Angeles, 1974.
            Cincinnati vs. Atlanta, 1995.
5-game series
  N.L.—44—Montreal vs. Los Angeles, 1981.
  A.L.—46—Minnesota vs. Anaheim, 2002.
6-game series
  N.L.—47—Florida vs. Atlanta, 1997.
  A.L.—60—Seattle vs. Cleveland, 1995.

7-game series
  N.L.—65—St. Louis vs. Atlanta, 1996.
  A.L.—83—Kansas City vs. Toronto, 1985.

Fewest total bases by both clubs, series
3-game series
  N.L.—61—St. Louis 45, Atlanta 16, 1982.
  A.L.—64—Detroit 43, Kansas City 21, 1984.
4-game series
  A.L.—69—Oakland 37, Baltimore 32, 1974.
  N.L.—91—Los Angeles 56, Pittsburgh 35, 1974.
5-game series
  N.L.—99—Los Angeles 55, Montreal 44, 1981.
  A.L.—101—Detroit 52, Oakland 49, 1972.
6-game series
  N.L.—123—Atlanta 76, Florida 47, 1997
  A.L.—142—Cleveland 77, New York 65, 1998.
7-game series
  N.L.—150—Atlanta 80, Pittsburgh 70, 1991.
  A.L.—173—Toronto 90, Kansas City 83, 1985.

Most total bases, game
A.L.—44—New York vs. Boston, October 16, 2004.
N.L.—34—Chicago vs. San Diego, October 2, 1984.
        Atlanta vs. St. Louis, October 14, 1996.

Most total bases by both clubs, game
N.L.—48—Chicago 31, Florida 17, October 8, 2003.
A.L.—70—New York 44, Boston 26, October 16, 2004.

Fewest total bases, game
N.L.—1—St. Louis vs. Houston, October 18, 2004.
A.L.—2—Baltimore vs. Oakland, October 8, 1974.
        Oakland vs. Baltimore, October 9, 1974.
        Kansas City vs. Toronto, October 12, 1985.
        Seattle vs. New York, October 14, 2000.

Fewest total bases by both clubs, game
A.L.—6—Detroit 3, Kansas City 3, October 5, 1984.
N.L.—7—Houston 6, St. Louis 1, October 18, 2004.

Most total bases, inning
A.L.—16—Baltimore vs. Minnesota, October 3, 1970, fourth inning.
N.L.—16—Pittsburgh vs. Atlanta, October 13, 1992, second inning.

Most total bases by both clubs, inning
A.L.—18—Baltimore 16, Minnesota 2, October 3, 1970, fourth inning.
N.L.—17—San Francisco 11, Pittsburgh 6, October 6, 1971, second inning.

EXTRA BASE HITS

Most extra base hits, total series
A.L.—188—New York; 12 series; 61 games.
N.L.—150—Atlanta; 11 series, 60 games.

Most extra base hits, series
3-game series
  N.L.—15—New York vs. Atlanta, 1969.
  A.L.—13—Baltimore vs. Minnesota, 1969, 1970.
4-game series
  N.L.—19—Los Angeles vs. Philadelphia, 1978.
  A.L.—15—Oakland vs. Boston, 1988.
5-game series
  A.L.—22—Minnesota vs. Detroit, 1987.
  N.L.—20—Chicago vs. San Diego, 1984.
6-game series
  N.L.—22—Philadelphia vs. Atlanta, 1993.
  A.L.—19—Toronto vs. Oakland, 1992.
7-game series
  A.L.—32—New York vs. Boston, 2004.
  N.L.—28—Pittsburgh vs. Atlanta, 1992.

Most extra base hits by both clubs, series
3-game series
  N.L.—29—New York 15, Atlanta 14, 1969.
  A.L.—24—Baltimore 12, Oakland 12, 1971.

4-game series
N.L.—29—Los Angeles 19, Philadelphia 10, 1978.
A.L.—22—Kansas City 13, New York 9, 1978.
5-game series
A.L.—33—Minnesota 22, Detroit 11, 1987.
New York 20, Baltimore 13, 1996.
Boston 20, New York 13, 1999.
N.L.—30—New York 17, St. Louis 13, 2000.
6-game series
N.L.—41—Philadelphia 22, Atlanta 19, 1993.
A.L.—33—Seattle 17, New York 16, 2000.
7-game series
N.L.—52—Chicago 27, Florida 25, 2003.
A.L.—55—New York 32, Boston 23, 2004.

Fewest extra base hits, series
3-game series
N.L.—1—Atlanta vs. St. Louis, 1982.
A.L.—2—Kansas City vs. Detroit, 1984.
4-game series
N.L.—4—Pittsburgh vs. Los Angeles, 1974.
A.L.—4—Baltimore vs. Oakland, 1974.
Chicago vs. Baltimore, 1983.
Oakland vs. Boston, 1990.
5-game series
N.L.—8—New York vs. Cincinnati, 1973.
Los Angeles vs. Montreal, 1981.
Montreal vs. Los Angeles, 1981.
San Diego vs. Chicago, 1984.
Arizona vs. Atlanta, 2001.
A.L.—7—Toronto vs. Minnesota, 1991.
6-game series
N.L.—9—New York vs. Houston, 1986.
Florida vs. Atlanta, 1997.
Atlanta vs. San Diego, 1998.
A.L.—10—Oakland vs. Toronto, 1992.
7-game series
N.L.—10—St. Louis vs. San Francisco, 1987.
St. Louis vs. Atlanta, 1996.
A.L.—17—Kansas City vs. Toronto, 1985.

Fewest extra base hits by both clubs, series
3-game series
N.L.—8—St. Louis 7, Atlanta 1, 1982.
A.L.—11—Detroit 9, Kansas City 2, 1984.
4-game series
A.L.—10—Boston 6, Oakland 4, 1990.
N.L.—15—Los Angeles 10, Philadelphia 5, 1977.
5-game series
N.L.—16—Los Angeles 8, Montreal 8, 1981.
A.L.—20—Detroit 11, Oakland 9, 1972.
Minnesota 13, Toronto 7, 1991.
6-game series
N.L.—20—Houston 11, New York 9, 1986.
A.L.—24—Toronto 13, Chicago 11, 1993.
7-game series
N.L.—27—San Francisco 17, St. Louis 10, 1987.
A.L.—37—Boston 19, California 18, 1986.

Most extra base hits, game
A.L.—13—New York vs. Boston, October 16, 2004 (eight doubles, one triple, four home runs).
N.L.—8—Cincinnati vs. Philadelphia, October 9, 1976 (five doubles, two triples, one home run).
Chicago vs. San Diego, October 2, 1984 (three doubles, five home runs).

Most extra base hits by both clubs, game
A.L.—20—New York 13 (eight doubles, one triple, four home runs), Boston 7 (five doubles, two home runs), October 16, 2004.
N.L.—12—Philadelphia 7 (three doubles, three triples, one home run), Atlanta 5 (five doubles), October 9, 1993.

RUNS BATTED IN

Most runs batted in, total series
N.L.—235—Atlanta; 11 series, 60 games.

A.L.—279—New York; 12 series, 61 games.

Most runs batted in, series
3-game series
A.L.—24—Baltimore vs. Minnesota, 1970.
N.L.—24—New York vs. Atlanta, 1969.
4-game series
A.L.—25—Baltimore vs. California, 1979.
N.L.—23—Pittsburgh vs. San Francisco, 1971.
5-game series
A.L.—33—Minnesota vs. Detroit, 1987.
N.L.—29—San Francisco vs. Chicago, 1989.
6-game series
N.L.—32—Atlanta vs. Philadelphia, 1993.
A.L.—30—Toronto vs. Oakland, 1992.
7-game series
A.L.—44—New York vs. Boston, 2004.
N.L.—43—Atlanta vs. St. Louis, 1996.

Most runs batted in by both clubs, series
3-game series
N.L.—39—New York 24, Atlanta 15, 1969.
A.L.—34—Baltimore 24, Minnesota 10, 1970.
4-game series
A.L.—39—Baltimore 25, California 14, 1979.
N.L.—37—Pittsburgh 23, San Francisco 14, 1971.
Los Angeles 21, Philadelphia 16, 1978.
5-game series
A.L.—54—Minnesota 33, Detroit 21, 1987.
N.L.—50—San Francisco 29, Chicago 21, 1989.
6-game series
N.L.—54—Atlanta 32, Philadelphia 22, 1993.
A.L.—53—Toronto 30, Oakland 23, 1992.
7-game series
A.L.—84—New York 44, Boston 40, 2004.
N.L.—80—Chicago 41, Florida 39, 2003.

Fewest runs batted in, series
3-game series
N.L.—3—Pittsburgh vs. Cincinnati, 1970.
Atlanta vs. St. Louis, 1982.
A.L.—4—Oakland vs. New York, 1981.
Kansas City vs. Detroit, 1984.
4-game series
A.L.—2—Chicago vs. Baltimore, 1983.
N.L.—4—Cincinnati vs. Atlanta, 1995.
5-game series
N.L.—8—Cincinnati vs. New York, 1973.
Montreal vs. Los Angeles, 1981.
A.L.—10—Oakland vs. Detroit, 1972.
Detroit vs. Oakland, 1972.
6-game series
A.L.—10—Seattle vs. Cleveland, 1995.
N.L.—17—Houston vs. New York, 1986.
Atlanta vs. San Diego, 1998.
7-game series
N.L.—11—Pittsburgh vs. Atlanta, 1991.
A.L.—23—Toronto vs. Kansas City, 1985.

Fewest runs batted in by both clubs, series
3-game series
N.L.—11—Cincinnati 8, Pittsburgh 3, 1970.
A.L.—18—Detroit 14, Kansas City 4, 1984.
4-game series
A.L.—18—Oakland 11, Baltimore 7, 1974.
N.L.—22—Philadelphia 15, Los Angeles 7, 1983.
5-game series
A.L.—20—Oakland 10, Detroit 10, 1972.
N.L.—23—Los Angeles 15, Montreal 8, 1981.
6-game series
A.L.—31—Cleveland 21, Seattle 10, 1995.
N.L.—36—New York 19, Houston 17, 1986.
7-game series
N.L.—30—Atlanta 19, Pittsburgh 11, 1991.
A.L.—49—Kansas City 26, Toronto 23, 1985.

Most runs batted in by pinch-hitters, series
A.L.—4—Baltimore vs. California, 1979 (4-game series).
Toronto vs. Kansas City, 1985 (7-game series).
Detroit vs. Minnesota, 1987 (5-game series).
New York vs. Boston, 1999 (5-game series).

N.L.—4—Philadelphia vs. Houston, 1980 (5-game series).

Most runs batted in by pinch-hitters on both clubs, series
A.L.—6—Detroit 4, Minnesota 2, 1987 (5-game series).
N.L.—5—Philadelphia 4, Houston 1, 1980 (5-game series).

Most runs batted in, game
A.L.—18—New York vs. Boston, October 16, 2004.
N.L.—14—Atlanta vs. Philadelphia, October 7, 1993.
Atlanta vs. St. Louis, October 14, 1996.
Atlanta vs. St. Louis, October 17, 1996.

Most runs batted in by both clubs, game
A.L.—25—New York 18, Boston 7, October 16, 2004.
N.L.—17—New York 11, Atlanta 6, October 5, 1969.
Atlanta 13, Pittsburgh 4, October 7, 1992.
Atlanta 14, Philadelphia 3, October 7, 1993.
(18—New York 9, Atlanta 9, October 19, 1999, 11 innings.)

Fewest runs batted in by both clubs, game
N.L.—0—Atlanta 0, New York 0, October 15, 1999.
A.L.—1—Held by many clubs.

Most runs batted in, inning
A.L.—9—Anaheim vs. Minnesota, October 13, 2002, seventh
inning.
N.L.—8—St. Louis vs. Los Angeles, October 13, 1985, second
inning.
Florida vs. Chicago, October 14, 2003, eighth inning.

Most runs batted in by both clubs, inning
A.L.—11—Anaheim 9, Minnesota 2, October 13, 2002, seventh
inning.
N.L.—8—St. Louis 8, Los Angeles 0, October 13, 1985, second
inning.
Florida 8, Chicago 0, October 14, 2003, eighth inning.

Most runs batted in by pinch-hitters, inning
A.L.—4—New York vs. Boston, October 17, 1999, ninth inning.
N.L.—2—Held by many clubs.

BASES ON BALLS

Most bases on balls, total series
A.L.—226—New York; 12 series, 61 games.
N.L.—215—Atlanta; 11 series, 60 games.

Most bases on balls, series
3-game series
N.L.—15—Cincinnati vs. Philadelphia, 1976.
A.L.—13—Baltimore vs. Minnesota, 1969.
Baltimore vs. Oakland, 1971.
4-game series
N.L.—30—Los Angeles vs. Pittsburgh, 1974.
A.L.—22—Oakland vs. Baltimore, 1974.
5-game series
N.L.—31—Houston vs. Philadelphia, 1980.
A.L.—27—New York vs. Seattle, 2000.
6-game series
A.L.—35—New York vs. Cleveland, 1998.
N.L.—31—Atlanta vs. New York, 1999.
7-game series
A.L.—33—New York vs. Boston, 2004.
N.L.—29—Atlanta vs. Pittsburgh, 1992.
Pittsburgh vs. Atlanta, 1992.

Most bases on balls by both clubs, series
3-game series
N.L.—27—Cincinnati 15, Philadelphia 12, 1976.
A.L.—25—Baltimore 13, Minnesota 12, 1969.
4-game series
N.L.—38—Los Angeles 30, Pittsburgh 8, 1974.
A.L.—28—Baltimore 16, Chicago 12, 1983.
Boston 18, Oakland 10, 1988.
5-game series
N.L.—44—Houston 31, Philadelphia 13, 1980.
A.L.—41—New York 23, Seattle 18, 2001.
6-game series
A.L.—53—Chicago 32, Toronto 21, 1993.
N.L.—53—San Diego 27, Atlanta 26, 1998.
7-game series
A.L.—61—New York, 33, Boston 28, 2004.

N.L.—58—Atlanta 29, Pittsburgh 29, 1992.

Fewest bases on balls, series
3-game series
A.L.—3—Boston vs. Oakland, 1975.
N.L.—6—Atlanta vs. St. Louis, 1982.
4-game series
A.L.—5—Baltimore vs. Oakland, 1974.
N.L.—5—Pittsburgh vs. San Francisco, 1971.
5-game series
A.L.—7—Minnesota vs. Anaheim, 2002.
N.L.—9—Pittsburgh vs. Cincinnati, 1972.
6-game series
N.L.—10—Cincinnati vs. Pittsburgh, 1990.
A.L.—15—Seattle vs. Cleveland, 1995.
7-game series
N.L.—11—St. Louis vs. Atlanta, 1996.
A.L.—16—Toronto vs. Kansas City, 1985.

Fewest bases on balls by both clubs, series
3-game series
A.L.—12—Oakland 9, Boston 3, 1975.
N.L.—18—St. Louis 12, Atlanta 6, 1982.
4-game series
N.L.—18—Los Angeles 9, Philadelphia 9, 1978.
A.L.—21—Kansas City 14, New York 7, 1978.
5-game series
A.L.—16—Anaheim 9, Minnesota 7, 2002.
N.L.—19—Cincinnati 10, Pittsburgh 9, 1972.
6-game series
N.L.—31—Houston 17, New York 14, 1986.
A.L.—40—Cleveland 25, Seattle 15, 1995.
7-game series
N.L.—33—San Francisco 17, St. Louis 16, 1987.
A.L.—38—Kansas City 22, Toronto 16, 1985.
New York 21, Boston 17, 2003.

Most bases on balls by pinch-hitters, series
N.L.—4—Los Angeles vs. New York, 1988 (7-game series).
A.L.—2—Held by many clubs.

Most bases on balls by pinch-hitters on both clubs, series
N.L.—6—Los Angeles 4, New York 2, 1988 (7-game series).
A.L.—3—California 2, Baltimore 1, 1979 (4-game series).
Toronto 2, Minnesota 1, 1991 (5-game series).
Boston 2, New York 1, 1999 (5-game series).

Most bases on balls, game
A.L.—11—Oakland vs. Baltimore, October 9, 1974.
New York vs. Cleveland, October 11, 1998.
N.L.—11—Los Angeles vs. Pittsburgh, October 9, 1974.

Most bases on balls by both clubs, game
A.L.—15—New York 10, Seattle 5, October 21, 2001.
N.L.—13—Atlanta 8, Pittsburgh 5, October 7, 1992.

Fewest bases on balls, game
A.L.-N.L.—0—Held by many clubs.

Fewest bases on balls by both clubs, game
A.L.—1—Oakland 1, Baltimore 0, October 8, 1974.
New York 1, Kansas City 0, October 9, 1976.
N.L.—1—New York 1, Atlanta 0, October 16, 1999.

Most bases on balls by pinch-hitters, game
N.L.—2—Pittsburgh vs. Cincinnati, October 7, 1975, 10
innings.
Los Angeles vs. New York, October 8, 1988.
(2—Los Angeles vs. New York, October 9, 1988, 12 innings.)
A.L.—2—California vs. Baltimore, October 4, 1979.
Baltimore vs. Chicago, October 7, 1983.

Most bases on balls by pinch-hitters on both clubs, game
N.L.—3—Los Angeles 2, New York 1, October 8, 1988.
(3—Pittsburgh 2, Cincinnati 1, October 7, 1975, 10 innings.)
A.L.—2—California 2, Baltimore 0, October 4, 1979.
Baltimore 2, Chicago 0, October 7, 1983.
Baltimore 1, Cleveland 1, October 9, 1997.
(2—Detroit 1, Oakland 1, October 11, 1972, 10 innings.)

Most bases on balls, inning
A.L.—4—Oakland vs. Baltimore, October 9, 1974, fifth inning
(consecutive).

N.L.—4—Philadelphia vs. Los Angeles, October 7, 1977, second inning (consecutive).
St. Louis vs. Los Angeles, October 12, 1985, first inning.
San Francisco vs. Chicago, October 9, 1989, eighth inning.

Most bases on balls by both clubs, inning
N.L.—6—St. Louis 4, Los Angeles 2, October 12, 1985, first inning.
A.L.—4—Made in many innings.

Most bases on balls by pinch-hitters, inning
N.L.—2—Pittsburgh vs. Cincinnati, October 7, 1975, ninth inning.
Los Angeles vs. New York, October 8, 1988, eighth inning.
A.L.—2—Baltimore vs. Chicago, October 7, 1983, ninth inning.

STRIKEOUTS

Most strikeouts, total series
N.L.—421—Atlanta; 11 series, 60 games.
A.L.—370—New York; 12 series, 61 games.

Most strikeouts, series
3-game series
N.L.—28—Cincinnati vs. Pittsburgh, 1975.
A.L.—27—Minnesota vs. Baltimore, 1969.
4-game series
A.L.—35—Oakland vs. Boston, 1988.
N.L.—33—Pittsburgh vs. San Francisco, 1971.
5-game series
A.L.—44—New York vs. Boston, 1999.
N.L.—42—Cincinnati vs. New York, 1973.
6-game series
A.L.—62—Cleveland vs. Baltimore, 1997.
N.L.—57—New York vs. Houston, 1986.
7-game series
N.L.—57—Pittsburgh vs. Atlanta, 1991.
Chicago vs. Florida, 2003.
A.L.—60—Boston vs. New York, 2003.

Most strikeouts by both clubs, series
3-game series
N.L.—46—Cincinnati 28, Pittsburgh 18, 1975.
A.L.—41—Minnesota 27, Baltimore 14, 1969.
Minnesota 22, Baltimore 19, 1970.
4-game series
N.L.—61—Pittsburgh 33, San Francisco 28, 1971.
A.L.—58—Oakland 35, Boston 23, 1988.
5-game series
A.L.—82—New York 44, Boston 38, 1999.
N.L.—71—Atlanta 39, Arizona 32, 2001.
6-game series
A.L.—109—Cleveland 62, Baltimore 47, 1997.
N.L.—105—Atlanta 54, Philadelphia 51, 1993.
7-game series
A.L.—109—Boston 60, New York 49, 2003.
N.L.—104—St. Louis 53, Atlanta 51, 1996.

Fewest strikeouts, series
3-game series
N.L.—9—Philadelphia vs. Cincinnati, 1976.
A.L.—10—New York vs. Oakland, 1981.
4-game series
A.L.—13—California vs. Baltimore, 1979.
N.L.—16—Los Angeles vs. Pittsburgh, 1974.
5-game series
A.L.—15—New York vs. Kansas City, 1976.
N.L.—19—Houston vs. Philadelphia, 1980.
6-game series
A.L.—29—Toronto vs. Oakland, 1992.
N.L.—31—Los Angeles vs. St. Louis, 1985.
7-game series
N.L.—28—Atlanta vs. Pittsburgh, 1992.
A.L.—31—Boston vs. California, 1986.

Fewest strikeouts by both clubs, series
3-game series
N.L.—25—Cincinnati 16, Philadelphia 9, 1976.
A.L.—26—Oakland 14, Boston 12, 1975.

4-game series
N.L.—33—Pittsburgh 17, Los Angeles 16, 1974.
A.L.—36—Baltimore 20, Oakland 16, 1974.
5-game series
A.L.—33—Kansas City 18, New York 15, 1976.
N.L.—48—Montreal 25, Los Angeles 23, 1981.
6-game series
A.L.—62—Oakland 33, Toronto 29, 1992.
N.L.—65—St. Louis 34, Los Angeles 31, 1985.
7-game series
N.L.—70—Pittsburgh 42, Atlanta 28, 1992.
A.L.—75—California 44, Boston 31, 1986.

Most strikeouts by pinch-hitters, series
N.L.—7—Cincinnati vs. New York, 1973 (5-game series).
A.L.—4—Minnesota vs. Baltimore, 1970 (3-game series).
Oakland vs. Detroit, 1972 (5-game series).
Anaheim vs. Minnesota, 2002 (5-game series).
Minnesota vs. Anaheim, 2002 (5-game series).

Most strikeouts by pinch-hitters on both clubs, series
N.L.—11—New York 6, Atlanta 5, 1999 (6-game series).
A.L.—8—Anaheim 4, Minnesota 4, 2002 (5-game series).

Most strikeouts, game
N.L.—15—Philadelphia vs. Atlanta, October 10, 1993.
Atlanta vs. Florida, October 12, 1997.
(15—Cincinnati vs. Pittsburgh, October 7, 1975, 10 innings.
New York vs. Houston, October 14, 1986, 12 innings.)
A.L.—15—Seattle vs. New York, October 14, 2000.
(21—Cleveland vs. Baltimore, October 11, 1997, 12 innings.)

Most strikeouts by pinch-hitters, game
A.L.—4—Oakland vs. Detroit, October 10, 1972.
N.L.—4—Pittsburgh vs. Atlanta, October 10, 1992.

Most strikeouts by both clubs, game
N.L.—25—Atlanta 15, Florida 10, October 12, 1997.
(32—Atlanta 19, New York 13, October 17, 1999, 15 innings.)
A.L.—22—New York 13, Seattle 9, October 10, 2000.
New York 12, Boston 10, October 13, 2003.
(33—Cleveland 21, Baltimore 12, October 11, 1997, 12 innings.)

Fewest strikeouts, game
N.L.—0—Pittsburgh vs. Los Angeles, October 6, 1974.
A.L.—1—Baltimore vs. Oakland, October 11, 1973.
New York vs. Kansas City, October 13, 1976.
Kansas City vs. New York, October 4, 1978.
Toronto vs. Kansas City, October 12, 1985.
Boston vs. Oakland, October 10, 1990.

Fewest strikeouts by both clubs, game
A.L.—3—Oakland 2, Baltimore 1, October 11, 1973.
Kansas City 2, New York 1, October 13, 1976.
N.L.—4—Philadelphia 2, Cincinnati 2, October 12, 1976.

Most consecutive strikeouts, game
A.L.—5—Cleveland vs. Baltimore, October 11, 1997 (one in fifth inning, three in sixth inning, one in seventh inning).
Boston vs. New York, October 12, 2004 (three in fourth inning, two in fifth inning).
N.L.—5—Atlanta vs. Philadelphia, October 6, 1993 (three in first inning, two in second inning).
Arizona vs. Atlanta, October 11, 2003 (three in eighth inning, two in ninth inning.)

Most strikeouts, inning
A.L.-N.L.—3—Held by many clubs.

Most strikeouts by both clubs, inning
A.L-N.L.—5—Occurred in many innings.

Most strikeouts by pinch-hitters, inning
A.L.—2—Oakland vs. Baltimore, October 5, 1971, ninth inning (consecutive).
N.L.—2—Cincinnati vs. New York, October 7, 1973, eighth inning (consecutive).
Pittsburgh vs. Atlanta, October 10, 1992, eighth inning.
Cincinnati vs. Atlanta, October 10, 1995, 10th inning (consecutive).
Atlanta vs. San Diego, October 10, 1998, sixth inning (consecutive).

New York vs. St. Louis, October 14, 2000, ninth inning (consecutive).

SACRIFICE HITS

Most sacrifice hits, total series
N.L.—31—Atlanta; 11 series, 60 games.
A.L.—22—Oakland; 10 series, 42 games.

Most sacrifice hits, series
N.L.—8—San Francisco vs. St. Louis, 2002 (5-game series).
A.L.—5—Boston vs. Oakland, 1975 (3-game series).
  California vs. Milwaukee, 1982 (5-game series).
  Chicago vs. Toronto, 1993 (6-game series).

Most sacrifice hits by both clubs, series ꞁ
N.L.—13—San Francisco 8, St. Louis 5, 2002 (5-game series).
A.L.—7—Oakland 4, Detroit 3, 1972 (5-game series).
  California 5, Milwaukee 2, 1982 (5-game series).
  California 4, Boston 3, 1986 (7-game series).

Fewest sacrifice hits, series
A.L.-N.L.—0—Held by many clubs.

Fewest sacrifice hits by both clubs, series
N.L.—0—Cincinnati 0, Pittsburgh 0, 1975 (3-game series).
A.L.—0—Baltimore 0, New York 0, 1996 (5-game series).

Most sacrifice hits, game
N.L.—3—Los Angeles vs. Montreal, October 17, 1981.
  St. Louis vs. Atlanta, October 9, 1982.
  San Francisco vs. St. Louis, October 12, 2002.
  St. Louis vs. Houston, October 21, 2004.
  (3—Pittsburgh vs. Cincinnati, October 3, 1979, 10 innings.
  Philadelphia vs. Houston, October 8, 1980, 10 innings.
  Atlanta vs. New York, October 19, 1999, 11 innings.)
A.L.—3—California vs. Milwaukee, October 10, 1982.
  (3—California vs. Boston, October 12, 1986, 11 innings.)

Most sacrifice hits by both clubs, game
N.L.—4—Los Angeles 3, Montreal 1, October 17, 1981.
  St. Louis 2, Atlanta 2, October 9, 1982.
  Atlanta 2, Philadelphia 2, October 13, 1993.
  (4—Pittsburgh 3, Cincinnati 1, October 3, 1979, 10 innings.
  Atlanta 3, New York 1, October 19, 1999, 11 innings.)
A.L.—3—California 3, Milwaukee 0, October 10, 1982.
  Oakland 2, Boston 1, October 6, 1990.
  (3—Boston 2, California 1, October 11, 1986, 11 innings.
  California 3, Boston 0, October 12, 1986, 11 innings.)

Most sacrifice hits, inning
N.L.—2—Philadelphia vs. Cincinnati, October 10, 1976, fourth inning.
A.L.—1—Held by many clubs.

SACRIFICE FLIES

Most sacrifice flies, total series
N.L.—15—Atlanta; 11 series, 60 games.

A.L.—14—New York; 12 series, 61 games.

Most sacrifice flies, series
A.L.—4—Kansas City vs. New York, 1976 (5-game series).
  Toronto vs. Oakland, 1992 (6-game series).
N.L.—4—San Diego vs. Chicago, 1984 (5-game series).
  St. Louis vs. San Francisco, 1987 (7-game series).

Most sacrifice flies by both clubs, series
N.L.—6—San Diego 4, Chicago 2, 1984 (5-game series).
A.L.—6—Toronto 4, Oakland 2, 1992 (6-game series).

Most sacrifice flies, game
N.L.—3—St. Louis vs. Atlanta, October 7, 1982.
A.L.—2—Held by many clubs.

Most sacrifice flies by both clubs, game
N.L.—3—St. Louis 3, Atlanta 0, October 7, 1982.
  St. Louis 2, San Francisco 1, October 11, 1987.
A.L.—2—Occurred many times.

Most sacrifice flies, inning
A.L.—2—Baltimore vs. Chicago, October 7, 1983, ninth inning.
  Detroit vs. Minnesota, October 7, 1987, eighth inning.
N.L.—2—San Diego vs. Chicago, October 7, 1984, sixth inning.

HIT BY PITCH

Most hit by pitch, total series
N.L.—13—Atlanta; 11 series, 60 games.
A.L.—23—New York; 12 series, 61 games.

Most hit by pitch, series
A.L.—7—New York vs. Boston, 2004 (7-game series).
N.L.—5—Houston vs. St. Louis, 2004 (7-game series).

Most hit by pitch by both clubs, series
A.L.—8—Minnesota 5, Detroit 3, 1987 (5-game series).
  New York 7, Boston 1, 2004 (7-game series).
N.L.—7—Houston 5, St. Louis 2, 2004 (7-game series).

Most hit by pitch, game
A.L.—3—Minnesota vs. Detroit, October 11, 1987.
  Cleveland vs. Baltimore, October 9, 1997.
N.L.—3—San Francisco vs. St. Louis, October 14, 2002.
  (3—Atlanta vs. New York, October 19, 1999, 11 innings.)

Most hit by pitch by both clubs, game
A.L.—4—Detroit 2, Minnesota 2, October 12, 1987.
  Cleveland 2, New York 2, October 11, 1998.
N.L.—3—Atlanta 2, Florida 1, October 7, 1997.
  San Francisco 3, St. Louis 0, October 14, 2002.
  (3—Atlanta 3, New York 0, October 19, 1999, 11 innings.)

Most hit by pitch, inning
A.L.—3—Cleveland vs. Baltimore, October 9, 1997, first inning.
N.L.—2—Atlanta vs. New York, October 19, 1999, first inning.

INDIVIDUAL BASERUNNING

STOLEN BASES

Most stolen bases, career
M.L.—17—Rickey Henderson, Oakland A.L., 1981, 1989, 1990, 1992; Toronto A.L., 1993; New York N.L., 1999; Seattle A.L.; 2000; seven series, 33 games.
A.L.—16—Rickey Henderson, Oakland, 1981, 1989, 1990, 1992; Toronto, 1993; Seattle, 2000; six series, 27 games.
N.L.—9—Dave Lopes, Los Angeles, 1974, 1977, 1978, 1981; Chicago, 1984; Houston, 1986; six series, 22 games.

Most stolen bases, series
3-game series
N.L.—4—Joe Morgan, Cincinnati, 1975.
A.L.—2—Juan Beniquez, Boston, 1975.
  Amos Otis, Kansas City, 1980.
  Rickey Henderson, Oakland, 1981.

4-game series
A.L.—4—Amos Otis, Kansas City, 1978.
N.L.—3—Dave Lopes, Los Angeles, 1974.
5-game series
A.L.—8—Rickey Henderson, Oakland, 1989.
N.L.—5—Dave Lopes, Los Angeles, 1981.
6-game series
A.L.—7—Willie Wilson, Oakland, 1992.
N.L.—3—Billy Hatcher, Houston, 1986.
  Barry Larkin, Cincinnati, 1990.
  Chipper Jones, Atlanta, 1999.
  Gerald Williams, Atlanta, 1999.
7-game series
N.L.—7—Ron Gant, Atlanta, 1991.
A.L.—1—Held by many players.

Most stolen bases, game
A.L.—4—Rickey Henderson, Oakland, October 4, 1989.

N.L.—3—Joe Morgan, Cincinnati, October 4, 1975.
Ken Griffey Sr., Cincinnati, October 5, 1975.
Ron Gant, Atlanta, October 10, 1991.
Edgar Renteria, St. Louis, October 12, 2000.
(3—Steve Sax, Los Angeles, October 9, 1988, 12 innings.)

Most stolen bases by pinch-runner, game
A.L.-N.L.—1—Held by many players.

Most times stealing home, game
A.L.—1—Reggie Jackson, Oakland, October 12, 1972, second inning (front end of double steal).
Marquis Grissom, Cleveland, October 11, 1997, 12th inning.
N.L.—1—Jeff Branson, Cincinnati, October 11, 1995, fifth inning.

Most stolen bases, inning
A.L.-N.L.—2—Held by many players.

CAUGHT STEALING

Most caught stealing, career
A.L.—6—Hal McRae, Kansas City, 1976, 1977, 1978, 1980, 1984, 1985; six series, 28 games.
N.L.—4—Willie McGee, St. Louis, 1982, 1985, 1987, 1996; four series, 22 games.
Vince Coleman, St. Louis, 1985, 1987; two series, 10 games.

Most caught stealing by pinch-runner, career
A.L.—2—Herb Washington, Oakland, 1974; one series, two games.

N.L.—Never accomplished.

Most caught stealing, series
A.L.—4—Devon White, Toronto, 1992 (no stolen bases; 6-game series).
N.L.—3—Willie McGee, St. Louis, 1985 (two stolen bases; 6-game series).
Kevin Bass, Houston, 1986 (two stolen bases; 6-game series).
Juan Pierre, Florida, 2003 (one stolen base; 7-game series).

Most caught stealing by pinch-runner, series
A.L.—2—Herb Washington, Oakland, 1974; two games.
N.L.—Never accomplished.

Most caught stealing, game
A.L.—2—Trot Nixon, Boston, October 13, 2003.
(2—Brooks Robinson, Baltimore, October 4, 1969, 12 innings.)
N.L.—1—Held by many players.
(2—Kevin Bass, Houston, October 15, 1986, 16 innings.)

Most caught stealing by pinch-runner, game
A.L.—1—Herb Washington, Oakland, October 6, 8, 1974.
Sandy Alomar Sr., New York, October 14, 1976.
Onix Concepcion, Kansas City, October 9, 1985.
N.L.—Never accomplished.

Most caught stealing, inning
A.L.-N.L.—1—Held by many players.

CLUB BASERUNNING

STOLEN BASES

Most stolen bases, total series
A.L.—54—Oakland; 10 series, 42 games.
N.L.—41—Atlanta; 11 series, 60 games.

Most stolen bases, series
3-game series
N.L.—11—Cincinnati vs. Pittsburgh, 1975.
A.L.—4—Detroit vs. Kansas City, 1984.
4-game series
A.L.—9—Oakland vs. Boston, 1990.
N.L.—5—Los Angeles vs. Pittsburgh, 1974.
5-game series
A.L.—13—Oakland vs. Toronto, 1989.
N.L.—7—Philadelphia vs. Houston, 1980.
6-game series
A.L.—16—Oakland vs. Toronto, 1992.
N.L.—14—Atlanta vs. New York, 1999.
7-game series
N.L.—10—Atlanta vs. Pittsburgh, 1991.
A.L.—5—New York vs. Boston, 2003.

Most stolen bases by both clubs, series
3-game series
N.L.—11—Cincinnati 11, Pittsburgh 0, 1975.
A.L.—4—New York 2, Oakland 2, 1981.
Detroit 4, Kansas City 0, 1984.
4-game series
A.L.—10—Oakland 9, Boston 1, 1990.
N.L.—6—Los Angeles 5, Pittsburgh 1, 1974.
Cincinnati 4, Atlanta 2, 1995.
5-game series
A.L.—24—Oakland 13, Toronto 11, 1989.
N.L.—11—Philadelphia 7, Houston 4, 1980.
6-game series
A.L.—23—Oakland 16, Toronto 7, 1992.
N.L.—21—Atlanta 14, New York 7, 1999.
7-game series
N.L.—16—Atlanta 10, Pittsburgh 6, 1991.
A.L.—7—New York 5, Boston 2, 2003.
Boston 4, New York 3, 2004.

Fewest stolen bases, series
A.L.-N.L.—0—Held by many clubs.

Fewest stolen bases by both clubs, series
3-game series
A.L.—0—Baltimore 0, Oakland 0, 1971.

N.L.—1—Cincinnati 1, Pittsburgh 0, 1970.
4-game series
N.L.—2—Los Angeles 2, Philadelphia 0, 1978.
A.L.—1—Oakland 1, Boston 0, 1988.
5-game series
N.L.—0—Cincinnati 0, New York 0, 1973.
A.L.—3—Milwaukee 2, California 1, 1982.
New York 3, Baltimore 0, 1996.
6-game series
N.L.—2—Philadelphia 2, Atlanta 0, 1993.
A.L.—7—New York 4, Seattle 3, 2000.
7-game series
A.L.—2—Boston 1, California 1, 1986.
N.L.—5—Atlanta 4, St. Louis 1, 1996.
Florida 4, Chicago 1, 2003.

Most stolen bases, game
N.L.—7—Cincinnati vs. Pittsburgh, October 5, 1975.
A.L.—6—Oakland vs. Toronto, October 4, 1989.
Oakland vs. Toronto, October 8, 1992.

Most stolen bases by both clubs, game
A.L.—8—Oakland 6, Toronto 2, October 4, 1989.
Oakland 6, Toronto 2, October 8, 1992.
N.L.—7—Cincinnati 7, Pittsburgh 0, October 5, 1975.
(8—Atlanta 6, New York 2, October 19, 1999, 11 innings.)

Longest game with no stolen bases
N.L.—16 innings—New York vs. Houston, October 15, 1986.
A.L.—14 innings—Boston vs. New York, October 18, 2004.
New York vs. Boston, October 18, 2004.

Longest game with no stolen bases by either club
N.L.—12 innings—New York 0, Cincinnati 0, October 9, 1973.
A.L.—14 innings—Boston 0, New York 0, October 18, 2004.

Most stolen bases, inning
A.L.—3—Oakland vs. Detroit, October 12, 1972, second inning.
Oakland vs. Toronto, October 8, 1992, fifth inning.
N.L.—2—Held by many clubs.

CAUGHT STEALING

Most caught stealing, series
3-game series
A.L.—5—Kansas City vs. New York, 1980.
N.L.—2—Pittsburgh vs. Cincinnati, 1970.

Cincinnati vs. Pittsburgh, 1979.
Atlanta vs. St. Louis, 1982.
4-game series
A.L.—3—Oakland vs. Baltimore, 1974.
Baltimore vs. Oakland, 1974.
Kansas City vs. New York, 1978.
Oakland vs. Boston, 1988, 1990.
N.L.—3—Cincinnati vs. Atlanta, 1995.
5-game series
A.L.—5—Kansas City vs. New York, 1976.
N.L.—3—Philadelphia vs. Houston, 1980.
Chicago vs. San Diego, 1984.
6-game series
N.L.—6—St. Louis vs. Los Angeles, 1985.
A.L.—5—Toronto vs. Oakland, 1992.
7-game series
A.L.—5—Boston vs. New York, 2003.
N.L.—4—San Francisco vs. St. Louis, 1987.
St. Louis vs. San Francisco, 1987.
Atlanta vs. Pittsburgh, 1991.
Houston vs. St. Louis, 2004.

Most caught stealing by both clubs, series
3-game series
A.L.—5—Kansas City 5, New York 0, 1980.
N.L.—3—Pittsburgh 2, Cincinnati 1, 1970.
4-game series
A.L.—6—Oakland 3, Baltimore 3, 1974.
N.L.—4—Cincinnati 3, Atlanta 1, 1995.
5-game series
A.L.—8—Kansas City 5, New York 3, 1976.
N.L.—5—Chicago 3, San Diego 2, 1984.
6-game series
N.L.—7—St. Louis 6, Los Angeles 1, 1985.
A.L.—7—Toronto 5, Oakland 2, 1992.
7-game series
N.L. 8—San Francisco 4, St. Louis 4, 1987.
A.L.—6—Kansas City 4, Toronto 2, 1985.
Boston 5, New York 1, 2003.

Fewest caught stealing, series
A.L.-N.L.—0—By many clubs.

Fewest caught stealing by both clubs, series
A.L.-N.L.—0—Occurred in many series.

Most caught stealing, game
A.L.-N.L.—2—Held by many clubs.

Most caught stealing by both clubs, game
A.L.—3—Baltimore 2, Oakland 1, October 10, 1973.
Kansas City 2, New York 1, October 12, 1976.
Milwaukee 2, California 1, October 9, 1982.
N.L.—3—Chicago 2, San Diego 1, October 7, 1984.
St. Louis 2, Los Angeles 1, October 12, 1985.

Most caught stealing, inning
N.L.—2—St. Louis vs. Los Angeles, October 10, 1985, first inning.
St. Louis vs. Los Angeles, October 12, 1985, second inning.
A.L.—1—Held by many clubs.

LEFT ON BASE

Most left on base, total series
A.L.—481—New York; 12 series, 61 games.
N.L.—441—Atlanta; 11 series, 60 games.

Most left on base, series
3-game series
N.L.—31—St. Louis vs. Atlanta, 1982.
A.L.—30—New York vs. Oakland, 1981.
4-game series
N.L.—44—Los Angeles vs. Pittsburgh, 1974.
A.L.—35—Chicago vs. Baltimore, 1983.
Oakland vs. Boston, 1990.
5-game series
N.L.—45—Houston vs. Philadelphia, 1980.
A.L.—45—Boston vs. New York, 1999.
6-game series
A.L.—56—Toronto vs. Chicago, 1993.
N.L.—52—Philadelphia vs. Atlanta, 1993.
San Diego vs. Atlanta, 1998.
7-game series
A.L.—69—New York vs. Boston, 2004.
N.L.—58—Atlanta vs. St. Louis, 1996.

Most left on base by both clubs, series
3-game series
A.L.—50—Baltimore 28, Minnesota 22, 1969.
New York 30, Oakland 20, 1981.
N.L.—49—Cincinnati 25, Pittsburgh 24, 1979.
4-game series
N.L.—68—Los Angeles 44, Pittsburgh 24, 1974.
A.L.—59—Chicago 35, Baltimore 24, 1983.
5-game series
N.L.—88—Houston 45, Philadelphia 43, 1980.
A.L.—87—Boston 45, New York 42, 1999.
6-game series
A.L.—106—Toronto 56, Chicago 50, 1993.
N.L.—99—Philadelphia 52, Atlanta 47, 1993.
7-game series
A.L.—122—New York 69, Boston 53, 2004.
N.L.—105—Pittsburgh 54, Atlanta 51, 1991.

Fewest left on base, series
3-game series
N.L.—12—Atlanta vs. St. Louis, 1982.
A.L.—14—Boston vs. Oakland, 1975.
4-game series
A.L.—16—Baltimore vs. Oakland, 1974.
N.L.—22—Los Angeles vs. Philadelphia, 1977.
5-game series
A.L.—22—Kansas City vs. New York, 1976.
N.L.—24—Pittsburgh vs. Cincinnati, 1972.
6-game series
N.L.—33—Cincinnati vs. Pittsburgh, 1990.
A.L.—38—Seattle vs. New York, 2000.
7-game series
N.L.—34—St. Louis vs. Atlanta, 1996.
A.L.—44—Kansas City vs. Toronto, 1985.

Fewest left on base by both clubs, series
3-game series
A.L.—33—Oakland 19, Boston 14, 1975.
N.L.—38—Pittsburgh 21, Cincinnati 17, 1975.
4-game series
A.L.—45—Baltimore 23, California 22, 1979.
N.L.—52—Los Angeles 28, Philadelphia 24, 1978.
5-game series
A.L.—53—California 29, Milwaukee 24, 1982.
N.L.—54—Cincinnati 30, Pittsburgh 24, 1972.
6-game series
N.L.—74—Pittsburgh 41, Cincinnati 33, 1990.
A.L.—87—New York 48, Cleveland 39, 1998.
New York 49, Seattle 38, 2000.
7-game series
N.L.—80—San Francisco 43, St. Louis 37, 1987.
A.L.—94—Toronto 50, Kansas City 44, 1985.
Boston 49, New York 45, 2003.

Most left on bases, game
N.L.—15—Philadelphia vs. Atlanta, October 10, 1993.
(19—Atlanta vs. New York, October 17, 1999; 15 innings.)
A.L.—15—New York vs. Seattle, October 15, 2000.
(18—New York vs. Boston, October 18, 2004, 14 innings.)

Most left on base by both clubs, game
N.L.—26—Philadelphia 15, Atlanta 11, October 10, 1993.
(31—Atlanta 19, New York 12, October 17, 1999, 15 innings.)
A.L.—25—Chicago 13, Toronto 12, October 5, 1993.
(30—New York 18, Boston 12, October 18, 2004, 14 innings.)

Fewest left on base, game
N.L.—0—Atlanta vs. New York, October 16, 1999.
A.L.—1—Baltimore vs. New York, October 11, 1996.

Fewest left on base by both clubs, game
N.L.—3—New York 3, Atlanta 0, October 16, 1999.
A.L.—6—Oakland 4, Detroit 2, October 8, 1972.
New York 5, Baltimore 1, October 11, 1996.
Boston 3, New York 3, October 11, 2003.

Most left on base, shutout defeat
A.L.—10—Oakland vs. Detroit, October 10, 1972 (lost 3-0).
(14—Baltimore vs. Cleveland, October 15, 1997 (lost 1-0),11 innings)
N.L.—10—Los Angeles vs. Pittsburgh, October 8, 1974 (lost 7-0).
San Diego vs. Chicago, October 2, 1984 (lost 13-0).
(11—Philadelphia vs. Houston, October 10, 1980 (lost 1-0), 11 innings)

INDIVIDUAL PITCHING

GAMES

Most games, career
A.L.—25—Mariano Rivera, New York, 1996, 1998 through 2001, 2003, 2004; seven series.
N.L.—18—Mark Wohlers, Atlanta, 1991, 1992, 1993, 1995, 1996, 1997; six series.

Most games, series
3-game series
A.L.-N.L.—3—Held by many pitchers.
4-game series
N.L.—4—Dave Giusti, Pittsburgh, 1971.
Mark Wohlers, Atlanta, 1995.
A.L.—4—Dennis Eckersley, Oakland, 1988.
5-game series
N.L.—5—Tug McGraw, Philadelphia, 1980.
A.L.—5—Jim Acker, Toronto, 1989.
6-game series
N.L.—6—John Rocker, Atlanta, 1998.
John Rocker, Atlanta, 1999.
A.L.—5—Paul Assenmacher, Cleveland, 1997.
Mike Jackson, Cleveland, 1997.
Paul Shuey, Cleveland, 1998.
Jose Paniagua, Seattle, 2000.
7-game series
N.L.—6—Mark Petkovsek, St. Louis, 1996.
Jason Isringhausen, St. Louis, 2004.
A.L.—6—Alan Embree, Boston, 2004.
Tom Gordon, New York, 2004.

Most consecutive games, series
N.L.—6—John Rocker, Atlanta, October 7, 8, 10, 11, 12, 14, 1998.
John Rocker, Atlanta, October 12, 13, 15, 16, 17, 19, 1999.
A.L.—5—Jim Acker, Toronto, October 3, 4, 6, 7, 8, 1989.
Paul Assenmacher, Cleveland, October 9, 11, 12, 13, 15, 1997.
Mike Jackson, Cleveland, October 9, 11, 12, 13, 15, 1997.
Alan Embree, Boston, October 12, 13, 16, 17, 18, 2004.
Tom Gordon, New York, October 12, 13, 16, 17, 18, 2004.

GAMES STARTED

Most games started, career
N.L.—15—Tom Glavine, Atlanta, 1991, 1992, 1993, 1995, 1996, 1997, 1998, 1999, 2001; nine series.
A.L.—11—Roger Clemens, Boston, 1986, 1988, 1990; New York, 1999, 2000, 2001, 2003; seven series.

Most opening games started, career
Both leagues—4—Don Gullett, Cincinnati N.L., 1972, 1975, 1976; New York A.L., 1977 (won 2, lost 2).
N.L.—4—Steve Carlton, Philadelphia, 1976, 1977, 1980, 1983 (won 2, lost 1).
Greg Maddux, Chicago, 1989; Atlanta, 1997, 1999, 2001 (won 1, lost 3).
A.L.—4—Dave Stewart, Oakland, 1988, 1989, 1990, 1992 (won 2).

Most games started, series
A.L.-N.L.—3—Held by many pitchers.

GAMES RELIEVED

Most games by relief pitcher, career
A.L.—25—Mariano Rivera, New York, 1996, 1998 through 2001, 2003, 2004; 38.2 innings.
N.L.—18—Mark Wohlers, Atlanta, 1991, 1992, 1993, 1995, 1996, 1997; 19 innings.

Most games by relief pitcher, series
N.L.—6—Mark Petkovsek, St. Louis, 1996 (7-game series).
John Rocker, Atlanta, 1998 (6-game series).
John Rocker, Atlanta, 1999 (6-game series).
Jason Isringhausen, St. Louis, 2004 (7-game series).
A.L.—6—Alan Embree, Boston, 2004 (7-game series).
Tom Gordon, New York, 2004 (7-game series).

COMPLETE GAMES

Most complete games pitched, career
A.L.—5—Jim Palmer, Baltimore, 1969, 1970, 1971, 1973, 1974.
N.L.—2—Held by many pitchers.

Most consecutive complete games pitched, career
A.L.—4—Jim Palmer, Baltimore, 1969 (1), 1970 (1), 1971 (1), 1973 (1; won four).
N.L.—2—Tommy John, Los Angeles, 1977 (1), 1978 (1; won two).
Mike Scott, Houston, 1986 (2; won two).
Danny Cox, St. Louis, 1987 (2; won one, lost one).
Tim Wakefield, Pittsburgh, 1992 (2; won two).

Most complete games, series
N.L.—2—Mike Scott, Houston, 1986 (6-game series).
Danny Cox, St. Louis, 1987 (7-game series).
Tim Wakefield, Pittsburgh, 1992 (7-game series).
A.L.—1—Held by many pitchers.

INNINGS

Most innings pitched, career
N.L.—95.1—John Smoltz, Atlanta, 1991, 1992, 1993, 1995, 1996, 1997, 1998, 1999, 2001; nine series, 17 games.
A.L.—75.1—Dave Stewart, Oakland, 1988, 1989, 1990, 1992; Toronto, 1993; five series, 10 games.

Most innings pitched, series
3-game series
A.L.—11—Dave McNally, Baltimore, 1969.
Ken Holtzman, Oakland, 1975.
N.L.—9.2—Dock Ellis, Pittsburgh, 1970.
4-game series
N.L.—17—Don Sutton, Los Angeles, 1974.
A.L.—16—Dave Stewart, Oakland, 1990.
5-game series
A.L.—19—Mickey Lolich, Detroit, 1972.
N.L.—17—Ray Burris, Montreal, 1981.
6-game series
N.L.—18—Mike Scott, Houston, 1986.
A.L.—16.2—Dave Stewart, Oakland, 1992.
7-game series
N.L.—24.2—Orel Hershiser, Los Angeles, 1988.
A.L.—22.2—Roger Clemens, Boston, 1986.

Most innings pitched, game
A.L.—11—Dave McNally, Baltimore, October 5, 1969 (complete game, won 1-0).
Ken Holtzman, Oakland, October 9, 1973 (complete game, won 2-1).
N.L.—10—Joe Niekro, Houston, October 10, 1980 (incomplete game, no decision).
Dwight Gooden, New York, October 14, 1986 (incomplete game, no decision).

GAMES WON

Most games won, career
A.L.—8—Dave Stewart, Oakland, 1988, 1989, 1990, 1992; Toronto, 1993; five series, 10 games (lost none).
N.L.—6—John Smoltz, Atlanta, 1991, 1992, 1993, 1995, 1996, 1997, 1998, 1999; eight series, 15 games (lost two).

For a complete list of pitchers with four or more victories, see page 448.

Most games won by undefeated pitcher, career
A.L.—8—Dave Stewart, Oakland, 1988, 1989, 1990, 1992; Toronto, 1993.
N.L.—3—Bruce Kison, Pittsburgh, 1971, 1972, 1974, 1975.
Jesse Orosco, New York, 1986; Los Angeles, 1988.

Most opening games won, career
N.L.—2—Don Gullett, Cincinnati, 1975, 1976.
Steve Carlton, Philadelphia, 1980, 1983.
John Smoltz, Atlanta, 1992, 1996.
A.L.—2—Dick Hall, Baltimore, 1969, 1970.
Tommy John, New York, 1981; California, 1982.
Dave Stewart, Oakland, 1989, 1990.
Jack Morris, Detroit, 1984; Minnesota, 1991.
Mariano Rivera, New York, 1996, 1999.

Most consecutive games won, career
A.L.—8—Dave Stewart, Oakland, October 9, 1988; October 3, 8, 1989; October 6, 10, 1990; October 12, 1992; Toronto, October 6, 12, 1993 (one complete).
N.L.—4—Steve Carlton, Philadelphia, October 6, 1978; October 7, 1980; October 4, 8, 1983 (one complete).
John Smoltz, Atlanta, October 6, 10, 1991; October 6, 10, 1992 (none complete).

Most consecutive complete games won, career
A.L.—4—Jim Palmer, Baltimore, October 6, 1969; October 5, 1970; October 5, 1971; October 6, 1973.
N.L.—2—Tommy John, Los Angeles, October 8, 1977; October 5, 1978.
Mike Scott, Houston, October 8, 12, 1986.
Tim Wakefield, Pittsburgh, October 9, 13, 1992.

Most games won, series
N.L.—3—Jesse Orosco, New York, 1986 (6-game series).
A.L.—2—Held by many pitchers.

Most games won by relief pitcher, series
N.L.—3—Jesse Orosco, New York, 1986 (6-game series).
A.L.—2—Sparky Lyle, New York, 1977 (5-game series).
Tom Henke, Toronto, 1985 (7-game series).
Jeff Reardon, Minnesota, 1987 (5-game series).
Francisco Rodriguez, Anaheim, 2002 (5-game series).

SAVES

Most saves, career
Both leagues—11—Dennis Eckersley, Oakland A.L., 1988, 1989, 1990, 1992; St. Louis N.L., 1996.
A.L.—10—Dennis Eckersley, Oakland, 1988, 1989, 1990, 1992.
Mariano Rivera, New York, 1996, 1998 through 2001, 2003, 2004.
N.L.—5—Tug McGraw, New York, 1969, 1973; Philadelphia, 1977, 1980.

Most saves, series
3-game series
  A.L.—2—Dick Drago, Boston, 1975.
  N.L.—2—Don Gullett, Cincinnati, 1970.
4-game series
  A.L.—4—Dennis Eckersley, Oakland, 1988.
  N.L.—3—Dave Giusti, Pittsburgh, 1971.
5-game series
  N.L.—3—Steve Bedrosian, San Francisco, 1989.
       Robb Nen, San Francisco, 2002.
  A.L.—3—Dennis Eckersley, Oakland, 1989.
       Rick Aguilera, Minnesota, 1991.
6-game series
  N.L.—3—Randy Myers, Cincinnati, 1990.
  A.L.—3—Tom Henke, Toronto, 1992.
7-game series
  N.L.—3—Alejandro Pena, Atlanta, 1991.
       Jason Isringhausen, St. Louis, 2004.
  A.L.—3—Scott Williamson, Boston, 2003.

GAMES LOST

Most games lost, career
N.L.—9—Tom Glavine, Atlanta, 1991, 1992, 1993, 1995, 1996, 1997, 1998, 1999, 2001; nine series, 15 games.
A.L.—4—Doyle Alexander, Baltimore, 1973; Toronto, 1985; Detroit, 1987; three series, five games (won none).

Most games lost by winless pitcher, career
N.L.—7—Jerry Reuss, Pittsburgh, 1974 (2), 1975; Los Angeles, 1981, 1983 (2), 1985.
A.L.—4—Doyle Alexander, Baltimore, 1973; Toronto, 1985; Detroit, 1987 (2).

Most consecutive games lost, career
N.L.—7—Jerry Reuss, Pittsburgh, 1974 (2), 1975; Los Angeles, 1981, 1983 (2), 1985.
A.L.—4—Doyle Alexander, Baltimore, 1973; Toronto, 1985; Detroit, 1987 (2).

Most games lost, series
N.L.—3—Doug Drabek, Pittsburgh, 1992.
A.L.—2—Held by many pitchers.

RUNS

Most runs allowed, career
N.L.—50—Greg Maddux, Chicago, 1989; Atlanta, 1993, 1995, 1996, 1997, 1998, 1999, 2001; eight series, 15 games.
A.L.—29—Roger Clemens, Boston, 1986, 1988, 1990; New York, 1999, 2000, 2001, 2003; seven series, 11 games.

Most runs allowed, series
3-game series
  A.L.—9—Jim Perry, Minnesota, 1970.
  N.L.—9—Phil Niekro, Atlanta, 1969.
4-game series
  N.L.—11—Gaylord Perry, San Francisco, 1971.
  A.L.—10—Dave Frost, California, 1979.
5-game series
  N.L.—12—Greg Maddux, Chicago, 1989.
  A.L.—10—Doyle Alexander, Detroit, 1987.
6-game series
  N.L.—10—Joaquin Andujar, St. Louis, 1985.
       Tommy Greene, Philadelphia, 1993.
  A.L.—10—Jack McDowell, Chicago, 1993.
7-game series
  A.L.—13—Kirk McCaskill, California, 1986.
  N.L.—11—Doug Drabek, Pittsburgh, 1992.
       Tom Glavine, Atlanta, 1992.
       Todd Stottlemyre, St. Louis, 1996.

Most runs allowed, game
N.L.—9—Phil Niekro, Atlanta, October 4, 1969.
A.L.—8—Jim Perry, Minnesota, October 3, 1970.
       Roger Clemens, Boston, October 7, 1986.
Hideki Irabu, New York, October 16, 1999.

Most runs allowed, inning
N.L.—8—Tom Glavine, Atlanta, October 13, 1992, second inning.
A.L.—6—Jim Perry, Minnesota, October 3, 1970, fourth inning.
Scott Erickson, Baltimore, October 13, 1996, third inning.

EARNED RUNS

Most earned runs allowed, career
N.L.—36—Greg Maddux, Chicago, 1989; Atlanta, 1993, 1995, 1996, 1997, 1998, 1999, 2001; eight series, 15 games.
A.L.—27—Roger Clemens, Boston, 1986, 1988, 1990; New York, 1999, 2000, 2001, 2003; seven series, 11 games.

Most earned runs allowed, series
3-game series
  A.L.—8—Jim Perry, Minnesota, 1970.
  N.L.—6—Jerry Koosman, New York, 1969.
       Pat Jarvis, Atlanta, 1969.
4-game series
  N.L.—10—Gaylord Perry, San Francisco, 1971.
  A.L.—9—Dave Frost, California, 1979.
5-game series
  N.L.—11—Greg Maddux, Chicago, 1989.
  A.L.—10—Doyle Alexander, Detroit, 1987.
6-game series
  N.L.—10—Tommy Greene, Philadelphia, 1993.
  A.L.—10—Jack McDowell, Chicago, 1993.

7-game series
A.L.—11—Roger Clemens, Boston, 1986.
N.L.—11—Todd Stottlemyre, St. Louis, 1996.

Most earned runs allowed, game
A.L.—7—Jim Perry, Minnesota, October 3, 1970.
Roger Clemens, Boston, October 7, 1986.
Jack McDowell, Chicago, October 5, 1993.
Hideki Irabu, New York, October 16, 1999.
N.L.—8—Greg Maddux, Chicago, October 4, 1989.

Most earned runs allowed, inning
N.L.—7—Tom Glavine, Atlanta, October 13, 1992, second inning.
A.L.—6—Jim Perry, Minnesota, October 3, 1970, fourth inning.

EARNED-RUN AVERAGE

Lowest earned-run average, career (30 or more innings)
A.L.—0.93—Mariano Rivera, New York, 1996, 1998 through 2001, 2003, 2004; seven series, 25 games (38.2 innings).
N.L.—1.83—Orel Hershiser, Los Angeles, New York, 1985 through 1988; New York, 1999; 4 series, 8 games (44.1

SHUTOUTS AND SCORELESS INNINGS

Most shutouts, series
A.L.-N.L.—1—Held by many pitchers.

For a complete list of shutouts, see page 442.

Most consecutive scoreless innings, career
N.L.—22.1—Steve Avery, Atlanta, October 10 (8.1 innings), October 16 (eight innings), 1991; October 7 (six innings), 1992.
A.L.—18—Ken Holtzman, Oakland, October 9, 1973 (nine innings); October 6 (nine innings), 1974.

Most consecutive scoreless innings, series
N.L.—16.1—Steve Avery, Atlanta, October 10, 16, 1991.
A.L.—11—Dave McNally, Baltimore, October 5, 1969.

HITS

Most hits allowed, career
N.L.—91—Tom Glavine, Atlanta, 1991, 1992, 1993, 1995 through 1999, 2001; nine series, 15 games.
A.L.—63—Andy Pettitte, New York, 1996, 1998 through 2001, 2003; six series, nine games.

Most consecutive hitless innings, career
A.L.—10—Dave McNally, Baltimore, October 5 (7 innings), 1969; October 4 (3 innings), 1970.
N.L.—7—Randy Johnson, Arizona, October 16 (7 innings), 2001.

Most hits allowed, series
3-game series
A.L.—12—Ken Holtzman, Oakland, 1975.
N.L.—10—Pat Jarvis, Atlanta, 1969.
4-game series
N.L.—19—Gaylord Perry, San Francisco, 1971.
A.L.—13—Dennis Leonard, Kansas City, 1978.
5-game series
A.L.—18—Larry Gura, Kansas City, 1976.
N.L.—16—Nolan Ryan, Houston, 1980.
Scott Garrelts, San Francisco, 1989.
Matt Morris, St. Louis, 2002.
6-game series
A.L.—18—Jack McDowell, Chicago, 1993.
N.L.—17—Orel Hershiser, Los Angeles, 1985.
7-game series
A.L.—22—Roger Clemens, Boston, 1986.
N.L.—19—Andy Benes, St. Louis, 1996.

Most hits allowed, game
A.L.—13—Jack McDowell, Chicago, October 5, 1993.
Hideki Irabu, New York, October 16, 1999.
N.L.—11—Kevin Brown, Florida, October 14, 1997.

Most consecutive hitless innings, game
A.L.—7—Dave McNally, Baltimore, October 5, 1969, pitched all innings of an 11-inning game.
N.L.—7—Randy Johnson, Arizona, October 16, 2001.

Fewest hits allowed, game
A.L.—1—Roger Clemens, New York, October 14, 2000.
N.L.—2—Ross Grimsley, Cincinnati, October 10, 1972.
Jon Matlack, New York, October 7, 1973.
Dave Dravecky, San Francisco, October 7, 1987.

Most hits allowed, inning
A.L.—6—Jim Perry, Minnesota, October 3, 1970; fourth inning.
Kirk McCaskill, California, October 14, 1966, third inning.
N.L.—6—Greg A. Harris, San Diego, October 2, 1984, fifth inning.
Tom Glavine, Atlanta, October 13, 1992, second inning.
Todd Stottlemyre, St. Louis, October 14, 1996, first inning.
Matt Morris, St. Louis, October 9, 2002, second inning.

Most consecutive hits allowed, inning (consecutive at-bats)
A.L.—6—Jim Perry, Minnesota, October 3, 1970, fourth inning (sacrifice fly during streak).
N.L.—6—Matt Morris, St. Louis, October 9, 2002, second inning.

Most consecutive hits allowed, inning (consecutive plate appearances)
N.L.—6—Matt Morris, St. Louis, October 9, 2002, second inning.
A.L.—5—Dave Beard, Oakland, October 14, 1981, fourth inning.
Jack Morris, Minnesota, October 8, 1991, sixth inning.

DOUBLES, TRIPLES AND HOME RUNS

Most doubles allowed, game
N.L.—6—Darryl Kile, St. Louis, October 15, 2000.
A.L.—4—Dave McNally, Baltimore, October 3, 1971.
Vida Blue, Oakland, October 3, 1971.
Charlie Leibrandt, Kansas City, October 12, 1985.
Hideki Irabu, New York, October 16, 1999.
Orlando Hernandez, New York, October 17, 2000.
Pedro Martinez, Boston, October 16, 2003.

Most triples allowed, game
A.L.—2—Ed Figueroa, New York, October 8, 1977.
N.L.—2—Steve Carlton, Philadelphia, October 9, 1976.
Larry Christenson, Philadelphia, October 4, 1978.
Tom Glavine, Atlanta, October 9, 1993.
Josh Beckett, Florida, October 7, 2003.
Carlos Zambrano, Chicago, October 7, 2003.

Most home runs allowed, career
A.L.—12—Catfish Hunter, Oakland, 1971 (4), 1972 (2), 1974 (3); New York 1978 (3).
N.L.—8—John Smoltz, Atlanta, 1991 (2), 1992, 1997, 1998 (2), 1999 (2).
Tom Glavine, Atlanta, 1991, 1992 (3), 1993, 1996 (2), 2001.

Most home runs allowed, series
3-game series
A.L.—4—Catfish Hunter, Oakland, 1971.
N.L.—3—Pat Jarvis, Atlanta, 1969.
4-game series
N.L.—4—Steve Blass, Pittsburgh, 1971.
A.L.—3—Catfish Hunter, Oakland, 1974; New York, 1978.
Mike Boddicker, Boston, 1988.
5-game series
N.L.—5—Eric Show, San Diego, 1984.
A.L.—4—Dave McNally, Baltimore, 1973.
Andy Pettitte, New York, 1996.
6-game series
A.L.—4—Andy Pettitte, New York, 1998.
N.L.—3—Tommy Greene, Philadelphia, 1993.

7-game series
 A.L.—4—Mike Mussina, New York, 2003.
 N.L.—4—Tim Wakefield, Pittsburgh, 1992.
  Carlos Zambrano, Chicago, 2003.

Most home runs allowed, game
A.L.—4—Catfish Hunter, Oakland, October 4, 1971.
 Dave McNally, Baltimore, October 7, 1973.
 Andy Pettitte, New York, October 9, 1998.
N.L.—3—Pat Jarvis, Atlanta, October 6, 1969.
 Eric Show, San Diego, October 2, 1984.
 Danny Cox, St. Louis, October 10, 1987.
 Carlos Zambrano, Chicago, October 7, 2003.

Most grand slams allowed, game
A.L.—1—Jim Perry, Minnesota, October 3, 1970, fourth inning.
 Moose Haas, Milwaukee, October 9, 1982, eighth inning.
 David Cone, New York, October 13, 1998, fifth inning.
 Rod Beck, Boston, October 17, 1999, ninth inning.
 Javier Vasquez, New York, October 20, 2004, second inning.
N.L.—1—Steve Carlton, Philadelphia, October 4, 1977, seventh inning.
 Jim Lonborg, Philadelphia, October 5, 1977, fourth inning.
 Greg Maddux, Chicago, October 4, 1989, fourth inning.
 Bob Walk, Pittsburgh, October 7, 1992, fifth inning.
 Greg Maddux, Atlanta, October 10, 1996, seventh inning.
 Dan Miceli, San Diego, October 11, 1998, seventh inning.

Most home runs allowed, inning
A.L.—3—Scott Erickson, Baltimore, October 13, 1996, third inning.
 Jaret Wright, Cleveland, October 12, 1997, third inning.
 Andy Pettitte, New York, October 9, 1998, fifth inning.
N.L.—3—Carlos Zambrano, Chicago, October 7, 2003, third inning.

Most consecutive home runs allowed, inning
A.L.-N.L.—2—Held by many pitchers.

TOTAL BASES

Most total bases allowed, career
N.L.—142—Tom Glavine, Atlanta, 1991, 1992, 1993, 1995, 1996, 1997, 1998, 1999, 2001; nine series, 15 games.
A.L.—112—Catfish Hunter, Oakland, 1971 through 1974; New York, 1970, 1978; six series, 10 games.

Most total bases allowed, game
A.L.—23—Hideki Irabu, New York, October 16, 1999.
N.L.—23—Carlos Zambrano, Chicago, October 7, 2003.

BASES ON BALLS

Most bases on balls, career
N.L.—37—Tom Glavine, Atlanta, 1991, 1992, 1993, 1995, 1996, 1997, 1998, 1999, 2001; nine series, 15 games.
A.L.—26—Orlando Hernandez, New York, 1998, 1999, 2000, 2001, 2004; five series, seven games.

Most bases on balls, series
3-game series
 A.L.—7—Dave Boswell, Minnesota, 1969.
 N.L.—5—Fred Norman, Cincinnati, 1975.
  Steve Carlton, Philadelphia, 1976.
4-game series
 A.L.—13—Mike Cuellar, Baltimore, 1974.
 N.L.—8—Jerry Reuss, Pittsburgh, 1974.
  Steve Carlton, Philadelphia, 1977.
5-game series
 A.L.—8—Jim Palmer, Baltimore, 1973.
  Paul Abbott, Seattle, 2001.
 N.L.—8—Steve Carlton, Philadelphia, 1980.
  Rick Sutcliffe, Chicago, 1984.
6-game series
 N.L.—11—Tom Glavine, Atlanta, 1997.
 A.L.—9—Jack Morris, Toronto, 1992.
  Juan Guzman, Toronto, 1993.
7-game series
 A.L.—10—Dave Stieb, Toronto, 1985.
 N.L.—10—John Smoltz, Atlanta, 1992.

Most bases on balls, game
A.L.—9—Mike Cuellar, Baltimore, October 9, 1974.
N.L.—8—Fernando Valenzuela, Los Angeles, October 14, 1985.

Most bases on balls, inning
A.L.—4—Mike Cuellar, Baltimore, October 9, 1974, fifth inning (consecutive).
N.L.—4—Burt Hooton, Los Angeles, October 7, 1977, second inning (consecutive).
 Bob Welch, Los Angeles, October 12, 1985, first inning.

Most consecutive bases on balls, inning
A.L.—4—Mike Cuellar, Baltimore, October 9, 1974, fifth inning.
N.L.—4—Burt Hooton, Los Angeles, October 7, 1977, second inning.

STRIKEOUTS

Most strikeouts, career
N.L.—89—John Smoltz, Atlanta, 1991, 1992, 1993, 1995, 1996, 1997, 1998, 1999, 2001; nine series, 17 games.
A.L.—66—Mike Mussina, Baltimore, 1996, 1997; New York, 2001, 2003, 2004; five series, nine games.

Most strikeouts, series
3-game series
 N.L.—14—John Candelaria, Pittsburgh, 1975.
 A.L.—12—Jim Palmer, Baltimore, 1970.
4-game series
 A.L.—14—Mike Boddicker, Baltimore, 1983.
 N.L.—13—Don Sutton, Los Angeles, 1974.
  Steve Carlton, Philadelphia, 1983.
  Pete Schourek, Cincinnati, 1995.
5-game series
 N.L.—19—Randy Johnson, Arizona, 2001.
 A.L.—15—Jim Palmer, Baltimore, 1973.
6-game series
 A.L.—25—Mike Mussina, Baltimore, 1997.
 N.L.—19—Mike Scott, Houston, 1986.
  Curt Schilling, Philadelphia, 1993.
7-game series
 N.L.—20—Dwight Gooden, New York, 1988.
 A.L.—18—Dave Stieb, Toronto, 1985.

Most strikeouts, game
A.L.—15—Mike Mussina, Baltimore, October 11, 1997, pitched first seven innings of nine-inning game.
 Roger Clemens, New York, October 14, 2000.
N.L.—15—Livan Hernandez, Florida, October 12, 1997.

For a complete list of pitchers with 10 or more strikeouts in a game, see page 448.

For a complete list of pitchers with 10 or more strikeouts in a game, see page 448.

Most strikeouts, game, relief pitcher
A.L.—8—Wes Gardner, Boston, October 8, 1988, pitched 4.2 innings.
N.L.—7—Nolan Ryan, New York, October 6, 1969, pitched seven innings.

Most consecutive strikeouts, game
N.L.—5—Curt Schilling, Philadelphia, October 6, 1993 (three in first inning, two in second inning).
A.L.—5—Mike Mussina, Baltimore, October 11, 1997 (one in fifth inning, three in sixth inning, one in seventh inning).
 Mike Mussina, New York, October 12, 2004 (three in fourth inning, two in fifth inning).

Most consecutive strikeouts from start of game
N.L.—5—Curt Schilling, Philadelphia, October 6, 1993 (three in first inning, two in second inning).
A.L.—4—Nolan Ryan, California, October 3, 1979.

Most strikeouts, inning
A.L.-N.L.—3—Held by many pitchers.

HIT BATSMEN, WILD PITCHES AND BALKS

Most hit batsmen, career
N.L.—5—Tom Glavine, Atlanta, 1992 (2), 1995, 1996, 1997.

Greg Maddux, Chicago, 1989; Atlanta, 1995, 1997, 1998, 2001.
A.L.—4—Frank Tanana, California, 1979; Detroit, 1987 (3).
Mike Boddicker, Baltimore, 1983 (2); Boston, 1990 (2).
David Wells, Baltimore, 1996; New York, 1998 (2), 2003.
Jeff Nelson, New York, 1998 (2), 1999, 2003.
Pedro Martinez, Boston, 2003 (1), 2004 (3).

Most hit batsmen, series
A.L.—3—Frank Tanana, Detroit, 1987 (5-game series).
Jimmy Key, Baltimore, 1997 (6-game series).
Pedro Martinez, Boston, 2004 (7-game series).
N.L.—3—Matt Morris, St. Louis, 2002 (5-game series).

Most hit batsmen, game
A.L.—3—Frank Tanana, Detroit, October 11, 1987.
Jimmy Key, Baltimore, October 9, 1997.
N.L.—3—Matt Morris, St. Louis, October 14, 2002.

Most hit batsmen, inning
A.L.—3—Jimmy Key, Baltimore, October 9, 1997, first inning.
N.L.—2—Al Leiter, New York, October 19, 1999, first inning.

Most wild pitches, career
M.L.—4—Orel Hershiser, Los Angeles N.L, 1985, 1988 (2);
Cleveland A.L., 1995.
Roger Clemens, Boston A.L., 1988, 1990; New York A.L.,
2001; Houston N.L., 2004.
A.L.—4—Tommy John, New York, 1980; California, 1982.
Juan Guzman, Toronto, 1991, 1992, 1993.

N.L.—4—Alejandro Pena, Los Angeles, 1983; Atlanta 1991.
Rick Ankiel, St. Louis, 2000.

Most wild pitches, series
N.L.—4—Rick Ankiel, St. Louis, 2000 (5-game series).
A.L.—3—Tommy John, California, 1982 (5-game series).
Juan Guzman, Toronto, 1993 (6-game series).

Most wild pitches, game
A.L.—3—Tommy John, California, October 9, 1982.
Juan Guzman, Toronto, October 5, 1993.
N.L.—2—Held by many pitchers.

Most wild pitches, inning
A.L.—2—Chris Zachary, Detroit, October 8, 1972, fifth inning.
Tommy John, California, October 9, 1982, fourth inning.
David West, Minnesota, October 11, 1991, fifth inning.
Juan Guzman, Toronto, October 5, 1993, first inning.
Mariano Rivera, New York, October 17, 2001, ninth inning.
N.L.—2—Jeff Calhoun, Houston, October 15, 1986, 16th
inning.
Sterling Hitchcock, San Diego, October 14, 1998, second
inning.
Rick Ankiel, St. Louis, October 12, 2000, first inning.
Rick Ankiel, St. Louis, October 16, 2000, seventh inning.

Most balks, game
A.L.-N.L.—1—Held by many pitchers.

CLUB PITCHING

APPEARANCES

Most appearances by pitchers, series
3-game series
A.L.—14—Minnesota vs. Baltimore, 1970.
N.L.—13—Cincinnati vs. Pittsburgh, 1979.
4-game series
A.L.—16—Oakland vs. Boston, 1988.
N.L.—16—Atlanta vs. Cincinnati, 1995.
5-game series
A.L.—24—Baltimore vs. New York, 1996.
N.L.—22—St. Louis vs. New York, 2000.
San Francisco vs. St. Louis, 2002.
6-game series
N.L.—30—New York vs. Atlanta, 1999.
A.L.—29—Cleveland vs. Baltimore, 1997.
7-game series
N.L.—32—St. Louis vs. Atlanta, 1996.
A.L.—28—New York vs. Boston, 2003.

Most appearances by pitchers of both clubs, series
3-game series
N.L.—25—Cincinnati 13, Pittsburgh 12, 1979.
A.L.—18—Minnesota 11, Baltimore 7, 1969.
Minnesota 14, Baltimore 4, 1970.
4-game series
N.L.—30—Atlanta 16, Cincinnati 14, 1995.
A.L.—26—Oakland 16, Boston 10, 1988.
Boston 15, Oakland 11, 1990.
5-game series
A.L.—41—Baltimore 24, New York 17, 1996.
N.L.—40—San Francisco 22, St. Louis 18, 2002.
6-game series
N.L.—55—Atlanta 28, San Diego 27, 1998.
A.L.—52—Cleveland 29, Baltimore 23, 1997.
7-game series
N.L.—56—Florida 28, Chicago 28, 2003.
A.L.—54—New York 28, Boston 26, 2003.

COMPLETE GAMES

Most complete games, series
3-game series
A.L.—2—Baltimore vs. Minnesota, 1969.
Baltimore vs. Minnesota, 1970.
Baltimore vs. Oakland, 1971.
N.L.—1—Cincinnati vs. Pittsburgh, 1975.
Pittsburgh vs. Cincinnati, 1979.
St. Louis vs. Atlanta, 1982.
4-game series
A.L.—2—Oakland vs. Baltimore, 1974.
N.L.—2—San Francisco vs. Pittsburgh, 1971.
Los Angeles vs. Philadelphia, 1977.
5-game series
N.L.—3—New York vs. Cincinnati, 1973.
A.L.—2—Baltimore vs. Oakland, 1973
Oakland vs. Baltimore, 1973.
California vs. Milwaukee, 1982.
6-game series
N.L.—2—Florida vs. Atlanta, 1997.
Houston vs. New York, 1986.
A.L.—1—Oakland vs. Toronto, 1992.
Toronto vs. Oakland, 1992.
Chicago vs. Toronto, 1993.
Cleveland vs. New York, 1998.
New York vs. Seattle, 2000.
7-game series
N.L.—3—Pittsburgh vs. Atlanta, 1992.
A.L.—1—Kansas City vs. Toronto, 1985.
Boston vs. California, 1986.
California vs. Boston, 1986.

Most complete games by both clubs, series
3-game series
A.L.—3—Baltimore 2, Oakland 1, 1971.
N.L.—1—Cincinnati 1, Pittsburgh 0, 1975.
Pittsburgh 1, Cincinnati 0, 1979.
St. Louis 1, Atlanta 0, 1982.
4-game series
A.L.—3—Oakland 2, Baltimore 1, 1974.

N.L.—2—San Francisco 2, Pittsburgh 0, 1971.
  Los Angeles 2, Philadelphia 0, 1977.
  Los Angeles 1, Philadelphia 1, 1978.
5-game series
  A.L.—4—Baltimore 2, Oakland 2, 1973.
  N.L.—23—New York 3, Cincinnati 0, 1973.
6-game series
  N.L.—3—Houston 2, New York 1, 1986.
    Florida 2, Atlanta 1, 1997.
  A.L.—2—Oakland 1, Toronto 1, 1992.
7-game series
  N.L.—4—St. Louis 2, San Francisco 2, 1987.
  A.L.—2—Boston 1, California 1, 1986.

SAVES

Most saves, series
3-game series
  N.L.—3—Cincinnati vs. Pittsburgh, 1970.
  A.L.—2—Boston vs. Oakland, 1975.
4-game series
  A.L.—4—Oakland vs. Boston, 1988.
  N.L.—3—Pittsburgh vs. San Francisco, 1971.
5-game series
  A.L.—3—Milwaukee vs. California, 1982.
    Minnesota vs. Detroit, 1987.
    Oakland vs. Toronto, 1989.
    Minnesota vs. Toronto, 1991.
    New York vs. Boston, 1999.
  N.L.—3—San Francisco vs. Chicago, 1989.
    San Francisco vs. St. Louis, 2002.
6-game series
  N.L.—4—Cincinnati vs. Pittsburgh, 1990.
  A.L.—3—Toronto vs. Oakland, 1992.
7-game series
  N.L.—3—St. Louis vs. San Francisco, 1987.
    Los Angeles vs. New York, 1988.
    Atlanta vs. Pittsburgh, 1991.
    St. Louis vs. Houston, 2004.
  A.L.—3—Boston vs. New York, 2003.

Most saves by both clubs, series
3-game series
  N.L.—3—Cincinnati 3, Pittsburgh 0, 1970.
  A.L.—2—Boston 2, Oakland 0, 1975.
4-game series
  A.L.—4—Oakland 4, Boston 0, 1988.
  N.L.—3—Pittsburgh 3, San Francisco 0, 1971.
5-game series
  N.L.—5—Houston 3, Philadelphia 2, 1980.
  A.L.—4—Minnesota 3, Toronto 1, 1991.
6-game series
  N.L.—6—Cincinnati 4, Pittsburgh 2, 1990.
  A.L.—4—Toronto 3, Oakland 1, 1992.
7-game series
  N.L.—5—Atlanta 3, Pittsburgh 2, 1991.
    St. Louis 3, Houston 2, 2004.
  A.L.—5—Boston 3, New York 2, 2003.

Fewest saves by one and both clubs, series
A.L.-N.L.—0—Held by many clubs.

RUNS AND SHUTOUTS

Most runs allowed, total series
N.L.—224—Atlanta; 11 series, 60 games.
A.L.—251—New York; 12 series, 61 games.

Most shutouts won, total series
N.L.—9—Atlanta, 1991 (3), 1995, 1996 (2), 1997, 1999, 2001.
A.L.—6—Baltimore, 1969, 1973, 1979, 1983 (2), 1997.

For a complete list of shutouts, see page 442.

Most shutouts won, series
N.L.—3—Atlanta vs. Pittsburgh, 1991 (7-game series).
A.L.—2—Oakland vs. Baltimore, 1974 (4-game series).
  Baltimore vs. Chicago, 1983 (4-game series).
  Cleveland vs. Seattle, 1995 (6-game series).

Most consecutive shutouts won, series
A.L.—2—Oakland vs. Baltimore, October 6, 8, 1974.
N.L.—2—St. Louis vs. San Francisco, October 13, 14, 1987.
  Atlanta vs. Pittsburgh, October 16, 17, 1991.

Most shutouts by both clubs, series
N.L.—4—Atlanta 3, Pittsburgh 1, 1991 (7-game series).
A.L.—2—Oakland 1, Detroit 1, 1972 (5-game series).
  Oakland 1, Baltimore 1, 1973 (5-game series).
  Oakland 2, Baltimore 0, 1974 (4-game series).
  Baltimore 2, Chicago 0, 1983 (4-game series).
  Cleveland 2, Seattle 0, 1995 (6-game series).
  Seattle 1, New York 1, 2000 (6-game series).

Largest score, shutout game
N.L.—15-0—Atlanta 15, St. Louis 0, October 17, 1996.
A.L.—8-0—Baltimore 8, California 0, October 6, 1979.

Longest shutout game
A.L.—11 innings—Baltimore 1, Minnesota 0, October 5, 1969.
  Cleveland 1, Baltimore 0, October 15, 1997.
N.L.—11 innings—Houston 1, Philadelphia 0, October 10, 1980.

Most consecutive innings shutting out opponent, total series
A.L.—30—Oakland vs. Baltimore, October 5 (sixth inning) through October 9 (eighth inning), 1974
N.L.—26—Pittsburgh vs. Atlanta, October 13 (second inning) through October 16 (eighth inning), 1991.

Most consecutive innings shutting out opponent, series
A.L.—30—Oakland vs. Baltimore, October 5 (sixth inning) through October 9 (eighth inning), 1974.
N.L.—26—Pittsburgh vs. Atlanta, October 13 (second inning) through October 16 (eighth inning), 1991.

WILD PITCHES AND BALKS

Most wild pitches, series
A.L.—5—Toronto vs. Chicago, 1993 (6-game series).
N.L.—5—St. Louis vs. New York, 2000 (5-game series).

Most wild pitches by both clubs, series
A.L.—7—Toronto 5, Chicago 2, 1993 (6-game series).
  Anaheim 4, Minnesota 3, 2002 (5-game series).
N.L.—7—St. Louis 5, New York 2, 2000 (5-game series).
  Florida 4, Chicago 3, 2003 (7-game series).

Most balks, series
A.L.—2—Baltimore vs. Chicago, 1983 (4-game series).
N.L.—2—Pittsburgh vs. Cincinnati, 1975 (3-game series).
  New York vs. Los Angeles, 1988 (7-game series).

Most balks by both clubs, series
N.L.—2—Pittsburgh 2, Cincinnati 0, 1975 (3-game series).
  Philadelphia 1, Los Angeles 1, 1977 (4-game series).
  New York 2, Los Angeles 0, 1988 (7-game series).
A.L.—2—Baltimore 2, Chicago 0, 1983 (4-game series).
  Boston 1, Oakland 1, 1988 (4-game series).

INDIVIDUAL FIELDING

FIRST BASEMEN
GAMES

Most games, career
M.L.—38—John Olerud, Toronto A.L., 1991, 1992, 1993; New York N.L., 1999; Seattle A.L., 2000, 2001; New York A.L., 2004; seven series (32 in A.L., 6 in N.L.).
A.L.—33—Tino Martinez, Seattle, 1995; New York, 1996, 1998 through 2001; six series.
N.L.—23—Fred McGriff, Atlanta, 1993, 1995, 1996, 1997; four series.

PUTOUTS, ASSISTS AND CHANCES ACCEPTED

Most putouts, career
M.L.—313—John Olerud, Toronto A.L., 1991, 1992, 1993; New York N.L., 1999; Seattle A.L., 2000, 2001; New York A.L., 2004; seven series, 38 games (254 in A.L., 59 in N.L.).
Tino Martinez, Seattle A.L., 1995; New York A.L., 1996, 1998 through 2001; St. Louis N.L., 2002; seven series, 37 games (256 in A.L., 32 in N.L.).
A.L.—256—Tino Martinez, Seattle, 1995; New York, 1996, 1998 through 2001; six series; 33 games.
N.L.—208—Steve Garvey, Los Angeles, 1974, 1977, 1978, 1981; San Diego, 1984; five series, 22 games.

Most putouts, series
3-game series
  N.L.—35—Keith Hernandez, St. Louis, 1982.
  A.L.—34—Boog Powell, Baltimore, 1969.
4-game series
  N.L.—44—Steve Garvey, Los Angeles, 1978.
  A.L.—44—Eddie Murray, Baltimore, 1979.
5-game series
  A.L.—55—Mike Epstein, Oakland, 1972.
  N.L.—53—Pete Rose, Philadelphia, 1980.
6-game series
  N.L.—67—Keith Hernandez, New York, 1986.
  A.L.—55—Rafael Palmeiro, Baltimore, 1997.
7-game series
  A.L.—72—Steve Balboni, Kansas City, 1985.
  N.L.—66—Derrek Lee, Florida, 2003.

Most putouts, game
N.L.—17—Andres Galarraga, Atlanta, October 14, 1998.
  (21—Glenn Davis, Houston, October 15, 1986, 16 innings.)
A.L.—15—Chris Chambliss, New York, October 14, 1976.
  Mark McGwire, Oakland, October 4, 1989.
  (16—John Olerud, Toronto, October 11, 1991, 10 innings.
  Herb Perry, Cleveland, October 13, 1995, 11 innings.)

Most putouts, inning
A.L.-N.L.—3—Held by many first basemen.

Most assists, career
Both leagues—33—Tino Martinez, Seattle A.L., 1995; New York A.L., 1996, 1998 through 2001; St. Louis N.L., 2002; seven series, 37 games (27 in A.L., 6 in N.L.).
A.L.—27—Tino Martinez, Seattle, 1995; New York, 1996, 1998 through 2001; six series, 33 games.
N.L.—17—Keith Hernandez, St. Louis, 1982; New York, 1986, 1988; three series, 16 games.

Most assists, series
3-game series
  A.L.—5—Rich Reese, Minnesota, 1969.
    Bob Watson, New York, 1980.
  N.L.—5—Tony Perez, Cincinnati, 1975.
    Chris Chambliss, Atlanta, 1982.
4-game series
  N.L.—5—Steve Garvey, Los Angeles, 1978.
  A.L.—3—Eddie Murray, Baltimore, 1979, 1983.
    Tom Paciorek, Chicago, 1983.
5-game series
  A.L.—8—Kent Hrbek, Minnesota, 1991.
  N.L.—7—Pete Rose, Philadelphia, 1980.
    Julio Franco, Atlanta, 2001.

6-game series
  N.L.—12—Keith Hernandez, New York, 1986.
  A.L.—9—John Olerud, Toronto, 1993.
7-game series
  A.L.—8—Kevin Millar, Boston, 2003.
  N.L.—7—Will Clark, San Francisco, 1987.

Most assists, game
N.L.—5—Tino Martinez, St. Louis, October 12, 2002.
  (7—Keith Hernandez, New York, October 15, 1986, 16 innings.)
A.L.—4—Steve Balboni, Kansas City, October 12, 1985.

Most assists, inning
A.L.-N.L.—2—Held by many first basemen.

Most chances accepted, career
Both leagues—343—John Olerud, Toronto A.L., 1991, 1992, 1993; New York N.L., 1999; Seattle A.L., 2000, 2001; New York A.L., 2004; seven series, 38 games (280 in A.L., 63 in N.L.).
A.L.—283—Tino Martinez, Seattle, 1995; New York, 1996, 1998 through 2001; six series; 33 games.
N.L.—221—Steve Garvey, Los Angeles, 1974, 1977, 1978, 1981; San Diego, 1984; five series, 22 games.

Most chances accepted, series
3-game series
  N.L.—36—Keith Hernandez, St. Louis, 1982.
  A.L.—34—Boog Powell, Baltimore, 1969.
4-game series
  N.L.—49—Steve Garvey, Los Angeles, 1978.
  A.L.—47—Eddie Murray, Baltimore, 1979.
5-game series
  N.L.—60—Pete Rose, Philadelphia, 1980.
  A.L.—57—Mike Epstein, Oakland, 1972.
6-game series
  N.L.—79—Keith Hernandez, New York, 1986.
  A.L.—57—John Olerud, Toronto, 1993.
    Rafael Palmeiro, Baltimore, 1997.
7-game series
  A.L.—79—Steve Balboni, Kansas City, 1985.
  N.L.—72—Derrek Lee, Florida, 2003.

Most chances accepted, game
N.L.—18—Steve Garvey, Los Angeles, October 6, 1978 (16 putouts, two assists).
  (27—Keith Hernandez, New York, October 15, 1986 (20 putouts, seven assists), 16 innings.)
A.L.—16—Steve Balboni, Kansas City, October 12, 1985 (12 putouts, four assists).
  George Hendrick, California, October 11, 1986, 11 innings (14 putouts, two assists).
  Kevin Millar, Boston, October 9, 2003 (12 putouts, four assists).
  (16—John Olerud, Toronto, October 11, 1991 (16 putouts), 10 innings.
  Herbert Perry, Cleveland, October 13, 1995 (16 putouts), 11 innings.)

Fewest chances offered, game
N.L.—2—Bob Robertson, Pittsburgh, October 2, 1971 (one putout, one assist).
A.L.—2—Carlos Quintana, Boston, October 6, 1990 (two putouts).

Most chances accepted, inning
A.L.-N.L.—3—Held by many first basemen.

ERRORS AND DOUBLE PLAYS

Most errors, career
N.L.—4—Andres Galarraga, Atlanta, 1998; one series, six games.
A.L.—3—Cecil Cooper, Boston, 1975; Milwaukee, 1982; two series, eight games.
  Eddie Murray, Baltimore, 1979, 1983; two series, eight games.
  Steve Balboni, Kansas City, 1984, 1985; two series, 10 games.

Most consecutive errorless games, career

Both leagues—24—Tino Martinez, New York A.L., St. Louis N.L., October 9, 1998 through October 13, 2002 (20 in A.L., 4 in N.L.)

A.L.—20—Tino Martinez, New York, October 9, 1998 through October 22, 2001.

N.L.—19—Steve Garvey, Los Angeles, San Diego, October 9, 1974 through October 7, 1984.

Most errors, series

N.L.—4—Andres Galarraga, Atlanta, 1998 (6-game series).
A.L.—2—Held by many first basemen.

Most chances accepted, errorless series

N.L.—79—Keith Hernandez, New York, 1986 (6-game series).
A.L.—64—Nick Johnson, New York, 2003 (7-game series).

Most errors, game

N.L.—1—Held by many first basemen.
(2-Andres Galarraga, Atlanta, October 7, 1998, 10 innings.
Brian R. Hunter, Atlanta, October 17, 1999, 15 innings.)
A.L.—1—Held by many first basemen.
(1—Held by many first basemen.)

Most double plays, career

M.L.—31—John Olerud, Toronto A.L., 1991, 1992, 1993; New York N.L., 1999; Seattle A.L., 2000, 2001; New York A.L., 2004; seven series, 38 games (26 in A.L., 5 in N.L.).

A.L.—27—Tino Martinez, Seattle, 1995; New York, 1996, 1998 through 2001; six series; 33 games.

N.L.—21—Steve Garvey, Los Angeles, 1974, 1977, 1978, 1981; San Diego, 1984; five series, 22 games.

Most double plays, series

N.L.—10—Will Clark, San Francisco, 1987 (7-game series).
A.L.—9—Nick Johnson, New York 2003 (7-game series).

Most double plays started, series

N.L.—2—Tino Martinez, St. Louis, 2002 (5-game series).
A.L.—1—Held by many first basemen.

Most double plays, game

N.L.—4—Will Clark, San Francisco, October 10, 1987.
A.L.—3—Held by many first basemen.

Most double plays started, game

N.L.—2—Tino Martinez, St. Louis, 2002 (5-game series).
A.L.—1—Held by many first basemen.

Most unassisted double plays, game

A.L.—1—Tino Martinez, New York, October 11, 1990.
Tino Martinez, New York, October 22, 2001.
Kevin Millar, Boston, October 13, 2003.
John Olerud, New York, October 16, 2004.
N.L.—1—John Mabry, St. Louis, October 14, 1996.

SECOND BASEMEN
GAMES

Most games, career

N.L.—31—Mark Lemke, Atlanta, 1991, 1992, 1993, 1995, 1996; five series.

A.L.—28—Roberto Alomar, Toronto, 1991, 1992, 1993; Baltimore, 1996, 1997; five series.

PUTOUTS, ASSISTS AND CHANCES ACCEPTED

Most putouts, career

A.L.—69—Roberto Alomar, Toronto, 1991, 1992, 1993; Baltimore, 1996, 1997; five series, 28 games.

N.L.—63—Joe Morgan, Cincinnati, 1972, 1973, 1975, 1976, 1979; Houston, 1980; Philadelphia, 1983; seven series, 27 games.

Most putouts, series

3-game series
   N.L.—12—Joe Morgan, Cincinnati, 1979.
   A.L.—12—Willie Randolph, New York, 1981.
4-game series
   A.L.—13—Bobby Grich, Baltimore, 1974.

N.L.—13—Mark Lemke, Atlanta, 1995.
5-game series
   N.L.—18—Manny Trillo, Philadelphia, 1980.
   A.L.—16—Bobby Grich, Baltimore, 1973.
6-game series
   N.L.—19—Jose Lind, Pittsburgh, 1990.
   A.L.—18—Joey Cora, Chicago, 1993.
7-game series
   A.L.—19—Marty Barrett, Boston, 1986.
   N.L.—20—Mark Grudzielanek, Chicago, 2003.

Most putouts, game

A.L.—7—Bobby Grich, Baltimore, October 6, 1974.
   (8—Roberto Alomar, Toronto, October 11, 1992, 11 innings.)
N.L.—6—Dave Cash, Philadelphia, October 12, 1976.
Dave Lopes, Los Angeles, October 13, 1981.
Jose Lind, Pittsburgh, October 12, 1990.
   (7—Steve Sax, Los Angeles, October 9, 1988, 12 innings.)

Most putouts, inning

N.L.—3—Joe Morgan, Cincinnati, October 10, 1976, eighth inning.
Ryne Sandberg, Chicago, October 4, 1984, fifth inning.
A.L.—3—Bobby Grich, Baltimore, October 11, 1973, third inning.
Dick Green, Oakland, October 8, 1974, seventh inning.

Most assists, career

A.L.—86—Roberto Alomar, Toronto, 1991, 1992, 1993; Baltimore, 1996, 1997; five series, 28 games.
N.L.—85—Joe Morgan, Cincinnati, 1972, 1973, 1975, 1976, 1979; Houston, 1980; Philadelphia, 1983; seven series, 27 games.

Most assists, series

3-games series
   N.L.—12—Tommy Helms, Cincinnati, 1970.
   A.L.—12—Willie Randolph, New York, 1981.
4-game series
   N.L.—18—Dave Lopes, Los Angeles, 1974.
   A.L.—14—Julio Cruz, Chicago, 1983.
5-game series
   N.L.—27—Joe Morgan, Cincinnati, 1973.
   A.L.—25—Roberto Alomar, Baltimore, 1996.
6-game series
   N.L.—21—Steve Sax, Los Angeles, 1985.
   A.L.—22—Carlos Baerga, Cleveland, 1995.
7-game series
   A.L.—28—Frank White, Kansas City, 1985.
   N.L.—24—Jose Lind, Pittsburgh, 1991.

Most assists, game

A.L.—9—Joey Cora, Chicago, October 6, 1993.
N.L.—8—Manny Trillo, Philadelphia, October 7, 1980.
Mark Grudzielanek, Chicago, October 8, 2003.
   (9—Wally Backman, October 14, 1986, 12 innings.)

Most assists, inning

A.L.—3—Tony Phillips, Oakland, October 4, 1989, fifth inning.
Joey Cora, Chicago, October 6, 1993, sixth inning.
N.L.—3—Mark Lemke, Atlanta, October 13, 1993, first inning.
Edgardo Alfonzo, New York, October 11, 2000, first inning.

Most chances accepted, career

A.L.—155—Roberto Alomar, Toronto, 1991, 1992, 1993; Baltimore, 1996, 1997; five series, 28 games.
N.L.—148—Joe Morgan, Cincinnati, 1972, 1973, 1975, 1976, 1979; Houston, 1980; Philadelphia, 1983; seven series, 27 games.

Most chances accepted, series

3-game series
   A.L.—24—Willie Randolph, New York, 1981.
   N.L.—23—Tommy Helms, Cincinnati, 1970.
           Joe Morgan, Cincinnati, 1979.
4-game series
   N.L.—29—Mark Lemke, Atlanta, 1995.
   A.L.—25—Bobby Grich, Baltimore, 1974.
5-game series
   N.L.—43—Manny Trillo, Philadelphia, 1980.

A.L.—40—Roberto Alomar, Baltimore, 1996.
6-game series
N.L.—38—Jose Lind, Pittsburgh, 1990.
A.L.—38—Joey Cora, Chicago, 1993.
7-game series
N.L.—43—Mark Grudzielanek, Chicago, 2003.
A.L.—40—Marty Barrett, Boston, 1986.

Most chances accepted, game
N.L.—13—Manny Trillo, Philadelphia, October 7, 1980 (five putouts, eight assists).
A.L.—12—Bobby Grich, Baltimore, October 6, 1974 (seven putouts, five assists, one error).
(13—Roberto Alomar, Toronto, October 11, 1992 (eight putouts, five assists), 11 innings.)

Fewest chances offered, game
A.L.—0—Danny Thompson, Minnesota, October 4, 1970.
Bobby Grich, California, October 10, 1986.
Adam Kennedy, Anaheim, October 8, 2002.
N.L.—0—Ryne Sandberg, Chicago, October 9, 1989.

Most chances accepted, inning
A.L.-N.L.—3—Held by many second basemen.

ERRORS AND DOUBLE PLAYS

Most errors, career
A.L.—5—Bobby Grich, Baltimore, 1973, 1974; California, 1979, 1982, 1986; five series, 21 games.
N.L.—4—Dave Lopes, Los Angeles, 1974, 1977, 1978, 1981; four series, 17 games.

Most consecutive errorless games, career
N.L.—27—Joe Morgan, Cincinnati, Houston, Philadelphia, October 7, 1972 through October 8, 1983.
A.L.—20—Willie Randolph, New York, Oakland, October 9, 1976 through October 10, 1990.

Most errors, series
A.L.—3—Joey Cora, Chicago, 1993 (6-game series).
N.L.—2—Held by many second basemen.

Most chances accepted, errorless series
A.L.—40—Marty Barrett, Boston, 1986 (7-game series).
N.L.—39—Joe Morgan, Cincinnati, 1973 (5-game series).

Most errors, game
A.L.—2—Dick Green, Oakland, October 8, 1974.
Lance Blankenship, Oakland, October 10, 1992.
(2—Dick Green, Oakland, October 9, 1973, 11 innings.)
N.L.—1—Held by many second basemen.

Most errors, inning
A.L.-N.L.—1—Held by many second basemen.

Most double plays, career
A.L.—20—Roberto Alomar, Toronto, 1991, 1992, 1993; Baltimore, 1996, 1997; five series, 28 games.
N.L.—15—Joe Morgan, Cincinnati, 1972, 1973, 1975, 1976, 1979; Houston, 1980; Philadelphia, 1983; seven series, 27 games.

Most double plays, series
A.L.—9—Alfonso Soriano, New York, 2003 (7-game series).
N.L.—7—Rodney Scott, Montreal, 1981 (5-game series).

Most double plays started, series
N.L.—5—Steve Sax, Los Angeles, 1988 (7-game series).
A.L.—4—Alfonso Soriano, New York, 2003 (7-game series).

Most double plays, game
N.L.—4—Dave Lopes, Los Angeles, October 13, 1981.
A.L.—3—Rob Wilfong, California, October 14, 1986.
Bip Roberts, Cleveland, October 11, 1997.
Alfonso Soriano, New York, October 13, 2003.

Most double plays started, game
N.L.—2—Held by many second basemen.
A.L.—1—Held by many second basemen.

Most unassisted double plays, game
N.L.—1—Joe Morgan, Cincinnati, October 10, 1976.
A.L.—Never accomplished.

THIRD BASEMEN
GAMES

Most games, career
N.L.—34—Terry Pendleton, St. Louis, 1985, 1987; Atlanta, 1991, 1992, 1993, 1996; six series.
Chipper Jones, Atlanta, 1995 through 2001, except 2000; six series.
A.L.—27—George Brett, Kansas City, 1976, 1977, 1978, 1980, 1984, 1985; six series.

PUTOUTS, ASSISTS AND CHANCES ACCEPTED

Most putouts, career
A.L.—25—Sal Bando, Oakland, 1971, 1972, 1973, 1974, 1975; five series, 20 games.
N.L.—25—Terry Pendleton, St. Louis, 1985, 1987; Atlanta, 1991, 1992, 1993, 1996; six series, 34 games.

Most putouts, series
3-game series
A.L.—6—Brooks Robinson, Baltimore, 1969.
Harmon Killebrew, Minnesota, 1969.
Sal Bando, Oakland, 1971.
N.L.—5—Tony Perez, Cincinnati, 1970.
4-game series
N.L.—7—Ron Cey, Los Angeles, 1977.
A.L.—7—Carney Lansford, Oakland, 1988.
5-game series
A.L.—9—Doug DeCinces, California, 1982.
N.L.—5—Richie Hebner, Pittsburgh, 1972.
Ron Cey, Los Angeles, 1981.
Graig Nettles, San Diego, 1984.
Matt Williams, San Francisco, 1989.
6-game series
N.L.—7—Chris Sabo, Cincinnati, 1990.
Terry Pendleton, Atlanta, 1993.
A.L.—6—Robin Ventura, Chicago, 1993.
Matt Williams, Cleveland, 1997.
7-game series
N.L.—11—Jeff King, Pittsburgh, 1992.
A.L.—7—George Brett, Kansas City, 1985.
Wade Boggs, Boston, 1986.
Bill Mueller, Boston, 2004.

Most putouts, game
A.L.—4—Carney Lansford, California, October 6, 1979.
Wade Boggs, Boston, October 10, 1990.
N.L.—3—Held by many players.

Most putouts, inning
A.L.-N.L.—2—Held by many third basemen.

Most assists, career
N.L.—66—Mike Schmidt, Philadelphia, 1976, 1977, 1978, 1980, 1983; five series, 20 games.
A.L.—49—Brooks Robinson, Baltimore, 1969, 1970, 1971, 1973, 1974; five series, 18 games.
George Brett, Kansas City, 1976, 1977, 1978, 1980, 1984, 1985; six series, 27 games.

Most assists, series
3-game series
A.L.—11—Sal Bando, Oakland, 1975.
N.L.—9—Mike Schmidt, Philadelphia, 1976.
4-game series
N.L.—18—Mike Schmidt, Philadelphia, 1978.
A.L.—13—Brooks Robinson, Baltimore, 1974.
Todd Cruz, Baltimore, 1983.
5-game series
N.L.—17—Mike Schmidt, Philadelphia, 1980.
A.L.—16—Sal Bando, Oakland, 1972.
6-game series
N.L.—19—Ray Knight, New York, 1986.
A.L.—18—Matt Williams, Cleveland, 1997.
7-game series
N.L.—19—Jeff King, Pittsburgh, 1992.
A.L.—18—Doug DeCinces, California, 1986.

Most assists, game
N.L.—8—Ron Cey, Los Angeles, October 16, 1981.

A.L.—6—Sal Bando, Oakland, October 8, 1972.
Todd Cruz, Baltimore, October 5, 1983.
Tom Brookens, Detroit, October 11, 1987.
Wade Boggs, New York, October 13, 1996.
Cal Ripken, Baltimore, October 8, 1997.
(7—Aurelio Rodriguez, Detroit, October 11, 1972,
10 innings.)

Most assists, inning
N.L.—3—Ron Cey, Los Angeles, October 4, 1977, fourth inning.
Ron Cey, Los Angeles, October 16, 1981, eighth inning.
A.L.—3—Todd Cruz, Baltimore, October 5, 1983, fifth inning.

Most chances accepted, career
N.L.—89—Terry Pendleton, St. Louis, 1985, 1987; Atlanta,
1991, 1992, 1993, 1996; six series, 34 games.
A.L.—72—Sal Bando, Oakland, 1971, 1972, 1973, 1974, 1975;
five series, 20 games.

Most chances accepted, series
3-game series
A.L.—16—Brooks Robinson, Baltimore, 1969.
N.L.—13—Mike Schmidt, Philadelphia, 1976.
4-game series
N.L.—21—Ron Cey, Los Angeles, 1977.
Mike Schmidt, Philadelphia, 1978.
A.L.—19—Todd Cruz, Baltimore, 1983.
5-game series
A.L.—22—Sal Bando, Oakland, 1972.
N.L.—21—Ron Cey, Los Angeles, 1981.
6-game series
N.L.—24—Terry Pendleton, St. Louis, 1985.
Ray Knight, New York, 1986.
A.L.—24—Matt Williams, Cleveland, 1997.
7-game series
N.L.—30—Jeff King, Pittsburgh, 1992.
A.L.—24—Doug DeCinces, California, 1986.

Most chances accepted, game
N.L.—10—Ron Cey, Los Angeles, October 16, 1981
(two putouts, eight assists).
A.L.—9—Todd Cruz, Baltimore, October 5, 1983 (three putouts,
six assists).
Wade Boggs, Boston, October 10, 1990 (four putouts,
five assists).

Fewest chances offered, game
A.L.-N.L.—0—Held by many players.

Most chances accepted, inning
A.L.-N.L.—3—Held by many third basemen.

ERRORS AND DOUBLE PLAYS

Most errors, career
A.L.—8—George Brett, Kansas City, 1976, 1977, 1978, 1980,
1984, 1985; six series, 27 games.
N.L.—5—Mike Schmidt, Philadelphia, 1976, 1977, 1978, 1980,
1983; five series, 20 games.

Most consecutive errorless games, career
N.L.—33—Terry Pendleton, St. Louis, Atlanta, October 10, 1985
through October 17, 1996.
A.L.—17—Sal Bando, Oakland, October 3, 1971 through
October 9, 1974.
Carney Lansford, California, Oakland, October 3, 1979
through October 8, 1992.

Most errors, series
A.L.—3—George Brett, Kansas City, 1976 (5-game series).
Doug DeCinces, California, 1982 (5-game series).
Kelly Gruber, Toronto, 1991 (5-game series).
N.L.—3—Matt Williams, Arizona, 2001 (5-game series).

Most chances accepted, errorless series
A.L.—22—Sal Bando, Oakland, 1972 (5-game series).
N.L.—22—Steve Buechele, Pittsburgh, 1991 (7-game series).
Terry Pendleton, Atlanta, 1992 (7-game series).
Aramis Ramirez, Chicago, 2003 (7-game series).

Most errors, game
A.L.—2—George Brett, Kansas City, October 9, 1976.
Doug DeCinces, California, October 9, 1982.

Darrell Evans, Detroit, October 11, 1987.
Kelly Gruber, Toronto, October 8, 1991.
N.L.—2—Ron Cey, Los Angeles, October 5, 1974.
Fernando Tatis, St. Louis, October 15, 2000.

Most errors, inning
A.L.—2—George Brett, Kansas City, October 9, 1976,
first inning.
N.L.—2—Fernando Tatis, St. Louis, October 15, 2000, sixth
inning.

Most double plays, career
N.L.—8—Terry Pendleton, St. Louis, 1985, 1987; Atlanta, 1991,
1992, 1993, 1996; six series, 34 games.
A.L.—7—Doug DeCinces, Baltimore, 1979; California, 1982,
1986; three series, 16 games.

Most double plays, series
N.L.—5—Jeff King, Pittsburgh, 1992 (7-game series).
A.L.—3—Carney Lansford, California, 1979 (4-game series).
Doug DeCinces, California, 1982 (5-game series).
Doug DeCinces, California, 1986 (7-game series).
Cal Ripken Jr., Baltimore, 1997 (6-game series).
Matt Williams, Cleveland, 1997 (6-game series).

Most double plays started, series
N.L.—5—Jeff King, Pittsburgh, 1992 (7-game series).
A.L.—3—Carney Lansford, California, 1979 (4-game series).
Doug DeCinces, California, 1986 (7-game series).
Cal Ripken Jr., Baltimore, 1997 (6-game series).
Matt Williams, Cleveland, 1997 (6-game series).

Most double plays, game
A.L.-N.L.—2—Held by many third basemen.

Most double plays started, game
A.L.-N.L.—2—Held by many third basemen.

Most unassisted double plays, game
N.L.—1—Mike Schmidt, Philadelphia, October 9, 1976.
Jeff King, Pittsburgh, October 14, 1992.
A.L.—Never accomplished.

SHORTSTOPS
GAMES

Most games, career
A.L.—41—Derek Jeter, New York, 1996, 1998 through 2001,
2003, 2004; seven series.
N.L.—29—Jeff Blauser, Atlanta, 1991, 1992, 1993, 1995, 1996,
1997; six series.

PUTOUTS, ASSISTS AND CHANCES ACCEPTED

Most putouts, career
A.L.—83—Derek Jeter, New York, 1996, 1998 through 2001,
2003, 2004; seven series, 41 games.
N.L.—42—Bill Russell, Los Angeles, 1974, 1977, 1978, 1981,
1983; five series, 21 games.

Most putouts, series
3-game series
A.L.—13—Leo Cardenas, Minnesota, 1969.
N.L.—6—Held by many shortstops.
4-game series
N.L.—13—Bill Russell, Los Angeles, 1974.
A.L.—9—Fred Patek, Kansas City, 1978.
5-game series
N.L.—19—Garry Templeton, San Diego, 1984.
A.L.—13—Fred Patek, Kansas City, 1976.
6-game series
N.L.—21—Barry Larkin, Cincinnati, 1990.
A.L.—16—Omar Vizquel, Cleveland, 1997.
7-game series
A.L.—23—Derek Jeter, New York, 2004.
N.L.—17—Alfredo Griffin, Los Angeles, 1988.

Most putouts, game
N.L.—7—Garry Templeton, San Diego, October 4, 1984.
A.L.—6—Mark Belanger, Baltimore, October 5, 1974.

Bucky Dent, New York, October 5, 1977.
Fred Patek, Kansas City, October 5, 1977.
Manny Lee, Toronto, October 8, 1992.
(7—Leo Cardenas, Minnesota, October 5, 1969, 11 innings.)

Most putouts, inning
A.L.—3—Mark Belanger, Baltimore, October 5, 1974, third inning.
Fred Patek, Kansas City, October 5, 1977, second inning.
N.L.—3—Chris Speier, Montreal, October 14, 1981, fifth inning.

Most assists, career
A.L.—104—Derek Jeter, New York, 1996, 1998 through 2001, 2003, 2004; seven series.
N.L.—70—Larry Bowa, Philadelphia, 1976, 1977, 1978, 1980; Chicago, 1984; five series, 21 games.

Most assists, series
3-game series
A.L.—14—Mark Belanger, Baltimore, 1970.
N.L.—14—Dave Concepcion, Cincinnati, 1979.
4-game series
A.L.—17—Bert Campaneris, Oakland, 1974.
N.L.—17—Larry Bowa, Philadelphia, 1977.
5-game series
A.L.—18—Fred Patek, Kansas City, 1976, 1977.
Cristian Guzman, Minnesota, 2002.
N.L.—16—Darrel Chaney, Cincinnati, 1972.
Chris Speier, Montreal, 1981.
6-game series
A.L.—26—Omar Vizquel, Cleveland, 1998.
N.L.—24—Rey Ordonez, New York, 1999.
7-game series
N.L.—26—Alex Gonzalez, Florida, 2003.
A.L.—25—Derek Jeter, New York, 2003.

Most assists, game
N.L.—9—Bill Russell, Los Angeles, October 5, 1978.
A.L.—9—Kiko Garcia, Baltimore, October 4, 1979.

Most assists, inning
A.L.-N.L.—3—Held by many shortstops.

Most chances accepted, career
A.L.—187—Derek Jeter, New York, 1996, 1998 through 2001, 2003, 2004; seven series, 41 games.
N.L.—107—Bill Russell, Los Angeles, 1974, 1977, 1978, 1981, 1983; five series, 21 games.

Most chances accepted, series
3-game series
A.L.—25—Leo Cardenas, Minnesota, 1969.
N.L.—17—Dave Concepcion, Cincinnati, 1979.
4-game series
N.L.—29—Bill Russell, Los Angeles, 1974.
A.L.—22—Kiko Garcia, Baltimore, 1979.
Luis Rivera, Boston, 1990.
5-game series
A.L.—31—Fred Patek, Kansas City, 1976.
N.L.—31—Chris Speier, Montreal, 1981.
6-game series
A.L.—37—Omar Vizquel, Cleveland, 1998.
N.L.—36—Barry Larkin, Cincinnati, 1990.
7-game series
A.L.—44—Derek Jeter, New York, 2003.
N.L.—32—Jay Bell, Pittsburgh, 1991.
Alex Gonzalez, Florida, 2003.

Most chances accepted, game
N.L.—13—Bill Russell, Los Angeles, October 8, 1974 (six putouts, seven assists).
A.L.—11—Kiko Garcia, Baltimore, October 4, 1979 (two putouts, nine assists).
Omar Vizquel, Cleveland, October 9, 1998 (four putouts, seven assists).
(11—Leo Cardenas, Minnesota, October 5, 1969 (six putouts, five assists), 11 innings.)

Fewest chances offered, game
A.L.-N.L.—0—Held by many shortstops.

Most chances accepted, inning
A.L.-N.L.—3—Held by many shortstops.

Most errors, career
A.L.—5—Spike Owen, Boston, 1986; one series, seven games.
Nomar Garciaparra, Boston, 1999, 2003; two series, 12 games.
N.L.—5—Jeff Blauser, Atlanta, 1991, 1992, 1993, 1995, 1996, 1997; six series, 29 games.

Most consecutive errorless games, career
A.L.—20—Derek Jeter, New York, October 10, 2000 through October 13, 2004.
N.L.—13—Bill Russell, Los Angeles, October 5, 1977 through October 4, 1983.
Rafael Belliard, Atlanta, October 10, 1991 through October 13, 1995.
Edgar Renteria, Florida, St. Louis, October 7, 1997 through October 10, 2002.

Most errors, series
A.L.—5—Spike Owen, Boston, 1986 (7-game series).
N.L.—3—Darrel Chaney, Cincinnati, 1972 (5-game series).

Most chances accepted, errorless series
A.L.—44—Derek Jeter, 2003, (7-game series).
N.L.—31—Rafael Santana, New York, 1986 (6-game series).
Rey Ordonez, New York, 1999 (6-game series).

Most errors, game
A.L.—2—Leo Cardenas, Minnesota, October 4, 1970.
Manny Lee, Toronto, October 11, 1992, 11 innings.
Nomar Garciaparra, Boston, October 13, 1999, 10 innings.
N.L.—2—Gene Alley, Pittsburgh, October 10, 1972.
Bill Russell, Los Angeles, October 4, 1977.
Kevin Elster, New York, October 9, 1988; 12 innings.
Rey Sanchez, Atlanta, October 20, 2001.

Most errors, inning
N.L.—2—Gene Alley, Pittsburgh, October 10, 1972, fourth inning.
Kevin Elster, New York, October 9, 1988, fifth inning.
A.L.—1—Held by many shortstops.

Most double plays, career
A.L.—30—Derek Jeter, New York, 1996, 1998 through 2001, 2003, 2004; seven series, 41 games.
N.L.—18—Bill Russell, Los Angeles, 1974, 1977, 1978, 1981, 1983; five series, 21 games.

Most double plays, series
A.L.—9—Derek Jeter, New York, 2003 (7-game series).
N.L.—7—Jose Uribe, San Francisco, 1987 (7-game series).
Alfredo Griffin, Los Angeles, 1988 (7-game series).

Most double plays started, series
A.L.—5—Omar Vizquel, Cleveland, 1997 (6-game series).
N.L.—3—Held by many shortstops.

Most double plays, game
A.L.—3—Bert Campaneris, Oakland, October 5, 1975.
Omar Vizquel, Cleveland, October 13, 1997.
Omar Vizquel, Cleveland, October 9, 1998.
Derek Jeter, New York, October 11, 2003.
(3—Omar Vizquel, Cleveland, October 11, 1997, 12 innings.)
N.L.—3—Bill Russell, Los Angeles, October 8, 1974.
Bill Russell, Los Angeles, October 5, 1983.
Jose Uribe, San Francisco, October 10, 1987.
Ozzie Smith, St. Louis, October 14, 1987.
(3—Jeff Blauser, Atlanta, October 10, 1995, 11 innings.)

Most double plays started, game
N.L.—3—Bill Russell, Los Angeles, October 5, 1983.
A.L.—3—Omar Vizquel, Cleveland, October 13, 1997.

Most unassisted double plays, game
A.L.-N.L.—1—Held by many shortstops.

OUTFIELDERS
GAMES

Most games, career
A.L.—41—Bernie Williams, New York, 1996, 1998 through 2001, 2003, 2004; seven series.
N.L.—31—Ron Gant, Atlanta, 1991, 1992, 1993; Cincinnati, 1995; St. Louis, 1996; five series.

PUTOUTS, ASSISTS AND CHANCES ACCEPTED

Most putouts, career
A.L.—103—Bernie Williams, New York, 1996, 1998 through 2001, 2003, 2004; seven series, 41 games.
N.L.—62—Garry Maddox, Philadelphia, 1976, 1977, 1978, 1980, 1983; five series, 17 games.
Ron Gant, Atlanta, 1991, 1992, 1993; Cincinnati, 1995; St. Louis, 1996; five series, 31 games.
Andruw Jones, Atlanta, 1996 through 2001, except 2000; five series, 27 games.

Most putouts, series
3-game series
N.L.—13—Cesar Geronimo, Cincinnati, 1975.
Dave Parker, Pittsburgh, 1975.
A.L.—12—Fred Lynn, Boston, 1975.
4-game series
N.L.—16—Garry Maddox, Philadelphia, 1978.
A.L.—14—Bill North, Oakland, 1974.
Rick Miller, California, 1979.
Jose Canseco, Oakland, 1990.
5-game series
N.L.—23—Garry Maddox, Philadelphia, 1980.
A.L.—22—Dave Henderson, Oakland, 1989.
6-game series
N.L.—18—Willie McGee, St. Louis, 1985.
A.L.—16—Devon White, Toronto, 1992.
Kenny Lofton, Cleveland, 1995.
Mike Cameron, Seattle, 2000.
7-game series
A.L.—28—Gary Pettis, California, 1986.
N.L.—26—Kenny Lofton, Chicago, 2003.

Most putouts by left fielder, game
A.L.—7—Roy White, New York, October 13, 1976.
N.L.—7—Rennie Stennett, Pittsburgh, October 7, 1972.
(7—Jose Cruz, Houston, October 10, 1980, 11 innings.)

Most putouts by center fielder, game
A.L.—9—Gary Pettis, California, October 10. 1986.
Darin Erstad, Anaheim, October 13, 2002.
N.L.—8—Al Oliver, Pittsburgh, October 7, 1972.
Don Hahn, New York, October 8, 1973.

Most putouts by right fielder, game
A.L.—9—Jesse Barfield, Toronto, October 11, 1985.
N.L.—8—Brian Jordan, Atlanta, October 21, 2001.

Most consecutive putouts, game
A.L.—4—Oscar Gamble, New York, October 15, 1981, 3 in sixth inning, 1 in seventh inning (right fielder).
Dan Gladden, Minnesota, October 9, 1991, 3 in eighth inning, 1 in ninth inning (left fielder).
Darin Erstad, Anaheim, October 13, 2002, 2 in third inning, 2 in fourth inning (center fielder).
N.L.—4—Andre Dawson, Montreal, October 19, 1981, 1 in sixth inning, 3 in seventh inning (center fielder).

Most putouts, inning
A.L.-N.L.—3—Held by many outfielders.

Most assists, career
Both leagues—6—Lonnie Smith, Philadelphia N.L., 1980; St. Louis N.L., 1982; Kansas City A.L., 1985; Atlanta N.L., 1991; four series, 19 games.
N.L.—5—Bake McBride, Philadelphia, 1977, 1978, 1980; three series, 11 games.
A.L.—3—Tony Oliva, Minnesota, 1969, 1970; two series, six games.
Reggie Jackson, Oakland, 1971, 1972, 1973, 1974, 1975; New York, 1977, 1978, 1980, 1981; nine series, 27 games.

Lonnie Smith, Kansas City, 1985; one series, seven games.

Most games played with no assists, career
A.L.—25—Manny Ramirez, Cleveland, 1995, 1997, 1998; Boston, 2003; four series.
N.L.—21—Willie McGee, St. Louis, 1982, 1985, 1987, 1996; four series.

Most assists, series
3-game series
N.L.—2—George Foster, Cincinnati, 1979.
A.L.—2—Tony Oliva, Minnesota, 1970.
Carl Yastrzemski, Boston, 1975.
Tony Armas, Oakland, 1981.
4-game series
N.L.—2—Bake McBride, Philadelphia, 1977.
A.L.—2—Rick Miller, California, 1979.
5-game series
N.L.—3—Bake McBride, Philadelphia, 1980.
A.L.—1—Held by many outfielders.
6-game series
N.L.—3—Melvin Mora, New York, 1999.
A.L.—2—Tim Raines Sr., Chicago, 1993.
7-game series
A.L.—3—Lonnie Smith, Kansas City, 1985.
N.L.—3—David Justice, Atlanta, 1992.

Most assists, game
A.L.—2—Tony Oliva, Minnesota, October 4, 1970.
N.L.—2—Rickey Henderson, New York, October 15, 1999.
(2—George Foster, Cincinnati, October 3, 1979, 10 innings. Bake McBride, Philadelphia, October 11, 1980, 10 innings.)

Most chances accepted, career
A.L.—105—Bernie Williams, New York, 1996, 1998 through 2001, 2003, 2004; seven series, 41 games.
N.L.—65—Ron Gant, Atlanta, 1991, 1992, 1993; Cincinnati, 1995; St. Louis, 1996; five series, 31 games.

Most chances accepted, series
3-game series
N.L.—14—Dave Parker, Pittsburgh, 1975.
A.L.—13—Fred Lynn, Boston, 1975.
4-game series
N.L.—16—Garry Maddox, Philadelphia, 1978.
A.L.—16—Rick Miller, California, 1979.
5-game series
N.L.—23—Garry Maddox, Philadelphia, 1980.
A.L.—22—Dave Henderson, Oakland, 1989.
6-game series
N.L.—18—Willie McGee, St. Louis, 1985.
A.L.—16—Devon White, Toronto, 1992.
Willie Wilson, Oakland, 1992.
Kenny Lofton, Cleveland, 1995.
Mike Cameron, Seattle, 2000.
7-game series
A.L.—28—Gary Pettis, California, 1986.
N.L.—27—Kenny Lofton, Chicago, 2003.

Most chances accepted by left fielder, game
A.L.—7—Roy White, New York, October 13, 1976 (seven putouts).
Clint Hurdle, Kansas City, October 6, 1978 (six putouts, one assist).
N.L.—7—Rennie Stennett, Pittsburgh, October 7, 1972 (seven putouts).
Jose Cruz, Houston, October 10, 1980 (seven putouts).
Kevin Mitchell, San Francisco, October 7, 1989 (six putouts, one assist).

Most chances accepted by center fielder, game
A.L.—9—Gary Pettis, California, October 10, 1986 (nine putouts).
Darin Erstad, Anaheim, October 13, 2002 (nine putouts).
N.L.—8—Al Oliver, Pittsburgh, October 7, 1972 (eight putouts).
Don Hahn, New York, October 8, 1973 (eight putouts).

Most chances accepted by right fielder, game
A.L.—9—Jesse Barfield, Toronto, October 11, 1985

(nine putouts).
N.L.—8—Brian Jordan, Atlanta, October 21, 2001 (eight putouts).

Longest game with no chances offered to outfielder
N.L.—12 innings—Don Hahn, New York, October 9, 1973.
Billy Hatcher, Houston, October 14, 1986.
A.L.—12 innings—Brian Giles, Cleveland, October 11, 1997.

Most chances accepted, inning
A.L.-N.L.—3—Held by many players.

ERRORS AND DOUBLE PLAYS

Most errors, career
M.L.—7—Rickey Henderson, Oakland A.L., 1981, 1989, 1990, 1992; Toronto A.L., 1993; New York N.L., 1999; Seattle A.L., 2000; seven series, 33 games (6 in A.L., 1 in N.L.).
A.L.—6—Rickey Henderson, Oakland, 1981, 1989, 1990, 1992; Toronto, 1993; Seattle, 2000; six series, 27 games.
N.L.—2—Reggie Smith, Los Angeles, 1977, 1978; two series, eight games.
Garry Maddox, Philadelphia, 1976 through 1978, 1980, 1983; five series, 17 games.
David Justice, Atlanta, 1991, 1992, 1993, 1995; four series, 23 games.
Willie McGee, St. Louis, 1982, 1985, 1987, 1996; four series, 21 games.
Marquis Grissom, Atlanta, 1995, 1996; two series, 11 games.
Kenny Lofton, Atlanta, 1997; San Francisco, 2002; two series, 11 games.

Most consecutive errorless games, career
M.L.—31—Paul O'Neill, Cincinnati N.L., New York A.L., October 4, 1990 through October 22, 2001.
A.L.—26—Paul O'Neill, New York, October 9, 1996 through October 22, 2001.
N.L.—27—Andruw Jones, Atlanta, October 9, 1996 through October 21, 2001.

Most errors, series
A.L.—3—Rickey Henderson, Oakland, 1992 (6-game series).
N.L.—2—Kenny Lofton, Atlanta, 1997 (6-game series).

Most chances accepted, errorless series
N.L.—27—Kenny Lofton, Chicago, 2003 (7-game series).
A.L.—22—Dave Henderson, Oakland, 1989 (5-game series).

Most errors, game
A.L.—2—Tony Oliva, Minnesota, October 6, 1969.
Ben Oglivie, Milwaukee, October 10, 1982.
Albert Belle, Cleveland, October 15, 1995.
N.L.—2—Wes Chamberlain, Philadelphia, October 11, 1993.

Most errors, inning
A.L.-N.L.—1—Held by many outfielders.

Most double plays, career
N.L.—3—Bake McBride, Philadelphia, 1977, 1978, 1980; three series, 11 games.
A.L.—2—Rick Miller, California, 1979; one series, four games.

Most double plays, series
A.L.—2—Rick Miller, California, 1979 (4-game series)
N.L.—1—Held by many outfielders.

Most double plays, game
A.L.—1—Held by many outfielders.
N.L.—1—Held by many outfielders.
(2—Bake McBride, Philadelphia, October 11, 1980, 10 innings.)

Most unassisted double plays, game
A.L.-N.L.—Never accomplished.

CATCHERS
GAMES

Most games, career
A.L.—33—Jorge Posada, New York, 1998 through 2001, 2003,

2004; six series.
N.L.—27—Javy Lopez, Atlanta, 1992, 1995, 1996, 1997, 1998, 2001; six series.

PUTOUTS, ASSISTS AND CHANCES ACCEPTED

Most putouts, career
A.L.—255—Jorge Posada, New York, 1998 through 2001, 2003, 2004; six series, 33 games. N.L.—183—Javy Lopez, Atlanta, 1992, 1995, 1996, 1997, 1998, 2001; six series, 27 games.

Most putouts, series
3-game series
N.L.—29—Manny Sanguillen, Pittsburgh, 1975.
A.L.—23—Rick Cerone, New York, 1981.
4-game series
N.L.—34—Dick Dietz, San Francisco, 1971.
A.L.—34—Rich Gedman, Boston, 1988.
5-game series
A.L.—44—Jason Varitek, Boston, 1999.
N.L.—42—Jerry Grote, New York, 1973.
6-game series
N.L.—59—Alan Ashby, Houston, 1986.
A.L.—51—Jorge Posada, New York, 2000.
7-game series
N.L.—62—Greg Olson, Atlanta, 1991.
A.L.—60—Jorge Posada, New York, 2003.

Most putouts, game
A.L.—15—Rick Dempsey, Baltimore, October 6, 1983.
Jorge Posada, New York, October 14, 2000.
(15—Chris Hoiles, Baltimore, October 11, 1997, caught first 8 inn of 12-inn game.)
Jason Varitek, Boston, October 18, 2004.
N.L.—15—Charles Johnson, Florida, October 12, 1997.
(16—Mike Piazza, New York, October 17, 1999, 15 inn.)

Most putouts, inning
A.L.-N.L.—3—many catchers.

Most assists, career
A.L.—19—Jorge Posada, New York, 1998 through 2001, 2003, 2004; six series, 33 games.
N.L.—18—Johnny Bench, Cincinnati, 1970, 1972, 1973, 1975, 1976, 1979; six series, 22 games.

Most assists, series
3-game series
A.L.—4—George Mitterwald, Minnesota, 1969.
Rick Cerone, New York, 1980.
N.L.—4—Johnny Bench, Cincinnati, 1975, 1976.
4-game series
A.L.—5—Rick Dempsey, Baltimore, 1983.
Rich Gedman, Boston, 1988.
N.L.—2—Held by many catchers.
5-game series
A.L.—6—Thurman Munson, New York, 1976.
N.L.—4—Terry Kennedy, San Diego, 1984.
Mike Matheny, St. Louis, 2002.
6-game series
A.L.—7—Terry Steinbach, Oakland, 1992.
N.L.—5—Gary Carter, New York, 1986.
7-game series
A.L.—6—Jorge Posada, New York, 2003.
N.L.—5—Tony Pena, St. Louis, 1987.
Don Slaught, Pittsburgh, 1991.
Damon Berryhill, Atlanta, 1992.

Most assists, game
N.L.—3—Johnny Bench, Cincinnati, October 5, 1975.
Mike Matheny, St. Louis, October 12, 2002.
(3—Johnny Bench, Cincinnati, October 3, 1970, 10 Inn.
Gary Carter, New York, October 15, 1986, 16 inn.)
A.L.—3—Rich Gedman, Boston, October 8, 1988.
Terry Steinbach, Oakland, October 10, 1992.
Pat Borders, Toronto, October 8, 1993.
Dan Wilson, Seattle, October 11, 2000.
Bengie Molina, Anaheim, October 8, 2002.

(3—Jorge Posada, New York, October 18, 2004, 14 inn.)

Most assists, inning
N.L.—2—Johnny Bench, Cincinnati, October 7, 1973, eighth
inning.
Mike Scioscia, Los Angeles, October 10, 1985, first inning.
Gary Carter, New York, October 15, 1986, 12th inning.
A.L.—2—Rich Gedman, Boston, October 8, 1988, first inning.

Most chances accepted, career
A.L.—274—Jorge Posada, New York, 1998 through 2001,
2003, 2004; six series, 33 games.
N.L.—193—Javy Lopez, Atlanta, 1992, 1995, 1996, 1997,
1998, 2001; six series, 27 games.

Most chances accepted, series
3-game series
N.L.—30—Manny Sanguillen, Pittsburgh, 1975.
A.L.—25—Rick Cerone, New York, 1981.
4-game series
A.L.—39—Rich Gedman, Boston, 1988.
N.L.—36—Dick Dietz, San Francisco, 1971.
5-game series
A.L.—45—Jason Varitek, Boston, 1999.
N.L.—43—Jerry Grote, New York, 1973.
6-game series
N.L.—60—Alan Ashby, Houston, 1986.
A.L.—54—Jorge Posada, New York, 2000.
7-game series
A.L.—66—Jorge Posada, New York, 2003.
N.L.—63—Greg Olson, Atlanta, 1991.

Most chances accepted, game
A.L.—16—Rick Dempsey, Baltimore, October 6, 1983 (15 po,
1 a).
(16—Chris Hoiles, Baltimore, October 11, 1997 (15 po, 1 a),
caught first 8 inn of 12-inn game).
Jorge Posada, New York, October 18, 2004 (13 po, 3 a), 14
inn.)
N.L.—16—Charles Johnson, Florida, October 12, 1997
(15 po, 1 a).
(18—Mike Piazza, New York, October 17, 1999 (16 po, 2), 15
inn.)

Fewest chances offered, game
A.L.-N.L.—2—many catchers.

Most chances accepted, inning
A.L.-N.L.—3—many catchers.

ERRORS AND PASSED BALLS

Most errors, career
N.L.—5—Manny Sanguillen, Pittsburgh, 1970, 1971, 1972,
1974, 1975; five series, 19 games.
A.L.—3—Don Slaught, Kansas City, 1984; one series, three
games.
Pat Borders, Toronto, 1989, 1991, 1992, 1993; four series,
18 games.
Sandy Alomar, Cleveland, 1995, 1997, 1998; three series, 16
games.

Most consecutive errorless games, career
A.L.—26—Jorge Posada, October 19, 1999 through October
20, 2004.
N.L.—18—Gary Carter, Montreal, New York, October 13, 1981
through October 12, 1988.

Most errors, series
A.L.—3—Don Slaught, Kansas City, 1984 (3-game series).
N.L.—3—Mike Piazza, New York, 1999 (6-game series).

Most chances accepted, errorless series
N.L.—63—Greg Olson, Atlanta, 1991 (7-game series).
A.L.—66—Jorge Posada, New York, 2003 (7-game series).

Most errors, game
A.L.—2—Thurman Munson, New York, October 10, 1976.
Don Slaught, Kansas City, October 5, 1984.
Sandy Alomar, Cleveland, October 10, 1998.
N.L.—2—Manny Sanguillen, Pittsburgh, October 6, 1974.
(2—Mike Piazza, New York, October 19, 1999, 11 innings.)

Most errors, inning
A.L.-N.L.—1—Held by many catchers.

Most passed balls, career
N.L.—4—Manny Sanguillen, Pittsburgh, 1970, 1971, 1972,
1974, 1975; five series, 19 games.
A.L.—5—Pat Borders, Toronto, 1989, 1991, 1992, 1993; four
series, 18 games.
Jason Varitek, Boston, 1999, 2003, 2004; three series, 18
games.

Most passed balls, series
A.L.—3—Pat Borders, Toronto, 1992 (6-game series).
N.L.—2—Manny Sanguillen, Pittsburgh, 1975 (3-game series).
Alan Ashby, Houston, 1986 (6-game series).
Don Slaught, Pittsburgh, 1992 (7-game series).
Darren Daulton, Philadelphia, 1993 (6-game series).
Paul Bako, Chicago, 2003 (7-game series).

Most passed balls, game
N.L.—2—Manny Sanguillen, Pittsburgh, October 4, 1975.
Alan Ashby, Houston, October 11, 1986.
Don Slaught, Pittsburgh, October 13, 1992.
A.L.—2—Pat Borders, Toronto, October 13, 19991.
Pat Borders, Toronto, October 14, 1992.
(3—Jason Varitek, Boston, October 18, 2004, 14 innings.)

Most passed balls, inning
A.L.—3—Jason Varitek, Boston, October 18, 2004, 13th inning.
N.L.—1—Held by many catchers.

DOUBLE PLAYS AND RUNNERS CAUGHT STEALING

Most double plays, career
A.L.—5—Jorge Posada, New York, 1998 through 2001, 2003,
2004; six series, 33 games.
N.L.—3—Manny Sanguillen, Pittsburgh, 1970, 1971, 1972,
1974, 1975; five series, 19 games.
Terry Kennedy, San Diego, 1984; San Francisco, 1989; two
series, 10 games.

Most double plays, series
A.L.—3—Jorge Posada, New York, 2003 (7-game series).
N.L.—2—Terry Kennedy, San Francisco, 1989 (5-game series).
Greg Olson, Atlanta, 1991 (7-game series).
Javy Lopez, Atlanta, 1997 (6-game series).
Mike Piazza, New York, 1999 (6-game series).

Most double plays started, series
A.L.—3—Jorge Posada, New York, 2003 (7-game series).
N.L.—1—Held by many catchers.

Most double plays, game
A.L.-N.L.—1—Held by many catchers.

Most double plays started, game
A.L.-N.L.—1—Held by many catchers.

Most unassisted double plays, game
A.L.-N.L.—Never accomplished.

Most runners caught stealing, career
A.L.—12—Thurman Munson, New York, 1976, 1977, 1978;
three series, 14 games.
N.L.—6—Mike Scioscia, Los Angeles, 1981, 1985, 1988;
three series, 18 games.

Most runners caught stealing, series
A.L.—5—Thurman Munson, New York, 1976 (5-game series).
Terry Steinbach, Oakland, 1992 (6-game series).
N.L.—4—Mike Scioscia, Los Angeles, 1985 (6-game series).

Most runners caught stealing, game
A.L.-N.L.—2—Held by many catchers.

Most runners caught stealing, inning
N.L.—2—Mike Scioscia, Los Angeles, October 10, 1985,
first inning.
A.L.—1—Held by many catchers.

PITCHERS
GAMES

Most games pitched, career
A.L.—24—Mariano Rivera, New York, 1996, 1998 through
2001, 2003, 2004; seven series.
N.L.—18—Mark Wohlers, Atlanta, 1991, 1992, 1993, 1995,
1996, 1997; six series.

Most games pitched, series
3-game series
  A.L.-N.L.—3—Held by many pitchers.
4-game series
  N.L.—4—Dave Giusti, Pittsburgh, 1971.
      Mark Wohlers, Atlanta, 1995.
  A.L.—4—Dennis Eckersley, Oakland, 1988.
5-game series
  N.L.—5—Tug McGraw, Philadelphia, 1980.
  A.L.—5—Jim Acker, Toronto, 1989.
6-game series
  N.L.—6—John Rocker, Atlanta, 1998.
      John Rocker, Atlanta, 1999.
  A.L.—5—Paul Assenmacher, Cleveland, 1997.
      Mike Jackson, Cleveland, 1997.
      Paul Shuey, Cleveland, 1998.
      Jose Paniagua, Seattle, 2000.
7-game series
  N.L.—6—Mark Petkovsek, St. Louis, 1996.
  A.L.—5—Alan Embree, Boston, 2003.
      Felix Heredia, New York, 2003.
      Mike Timlin, Boston, 2003.

PUTOUTS, ASSISTS AND CHANCES ACCEPTED

Most putouts, career
A.L.—12—Mariano Rivera, New York, 1996, 1998 through
2001, 2003, 2004; seven series, 24 games.
N.L.—11—Greg Maddux, Chicago, 1989; Atlanta, 1993, 1995,
1996, 1997, 1998, 1999, 2001; eight series, 15 games.

Most putouts, series
3-game series
  N.L.—4—Don Gullett, Cincinnati, 1975.
  A.L.—2—Rick Wise, Boston, 1975.
      Rudy May, New York, 1980.
      Milt Wilcox, Detroit, 1984.
4-game series
  A.L.—3—Catfish Hunter, Oakland, 1974.
  N.L.—2—Juan Marichal, San Francisco, 1971.
      Don Sutton, Los Angeles, 1974.
      Jeff Brantley, Cincinnati, 1995.
5-game series
  A.L.—4—Mariano Rivera, 2001.
  N.L.—2—Tug McGraw, New York, 1973.
      Dick Ruthven, Philadelphia, 1980.
      Miguel Batista, Arizona, 2001.
      Tom Glavine, Atlanta, 2001.
      Greg Maddux, Atlanta, 2001.
      Kirk Rueter, San Francisco, 2002.
6-game series
  N.L.—4—Greg Maddux, Atlanta, 1993.
      Andy Ashby, San Diego, 1998.
  A.L.—4—Brett Tomko, Seattle, 2000.
7-game series
  N.L.—4—Danny Cox, St. Louis, 1987.
  A.L.—4—Derek Lowe, Boston, 2004.

Most putouts, game
N.L.—4—Don Gullett, Cincinnati, October 4, 1975.
A.L.—3—Tommy John, California, October 5, 1982.
  Charlie Leibrandt, Kansas City, October 12, 1985.
  Charles Nagy, Cleveland, October 7, 1998.
  Derek Lowe, Boston, October 20, 2004.

Most putouts, inning
A.L.—2—Mike Torrez, New York, October 7, 1977, second
inning.

Charlie Leibrandt, Kansas City, October 12, 1985, fifth inning.
Mike Witt, California, October 12, 1986, first inning.
Mariano Rivera, New York, October 17, 2001, ninth inning.
N.L.—2—Don Gullett, Cincinnati, October 4, 1975, third inning.
  Roger McDowell, New York, October 15, 1986, 10th inning.

Most assists, career
N.L.—25—Greg Maddux, Chicago, 1989; Atlanta, 1993, 1995,
1996, 1997, 1998, 1999, 2001; eight series, 15 games.
A.L.—12—Mike Cuellar, Baltimore, 1969, 1970, 1971, 1973,
1974; five series, six games.

Most assists, series
3-game series
  A.L.—4—Dave Boswell, Minnesota, 1969.
      Paul Lindblad, Oakland, 1975.
  N.L.—3—Phil Niekro, Atlanta, 1969.
      Dock Ellis, Pittsburgh, 1970.
      Pat Zachry, Cincinnati, 1976.
4-game series
  A.L.—5—Mike Cuellar, Baltimore, 1974.
  N.L.—5—Steve Carlton, Philadelphia, 1983.
5-game series
  N.L.—4—Darryl Kile, St. Louis, 2000.
  A.L.—3—Held by many pitchers.
6-game series
  N.L.—7—Greg Maddux, Atlanta, 1997.
  A.L.—5—Scott Erickson, Baltimore, 1997.
7-game series
  A.L.—7—Charlie Leibrandt, Kansas City, 1985.
  N.L.—5—Danny Cox, St. Louis, 1987.

Most assists, game
A.L.—5—Charlie Leibrandt, Kansas City, October 12, 1985.
N.L.—4—Juan Marichal, San Francisco, October 5, 1971.
  Greg Maddux, Atlanta, October 7, 1997.
  Andy Ashby, San Diego, October 7, 1998.
  Greg Maddux, Atlanta, October 12, 1999.
  Kenny Rogers, New York, October 13, 1999.

Most assists, inning
N.L.—3—Pat Zachry, Cincinnati, October 10, 1976,
fourth inning.
A.L.—2—Held by many pitchers.

Most chances accepted, career
N.L.—35—Greg Maddux, Chicago, 1989; Atlanta, 1993, 1995,
1996, 1997, 1998, 1999, 2001; eight series, 15 games.
A.L.—22—Mariano Rivera, New York, 1996, 1998 through
2001, 2003, 2004; seven series, 24 games.

Most chances accepted, series
3-game series
  N.L.—5—Don Gullett, Cincinnati, 1975.
  A.L.—5—Dave Boswell, Minnesota, 1969.
      Rick Wise, Boston, 1975.
      Paul Lindblad, Oakland, 1975.
4-game series
  N.L.—6—Juan Marichal, San Francisco, 1971.
      Steve Carlton, Philadelphia, 1983.
  A.L.—5—Catfish Hunter, Oakland, 1974.
      Mike Cuellar, Baltimore, 1974.
      Larry Gura, Kansas City, 1978.
5-game series
  N.L.—5—Darryl Kile, St. Louis, 2000.
      Tom Glavine, Atlanta, 2001.
      Greg Maddux, Atlanta, 2001.
      Kirk Rueter, San Francisco, 2002.
  A.L.—5—Mike Flanagan, Toronto, 1989.
      Jack Morris, Minnesota, 1991.
      Mariano Rivera, New York, 2001.
6-game series
  N.L.—9—Greg Maddux, Atlanta, 1993.
  A.L.—5—Scott Erickson, Baltimore, 1997.
7-game series
  A.L.—10—Charlie Leibrandt, Kansas City, 1985.
  N.L.—9—Danny Cox, St. Louis, 1987.

Most chances accepted, game
A.L.—8—Charlie Leibrandt, Kansas City, October 12, 1985.

N.L.—6—Juan Marichal, San Francisco, October 5, 1971.

Most chances accepted, inning
N.L.—3—Pat Zachry, Cincinnati, October 10, 1976, fourth inning.
A.L.—3—Mariano Rivera, New York, October 17, 2001, ninth inning.

ERRORS AND DOUBLE PLAYS

Most errors, career
N.L.—3—Greg Maddux, Chicago, 1989; Atlanta, 1993, 1995, 1996, 1997, 1998, 1999, 2001; eight series, 15 games.
A.L.—1—Held by many pitchers.

Most consecutive errorless games, career
A.L.—25—Mariano Rivera, New York, October 9, 1996 through October 20, 2004.
N.L.—18—Mark Wohlers, Atlanta, October 9, 1991 through October 8, 1997.

Most errors, series
N.L.—2—Joaquin Andujar, St. Louis, 1985.
A.L.—1—Held by many pitchers.

Most chances accepted, errorless series
A.L.—10—Charlie Leibrandt, Kansas City, 1985 (7-game series).
N.L.—9—Danny Cox, St. Louis, 1987 (7-game series).

Most errors, game
A.L.-N.L.—1—Held by many pitchers.

Most double plays, career
N.L.—3—Greg Maddux, Chicago, 1989; Atlanta, 1993 through 2001, except 1994 and 2000; eight series, 15 games.
A.L.—2—Mike Flanagan, Baltimore, 1979, 1983; Toronto, 1989; three series, three games.

Jeff Nelson, Seattle, 1995, 2001; New York, 1997 through 2000; six series, 15 games.
Mariano Rivera, New York, 1996, 1998 through 2001, 2003, 2004; seven series, 24 games.

Most double plays started, career
N.L.—3—Greg Maddux, Chicago, 1989; Atlanta, 1993 through 2001, except 1994 and 2000; eight series, 15 games.
A.L.—2—Mike Flanagan, Baltimore, 1979, 1983; Toronto, 1989; three series, three games.
Jeff Nelson, Seattle, 1995, 2001; New York, 1997 through 2000; six series, 15 games.
Mariano Rivera, New York, 1996, 1998 through 2001, 2003, 2004; seven series, 24 games.

Most double plays, series
A.L.—2—Mike Flanagan, Toronto, 1989 (5-game series).
Jeff Nelson, Seattle, 1995 (6-game series).
N.L.—2—Danny Cox, St. Louis, 1987 (7-game series).
Pat Mahomes, New York, 1999 (6-game series).
Greg Maddux, Atlanta, 2001 (5-game series).

Most double plays started, series
A.L.—2—Mike Flanagan, Toronto, 1989 (5-game series).
Jeff Nelson, Seattle, 1995 (6-game series).
N.L.—2—Pat Mahomes, New York, 1999 (6-game series).
Greg Maddux, Atlanta, 2001 (5-game series).

Most double plays, game
A.L.—2—Mike Flanagan, Toronto, October 7, 1989.
Jeff Nelson, Seattle, October 14, 1995.
N.L.—2—Danny Cox, St. Louis, October 14, 1987.
Greg Maddux, Atlanta, October 16, 2001.

Most unassisted double plays, game
A.L.-N.L.—Never accomplished.

CLUB FIELDING

AVERAGE

Highest fielding average, series
3-game series
　A.L.—1.000—Baltimore vs. Minnesota, 1970.
　　　　　　Oakland vs. Baltimore, 1971.
　N.L.—1.000—Pittsburgh vs. Cincinnati, 1979.
4-game series
　A.L.—.993—New York vs. Kansas City, 1978.
　　　　　　Boston vs. Oakland, 1988.
　　　　　　Oakland vs. Boston, 1990.
　N.L.—.993—Los Angeles vs. Philadelphia, 1983.
5-game series
　A.L.—.995—New York vs. Baltimore, 1996.
　N.L.—.995—San Francisco vs. St. Louis, 2002.
6-game series
　N.L.—.996—New York vs. Houston, 1986.
　　　　　　San Diego vs. Atlanta, 1998.
　A.L.—.995—New York vs. Seattle, 2000.
7-game series
　N.L.—.996—St. Louis vs Houston, 2004.
　A.L.—.996—Boston vs. New York, 2004.

For a list of fielding statistics by teams each series, see page 451.

Highest fielding average by both clubs, series
3-game series
　N.L.—.996—Pittsburgh 1.000, Cincinnati .992, 1979.
　A.L.—.995—Oakland 1.000, Baltimore .991, 1971.
4-game series
　A.L.—.986—Boston .993, Oakland .979, 1988.
　N.L.—.985—Cincinnati .987, Atlanta .983, 1995.
5-game series
　N.L.—.994—San Francisco .995, St. Louis .994, 2002.
　A.L.—.987—New York .995, Baltimore .980, 1996.

6-game series
　A.L.—.991—New York .995, Seattle .986, 2000.
　N.L.—.985—New York .996, Houston .973, 1986.
7 game series
　N.L.—.994—St. Louis .996, Houston .992, 2004.
　A.L.—.991—Boston .996, New York .986, 2004.

Lowest fielding average, series
3 game series
　A.L.—.940—Kansas City vs. Detroit, 1984.
　N.L.—.950—Atlanta vs. New York, 1969.
4-game series
　N.L.—.957—Los Angeles vs. Pittsburgh, 1974.
　A.L.—.968—Boston vs. Oakland, 1990.
5-game series
　A.L.—.945—Boston vs. New York, 1999.
　N.L.—.962—St. Louis vs. New York, 2000.
6-game series
　A.L.—.966—Toronto vs. Oakland, 1992.
　N.L.—.968—Philadelphia vs. Atlanta, 1993.
7-game series
　N.L.—.969—New York vs. Los Angeles, 1988.
　A.L.—.971—California vs. Boston, 1986.

Lowest fielding average by both clubs, series
3-game series
　A.L.—.958—Boston .966, Oakland .950, 1975.
　N.L.—.965—New York .981, Atlanta .950, 1969.
4-game series
　N.L.—.964—Pittsburgh .973, Los Angeles .957, 1974.
　A.L.—.978—California .986, Baltimore .970, 1979.
5-game series
　A.L.—.961—New York .977, Boston .945, 1999.
　N.L.—.970—New York .978, St. Louis .962, 2000.
6-game series
　A.L.—.967—Oakland .969, Toronto .966, 1992.
　N.L.—.971—Atlanta .971, New York .970, 1999.
7-game series
　A.L.—.973—Boston .975, California .971, 1986.
　N.L.—.975—New York .969, Los Angeles .981, 1988.

PUTOUTS

Most putouts, total series
N.L.—1,620—Atlanta; 11 series, 60 games.
A.L.—1,664—New York; 12 series, 61 games.

Most putouts, series
3-game series
    A.L.—96—Baltimore vs. Minnesota, 1969.
    N.L.—90—Pittsburgh vs. Cincinnati, 1979.
4-game series
    N.L.—117—Atlanta vs. Cincinnati, 1995.
    A.L.—111—Baltimore vs. Chicago, 1983.
5-game series
    N.L.—148—Philadelphia vs. Houston, 1980.
    A.L.—141—New York vs. Baltimore, 1996.
6-game series
    N.L.—189—New York vs. Houston, 1986.
    A.L.—174—Baltimore vs. Cleveland, 1997.
             Cleveland vs. Baltimore, 1997.
7-game series
    A.L.—209—New York vs. Boston, 2004.
    N.L.—198— Florida vs. Chicago, 2003.
             Chicago vs. Florida, 2003.

Most putouts by both clubs, series
3-game series
    A.L.—190—Baltimore 96, Minnesota 94, 1969.
    N.L.—177—Pittsburgh 90, Cincinnati 87, 1979.
4-game series
    N.L.—228—Atlanta 117, Cincinnati 111, 1995.
    A.L.—219—Baltimore 111, Chicago 108, 1983.
5-game series
    N.L.—295—Philadelphia 148, Houston 147, 1980.
    A.L.—279—New York 141, Baltimore 138, 1996.
6-game series
    N.L.—377—New York 189, Houston 188, 1986.
    A.L.—348—Baltimore 174, Cleveland 174, 1997.
7-game series
    A.L.—416—New York 209, Boston 207, 2004.
    N.L.—396—Florida 198, Chicago 198, 2003.

Fewest putouts, series
3-game series
    A.L.—75—Oakland vs. Baltimore, 1971.
             Oakland vs. Boston, 1975.
             New York vs. Kansas City, 1980.
             Oakland vs. New York, 1981.
    N.L.—76—Atlanta vs. St. Louis, 1982.
4-game series
    A.L.—102—Kansas City vs. New York, 1978.
             Boston vs. Oakland, 1988, 1990.
    N.L.—102—San Francisco vs. Pittsburgh, 1971.
             Los Angeles vs. Philadelphia, 1983.
5-game series
    A.L.—126—California vs. Milwaukee, 1982.
    N.L.—126—Chicago vs. San Francisco, 1989.
6-game series
    N.L.—154—Los Angeles vs. St. Louis, 1985.
    A.L.—156—Seattle vs. New York, 2000.
7-game series
    N.L.—180—San Francisco vs. St. Louis, 1987.
             St. Louis vs. Atlanta, 1996.
    A.L.—186—Toronto vs. Kansas City, 1985.

Fewest putouts by both clubs, series
3-game series
    A.L.—156—Baltimore 81, Oakland 75, 1971.
             Boston 81, Oakland 75, 1975.
             Kansas City 81, New York 75, 1980.
             New York 81, Oakland 75, 1981.
    N.L.—157—St. Louis 81, Atlanta 76, 1982.
4-game series
    A.L.—207—New York 105, Kansas City 102, 1978.
    N.L.—207—Pittsburgh 105, San Francisco 102, 1971.
             Philadelphia 105, Los Angeles 102, 1983.
5-game series
    A.L.—255—Milwaukee 129, California 126, 1982.
    N.L.—256—Chicago 129, San Diego 127, 1984.

6-game series
    N.L.—310—St. Louis 156, Los Angeles 154, 1985.
    A.L.—315—New York 159, Seattle 156, 2000.
7-game series
    N.L.—363—St. Louis 183, San Francisco 180, 1987.
             Atlanta 183, St. Louis 180, 1996.
    A.L.—374—Kansas City 188, Toronto 186, 1985.

Most putouts by outfield, game
N.L.—18—Pittsburgh vs. Cincinnati, October 7, 1972.
A.L.—14—Boston vs. Oakland, October 4, 1975.
    New York vs. Kansas City, October 13, 1976.
    Anaheim vs. Minnesota, October 13, 2002.

Most putouts by outfield of both clubs, game
A.L.—26—New York 14, Kansas City 12, October 13, 1976.
N.L.—25—Pittsburgh 18, Cincinnati 7, October 7, 1972.

Fewest putouts by outfield, game
N.L.—1—Atlanta vs. New York, October 4, 1969.
    Cincinnati vs. Pittsburgh, October 5, 1970.
    Montreal vs. Los Angeles, October 16, 1981.
    (3—Cincinnati vs. Pittsburgh, October 3, 1970,
      10 innings.
    Florida vs. Chicago, October 7, 2003, 11 innings.)
A.L.—1—Minnesota vs. Anaheim, October 13, 2002; fielded
    eight innings.
    (3—Baltimore vs. Cleveland, October 11, 1997,
    fielded 11.1 innings of 12-inning game.)

Fewest putouts by outfield of both clubs, game
N.L.—5—Pittsburgh 4, Cincinnati 1, October 5, 1970.
    (10—Chicago 7, Florida 3, October 7, 2003, 11 innings.)
A.L.—6—New York 4, Boston 2, October 9, 2003.
    (9—Cleveland 6, Baltimore 3, October 11, 1997, 12 innings.)

Most putouts by outfield, inning
A.L.-N.L.—3—Held by many clubs.

Most putouts by outfield of both clubs, inning
A.L.—6—Baltimore 3, Oakland 3, October 11, 1973,
    seventh inning.
N.L.—5—New York 3, Atlanta 2, October 5, 1969, seventh
    inning.
    Pittsburgh 3, Cincinnati 2, October 7, 1972, third inning.
    Los Angeles 3, Philadelphia 2, October 7, 1978, third inning.
    St. Louis 3, Atlanta 2, October 9, 1996, sixth inning.

Most putouts by catchers of both clubs, inning
A.L.-N.L.—5—Occurred in many innings.

ASSISTS

Most assists, total series
N.L.—613—Atlanta; 11 series, 60 games.
A.L.—598—New York; 12 series, 61 games.

Most assists, series
3-game series
    A.L.—41—New York vs. Kansas City, 1980.
    N.L.—39—Cincinnati vs. Pittsburgh, 1970, 1979.
             Atlanta vs. St. Louis, 1982.
4-game series
    N.L.—54—Atlanta vs. Cincinnati, 1995.
    A.L.—52—Baltimore vs. California, 1979.
5-game series
    N.L.—71—Philadelphia vs. Houston, 1980.
    A.L.—60—New York vs. Kansas City, 1976.
6-game series
    N.L.—94—New York vs. Houston, 1986.
    A.L.—77—Cleveland vs. New York, 1998.
7-game series
    A.L.—87—Kansas City vs. Toronto, 1985.
    N.L.—81—Chicago vs. Florida, 2003.

Most assists by both clubs, series
3-game series
    N.L.—76—Cincinnati 39, Pittsburgh 37, 1970.

A.L.—73—Oakland 40, Boston 33, 1975.
4-game series
  A.L.—100—Chicago 51, Baltimore 49, 1983.
  N.L.—97—Atlanta 54, Cincinnati 43, 1995.
5-game series
  N.L.—123—Philadelphia 71, Houston 52, 1980.
  A.L.—111—New York 60, Kansas City 51, 1976.
6-game series
  N.L.—160—New York 94, Houston 66, 1986.
  A.L.—131—Cleveland 77, New York 54, 1998.
7-game series
  A.L.—151—California 78, Boston 73, 1986.
  N.L.—151—Chicago 81, Florida 70, 2003.

Fewest assists, series
3-game series
  A.L.—15—Oakland vs. Baltimore, 1971.
  N.L.—20—Pittsburgh vs. Cincinnati, 1975.
4-game series
  A.L.—30—Oakland vs. Boston, 1988.
  N.L.—32—Pittsburgh vs. San Francisco, 1971.
5-game series
  N.L.—38—Pittsburgh vs. Cincinnati, 1972.
  A.L.—38—New York vs. Boston, 1999.
        Anaheim vs. Minnesota, 2002.
6-game series
  N.L.—45—Cincinnati vs. Pittsburgh, 1980.
  A.L.—54—New York vs. Cleveland, 1998.
        New York vs. Seattle, 2000.
7-game series
  N.L.—55—Atlanta vs. St. Louis, 1996.
  A.L.—61—Toronto vs. Kansas City, 1985.

Fewest assists by both clubs, series
3-game series
  A.L.—46—Baltimore 31, Oakland 15, 1971.
  N.L.—51—Cincinnati 31, Pittsburgh 20, 1975.
4-game series
  A.L.—64—Boston 34, Oakland 30, 1988.
  N.L.—69—San Francisco 37, Pittsburgh 32, 1971.
5-game series
  A.L.—78—New York 40, Boston 38, 1999.
  N.L.—88—St. Louis 49, New York 39, 2000.
6-game series
  N.L.—101—Atlanta 54, Philadelphia 47, 1993.
  A.L.—112—Seattle 58, New York 54, 2000.
7-game series
  N.L.—117—St. Louis 62, Atlanta 55, 1996.
  A.L.—140—New York 73, Boston 67, 2003.
        Boston 66, New York 74, 2004.

Most assists, game
N.L.—21—Los Angeles vs. Philadelphia, October 5, 1978.
  (31—New York vs. Houston, October 15, 1986, 16 inn.)
A.L.—19—Boston vs. New York, October 9, 2003.
  (18—Toronto vs. Oakland, October 11, 1992, 11 inn.)

Most assists by both clubs, game
A.L.—33—Boston 18, Oakland 15, October 7, 1975.
N.L.—30—Los Angeles 21, Philadelphia 9, October 5, 1978.
  (56—New York 31, Houston 25, October 15, 1986, 16 inn).

Fewest assists, game
A.L.—2—Boston vs. Oakland, October 4, 1975.
  Boston vs. New York, October 13, 2003.
N.L.—2—Pittsburgh vs. Cincinnati, October 7, 1972.
  (2—Pittsburgh vs. Cincinnati, October 7, 1975, 10 inn.)

Fewest assists by both clubs, game
A.L.—6—Anaheim 5, Minnesota 1, October 11, 2002.
N.L.—7—Atlanta 4, St. Louis 3, October 9, 1996.

Most assists by outfield, game
N.L.—3—New York vs. Atlanta, October 15, 1999.
  (3—Philadelphia vs. Houston, October 11, 1980, 10 inn.)
A.L.—2—Minnesota vs. Baltimore, October 4, 1970.
  Boston vs. Oakland, October 5, 1975.
  Baltimore vs. California, October 5, 1979.

New York vs. Boston, October 16, 2004.

Most assists by outfield of both clubs, game
N.L.—3—Pittsburgh 2, Cincinnati 1, October 9, 1972.
  New York 3, Atlanta 0, October 15, 1999.
  (4—Philadelphia 3, Houston 1, October 11, 1980, 10 inn.)
A.L.—3—Minnesota 2, Baltimore 1, October 4, 1970.
  Boston 2, Oakland 1, October 5, 1975.
  Baltimore 2, California 1, October 5, 1979.

Most assists by outfield, inning
N.L.—2—Cincinnati vs. New York, October 10, 1973, 5th inn.
A.L.—1—many clubs.

CHANCES OFFERED

Fewest chances offered to outfield, game
N.L.—1—Cincinnati vs. Pittsburgh, October 5, 1970.
  Montreal vs. Los Angeles, October 16, 1981.
  (3—Cincinnati vs. Pittsburgh, October 3, 1970, 10 innings.
  Florida vs. Chicago, October 7, 2003, 11 innings.)
A.L.—1—Minnesota vs. Anaheim, October 13, 2002; fielded
  eight innings.
  (3—Baltimore vs. Cleveland, October 11, 1997, fielded 11.1
  innings of 12-inning game.)

Fewest chances offered to outfields of both clubs, game
N.L.—5—Pittsburgh 4, Cincinnati 1, October 5, 1970.
  (10—Chicago 7, Florida 3, October 7, 2003, 11 innings.)
A.L.—7—Minnesota 4, Baltimore 3, October 3, 1970.
  New York 4, Boston 3, October 9, 2003.
  Boston 5, New York 2, October 14, 2003.
  (9—Cleveland 6, Baltimore 3, October 11, 1997, 12 innings.)

ERRORS

Most errors, total series
N.L.—51—Atlanta; 11 series, 60 games.
A.L.—33—Oakland; 10 series, 42 games.
        New York, 12 series, 61 games.

Most errors, series
3-game series
  A.L.—7—Kansas City vs. Detroit, 1984.
  N.L.—6—Atlanta vs. New York, 1969.
4-game series
  N.L.—7—Los Angeles vs. Pittsburgh, 1974.
  A.L.—5—Baltimore vs. California, 1979.
        Boston vs. Oakland, 1990.
5-game series
  A.L.—10—Boston vs. New York, 1999.
  N.L.—7—St. Louis vs. New York, 2000.
        Atlanta vs. Arizona, 2001.
6-game series
  A.L.—8—Toronto vs. Oakland, 1992.
  N.L.—8—Atlanta vs. San Diego, 1998.
        New York vs. Atlanta, 1999.
7-game series
  A.L.—8—California vs. Boston, 1986.
  N.L.—8—New York vs. Los Angeles, 1988.

Most errors by both clubs, series
3-game series
  A.L.—10—Oakland 6, Boston 4, 1975.
  N.L.—8—Atlanta 6, New York 2, 1969.
4-game series
  N.L.—11—Los Angeles 7, Pittsburgh 4, 1974.
  A.L.—7—Baltimore 5, California 2, 1979.
5-game series
  A.L.—14—Boston 10, New York 4, 1999.
  N.L.—11—St. Louis 7, New York 4, 2000.
6-game series
  A.L.—15—Toronto 8, Oakland 7, 1992.
  N.L.—15—New York 8, Atlanta 7, 1999.
7-game series
  A.L.—15—California 8, Boston 7, 1986.
  N.L.—13—New York 8, Los Angeles 5, 1988.

Fewest errors, series

3-game series
A.L.—0—Baltimore vs. Minnesota, 1970.
  Oakland vs. Baltimore, 1971.
N.L.—0—Pittsburgh vs. Cincinnati, 1970.
4-game series
A.L.—1—New York vs. Kansas City, 1978.
  Boston vs. Oakland, 1988.
  Oakland vs. Boston, 1990.
N.L.—1—Los Angeles vs. Philadelphia, 1983.
5-game series
N.L.—1—San Diego vs. Chicago, 1984.
  San Francisco vs. St. Louis, 2002.
  St. Louis vs. San Francisco, 2002.
A.L.—1—New York vs. Baltimore, 1996.
  Seattle vs. New York, 2001.
6-game series
N.L.—1—New York vs. Houston, 1986.
  San Diego vs. Atlanta, 1998.
A.L.—1—New York vs. Seattle, 2000.
7-game series
N.L.—1—St. Louis vs. Houston, 2004.
A.L.—1—Boston vs. New York, 2004.

Fewest errors by both clubs, series

3-game series
A.L.—1—Baltimore 1, Oakland 0, 1971.
N.L.—1—Cincinnati 1, Pittsburgh 0, 1979.
4-game series
A.L.—4—Oakland 3, Boston 1, 1988.
N.L.—5—Atlanta 3, Philadelphia 2, 1995.
5-game series
N.L.—2—San Francisco 1, St. Louis 1, 2002.
A.L.—5—Oakland 3, Toronto 2, 1989.
  Baltimore 4, New York 1, 1996.
  New York 4, Seattle 1, 2001.
6-game series
A.L.—4—Seattle 3, New York 1, 2000.
N.L.—7—Pittsburgh 5, Cincinnati 2, 1990.
  Atlanta 4, Florida 3, 1997.
7-game series
N.L.—3—Houston 2, St. Louis 1, 2004.
A.L.—5—New York 4, Boston 1, 2004.

Most errors, game

A.L.—5—New York vs. Kansas City, October 10, 1976.
N.L.—5—Los Angeles vs. Pittsburgh, October 8, 1974.

Most errors by both clubs, game

A.L.—7—Oakland 4, Boston 3, October 4, 1975.
N.L.—5—Los Angeles 5, Pittsburgh 0, October 8, 1974.

Most errors by infield, game

A.L.—3—California vs. Boston, October 8, 1986.
  Oakland vs. Toronto, October 10, 1992.
  (3—Oakland vs. Baltimore, October 9, 1973, 11 innings.)
N.L.—3—Atlanta vs. Arizona, October 20, 2001.

Most errors by infields of both clubs, game

A.L.—5—California 3, Boston 2, October 8, 1986.
N.L.—3—Atlanta 2, New York 1, October 5, 1969.
  Pittsburgh 2, Cincinnati 1, October 10, 1972.
  Pittsburgh 2, Atlanta 1, October 14, 1991.
  St. Louis 2, Atlanta 1, October 10, 1996.
  Atlanta 3, Arizona 0, October 20, 2001.
  (3—New York 2, Los Angeles 1, October 9, 1988, 12 innings.
  Atlanta 2, New York 1, October 17, 1999, 15 innings.)

Most errors by outfield, game

A.L.—2—Minnesota vs. Baltimore, October 6, 1969.
  Oakland vs. Boston, October 4, 1975.
  Milwaukee vs. California, October 10, 1982.
  Cleveland vs. Seattle, October 15, 1995.
  Cleveland vs. Baltimore, October 9, 1997.
  New York vs. St. Louis, October 11, 2000.
N.L.—1—Held by many clubs.

Most errors by outfields of both clubs, game

A.L.—3—Oakland 2, Boston 1, October 4, 1975.
  Cleveland 2, Seattle 1, October 15, 1995.
N.L.—2—Philadelphia 1, Atlanta 1, October 13, 1993.
  New York 1, Atlanta 1, October 12, 1999.
  New York 2, St. Louis 0, October 11, 2000.
  (2—Atlanta 1, Pittsburgh 1, October 13, 1991, 10 innings.)

Longest errorless game

N.L.—16 innings—New York vs. Houston, October 15, 1986.
A.L.—12 innings—Cleveland vs. Baltimore, October 11, 1997.

Longest errorless game by both clubs

N.L.—11 innings—Pittsburgh vs. Cincinnati, October 2, 1979.
  Atlanta vs. Cincinnati, October 16, 1995.
  Florida vs. Chicago, October 10, 2003.
A.L.—11 innings—California vs. Boston, October 12, 1986.
  Cleveland vs. Baltimore, October 15, 1997.

Most errors, inning

A.L.—3—Oakland vs. Boston, October 4, 1975, first inning.
  California vs. Boston, October 8, 1986, seventh inning.
N.L.—3—Atlanta vs. Arizona, October 20, 2001, third inning.

PASSED BALLS

Most passed balls, total series

N.L.—6—Pittsburgh; nine series, 42 games.
  Atlanta; 11 series, 60 games.
A.L.—6—Boston, 7 series, 47 games.

Most passed balls, series

A.L.—3—Toronto vs. Oakland, 1992 (6-game series).
  Boston vs. New York, 2003 (7-game series).
  Boston vs. New York, 2004 (7-game series).
N.L.—2—many series.

Most passed balls by both clubs, series

A.L.—4—Boston 3, New York 1, 2004 (7-game series).
N.L.—3—Chicago 2, San Francisco 1, 1989 (5-game series).
  Pittsburgh 2, Atlanta 1, 1992 (7-game series).

Most passed balls, game

N.L.—2—Pittsburgh vs. Cincinnati, October 4, 1975.
  Houston vs. New York, October 11, 1986.
  Pittsburgh vs. Atlanta, October 13, 1992.
A.L.—2—Toronto vs. Oakland, October 14, 1992.
  (3—Boston vs. New York, October 18, 2004.)

Most passed balls, inning

A.L.—3—Boston vs. New York, October 18, 2004, 13th inning.
N.L.—1—Held by many clubs.

DOUBLE AND TRIPLE PLAYS

Most double plays, total series

N.L.—47—Atlanta; 11 series, 60 games.
A.L.—59—New York; 12 series, 61 games.

Most double plays, series

3-game series
A.L.—6—New York vs. Oakland, 1981.
N.L.—4—Atlanta vs. New York, 1969.
4-game series
N.L.—8—Los Angeles vs. Pittsburgh, 1974.
A.L.—7—California vs. Baltimore, 1979.
5-game series
N.L.—8—Montreal vs. Los Angeles, 1981.
A.L.—7—Baltimore vs. New York, 1996.
  New York vs. Boston, 1999.
6-game series
A.L.—11—Cleveland vs. Baltimore, 1997.
N.L.—9—New York vs. Atlanta, 1999.
7-game series
N.L.—10—San Francisco vs. St. Louis, 1987.
A.L.—12—New York vs. Boston, 2003.

Most double plays by both clubs, series

3-game series
A.L.—8—Minnesota 5, Baltimore 3, 1970.
N.L.—6—Atlanta 4, New York 2, 1969.

Cincinnati 3, Philadelphia 3, 1976.
4-game series
  A.L.—12—California 7, Baltimore 5, 1979.
  N.L.—11—Atlanta 7, Cincinnati 4, 1995.
5-game series
  N.L.—13—Montreal 8, Los Angeles 5, 1981.
  A.L.—9—Oakland 5, Detroit 4, 1972.
      Toronto 5, Oakland 4, 1989.
      Seattle 5, New York 4, 2001.
6-game series
  A.L.—15—Cleveland 11, Baltimore 4, 1997.
  N.L.—13—New York 9, Atlanta 4, 1999.
7-game series
  N.L.—15—San Francisco 10, St. Louis 5, 1987.
  A.L.—17—New York 12, Boston 5, 2003.

Fewest double plays, series

3-game series
  N.L.—0—Atlanta vs. St. Louis, 1982.
  A.L.—0—Detroit vs. Kansas City, 1984.
4-game series
  N.L.—0—Philadelphia vs. Los Angeles, 1983.
  A.L.—2—New York vs. Kansas City, 1978.
      Boston vs. Oakland, 1988.
5-game series
  A.L.—0—Boston vs. New York, 1999.
  N.L.—1—Chicago vs. San Francisco, 1989.
      New York vs. St. Louis, 2000.
6-game series
  N.L.—1—Atlanta vs. Philadelphia, 1993.
  A.L.—4—Cleveland vs. Seattle, 1995.
      Baltimore vs. Cleveland, 1997.
      Seattle vs. New York, 2000.
7-game series
  N.L.—2—New York vs. Los Angeles, 1988.

Houston vs. St. Louis, 2004.
  A.L.—4—Toronto vs. Kansas City, 1985.
      Boston vs. New York, 2004.

Fewest double plays by both clubs, series

3-game series
  A.L.—2—Kansas City 2, Detroit 0, 1984.
  N.L.—3—St. Louis 3, Atlanta 0, 1982.
4-game series
  N.L.—3—Los Angeles 3, Philadelphia 0, 1983.
  A.L.—6—Kansas City 4, New York 2, 1978.
5-game series
  A.L.—4—Kansas City 2, New York 2, 1977.
      Minnesota 3, Detroit 1, 1987.
  N.L.—4—St. Louis 3, New York 1, 2000.
6-game series
  N.L.—3—Philadelphia 2, Atlanta 1, 1993.
  A.L.—9—New York 5, Seattle 4, 2000.
7-game series
  N.L.—7—St. Louis 5, Houston 2, 2004.
  A.L.—10—Boston 5, California 5, 1986.

Most double plays, game

N.L.—4—Los Angeles vs. Montreal, October 13, 1981.
  San Francisco vs. St. Louis, October 10, 1987.
    (5—Atlanta vs. Cincinnati, October 10, 1995, 11 innings.)
A.L.—4—Oakland vs. Boston, October 5, 1975.
    (4—Cleveland vs. Baltimore, October 11, 1997, 12 innings.)

Most double plays by both clubs, game

A.L.—6—Oakland 4, Boston 2, October 5, 1975.
N.L.—5—Pittsburgh 3, Cincinnati 2, October 5, 1975.
    (6—Atlanta 5, Cincinnati 1, October 10, 1995, 11 innings.)

Most triple plays, series

A.L.-N.L.—Never accomplished.

MISCELLANEOUS

CLUB AND DIVISION
ONE-RUN DECISIONS

Most one-run games won, series

N.L.—3—New York vs. Houston, 1986 (6-game series).
  Atlanta vs. New York, 1999 (6-game series).
A.L.—4—Cleveland vs. Baltimore, 1997 (6-game series).

Most one-run games by both clubs, series

N.L.—5—Atlanta (won three) vs. New York (won two), 1999 (6-game series).
A.L.—4—Cleveland (won four) vs. Baltimore, 1997 (6-game series).

LENGTH OF GAMES
BY INNINGS

Longest game

N.L.—16 innings—New York 7, Houston 6, October 15, 1986 (at Houston).
A.L.—14 innings—Boston 5, New York 4, October 18, 2004 (at Boston).

For a complete list of extra-inning games,
see page 443.

Most extra-inning games, total series

A.L.—8—Baltimore; nine series, 37 games (won four, lost four).
N.L.—8—Atlanta; 11 series, 60 games (won three, lost five).

Most extra-inning games won, total series

A.L.—4—Baltimore; nine series, 37 games; lost four.
N.L.—4—Philadelphia; six series, 26 games; lost none.

Most extra-inning games lost, total series

N.L.—5—Atlanta; 11 series, 60 games; won three.

A.L.—4—Baltimore; nine series, 37 games; won four.

Most extra-inning games, series

N.L.—4—Philadelphia vs. Houston, 1980 (5-game series).
A.L.—2—Occurred often.

BY TIME

Longest nine-inning game

A.L.—4 hours, 20 minutes—New York 19, Boston 8, October 16, 2004 (at Boston).
N.L.—3 hours, 59 minutes—New York 6, St. Louis 5, October 12, 2000 (at St. Louis).

Longest extra-inning game

A.L.—5 hours, 49 minutes—Boston 5, New York 4, October 18, 2004, 14 innings (at Boston).
N.L.—5 hours, 46 minutes—New York 4, Atlanta 3, October 17, 1999, 15 innings (at New York).

Shortest game

A.L.—1 hour, 57 minutes—Oakland 1, Baltimore 0, October 8, 1974 (at Baltimore).
N.L.—1 hour, 57 minutes—Pittsburgh 5, Cincinnati 1, October 7, 1972 (at Pittsburgh).

SERIES STARTING AND FINISHING DATES

Earliest date for series game

N.L.—October 2, 1971—Pittsburgh at San Francisco.
  October 2, 1979—Pittsburgh at Cincinnati, 11 innings.
  October 2, 1984—San Diego at Chicago.
A.L.—October 2, 1984—Detroit at Kansas City.

Earliest date for series final game

N.L.—October 5, 1970—Pittsburgh at Cincinnati (3-game series).
  October 5, 1979—Cincinnati at Pittsburgh (3-game series).

A.L.—October 5, 1970—Minnesota at Baltimore (3-game series).
  October 5, 1971—Baltimore at Oakland (3-game series).
  October 5, 1984—Kansas City at Detroit (3-game series).

Latest date for series start
A.L.—October 17, 2001—New York at Seattle.
N.L.—October 16, 2001—Atlanta at Arizona.

Latest date for series finish
A.L.—October 22, 2001—Seattle at New York (5-game series).
N.L.—October 21, 2001—Arizona at Atlanta (5-game series).
  Houston at St. Louis (7-game series).

SERIES AND GAMES WON

Most series won
A.L.—10—New York, 1976, 1977, 1978, 1981, 1996, 1998, 1999, 2000, 2001, 2003 (lost two).
N.L.—5—Los Angeles, 1974, 1977, 1978, 1981, 1988 (lost two).
  Cincinnati, 1970, 1972, 1975, 1976, 1990 (lost three).
  Atlanta, 1991, 1992, 1995, 1996, 1999 (lost six).

For complete lists of results, and series played by all teams, see page 442.

Most consecutive years winning series
A.L.—4—New York, 1998 through 2001.
N.L.—2—Cincinnati, 1975, 1976.
  Los Angeles, 1977, 1978.
  Atlanta, 1991, 1992; 1995, 1996.

Most consecutive series won, division
N.L.—5—West Division, 1974, 1975, 1976, 1977, 1978.
  West Division, 1988, 1989, 1990, 1991, 1992.
A.L.—5—East Division, 1975, 1976, 1977, 1978, 1979.
  West Division, 1987, 1988, 1989, 1990, 1991.

Most times winning series in four consecutive games (since 1985)
A.L.—2—Oakland, 1988, 1990.
N.L.—1—Atlanta, 1995.

Most times winning series in three consecutive games (1969-1984)
A.L.—3—Baltimore, 1969, 1970, 1971.
N.L.—3—Cincinnati, 1970, 1975, 1976.

Winning series after winning first game
A.L—Accomplished 21 times.
N.L.—Accomplished 25 times.

Winning series after losing first game
A.L.—Accomplished 14 times.
N.L.—Accomplished 10 times.

Winning series after trailing two games to one
N.L.—Cincinnati vs. Pittsburgh, 1972 (5-game series).
  Philadelphia vs. Houston, 1980 (5-game series).
  Los Angeles vs. Montreal, 1981 (5-game series).
  San Diego vs. Chicago, 1984 (5-game series).
  St. Louis vs. Los Angeles, 1985 (6-game series).
  Los Angeles vs. New York, 1988 (7-game series).
  Philadelphia vs. Atlanta, 1993 (6-game series).
  Atlanta vs. St. Louis, 1996 (7-game series).
  Florida vs. Chicago, 2003 (7-game series).
A.L.—New York vs. Kansas City, 1977 (5-game series).
  Milwaukee vs. California, 1982 (5-game series).
  Kansas City vs. Toronto, 1985 (7-game series).
  Boston vs. California, 1986 (7-game series).
  Cleveland vs. Seattle, 1995 (6-game series).
  New York vs. Cleveland, 1998 (6-game series).

Winning series after trailing three games to one
A.L.—Kansas City vs. Toronto, 1985.
  Boston vs. California, 1986.
  Boston vs. New York, 2004.
N.L.—Atlanta vs. St. Louis, 1996.
  Florida vs. Chicago, 2003.

Winning series after losing first two games
A.L.—Milwaukee vs. California, 1982 (5-game series).

Kansas City vs. Toronto, 1985 (7-game series).
  Boston vs. New York, 2004 (7-game series).
N.L.—San Diego vs. Chicago, 1984 (5-game series).
  St. Louis vs. Los Angeles, 1985 (6-game series).

Winning series after losing first three games
A.L.—Boston vs. New York, 2004 (7-game series).
N.L.—Never accomplished.

Most games won, total series
A.L.—39—New York; 12 series; won 39, lost 22.
N.L.—27—Atlanta; 11 series; won 27, lost 33.

For complete lists of results, and games played by all teams, see page 442.

Most consecutive games won, total series
A.L.—10—Baltimore, 1969 (3), 1970 (3), 1971 (3), 1973 (first 1).
N.L.—6—Cincinnati, 1975 (3), 1976 (3).

Most consecutive games won, division
A.L.—9—East Division, 1969 (3), 1970 (3), 1971 (3).
N.L.—7—West Division, 1974 (last 1), 1975 (3), 1976 (3).

SERIES AND GAMES LOST

Most series lost
N.L.—7—Pittsburgh, 1970, 1972, 1974, 1975, 1990, 1991, 1992; won two.
A.L.—4—Kansas City, 1976, 1977, 1978, 1984; won two.
  Oakland, 1971, 1975, 1981, 1992; won six.
  Baltimore, 1973, 1974, 1996, 1997; won five.
  Boston, 1988, 1990, 1999, 2003; won two.

For complete lists of results, and series played by all teams, see page 442.

Most consecutive years losing series
A.L.—3—Kansas City, 1976, 1977, 1978.
N.L.—3—Philadelphia, 1976, 1977, 1978.
  Pittsburgh, 1990, 1991, 1992.

Most games lost, total series
N.L.—33—Atlanta; 11 series; won 27, lost 33.
A.L.—22—New York; 12 series; won 39, lost 22.

For complete lists of results, and games played by all teams, see page 442.

Most consecutive games lost, total series
A.L.—10—Boston, 1988 (4), 1990 (4), 1999 (2).
N.L.—7—Atlanta, 1969 (3), 1982 (3), 1991 (1).

ATTENDANCE

Largest attendance, series
3-game series
  N.L.—180,338—Cincinnati vs. Philadelphia, 1976.
  A.L.—151,539—Oakland vs. New York, 1981.
4-game series
  N.L.—240,584—Philadelphia vs. Los Angeles, 1977.
  A.L.—195,748—Baltimore vs. Chicago, 1983.
5-game series
  A.L.—284,691—California vs. Milwaukee, 1982.
  N.L.—271,558—New York vs. St. Louis, 2000.
6-game series
  N.L.—343,046—Philadelphia vs. Atlanta, 1993.
  A.L.—309,828—New York vs. Seattle, 2000.
7-game series
  N.L.—396,597—St. Louis vs. San Francisco, 1987.
  A.L.—329,600—New York vs. Boston, 2004.

For a list of attendance each series, see page 444.

Smallest attendance, series
3-game series
  A.L.—81,945—Baltimore vs. Minnesota, 1970.

N.L.—112,943—Pittsburgh vs. Cincinnati, 1970.
4-game series
A.L.—144,615—Baltimore vs. Oakland, 1974.
N.L.—157,348—San Francisco vs. Pittsburgh, 1971.
5-game series
A.L.—175,833—Baltimore vs. Oakland, 1973.
N.L.—206,630—Arizona vs. Atlanta, 2001.
6-game series
A.L.—282,431—Cleveland vs. Baltimore, 1997.
N.L.—299,316—New York vs. Houston, 1986.
7-game series
A.L.—264,167—Kansas City vs. Toronto, 1985.
N.L.—337,655—Houston vs. St. Louis, 2004.

Largest attendance, game
N.L.—65,829—At Florida, October 11, 2003 (Chicago 8, Florida 3).
A.L.—64,406—At California, October 5, 1982 (California 8, Milwaukee 3).

Smallest attendance, game
A.L.—24,265—At Oakland, October 11, 1973 (Oakland 3, Baltimore 0).
N.L.—33,088—At Pittsburgh, October 3, 1970 (Cincinnati 3, Pittsburgh 0).

Largest attendance by each club, game

AMERICAN LEAGUE

Club	Attendance	Date
Baltimore	52,787	Oct. 3,1979
Boston	35,578	Oct. 4, 1975
		Oct. 5, 1975
California/Anaheim	64,406	Oct. 5, 1982
Chicago	46,635	Oct. 7, 1983
Cleveland	45,081	Oct. 12, 1997
Detroit	52,168	Oct. 5, 1984
Kansas City	42,633	Oct. 9, 1980
Milwaukee	54,968	Oct. 10, 1982
Minnesota	55,990	Oct. 9, 2002
New York	57,181	Oct. 13, 1999
Oakland	49,444	Oct. 4, 1989
Seattle	58,489	Oct. 17, 1995
Toronto	51,889	Oct. 9, 1993

NATIONAL LEAGUE

Club	Attendance	Date
Arizona	49,334	Oct. 17, 2001
Atlanta	52,335	Oct. 19, 1999
Chicago	39,577	Oct. 14, 2003
Cincinnati	56,079	Oct. 12, 1990
Florida	65,829	Oct. 11, 2003
Houston	42,896	Oct. 17, 2004
Los Angeles	55,973	Oct. 5, 1977
Montreal	54,499	Oct. 17, 1981
New York	55,911	Oct. 15, 1999
Philadelphia	65,476	Oct. 8, 1980
Pittsburgh	57,533	Oct. 10, 1991
St. Louis	52,140	Oct. 21, 2004
San Diego	62,779	Oct. 10, 1998
San Francisco	62,084	Oct. 9, 1989

Smallest attendance by each club, game

AMERICAN LEAGUE

Club	Attendance	Date
Baltimore	27,608	Oct. 5, 1970
Boston	32,786	Oct. 8, 1986
California/Anaheim	43,199	Oct. 5, 1979
		Oct. 6, 1979
Chicago	45,477	Oct. 8, 1983
Cleveland	43,607	Oct. 16, 1995
Detroit	37,615	Oct. 11, 1972
Kansas City	40,046	Oct. 13, 1985
Milwaukee	50,135	Oct. 8, 1982
Minnesota	26,847	Oct. 3, 1970
New York	48,497	Oct. 14, 1981
Oakland	24,265	Oct. 11, 1973
Seattle	47,644	Oct. 17, 2001
Toronto	32,084	Oct. 16, 1985

NATIONAL LEAGUE

Club	Attendance	Date
Arizona	37,729	Oct. 16, 2001
Atlanta	35,652	Oct. 21, 2001
Chicago	36,282	Oct. 2, 1984
		Oct. 3, 1984
Cincinnati	39,447	Oct. 10, 1972
Florida	51,982	Oct. 12, 1997
Houston	44,131	Oct. 8, 1986
Los Angeles	40,060	Oct. 4, 1983
Montreal	36,491	Oct. 19, 1981
New York	44,672	Oct. 8, 1988
Philadelphia	53,490	Oct. 7, 1983
Pittsburgh	33,088	Oct. 3, 1970
St. Louis	52,175	Oct. 9, 2002
San Diego	58,346	Oct. 4, 1984
San Francisco	40,977	Oct. 2, 1971

NON-PLAYING PERSONNEL

MANAGERS

Most series by manager
M.L.—10—Bobby Cox, Toronto A.L., 1985; Atlanta N.L., 1991 through 2001, except 1994 and 2000 (won five, lost five).
N.L.—9—Bobby Cox, Atlanta, 1991 through 2001, except 1994 and 2000 (won five, lost four).
A.L.—7—Joe Torre, New York, 1996, 1998, 1999, 2000, 2001, 2003, 2004 (won six, lost one).

For a complete list of managers and their records, see page 453.

Most championship series winners managed
M.L.—5—Sparky Anderson, Cincinnati N.L., 1970, 1972, 1975, 1976; Detroit A.L., 1984.
N.L.—5—Bobby Cox, Atlanta, 1991, 1992, 1995, 1996, 1999.
A.L.—6—Joe Torre, New York, 1996, 1998 through 2001, 2003.

Most championship series losers managed
Both leagues—5—Bobby Cox, Toronto A.L., 1985; Atlanta N.L., 1993, 1997, 1998, 2001.
Tony La Russa, Chicago A.L., 1983; Oakland A.L., 1992; St. Louis N.L., 1996, 2000, 2002.

A.L.—3—Whitey Herzog, Kansas City, 1976, 1977, 1978.
Billy Martin, Minnesota, 1969; Detroit, 1972; Oakland, 1981.
Lou Piniella, Seattle, 1995, 2000, 2001.
N.L.—4—Bobby Cox, Atlanta, 1993, 1997, 1998, 2001.

Most different clubs managed, league
A.L.—4—Billy Martin, Minnesota 1970; Detroit 1972; New York 1976, 1977; Oakland 1981.
N.L.—2—Bill Virdon, Pittsburgh 1972; Houston 1980.
Dave Johnson, New York 1986, 1988; Cincinnati 1995.

UMPIRES

Most series umpired
10—Jerry Crawford; 55 games.
　　Bruce Froemming; 52 games.

Most games umpired
56—Jerry Crawford; 10 series.

CHAMPIONSHIP SERIES Non-playing personnel

GENERAL REFERENCE

SERIES WON AND LOST BY TEAMS

AMERICAN LEAGUE

	W	L	Pct.
Milwaukee	1	0	1.000
New York	10	2	.833
Cleveland	2	1	.667
Oakland	6	4	.600
Baltimore	5	4	.556
Boston	3	4	.429
Minnesota	2	3	.400
Toronto	2	3	.400
Detroit	1	2	.333
Kansas City	2	4	.333
California/Anaheim	1	3	.250
Chicago	0	2	.000
Seattle	0	3	.000

Total series: 35

NATIONAL LEAGUE

	W	L	Pct.
Florida	2	0	1.000
San Diego	2	0	1.000
Arizona	1	0	1.000
Los Angeles	5	2	.714
New York	4	2	.667
Cincinnati	5	3	.625
St. Louis	4	3	.571
Philadelphia	3	3	.500
San Francisco	2	2	.500
Atlanta	5	6	.455
Pittsburgh	2	7	.222
Montreal	0	1	.000
Houston	0	3	.000
Chicago	0	3	.000

Total series: 35

GAMES WON AND LOST BY TEAMS

AMERICAN LEAGUE

	W	L	Pct.
New York	39	22	.639
Milwaukee	3	2	.600
Baltimore	21	16	.568
Cleveland	10	8	.556
Oakland	23	19	.548
California/Anaheim	10	11	.476
Detroit	6	7	.462
Toronto	13	16	.448
Kansas City	12	15	.444
Minnesota	9	12	.429
Boston	15	22	.405
Seattle	5	12	.294
Chicago	3	7	.300

Total games: 169

NATIONAL LEAGUE

	W	L	Pct.
Arizona	4	1	.800
San Diego	7	4	.636
Florida	8	5	.615
New York	19	13	.594
San Francisco	12	9	.571
Cincinnati	18	14	.563
Los Angeles	19	15	.559
St. Louis	20	20	.500
Philadelphia	12	14	.462
Atlanta	27	33	.450
Pittsburgh	17	25	.405
Montreal	2	3	.400
Houston	7	11	.389
Chicago	6	11	.353

Total games: 178

HOME AND ROAD GAMES BY TEAMS

AMERICAN LEAGUE

	Years	Games	Home	Away
New York	12	61	31	30
Oakland	10	42	19	23
Baltimore	9	37	19	18
Boston	7	37	19	18
Toronto	5	29	16	13
Kansas City	6	27	14	13
Minnesota	5	21	9	12
California/Anaheim	4	21	10	11
Cleveland	3	18	9	9
Seattle	3	17	8	9
Detroit	3	13	7	6
Chicago	2	10	5	5
Milwaukee	1	5	3	2

NATIONAL LEAGUE

	Years	Games	Home	Away
Atlanta	11	60	30	30
Pittsburgh	9	42	20	22
St. Louis	7	40	20	20
Los Angeles	7	34	17	17
Cincinnati	8	32	16	16
New York	6	32	16	16
Philadelphia	6	26	13	13
San Francisco	4	21	11	10
Houston	3	18	9	9
Chicago	3	17	8	9
Florida	2	13	6	7
San Diego	2	11	6	5
Arizona	1	5	2	3
Montreal	1	5	3	2

SHUTOUTS

AMERICAN LEAGUE

Oct. 5, 1969   Dave McNally, Baltimore 1, Minnesota 0, 11 innings (three hits).

Oct. 8, 1972   Blue Moon Odom, Oakland 5, Detroit 0 (three hits).

Oct. 10, 1972   Joe Coleman, Detroit 3, Oakland 0 (seven hits).

Oct. 6, 1973   Jim Palmer, Baltimore 6, Oakland 0 (five hits).

Oct. 11, 1973 Catfish Hunter, Oakland 3, Baltimore 0 (five hits).
Oct. 6, 1974 Ken Holtzman, Oakland 5, Baltimore 0 (five hits).
Oct. 8, 1974 Vida Blue, Oakland 1, Baltimore 0 (two hits).
Oct. 6, 1979 Scott McGregor, Baltimore 8, California 0 (six hits).
Oct. 15, 1981 Dave Righetti, Ron Davis and Rich Gossage, New York 4, Oakland 0 (five hits).
Oct. 6, 1983 Mike Boddicker, Baltimore 4, Chicago 0 (five hits).
Oct. 8, 1983 Storm Davis and Tippy Martinez, Baltimore 3, Chicago 0, 10 innings (10 hits).
Oct. 5, 1984 Milt Wilcox and Willie Hernandez, Detroit 1, Kansas City 0 (three hits).
Oct. 13, 1985 Danny Jackson, Kansas City 2, Toronto 0 (eight hits).
Oct. 14, 1995 Ken Hill, Jim Poole, Chad Ogea and Alan Embree, Cleveland 7, Seattle 0 (six hits).
Oct. 17, 1995 Dennis Martinez, Julian Tavares and Jose Mesa, Cleveland 4, Seattle 0 (four hits).
Oct. 8, 1997 Scott Erickson and Randy Myers, Baltimore 3, Cleveland 0 (four hits).
Oct. 15, 1997 Charles Nagy, Paul Assenmacher, Mike Jackson, Brian Anderson and Jose Mesa, Cleveland 1, Baltimore 0, 11 innings (10 hits).
Oct. 10, 1998 Orlando Hernandez, New York 4, Cleveland 0, (four hits).
Oct. 10, 2000 Freddy Garcia, Jose Paniagua, Arthur Rhodes and Kazuhiro Sasaki, Seattle 2, New York 0 (six hits).
Oct. 14, 2000 Roger Clemens, New York 5, Seattle 0 (one hit).

Total number of shutouts: 20

NATIONAL LEAGUE

Oct. 3, 1970 Gary Nolan and Clay Carroll, Cincinnati 3, Pittsburgh 0, 10 innings (eight hits).
Oct. 7, 1973 Jon Matlack, New York 5, Cincinnati 0 (two hits).
Oct. 5, 1974 Don Sutton, Los Angeles 3, Pittsburgh 0 (four hits).
Oct. 8, 1974 Bruce Kison and Ramon Hernandez, Pittsburgh 7, Los Angeles 0 (four hits).
Oct. 4, 1978 Tommy John, Los Angeles 4, Philadelphia 0 (four hits).
Oct. 10, 1980 Joe Niekro and Dave Smith, Houston 1, Philadelphia 0, 11 innings (seven hits).
Oct. 14, 1981 Ray Burris, Montreal 3, Los Angeles 0 (five hits).
Oct. 7, 1982 Bob Forsch, St. Louis 7, Atlanta 0 (three hits).
Oct. 4, 1983 Steve Carlton and Al Holland, Philadelphia 1, Los Angeles 0 (seven hits).
Oct. 2, 1984 Rick Sutcliffe and Warren Brusstar, Chicago 13, San Diego 0 (six hits).
Oct. 8, 1986 Mike Scott, Houston 1, New York 0 (five hits).
Oct. 7, 1987 Dave Dravecky, San Francisco 5, St. Louis 0 (two hits).
Oct. 13, 1987 John Tudor, Todd Worrell and Ken Dayley, St. Louis 1, San Francisco 0 (six hits).
Oct. 14, 1987 Danny Cox, St. Louis 6, San Francisco 0 (eight hits).
Oct. 12, 1988 Orel Hershiser, Los Angeles 6, New York 0 (five hits).
Oct. 10, 1991 Steve Avery and Alejandro Pena, Atlanta 1, Pittsburgh 0 (six hits).
Oct. 14, 1991 Zane Smith and Roger Mason, Pittsburgh 1, Atlanta 0 (nine hits).
Oct. 16, 1991 Steve Avery and Alejandro Pena, Atlanta 1, Pittsburgh 0 (four hits).

Oct. 17, 1991 John Smoltz, Atlanta 4, Pittsburgh 0 (six hits).
Oct. 14, 1995 Steve Avery, Greg McMichael, Alejandro Pena and Mark Wohlers, Atlanta 6, Cincinnati 0 (three hits).
Oct. 14, 1996 John Smoltz, Mike Bielecki, Terrell Wade and Brad Clontz, Atlanta 14, St. Louis 0 (seven hits).
Oct. 17, 1996 Tom Glavine, Mike Bielecki and Steve Avery, Atlanta, 15, St. Louis 0 (four hits).
Oct. 11, 1997 Denny Neagle, Atlanta 4, Florida 0 (four hits).
Oct. 8, 1998 Kevin Brown, San Diego 3, Atlanta 0 (three hits).
Oct. 14, 1998 Sterling Hitchcock, Brian Boehringer, Mark Langston, Joey Hamilton and Trevor Hoffman, San Diego 5, Atlanta 0 (two hits).
Oct. 15, 1999 Tom Glavine, Mike Remlinger and John Rocker, Atlanta 1, New York 0 (seven hits).
Oct. 16, 2000 Mike Hampton, New York 7, St. Louis 0 (three hits).
Oct. 16, 2001 Randy Johnson, Arizona 2, Atlanta 0 (three hits).
Oct. 12, 2003 Josh Beckett, Florida 4, Chicago 0 (two hits).
Oct. 18, 2004 Brandon Backe and Brad Lidge, Houston 3, St. Louis 0 (one hit).

Total number of shutouts: 30

EXTRA-INNING GAMES

AMERICAN LEAGUE

Oct. 4, 1969 12 innings, Baltimore 4, Minnesota 3.
Oct. 5, 1969 11 innings, Baltimore 1, Minnesota 0.
Oct. 7, 1972 11 innings, Oakland 3, Detroit 2.
Oct. 11, 1972 10 innings, Detroit 4, Oakland 3.
Oct. 9, 1973 11 innings, Oakland 2, Baltimore 1.
Oct. 3, 1979 10 innings, Baltimore 6, California 2.
Oct. 8, 1983 10 innings, Baltimore 3, Chicago 0.
Oct. 3, 1984 11 innings, Detroit 5, Kansas City 3.
Oct. 9, 1985 10 innings, Toronto 6, Kansas City 5.
Oct. 11, 1986 11 innings, California 4, Boston 3.
Oct. 12, 1986 11 innings, Boston 7, California 6.
Oct. 11, 1991 10 innings, Minnesota 3, Toronto 2.
Oct. 11, 1992 11 innings, Toronto 7, Oakland 6.
Oct. 13, 1995 11 innings, Seattle 5, Cleveland 2.
Oct. 9, 1996 11 innings, New York 5, Baltimore 4.
Oct. 11, 1997 12 innings, Cleveland 2, Baltimore 1.
Oct. 15, 1997 11 innings, Cleveland 1, Baltimore 0.
Oct. 7, 1998 12 innings, Cleveland 4, New York 1.
Oct. 13, 1999 10 innings, New York 4, Boston 3.
Oct. 16, 2003 11 innings, New York 6, Boston 5.
Oct. 17, 2004 12 innings, Boston 6, New York 4.
Oct. 18, 2004 14 innings, Boston 5, New York 4.

Total number of extra-inning games: 22

NATIONAL LEAGUE

Oct. 3, 1970 10 innings, Cincinnati 3, Pittsburgh 0.
Oct. 9, 1973 12 innings, Cincinnati 2, New York 1.
Oct. 7, 1975 10 innings, Cincinnati 5, Pittsburgh 3.
Oct. 7, 1978 10 innings, Los Angeles 4, Philadelphia 3.
Oct. 2, 1979 11 innings, Pittsburgh 5, Cincinnati 2.
Oct. 3, 1979 10 innings, Pittsburgh 3, Cincinnati 2.
Oct. 8, 1980 10 innings, Houston 7, Philadelphia 4.
Oct. 10, 1980 11 innings, Houston 1, Philadelphia 0.
Oct. 11, 1980 10 innings, Philadelphia 5, Houston 3.
Oct. 12, 1980 10 innings, Philadelphia 8, Houston 7.
Oct. 14, 1986 12 innings, New York 2, Houston 1.
Oct. 15, 1986 16 innings, New York 7, Houston 6.

Oct. 9, 1988   12 innings, Los Angeles 5, New York 4.
Oct. 13, 1991 10 innings, Pittsburgh 3, Atlanta 2.
Oct. 6, 1993   10 innings, Philadelphia 4, Atlanta 3.
Oct. 11, 1993 10 innings, Philadelphia 4, Atlanta 3.
Oct. 10, 1995 11 innings, Atlanta 2, Cincinnati 1.
Oct. 11, 1995 10 innings, Atlanta 6, Cincinnati 2.
Oct. 7, 1998   10 innings, San Diego 3, Atlanta 2.
Oct. 17, 1999 15 innings, New York 4, Atlanta 3.
Oct. 19, 1999 11 innings, Atlanta 10, New York 9.
Oct. 7, 2003   11 innings, Florida 9, Chicago 8.
Oct. 10, 2003 11 innings, Chicago 5, Florida 4.
Oct. 20, 2004 12 innings, St. Louis 6, Houston 4.

Total number of extra-inning games: 24

ATTENDANCE

AMERICAN LEAGUE

Year	Games	Total
1969	3	113,763
1970	3	81,945
1971	3	110,800
1972	5	189,671
1973	5	175,833
1974	4	144,615
1975	3	120,514
1976	5	252,152
1977	5	234,713
1978	4	194,192
1979	4	191,293
1980	3	141,819
1981	3	151,539
1982	5	284,691
1983	4	195,748
1984	3	136,160
1985	7	264,167
1986	7	324,430
1987	5	257,631
1988	4	167,376
1989	5	249,247
1990	4	168,340
1991	5	263,987
1992	6	293,086
1993	6	292,921
1995	6	304,634
1996	5	259,254
1997	6	282,431
1998	6	323,007
1999	5	214,726
2000	6	309,828
2001	5	264,697
2002	5	245,451
2003	7	328,559
2004	7	329,600

NATIONAL LEAGUE

Year	Games	Total
1969	3	153,587
1970	3	112,943
1971	4	157,348
1972	5	234,814
1973	5	262,548
1974	4	200,262
1975	3	155,740
1976	3	180,338
1977	4	240,584
1978	4	234,269
1979	3	152,246
1980	5	264,950
1981	5	250,098
1982	3	158,589
1983	4	223,914
1984	5	247,623
1985	6	326,824
1986	6	299,316
1987	7	396,597
1988	7	373,695
1989	5	264,617
1990	6	310,528
1991	7	369,443
1992	7	374,599
1993	6	343,046
1995	4	188,497
1996	7	375,202
1997	6	309,352
1998	6	306,259
1999	6	308,637
2000	5	271,558
2001	5	206,630
2002	5	231,896
2003	7	354,503
2004	7	337,655

INDIVIDUAL BATTING

LEADING BATTERS

(Playing in all games, each series, with four or more hits)

AMERICAN LEAGUE

Year	Player, Club	AB	H	TB	Avg.
1969	Brooks Robinson, Baltimore	14	7	8	.500
1970	Brooks Robinson, Baltimore	12	7	9	.583
1971	Brooks Robinson, Baltimore	11	4	8	.364
	Sal Bando, Oakland	11	4	9	.364
1972	Matty Alou, Oakland	21	8	12	.381
1973	Bert Campaneris, Oakland	21	7	14	.333
1974	Ray Fosse, Oakland	12	4	8	.333
1975	Sal Bando, Oakland	12	6	8	.500
1976	Chris Chambliss, New York	21	11	20	.524
1977	Hal McRae, Kansas City	18	8	14	.444
1978	Reggie Jackson, New York	13	6	13	.462
1979	Eddie Murray, Baltimore	12	5	8	.417
1980	Frank White, Kansas City	11	6	10	.545
1981	Graig Nettles, New York	12	6	11	.500
	Jerry Mumphrey, New York	12	6	7	.500
1982	Fred Lynn, California	18	11	16	.611
1983	Cal Ripken Jr., Baltimore	15	6	8	.400
1984	Kirk Gibson, Detroit	12	5	9	.417
1985	Cliff Johnson, Toronto	19	7	9	.368
1986	Bob Boone, California	22	10	13	.455
1987	Tom Brunansky, Minnesota	17	7	17	.412
1988	Ron Hassey, Oakland	8	4	8	.500

Year	Player, Club	AB	H	TB	Avg.
1989	Rickey Henderson, Oakland	15	6	15	.400
1990	Wade Boggs, Boston	16	7	11	.438
	Carney Lansford, Oakland	16	7	8	.438
1991	Roberto Alomar, Toronto	19	9	9	.474
1992	Harold Baines, Oakland	25	11	16	.440
1993	Tim Raines Sr., Chicago	27	12	14	.444
	Devon White, Toronto	27	12	18	.444
1994	No series played.				
1995	Kenny Lofton, Cleveland	24	11	15	.458
1996	Bernie Williams, New York	19	9	18	.474
1997	Brady Anderson, Baltimore	25	9	17	.360
1998	Omar Vizquel, Cleveland	25	11	13	.440
1999	Jose Offerman, Boston	24	11	13	.458
2000	Bernie Williams, New York	23	10	14	.435
2001	Paul O'Neill, New York	12	5	11	.417
2002	Dustan Mohr, Minnesota	12	5	6	.417
2003	Todd Walker, Boston	27	10	19	.370
2004	Hideki Matsui, New York	34	14	28	.412

NATIONAL LEAGUE

Year	Player, Club	AB	H	TB	Avg.
1969	Art Shamsky, New York	13	7	7	.538
1970	Willie Stargell, Pittsburgh	12	6	7	.500
1971	Bob Robertson, Pittsburgh	16	7	20	.438
1972	Pete Rose, Cincinnati	20	9	13	.450
1973	Pete Rose, Cincinnati	21	8	15	.381
1974	Willie Stargell, Pittsburgh	15	6	12	.400
1975	Richie Zisk, Pittsburgh	10	5	6	.500
1976	Jay Johnstone, Philadelphia	9	7	10	.778
1977	Bob Boone, Philadelphia	10	4	4	.400
1978	Dusty Baker, Los Angeles	15	7	9	.467
1979	Willie Stargell, Pittsburgh	11	5	13	.455
1980	Terry Puhl, Houston	19	10	12	.526
1981	Gary Carter, Montreal	16	7	8	.438
1982	Darrell Porter, St. Louis	9	5	8	.556
	Ozzie Smith, St. Louis	9	5	5	.556
1983	Mike Schmidt, Philadelphia	15	7	12	.467
1984	Steve Garvey, San Diego	20	8	12	.400
1985	Ozzie Smith, St. Louis	23	10	16	.435
1986	Lenny Dykstra, New York	23	7	13	.304
1987	Jeffrey Leonard, San Francisco	24	10	22	.417
1988	Lenny Dykstra, New York	14	6	12	.439
1989	Will Clark, San Francisco	20	13	24	.650
1990	Mariano Duncan, Cincinnati	20	6	9	.300
1991	Jay Bell, Pittsburgh	29	12	17	.414
1992	Mark Lemke, Atlanta	21	7	8	.333
1993	Fred McGriff, Atlanta	23	10	15	.435
1994	No series played.				
1995	Chipper Jones, Atlanta	16	7	10	.438
	Fred McGriff, Atlanta	16	7	11	.438
1996	Javy Lopez, Atlanta	24	13	24	.542
1997	Keith Lockhart, Atlanta	16	8	11	.500
1998	Michael Tucker, Atlanta	13	5	9	.385
1999	Eddie Perez, Atlanta	20	10	18	.500
	Roger Cedeno, New York	12	6	7	.500
2000	Edgardo Alfonzo, New York	18	8	11	.444
2001	Craig Counsell, Arizona	21	8	11	.381
2002	David Bell, San Francisco	17	7	11	.412
2003	Jeff Conine, Florida	24	11	17	.458
2004	Albert Pujols, St. Louis	28	14	28	.500

.500 HITTERS

(Playing in all games and having nine or more at-bats)

AMERICAN LEAGUE

Player, Club	Year	AB	H	TB	Avg.
Fred Lynn, California	1982	18	11	16	.611
Brooks Robinson, Baltimore	1970	12	7	9	.583
Frank White, Kansas City	1980	11	6	10	.545
Chris Chambliss, New York	1976	21	11	20	.524
Brooks Robinson, Baltimore	1969	14	7	8	.500
Tony Oliva, Minnesota	1970	12	6	11	.500
Sal Bando, Oakland	1975	12	6	8	.500
Bob Watson, New York	1980	12	6	11	.500
Graig Nettles, New York	1981	12	6	11	.500
Jerry Mumphrey, New York	1981	12	6	7	.500

Total number of occurrences: 10

NATIONAL LEAGUE

Player, Club	Year	AB	H	TB	Avg.
Jay Johnstone, Philadelphia	1976	9	7	10	.778
Will Clark, San Francisco	1989	20	13	24	.650
Mark Grace, Chicago	1989	17	11	19	.647
Darrell Porter, St. Louis	1982	9	5	8	.556
Ozzie Smith, St. Louis	1982	9	5	5	.556
Javy Lopez, Atlanta	1996	24	13	24	.542
Art Shamsky, New York	1969	13	7	7	.538
Terry Puhl, Houston	1980	19	10	12	.526
Albert Pujols, St. Louis	2004	28	14	28	.500
Keith Lockhart, Atlanta	1997	16	8	11	.500
Eddie Perez, Atlanta	1999	20	10	18	.500
Willie Stargell, Pittsburgh	1970	12	6	7	.500
Roger Cedeno, New York	1999	12	6	7	.500
Richie Zisk, Pittsburgh	1975	10	5	6	.500

Total number of occurrences: 14

HOME RUNS

AMERICAN LEAGUE

1969—4—Baltimore (East), Frank Robinson, Mark Belanger, Boog Powell, Paul Blair.

1—Minnesota (West), Tony Oliva.

1970—6—Baltimore (East), Dave Johnson 2, Mike Cuellar, Don Buford, Boog Powell, Frank Robinson.

3—Minnesota (West), Harmon Killebrew 2, Tony Oliva.

1971—4—Baltimore (East), Boog Powell 2, Brooks Robinson, Elrod Hendricks.

3—Oakland (West), Reggie Jackson 2, Sal Bando.

1972—4—Detroit (East), Norm Cash, Al Kaline, Bill Freehan, Dick McAuliffe.

1—Oakland (West), Mike Epstein.

1973—5—Oakland (West), Sal Bando 2, Bert Campaneris 2, Joe Rudi.

3—Baltimore (East), Earl Williams, Andy Etchebarren, Bobby Grich.

1974—3—Baltimore (East), Paul Blair, Brooks Robinson, Bobby Grich.

3—Oakland (West), Sal Bando 2, Ray Fosse.

1975—2—Boston (East), Carl Yastrzemski, Rico Petrocelli.

1—Oakland (West), Reggie Jackson.

1976—4—New York (East), Graig Nettles 2, Chris Chambliss 2.

2—Kansas City (West), John Mayberry, George Brett.

1977—3—Kansas City (West), Hal McRae, John Mayberry, Al Cowens.

2—New York (East), Thurman Munson, Cliff Johnson.

1978—5—New York (East), Reggie Jackson 2, Thurman Munson, Graig Nettles, Roy White.

4—Kansas City (West), George Brett 3, Fred Patek.

1979—3—Baltimore (East), John Lowenstein, Eddie Murray, Pat Kelly.

3—California (West), Dan Ford 2, Don Baylor.

1980—3—New York (East), Rick Cerone, Lou Piniella, Graig Nettles.

3—Kansas City (West), George Brett 2, Frank White.

1981—3—New York (East), Lou Piniella, Graig Nettles, Willie Randolph.

0—Oakland (West).

1982—5—Milwaukee (East), Paul Molitor 2, Gorman Thomas, Mark Brouhard, Ben Oglivie.

4—California (West), Fred Lynn, Reggie Jackson, Bob Boone, Don Baylor.

1983—3—Baltimore (East), Gary Roenicke, Eddie Murray, Tito Landrum.

0—Chicago (West).

1984—4—Detroit (East), Kirk Gibson, Larry Herndon, Lance Parrish, Alan Trammell.

0—Kansas City (West).

1985—7—Kansas City (West), George Brett 3, Pat Sheridan 2, Willie Wilson, Jim Sundberg.

2—Toronto (East), Jesse Barfield, Rance Mulliniks.

1986—7—California (West), Bob Boone, Doug DeCinces, Brian Downing, Bobby Grich, Wally Joyner, Gary Pettis, Dick Schofield.

6—Boston (East), Jim Rice 2, Don Baylor, Dwight Evans, Rich Gedman, Dave Henderson.

1987—8—Minnesota (West), Tom Brunansky 2, Gary Gaetti 2, Greg Gagne 2, Kent Hrbek, Kirby Puckett.

7—Detroit (East), Chet Lemon 2, Kirk Gibson, Mike Heath, Matt Nokes, Pat Sheridan, Lou Whitaker.

1988—7—Oakland (West), Jose Canseco 3, Ron Hassey, Dave Henderson, Carney Lansford, Mark McGwire.

2—Boston (East), Rich Gedman, Mike Greenwell.

1989—7—Oakland (West), Rickey Henderson 2, Dave Parker 2, Jose Canseco, Dave Henderson, Mark McGwire.

3—Toronto (East), George Bell, Lloyd Moseby, Ernie Whitt.

1990—1—Boston (East), Wade Boggs.

0—Oakland (West).

1991—3—Minnesota (West), Kirby Puckett 2, Mike Pagliarulo.

1—Toronto (East), Joe Carter.

1992—10—Toronto (East), Roberto Alomar 2, Candy Maldonado 2, Dave Winfield 2, Pat Borders, Joe Carter, Kelly Gruber, John Olerud.

4—Oakland (West), Harold Baines, Mark McGwire, Ruben Sierra, Terry Steinbach.

1993—5—Chicago (West), Ellis Burks, Lance Johnson, Warren Newson, Frank Thomas, Robin Ventura.

2—Toronto (East), Paul Molitor, Devon White.

1994—No series played.

1995—7—Cleveland (Central), Manny Ramirez 2, Jim Thome 2, Carlos Baerga, Albert Belle, Eddie Murray.

5—Seattle (West), Jay Buhner 3, Mike Blowers, Ken Griffey Jr.

1996—10—New York (East), Darryl Strawberry 3, Cecil Fielder 2, Bernie Williams 2, Derek Jeter 2, Jim Leyritz, Paul O'Neill.

9—Baltimore (East), Todd Zeile 3, Rafael Palmeiro 2, Brady Anderson, Bobby Bonilla, Chris Hoiles, Eddie Murray.

1997—7—Baltimore (East), Brady Anderson 2, Roberto Alomar, Harold Baines, Eric Davis, Rafael Palmeiro, Cal Ripken Jr.

5—Cleveland (Central), Manny Ramirez 2, Sandy Alomar Jr., Tony Fernandez, Marquis Grisson.

1998—9—Cleveland (Central), Jim Thome 4, Manny Ramirez 2, David Justice, Kenny Lofton, Mark Whiten.

4—New York (East), Scott Brosius, Chili Davis, Paul O'Neill, Jorge Posada.

1999—8—New York (East), Scott Brosius 2, Derek Jeter, Ricky Ledee, Tino Martinez, Jorge Posada, Darryl Strawberry, Bernie Williams.

5—Boston (East), Nomar Garciaparra 2, Brian Daubach, John Valentin, Jason Varitek.

2000—6—New York (East), Derek Jeter 2, David Justice 2, Tino Martinez, Bernie Williams.

5—Seattle (West), Alex Rodriguez 2, Carlos Guillen, Edgar Martinez, John Olerud.

2001—7—New York (East), Bernie Williams 3, Paul O'Neill 2, Tino Martinez, Alfonso Soriano.

5—Seattle (West), Bret Boone 2, Jay Buhner, Stan Javier, John Olerud.

2002—8—Anaheim (West), Adam Kennedy 3, Garret Anderson, Darin Erstad, Brad Fullmer, Troy Glaus, Scott Spiezio.

0—Minnesota (Central).

2003—12—Boston (East), Trot Nixon 3, David Ortiz 2, Manny Ramirez 2, Jason Varitek 2, Todd Walker 2, Kevin Millar.

8—New York (East), Jason Giambi 3, Aaron Boone, Derek Jeter, Nick Johnson, Jorge Posada, Ruben Sierra.

2004—10—Boston (East), David Ortiz 3, Mark Bellhorn 2, Johnny Damon 2, Jason Varitek 2, Trot Nixon.

9—New York (East), Hideki Matsui 2, Alex Rodriguez 2, Bernie Williams 2, Kenny Lofton, John Olerud, Gary Sheffield.

Total number of home runs: 315

NATIONAL LEAGUE

1969—6—New York (East), Tommie Agee 2, Ken Boswell 2, Cleon Jones, Wayne Garrett.

5—Atlanta (West), Hank Aaron 3, Tony Gonzalez, Orlando Cepeda.

1970—3—Cincinnati (West), Bobby Tolan, Tony Perez, Johnny Bench.

0—Pittsburgh (East).

1971—8—Pittsburgh (East), Bob Robertson 4, Richie Hebner 2, Gene Clines, Al Oliver.

5—San Francisco (West), Willie McCovey 2, Tito Fuentes, Willie Mays, Chris Speier.

1972—4—Cincinnati (West), Joe Morgan 2, Cesar Geronimo, Johnny Bench.

3—Pittsburgh (East), Al Oliver, Manny Sanguillen, Roberto Clemente.

1973—5—Cincinnati (West), Pete Rose 2, Johnny Bench, Denis Menke, Tony Perez.

3—New York (East), Rusty Staub 3.

1974—3—Los Angeles (West), Steve Garvey 2, Ron Cey.

3—Pittsburgh (East), Willie Stargell 2, Richie Hebner.

1975—4—Cincinnati (West), Don Gullett, Tony Perez, Dave Concepcion, Pete Rose.

1—Pittsburgh (East), Al Oliver.

1976—3—Cincinnati (West), George Foster 2, Johnny Bench.

1—Philadelphia (East), Greg Luzinski.

1977—3—Los Angeles (West), Dusty Baker 2, Ron Cey.

2—Philadelphia (East), Greg Luzinski, Bake McBride.

1978—8—Los Angeles (West), Steve Garvey 4, Dave Lopes 2, Steve Yeager, Ron Cey.

5—Philadelphia (East), Greg Luzinski 2, Jerry Martin, Steve Carlton, Bake McBride.

1979—4—Pittsburgh (East), Willie Stargell 2, Phil Garner, Bill Madlock.

2—Cincinnati (West), George Foster, Johnny Bench.

1980—1—Philadelphia (East), Greg Luzinski.

0—Houston (West).

1981—4—Los Angeles (West), Pedro Guerrero, Mike Scioscia, Steve Garvey, Rick Monday.

1—Montreal (East), Jerry White.

1982—1—St. Louis (East), Willie McGee.

0—Atlanta (West).

1983—5—Philadelphia (East), Gary Matthews 3, Mike Schmidt, Sixto Lezcano.

2—Los Angeles (West), Mike A. Marshall, Dusty Baker.

1984—9—Chicago (East), Jody Davis 2, Leon Durham 2, Gary Matthews 2, Ron Cey, Bob Dernier, Rick Sutcliffe.

2—San Diego (West), Steve Garvey, Kevin McReynolds.

1985—5—Los Angeles (West), Bill Madlock 3, Greg Brock, Mike A. Marshall.

3—St. Louis (East), Jack Clark, Tom Herr, Ozzie Smith.

1986—5—Houston (West), Alan Ashby, Glenn Davis, Bill Doran, Billy Hatcher, Dickie Thon.

3—New York (East), Darryl Strawberry 2, Lenny Dykstra.

1987—9—San Francisco (West), Jeffrey Leonard 4, Bob Brenly, Will Clark, Kevin Mitchell, Harry Spilman, Robby Thompson.

2—St. Louis (East), Jim Lindeman, Jose Oquendo.

1988—5—New York (East), Kevin McReynolds 2, Lenny Dykstra, Keith Hernandez, Darryl Strawberry.

3—Los Angeles (West), Kirk Gibson 2, Mike Scioscia.

1989—8—San Francisco (West), Will Clark 2, Kevin Mitchell 2, Robby Thompson 2, Matt Williams 2.

3—Chicago (East), Mark Grace, Luis Salazar, Ryne Sandberg.

1990—4—Cincinnati (West), Mariano Duncan, Billy Hatcher, Paul O'Neill, Chris Sabo.

3—Pittsburgh (East), Jay Bell, Sid Bream, Jose Lind.

1991—5—Atlanta (West), Sid Bream, Ron Gant, Brian Hunter, David Justice, Greg Olson.

3—Pittsburgh (East), Jay Bell, Orlando Merced, Andy Van Slyke.

1992—6—Atlanta (West), Ron Gant 2, David Justice 2, Jeff Blauser, Sid Bream.

5—Pittsburgh (East), Jay Bell, Barry Bonds, Jose Lind, Lloyd McClendon, Don Slaught.

1993—7—Philadelphia (East), Lenny Dykstra 2, Dave Hollins 2, Darren Daulton, Pete Incaviglia, John Kruk.

5—Atlanta (West), Jeff Blauser 2, Damon Berryhill,

Fred McGriff, Terry Pendleton.

1994—No series played.

1995—4—Atlanta (East), Mike Devereaux, Chipper Jones, Javy Lopez, Charlie O'Brien.

0—Cincinnati (Central).

1996—8—Atlanta (East), Javy Lopez 2, Fred McGriff 2, Marquis Grissom, Andruw Jones, Ryan Klesko, Mark Lemke.

4—St. Louis (Central), Ron Gant 2, Gary Gaetti, Brian Jordan.

1997—6—Atlanta (East), Chipper Jones 2, Ryan Klesko 2, Jeff Blauser, Michael Tucker.

1—Florida (East), Gary Sheffield.

1998—5—San Diego (West), Ken Caminiti 2, Jim Leyritz, Greg Myers, John Vander Wal.

4—Atlanta (East), Andres Galarraga, Andruw Jones, Javy Lopez, Michael Tucker.

1999—5—Atlanta (East), Brian Jordan 2, Eddie Perez 2, Ryan Klesko.

4—New York (East), John Olerud 2, Melvin Mora, Mike Piazza.

2000—4—New York (East), Mike Piazza 2, Jay Payton, Todd Zeile.

2—St. Louis (Central), Will Clark, Jim Edmonds.

2001—5—Atlanta (East), Julio Franco, Marcus Giles, Andruw Jones, Javy Lopez, B.J. Surhoff.

2—Arizona (West), Erubiel Durazo, Luis Gonzalez.

2002—7—San Francisco (West), Rich Aurilia 2, Benito Santiago 2, David Bell, Barry Bonds, Kenny Lofton.

7—St. Louis (Central), Miguel Cairo, J.D. Drew, Jim Edmonds, Eli Marrero, Mike Matheny, Eduardo Perez, Albert Pujols.

2003—13—Chicago (Central), Alex S. Gonzalez 3, Aramis Ramirez 3, Moises Alou 2, Sammy Sosa 2, Troy O'Leary, Randall Simon, Kerry Wood.

10—Florida (East), Miguel Cabrera 3, Mike Lowell 2, Ivan Rodriguez 2, Jeff Conine, Juan Encarnacion, Derrek Lee.

2004—14—Houston (Central), Carlos Beltran 4, Lance Berkman 3, Jeff Kent 3, Mike Lamb 2, Craig Biggio, Morgan Ensberg.

11—St. Louis (Central), Albert Pujols 4, Scott Rolen 3, Jim Edmonds 2, Larry Walker 2.

Total number of home runs: 306

PLAYERS WITH FOUR HOME RUNS

BOTH LEAGUES

Player	Series	No.
Darryl Strawberry	4	7
David Justice	8	6
John Olerud	7	6
Paul O'Neill	6	5
Kirk Gibson	3	4
Todd Zeile	2	4

Total number of players: 6

AMERICAN LEAGUE

Player	Series	No.
George Brett	6	9
Bernie Williams	7	9

Player	Series	No.
Manny Ramirez	5	8
Jim Thome	3	6
Reggie Jackson	11	6
David Ortiz	3	5
Jason Varitek	3	5
Sal Bando	5	5
Graig Nettles	6	5
Derek Jeter	7	5
Darryl Strawberry	2	4
Jay Buhner	3	4
Jose Canseco	3	4
Trot Nixon	3	4
Alex Rodriguez	3	4
Eddie Murray	4	4
Paul O'Neill	5	4
Boog Powell	5	4
John Olerud	6	4

Total number of players: 19

NATIONAL LEAGUE

Player	Series	No.
Steve Garvey	5	8
Gary Matthews	2	5
Albert Pujols	2	5
Greg Luzinski	4	5
Ron Gant	5	5
Johnny Bench	6	5
Javy Lopez	6	5
Carlos Beltran	1	4
Jeffrey Leonard	2	4
Bill Madlock	2	4
Will Clark	3	4
Lenny Dykstra	3	4
Ron Cey	5	4
Ryan Klesko	5	4
Bob Robertson	5	4
Jeff Blauser	6	4
Willie Stargell	6	4

Total number of players: 17

INDIVIDUAL PITCHING
PITCHERS WITH FOUR VICTORIES
BOTH LEAGUES

Pitcher, Club	Yrs.	W	L
Tim Wakefield, Pit. N.L., Bos. A.L.	3	5	1
Bruce Kison, Pit. N.L., Cal. A.L.	5	4	0
Orel Hershiser, L.A. N.L., Cle. A.L., N.Y. N.L.	5	4	0
Tommy John, L.A. N.L., N.Y. A.L., Cal. A.L.	5	4	1
Don Sutton, L.A. N.L., Mil. A.L., Cal A.L.	5	4	1
David Wells, Tor. A.L., Cin. N.L., Bal. A.L., N.Y. A.L.	6	4	1
David Cone, N.Y. N.L., Tor. A.L., N.Y. A.L.	6	4	2
Roger Clemens, Bos. A.L., N.Y. A.L, Hou. N.L.	8	4	4

Total number of pitchers: 8

AMERICAN LEAGUE

Pitcher, Club	Yrs.	W	L
Dave Stewart, Oakland, Toronto	5	8	0
Juan Guzman, Toronto	3	5	0
Mariano Rivera, New York	6	4	0
David Wells, Toronto, Baltimore, New York	5	4	0
Andy Pettitte, New York	6	6	1
Orlando Hernandez, New York	4	4	1
Jim Palmer, Baltimore	6	4	1
Catfish Hunter, Oakland, New York	6	4	3

Total number of pitchers: 8

NATIONAL LEAGUE

Pitcher, Club	Yrs.	W	L
Steve Avery, Atlanta	5	4	1
John Smoltz, Atlanta	9	6	2
Steve Carlton, Philadelphia	5	4	2
Tom Glavine, Atlanta	9	5	9
Greg Maddux, Chicago, Atlanta	8	4	8

Total number of pitchers: 5

10-STRIKEOUT GAMES BY PITCHERS
AMERICAN LEAGUE

Date	Pitcher, Club	No.
Oct. 5, 1969	Dave McNally, Bal. vs. Min. (11 inn.)	11
Oct. 5, 1970	Jim Palmer, Bal. vs. Min.	12
Oct. 10, 1972	Joe Coleman, Det. vs. Oak.	14
Oct. 6, 1973	Jim Palmer, Bal. vs. Oak.	12
Oct. 9, 1973	Mike Cuellar, Bal. vs. Oak. (10 inn.)	11
Oct. 6, 1983	Mike Boddicker, Bal. vs. Chi.	14
Oct. 11, 1997	Mike Mussina, Bal. vs. Cle. (7 inn.)	15
Oct. 15, 1997	Mike Mussina, Bal. vs. Cle. (8 inn.)	10
Oct. 11, 1998	David Wells, N.Y. vs. Cle. (7.1 inn.)	11
Oct. 16, 1999	Pedro Martinez, Bos. vs. N.Y. (7 inn.)	12
Oct. 14, 2000	Roger Clemens, N.Y. vs. Sea.	15
Oct, 13, 2003	Mike Mussina, N.Y. vs. Bos.	10

Total number of occurrences: 12

NATIONAL LEAGUE

Date	Pitcher, Club	No.
Oct. 6, 1973	Tom Seaver, N.Y. vs. Cin. (8.1 inn.)	13
Oct. 7, 1975	John Candelaria, Pit. vs. Cin. (7.2 inn.)	14
Oct. 8, 1986	Mike Scott, Hou. vs. N.Y.	14
Oct. 14, 1986	Nolan Ryan, Hou. vs. N.Y.	12
Oct. 4, 1988	Dwight Gooden, N.Y. vs. L.A.	10
Oct. 5, 1988	Tim Belcher, L.A. vs. N.Y.	10
Oct. 6, 1993	Curt Schilling, Phi. vs. Atl. (8 inn.)	10
Oct. 10, 1993	John Smoltz, Atl. vs. Phi. (6.1 inn.)	10
Oct. 12, 1997	Livan Hernandez, Fla. vs. Atl.	15
Oct. 8, 1998	Kevin Brown, S.D. vs. Atl.	11
Oct. 16, 2001	Randy Johnson, Ari. vs. Atl.	11
Oct. 19, 2001	Curt Schilling, Ari. vs. Atl.	12
Oct. 12, 2003	Josh Beckett, Fla. vs. Chi.	11

Total number of occurrences: 13

CLUB BATTING
AMERICAN LEAGUE

Year	Team, Division	G	AB	R	H	TB	2B	3B	HR	SH	SF	SB	BB	SO	RBI	Avg.	LOB
1969	Baltimore, East	3	123	16	36	58	8	1	4	2	0	0	13	14	15	.293	28
	Minnesota, West	3	110	5	17	25	3	1	1	0	1	2	12	27	5	.155	22
1970	Baltimore, East	3	109	27	36	61	7	0	6	1	2	1	12	19	24	.330	20
	Minnesota, West	3	101	10	24	39	4	1	3	1	0	0	9	22	10	.238	20
1971	Baltimore, East	3	95	15	26	47	7	1	4	0	1	0	13	22	14	.274	19
	Oakland, West	3	96	7	22	41	8	1	3	2	0	0	5	16	7	.229	15

Year	Team, Division	G	AB	R	H	TB	2B	3B	HR	SH	SF	SB	BB	SO	RBI	Avg.	LOB
1972	Detroit, East 5		162	10	32	52	6	1	4	3	0	0	13	25	10	.198	30
	Oakland, West 5		170	13	38	49	8	0	1	4	1	7	12	35	10	.224	38
1973	Baltimore, East.......5		171	15	36	52	7	0	3	0	0	1	16	25	15	.211	36
	Oakland, West 5		160	15	32	54	5	1	5	4	1	3	17	39	15	.200	34
1974	Baltimore, East.......4		124	7	22	32	1	0	3	2	0	0	5	20	7	.177	16
	Oakland, West 4		120	11	22	37	4	1	3	2	1	3	22	16	11	.183	30
1975	Boston, East 3		98	18	31	45	8	0	2	5	1	3	3	12	14	.316	14
	Oakland, West 3		98	7	19	28	6	0	1	0	0	0	9	14	7	.194	19
1976	New York, East.......5		174	23	55	84	13	2	4	2	1	4	16	15	21	.316	41
	Kansas City, West...5		162	24	40	60	6	4	2	0	4	5	11	18	24	.247	22
1977	New York, East.......5		175	21	46	64	12	0	2	1	2	2	9	16	17	.263	34
	Kansas City, West...5		163	22	42	66	9	3	3	2	2	5	15	22	21	.258	28
1978	New York, East.......4		140	19	42	62	3	1	5	0	1	0	7	18	18	.300	27
	Kansas City, West...4		133	17	35	59	6	3	4	1	2	6	14	21	16	.263	28
1979	Baltimore, East.......4		133	26	37	53	5	1	3	1	3	5	18	24	25	.278	23
	California, West......4		137	15	32	48	7	0	3	0	2	2	7	13	14	.234	22
1980	New York, East.......3		102	6	26	44	7	1	3	1	0	0	6	16	5	.255	22
	Kansas City, West...3		97	14	28	45	6	1	3	0	0	3	9	15	14	.289	18
1981	New York, East.......3		107	20	36	49	4	0	3	2	1	2	13	10	20	.336	30
	Oakland, West 3		99	4	22	28	4	1	0	0	0	2	6	23	4	.222	20
1982	Milwaukee, East 5		151	23	33	52	4	0	5	2	3	2	15	28	20	.219	24
	California, West......5		157	23	40	62	8	1	4	5	2	1	16	34	23	.255	29
1983	Baltimore, East.......4		129	19	28	46	9	0	3	1	3	2	16	24	17	.217	24
	Chicago, West 4		133	3	28	32	4	0	0	1	0	4	12	26	2	.211	35
1984	Detroit, East 3		107	14	25	43	4	1	4	2	1	4	8	17	14	.234	20
	Kansas City, West...3		106	4	18	21	1	1	0	0	0	0	6	21	4	.170	21
1985	Toronto, East..........7		242	25	65	90	19	0	2	0	2	2	16	37	23	.269	50
	Kansas City, West...7		227	26	51	83	9	1	7	4	2	2	22	51	26	.225	44
1986	Boston, East 7		254	41	69	102	11	2	6	3	2	1	19	31	35	.272	48
	California, West......7		256	30	71	103	11	0	7	4	2	1	20	44	29	.277	60
1987	Detroit, East 5		167	23	40	65	4	0	7	2	2	5	18	35	21	.240	37
	Minnesota, West 5		171	34	46	85	13	1	8	2	2	4	20	25	33	.269	37
1988	Boston, East..........4		126	11	26	36	4	0	2	2	2	0	18	23	10	.206	30
	Oakland, West 4		137	20	41	70	8	0	7	0	1	1	10	35	20	.299	26
1989	Toronto, East..........5		165	21	40	54	5	0	3	0	3	11	15	24	19	.242	30
	Oakland, West 5		158	26	43	75	9	1	7	3	2	13	20	32	23	.272	29
1990	Boston, East..........4		126	4	23	31	5	0	1	1	2	1	6	16	4	.183	23
	Oakland, West 4		127	20	38	42	4	0	0	4	3	9	19	21	18	.299	35
1991	Toronto, East..........5		173	19	43	52	6	0	1	3	1	7	15	30	18	.249	35
	Minnesota, West 5		181	27	50	70	9	1	3	1	2	8	15	37	25	.276	38
1992	Toronto, East..........6		210	31	59	99	8	1	10	1	4	7	23	29	30	.281	45
	Oakland, West 6		207	24	52	71	5	1	4	3	2	16	24	33	23	.251	48
1993	Toronto, East..........6		216	26	65	85	8	3	2	1	1	7	21	36	24	.301	56
	Chicago, West 6		194	23	46	68	5	1	5	5	1	3	32	43	22	.237	50
1994	No series played.																
1995	Cleveland, East.......6		206	23	53	86	6	3	7	1	2	9	25	37	21	.257	50
	Seattle, West 6		201	12	37	60	8	0	5	1	0	9	15	46	10	.184	43
1996	New York, East.......5		183	27	50	91	9	1	10	0	0	3	20	37	24	.273	40
	Baltimore, East.......5		176	19	39	70	4	0	9	0	3	0	15	33	19	.222	34
1997	Baltimore, East.......6		218	19	54	86	11	0	7	1	0	3	23	47	19	.248	50
	Cleveland, Central ..6		207	18	40	63	8	0	5	2	0	5	23	62	15	.193	44
1998	New York, East.......6		197	27	43	65	8	1	4	3	3	9	35	42	25	.218	48
	Cleveland, Central ..6		205	20	45	77	3	1	9	0	1	6	16	51	19	.220	39
1999	New York, East.......5		176	23	42	72	4	1	8	2	0	3	18	44	21	.239	42
	Boston, East..........5		184	21	54	86	13	2	5	1	0	4	15	38	19	.293	45
2000	New York, East.......6		204	31	57	85	10	0	6	1	3	4	25	41	31	.279	49
	Seattle, West 6		191	18	41	68	12	0	5	2	1	3	21	48	18	.215	38
2001	New York, East.......5		159	25	42	70	7	0	7	4	1	3	23	31	24	.264	34
	Seattle, West 5		171	22	36	59	4	2	5	1	0	3	18	35	20	.211	34
2002	Anaheim, West.......5		171	29	49	82	5	2	8	2	0	3	9	26	26	.287	29

CHAMPIONSHIP SERIES *General reference*

Year	Team, Division	G	AB	R	H	TB	2B	3B	HR	SH	SF	SB	BB	SO	RBI	Avg.	LOB
	Minnesota, Central	.5	160	12	37	46	9	0	0	2	2	1	7	38	11	.231	28
2003	New York, East	7	238	30	54	90	12	0	8	0	1	5	21	49	29	.227	45
	Boston, East	7	250	29	68	117	9	2	12	0	0	2	17	60	26	.272	49
2004	Boston, East	7	271	41	75	119	12	1	10	1	2	4	28	53	40	.277	53
	New York, East	7	277	45	78	131	20	3	9	3	1	3	33	51	44	.282	69

NATIONAL LEAGUE

Year	Team, Division	G	AB	R	H	TB	2B	3B	HR	SH	SF	SB	BB	SO	RBI	Avg.	LOB
1969	New York, East	3	113	27	37	65	8	1	6	1	0	5	10	25	24	.327	19
	Atlanta, West	3	106	15	27	51	9	0	5	0	1	1	11	20	15	.255	23
1970	Pittsburgh, East	3	102	3	23	29	6	0	0	2	0	0	12	19	3	.225	29
	Cincinnati, West	3	100	9	22	36	3	1	3	0	0	1	8	12	8	.220	18
1971	Pittsburgh, East	4	144	24	39	67	4	0	8	1	0	2	5	33	23	.271	26
	San Francisco, West	4	132	15	31	51	5	0	5	4	0	2	16	28	14	.235	33
1972	Pittsburgh, East	5	158	15	30	47	6	1	3	2	0	0	9	27	14	.190	24
	Cincinnati, West	5	166	19	42	67	9	2	4	3	1	4	10	28	16	.253	30
1973	New York, East	5	168	23	37	51	5	0	3	3	1	0	19	28	22	.220	30
	Cincinnati, West	5	167	8	31	52	6	0	5	3	1	0	13	42	8	.186	35
1974	Pittsburgh, East	4	129	10	25	35	1	0	3	2	0	1	8	17	10	.194	24
	Los Angeles, West	.4	138	20	37	56	8	1	3	1	0	5	30	16	19	.268	44
1975	Pittsburgh, East	3	101	7	20	26	3	0	1	0	0	0	10	18	7	.198	21
	Cincinnati, West	3	102	19	29	45	4	0	4	0	3	11	9	28	18	.284	17
1976	Philadelphia, East	3	100	11	27	40	8	1	1	3	2	0	12	9	11	.270	25
	Cincinnati, West	3	99	19	25	45	5	3	3	1	3	5	15	16	17	.253	20
1977	Philadelphia, East	4	138	14	31	40	3	0	2	2	0	1	11	21	12	.225	32
	Los Angeles, West	.4	133	22	35	52	6	1	3	2	0	3	14	22	20	.263	22
1978	Philadelphia, East	4	140	17	35	37	3	2	5	2	1	0	9	21	16	.250	24
	Los Angeles, West	.4	147	21	42	80	8	3	8	2	0	2	9	22	21	.286	28
1979	Pittsburgh, East	3	105	15	28	47	3	2	4	5	3	4	13	13	14	.267	24
	Cincinnati, West	3	107	5	23	35	4	1	2	1	1	4	11	26	5	.215	25
1980	Philadelphia, East	5	190	20	55	68	8	1	1	5	1	7	13	37	19	.291	43
	Houston, West	5	172	19	40	57	7	5	0	7	2	4	31	19	18	.233	45
1981	Montreal, East	5	158	10	34	44	7	0	1	3	0	2	12	25	8	.215	31
	Los Angeles, West	.5	163	15	38	55	3	1	4	4	0	5	12	23	15	.233	33
1982	St. Louis, East	3	103	17	34	45	4	2	1	5	3	1	12	16	16	.330	31
	Atlanta, West	3	89	5	15	16	1	0	0	2	1	1	6	15	3	.169	12
1983	Philadelphia, East	4	130	16	34	53	4	0	5	3	1	2	15	22	15	.262	31
	Los Angeles, West	.4	129	8	27	40	5	1	2	2	0	3	11	31	7	.209	31
1984	Chicago, East	5	162	26	42	80	11	0	9	1	2	6	20	28	25	.259	32
	San Diego, West	5	155	22	41	54	5	1	2	2	4	2	14	22	20	.265	27
1985	St. Louis, East	6	201	29	56	77	10	1	3	2	1	6	30	34	26	.279	51
	Los Angeles, West	.6	197	23	46	75	12	1	5	1	1	4	19	31	23	.234	40
1986	New York, East	6	227	21	43	60	4	2	3	1	3	4	14	57	19	.189	36
	Houston, West	6	225	17	49	70	6	0	5	2	0	8	17	40	17	.218	39
1987	St. Louis, East	7	215	23	56	74	4	4	2	5	4	4	16	42	22	.260	37
	San Francisco, West	.7	226	23	54	90	7	1	9	3	1	5	17	51	20	.239	43
1988	New York, East	7	240	27	58	87	12	1	5	3	1	6	28	42	27	.242	54
	Los Angeles, West	.7	243	31	52	70	7	1	3	1	2	9	25	54	30	.214	50
1989	Chicago, East	5	175	22	53	77	9	3	3	3	2	3	16	27	21	.303	43
	San Francisco, West	5	165	30	44	78	6	2	8	2	1	2	17	29	29	.267	30
1990	Pittsburgh, East	6	186	15	36	58	9	2	3	0	1	6	27	49	14	.194	41
	Cincinnati, West	6	192	20	49	70	9	0	4	3	3	6	10	37	20	.255	33
1991	Pittsburgh, East	7	228	12	51	70	10	0	3	4	1	6	22	57	11	.224	54
	Atlanta, West	7	229	19	53	80	10	1	5	5	1	10	22	42	19	.231	51
1992	Pittsburgh, East	7	231	35	59	100	20	3	5	3	3	1	29	42	32	.255	50
	Atlanta, West	7	234	34	57	90	11	2	6	2	2	5	29	28	32	.244	51
1993	Philadelphia, East	6	207	23	47	87	11	4	7	3	2	2	26	51	22	.227	52
	Atlanta, West	6	215	33	59	88	14	0	5	5	2	0	22	54	32	.274	47
1994	No series played.																
1995	Atlanta, East	4	149	19	42	62	6	1	4	1	0	2	16	22	17	.282	36

Year	Team, Division	G	AB	R	H	TB	2B	3B	HR	SH	SF	SB	BB	SO	RBI	Avg.	LOB
	Cincinnati, Central ..4		134	5	28	35	5	1	0	1	1	4	12	31	4	.209	28
1996	Atlanta, East 7		249	44	77	118	11	3	8	2	3	4	25	51	43	.309	58
	St. Louis, Central ...7		221	18	45	65	4	2	4	1	1	1	11	53	15	.204	34
1997	Atlanta, East 6		194	21	49	76	5	2	6	5	3	1	16	49	21	.253	40
	Florida, East 6		181	20	36	47	8	0	1	5	0	2	23	52	20	.199	36
1998	San Diego, West.....6		208	24	53	75	7	0	5	2	0	2	27	48	20	.255	52
	Atlanta, East 6		200	18	47	65	4	1	4	2	1	3	26	54	17	.235	46
1999	Atlanta, East 6		206	24	46	72	9	1	5	7	1	14	31	47	22	.223	47
	New York, East 6		225	21	49	70	9	0	4	3	2	7	14	49	21	.218	42
2000	New York, East 5		164	31	43	69	12	1	4	3	3	2	27	24	27	.262	40
	St. Louis, Central ...5		177	21	47	64	11	0	2	4	2	3	11	39	18	.266	39
2001	Atlanta, East 5		169	15	35	56	6	0	5	0	0	0	11	39	14	.207	30
	Arizona, West 5		172	22	40	52	6	0	2	2	0	3	18	32	19	.233	39
2002	San Fran., West......5		158	23	39	67	3	2	7	8	2	1	21	36	23	.247	38
	St. Louis, Central ...5		171	16	44	73	8	0	7	5	2	1	10	23	16	.257	39
2003	Florida, East 7		256	40	68	116	12	3	10	3	2	4	28	45	39	.266	53
	Chicago, Central.....7		252	42	65	122	10	4	13	7	1	1	23	57	41	.258	45
2004	St. Louis, Central ...7		235	34	60	107	12	1	11	6	1	2	17	56	33	.255	40
	Houston, Central 7		233	31	53	105	10	0	14	1	1	6	25	42	30	.227	44

CLUB FIELDING AND PLAYERS USED

AMERICAN LEAGUE

Year	Team, Division	G	PO	A	E	DP	PB	Fielding Avg.	Players Used	Pitchers Used
1969	Baltimore, East	3	96	31	1	2	0	.992	20	7
	Minnesota, West	3	94	34	5	3	0	.962	22	9
1970	Baltimore, East	3	81	29	0	3	0	1.000	14	4
	Minnesota, West	3	78	28	6	5	0	.946	24	9
1971	Baltimore, East	3	81	31	1	3	0	.991	15	4
	Oakland, West	3	75	15	0	4	0	1.000	20	7
1972	Detroit, East	5	139	48	7	4	0	.964	24	8
	Oakland, West	5	138	60	3	5	1	.985	25	8
1973	Baltimore, East	5	135	51	2	2	1	.989	23	7
	Oakland, West	5	138	47	4	4	0	.979	22	6
1974	Baltimore, East	4	105	50	4	4	0	.975	22	7
	Oakland, West	4	108	43	2	4	1	.987	20	5
1975	Boston, East	3	81	33	4	3	0	.966	14	5
	Oakland, West	3	75	40	6	4	0	.950	22	7
1976	New York, East	5	132	60	6	3	1	.970	22	6
	Kansas City, West	5	129	51	4	5	0	.978	24	9
1977	New York, East	5	132	51	2	2	0	.989	18	6
	Kansas City, West	5	132	54	5	4	0	.974	22	8
1978	New York, East	4	105	35	1	2	1	.993	21	8
	Kansas City, West	4	102	36	4	4	1	.972	20	7
1979	Baltimore, East	4	109	52	5	5	1	.970	20	5
	California, West	4	107	37	2	7	0	.986	23	9
1980	New York, East	3	75	42	1	2	0	.991	20	6
	Kansas City, West	3	81	29	1	3	0	.991	15	4
1981	New York, East	3	81	30	1	6	1	.991	22	6
	Oakland, West	3	75	33	4	1	0	.964	24	8
1982	Milwaukee, East	5	129	45	8	5	0	.956	20	8
	California, West	5	126	46	4	3	1	.977	20	7
1983	Baltimore, East	4	111	49	2	4	0	.988	22	6
	Chicago, West	4	108	51	3	5	0	.981	23	9
1984	Detroit, East	3	87	27	1	0	0	.991	20	5
	Kansas City, West	3	84	26	7	2	0	.940	22	6
1985	Toronto, East	7	186	61	4	4	0	.984	24	8
	Kansas City, West	7	188	87	6	7	0	.979	22	7
1986	Boston, East	7	196	73	7	5	0	.975	20	7

Year	Team, Division	G	PO	A	E	DP	PB	Fielding Avg.	Players Used	Pitchers Used
	California, West	7	192	78	8	5	2	.971	24	9
1987	Detroit, East	5	129	56	5	1	1	.974	24	10
	Minnesota, West	5	132	41	3	3	0	.983	21	7
1988	Boston, East	4	102	34	1	2	1	.993	20	7
	Oakland, West	4	108	30	3	5	1	.979	22	9
1989	Toronto, East	5	129	40	2	5	1	.988	22	9
	Oakland, West	5	132	45	3	4	1	.983	22	8
1990	Boston, East	4	102	47	5	6	1	.968	23	10
	Oakland, West	4	108	43	1	3	0	.993	21	6
1991	Toronto, East	5	135	49	7	4	0	.963	23	10
	Minnesota, West	5	138	51	4	3	0	.979	23	8
1992	Toronto, East	6	165	60	8	7	3	.966	21	9
	Oakland, West	6	162	55	7	5	0	.969	25	11
1993	Toronto, East	6	162	57	2	7	0	.991	19	10
	Chicago, West	6	159	56	7	5	0	.968	22	9
1994	no series played.									
1995	Cleveland, East	6	165	66	7	4	0	.971	25	11
	Seattle, West	6	162	59	6	7	1	.974	25	10
1996	New York, East	5	141	44	1	1	0	.995	24	9
	Baltimore, East	5	138	58	4	7	0	.980	23	10
1997	Baltimore, East	6	174	60	5	4	0	.979	23	9
	Cleveland, Central	6	174	61	5	11	0	.979	23	11
1998	New York, East	6	168	54	2	5	0	.991	24	9
	Cleveland, Central	6	165	77	7	7	0	.972	25	11
1999	New York, East	5	135	38	4	7	1	.977	25	10
	Boston, East	5	132	40	10	0	0	.945	24	10
2000	New York, East	6	159	54	1	5	0	.995	22	10
	Seattle, West	6	156	58	3	4	1	.986	25	10
2001	New York, East	5	135	47	4	4	0	.978	24	9
	Seattle, West	5	130	45	1	5	0	.994	25	11
2002	Anaheim, West	5	132	38	2	4	0	.988	24	9
	Minnesota, Central	5	126	43	4	4	0	.977	25	11
2003	New York, East	7	192	73	5	12	0	.981	22	9
	Boston, East	7	189	67	3	5	3	.988	23	10
2004	Boston, East	7	207	66	1	4	3	.996	25	11
	New York, East	7	209	74	4	9	1	.986	23	11

NATIONAL LEAGUE

Year	Team, Division	G	PO	A	E	DP	PB	Fielding Avg.	Players Used	Pitchers Used
1969	New York, East	3	81	23	2	2	1	.981	17	6
	Atlanta, West	3	78	37	6	4	1	.950	23	9
1970	Pittsburgh, East	3	81	37	2	3	0	.983	18	5
	Cincinnati, West	3	84	39	1	1	0	.992	20	7
1971	Pittsburgh, East	4	105	32	3	3	1	.979	21	7
	San Francisco, West	4	102	37	4	1	1	.972	22	9
1972	Pittsburgh, East	5	131	38	4	3	0	.977	23	10
	Cincinnati, West	5	132	53	4	3	1	.979	21	8
1973	New York, East	5	142	44	4	3	0	.979	17	6
	Cincinnati, West	5	138	59	2	3	0	.990	24	9
1974	Pittsburgh, East	4	105	37	4	2	1	.973	22	8
	Los Angeles, West	4	108	46	7	8	1	.957	22	7
1975	Pittsburgh, East	3	78	20	2	3	2	.980	24	10
	Cincinnati, West	3	84	31	1	2	0	.991	18	7
1976	Philadelphia, East	3	79	34	2	3	0	.983	22	7
	Cincinnati, West	3	81	32	2	3	0	.983	18	6
1977	Philadelphia, East	4	105	49	3	3	1	.981	21	7
	Los Angeles, West	4	108	44	5	3	0	.968	23	9
1978	Philadelphia, East	4	110	46	4	4	0	.975	22	8
	Los Angeles, West	4	111	50	3	4	0	.982	22	9
1979	Pittsburgh, East	3	90	34	0	2	0	1.000	20	8
	Cincinnati, West	3	87	39	1	2	0	.992	20	9
1980	Philadelphia, East	5	148	71	6	7	0	.973	23	9
	Houston, West	5	147	52	3	4	1	.985	24	7

Year	Team, Division	G	PO	A	E	DP	PB	Fielding Avg.	Players Used	Pitchers Used
1981	Montreal, East	5	132	52	4	8	0	.979	19	7
	Los Angeles, West	5	132	53	2	5	1	.989	23	9
1982	St. Louis, East	3	81	35	2	3	0	.983	15	5
	Atlanta, West	3	76	39	1	0	1	.991	20	8
1983	Philadelphia, East	4	105	36	5	0	0	.966	20	5
	Los Angeles, West	4	102	38	1	3	1	.993	22	8
1984	Chicago, East	5	127	49	3	6	1	.983	23	8
	San Diego, West	5	129	43	1	4	0	.994	24	10
1985	St. Louis, East	6	156	54	4	4	1	.981	23	9
	Los Angeles, West	6	154	72	6	3	0	.974	25	9
1986	New York, East	6	189	94	1	6	0	.996	22	8
	Houston, West	6	188	66	7	3	2	.973	21	8
1987	St. Louis, East	7	183	67	3	5	0	.988	23	8
	San Francisco, West	7	180	77	6	10	1	.977	23	10
1988	New York, East	7	192	62	8	2	0	.969	22	8
	Los Angeles, West	7	195	61	5	9	1	.981	24	9
1989	Chicago, East	5	126	40	3	1	2	.982	24	9
	San Francisco, West	5	132	49	5	7	1	.973	24	9
1990	Pittsburgh, East	6	156	71	5	4	0	.978	21	8
	Cincinnati, West	6	159	45	2	3	0	.990	23	8
1991	Pittsburgh, East	7	189	75	6	3	0	.978	25	11
	Atlanta, West	7	189	62	4	6	0	.984	23	9
1992	Pittsburgh, East	7	182	63	5	6	2	.980	25	10
	Atlanta, West	7	183	74	2	3	1	.992	25	10
1993	Philadelphia, East	6	165	47	7	2	2	.968	25	10
	Atlanta, West	6	163	54	5	1	0	.977	23	8
1994	no series played.									
1995	Atlanta, East	4	117	54	3	7	0	.983	22	8
	Cincinnati, West	4	111	43	2	4	1	.987	25	10
1996	Atlanta, East	7	183	55	4	6	0	.983	24	10
	St. Louis, Central	7	180	61	6	4	0	.976	25	10
1997	Atlanta, East	6	156	57	4	7	0	.982	22	8
	Florida, East	6	159	57	3	4	0	.986	24	10
1998	San Diego, West	6	165	60	1	6	0	.996	24	10
	Atlanta, East	6	162	74	8	6	1	.967	24	9
1999	Atlanta, East	6	181	55	7	4	1	.971	25	9
	New York, East	6	178	82	8	9	0	.970	25	11
2000	New York, East	5	135	39	4	1	0	.978	24	10
	St. Louis, Central	5	129	49	7	3	1	.962	25	10
2001	Atlanta, East	5	132	52	7	5	1	.963	24	10
	Arizona, West	5	135	43	3	3	0	.983	23	9
2002	San Francisco, West	5	135	49	1	4	0	.995	23	10
	St. Louis, Central	5	131	40	1	4	0	.994	22	10
2003	Florida, East	7	198	70	3	4	0	.989	25	11
	Chicago, Central	7	198	81	4	6	2	.986	24	10
2004	St. Louis, Central	7	190	66	1	5	0	.996	25	11
	Houston, Central	7	187	71	2	2	1	.992	23	9

MANAGERIAL RECORDS

AMERICAN LEAGUE

	Series W	Series L	Games W	Games L		Series W	Series L	Games W	Games L
Joe Altobelli, Baltimore	1	0	3	1	Whitey Herzog, Kansas City	0	3	5	9
Sparky Anderson, Detroit	1	1	4	4	Dick Howser, New York, Kansas City	1	2	4	9
Bobby Cox, Toronto	0	1	3	4	Darrell Johnson, Boston	1	0	3	0
Alvin Dark, Oakland	1	1	3	4	Dave Johnson, Baltimore	0	2	3	8
Terry Francona, Boston	1	0	4	3	Tom Kelly, Minnesota	2	0	8	2
Jim Fregosi, California	0	1	1	3	Harvey Kuenn, Milwaukee	1	0	3	2
Jim Frey, Kansas City	1	0	3	0	Gene Lamont, Chicago	0	1	2	4
Ron Gardenhire, Minnesota	0	1	1	4	Tony La Russa, Chicago, Oakland	3	2	15	8
Cito Gaston, Toronto	2	2	10	12	Bob Lemon, New York	2	0	6	1
Mike Hargrove, Cleveland	2	1	10	8	Grady Little, Boston	0	1	3	4

	Series W	L	Games W	L
Billy Martin, Minnesota, Detroit, New York, Oakland	2	3	8	13
Gene Mauch, California	0	2	5	7
John McNamara, Boston	1	0	4	3
Joe Morgan, Boston	0	2	0	8
Lou Piniella, Seattle	0	3	5	12
Bill Rigney, Minnesota	0	1	0	3
Mike Scioscia, Anaheim	1	0	4	1
Joe Torre, New York	6	1	27	14
Earl Weaver, Baltimore	4	2	15	7
Dick Williams, Oakland	2	1	6	7
Jimy Williams, Boston	0	1	1	4

Total number of managers: 31

NATIONAL LEAGUE

	Series W	L	Games W	L
Walter Alston, Los Angeles	1	0	3	1
Sparky Anderson, Cincinnati	4	1	14	5
Dusty Baker, San Francisco, Chicago	1	1	7	5
Yogi Berra, New York	1	0	3	2
Bruce Bochy, San Diego	1	0	4	2
Bob Brenly, Arizona	1	0	4	1
Bobby Cox, Atlanta	5	4	27	27
Roger Craig, San Francisco	1	1	7	5
Jim Fanning, Montreal	0	1	2	3
Jim Fregosi, Philadelphia	1	0	4	2
Jim Frey, Chicago	0	1	2	3
Charlie Fox, San Francisco	0	1	1	3
Phil Garner, Houston	0	1	3	4
Dallas Green, Philadelphia	1	0	3	2
Lum Harris, Atlanta	0	1	0	3
Whitey Herzog, St. Louis	3	0	11	5
Gil Hodges, New York	1	0	3	0
Dave Johnson, New York, Cincinnati	1	2	7	10
Hal Lanier, Houston	0	1	2	4
Tony La Russa, St. Louis	1	3	9	15

	Series W	L	Games W	L
Tom Lasorda, Los Angeles	4	2	16	14
Jim Leyland, Pittsburgh, Florida	1	3	12	14
Jack McKeon, Florida	1	0	4	3
John McNamara, Cincinnati	0	1	0	3
Danny Murtaugh, Pittsburgh	1	3	4	10
Paul Owens, Philadelphia	1	0	3	1
Danny Ozark, Philadelphia	0	3	2	9
Lou Piniella, Cincinnati	1	0	4	2
LChuck Tanner, Pittsburgh	1	0	3	0
Joe Torre, Atlanta	0	1	0	3
Bobby Valentine, New York	1	1	6	5
Bill Virdon, Pittsburgh, Houston	0	2	4	6
Dick Williams, San Diego	1	0	3	2
Don Zimmer, Chicago	0	1	1	4

Total number of managers: 34

COMBINED RECORDS FOR BOTH LEAGUES

	Series W	L	Games W	L
Sparky Anderson, Cincinnati N.L., Detroit A.L.	5	2	18	9
Bobby Cox, Toronto A.L., Atlanta N.L.	5	5	30	31
Jim Fregosi, California A.L., Philadelphia N.L.	1	1	5	5
Jim Frey, Kansas City A.L., Chicago N.L.	1	1	5	3
Whitey Herzog, Kansas City A.L., St. Louis N.L.	3	3	16	14
Dave Johnson, New York N.L., Cincinnati N.L., Baltimore A.L.	1	4	10	18
Tony La Russa, Chicago A.L., Oakland A.L., St. Louis N.L.	4	5	24	23
John McNamara, Cincinnati N.L., Boston A.L.	1	1	4	6
Lou Piniella, Cincinnati N.L., Seattle A.L.	1	3	9	14
Joe Torre, Atlanta N.L., New York A.L.	6	2	27	17
Dick Williams, Oakland A.L., San Diego N.L.	3	1	9	9

Total number of managers: 11

WORLD SERIES

Results: World Series Champions

Service (Individual, Club)

Batting (Individual, Club)

Baserunning (Individual, Club)

Pitching (Individual, Club)

Fielding (Individual, Club)

Miscellaneous

Non-Playing Personnel

General Reference

WORLD SERIES CHAMPIONS

Year	Winner	Loser	Games	Year	Winner	Loser	Games
1903	Boston A.L.	Pittsburgh N.L.	5-3	1954	New York N.L.	Cleveland A.L.	4-0
1904	no series played			1955	Brooklyn N.L.	New York A.L.	4-3
1905	New York N.L.	Philadelphia A.L.	4-1	1956	New York A.L.	Brooklyn N.L.	4-3
1906	Chicago A.L.	Chicago N.L.	4-2	1957	Milwaukee N.L.	New York A.L.	4-3
1907	Chicago N.L.	Detroit A.L.	*4-0	1958	New York A.L.	Milwaukee N.L.	4-3
1908	Chicago N.L.	Detroit A.L.	4-1	1959	Los Angeles N.L.	Chicago A.L.	4-2
1909	Pittsburgh N.L.	Detroit A.L.	4-3	1960	Pittsburgh N.L.	New York A.L.	4-3
1910	Philadelphia A.L.	Chicago N.L.	4-1	1961	New York A.L.	Cincinnati N.L.	4-1
1911	Philadelphia A.L.	New York N.L.	4-2	1962	New York A.L.	San Francisco N.L.	4-3
1912	Boston A.L.	New York N.L.	*4-3	1963	Los Angeles N.L.	New York A.L.	4-0
1913	Philadelphia A.L.	New York N.L.	4-1	1964	St. Louis N.L.	New York A.L.	4-3
1914	Boston N.L.	Philadelphia A.L.	4-0	1965	Los Angeles N.L.	Minnesota A.L.	4-3
1915	Boston A.L.	Philadelphia N.L.	4-1	1966	Baltimore A.L.	Los Angeles N.L.	4-0
1916	Boston A.L.	Brooklyn N.L.	4-1	1967	St. Louis N.L.	Boston A.L.	4-3
1917	Chicago A.L.	New York N.L.	4-2	1968	Detroit A.L.	St. Louis N.L.	4-3
1918	Boston A.L.	Chicago N.L.	4-2	1969	New York N.L.	Baltimore A.L.	4-1
1919	Cincinnati N.L.	Chicago A.L.	5-3	1970	Baltimore A.L.	Cincinnati N.L.	4-1
1920	Cleveland A.L.	Brooklyn N.L.	5-2	1971	Pittsburgh N.L.	Baltimore A.L.	4-3
1921	New York N.L.	New York A.L.	5-3	1972	Oakland A.L.	Cincinnati N.L.	4-3
1922	New York N.L.	New York A.L.	*4-0	1973	Oakland A.L.	New York N.L.	4-3
1923	New York A.L.	New York N.L.	4-2	1974	Oakland A.L.	Los Angeles N.L.	4-1
1924	Washington A.L.	New York N.L.	4-3	1975	Cincinnati N.L.	Boston A.L.	4-3
1925	Pittsburgh N.L.	Washington A.L.	4-3	1976	Cincinnati N.L.	New York A.L.	4-0
1926	St. Louis N.L.	New York A.L.	4-3	1977	New York A.L.	Los Angeles N.L.	4-2
1927	New York A.L.	Pittsburgh N.L.	4-0	1978	New York A.L.	Los Angeles N.L.	4-2
1928	New York A.L.	St. Louis N.L.	4-0	1979	Pittsburgh N.L.	Baltimore A.L.	4-3
1929	Philadelphia A.L.	Chicago N.L.	4-1	1980	Philadelphia N.L.	Kansas City A.L.	4-2
1930	Philadelphia A.L.	St. Louis N.L.	4-2	1981	Los Angeles N.L.	New York A.L.	4-2
1931	St. Louis N.L.	Philadelphia A.L.	4-3	1982	St. Louis N.L.	Milwaukee A.L.	4-3
1932	New York A.L.	Chicago N.L.	4-0	1983	Baltimore A.L.	Philadelphia N.L.	4-1
1933	New York N.L.	Washington A.L.	4-1	1984	Detroit A.L.	San Diego N.L.	4-1
1934	St. Louis N.L.	Detroit A.L.	4-3	1985	Kansas City A.L.	St. Louis N.L.	4-3
1935	Detroit A.L.	Chicago N.L.	4-2	1986	New York N.L.	Boston A.L.	4-3
1936	New York A.L.	New York N.L.	4-2	1987	Minnesota A.L.	St. Louis N.L.	4-3
1937	New York A.L.	New York N.L.	4-1	1988	Los Angeles N.L.	Oakland A.L.	4-1
1938	New York A.L.	Chicago N.L.	4-0	1989	Oakland A.L.	San Francisco N.L.	4-0
1939	New York A.L.	Cincinnati N.L.	4-0	1990	Cincinnati N.L.	Oakland A.L.	4-0
1940	Cincinnati N.L.	Detroit A.L.	4-3	1991	Minnesota A.L.	Atlanta N.L.	4-3
1941	New York A.L.	Brooklyn N.L.	4-1	1992	Toronto A.L.	Atlanta N.L.	4-2
1942	St. Louis N.L.	New York A.L.	4-1	1993	Toronto A.L.	Philadelphia N.L.	4-2
1943	New York A.L.	St. Louis N.L.	4-1	1994	no series played		
1944	St. Louis N.L.	St. Louis A.L.	4-2	1995	Atlanta N.L.	Cleveland A.L.	4-2
1945	Detroit A.L.	Chicago N.L.	4-3	1996	New York A.L.	Atlanta N.L.	4-2
1946	St. Louis N.L.	Boston A.L.	4-3	1997	Florida N.L.	Cleveland A.L.	4-3
1947	New York A.L.	Brooklyn N.L.	4-3	1998	New York A.L.	San Diego N.L.	4-0
1948	Cleveland A.L.	Boston N.L.	4-2	1999	New York A.L.	Atlanta N.L.	4-0
1949	New York A.L.	Brooklyn N.L.	4-1	2000	New York A.L.	New York N.L.	4-1
1950	New York A.L.	Philadelphia N.L.	4-0	2001	Arizona N.L.	New York A.L.	4-3
1951	New York A.L.	New York N.L.	4-2	2002	Anaheim A.L.	San Francisco N.L.	4-3
1952	New York A.L.	Brooklyn N.L.	4-3	2003	Florida N.L.	New York A.L.	4-2
1953	New York A.L.	Brooklyn N.L.	4-2	2004	Boston A.L.	St. Louis N.L.	4-0

*includes one tie

INDIVIDUAL SERVICE

ALL PLAYERS
SERIES AND CLUBS

Most series played
14—Yogi Berra, New York A.L., 1947, 1949, 1950, 1951, 1952, 1953, 1955, 1956, 1957, 1958, 1960, 1961, 1962, 1963, 75 games (65 consecutive).

Most series eligible, but did not play
6—Charlie Silvera, New York A.L., 1950, 1951, 1952, 1953, 1955, 1956, 37 games (played one game in 1949).

Most consecutive series played (17 times)
5—Hank Bauer, New York A.L., 1949 through 1953.
Yogi Berra, New York A.L., 1949 through 1953.
Ed Lopat, New York A.L., 1949 through 1953.
Johnny Mize, New York A.L., 1949 through 1953.
Vic Raschi, New York A.L., 1949 through 1953.
Allie Reynolds, New York A.L., 1949 through 1953.
Phil Rizzuto, New York A.L., 1949 through 1953.
Gene Woodling, New York A.L., 1949 through 1953.
Johnny Blanchard, New York A.L., 1960 through 1964.
Clete Boyer, New York A.L., 1960 through 1964.
Ralph Terry, New York A.L., 1960 through 1964.
Whitey Ford, New York A.L., 1960 through 1964.
Elston Howard, New York A.L., 1960 through 1964.
Hector Lopez, New York A.L., 1960 through 1964.
Mickey Mantle, New York A.L., 1960 through 1964.
Roger Maris, New York A.L., 1960 through 1964.
Bobby Richardson, New York A.L., 1960 through 1964.

Most series played with one club
14—Yogi Berra, New York A.L., 1947, 1949, 1950, 1951, 1952, 1953, 1955, 1956, 1957, 1958, 1960, 1961, 1962, 1963, 75 games (65 consecutive).

Most series playing in all games
10—Joe DiMaggio, New York A.L., 1936, 1937, 1938, 1939, 1941, 1942, 1947, 1949, 1950, 1951, 51 games.

Most times on series-winning club (playing one or more games each series)
10—Yogi Berra, New York A.L., 1947, 1949, 1950, 1951, 1952, 1953, 1956, 1958, 1961, 1962.

Most times on series-losing club (playing one or more games each series)
6—Pee Wee Reese, Brooklyn N.L., 1941, 1947, 1949, 1952, 1953, 1956.
Elston Howard, New York A.L., 1955, 1957, 1960, 1963, 1964; Boston A.L., 1967.

Most series played in first four major league seasons
4—Joe DiMaggio, New York A.L., 1936 through 1939.
Elston Howard, New York A.L., 1955 through 1958.
Johnny Kucks, New York A.L., 1955 through 1958.
Orlando Hernandez, New York A.L., 1998 through 2001.

Most clubs, career
4—Lonnie Smith, Philadelphia N.L., 1980; St. Louis N.L., 1982; Kansas City A.L., 1985; Atlanta N.L., 1991, 1992.

BY POSITION (EXCEPT PITCHERS)

Most series by first baseman
8—Bill Skowron, New York A.L., 1955, 1956, 1957, 1958, 1960, 1961, 1962; Los Angeles N.L., 1963, 37 games.

Most series by second baseman
7—Frankie Frisch, New York N.L., 1922, 1923, 1924; St. Louis N.L., 1928, 1930, 1931, 1934, 42 games.

Most series by third baseman
6—Red Rolfe, New York A.L., 1936, 1937, 1938, 1939, 1941, 1942, 28 games.

Most series by shortstop
9—Phil Rizzuto, New York A.L., 1941, 1942, 1947, 1949, 1950, 1951, 1952, 1953, 1955, 52 games.

Most series by outfielder
12—Mickey Mantle, New York A.L., 1951, 1952, 1953, 1955, 1956, 1957, 1958, 1960, 1961, 1962, 1963, 1964, 63 games.

Most series by catcher
12—Yogi Berra, New York A.L., 1947, 1949, 1950, 1951, 1952, 1953, 1955, 1956, 1957, 1958, 1960, 1962, 63 games.

YOUNGEST AND OLDEST NON-PITCHERS

Youngest World Series non-pitcher
18 years, 10 months, 13 days—Fred Lindstrom, New York N.L., October 4, 1924.

Oldest World Series non-pitcher
43 years, 7 months, 12 days—Sam Rice, Washington A.L., October 4, 1933.

YEARS BETWEEN SERIES (INCLUDES PITCHERS)

Most years between first and second series
17—Jim Kaat, Minnesota A.L., 1965; St. Louis N.L., 1982.

Most years between first and last series
22—Willie Mays, New York Giants N.L., 1951; New York Mets N.L., 1973.

Most years played in majors before playing in series
21—Joe Niekro, Minnesota A.L., October 21, 1987.
Mike Morgan, Arizona N.L., October 27, 2001.

POSITIONS

Most positions played, career
4—Babe Ruth, Boston A.L., 1915, 1916, 1918; New York A.L., 1921, 1922, 1923, 1926, 1927, 1928, 1932, 41 games (pitcher, left field, right field, first base).
Jackie Robinson, Brooklyn N.L., 1947, 1949, 1952, 1953, 1955, 1956, 38 games (first base, second base, left field, third base).
Elston Howard, New York A.L., 1955, 1956, 1957, 1958, 1960, 1961, 1962, 1963, 1964; Boston A.L., 1967, 54 games (left field, right field, first base, catcher).
Tony Kubek, New York A.L., 1957, 1958, 1960, 1961, 1962, 1963, 37 games (left field, third base, center field, shortstop).
Pete Rose, Cincinnati N.L., 1970, 1972, 1975, 1976; Philadelphia N.L., 1980, 1983, 34 games (right field, left field, third base, first base).

Most positions played, series
3—Held by many players.

PITCHERS
SERIES

Most series pitched
11—Whitey Ford, New York A.L., 1950, 1953, 1955, 1956, 1957, 1958, 1960, 1961, 1962, 1963, 1964, 22 games.

Most series pitched by relief pitcher
6—Johnny Murphy, New York A.L., 1936, 1937, 1938, 1939, 1941, 1943, eight games as a relief pitcher.
Mike Stanton, Atlanta N.L., 1991, 1992; New York A.L., 1998 through 2001, 20 games as a relief pitcher.
Mariano Rivera, New York A.L., 1996, 1998 through 2001, 2003, 20 games as a relief pitcher.

YOUNGEST AND OLDEST PITCHERS

Youngest World Series pitcher
19 years, 20 days—Ken Brett, Boston A.L., October 8, 1967.

Oldest World Series pitcher
46 years, 2 months, 29 days—Jack Quinn, Philadelphia A.L., October 4, 1930.

CLUB SERVICE

PLAYERS USED

Most players, series
4-game series
25—Oakland A.L. vs. Cincinnati N.L., 1990.
　　Atlanta N.L. vs. New York A.L., 1999.
5-game series
25—Brooklyn N.L. vs. New York A.L., 1949.
　　New York N.L. vs. New York A.L., 2000.
6-game series
25—Los Angeles N.L. vs. New York A.L., 1977.
　　New York A.L. vs. Atlanta N.L., 1996.
7-game series
26—Detroit A.L. vs. Chicago N.L., 1945.
　　Boston A.L. vs. St. Louis N.L., 1946.
　　Florida N.L. vs. Cleveland A.L., 1997.
　　Anaheim A.L. vs. San Francisco N.L., 2002.
8-game series
19—Chicago A.L. vs. Cincinnati N.L., 1919.
　　New York A.L. vs. New York N.L., 1921.

For a list of players and pitchers used each series, see page 508.

Most players used by both clubs, series
4-game series
48—Atlanta N.L. 25, New York A.L. 23, 1999.
5-game series
47—New York N.L. 25, New York A.L. 22, 2000.
6-game series
49—New York A.L. 25, Atlanta N.L. 24, 1996.
7-game series
51—Detroit A.L. 26, Chicago N.L. 25, 1945.
8-game series
36—Chicago A.L. 19, Cincinnati N.L. 17, 1919.

Fewest players, series
4-game series
13—Los Angeles N.L. vs. New York A.L., 1963.
　　Baltimore A.L. vs. Los Angeles N.L., 1966.
5-game series
12—New York N.L. vs. Philadelphia A.L., 1905.
　　Philadelphia A.L. vs. Chicago N.L., 1910.
　　Philadelphia A.L. vs. New York N.L., 1913.
6-game series
14—Chicago N.L. vs. Chicago A.L., 1906.
　　Philadelphia A.L. vs. New York N.L., 1911.
7-game series
16—Detroit A.L. vs. Pittsburgh N.L., 1909.
8-game series
13—Boston A.L. vs. Pittsburgh N.L., 1903.
　　New York N.L. vs. New York A.L., 1921.

Fewest players used by both clubs, series
4-game series
31—Philadelphia A.L. 16, Boston N.L. 15, 1914.
5-game series
25—Philadelphia A.L. 13, New York N.L. 12, 1905.
6-game series
29—New York N.L. 15, Philadelphia A.L. 14, 1911.
7-game series
33—Pittsburgh N.L. 17, Detroit A.L. 16, 1909.
8-game series
27—Pittsburgh N.L. 14, Boston A.L. 13, 1903.

Most times one club using only nine players in game, series
5-game series
5—Philadelphia A.L. vs. Chicago N.L., 1910.
　　Philadelphia A.L. vs. New York N.L., 1913.

7-game series
5—New York A.L. vs. Brooklyn N.L., 1956.
8-game series
6—Pittsburgh N.L. vs. Boston A.L., 1903.

Most times both clubs using only nine players in game, series
7-game series
7—New York A.L. 5, Brooklyn N.L. 2, 1956.
8-game series
11—Pittsburgh N.L. 6, Boston A.L. 5, 1903.

Most players, game
21—New York A.L. vs. Brooklyn N.L., October 5, 1947.
　　Cincinnati N.L. vs. New York A.L., October 9, 1961.
　　(23—Minnesota A.L. vs. Atlanta N.L., October 22, 1991, 12 innings.)

Most players used by both clubs, game
38—New York A.L. 21, Brooklyn N.L. 17, October 5, 1947.
　　(42—Minnesota A.L. 23, Atlanta N.L. 19, October 22, 1991, 12 innings.)

PINCH-HITTERS

Most times pinch-hitters used, series
23—Baltimore A.L. vs. Pittsburgh N.L., 1979 (7-game series).

Most pinch-hitters used by both clubs, series
37—Minnesota A.L. 21, Atlanta N.L. 16, 1991 (7-game series).

Fewest times pinch-hitters used, series
0—Held by many clubs. Last club—Cincinnati N.L. vs. New York A.L., 1976 (4-game series).

Fewest pinch-hitters used by both clubs, series
2—New York N.L. 1, Philadelphia A.L. 1, 1905 (5-game series).

Most pinch-hitters, game
6—Los Angeles N.L. vs. Chicago A.L., October 6, 1959.
　　(8—Minnesota A.L. vs. Atlanta N.L., October 22, 1991, 12 innings.)

Most pinch-hitters used by both clubs, game
8—Oakland A.L. 5, New York N.L. 3, October 14, 1973.
　　Baltimore A.L. 4, Philadelphia N.L. 4, October 15, 1983.
　　(12—Minnesota A.L. 8, Atlanta N.L. 4, October 22, 1991, 12 innings.)

Most pinch-hitters, inning
4—New York N.L. vs. Oakland A.L. October 13, 1973, ninth inning.
　　Baltimore A.L. vs. Philadelphia N.L., October 15, 1983, sixth inning.
　　Minnesota A.L. vs. St. Louis N.L., October 22, 1987, ninth inning.
　　Atlanta N.L. vs. New York A.L., October 23, 1999, eighth inning.
　　New York N.L. vs. New York A.L., October 25, 2000, seventh inning.

PINCH-RUNNERS

Most times pinch-runners used, series
8—Oakland A.L. vs. Cincinnati N.L., 1972 (7-game series).

Most pinch-runners used by both clubs, series
10—Oakland A.L. 8, Cincinnati N.L. 2, 1972 (7-game series).

Fewest times pinch-runners used, series
0—Held by many clubs.

Most pinch-runners, game
2—Made in many games.

Most pinch-runners used by both clubs, game
4—St. Louis N.L. 2, Kansas City A.L. 2, October 26, 1985.

Most pinch-runners, inning
2—Held by many clubs.

Most pinch-runners used by both clubs, inning
2—Made in many games.

NUMBER OF PLAYERS USED BY POSITION
FIRST BASEMEN

Most first basemen, series
4—New York A.L. vs. Milwaukee N.L., 1957 (7-game series).
   Oakland A.L. vs. New York N.L., 1973 (7-game series).

Most first basemen used by both clubs, series
6—New York A.L. 4, Milwaukee N.L. 2, 1957 (7-game series).

Most first basemen, game
3—New York A.L. vs. Milwaukee N.L., October 2, 1957.
   New York A.L. vs. Milwaukee N.L., October 5, 1957.
   (3—Florida N.L. vs. Cleveland A.L., October 26, 1997,
   11 innings.)

Most first basemen used by both clubs, game
5—New York A.L. 3, Milwaukee N.L. 2, October 2, 1957.
   New York A.L. 3, Milwaukee N.L. 2, October 5, 1957.

SECOND BASEMEN

Most second basemen, series
3—Held by many clubs. Last club—St. Louis N.L. vs. Boston
   A.L., 2004 (4-game series).

Most second basemen used by both clubs, series
5—Oakland A.L. 3, San Francisco N.L. 2, 1989 (4-game series).

Most second basemen, game
3—St. Louis N.L. vs. New York A.L., October 7, 1964.
   (3—Oakland A.L. vs. New York N.L., October 14, 1973,
   12 innings.)

Most second basemen used by both clubs, game
4—Made in many games. Last game—Boston A.L. 2, St. Louis
   N.L. 2, October 27, 2004.

THIRD BASEMEN

Most third basemen, series
3—Held by many clubs. Last club—New York A.L. vs. Atlanta
   N.L., 1996 (6-game series).

Most third basemen used by both clubs, series
6—Oakland A.L. 3, San Francisco N.L. 3, 1989 (4-game series).

Most third basemen, game
3—Held by many clubs. Last club—Minnesota A.L. vs. Atlanta
   N.L., October 23, 1991.
   (3—Held by many clubs. Last club—New York A.L. vs.
   Atlanta N.L., October 23, 1996, 10 innings.)

Most third basemen used by both clubs, game
4—Made in many games.
   (5—New York A.L. 3, Atlanta N.L. 2, October 23, 1996,
   10 innings.)

SHORTSTOPS

Most shortstops, series
3—Held by many clubs. Last club—Atlanta N.L. vs. New York
   A.L., 1999 (4-game series).

Most shortstops used by both clubs, series
5—Chicago N.L. 3, Detroit A.L. 2, 1945 (7-game series).
   New York A.L. 3, Pittsburgh N.L. 2, 1960 (7-game series).
   Minnesota A.L. 3, Atlanta N.L. 2, 1991 (7-game series).

Most shortstops, game
3—New York A.L. vs. Pittsburgh N.L., October 13, 1960.
   Cincinnati N.L. vs. Baltimore A.L., October 14, 1970.
   (3—Minnesota A.L. vs. Atlanta N.L. October 27, 1991,
   10 innings.)
   Atlanta N.L. vs. New York A.L., October 23, 1996, 10 innings.)

Most shortstops used by both clubs, nine-inning game
4—Made in many games.
   (5—Minnesota A.L. 3, Atlanta N.L. 2, October 27, 1991,
   10 innings.)

LEFT FIELDERS

Most left fielders, series
4—Held by many clubs. Last club—St. Louis N.L. vs. Boston

A.L., 2004 (4-game series).

Most left fielders used by both clubs, series
7—Oakland A.L. 4, Los Angeles N.L. 3, 1988 (5-game series).
   New York A.L. 4, Arizona N.L. 3, 2001 (7-game series).

Most left fielders, game
3—Held by many clubs. Last club—Atlanta N.L. vs. Cleveland
   A.L., October 22, 1995.
   (3—Held by many clubs. Last club—New York A.L. vs. New
   York N.L., October 21, 2000, 12 innings.)

Most left fielders used by both clubs, game
5—Brooklyn N.L. 3, New York A.L. 2, October 5, 1947.
   (5—New York A.L. 3, New York N.L. 2, October 21, 2000,
   12 innings.)

CENTER FIELDERS

Most center fielders, series
4—Los Angeles N.L. vs. Chicago A.L., 1959 (6-game series).

Most center fielders used by both clubs, series
6—New York A.L. 3, Los Angeles N.L. 3, 1981 (6-game series).

Most center fielders, game
2—Held by many clubs.
   (3—New York N.L. vs. New York A.L., October 5, 1922,
   10 innings.)

Most center fielders used by both clubs, game
4—Made in many games. Last game—New York A.L. 2, Los
   Angeles N.L. 2, October 25, 1981.

RIGHT FIELDERS

Most right fielders, series
5—Los Angeles N.L. vs. Chicago A.L., 1959 (6-game series).
   New York A.L. vs. Florida N.L., 2003 (6-game series).

Most right fielders used by both clubs, series
9—Los Angeles N.L. 5, Chicago A.L. 4, 1959 (6-game series).

Most right fielders, game
3—Held by many clubs.

Most right fielders used by both clubs, game
5—Los Angeles N.L. 3, Chicago A.L. 2, October 8, 1959.
   San Francisco N.L. 3, Anaheim A.L. 2, October 24, 2002.

CATCHERS

Most catchers, series
4—Los Angeles N.L. vs. New York A.L., 1978 (6-game series).

Most catchers used by both clubs, series
6—New York A.L. 3, Pittsburgh N.L. 3, 1927 (4-game series).
   Los Angeles N.L. 4, New York A.L. 2, 1978 (6-game series).
   New York A.L. 3, Pittsburgh N.L. 3, 1960 (7-game series).

Most catchers, game
3—Los Angeles N.L. vs. New York A.L., October 13, 1978.
   (3—Philadelphia N.L. vs. New York A.L., October 5, 1950,
   10 innings.)

Most catchers used by both clubs, game
4—Made in many games.

PITCHERS

Most pitchers, series
4-game series
   11—St. Louis N.L. vs. Boston A.L., 2004.
5-game series
   10—San Diego N.L. vs. Detroit A.L., 1984.
   Oakland A.L. vs. Los Angeles N.L., 1988.
   New York N.L. vs. New York A.L., 2000.
6-game series
   10—Held by many clubs. Last clubs—Atlanta N.L. vs. New
   York A.L., 1996; New York A.L. vs. Atlanta N.L., 1996.
7-game series
   11—Boston A.L. vs. St. Louis N.L., 1946.
   Cleveland A.L. vs. Florida N.L., 1997.
   San Francisco N.L. vs. Anaheim A.L., 2002.
8-game series
   8—New York A.L. vs. New York N.L., 1921.

For a list of players and pitchers used each
series, see page 508.

Most pitchers used by both clubs, series
4-game series
19—San Diego N.L. 10, New York A.L. 9, 1998.
   St. Louis N.L. 11, Boston A.L. 8, 2004.
5-game series
18—Baltimore A.L. 9, Cincinnati N.L. 9, 1970.
   New York N.L. 10, New York A.L. 8, 2000.
6-game series
20—Toronto A.L. 10, Philadelphia N.L. 10, 1993.
   Atlanta N.L. 10, New York A.L. 10, 1996.
7-game series
21—Cleveland A.L. 11, Florida N.L. 10, 1997.
   San Francisco N.L. 11, Anaheim A.L. 10, 2002.
8-game series
12—New York A.L. 8, New York N.L. 4, 1921.
Fewest pitchers, series
2—Philadelphia A.L. vs. Chicago N.L. 1910 (5-game series).
Fewest pitchers used by both clubs, series
6—Philadelphia A.L. 3, New York N.L. 3, 1905 (5-game series).
Most different starting pitchers, series
6—Brooklyn N.L. vs. New York A.L., 1947.
   Brooklyn N.L. vs. New York A.L., 1955.
   Pittsburgh N.L. vs. Baltimore A.L., 1971.
Most different starting pitchers used by both clubs, series
11—Brooklyn N.L. 6, New York A.L. 5, 1955.
Most pitchers, game
8—Cincinnati N.L. vs. New York A.L., October 9, 1961.
   St. Louis N.L. vs. Boston A.L., October 11, 1967.
   (8—Cincinnati N.L. vs. Boston A.L., October 21, 1975,
    12 innings.)
Most pitchers used by winning club, game
6—Cincinnati N.L. vs. Oakland A.L., October 20, 1972 (won 5-4).
   (7—Toronto A.L. vs. Atlanta N.L., October 24, 1992 (won
    4-3), 11 innings.)
Most pitchers used by losing club, game
8—Cincinnati N.L. vs. New York A.L., October 9, 1961 (lost 13-5).

St. Louis N.L. vs. Boston A.L., October 11, 1967 (lost 8-4).
(8—Cincinnati N.L. vs. Boston A.L., October 21, 1975 (lost
 7-6), 12 innings.)
Most pitchers used by both clubs, game
11—St. Louis N.L. 8, Boston A.L. 3, October 11, 1967.
   San Francisco N.L. 6, Oakland A.L. 5, October 28, 1989.
   St. Louis N.L. 6, Boston A.L. 5, October 23, 2004.
   (13—Minnesota A.L. 7, Atlanta N.L. 6, October 22, 1991,
    12 innings.
   New York A.L. 7, Atlanta N.L. 6, October 23, 1996,
    10 innings.)
Most pitchers, inning
5—Baltimore A.L. vs. Pittsburgh N.L., October 17, 1979, ninth inning.
   St. Louis N.L. vs. Kansas City A.L., October 27, 1985, fifth inning.

SERIES

Most series played
39—New York A.L., 1921, 1922, 1923, 1926, 1927, 1928, 1932,
   1936, 1937, 1938, 1939, 1941, 1942, 1943, 1947,
   1949, 1950, 1951, 1952, 1953, 1955, 1956, 1957,
   1958, 1960, 1961, 1962, 1963, 1964, 1976, 1977,
   1978, 1981, 1996, 1998, 1999, 2000, 2001, 2003 (won
   26, lost 13).
18—Brooklyn/Los Angeles N.L., 1916, 1920, 1941, 1947, 1949,
   1952, 1953, 1955, 1956, 1959, 1963, 1965, 1966,
   1974, 1977, 1978, 1981, 1988 (won 6, lost 12).

For a complete list of series won and lost by
teams, see page 498.

Most consecutive series played between same clubs
3—New York N.L. vs. New York A.L., 1921, 1922, 1923.

INDIVIDUAL BATTING

GAMES

Most games, career
75—Yogi Berra, New York A.L., 1947, 1949, 1950, 1951, 1952,
   1953, 1955, 1956, 1957, 1958, 1960, 1961, 1962,
   1963 (14 series, 65 consecutive games).

Most games with one club, career
75—Yogi Berra, New York A.L., 1947, 1949, 1950, 1951, 1952,
   1953, 1955, 1956, 1957, 1958, 1960, 1961, 1962,
   1963 (14 series, 65 consecutive games).

Most consecutive games played (in consecutive years)
30—Bobby Richardson, New York A.L., October 5, 1960
   through October 15, 1964.

Most games by pinch-hitter, career
12—Luis Polonia, Oakland A.L., 1988 (2); Atlanta N.L., 1995 (2),
   1996 (6); New York A.L., 2000 (2).

Most games by pinch-runner, career
9—Allan Lewis, Oakland A.L., 1972, 1973; two series (three runs).

Most games by pinch-hitter, series
6—Luis Polonia, Atlanta N.L., 1996.

Most games by pinch-runner, series
6—Allan Lewis, Oakland A.L., 1972 (scored two runs).

BATTING AVERAGE

Highest batting average, career (50 or more PA)
.418—Pepper Martin, St. Louis N.L., 1928, 1931, 1934; three
   series, 15 games (55 at-bats, 23 hits).
   Paul Molitor, Milwaukee A.L., 1982; Toronto A.L., 1993;
   two series, 13 games (55 at-bats, 23 hits).

For a yearly list of batting leaders and a
complete list of .500 hitters, see page 501.

Highest batting average, series
4-game series—.750—Billy Hatcher, Cincinnati N.L., 1990.
5-game series—.500—Larry McLean, New York N.L., 1913.
   Joe Gordon, New York A.L., 1941.
6-game series—.500—Dave Robertson, New York N.L., 1917.
   Billy Martin, New York A.L., 1953.
   Paul Molitor, Toronto A.L., 1993.
7-game series—.500—Pepper Martin, St. Louis N.L., 1931.
   Johnny Lindell, New York A.L., 1947
   (played only six games).
   Phil Garner, Pittsburgh N.L., 1979.
8-game series—.400—Buck Herzog, New York N.L., 1912.

Most series leading club in batting average
3—Home Run Baker, Philadelphia A.L., 1911, 1913, 1914.
   Pee Wee Reese, Brooklyn N.L., 1947, 1949, 1952 (tied).
   Duke Snider, Brooklyn N.L., 1952 (tied), 1955, 1956 (tied).
   Gil Hodges, Brooklyn N.L., Los Angeles N.L., 1953, 1956
   (tied), 1959.
   Steve Garvey, Los Angeles N.L., 1974, 1977, 1981.

Most series batting .300 or over
6—Babe Ruth, New York A.L., 1921, 1923, 1926, 1927, 1928,
   1932.

ON-BASE PERCENTAGE (SINCE 1954)

Highest on-base percentage, career (50 or more PA)
.475—Paul Molitor, Milwaukee A.L., 1982; Toronto A.L., 1993;
   two series, 13 games (55 at-bats, 23 hits, five walks,
   one hit by pitch).

Highest on-base percentage, series
4-game series—.800—Billy Hatcher, Cincinnati N.L., 1990.
5-game series—.563—Al Weis, New York N.L., 1969.
6-game series—.500—Bob Boone, Philadelphia N.L., 1980.
   Lenny Dykstra, Philadelphia N.L., 1993.

John Kruk, Philadelphia N.L., 1993.
Andruw Jones, Atlanta N.L., 1996
7-game series—.700—Barry Bonds, San Francisco N.L., 2002.

SLUGGING AVERAGE

Highest slugging average, career (50 or more PA)
.755—Reggie Jackson, Oakland A.L., 1973, 1974; New York
A.L., 1977, 1978, 1981; five series, 30 games (98 at-
bats, 35 hits, seven doubles, one triple, 10 home runs,
74 total bases).

Highest slugging average, series
4-game series—1.727—Lou Gehrig, New York A.L., 1928.
5-game series—1.071—Donn Clendenon, New York N.L., 1969.
6-game series—1.250—Reggie Jackson, New York A.L., 1977.
7-game series—1.294—Barry Bonds, San Francisco N.L., 2002.
8-game series—.600—Buck Herzog, New York N.L., 1912.

AT-BATS AND PLATE APPEARANCES

Most at-bats, career
259—Yogi Berra, New York A.L., 1947, 1949, 1950, 1951,
1952, 1953, 1955, 1956, 1957, 1958, 1960, 1961,
1962, 1963; 14 series, 75 games.

Most at-bats, series
4-game series—19—Mark Koenig, New York A.L., 1928.
Rickey Henderson, Oakland A.L., 1989.
Paul O'Neill, New York A.L., 1990.
5-game series—23—Hal Janvrin, Boston A.L., 1916.
Joe Moore, New York N.L., 1937.
Bobby Richardson, New York A.L., 1961.
6-game series—29—Mariano Duncan, Philadelphia N.L., 1993.
7-game series—33—Bucky Harris, Washington A.L., 1924.
Sam Rice, Washington A.L., 1925.
Omar Moreno, Pittsburgh N.L., 1979.
Devon White, Florida N.L., 1997.
8-game series—36—Jimmy Collins, Boston A.L., 1903.

Most at-bats, game
6—Held by many players. Last players—Johnny Damon,
Boston A.L., October 23, 2004.
(7—Don Halm, New York N.L., October 14, 1973, 12
innings.)

Most times faced pitcher with no at-bats, game
5—Fred Clarke, Pittsburgh N.L., October 16, 1909 (four bases
on balls, one sacrifice hit).

Most at-bats, inning
2—Held by many players. Last players—Matt Williams, Arizona
N.L., November 3, 2001, third inning; Reggie Sanders,
Arizona N.L., November 3, 2001, third inning.

Most times faced pitcher, inning
2—Held by many players. Last players—Greg Colbrunn,
Arizona N.L., November 3, 2001, third inning; Matt
Williams, Arizona N.L., November 3, 2001, third inning;
Reggie Sanders, Arizona N.L., November 3, 2001, third
inning.

Most at-bats by pinch-hitter, inning
2—George H. Burns, Philadelphia A.L., October 12, 1929, seventh
inning.

Most times faced pitcher twice in an inning, career
3—Joe DiMaggio, New York A.L., October 6, 1936, ninth inning;
October 6, 1937, sixth inning; September 30, 1947, fifth
inning.

Most times faced pitcher twice in an inning, series
2—Stan Musial, St. Louis N.L., September 30, ninth inning;
October 4, 1942, fourth inning.

RUNS

Most runs, career
42—Mickey Mantle, New York A.L., 1951, 1952, 1953, 1955,
1956, 1957, 1958, 1960, 1961, 1962, 1963, 1964; 12
series, 65 games.

Most runs, series
4-game series—9—Babe Ruth, New York A.L., 1928.
Lou Gehrig, New York A.L., 1932.
5-game series—6—Home Run Baker, Philadelphia A.L., 1910.
Dan Murphy, Philadelphia A.L., 1910.
Harry Hooper, Boston A.L., 1916.
Al Simmons, Philadelphia A.L., 1929.
Lee May, Cincinnati N.L., 1970.
Boog Powell, Baltimore A.L., 1970.
Lou Whitaker, Detroit A.L., 1984.
Derek Jeter, New York A.L., 2000.
6-game series—10—Reggie Jackson, New York A.L., 1977.
Paul Molitor, Toronto A.L., 1993.
7-game series—8—Tommy Leach, Pittsburgh N.L., 1909.
Pepper Martin, St. Louis N.L., 1934.
Billy Johnson, New York A.L., 1947.
Mickey Mantle, New York A.L., 1960.
Bobby Richardson, New York A.L., 1960.
Mickey Mantle, New York A.L., 1964.
Lou Brock, St. Louis N.L., 1967.
Jim Thome, Cleveland A.L., 1997.
Matt Williams, Cleveland A.L., 1997.
Barry Bonds, San Francisco N.L., 2002.
8-game series—8—Fred Parent, Boston A.L., 1903.

Most series with one or more runs
12—Yogi Berra, New York A.L., 1947, 1949, 1950, 1951, 1952,
1953, 1955, 1956, 1957, 1958, 1960, 1961.

Most at-bats without scoring a run, series
33—Devon White, Florida N.L., 1997 (7-game series).

Most consecutive games with one or more runs, career
9—Babe Ruth, New York A.L., 1927 (last 2), 1928 (4),
1932(first 3).

Most runs, game
4—Babe Ruth, New York A.L., October 6, 1926.
Earle Combs, New York A.L., October 2, 1932.
Frank Crosetti, New York A.L., October 2, 1936.
Enos Slaughter, St. Louis N.L., October 10, 1946.
Reggie Jackson, New York A.L., October 18, 1977.
Kirby Puckett, Minnesota A.L., October 24, 1987.
Carney Lansford, Oakland A.L., October 27, 1989.
Lenny Dykstra, Philadelphia N.L., October 20, 1993.
Jeff Kent, San Francisco N.L., October 24, 2002.

Most runs, inning
2—Frankie Frisch, New York N.L., October 7, 1921, seventh
inning.
Al Simmons, Philadelphia A.L., October 12, 1929, seventh
inning.
Jimmie Foxx, Philadelphia A.L., October 12, 1929, seventh
inning.
Dick McAuliffe, Detroit A.L., October 9, 1968, third inning.
Mickey Stanley, Detroit A.L., October 9, 1968, third inning.
Al Kaline, Detroit A.L., October 9, 1968, third inning.
Greg Colbrunn, Arizona N.L., November 3, 2001, third
inning.

HITS
CAREER AND SERIES

Most hits, career
71—Yogi Berra, New York A.L., 1947, 1949, 1950, 1951, 1952,
1953, 1955, 1956, 1957, 1958, 1960, 1961, 1962,
1963; 14 series, 75 games.

Most hits by pinch-hitter, career
3—Ken O'Dea, Chicago N.L., 1935 (1), 1938 (0); St. Louis N.L.,
1942 (1), 1943 (0), 1944 (1), 5 series, 8 games.
Bobby Brown, New York A.L., 1947 (3), 1949 (0), 1950 (0),

1951 (0), four series, seven games.
Johnny Mize, New York A.L., 1949 (2), 1950 (0), 1951 (0), 1952 (1), 1953 (0), five series, eight games.
Dusty Rhodes, New York N.L., 1954 (3), one series, three games.
Carl Furillo, Brooklyn N.L., 1947 (2), 1949 (0); Los Angeles N.L., 1959 (1), three series, seven games.
Bob Cerv, New York A.L., 1955 (1), 1956 (1), 1960 (1), three series, three games.
John Blanchard, New York A.L., 1960 (1), 1961 (1), 1962 (0), 1964 (1), four series, 10 games.
Carl Warwick, St. Louis N.L., 1964 (3), one series, five games.
Gonzalo Marquez, Oakland A.L., 1972 (3), one series, five games.
Ken Boswell, New York N.L., 1973 (3), one series, three games.

Most series with one or more hits
12—Yogi Berra, New York A.L., 1947, 1949, 1950, 1951, 1952, 1953, 1955, 1956, 1957, 1958, 1960, 1961.
Mickey Mantle, New York A.L., 1951, 1952, 1953, 1955, 1956, 1957, 1958, 1960, 1961, 1962, 1963, 1964.

Most consecutive games with one or more hits, career
17—Hank Bauer, New York A.L., 1956 (7), 1957 (7), 1958 (first 3).

Most hits, series
4-game series—10—Babe Ruth, New York A.L., 1928.
5-game series—9—Home Run Baker, Philadelphia A.L., 1910.
Eddie Collins, Philadelphia A.L., 1910.
Home Run Baker, Philadelphia A.L., 1913.
Heinie Groh, New York N.L., 1922.
Joe Moore, New York N.L., 1937.
Bobby Richardson, New York A.L., 1961.
Paul Blair, Baltimore A.L., 1970.
Brooks Robinson, Baltimore A.L., 1970.
Alan Trammell, Detroit A.L., 1984.
Derek Jeter, New York A.L., 2000.
Paul O'Neill, New York A.L., 2000.
6-game series—12—Billy Martin, New York A.L., 1953.
Paul Molitor, Toronto A.L., 1993.
Roberto Alomar, Toronto A.L., 1993.
Marquis Grissom, Atlanta N.L., 1996.
7-game series—13—Bobby Richardson, New York A.L., 1964.
Lou Brock, St. Louis N.L., 1968.
Marty Barrett, Boston A.L., 1986.
8-game series—12—Buck Herzog, New York N.L., 1912.
Joe Jackson, Chicago A.L., 1919.

Most hits by pinch-hitter, series
3—Bobby Brown, New York A.L., 1947 (consecutive; four games; one base on balls, one single, two doubles, three runs batted in).
Dusty Rhodes, New York N.L., 1954 (consecutive; three games; one home run, two singles, six runs batted in).
Carl Warwick, St. Louis N.L., 1964 (consecutive; five games; two singles, walk, single, one run batted in).
Gonzalo Marquez, Oakland A.L., 1972 (consecutive; three games; three singles, one run batted in).
Ken Boswell, New York N.L., 1973 (consecutive; three games; three singles).

Most consecutive hits, career
7—Thurman Munson, New York A.L., October 19 (2), October 21 (4), 1976, October 11 (1), 1977.
Billy Hatcher, Cincinnati N.L., October 16 (3), 17 (4), 1990.

Most consecutive hits, series
7—Billy Hatcher, Cincinnati N.L., October 16 (3), 17 (4), 1990.

Most games with four or more hits, series
2—Robin Yount, Milwaukee A.L., October 12 (4), 16 (4), 1982.

Collecting one or more hits in each game, series
Held by many players.

Most at-bats without a hit, career
22—George Earnshaw, Philadelphia A.L., 1929 (5), 1930 (9), 1931 (8).

Most at-bats without a hit, series
22—Dal Maxvill, St. Louis N.L., 1968 (7-game series).

Most consecutive hitless times at bat, career
31—Marv Owen, Detroit A.L., 1934 (last 12), 1935 (first 19).

GAME AND INNING

Most hits, game
5—Paul Molitor, Milwaukee A.L., October 12, 1982.

Most times reached first base safely, game (batting 1.000)
5—Babe Ruth, New York A.L., October 6, 1926 (three home runs, two bases on balls).
Babe Ruth, New York A.L., October 10, 1926 (one home run, four bases on balls).
Lou Brock, St. Louis N.L., October 4, 1967 (four singles, one base on balls).
Brooks Robinson, Baltimore A.L., October 11, 1971 (three singles, two bases on balls).
Rusty Staub, New York N.L., October 17, 1973 (three singles, one home run, one base on balls).
Kiko Garcia, Baltimore A.L., October 12, 1979 (two singles, one double, one triple, one base on balls).
Reggie Jackson, New York A.L., October 24, 1981 (two singles, one home run, two bases on balls).
George Brett, Kansas City A.L., October 22, 1985 (two singles, three bases on balls).
Kirby Puckett, Minnesota A.L., October 24, 1987 (four singles, one base on balls).
Billy Hatcher, Cincinnati N.L., October 17, 1990 (one single, two doubles, one triple, one base on balls).
Matt Williams, Cleveland A.L., October 22, 1997 (two singles, one home run, two bases on balls).
Tim Salmon, Anaheim A.L., October 20, 2002 (two singles, two home runs, one base on balls).
Bengie Molina, Anaheim A.L., October 22, 2002 (two singles, three bases on balls).

Most hits accounting for all club's hits, game
3—Irish Meusel, New York N.L., October 14, 1923 (one single, one double, one triple).
Dave Parker, Oakland A.L., October 16, 1988 (three singles).

Most at-bats with no hits, game
5—Held by many players.
(6—Travis Jackson, New York N.L., October 10, 1924, 12 innings.
Hughie Critz, New York N.L., October 6, 1933, 11 innings.
Felix Millan, New York N.L., October 14, 1973, 12 innings.
Mickey Rivers, New York A.L., October 11, 1977, 12 innings.
Ron Gant, Atlanta N.L., October 22, 1991, 12 innings.
Devon White, Florida N.L., October 26, 1997, 11 innings.
Craig Counsell, Arizona N.L., November 1, 2001, 12 innings.)

Most hits in two consecutive games, series
7—Frank Isbell, Chicago A.L., October 13 (4), 14 (3), 1906.
Fred Lindstrom, New York N.L., October 7 (3), 8 (4), 1924.
Monte Irvin, New York N.L., October 4 (4), 5 (3), 1951.
Thurman Munson, New York A.L., October 19 (3), 21 (4), 1976.
Paul Molitor, Milwaukee A.L., October 12 (5), 13 (2), 1982.
Billy Hatcher, Cincinnati N.L., October 16 (3), 17 (4), 1990.

Most hits, inning (18 times)
2—Ross Youngs, New York N.L., October 7, 1921, seventh inning.
Al Simmons, Philadelphia A.L., October 12, 1929, seventh inning.
Jimmie Foxx, Philadelphia A.L., October 12, 1929, seventh inning.
Jimmie Dykes, Philadelphia A.L., October 12, 1929, seventh inning.
Joe Moore, New York N.L., October 4, 1933, sixth inning.
Dizzy Dean, St. Louis N.L., October 9, 1934, third inning.
Joe DiMaggio, New York A.L., October 6, 1936, ninth inning.
Hank Leiber, New York N.L., October 9, 1937, second inning.
Stan Musial, St. Louis N.L., October 4, 1942, fourth inning.
Elston Howard, New York A.L., October 6, 1960, sixth inning.
Bobby Richardson, New York A.L., October 6, 1960, sixth inning.
Bob Cerv, New York A.L., October 8, 1960, first inning.
Frank Quilici, Minnesota A.L., October 6, 1965, third inning.
Al Kaline, Detroit A.L., October 9, 1968, third inning.
Norm Cash, Detroit A.L., October 9, 1968, third inning.

Merv Rettenmund, Baltimore A.L., October 11, 1971, fifth
inning.
Gary Gaetti, Minnesota A.L., October 17, 1987, fourth inning.
Matt Williams, Arizona N.L., November 3, 2001, third inning.

SINGLES

Most singles, career
49—Yogi Berra, New York A.L., 1947, 1949, 1950, 1951, 1952,
1953, 1955, 1956, 1957, 1958, 1960, 1961, 1962,
1963; 14 series, 75 games.

Most singles, series
4-game series—9—Thurman Munson, New York A.L., 1976.
5-game series—8—Frank Chance, Chicago N.L., 1908.
Home Run Baker, Philadelphia A.L., 1913.
Heinie Groh, New York N.L., 1922.
Joe Moore, New York N.L., 1937.
Bobby Richardson, New York A.L., 1961.
Paul Blair, Baltimore A.L., 1970.
Steve Garvey, Los Angeles N.L., 1974.
6-game series—10—Red Rolfe, New York A.L., 1936.
Monte Irvin, New York N.L., 1951.
7-game series—12—Sam Rice, Washington A.L., 1925.
8-game series—9—Jimmy Sebring, Pittsburgh N.L., 1903.
Chief Meyers, New York N.L., 1912.

Most singles, game
5—Paul Molitor, Milwaukee A.L., October 12, 1982.

Most singles, inning
2—Jimmie Foxx, Philadelphia A.L., October 12, 1929, seventh
inning.
Joe Moore, New York N.L., October 4, 1933, sixth inning.
Joe DiMaggio, New York A.L., October 6, 1936, ninth inning.
Hank Leiber, New York N.L., October 9, 1937, second inning.
Bob Cerv, New York A.L., October 8, 1960, first inning.
Al Kaline, Detroit A.L., October 9, 1968, third inning.
Norm Cash, Detroit A.L., October 9, 1968, third inning.
Merv Rettenmund, Baltimore A.L., October 11, 1971, fifth
inning.

DOUBLES

Most doubles, career
10—Frankie Frisch, New York N.L. (5), 1921, 1922, 1923, 1924;
St. Louis N.L. (5), 1928, 1930, 1931, 1934; eight
series, 50 games.
Yogi Berra, New York A.L., 1947, 1949, 1950, 1951, 1952,
1953, 1955, 1956, 1957, 1958, 1960, 1961, 1962,
1963; 14 series, 75 games.

Most doubles, series
4-game series—4—Billy Hatcher, Cincinnati, N.L., 1990.
5-game series—4—Eddie Collins, Philadelphia A.L., 1910.
Rick Dempsey, Baltimore A.L., 1983.
6-game series—5—Chick Hafey, St. Louis N.L., 1930.
7-game series—6—Pete Fox, Detroit A.L., 1934.
8-game series—4—Red Murray, New York N.L., 1912.
Buck Herzog, New York N.L., 1912.
Buck Weaver, Chicago A.L., 1919.
George J. Burns, New York N.L., 1921.

Most doubles, game
4—Frank Isbell, Chicago A.L., October 13, 1906.

Most doubles batting in three runs, game
1—Frankie Frisch, St. Louis N.L., October 9, 1934, third inning.
Paul Richards, Detroit A.L., October 10, 1945, first inning.
Lou Brock, St. Louis N.L., October 6, 1968, eighth inning.
Terry Pendleton, St. Louis N.L., October 20, 1985, ninth
inning.
Garret Anderson, Anaheim A.L., October 27, 2002, third
inning.

Most doubles, inning
2—Matt Williams, Arizona N.L., November 3, 2001, third inning.

TRIPLES

Most triples, career
4—Tommy Leach, Pittsburgh N.L., 1903, 1909; two series, 15
games.
Tris Speaker, Boston A.L. (3), 1912, 1915; Cleveland A.L.
(1), 1920; three series, 20 games.
Billy Johnson, New York A.L., 1943, 1947, 1949, 1950; four
series, 18 games.

Most games without a triple, career
75—Yogi Berra, New York A.L.; 14 series, 259 at-bats.

Most triples, series
4-game series—2—Lou Gehrig, New York A.L., 1927.
Tommy Davis, Los Angeles N.L., 1963.
Rickey Henderson, Oakland A.L., 1989.
5-game series—2—Eddie Collins, Philadelphia A.L., 1913.
Bobby Brown, New York A.L., 1949.
Paul O'Neill, New York A.L., 2000.
6-game series—2—George Rohe, Chicago A.L., 1906.
Bob Meusel, New York A.L., 1923.
Billy Martin, New York A.L., 1953.
Paul Molitor, Toronto A.L., 1993.
Devon White, Toronto A.L., 1993.
7-game series—3—Billy Johnson, New York A.L., 1947.
Mark Lemke, Atlanta N.L., 1991.
8-game series—4—Tommy Leach, Pittsburgh N.L., 1903.

Most triples, game
2—Tommy Leach, Pittsburgh N.L., October 1, 1903.
Patsy Dougherty, Boston A.L., October 7, 1903.
Dutch Ruether, Cincinnati N.L., October 1, 1919.
Bobby Richardson, New York A.L., October 12, 1960.
Tommy Davis, Los Angeles N.L., October 3, 1963.
Mark Lemke, Atlanta N.L., October 24, 1991.

Most bases-loaded triples, game
1—George Rohe, Chicago A.L., October 11, 1906, sixth inning.
Ross Youngs, New York N.L., October 7, 1921, seventh inning.
Billy Johnson, New York A.L., October 7, 1943, eighth inning.
Bobby Brown, New York A.L., October 8, 1949, fifth inning.
Hank Bauer, New York A.L., October 10, 1951, sixth inning.
Billy Martin, New York A.L., September 30, 1953, first inning.
Kiko Garcia, Baltimore A.L., October 12, 1979, fourth inning.
Milt Thompson, Philadelphia N.L., October 20, 1993, first
inning.

Most triples, inning
1—Held by many players.

HOME RUNS
CAREER AND SERIES

Most home runs, career
18—Mickey Mantle, New York A.L., 1951, 1952, 1953, 1955,
1956, 1957, 1958, 1960, 1961, 1962, 1963, 1964; 12
series, 65 games.

For a list of all home runs each series and a
complete list of players with five or more
career home runs, see page 503.

Most home runs by pitcher, career
2—Bob Gibson, St. Louis N.L., 1964 (0), 1967 (1), 1968 (1);
three series, nine games.
Dave McNally, Baltimore A.L., 1966 (0), 1969 (1), 1970 (1),
1971 (0); four series, nine games.

Most games without a home run, career
50—Frankie Frisch, New York N.L., St. Louis N.L.; eight series,
197 at-bats.

Most series with one or more home runs
9—Yogi Berra, New York A.L., 1947 (1), 1950 (1), 1952 (2),

1953 (1), 1955 (1), 1956 (3), 1957 (1), 1960 (1), 1961 (1).
Mickey Mantle, New York A.L., 1952 (2), 1953 (2), 1955 (1), 1956 (3), 1957 (1), 1958 (2), 1960 (3), 1963 (1), 1964 (3).

Most home runs, four consecutive games (homering in each game)
6—Reggie Jackson, New York A.L., 1977 (5), last three games; 1978 (1), first game.

Hitting home runs for both leagues
Bill Skowron, A.L. (7), N.L. (1).
Frank Robinson, N.L. (1), A.L. (7).
Roger Maris, A.L. (5), N.L. (1).
Reggie Smith, A.L. (2), N.L. (4).
Enos Slaughter, N.L. (2), A.L. (1).
Kirk Gibson, A.L. (2), N.L. (1).
Matt Williams, N.L. (2), A.L. (1).

Most home runs, series
4-game series—4—Lou Gehrig, New York A.L., 1928.
5-game series—3—Donn Clendenon, New York N.L., 1969.
6-game series—5—Reggie Jackson, New York, 1977.
7-game series—4—Babe Ruth, New York A.L., 1926.
          Duke Snider, Brooklyn N.L., 1952.
          Duke Snider, Brooklyn N.L., 1955.
          Hank Bauer, New York A.L., 1958.
          Gene Tenace, Oakland A.L., 1972.
          Barry Bonds, San Francisco N.L., 2002.
8-game series—2—Patsy Dougherty, Boston A.L., 1903.

Most home runs by pinch-hitter, series
2—Chuck Essegian, Los Angeles N.L., 4 games, 1959.
   Bernie Carbo, Boston A.L., 3 games, 1975.

Most home runs by rookie, series
3—Charlie Keller, New York A.L., 1939.

Most series with two or more home runs
6—Mickey Mantle, New York A.L., 1952 (2), 1953 (2), 1956 (3), 1958 (2), 1960 (3), 1964 (3).

Most series with three or more home runs
3—Babe Ruth, New York A.L., 1923 (3), 1926 (4), 1928 (3).
   Mickey Mantle, New York A.L., 1956 (3), 1960 (3), 1964 (3).

Most series with four or more home runs
2—Duke Snider, Brooklyn N.L., 1952, 1955.

Most home runs, two consecutive series (two consecutive years)
7—Reggie Jackson, New York A.L., 1977 (5), 1978 (2).

Most home runs, three consecutive series (three consecutive years)
9—Babe Ruth, New York A.L., 1926 (4), 1927 (2), 1928 (3).

Most home runs in three consecutive games, series (homering each game)
5—Reggie Jackson, New York A.L., October 15 (1), 16 (1), 18 (3), 1977.

Most home runs in two consecutive games, series (homering each game)
4—Reggie Jackson, New York A.L., October 16 (1), 18 (3), 1977.

Most consecutive home runs in two consecutive games, series
4—Reggie Jackson, New York A.L., October 16 (1), 18 (3), 1977 (one base on balls included).

Most series with two or more home runs in a game
4—Babe Ruth, New York A.L., 1923, 1926, 1928, 1932 (two home runs in one game twice, three home runs in one game twice).

GAME AND INNING

Most home runs, game (3 homers, 3 times; 2 homers, 39 times; *consecutive)
3—Babe Ruth, New York A.L., October 6, 1926 (two consecutive).
   Babe Ruth, New York A.L., October 9, 1928, (two consecutive).
   Reggie Jackson, New York A.L., October 18, 1977 (each on first pitch).*

2—Patsy Dougherty, Boston A.L., October 2, 1903.
   Harry Hooper, Boston A.L., October 13, 1915.
   Benny Kauff, New York N.L., October 11, 1917.
   Babe Ruth, New York A.L., October 11, 1923.*
   Lou Gehrig, New York A.L., October 7, 1928.*
   Lou Gehrig, New York A.L., October 1, 1932.*
   Babe Ruth, New York A.L., October 1, 1932.
   Tony Lazzeri, New York A.L., October 2, 1932.
   Charlie Keller, New York A.L., October 7, 1939.
   Bob Elliott, Boston N.L., October 10, 1948.*
   Duke Snider, Brooklyn N.L., October 6, 1952.*
   Joe Collins, New York A.L., September 28, 1955.*
   Duke Snider, Brooklyn N.L., October 2, 1955.*
   Yogi Berra, New York A.L., October 10, 1956.*
   Tony Kubek, New York A.L., October 5, 1957.
   Mickey Mantle, New York A.L., October 2, 1958.
   Ted Kluszewski, Chicago A.L., October 1, 1959.*
   Charlie Neal, Los Angeles N.L., October 2, 1959.*
   Mickey Mantle, New York A.L., October 6, 1960.
   Carl Yastrzemski, Boston A.L., October 5, 1967.
   Rico Petrocelli, Boston A.L., October 11, 1967.*
   Gene Tenace, Oakland A.L., October 14, 1972.*
   Tony Perez, Cincinnati N.L., October 16, 1975.*
   Johnny Bench, Cincinnati N.L., October 21, 1976.
   Dave Lopes, Los Angeles N.L., October 10, 1978.*
   Willie Aikens, Kansas City A.L., October 14, 1980.
   Willie Aikens, Kansas City A.L., October 18, 1980.
   Willie McGee, St. Louis N.L., October 15, 1982.*
   Eddie Murray, Baltimore A.L., October 16, 1983.*
   Alan Trammell, Detroit A.L., October 13, 1984.*
   Kirk Gibson, Detroit A.L., October 14, 1984.
   Gary Carter, New York N.L., October 22, 1986.
   Dave Henderson, Oakland A.L., October 27, 1989.*
   Chris Sabo, Cincinnati N.L., October 19, 1990.*
   Andruw Jones, Atlanta N.L., October 20, 1996.*
   Scott Brosius, New York A.L., October 20, 1998.*
   Chad Curtis, New York A.L., October 26, 1999 (10 innings).
   Troy Glaus, Anaheim A.L., October 19, 2002.
   Jeff Kent, San Francisco N.L., October 24, 2002.*

Most home runs by rookie, game
2—Charlie Keller, New York A.L., October 7, 1939.
   Tony Kubek, New York A.L., October 5, 1957.
   Willie McGee, St. Louis N.L., October 15, 1982.
   Andruw Jones, Atlanta N.L., October 20, 1996.

Hitting home runs in first two World Series at-bats
Gene Tenace, Oakland A.L., October 14, 1972, second and fifth innings.
Andruw Jones, Atlanta N.L., October 20, 1996, second and third innings.

Hitting home run in first World Series at-bat (27 times; *not first plate appearance)
Joe Harris, Washington A.L., vs. Pittsburgh N.L., October 7, 1925, second inning.
George Watkins, St. Louis N.L., vs. Philadelphia A.L., October 2, 1930, second inning.
Mel Ott, New York N.L., vs. Washington A.L., October 3, 1933, first inning.
George Selkirk, New York A.L., vs. New York N.L., September 30, 1936, third inning.
Dusty Rhodes, New York N.L., vs. Cleveland A.L., September 29, 1954, 10th inning.
Elston Howard, New York A.L., vs. Brooklyn N.L. September 28, 1955, second inning.
Roger Maris, New York A.L., vs. Pittsburgh N.L., October 5, 1960, first inning.
Don Mincher, Minnesota A.L., vs. Los Angeles N.L., October 6, 1965, second inning.
Brooks Robinson, Baltimore A.L., vs. Los Angeles N.L., October 5, 1966, first inning.
Jose R. Santiago, Boston A.L., vs. St. Louis N.L., October 4, 1967, third inning.
Mickey Lolich, Detroit A.L., vs. St. Louis N.L., October 3, 1968, third inning.
Don Buford, Baltimore A.L., vs. New York N.L., October 11, 1969, first inning.
Gene Tenace, Oakland A.L., vs. Cincinnati N.L., October 14, 1972, second inning.
Jim Mason, New York A.L., vs. Cincinnati N.L., October 19, 1976, seventh inning.

Doug DeCinces, Baltimore A.L. vs. Pittsburgh N.L., October 10, 1979, first inning.
Amos Otis, Kansas City A.L. vs. Philadelphia N.L., October 14, 1980, second inning.
Bob Watson, New York A.L. vs. Los Angeles N.L., October 20, 1981, first inning.
Jim Dwyer, Baltimore A.L. vs. Philadelphia N.L., October 11, 1983, first inning.
Mickey Hatcher, Los Angeles N.L. vs. Oakland A.L., October 15, 1988, first inning.
Jose Canseco, Oakland A.L. vs. Los Angeles N.L., October 15, 1988, second inning.*
Bill Bathe, San Francisco N.L. vs. Oakland A.L., October 27, 1989, ninth inning.
Eric Davis, Cincinnati N.L. vs. Oakland A.L., October 16, 1990, first inning.
Ed Sprague Jr., Toronto A.L. vs. Atlanta N.L., October 18, 1992, ninth inning.
Fred McGriff, Atlanta N.L. vs. Cleveland A.L., October 21, 1995, second inning.
Andruw Jones, Atlanta N.L. vs. New York A.L., October 20, 1996, second inning.
Barry Bonds, San Francisco N.L. vs. Anaheim A.L., October 19, 2002, second inning.
Troy Glaus, Anaheim A.L. vs. San Francisco N.L., October 19, 2002, second inning.

Hitting a home run to win a 1-0 game
Casey Stengel, New York N.L., October 12, 1923, seventh inning.
Tommy Henrich, New York A.L., October 5, 1949, ninth inning.
Paul Blair, Baltimore A.L., October 8, 1966, fifth inning.
Frank Robinson, Baltimore A.L., October 9, 1966, fourth inning.
David Justice, Atlanta N.L., October 28, 1995, sixth inning.

Homering as leadoff batter at start of game (16 times)
Patsy Dougherty, Boston A.L., October 2, 1903.
Davy Jones, Detroit A.L., October 13, 1909.
Phil Rizzuto, New York A.L., October 5, 1942.
Dale Mitchell, Cleveland A.L., October 10, 1948.
Gene Woodling, New York A.L., October 4, 1953.
Al Smith, Cleveland A.L., September 30, 1954.
Billy Bruton, Milwaukee N.L., October 2, 1958.
Lou Brock, St. Louis N.L., October 6, 1968.
Don Buford, Baltimore A.L., October 11, 1969.
Tommie Agee, New York N.L., October 14, 1969.
Pete Rose, Cincinnati N.L., October 20, 1972.
Wayne Garrett, New York N.L., October 16, 1973.
Dave Lopes, Los Angeles N.L., October 17, 1978.
Lenny Dykstra, New York N.L., October 21, 1986.
Rickey Henderson, Oakland A.L., October 28, 1989.
Derek Jeter, New York A.L., October 25, 2000.

Home runs by pitcher, game (14 times)
Jim Bagby Sr., Cleveland A.L., October 10, 1920 (two on base).
Rosy Ryan, New York N.L., October 6, 1924 (none on base).
Jack Bentley, New York N.L., October 8, 1924 (one on base).
Jesse Haines, St. Louis N.L., October 5, 1926 (one on base).
Bucky Walters, Cincinnati N.L., October 7, 1940 (none on base).
Lew Burdette, Milwaukee N.L., October 2, 1958 (two on base).
Mudcat Grant, Minnesota A.L., October 13, 1965 (two on base).
Jose R. Santiago, Boston A.L., October 4, 1967 (none on base).
Bob Gibson, St. Louis N.L., October 12, 1967 (none on base).
Mickey Lolich, Detroit A.L., October 3, 1968 (none on base).
Bob Gibson, St. Louis N.L., October 6, 1968 (none on base).
Dave McNally, Baltimore A.L., October 16, 1969 (one on base).
Dave McNally, Baltimore A.L., October 13, 1970 (three on base).
Ken Holtzman, Oakland A.L., October 16, 1974 (none on base).

Home runs by pinch-hitter (17 times)
Yogi Berra, New York A.L., October 2, 1947, seventh inning (none on base).
Johnny Mize, New York A.L., October 3, 1952, ninth inning (none on base).
George Shuba, Brooklyn N.L., September 30, 1953, sixth inning (one on base).
Dusty Rhodes, New York N.L., September 29, 1954, 10th inning (two on base).
Hank Majeski, Cleveland A.L., October 2, 1954, fifth inning (two on base).

Bob Cerv, New York A.L., October 2, 1955, seventh inning (none on base).
Chuck Essegian, Los Angeles N.L., October 2, 1959, seventh inning (none on base).
Chuck Essegian, Los Angeles N.L., October 8, 1959, ninth inning (none on base).
Elston Howard, New York A.L., October 5, 1960, ninth inning (one on base).
John Blanchard, New York A.L., October 7, 1961, eighth inning (none on base).
Bernie Carbo, Boston A.L., October 14, 1975, seventh inning (none on base).
Bernie Carbo, Boston A.L., October 21, 1975, eighth inning (two on base).
Jay Johnstone, Los Angeles N.L., October 24, 1981, sixth inning (one on base).
Kirk Gibson, Los Angeles N.L., October 15, 1988, ninth inning (one on base).
Bill Bathe, San Francisco N.L., October 27, 1989, ninth inning (two on base).
Chili Davis, Minnesota A.L., October 22, 1991, eighth inning (one on base).
Ed Sprague Jr., Toronto A.L., October 18, 1992, ninth inning (one on base).
Jim Leyritz, New York A.L., October 27, 1999, eighth inning (none on base).

Grand slams (17)
Elmer Smith, Cleveland A.L., October 10, 1920, first inning.
Tony Lazzeri, New York A.L., October 2, 1936, third inning.
Gil McDougald, New York A.L., October 9, 1951, third inning.
Mickey Mantle, New York A.L., October 4, 1953, third inning.
Yogi Berra, New York A.L., October 5, 1956, second inning.
Bill Skowron, New York A.L., October 10, 1956, seventh inning.
Bobby Richardson, New York A.L., October 8, 1960, first inning.
Chuck Hiller, San Francisco N.L., October 8, 1962, seventh inning.
Ken Boyer, St. Louis N.L., October 11, 1964, sixth inning.
Joe Pepitone, New York A.L., October 14, 1964, eighth inning.
Jim Northrup, Detroit A.L., October 9, 1968, third inning.
Dave McNally, Baltimore A.L., October 13, 1970, sixth inning.
Dan Gladden, Minnesota A.L., October 17, 1987, fourth inning.
Kent Hrbek, Minnesota A.L., October 24, 1987, sixth inning.
Jose Canseco, Oakland A.L., October 15, 1988, second inning.
Lonnie Smith, Atlanta N.L., October 22, 1992, fifth inning.
Tino Martinez, New York A.L., October 17, 1998, seventh inning.

Most home runs, inning
1—Held by many players.

Most home runs, two consecutive innings (10 times)
2—Babe Ruth, New York A.L., October 11, 1923, fourth and fifth innings.
Babe Ruth, New York A.L., October 9, 1928, seventh and eighth innings.
Ted Kluszewski, Chicago A.L., October 1, 1959, third and fourth innings.
Reggie Jackson, New York A.L., October 18, 1977, fourth and fifth innings.
Willie Aikens, Kansas City A.L., October 18, 1980, first and second innings.
Dave Henderson, Oakland A.L., October 27, 1989, fourth and fifth innings.
Chris Sabo, Cincinnati N.L., October 19, 1990, second and third innings.
Andruw Jones, Atlanta N.L., October 20, 1996, second and third innings.
Scott Brosius, New York A.L., October 20, 1998, seventh and eighth innings.
Jeff Kent, San Francisco N.L., October 24, 2002, sixth and seventh innings.

TOTAL BASES

Most total bases, career
123—Mickey Mantle, New York A.L., 1951, 1952, 1953, 1955, 1956, 1957, 1958, 1960, 1961, 1962, 1963, 1964; 12 series, 65 games.

Most total bases, series
4-game series—22—Babe Ruth, New York A.L., 1928.
5-game series—19—Derek Jeter, New York A.L., 2000.

6-game series—25—Reggie Jackson, New York A.L., 1977.
7-game series—25—Willie Stargell, Pittsburgh N.L., 1979.
8-game series—18—Buck Herzog, New York N.L., 1912.
        Joe Jackson, Chicago A.L., 1919.

Most total bases by pinch-hitter, series
8—Chuck Essegian, Los Angeles N.L., 1959; four games (two home runs).
    Bernie Carbo, Boston A.L., 1975; three games (two home runs).

Most total bases, game
12—Babe Ruth, New York A.L., October 6, 1926 (three home runs).
    Babe Ruth, New York A.L., October 9, 1928 (three home runs).
    Reggie Jackson, New York A.L., October 18, 1977 (three home runs).

Most total bases, inning
5—Ross Youngs, New York N.L., October 7, 1921, seventh inning (double and triple).
    Al Simmons, Philadelphia A.L., October 12, 1929, seventh inning (home run and single).

EXTRA BASE HITS

Most extra base hits, career
26—Mickey Mantle, New York A.L., 1951, 1952, 1953, 1955, 1956, 1957, 1958, 1960, 1961, 1962, 1963, 1964; 12 series, 65 games.

Most extra base hits, series
4-game series—6—Babe Ruth, New York A.L., 1928.
5-game series—5—Rick Dempsey, Baltimore A.L., 1983.
                Derek Jeter, New York A.L., 2000.
6-game series—6—Reggie Jackson, New York A.L., 1977.
                Paul Molitor, Toronto A.L., 1993.
                Devon White, Toronto A.L., 1993.
7-game series—7—Willie Stargell, Pittsburgh N.L., 1979.
8-game series—5—Red Murray, New York N.L., 1912.
                Buck Herzog, New York N.L., 1912.
                Buck Weaver, Chicago A.L., 1919.
                George J. Burns, New York N.L., 1921.

Most extra base hits, game
4—Frank Isbell, Chicago A.L., October 13, 1906 (four doubles).

Most extra base hits in two consecutive games, series
5—Lou Brock, St. Louis N.L., October 6 (3—double, triple, home run); October 7 (2—two doubles), 1968.

Most extra base hits, inning
2—Ross Youngs, New York N.L., October 7, 1921, seventh inning (double and triple).

RUNS BATTED IN

Most runs batted in, career
40—Mickey Mantle, New York A.L., 1951, 1952, 1953, 1955, 1956, 1957, 1958, 1960, 1961, 1962, 1963, 1964; 12 series, 65 games.

Most series with one or more runs batted in
11—Yogi Berra, New York A.L., 1947, 1949, 1950, 1952, 1953, 1955, 1956, 1957, 1958, 1960, 1961.

Most consecutive games with one or more RBIs, career
8—Lou Gehrig, New York A.L., 1928 (4), 1932 (4); total of 17 runs batted in.
    Reggie Jackson, New York A.L., 1977 (4), 1978 (4); total of 14 runs batted in.

Most runs batted in, series
4-game series—9—Lou Gehrig, New York A.L., 1928.
5-game series—8—Dan Murphy, Philadelphia A.L., 1910.
                Lee May, Cincinnati N.L., 1970.
6-game series—10—Ted Kluszewski, Chicago A.L., 1959.
7-game series—12—Bobby Richardson, New York A.L., 1960.
8-game series—8—Tommy Leach, Pittsburgh N.L., 1903.
                Pat Duncan, Cincinnati N.L., 1919.

Most runs batted in by pinch-hitter, series
6—Dusty Rhodes, New York N.L., 1954; three games.

Most at-bats without a run batted in, series
34—Fred Clarke, Pittsburgh N.L., 1903; eight games.
    Buck Weaver, Chicago A.L., 1919; eight games.

Most runs batted in, game
6—Bobby Richardson, New York A.L., October 8, 1960.

Most runs batted in accounting for all club's runs, game
4—Hank Bauer, New York A.L., October 4, 1958 (won 4-0).
    Ken Boyer, St. Louis N.L., October 11, 1964 (won 4-3).
    Ron Cey, Los Angeles N.L., October 11, 1978 (won 4-3).
    Alan Trammell, Detroit A.L., October 13, 1984 (won 4-2).
    Jose Canseco, Oakland A.L., October 15, 1988 (lost 5-4).

Most runs batted in, inning (17 times)
4—Elmer Smith, Cleveland A.L., October 10, 1920, first inning.
    Tony Lazzeri, New York A.L., October 2, 1936, third inning.
    Gil McDougald, New York A.L., October 9, 1951, third inning.
    Mickey Mantle, New York A.L., October 4, 1953, third inning.
    Yogi Berra, New York A.L., October 5, 1956, second inning.
    Bill Skowron, New York A.L., October 10, 1956, seventh inning.
    Bobby Richardson, New York A.L., October 8, 1960, first inning.
    Chuck Hiller, San Francisco N.L., October 8, 1962, seventh inning.
    Ken Boyer, St. Louis N.L., October 11, 1964, sixth inning.
    Joe Pepitone, New York A.L., October 14, 1964, eighth inning.
    Jim Northrup, Detroit A.L., October 9, 1968, third inning.
    Dave McNally, Baltimore A.L., October 13, 1970, sixth inning.
    Dan Gladden, Minnesota A.L., October 17, 1987, fourth inning.
    Kent Hrbek, Minnesota A.L., October 24, 1987, sixth inning.
    Jose Canseco, Oakland A.L., October 15, 1988, second inning.
    Lonnie Smith, Atlanta N.L., October 22, 1992, fifth inning.
    Tino Martinez, New York A.L., October 17, 1998, seventh inning.

BASES ON BALLS

Most bases on balls, career
43—Mickey Mantle, New York A.L., 1951, 1952, 1953, 1955, 1956, 1957, 1958, 1960, 1961, 1962, 1963, 1964; 12 series, 65 games.

Most bases on balls, series
4-game series—7—Hank Thompson, New York N.L., 1954.
5-game series—7—Jimmy Sheckard, Chicago N.L., 1910.
                   Mickey Cochrane, Philadelphia A.L., 1929.
                   Joe Gordon, New York A.L., 1941.
6-game series—9—Willie Randolph, New York A.L., 1981.
7-game series—13—Barry Bonds, San Francisco N.L., 2002.
8-game series—7—Josh Devore, New York N.L., 1912.
                Ross Youngs, New York N.L., 1921.

Most series with one or more bases on balls, career
13—Yogi Berra, New York A.L., 1947, 1949, 1950, 1951, 1952, 1953, 1955, 1956, 1957, 1958, 1960, 1961, 1962.

Most bases on balls by pinch-hitter, series
3—Bennie Tate, Washington A.L., 1924; three games.

Most at-bats without a base on balls, series
34—Buck Weaver, Chicago A.L., 1919 (8-game series).

Most at-bats without a base on balls or strikeout, series
29—Billy Southworth, St. Louis N.L., 1926 (7-game series).

Most consecutive bases on balls, one series
5—Lou Gehrig, New York A.L., October 7 (2), October 9 (3), 1928.

Most bases on balls, game
4—Fred Clarke, Pittsburgh N.L., October 16, 1909.
    Babe Ruth, New York A.L., October 10, 1926.
    Doug DeCinces, Baltimore A.L., October 13, 1979.
    (4—Dick Hoblitzell, Boston A.L., October 9, 1916, 14 innings.
    Ross Youngs, New York N.L., October 10, 1924, 12 innings.
    Jackie Robinson, Brooklyn N.L., October 5, 1952, 11 innings.)

Most bases on balls with bases filled, game
2—Jim Palmer, Baltimore A.L., October 11, 1971, fourth and fifth innings.

Most bases on balls, two consecutive games
6—Jimmy Sheckard, Chicago N.L., October 18 (3), October 20 (3), 1910.

Most bases on balls, inning
2—Lefty Gomez, New York A.L., October 6, 1937, sixth inning.
Dick McAuliffe, Detroit A.L., October 9, 1968, third inning.

STRIKEOUTS

Most strikeouts, career
54—Mickey Mantle, New York A.L., 1951, 1952, 1953, 1955, 1956, 1957, 1958, 1960, 1961, 1962, 1963, 1964; 12 series, 65 games.

Most strikeouts, series
4-game series—7—Bob Meusel, New York A.L., 1927.
Ken Caminiti, San Diego N.L., 1998.
5-game series—9—Carmelo Martinez, San Diego N.L., 1984.
6-game series—12—Willie Wilson, Kansas City A.L., 1980.
7-game series—11—Eddie Mathews, Milwaukee N.L., 1958.
Wayne Garrett, New York N.L., 1973.
Luis Gonzalez, Arizona N.L., 2001.
Damian Miller, Arizona N.L., 2001.
8-game series—10—George Kelly, New York N.L., 1921.

Most series with one or more strikeouts
12—Mickey Mantle, New York A.L., 1951, 1952, 1953, 1955, 1956, 1957, 1958, 1960, 1961, 1963, 1964.

Most consecutive strikeouts, career
8—Vida Blue, Oakland A.L., October 14 (2), 18 (2), 1973; October 13 (2), 17 (2), 1974.
David Justice, New York A.L., October 27 (3), 30, (2), 31 (3), 2001.

Most consecutive strikeouts, one series
8—David Justice, New York A.L., October 27 (3), 30, (2), 31 (3), 2001.

Most strikeouts by pinch-hitter, series
3—Gabby Hartnett, Chicago N.L., 1929; three games.
Rollie Hemsley, Chicago N.L., 1932; three games.
Otto Velez, New York A.L., 1976; three games.
Luis Polonia, Atlanta N.L., 1996; six games.

Most at-bats without a strikeout, series
30—Tim Foli, Pittsburgh N.L., 1979 (7-game series).

Most strikeouts, game
5—George Pipgras, New York A.L., October 1, 1932 (consecutive).

Most strikeouts, inning
2—Edgar Renteria, Florida N.L., October 23, 1997, sixth inning.

SACRIFICE HITS

Most sacrifice hits, career
6—Eddie Collins, Philadelphia A.L. (5), 1910, 1911, 1913, 1914; Chicago A.L. (1), 1917, 1919; six series, 34 games.
Wally Schang, Philadelphia A.L. (0), 1913, 1914; Boston A.L. (0), 1918; New York A.L. (6), 1921 through 1923; six series, 32 games.

Most sacrifice hits, series
4-game series—2—Rube Oldring, Philadelphia A.L., 1914.
Joe Dugan, New York A.L., 1927.
Andy Seminick, Philadelphia A.L., 1950.
Davey Williams, New York N.L., 1954.
Willie Davis, Los Angeles N.L., 1963.
5-game series—4—Duffy Lewis, Boston A.L., 1916.
6-game series—3—Jimmy Sheckard, Chicago N.L., 1906.
Harry Steinfeldt, Chicago N.L., 1906.
Joe Tinker, Chicago N.L., 1906.
Bill Lee, Chicago N.L., 1935.
7-game series—4—Fred Clarke, Pittsburgh N.L., 1909.
Bucky Harris, Washington A.L., 1925.
Don Johnson, Chicago N.L., 1945.
8-game series—5—Jake Daubert, Cincinnati N.L., 1919.

Most sacrifice hits, game
3—Joe Tinker, Chicago N.L., October 12, 1906.
Craig Counsell, Arizona N.L., October 31, 2001.

Most sacrifice hits, inning
1—Held by many players.

SACRIFICE FLIES

Most sacrifice flies, career
4—Joe Carter, Toronto A.L., 1992 (1), 1993 (3); two series, 12 games.

Most sacrifice flies, series
3—Joe Carter, Toronto A.L., 1993 (6-game series).

Most sacrifice flies, game
2—Glenn Wright, Pittsburgh N.L., October 5, 1927.
Wes Westrum, New York N.L., October 2, 1954.
Manny Ramirez, Cleveland A.L., October 25, 1997.
Mike Matheny, St. Louis N.L., October 23, 2004.

Most sacrifice flies, inning
1—Held by many players.

Most runs batted in on sacrifice fly
2—Tommy Herr, St. Louis N.L., October 16, 1982, second inning.

HIT BY PITCH

Most hit by pitch, career
3—Frank Chance, Chicago N.L., 1906 (2), 1907 (1).
Honus Wagner, Pittsburgh N.L., 1903 (1), 1909 (2).
Fred Snodgrass, New York N.L., 1911 (2), 1912 (1).
Max Carey, Pittsburgh N.L., 1925 (3).
Yogi Berra, New York A.L., 1953 (2), 1955 (1).
Elston Howard, New York A.L., 1960 (1), 1962 (1), 1964 (1).
Frank Robinson, Cincinnati N.L., 1961 (2); Baltimore A.L., 1971 (1).
Bert Campaneris, Oakland A.L., 1973 (2), 1974 (1).
Reggie Jackson, New York A.L., 1977 (1), 1978 (2).
Derek Jeter, New York A.L., 1996 (1), 2001 (1), 2003 (1).

Most hit by pitch, series
3—Max Carey, Pittsburgh N.L., 1925 (7-game series).

Most hit by pitch, game
2—Max Carey, Pittsburgh N.L., October 7, 1925.
Yogi Berra, New York A.L., October 2, 1953.
Frank Robinson, Cincinnati N.L., October 8, 1961.
(2—Todd Pratt, New York N.L., October 21, 2000, 12 innings.)

Most hit by pitch, inning
1—Held by many players.

grounding into double play, career
7—Joe DiMaggio, New York A.L., 1936, 1937, 1938, 1939, 1941, 1942, 1947, 1949, 1950, 1951; 10 series, 51 games.
Paul O'Neill, Cincinnati N.L., 1990; New York A.L., 1996, 1998 through 2001; 6 series, 27 games.

Most grounding into double play, series
5—Irv Noren, New York A.L., 1955 (7-game series).

Most grounding into double play, game
3—Willie Mays, New York N.L., October 8, 1951.

REACHING ON ERRORS OR INTERFERENCE

Most times reaching first base on error, game
3—Fred Clarke, Pittsburgh N.L., October 10, 1903.

Most times awarded first base on catcher's interference, game
1—Roger Peckinpaugh, Washington A.L., October 15, 1925, first inning.
Bud Metheny, New York A.L., October 6, 1943, sixth inning.
Ken Boyer, St. Louis N.L., October 12, 1964, first inning.
Pete Rose, Cincinnati N.L., October 10, 1970, fifth inning.
George Hendrick, St. Louis N.L., October 15, 1982, ninth inning.

CLUB BATTING

GAMES

Most games played, total series
219—New York A.L.; 39 series (won 130, lost 88, tied 1).

For summaries of series won and lost, games, and home and road games played by all teams, see page 498. For a yearly list of batting statistics by teams, see page 506.

BATTING AVERAGE

Highest batting average, series
4-game series
.317—Cincinnati N.L. vs. Oakland A.L., 1990.
5-game series
.316—Philadelphia A.L. vs. Chicago N.L., 1910.
6-game series
.311—Toronto A.L. vs. Philadelphia N.L., 1993.
7-game series
.338—New York A.L. vs. Pittsburgh N.L., 1960.
8-game series
.270—New York N.L. vs. Boston A.L., 1912.

Highest batting average by both clubs, series
4-game series
.283—New York A.L. .313, Chicago N.L. .253, 1932.
5-game series
.272—Philadelphia A.L. .316, Chicago N.L. .222, 1910.
6-game series
.292—Philadelphia N.L. .294, Kansas City A.L. .290, 1980.
   Toronto A.L. .311, Philadelphia N.L. .274, 1993.
7-game series
.300—New York A.L. .338, Pittsburgh N.L. .256, 1960.
8-game series
.245—New York N.L. .270, Boston A.L. .220, 1912.

Highest batting average by series loser
.338—New York A.L. vs. Pittsburgh N.L., 1960 (7-game series).

Lowest batting average, series
4-game series
.142—Los Angeles N.L. vs. Baltimore A.L., 1966.
5-game series
.146—Baltimore A.L. vs. New York N.L., 1969.
6-game series
.175—New York N.L. vs. Philadelphia A.L., 1911.
7-game series
.183—New York A.L. vs. Arizona N.L., 2001.
8-game series
.207—New York A.L. vs. New York N.L., 1921.

Lowest batting average by both clubs, series
4-game series
.171—Los Angeles N.L. .142, Baltimore A.L. .200, 1966.
5-game series
.184—Baltimore A.L. .146, New York N.L. .220, 1969.
6-game series
.197—Chicago A.L. .198, Chicago N.L. .196, 1906.
7-game series
.209—Oakland A.L. .209, Cincinnati N.L. .209, 1972.
8-game series
.239—Cincinnati N.L. .255, Chicago A.L. .224, 1919.

Lowest batting average by series winner
.186—Boston A.L. vs. Chicago N.L., 1918 (6-game series).

ON-BASE PERCENTAGE (SINCE 1954)

Highest on-base percentage, series
4-game series
.404—Boston A.L. vs. St. Louis N.L., 2004.

5-game series
.366—Baltimore A.L. vs. Cincinnati N.L., 1970.
6-game series
.382—Toronto A.L. vs. Philadelphia N.L., 1993.
7-game series
.386—Cleveland A.L. vs Florida N.L., 1997.

Highest on-base percentage by both clubs, series
4-game series
.350—New York A.L. .398, San Diego N.L. .297, 1998.
5-game series
.331—Detroit A.L. .355, San Diego N.L. .306, 1984.
6-game series
.378—Toronto A.L. .382, Philadelphia N.L. .375, 1993.
7-game series
.375—Cleveland A.L. .386, Florida N.L. .363, 1997.

Lowest on-base percentage, series
4-game series
.207—New York A.L. vs. Los Angeles N.L., 1963.
5-game series
.220—Baltimore A.L. vs. New York N.L., 1969.
6-game series
.273—Cleveland A.L. vs. Atlanta N.L., 1995.
7-game series
.240—New York A.L. vs. Arizona N.L., 2001.

Lowest on-base percentage by both clubs, series
4-game series
.242—Los Angeles N.L. .279, New York A.L. .207, 1963.
5-game series
.243—Baltimore A.L. .258, Philadelphia N.L. .228, 1983.
6-game series
.287—New York A.L. .288, Los Angeles N.L. .286, 1977.
7-game series
.271—New York A.L. .273, San Francisco N.L. .268, 1962.

SLUGGING AVERAGE

Highest slugging average, series
4-game series
.582—Oakland A.L. vs. San Francisco N.L., 1989.
5-game series
.509—Baltimore A.L. vs. Cincinnati N.L., 1970.
6-game series
.510—Toronto A.L. vs. Philadelphia N.L., 1993.
7-game series
.528—New York A.L. vs. Pittsburgh N.L., 1960.
8-game series
.401—Boston A.L. vs. Pittsburgh N.L., 1903.

Highest slugging average by both clubs, series
4-game series
.468—Oakland A.L. .582, San Francisco N.L. .343, 1989.
5-game series
.433—Baltimore A.L. .509, Cincinnati N.L. .354, 1970.
6-game series
.467—Toronto A.L. .510, Philadelphia N.L. .425, 1993.
7-game series
.481—San Francisco N.L. .498, Anaheim A.L. .465, 2002.
8-game series
.344—New York N.L. .361, Boston A.L. .326, 1912.

Lowest slugging average, series
4-game series
.192—Los Angeles N.L. vs. Baltimore A.L., 1966.
5-game series
.194—Philadelphia A.L. vs. New York N.L., 1905.
6-game series
.233—Boston A.L. vs. Chicago N.L., 1918.
7-game series
.237—Brooklyn N.L. vs. Cleveland A.L., 1920.
8-game series
.270—New York A.L. vs. New York N.L., 1921.

Lowest slugging average by both clubs, series
4-game series
.267—Baltimore A.L. .342, Los Angeles N.L. .192, 1966.
5-game series
.224—New York N.L. .255, Philadelphia A.L. .194, 1905.
6-game series
.241—Chicago N.L. .250, Boston A.L. .233, 1918.
7-game series
.285—Cleveland A.L. .332, Brooklyn N.L. .237, 1920.
8-game series
.323—New York N.L. .371, New York A.L. .270, 1921.

AT-BATS AND PLATE APPEARANCES

Most at-bats, total series
7,345—New York A.L.; 39 series, 219 games.

Most at-bats, series
4-game series
146—Chicago N.L. vs. New York A.L., 1932.
Oakland A.L. vs. San Francisco N.L., 1989.
5-game series
179—New York A.L. vs. New York N.L., 2000.
6-game series
222—New York A.L. vs. Los Angeles N.L., 1978.
7-game series
269—New York A.L. vs. Pittsburgh N.L., 1960.
8-game series
282—Boston A.L. vs. Pittsburgh N.L., 1903.

Most at-bats by both clubs, series
4-game series
290—Chicago N.L. 146, New York A.L. 144, 1932.
5-game series
354—New York A.L. 179, New York N.L. 175, 2000.
6-game series
421—New York A.L. 222, Los Angeles N.L. 199, 1978.
7-game series
512—St. Louis N.L. 262, Detroit A.L. 250, 1934.
8-game series
552—Boston A.L. 282, Pittsburgh N.L. 270, 1903.

Fewest at-bats, series
4-game series
117—Los Angeles N.L. vs. New York A.L., 1963.
5-game series
142—Oakland A.L. vs. Los Angeles N.L., 1974.
6-game series
172—Boston A.L. vs. Chicago N.L., 1918.
7-game series
215—Brooklyn N.L. vs. Cleveland A.L., 1920.
Brooklyn N.L. vs. New York A.L., 1956.
Minnesota A.L. vs. Los Angeles N.L., 1965.
8-game series
241—New York A.L. vs. New York N.L., 1921.

Fewest at-bats by both clubs, series
4-game series
240—Baltimore A.L. 120, Los Angeles N.L. 120, 1966.
5-game series
300—Los Angeles N.L. 158, Oakland A.L. 142, 1974.
6-game series
348—Chicago N.L. 176, Boston A.L. 172, 1918.
7-game series
432—Cleveland A.L. 217, Brooklyn N.L. 215, 1920.
8-game series
505—New York N.L. 264, New York A.L. 241, 1921.

Most at-bats, game
46—Arizona N.L. vs. New York A.L., November 3, 2001.
(54—New York N.L. vs. Oakland A.L., October 14, 1973, 12 innings.)

Most at-bats by both clubs, game
85—Toronto A.L. 44, Philadelphia 41, October 20, 1993.
(101—New York N.L. 54, Oakland A.L. 47, October 14, 1973, 12 innings.)

Fewest at-bats, game
25—Philadelphia A.L. vs. Boston N.L., October 10, 1914.
Atlanta N.L. vs. Cleveland A.L., October 21, 1995 (batted eight innings).

Fewest at-bats by both clubs, game
54—Chicago N.L. 27, Chicago A.L. 27, October 12, 1906.

Most at-bats, inning
13—Philadelphia A.L. vs. Chicago N.L., October 12, 1929, seventh inning.

Most at-bats by both clubs, inning
17—Philadelphia A.L. 13, Chicago N.L. 4, October 12, 1929, seventh inning.

Most batters facing pitcher, inning
15—Philadelphia A.L. vs. Chicago N.L., October 12, 1929, seventh inning.
Detroit A.L. vs. St. Louis N.L., October 9, 1968, third inning.

Most batters facing pitcher by both clubs, inning
20—Philadelphia A.L. 15, Chicago N.L. 5, October 12, 1929, seventh inning.

RUNS
SERIES AND GAME

Most runs, total series
957—New York A.L.; 39 series, 219 games.

Most runs, series
4-game series
37—New York A.L. vs. Chicago N.L., 1932.
5-game series
35—Philadelphia A.L. vs. Chicago N.L., 1910.
6-game series
45—Toronto A.L. vs. Philadelphia N.L., 1993.
7-game series
55—New York A.L. vs. Pittsburgh N.L., 1960.
8-game series
39—Boston A.L. vs. Pittsburgh N.L., 1903.

Most runs by both clubs, series
4-game series
56—New York A.L. 37, Chicago N.L. 19, 1932.
5-game series
53—Baltimore A.L. 33, Cincinnati N.L. 20, 1970.
6-game series
81—Toronto A.L. 45, Philadelphia N.L. 36, 1993.
7-game series
85—San Francisco N.L. 44, Anaheim A.L. 41, 2002.
8-game series
63—Boston A.L. 39, Pittsburgh N.L. 24, 1903.

Most runs by series loser
55—New York A.L. vs. Pittsburgh N.L., 1960 (7-game series).

Fewest runs, series
4-game series
2—Los Angeles N.L. vs. Baltimore A.L. 1966.
5-game series
3—Philadelphia A.L. vs. New York N.L. 1905.
6-game series
9—Boston A.L. vs. Chicago N.L., 1918.
7-game series
8—Brooklyn N.L. vs. Cleveland A.L., 1920.
8-game series
20—Chicago A.L. vs. Cincinnati N.L., 1919.

Fewest runs by both clubs, series
4-game series
15—Baltimore A.L. 13, Los Angeles N.L. 2, 1966.
5-game series
18—New York N.L. 15, Philadelphia A.L. 3, 1905.
6-game series
19—Chicago N.L. 10, Boston A.L. 9, 1918.
7-game series
29—Cleveland A.L. 21, Brooklyn N.L. 8, 1920.
8-game series
51—New York N.L. 29, New York A.L. 22, 1921.

Most runs, game
18—New York A.L. vs. New York N.L., October 2, 1936 (won 18-4).

Most runs by pinch-hitters, game
3—New York A.L. vs. Brooklyn N.L., October 2, 1947.

Most earned runs, game
17—New York A.L. vs. New York N.L., October 2, 1936 (won 18-4).

Most runs by both clubs, game
29—Toronto A.L. 15, Philadelphia N.L. 14, October 20, 1993.

Largest score, shutout game
12-0—New York A.L. 12, Pittsburgh N.L. 0, October 12, 1960.

Most players scoring one or more runs, game
9—St. Louis N.L. vs. Detroit A.L., October 9, 1934.
New York A.L. vs. New York N.L., October 2, 1936.
Milwaukee N.L. vs. New York A.L., October 2, 1958.
New York A.L. vs. Pittsburgh N.L., October 6, 1960.
Pittsburgh N.L. vs. New York A.L., October 13, 1960.
St. Louis N.L. vs. Milwaukee A.L., October 19, 1982.
Toronto A.L. vs. Philadelphia N.L., October 20, 1993.

Most players from both clubs scoring one or more runs, game
16—Toronto A.L. 9, Philadelphia N.L. 7, October 20, 1993.
Boston A.L. 8, St. Louis N.L. 8, October 23, 2004.

INNING

Most runs, inning
10—Philadelphia A.L. vs. Chicago N.L., October 12, 1929, seventh inning.
Detroit A.L. vs. St. Louis N.L., October 9, 1968, third inning.

Most runs by both clubs, inning
11—Philadelphia A.L. 10, Chicago N.L. 1, October 12, 1929, seventh inning.
Brooklyn N.L. 6, New York A.L. 5, October 5, 1956, second inning.

Most runs, extra inning
4—New York N.L. vs. Oakland A.L., October 14, 1973, 12th inning.

Most runs, two consecutive innings
12—Detroit A.L. vs. St. Louis N.L., October 9, 1968 (2 in second inning, 10 in third inning).

Most innings scored, game
6—New York A.L. vs. St. Louis N.L., October 6, 1926.
New York A.L. vs. Brooklyn N.L., October 1, 1947.
New York A.L. vs. Pittsburgh N.L., October 6, 1960.
Philadelphia N.L. vs. Toronto A.L., October 20, 1993.

Most innings scored by both clubs, game
10—Philadelphia N.L. 6, Toronto A.L. 4, October 20, 1993.

Most runs, first inning
7—Milwaukee N.L. vs. New York A.L., October 2, 1958.

Most runs, second inning
6—New York A.L. vs. New York N.L., October 13, 1923.
New York N.L. vs. New York A.L., October 9, 1937.
Brooklyn N.L. vs. New York A.L., October 2, 1947.
Brooklyn N.L. vs. New York A.L., October 5, 1956.

Most runs, third inning
10—Detroit A.L. vs. St. Louis N.L., October 9, 1968.

Most runs, fourth inning
7—Minnesota A.L. vs. St. Louis N.L., October 17, 1987.

Most runs, fifth inning
6—Baltimore A.L. vs. Pittsburgh N.L., October 11, 1971.
Kansas City A.L. vs. St. Louis N.L., October 27, 1985.

Most runs, sixth inning
7—New York A.L. vs. New York N.L., October 6, 1937.
New York A.L. vs. Pittsburgh N.L., October 6, 1960.

Most runs, seventh inning
10—Philadelphia A.L. vs. Chicago N.L., October 12, 1929.

Most runs, eighth inning
6—Chicago N.L. vs. Detroit A.L., October 11, 1908.
Baltimore A.L. vs. Pittsburgh N.L., October 13, 1979.
Toronto A.L. vs. Philadelphia N.L., October 20, 1993.

Most runs, ninth inning
7—New York A.L. vs. New York N.L., October 6, 1936.

Most runs with none on base and two out in ninth inning
4—New York A.L. vs. Brooklyn N.L., October 5, 1941.

Most runs, 10th inning
3—New York N.L. vs. Philadelphia A.L., October 8, 1913.
New York A.L. vs. Cincinnati N.L., October 8, 1939.
New York N.L. vs. Cleveland A.L., September 29, 1954.
Milwaukee N.L. vs. New York A.L., October 6, 1957.
St. Louis N.L. vs. New York A.L., October 12, 1964.
New York N.L. vs. Boston A.L., October 25, 1986.

Most runs, 11th inning
2—Philadelphia A.L. vs. New York N.L., October 17, 1911.
Toronto A.L. vs. Atlanta N.L., October 24, 1992.

Most runs, 12th inning
4—New York N.L. vs. Oakland A.L., October 14, 1973.

Most runs, 13th inning
none

Most runs, 14th inning
1—Boston A.L. vs Brooklyn N.L., October 9, 1916.

GAMES BEING SHUT OUT

Most times shut out, total series
15—New York A.L.

Most times shut out, series
4—Philadelphia A.L. vs. New York N.L., 1905.

Most consecutive times shut out, series
3—Philadelphia A.L. vs. New York N.L., October 12, 13, 14, 1905.
Los Angeles N.L. vs. Baltimore A.L., October 6, 8, 9, 1966.

Most consecutive games without being shut out, total series
42—New York A.L., October 6, 1926 through October 1, 1942.

HITS
SERIES

Most hits, total series
1,834—New York A.L.; 39 series, 219 games.

Most hits, series
4-game series
45—New York A.L. vs. Chicago N.L., 1932.
Cincinnati N.L. vs. Oakland A.L., 1990.
5-game series
56—Philadelphia A.L. vs. Chicago N.L., 1910.
6-game series
68—New York A.L. vs. Los Angeles N.L., 1978.
7-game series
91—New York A.L. vs. Pittsburgh N.L., 1960.
8-game series
74—New York N.L. vs. Boston A.L., 1912.

Most hits by both clubs, series
4-game series
82—New York A.L. 45, Chicago N.L. 37, 1932.
5-game series
91—Philadelphia A.L. 56, Chicago N.L. 35, 1910.
6-game series
122—Toronto A.L. 64, Philadelphia N.L. 58, 1993.
7-game series
151—New York A.L. 91, Pittsburgh N.L. 60, 1960.
8-game series
135—Boston A.L. 71, Pittsburgh N.L. 64, 1903.

Fewest hits, series
4-game series
17—Los Angeles N.L. vs. Baltimore A.L., 1966.

5-game series
23—Baltimore A.L. vs. New York N.L., 1969.
6-game series
32—Boston A.L. vs. Chicago N.L., 1918.
7-game series
40—St. Louis N.L. vs. Kansas City A.L., 1985.
8-game series
50—New York A.L. vs. New York N.L., 1921.

Fewest hits by both clubs, series
4-game series
41—Baltimore A.L. 24, Los Angeles N.L. 17, 1966.
5-game series
57—New York N.L. 32, Philadelphia A.L. 25, 1905.
6-game series
69—Chicago N.L. 37, Boston A.L. 32, 1918.
7-game series
92—Oakland A.L. 46, Cincinnati N.L. 46, 1972.
8-game series
121—New York N.L. 71, New York A.L. 50, 1921.

Most hits by pinch-hitters, series
6—New York A.L. vs. Brooklyn N.L., 1947 (7-game series).
New York A.L. vs. Pittsburgh N.L., 1960 (7-game series).
Oakland A.L. vs. Cincinnati N.L., 1972 (7-game series).
Baltimore A.L. vs. Pittsburgh N.L., 1979 (7-game series).

Most hits by pinch-hitters for both clubs, series
11—New York A.L. 6, Brooklyn N.L. 5, 1947 (7-game series).

Most players with one or more hits in each game, series
4—New York A.L. vs. Los Angeles N.L., 1978 (6-game series).

Most consecutive hitless innings, series
9—Brooklyn N.L. vs. New York A.L., October 8, 1956 (all 27 batters).

Most hits, game
22—Arizona N.L. vs. New York A.L., November 3, 2001.

Most hits by losing club, game
17—Pittsburgh N.L. vs. Baltimore A.L., October 13, 1979.

Most hits by pinch-hitters, game
3—Oakland A.L. vs. Cincinnati N.L., October 19, 1972.
Baltimore A.L. vs. Pittsburgh N.L., October 13, 1979.

Most hits by both clubs, game
32—New York A.L. 19, Pittsburgh N.L. 13, October 6, 1960.
Toronto A.L. 18, Philadelphia 14, October 20, 1993.

Fewest hits, game
0—Brooklyn N.L. vs. New York A.L., October 8, 1956.

Fewest hits by both clubs, game
5—New York A.L. 3, New York N.L. 2, October 6, 1921.
New York A.L. 5, Brooklyn N.L. 0, October 8, 1956.
Atlanta N.L. 3, Cleveland A.L. 2, October 21, 1995.

Most players with one or more hits, game
11—New York A.L. vs. St. Louis N.L., October 9, 1928.
New York A.L. vs. Pittsburgh N.L., October 6, 1960.

Most players with one or more hits for either club, game
19—New York A.L. 11, Pittsburgh N.L. 8, October 6, 1960.

Most players with one or more hits and runs, game
9—New York A.L. vs. New York N.L., October 2, 1936.
New York A.L. vs. Pittsburgh N.L., October 6, 1960.

Most hits, inning
10—Philadelphia A.L. vs. Chicago N.L., October 12, 1929, seventh inning.

Most hits by pinch-hitters, inning
3—Oakland A.L. vs. Cincinnati N.L., October 19, 1972, ninth inning.

Most hits by both clubs, inning
12—Philadelphia A.L. 10, Chicago N.L. 2, October 12, 1929, seventh inning.

Most consecutive hits, inning
8—New York N.L. vs. New York A.L., October 7, 1921, seventh inning. (base on balls and sacrifice during streak.)

Most consecutive hits, inning (consecutive plate appearances)
6—Chicago N.L. vs. Detroit A.L., October 10, 1908, ninth inning (6 singles).

Most singles, total series
1,308—New York A.L.; 39 series, 219 games.

Most singles, series
4-game series
32—New York A.L. vs. San Diego N.L., 1998.
5-game series
46—New York N.L. vs. New York A.L., 1922.
6-game series
57—New York A.L. vs. Los Angeles N.L., 1978.
7-game series
64—New York A.L. vs. Pittsburgh N.L., 1960.
8-game series
55—New York N.L. vs. Boston A.L., 1912.

Most singles by both clubs, series
4-game series
55—New York A.L. 31, Chicago N.L. 24, 1932.
5-game series
70—New York N.L. 39, Washington A.L. 31, 1933.
6-game series
95—New York A.L. 57, Los Angeles N.L. 38, 1978.
7-game series
109—New York A.L. 64, Pittsburgh N.L. 45, 1960.
8-game series
96—Boston A.L. 49, Pittsburgh N.L. 47, 1903.

Fewest singles, series
4-game series
13—Philadelphia A.L. vs. Boston N.L., 1914.
Los Angeles N.L. vs. Baltimore A.L., 1966.
5-game series
19—Brooklyn N.L. vs. New York A.L., 1941.
Baltimore A.L. vs. New York N.L., 1969.
6-game series
17—Philadelphia A.L. vs. St. Louis N.L., 1930.
7-game series
27—Minnesota A.L. vs. Los Angeles N.L., 1965.
St. Louis N.L. vs. Kansas City A.L., 1985.
8-game series
39—Boston A.L. vs. New York N.L., 1912.

Fewest singles by both clubs, series
4-game series
29—Baltimore A.L. 16, Los Angeles N.L. 13, 1966.
5-game series
40—New York N.L. 21, Baltimore A.L. 19, 1969.
6-game series
42—St. Louis N.L. 25, Philadelphia A.L. 17, 1930.
7-game series
66—St. Louis N.L. 33, Boston A.L. 33, 1967.
8-game series
92—Cincinnati N.L. 47, Chicago A.L. 45, 1919.
New York N.L. 52, New York A.L. 40, 1921.

Most singles, game
16—New York A.L. vs. Los Angeles N.L., October 15, 1978.
Arizona N.L. vs. New York A.L., November 3, 2001.

Most singles by both clubs, game
24—New York A.L. 16, Los Angeles N.L. 8, October 15, 1978.

Fewest singles, game
0—Philadelphia A.L. vs. St. Louis N.L., October 1, 1930 (batted eight innings).
Philadelphia A.L. vs. St. Louis N.L., October 8, 1930 (batted eight innings).
Brooklyn N.L. vs. New York A.L., October 3, 1947 (batted 8.2 innings).
New York A.L. vs. Brooklyn N.L., October 4, 1952 (batted eight innings).
Brooklyn N.L. vs. New York A.L., October 8, 1956.

St. Louis N.L. vs. Boston A.L., October 5, 1967.

Fewest singles by both clubs, game
2—St. Louis N.L. 2, Philadelphia A.L. 0, October 8, 1930.

Most singles, inning
7—Philadelphia A.L. vs. Chicago N.L., October 12, 1929, seventh inning.
New York N.L. vs. Washington A.L., October 4, 1933, sixth inning.
Brooklyn N.L. vs. New York A.L., October 8, 1949, sixth inning.

Most singles by both clubs, inning
8—Philadelphia A.L. 7, Chicago N.L. 1, October 12, 1929, seventh inning.
New York N.L. 7, Washington A.L. 1, October 4, 1933, sixth inning.
Brooklyn N.L. 7, New York A.L. 1, October 8, 1949, sixth inning.

DOUBLES

Most doubles, total series
264—New York A.L; 39 series, 219 games.

Most doubles, series
4-game series
11—Boston A.L. vs. St. Louis N.L., 2004.
5-game series
19—Philadelphia A.L. vs. Chicago N.L., 1910.
6-game series
15—Philadelphia A.L. vs. New York N.L., 1911.
7-game series
19—St. Louis N.L. vs. Boston A.L., 1946.
8-game series
14—Boston A.L. vs. New York N.L., 1912.
New York N.L. vs. Boston A.L., 1912.

Most doubles by both clubs, series
4-game series
19—Boston A.L. 11, St. Louis 8, 2004.
5-game series
30—Philadelphia A.L. 19, Chicago N.L. 11, 1910.
6-game series
26—Philadelphia A.L. 15, New York N.L. 11, 1911.
7-game series
29—Detroit A.L. 16, Pittsburgh N.L. 13, 1909.
8-game series
28—Boston A.L. 14, New York N.L. 14, 1912.

Fewest doubles, series
4-game series
3—Cincinnati N.L. vs. New York A.L., 1939.
New York A.L. vs. Philadelphia N.L., 1950.
New York N.L. vs. Cleveland A.L., 1954.
Los Angeles N.L. vs. New York A.L., 1963.
New York A.L. vs. Los Angeles N.L., 1963.
Baltimore A.L. vs. Los Angeles N.L., 1966.
Los Angeles N.L. vs. Baltimore A.L., 1966.
New York A.L. vs. Cincinnati N.L., 1976.
5-game series
1—Detroit A.L. vs. Chicago N.L., 1907.
Baltimore A.L. vs. New York N.L., 1969.
6-game series
2—Boston A.L. vs. Chicago N.L., 1918.
New York N.L. vs. New York A.L., 1923.
7-game series
3—Baltimore A.L. vs. Pittsburgh N.L., 1971.
8-game series
4—Boston A.L. vs. Pittsburgh N.L., 1903.

Fewest doubles by both clubs, series
4-game series
6—Los Angeles N.L. 3, New York A.L. 3, 1963.
Baltimore A.L. 3, Los Angeles N.L. 3, 1966.
5-game series
6—Philadelphia N.L. 4, Boston A.L. 2, 1915.
6-game series
7—Chicago N.L. 5, Boston A.L. 2, 1918.

7-game series
11—St. Louis N.L. 7, Detroit A.L. 4, 1968.
8-game series
11—Pittsburgh N.L. 7, Boston A.L. 4, 1903.

Most doubles, game
8—Chicago A.L. vs. Chicago N.L., October 13, 1906.
Pittsburgh N.L. vs. Washington A.L., October 15, 1925.

Most doubles by both clubs, game
11—Chicago A.L. 8, Chicago N.L. 3, October 13, 1906.

Most doubles, inning
3—Chicago A.L. vs. Chicago N.L., October 13, 1906, fourth inning.
Philadelphia A.L. vs. Chicago N.L., October 18, 1910, seventh inning.
Philadelphia A.L. vs. New York N.L., October 24, 1911, fourth inning (consecutive).
Pittsburgh N.L. vs. Washington A.L., October 15, 1925, eighth inning.
St. Louis N.L. vs. Detroit A.L., October 9, 1934, third inning.
Brooklyn N.L. vs. New York A.L., October 2, 1947, second inning.
Brooklyn N.L. vs. New York A.L., October 5, 1947, third inning (consecutive).
New York A.L. vs. Brooklyn N.L., October 8, 1949, fourth inning.
Chicago A.L. vs. Los Angeles N.L., October 1, 1959, third inning.
Arizona N.L. vs. New York A.L., November 3, 2001, third inning.

TRIPLES

Most triples, total series
52—New York A.L.; 39 series, 219 games.

Most triples, series
4-game series
3—Cincinnati N.L. vs. New York A.L., 1976.
Oakland A.L. vs. San Francisco N.L., 1989.
5-game series
6—Boston A.L. vs. Brooklyn N.L., 1916.
6-game series
5—Toronto A.L. vs. Philadelphia N.L., 1993.
7-game series
5—St. Louis N.L. vs. Detroit A.L., 1934.
New York A.L. vs. Brooklyn N.L., 1947.
8-game series
16—Boston A.L. vs. Pittsburgh N.L., 1903.

Most triples by both clubs, series
4-game series
4—Cincinnati N.L. 3, New York A.L. 1, 1976.
Oakland A.L. 3, San Francisco N.L. 1, 1989.
5-game series
11—Boston A.L. 6, Brooklyn N.L. 5, 1916.
6-game series
7—New York A.L. 4, New York N.L. 3, 1923.
Toronto A.L. 5, Philadelphia N.L. 2, 1993.
7-game series
8—Atlanta N.L. 4, Minnesota A.L. 4, 1991.
8-game series
25—Boston A.L. 16, Pittsburgh N.L. 9, 1903.

Fewest triples, series
4-game series
0—Held by many clubs. Last club—St. Louis N.L., 2004.
5-game series
0—Held by many clubs. Last club—Oakland A.L., 1988.
6-game series
0—Held by many clubs. Last club—Florida N.L., 2003.
7-game series
0—Held by many clubs. Last clubs—Arizona N.L., 2001; New York A.L., 2001.
8-game series
1—New York A.L. vs. New York N.L., 1921.

Fewest triples by both clubs, series
4-game series
1—St. Louis N.L. 1, New York A.L. 0, 1928.

Cleveland A.L. 1, New York N.L. 0, 1954.
Baltimore A.L. 1, Los Angeles N.L. 0, 1966.
San Diego N.L. 1, New York A.L. 0, 1998.
Atlanta N.L. 1, New York A.L. 0, 1999.
5-game series
0—New York N.L. 0, Philadelphia A.L. 0, 1905.
New York N.L. 0, Washington A.L. 0, 1933.
- New York N.L. 0, Baltimore A.L. 0, 1969.
Detroit A.L. 0, San Diego N.L. 0, 1984.
6-game series
0—Cleveland A.L. 0, Boston N.L. 0, 1948.
New York A.L. 0, Los Angeles N.L. 0, 1978.
Toronto A.L. 0, Atlanta N.L. 0, 1992.
7-game series
0—St. Louis N.L. 0, Philadelphia A.L. 0, 1931.
Arizona N.L. 0, New York A.L. 0, 2001.
8-game series
5—New York N.L. 4, New York A.L. 1, 1921.

Most triples, game
5—Boston A.L. vs. Pittsburgh N.L., October 7, 1903.
Boston A.L. vs. Pittsburgh N.L., October 10, 1903.

Most triples by both clubs, game
7—Boston A.L. 5, Pittsburgh N.L. 2, October 10, 1903.

Most triples, inning
2—Boston A.L. vs. Pittsburgh N.L., October 7, 1903, eighth
inning.
Boston A.L. vs. Pittsburgh N.L., October 10, 1903, first
inning, also fourth inning.
Boston A.L. vs. New York N.L., October 12, 1912, third inning.
Philadelphia A.L. vs. New York N.L., October 7, 1913,
fourth inning.
Boston A.L. vs. Chicago N.L., September 6, 1918, ninth inning.
New York A.L. vs. Brooklyn N.L., October 1, 1947, third inning.
New York A.L. vs. Brooklyn N.L., September 30, 1953,
first inning.
Detroit A.L. vs. St. Louis N.L., October 7, 1968, fourth inning.

HOME RUNS
SERIES

Most home runs, total series
210—New York A.L.; 39 series, 219 games.

Most grand slams, total series
8—New York A.L.; 30 series, 219 games.

Most home runs by pinch-hitters, total series
7—New York A.L.; 39 series, 219 games.

Most home runs, series
4-game series
9—New York A.L. vs. St. Louis N.L., 1928.
Oakland A.L. vs. San Francisco N.L., 1989.
5-game series
10—Baltimore A.L. vs. Cincinnati N.L., 1970.
6-game series
9—New York A.L. vs. Brooklyn N.L., 1953.
Los Angeles N.L. vs. New York A.L., 1977.
7-game series
14—San Francisco N.L. vs. Anaheim A.L., 2002.
8-game series
2—Boston A.L. vs. Pittsburgh N.L., 1903.
New York A.L. vs. New York N.L., 1921.
New York N.L. vs. New York A.L., 1921.

Most home runs by both clubs, series
4-game series
13—Oakland A.L. 9, San Francisco N.L. 4, 1989.
5-game series
15—Baltimore A.L. 10, Cincinnati N.L. 5, 1970.
6-game series
17—New York A.L. 9, Brooklyn N.L. 8, 1953.
Los Angeles N.L. 9, New York A.L. 8, 1977.
7-game series
21—San Francisco N.L. 14, Anaheim A.L. 7, 2002.

8-game series
4—New York N.L. 2, New York A.L. 2, 1921.

Most grand slams, series
2—New York A.L. vs. Brooklyn N.L., 1956.
Minnesota A.L. vs. St. Louis N.L., 1987.

Most grand slams by both clubs, series
2—New York A.L. 2, Brooklyn N.L. 0, 1956.
St. Louis N.L. 1, New York A.L. 1, 1964.
Minnesota A.L. 2, St. Louis N.L. 0, 1987.

Most home runs by pinch-hitters, series
2—Los Angeles N.L. vs. Chicago A.L., 1959.
Boston A.L. vs. Cincinnati N.L., 1975.

Most home runs by pinch-hitters for both clubs, series
2—New York N.L. 1, Cleveland A.L. 1, 1954.
Los Angeles N.L. 2, Chicago A.L. 0, 1959.
Boston A.L. 2, Cincinnati N.L. 0, 1975.

Most home runs by pitchers as batters, series
2—New York N.L. vs. Washington A.L., 1924.

Most home runs by pitchers as batters for both clubs, series
2—New York N.L. 2, Washington A.L. 0, 1924.
Boston A.L. 1, St. Louis N.L. 1, 1967.
Detroit A.L. 1, St. Louis N.L. 1, 1968.

Fewest home runs, series
4-game series
0—Held by many clubs.
5-game series
0—Held by many clubs.
6-game series
0—Chicago N.L. vs. Chicago A.L., 1906.
Chicago A.L. vs. Chicago N.L., 1906.
New York N.L. vs. Philadelphia A.L., 1911.
Boston A.L. vs. Chicago N.L., 1918.
Chicago N.L. vs. Boston A.L., 1918.
7-game series
0—Brooklyn N.L. vs. Cleveland A.L., 1920.
8-game series
0—Cincinnati N.L. vs. Chicago A.L., 1919.

Fewest home runs by both clubs, series
4-game series
1—Boston N.L. 1, Philadelphia A.L. 0, 1914.
5-game series
0—New York N.L. 0, Philadelphia A.L. 0, 1905.
Chicago N.L. 0, Detroit A.L. 0, 1907.
6-game series
0—Chicago A.L. 0, Chicago N.L. 0, 1906.
Boston A.L. 0, Chicago N.L. 0, 1918.
7-game series
2—Cleveland A.L. 2, Brooklyn N.L. 0, 1920.
8-game series
1—Chicago A.L. 1, Cincinnati N.L. 0, 1919.

GAME

Most home runs, game
5—New York A.L. vs. St. Louis N.L., October 9, 1928.
Oakland A.L. vs. San Francisco N.L., October 27, 1989.

Most home runs by both clubs, game
7—Oakland A.L. 5, San Francisco N.L. 2, October 27, 1989.

Most consecutive games with one or more home runs, total series
9—New York A.L., last 2 games vs. Chicago N.L. in 1932 (seven
home runs), all 6 games vs. New York N.L. in 1936
(seven home runs) and first game vs. New York N.L. in
1937 (one home run; total 15 home runs).
New York A.L., all 7 games vs. Brooklyn N.L. in 1952 (10
home runs) and first 2 games vs. Brooklyn N.L. in 1953
(four home runs; total 14 home runs).

Most consecutive games with one or more home runs, series
7—Washington A.L. vs. Pittsburgh N.L., October 7 through 15,

1925 (eight home runs).
New York A.L. vs. Brooklyn N.L., October 1 through 7, 1952 (10 home runs).

INNING

Most home runs, inning (two or more home runs, 38 times)
3—Boston A.L. vs. St. Louis N.L., October 11, 1967, fourth inning, Yastrzemski, Smith, Petrocelli (two consecutive).
2—New York N.L. vs. New York A.L., October 11, 1921, second inning.
Washington A.L. vs. Pittsburgh N.L., October 11, 1925, third inning.
New York A.L. vs. St. Louis N.L., October 9, 1928, seventh inning.
New York A.L. vs. St. Louis N.L., October 9, 1928, eighth inning.
Philadelphia A.L. vs. Chicago N.L., October 12, 1929, seventh inning.
New York A.L. vs. Chicago N.L., October 1, 1932, fifth inning.
New York A.L. vs. Chicago N.L., October 2, 1932, ninth inning.
New York A.L. vs. Cincinnati N.L., October 7, 1939, fifth inning.
New York A.L. vs. Cincinnati N.L., October 8, 1939, seventh inning.
Detroit A.L. vs. Cincinnati N.L., October 4, 1940, seventh inning.
Brooklyn N.L. vs. New York A.L., October 7, 1949, ninth inning.
Brooklyn N.L. vs. New York A.L., September 30, 1953, sixth inning.
Brooklyn N.L. vs. New York A.L., October 1, 1955, fourth inning.
Milwaukee N.L. vs. New York A.L., October 6, 1957, fourth inning.
Milwaukee N.L. vs. New York A.L., October 2, 1958, first inning.
New York A.L. vs. Milwaukee N.L., October 2, 1958, ninth inning.
Los Angeles N.L. vs. Chicago A.L., October 2, 1959, seventh inning.
New York A.L. vs. St. Louis N.L., October 14, 1964, sixth inning.
New York A.L. vs. St. Louis N.L., October 15, 1964, ninth inning.
Baltimore A.L. vs. Los Angeles N.L., October 5, 1966, first inning.
Baltimore A.L. vs. New York N.L., October 16, 1969, third inning.
Oakland A.L. vs. New York N.L., October 21, 1973, third inning.
Cincinnati N.L. vs. Boston A.L., October 14, 1975, fifth inning.
New York A.L. vs. Los Angeles N.L., October 16, 1977, eighth inning.
Los Angeles N.L. vs. New York A.L., October 10, 1978, second inning.
Los Angeles N.L. vs. New York A.L., October 25, 1981, seventh inning.
Boston A.L. vs. New York N.L., October 27, 1986, second inning.
Oakland A.L. vs. San Francisco N.L., October 27, 1989, fourth and fifth innings.
Philadelphia N.L. vs. Toronto A.L., October 20, 1993, fifth inning.
Florida N.L. vs. Cleveland A.L., October 18, 1997, fourth inning.
San Diego N.L. vs. New York A.L., October 17, 1998, fifth inning.
New York A.L. vs. San Diego N.L., October 17, 1998, seventh inning.
New York N.L. vs. New York A.L., October 22, 2000, ninth inning.
Arizona N.L. vs. New York A.L., November 1, 2001, fifth inning.
San Francisco N.L. vs. Anaheim A.L., October 19, 2002, second inning.
San Francisco N.L. vs. Anaheim A.L., October 20, 2002, second inning.
San Francisco N.L. vs. Anaheim A.L., October 22, 2002, fifth inning.
New York A.L. vs. Florida N.L., October 21, 2003, ninth inning.

Most home runs by both clubs, inning
3—New York N.L. 2, New York A.L. 1, October 11, 1921, second inning.
Boston A.L. 3, St. Louis N.L. 0, October 11, 1967, fourth inning.
San Francisco N.L. 2, Anaheim A.L. 1, October 19, 2002, second inning.
San Francisco N.L. 2, Anaheim A.L. 1, October 20, 2002, second inning.

Most consecutive home runs, inning (13 times)
2—Washington A.L. vs. Pittsburgh N.L., October 11, 1925, third inning.
New York A.L. vs. St. Louis N.L., October 9, 1928, seventh inning.
New York A.L. vs. Chicago N.L., October 1, 1932, fifth inning.
New York A.L. vs. St. Louis N.L., October 14, 1964, sixth inning.
Baltimore A.L. vs. Los Angeles N.L., October 5, 1966, first inning.
Boston A.L. vs. St. Louis N.L., October 11, 1967, fourth inning.
Cincinnati N.L. vs. Boston A.L., October 14, 1975, fifth inning.
New York A.L. vs. Los Angeles N.L., October 16, 1977, eighth inning.
Los Angeles N.L. vs. New York A.L., October 25, 1981, seventh inning.
Boston A.L. vs. New York N.L., October 27, 1986, second inning.
Florida N.L. vs. Cleveland A.L., October 18, 1997, fourth inning.
San Diego N.L. vs. New York A.L., October 17, 1998, fifth inning.
San Francisco N.L. vs. Anaheim A.L., October 20, 2002, second inning.

Most times hitting two home runs in an inning, total series
12—New York A.L., 1928 (2), 1932 (2), 1939 (2), 1958 (1), 1964 (2), 1977 (1), 1998 (1), 2003 (1).

Most times hitting two home runs in an inning, series
3—San Francisco N.L., 2002.

Most times hitting two home runs in an inning, game
2—New York A.L. vs. St. Louis N.L., October 9, 1928, seventh and eighth innings.
Oakland A.L. vs. San Francisco N.L., October 27, 1989, fourth and fifth innings.

TOTAL BASES

Most total bases, total series
2,832—New York A.L.; 39 series, 219 games.

Most total bases, series
4-game series
85—Oakland A.L. vs. San Francisco N.L., 1989.
5-game series
87—Baltimore A.L. vs. Cincinnati N.L., 1970.
6-game series
105—Toronto A.L. vs. Philadelphia N.L., 1993.
7-game series
142—New York A.L. vs. Pittsburgh N.L., 1960.
8-game series
113—Boston A.L. vs. Pittsburgh N.L., 1903.

Most total bases by both clubs, series
4-game series
133—New York A.L. 75, Chicago N.L. 58, 1932.
5-game series
145—Baltimore A.L. 87, Cincinnati N.L. 58, 1970.
6-game series
200—Brooklyn N.L. 103, New York A.L. 97, 1953.
7-game series
231—San Francisco N.L. 117, Anaheim A.L. 114, 2002.
8-game series
205—Boston A.L. 113, Pittsburgh N.L. 92, 1903.

Fewest total bases, series
4-game series
23—Los Angeles N.L. vs. Baltimore A.L., 1966.
5-game series
30—Philadelphia A.L. vs. New York N.L., 1905.
6-game series
40—Boston A.L. vs. Chicago N.L., 1918.
7-game series
51—Brooklyn N.L. vs. Cleveland A.L., 1920.
8-game series
65—New York A.L. vs. New York N.L., 1921.

Fewest total bases by both clubs, series
4-game series
64—Baltimore A.L. 41, Los Angeles N.L. 23, 1966.
5-game series
69—New York N.L. 39, Philadelphia A.L. 30, 1905.
6-game series
84—Chicago N.L. 44, Boston A.L. 40, 1918.
7-game series
123—Cleveland A.L. 72, Brooklyn N.L. 51, 1920.
8-game series
163—New York N.L. 98, New York A.L. 65, 1921.

Most total bases, game
34—Atlanta N.L. vs. Minnesota A.L., October 24, 1991.

Most total bases by both clubs, game
50—San Francisco N.L. 25, Anaheim A.L. 25, October 20, 2002.

Fewest total bases, game
0—Brooklyn N.L. vs. New York A.L., October 8, 1956.

Fewest total bases by both clubs, game
5—New York A.L. 3, New York N.L. 2, October 6, 1921.

Most total bases, inning
17—Philadelphia A.L. vs. Chicago N.L., October 12, 1929,
    seventh inning.

Most total bases by both clubs, inning
21—Philadelphia A.L. 17, Chicago N.L. 4, October 12, 1929,
    seventh inning.

EXTRA BASE HITS

Most extra base hits, total series
526—New York A.L.; 39 series, 219 games.

Most extra base hits, series
4-game series
20—Oakland A.L. vs. San Francisco N.L., 1989.
5-game series
21—Philadelphia A.L. vs. Chicago N.L., 1910.
6-game series
24—Toronto A.L. vs. Philadelphia N.L., 1993.
7-game series
27—New York A.L. vs. Pittsburgh N.L., 1960.
8-game series
22—Boston A.L. vs. Pittsburgh N.L., 1903.

Most extra base hits by both clubs, series
4-game series
29—Oakland A.L. 20, San Francisco N.L. 9, 1989.
5-game series
33—Philadelphia A.L. 21, Chicago N.L. 12, 1910.
6-game series
41—Brooklyn N.L. 22, New York A.L. 19, 1953.
7-game series
45—Anaheim A.L. 23, San Francisco N.L. 22, 2002.
8-game series
40—Boston A.L. 21, New York N.L. 19, 1912.

Fewest extra base hits, series
4-game series
4—Cincinnati N.L. vs. New York A.L., 1939.
    Los Angeles N.L. vs. Baltimore A.L., 1966.
5-game series
3—Detroit A.L. vs. Chicago N.L., 1907.
6-game series
5—Boston A.L. vs. Chicago N.L., 1918.
7-game series
6—Brooklyn N.L. vs. Cleveland A.L., 1920.

8-game series
10—New York A.L. vs. New York N.L., 1921.

Fewest extra base hits by both clubs, series
4-game series
12—Baltimore A.L. 8, Los Angeles N.L. 4, 1966.
5-game series
10—Chicago N.L. 7, Detroit A.L. 3, 1907.
6-game series
11—Chicago N.L. 6, Boston A.L. 5, 1918.
7-game series
19—Cleveland A.L. 13, Brooklyn N.L. 6, 1920.
8-game series
29—New York N.L. 19, New York A.L. 10, 1921.

Most extra base hits, game
9—Pittsburgh N.L. vs. Washington A.L., October 15, 1925 (8
    doubles, 1 triple).

Most extra base hits by both clubs, game
11—Chicago A.L. 8 (eight doubles), Chicago N.L. 3 (3 doubles),
    October 13, 1906.
    Pittsburgh N.L. 9 (8 doubles, 1 triple), Washington A.L. 2
    (1 double, 1 home run), October 15, 1925.
    New York A.L. 7 (4 doubles, 1 triple, 2 home runs),
    Cincinnati N.L. 4 (2 doubles, 2 home runs), October
    9, 1961.
    Oakland A.L. 7 (2 doubles, 5 home runs), San Francisco
    N.L. 4 (2 doubles, 2 home runs), October 27, 1989.
    Atlanta N.L. 8 (2 doubles, 3 triples, 3 home runs),
    Minnesota A.L. 3 (1 double, 2 triples), October 24,
    1991, 12 innings.

Longest extra-inning game without an extra base hit
12 innings—Chicago N.L. vs. Detroit A.L., October 8, 1907.
    Detroit A.L. vs. Chicago N.L., October 8, 1907.

**Longest extra-inning game without an extra base hit by either
club**
12 innings—Chicago N.L. 0, Detroit A.L. 0, October 8, 1907.

RUNS BATTED IN

Most runs batted in, total series
905—New York A.L.; 39 series, 219 games.

Most runs batted in, series
4-game series
36—New York A.L. vs. Chicago N.L., 1932.
5-game series
32—Baltimore A.L. vs. Cincinnati N.L., 1970.
6-game series
45—Toronto A.L. vs. Philadelphia N.L., 1993.
7-game series
54—New York A.L. vs. Pittsburgh N.L., 1960.
8-game series
35—Boston A.L. vs. Pittsburgh N.L., 1903.

Most runs batted in by both clubs, series
4-game series
52—New York A.L. 36, Chicago N.L. 16, 1932.
5-game series
52—Baltimore A.L. 32, Cincinnati N.L. 20, 1970.
6-game series
80—Toronto A.L. 45, Philadelphia N.L. 35, 1993.
7-game series
80—New York A.L. 54, Pittsburgh N.L. 26, 1960.
    San Francisco N.L. 42, Anaheim A.L. 38, 2002.
8-game series
58—Boston A.L. 35, Pittsburgh N.L. 23, 1903.

Fewest runs batted in, series
4-game series
2—Los Angeles N.L. vs. Baltimore A.L., 1966.
5-game series
2—Philadelphia A.L. vs. New York N.L., 1905.
6-game series
6—Boston A.L. vs. Chicago N.L., 1918.
7-game series
8—Brooklyn N.L. vs. Cleveland A.L., 1920.
8-game series
17—Chicago A.L. vs. Cincinnati N.L., 1919.

Fewest runs batted in by both clubs, series
4-game series
   12—Los Angeles N.L. 2, Baltimore A.L. 10, 1966.
5-game series
   15—Philadelphia A.L. 2, New York N.L. 13, 1905.
6-game series
   16—Boston A.L. 6, Chicago N.L. 10, 1918.
7-game series
   26—Brooklyn N.L. 8, Cleveland A.L. 18, 1920.
8-game series
   46—Boston A.L. 21, New York N.L. 25, 1912.

Most runs batted in, game
18—New York A.L. vs. New York N.L., October 2, 1936.

Most runs batted in by both clubs, game
29—Toronto A.L. 15, Philadelphia N.L. 14, October 20, 1993.

Fewest runs batted in, game
0—Held by many clubs.

Most runs batted in, inning
10—Philadelphia A.L. vs. Chicago N.L., October 12, 1929, seventh inning.
   Detroit A.L. vs. St. Louis N.L., October 9, 1968, third inning.

Most runs batted in by both clubs, inning
11—Philadelphia A.L. 10, Chicago N.L. 1, October 12, 1929, seventh inning.
   Brooklyn N.L. 6, New York A.L. 5, October 5, 1956, second inning.

Fewest runs batted in by both clubs, game
0—New York N.L. 0, Philadelphia A.L. 0, October 13, 1905.
   New York N.L. 0, New York A.L. 0, October 13, 1921.
   Chicago A.L. 0, Los Angeles N.L. 0, October 6, 1959.
   New York A.L. 0, San Francisco N.L. 0, October 16, 1962.

BASES ON BALLS

Most bases on balls, total series
769—New York A.L.; 39 series, 219 games.

Most bases on balls, series
4-game series
   24—Boston A.L. vs. St. Louis N.L., 2004.
5-game series
   25—New York A.L. vs. New York N.L., 2000.
6-game series
   34—Philadelphia N.L. vs. Toronto A.L., 1993.
7-game series
   40—Cleveland A.L. vs. Florida N.L., 1997.
8-game series
   27—New York A.L. vs. New York N.L., 1921.

Most bases on balls by both clubs, series
4-game series
   36—Boston A.L. 24, St. Louis N.L. 12, 2004.
5-game series
   37—New York A.L. 23, Brooklyn N.L. 14, 1941.
6-game series
   59—Philadelphia N.L. 34, Toronto A.L. 25, 1993.
7-game series
   76—Cleveland A.L. 40, Florida N.L. 36, 1997.
8-game series
   49—New York A.L. 27, New York N.L. 22, 1921.

Fewest bases on balls, series
4-game series
   4—Pittsburgh N.L. vs. New York A.L., 1927.
5-game series
   5—Philadelphia A.L. vs. New York N.L., 1905.
6-game series
   4—Philadelphia A.L. vs. New York N.L., 1911.
7-game series
   9—St. Louis N.L. vs. Philadelphia A.L., 1931.
8-game series
   13—Boston A.L. vs. Pittsburgh N.L., 1903.

Fewest bases on balls by both clubs, series
4-game series
   15—New York A.L. 9, Cincinnati N.L. 6, 1939.

5-game series
   15—New York N.L. 8, Philadelphia A.L. 7, 1913.
6-game series
   17—Chicago A.L. 11, New York N.L. 6, 1917.
7-game series
   30—New York A.L. 18, Pittsburgh N.L. 12, 1960.
8-game series
   27—Pittsburgh N.L. 14, Boston A.L. 13, 1903.

Most bases on balls, game
11—Brooklyn N.L. vs. New York A.L., October 5, 1956.
   New York A.L. vs. Milwaukee N.L., October 5, 1957.
   Detroit A.L. vs. San Diego N.L., October 12, 1984.

Most bases on balls by both clubs, game
19—New York A.L. 11, Milwaukee N.L. 8, October 5, 1957.

Longest game with no bases on balls
12 innings—St. Louis N.L. vs. Detroit A.L., October 4, 1934.

Fewest bases on balls by both clubs, game
0—Philadelphia A.L. 0, New York N.L. 0, October 16, 1911.
   New York N.L. 0, Chicago A.L. 0, October 10, 1917.
   New York N.L. 0, New York A.L. 0, October 9, 1921.
   Boston A.L. 0, St. Louis N.L. 0, October 7, 1967.
   Philadelphia N.L. 0, Baltimore A.L. 0, October 11, 1983.

Most bases on balls, inning
5—New York A.L. vs. St. Louis N.L., October 6, 1926, fifth inning.

Most bases on balls by both clubs, inning
6—New York A.L. 3, New York N.L. 3, October 7, 1921, third inning.
   New York A.L. 5, St. Louis N.L. 1, October 6, 1926, fifth inning.
   St. Louis N.L. 4, Boston A.L. 2, October 23, 2004, fourth inning.

Most bases on balls by pinch-hitters, inning
2—New York A.L. vs. New York N.L., October 15, 1923, eighth inning.
   Baltimore A.L. vs. Philadelphia N.L., October 15, 1983, sixth inning.

STRIKEOUTS

Most strikeouts, total series
1,242—New York A.L.; 39 series, 219 games.

Most strikeouts, series
4-game series
   37—New York A.L. vs. Los Angeles N.L., 1963.
5-game series
   50—Chicago N.L. vs. Philadelphia A.L., 1929.
6-game series
   50—Philadelphia N.L. vs. Toronto A.L., 1993.
7-game series
   70—Arizona N.L. vs. New York A.L., 2001.
8-game series
   45—Pittsburgh N.L. vs. Boston A.L., 1903.

Most strikeouts by both clubs, series
4-game series
   62—New York A.L. 37, Los Angeles N.L. 25, 1963.
5-game series
   88—New York N.L. 48, New York A.L., 40, 2000.
6-game series
   97—New York A.L. 49, Florida N.L. 48, 2003.
7-game series
   133—Arizona N.L. 70, New York A.L. 63, 2001.
8-game series
   82—New York A.L. 44, New York N.L. 38, 1921.

Fewest strikeouts, series
4-game series
   7—Pittsburgh N.L. vs. New York A.L., 1927.
5-game series
   15—New York N.L. vs. New York A.L., 1922.
6-game series
   14—Chicago N.L. vs. Boston A.L., 1918.
7-game series
   20—Brooklyn N.L. vs. Cleveland A.L., 1920.
8-game series
   22—Cincinnati N.L. vs. Chicago A.L., 1919.

Fewest strikeouts by both clubs, series
4-game series
32—New York A.L. 25, Pittsburgh N.L. 7, 1927.
Cincinnati N.L. 16, New York A.L. 16, 1976.
5-game series
35—New York N.L. 19, Philadelphia A.L. 16, 1913.
New York A.L. 20, New York N.L. 15, 1922.
6-game series
35—Boston A.L. 21, Chicago N.L. 14, 1918.
7-game series
41—Cleveland A.L. 21, Brooklyn N.L. 20, 1920.
8-game series
52—Chicago A.L. 30, Cincinnati N.L. 22, 1919.

Most strikeouts, game
17—Detroit A.L. vs. St. Louis N.L., October 2, 1968.

Most strikeouts by pinch-hitters, game
4—St. Louis A.L. vs. St. Louis N.L., October 8, 1944
(consecutive) and October 9, 1944 (consecutive).

Most consecutive strikeouts, game
6—Chicago A.L. vs. Cincinnati N.L., October 6, 1919 (3 in second
inning, 3 in third inning).
Los Angeles N.L. vs. Baltimore A.L., October 5, 1966 (3 in
fourth inning, 3 in fifth inning).
Kansas City A.L. vs. St. Louis N.L., October 24, 1985 (3 in
sixth inning, 3 in seventh inning).

Most strikeouts by both clubs, game
25—New York A.L. 15, Los Angeles N.L. 10, October 2, 1963.
New York N.L. 13, New York A.L. 12, October 24, 2000.
(25—Oakland A.L. 15, New York N.L. 10, October 14,
1973, 12 innings.)

Fewest strikeouts, game
0—Chicago N.L. vs. Boston A.L., September 6, 1918 (batted
eight innings).
Chicago N.L. vs. Boston A.L., September 9, 1918.
New York A.L. vs. New York N.L., October 6, 1921 (batted
eight innings).
New York A.L. vs. Philadelphia N.L., October 4, 1950.
Brooklyn N.L. vs. New York A.L., October 3, 1952.
Pittsburgh N.L. vs. New York A.L., October 6, 1960.
Pittsburgh N.L. vs. New York A.L., October 13, 1960.
New York A.L. vs. Pittsburgh N.L., October 13, 1960.
Anaheim A.L. vs. San Francisco N.L., October 20, 2002
(batted eight innings).

Fewest strikeouts by both clubs, game
0—Pittsburgh N.L. 0, New York A.L. 0, October 13, 1960.

Most strikeouts, inning
4—Detroit A.L. vs. Chicago N.L., October 14, 1908, first inning.

Most strikeouts by pinch-hitters, Inning
3—St. Louis A.L. vs. St. Louis N.L., October 8, 1944,
ninth inning.

Most strikeouts by both clubs, inning
6—Cincinnati N.L. 3, Oakland A.L. 3, October 18, 1972,
fifth inning.
Kansas City A.L. 3, St. Louis N.L. 3, October 24, 1985,
seventh inning.
New York A.L. 3, New York N.L. 3, October 24, 2000, second
inning.

SACRIFICE HITS

Most sacrifice hits, total series
93—New York A.L.; 39 series, 216 games.

Most sacrifice hits, series
13—Chicago N.L. vs. Chicago A.L., 1906 (6-game series).

Most sacrifice hits by both clubs, series
29—Chicago N.L. 13, Chicago A.L. 6, 1906 (6-game series).

Fewest sacrifice hits, series
0—Held by many clubs. Last club—Atlanta N.L. vs. New York A.L.,
1999.

Fewest sacrifice hits by both clubs, series
0—New York A.L. 0, Brooklyn N.L. 0, 1941 (5-game series).

Cincinnati N.L. 0, New York A.L. 0, 1976 (4-game series).
Baltimore A.L. 0, Philadelphia N.L. 0, 1983 (5-game series).
Oakland A.L. 0, San Francisco N.L. 0, 1989 (4-game series).

Most sacrifice hits, game
5—Chicago N.L. vs. Chicago A.L., October 12, 1906.

Most sacrifice hits by both clubs, game
6—Chicago N.L. 5, Chicago A.L. 1, October 12, 1906.
Chicago N.L. 4, Detroit A.L. 2, October 10, 1908.

Most sacrifice hits, inning
2—Held by many teams

SACRIFICE FLIES

Most sacrifice flies, total series
35—New York A.L.; 26 series, 150 games.

Most sacrifice flies, series
7—Toronto A.L. vs. Philadelphia N.L., 1993 (6-game series).

Most sacrifice flies by both clubs, series
8—Toronto A.L. 7, Philadelphia N.L. 1, 1993 (6-game series).

Most sacrifice flies, game
3—New York A.L. vs. Pittsburgh N.L., October 6, 1927.
Toronto A.L. vs. Philadelphia N.L., October 19, 1993.

Most sacrifice flies by both clubs, game
5—New York A.L. 3, Pittsburgh N.L. 2, October 6, 1927.

Most sacrifice flies, inning
2—Baltimore A.L. vs. Pittsburgh N.L., October 13, 1971,
first inning.

HIT BY PITCH

Most hit by pitch, total series
49—New York A.L.; 39 series, 219 games.

Most hit by pitch, series
6—Pittsburgh N.L. vs. Detroit A.L., 1909 (7-game series).
Arizona N.L. vs. New York A.L., 2001 (7-game series).

Most hit by pitch by both clubs, series
10—Pittsburgh N.L. 6, Detroit A.L. 4, 1909 (7-game series).

Fewest hit by pitch, series
0—Held by many clubs.

Most hit by pitch, game
3—Detroit A.L. vs. St. Louis N.L., October 9, 1968.
Baltimore A.L. vs. Pittsburgh N.L., October 13, 1971.

Most hit by pitch by both clubs, game
3—Philadelphia N.L. 2, Boston A.L. 1, October 13, 1915.
Cincinnati N.L. 2, Chicago A.L. 1, October 9, 1919.
Pittsburgh N.L. 2, Washington A.L. 1, October 7, 1925.
Detroit A.L. 3, St. Louis N.L. 0, October 9, 1968.
Baltimore A.L. 3, Pittsburgh N.L. 0, October 13, 1971.
New York N.L. 2, Oakland A.L. 1, October 14, 1973.
Minnesota A.L. 2, St. Louis N.L. 1, October 21, 1987.

Most hit by pitch, inning
2—Pittsburgh N.L. vs. Detroit A.L., October 11, 1909, second
inning (consecutive).
Detroit A.L. vs. St. Louis N.L., October 9, 1968,
eighth inning.
Pittsburgh N.L. vs. Baltimore A.L., October 17, 1979, ninth
inning (consecutive).

REACHING BASE ON ERRORS

Most first on error, game
5—Chicago N.L. vs. Chicago A.L., October 13, 1906.

Most first on error by both clubs, game
6—Pittsburgh N.L. 4, Boston A.L. 2, October 10, 1903.
Chicago N.L. 4, Philadelphia A.L. 2, October 18, 1910.
New York N.L. 4, Philadelphia A.L. 2, October 26, 1911.

INDIVIDUAL BASERUNNING

STOLEN BASES

Most stolen bases, career

14—Eddie Collins, Philadelphia A.L. (10), 1910, 1911, 1913, 1914; Chicago A.L. (4), 1917, 1919; six series, 34 games.
Lou Brock, St. Louis N.L., 1964 (0), 1967 (7), 1968 (7); three series, 21 games.

Most stolen bases, series

4-game series—3—Rickey Henderson, Oakland A.L., 1989, 1990.
Derek Jeter, New York A.L., 1999.
5-game series—6—Jimmy Slagle, Chicago N.L., 1907.
6-game series—6—Kenny Lofton, Cleveland A.L., 1995.
7-game series—7—Lou Brock, St. Louis N.L., 1967.
Lou Brock, St. Louis N.L., 1968.
8-game series—4—Josh Devore, New York N.L., 1912.

Most stolen bases, game

3—Honus Wagner, Pittsburgh N.L., October 11, 1909.
Willie Davis, Los Angeles N.L., October 11, 1965.
Lou Brock, St. Louis N.L., October 12, 1967.
Lou Brock, St. Louis N.L., October 5, 1968.

Most times stealing home, game (14 times; *part of double steal)

1—Bill Dahlen, New York N.L., October 12, 1905, fifth inning.*
George Davis, Chicago A.L., October 13, 1906, third inning.*
Jimmy Slagle, Chicago N.L., October 11, 1907, seventh inning.
Ty Cobb, Detroit A.L., October 9, 1909, third inning.
Buck Herzog, New York N.L., October 14, 1912, first inning.*
Butch Schmidt, Boston N.L., October 9, 1914, eighth inning.*
Mike McNally, New York A.L., October 5, 1921, fifth inning.
Bob Meusel, New York A.L., October 6, 1921, eighth inning.
Bob Meusel, New York A.L., October 7, 1928, sixth inning.*
Hank Greenberg, Detroit A.L., October 6, 1934, eighth inning.*
Monte Irvin, New York N.L., October 4, 1951, first inning.
Jackie Robinson, Brooklyn N.L., September 28, 1955, eighth inning.

Tim McCarver, St. Louis N.L., October 15, 1964, fourth inning.*
Brad Fullmer, Anaheim A.L., October 20, 2002, first inning.*

Most stolen bases, inning (nine times)

2—Jimmy Slagle, Chicago N.L., October 8, 1907, 10th inning.
George Browne, New York N.L., October 12, 1905, ninth inning.
Ty Cobb, Detroit A.L., October 12, 1908, ninth inning.
Eddie Collins, Chicago A.L., October 7, 1917, sixth inning.
Babe Ruth, New York A.L., October 6, 1921, fifth inning.
Lou Brock, St. Louis N.L., October 12, 1967, fifth inning.
Dave Lopes, Los Angeles N.L., October 15, 1974, first inning.
Kenny Lofton, Cleveland A.L., October 21, 1995, first inning.
Omar Vizquel, Cleveland A.L., October 26, 1997, fifth inning.

CAUGHT STEALING

Most caught stealing, career

9—Frank Schulte, Chicago N.L., 1906, 1907, 1908, 1910; four series, 21 games.

Most caught stealing, series

5—Frank Schulte, Chicago N.L., 1910 (5-game series).

Most times caught stealing, game

2—Frank Schulte, Chicago N.L., October 17, 1910.
Frank Schulte, Chicago N.L., October 23, 1910.
Fred Luderus, Philadelphia N.L., October 8, 1915.
Jimmy Johnston, Brooklyn N.L., October 9, 1916.
Mickey Livingston, Chicago N.L., October 3, 1945.
Billy Martin, New York A.L., September 28, 1955.

Most times caught stealing, inning

1—Held by many players.

Most times picked off base, game

2—Max Flack, Chicago N.L., September 9, 1918 (first base in first inning, second base in third inning).

CLUB BASERUNNING

STOLEN BASES

Most stolen bases, total series

74—New York A.L.; 39 series, 219 games.

Most stolen bases, series

4-game series—9—Boston N.L. vs. Philadelphia A.L., 1914.
5-game series—18—Chicago N.L. vs. Detroit A.L., 1907.
6-game series—15—Atlanta N.L. vs. Toronto A.L., 1992.
7-game series—18—Pittsburgh N.L. vs. Detroit A.L., 1909.
8-game series—12—New York N.L. vs. Boston A.L., 1912.

Most stolen bases by both clubs, series

4-game series—11—Boston N.L. 9, Philadelphia A.L. 2, 1914.
5-game series—25—Chicago N.L. 18, Detroit A.L. 7, 1907.
6-game series—20—Atlanta N.L. 15, Toronto A.L. 5, 1992.
7-game series—24—Pittsburgh N.L. 18, Detroit A.L. 6, 1909.
8-game series—18—New York N.L. 12, Boston A.L. 6, 1912.

Fewest stolen bases, series

4-game series—0—Held by many clubs.
5-game series—0—Held by many clubs.
6-game series—0—Held by many clubs.
7-game series—0—Philadelphia A.L. vs. St. Louis N.L., 1931.
Detroit A.L. vs. Cincinnati N.L., 1940.

New York A.L. vs. Pittsburgh N.L., 1960.
Detroit A.L. vs. St. Louis N.L., 1968.
New York N.L. vs. Oakland A.L., 1973.
Boston A.L. vs. Cincinnati N.L., 1975.
Pittsburgh N.L. vs. Baltimore A.L., 1979.
Boston A.L. vs. New York N.L., 1986.
8-game series—5
Boston A.L. vs. Pittsburgh N.L., 1903.
Chicago A.L. vs. Cincinnati N.L., 1919.

Fewest stolen bases by both clubs, series

4-game series—1—Cincinnati N.L. 1, New York A.L. 0, 1939.
New York N.L. 1, Cleveland A.L. 0, 1954.
Los Angeles N.L. 1, Baltimore A.L. 0, 1966.
St. Louis N.L. 1, Boston A.L. 0, 2004.
5-game series—1—Chicago N.L. 1, Philadelphia A.L. 0, 1929.
Washington A.L. 1, New York N.L. 0, 1933.
New York N.L. 1, New York A.L. 0, 1937.
New York A.L. 1, Cincinnati N.L. 0, 1961.
Cincinnati N.L. 1, Baltimore A.L. 0, 1970.
New York A.L. 1, New York N.L. 0, 2000.
6-game series—0—St. Louis N.L. 0, St. Louis A.L. 0, 1944.
7-game series—1—Cincinnati N.L. 1, Detroit A.L. 0, 1940.
8-game series—12—Pittsburgh N.L. 7, Boston A.L. 5, 1903.
Cincinnati N.L. 7, Chicago A.L. 5, 1919.

Most stolen bases, game

5—New York N.L. vs. Philadelphia A.L., October 12, 1905.
    Chicago N.L. vs. Chicago A.L., October 10, 1906.
    Chicago N.L. vs. Detroit A.L., October 9, 1907.
    St. Louis N.L. vs. Minnesota A.L., October 22, 1987.
    Atlanta N.L. vs. Toronto A.L., October 18, 1992.
    (7—Chicago N.L. vs. Detroit A.L., October 8, 1907, 12
    innings.)

Most stolen bases by both clubs, game

6—New York N.L. 5, Philadelphia A.L. 1, October 12, 1905.
    Pittsburgh N.L. 4, Detroit A.L. 2, October 13, 1909.
    New York N.L. 3, Philadelphia A.L. 3, October 9, 1913.
    St. Louis N.L. 5, Minnesota A.L. 1, October 22, 1987.
    (11—Chicago N.L. 7, Detroit A.L. 4, October 8, 1907, 12
    innings.)

Longest game with no stolen bases

14 innings—Boston A.L. vs. Brooklyn N.L., October 9, 1916.
            Brooklyn N.L. vs. Boston A.L., October 9, 1916.

Longest game with no stolen bases by either club

14 innings—Boston A.L. vs. Brooklyn N.L., October 9, 1916.

Most stolen bases, inning

3—Pittsburgh N.L. vs. Boston A.L., October 1, 1903, first
    inning.
    New York N.L. vs. Philadelphia A.L., October 12, 1905, ninth
    inning.
    Chicago N.L. vs. Detroit A.L., October 8, 1907, 10th inning.
    Chicago N.L. vs. Detroit A.L., October 11, 1908, eighth inning.
    New York N.L. vs. Boston A.L., October 14, 1912, first inning.
    Chicago A.L. vs. New York N.L., October 7, 1917, sixth inning.

CAUGHT STEALING

Most caught stealing, series

4-game series—5—Boston N.L. vs. Philadelphia A.L., 1914.
                Cincinnati N.L. vs. New York, A.L., 1976.
5-game series—8—Chicago N.L. vs. Philadelphia A.L. 1910.
6-game series—13—New York N.L. vs. Philadelphia A.L. 1911.
7-game series—7—Cleveland A.L. vs. Brooklyn N.L., 1920.
                Washington A.L. vs. Pittsburgh N.L., 1925.
                St. Louis N.L. vs. Detroit A.L., 1968.
8-game series—11—New York N.L. vs. Boston A.L., 1912.

Most caught stealing by both clubs, series

4-game series—7—Cincinnati N.L. 5, New York A.L. 2, 1976.
5-game series—15—Chicago N.L. 8, Philadelphia A.L. 7, 1910.
6-game series—19—New York N.L. 13, Philadelphia A.L. 6, 1911.
7-game series—11—Pittsburgh N.L. 6, Detroit A.L. 5, 1909.
8-game series—16—New York N.L. 11, Boston A.L. 5, 1912.

Fewest caught stealing, series

0—Held by many clubs.

Fewest caught stealing by both clubs, series

4-game series—0—Boston A.L. 0, St. Louis N.L. 0, 2004.
5-game series—0—New York A.L. 0, Brooklyn N.L. 0, 1949.
6-game series—1—St. Louis N.L. 1, St. Louis A.L. 0, 1944.
                Cleveland A.L. 1, Boston N.L. 0, 1948.
7-game series—0—St. Louis N.L. 0, New York A.L. 0, 1964.
8-game series—6—Pittsburgh N.L. 4, Boston A.L. 2, 1903.

Most caught stealing, game

3—Made in many games. Last time—Los Angeles N.L. vs.
    Oakland A.L., October 19, 1988.
    (5—New York N.L. vs. Philadelphia A.L., October 17, 1911
    (0 stolen bases), 11 innings.)

Most caught stealing by both clubs, game

5—Philadelphia A.L. 3, Chicago N.L. 2, October 17, 1910.

Most caught stealing, inning

2—Made in many innings.

LEFT ON BASE

Most left on base, total series

1,518—New York A.L.; 39 series, 219 games.

Most left on base, series

4-game series—41—Boston A.L. vs. St. Louis N.L., 2004.
5-game series—52—New York A.L. vs. New York N.L., 2000.
6-game series—55—New York A.L. vs. Los Angeles N.L., 1981.
7-game series—72—New York N.L. vs. Oakland A.L., 1973.
8-game series—55—Boston A.L. vs. Pittsburgh N.L., 1903.
                Boston A.L. vs. New York N.L., 1912.

Most left on base by both clubs, series

4-game series—65—Cleveland A.L. 37, New York N.L. 28, 1954.
                Boston A.L. 41, St. Louis N.L. 24, 2004.
5-game series—88—New York A.L. 52, New York N.L. 36, 2000.
6-game series—101—New York A.L. 55, Los Angeles N.L. 46,
                1981.
7-game series—130—New York N.L. 72, Oakland A.L. 58, 1973.
8-game series—108—Boston A.L. 55, New York N.L. 53, 1912.

Fewest left on base, series

4-game series—16—New York A.L. vs. Cincinnati N.L., 1939.
5-game series—23—Philadelphia N.L. vs Boston A.L., 1915.
                Philadelphia N.L. vs. Baltimore A.L., 1983.
6-game series—29—Philadelphia N.L. vs. New York A.L., 1911.
7-game series—36—Minnesota A.L. vs. Los Angeles N.L., 1965.
8-game series—43—New York A.L. vs. New York N.L., 1921.

Fewest left on base by both clubs, series

4-game series—39—Cincinnati N.L. 23, New York A.L. 16, 1939.
5-game series—51—Baltimore A.L. 28, Philadelphia N.L. 23, 1983.
6-game series—60—New York N.L. 31, Philadelphia A.L. 29, 1911.
7-game series—82—Cleveland A.L. 43, Brooklyn N.L. 39, 1920.
                Brooklyn N.L. 42, New York A.L. 40, 1956.
                New York A.L. 43, San Francisco N.L. 39,
    1962.
8-game series—97—New York N.L. 54, New York A.L. 43, 1921.

Most left on base, game

15—Anaheim A.L. vs. San Francisco N.L., October 22, 2002.
    (15—New York N.L. vs. Oakland A.L., October 14, 1973,
    12 innings.
    Philadelphia N.L. vs. Kansas City A.L., October 17, 1980,
    10 innings.
    New York A.L. vs. New York N.L., October 21, 2000,
    12 innings.)

Most left on base, shutout defeat

11—Philadelphia A.L. vs. St. Louis N.L., October 4, 1930 (lost 5-0).
    St. Louis N.L. vs. New York A.L., October 11, 1943 (lost 2-0).
    Los Angeles N.L. vs. Chicago A.L., October 6, 1959 (lost 1-0).
    Baltimore A.L. vs. New York N.L., October 14, 1969 (lost 5-0).

Most left on base by both clubs, game

24—Detroit A.L. 14, San Diego N.L. 10, October 12, 1984.
    (27—New York N.L. 15, Oakland A.L. 12, October 14,
    1973, 12 innings.)

Fewest left on base, game

0—Brooklyn N.L. vs. New York A.L., October 8, 1956.
    Los Angeles N.L. vs. New York A.L., October 6, 1963 (batted
    eight innings).

Fewest left on base by both clubs, game

3—New York A.L. 3, Brooklyn N.L. 0, October 8, 1956.

INDIVIDUAL PITCHING

GAMES

Most games, career
22—Whitey Ford, New York A.L., 1950, 1953, 1955, 1956,
1957, 1958, 1960, 1961, 1962, 1963, 1964; 11 series.

Most games, series
4-game series—4—Jeff Nelson, New York A.L., 1999 (2.2
innings).
Keith Foulke, Boston A.L., 2004 (5.0
innings)
5-game series—5—Mike G. Marshall, Los Angeles N.L., 1974
(9.0 innings).
6-game series—6—Dan Quisenberry, Kansas City A.L., 1980
(10.1 innings).
7-game series—7—Darold Knowles, Oakland A.L., 1973
(6.1 innings).
8-game series—5—Deacon Phillippe, Pittsburgh N.L., 1903
(44 innings).

Most consecutive games, series
7—Darold Knowles, Oakland A.L., October 13, 14, 16, 17, 18,
20, 21, 1973.

GAMES STARTED

Most games started, career
22—Whitey Ford, New York A.L., 1950, 1953, 1955, 1956,
1957, 1958, 1960, 1961, 1962, 1963, 1964; 11 series.

Most opening games started, career
8—Whitey Ford, New York A.L., 1955, 1956, 1957, 1958, 1961,
1962, 1963, 1964 (won 4, lost 3).

Most consecutive games started, series
2—Deacon Phillippe, Pittsburgh N.L., October 3, 6, 1903.
Deacon Phillippe, Pittsburgh N.L., October 10, 13, 1903.
Jack Coombs, Philadelphia A.L., October 18, 20, 1910.
Christy Mathewson, New York N.L., October 17, 24, 1911.
George Earnshaw, Philadelphia A.L., October 9, 11, 1929.
George Earnshaw, Philadelphia A.L., October 6, 8, 1930.

Most series with three games started, career
3—Bob Gibson, St. Louis N.L., 1964, 1967, 1968.

Most games started, series
5—Deacon Phillippe, Pittsburgh N.L., 1903 (8-game series).

Oldest pitcher to start a game
45 years, 3 months, 7 days—Jack Quinn, Philadelphia A.L.,
October 12, 1929 (pitched five innings).

GAMES RELIEVED

Most games by relief pitcher, career
20—Mike Stanton, Atlanta N.L., 1991, 1992; New York A.L.,
1998 through 2001 (23.1 innings).
Mariano Rivera, New York A.L., 1996, 1998 through 2001,
2003 (31.0 innings).

Most games pitched by relief pitcher, series
7—Darold Knowles, Oakland A.L., 1973 (7-game series).

COMPLETE GAMES

Most complete games pitched, career
10—Christy Mathewson, New York N.L. 1905, 1911, 1912, 1913.

Most consecutive complete games pitched, career
8—Bob Gibson, St. Louis N.L., 1964, 1967, 1968 (won 7, lost 1).

Most consecutive complete games won, career
7—Bob Gibson, St. Louis N.L., October 12, 15, 1964; October
4, 8, 12, 1967; October 2, 6, 1968.

Most complete games, series
5—Deacon Phillippe, Pittsburgh N.L., 1903 (8-game series).

Youngest pitcher to pitch a complete game
20 years, 10 months, 12 days—Joe Bush, Philadelphia A.L.,
October 9, 1913 (Philadelphia A.L. 8, New York N.L. 2).

Youngest pitcher to win a complete game
20 years, 10 months, 12 days—Joe Bush, Philadelphia A.L.,
October 9, 1913 (Philadelphia A.L. 8, New York N.L. 2).

Oldest pitcher to pitch a complete game
39 years, 7 months, 13 days—Grover Alexander, St. Louis N.L.,
October 9, 1926 (St. Louis N.L. 10, New York A.L. 2).

INNINGS

Most innings pitched, career
146—Whitey Ford, New York A.L., 1950, 1953, 1955 through
1964, except 1959; 11 series, 22 games.

Most innings pitched, series
4-game series—18—Dick Rudolph, Boston N.L., 1914.
Waite Hoyt, New York A.L., 1928.
Red Ruffing, New York A.L., 1938.
Sandy Koufax, Los Angeles N.L., 1963.
5-game series—27—Christy Mathewson, New York N.L., 1905.
Jack Coombs, Philadelphia A.L., 1910.
6-game series—27—Christy Mathewson, New York N.L. 1911.
Red Faber, Chicago A.L., 1917.
Hippo Vaughn, Chicago N.L., 1918.
7-game series—32—George Mullin, Detroit A.L., 1909.
8-game series—44—Deacon Phillippe, Pittsburgh N.L., 1903.

Most innings pitched, game
14—Babe Ruth, Boston A.L., October 9, 1916 (complete game,
won 2-1).

GAMES WON

Most games won, career
10—Whitey Ford, New York A.L., 1950, 1953, 1955, 1956,
1957, 1958, 1960, 1961, 1962, 1963, 1964; 11 series,
22 games (lost 8).

For a complete list of pitchers with five or
more victories, see page 505.

Most consecutive games won, career
7—Bob Gibson, St. Louis N.L., October 12, 15, 1964; October
4, 8, 12, 1967; October 2, 6, 1968 (seven complete).

Most games won by undefeated pitcher, career
6—Lefty Gomez, New York A.L., 1932, 1936, 1937, 1938.

Most series-opening games won, career
5—Red Ruffing, New York A.L., 1932, 1938, 1939, 1941, 1942,
four complete (lost complete-game opener in 1936).

Most games won, series
4-game series—2—Held by many pitchers.
5-game series—3—Christy Mathewson, New York N.L., 1905.
Jack Coombs, Philadelphia A.L., 1910.
6-game series—3—Red Faber, Chicago A.L., 1917.
7-game series—3—Babe Adams, Pittsburgh N.L., 1909.
Stan Coveleski, Cleveland A.L., 1920.
Harry Brecheen, St. Louis N.L., 1946.
Lew Burdette, Milwaukee N.L., 1957.
Bob Gibson, St. Louis N.L., 1967.
Mickey Lolich, Detroit A.L., 1968.
Randy Johnson, Arizona N.L., 2001.
8-game series—3—Bill Dinneen, Boston A.L., 1903.
Deacon Phillippe, Pittsburgh N.L., 1903.
Joe Wood, Boston A.L., 1912.

Most games won by relief pitcher, series
2—Jesse Barnes, New York N.L., 1921 (8-game series).
Hugh Casey, Brooklyn N.L., 1947 (7-game series).

Larry Sherry, Los Angeles N.L., 1959 (6-game series).
Ross Grimsley, Cincinnati N.L., 1972 (6-game series).
Rawly Eastwick, Cincinnati N.L., 1975 (7-game series).
Duane Ward, Toronto A.L., 1992 (6-game series).
Mike Stanton, New York A.L., 2000 (5-game series).

Most games won by undefeated pitcher, series
4-game series—2—Held by many pitchers.
5-game series—3—Christy Mathewson, New York N.L., 1905.
                Jack Coombs, Philadelphia A.L., 1910.
6-game series—2—Held by many pitchers.
7-game series—3—Babe Adams, Pittsburgh N.L., 1909.
                Stan Coveleski, Cleveland A.L., 1920.
                Harry Brecheen, St. Louis N.L., 1946.
                Lew Burdette, Milwaukee N.L., 1957.
                Bob Gibson, St. Louis N.L., 1967.
                Mickey Lolich, Detroit A.L., 1968.
                Randy Johnson, Arizona N.L., 2001.
8-game series—2—Rube Marquard, New York N.L., 1912.
                Hod Eller, Cincinnati N.L., 1919.
                Dickie Kerr, Chicago A.L., 1919.
                Jesse Barnes, New York N.L., 1921.

SAVES (SINCE 1969)

Most saves, career
9—Mariano Rivera, New York A.L., 1996, 1998 through 2001, 2003.

Most saves, series
4—John Wetteland, New York A.L., 1996 (6-game series).

GAMES LOST

Most games lost, career
8—Whitey Ford, New York A.L., 1950, 1953, 1955, 1956, 1957, 1958, 1960, 1961, 1962, 1963, 1964; 11 series, 22 games (won 10).

Most consecutive games lost, career
5—Joe Bush, Philadelphia A.L., 1914 (1), Boston A.L., 1918 (1), New York A.L., 1922 (2), 1923 (1).

Most games lost by winless pitcher, career
4—Ed Summers, Detroit A.L., 1908 (2), 1909 (2).
    Willie Sherdel, St. Louis N.L., 1926 (2), 1928 (2).
    Don Newcombe, Brooklyn N.L., 1949 (2), 1955 (1), 1956 (1).
    Charlie Leibrandt, Kansas City A.L., 1985 (1); Atlanta N.L., 1991 (2), 1992 (1).

Most games lost, series
4-game series—2—Held by many pitchers.
5-game series—2—Held by many pitchers.
6-game series—3—George Frazier, New York A.L., 1981.
7-game series—2—Held by many pitchers
8-game series—3—Lefty Williams, Chicago A.L., 1919.

RUNS, EARNED RUNS AND ERA

Most runs allowed, career
51—Whitey Ford, New York A.L., 1950, 1953, 1955, 1956, 1957, 1958, 1960, 1961, 1962, 1963, 1964; 11 series; 22 games.

Most runs allowed, series
4-game series—11—Grover Alexander, St. Louis N.L., 1928.
                Bob Lemon, Cleveland A.L., 1954.
5-game series—16—Mordecai Brown, Chicago N.L., 1910.
6-game series—10—Slim Sallee, New York N.L., 1917.
                Red Ruffing, New York A.L., 1936.
                Don Gullett, New York A.L., 1977.
                Don Sutton, Los Angeles N.L., 1978.
                Jack Morris, Toronto A.L., 1992.
7-game series—17—Lew Burdette, Milwaukee N.L., 1958.
8-game series—19—Deacon Phillippe, Pittsburgh N.L., 1903.

Most runs allowed, game
10—Bill Kennedy, Pittsburgh N.L., October 7, 1903.

Most runs allowed, inning
7—Hooks Wiltse, New York N.L., October 26, 1911, seventh inning.

Carl Hubbell, New York N.L., October 6, 1937, sixth inning.

Most earned runs allowed, career
44—Whitey Ford, New York A.L., 1950, 1953, 1955, 1956, 1957, 1958, 1960, 1961, 1962, 1963, 1964; 11 series; 22 games.

Most earned runs allowed, game
8—Jay Witasick, New York A.L., November 3, 2001.

Most earned runs allowed, inning
6—Hooks Wiltse, New York N.L., October 26, 1911, seventh inning.
    Danny Cox, St. Louis N.L., October 18, 1987, fourth inning.
    Jay Witasick, New York A.L., November 3, 2001, third inning.

Lowest earned-run average, career (30 or more innings)
0.83—Harry Breechen, St. Louis N.L., 1943, 1944, 1946; 3 series; 3 games (32.2 innings).

Lowest earned-run average, series (14 or more innings)
0.00—Christy Mathewson, New York N.L., 1905 (27 innings).
    Waite Hoyt, New York A.L., 1921 (27 innings).
    Carl Hubbell, New York N.L., 1933 (20 innings).
    Whitey Ford, New York A.L., 1960 (18 innings).
    Joe McGinnity, New York N.L., 1905 (17 innings).
    Duster Mails, Cleveland A.L., 1920 (15.2 innings).
    Rube Benton, New York N.L., 1917 (14 innings).
    Whitey Ford, New York A.L., 1961 (14 innings).

SHUTOUTS AND SCORELESS INNINGS

Most shutouts won, career
4—Christy Mathewson, New York N.L., 1905 (3), 1913 (1).

For a complete list of shutouts, see page 498.

Most shutouts won, series
3—Christy Mathewson, New York N.L., October 9, 12, 14, 1905 (consecutive).

Most 1-0 shutouts won, career
2—Art Nehf, New York N.L., October 13, 1921, October 12, 1923.

Most shutouts lost, career
3—Eddie Plank, Philadelphia A.L., 1905 (2), 1914 (1).

Most 1-0 shutouts lost, career
2—Eddie Plank, Philadelphia A.L., October 13, 1905, October 10, 1914.

Youngest pitcher to win a complete game shutout
20 years, 11 months, 21 days—Jim Palmer, Baltimore A.L., October 6, 1966; Baltimore A.L., 6, Los Angeles N.L., 0.

Oldest pitcher to win a complete game shutout
38 years, 1 month, 18 days—Randy Johnson, Arizona N.L., October 28, 2001; Arizona N.L. 4, New York A.L. 0.

Most consecutive scoreless innings, career
33—Whitey Ford, New York A.L., October 8, 1960 (9); October 12, 1960 (9); October 4, 1961 (9) innings; October 8, 1961 (5); October 4, 1962 (1).

Most consecutive scoreless innings, series
27—Christy Mathewson, New York N.L., October 9, 12, 14, 1905.

Retiring side on three pitched balls
Christy Mathewson, New York N.L., October 9, 1912, 11th inning.
Christy Mathewson, New York N.L., October 16, 1912, fifth inning.
Rube Walberg, Philadelphia A.L., October 14, 1929, seventh inning.
Tiny Bonham, New York A.L., October 6, 1941, seventh inning.

HITS

Most hits allowed, series
132—Whitey Ford, New York A.L., 1950, 1953, 1955, 1956, 1957, 1958, 1960, 1961, 1962, 1963, 1964; 11 series, 22 games.

Most hits allowed, series

4-game series—17—Red Ruffing, New York A.L., 1938.
5-game series—23—Jack Coombs, Philadelphia A.L., 1910.
Mordecai Brown, Chicago N.L., 1910.
6-game series—25—Christy Mathewson, New York N.L., 1911.
7-game series—30—Walter Johnson, Washington A.L., 1924.
8-game series—38—Deacon Phillippe, Pittsburgh N.L., 1903.

Most hits allowed, game

15—Walter Johnson, Washington A.L., October 15, 1925.

Fewest hits allowed, game

0—Don Larsen, New York A.L., October 8, 1956 (perfect game).

One and two-hit games of nine innings (pitching complete game)

1 hit—Ed Reulbach, Chicago N.L., October 10, 1906 (hit came
with none out in seventh).
Claude Passeau, Chicago N.L., October 5, 1945 (hit came
with two out in second).
Bill Bevens, New York A.L., October 3, 1947 (hit came with
two out in ninth).
Jim Lonborg, Boston A.L., October 5, 1967 (hit came with
two out in eighth).

2 hits—Ed Walsh, Chicago A.L., October 11, 1906.
Mordecai Brown, Chicago N.L., October 12, 1906.
Eddie Plank, Philadelphia A.L., October 11, 1913.
Bill James, Boston N.L., October 10, 1914.
Waite Hoyt, New York A.L., October 6, 1921.
Burleigh Grimes, St. Louis N.L., October 5, 1931.
George Earnshaw, Philadelphia A.L., October 6, 1931.
Monte Pearson, New York A.L., October 5, 1939.
Mort Cooper, St. Louis N.L., October 4, 1944.
Bob Feller, Cleveland A.L., October 6, 1948.
Allie Reynolds, New York A.L., October 5, 1949.
Vic Raschi, New York A.L., October 4, 1950.
Warren Spahn, Milwaukee N.L., October 5, 1958.
Whitey Ford, New York A.L., October 4, 1961.
Nelson Briles, Pittsburgh N.L., October 14, 1971.
Greg Maddux, Atlanta N.L., October 21, 1995.

Fewest hits allowed, two consecutive complete games

4—Jim Lonborg, Boston A.L., October 5 (1), October 9 (3), 1967.

Fewest hits allowed, three consecutive complete games

14—Christy Mathewson, New York N.L., October 5 (4), October
12 (4), October 14 (6), 1905.
Bob Gibson, St. Louis N.L., October 4 (6), October 8 (5),
October 12 (3), 1967.

Most consecutive hitless innings, career

11—Don Larsen, New York A.L., October 8, 1956 (9), October
5, 1957 (2).

Most consecutive hitless innings, game

9—Don Larsen, New York A.L., October 8, 1956.

**Most consecutive innings allowing no players to reach first
base, career**

11—Don Larsen, New York A.L., October 8, 1956 (9), October
5, 1957 (2).

**Most consecutive innings allowing no players to reach first
base, series**

9—Don Larsen, New York A.L., October 8, 1956.

**Most consecutive innings allowing no player to reach first
base, game**

9—Don Larsen, New York A.L., October 8, 1956 (perfect game).

Most hits allowed, inning

8—Jay Witasick, New York A.L., November 3, 2001, third
inning.

**Most consecutive hits allowed, inning (consecutive plate
appearances)**

6—Ed Summers, Detroit A.L., October 10, 1908, ninth inning (6
singles).

DOUBLES, TRIPLES AND HOME RUNS

Most doubles allowed, game

8—Walter Johnson, Washington A.L., October 15, 1925.

Most triples allowed, game

5—Deacon Phillippe, Pittsburgh N.L., October 10, 1903.

Most home runs allowed, career

9—Catfish Hunter, Oakland A.L., 1972, 1973, 1974; New York
A.L., 1976, 1977, 1978; six series, 12 games.

Most home runs allowed, series

4-game series—4—Willie Sherdel, St. Louis N.L., 1928.
Charlie Root, Chicago N.L., 1932.
Junior Thompson, Cincinnati N.L., 1939.
Scott Garrelts, San Francisco N.L., 1989.
5-game series—4—Gary Nolan, Cincinnati N.L., 1970.
Charles Hudson, Philadelphia N.L., 1983.
6-game series—4—Allie Reynolds, New York A.L., 1953.
7-game series—5—Lew Burdette, Milwaukee N.L., 1958.
Dick Hughes, St. Louis N.L., 1967.
8-game series—2—Babe Adams, Pittsburgh N.L., 1909.
Harry Harper, New York A.L., 1921.

Most home runs allowed, game

4—Charlie Root, Chicago N.L., October 1, 1932.
Junior Thompson, Cincinnati N.L., October 7, 1939.
Dick Hughes, St. Louis N.L., October 11, 1967.

Most home runs allowed, inning

3—Dick Hughes, St. Louis N.L., October 11, 1967, fourth inning.

Most consecutive home runs allowed, inning (13 times)

2—Emil Yde, Pittsburgh N.L., October 11, 1925, third inning.
Bill Sherdel, St. Louis N.L., October 9, 1928, seventh inning.
Charlie Root, Chicago N.L., October 1, 1932, fifth inning.
Curt Simmons, St. Louis N.L., October 14, 1964, sixth inning.
Don Drysdale, Los Angeles N.L., October 5, 1966, first inning.
Dick Hughes, St. Louis N.L., October 11, 1967, fourth inning.
Rick Wise, Boston A.L., October 14, 1975, fifth inning.
Don Sutton, Los Angeles N.L., October 16, 1977, eighth inning.
Ron Guidry, New York A.L., October 25, 1981, seventh inning.
Ron Darling, New York N.L., October 27, 1986, second inning.
Orel Hershiser, Cleveland A.L., October 18, 1997, fourth inning.
David Wells, New York A.L., October 17, 1998, fifth inning.
Kevin Appier, Anaheim A.L., October 20, 2002, second inning.

TOTAL BASES

Most total bases allowed, career

184—Whitey Ford, New York A.L., 1950, 1953, 1955, 1956,
1957, 1958, 1960, 1961, 1962, 1963, 1964; 11 series,
22 games.

Most total bases allowed, game

25—Walter Johnson, Washington A.L., October 15, 1925.

BASES ON BALLS

Most bases on balls, career

34—Whitey Ford, New York A.L., 1950, 1953, 1955, 1956,
1957, 1958, 1960, 1961, 1962, 1963, 1964; 11 series,
22 games.

Most innings pitched without allowing a base on balls, series

26—Carl Mays, New York A.L., 1921.

Most bases on balls, series

4-game series—8—Bob Lemon, Cleveland A.L., 1954.
5-game series—14—Jack Coombs, Philadelphia A.L., 1910.
6-game series—11—Lefty Tyler, Chicago N.L., 1918.
Lefty Gomez, New York A.L., 1936.

Allie Reynolds, New York A.L., 1951.
7-game series—11—Walter Johnson, Washington A.L., 1924.
Bill Bevens, New York A.L., 1947.
8-game series—13—Art Nehf, New York N.L., 1921.

Most bases on balls, game
10—Bill Bevens, New York A.L., October 3, 1947.

Longest game without allowing base on balls
12 innings—Schoolboy Rowe, Detroit A.L., October 4, 1934.

Most bases on balls, inning
4—Bill Donovan, Detroit A.L., October 16, 1909, second inning.
Art Reinhart, St. Louis N.L., October 6, 1926, fifth inning
(one base on balls with bases full).
Guy Bush, Chicago N.L., September 28, 1932, sixth inning.
Don Gullett, Cincinnati N.L., October 22, 1975, third inning
(two bases on balls with bases full).
Tom Glavine, Atlanta N.L., October 24, 1991, sixth inning
(two bases on balls with bases full).
Todd Stottlemyre, Toronto A.L., October 20, 1993, first
inning (one base on balls with bases full).
Al Leiter, Florida N.L., October 21, 1997, fourth inning (one
base on balls with bases full).
Tim Wakefield, Boston A.L., October 23, 2004, fourth
inning.

Most consecutive bases on balls, inning
3—Bob Shawkey, New York A.L., October 7, 1921, fourth inning
(two bases on balls with bases full).
Art Reinhart, St. Louis N.L., October 6, 1926, fifth inning
(one base on balls with bases full).
Guy Bush, Chicago N.L., September 28, 1932, sixth inning.
Joe Hoerner, St. Louis N.L., October 3, 1968, ninth inning
(two bases on balls with bases full).
Tom Glavine, Atlanta N.L., October 24, 1991, sixth inning
(two bases on balls with bases full).
Todd Stottlemyre, Toronto A.L., October 20, 1993, first
inning (one base on balls with bases full).
Charles Nagy, Cleveland A.L., October 21, 1997, third inning
(one base on balls with bases full).
Jarrod Washburn, Anaheim A.L., October 24, 2002, first
inning (one base on balls with bases full).
Tim Wakefield, Boston A.L., October 23, 2004, fourth
inning.

STRIKEOUTS

Most strikeouts, career
94—Whitey Ford, New York A.L., 1950, 1953, 1955, 1956,
1957, 1958, 1960, 1961, 1962, 1963, 1964; 11 series,
22 games.

Most strikeouts, series
4-game series—23—Sandy Koufax, Los Angeles N.L., 1963.
5-game series—18—Christy Mathewson, New York N.L., 1905.
6-game series—20—Chief Bender, Philadelphia A.L., 1911.
7-game series—35—Bob Gibson, St. Louis N.L., 1968.
8-game series—28—Bill Dinneen, Boston A.L., 1903.

Most strikeouts, game
17—Bob Gibson, St. Louis N.L., October 2, 1968.

For a complete list of pitchers with 10 or
more strikeouts in a game, see page 505.

Most games with 10 or more strikeouts, career
5—Bob Gibson, St. Louis N.L., 1964 (1), 1967 (2), 1968 (2).

Most strikeouts by losing pitcher, game
12—Orlando Hernandez, New York A.L., October 24, 2000,
pitched first 7.1 innings.
(12—Walter Johnson, Washington A.L., October 4, 1924,
12 innings.)

Most strikeouts by relief pitcher, game
11—Moe Drabowsky, Baltimore A.L., October 5, 1966, pitched
6.2 innings.

Most consecutive strikeouts, game
6—Hod Eller, Cincinnati N.L., October 6, 1919 (three in second
inning, three in third inning).
Moe Drabowsky, Baltimore A.L., October 5, 1966 (three in
fourth inning, three in fifth inning).
Todd Worrell, St. Louis N.L., October 24, 1985 (three in
sixth inning, three in seventh inning).

Most consecutive strikeouts at start of game
5—Mort Cooper, St. Louis N.L., October 11, 1943.
Sandy Koufax, Los Angeles N.L., October 23, 1963.

Most innings with one or more strikeouts, game
9—Ed Walsh, Chicago A.L., October 11, 1906 (12 strikeouts).
Bob Gibson, St. Louis N.L., October 2, 1968 (17 strikeouts).

Most strikeouts, inning
4—Orval Overall, Chicago N.L., October 14, 1908, first inning.

HIT BATSMEN, WILD PITCHES AND BALKS

Most hit batsmen, career
4—Bill Donovan, Detroit A.L., 1907 (3), 1908 (0), 1909 (1).
Eddie Plank, Philadelphia A.L., 1905 (1), 1911 (1), 1913 (1),
1914 (1).

Most hit batsmen, series
3—Bill Donovan, Detroit A.L., 1907 (5-game series).
Bruce Kison, Pittsburgh N.L., 1971 (7-game series).

Most hit batsmen, game
3—Bruce Kison, Pittsburgh N.L., October 13, 1971, 6.1 innings.

Most hit batsmen, inning
2—Ed Willett, Detroit A.L., October 11, 1909, second inning
(consecutive).
Wayne Granger, St. Louis N.L., October 9, 1968, eighth
inning.

Most wild pitches, career
5—Hal Schumacher, New York N.L., 1933 (2), 1936 (2), 1937 (1).
Jack Morris, Detroit A.L., 1984 (2); Minnesota A.L., 1991 (2);
Toronto A.L., 1992 (1).

Most wild pitches, series
3—Jeff Tesreau, New York N.L., 1912.
John Stuper, St. Louis N.L., 1982.

Most wild pitches, game
2—Jeff Tesreau, New York N.L., October 15, 1912.
Jeff Pfeffer, Brooklyn N.L., October 12, 1916.
Bob Shawkey, New York A.L., October 5, 1922.
Vic Aldridge, Pittsburgh N.L., October 15, 1925.
Johnny Miljus, Pittsburgh N.L., October 8, 1927.
Tex Carleton, Chicago N.L., October 9, 1938.
Jim Bouton, New York A.L., October 5, 1963.
John Stuper, St. Louis N.L., October 13, 1982.
George Medich, Milwaukee A.L., October 19, 1982.
Jack Morris, Detroit A.L., October 13, 1984.
Ron Darling, New York N.L., October 18, 1986.
Mike Moore, Oakland A.L., October 15, 1989.
John Smoltz, Atlanta N.L., October 18, 1992.
Glendon Rusch, New York N.L., October 21, 2000.

Most wild pitches, inning
2—Bob Shawkey, New York A.L., October 5, 1922, fifth inning.
Vic Aldridge, Pittsburgh N.L., October 15, 1925, first inning.
Johnny Miljus, Pittsburgh N.L., October 8, 1927, ninth
inning.
Tex Carleton, Chicago N.L., October 9, 1938, eighth inning.
Doc Medich, Milwaukee A.L., October 19, 1982, sixth inning.

Most balks, career
2—Dave Stewart, Oakland, 1988; Toronto, 1993.

Most balks, series, game or inning
1—Held by many pitchers.

CLUB PITCHING

APPEARANCES

Most appearances by pitchers, series
4-game series—19—San Francisco N.L. vs. Oakland A.L., 1989.
5-game series—21—New York N.L. vs. New York A.L., 2000.
6-game series—27—New York A.L. vs. Atlanta N.L., 1996.
7-game series—33—Cleveland A.L. vs. Florida N.L., 1997.
          San Francisco N.L. vs. Anaheim A.L., 2002.
8-game series—14—Boston A.L. vs. New York N.L., 1912.

Most appearances by pitchers from both clubs, series
4-game series—32—San Francisco N.L. 19, Oakland A.L. 13, 1989.
5-game series—38—New York N.L. 21, New York A.L. 17, 2000.
6-game series—48—New York A.L. 27, Atlanta N.L. 21, 1996.
7-game series—60—Cleveland A.L. 33, Florida N.L. 27, 1997.
          San Francisco N.L. 33, Anaheim A.L. 27, 2002.
8-game series—25—Chicago A.L. 13, Cincinnati N.L. 12, 1919.

COMPLETE GAMES

Most complete games, series
4-game series
  A.L.—4—New York vs. St. Louis, 1928.
  N.L.—3—Boston vs. Philadelphia, 1914.
       Los Angeles vs. New York, 1963.
5-game series
  A.L.—5—Philadelphia vs. New York, 1905.
       Philadelphia vs. Chicago, 1910.
       Philadelphia vs. New York, 1913.
       Boston vs. Philadelphia, 1915.
  N.L.—4—New York vs. Philadelphia, 1905.
       Chicago vs. Detroit, 1907.
       Philadelphia vs. Boston, 1915.
       New York vs. New York, 1922.
6-game series
  A.L.—5—Philadelphia vs. New York, 1911.
       Boston vs. Chicago, 1918.
       Detroit vs. Chicago, 1935.
  N.L.—4—Chicago vs. Chicago, 1906.
       Chicago vs. Boston, 1918.
       St. Louis vs. Philadelphia, 1930.
7-game series
  A.L.—5—New York vs. Brooklyn, 1956.
  N.L.—4—Accomplished nine times; last time, St. Louis vs.
       Boston, 1967.
8-game series
  A.L.—7—Boston vs. Pittsburgh, 1903.
  N.L.—6—Pittsburgh vs. Boston, 1903.
       New York vs. Boston, 1912.

Most complete games from both clubs, series
4-game series—5—Boston N.L. 3, Philadelphia A.L. 2, 1914.
5-game series—9—Philadelphia A.L. 5, New York N.L. 4, 1905.
        Boston A.L. 5, Philadelphia N.L. 4, 1915
6-game series—9—Boston A.L. 5, Chicago N.L. 4, 1918.
7-game series—8—Pittsburgh N.L. 4, Detroit A.L. 4, 1909.
        Pittsburgh N.L. 4, Washington A.L. 4, 1925.
        St. Louis N.L. 4, Detroit A.L. 4, 1934.
        Cincinnati N.L. 4, Detroit A.L. 4, 1940.
        New York A.L. 5, Brooklyn 3, 1956.
        Cincinnati N.L. 4, Detroit A.L. 4, 1940
8-game series—13—Boston A.L. 7 vs. Pittsburgh N.L., 1903.

Fewest complete games, series
0—Held by many clubs.

Fewest complete games by both clubs, series
0—Occurred many times. Last time—Boston A.L. 0, St. Louis

N.L., 2004 (4-gam-series).

SAVES (SINCE 1969)

Most saves, series
4-game series—3—New York A.L. vs. San Diego N.L., 1998.
5-game series—3—Oakland A.L. vs. Los Angeles N.L., 1974.
6-game series—4—New York A.L. vs. Atlanta N.L., 1996.
7-game series—4—Oakland A.L. vs. New York N.L., 1973.

Most saves by both clubs, series
4-game series—3—New York A.L. 3, San Diego N.L. 0, 1998.
5-game series—4—Oakland A.L. 3, Los Angeles N.L. 1, 1974.
6-game series—4—Philadelphia N.L. 3, Kansas City A.L. 1, 1980.
        Toronto A.L. 3, Atlanta N.L. 1, 1992.
        Atlanta N.L. 3, Cleveland A.L. 1, 1995.
        New York A.L. 4, Atlanta N.L. 0, 1996.
7-game series—7—Oakland A.L. 4, New York N.L. 3, 1973.

Fewest saves, series
0—Held by many clubs.

Fewest saves by both clubs, series
0—New York A.L. 0, Los Angeles N.L. 0, 1977 (6-game series).

RUNS AND SHUTOUTS

Most runs allowed, total series
769—New York A.L.; 39 series, 219 games.

Most shutouts won, total series
17—New York A.L.

For a complete list of shutouts, see page 498.

Most shutouts won, series
4—New York N.L. vs. Philadelphia A.L., 1905.

Most consecutive shutouts won, series
3—New York N.L. vs. Philadelphia A.L., October 12, 13, 14, 1905.
    Baltimore A.L., vs. Los Angeles N.L., October 6, 8, 9, 1966.

Most shutouts by both clubs, series
5—New York N.L. 4, Philadelphia A.L. 1, 1905.

Fewest shutouts, series
0—Held by many clubs in series of all lengths.

Fewest shutouts by both clubs, series
0—Held by many clubs in series of all lengths.

Longest shutout game
10 innings—New York N.L. 3, Philadelphia A.L. 0, October 8, 1913.
       Brooklyn N.L. 1, New York A.L. 0, October 9, 1956.
       Minnesota A.L. 1, Atlanta N.L. 0, October 27, 1991.

Largest score, shutout game
12-0—New York A.L. 12, Pittsburgh N.L. 0, October 12, 1960.

Most consecutive innings shut out opponents, total series
39—Baltimore A.L., October 5, 1966, fourth inning, through
    October 11, 1969, first six innings.

Most consecutive innings shut out opponent, series
33—Baltimore A.L. vs. Los Angeles N.L., October 5, fourth
    inning, through end of game, October 6, 8, 9, 1966.

1-0 GAMES

Most 1-0 games won, total series
4—New York A.L.; 39 series, 219 games.

Most 1-0 games won, series
2—Baltimore A.L. vs. Los Angeles N.L., 1966.

Most 1-0 games won by both clubs, series
2—New York A.L. 1, Brooklyn N.L. 1, 1949.
Baltimore A.L. 2, Los Angeles N.L. 0, 1966.

WILD PITCHES AND BALKS

Most wild pitches, series
5—Pittsburgh N.L. vs. New York A.L., 1960.

Most wild pitches by both clubs, series
8—New York A.L. 4, Brooklyn N.L. 4, 1947.

Fewest wild pitches by both clubs, series
0—Made in series of all lengths.

Most balks, series
2—Cleveland A.L. vs. Boston N.L., 1948.
Minnesota A.L. vs. St. Louis N.L., 1987.

Most balks by both clubs, series
2—Cleveland A.L. 2, Boston N.L. 0, 1948.
Minnesota A.L. 2, St. Louis N.L. 0, 1987.
Los Angeles N.L. 1, Oakland A.L. 1, 1988.

Fewest balks by both clubs, series
0—Made in series of all lengths.

INDIVIDUAL FIELDING

FIRST BASEMEN
GAMES

Most games, career
38—Gil Hodges, Brooklyn N.L., 1949, 1952, 1953, 1955, 1956;
Los Angeles N.L., 1959; six series.

PUTOUTS, ASSISTS AND CHANCES ACCEPTED

Most putouts, career
326—Gil Hodges, Brooklyn N.L., 1949, 1952, 1953, 1955,
1956; Los Angeles N.L., 1959; six series, 38 games.

Most putouts, series
4-game series—52—Butch Schmidt, Boston N.L., 1914.
5-game series—69—Dick Hoblitzel, Boston A.L., 1916.
6-game series—79—Jiggs Donahue, Chicago A.L., 1906.
7-game series—79—Jim Bottomley, St. Louis N.L., 1926.
8-game series—92—Wally Pipp, New York A.L., 1921.

Most putouts, game
19—George Kelly, New York N.L., October 15, 1923.
Fred McGriff, Atlanta N.L., October 21, 1995.

Most putouts, inning
3—Held by many first basemen.

Most assists, career
29—Bill Skowron, New York A.L., 1955, 1956, 1957, 1958,
1960, 1961, 1962; Los Angeles N.L., 1963; eight series,
37 games.

Most assists, series
4-game series—6—Vic Wertz, Cleveland A.L., 1954.
Joe Pepitone, New York A.L., 1963.
5-game series—5—Claude Rossman, Detroit A.L., 1908.
Dolph Camilli, Brooklyn N.L., 1941.
Ray Sanders, St. Louis N.L., 1943.
Bill Skowron, New York A.L., 1961.
6-game series—9—Fred Merkle, Chicago N.L., 1918.
7-game series—10—Cecil Cooper, Milwaukee A.L., 1982.
8-game series—7—George Kelly, New York N.L., 1921.

Most assists, game
4—Marv Owen, Detroit A.L., October 6, 1935.
Don Mincher, Minnesota A.L., October 7, 1965.

Most assists, inning
2—Held by many first basemen.

Most chances accepted, career
350—Gil Hodges, Brooklyn N.L., 1949, 1952, 1953, 1955,
1956; Los Angeles N.L., 1959; six series, 38 games.

Most chances accepted, series
4-game series—55—Butch Schmidt, Boston N.L., 1914.
5-game series—73—Dick Hoblitzel, Boston A.L., 1916.

6-game series—87—Jiggs Donahue, Chicago A.L., 1906.
7-game series—81—Cecil Cooper, Milwaukee A.L., 1982.
8-game series—93—George Kelly, New York N.L., 1921.
Wally Pipp, New York A.L., 1921.

Most chances accepted, game
20—Fred McGriff, Atlanta N.L., October 21, 1995 (19 putouts, 1
assist).

Fewest chances offered, game
2—Wally Pipp, New York A.L., October 11, 1921 (2 putouts).
Orlando Cepeda, St. Louis N.L., October 2, 1968 (1 putout,
1 assist).

Most chances accepted, inning
3—Held by many first basemen.

ERRORS AND DOUBLE PLAYS

Most errors, career
8—Fred Merkle, New York N.L., 1911, 1912, 1913 (7); Brooklyn
N.L., 1916 (1), Chicago N.L., 1918 (0); five series,
26 games.

Most consecutive errorless games, career
32—Bill Skowron, New York A.L., Los Angeles N.L., October 10,
1956 through October 6, 1963.

Most errors, series
4-game series—2—Mark McGwire, Oakland A.L., 1990.
Brian R. Hunter, Atlanta N.L., 1999.
5-game series—3—Frank Chance, Chicago N.L., 1908.
Harry Davis, Philadelphia A.L., 1910.
6-game series—3—Hank Greenberg, Detroit A.L., 1935.
7-game series—5—Bill Abstein, Pittsburgh N.L., 1909.
8-game series—3—Fred Merkle, New York N.L., 1912.

Most chances accepted, errorless series
93—George Kelly, New York N.L., 1921 (8-game series).
Wally Pipp, New York A.L., 1921 (8-game series).

Most errors, game
2—Held by many first basemen.

Most errors, inning
2—Hank Greenberg, Detroit A.L., October 3, 1935, fifth inning.
Johnny McCarthy, New York N.L., October 8, 1937,
fifth inning.
Frank Torre, Milwaukee N.L., October 9, 1958, second inning.
Brian R. Hunter, Atlanta N.L., October 23, 1999, eighth inning.

Most double plays, career
31—Gil Hodges, Brooklyn N.L., 1949, 1952, 1953, 1955, 1956;
Los Angeles N.L., 1959; six series, 38 games.

Most double plays, series
11—Gil Hodges, Brooklyn N.L., 1955 (7-game series).

Most double plays started, series
3—Gil Hodges, Brooklyn N.L., 1955 (7-game series).

Most double plays, game
4—Stuffy McInnis, Philadelphia A.L., October 9, 1914.
Joe Collins, New York A.L., October 8, 1951.
Gene Tenace, Oakland A.L., October 17, 1973.
Pete Rose, Philadelphia N.L., October 15, 1980.

Most double plays started, game
2—Eddie Murray, Baltimore A.L., October 11, 1979.

Most unassisted double plays, game
1—Held by many first basemen.

SECOND BASEMEN
GAMES

Most games, career
42—Frankie Frisch, New York N.L. (18), 1922, 1923, 1924; St. Louis N.L. (24), 1928, 1930, 1931, 1934; seven series.

PUTOUTS, ASSISTS AND CHANCES ACCEPTED

Most putouts, career
104—Frankie Frisch, New York N.L., St. Louis N.L., 1922, 1923, 1924, 1928, 1930, 1931, 1934; seven series, 42 games.

Most putouts, series
4-game series—14—Willie Randolph, Oakland A.L., 1990.
5-game series—20—Joe Gordon, New York A.L., 1943.
6-game series—26—Dave Lopes, Los Angeles N.L., 1981.
7-game series—26—Bucky Harris, Washington A.L., 1924.
8-game series—22—Morrie Rath, Cincinnati N.L., 1919.

Most putouts, game
8—Bucky Harris, Washington A.L., October 8, 1924.
Dave Lopes, Los Angeles N.L., October 16, 1974.
(9—Hughie Critz, New York N.L., October 6, 1933, 11 innings.)

Most putouts, inning
3—Larry Doyle, New York N.L., October 9, 1913, seventh inning.
Bill Wambsganss, Cleveland A.L., October 10, 1920, fifth inning.
Johnny Rawlings, New York N.L., October 11, 1921, ninth inning.
Dave Lopes, Los Angeles N.L., October 16, 1974, sixth inning.
Dave Lopes, Los Angeles N.L., October 21, 1981, fourth inning.

Most assists, career
135—Frankie Frisch, New York N.L., St. Louis N.L., 1922, 1923, 1924, 1928, 1930, 1931, 1934; seven series, 42 games.

Most assists, series
4-game series—18—Tony Lazzeri, New York A.L., 1927.
5-game series—23—Joe Gordon, New York A.L., 1943.
6-game series—27—Aaron Ward, New York A.L., 1923.
7-game series—33—Jim Gantner, Milwaukee A.L., 1982.
8-game series—34—Aaron Ward, New York A.L., 1921.

Most assists, game
8—Claude Ritchey, Pittsburgh, N.L., October 10, 1903.
Germany Schaefer, Detroit A.L., October 12, 1907.
Hal Janvrin, Boston A.L., October 7, 1916.
Eddie Collins, Chicago A.L., October 15, 1917.
Bucky Harris, Washington A.L., October 7, 1924.
Joe Gordon, New York A.L., October 5, 1943.
Bobby Doerr, Boston A.L., October 9, 1946.
Mark Lemke, Atlanta N.L., October 21, 1995.

Most assists, inning
3—Eddie Collins, Philadelphia A.L., October 12, 1914, fourth inning.
Pete Kilduff, Brooklyn N.L., October 10, 1920, third inning.
Aaron Ward, New York A.L., October 12, 1921, sixth inning.
Joe Gordon, New York A.L., October 11, 1943, eighth inning.
Jackie Robinson, Brooklyn N.L., October 8, 1949, seventh inning.
Phil Garner, Pittsburgh N.L., October 13, 1979, ninth inning.

Marty Barrett, Boston A.L., October 23, 1986; first inning.

Most chances accepted, career
239—Frankie Frisch, New York N.L., St. Louis N.L., 1922, 1923, 1924, 1928, 1930, 1931, 1934; seven series, 42 games.

Most chances accepted, series
4-game series—28—Tony Lazzeri, New York A.L., 1927.
5-game series—43—Joe Gordon, New York A.L., 1943.
6-game series—40—Dave Lopes, Los Angeles N.L., 1981.
7-game series—54—Bucky Harris, Washington A.L., 1924.
8-game series—52—Eddie Collins, Chicago A.L., 1919.
Aaron Ward, New York A.L., 1921.

Most chances accepted, game
13—Claude Ritchey, Pittsburgh N.L., October 10, 1903 (5 putouts, 8 assists).
Bucky Harris, Washington A.L., October 11, 1925 (6 putouts, 7 assists).
Dave Lopes, Los Angeles N.L., October 16, 1974 (8 putouts, 5 assists).
(14—Hughie Critz, New York N.L., October 6, 1933 (9 putouts, 5 assists), 11 innings.)

Fewest chances offered, game
0—Charlie Pick, Chicago N.L., September 7, 1918.
Max Bishop, Philadelphia A.L., October 6, 1931.
Jerry Coleman, New York A.L., October 8, 1949.
Willie Randolph, New York A.L., October 25, 1981.
Frank White, Kansas City A.L., October 20, 1985.
Mariano Duncan, Cincinnati N.L., October 19, 1990.

Most chances accepted, inning
3—Held by many second basemen.

ERRORS AND DOUBLE PLAYS

Most errors, career
8—Larry Doyle, New York N.L., 1911, 1912, 1913; three series, 19 games.
Eddie Collins, Philadelphia A.L., 1910, 1911, 1913, 1914, Chicago A.L., 1917, 1919; six series, 34 games.

Most consecutive errorless games, career
23—Billy Martin, New York A.L., October 5, 1952 through October 10, 1956.

Most errors, series
4-game series—2—Tony Lazzeri, New York A.L., 1928.
Joe Gordon, New York A.L., 1938.
Billy Herman, Chicago N.L., 1938.
Joe Morgan, Cincinnati N.L., 1976.
5-game series—4—Danny Murphy, Philadelphia A.L., 1905.
6-game series—6—Dave Lopes, Los Angeles N.L., 1981.
7-game series—5—Jim Gantner, Milwaukee A.L., 1982.
8-game series—4—Larry Doyle, New York N.L., 1912.

Most chances accepted, errorless series
49—Bobby Doerr, Boston A.L., 1946 (7-game series).

Most errors, game
3—Danny Murphy, Philadelphia A.L., October 12, 1905.
Buddy Myer, Washington A.L., October 3, 1933.
Dave Lopes, Los Angeles N.L., October 25, 1981.

Most errors, inning
2—Danny Murphy, Philadelphia A.L., October 12, 1905, fifth inning.
Mike Andrews, Oakland A.L., October 14, 1973, 12th inning.
Dave Lopes, Los Angeles N.L., October 25, 1981, fourth inning.

Most double plays, career
24—Frankie Frisch, New York N.L., St. Louis N.L., 1922, 1923, 1924, 1928, 1930, 1931, 1934; seven series, 42 games.

Most double plays, series
9—Phil Garner, Pittsburgh N.L., 1979 (7-game series).

Most double plays started, series
5—Billy Herman, Chicago N.L., 1932 (4-game series).
Tom Herr, St. Louis N.L., 1985 (7-game series).

Most double plays, game
3—Held by many second basemen.

Most double plays started, game
3—Dick Green, Oakland A.L., October 15, 1974.

Most unassisted double plays, game
1—Hobe Ferris, Boston A.L., October 2, 1903.
Larry Doyle, New York N.L., October 9, 1913.
Buck Herzog, New York N.L., October 7, 1917.
Frank White, Kansas City A.L., October 17, 1980.
Mark Lemke, Atlanta N.L., October 27, 1991, 10 innings.

Unassisted triple play
1—Bill Wambsganss, Cleveland A.L., October 10, 1920.

THIRD BASEMEN
GAMES

Most games, career
31—Gil McDougald, New York A.L., 1951, 1952, 1953, 1955, 1960; five series.

PUTOUTS, ASSISTS AND CHANCES ACCEPTED

Most putouts, career
37—Home Run Baker, Philadelphia A.L., New York A.L., 1910, 1911, 1913, 1914, 1921; five series, 22 games.

Most putouts, series
4-game series—10—Home Run Baker, Philadelphia A.L., 1914.
5-game series—10—Harry Steinfeldt, Chicago N.L., 1907.
6-game series—14—Red Rolfe, New York A.L. 1936.
7-game series—13—Whitey Kurowski, St. Louis N.L., 1946.
8-game series—13—Frankie Frisch, New York N.L., 1921.

Most putouts, game
4—Art Devlin, New York N.L., October 13, 1905.
Bill Coughlin, Detroit A.L., October 10, 1907.
Bobby Byrne, Pittsburgh N.L., October 9, 1909.
Tommy Leach, Pittsburgh N.L., October 16, 1909.
Home Run Baker, Philadelphia A.L., October 24, 1911.
Heinie Zimmerman, New York N.L., October 7, 1917.
Jimmie Dykes, Philadelphia A.L., October 2, 1930.
Bob Elliott, Boston N.L., October 11, 1948.
Willie Jones, Philadelphia N.L. October 4, 1950.
Bill Mueller, Boston A.L., October 24, 2004.

Most putouts, inning
2—Held by many third basemen.

Most assists, career
68—Graig Nettles, New York A.L., 1976, 1977, 1978, 1981; San Diego N.L., 1984; five series, 24 games.

Most assists, series
4-game series—15—Home Run Baker, Philadelphia A.L., 1914.
5-game series—18—Larry Gardner, Boston A.L., 1916.
6-game series—20—Graig Nettles, New York A.L., 1977.
7-game series—30—Pinky Higgins, Detroit A.L., 1940.
8-game series—24—Frankie Frisch, New York N.L., 1921.

Most assists, game
9—Pinky Higgins, Detroit A.L., October 5, 1940.

Most assists, inning
3—Jose Pagan, Pittsburgh N.L., October 14, 1971, ninth inning.
Sal Bando, Oakland A.L., October 16, 1974, sixth inning.
Wade Boggs, Boston A.L., October 19, 1986, third inning.
Terry Pendleton, Atlanta N.L., October 27, 1991, seventh inning.

Most chances accepted, career
96—Graig Nettles, New York A.L., 1976, 1977, 1978, 1981; San Diego N.L., 1984; five series, 24 games.

Most chances accepted, series
4-game series—25—Home Run Baker, Philadelphia A.L., 1914.
5-game series—25—Larry Gardner, Boston A.L., 1916.
6-game series—27—Bobby Thomson, New York N.L., 1951.
7-game series—34—Pinky Higgins, Detroit A.L., 1940.

8-game series—37—Frankie Frisch, New York N.L., 1921.

Most chances accepted, game
10—Pinky Higgins, Detroit A.L., October 5, 1940 (1 putout, 9 assists).
Chris Sabo, Cincinnati N.L., October 19, 1990 (3 putouts, 7 assists).

Fewest chances offered, game
0—Held by many third basemen.

Most chances accepted, inning
4—Eddie Mathews, Milwaukee N.L., October 5, 1957, third inning.

ERRORS AND DOUBLE PLAYS

Most errors, career
8—Larry Gardner, Boston A.L., 1912, 1915, 1916 (6); Cleveland A.L., 1920 (2); four series, 25 games.

Most consecutive errorless games, career
22—Ron Cey, Los Angeles N.L., October 13, 1974 through October 28, 1981.

Most errors, series
4-game series—3—Bill Mueller, Boston A.L., 2004.
5-game series—4—Harry Steinfeldt, Chicago N.L., 1910.
6-game series—3—George Rohe, Chicago A.L., 1906.
Buck Herzog, New York N.L., 1911.
Travis Jackson, New York N.L., 1936.
Bob Elliott, Boston N.L., 1948.
Aaron Boone, New York N.L., 2003.
7-game series—4—Pepper Martin, St. Louis N.L., 1934.
Gil McDougald, New York A.L., 1952.
8-game series—4—Tommy Leach, Pittsburgh N.L., 1903.
Larry Gardner, Boston A.L., 1912.

Most chances accepted, errorless series
29—Denis Menke, Cincinnati N.L., 1972 (7-game series).

Most errors, game
3—Pepper Martin, St. Louis N.L., October 6, 1934.
Bill Mueller, Boston A.L., October 24, 2004.

Most errors, inning
2—Harry Steinfeldt, Chicago N.L., October 18, 1910, third inning.
Doug DeCinces, Baltimore A.L., October 10, 1979, sixth inning.

Most double plays, career
7—Graig Nettles, New York A.L., 1976, 1977, 1978, 1981; San Diego N.L., 1984; five series, 24 games.

Most double plays, series
4—Jim Davenport, San Francisco N.L., 1962 (7-game series).
Bill Madlock, Pittsburgh N.L., 1979 (7-game series).

Most double plays started, series
4—Jim Davenport, San Francisco N.L., 1962 (7-game series).

Most double plays, game
2—Held by many third basemen.

Most double plays started, game
2—Fred McMullin, Chicago A.L., October 13, 1917.
Ossie Bluege, Washington A.L., October 5, 1924.
Whitey Kurowski, St. Louis N.L., October 13, 1946.
Clete Boyer, New York A.L., October 12, 1960.
Dalton Jones, Boston A.L., October 4, 1967.
Graig Nettles, New York A.L., October 19, 1976.
Bobby Bonilla, Florida N.L., October 19, 1997.
Bill Mueller, Boston A.L., October 24, 2004.

Most unassisted double plays, game
1—Bill Mueller, Boston A.L., October 24, 2004.

SHORTSTOPS
GAMES

Most games, career
52—Phil Rizzuto, New York A.L., 1941, 1942, 1947, 1949, 1950, 1951, 1952, 1953, 1955; nine series.

PUTOUTS, ASSISTS AND CHANCES ACCEPTED

Most putouts, career
107—Phil Rizzuto, New York A.L., 1941, 1942, 1947, 1949,
1950, 1951, 1952, 1953, 1955; nine series, 52 games.

Most putouts, series
4-game series—16—Frank Crosetti, New York A.L., 1938.
5-game series—15—Joe Tinker, Chicago N.L., 1907.
Phil Rizzuto, New York A.L., 1942.
6-game series—16—Billy Jurges, Chicago N.L., 1935.
7-game series—22—Ozzie Smith, St. Louis N.L., 1982.
8-game series—24—Heinie Wagner, Boston A.L., 1912.

Most putouts, game
7—Buck Weaver, Chicago A.L., October 7, 1917.
Phil Rizzuto, New York A.L., October 5, 1942.

Most putouts, inning
3—Mickey Stanley, Detroit A.L., October 10, 1968, sixth inning.

Most assists, career
143—Phil Rizzuto, New York A.L., 1941, 1942, 1947, 1949,
1950, 1951, 1952, 1953, 1955; nine series, 52 games.

Most assists, series
4-game series—21—Jack Barry, Philadelphia A.L., 1914.
5-game series—25—Everett Scott, Boston A.L., 1916.
6-game series—26—Bill Russell, Los Angeles N.L., 1981.
7-game series—32—Tim Foli, Pittsburgh N.L., 1979.
8-game series—30—Freddy Parent, Boston A.L., 1903.

Most assists, game
9—Roger Peckinpaugh, New York A.L., October 5, 1921.
(10—Johnny Logan, Milwaukee N.L., October 6, 1957, 10
innings.)

Most assists, inning
3—Dave Bancroft, New York N.L., October 8, 1922, third inning.
Ossie Bluege, Washington, A.L., October 7, 1924,
sixth inning.
Glenn Wright, Pittsburgh N.L., October 8, 1927,
second inning.
Blondy Ryan, New York N.L., October 7, 1933, third inning.
Phil Rizzuto, New York A.L., October 3, 1942,
second inning.
Ernie Bowman, San Francisco N.L., October 8, 1962,
ninth inning.
Bud Harrelson, New York N.L., October 14, 1969, fifth inning.
Mark Belanger, Baltimore A.L., October 16, 1971,
seventh inning.
Bud Harrelson, New York N.L., October 13, 1973,
seventh inning.
Tim Foli, Pittsburgh N.L., October 12, 1979, second inning.

Most chances accepted, career
250—Phil Rizzuto, New York A.L., 1941, 1942, 1947, 1949,
1950, 1951, 1952, 1953, 1955; nine series, 52 games.

Most chances accepted, series
4-game series—27—Maury Wills, Los Angeles N.L., 1966.
5-game series—38—Joe Tinker, Chicago N.L., 1907.
6-game series—37—Phil Rizzuto, New York A.L., 1951.
7-game series—42—Charlie Gelbert, St. Louis N.L., 1931.
8-game series—51—Swede Risberg, Chicago A.L., 1919.

Most chances accepted, game
13—Buck Weaver, Chicago A.L., October 7, 1917 (7 putouts, 6
assists).

Fewest chances offered, game
0—Dave Bancroft, Philadelphia N.L., October 12, 1915 (fielded
eight innings).
Joe Boley, Philadelphia A.L., October 8, 1929.
Pee Wee Reese, Brooklyn N.L., October 1, 1947 (fielded
eight innings).
Phil Rizzuto, New York A.L., October 7, 1949.
Zoilo Versalles, Minnesota A.L., October 7, 1965 (fielded
eight innings).
Rico Petrocelli, Boston A.L., October 4, 1967.

Bert Campaneris, Oakland A.L., October 18, 1972.
Dave Concepcion, Cincinnati N.L., October 16, 1975.
Ozzie Smith, St. Louis N.L., October 23, 1985.
Omar Vizquel, Cleveland A.L., October 19, 1997.

Most chances accepted, inning
3—Held by many shortstops.

ERRORS AND DOUBLE PLAYS

Most errors, career
12—Art Fletcher, New York N.L., 1911, 1912, 1913, 1917; four
series, 25 games.

Most consecutive errorless games, career
26—Derek Jeter, New York A.L., October 26, 1996 through
October 23, 2003.

Most errors, series
4-game series—4—Frank Crosetti, New York A.L., 1932.
5-game series—4—Ivy Olson, Brooklyn N.L., 1916.
Woody English, Chicago N.L., 1929.
6-game series—4—Art Fletcher, New York N.L., 1911.
Buck Weaver, Chicago A.L., 1917.
7-game series—8—Roger Peckinpaugh, Washington A.L., 1925.
8-game series—6—Honus Wagner, Pittsburgh N.L., 1903.

Most chances accepted, errorless series
42—Charlie Gelbert, St. Louis N.L., 1931 (7-game series).

Most errors, game
3—Jack Barry, Philadelphia A.L., October 26, 1911.
Art Fletcher, New York N.L., October 9, 1912.
Buck Weaver, Chicago A.L., October 13, 1917.

Most errors, inning
2—Roger Peckinpaugh, Washington A.L., October 8, 1925,
eighth inning.
Woody English, Chicago N.L., October 8, 1929, ninth inning.
Dick Bartell, New York N.L., October 9, 1937, third inning.
Pee Wee Reese, Brooklyn N.L., October 2, 1941, eighth
inning.

Most double plays, career
32—Phil Rizzuto, New York A.L., 1941, 1942, 1947, 1949,
1950, 1951, 1952, 1953, 1955; nine series, 52 games.

Most double plays, series
8—Phil Rizzuto, New York A.L., 1951 (6-game series).

Most double plays started, series
7—Larry Bowa, Philadelphia N.L., 1980 (6-game series).

Most unassisted double plays, series
2—Joe Tinker, Chicago N.L., October 10, 11, 1907.

Most double plays, game
4—Phil Rizzuto, New York A.L., October 8, 1951.

Most double plays started, game
3—Phil Rizzuto, New York A.L., October 10, 1951.
Maury Wills, Los Angeles N.L., October 11, 1965.
Larry Bowa, Philadelphia N.L., October 15, 1980.

Most unassisted double plays, game
1—Joe Tinker, Chicago N.L., October 10, 1907
Joe Tinker, Chicago N.L., October 11, 1907.
Charlie Gelbert, St. Louis N.L., October 2, 1930.
Eddie Kasko, Cincinnati N.L., October 7, 1961.
(1—Greg Gagne, Minnesota A.L., October 26, 1991, 11
innings.)

OUTFIELDERS
GAMES

Most games, career
63—Mickey Mantle, New York A.L., 1951, 1952, 1953, 1955, 1956,
1957, 1958, 1960, 1961, 1962, 1963, 1964; 12 series.

PUTOUTS, ASSISTS AND CHANCES ACCEPTED

Most putouts, career
150—Joe DiMaggio, New York A.L., 1936, 1937, 1938, 1939, 1941, 1942, 1947, 1949, 1950, 1951; 10 series, 51 games.

Most putouts, series
4-game series—16—Earle Combs, New York A.L., 1927.
5-game series—20—Joe DiMaggio, New York A.L., 1942.
6-game series—24—Mickey Rivers, New York A.L., 1977.
7-game series—25—Dan Gladden, Minnesota A.L., 1991.
8-game series—30—Edd Roush, Cincinnati N.L., 1919.

Most putouts, game
8—Edd Roush, Cincinnati N.L., October 1, 1919.
George Foster, Cincinnati N.L., October 21, 1976.

Most putouts by left fielder, game
8—George Foster, Cincinnati N.L., October 21, 1976.

Most putouts by center fielder, game
8—Edd Roush, Cincinnati N.L., October 1, 1919.
(9—Amos Otis, Kansas City A.L., October 17, 1980, 10 innings.)

Most putouts by right fielder, game
7—Red Murray, New York N.L., October 14, 1912.
Bing Miller, Philadelphia A.L., October 5, 1930.
Ray Blades, St. Louis N.L., October 5, 1930.
Tony Oliva, Minnesota A.L., October 6, 1965.
Al Kaline, Detroit A.L., October 9, 1968.
Frank Robinson, Baltimore A.L., October 14, 1969.

Most consecutive putouts, game
4—Mike Donlin, New York N.L., October 13, 1905 (1 in third inning, 3 in fourth inning, center field).
Dode Paskert, Philadelphia N.L., October 11, 1915 (3 in fourth inning, 1 in fifth inning, center field).
Charlie Keller, New York A.L., October 1, 1941 (1 in second inning, 3 in third inning, left field).
Monte Irvin, New York N.L., September 29, 1954 (1 in eighth inning, 3 in ninth inning, left field; Irvin dropped fly for error after second putout in ninth inning).
Tommie Agee, New York N.L., October 14, 1969 (3 in seventh inning, 1 in eighth inning, center field).
Ben Oglivie, Milwaukee A.L., October 19, 1982 (1 in sixth inning, 3 in seventh inning, left field).

Most putouts by left fielder, inning
3—Charlie Keller, New York A.L., October 1, 1941, third inning.
Monte Irvin, New York N.L., September 29, 1954, ninth inning.
Tommy Davis, Los Angeles N.L., October 3, 1963, seventh inning.
Ben Oglivie, Milwaukee A.L., October 19, 1982, seventh inning.
Deion Sanders, Atlanta N.L., October 22, 1992, fifth inning.

Most putouts by center fielder, inning
3—Mike Donlin, New York N.L., October 13, 1905, fourth inning.
Dode Paskert, Philadelphia N.L., October 11, 1915, fourth inning.
Ernie Orsatti, St. Louis N.L., October 8, 1934, fifth inning.
Joe DiMaggio, New York A.L., October 2, 1936, ninth inning, and October 7, 1937, sixth inning.
Roger Maris, New York A.L., October 11, 1964, third inning.
Reggie Smith, Boston A.L., October 11, 1967, seventh inning.
Tommie Agee, New York N.L., October 14, 1969, seventh inning.
Willie McGee, St. Louis N.L., October 22, 1987, eighth inning.
Andruw Jones, Atlanta N.L., October 24, 1999, seventh inning.
Kenny Lofton, San Francisco N.L., October 22, 2002, seventh inning.

Most putouts by right fielder, inning
3—Mel Ott, New York N.L., October 4, 1933, seventh inning.
Bob Hazle, Milwaukee N.L., October 10, 1957, fourth inning.
Ron Swoboda, New York N.L., October 15, 1969, ninth inning.
Charlie Moore, Milwaukee A.L., October 12, 1982, eighth inning.

Most assists, career
5—Harry Hooper, Boston A.L., 1912, 1915, 1916, 1918; four series, 24 games.
Ross Youngs, New York N.L., 1921, 1922, 1923, 1924; four series, 26 games.

Most games by outfielder with no assists, career
51—Joe DiMaggio, New York A.L., 1936, 1937, 1938, 1939, 1941, 1942, 1947, 1949, 1950, 1951; 10 series.

Most assists, series
4-game series—2—Joe Connally, Boston, N.L., 1914.
5-game series—2—Held by many outfielders.
6-game series—2—Held by many outfielders.
7-game series—4—Edgar Rice, Washington A.L., 1924.
8-game series—3—Patsy Dougherty, Boston A.L., 1903.
Harry Hooper, Boston A.L., 1912.
Edd Roush, Cincinnati N.L., 1919.

Most assists, game
2—Held by many outfielders.

Most chances accepted, career
150—Joe DiMaggio, New York A.L., 1936, 1937, 1938, 1939, 1941, 1942, 1947, 1949, 1950, 1951; 10 series, 51 games.

Most chances accepted, series
4-game series—16—Earle Combs, New York A.L., 1927.
5-game series—20—Joe DiMaggio, New York A.L., 1942.
6-game series—25—Mickey Rivers, New York A.L., 1977.
7-game series—26—Andy Pafko, Chicago N.L., 1945.
Dan Gladden, Minnesota A.L., 1991.
8-game series—33—Edd Roush, Cincinnati N.L., 1919.

Most chances accepted by left fielder, game
8—George Foster, Cincinnati N.L., October 21, 1976 (8 putouts).

Most chances accepted by center fielder, game
8—Edd Roush, Cincinnati N.L., October 1, 1919 (8 putouts).
Hank Leiber, New York N.L., October 2, 1936 (7 putouts, 1 assist).
(9—Edd Roush, Cincinnati N.L., October 7, 1919 (seven putouts, two assists), 10 innings.
Amos Otis, Kansas City A.L., October 17, 1980 (nine putouts), 10 innings.)

Most chances accepted by right fielder, game
7—Red Murray, New York N.L., October 14, 1912 (7 putouts).
Bing Miller, Philadelphia A.L., October 5, 1930 (7 putouts).
Ray Blades, St. Louis N.L., October 5, 1930 (7 putouts).
Tony Oliva, Minnesota A.L., October 6, 1965 (7 putouts).
Al Kaline, Detroit A.L., October 9, 1968 (7 putouts).
Frank Robinson, Baltimore A.L., October 14, 1969 (7 putouts).

Longest game with no chances offered
12 innings—Ty Cobb, Detroit A.L., right field, October 8, 1907 (right field).
Earl McNeely, Washington A.L., October 10, 1924 (center field).
Joe Medwick, St. Louis N.L., October 4, 1934 (played 11.1 innings in left field).
Don Hahn, New York N.L., October 14, 1973 (center and right field).
Cleon Jones, New York N.L., October 14, 1973 (left field).
Ken Griffey Sr., Cincinnati N.L., October 21, 1975 (played 11 innings in right field).

Most chances accepted, inning
3—Held by many outfielders.

ERRORS AND DOUBLE PLAYS

Most errors, career
4—Ross Youngs, New York N.L., 1921, 1922, 1923, 1924; four series, 26 games.

Most consecutive errorless games, career
45—Joe DiMaggio, New York A.L., October 6, 1937 through October 10, 1951.

Most errors, series
4-game series—3—Willie Davis, Los Angeles N.L., 1966.

5-game series—2—Held by many outfielders.
6-game series—3—Red Murray, New York N.L., 1911.
Shano Collins, Chicago A.L., 1917.
7-game series—2—Zack Wheat, Brooklyn N.L., 1920.
Ernie Orsatti, St. Louis N.L., 1934.
Goose Goslin, Detroit A.L., 1934.
Mickey Mantle, New York A.L., 1964.
Jim Northrup, Detroit A.L., 1968.
8-game series—2—Held by many outfielders.

Most chances accepted, errorless series
25—Mickey Rivers, New York A.L., 1977 (6-game series).

Most errors, game
3—Willie Davis, Los Angeles N.L., October 6, 1966.

Most errors, inning
3—Willie Davis, Los Angeles N.L., October 6, 1966, fifth inning.

Most double plays, career
2—Held by many outfielders.

Most double plays, series
2—Danny Murphy, Philadelphia A.L., 1910 (5-game series).
Tris Speaker, Boston A.L., 1912 (8-game series).
Edd Roush, Cincinnati N.L., 1919 (8-game series).
Elston Howard, New York A.L., 1958 (7-game series).

Most double plays started, series
2—Danny Murphy, Philadelphia A.L., 1910 (5-game series).
Tris Speaker, Boston A.L., 1912 (8-game series).
Edd Roush, Cincinnati N.L., 1919 (8-game series).
Elston Howard, New York A.L., 1958 (7-game series).

Most double plays, game
1—Accomplished by many outfielders.
(2—Edd Roush, Cincinnati N.L., October 7, 1919, 10 innings.)

Most double plays started, game
1—Accomplished by many outfielders.
(2—Edd Roush, Cincinnati N.L., October 7, 1919, 10 innings.)

Most unassisted double plays, game
1—Tris Speaker, Boston A.L., October 15, 1912.

CATCHERS
GAMES

Most games, career
63—Yogi Berra, New York A.L., 1947, 1949, 1950, 1951, 1952, 1953, 1955, 1956, 1957, 1958, 1960, 1962; 12 series.

PUTOUTS, ASSISTS AND CHANCES ACCEPTED

Most putouts, career
421—Yogi Berra, New York A.L., 1947, 1949, 1950, 1951, 1952, 1953, 1955, 1956, 1957, 1958, 1960, 1962; 12 series, 63 games.

Most putouts, series
4-game series—43—John Roseboro, Los Angeles N.L., 1963.
5-game series—59—Mickey Cochrane, Philadelphia A.L., 1929.
6-game series—55—Walker Cooper, St. Louis N.L., 1944.
7-game series—69—Jorge Posada, New York A.L., 2001.
8-game series—54—Lou Criger, Boston A.L., 1903.

Most putouts, game
18—John Roseboro, Los Angeles N.L., October 2, 1963 (15 strikeouts).

Fewest putouts, game
1—Held by many catchers.

Most putouts, inning
3—Held by many catchers.

Most assists, career
36—Yogi Berra, New York A.L., 1947, 1949, 1950, 1951, 1952, 1953, 1955, 1956, 1957, 1958, 1960, 1962; 12 series, 63 games.

Most assists, series
4-game series—7—Thurman Munson, New York A.L., 1976.
5-game series—9—Boss Schmidt, Detroit A.L., 1907.
Johnny Kling, Chicago N.L., 1907.
Ed Burns, Philadelphia N.L., 1915.
6-game series—12—Chief Meyers, New York N.L., 1911.
7-game series—11—Boss Schmidt, Detroit A.L., 1909.
8-game series—15—Ray Schalk, Chicago A.L., 1919.

Most assists, game
4—Johnny Kling, Chicago N.L., October 9, 1907.
Boss Schmidt, Detroit A.L., October 11, 1907.
Boss Schmidt, Detroit A.L., October 14, 1908.
George Gibson, Pittsburgh N.L., October 12, 1909.
Bill Rariden, New York N.L., October 10, 1917.
Sam Agnew, Boston A.L., September 6, 1918.
Bill DeLancey, St. Louis N.L., October 8, 1934.
(6—Jack Lapp, Philadelphia A.L., October 17, 1911, 11 innings.)

Most assists, inning
2—Held by many catchers.

Most chances accepted, career
457—Yogi Berra, New York A.L., 1947, 1949, 1950, 1951, 1952, 1953, 1955, 1956, 1957, 1958, 1960, 1962; 12 series, 63 games.

Most chances accepted, series
4-game series—43—John Roseboro, Los Angeles N.L., 1963.
5-game series—61—Mickey Cochrane, Philadelphia A.L., 1929.
6-game series—56—Johnny Kling, Chicago N.L., 1906.
Roy Campanella, Brooklyn N.L., 1953.
7-game series—73—Jorge Posada, New York A.L., 2001.
8-game series—62—Lou Criger, Boston A.L., 1903.

Most chances accepted, game
18—John Roseboro, Los Angeles N.L., October 2, 1963, (18 putouts, 15 strikeouts).
Tim McCarver, St. Louis N.L., October 2, 1968 (17 putouts, 1 assist, 17 strikeouts).

Fewest chances offered, game
1—Wally Schang, Philadelphia A.L., October 11, 1913 (strikeout).
Wally Schang, New York A.L., October 11, 1923 (strikeout).
Muddy Ruel, Washington A.L., October 5, 1924 (strikeout).
Mickey Cochrane, Detroit A.L., October 6, 1934 (strikeout).
Gabby Hartnett, Chicago N.L., October 2, 1935 (strikeout).
Sherm Lollar, Chicago A.L., October 6, 1959 (strikeout).
Elston Howard, New York A.L., October 6, 1960.
(0—Benito Santiago, San Francisco N.L., October 20, 2002, caught eight innings.)

Most chances accepted, inning
4—Tim McCarver, St. Louis N.L., October 9, 1967, ninth inning (3 putouts, 1 assist; 2 strikeouts).

ERRORS AND PASSED BALLS

Most errors, career
7—Boss Schmidt, Detroit A.L., 1907, 1908, 1909; three series, 13 games.

Most consecutive errorless games, career
30—Yogi Berra, New York A.L., October 4, 1952 through October 9, 1957.

Most errors, series
4-game series—3—Joe Oliver, Cincinnati N.L., 1990.
5-game series—2—Boss Schmidt, Detroit A.L., 1907.
Walker Cooper, St. Louis N.L., 1943.
Joe Ferguson, Los Angeles N.L., 1974.
6-game series—2—Ray Schalk, Chicago A.L., 1917.
7-game series—5—Boss Schmidt, Detroit A.L., 1909.
8-game series—3—Lou Criger, Boston A.L., 1909.

Most chances accepted, errorless series
71—Jerry Grote, New York N.L., 1973 (7-game series).

Most errors, game
2—Lou Criger, Boston A.L., October 1, 1903.
Jimmie Wilson, St. Louis N.L., October 7, 1928.

Joe Ferguson, Los Angeles N.L., October 15, 1974.
Carlton Fisk, Boston A.L., October 14, 1975, 9.1 innings.

Most errors, inning
2—Lou Criger, Boston A.L., October 1, 1903, first inning.
Jimmie Wilson, St. Louis N.L., October 7, 1928, sixth inning.

Most passed balls, career
5—Johnny Kling, Chicago N.L., 1906 (3), 1907, 1908.

Most passed balls, series
3—Johnny Kling, Chicago N.L., 1906.
Smoky Burgess, Pittsburgh N.L., 1960.
Elston Howard, New York A.L., 1964.

Most passed balls, game
2—Johnny Kling, Chicago N.L., October 9, 1906.
Bill Killefer, Chicago N.L., September 9, 1918.
Paul Richards, Detroit A.L., October 3, 1945.
Bruce Edwards, Brooklyn N.L., October 4, 1947.
Smoky Burgess, Pittsburgh N.L., October 6, 1960.
Elston Howard, New York A.L., October 7, 1964.

Most passed balls, inning
1—Held by many catchers.

DOUBLE PLAYS, RUNNERS CAUGHT STEALING

Most double plays, career
6—Yogi Berra, New York A.L., 1947, 1949, 1950, 1951, 1952,
1953, 1955, 1956, 1957, 1958, 1960, 1962; 12 series,
63 games.
Johnny Bench, Cincinnati N.L., 1970 (1), 1972 (2), 1975
(3), 1976 (0); four series, 23 games.

Most double plays, series
3—Johnny Kling, Chicago N.L., 1906 (6-game series).
Boss Schmidt, Detroit A.L., 1909 (7-game series).
Wally Schang, New York A.L., 1921 (8-game series).
Johnny Bench, Cincinnati N.L., 1975 (7 game series).

Most double plays started, series
3—Wally Schang, New York A.L., 1921 (8-game series).

Most double plays, game
2—Boss Schmidt, Detroit A.L., October 14, 1909.
Wally Schang, New York A.L., October 11, 1921.
Gabby Hartnett, Chicago N.L., September 29, 1932.
Del Rice, Milwaukee N.L., October 9, 1957.
Rich Gedman, Boston A.L., October 22, 1986.

Most double plays started, game
2—Boss Schmidt, Detroit A.L., October 14, 1909.
Wally Schang, New York A.L., October 11, 1921.

Most unassisted double plays, game
Never accomplished.

Most runners caught stealing, career
20—Wally Schang, Philadelphia A.L., 1913, 1914; Boston A.L.,
1918; New York A.L., 1921, 1922, 1923, six series,
32 games.

Most runners caught stealing, series
10—Ray Schalk, Chicago A.L., 1919 (8-game series).

Most runners caught stealing, game
3—Performed nine times by eight catchers. Last time—Terry
Steinbach, Oakland A.L., October 19, 1988.
(5—Jack Lapp, Philadelphia A.L., October 17, 1911, 11
innings.)

Most runners caught stealing, inning
2—Jack Lapp, Philadelphia A.L., October 17, 1911, 10th inning.
Aaron Robinson, New York A.L., October 6, 1947, first inning.
Bill Carrigan, Boston A.L., October 9, 1912, 11th inning.
Roy Campanella, Brooklyn N.L., October 2, 1952,
first inning.

PITCHERS
GAMES

Most games, career
22—Whitey Ford, New York A.L., 1950, 1953, 1955, 1956,
1957, 1958, 1960, 1961, 1962, 1963, 1964; 11 series.

Most games, series
4-game series—4—Jeff Nelson, New York A.L., 1999, 2.2
innings.
5-game series—5—Mike G. Marshall, Los Angeles N.L., 1974,
nine innings.
6-game series—6—Dan Quisenberry, Kansas City A.L., 1980,
10.1 innings.
7-game series—7—Darold Knowles, Oakland A.L., 1973,
6.1 innings.
8-game series—5—Deacon Phillippe, Pittsburgh N.L., 1903,
44 innings.

PUTOUTS, ASSISTS AND CHANCES ACCEPTED

Most putouts, career
11—Whitey Ford, New York A.L., 1950, 1953, 1955, 1956,
1957, 1958, 1960, 1961, 1962, 1963, 1964; 11 series,
22 games.

Most putouts, series
4-game series—3—Whitey Ford, New York A.L., 1963.
5-game series—5—Jack Morris, Detroit, A.L., 1984.
6-game series—6—Nick Altrock, Chicago A.L., 1906.
Hippo Vaughn, Chicago N.L., 1918.
7-game series—5—Jim Kaat, Minnesota A.L., 1965.
8-game series—2—Deacon Phillippe, Pittsburgh N.L., 1903.
Phil Douglas, New York N.L., 1921.

Most putouts, game
5—Jim Kaat, Minnesota A.L., October 7, 1965.

Most putouts, inning
2—Johnny Beazley, St. Louis N.L., October 5, 1942, eighth inning.
Bob Turley, New York A.L., October 9, 1957, seventh inning.
Whitey Ford, New York A.L., October 8, 1960, ninth inning.
Bob Purkey, Cincinnati N.L., October 7, 1961, ninth inning.
John Denny, Philadelphia N.L., October 15, 1983, fifth inning.
Dave Stewart, Oakland A.L., October 16, 1990, third inning.

Most assists, career
34—Christy Mathewson, New York N.L., 1905, 1911, 1912,
1913; four series, 11 games.

Most assists, series
4-game series—5—Joe Bush, Philadelphia A.L., 1914.
Lefty Tyler, Boston N.L., 1914.
Bill James, Boston N.L., 1914.
Wilcy Moore, New York A.L., 1927.
Monte Pearson, New York A.L., 1939.
5-game series—10—Mordecai Brown, Chicago N.L., 1910.
6-game series—12—Mordecai Brown, Chicago N.L., 1906.
7-game series—12—George Mullin, Detroit A.L., 1909.
8-game series—12—Christy Mathewson, New York N.L., 1912.

Most assists, game
8—Nick Altrock, Chicago A.L., October 12, 1906.
Lon Warneke, Chicago N.L., October 2, 1935.

Most assists, inning
3—Eddie Plank, Philadelphia A.L., October 13, 1905,
eighth inning.
Rube Marquard, New York N.L., October 7, 1913,
fourth inning.
Lon Warneke, Chicago N.L., October 2, 1935, third inning.
Johnny Murphy, New York A.L., October 8, 1939,
eighth inning.
Bob Rush, Milwaukee N.L., October 4, 1958, third inning.

Most chances accepted, career
40—Christy Mathewson, New York N.L., 1905, 1911, 1912,
1913; four series, 11 games.

Most chances accepted, series
4-game series—6—Lefty Tyler, Boston N.L., 1914.
    Red Ruffing, New York A.L., 1938.
5-game series—10—Christy Mathewson, New York N.L., 1905.
    Mordecai Brown, Chicago N.L., 1910.
6-game series—17—Nick Altrock, Chicago A.L., 1906.
    Hippo Vaughn, Chicago N.L., 1918.
7-game series—12—George Mullin, Detroit A.L., 1909.
8-game series—13—Christy Mathewson, New York N.L., 1912.

Most chances accepted, game
11—Nick Altrock, Chicago A.L., October 12, 1906 (3 putouts, 8 assists).

Most chances accepted, inning
3—Held by many pitchers.

ERRORS AND DOUBLE PLAYS

Most errors, career
3—Deacon Phillippe, Pittsburgh N.L., 1903, 1909; two series, seven games.
    Ed Cicotte, Chicago A.L., 1917, 1919; two series, six games.
    Max Lanier, St. Louis N.L., 1942, 1943, 1944; three series, seven games.

Most errors, series
4-game series—1—Held by many pitchers.
5-game series—2—Jack Coombs, Philadelphia A.L., 1910.
    Max Lanier, St. Louis N.L., 1942.
6-game series—2—Nels Potter, St. Louis A.L., 1944.
7-game series—2—Deacon Phillippe, Pittsburgh N.L., 1909.
    Allie Reynolds, New York A.L., 1952.
8-game series—2—Ed Cicotte, Chicago A.L., 1919.

Most chances accepted, errorless series
17—Nick Altrock, Chicago A.L., 1906 (6-game series).
    Hippo Vaughn, Chicago N.L., 1918 (6-game series).

Most errors, game
2—Deacon Phillippe, Pittsburgh N.L., October 12, 1909.

Jack Coombs, Philadelphia A.L., October 18, 1910.
Ed Cicotte, Chicago A.L., October 4, 1919.
Max Lanier, St. Louis N.L., September 30, 1942.
Nels Potter, St. Louis A.L., October 5, 1944.

Most errors, inning
2—Jack Coombs, Philadelphia A.L., October 18, 1910, fifth inning.
    Ed Cicotte, Chicago A.L., October 4, 1919, fifth inning.
    Max Lanier, St. Louis N.L., September 30, 1942, ninth inning.
    Nels Potter, St. Louis A.L., October 5, 1944, third inning.

Most consecutive errorless games, career
20—Mike Stanton, Atlanta N.L., New York A.L., October 19, 1991 through November 4, 2001.

Most double plays, career
3—Chief Bender, Philadelphia A.L., 1905, 1910, 1911, 1913, 1914; five series, 10 games.
    Joe Bush, Philadelphia A.L., Boston A.L., New York A.L., 1913, 1914, 1918, 1922, 1923; five series, nine games.
    Allie Reynolds, New York A.L., 1947, 1949, 1950, 1951, 1952, 1953; six series, 15 games.

Most double plays, series
2—Held by many pitchers.

Most double plays started, series
2—Held by many pitchers.

Most double plays, game
2—Chief Bender, Philadelphia A.L., October 9, 1914.
    Joe Bush, New York A.L., October 8, 1922.
    Allie Reynolds, New York A.L., October 8, 1951

Most double plays started, game
2—Chief Bender, Philadelphia A.L., October 9, 1914.
    Joe Bush, New York A.L., October 8, 1922.
    Allie Reynolds, New York A.L., October 8, 1951.

Most unassisted double plays, nine-inning game
Never accomplished

CLUB FIELDING

AVERAGE

Highest fielding average, series
4-game series—1.000—Baltimore A.L. vs. Los Angeles N.L., 1966.
5-game series—1.000—New York A.L. vs. New York N.L., 1937.
6-game series—.996—Boston A.L. vs. Chicago N.L., 1918.
    St. Louis N.L. vs. St. Louis A.L., 1944.
    Los Angeles N.L. vs. New York A.L., 1977.
7-game series—.993—Cincinnati N.L. vs. Boston A.L., 1975.
8-game series—.984—New York N.L. vs. New York A.L., 1921.

For a list of fielding statistics by teams each series, see page 508.

Highest fielding average by both clubs, series
4-game series—.986—New York A.L. .993, Los Angeles N.L. .979, 1963.
5-game series—.986—Oakland A.L. .989, Los Angeles N.L. .983, 1988.
6-game series—.991—Los Angeles N.L. .996, New York A.L. .987, 1977.
7-game series—.990—St. Louis N.L. .992, Kansas City A.L. .989, 1985.
8-game series—.983—New York N.L. .984, New York A.L. .981, 1921.

Lowest fielding average, series
4-game series—.949—New York A.L. vs. Chicago N.L., 1932.
5-game series—.942—Brooklyn N.L. vs. Boston A.L., 1916.
6-game series—.938—New York N.L. vs. Philadelphia A.L., 1911.
7-game series—.934—Detroit A.L. vs. Pittsburgh N.L., 1909.
8-game series—.944—Pittsburgh N.L. vs. Boston A.L., 1903.

Lowest fielding average by both clubs, series
4-game series—.954—Chicago N.L. .959, New York A.L. .949, 1932.
5-game series—.946—Philadelphia A.L. .947, Chicago N.L. .946, 1910.
6-game series—.947—Philadelphia A.L. .956, New York N.L. .938, 1911.
7-game series—.941—Pittsburgh N.L. .947, Detroit A.L. .934, 1909.
8-game series—.951—Boston A.L. .957, Pittsburgh N.L. .944, 1903.

PUTOUTS

Most putouts, total series
5,763—New York A.L.; 39 series, 219 games.

Most putouts, series
4-game series—117—Boston N.L. vs. Philadelphia A.L., 1914.
5-game series—147—Boston A.L. vs. Brooklyn N.L., 1916.
6-game series—168—New York A.L. vs. Los Angeles N.L., 1977.
    Florida N.L. vs. New York A.L., 2003.
7-game series—202—Minnesota A.L. vs. Atlanta N.L., 1991.
8-game series—222—Boston A.L. vs. New York N.L., 1912.

Most putouts by both clubs, series
4-game series—228
    Boston N.L. 117, Philadelphia A.L. 111, 1914.
5-game series—289
    Boston A.L. 147, Brooklyn N.L. 142, 1916.
6-game series—333
    New York A.L. 168, Los Angeles N.L. 165, 1977.
    Florida N.L. 168, New York A.L. 165, 2003.
7-game series—401
    Washington A.L. 201, New York N.L. 200, 1924.

8-game series—443
Boston A.L. 222, New York N.L. 221, 1912.

Fewest putouts, series
4-game series—102
St. Louis N.L. vs. New York A.L., 1928.
Chicago N.L. vs. New York A.L., 1932.
Chicago N.L. vs. New York A.L., 1938.
New York A.L. vs. Los Angeles N.L., 1963.
Los Angeles N.L. vs. Baltimore A.L., 1966.
San Francisco N.L. vs. Oakland A.L., 1989.
San Diego N.L. vs. New York A.L., 1998.
St. Louis N.L. vs. Boston A.L., 2004.
5-game series—126
Los Angeles N.L. vs. Oakland A.L., 1974.
San Diego N.L. vs. Detroit A.L., 1984.
6-game series—153
New York N.L. vs. Chicago A.L., 1917.
St. Louis N.L. vs. Philadelphia A.L., 1930.
New York A.L. vs. Los Angeles N.L., 1981.
7-game series—177
Brooklyn N.L. vs. Cleveland A.L., 1920.
St. Louis N.L. vs. Minnesota A.L., 1987.
8-game series—210
Pittsburgh N.L. vs. Boston A.L., 1903.
New York A.L. vs. New York N.L., 1921.

Fewest putouts by both clubs, series
4-game series—210
New York A.L. 108, St. Louis N.L. 102, 1928.
New York A.L. 108, Chicago N.L. 102, 1932.
New York A.L. 108, Chicago N.L. 102, 1938.
Los Angeles N.L. 108, New York A.L. 102, 1963.
Baltimore A.L. 108, Los Angeles N.L. 102, 1966.
Oakland A.L. 108, San Francisco N.L. 102, 1989.
New York A.L. 108, San Diego N.L. 102, 1998.
Boston A.L. 108, St. Louis N.L. 102, 2004.
5-game series—258
Oakland A.L. 132, Los Angeles N.L. 126, 1974.
Detroit A.L. 132, San Diego N.L. 126, 1984.
6-game series—309
Chicago A.L. 156, New York N.L. 153, 1917.
Philadelphia A.L. 156, St. Louis N.L. 153, 1930.
Los Angeles N.L. 156, New York A.L. 153, 1981.
7-game series—357
Minnesota A.L. 180, St. Louis N.L 177, 1987.
8-game series—422
New York N.L. 212, New York A.L. 210, 1921.

Most putouts by outfield, game
15—New York N.L. vs. Boston A.L., October 14, 1912.
Boston N.L. vs. Cleveland A.L., October 6, 1948.
(16—Brooklyn N.L. vs. New York A.L., October 5, 1952,
11 innings.)

Most putouts by outfields of both clubs, game
23—Pittsburgh N.L. 13, New York A.L. 10, October 6, 1927.
(23—Brooklyn N.L. 16, New York A.L. 7, October 5, 1952,
11 innings.)

Fewest putouts by outfield, game
0—New York N.L. vs. New York A.L., October 5, 1921.
New York N.L. vs. New York A.L., September 30, 1936.
Cleveland A.L. vs. Atlanta N.L., October 21, 1995 (fielded
eight innings).
(1—New York N.L. vs. Oakland A.L., October 14, 1973, 12
innings.)

Fewest putouts by outfields of both clubs, game
2—Atlanta N.L. 2, Cleveland A.L. 0, October 21, 1995
(Cleveland fielded eight innings).
3—New York A.L. 2, Brooklyn N.L. 1, October 10, 1956.

Most putouts by outfield, inning
3—Made in many games.

Most putouts by outfields of both clubs, inning
6—Kansas City A.L. 3, St. Louis N.L. 3, October 27, 1985,
seventh inning.

Most putouts by catchers of both clubs, inning
6—Chicago A.L. 3, Cincinnati N.L. 3, October 6, 1919,
second inning.
Cincinnati N.L. 3, Oakland A.L. 3, October 18, 1972,
fifth inning.

St. Louis N.L. 3, Kansas City A.L. 3, October 24, 1985,
seventh inning.
New York N.L. 3, New York A.L. 3, October 24, 2000, second inning.

ASSISTS

Most assists, total series
2,312—New York A.L.; 39 series, 219 games.

Most assists, series
4-game series—67—Philadelphia A.L. vs. Boston N.L., 1914.
5-game series—90—Boston A.L. vs. Brooklyn N.L., 1916.
6-game series—99—Chicago A.L. vs. Chicago N.L., 1906.
7-game series—99—Washington A.L. vs. New York N.L., 1924.
St. Louis N.L. vs. New York A.L., 1926.
8-game series—116—Chicago A.L. vs. Cincinnati N.L., 1919.

Most assists by both clubs, series
4-game series—129—Philadelphia A.L. 67, Boston N.L. 62, 1914.
5-game series—160—Boston A.L. 90, Brooklyn N.L. 70, 1916.
6-game series—183—Chicago A.L. 99, Chicago N.L. 84, 1906.
7-game series—193—Washington A.L. 99, New York N.L.
94, 1924.
8-game series—212—Chicago A.L. 116, Cincinnati N.L. 96, 1919.

Fewest assists, series
4-game series—28—New York A.L. vs. St. Louis N.L., 1928.
5-game series—36—Los Angeles N.L. vs. Oakland A.L., 1988.
6-game series—41—Philadelphia A.L. vs. St. Louis N.L., 1930.
7-game series—48—St. Louis N.L. vs. Detroit A.L., 1968.
8-game series—96—Pittsburgh N.L. vs. Boston A.L., 1903.
Cincinnati N.L. vs. Chicago A.L., 1919.

Fewest assists by both clubs, series
4-game series—64—St. Louis N.L. 36, New York A.L. 28, 1928.
5-game series—79—Oakland A.L. 43, Los Angeles N.L. 36, 1988.
6-game series—96—St. Louis N.L. 55, Philadelphia A.L. 41, 1930.
7-game series—120—Detroit A.L. 72, St. Louis N.L. 48, 1968.
8-game series—198—Boston A.L. 102, Pittsburgh N.L. 96, 1903.

Most assists, game
21—Chicago A.L. vs. New York N.L., October 7, 1917.
Boston A.L. vs. Chicago N.L., September 9, 1910.

Most assists by both clubs, game
38—Chicago A.L. 20, Chicago N.L. 18, October 12, 1906.

Fewest assists, game
2—St. Louis N.L. vs. Detroit A.L., October 2, 1968.

Fewest assists by both clubs, game
8—Philadelphia A.L. 5, St. Louis N.L. 3, October 2, 1930.
Boston A.L. 5, Cincinnati N.L. 3, October 16, 1975.

Fewest assists by infield, game
1—St. Louis N.L. vs. Detroit A.L., October 2, 1968.

Most assists by outfield, inning
2—Boston A.L. vs. St. Louis N.L., October 10, 1946, fifth inning.

CHANCES OFFERED

Fewest chances offered to outfield, game
0—New York N.L. vs. New York A.L., September 30, 1936.
Cleveland A.L. vs. Atlanta N.L., October 21, 1995 (fielded
eight innings.
(1—New York N.L. vs. Oakland A.L., October 14, 1973,
12 innings.)

Fewest chances offered to outfield by both clubs, game
2—Atlanta N.L. 2, Cleveland A.L. 0, October 21, 1995
(Cleveland fielded eight innings).
3—New York A.L., 2, Brooklyn N.L., 1, October 10, 1956.

Fewest chances offered to infield, game (excluding first base)
2—Philadelphia A.L. vs. St. Louis N.L., October 6, 1931.

ERRORS

Most errors, total series
163—New York A.L.; 39 series, 219 games.

Most errors, series
4-game series—8—New York A.L. vs. Chicago N.L., 1932.
Boston A.L. vs. St. Louis N.L., 2004.
5-game series—13—Brooklyn N.L. vs. Boston A.L., 1916.
6-game series—16—New York N.L. vs. Philadelphia A.L., 1911.
7-game series—19—Detroit A.L. vs. Pittsburgh N.L., 1909.
8-game series—18—Pittsburgh N.L. vs. Boston A.L., 1903.

Most errors by both clubs, series
4-game series—14—New York A.L. 8, Chicago N.L. 6, 1932.
5-game series—23—Chicago N.L. 12, Philadelphia A.L. 11, 1910.
6-game series—27—New York N.L. 16, Philadelphia A.L. 11, 1911.
7-game series—34—Detroit A.L. 19, Pittsburgh N.L. 15, 1909.
8-game series—32—Pittsburgh N.L. 18, Boston A.L. 14, 1903.

Fewest errors, series
4-game series—0—Baltimore A.L. vs. Los Angeles N.L., 1966.
5-game series—0—New York A.L. vs. New York N.L., 1937.
6-game series—1—Boston A.L. vs. Chicago N.L., 1918.
St. Louis N.L. vs. St. Louis A.L., 1944.
New York A.L. vs. Brooklyn N.L., 1953.
Los Angeles N.L. vs. New York A.L., 1977.
7-game series—2—Held by many clubs.
8-game series—5—New York N.L. vs. New York A.L., 1921.

Fewest errors by both clubs, series
4-game series—4—Los Angeles N.L. 3, New York A.L. 1, 1963.
5-game series—5—Los Angeles N.L. 3, Oakland A.L. 2, 1988.
6-game series—4—New York A.L. 3, Los Angeles N.L. 1, 1977.
7-game series—5—Kansas City A.L. 3, St. Louis N.L. 2, 1985.
8-game series—11—New York A.L. 6, New York N.L. 5, 1921.

Most errors, game
6—Chicago A.L. vs. Chicago N.L., October 13, 1906.
Pittsburgh N.L. vs. Detroit A.L., October 12, 1909.
Chicago A.L. vs. New York N.L., October 13, 1917.
Los Angeles N.L. vs. Baltimore A.L., October 6, 1966.

Most errors by both clubs, game
9—Chicago A.L. 6, New York N.L. 3, October 13, 1917.

Most errors by outfield, game
4—Los Angeles N.L. vs. Baltimore A.L., October 6, 1966.

Most errors by outfields of both clubs, game
4—Los Angeles N.L. 4, Baltimore A.L. 0, October 6, 1966.

Most errors by infield, game
5—Chicago A.L. vs. Chicago N.L., October 13, 1906.
New York N.L. vs. Philadelphia A.L., October 17, 1911,
11 innings.
Detroit A.L. vs. St. Louis N.L., October 3, 1934.

Most errors by infields of both clubs, game
7—New York N.L. 5, Philadelphia A.L. 2, October 17, 1911,
11 innings.
Chicago A.L. 4, New York N.L. 3, October 13, 1917.

Most errors, inning
3—Chicago A.L., October 13, 1917, fourth inning.
New York N.L., October 8, 1937, fifth inning.
New York N.L., October 9, 1937, third inning.
Cincinnati N.L., October 8, 1939, 10th inning.
Los Angeles N.L., October 1, 1959, third inning.
Los Angeles N.L., October 6, 1966, fifth inning.
Cleveland A.L., October 21, 1997, ninth inning.

Most errorless games, total series
102—New York A.L; 39 series, 219 games.

Most consecutive errorless games, total series
7—Philadelphia A.L. vs. St. Louis N.L., October 6, 7, 1930;
October 1, 2, 5, 6, 7, 1931.

Most errorless games, series
4-game series—4—Baltimore A.L. vs. Los Angeles N.L., 1966.
5-game series—5—New York A.L. vs. New York N.L., 1937.
6-game series—5—Boston A.L. vs. Chicago N.L., 1918.
St. Louis N.L. vs. St. Louis A.L., 1944.
New York A.L. vs. Brooklyn N.L., 1953.
Los Angeles N.L. vs. New York A.L., 1977.
7-game series—6—Arizona N.L. vs. New York A.L., 2001.
8-game series—5—New York N.L. vs. New York A.L., 1921.

Most consecutive errorless games, series
5—Philadelphia A.L. vs. St. Louis N.L., October 1, 2, 5, 6, 7,
1931 (first five games).
New York A.L. vs. New York N.L., October 6, 7, 8, 9, 10,
1937 (full series).
New York A.L. vs. Brooklyn N.L., September 29, 30, October
1, 2, 3, 1955.

Most errorless games by both clubs, series
4-game series—7—Baltimore A.L. 4, Los Angeles N.L. 3, 1966.
5-game series—7—New York A.L. 5, New York N.L. 2, 1937.
6-game series—9—Los Angeles N.L. 5, New York A.L. 4, 1977.
7-game series—10—St. Louis N.L. 5, Kansas City A.L. 5, 1985.
8-game series—8—New York N.L. 5, New York A.L. 3, 1921.

Fewest errorless games, series
0—Held by many clubs.

Longest errorless game
12 innings—Detroit A.L. vs. St. Louis N.L., October 4, 1934.
New York A.L. vs. Los Angeles N.L., October 11, 1977.
New York A.L. vs. New York N.L., October 21, 2000.
Arizona N.L. vs. New York A.L., November 1, 2001.
Florida N.L. vs. New York A.L., October 23, 2003.

Longest errorless game by both clubs
12 innings—New York A.L. vs. Los Angeles N.L., October 11,
1977 (Los Angeles fielded 11 innings).
New York A.L. vs. New York N.L., October 21, 2000 (New
York N.L. fielded 11.2 innings).
Florida N.L. vs. New York A.L., October 23, 2003 (New York
fielded 11 innings).

PASSED BALLS

Most passed balls, total series
15—New York A.L.; 39 series, 219 games.

Most passed balls, series
3—Chicago N.L. vs. Chicago A.L., 1906.
Pittsburgh N.L. vs. New York A.L., 1960.
New York A.L. vs. St. Louis N.L., 1964.

Most passed balls by both clubs, series
4—Chicago N.L., 3, Chicago A.L., 1, 1906 (6-game series).
New York A.L. 2, Brooklyn N.L. 2, 1947 (7-game series).

Fewest passed balls, series
0—Held by many clubs.

Fewest passed balls by both clubs, series
0—Held by many clubs.

DOUBLE AND TRIPLE PLAYS

Most double plays, total series
193—New York A.L.; 39 series, 219 games.

Most double plays, series
4-game series—7
Chicago N.L. vs. New York A.L., 1932.
New York A.L. vs. Los Angeles N.L., 1963.
5-game series—7
New York A.L. vs. New York N.L., 1922.
New York A.L. vs. Brooklyn N.L., 1941.
Cincinnati N.L. vs. New York A.L., 1961.
6-game series—10—New York A.L. vs. New York N.L., 1951.
7-game series—12—Brooklyn N.L. vs. New York A.L., 1955.
8-game series—9—Chicago A.L. vs. Cincinnati N.L., 1919.

Most double plays by both clubs, series
4-game series—10—New York A.L. 6, Cincinnati N.L. 4, 1976.
5-game series—12—New York A.L. 7, Brooklyn N.L. 5, 1941.
6-game series—16—Philadelphia N.L. 8, Kansas City A.L. 8, 1980.
7-game series—19—Brooklyn N.L. 12, New York A.L. 7, 1955.
8-game series—16—Chicago A.L. 9, Cincinnati N.L. 7, 1919.

Fewest double plays, series
4-game series—1—New York A.L. vs. Chicago N.L., 1932.
Cincinnati N.L. vs. New York A.L., 1939.

Philadelphia N.L. vs. New York A.L., 1950.
Los Angeles N.L. vs. New York A.L., 1963.
Oakland A.L. vs. San Francisco N.L., 1989.
5-game series—0—New York N.L. vs. Baltimore A.L., 1969.
6-game series—2—Chicago A.L. vs. Chicago N.L., 1906.
New York N.L. vs. Philadelphia A.L., 1911.
Philadelphia A.L. vs. New York N.L., 1911.
Philadelphia A.L. vs. St. Louis N.L., 1930.
New York A.L. vs. New York N.L., 1936.
Chicago A.L. vs. Los Angeles N.L., 1959.
New York A.L. vs. Los Angeles N.L., 1977,
New York A.L. vs. Los Angeles N.L., 1981.
7-game series—2—St. Louis N.L. vs. Detroit A.L., 1934.
Baltimore A.L. vs. Pittsburgh N.L., 1971.
St. Louis N.L. vs. Minnesota A.L., 1987.
8-game series—4—New York A.L. vs. Boston A.L., 1912.

Fewest double plays by both clubs, series
4-game series—4—New York N.L. 2, Cleveland A.L. 2, 1954.
San Francisco N.L. 3, Oakland A.L. 1, 1989.
5-game series—4—New York N.L. 2, Philadelphia A.L. 2, 1905.

Baltimore A.L. 4, New York N.L. 0, 1969.
New York N.L. 3, New York A.L. 1, 2000.
6-game series—4—Philadelphia A.L. 2, New York N.L. 2, 1911.
7-game series—6—Minnesota A.L. 4, St. Louis N.L. 2, 1987.
8-game series—9—Boston A.L. 5, New York N.L. 4, 1912.

Most double plays, game
4—Philadelphia A.L. vs. Boston N.L., October 9, 1914.
Boston A.L. vs. Brooklyn N.L., October 7, 1916.
Chicago N.L. vs. New York A.L., September 29, 1932.
Cleveland A.L. vs. Boston N.L., October 11, 1948.
New York A.L. vs. New York N.L., October 8, 1951.
Oakland A.L. vs. New York N.L., October 17, 1973.
Philadelphia N.L. vs. Kansas City A.L., October 15, 1980.

Most double plays by both clubs, game
6—New York A.L. 3, Brooklyn N.L. 3, September 29, 1955.
Philadelphia N.L. 4, Kansas City A.L. 2, October 15, 1980.

Most triple plays, series
1—Cleveland A.L. vs. Brooklyn N.L., 1920.

MISCELLANEOUS

CLUB

ONE-RUN DECISIONS

Most one-run games, total series
69—New York A.L.; 39 series; won 36 lost 33.

Most one-run games won, total series
36—New York A.L.; 39 series.

Most one-run games lost, total series
33—New York A.L.; 39 series.

Most one-run games won, series
4—Boston A.L. vs. Philadelphia N.L., 1915 (lost one).
Boston A.L. vs. Chicago N.L., 1918 (lost none).
Oakland A.L. vs. Cincinnati N.L., 1972 (lost two).

Most one-run games by both clubs, series
4-game series—3—New York A.L. (won three) vs. Philadelphia N.L., 1950.
5-game series—4—Boston A.L. (won four) vs. Philadelphia N.L., 1915.
Oakland A.L. (won three) vs. Los Angeles N.L. (won one), 1974.
6-game series—5—Atlanta N.L. (won three) vs. Cleveland A.L. (won two), 1995.
7-game series—6—Oakland A.L. (won four) vs. Cincinnati N.L (won two), 1972.
8-game series—4—Boston A.L. (won three) vs. New York N.L. (won one), 1912.

Most one-run games won, series
4-game series—3—New York A.L. vs. Philadelphia N.L., 1950.
5-game series—4—Boston A.L. vs. Philadelphia N.L., 1915.
6-game series—4—Boston A.L. vs. Chicago N.L., 1918.
Toronto A.L. vs. Atlanta N.L., 1992.
7-game series—4—Oakland A.L. vs. Cincinnati N.L., 1972.
8-game series—3—Boston A.L. vs. New York N.L., 1912.

Most consecutive one-run games won, total series
6—Boston A.L., 1915 (last 4), 1916 (first 2).

Most consecutive one-run games lost, total series
7—Philadelphia N.L., 1915 (last 4), 1950 (first 3).

LENGTH OF GAMES

BY INNINGS

Longest game
14 innings—Boston A.L. 2, Brooklyn N.L. 1, October 9, 1916 (at Boston).

For a complete list of extra-inning games, see page 500.

Longest tie game
12 innings—Chicago N.L. 3, Detroit A.L. 3, October 8, 1907 (at Chicago).

Most extra-inning games, total series
19—New York A.L.; 39 series (won 11, lost seven, tied one).

Most extra-inning games won, total series
11—New York A.L.; 39 series (won 11, lost seven, tied one).

Most extra-inning games lost, total series
7—New York A.L.; 39 series (won 11 lost seven, tied one).

Most extra-inning games, series
4-game series—1—Boston N.L. vs. Philadelphia A.L., 1914.
New York A.L. vs. Cincinnati N.L., 1939.
New York A.L. vs. Philadelphia N.L., 1950.
New York A.L. vs. Cleveland A.L., 1954.
5-game series—2—New York N.L. vs. Washington A.L., 1933.
6-game series—2—Philadelphia A.L. vs. New York N.L., 1911.
7-game series—3—Minnesota A.L. vs. Atlanta N.L., 1991.
8-game series—2—Boston A.L. vs. New York N.L., 1912.

BY TIME

Longest average time per game, series
4-game series—3 hours, 14 minutes—New York A.L. vs. San Diego N.L., 1998.
5-game series—3 hours, 46 minutes—New York A.L. vs. New York N.L., 2000.
6-game series—3 hours, 29 minutes—Toronto A.L. vs. Philadelphia N.L., 1993.
7-game series—3 hours, 37 minutes—Anaheim A.L. vs. San Francisco N.L., 2002.
8-game series—2 hours, 14 minutes—Boston A.L. vs. New York N.L., 1912.

Shortest average time per game, series
4-game series—1 hour, 46 minutes—New York A.L. vs. Cincinnati N.L., 1939.
5-game series—1 hour, 46 minutes—Detroit A.L. vs. Chicago N.L., 1908.
6-game series—1 hour, 49 minutes—Philadelphia A.L. vs. St. Louis N.L., 1930.
7-game series—1 hour, 47 minutes—Cleveland A.L. vs. Brooklyn N.L., 1920.
8-game series—1 hour, 48 minutes—Boston A.L. vs. Pittsburgh N.L., 1903.

Shortest game
1 hour, 25 minutes—Chicago N.L., 2, Detroit A.L., 0, October 14, 1908 (at Detroit).

Longest 9-inning day game
3 hours, 48 minutes—Baltimore A.L., 9, Pittsburgh N.L., 6, October 13, 1979 (at Pittsburgh).

Longest 9-inning night game
4 hours, 14 minutes—Toronto A.L., 15, Philadelphia N.L., 14, October 20, 1993 (at Philadelphia).

Longest extra-inning day game
4 hours, 13 minutes—New York N.L., 10, Oakland A.L., 7, October 14, 1973, 12 innings (at Oakland).

Longest extra-inning night game
4 hours, 51 minutes—New York A.L. 4, New York N.L. 3, October 21, 2000, 12 innings (at New York A.L.).

SERIES STARTING AND FINISHING DATES

Earliest date for series game (except 1918)
September 28, 1932—Chicago N.L. at New York A.L.
September 28, 1955—Brooklyn N.L. at New York A.L.

Earliest date for series final game (except 1918)
October 2, 1932—New York A.L. at Chicago N.L. (4-game series).
October 2, 1954—New York N.L. at Cleveland A.L. (4-game series).

Latest date for series start
October 27, 2001—New York A.L. at Arizona N.L.

Latest date for series finish
November 4, 2001—New York A.L. at Arizona N.L. (7-game series).

NIGHT GAMES

First night game
October 13, 1971—Pittsburgh N.L., 4, Baltimore A.L., 3 (at Pittsburgh).

First year the entire series played at night
1985—St. Louis N.L. vs. Kansas City A.L., October 19 through 27 (7-game series).

SERIES AND GAMES WON

Most series won
26—New York A.L., 1923, 1927, 1928, 1932, 1936, 1937, 1938, 1939, 1941, 1943, 1947, 1949, 1950, 1951, 1952, 1953, 1956, 1958, 1961, 1962, 1977, 1978, 1996, 1998, 1999, 2000 (lost 12).

For complete lists of results, and series played by all teams, see page 452.

Most consecutive series won
8—New York A.L., 1927, 1928, 1932, 1936, 1937, 1938, 1939, 1941.

Most consecutive years winning series
5—New York A.L., 1949, 1950, 1951, 1952, 1953.

Most times winning series in four consecutive games
8—New York A.L., 1927, 1928, 1932, 1938, 1939, 1950, 1998, 1999.

Winning series after winning first game
Accomplished 61 times.

Winning series after losing first game
Accomplished 39 times.

Winning series after winning one game and losing three
Boston A.L. vs. Pittsburgh N.L., 1903 (8-game series; needed five wins).
Pittsburgh N.L. vs. Washington A.L., 1925 (7-game series).
New York A.L. vs. Milwaukee N.L., 1958 (7-game series).
Detroit A.L. vs. St. Louis N.L., 1968 (7-game series).
Pittsburgh N.L. vs. Baltimore A.L., 1979 (7-game series).
Kansas City A.L. vs. St. Louis N.L., 1985 (7-game series).

Winning series after losing first two games
New York N.L. vs. New York A.L., 1921 (8-game series; needed five wins).
Brooklyn N.L. vs. New York A.L., 1955 (7-game series).
New York A.L. vs. Brooklyn N.L., 1956 (7-game series).
New York A.L. vs. Milwaukee N.L., 1958 (7-game series).
Los Angeles N.L. vs. Minnesota A.L., 1965 (7-game series).
Pittsburgh N.L. vs. Baltimore A.L., 1971 (7-game series).
New York A.L. vs. Los Angeles N.L., 1978 (6-game series).
Los Angeles N.L. vs. New York A.L., 1981 (6-game series).
Kansas City A.L. vs. St. Louis N.L., 1985 (7-game series).
New York N.L. vs. Boston A.L., 1986 (7-game series).
New York A.L. vs. Atlanta N.L., 1996 (6-game series).

Winning series after losing first three games
Never accomplished.

Most games won, total series
130—New York A.L.; 39 series; lost 88, tied one.

For complete lists of results, and games played by all teams, see page 452.

Most consecutive games won, total series
14—New York A.L., 1996 (last 4), 1998 (4), 1999 (4), 2000 (first 2).

SERIES AND GAMES LOST

Most series lost
13—New York A.L., 1921, 1922, 1926, 1942, 1955, 1957, 1960, 1963, 1964, 1976, 1981, 2001, 2003 (won 26).

Most consecutive series lost
7—Chicago N.L., 1910, 1918, 1929, 1932, 1935, 1938, 1945.
Brooklyn N.L., 1916, 1920, 1941, 1947, 1949, 1952, 1953.

Most consecutive years losing series
3—Detroit A.L., 1907, 1908, 1909.
New York N.L., 1911, 1912, 1913.

Most games lost, total series
88—New York A.L.; 39 series.

For complete lists of results, and games played by all teams, see page 452.

Most consecutive games lost, total series
8—New York A.L., 1921 (last 3), 1922 (4; one tie during streak), 1923 (first 1).
Philadelphia N.L., 1915 (last 4), 1950 (4).
Atlanta N.L., 1996 (last 4), 1999 (4).

ATTENDANCE

Largest attendance, series
4-game series—251,507—New York N.L. vs. Cleveland A.L., 1954.
5-game series—304,139—Baltimore A.L. vs. Philadelphia N.L., 1983.
6-game series—420,784—Los Angeles N.L. vs. Chicago A.L., 1959.
7-game series—403,617—Florida N.L. vs. Cleveland A.L., 1997.

8-game series—269,976—New York N.L. vs. New York A.L., 1921.

For list of attendance by series each series, see page 500.

Smallest attendance, series
4-game series—111,009—Boston N.L. vs. Philadelphia A.L., 1914.
5-game series—62,232—Chicago N.L. vs. Detroit A.L., 1908.
6-game series—99,845—Chicago A.L. vs. Chicago N.L., 1906.
7-game series—145,295—Pittsburgh N.L. vs. Detroit A.L., 1909.
8-game series—100,429—Pittsburgh N.L. vs. Boston A.L., 1903.

Largest attendance, game
92,706—At Los Angeles, October 6, 1959, Chicago A.L. 1, Los Angeles N.L. 0.

Smallest attendance, game
6,210—At Detroit, October 14, 1908; Chicago N.L. 2, Detroit A.L. 0.

LEAGUE
SERIES AND GAMES WON AND LOST

Most consecutive series won, league
7—American League, 1947, 1948, 1949, 1950, 1951, 1952, 1953.

Most consecutive series lost, league
7—National League, 1947, 1948, 1949, 1950, 1951, 1952, 1953.

Most consecutive games won, league
10—American League, 1927 (4) 1928 (4), 1929 (first 2).
American League, 1937 (last 1), 1938 (4), 1939 (4), 1940 (first 1).
American League, 1998 (4), 1999 (4), 2000 (first 2).

SHUTOUTS

Most consecutive series with shutouts
9—1955 through 1963.

Most consecutive series ending in shutouts
3—1907, 1908, 1909.
1955, 1956, 1957.

Most consecutive series without shutouts
3—1910, 1911, 1912.
1927, 1928, 1929.
1936, 1937, 1938.
1976, 1977, 1978.

NON-PLAYING PERSONNEL

MANAGERS AND COACHES

Most series by manager
10—Casey Stengel, New York A.L., 1949, 1950, 1951, 1952, 1953, 1955, 1956, 1957, 1958, 1960 (won seven, lost three).

For a complete list of managers and their records, see page 511.

Most series by coach
15—Frank Crosetti, New York A.L., 1947, 1949, 1950, 1951, 1952, 1953, 1955, 1956, 1957, 1958, 1960, 1961, 1962, 1963, 1964 (10 World Series winners).

Most series eligible as player and coach
23—Frank Crosetti, New York A.L., 1932, 1936, 1937, 1938, 1939, 1941, 1942, 1943 (eight series as player, seven winners); 1947, 1949, 1950, 1951, 1952, 1953, 1955, 1956, 1957, 1958, 1960, 1961, 1962, 1963, 1964 (15 series as coach, 10 winners).

Most series winners managed
7—Joe McCarthy, New York A.L., 1932, 1936, 1937, 1938, 1939, 1941, 1943.
Casey Stengel, New York A.L., 1949, 1950, 1951, 1952, 1953, 1956, 1958.

Most consecutive years managing series winners
5—Casey Stengel, New York A.L., 1949, 1950, 1951, 1952, 1953 (his first five years as New York A.L. manager).

Most consecutive series winners managed, career
6—Joe McCarthy, New York A.L., 1932, 1936, 1937, 1938, 1939, 1941.

Most series losers managed
6—John McGraw, New York N.L., 1911, 1912, 1913, 1917, 1923, 1924.

Most consecutive years managing series losers
3—Hughey Jennings, Detroit A.L., 1907, 1908, 1909.
John McGraw, New York N.L., 1911, 1912, 1913.

Most consecutive series losers managed, career
4—John McGraw, New York N.L., 1911, 1912, 1913, 1917.

Most different series winners managed
2—Bill McKechnie, Pittsburgh N.L., 1925; Cincinnati N.L., 1940.
Bucky Harris, Washington A.L., 1924; New York A.L., 1947.
Sparky Anderson, Cincinnati N.L., 1975, 1976; Detroit A.L., 1984.

Most different clubs managed
3—Bill McKechnie, Pittsburgh N.L., 1925; St. Louis N.L., 1928; Cincinnati N.L., 1939, 1940.
Dick Williams, Boston A.L., 1967; Oakland A.L., 1972, 1973; San Diego N.L., 1984.

Most games by manager
63—Casey Stengel, New York A.L., 10 series.

Most games won by manager
37—Casey Stengel, New York A.L., 10 series.

Most games lost by manager
28—John McGraw, New York N.L., 10 series.

Youngest manager
26 years, 11 months, 21 days—Joe Cronin, Washington A.L. vs. New York N.L., October 3, 1933.

Youngest manager of a series winner
27 years, 11 months, 2 days—Bucky Harris, Washington A.L. vs. New York N.L., October 10, 1924.

UMPIRES

Most series umpired
18—Bill Klem, 1908, 1909, 1911, 1912, 1913, 1914, 1915, 1917, 1918, 1920, 1922, 1924, 1926, 1929, 1931, 1932, 1934, 1940.

Most consecutive series umpired
5—Bill Klem, 1911, 1912, 1913, 1914, 1915.

Most games umpired
104—Bill Klem, 18 series.

GENERAL REFERENCE

SERIES WON AND LOST BY TEAMS

AMERICAN LEAGUE

	W	L	Pct.
Toronto	2	0	1.000
Anaheim	1	0	1.000
New York	26	13	.667
Oakland	4	2	.667
Minnesota	2	1	.667
Philadelphia	5	3	.625
Boston	6	4	.600
Baltimore	3	3	.500
Chicago	2	2	.500
Kansas City	1	1	.500
Detroit	4	5	.444
Cleveland	2	3	.400
Washington	1	2	.333
Milwaukee	0	1	.000
St. Louis	0	1	.000
Totals	59	41	.590

NATIONAL LEAGUE

	W	L	Pct.
Florida	2	0	1.000
Arizona	1	0	1.000
Pittsburgh	5	2	.714
St. Louis	9	7	.563
Cincinnati	5	4	.556
Los Angeles	5	4	.555
New York Mets	2	2	.500
Boston	1	1	.500
Milwaukee	1	1	.500
New York Giants	5	9	.357
Atlanta	1	4	.200
Philadelphia	1	4	.200
Chicago	2	8	.200
Brooklyn	1	8	.111
San Diego	0	2	.000
San Francisco	0	3	.000
Totals	41	59	.410

GAMES WON AND LOST BY TEAMS

*includes one tie per asterisk

AMERICAN LEAGUE

	W	L	Pct.
Toronto	8	4	.667
New York*	130	88	.596
Boston*	37	26	.587
Baltimore	19	14	.576
Anaheim	4	3	.571
Philadelphia	24	19	.558
Oakland	17	15	.531
Minnesota	11	10	.524
Chicago	13	13	.500
Detroit*	26	29	.473
Cleveland	14	16	.467
Kansas City	6	7	.462
Milwaukee	3	4	.429
Washington	8	11	.421
St. Louis	2	4	.333
Totals	322	263	.550

NATIONAL LEAGUE

	W	L	Pct.
Boston	6	4	.600
Florida	8	5	.615
Arizona	4	3	.571
Los Angeles	25	24	.510
Cincinnati	26	25	.510
New York Mets	12	12	.500

	W	L	Pct.
Milwaukee	7	7	.500
Pittsburgh	23	24	.489
New York Giants**	39	41	.488
St. Louis	48	52	.480
Atlanta	11	18	.379
Chicago*	19	33	.365
Brooklyn	20	36	.357
San Francisco	6	12	.333
Philadelphia	8	18	.308
San Diego	1	8	.111
Totals	263	322	.450

HOME AND ROAD GAMES BY TEAMS

AMERICAN LEAGUE

	Years	Games	Home	Away
New York	39	219	106	113
Boston	10	64	33	31
Detroit	9	56	28	28
Philadelphia	8	43	20	23
Baltimore	6	33	17	16
Oakland	6	32	17	15
Cleveland	5	30	15	15
Chicago	4	26	13	13
Minnesota	3	21	12	9
Washington	3	19	10	9
Kansas City	2	13	7	6
Toronto	2	12	6	6
Anaheim	1	7	4	3
Milwaukee	1	7	3	4
St. Louis	1	6	3	3
Totals	100	588	294	294

NATIONAL LEAGUE

	Years	Games	Home	Away
St. Louis	16	100	49	51
New York Giants	14	82	41	41
Chicago	10	53	27	26
Brooklyn	9	56	28	28
Cincinnati	9	51	26	25
Los Angeles	9	49	23	26
Pittsburgh	7	47	23	24
Philadelphia	5	26	14	12
Atlanta	5	29	14	15
New York Mets	4	24	13	11
San Francisco	3	18	9	9
Milwaukee	2	14	7	7
Florida	2	13	7	6
Boston	2	10	5	5
San Diego	2	9	4	5
Arizona	1	7	4	3
Totals	100	588	294	294

TIE GAMES

Oct. 8, 1907—12 inn, Chicago N.L. 3, Detroit A.L. 3
Oct. 9, 1912—11 inn, Boston A.L. 6, New York N.L. 6
Oct. 5, 1922—10 inn, New York A.L. 3, New York N.L. 3
Total number of ties: 3

SHUTOUTS

Oct. 2, 1903	Bill Dinneen, Boston A.L. 3, Pittsburgh N.L. 0 (three hits).
Oct. 13, 1903	Bill Dinneen, Boston A.L. 3, Pittsburgh N.L. 0 (four hits).
Oct. 9, 1905	Christy Mathewson, New York N.L. 3, Philadelphia A.L. 0 (four hits).
Oct. 10, 1905	Chief Bender, Philadelphia A.L. 3, New York N.L. 0 (four hits).
Oct. 12, 1905	Christy Mathewson, New York N.L. 9, Philadelphia A.L. 0 (four hits).

Oct. 13, 1905 Joe McGinnity, New York N.L. 1, Philadelphia A.L. 0 (five hits).

Oct. 14, 1905 Christy Mathewson, New York N.L. 2, Philadelphia A.L. 0 (six hits).

Oct. 11, 1906 Ed Walsh, Chicago A.L. 3, Chicago N.L. 0 (two hits).

Oct. 12, 1906 Mordecai Brown, Chicago N.L. 1, Chicago A.L. 0 (two hits).

Oct. 12, 1907 Mordecai Brown, Chicago N.L. 2, Detroit A.L. 0 (seven hits).

Oct. 13, 1908 Mordecai Brown, Chicago N.L. 3, Detroit A.L. 0 (four hits).

Oct. 14, 1908 Orval Overall, Chicago N.L. 2, Detroit A.L. 0 (three hits).

Oct. 12, 1909 George Mullin, Detroit A.L. 5, Pittsburgh N.L. 0 (five hits).

Oct. 16, 1909 Babe Adams, Pittsburgh N.L. 8, Detroit A.L. 0 (six hits).

Oct. 8, 1913 Christy Mathewson, New York N.L. 3, Philadelphia A.L. 0, 10 innings (eight hits).

Oct. 10, 1914 Bill James, Boston N.L. 1, Philadelphia A.L. 0 (two hits).

Oct. 10, 1917 Rube Benton, New York N.L. 2, Chicago A.L. 0 (five hits).

Oct. 11, 1917 Ferdie Schupp, New York N.L. 5, Chicago A.L. 0 (seven hits).

Sept. 5, 1918 Babe Ruth, Boston A.L. 1, Chicago N.L. 0 (six hits).

Sept. 10, 1918 Hippo Vaughn, Chicago N.L. 3, Boston A.L. 0 (five hits).

Oct. 3, 1919 Dickie Kerr, Chicago A.L. 3, Cincinnati N.L. 0 (three hits).

Oct. 4, 1919 Jimmy Ring, Cincinnati N.L. 2, Chicago A.L. 0 (three hits).

Oct. 6, 1919 Hod Eller, Cincinnati N.L. 5, Chicago A.L. 0 (three hits).

Oct. 6, 1920 Burleigh Grimes, Brooklyn N.L. 3, Cleveland A.L. 0 (seven hits).

Oct. 11, 1920 Duster Mails, Cleveland A.L. 1, Brooklyn N.L. 0 (three hits).

Oct. 12, 1920 Stan Coveleski, Cleveland A.L. 3, Brooklyn N.L. 0 (five hits).

Oct. 5, 1921 Carl Mays, New York A.L. 3, New York N.L. 0 (five hits).

Oct. 6, 1921 Waite Hoyt, New York A.L. 3, New York N.L. 0 (two hits).

Oct. 13, 1921 Art Nehf, New York N.L. 1, New York A.L. 0 (four hits).

Oct. 6, 1922 Jack Scott, New York N.L. 3, New York A.L. 0 (four hits).

Oct. 12, 1923 Art Nehf, New York N.L. 1, New York A.L. 0 (six hits).

Oct. 11, 1925 Walter Johnson, Washington A.L. 4, Pittsburgh N.L. 0 (six hits).

Oct. 5, 1926 Jesse Haines, St. Louis N.L. 4, New York A.L. 0 (five hits).

Oct. 4, 1930 Bill Hallahan, St. Louis N.L. 5, Philadelphia A.L. 0 (seven hits).

Oct. 6, 1930 George Earnshaw and Lefty Grove, Philadelphia A.L. 2, St. Louis N.L. 0 (three hits).

Oct. 2, 1931 Bill Hallahan, St. Louis N.L. 2, Philadelphia A.L. 0 (three hits).

Oct. 6, 1931 George Earnshaw, Philadelphia A.L. 3, St. Louis N.L. 0 (two hits).

Oct. 5, 1933 Earl Whitehill, Washington A.L. 4, New York N.L. 0 (five hits).

Oct. 9, 1934 Dizzy Dean, St. Louis N.L. 11, Detroit A.L. 0 (six hits).

Oct. 2, 1935 Lon Warneke, Chicago N.L. 3, Detroit A.L. 0 (four hits).

Oct. 5, 1939 Monte Pearson, New York A.L. 4, Cincinnati N.L. 0 (two hits).

Oct. 6, 1940 Bobo Newsom, Detroit A.L. 8, Cincinnati N.L. 0 (three hits).

Oct. 7, 1940 Bucky Walters, Cincinnati N.L. 4, Detroit A.L. 0 (five hits).

Oct. 3, 1942 Ernie White, St. Louis N.L. 2, New York A.L. 0 (six hits).

Oct. 11, 1943 Spud Chandler, New York A.L. 2, St. Louis N.L. 0 (10 hits).

Oct. 8, 1944 Mort Cooper, St. Louis N.L. 2, St. Louis A.L. 0 (seven hits).

Oct. 3, 1945 Hank Borowy, Chicago N.L. 9, Detroit A.L. 0 (six hits).

Oct. 5, 1945 Claude Passeau, Chicago N.L. 3, Detroit A.L. 0 (one hit).

Oct. 7, 1946 Harry Brecheen, St. Louis N.L. 3, Boston A.L. 0 (four hits).

Oct. 9, 1946 Boo Ferriss, Boston A.L. 4, St. Louis N.L. 0 (six hits).

Oct. 6, 1948 Johnny Sain, Boston N.L. 1, Cleveland A.L. 0 (four hits).

Oct. 8, 1948 Gene Bearden, Cleveland A.L. 2, Boston N.L. 0 (five hits).

Oct. 5, 1949 Allie Reynolds, New York A.L. 1, Brooklyn N.L. 0 (two hits).

Oct. 6, 1949 Preacher Roe, Brooklyn N.L. 1, New York A.L. 0 (six hits).

Oct. 4, 1950 Vic Raschi, New York A.L. 1, Philadelphia N.L. 0 (two hits).

Oct. 4, 1952 Allie Reynolds, New York A.L. 2, Brooklyn N.L. 0 (four hits).

Oct. 4, 1955 Johnny Podres, Brooklyn N.L. 2, New York A.L. 0 (eight hits).

Oct. 8, 1956 Don Larsen, New York A.L. 2, Brooklyn N.L. 0 (no hits).

Oct. 9, 1956 Clem Labine, Brooklyn N.L. 1, New York A.L. 0, 10 innings (seven hits).

Oct. 10, 1956 Johnny Kucks, New York A.L. 9, Brooklyn N.L. 0 (three hits).

Oct. 7, 1957 Lew Burdette, Milwaukee N.L. 1, New York A.L. 0 (seven hits).

Oct. 10, 1957 Lew Burdette, Milwaukee N.L. 5, New York A.L. 0 (seven hits).

Oct. 4, 1958 Don Larsen and Ryne Duren, New York A.L. 4, Milwaukee N.L. 0 (six hits).

Oct. 5, 1958 Warren Spahn, Milwaukee N.L. 3, New York A.L., 0 (two hits).

Oct. 6, 1958 Bob Turley, New York A.L. 7, Milwaukee N.L. 0 (five hits).

Oct. 1, 1959 Early Wynn and Gerry Staley, Chicago A.L. 11, Los Angeles N.L. 0 (eight hits).

Oct. 6, 1959 Bob Shaw, Billy Pierce and Dick Donovan, Chicago A.L. 1, Los Angeles N.L. 0 (nine hits).

Oct. 8, 1960 Whitey Ford, New York A.L. 10, Pittsburgh N.L. 0 (four hits).

Oct. 12, 1960 Whitey Ford, New York A.L. 12, Pittsburgh N.L. 0 (seven hits).

Oct. 4, 1961 Whitey Ford, New York A.L. 2, Cincinnati N.L. 0 (two hits).

Oct. 8, 1961 Whitey Ford and Jim Coates, New York A.L. 7, Cincinnati N.L. 0 (five hits).

Oct. 5, 1962 Jack Sanford, San Francisco N.L. 2, New York A.L. 0 (three hits).

Oct. 16, 1962 Ralph Terry, New York A.L. 1, San Francisco N.L. 0 (four hits).

Oct. 5, 1963 Don Drysdale, Los Angeles N.L. 1, New York A.L. 0 (three hits).

Oct. 9, 1965 Claude Osteen, Los Angeles N.L. 4, Minnesota A.L. 0 (five hits).

Oct. 11, 1965 Sandy Koufax, Los Angeles N.L. 7, Minnesota A.L. 0 (four hits).

Oct. 14, 1965 Sandy Koufax, Los Angeles N.L. 2, Minnesota A.L. 0 (three hits).

Oct. 6, 1966 Jim Palmer, Baltimore A.L. 6, Los Angeles N.L. 0 (four hits).

Oct. 8, 1966 Wally Bunker, Baltimore A.L. 1, Los Angeles N.L. 0 (six hits).

Oct. 9, 1966 Dave McNally, Baltimore A.L. 1, Los Angeles N.L. 0 (four hits).

Oct. 5, 1967 Jim Lonborg, Boston A.L. 5, St. Louis N.L. 0 (one hit).

Oct. 8, 1967 Bob Gibson, St. Louis N.L. 6, Boston A.L. 0 (five hits).

Oct. 2, 1968 Bob Gibson, St. Louis N.L. 4, Detroit A.L. 0 (five hits).

Oct. 14, 1969	Gary Gentry and Nolan Ryan, New York N.L. 5, Baltimore A.L. 0 (four hits).
Oct. 14, 1971	Nelson Briles, Pittsburgh N.L. 4, Baltimore A.L. 0 (two hits).
Oct. 18, 1972	Jack Billingham and Clay Carroll, Cincinnati N.L. 1, Oakland A.L. 0 (three hits).
Oct. 18, 1973	Jerry Koosman and Tug McGraw, New York N.L. 2, Oakland A.L. 0 (three hits).
Oct. 11, 1975	Luis Tiant, Boston A.L. 6, Cincinnati N.L. 0 (five hits).
Oct. 16, 1979	John Candelaria and Kent Tekulve, Pittsburgh N.L. 4, Baltimore A.L. 0 (seven hits).
Oct. 21, 1981	Tommy John and Rich Gossage, New York A.L., 3 Los Angeles N.L. 0 (four hits).
Oct. 12, 1982	Mike Caldwell, Milwaukee A.L. 10, St. Louis N.L. 0 (three hits).
Oct. 16, 1983	Scott McGregor, Baltimore A.L. 5, Philadelphia N.L. 0 (five hits).
Oct. 23, 1985	John Tudor, St. Louis N.L. 3, Kansas City A.L. 0 (five hits).
Oct. 27, 1985	Bret Saberhagen, Kansas City A.L. 11, St. Louis N.L. 0 (five hits).
Oct. 18, 1986	Bruce Hurst and Calvin Schiraldi, Boston A.L. 1, New York N.L. 0 (five hits).
Oct. 16, 1988	Orel Hershiser, Los Angeles N.L. 6, Oakland A.L. 0 (three hits).
Oct. 14, 1989	Dave Stewart, Oakland A.L. 5, San Francisco N.L. 0 (five hits).
Oct. 16, 1990	Jose Rijo, Rob Dibble and Randy Myers, Cincinnati N.L. 7, Oakland A.L. 0 (nine hits).
Oct. 27, 1991	Jack Morris, Minnesota A.L. 1, Atlanta N.L. 0, 10 innings (seven hits).
Oct. 21, 1993	Curt Schilling, Philadelphia N.L. 2, Toronto A.L. 0 (five hits).
Oct. 28, 1995	Tom Glavine, Atlanta N.L. 1, Cleveland A.L. 0 (one hit).
Oct. 21, 1996	Greg Maddux, Atlanta N.L. 4, New York A.L. 0 (seven hits).
Oct. 24, 1996	Andy Pettitte and John Wetteland, New York A.L. 1, Atlanta N.L. 0 (five hits).
Oct. 21, 1998	Andy Pettitte, Jeff Nelson and Mariano Rivera, New York A.L. 3, San Diego N.L. 0 (seven hits).
Oct. 28, 2001	Randy Johnson, Arizona N.L. 4, New York A.L. 0 (three hits).
Oct. 25, 2003	Josh Beckett, Florida N.L. 2, New York A.L. 0 (two hits).
Oct. 27, 2004	Derek Lowe, Bronson Arroyo, Alan Embree, Keith Foulke, Boston A.L. 3, St. Louis N.L. 0 (four hits).

Total number of shutouts: 107

EXTRA-INNING GAMES

Oct. 8, 1907	12 innings, Chicago N.L. 3, Detroit A.L. 3 (tie).
Oct. 22, 1910	10 innings, Chicago N.L. 4, Philadelphia A.L. 3.
Oct. 17, 1911	11 innings, Philadelphia A.L. 3, New York N.L. 2.
Oct. 25, 1911	10 innings, New York N.L. 4, Philadelphia A.L. 3.
Oct. 9, 1912	11 innings, Boston A.L., 6, New York N.L. 6 (tie).
Oct. 16, 1912	10 innings, Boston A.L. 3, New York N.L. 2.
Oct. 8, 1913	10 innings, New York N.L. 3, Philadelphia A.L. 0.
Oct. 12, 1914	12 innings, Boston N.L. 5, Philadelphia A.L. 4.
Oct. 9, 1916	14 innings, Boston A.L. 2, Brooklyn N.L. 1.
Oct. 7, 1919	10 innings, Chicago A.L. 5, Cincinnati N.L. 4.
Oct. 5, 1922	10 innings, New York N.L. 3, New York A.L. 3 (tie).
Oct. 4, 1924	12 innings, New York N.L. 4, Washington A.L. 3.
Oct. 10, 1924	12 innings, Washington A.L. 4, New York N.L. 3.
Oct. 7, 1926	10 innings, New York A.L. 3, St. Louis N.L. 2.
Oct. 6, 1933	11 innings, New York N.L. 2, Washington A.L. 1.
Oct. 7, 1933	10 innings, New York N.L. 4, Washington A.L. 3.
Oct. 4, 1934	12 innings, Detroit A.L. 3, St. Louis N.L. 2.
Oct. 4, 1935	11 innings, Detroit A.L. 6, Chicago N.L. 5.
Oct. 5, 1936	10 innings, New York N.L. 5, New York A.L. 4.
Oct. 8, 1939	10 innings, New York A.L. 7, Cincinnati N.L. 4.
Oct. 5, 1944	11 innings, St. Louis N.L. 3, St. Louis A.L. 2.
Oct. 8, 1945	12 innings, Chicago N.L. 8, Detroit A.L. 7.
Oct. 6, 1946	10 innings, Boston A.L. 3, St. Louis N.L. 2.
Oct. 5, 1950	10 innings, New York A.L. 2, Philadelphia N.L. 1.
Oct. 5, 1952	11 innings, Brooklyn N.L. 6, New York A.L. 5.

Sept. 29, 1954	10 innings, New York N.L. 5, Cleveland A.L. 2.
Oct. 9, 1956	10 innings, Brooklyn N.L. 1, New York A.L. 0.
Oct. 6, 1957	10 innings, Milwaukee N.L. 7, New York A.L. 5.
Oct. 1, 1958	10 innings, Milwaukee N.L. 4, New York A.L. 3.
Oct. 8, 1958	10 innings, New York A.L. 4, Milwaukee N.L. 3.
Oct. 12, 1964	10 innings, St. Louis N.L. 5, New York A.L. 2.
Oct. 15, 1969	10 innings, New York N.L. 2, Baltimore A.L. 1.
Oct. 16, 1971	10 innings, Baltimore A.L. 3, Pittsburgh N.L. 2.
Oct. 14, 1973	12 innings, New York N.L. 10, Oakland A.L. 7.
Oct. 16, 1973	11 innings, Oakland A.L. 3, New York N.L. 2.
Oct. 14, 1975	10 innings, Cincinnati N.L. 6, Boston A.L. 5.
Oct. 21, 1975	12 innings, Boston A.L. 7, Cincinnati N.L. 6.
Oct. 11, 1977	12 innings, New York A.L. 4, Los Angeles N.L. 3.
Oct. 14, 1978	10 innings, New York A.L. 4, Los Angeles N.L. 3.
Oct. 17, 1980	10 innings, Kansas City A.L. 4, Philadelphia N.L. 3.
Oct. 25, 1986	10 innings, New York N.L. 6, Boston A.L. 5.
Oct. 17, 1990	10 innings, Cincinnati N.L. 5, Oakland A.L. 4.
Oct. 22, 1991	12 innings, Atlanta N.L. 5, Minnesota A.L. 4.
Oct. 26, 1991	11 innings, Minnesota A.L. 4, Atlanta N.L. 3.
Oct. 27, 1991	10 innings, Minnesota A.L. 1, Atlanta N.L. 0.
Oct. 24, 1992	11 innings, Toronto A.L. 4, Atlanta N.L. 3.
Oct. 24, 1995	11 innings, Cleveland A.L. 7, Atlanta N.L. 6.
Oct. 23, 1996	10 innings, New York A.L. 8, Atlanta N.L. 6.
Oct. 26, 1997	11 innings, Florida N.L. 3, Cleveland A.L. 2.
Oct. 26, 1999	10 innings, New York A.L. 6, Atlanta N.L. 5.
Oct. 21, 2000	12 innings, New York A.L. 4, New York N.L. 3.
Oct. 31, 2001	10 innings, New York A.L. 4, Arizona N.L. 3.
Nov. 1, 2001	12 innings, New York A.L. 3, Arizona N.L. 2.
Oct. 22, 2003	12 innings, Florida N.L. 4, New York A.L. 3

Total number of occurrences: 53

ATTENDANCE

Year	Games	Total
1903	8	100,429
1905	5	91,723
1906	6	99,845
1907	5	78,068
1908	5	62,232
1909	7	145,295
1910	5	124,222
1911	6	179,851
1912	8	252,037
1913	5	151,000
1914	4	111,009
1915	5	143,351
1916	5	162,859
1917	6	186,654
1918	6	128,483
1919	8	236,928
1920	7	178,737
1921	8	269,976
1922	5	185,947
1923	6	301,430
1924	7	283,665
1925	7	282,848
1926	7	328,051
1927	4	201,705
1928	4	199,072
1929	5	190,490
1930	6	212,619
1931	7	231,567
1932	4	191,998
1933	5	163,076
1934	7	281,510
1935	6	286,672
1936	6	302,924
1937	5	238,142
1938	4	200,833
1939	4	183,849
1940	7	281,927
1941	5	235,773
1942	5	277,101
1943	5	277,312
1944	6	206,708
1945	7	333,457
1946	7	250,071
1947	7	389,763

Year	Games	Total
1948	6	358,362
1949	5	236,716
1950	4	196,009
1951	6	341,977
1952	7	340,706
1953	6	307,350
1954	4	251,507
1955	7	362,310
1956	7	345,903
1957	7	394,712
1958	7	393,909
1959	6	420,784
1960	7	349,813
1961	5	223,247
1962	7	376,864
1963	4	247,279
1964	7	321,807
1965	7	364,326
1966	4	220,791
1967	7	304,085
1968	7	379,670
1969	5	272,378
1970	5	253,183
1971	7	351,091
1972	7	363,149
1973	7	358,289
1974	5	260,004
1975	7	308,272
1976	4	223,009
1977	6	337,708
1978	6	337,304
1979	7	367,597
1980	6	324,516
1981	6	338,081
1982	7	384,570
1983	5	304,139
1984	5	271,820
1985	7	327,494
1986	7	321,774
1987	7	387,138
1988	5	259,984
1989	4	222,843
1990	4	208,544
1991	7	373,160
1992	6	311,400
1993	6	344,394
1994		no World Series
1995	6	286,385
1996	6	324,685
1997	7	403,617
1998	4	243,498
1999	4	216,114
2000	5	277,853
2001	7	366,289
2002	7	306,414
2003	7	364,932
2004	4	174,088

INDIVIDUAL BATTING
LEADING BATTERS

(Playing in all games, each series; capitalized name denotes leader or tied for series lead, both teams)

AMERICAN LEAGUE

Year	Player, Club	AB	H	TB	Avg.
1903	Chick Stahl, Boston	33	10	17	.303
1904	no series played				
1905	Topsy Hartsel, Philadelphia	17	5	6	.294
1906	GEORGE ROHE, Chicago	21	7	12	.333
	JIGGS DONAHUE, Chicago	18	6	10	.333
1907	Claude Rossman, Detroit	20	8	10	.400
1908	Ty Cobb, Detroit	19	7	8	.368
1909	Jim Delahanty, Detroit	26	9	13	.346
1910	EDDIE COLLINS, Philadelphia	21	9	13	.429

Year	Player, Club	AB	H	TB	Avg.
1911	HOME RUN BAKER, Philadelphia	24	9	17	.375
1912	Tris Speaker, Boston	30	9	14	.300
1913	Home Run Baker, Philadelphia	20	9	12	.450
1914	Home Run Baker, Philadelphia	16	4	6	.250
1915	DUFFY LEWIS, Boston	18	8	12	.444
1916	DUFFY LEWIS, Boston	17	6	10	.353
1917	Eddie Collins, Chicago	22	9	10	.409
1918	Stuffy McInnis, Boston	20	5	5	.250
	George Whiteman, Boston	20	5	7	.250
1919	JOE JACKSON, Chicago	32	12	18	.375
1920	STEVE O'NEILL, Cleveland	21	7	10	.333
1921	Wally Schang, New York	21	6	9	.296
1922	Bob Meusel, New York	20	6	7	.300
1923	AARON WARD, New York	24	10	13	.417
1924	JOE JUDGE, Washington	26	10	11	.385
1925	Bucky Harris, Washington	25	11	22	.440
1926	Earle Combs, New York	28	10	12	.357
1927	MARK KOENIG, New York	18	9	11	.500
1928	BABE RUTH, New York	16	10	22	.625
1929	Jimmie Dykes, Philadelphia	19	8	9	.421
1930	AL SIMMONS, Philadelphia	22	8	16	.364
1931	Jimmie Foxx, Philadelphia	23	8	11	.348
1932	LOU GEHRIG, New York	17	9	19	.529
1933	Fred Schulte, Washington	21	7	21	.333
1934	CHARLIE GEHRINGER, Detroit	29	11	15	.379
1935	PETE FOX, Detroit	26	10	15	.385
1936	JAKE POWELL, New York	22	10	14	.455
1937	TONY LAZZERI, New York	15	6	11	.400
1938	Bill Dickey, New York	15	6	9	.400
	Joe Gordon, New York	15	6	11	.400
1939	CHARLIE KELLER, New York	16	7	19	.438
1940	Bruce Campbell, Detroit	25	9	13	.360
1941	JOE GORDON, New York	14	7	13	.500
1942	PHIL RIZZUTO, New York	21	8	11	.381
1943	Billy Johnson, New York	20	6	9	.300
1944	GEORGE McQUINN, St. Louis	16	7	12	.438
1945	Roger Cramer, Detroit	29	11	11	.379
1946	Rudy York, Boston	23	6	15	.261
1947	TOMMY HENRICH, New York	31	10	15	.323
1948	Larry Doby, Cleveland	22	7	11	.318
1949	Tommy Henrich, New York	19	5	8	.263
1950	GENE WOODLING, New York	14	6	6	.429
1951	Phil Rizzuto, New York	25	8	11	.320
1952	GENE WOODLING, New York	23	8	14	.348
1953	BILLY MARTIN, New York	24	12	23	.500
1954	VIC WERTZ, Cleveland	16	8	15	.500
1955	YOGI BERRA, New York	24	10	14	.417
1956	YOGI BERRA, New York	25	9	20	.360
1957	Jerry Coleman, New York	22	8	10	.364
1958	Hank Bauer, New York	31	10	22	.323
1959	TED KLUSZEWSKI, Chicago	23	9	19	.391
1960	MICKEY MANTLE, New York	25	10	20	.400
1961	BOBBY RICHARDSON, New York	23	9	10	.391
1962	Tom Tresh, New York	28	9	13	.321
1963	Elston Howard, New York	15	5	5	.333
1964	Bobby Richardson, New York	32	13	15	.406
1965	Zoilo Versalles, Minnesota	28	8	14	.286
	Harmon Killebrew, Minnesota	21	6	9	.286
1966	BOOG POWELL, Baltimore	14	5	6	.357
1967	Carl Yastrzemski, Boston	25	10	21	.400
1968	Norm Cash, Detroit	26	10	13	.385
1969	Boog Powell, Baltimore	19	5	5	.263
1970	PAUL BLAIR, Baltimore	19	9	10	.474
1971	Brooks Robinson, Baltimore	22	7	7	.318
1972	Gene Tenace, Oakland	23	8	21	.348
1973	Joe Rudi, Oakland	27	9	11	.333
1974	Bert Campaneris, Oakland	17	6	8	.353
1975	Carl Yastrzemski, Boston	29	9	9	.310
1976	Thurman Munson, New York	17	9	9	.529
1977	REGGIE JACKSON, New York	20	9	25	.450
1978	BRIAN DOYLE, New York	16	7	8	.438
1979	Ken Singleton, Baltimore	28	10	11	.357
1980	AMOS OTIS, Kansas City	23	11	22	.478
1981	LOU PINIELLA, New York	16	7	8	.438
1982	ROBIN YOUNT, Milwaukee	29	12	18	.414
1983	JOHN SHELBY, Baltimore	9	4	4	.444

Year	Player, Club	AB	H	TB	Avg.
1984	ALAN TRAMMELL, Detroit	20	9	16	.450
1985	GEORGE BRETT, Kansas City	27	10	11	.370
1986	MARTY BARRETT, Boston	30	13	15	.433
1987	Kirby Puckett, Minnesota	28	10	13	.357
1988	Dave Henderson, Oakland	20	6	8	.300
1989	RICKEY HENDERSON, Oakland	19	9	17	.474
1990	Rickey Henderson, Oakland	15	5	10	.333
1991	BRIAN HARPER, Minnesota	21	8	10	.381
1992	PAT BORDERS, Toronto	20	9	15	.450
1993	PAUL MOLITOR, Toronto	24	12	24	.500
1994	no series played				
1995	Albert Belle, Cleveland	17	4	10	.235
1996	Cecil Fielder, New York	23	9	11	.391
1997	Matt Williams, Cleveland	26	10	14	.385
1998	RICKY LEDEE, New York	10	6	9	.600
1999	Scott Brosius, New York	16	6	7	.375
2000	PAUL O'NEILL, New York	19	9	15	.474
2001	Alfonso Soriano, New York	25	6	9	.240
2002	Troy Glaus, Anaheim	26	10	22	.385
2003	BERNIE WILLIAMS, New York	25	10	18	.400
2004	BILL MUELLER, Boston	14	6	8	.429

NATIONAL LEAGUE

Year	Player, Club	AB	H	TB	Avg.
1903	JIMMY SEBRING, Pittsburgh	30	11	16	.367
1904—no series played					
1905	MIKE DONLIN, New York	19	6	7	.316
1906	Solly Hofman, Chicago	23	7	8	.304
1907	HARRY STEINFELDT, Chicago	17	8	11	.471
1908	FRANK CHANCE, Chicago	19	8	8	.421
1909	TOMMY LEACH, Pittsburgh	25	9	14	.360
1910	Frank Schulte, Chicago	17	6	9	.353
	Frank Chance, Chicago	17	6	9	.353
1911	Larry Doyle, New York	23	7	12	.304
1912	BUCK HERZOG, New York	30	12	18	.400
1913	LARRY McLEAN, New York	12	6	6	.500
1914	HANK GOWDY, Boston	11	6	14	.545
1915	Fred Luderus, Philadelphia	16	7	12	.438
1916	Ivy Olson, Brooklyn	16	4	6	.250
1917	DAVE ROBERTSON, New York	22	11	14	.500
1918	CHARLIE PICK, Chicago	18	7	8	.389
1919	Greasy Neale, Cincinnati	28	10	13	.357
1920	ZACH WHEAT, Brooklyn	27	9	11	.333
1921	IRISH MEUSEL, New York	29	10	17	.345
1922	HEINIE GROH, New York	19	9	11	.474
1923	CASEY STENGEL, New York	12	5	11	.417
1924	Frankie Frisch, New York	30	10	16	.333
	Fred Lindstrom, New York	30	10	12	.333
1925	MAX CAREY, Pittsburgh	24	11	15	.458
1926	TOMMY THEVENOW, St. Louis	24	10	14	.417
1927	Lloyd Waner, Pittsburgh	15	6	9	.400
1928	Rabbit Maranville, St. Louis	13	4	5	.308
1929	Hack Wilson, Chicago	17	8	10	.471
1930	Charlie Gelbert, St. Louis	17	6	8	.353
1931	PEPPER MARTIN, St. Louis	24	12	19	.500
1932	Riggs Stephenson, Chicago	18	8	9	.444
1933	MEL OTT, New York	18	7	13	.389
1934	JOE MEDWICK, St. Louis	29	11	16	.379
1935	Billy Herman, Chicago	24	8	15	.333
1936	Dick Bartell, New York	21	8	14	.381
1937	Joe Moore, New York	23	9	10	.391
1938	STAN HACK, Chicago	17	8	9	.471
1939	Frank McCormick, Cincinnati	15	6	7	.400
1940	BILL WERBER, Cincinnati	27	10	14	.370
1941	Joe Medwick, Brooklyn	17	4	5	.235
1942	Jimmy Brown, St. Louis	20	6	6	.300
1943	MARTY MARION, St. Louis	14	5	10	.357
1944	Emil Verban, St. Louis	17	7	7	.412
1945	PHIL CAVARRETTA, Chicago	26	11	16	.423
1946	HARRY WALKER, St. Louis	17	7	9	.412
1947	Pee Wee Reese, Brooklyn	23	7	8	.304
1948	BOB ELLIOTT, Boston	21	7	13	.333
1949	PEE WEE REESE, Brooklyn	19	6	10	.316
1950	GRANNY HAMNER, Philadelphia	14	6	10	.429
1951	MONTE IRVIN, New York	24	11	13	.458
1952	Duke Snider, Brooklyn	29	10	24	.345
	Pee Wee Reese, Brooklyn	29	10	13	.345
1953	Gil Hodges, Brooklyn	22	8	11	.364
1954	Alvin Dark, New York	17	7	7	.412
1955	Duke Snider, Brooklyn	25	8	21	.320
1956	Duke Snider, Brooklyn	23	7	11	.304
	Gil Hodges, Brooklyn	23	7	12	.304
1957	HANK AARON, Milwaukee	28	11	22	.393
1958	BILL BRUTON, Milwaukee	17	7	10	.412
1959	GIL HODGES, Los Angeles	23	9	14	.391
1960	Bill Mazeroski, Pittsburgh	25	8	16	.320
1961	Wally Post, Cincinnati	18	6	10	.333
1962	JOSE PAGAN, San Francisco	19	7	10	.368
1963	TOMMY DAVIS, Los Angeles	15	6	10	.400
1964	TIM McCARVER, St. Louis	23	11	17	.478
1965	RON FAIRLY, Los Angeles	29	11	20	.379
1966	Lou Johnson, Los Angeles	15	4	5	.267
1967	LOU BROCK, St. Louis	29	12	19	.414
1968	LOU BROCK, St. Louis	28	13	24	.464
1969	AL WEIS, New York	11	5	8	.455
1970	Lee May, Cincinnati	18	7	15	.389
1971	ROBERTO CLEMENTE, Pittsburgh	29	12	22	.414
1972	TONY PEREZ, Cincinnati	23	10	12	.435
1973	RUSTY STAUB, New York	26	11	16	.423
1974	STEVE GARVEY, Los Angeles	21	8	8	.381
1975	PETE ROSE, Cincinnati	27	10	13	.370
1976	JOHNNY BENCH, Cincinnati	15	8	17	.533
1977	Steve Garvey, Los Angeles	24	9	15	.375
1978	Bill Russell, Los Angeles	26	11	13	.423
1979	PHIL GARNER, Pittsburgh	24	12	16	.500
1980	Bob Boone, Philadelphia	17	7	9	.412
1981	Steve Garvey, Los Angeles	24	10	11	.417
1982	George Hendrick, St. Louis	28	9	9	.321
	Lonnie Smith, St. Louis	28	9	15	.321
1983	Bo Diaz, Philadelphia	15	5	6	.333
1984	Kurt Bevacqua, San Diego	17	7	15	.412
1985	Tito Landrum, St. Louis	25	9	14	.360
1986	Lenny Dykstra, New York	27	8	14	.296
1987	TONY PENA, St. Louis	22	9	10	.409
1988	MICKEY HATCHER, Los Angeles	19	7	14	.368
1989	Ken Oberkfell, San Francisco	6	2	2	.333
1990	BILLY HATCHER, Cincinnati	12	9	15	.750
1991	Rafael Belliard, Atlanta	16	6	7	.375
1992	Otis Nixon, Atlanta	27	8	9	.296
1993	Lenny Dykstra, Philadelphia	23	8	21	.348
	John Kruk, Philadelphia	23	8	9	.348
1994	no series played				
1995	MARQUIS GRISSOM, Atlanta	25	9	10	.360
1996	MARQUIS GRISSOM, Atlanta	27	12	16	.444
1997	DARREN DAULTON, Florida	18	7	12	.389
1998	Tony Gwynn, San Diego	16	8	11	.500
1999	BRET BOONE, Atlanta	13	7	11	.538
2000	Todd Zeile, New York	20	8	10	.400
2001	STEVE FINLEY, Arizona	19	7	10	.368
2002	BARRY BONDS, San Francisco	17	8	22	.471
2003	Jeff Conine, Florida	21	7	8	.333
2004	Larry Walker, St. Louis	14	5	13	.357

.500 HITTERS

(Playing in all games and having 10 or more at-bats)

Player, Club	Year	AB	H	TB	Avg.
Billy Hatcher, Cincinnati N.L.	1990	12	9	15	.750
Babe Ruth, New York A.L.	1928	16	10	22	.625
Ricky Ledee, New York A.L.	1998	10	6	9	.600
Chris Sabo, Cincinnati N.L.	1990	16	9	16	.563
Hank Gowdy, Boston N.L.	1914	11	6	14	.545
Lou Gehrig, New York A.L.	1928	11	6	19	.545
Bret Boone, Atlanta N.L.	1999	13	7	11	.538
Johnny Bench, Cincinnati N.L.	1976	15	8	17	.533
Lou Gehrig, New York A.L.	1932	17	9	19	.529
Thurman Munson, New York A.L.	1976	17	9	9	.529
Larry McLean, New York N.L.	1913	12	6	6	.500
Dave Robertson, New York N.L.	1917	22	11	14	.500
Mark Koenig, New York A.L.	1927	18	9	11	.500
Pepper Martin, St. Louis N.L.	1931	24	12	19	.500
Joe Gordon, New York A.L.	1941	14	7	13	.500
Billy Martin, New York A.L.	1953	24	12	23	.500

Player, Club	Year	AB	H	TB	Avg.
Vic Wertz, Cleveland A.L.	1954	16	8	15	.500
Phil Garner, Pittsburgh N.L.	1979	24	12	16	.500
Paul Molitor, Toronto A.L.	1993	24	12	24	.500
Tony Gwynn, San Diego N.L.	1998	16	8	11	.500

Total number of occurrences: 20

HOME RUNS

AMERICAN LEAGUE

1903—2—Boston, Patsy Dougherty 2.
1904—no series played
1905—0—Philadelphia.
1906—0—Chicago.
1907—0—Detroit.
1908—0—Detroit.
1909—2—Detroit, Davy Jones, Sam Crawford.
1910—1—Philadelphia, Danny Murphy.
1911—3—Philadelphia, Home Run Baker 2, Rube Oldring.
1912—1—Boston, Larry Gardner.
1913—2—Philadelphia, Home Run Baker, Wally Schang.
1914—0—Philadelphia.
1915—2—Boston, Harry Hooper 2, Duffy Lewis.
1916—2—Boston, Larry Gardner 2.
1917—1—Chicago, Happy Felsch.
1918—0—Boston.
1919—1—Chicago, Joe Jackson.
1920—2—Cleveland, Elmer Smith, Jim Bagby.
1921—2—New York, Babe Ruth, Chick Fewster.
1922—2—New York, Aaron Ward 2.
1923—5—New York, Babe Ruth 3, Aaron Ward, Joe Dugan.
1924—5—Washington, Goose Goslin 3, Bucky Harris 2.
1925—8—Washington, Bucky Harris 3, Goose Goslin 3, Joe Judge, Roger Peckinpaugh.
1926—4—New York, Babe Ruth 4.
1927—2—New York, Babe Ruth 2.
1928—9—New York, Lou Gehrig 4, Babe Ruth 3, Bob Meusel, Cedric Durst.
1929—6—Philadelphia, Jimmie Foxx 2, Al Simmons 2, Mule Haas 2.
1930—6—Philadelphia, Mickey Cochrane 2, Al Simmons 2, Jimmie Foxx, Jimmie Dykes.
1931—3—Philadelphia, Al Simmons 2, Jimmie Foxx.
1932—8—New York, Lou Gehrig 3, Babe Ruth 2, Tony Lazzeri 2, Earle Combs.
1933—2—Washington, Goose Goslin, Fred Schulte.
1934—2—Detroit, Hank Greenberg, Charlie Gehringer.
1935—1—Detroit, Hank Greenberg.
1936—7—New York, Lou Gehrig 2, George Selkirk 2, Tony Lazzeri, Bill Dickey, Jake Powell.
1937—4—New York, Tony Lazzeri, Lou Gehrig, Myril Hoag, Joe DiMaggio.
1938—5—New York, Frank Crosetti, Joe DiMaggio, Joe Gordon, Bill Dickey, Tommy Henrich.
1939—7—New York, Charlie Keller 3, Bill Dickey 2, Babe Dahlgren, Joe DiMaggio.
1940—4—Detroit, Bruce Campbell, Rudy York, Pinky Higgins, Hank Greenberg.
1941—2—New York, Joe Gordon, Tommy Henrich.
1942—3—New York, Charlie Keller 2, Phil Rizzuto.
1943—2—New York, Joe Gordon, Bill Dickey.
1944—1—St. Louis, George McQuinn.
1945—2—Detroit, Hank Greenberg 2.
1946—4—Boston, Rudy York 2, Bobby Doerr, Leon Culberson.
1947—4—New York, Joe DiMaggio 2, Tommy Henrich, Yogi Berra.
1948—4—Cleveland, Larry Doby, Dale Mitchell, Jim Hegan, Joe Gordon.
1949—2—New York, Tommy Henrich, Joe DiMaggio.
1950—2—New York, Joe DiMaggio, Yogi Berra.
1951—5—New York, Joe Collins, Gene Woodling, Joe DiMaggio, Gil McDougald, Phil Rizzuto.
1952—10—New York, Johnny Mize 3, Mickey Mantle 2, Yogi Berra 2, Gil McDougald, Billy Martin, Gene Woodling.
1953—9—New York, Mickey Mantle 2, Gil McDougald 2, Billy Martin 2, Yogi Berra, Joe Collins, Gene Woodling.
1954—3—Cleveland, Al Smith, Vic Wertz, Hank Majeski
1955—8—New York, Joe Collins 2, Yogi Berra, Bob Cerv, Elston Howard, Mickey Mantle, Gil McDougald, Bill Skowron.
1956—12—New York, Mickey Mantle 3, Yogi Berra 3, Billy Martin 2, Enos Slaughter, Hank Bauer, Elston Howard, Bill Skowron.
1957—7—New York, Hank Bauer 2, Tony Kubek 2, Mickey Mantle, Yogi Berra, Elston Howard.
1958—10—New York, Hank Bauer 4, Gil McDougald 2, Mickey Mantle 2, Bill Skowron 2.
1959—4—Chicago, Ted Kluszewski 3, Sherm Lollar.
1960—10—New York, Mickey Mantle 3, Roger Maris 2, Bill Skowron 2, Yogi Berra, Elston Howard, Bobby Richardson.
1961—7—New York, Johnny Blanchard 2, Yogi Berra, Elston Howard, Hector Lopez, Roger Maris, Bill Skowron.
1962—3—New York, Tom Tresh, Roger Maris, Clete Boyer.
1963—2—New York, Tom Tresh, Mickey Mantle.
1964—10—New York, Mickey Mantle 3, Phil Linz 2, Tom Tresh 2, Roger Maris, Joe Pepitone, Clete Boyer.
1965—6—Minnesota, Zoilo Versalles, Tony Oliva, Harmon Killebrew, Don Mincher, Bob Allison, Mudcat Grant.
1966—4—Baltimore, Frank Robinson 2, Brooks Robinson, Paul Blair.
1967—8—Boston, Carl Yastrzemski 3, Reggie Smith 2, Rico Petrocelli 2, Jose Santiago.
1968—8—Detroit, Al Kaline 2, Jim Northrup 2, Norm Cash, Willie Horton, Mickey Lolich, Dick McAuliffe.
1969—3—Baltimore, Don Buford, Dave McNally, Frank Robinson.
1970—10—Baltimore, Boog Powell 2, Frank Robinson 2, Brooks Robinson 2, Don Buford, Elrod Hendricks, Dave McNally, Merv Rettenmund.
1971—5—Baltimore, Don Buford 2, Frank Robinson 2, Merv Rettenmund.
1972—5—Oakland, Gene Tenace 4, Joe Rudi.
1973—2—Oakland, Bert Campaneris, Reggie Jackson.
1974—4—Oakland, Ray Fosse, Ken Holtzman, Reggie Jackson, Joe Rudi.
1975—6—Boston, Bernie Carbo 2, Carlton Fisk 2, Dwight Evans, Fred Lynn.
1976—1—New York, Jim Mason.
1977—8—New York, Reggie Jackson 5, Chris Chambliss, Thurman Munson, Willie Randolph.
1978—3—New York, Reggie Jackson 2, Roy White.
1979—4—Baltimore, Doug DeCinces, Eddie Murray, Benny Ayala, Rich Dauer.
1980—8—Kansas City, Willie Aikens 4, Amos Otis 3, George Brett.
1981—6—New York, Willie Randolph 2, Bob Watson 2, Rich Cerone, Reggie Jackson.
1982—5—Milwaukee, Ted Simmons 2, Cecil Cooper, Ben Oglivie, Robin Yount.
1983—6—Baltimore, Eddie Murray 2, Jim Dwyer, John Lowenstein, Dan Ford, Rick Dempsey.
1984—7—Detroit, Kirk Gibson 2, Alan Trammell 2, Marty Castillo, Larry Herndon, Lance Parrish.
1985—2—Kansas City, Frank White, Darryl Motley.
1986—5—Boston, Dwight Evans 2, Dave Henderson 2, Rich Gedman.
1987—7—Minnesota, Don Baylor, Gary Gaetti, Greg Gagne, Dan Gladden, Kent Hrbek, Tim Laudner, Steve Lombardozzi.
1988—2—Oakland, Jose Canseco, Mark McGwire.
1989—9—Oakland, Dave Henderson 2, Jose Canseco, Rickey Henderson, Carney Lansford, Dave Parker, Tony Phillips, Terry Steinbach, Walt Weiss.
1990—3—Oakland, Harold Baines, Jose Canseco, Rickey Henderson.
1991—8—Minnesota, Chili Davis 2, Kirby Puckett 2, Greg Gagne, Kent Hrbek, Scott Leius, Mike Pagliarulo.
1992—6—Toronto, Joe Carter 2, Pat Borders, Kelly Gruber, Candy Maldonado, Ed Sprague.
1993—6—Toronto, Joe Carter 2, Paul Molitor 2, John Olerud, Devon White.
1994—no series played

1995—5—Cleveland, Albert Belle 2, Eddie Murray, Manny Ramirez, Jim Thome.
1996—2—New York, Jim Leyritz, Bernie Williams.
1997—7—Cleveland, Sandy Alomar Jr. 2, Manny Ramirez 2, Jim Thome 2, Matt Williams.
1998—6—New York, Scott Brosius 2, Chuck Knoblauch, Tino Martinez, Jorge Posada, Bernie Williams.
1999—5—New York, Chad Curtis 2, Chuck Knoblauch, Jim Leyritz, Tino Martinez.
2000—4—New York, Derek Jeter 2, Scott Brosius, Bernie Williams.
2001—6—New York, Scott Brosius, Derek Jeter, Tino Martinez, Jorge Posada, Alfonso Soriano, Shane Spencer.
2002—7—Anaheim, Troy Glaus 3, Tim Salmon 2, Darin Erstad, Scott Spiezio.
2003—6—New York, Bernie Williams 2, Aaron Boone, Jason Giambi, Hideki Matsui, Alfonso Soriano.
2004—4—Boston, Mark Bellhorn, Johnny Damon, David Ortiz, Manny Ramirez.

Total number of home runs: 447

NATIONAL LEAGUE

1903—1—Pittsburgh, Jimmy Sebring.
1904—no series played
1905—0—New York.
1906—0—Chicago.
1907—0—Chicago.
1908—1—Chicago, Joe Tinker.
1909—2—Pittsburgh, Fred Clarke 2.
1910—0—Chicago.
1911—0—New York.
1912—1—New York, Larry Doyle.
1913—1—New York, Fred Merkle.
1914—1—Boston, Hank Gowdy.
1915—1—Philadelphia, Fred Luderus.
1916—1—Brooklyn, Hy Myers.
1917—2—New York, Benny Kauff 2.
1918—0—Chicago.
1919—0—Cincinnati.
1920—0—Brooklyn.
1921—2—New York, Frank Snyder, Irish Meusel.
1922—1—New York, Irish Meusel.
1923—5—New York, Casey Stengel 2, Irish Meusel, Ross Youngs, Frank Snyder.
1924—4—New York, George Kelly, Bill Terry, Rosy Ryan, Jack Bentley.
1925—4—Pittsburgh, Pie Traynor, Glenn Wright, Kiki Cuyler, Eddie Moore.
1926—4—St. Louis, Billy Southworth, Tommy Thevenow, Jesse Haines, Les Bell.
1927—0—Pittsburgh.
1928—1—St. Louis, Jim Bottomley.
1929—1—Chicago, Charlie Grimm.
1930—2—St. Louis, George Watkins, Taylor Douthit.
1931—2—St. Louis, Pepper Martin, George Watkins.
1932—3—Chicago, Kiki Cuyler, Gabby Hartnett, Frank Demaree.
1933—3—New York, Mel Ott 2, Bill Terry.
1934—2—St. Louis, Joe Medwick, Bill DeLancey.
1935—5—Chicago, Frank Demaree 2, Gabby Hartnett, Chuck Klein, Billy Herman.
1936—4—New York, Dick Bartell, Jimmy Ripple, Mel Ott, Joe Moore.
1937—1—New York, Mel Ott.
1938—2—Chicago, Joe Marty, Ken O'Dea.
1939—0—Cincinnati.
1940—2—Cincinnati, Jimmy Ripple, Bucky Walters.
1941—1—Brooklyn, Pete Reiser.
1942—2—St. Louis, Enos Slaughter, Whitey Kurowski.
1943—2—St. Louis, Marty Marion, Ray Sanders.
1944—3—St. Louis, Stan Musial, Ray Sanders, Danny Litwhiler.
1945—1—Chicago, Phil Cavarretta.

1946—1—St. Louis, Enos Slaughter.
1947—1—Brooklyn, Dixie Walker.
1948—4—Boston, Bob Elliott 2, Marv Rickert, Bill Salkeld.
1949—4—Brooklyn, Pee Wee Reese, Luis Olmo, Roy Campanella, Gil Hodges.
1950—0—Philadelphia.
1951—2—New York, Alvin Dark, Whitey Lockman.
1952—6—Brooklyn, Duke Snider 4, Jackie Robinson, Pee Wee Reese.
1953—8—Brooklyn, Jim Gilliam 2, Roy Campanella, Billy Cox, Carl Furillo, Gil Hodges, George Shuba, Duke Snider.
1954—2—New York, Dusty Rhodes 2.
1955—9—Brooklyn, Duke Snider 4, Roy Campanella 2, Sandy Amoros, Carl Furillo, Gil Hodges.
1956—3—Brooklyn, Duke Snider, Jackie Robinson, Gil Hodges.
1957—8—Milwaukee, Hank Aaron 3, Frank Torre 2, Eddie Mathews, Johnny Logan, Del Crandall.
1958—3—Milwaukee, Del Crandall, Bill Bruton, Lew Burdette.
1959—7—Los Angeles, Charlie Neal 2, Chuck Essegian 2, Wally Moon, Duke Snider, Gil Hodges.
1960—4—Pittsburgh, Bill Mazeroski 2, Rocky Nelson, Hal Smith.
1961—3—Cincinnati, Gordy Coleman, Wally Post, Frank Robinson.
1962—5—San Francisco, Chuck Hiller, Willie McCovey, Tom Haller, Ed Bailey, Jose Pagan.
1963—3—Los Angeles, John Roseboro, Bill Skowron, Frank Howard.
1964—5—St. Louis, Ken Boyer 2, Lou Brock, Mike Shannon, Tim McCarver.
1965—5—Los Angeles, Ron Fairly 2, Lou Johnson 2, Wes Parker.
1966—1—Los Angeles, Jim Lefebvre.
1967—5—St. Louis, Lou Brock, Bob Gibson, Julian Javier, Roger Maris, Mike Shannon.
1968—7—St. Louis, Lou Brock 2, Orlando Cepeda 2, Bob Gibson, Tim McCarver, Mike Shannon.
1969—6—New York, Donn Clendenon 3, Tommie Agee, Ed Kranepool, Al Weis.
1970—5—Cincinnati, Lee May 2, Johnny Bench, Pete Rose, Bobby Tolan.
1971—5—Pittsburgh, Bob Robertson 2, Roberto Clemente 2, Richie Hebner.
1972—3—Cincinnati, Johnny Bench, Denis Menke, Pete Rose.
1973—4—New York, Wayne Garrett 2, Cleon Jones, Rusty Staub.
1974—4—Los Angeles, Bill Buckner, Willie Crawford, Joe Ferguson, Jim Wynn.
1975—7—Cincinnati, Tony Perez 3, Cesar Geronimo 2, Johnny Bench, David Concepcion.
1976—4—Cincinnati, Johnny Bench 2, Dan Driessen, Joe Morgan.
1977—9—Los Angeles, Reggie Smith 3, Steve Yeager 2, Dusty Baker, Ron Cey, Steve Garvey, Dave Lopes.
1978—6—Los Angeles, Dave Lopes 3, Dusty Baker, Ron Cey, Reggie Smith.
1979—3—Pittsburgh, Willie Stargell 3.
1980—3—Philadelphia, Mike Schmidt 2, Bake McBride.
1981—6—Los Angeles, Pedro Guerrero 2, Steve Yeager 2, Ron Cey, Jay Johnstone.
1982—4—St. Louis, Willie McGee 2, Keith Hernandez, Darrell Porter.
1983—4—Philadelphia, Joe Morgan, Garry Maddox, Gary Matthews.
1984—3—San Diego, Kurt Bevacqua 2, Terry Kennedy.
1985—2—St. Louis, Tito Landrum, Willie McGee.
1986—7—New York, Gary Carter 2, Lenny Dykstra 2, Ray Knight, Darryl Strawberry, Tim Teufel.
1987—2—St. Louis, Tom Herr, Tom Lawless.
1988—5—Los Angeles, Mickey Hatcher 2, Mike Davis, Kirk Gibson, Mike A. Marshall.
1989—4—San Francisco, Bill Bathe, Greg Litton, Kevin

Mitchell, Matt Williams.
1990—3—Cincinnati, Chris Sabo 2, Eric Davis.
1991—8—Atlanta, Lonnie Smith 3, David Justice 2, Terry
　　　　　Pendleton 2, Brian Hunter.
1992—3—Atlanta, Damon Berryhill, David Justice, Lonnie
　　　　　Smith.
1993—7—Philadelphia, Lenny Dykstra 4, Darren Daulton, Jim
　　　　　Eisenreich, Milt Thompson.
1994—no series played
1995—8—Atlanta, Ryan Klesko 3, Fred McGriff 2, David
　　　　　Justice, Javier Lopez, Luis Polonia.
1996—4—Atlanta, Andruw Jones 2, Fred McGriff 2.
1997—8—Florida, Moises Alou 3, Bobby Bonilla, Darren Daulton,
　　　　　Jim Eisenreich, Charles Johnson, Gary Sheffield.
1998—3—San Diego, Greg Vaughn 2, Tony Gwynn.
1999—1—Atlanta, Chipper Jones.
2000—4—New York, Mike Piazza 2, Jay Payton, Robin Ventura.
2001—6—Arizona, Rod Barajas, Craig Counsell, Steve Finley,
　　　　　Luis Gonzalez, Mark Grace, Matt Williams.
2002—14—San Francisco, Barry Bonds 4, Jeff Kent 3, Rich
　　　　　Aurilia 2, Reggie Sanders 2, David Bell, Shawon
　　　　　Dunston, J.T. Snow.
2003—2—Florida, Miguel Cabrera, Alex Gonzalez.
2004—2—St. Louis, Larry Walker 2.

Total number of home runs: 333

PLAYERS WITH FIVE HOME RUNS

Player	Series	No.
Mickey Mantle	12	18
Babe Ruth	10	15
Yogi Berra	14	12
Duke Snider	6	11
Reggie Jackson	5	10
Lou Gehrig	7	10
Frank Robinson	5	8
Bill Skowron	8	8
Joe DiMaggio	10	8
Goose Goslin	5	7
Gil McDougald	8	7
Hank Bauer	9	7
Lenny Dykstra	2	6
Al Simmons	4	6
Reggie Smith	4	6
Roger Maris	7	6
Charlie Keller	4	5
Hank Greenberg	4	5
Johnny Bench	4	5
Billy Martin	5	5
Bernie Williams	6	5
Gil Hodges	7	5
Bill Dickey	8	5
Elston Howard	9	5

Total number of players: 24

INDIVIDUAL PITCHING
PITCHERS WITH FIVE VICTORIES

Pitcher, Club	Yrs.	W	L
Whitey Ford, New York A.L.	11	10	8
Red Ruffing, New York A.L.	7	7	2
Allie Reynolds, New York A.L.	6	7	2
Bob Gibson, St. Louis N.L.	3	7	2
Lefty Gomez, New York A.L.	4	6	0
Chief Bender, Philadelphia A.L.	5	6	4
Waite Hoyt, New York A.L., Philadelphia A.L.	6	6	4
Jack Coombs, Philadelphia A.L., Brooklyn N.L.	3	5	0
Herb Pennock, New York A.L.	3	5	0
Vic Raschi, New York A.L.	5	5	3
Catfish Hunter, Oakland A.L., New York A.L.	6	5	3
Mordecai Brown, Chicago N.L.	4	5	4
Christy Mathewson, New York N.L.	5	5	5

Total number of pitchers: 13

10-STRIKEOUT GAMES BY PITCHERS

Date	Pitcher, Club	No.
Oct. 1,1903	Deacon Phillippe, Pit. N.L. vs. Bos. A.L.	10
Oct. 2,1903	Bill Dinneen, Bos. A.L. vs. Pit. N.L.	11
Oct. 11,1906	Ed Walsh, Chi. A.L. vs. Chi. N.L.	12
Oct. 8,1907	Bill Donovan, Det. A.L. vs. Chi. N.L. (12 innings)	12
Oct. 14,1908	Orval Overall, Chi. N.L. vs. Det. A.L.	10

Date	Pitcher, Club	No.
Oct. 12,1909	George Mullin, Det. A.L. vs. Pit. N.L.	10
Oct. 14,1911	Chief Bender, Phi. A.L. vs. N.Y. N.L. (eight innings)	11
Oct. 8,1912	Joe Wood, Bos. A.L. vs. N.Y. N.L.	11
Oct. 11,1921	Jesse Barnes, N.Y. N.L. vs. N.Y. A.L.	10
Oct. 24,1924	Walter Johnson, Was. A.L. vs. N.Y. N.L. (12 innings)	12
Oct. 7,1925	Walter Johnson, Was. A.L. vs. Pit. N.L.	10
Oct. 3,1926	Grover Alexander, St.L. N.L. vs. N.Y. A.L.	10
Oct. 8,1929	Howard Ehmke, Phi. A.L. vs. Chi. N.L.	13
Oct. 11,1929	George Earnshaw, Phi. A.L. vs. Chi. N.L.	10
Sept.28,1932	Red Ruffing, N.Y. A.L. vs. Chi. N.L.	10
Oct. 3,1933	Carl Hubbell, N.Y. N.L. vs. Was. A.L.	10
Oct. 5,1936	Hal Schumacher, N.Y. N.L. vs. N.Y. A.L. (10 innings)	10
Oct. 6,1944	Jack Kramer, St.L. A.L. vs. St.L. N.L.	10
Oct. 8,1944	Denny Galehouse, St.L. A.L. vs. St.L. N.L.	10
Oct. 8,1944	Mort Cooper, St.L. N.L. vs. St.L. A.L.	12
Oct. 10,1945	Hal Newhouser, Det. A.L. vs. Chi. N.L.	10
Oct. 5,1949	Don Newcombe, Bkn. N.L. vs. N.Y. A.L. (eight innings)	11
Oct. 4,1952	Allie Reynolds, N.Y. A.L. vs. Bkn. N.L.	10
Oct. 2,1953	Carl Erskine, Bkn. N.L. vs. N.Y. A.L.	14
Oct. 3,1956	Sal Maglie, Bkn. N.L. vs. N.Y. A.L.	10
Oct. 9,1956	Bob Turley, N.Y. A.L. vs. Bkn. N.L.	11
Oct. 6,1958	Bob Turley, N.Y. A.L. vs. Mil. N.L.	10
Oct. 10,1962	Jack Sanford, S.F. N.L. vs. N.Y. A.L.	10
Oct. 2,1963	Sandy Koufax, L.A. N.L. vs. N.Y. A.L.	15
Oct. 12,1964	Bob Gibson, St.L. N.L. vs. N.Y. A.L. (10 innings)	13
Oct. 10,1965	Don Drysdale, L.A. N.L. vs. Min. A.L.	11
Oct. 11,1965	Sandy Koufax, L.A. N.L. vs. Min. A.L.	10
Oct. 14,1965	Sandy Koufax, L.A. N.L. vs. Min. A.L.	10
Oct. 5,1966	Moe Drabowsky, Bal. A.L. vs. L.A. N.L.	11
Oct. 4,1967	Bob Gibson, St.L. N.L. vs. Bos. A.L.	10
Oct. 12,1967	Bob Gibson, St.L. N.L. vs. Bos. A.L.	10
Oct. 2,1968	Bob Gibson, St.L. N.L. vs. Det. A.L.	17
Oct. 6,1968	Bob Gibson, St.L. N.L. vs. Det. A.L.	10
Oct. 11,1971	Jim Palmer, Bal. A.L. vs. Pit. N.L.	10
Oct. 18,1972	Blue Moon Odom, Oak. A.L. vs. Cin. N.L. (seven innings)	11
Oct. 16,1973	Tom Seaver, N.Y. N.L. vs. Oak. A.L. (eight innings)	12
Oct. 15,1980	Steve Carlton, Phi. N.L. vs. K.C. A.L. (eight innings)	10
Oct. 24,1996	John Smoltz, Atl. N.L. vs. N.Y. A.L. (eight innings)	10
Oct. 23,1999	Orlando Hernandez, N.Y. A.L. vs. Atl. N.L. (seven innings)	10
Oct. 27,1999	John Smoltz, Atl. N.L. vs. N.Y. A.L. (seven innings)	11
Oct. 24,2000	Orlando Hernandez, N.Y. A.L. vs. N.Y. N.L.	12
Oct. 28,2001	Randy Johnson, Ariz. N.L. vs. N.Y. A.L.	11
Nov. 1,2001	Mike Mussina, N.Y. A.L. vs. Ariz. N.L. (eight innings)	10
Nov. 3,2001	Roger Clemens, N.Y. A.L. vs. Ariz. N.L. (6.1 innings)	10
Oct. 21,2003	Josh Beckett, Fla. N.L. vs. N.Y. A.L. (7.1 innings)	10

Total number of performances: 50

INDIVIDUAL FIELDING
UNASSISTED TRIPLE PLAYS

Bill Wambsganss, second baseman, Cleveland A.L. vs. Brooklyn N.L. at Cleveland, October 10, 1920, fifth inning. Wambsganss caught Clarence Mitchell's line drive, stepped on second to retire Pete Kilduff, then tagged Otto Miller coming from first. (This unassisted triple play was made with runners on first and second bases only.)

Total number of occurrences: 1

CLUB BATTING

Year	Club, League	G	AB	R	H	TB	2B	3B	HR	SB	BB	SO	RBI	Avg.	LOB
1903	Pittsburgh N.L.	8	270	24	64	92	7	9	1	7	14	45	23	.237	51
	Boston A.L.	8	282	39	71	113	4	16	2	5	13	27	35	.252	55
1904	No series played.														
1905	New York N.L.	5	153	15	32	39	7	0	0	11	15	26	13	.209	31
	Philadelphia A.L.	5	155	3	25	30	5	0	0	2	5	25	2	.161	26
1906	Chicago N.L.	6	184	18	36	45	9	0	0	8	18	27	11	.196	37
	Chicago A.L.	6	187	22	37	53	10	3	0	6	18	35	19	.198	33
1907	Chicago N.L.	5	167	19	43	51	6	1	0	18	12	25	16	.257	35
	Detroit A.L.	5	173	6	36	41	1	2	0	7	9	21	6	.208	36
1908	Chicago N.L.	5	164	24	48	59	4	2	1	13	13	26	21	.293	30
	Detroit A.L.	5	158	15	32	37	5	0	0	5	12	26	14	.203	27
1909	Pittsburgh N.L.	7	223	34	49	70	12	1	2	18	20	34	26	.220	44
	Detroit A.L.	7	234	28	55	77	16	0	2	6	20	22	25	.235	50
1910	Chicago N.L.	5	158	15	35	48	11	1	0	3	18	31	13	.222	31
	Philadelphia A.L.	5	177	35	56	80	19	1	1	7	17	24	29	.316	36
1911	New York N.L.	6	189	13	33	46	11	1	0	4	14	44	10	.175	31
	Philadelphia A.L.	6	205	27	50	74	15	0	3	4	4	31	21	.244	29
1912	New York N.L.	8	274	31	74	99	14	4	1	12	22	39	25	.270	53
	Boston A.L.	8	273	25	60	89	14	6	1	6	19	36	21	.220	55
1913	New York N.L.	5	164	15	33	41	3	1	1	5	8	19	15	.201	24
	Philadelphia A.L.	5	174	23	46	64	4	4	2	5	7	16	21	.264	30
1914	Boston N.L.	4	135	16	33	46	6	2	1	9	15	18	14	.244	27
	Philadelphia A.L.	4	128	6	22	31	9	0	0	2	13	28	5	.172	21
1915	Philadelphia N.L.	5	148	10	27	36	4	1	1	2	10	25	9	.182	23
	Boston A.L.	5	159	12	42	57	2	2	3	1	11	25	11	.264	35
1916	Brooklyn N.L.	5	170	13	34	49	2	5	1	1	14	19	11	.200	32
	Boston A.L.	5	164	21	39	64	7	6	2	1	18	25	18	.238	31
1917	New York N.L.	6	199	17	51	70	5	4	2	4	6	27	16	.256	37
	Chicago A.L.	6	197	21	54	63	6	0	1	6	11	28	18	.274	37
1918	Chicago N.L.	6	176	10	37	44	5	1	0	3	18	14	10	.210	31
	Boston A.L.	6	172	9	32	40	2	3	0	3	16	21	6	.186	32
1919	Cincinnati N.L.	8	251	35	64	88	10	7	0	7	25	22	34	.255	46
	Chicago A.L.	8	263	20	59	78	10	3	1	5	15	30	17	.224	52
1920	Brooklyn N.L.	7	215	8	44	51	5	1	0	1	10	20	8	.205	39
	Cleveland A.L.	7	217	21	53	72	9	2	2	2	21	21	18	.244	43
1921	New York N.L.	8	264	29	71	98	13	4	2	7	22	38	28	.269	54
	New York A.L.	8	241	22	50	65	7	1	2	6	27	44	20	.207	43
1922	New York N.L.	5	162	18	50	57	2	1	1	1	12	15	18	.309	32
	New York A.L.	5	158	11	32	46	6	1	2	2	8	20	11	.203	25
1923	New York N.L.	6	201	17	47	70	2	3	5	1	12	18	17	.234	35
	New York A.L.	6	205	30	60	91	8	4	5	1	20	22	29	.293	43
1924	New York N.L.	7	253	27	66	91	9	2	4	3	25	40	22	.261	59
	Washington A.L.	7	248	26	61	85	9	0	5	5	29	34	23	.246	57
1925	Pittsburgh N.L.	7	230	25	61	89	12	2	4	7	17	32	25	.265	54
	Washington A.L.	7	225	26	59	91	8	0	8	2	17	32	25	.262	46
1926	St. Louis N.L.	7	239	31	65	91	12	1	4	2	11	30	30	.272	43
	New York A.L.	7	223	21	54	78	10	1	4	1	31	31	19	.242	55
1927	Pittsburgh N.L.	4	130	10	29	37	6	1	0	0	4	7	10	.223	23
	New York A.L.	4	136	23	38	54	6	2	2	2	13	25	19	.279	29
1928	St. Louis N.L.	4	131	10	27	37	5	1	1	3	11	29	9	.206	27
	New York A.L.	4	134	27	37	71	7	0	9	4	13	12	25	.276	24
1929	Chicago N.L.	5	173	17	43	56	6	2	1	1	13	50	15	.249	36
	Philadelphia A.L.	5	171	26	48	71	5	0	6	0	13	27	26	.281	35
1930	St. Louis N.L.	6	190	12	38	56	10	1	2	1	11	33	11	.200	37
	Philadelphia A.L.	6	178	21	35	67	10	2	6	0	24	32	21	.197	36
1931	St. Louis N.L.	7	229	19	54	71	11	0	2	8	9	41	17	.236	40
	Philadelphia A.L.	7	227	22	50	64	5	0	3	0	28	46	20	.220	52
1932	Chicago N.L.	4	146	19	37	58	8	2	3	2	11	24	16	.253	31
	New York A.L.	4	144	37	45	75	6	0	8	0	23	26	36	.313	33
1933	New York N.L.	5	176	16	47	61	5	0	3	0	11	21	16	.267	39
	Washington A.L.	5	173	11	37	47	4	0	2	1	13	25	11	.214	41
1934	St. Louis N.L.	7	262	34	73	103	14	5	2	2	11	31	32	.279	49
	Detroit A.L.	7	250	23	56	76	12	1	2	4	25	43	20	.224	64
1935	Chicago N.L.	6	202	18	48	73	6	2	5	1	11	29	17	.238	33
	Detroit A.L.	6	206	21	51	67	11	1	1	1	25	27	18	.248	51

Year	Club, League	G	AB	R	H	TB	2B	3B	HR	SB	BB	SO	RBI	Avg.	LOB
1936	New York N.L.	6	203	23	50	71	9	0	4	0	21	33	20	.246	46
	New York A.L.	6	215	43	65	96	8	1	7	1	26	35	41	.302	43
1937	New York N.L.	5	169	12	40	49	6	0	1	1	11	21	12	.237	36
	New York A.L.	5	169	28	42	68	6	4	4	0	21	21	25	.249	36
1938	Chicago N.L.	4	136	9	33	45	4	1	2	0	6	26	8	.243	26
	New York A.L.	4	135	22	37	60	6	1	5	3	11	16	21	.274	24
1939	Cincinnati N.L.	4	133	8	27	32	3	1	0	1	6	22	8	.203	23
	New York A.L.	4	131	20	27	54	4	1	7	0	9	20	18	.206	16
1940	Cincinnati N.L.	7	232	22	58	78	14	0	2	1	15	30	21	.250	49
	Detroit A.L.	7	228	28	56	83	9	3	4	0	30	30	24	.246	50
1941	Brooklyn N.L.	5	159	11	29	43	7	2	1	0	14	21	11	.182	27
	New York A.L.	5	166	17	41	54	5	1	2	2	23	18	16	.247	42
1942	St. Louis N.L.	5	163	23	39	53	4	2	2	0	17	19	23	.239	32
	New York A.L.	5	178	18	44	59	6	0	3	3	8	22	14	.247	34
1943	St. Louis N.L.	5	165	9	37	48	5	0	2	1	11	26	8	.224	37
	New York A.L.	5	159	17	35	50	5	2	2	2	12	30	14	.220	29
1944	St. Louis N.L.	6	204	16	49	69	9	1	3	0	19	43	15	.240	51
	St. Louis A.L.	6	197	12	36	50	9	1	1	0	23	49	9	.183	-44
1945	Chicago N.L.	7	247	29	65	90	16	3	1	2	19	48	27	.263	50
	Detroit A.L.	7	242	32	54	70	10	0	2	3	33	22	32	.223	53
1946	St. Louis N.L.	7	232	28	60	86	19	2	1	3	19	30	27	.259	50
	Boston A.L.	7	233	20	56	77	7	1	4	2	22	28	18	.240	53
1947	Brooklyn N.L.	7	226	29	52	70	13	1	1	7	30	32	26	.230	46
	New York A.L.	7	238	38	67	100	11	5	4	2	38	37	36	.282	63
1948	Boston N.L.	6	187	17	43	61	6	0	4	1	16	19	16	.230	34
	Cleveland A.L.	6	191	17	38	57	7	0	4	2	12	26	16	.199	34
1949	Brooklyn N.L.	5	162	14	34	55	7	1	4	1	15	38	14	.210	31
	New York A.L.	5	164	21	37	57	10	2	2	2	18	27	20	.226	32
1950	Philadelphia N.L.	4	128	5	26	34	6	1	0	1	7	24	3	.203	26
	New York A.L.	4	135	11	30	41	3	1	2	1	13	12	10	.222	33
1951	New York N.L.	6	194	18	46	61	7	1	2	2	25	22	15	.237	45
	New York A.L.	6	199	29	49	75	7	2	5	0	26	23	25	.246	41
1952	Brooklyn N.L.	7	233	20	50	75	7	0	6	5	24	49	18	.215	52
	New York A.L.	7	232	26	50	89	5	2	10	1	31	32	24	.216	48
1953	Brooklyn N.L.	6	213	27	64	103	13	1	8	2	15	30	26	.300	49
	New York A.L.	6	201	33	56	97	6	4	9	2	25	43	32	.279	47
1954	New York N.L.	4	130	21	33	42	3	0	2	1	17	24	20	.254	28
	Cleveland A.L.	4	137	9	26	42	5	1	3	0	16	23	9	.190	37
1955	Brooklyn N.L.	7	223	31	58	95	8	1	9	2	33	38	30	.260	55
	New York A.L.	7	222	26	55	87	4	2	8	3	22	39	25	.248	41
1956	Brooklyn N.L.	7	215	25	42	61	8	1	3	1	32	47	24	.195	42
	New York A.L.	7	229	33	58	100	6	0	12	2	21	43	33	.253	40
1957	Milwaukee N.L.	7	225	23	47	79	6	1	8	1	22	40	22	.209	46
	New York A.L.	7	230	25	57	87	7	1	7	1	22	34	25	.248	45
1958	Milwaukee N.L.	7	240	25	60	81	10	1	3	1	27	56	24	.250	58
	New York A.L.	7	233	29	49	86	5	1	10	1	21	42	29	.210	40
1959	Los Angeles N.L.	6	203	21	53	79	3	1	7	5	12	27	19	.261	42
	Chicago A.L.	6	199	23	52	74	10	0	4	2	20	33	19	.261	43
1960	Pittsburgh N.L.	7	234	27	60	83	11	0	4	2	12	26	26	.256	42
	New York A.L.	7	269	55	91	142	13	4	10	0	18	40	54	.338	51
1961	Cincinnati N.L.	5	170	13	35	52	8	0	3	0	8	27	11	.206	33
	New York A.L.	5	165	27	42	73	8	1	7	1	24	25	26	.255	34
1962	San Francisco N.L.	7	226	21	51	80	10	2	5	1	12	39	19	.226	39
	New York A.L.	7	221	20	44	61	6	1	3	4	21	39	17	.199	43
1963	Los Angeles N.L.	4	117	12	25	41	3	2	3	2	11	25	12	.214	17
	New York A.L.	4	129	4	22	31	3	0	2	0	5	37	4	.171	24
1964	St. Louis N.L.	7	240	32	61	90	8	3	5	3	18	39	29	.254	47
	New York A.L.	7	239	33	60	101	11	0	10	2	25	54	33	.251	47
1965	Los Angeles N.L.	7	234	24	64	91	10	1	5	9	13	31	21	.274	52
	Minnesota A.L.	7	215	20	42	71	7	2	6	2	19	54	19	.195	36
1966	Los Angeles N.L.	4	120	2	17	23	3	0	1	1	13	28	2	.142	24
	Baltimore A.L.	4	120	13	24	41	3	1	4	0	11	17	10	.200	18
1967	St. Louis N.L.	7	229	25	51	81	11	2	5	7	17	30	24	.223	40
	Boston A.L.	7	222	21	48	80	6	1	8	1	17	49	19	.216	43
1968	St. Louis N.L.	7	239	27	61	95	7	3	7	11	21	40	27	.255	49
	Detroit A.L.	7	231	34	56	90	4	3	8	0	27	59	33	.242	44
1969	New York N.L.	5	159	15	35	61	8	0	6	1	15	35	13	.220	34
	Baltimore A.L.	5	157	9	23	33	1	0	3	1	15	28	9	.146	29
1970	Cincinnati N.L.	5	164	20	35	58	6	1	5	1	15	23	20	.213	28
	Baltimore A.L.	5	171	33	50	87	7	0	10	0	20	33	32	.292	31
1971	Pittsburgh N.L.	7	238	23	56	84	9	2	5	5	26	47	21	.235	63
	Baltimore A.L.	7	219	24	45	65	3	1	5	1	20	35	22	.205	39
1972	Cincinnati N.L.	7	220	21	46	65	8	1	3	12	27	46	21	.209	49
	Oakland A.L.	7	220	16	46	65	4	0	5	1	21	37	16	.209	45
1973	New York N.L.	7	261	24	66	89	7	2	4	0	26	36	16	.253	72
	Oakland A.L.	7	241	21	51	75	12	3	2	3	28	62	20	.212	58

Year	Club, League	G	AB	R	H	TB	2B	3B	HR	SB	BB	SO	RBI	Avg.	LOB
1974	Los Angeles N.L. 5		158	11	36	54	4	1	4	3	16	32	10	.228	36
	Oakland A.L. 5		142	16	30	46	4	0	4	3	16	42	14	.211	26
1975	Cincinnati N.L. 7		244	29	59	95	9	3	7	9	25	30	29	.242	50
	Boston A.L. 7		239	30	60	89	7	2	6	0	30	40	30	.251	52
1976	Cincinnati N.L. 4		134	22	42	70	10	3	4	7	12	16	21	.313	22
	New York A.L. 4		135	8	30	38	3	1	1	1	12	16	8	.222	33
1977	Los Angeles N.L. 6		208	28	48	86	5	3	9	2	16	36	28	.231	31
	New York A.L. 6		205	26	50	84	10	0	8	1	11	37	25	.244	32
1978	Los Angeles N.L. 6		199	23	52	78	8	0	6	5	20	31	22	.261	38
	New York A.L. 6		222	36	68	85	8	0	3	5	16	40	34	.306	47
1979	Pittsburgh N.L. 7		251	32	81	110	18	1	3	0	16	35	32	.323	60
	Baltimore A.L. 7		233	26	54	78	10	1	4	2	26	41	23	.232	49
1980	Philadelphia N.L. 6		201	27	59	81	13	0	3	3	15	17	26	.294	41
	Kansas City A.L. 6		207	23	60	97	9	2	8	6	26	49	22	.290	54
1981	Los Angeles N.L. 6		198	27	51	77	6	1	6	6	20	44	26	.258	46
	New York A.L. 6		193	22	46	74	8	1	6	4	33	24	22	.238	55
1982	St. Louis N.L. 7		245	39	67	101	16	3	4	7	20	26	34	.273	49
	Milwaukee A.L. 7		238	33	64	95	12	2	5	1	19	28	29	.269	44
1983	Philadelphia N.L. 5		159	9	31	49	4	1	4	1	7	29	9	.195	23
	Baltimore A.L. 5		164	18	35	61	8	0	6	1	10	37	17	.213	28
1984	San Diego N.L. 5		166	15	44	60	7	0	3	2	11	26	14	.265	34
	Detroit A.L. 5		158	23	40	65	4	0	7	7	24	27	23	.253	39
1985	St. Louis N.L. 7		216	13	40	58	10	1	2	2	28	42	13	.185	38
	Kansas City A.L. 7		236	28	68	90	12	2	2	7	18	56	26	.288	56
1986	New York N.L. 7		240	32	65	92	6	0	7	7	21	43	29	.271	50
	Boston A.L. 7		248	27	69	99	11	2	5	0	28	53	26	.278	69
1987	St. Louis N.L. 7		232	26	60	74	8	0	2	12	13	44	25	.259	43
	Minnesota A.L. 7		238	38	64	101	10	3	7	6	29	36	38	.269	56
1988	Los Angeles N.L. 5		167	21	41	66	8	1	5	4	13	36	19	.246	30
	Oakland A.L. 5		158	11	28	37	3	0	2	3	17	41	11	.177	34
1989	San Francisco N.L..........4		134	14	28	46	4	1	4	2	8	27	14	.209	21
	Oakland A.L. 4		146	32	44	85	8	3	9	4	18	22	30	.301	31
1990	Cincinnati N.L. 4		142	22	45	67	9	2	3	2	15	9	22	.317	32
	Oakland A.L. 4		135	8	28	41	4	0	3	7	12	28	8	.207	31
1991	Atlanta N.L. 7		249	29	63	105	10	4	8	5	26	39	29	.253	52
	Minnesota A.L. 7		241	24	56	96	8	4	8	7	21	48	24	.232	47
1992	Atlanta N.L. 6		200	20	44	59	6	0	3	15	20	48	19	.220	40
	Toronto A.L. 6		196	17	45	71	8	0	6	5	18	33	17	.230	38
1993	Philadelphia N.L. 6		212	36	58	90	7	2	7	7	34	50	35	.274	54
	Toronto A.L. 6		206	45	64	105	13	5	6	7	25	30	45	.311	39
1994	no series played														
1995	Atlanta N.L. 6		193	23	47	81	10	0	8	5	25	34	23	.244	44
	Cleveland A.L. 6		195	19	35	59	7	1	5	8	25	37	17	.179	39
1996	Atlanta N.L. 6		201	26	51	74	9	1	4	3	23	36	26	.254	41
	New York A.L. 6		199	18	43	57	6	1	2	4	26	43	16	.216	48
1997	Florida N.L. 7		250	37	68	106	12	1	8	4	36	48	34	.272	62
	Cleveland A.L. 7		247	44	72	107	12	1	7	5	40	51	42	.291	59
1998	San Diego N.L. 4		134	13	32	50	7	1	3	1	12	29	11	.239	27
	New York A.L. 4		139	26	43	66	5	0	6	1	20	29	25	.309	34
1999	Atlanta N.L. 4		130	9	26	36	5	1	1	1	15	26	9	.200	25
	New York A.L. 4		137	21	37	57	5	0	5	5	13	31	20	.270	27
2000	New York N.L. 5		175	16	40	60	8	0	4	0	11	48	15	.229	36
	New York A.L. 5		179	19	47	73	8	3	4	1	25	40	18	.263	52
2001	Arizona N.L. 7		246	37	65	97	14	0	6	2	17	70	36	.264	49
	New York A.L. 7		229	14	42	66	6	0	6	1	16	63	14	.183	38
2002	San Francisco N.L. 7		235	44	66	117	7	1	14	5	30	50	42	.281	47
	Anaheim A.L. 7		245	41	76	114	15	1	7	6	23	38	38	.310	54
2003	Florida N.L. 6		203	17	47	61	8	0	2	2	14	48	17	.232	43
	New York A.L. 6		207	21	54	84	10	1	6	2	22	49	21	.261	47
2004	Boston A.L. 4		138	24	39	66	1	2	4	0	24	20	24	.283	41
	St. Louis N.L. 4		126	12	24	38	8	0	2	1	12	32	8	.190	24

CLUB FIELDING AND PLAYERS USED

Year	Club, League	G	PO	A	E	DP	PB	Fielding Avg.	Players Used	Pitchers Used	PH	PR
1903	Pittsburgh N.L. 8		210	96	18	5	0	.944	14	5	1	0
	Boston A.L. 8		213	102	14	6	2	.957	13	3	4	0
1904	No series played.											
1905	New York N.L. 5		135	78	6	2	0	.973	12	3	1	0
	Philadelphia A.L...........5		129	56	9	2	0	.954	13	3	1	0
1906	Chicago N.L. 6		159	84	7	4	3	.972	14	4	4	0
	Chicago A.L. 6		162	99	14	2	1	.949	16	4	2	1
1907	Chicago N.L. 5		144	65	10	6	1	.954	15	4	2	0
	Detroit A.L. 5		138	70	9	2	0	.959	14	4	1	1

Year	Club, League	G	PO	A	E	DP	PB	Fielding Avg.	Players Used	Pitchers Used	PH	PR
1908	Chicago N.L.	5	135	74	5	4	1	.977	13	4	1	0
	Detroit A.L.	5	131	63	10	5	1	.951	16	5	4	1
1909	Pittsburgh N.L.	7	182	88	15	3	0	.947	17	6	3	0
	Detroit A.L.	7	183	87	19	4	1	.934	16	5	5	0
1910	Chicago N.L.	5	132	77	12	3	0	.946	18	7	6	1
	Philadelphia A.L.	5	136	59	11	6	0	.947	12	2	0	0
1911	New York N.L.	6	162	79	16	2	1	.938	15	5	4	0
	Philadelphia A.L.	6	167	72	11	2	0	.956	14	3	0	1
1912	New York N.L.	8	221	108	17	4	0	.951	17	5	5	3
	Boston A.L.	8	222	101	14	5	0	.958	17	5	5	1
1913	New York N.L.	5	135	67	7	1	1	.967	20	5	6	5
	Philadelphia A.L.	5	138	54	5	6	0	.975	12	3	0	0
1914	Boston N.L.	4	117	62	4	4	0	.978	15	3	3	1
	Philadelphia A.L.	4	111	66	3	4	1	.983	16	6	1	0
1915	Philadelphia N.L.	5	131	54	3	3	0	.984	16	4	2	2
	Boston A.L.	5	132	58	4	2	0	.979	17	3	3	1
1916	Brooklyn N.L.	5	142	70	13	2	2	.942	20	7	6	1
	Boston A.L.	5	147	90	6	5	1	.975	20	5	3	1
1917	New York N.L.	6	153	72	11	3	1	.953	17	6	3	0
	Chicago A.L.	6	156	82	12	7	1	.952	16	5	6	0
1918	Chicago N.L.	6	156	76	5	7	2	.979	17	4	8	2
	Boston A.L.	6	159	88	1	4	1	.996	15	4	5	0
1919	Cincinnati N.L.	8	216	96	12	7	0	.963	17	6	3	1
	Chicago A.L.	8	213	116	12	9	1	.965	19	7	6	0
1920	Brooklyn N.L.	7	177	91	6	5	2	.978	21	7	7	3
	Cleveland A.L.	7	182	89	12	8	0	.958	20	5	12	1
1921	New York N.L.	8	212	102	5	5	2	.984	13	4	2	0
	New York A.L.	8	210	106	6	8	0	.981	19	8	3	2
1922	New York N.L.	5	138	70	6	4	0	.972	16	5	3	1
	New York A.L.	5	129	62	1	7	1	.995	17	5	4	0
1923	New York N.L.	6	159	80	6	8	0	.976	22	8	9	3
	New York A.L.	6	162	77	3	6	0	.988	17	5	4	2
1924	New York N.L.	7	200	94	6	4	0	.980	21	9	7	3
	Washington A.L.	7	201	99	12	10	1	.962	21	8	8	2
1925	Pittsburgh N.L.	7	182	89	7	4	0	.980	18	7	5	2
	Washington A.L.	7	180	75	9	8	1	.966	21	6	7	4
1926	St. Louis N.L.	7	189	99	5	6	0	.983	19	8	6	0
	New York A.L.	7	189	82	7	3	1	.975	19	7	7	2
1927	Pittsburgh N.L.	4	104	46	6	2	0	.962	21	7	5	1
	New York A.L.	4	108	44	3	4	0	.981	15	4	1	0
1928	St. Louis N.L.	4	102	36	5	3	0	.965	20	6	6	1
	New York A.L.	4	108	28	6	3	0	.958	16	3	4	0
1929	Chicago N.L.	5	131	44	7	4	0	.962	19	6	8	0
	Philadelphia A.L.	5	135	40	4	2	6	.978	17	6	3	0
1930	St. Louis N.L.	6	153	55	5	4	1	.977	21	7	7	0
	Philadelphia A.L.	6	156	41	3	2	0	.985	15	5	3	0
1931	St. Louis N.L.	7	186	73	4	7	0	.985	21	6	6	1
	Philadelphia A.L.	7	183	69	2	4	0	.992	20	6	8	1
1932	Chicago N.L.	4	102	40	6	7	0	.959	22	8	6	1
	New York A.L.	4	108	41	8	1	0	.949	16	6	6	1
1933	New York N.L.	5	141	67	4	5	0	.981	15	5	2	0
	Washington A.L.	5	138	65	4	4	0	.981	10	7	5	1
1934	St. Louis N.L.	7	196	73	15	2	0	.947	20	8	5	2
	Detroit A.L.	7	195	70	12	6	0	.957	17	6	4	0
1935	Chicago N.L.	6	164	74	6	5	0	.975	18	7	5	0
	Detroit A.L.	6	165	72	9	7	1	.963	15	5	2	0
1936	New York N.L.	6	159	62	7	7	0	.969	22	8	10	2
	New York A.L.	6	162	57	6	2	0	.973	16	6	2	2
1937	New York N.L.	5	129	46	9	5	0	.951	20	7	7	0
	New York A.L.	5	132	47	0	2	0	1.000	17	7	1	0
1938	Chicago N.L.	4	102	35	3	3	0	.979	20	8	8	0
	New York A.L.	4	108	39	6	4	0	.961	14	4	1	0
1939	Cincinnati N.L.	4	106	34	4	1	0	.972	18	5	3	2
	New York A.L.	4	111	50	2	5	0	.988	15	7	0	0
1940	Cincinnati N.L.	7	183	67	8	9	1	.969	23	9	9	1
	Detroit A.L.	7	180	80	4	4	0	.985	20	8	6	0
1941	Brooklyn N.L.	5	132	60	4	5	0	.980	20	7	6	0
	New York A.L.	5	135	55	2	7	0	.990	18	7	2	1
1942	St. Louis N.L.	5	135	45	10	3	0	.947	18	6	4	1
	New York A.L.	5	132	45	5	2	0	.973	20	7	4	2
1943	St. Louis N.L.	5	129	53	10	4	0	.948	20	6	6	1
	New York A.L.	5	135	63	5	3	0	.975	16	5	2	0
1944	St. Louis N.L.	6	165	59	1	3	1	.996	20	8	7	0
	St. Louis A.L.	6	163	60	10	4	0	.957	22	7	13	1

Year	Club, League	G	PO	A	E	DP	PB	Fielding Avg.	Players Used	Pitchers Used	PH	PR
1945	Chicago N.L.	7	195	78	6	5	1	.978	25	8	14	3
	Detroit A.L.	7	197	85	5	4	2	.983	26	9	11	1
1946	St. Louis N.L.	7	186	68	4	7	1	.984	19	7	5	0
	Boston A.L.	7	183	76	10	8	0	.963	26	11	10	3
1947	Brooklyn N.L.	7	180	71	8	8	2	.969	24	8	19	5
	New York A.L.	7	185	70	4	4	2	.985	24	9	11	0
1948	Boston N.L.	6	156	54	6	3	0	.972	20	6	8	4
	Cleveland A.L.	6	159	72	3	9	0	.987	23	8	3	0
1949	Brooklyn N.L.	5	132	40	5	1	0	.972	25	9	11	0
	New York A.L.	5	135	44	3	5	0	.984	20	5	4	2
1950	Philadelphia N.L.	4	107	35	4	1	0	.973	20	5	6	4
	New York A.L.	4	111	41	2	4	0	.987	18	5	2	2
1951	New York N.L.	6	156	65	10	4	0	.957	24	9	10	2
	New York A.L.	6	159	67	4	10	1	.982	21	8	5	2
1952	Brooklyn N.l.	7	192	71	4	4	0	.985	19	6	8	1
	New York A.L.	7	192	66	10	7	1	.963	19	8	6	1
1953	Brooklyn N.L.	6	154	62	7	3	0	.969	23	10	8	0
	New York A.L.	6	156	60	1	5	0	.995	20	9	7	0
1954	New York N.L.	4	111	40	7	2	0	.955	15	6	3	0
	Cleveland A.L.	4	106	40	4	2	0	.973	24	7	16	2
1955	Brooklyn N.L.	7	180	84	6	12	0	.978	22	10	6	1
	New York A.L.	7	180	72	2	7	0	.992	24	9	12	3
1956	Brooklyn N.L.	7	183	69	2	8	0	.992	21	8	9	0
	New York A.L.	7	185	66	6	7	0	.977	22	8	6	0
1957	Milwaukee N.L.	7	186	93	3	10	1	.989	23	8	9	2
	New York A.L.	7	187	72	6	5	0	.977	23	9	10	2
1958	Milwaukee N.L.	7	189	78	7	5	0	.974	19	6	8	5
	New York A.L.	7	191	65	3	5	1	.988	22	9	9	0
1959	Los Angeles N.L.	6	159	69	4	7	0	.983	24	9	13	4
	Chicago A.L.	6	156	62	4	2	1	.982	21	7	9	2
1960	Pittsburgh N.L.	7	186	67	4	7	3	.984	25	10	9	2
	New York A.L.	7	183	93	8	9	0	.972	25	10	11	3
1961	Cincinnati N.L.	5	132	42	4	7	1	.978	24	9	15	1
	New York A.L.	5	135	50	5	1	1	.974	18	6	4	1
1962	San Francisco N.L.	7	183	67	8	9	1	.969	21	7	7	1
	New York A.L.	7	183	67	5	5	0	.980	18	6	4	0
1963	Los Angeles N.L.	4	108	31	3	1	0	.979	13	4	1	0
	New York A.L.	4	102	49	1	7	0	.993	20	7	7	0
1964	St. Louis N.L.	7	189	64	4	6	0	.984	21	8	12	3
	New York A.L.	7	186	82	9	6	3	.968	21	9	8	1
1965	Los Angeles N.L.	7	180	72	6	7	0	.977	20	7	7	1
	Minnesota A.L.	7	180	58	5	3	0	.979	21	9	7	0
1966	Los Angeles N.L.	4	102	44	6	4	0	.961	23	8	8	1
	Baltimore A.L.	4	108	33	0	4	0	1.000	13	4	0	0
1967	St. Louis N.L.	7	183	66	4	3	0	.984	23	10	8	1
	Boston A.L.	7	183	66	4	4	1	.984	25	10	13	1
1968	St. Louis N.L.	7	186	48	2	7	0	.992	25	10	8	1
	Detroit A.L.	7	186	72	11	4	0	.959	24	9	8	1
1969	New York N.L.	5	135	42	2	0	0	.989	21	6	4	1
	Baltimore A.L.	5	129	51	4	4	0	.978	21	7	5	3
1970	Cincinnati N.L.	5	129	50	3	4	0	.984	24	9	13	0
	Baltimore A.L.	5	135	43	5	3	0	.973	21	9	3	0
1971	Pittsburgh N.L.	7	185	70	3	7	1	.988	25	10	8	1
	Baltimore A.L.	7	183	69	9	2	0	.966	21	10	6	1
1972	Cincinnati N.L.	7	187	89	5	5	0	.982	22	8	16	2
	Oakland A.L.	7	186	65	9	4	0	.965	23	8	13	8
1973	New York N.L.	7	195	72	10	3	1	.964	22	7	15	3
	Oakland A.L.	7	198	79	9	8	1	.969	24	8	20	4
1974	Los Angeles N.L.	5	126	50	6	5	0	.967	19	6	9	2
	Oakland A.L.	5	132	51	5	6	0	.973	20	5	6	4
1975	Cincinnati N.L.	7	195	76	2	8	0	.993	22	9	8	0
	Boston A.L.	7	196	72	6	6	0	.978	23	10	13	0
1976	Cincinnati N.L.	4	108	36	5	4	0	.966	16	7	0	0
	New York A.L.	4	104	41	2	6	0	.986	21	7	9	0
1977	Los Angeles N.L.	6	165	69	1	4	0	.996	25	9	10	1
	New York A.L.	6	168	68	3	2	1	.987	20	7	6	0
1978	Los Angeles N.L.	6	158	64	7	4	0	.969	23	8	4	0
	New York A.L.	6	159	54	2	9	1	.991	24	8	5	2
1979	Pittsburgh N.L.	7	186	79	9	11	0	.967	24	9	11	1
	Baltimore A.L.	7	186	85	9	5	0	.968	25	9	23	2
1980	Philadelphia N.L.	6	161	68	2	8	0	.991	22	10	4	3
	Kansas City A.L.	6	156	72	7	8	0	.970	21	7	3	3
1981	Los Angeles N.L.	6	156	65	9	6	0	.961	24	10	14	2
	New York A.L.	6	153	55	4	2	1	.981	24	9	10	5
1982	St. Louis N.L.	7	183	74	7	9	0	.973	22	8	8	3
	Milwaukee A.L.	7	180	81	11	3	0	.960	21	9	2	1

Year	Club, League	G	PO	A	E	DP	PB	Fielding Avg.	Players Used	Pitchers Used	PH	PR
1983	Philadelphia N.L. 5		132	42	3	3	0	.983	23	8	12	3
	Baltimore A.L.............5		135	51	4	5	0	.979	23	7	13	2
1984	San Diego N.L.............5		126	40	4	5	0	.976	24	10	4	3
	Detroit A.L...............5		132	52	4	2	0	.979	22	7	10	1
1985	St. Louis N.L. 7		184	60	2	9	1	.992	24	9	8	2
	Kansas City A.L. 7		186	80	3	3	1	.989	22	6	13	3
1986	New York N.L. 7		189	63	5	4	0	.981	22	8	11	2
	Boston A.L...............7		188	79	4	7	1	.985	21	8	6	3
1987	St. Louis N.L. 7		177	69	6	2	1	.976	24	9	4	1
	Minnesota A.L. 7		180	74	3	4	0	.988	24	9	15	2
1988	Los Angeles N.L. 5		133	36	3	3	1	.983	22	7	11	0
	Oakland A.L..............5		131	43	2	2	1	.989	24	10	4	3
1989	San Francisco N.L. ...4		102	40	4	3	0	.973	24	9	10	0
	Oakland A.L..............4		108	35	1	1	1	.993	19	6	4	0
1990	Cincinnati N.L...........4		111	42	4	2	0	.975	21	8	6	0
	Oakland A.L..............4		106	46	5	5	0	.968	25	10	8	1
1991	Atlanta N.L...............7		196	86	5	9	0	.983	25	10	16	1
	Minnesota A.L. 7		202	75	5	6	1	.982	25	9	21	2
1992	Atlanta N.L...............6		163	68	2	7	0	.991	22	8	7	3
	Toronto A.L..............6		165	47	4	5	0	.981	23	10	8	0
1993	Philadelphia N.L. 6		157	54	2	5	1	.991	23	10	7	1
	Toronto A.L..............6		159	45	7	5	0	.967	23	10	3	3
1994	No series played.											
1995	Atlanta N.L...............6		162	69	6	2	0	.975	23	10	9	0
	Cleveland A.L............6		159	73	6	8	1	.975	23	9	6	2
1996	Atlanta N.L...............6		162	73	4	6	0	.983	24	10	10	3
	New York A.L.............6		165	63	5	7	0	.979	25	10	8	1
1997	Florida N.L...............7		192	82	8	9	0	.972	25	10	17	2
	Cleveland A.L............7		191	64	5	8	0	.981	23	11	5	0
1998	San Diego N.L. 4		102	41	3	5	0	.979	24	10	9	2
	New York A.L.............4		108	36	2	4	1	.986	21	9	3	2
1999	Atlanta N.L...............4		105	31	4	4	0	.971	25	9	11	1
	New York A.L. 4		111	48	1	5	0	.994	23	9	4	1
2000	New York N.L. 5		140	47	5	3	0	.974	25	10	11	2
	New York A.L.............5		141	46	2	1	1	.989	22	8	8	1
2001	Arizona N.L. 7		195	61	3	6	0	.988	25	10	5	4
	New York A.L.............7		190	75	8	7	0	.971	25	10	8	2
2002	San Francisco N.L. ...7		180	70	5	7	1	.980	24	11	11	0
	Anaheim A.L..............7		183	56	5	6	1	.980	25	10	9	2
2003	Florida N.L...............6		168	57	2	8	0	.991	20	9	3	0
	New York A.L.............6		165	66	5	6	0	.979	23	9	12	3
2004	St. Louis N.L. 4		102	37	1	3	0	.993	25	11	5	1
	Boston A.L...............4		108	32	8	5	1	.946	21	8	5	3

MANAGERIAL RECORDS

AMERICAN LEAGUE

	Series W	L	Games W	L
Joe Altobelli, Baltimore.....................1	1	0	4	1
Sparky Anderson, Detroit........................1	1	0	4	1
Del Baker, Detroit..............................0	0	1	3	4
Ed Barrow, Boston...............................1	1	0	4	2
Hank Bauer, Baltimore 1	1	0	4	0
Yogi Berra, New York...........................0	0	1	3	4
Lou Boudreau, Cleveland........................1	1	0	4	2
Bill Carrigan, Boston...........................2	2	0	8	2
Mickey Cochrane, Detroit........................1	1	1	7	6
Jimmy Collins, Boston...........................1	1	0	5	3
Joe Cronin, Washington, Boston 0	0	2	4	8
Alvin Dark, Oakland 1	1	0	4	1
Terry Francona, Boston..........................1	1	0	4	0
Jim Frey, Kansas City 0	0	1	2	4
Cito Gaston, Toronto............................2	2	0	8	4
Kid Gleason, Chicago............................0	0	1	3	5
Mike Hargrove, Cleveland 0	0	2	5	8
Bucky Harris, Washington, New York........2	2	1	11	10
Ralph Houk, New York...........................2	2	1	8	8
Dick Howser, Kansas City 1	1	0	4	3
Miller Huggins, New York*.....................3	3	3	18	15
Hughey Jennings, Detroit*.....................0	0	3	4	12

	Series W	L	Games W	L
Darrell Johnson, Boston.........................0	0	1	3	4
Fielder Jones, Chicago..........................1	1	0	4	2
Tom Kelly, Minnesota...........................2	2	0	8	6
Harvey Kuenn, Milwaukee.......................0	0	1	3	4
Tony La Russa, Oakland 1	1	2	5	8
Bob Lemon, New York............................1	1	1	6	6
Al Lopez, Cleveland, Chicago..................0	0	2	2	8
Connie Mack, Philadelphia......................5	5	3	24	19
Billy Martin, New York..........................1	1	1	4	6
Joe McCarthy, New York.........................7	7	1	29	9
John McNamara, Boston 0	0	1	3	4
Sam Mele, Minnesota 0	0	1	3	4
Steve O'Neill, Detroit..........................1	1	0	4	3
Pants Rowland, Chicago..........................1	1	0	4	2
Mike Scioscia, Anaheim.........................1	1	0	4	3
Luke Sewell, St. Louis..........................0	0	1	2	4
Mayo Smith, Detroit.............................1	1	0	4	3
Tris Speaker, Cleveland 1	1	0	5	2
Jake Stahl, Boston*.............................1	1	0	4	3
Joe Torre, New York 4	4	2	21	11
Casey Stengel, New York........................7	7	3	37	26
Earl Weaver, Baltimore..........................1	1	3	11	13
Dick Williams, Boston, Oakland................2	2	1	11	10

Total number of managers: 45

*includes one tie per asterisk

NATIONAL LEAGUE

	Series W	L	Games W	L
Walter Alston, Brooklyn, Los Angeles	4	3	20	20
Sparky Anderson, Cincinnati	2	2	12	11
Dusty Baker, San Francisco	0	1	3	4
Yogi Berra, New York	0	1	3	4
Bruce Bochy, San Diego	0	1	0	4
Bob Brenly, Arizona	1	0	4	3
Donie Bush, Pittsburgh	0	1	0	4
Frank Chance, Chicago*	2	2	11	9
Fred Clarke, Pittsburgh	1	1	7	8
Bobby Cox, Atlanta	1	4	11	18
Roger Craig, San Francisco	0	1	0	4
Alvin Dark, San Francisco	0	1	3	4
Charlie Dressen, Brooklyn	0	2	5	8
Leo Durocher, Brooklyn, New York	1	2	7	8
Eddie Dyer, St. Louis	1	0	4	3
Jim Fregosi, Philadelphia	0	1	2	4
Frank Frisch, St. Louis	1	0	4	3
Dallas Green, Philadelphia	1	0	4	2
Chuck Grimm, Chicago	0	3	5	12
Fred Haney, Milwaukee	1	1	7	7
Gabby Hartnett, Chicago	0	1	0	4
Whitey Herzog, St. Louis	1	2	10	11
Gil Hodges, New York	1	0	4	1
Rogers Hornsby, St. Louis	1	0	4	3
Fred Hutchinson, Cincinnati	0	1	1	4
Dave Johnson, New York	1	0	4	3
Johnny Keane, St. Louis	1	0	4	3
Tony La Russa, St. Louis	0	1	0	4
Tom Lasorda, Los Angeles	2	2	12	11
Jim Leyland, Florida	1	0	4	3
Joe McCarthy, Chicago	0	1	1	4
John McGraw, New York**	3	6	26	28
Bill McKechnie, Pittsburgh, St. Louis, Cincinnati	2	2	8	14
Jack McKeon, Florida	1	0	4	2
Fred Mitchell, Chicago	0	1	2	4
Pat Moran, Philadelphia, Cincinnati	1	1	6	7
Danny Murtaugh, Pittsburgh	2	0	8	6
Paul Owens, Philadelphia	0	1	1	4
Lou Piniella, Cincinnati	1	0	4	0
Wilbert Robinson, Brooklyn	0	2	3	9
Eddie Sawyer, Philadelphia	0	1	0	4
Red Schoendienst, St. Louis	1	1	7	7
Burt Shotton, Brooklyn	0	2	4	8
Billy Southworth, St. Louis, Boston	2	2	11	11
George Stallings, Boston	1	0	4	0
Gabby Street, St. Louis	1	1	6	7
Chuck Tanner, Pittsburgh	1	0	4	3
Bill Terry, New York	1	2	7	9
Bobby Valentine, New York	0	1	1	4
Dick Williams, San Diego	0	1	1	4

Total number of managers: 49

COMBINED RECORDS FOR BOTH LEAGUES

	Series W	L	Games W	L
Sparky Anderson, Cincinnati N.L., Detroit A.L.	3	2	16	12
Yogi Berra, New York A.L., New York N.L.	0	2	6	8
Alvin Dark, San Francisco N.L., Oakland A.L.	1	1	7	5
Tony La Russa, Oakland A.L., St. Louis N.L.	1	3	5	12
Joe McCarthy, Chicago N.L., New York A.L.	7	2	30	13
Dick Williams, Boston A.L., Oakland A.L., San Diego N.L.	2	2	12	14

Total number of managers: 6

ALL-STAR GAME

Results

Service (Individual, Club)

Batting (Individual, Club)

Baserunning (Individual, Club)

Pitching (Individual, Club)

Fielding (Individual, Club)

Miscellaneous

Non-Playing Personnel

General Reference

RESULTS

Year	Date	Site	Winner	Manager	Loser	Manager	Score
1933	July 6	Comiskey Park, Chicago	A.L.	Connie Mack, Phi.	N.L.	John McGraw, N.Y.	4-2
1934	July 10	Polo Grounds, New York	A.L.	Joe Cronin, Was.	N.L.	Bill Terry, N.Y.	9-7
1935	July 8	Cleveland Stadium, Cleveland	A.L.	Mickey Cochrane, Det.	N.L.	Frankie Frisch, St.L.	4-1
1936	July 7	Braves Field, Boston	N.L.	Charley Grimm, Chi.	A.L.	Joe McCarthy, N.Y.	4-3
1937	July 7	Griffith Stadium, Washington	A.L.	Joe McCarthy, N.Y.	N.L.	Bill Terry, N.Y.	8-3
1938	July 6	Crosley Field, Cincinnati	N.L.	Bill Terry, N.Y.	A.L.	Joe McCarthy, N.Y.	4-1
1939	July 11	Yankee Stadium, New York	A.L.	Joe McCarthy, N.Y.	N.L.	Gabby Hartnett, Chi.	3-1
1940	July 9	Sportsman's Park, St. Louis	N.L.	Bill McKechnie, Cin.	A.L.	Joe Cronin, Bos.	4-0
1941	July 8	Briggs Stadium, Detroit	A.L.	Del Baker, Det.	N.L.	Bill McKechnie, Cin.	7-5
1942	July 6	Polo Grounds, New York	A.L.	Joe McCarthy, N.Y.	N.L.	Leo Durocher, Bkn.	3-1
1943	July 13	Shibe Park, Philadelphia	A.L.	Joe McCarthy, N.Y.	N.L.	Billy Southworth, St.L.	5-3
1944	July 11	Forbes Field, Pittsburgh	N.L.	Billy Southworth, St.L.	A.L.	Joe McCarthy, N.Y.	7-1
1945		game canceled because of travel restrictions during World War II					
1946	July 9	Fenway Park, Boston	A.L.	Steve O'Neill, Det.	N.L.	Charley Grimm, Chi.	12-0
1947	July 8	Wrigley Field, Chicago	A.L.	Joe Cronin, Bos.	N.L.	Eddie Dyer, St.L.	2-1
1948	July 13	Sportsman's Park, St. Louis	A.L.	Bucky Harris, N.Y.	N.L.	Leo Durocher, Bkn.	5-2
1949	July 12	Ebbets Field, Brooklyn	A.L.	Lou Boudreau, Cle.	N.L.	Billy Southworth, Bos.	11-7
1950	July 11	Comiskey Park, Chicago	N.L.	Burt Shotton, Bkn.	A.L.	Casey Stengel, N.Y.	4-3, 14 inn
1951	July 10	Briggs Stadium, Detroit	N.L.	Eddie Sawyer, Phi.	A.L.	Casey Stengel, N.Y.	8-3
1952	July 8	Shibe Park, Philadelphia	N.L.	Leo Durocher, N.Y.	A.L.	Casey Stengel, N.Y.	3-2, 5 inn
1953	July 14	Crosley Field, Cincinnati	N.L.	Charlie Dressen, Bkn.	A.L.	Casey Stengel, N.Y.	5-1
1954	July 13	Cleveland Stadium, Cleveland	A.L.	Casey Stengel, N.Y.	N.L.	Walter Alston, Bkn.	11-9
1955	July 12	County Stadium, Milwaukee	N.L.	Leo Durocher, N.Y.	A.L.	Al Lopez, Cle.	6-5, 12 inn
1956	July 10	Griffith Stadium, Washington	N.L.	Walter Alston, Bkn.	A.L.	Casey Stengel, N.Y.	7-3
1957	July 9	Busch Stadium, St. Louis	A.L.	Casey Stengel, N.Y.	N.L.	Walter Alston, Bkn.	6-5
1958	July 8	Memorial Stadium, Baltimore	A.L.	Casey Stengel, N.Y.	N.L.	Fred Haney, Mil.	4-3
1959	July 7	Forbes Field, Pittsburgh	N.L.	Fred Haney, Mil.	A.L.	Casey Stengel, N.Y.	5-4
	August 3	Memorial Coliseum, Los Angeles	A.L.	Casey Stengel, N.Y.	N.L.	Fred Haney, Mil.	5-3
1960	July 11	Municipal Stadium, Kansas City	N.L.	Walter Alston, L.A.	A.L.	Al Lopez, Chi.	5-3
	July 13	Yankee Stadium, New York	N.L.	Walter Alston, L.A.	A.L.	Al Lopez, Chi.	6-0
1961	July 11	Candlestick Park, San Francisco	N.L.	Danny Murtaugh, Pit.	A.L.	Paul Richards, Bal.	5-4, 10 inn
	July 31	Fenway Park, Boston		Paul Richards, Bal. (A.L.), Danny Murtaugh, Pit. (N.L.)			1-1, tie
1962	July 10	District of Columbia Stad., Was.	N.L.	Fred Hutchinson, Cin.	A.L.	Ralph Houk, N.Y.	3-1
	July 30	Wrigley Field, Chicago	A.L.	Ralph Houk, N.Y.	N.L.	Fred Hutchinson, Cin.	9-4
1963	July 9	Cleveland Stadium, Cleveland	N.L.	Alvin Dark, S.F.	A.L.	Ralph Houk, N.Y.	5-3
1964	July 7	Shea Stadium, New York	N.L.	Walter Alston, L.A.	A.L.	Al Lopez, Chi.	7-4
1965	July 13	Metropolitan Stad., Bloomington	N.L.	Gene Mauch, Phi.	A.L.	Al Lopez, Chi.	6-5
1966	July 12	Busch Memorial Stad., St. Louis	N.L.	Walter Alston, L.A.	A.L.	Sam Mele, Min.	2-1, 10 inn
1967	July 11	Anaheim Stadium, Anaheim	N.L.	Walter Alston, L.A.	A.L.	Hank Bauer, Bal.	2-1, 15 inn
1968	July 9	Astrodome, Houston	N.L.	Red Schoendienst, St.L.	A.L.	Dick Williams, Bos.	1-0
1969	July 23	Robt. F. Kennedy Mem. Stad., Was.	N.L.	Red Schoendienst, St.L.	A.L.	Mayo Smith, Det.	9-3
1970	July 14	Riverfront Stadium, Cincinnati	N.L.	Gil Hodges, N.Y.	A.L.	Earl Weaver, Bal.	5-4, 12 inn
1971	July 13	Tiger Stadium, Detroit	A.L.	Earl Weaver, Bal.	N.L.	Sparky Anderson, Cin.	6-4
1972	July 25	Atlanta Stadium, Atlanta	N.L.	Danny Murtaugh, Pit.	A.L.	Earl Weaver, Bal.	4-3, 10 inn
1973	July 24	Royals Stadium, Kansas City	N.L.	Sparky Anderson, Cin.	A.L.	Dick Williams, Oak.	7-1
1974	July 23	Three Rivers Stadium, Pittsburgh	N.L.	Yogi Berra, N.Y.	A.L.	Dick Williams, Cal.	7-2
1975	July 15	County Stadium, Milwaukee	N.L.	Walter Alston, L.A.	A.L.	Alvin Dark, Oak.	6-3
1976	July 13	Veterans Stadium, Philadelphia	N.L.	Sparky Anderson, Cin.	A.L.	Darrell Johnson, Bos.	7-1
1977	July 19	Yankee Stadium, New York	N.L.	Sparky Anderson, Cin.	A.L.	Billy Martin, N.Y.	7-5
1978	July 11	San Diego Stadium, San Diego	N.L.	Tom Lasorda, L.A.	A.L.	Billy Martin, N.Y.	7-3
1979	July 17	Kingdome, Seattle	N.L.	Tom Lasorda, L.A.	A.L.	Bob Lemon, N.Y.	7-6
1980	July 8	Dodger Stadium, Los Angeles	N.L.	Chuck Tanner, Pit.	A.L.	Earl Weaver, Bal.	4-2
1981	August 9	Cleveland Stadium, Cleveland	N.L.	Dallas Green, Phi.	A.L.	Jim Frey, K.C.	5-4
1982	July 13	Olympic Stadium, Montreal	N.L.	Tom Lasorda, L.A.	A.L.	Billy Martin, N.Y.	4-1
1983	July 6	Comiskey Park, Chicago	A.L.	Harvey Kuenn, Mil.	N.L.	Whitey Herzog, St.L.	13-3
1984	July 10	Candlestick Park, San Francisco	N.L.	Paul Owens, Phi.	A.L.	Joe Altobelli, Bal.	3-1
1985	July 16	Metrodome, Minneapolis	N.L.	Dick Williams, S.D.	A.L.	Sparky Anderson, Det.	6-1
1986	July 15	Astrodome, Houston	A.L.	Dick Howser, K.C.	N.L.	Whitey Herzog, St.L.	3-2
1987	July 14	Oakland Coliseum, Oakland	N.L.	Dave Johnson, N.Y.	A.L.	John McNamara, Bos.	2-0, 13 inn

ALL-STAR GAME Results

Year	Date	Site	Winner	Manager	Loser	Manager	Score
1988	July 12	Riverfront Stadium, Cincinnati.......A.L.		Tom Kelly, Min.	N.L.	Whitey Herzog, St.L.	2-1
1989	July 11	Anaheim Stadium, Anaheim...........A.L.		Tony La Russa, Oak.	N.L.	Tom Lasorda, L.A.	5-3
1990	July 10	Wrigley Field, Chicago ...................A.L.		Tony La Russa, Oak.	N.L.	Roger Craig, S.F.	2-0
1991	July 9	SkyDome, Toronto ........................A.L.		Tony La Russa, Oak.	N.L.	Lou Piniella, Cin.	4-2
1992	July 14	Jack Murphy Stadium, San Diego .A.L.		Tom Kelly, Min.	N.L.	Bobby Cox, Atl.	13-6
1993	July 13	Oriole Park at Camden Yards, Bal. A.L.		Cito Gaston, Tor.	N.L.	Bobby Cox, Atl.	9-3
1994	July 12	Three Rivers Stadium, Pittsburgh..N.L.		Jim Fregosi, Phi.	A.L.	Cito Gaston, Tor.	8-7, 10 inn
1995	July 11	The Ballpark in Arlington, Texas ....N.L.		Felipe Alou, Mon.	A.L.	Buck Showalter, N.Y.	3-2
1996	July 9	Veterans Stadium, Philadelphia .....N.L.		Bobby Cox, Atl.	A.L.	Mike Hargrove, Cle.	6-0
1997	July 8	Jacobs Field, Cleveland..................A.L.		Joe Torre, N.Y.	N.L.	Bobby Cox, Atl.	3-1
1998	July 7	Coors Field, Colorado ....................A.L.		Mike Hargrove, Cle.	N.L.	Jim Leyland, Fla.	13-8
1999	July 13	Fenway Park, Boston .....................A.L.		Joe Torre, N.Y.	N.L.	Bruce Bochy, S.D.	4-1
2000	July 11	Turner Field, Atlanta......................A.L.		Joe Torre, N.Y.	N.L.	Bobby Cox, Atl.	6-3
2001	July 10	Safeco Field, Seattle......................A.L.		Joe Torre, N.Y.	N.L.	Bobby Valentine, N.Y.	4-1
2002	July 9	Miller Park, Milwaukee...................		Joe Torre, N.Y. (A.L.), Bob Brenly, Ari. (N.L.)			7-7, tie, 11 inn
2003	July 15	U.S. Cellular Field, Chicago............A.L.		Mike Scioscia, Ana.	N.L.	Dusty Baker, Chi.	7-6
2004	July 13	Minute Maid Park, Houston ...........A.L.		Joe Torre, N.Y.	N.L.	Jack McKeon, Fla.	9-4

Overall record: N.L. wins, 40; A.L. wins, 33; two ties

SERVICE

INDIVIDUAL
CLUBS

Most clubs represented, career
5—Gary Sheffield, San Diego N.L., 1992; Florida N.L., 1993, 1996; Los Angeles N.L., 1998, 1999, 2000; Atlanta N.L., 2003; New York A.L., 2004 (7 G)

PLAYING ON WINNING AND LOSING CLUBS

Most times playing on winning club
17—Willie Mays, N.L., 1955, 1956, 1959 (1st), 1960 (both), 1961 (1st), 1962 (1st), 1963 through 1970, 1972, 1973 (1 tie—1961, 2nd)
Hank Aaron, N.L., 1955, 1956, 1959 (1st), 1960, 1960, 1961 (1st, 1963 through 1970, 1972 through 1974 (1 tie—1961, 2nd)

Most times playing on losing club
15—Brooks Robinson, A.L., 1960, 1960, 1961 (1st), 1962 (1st), 1963 through 1970, 1972 through 1974 (1 tie—1961, 2nd)

YOUNGEST AND OLDEST PLAYERS

Youngest player
19 years, 7 months, 24 days—Dwight Gooden, N.L., 1984

Oldest player
47 years, 7 days—Satchel Paige, A.L., 1953

POSITIONS

Most fielding positions played, career
5—Pete Rose, N.L. (2B, LF, RF, 3B, 1B; 16 G)

Most fielding positions played, game
2—many players

CLUB
PLAYERS USED

Most players, game
29—N.L., August 9, 1981
A.L., July 11, 2000
A.L., July 10, 2001
N.L., July 10, 2001
(30—A.L., July 9, 2002, 11 inn
N.L., July 9, 2002, 11 inn)

Most players by both clubs, game
58—N.L. 29, A.L. 29, July 10, 2001
(60—A.L. 30, N.L. 30, July 9, 2002, 11 inn)

Fewest players, game
11—A.L., July 6, 1942

Fewest players by both clubs, game
27—A.L. 15, N.L. 12, July 1, 1938

PINCH-HITTERS

Most pinch-hitters, game
8—N.L., July 9, 1957

Most pinch-hitters by both clubs, game
11—N.L. 7, A.L. 4, July 24, 1973
N.L. 7, A.L. 4, August 9, 1981
(11—N.L. 6, A.L. 5, July 11, 1967, 15 inn)

Fewest pinch-hitters, game
0—A.L., July 8, 1935
N.L., July 9, 1940
A.L., July 8, 1980

Fewest pinch-hitters by both clubs, game
1—A.L. 1, N.L. 0, July 9, 1940

INDIVIDUAL BATTING

GAMES

Most games played
24—Stan Musial, N.L., 1943, 1944, 1946 through 1958, 1959 (both), 1960 (both), 1961 (both), 1962 (1962), 1963 (consecutive)
Willie Mays, N.L., 1954 through 1958, 1959 (both), 1960, (both), 1961 (both), 1962 (both), 1963 through 1973 (consecutive)
Hank Aaron, N.L., 1955 through 1958, 1959 (both), 1960 (both), 1961 (both), 1962 (2nd), 1963 through 1974 (23 G); A.L., 1975 (1 G)

Most games by pinch-hitter
10—Stan Musial, 1947, 1955, 1959 (1st), 1960 (both), 1961 (both), 1962 (both) 1963 (10 PH AB)

BATTING AVERAGE AND AT-BATS

Highest batting average, career (five or more games)
.700—Derek Jeter, A.L., 1998 through 2002, 2004 (6 G, 10 AB, 7 H)

Most at-bats, career
75—Willie Mays, N.L., 1954 through 1958, 1959 (both), 1960 (both), 1961 (both), 1962 (both), 1963 through 1973 (24 G)

Most at-bats, game
5—many players. Last players—Cal Ripken, A.L., July 12, 1994; Ivan Rodriguez, A.L., July 12, 1994; Tony Gwynn, N.L., July 12, 1994
(7—Willie Jones, N.L., July 11, 1950, 14 inn)

Most at-bats, inning
2—Jim Rice, A.L., July 6, 1983, 3rd

Most times faced pitcher, inning
2—Babe Ruth, A.L., July 10, 1934, 5th
Lou Gehrig, A.L., July 10, 1934, 5th
Jim Rice, A.L., July 6, 1983, 3rd

RUNS

Most runs, career
20—Willie Mays, N.L., 1954 through 1958, 1959 (both), 1960 (both), 1961 (both), 1962 (both), 1963 through 1973 (24 G)

Most runs, game
4—Ted Williams, A.L., July 9, 1946

Most runs, inning
1—many players

HITS

Most hits, career
23—Willie Mays, N.L., 1954 through 1958, 1959 (both), 1960 (both), 1961 (both), 1962 (both), 1963 through 1973 (24 G)

Most hits by pinch-hitter, career
3—Stan Musial, N.L., 1943, 1944, 1946 through 1958, 1959 (both), 1960 (both), 1961 (both), 1962 (both), 1963 (24 G)

Most consecutive games batted safely
7—Mickey Mantle, A.L., 1954 through 1958, 1959 (2nd), 1960, (2nd); pinch-ran in 1959 (1st), and received 2 BB in 1960 (1st)
Joe Morgan, N.L., 1970, 1972 through 1977 (not on team in 1971)

Dave Winfield, A.L., 1982 through 1988

Most at-bats without a hit, career
10—Terry Moore, N.L., 1939 through 1942 (4 G)

Most hits, game
4—Joe Medwick, N.L., July 7, 1937 (2 singles, 2 doubles; consecutive)
Ted Williams, A.L., July 9, 1946 (2 singles, 2 HR, also 1 BB; consecutive)
(4—Carl Yastrzemski, A.L., July 14, 1970 (3 singles, 1 double), 12 inn)

Most times reached first base safely, game
5—Charlie Gehringer, A.L., July 10, 1934 (3 BB, 2 singles)
Phil Cavarretta, N.L., July 11, 1944 (3 BB, 1 single, 1 triple)
Ted Williams, A.L., July 9, 1946 (2 singles, 2 HR, 1 BB)

Most hits, inning
1—many players

SINGLES

Most singles, game
3—Charlie Gehringer, A.L., July 7, 1937
Billy Herman, N.L., July 9, 1940
Stan Hack, N.L., July 13, 1943
Bobby Avila, A.L., July 13, 1954
Ken Boyer, N.L., July 10, 1956
Harmon Killebrew, A.L., July 7, 1964
Rickey Henderson, A.L., July 13, 1982
Ivan Rodriguez, A.L., July 7, 1998
Derek Jeter, A.L., July 13, 2004
(3—Carl Yastrzemski, A.L., July 14, 1970, 12 inn)

Most singles, inning
1—many players

DOUBLES

Most doubles, career
7—Dave Winfield, N.L., 1977 through 1980; A.L., 1981 through 1988 (12 G)

Most doubles, game
2—Joe Medwick, N.L., July 7, 1937
Al Simmons, A.L., July 10, 1934
Ted Kluszewski, N.L., July 10, 1956
Ernie Banks, N.L., July 7, 1959
Barry Bonds, N.L., July 13, 1993
Paul Konerko, A.L., July 9, 2002
Damian Miller, A.L., July 9, 2002
Albert Pujols, N.L., July 13, 2004

Most doubles, inning
1—many players

Most doubles driving in three runs, inning
none

TRIPLES

Most triples, career
3—Willie Mays, N.L., 1954 through 1958, 1959 (both), 1960 (both), 1961 (both), 1962 (both), 1963 through 1973 (24 G)
Brooks Robinson, A.L., 1960 (both), 1961 (both), 1962 (both), 1963 through 1974 (18 G)

Most triples, game
2—Rod Carew, A.L., July 11, 1978

Most triples, inning
1—many players

Most triples driving in three runs, inning

HOME RUNS

Most home runs, career
6—Stan Musial, N.L., 1943, 1944, 1946 through 1958, 1959 (both), 1960 (both), 1961 (both), 1962 (both), 1963 (24 G)

For a complete list of All-Star Game home runs, see page 532.

Most home runs, game
2—Arky Vaughan, N.L., July 8, 1941 (consecutive)
Ted Williams, A.L., July 9, 1946
Al Rosen, A.L., July 13, 1954 (consecutive)
Willie McCovey, N.L., July 23, 1969 (consecutive)
Gary Carter, N.L., August 9, 1981 (consecutive)

Home runs by pinch-hitter, game (17)
Mickey Owen, N.L., July 6, 1942, 8th
Gus Bell, N.L., July 13, 1954, 8th
Larry Doby, A.L., July 14, 1954, 8th
Willie Mays, N.L., July 10, 1956, 4th
Stan Musial, N.L., July 13, 1960, 7th
Harmon Killebrew, A.L., July 11, 1961, 6th
George Altman, N.L., July 11, 1961, 8th
Pete Runnels, A.L., July 30, 1962, 3rd
Reggie Jackson, A.L., July 13, 1971, 3rd
Cookie Rojas, A.L., July 25, 1972, 8th
Willie Davis, N.L., July 24, 1973, 6th
Carl Yastrzemski, A.L., July 15, 1975, 6th
Lee Mazzilli, N.L., July 17, 1979, 8th
Frank White, A.L., July 15, 1986, 7th
Fred McGriff, N.L., July 12, 1994, 9th
Jeff Conine, N.L., July 11, 1995, 8th
Hank Blalock, A.L., July 15, 2003, 8th

Home runs as leadoff batter, start of game (5)
Frankie Frisch, N.L., July 10, 1934
Lou Boudreau, A.L., July 6, 1942
Willie Mays, N.L., July 13, 1965
Joe Morgan, N.L., July 19, 1977
Bo Jackson, A.L., July 11, 1989

Hitting home run in first at-bat (12)
Max West, N.L., July 9, 1940, 1st
Hoot Evers, A.L., July 13, 1948, 2nd
Jim Gilliam, N.L., Aug. 3, 1959, 7th
George Altman, N.L., July 11, 1961, 8th
Johnny Bench, N.L., July 23, 1969, 2nd
Dick Dietz, N.L., July 14, 1970, 9th
Lee Mazzilli, N.L., July 17, 1979, 8th
Terry Steinbach, A.L., July 12, 1988, 3rd
Bo Jackson, A.L., July 11, 1989, 1st
Jeff Conine, N.L., July 11, 1995, 8th
Javy Lopez, N.L., July 8, 1997, 7th
Hank Blalock, A.L., July 15, 2003, 8th

Most grand slams, game
1—Fred Lynn, A.L., July 6, 1983, 3rd

Most home runs, inning
1—many players

TOTAL BASES

Most total bases, career
40—Stan Musial, N.L., 1943, 1944, 1946 through 1958, 1959 (both), 1960 (both), 1961 (both), 1962 (both), 1963 (24 G)
Willie Mays, N.L., 1954 through 1958, 1959 (both), 1960 (both), 1961 (both), 1962 (both), 1963 through 1973 (24 G)

Most total bases, game
10—Ted Williams, A.L., July 9, 1946

Most total bases, inning
4—many players

EXTRA BASE HITS

Most extrra base hits, career
8—Stan Musial, N.L., 1943, 1944, 1946 through 1958, 1959 (both), 1960 (both), 1961 (both), 1962 (both), 1963 (24 G; 2 doubles, 6 HR)
Willie Mays, N.L., 1954 through 1958, 1959 (both), 1960 (both), 1961 (both), 1962 (both), 1963 through 1973 (24 G; 2 doubles, 3 triples, 3 HR)

Most extra base hits, game
2—many players

Most extra base hits, inning
1—many players

RUNS BATTED IN

Most runs batted in, career
12—Ted Williams, A.L., 1940 through 1942, 1946 through 1951, 1954 through 1958, 1959 (both), 1960 (both), (18 G)

Most runs batted in, game
5—Ted Williams A.L., July 9, 1946
Al Rosen, A.L., July 13, 1954

Most runs batted in, inning
4—Fred Lynn, A.L., July 6, 1983, 3rd

BASES ON BALLS

Most bases on balls, career
11—Ted Williams, A.L., 1940 through 1942, 1946 through 1951, 1954 through 1958, 1959 (both), 1960 (both) (18 G)

Most bases on balls, game
3—Charlie Gehringer, A.L., July 10, 1934.
Phil Cavarretta, N.L., July 11, 1944 (also 1 single, 1 triple)

Most bases on balls, inning
1—many players

STRIKEOUTS

Most strikeouts, career
17—Mickey Mantle, A.L., 1953 through 1958, 1959 (both), 1960 (both), 1961 (both), 1962 (1st), 1964, 1967, 1968 (16 G)

Most strikeouts, game
3—Lou Gehrig, A.L., July 10, 1934
Bob L. Johnson, A.L., July 8, 1935
Stan Hack, N.L., July 11, 1939
Joe Gordon, A.L., July 6, 1942
Ken Keltner, A.L., July 13, 1943
Jim Hegan, A.L., July 11, 1950.
Mickey Mantle, A.L., July 10, 1956
Johnny Roseboro, N.L., July 31, 1961
Willie McCovey, N.L., July 9, 1968
Johnny Bench, N.L., July 14, 1970
Albert Belle, A.L., July 9, 1996
Craig Biggio, N.L., July 7, 1998
(4—Roberto Clemente, N.L. (consecutive), July 11, 1967)

Most strikeouts, inning
1—many players

SACRIFICE HITS AND FLIES

Most sacrifice hits, career
1—many players

Most sacrifice hits, game or inning
1—many players

Most sacrifice flies, career
3—George Brett, A.L., 1976 through 1979, 1981 through 1985, 1988 (10 G)

Most sacrifice flies, game or inning
1—many players

ALL-STAR GAME Individual batting

HIT BY PITCH, GROUNDING INTO DOUBLE PLAYS

Most hit by pitch, career
1—many players

Most grounding into double plays, career
3—Joe DiMaggio, A.L., 1936 through 1942, 1947 through 1950 (11 G)
   Pete Rose N.L., 1965, 1967, 1969 through 1971, 1973
      through 1982, 1985 (16 G)

Most grounding into double plays, game
2—Bobby Richardson, A.L., July 9, 1963

REACHING ON ERRORS OR INTERFERENCE

Most times reaching base on catcher's interference, game
1—Paul Molitor, A.L., July 9, 1991

CLUB BATTING

BATTING AVERAGE

Highest batting average, game
.442—A.L., July 7, 1998 (43 AB, 19 H)

Lowest batting average, game
.069—N.L., July 10, 1990 (29 AB, 2 H)

AT-BATS AND PLATE APPEARANCES

Most at-bats, game
44—A.L., July 14, 1992

Most at-bats by both clubs, game
83—A.L. 44, N.L. 39, July 14, 1992

Fewest at-bats, game
27—N.L., July 9, 1968 (batted 8 inn)
29—many clubs; Last club: N.L., July 10, 2001

Fewest at-bats by both clubs, game
57—A.L. 30, N.L. 27, July 9, 1968

Most consecutive batters facing pitcher with none reaching base, game
20—A.L., July 9, 1968 (Jim Fregosi doubled to start game, then 20 consecutive batters were retired before Tony Oliva doubled in 7th inn)

Most batters facing pitcher, inning
11—A.L., July 10, 1934, 5th

Most batters facing pitcher by both clubs, inning
19—A.L. 11, N.L. 8, July 10, 1934, 5th

RUNS

Most runs, game
13—A.L., July 6, 1983
     A.L., July 14, 1992
     A.L., July 7, 1998

Most runs by both clubs, game
21—A.L. 13, N.L. 8, July 7, 1998

Most runs, inning
7—A.L., July 6, 1983, 3rd

Most runs by both clubs, inning
9—A.L. 6, N.L. 3, July 10, 1934, 5th

Most innings scored, game
6—A.L., July 7, 1998

Most innings scored by both clubs, game
10—A.L. 6, N.L. 4, July 7, 1998

Most consecutive scoreless innings by one league, total games
19—A.L.; 1967 (last 9 inn); 1968 (all 9 inn); 1969 (1st inn)

EARNED RUNS

Most earned runs, game
13—A.L., July 14, 1992

Most earned runs by both clubs, game
20—A.L. 11, N.L. 9, July 13, 1954

Fewest earned runs, game
0—N.L., July 11, 1939; A.L., July 9, 1940; N.L., July 9, 1946; A.L., July 13, 1960; A.L., July 9, 1968; N.L., July 9, 1968; A.L., July 16, 1985; A.L., July 14, 1987; N.L., July 10, 1990; A.L., July 9, 1996

Fewest earned runs by both clubs, game
0— A.L. 0, N.L. 0, July 9, 1968

HITS

Most hits, game
19—A.L., July 14, 1992

Most hits by both clubs, game
31—A.L. 17, N.L. 14, July 13, 1954
     A.L. 19, N.L. 12, July 14, 1992
     A.L. 19, N.L. 12, July 7, 1998

Fewest hits, game
2—N.L., July 10, 1990

Fewest hits by both clubs, game
8—N.L. 5, A.L. 3, July 9, 1968

SINGLES

Most singles, game
16—A.L., July 7, 1998

Most singles by both clubs, game
26—A.L. 16, N.L. 10, July 7, 1998

Fewest singles, game
0—A.L., July 9, 1968
    N.L., July 11, 1995

Fewest singles by both clubs, game
4—N.L. 4, A.L. 0, July 9, 1968

DOUBLES

Most doubles, game
5—A.L., July 10, 1934
    A.L., July 12, 1949

Most doubles by both clubs, game
7—A.L. 5, N.L. 2, July 12, 1949
    A.L. 4, N.L. 3, July 13, 1993

Fewest doubles, game
0—many games

Fewest doubles by both clubs, game
0—July 6, 1942; July 9, 1946; July 13, 1948; July 8, 1958, July 13, 1976

TRIPLES

Most triples, game
2—A.L., July 10, 1934; A.L., July 10, 1951; N.L., July 13, 1976; A.L., July 11, 1978; A.L., July 6, 1983

Most triples by both clubs, game
3—A.L. 2, N.L. 1, July 11, 1978

Fewest triples, game
0—many games

Fewest triples by both clubs, game
0—many games

HOME RUNS

Most home runs, game
4—N.L., July 10, 1951; A.L., July 13, 1954; N.L., July 13, 1960; N.L., August 9, 1981

Most home runs by both clubs, game
6—N.L. 4, A.L. 2, July 10, 1951
    A.L. 4, N.L. 2, July 13, 1954
    A.L. 3, N.L. 3, July 13, 1971

Most home runs accounting for all runs by both clubs, game
3—N.L. 2, A.L. 1, July 11, 1967, 15 inn

Fewest home runs, game
0—many games

Fewest home runs by both clubs, game
0—many games

Most consecutive games, one or more home runs
9—N.L., 1969 through 1977

Most consecutive home runs from start of game
2—A.L., July 11, 1989 (Jackson, Boggs)

Most home runs, inning (13 times; *consecutive)
2—A.L., July 6, 1942, 1st (Boudreau, York)
  N.L., July 10, 1951, 4th (Musial, Elliott)
  A.L., July 13, 1954, 3rd* (Rosen, Boone)
  A.L., July 10, 1956, 6th* (Williams, Mantle)
  N.L., July 7, 1964, 4th (Williams, Boyer)
  N.L., July 13, 1965, 1st (Mays, Torre)
  A.L., July 13, 1965, 5th (McAuliffe, Killebrew)
  A.L., July 13, 1971, 3rd (Jackson, F. Robinson)
  N.L., July 15, 1975, 2nd* (Garvey, Wynn)
  N.L., July 19, 1977, 1st (Morgan, Luzinski)
  A.L., July 6, 1983, 3rd (Rice, Lynn)
  A.L., July 11, 1989, 1st* (Jackson, Boggs)
  A.L., July 10, 2001, 6th* (Jeter, Ordonez)

Most home runs by both clubs, inning
3—N.L. 2 (Musial, Elliott), A.L. 1 (Wertz), July 10, 1951, 4th
  A.L. 2 (Jackson, F. Robinson), N.L. 1 (Aaron), July 13, 1971, 3rd

TOTAL BASES

Most total bases, game
29—A.L., July 13, 1954

Most total bases by both clubs, game
52—A.L. 29, N.L. 23, July 13, 1954

Fewest total bases, game
2—N.L., July 10, 1990

Fewest total bases by both clubs, game
12—A.L. 6, N.L. 6, 1968

EXTRA BASE HITS

Most extra base hits, game
7—A.L., July 10, 1934 (5 doubles, 2 triples)
  A.L., July 8, 1993 (3 doubles, 2 triples, 2 HR)

Most extra base hits by both clubs, game
10—N.L. 5 (1 double, 4 HR); A.L. 5 (1 double, 2 triples, 2 HR), July 10, 1951
  A.L. 6 (4 doubles, 2 HR); N.L. 4 (3 doubles, 1 HR), July 13, 1993

Fewest extra base hits, game
0—A.L., July 11, 1944; N.L., July 9, 1946; A.L., July 14, 1953; N.L., July 8, 1958; A.L., July 8, 1958; N.L., July 9, 1963; A.L., July 16, 1985; N.L., July 12, 1988; N.L., July 11, 1989; N.L., July 10, 1990; A.L., July 13, 1999

Fewest extra base hits by both clubs, game
0—July 8, 1958

RUNS BATTED IN

Most runs batted in, game
13—A.L., July 6, 1983
  A.L., July 14, 1992

Most runs batted in by both clubs, game
20—A.L. 11, N.L. 9, July 13, 1954

Fewest runs batted in, game
0—A.L., July 9, 1940; N.L., July 9, 1946; A.L., July 13, 1960; A.L., July 12, 1966; A.L., July 9, 1968; N.L., July 9, 1968; A.L., July 14, 1987; N.L., July 12, 1988; N.L., July 10, 1990; A.L., July 9, 1996

Fewest runs batted in, game, both clubs
0—A.L. 0, N.L. 0, July 9, 1968

BASES ON BALLS

Most bases on balls, game
9—A.L., July 10, 1934

Most bases on balls by both clubs, game
13—N.L. 8, A.L. 5, July 12, 1949

Fewest bases on balls, game
0—N.L., July 6, 1933; N.L., July 7, 1937; N.L., July 6, 1938; A.L., July 6, 1942; A.L., July 10, 1956; N.L., July 11, 1967, 15 innings; A.L., July 9, 1968; N.L., July 15, 1975; A.L., July 9, 1996; N.L., July 9, 1996; A.L., July 10, 2001

Fewest bases on balls by both clubs, ame
0—A.L. 0, N.L. 0, July 9, 1996
  (2—A.L. 2, N.L. 0, July 11, 1967, 15 inn)

STRIKEOUTS

Most strikeouts, game
12—A.L., July 10, 1934; N.L., July 10, 1956; A.L., August 3, 1959; A.L., July 15, 1986; N.L., July 13, 1999
  (17—A.L., July 11, 1967, 15 inn)

Most strikeouts by both clubs, game
22—A.L. 12, A.L. 10, July 13, 1999
  (30—A.L. 17, N.L. 13, July 11, 1967, 15 inn)

Fewest strikeouts, game
0—N.L., July 7, 1937

Fewest strikeouts by both clubs, game
6—A.L. 4, N.L. 2, July 8, 1958

SACRIFICE HITS

Most sacrifice hits, game
3—N.L., July 11, 1944.
  (3—N.L. 3, A.L. 0, July 11, 1944)

Fewest sacrifice hits, game
0—many games

Fewest sacrifice hits by both clubs, game
0—many games

HIT BY PITCH

Most hit by pitch, game
2—A.L., July 10, 1962

Most hit by pitch by both clubs, game
2—A.L. 2, N.L. 0, July 10, 1962
  A.L. 1, N.L. 1, July 15, 1975
  A.L. 1, N.L. 1, July 19, 1977

BASERUNNING

Most stolen bases, career
6—Willie Mays, N.L., 1954 through 1958, 1959 (both), 1960 (both), 1961 (both), 1962 (both), 1963 through 1973 (24 G)

Most stolen bases, game
2—Willie Mays, N.L., July 9, 1963
    Kelly Gruber, A.L., July 10, 1990
    Roberto Alomar, A.L., July 14, 1992
    Kenny Lofton, A.L., July 9, 1996

Stealing home, game
Pie Traynor, N.L., July 10, 1934, 5th (front end of a double steal with Mel Ott)

Most times caught stealing, game
1—many players
    (2—Tony Oliva, A.L., July 11, 1967, 15 inn)

CLUB

Most stolen bases, game
5—A.L., July 7, 1998

Most stolen bases by both clubs, game
5—A.L. 3, N.L. 2, July 16, 1985
    A.L. 4, N.L. 1, July 10, 1990
    A.L. 5, N.L. 0, July 7, 1998
    A.L. 3, N.L. 2, July 9, 2002

Fewest stolen bases, game
0—many games

Fewest stolen bases by both clubs, game
0—many games

Most left on base, game
12—A.L., July 10, 1934
     N.L., July 12, 1949
     A.L., July 13, 1960

Most left on base by both clubs, game
20—N.L. 12, A.L. 8, July 12, 1949

Fewest left on bases, game
0—N.L., July 11, 1995

Fewest left on base by both clubs, game
4—N.L. 2, A.L. 2, July 13, 1971

ALL-STAR GAME *Baserunning*

PITCHING

GAMES

Most games pitched
9—Roger Clemens, A.L., 1986, 1988, 1991, 1992, 1997, 1998, 2001, 2003; N.L., 2004
Most consecutive games pitched
6—Ewell Blackwell, N.L., 1946 through 1951
Early Wynn, A.L., 1955 through 1958, 1959 (both)

GAMES STARTED

Most games started
5—Lefty Gomez, A.L., 1933 through 1935, 1937, 1938.
Robin Roberts, N.L., 1950, 1951, 1953 through 1955.
Don Drysdale, N.L. 1959 (both), 1962 (1st), 1964, 1968

INNINGS

Most innings pitched, career
19.1—Don Drysdale, N.L., 1959 (both), 1962 (1st), 1963, 1964, 1965, 1967, 1968 (8 G)
Most innings, game
6—Lefty Gomez, A.L., July 8, 1935

GAMES WON AND LOST

Most games won
3—Lefty Gomez, A.L., 1933, 1935, 1937
Most games lost
2—Mort Cooper, N.L., 1942, 1943
Claude Passeau, N.L., 1941, 1946
Whitey Ford, A.L., 1959 (1st), 1960 (2nd)
Luis Tiant, A.L., 1968, 1974
Catfish Hunter, A.L., 1967, 1975
Dwight Gooden, N.L., 1986, 1988

RUNS AND EARNED RUNS

Most runs allowed, career
13—Whitey Ford, A.L., 1954 through 1956, 1959 (1st), 1960 (2nd), 1961 (1st)
Most earned runs allowed, career
11—Whitey Ford, A.L., 1954 through 1956, 1959 (1st), 1960 (2nd), 1961 (1st)
Most runs allowed, game
7—Atlee Hammaker, N.L., July 6, 1983
Most earned runs allowed, game
7—Atlee Hammaker, N.L., July 6, 1983
Most runs allowed, inning
7—Atlee Hammaker, N.L., July 6, 1983, 3rd
Most earned runs allowed, inning
7—Atlee Hammaker, N.L., July 6, 1983, 3rd

HITS

Most hits allowed, total games
19—Whitey Ford, A.L., 1954 through 1956, 1959 (1st), 1960 (2nd), 1961 (1st)
Most hits allowed, game
9—Tom Glavine, N.L., July 14, 1992
Most hits allowed, inning
7—Tom Glavine, N.L., July 14, 1992, 1st (consecutive)

HOME RUNS

Most home runs allowed, career

4—Vida Blue, A.L., 1971, 1975
Catfish Hunter, A.L., 1967, 1970, 1973 through 1976
Most home runs allowed, game
3—Jim Palmer, A.L., July 19, 1977
Most home runs allowed, inning (12 times; *consecutive)
2—Mort Cooper, N.L., July 6, 1942, 1st
Eddie Lopat, A.L., July 10, 1951, 4th
Robin Roberts, N.L., July 13, 1954, 3rd*
Warren Spahn, N.L., July 10, 1956, 6th*
John Wyatt, A.L., July 7, 1964, 4th
Milt Pappas, A.L., July 13, 1965, 1st
Jim Maloney, N.L., July 13, 1965, 5th
Dock Ellis, N.L., July 13, 1971, 3rd
Vida Blue, A.L., July 15, 1975, 2nd*
Jim Palmer, A.L., July 19, 1977, 1st
Atlee Hammaker, A.L., July 6, 1983, 3rd
Rick Reuschel, N.L., July 11, 1989, 1st*
Jon Lieber, N.L., July 10, 2001, 6th*

BASES ON BALLS

Most bases on balls, career
7—Jim Palmer, A.L., 1970 through 1972, 1977, 1978
Most bases on balls, game
5—Bill Hallahan, N.L., July 6, 1933 (2 IP)
Most bases on balls, inning (*consecutive)
3—Early Wynn, A.L., August 3, 1959, 5th
Jim Palmer, A.L., July 11, 1978, 3rd*
Jim Kern, A.L., July 17, 1979, 9th
Dan Petry, A.L., July 16, 1985, 9th
Kevin Brown, N.L., July 11, 2000, 3rd

STRIKEOUTS

Most strikeouts, career
10—Don Drysdale, N.L., 1959 (both), 1962 (1st), 1963 through 1965, 1967, 1968 (8 G)
Most strikeouts, game
6—Carl Hubbell, N.L., July 10, 1934 (3 IP)
Johnny Vander Meer, N.L., July 13, 1943 (2.2 IP)
Larry Jansen, N.L., July 11, 1950 (5 IP)
Ferguson Jenkins, N.L., July 11, 1967 (3 IP)
Most consecutive strikeouts, game
5—Carl Hubbell, N.L., July 10, 1934; 3 in 1st, 2 in 2nd (Ruth, Gehrig, Foxx, Simmons, Cronin)
Fernando Valenzuela, N.L., July 15, 1986; 3 in 4th 2 in 5th (Mattingly, Ripken, Barfield, Whitaker, Higuera)
Most consecutive strikeouts from start of game
4—Pedro Martinez, A.L., July 13, 1999; 3in 1st, 1 in 2nd (Larkin, Walker, Sosa, McGwire)

HIT BATSMEN, WILD PITCHES AND BALKS

Most hit batsmen, inning or game
1—many pitchers
Most wild pitches, career
2—Ewell Blackwell, N.L., 1946 through 1951
Robin Roberts, N.L., 1950, 1951, 1953 through 1955
Tom Brewer, A.L., 1956
Juan Marichal, N.L., 1962 (both), 1964 through 1968, 1971
Dave Stieb, A.L., 1980, 1981
Steve Rogers, N.L., 1978, 1979, 1982
John Smoltz, N.L., 1989, 1992, 1993
Most wild pitches, game
2—Tom Brewer, A.L., July 10, 1956, 6th and 7th
Juan Marichal, N.L., July 30, 1962, 9th
Dave Stieb, A.L., July 8, 1980, 7th
John Smoltz, N.L., July 13, 1993, 6th

INDIVIDUAL FIELDING

Most wild pitches, inning
2—Juan Marichal, N.L., July 30, 1962, 9th
  Dave Stieb, A.L., July 8, 1980, 7th
  John Smoltz, N.L., July 13, 1993, 6th

Most balks, career
2—Dwight Gooden, N.L., 1986, 1988

Most balks, inning or game
1—Bob Friend, N.L., July 11, 1960
  Stu Miller, N.L., July 11, 1961
  Steve Busby, A.L., July 15, 1975
  Jim Kern, A.L., July 17, 1979
  Dwight Gooden, N.L., July 15, 1986; July 12, 1988
  Charlie Hough, A.L., July 15, 1986

FIRST BASEMEN

Most games
10—Steve Garvey, N.L., 1974 through 1981, 1984, 1985

Most putouts, career
53—Lou Gehrig, A.L., 1933 through 1938

Most putouts, game
14—George McQuinn, A.L., July 13, 1948
  (14—Harmon Killebrew, A.L., July 11, 1967, 15 inn)

Most assists, career
6—Steve Garvey, N.L., 1974 through 1981, 1984, 1985

Most assists, game
3—Rudy York, A.L., July 6, 1942
  Bill White, N.L., July 9, 1963

Most chances accepted, career
55—Lou Gehrig, A.L., 1933 through 1938
  Steve Garvey, N.L., 1974 through 1981, 1984, 1985

Most chances accepted, game
14—Rudy York, A.L., July 6, 1942
  George McQuinn, A.L., July 13, 1948
  (15—Harmon Killebrew, A.L., July 11, 1967, 15 inn)

Most errors, career
2—Lou Gehrig, A.L., 1933 through 1938

Most errors, game and inning
1—many players

Most double plays, career
6—Bill White, N.L., 1960, 1960, 1961, 1961, 1963
  Harmon Killebrew, A.L., 1965, 1967, 1968, 1971

Most double plays, game
3—Stan Musial, N.L., July 8, 1958

Most unassisted double plays, game
1—Pete Runnels, A.L., August 3, 1959, 2nd
  Lee May, N.L., July 25, 1972, 3rd

SECOND BASEMEN

Most games
13—Nellie Fox, A.L., 1951, 1953 through 1958, 1959 (both),
  1960 (both), 1961 (1st), 1963

Most putouts, career
25—Nellie Fox, A.L., 1951, 1953 through 1958, 1959 (both),
  1960 (both), 1961 (1st), 1963

Most putouts, game
5—Frankie Frisch, N.L., July 6, 1933
  (7—Juan Samuel, N.L., July 14, 1987, 13 inn)

Most assists, career
23—Billy Herman, N.L., 1934 through 1938, 1940 through 1943

Most assists, game
6—Willie Randolph, A.L., July 19, 1977

Most chances accepted, career
39—Nellie Fox, A.L., 1951, 1953 through 1958, 1959 (both),
  1960 (both), 1961 (1st), 1963

Most chances accepted, game
9—Bill Mazeroski, N.L., July 8, 1958.
  (9—Juan Samuel, N.L., July 14, 1987, 13 inn)

Most errors, career
2—Billy Herman, N.L., 1934 through 1938, 1940 through 1943
  Nellie Fox, A.L., 1951, 1953 through 1958, 1959 (both),
  1960 (both), 1961, 1963
  Willie Randolph, A.L., 1977, 1980, 1981, 1987, 1989
  Steve Sax, N.L., 1982, 1983, 1986, 1989, 1990

Most errors, game
2—Billy Herman, N.L., July 13, 1943
  Willie Randolph, A.L., July 8, 1980

Most double plays, career
5—Roberto Alomar, N.L., 1990; A.L. 1991 through 2001

Most double plays, game
3—Billy Herman, N.L., July 13, 1943
  Bill Mazeroski, N.L., July 8, 1958

Most unassisted double plays, game
none

THIRD BASEMEN

Most games
18—Brooks Robinson, A.L., 1960 (both), 1961 (both), 1962
  (both), 1963 through 1974 (consecutive)

Most putouts, career
11—Brooks Robinson, A.L., 1960 (both), 1961 (both), 1962
  (both), 1963 through 1974

Most putouts, game
4—George Kell, A.L., July 10, 1951
  (4—Brooks Robinson, A.L., July 12, 1966, 9.1 inn)

Most assists, career
32—Brooks Robinson, A.L., 1960, 1960, 1961, 1961, 1962,
  1962, 1963 through 1974

Most assists, game
6—Ken Keltner, A.L., July 13, 1948
  Frank Malzone, A.L., August 3, 1959

Most chances accepted, career
43—Brooks Robinson, A.L., 1960 (both), 1961 (both), 1962
  (both), 1963 through 1974

Most chances accepted, game
7—Ken Keltner, A.L., July 13, 1948
  Frank Malzone, A.L., August 3, 1959
  (8—Brooks Robinson, A.L., July 12, 1966, 9.1 inn

Most errors, career
6—Eddie Mathews, N.L., 1953, 1955, 1957, 1959 (1st), 1960
  (both), 1961 (both), 1962 (2nd)

Most errors, game
2—Red Rolfe, A.L., July 7, 1937
  Eddie Mathews, N.L., July 11, 1960; July 30, 1962

(2—Ken Boyer, N.L., July 11, 1961, 10 inn)

Most errors, inning
2—Eddie Mathews, N.L., July 30, 1962, 9th

Most double plays, career
3—Frank Malzone, A.L., 1957, 1958, 1959 (both), 1960 (both), 1963
   Brooks Robinson, A.L., 1960 (both), 1961 (both), 1962 (both), 1963 through 1974
   George Brett, A.L., 1976 through 1979, 1981 through 1983

Most double plays, game
1—many players

Most unassisted double plays, game
none

SHORTSTOPS

Most games
15—Cal Ripken Jr., A.L., 1983 through 1996, 2001

Most putouts, career
16—Ozzie Smith, N.L., 1981 through 1992, 1994, 1996

Most putouts, game
5—Chico Carrasquel, A.L., July 13, 1954

Most assists, career
24—Joe Cronin, A.L., 1933 through 1935, 1937 through 1939, 1941

Most assists, game
8—Joe Cronin, A.L., July 10, 1934

Most chances accepted, career
39—Ozzie Smith, N.L., 1981 through 1992, 1994, 1996

Most chances accepted, game
10—Joe Cronin, A.L., July 10, 1934
    Marty Marion, N.L., July 9, 1946

Most errors, career
2—Joe Cronin, A.L., 1933 through 1935, 1937 through 1939, 1941
   Ernie Banks, N.L., 1955, 1957, 1958, 1959 (both), 1960 (both), 1961 (2nd)
   Nomar Garciaparra, A.L., 1997, 1999, 2000

Most errors, game
2—Nomar Garciaparra, A.L., July 11, 2000

Most double plays, career
6—Ernie Banks, N.L., 1955, 1957, 1958, 1959 (both), 1960 (both), 1961 (2nd)

Most double plays, game
2—Lou Boudreau, A.L., July 6, 1942
   Marty Marion, N.L., July 9, 1946
   Eddie Joost, A.L., July 12, 1949
   Ernie Banks, N.L., July 8, 1958; July 13, 1960
   Eddie Kasko, N.L., July 31, 1961
   Luis Aparicio, A.L., July 30, 1962
   Dick Groat, N.L., July 9, 1963
   Tony Fernandez, A.L., July 11, 1989

Most unassisted double plays, game
none

OUTFIELDERS

Most games
22—Willie Mays, N.L., 1954 through 1958, 1959 (both), 1960 (both), 1961 (both), 1962 (both), 1963 through 1972

Most putouts, career

55—Willie Mays, N.L., 1954 through 1958, 1959 (both), 1960 (both), 1961 (both), 1962 (both), 1963 through 1972

Most putouts, left fielder, game
5—Sammy West, A.L., July 7, 1937
   Frank Robinson, N.L., July 9, 1957
   Joe Rudi, A.L., July 15, 1975

Most putouts, center fielder, game
7—Chet Laabs, A.L., July 13, 1943
   Willie Mays, N.L., July 7, 1964
   (9—Larry Doby, A.L., July 11, 1950, 14 inn)

Most putouts, right fielder, game
4—Charlie Keller, A.L., July 9, 1940
   Enos Slaughter, N.L., July 14, 1953
   Darryl Strawberry, N.L., July 12, 1988
   (6—Roberto Clemente, N.L., July 11, 1967, 15 inn)

Most assists, career
3—Stan Musial, N.L., 1943, 1944, 1946, 1948, 1949, 1951 through 1956, 1962 (2nd)

Most assists, left fielder, game
1—many players

Most assists, center fielder, game
1—many players

Most assists, right fielder, game
2—Dave Parker, N.L., July 17, 1979
   Tony Gwynn, N.L., July 14, 1992

Most chances accepted, career
55—Willie Mays, N.L., 1954 through 1958, 1959 (both), 1960 (both), 1961 (both), 1962 (both), 1963 through 1972

Most chances accepted, left fielder, game
5—Samny West, A.L., July 7, 1937
   Joe Rudi, A.L., July 15, 1975

Most chances accepted, center fielder, game
7—Chet Laabs, A.L., July 13, 1943
   Willie Mays, N.L., July 7, 1964
   (9—Larry Doby, A.L., July 11, 1950, 14 inn)

Most chances accepted, right fielder, game
4—Charlie Keller, A.L., July 9, 1940
   Enos Slaughter, N.L., July 14, 1953
   Darryl Strawberry, N.L., July 12, 1988

Most errors, career
2—Pete Reiser, N.L., 1941, 1942
   Joe DiMaggio, A.L., 1936 through 1942, 1947, 1949, 1950

Most errors, left fielder, game
1—many players

Most errors, center fielder, game
2—Pete Reiser, N.L., July 8, 1941

Most errors, right fielder, game
1—many players

Most double plays, career
1—Stan Spence, A.L., 1944, 1946, 1947
   Tommy Davis, N.L., 1962, 1962, 1963
   Darryl Strawberry, N.L., 1984 through 1988, 1990

Most double plays, left fielder, game
1—Tommy Davis, N.L., July 9, 1963

Most double plays, center fielder, game
none

Most double plays, right fielder, game
1—Stan Spence, A.L., July 11, 1944
   Darryl Strawberry, N.L., July 10, 1990

Most unassisted double plays, game

CATCHERS

Most games
14—Yogi Berra, A.L., 1949 through 1958, 1959 (2nd), 1960 (both), 1961 (1st)

Most innings, game
15—Bill Freehan, A.L., July 11, 1967 (complete game)

Most putouts, career
61—Yogi Berra, A.L., 1949 through 1958, 1959 (2nd), 1960 (both), 1961 (1st)

Most putouts, game
10—Bill Dickey, A.L., July 11, 1939
Yogi Berra, A.L., July 10, 1956
Del Crandall, N.L., July 7, 1959
Johnny Bench, N.L., July 15, 1975
Ivan Rodriguez, A.L., July 13, 1999
(13—Roy Campanella, N.L., July 11, 1950, 14 inn
Smoky Burgess, N.L., July 11, 1961, 10 inn
Bill Freehan, A.L., July 11, 1967, 15 inn)

Most assists, career
7—Yogi Berra, A.L., 1949 through 1958, 1959 (2nd), 1960 (both), 1961 (1st)

Most assists, game
3—Lance Parrish, A.L., July 13, 1982

Most chances accepted, career
68—Yogi Berra, A.L., 1949 through 1958, 1959, 1960, 1960, 1961

Most chances accepted, game
11—Yogi Berra, A.L., July 10, 1956
Johnny Bench, N.L., July 15, 1975
Ivan Rodriguez, A.L., July 13, 1999
(15—Roy Campanella, N.L., July 11, 1950, 14 inn)

Most errors, career
2—Smoky Burgess, N.L., 1954, 1955, 1960 (both), 1961 (both)

Most errors, game
1—many players

Most passed balls, career and game
1—many catchers

Most double plays, career
2—Ivan Rodriguez, A.L., 1992 through 2001

Most double plays, game
1—many catchers

Most unassisted double plays, game
none

PITCHERS

Most games
9—Roger Clemens, A.L., 1986, 1988, 1991, 1992, 1997, 1998, 2001, 2003; N.L., 2004

Most putouts, career
3—Spud Chandler, A.L., 1942

Most putouts, game
3—Spud Chandler, A.L., July 6, 1942

Most assists, career
5—Johnny Vander Meer, N.L., 1938, 1942, 1943

Most assists, game
3—Johnny Vander Meer, N.L., July 6, 1938
Don Drysdale, N.L., July 7, 1964
Mickey Lolich, A.L., July 13, 1971

Most chances accepted, career
5—Mel Harder, A.L., 1934, 1935, 1936, 1937
Johnny Vander Meer, N.L., 1938, 1942, 1943
Don Drysdale, N.L., 1959 (both), 1962 (1st), 1963 through 1965, 1967, 1968

Most chances accepted, game
4—Spud Chandler, A.L., July 6, 1942

Most errors, career and game
1—many pitchers

Most double plays, career and game
1—many pitchers

Most unassisted double plays, game

CLUB FIELDING

NUMBER OF PLAYERS AT POSITIONS
INFIELDERS

Most infielders, game
10—N.L., July 13, 1960
　　N.L., July 13, 1976
　　A.L., July 11, 2000
　　A.L., July 10, 2001

Most infielders by both clubs, game
19—A.L. 10, N.L. 9, July 11, 2000

Most first basemen, game
3—N.L., July 9, 1946.
　　N.L., July 13, 1960
　　N.L., July 24, 1973
　　A.L., July 11, 2000
　　A.L., July 10, 2001

Most first basemen by both clubs, game
5—N.L. 3, A.L. 2, July 9, 1946
　　N.L. 3, A.L. 2, July 13, 1960
　　A.L. 3, N.L. 2, July 11, 2000
　　N.L. 3, A.L. 2, July 10, 2001

Most second basemen, game
3—N.L., July 13, 1960
　　N.L., August 9, 1981
　　A.L., July 14, 1992
　　A.L., July 8, 1997.
　　N.L., July 11, 2000

Most second basemen by both clubs, game
5—N.L. 3, A.L. 2, July 13, 1960
　　N.L. 3, A.L. 2, August 9, 1981
　　A.L. 3, N.L. 2, July 14, 1992
　　A.L. 3, N.L. 2, July 8, 1997
　　N.L. 3, A.L. 2, July 11, 2000

Most third basemen, game
3—many clubs

Most third basemen by both clubs, game
6—A.L. 3, N.L. 3, July 10, 2001

Most shortstops, game
3—many clubs

Most shortstops by both clubs, game
6—A.L. 3, N.L. 3, July 13, 1976

OUTFIELDERS

Most outfielders, game
8—N.L., July 24, 1973

Most outfielders by both clubs, game
14—N.L. 7, A.L. 7, July 8, 1980

Most right fielders, game
4—N.L., July 13, 1976

Most right fielders by both clubs, game
6—N.L. 4, A.L. 2, July 13, 1976

Most center fielders, game
3—many times

Most center fielders by both clubs, game
5—many times

Most left fielders, game
3—many times

Most left fielders by both clubs, game
5—many times
　　(6—N.L. 3, A.L. 3, July 14, 1970, 12 inn)

BATTERY

Most catchers, game
3—many times

Most catchers by both clubs, game
6—many times

Most pitchers, game
10—A.L., July 14, 1992

Most pitchers by both clubs, game
18—A.L. 10, N.L. 8, July 14, 1992
　　A.L. 9, N.L. 9, July 10, 2001

Fewest pitchers, game
2—A.L., July 8, 1935
　　A.L., July 6, 1942

Fewest pitchers by both clubs, game
6—many times

PUTOUTS, ASSISTS

Most players with one or more putouts, game
14—N.L., July 13, 1976
　　A.L., July 6, 1983
　　A.L., July 14, 1992
　　A.L., July 10, 2001

Most players with one or more putouts by both clubs, game
25—N.L. 14, A.L. 11, July 13, 1976
　　A.L. 13, N.L. 12, July 16, 1985
　　A.L. 14, N.L. 11, July 14, 1992

Most assists, game
16—A.L., July 6, 1942
　　A.L., August 9, 1981

Most assists by both clubs, game
26—A.L. 15, N.L. 11, July 12, 1949
　　A.L. 16, N.L. 10, August 9, 1981
　　A.L. 14, N.L. 12, July 8, 1997

Fewest assists, game
5—N.L., July 10, 1934
　　N.L., July 9, 1957
　　N.L., July 23, 1969
　　N.L., July 13, 1999
　　A.L., July 15, 2003
　　(3—N.L., July 15, 2003, fielded 8 inn)

Fewest assists by both clubs, game
8—A.L. 5, N.L. 3, July 15, 2003

Most players one or more assists, game
10—N.L., July 24, 1973

Most players one or more assists by both clubs, game
19—N.L. 10, A.L. 9, July 24, 1973

ERRORS, DOUBLE PLAYS

Most errors, game
5—N.L., July 12, 1949
　　N.L., July 11, 1961

Most errors by both clubs, game
6—N.L. 5, A.L. 1, July 12, 1949
　　(7—N.L. 5, A.L. 2, July 11, 1961, 10 inn)

Fewest errors, game
0—many times

Fewest errors by both clubs, game
0—many times

Most consecutive errorless games
11—N.L., 1963 through 1973

Most double plays, game
3—many times

Most double plays by both clubs, game
4—many times

Fewest double plays, game
0—many times

Fewest double plays by both clubs, game
0—many times

MISCELLANEOUS

EARLIEST AND LATEST GAME DATES

Earliest date for All-Star Game
July 6, 1933 at Comiskey Park, Chicago
July 6, 1938 at Crosley Field, Cincinnati
July 6, 1942 at Polo Grounds, New York
July 6, 1983 at Comiskey Park, Chicago

Latest date for All-Star Game
August 9, 1981 at Municipal Stadium, Cleveland

NIGHT GAMES

First night game
July 13, 1943 at Shibe Park, Philadelphia

LENGTH OF GAMES

Longest game, by innings
15 inn—at Anaheim Stadium, California, July 11, 1967

Shortest game, by innings
5 inn—at Shibe Park, Philadelphia, July 8, 1952 (rain)

Longest 9-inning game, by time
3:38—at Coors Field, Colorado, July 7, 1998

Shortest 9-inning game, by time
1:53—at Sportsman's Park, St. Louis, July 9, 1940

Longest extra-inning game, by time
3:41—at Anaheim Stadium, California, July 11, 1967, 15 inn

GAMES WON AND LOST

All-Star games won
40—National League (lost 33, tied 2)
33—American League (lost 40, tied 2)

For a complete list of All-Star Game results,
see page 514.

Most consecutive All-Star games won
11—National League, 1972 through 1982

Most consecutive All-Star games lost
11—American League, 1972 through 1982

ATTENDANCE

Largest attendance, game
72,086—at Municipal Stadium, Cleveland, August 9, 1981

Smallest attendance, game
25,556—at Braves Field, Boston, July 7, 1936

NON-PLAYING PERSONNEL

MANAGERS
GAMES

Most All-Star games managed
10—Casey Stengel, A.L., 1950 through 1954, 1956, 1957, 1958, 1959 (both), (won 4, lost 6)

Most consecutive All-Star games managed
5—Casey Stengel, A.L., 1950, through 1954; also 1956, 1957, 1958, 1959 (both)

GAMES WON

Most All-Star games won as manager
7—Walter Alston, N.L., 1956, 1960 (both), 1964, 1966, 1967, 1975 (lost 2)

Most All-Star games won as undefeated manager
5—Joe Torre, A.L., 1997, 1999 through 2001, 2004 (tie in 2003)

Most consecutive victories as All-Star manager
6—Walter Alston, N.L., 1960 (both), 1964, 1966, 1967, 1975

Most consecutive years managing All-Star winners
3—Tony La Russa, A.L., 1989 though 1991
    Joe Torre, A.L., 1999 through 2001

Most All-Star games won as manager, one season
2—Walter Alston, N.L., July 11, July 13, 1960

GAMES LOST

Most All-Star games lost as manager
6—Casey Stengel, A.L., 1950 through 1953, 1956, 1959 (1st), (won 4)

Most All-Star games lost as winless manager
5—Al Lopez, A.L., 1955, 1960 (both), 1964, 1965

Most consecutive defeats as All-Star manager
5—Al Lopez, A.L., 1955, 1960 (both), 1964, 1965

Most consecutive years managing All-Star losers
4—Casey Stengel, A.L., 1950 through 1953

Most All-Star games lost as manager, one season
2—Al Lopez, A.L., July 11, July 13, 1960

UMPIRES

Most games umpired
7—Bill Summers, A.L., 1936, 1941, 1946, 1949, 1952, 1955, 1959 (2nd)
    Al Barlick, N.L., 1942, 1949, 1952, 1955, 1959 (1st), 1966, 1970

Most consecutive games umpired
2—many umpires

GENERAL REFERENCE

HOME RUNS (161)

(Numbers in parentheses indicate cumulative totals by batters or pitchers)

Player	Date	Inning	On	Pitcher
Babe Ruth, A.L.	July 6, 1933	3	1	Bill Hallahan
Frankie Frisch, N.L.	July 6, 1933	6	0	Alvin Crowder
Frankie Frisch, N.L. (2)	July 10, 1934	1	0	Lefty Gomez
Joe Medwick, N.L.	July 10, 1934	3	2	Lefty Gomez (2)
Jimmie Foxx, A.L.	July 8, 1935	1	1	Bill Walker
Augie Galan, N.L.	July 7, 1936	5	0	Schoolboy Rowe
Lou Gehrig, A.L.	July 7, 1936	7	0	Curt Davis
Lou Gehrig, A.L. (2)	July 7, 1937	3	1	Dizzy Dean
Joe DiMaggio, A.L.	July 11, 1939	5	0	Bill C. Lee
Max West, N.L.	July 9, 1940	1	2	Red Ruffing
Arky Vaughan, N.L.	July 8, 1941	7	1	Sid Hudson
Arky Vaughan, N.L. (2)	July 8, 1941	8	1	Eddie Smith
Ted Williams, A.L.	July 8, 1941	9	2	Claude Passeau
Lou Boudreau, A.L.	July 6, 1942	1	0	Mort Cooper
Rudy York, A.L.	July 6, 1942	1	1	Mort Cooper (2)
Mickey Owen, N.L.	July 6, 1942	8	0	Al Benton
Bobby Doerr, A.L.	July 13, 1943	2	2	Mort Cooper (3)
Vince DiMaggio, N.L.	July 13, 1943	9	0	Cecil Hughson
Charlie Keller, A.L.	July 9, 1946	1	1	Claude Passeau
Ted Williams, A.L. (2)	July 9, 1946	4	0	Kirby Higbe
Ted Williams, A.L. (3)	July 9, 1946	8	2	Rip Sewell
Johnny Mize, N.L.	July 8, 1947	4	0	Spec Shea
Stan Musial, N.L.	July 13, 1948	1	1	Walt Masterson
Hoot Evers, A.L.	July 13, 1948	2	0	Ralph Branca
Stan Musial, N.L. (2)	July 12, 1949	1	1	Mel Parnell
Ralph Kiner, N.L.	July 12, 1949	6	1	Lou Brissie
Ralph Kiner, N.L. (2)	July 11, 1950	9	0	Art Houtteman
Red Schoendienst, N.L.	July 11, 1950	14	0	Ted Gray
Stan Musial, N.L. (3)	July 10, 1951	4	0	Eddie Lopat
Bob Elliott, N.L.	July 10, 1951	4	1	Eddie Lopat (2)
Vic Wertz, A.L.	July 10, 1951	4	0	Sal Maglie
George Kell, A.L.	July 10, 1951	5	0	Sal Maglie (2)
Gil Hodges, N.L.	July 10, 1951	6	1	Fred Hutchinson
Ralph Kiner, N.L. (3)	July 10, 1951	8	0	Mel Parnell (2)
Jackie Robinson, N.L.	July 8, 1952	1	0	Vic Raschi
Hank Sauer, N.L.	July 8, 1952	4	1	Bob Lemon
Al Rosen, A.L.	July 13, 1954	3	2	Robin Roberts
Ray Boone, A.L.	July 13, 1954	3	0	Robin Roberts (2)
Ted Kluszewski, N.L.	July 13, 1954	5	1	Bob Porterfield
Al Rosen, A.L. (2)	July 13, 1954	5	1	Johnny Antonelli
Gus Bell, N.L.	July 13, 1954	8	1	Bob Keegan
Larry Doby, A.L.	July 13, 1954	8	0	Gene Conley
Mickey Mantle, A.L.	July 12, 1955	1	2	Robin Roberts (3)
Stan Musial, N.L. (4)	July 12, 1955	12	0	Frank Sullivan
Willie Mays, N.L.	July 10, 1956	4	1	Whitey Ford
Ted Williams, A.L. (4)	July 10, 1956	6	1	Warren Spahn
Mickey Mantle, A.L. (2)	July 10, 1956	6	0	Warren Spahn (2)
Stan Musial, N.L. (5)	July 10, 1956	7	0	Tom Brewer
Eddie Mathews, N.L.	July 7, 1959	1	0	Early Wynn
Al Kaline, A.L.	July 7, 1959	4	0	Lew Burdette
Frank Malzone, A.L.	Aug. 3, 1959	2	0	Don Drysdale
Yogi Berra, A.L.	Aug. 3, 1959	3	1	Don Drysdale (2)
Frank Robinson, N.L.	Aug. 3, 1959	5	0	Early Wynn (2)
Jim Gilliam, N.L.	Aug. 3, 1959	7	0	Billy O'Dell
Rocky Colavito, A.L.	Aug. 3, 1959	8	0	Roy Face
Ernie Banks, N.L.	July 11, 1960	1	1	Bill Monbouquette
Del Crandall, N.L.	July 11, 1960	2	1	Bill Monbouquette (2)
Al Kaline, A.L. (2)	July 11, 1960	8	0	Bob Buhl
Eddie Mathews, N.L. (2)	July 13, 1960	2	1	Whitey Ford (2)
Willie Mays, N.L. (2)	July 13, 1960	3	0	Whitey Ford (3)
Stan Musial, N.L. (6)	July 13, 1960	7	0	Gerry Staley
Ken Boyer, N.L.	July 13, 1960	9	1	Gary Bell
Harmon Killebrew, A.L.	July 11, 1961	6	0	Mike McCormick
George Altman, N.L.	July 11, 1961	8	0	Mike Fornieles
Rocky Colavito, A.L. (2)	July 31, 1961	1	0	Bob Purkey
Pete Runnels, A.L.	July 30, 1962	3	0	Art Mahaffey
Leon Wagner, A.L.	July 30, 1962	4	1	Art Mahaffey (2)
Rocky Colavito, A.L. (3)	July 30, 1962	7	2	Dick Farrell

Player	Date	Inning	On	Pitcher
Johnny Roseboro, N.L.	July 30, 1962	9	0	Milt Pappas
Billy Williams, N.L.	July 7, 1964	4	0	John Wyatt
Ken Boyer, N.L. (2)	July 7, 1964	4	0	John Wyatt (2)
Johnny Callison, N.L.	July 7, 1964	9	2	Dick Radatz
Willie Mays, N.L. (3)	July 13, 1965	1	0	Milt Pappas (2)
Joe Torre, N.L.	July 13, 1965	1	1	Milt Pappas (3)
Willie Stargell, N.L.	July 13, 1965	2	1	Mudcat Grant
Dick McAuliffe, A.L.	July 13, 1965	5	1	Jim Maloney
Harmon Killebrew, A.L. (2)	July 13, 1965	5	1	Jim Maloney (2)
Dick Allen, N.L.	July 11, 1967	2	0	Dean Chance
Brooks Robinson, A.L.	July 11, 1967	6	0	Ferguson Jenkins
Tony Perez, N.L.	July 11, 1967	15	0	Catfish Hunter
Johnny Bench, N.L.	July 23, 1969	2	1	Mel Stottlemyre
Frank Howard, A.L.	July 23, 1969	2	0	Steve Carlton
Willie McCovey, N.L.	July 23, 1969	3	1	Blue Moon Odom
Bill Freehan, A.L.	July 23, 1969	3	0	Steve Carlton (2)
Willie McCovey, N.L. (2)	July 23, 1969	4	0	Denny McLain
Dick Dietz, N.L.	July 14, 1970	9	0	Catfish Hunter (2)
Johnny Bench, N.L. (2)	July 13, 1971	2	1	Vida Blue
Hank Aaron, N.L.	July 13, 1971	3	0	Vida Blue (2)
Reggie Jackson, A.L.	July 13, 1971	3	1	Dock Ellis
Frank Robinson, A.L. (2)	July 13, 1971	3	1	Dock Ellis (2)
Harmon Killebrew, A.L. (3)	July 13, 1971	6	1	Ferguson Jenkins
Roberto Clemente, N.L.	July 13, 1971	8	0	Mickey Lolich
Hank Aaron, N.L. (2)	July 25, 1972	6	1	Gaylord Perry
Cookie Rojas, A.L.	July 25, 1972	8	1	Bill Stoneman
Johnny Bench, N.L. (3)	July 24, 1973	4	0	Bill Singer
Bobby Bonds, N.L.	July 24, 1973	5	1	Bill Singer (2)
Willie Davis, N.L.	July 24, 1973	6	1	Nolan Ryan
Reggie Smith, N.L.	July 23, 1974	7	0	Catfish Hunter (3)
Steve Garvey, N.L.	July 15, 1975	2	0	Vida Blue (3)
Jimmy Wynn, N.L.	July 15, 1975	2	0	Vida Blue (4)
Carl Yastrzemski, A.L.	July 15, 1975	6	2	Tom Seaver
George Foster, N.L.	July 13, 1976	3	1	Catfish Hunter (4)
Fred Lynn, A.L.	July 13, 1976	4	0	Tom Seaver (2)
Cesar Cedeno, N.L.	July 13, 1976	8	1	Frank Tanana
Joe Morgan, N.L.	July 19, 1977	1	0	Jim Palmer
Greg Luzinski, N.L.	July 19, 1977	1	1	Jim Palmer (2)
Steve Garvey, N.L. (2)	July 19, 1977	3	0	Jim Palmer (3)
George Scott, A.L.	July 19, 1977	9	1	Rich Gossage
Fred Lynn, A.L. (2)	July 17, 1979	1	1	Steve Carlton (3)
Lee Mazzilli, N.L.	July 17, 1979	8	0	Jim Kern
Fred Lynn, A.L. (3)	July 8, 1980	5	1	Bob Welch
Ken Griffey Sr., N.L.	July 8, 1980	5	0	Tommy John
Ken Singleton, A.L.	Aug. 9, 1981	2	0	Tom Seaver (3)
Gary Carter, N.L.	Aug. 9, 1981	5	0	Ken Forsch
Dave Parker, N.L.	Aug. 9, 1981	6	0	Mike Norris
Gary Carter, N.L. (2)	Aug. 9, 1981	7	0	Ron Davis
Mike Schmidt, N.L.	Aug. 9, 1981	8	1	Rollie Fingers
Dave Concepcion, N.L.	July 13, 1982	2	1	Dennis Eckersley
Jim Rice, A.L.	July 6, 1983	3	0	Atlee Hammaker
Fred Lynn, A.L. (4)	July 6, 1983	3	3	Atlee Hammaker (2)
George Brett, A.L.	July 10, 1984	2	0	Charlie Lea
Gary Carter, N.L. (3)	July 10, 1984	2	0	Dave Stieb
Dale Murphy, N.L.	July 10, 1984	8	0	Guillermo Hernandez
Lou Whitaker, A.L.	July 15, 1986	2	1	Dwight Gooden
Frank White, A.L.	July 15, 1986	7	0	Mike Scott
Terry Steinbach, A.L.	July 12, 1988	3	0	Dwight Gooden (2)
Bo Jackson, A.L.	July 11, 1989	1	0	Rick Reuschel
Wade Boggs, A.L.	July 11, 1989	1	0	Rick Reuschel (2)
Cal Ripken Jr., A.L.	July 9, 1991	3	2	Dennis Martinez
Andre Dawson, N.L.	July 9, 1991	4	0	Roger Clemens
Ken Griffey Jr., A.L.	July 14, 1992	3	0	Greg Maddux
Ruben Sierra, A.L.	July 14, 1992	6	1	Bob Tewksbury
Will Clark, N.L.	July 14, 1992	8	2	Rick Aguilera
Gary Sheffield, N.L.	July 13, 1993	1	1	Mark Langston
Kirby Puckett, A.L.	July 13, 1993	2	0	Terry Mulholland
Roberto Alomar, A.L.	July 13, 1993	3	0	Andy Benes
Marquis Grissom, N.L.	July 12, 1994	6	0	Randy Johnson
Fred McGriff, N.L.	July 12, 1994	9	1	Lee Smith
Frank Thomas, A.L.	July 11, 1995	4	1	John Smiley
Craig Biggio, N.L.	July 11, 1995	6	0	Dennis Martinez (2)
Mike Piazza, N.L.	July 11, 1995	7	0	Kenny Rogers
Jeff Conine, N.L.	July 11, 1995	8	0	Steve Ontiveros
Mike Piazza, N.L. (2)	July 9, 1996	2	0	Charles Nagy

Player	Date	Inning	On	Pitcher
Ken Caminiti, N.L.	July 9, 1996	6	0	Roger Pavlik
Edgar Martinez, A.L.	July 8, 1997	2	0	Greg Maddux (2)
Javy Lopez, N.L.	July 8, 1997	7	0	Jose Rosado
Sandy Alomar Jr., A.L.	July 8, 1997	7	1	Shawn Estes
Alex Rodriguez, A.L.	July 7, 1998	5	0	Andy Ashby
Barry Bonds, N.L.	July 7, 1998	5	2	Bartolo Colon
Roberto Alomar, A.L. (2)	July 7, 1998	7	0	Trevor Hoffman
Chipper Jones, N.L.	July 11, 2000	3	0	James Baldwin
Cal Ripken Jr., A.L. (2)	July 10, 2001	3	0	Chan Ho Park
Derek Jeter, A.L.	July 10, 2001	6	0	Jon Lieber
Magglio Ordonez, A.L.	July 10, 2001	6	0	Jon Lieber (2)
Barry Bonds, N.L. (2)	July 9, 2002	3	1	Roy Halladay
Alfonso Soriano, A.L.	July 9, 2002	5	0	Eric Gagne
Todd Helton, N.L.	July 15, 2003	5	1	Shigetoshi Hasegawa
Garrett Anderson, A.L.	July 15, 2003	6	1	Woody Williams
Andruw Jones, A.L.	July 15, 2003	7	0	Mark Mulder
Jason Giambi, A.L.	July 15, 2003	7	0	Billy Wagner
Hank Blalock, A.L.	July 15, 2003	8	1	Eric Gagne (2)
Manny Ramirez, A.L.	July 13, 2004	1	1	Roger Clemens (2, 1st in N.L.)
Alfonso Soriano, A.L.	July 13, 2004	1	2	Roger Clemens (3, 2nd in N.L.)
David Ortiz, A.L.	July 13, 2004	6	1	Carl Pavano

MANAGERIAL RECORDS

AMERICAN LEAGUE

	Games W	L
Joe Altobelli, Baltimore	0	1
Sparky Anderson, Detroit	0	1
Del Baker, Detroit	1	0
Hank Bauer, Baltimore	0	1
Lou Boudreau, Cleveland	1	0
Mickey Cochrane, Detroit	1	0
Joe Cronin, Boston, Washington	2	1
Alvin Dark, Oakland	0	1
Jim Frey, Kansas City	0	1
Cito Gaston, Toronto	1	1
Mike Hargrove, Cleveland	1	1
Bucky Harris, New York	1	0
Ralph Houk, New York	1	2
Dick Howser, Kansas City	1	0
Darrell Johnson, Boston	0	1
Tom Kelly, Minnesota	2	0
Harvey Kuenn, Milwaukee	1	0
Tony La Russa, Oakland	3	0
Bob Lemon, New York	0	1
Al Lopez, Cleveland-Chicago	0	5
Connie Mack, Philadelphia	1	0
Billy Martin, New York	0	3
Joe McCarthy, New York	4	3
John McNamara, Boston	0	1
Sam Mele, Minnesota	0	1
Steve O'Neill, Detroit	1	0
Paul Richards, Baltimore*	0	1
Mike Scioscia, Anaheim	1	0
Buck Showalter, New York	0	1
Mayo Smith, Detroit	0	1
Casey Stengel, New York	4	6
Joe Torre, New York*	5	0
Earl Weaver, Baltimore	1	3
Dick Williams, Boston, Oakland, California	0	3

Total number of managers: 34
*includes one tie per asterisk

NATIONAL LEAGUE

	Games W	L
Felipe Alou, Montreal	1	0
Walter Alston, Brooklyn, Los Angeles	7	2
Sparky Anderson, Cincinnati	3	1
Dusty Baker, Chicago	0	1

	Games W	L
Yogi Berra, New York	1	0
Bruce Bochy, San Diego	0	1
Bob Brenly, Arizona*	0	0
Bobby Cox, Atlanta	1	4
Roger Craig, San Francisco	0	1
Alvin Dark, San Francisco	1	0
Charlie Dressen, Brooklyn	1	0
Leo Durocher, Brooklyn	2	2
Eddie Dyer, St. Louis	0	1
Jim Fregosi, Philadelphia	1	0
Frankie Frisch, St. Louis	0	1
Dallas Green, Philadelphia	1	0
Charley Grimm, Chicago	1	1
Fred Haney, Milwaukee	1	2
Gabby Hartnett, Chicago	0	1
Whitey Herzog, St. Louis	0	3
Gil Hodges, New York	1	0
Fred Hutchinson, Cincinnati	1	1
Dave Johnson, New York	1	0
Tom Lasorda, Los Angeles	3	1
Jim Leyland, Florida	0	1
Gene Mauch, Philadelphia	1	0
John McGraw, New York	0	1
Bill McKechnie, Cincinnati	1	1
Jack McKeon, Florida	0	1
Danny Murtaugh, Pittsburgh*	2	0
Paul Owens, Philadelphia	1	0
Lou Piniella, Cincinnati	0	1
Eddie Sawyer, Philadelphia	1	0
Red Schoendienst, St. Louis	2	0
Burt Shotton, Brooklyn	1	0
Billy Southworth, St. Louis	1	2
Chuck Tanner, Pittsburgh	1	0
Bill Terry, New York	1	2
Bobby Valentine, New York	0	1
Dick Williams, San Diego	1	0

Total number of managers: 40

COMBINED RECORDS FOR BOTH LEAGUES

	Games W	L
Sparky Anderson, Cincinnati N.L., Detroit A.L.	3	2
Alvin Dark, San Francisco N.L., Oakland A.L.	1	1
Dick Williams, Boston, Oakland, California	1	3

Total number of managers: 3

INDEX

INDEX

INDEX

INDEX

INDEX

DIVISION SERIES

CHAMPIONSHIP SERIES

INDEX

INDEX

WORLD SERIES

ALL-STAR GAME

INDEX